D0992835

MANAGING MARKETING IN THE 21st CENTURY

Developing & Implementing the Market Strategy

4th edition

www.wessexlearning.com

For complimentary material, see Axcess Capon codes at www.axcessvids.com

IMPORTANT NOTE TO PURCHASERS

The material within these covers comprises two separate sets of items:

- All the typical contents of a textbook — words, tables, figures — that you associate with a regular book. You purchased these items at a highly advantageous price — much lower than competitor books from traditional publishers. We hope you find the price/value relationship to your advantage.

- Complimentary access to additional learning materials. These materials comprise audio and video interviews, specially produced documents, and links to publicly available content. You did not purchase this access; this access is provided to you separately at no charge. All such items are noted in the book by four-digit alphanumeric codes and are easily accessible at *www.axcessvids.com* from your PC, tablet, or smartphone. All codes in this book are valid for 2016 and 2017. Some codes will change on January 1, 2018. After that date, previous new-book purchasers may secure updated codes by sending original proof of purchase to *contact@mm21c.com*.

Thank you and enjoy.

Wessex Press

ALSO BY NOEL CAPON*

MARKETING
Capon's Marketing Video Book
Financial Analysis for Marketing Decisions — Video
Capon's Marketing Framework (4th Edition)
The Virgin Marketer: Create Your Market Plan (4th Edition)
† *The Marketing Mavens*, Crown Business
Total Integrated Marketing
(with J.M. Hulbert and N. Piercy), Free Press, Kogan Page
The Marketing of Financial Services: A Book of Cases,
Prentice Hall

MARKETING – SPECIAL GEOGRAPHIC EDITIONS
ASIA PACIFIC
Capon's Marketing Principles (with S. Khan), SJ Learning
The Asian Marketing Casebook
(with W. Van Honacker), Pearson

BRAZIL
Managing Marketing for Brazilian Decision Makers
(with C.F. dos Santos Rocha)
Managing Marketing for Brazilian Decision Makers:
   Creating Your Marketing Plan
(with C.F. dos Santos Rocha)

CHINA
† *Marketing for China's Managers: Current and Future*
(3rd Edition) (with Y. Zheng), Renmin University Press

EUROPE
Frameworks for Strategic Marketing (with F. Go), Routledge
Creating Your Market Plan (with F. Go), Routledge

INDIA
Managing Marketing: A Concise Approach
(with S.S. Singh), Wiley (India)
Managing Marketing: An Applied Approach
(with S.S. Singh), Wiley (India)
The Marketing Toolkit
(with S.S. Singh), Wiley (India)

MIDDLE EAST
Marketing for Middle-Eastern Managers
(with O. Ramzy)

RUSSIA
‡ *Managing Marketing in the 21st Century*
(with V. Kolchanov), Piter Press
‡ *The Virgin Marketer*
(with V. Kolchanov), Piter Press

SPANISH LATIN AMERICA
§ *Managing Marketing in the 21st Century* (with N. Urcelay)
§ *Capon's Marketing Framework* (with N. Urcelay)
§ *The Virgin Marketer* (with N. Urcelay)

SALES AND ACCOUNT MANAGEMENT
Managing Global Accounts Video Book
Case Studies in Key, Strategic, and
   Global Account Management (with C. Senn)
Sales Eats First (with G.S. Tubridy)
Strategic Account Strategy
Managing Global Accounts
(with D. Potter and F. Schindler),
Thomson-Southwestern, Wessex
Key Account Management and Planning, Free Press

SALES AND ACCOUNT MANAGEMENT –
SPECIAL GEOGRAPHIC EDITIONS
Key Account Management and Planning
(with Y. Zheng), Huazhan Press
Sales Eats First (with G.S. Tubridy and Y. Zheng), CITIC Press

MANAGEMENT
Corporate Strategic Planning
(with J.U. Farley and J.M. Hulbert), Columbia University Press
Planning the Development of Builders, Leaders
   and Managers for 21st Century Business:
   Curriculum Change at Columbia Business School, Kluwer
Toward an Integrative Explanation of
   Corporate Financial Performance
(with J.U. Farley and S. Hoenig), Kluwer

---

* published by Wessex Press, unless otherwise stated
† also published in Chinese
‡ published in Russian
§ published in Spanish
# also published in German

MANAGING MARKETING IN THE 21st CENTURY

Developing & Implementing the Market Strategy

4th edition

Noel Capon

Graduate School of Business

Columbia University

New York, NY, USA

© Copyright 2017 by Wessex Press, Inc. All rights reserved.

Library of Congress Cataloging-in-Publication Data

Capon, Noel
  Managing Marketing in the 21st Century / Noel Capon – 4th edition
  p. cm.
  ISBN 978-0-9907405-9-9 (hardcover/color)
        978-0-9864023-0-2 (softcover/color)
        978-0-9864023-1-9 (softcover/B&W)
  1. Managing—Marketing.   I. Title: Managing marketing in the twenty-first century.

Copy Editor: Christy Goldfinch
Permissions Editor: Sandra Lord
Book / Cover Design: Anna Botelho
Indexer: Judi Gibbs

Acknowledgments are a continuation of the copyright page; they are on pages xxxix and xl.

Copyright © 2017 by Wessex Press, Inc., 1204 Broadway, New York, New York, 10001, USA. All rights reserved.
This publication is protected by copyright and permission should be obtained from the publisher prior to any
prohibited reproduction, storage in a retrieval system, or transmission in any form or by any means, electronic,
mechanical, photocopying, recording, or likewise. For information regarding permission, write to Wessex Press, Inc.
at *contact@wessexlearning.com.*

This book contains references to the products of SAP AG, Dietmar-Hopp-allee 16, 69190 Walldorf, Germany.
The names of these products are registered and/or unregistered trademarks of SAP AG. SAP AG is neither the
author nor the publisher of this book and is not responsible for its content.

DEDICATION

To Deanna Kuhn

ABOUT THE AUTHOR

 NOEL CAPON is R. C. Kopf Professor of International Marketing and past Chair of the Marketing Division, Graduate School of Business, Columbia University. Educated primarily in Great Britain, Professor Capon earned B.Sc. and Ph.D. degrees in Chemistry from University College, London University. He also received degrees in Business Administration from Manchester (Dip. BA), Harvard (MBA), and Columbia Business Schools (Ph.D.).

Professor Capon joined the Columbia Business School faculty in 1979. Previously he served on the faculty of, and received tenure from, the University of California – Graduate School of Management, UCLA. He has taught and/or held faculty positions at Harvard Business School; Australia — Monash University; England — Bradford Management Centre, London Business School, Manchester Business School; France — INSEAD; Hong Kong — Hong Kong University of Science and Technology (HKUST); China — China European International Business School (CEIBS — Shanghai); and India — Indian School of Business (ISB — Hyderabad).

Professor Capon has published more than 60 refereed articles and book chapters, and is editor for sections on Marketing, and Sales Management and Distribution, in the *AMA Management Handbook* (1994). He has published more than 30 books plus three video books (see *Also by Noel Capon* — page ii).

Professor Capon teaches on Columbia's full-time MBA and Executive MBA (EMBA) programs and its partner program with Hong Kong University and London Business School. He is a pioneer in developing video teaching materials and teaching via the *flipped classroom*. Professor Capon was Founding Director of *Managing Strategic Accounts* and the *Global Account Manager Certification* program in conjunction with St. Gallen University (Switzerland). He is a director of the *Strategic Account Management Association* (SAMA). He founded the *Advanced Marketing Management* Program in conjunction with CEIBS. Professor Capon also designs, directs, and teaches in numerous custom programs for major corporations globally. In 2001, Professor Capon cofounded *The Chief Sales Executive Forum*, offering multiple educational opportunities for sales and account management leaders. Capon is Chair of Wessex Press and of Lunacap Ventures, a venture capital firm.

FOREWORD

Having been active in business education for more than three decades, I believe the traditional textbook system must change, and must change radically. *Managing Marketing in the 21st Century* is my attempt to usher in a new model and bring considerable additional value to both marketing instructors and their students.

Whether you are an instructor or student, I encourage you to search *amazon.com* or *barnesandnoble.com* for a marketing textbook for your graduate or senior undergraduate marketing course. Or just go to your college bookstore. You will find the prices of most marketing textbooks well over $200. Of course, preowned books are somewhat cheaper, but these rapidly become out of date in the typical three-year new-edition cycle.

Even for students in the U.S. and advanced western countries, $200 to $300 per textbook is a pretty big nut to swallow. When we consider emerging-economy countries, a new marketing textbook is far out of reach for the average student. Such high prices are not only an issue for individual faculty members and their students. There is, perhaps, a more basic societal problem. Many political scientists believe that, over the long run, there is a strong relationship between market freedom and political freedom. What could be more fundamental to learning how to participate in free markets than a marketing textbook? Excessively priced marketing textbooks deprive people all over the world of learning about the tools they need to operate in free-market economies. Arguably, they also inhibit the growth of political freedom.

I have spent most of my career at Columba Business School in Manhattan, New York. Situated in the world's financial capital, Columbia University has long played a global role in creating and disseminating knowledge. I have spent time at major business schools around the world, and have worked with corporations large and small in several continents and many countries. These experiences have helped me accumulate the ability to bridge theory and practice. I also firmly believe I have a professional responsibility to deliver the intellectual capital expressed in this volume to faculty and students, no matter where they are located.

Please do not misunderstand; many conventional marketing textbooks have fine content. Indeed, my friends and professional colleagues wrote them. But the traditional textbook model must change. There is simply no reason why students should pay such excessive prices for their textbooks, nor why publishers should earn gross margins in excess of 75 percent.

Wessex Press offers the fourth edition of *Managing Marketing in the 21st Century* at a fraction of the price of traditional textbooks. This state-of-the-art marketing textbook is available to you as a printed book, and/or as a downloadable PDF e-book — at *www.wessexlearning*. Just go to the website and you will find out how to secure the version that best suits your needs. *Managing Marketing in the 21st Century* is also available for reading on iPad and Kindle. And to assist your learning, Wessex Press also provides a student study guide and a series of flash cards.

Managing Marketing in the 21st Century

SECTION I: MARKETING AND THE FIRM

CHAPTER 1
Introduction to Managing Marketing

CHAPTER 2
The Value of Customers

SECTION II: FUNDAMENTAL INSIGHTS FOR STRATEGIC MARKETING

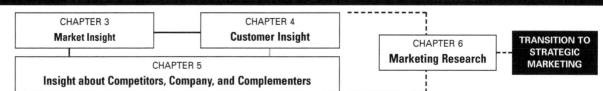

CHAPTER 3
Market Insight

CHAPTER 4
Customer Insight

CHAPTER 5
Insight about Competitors, Company, and Complementers

CHAPTER 6
Marketing Research

TRANSITION TO STRATEGIC MARKETING

SECTION III: STRATEGIC MARKETING

IMPERATIVE 1
Determine and Recommend Which Markets to Address

CHAPTER 7
Identifying and Choosing Opportunities

IMPERATIVE 2
Identify and Target Market Segments

CHAPTER 8
Market Segmentation and Targeting

IMPERATIVE 3
Set Strategic Direction and Positioning

CHAPTER 9
Market Strategy – Integrating Firm Efforts for Marketing Success

CHAPTER 10
Managing through the Life Cycle

CHAPTER 11
Managing Brands

SECTION IV: IMPLEMENTING THE MARKET STRATEGY

IMPERATIVE 4
Design the Market Offer

PART A: PROVIDING CUSTOMER VALUE

CHAPTER 12
Managing the Product Line

CHAPTER 13
Managing Services and Customer Service

CHAPTER 14
Developing New Products

PART B: COMMUNICATING CUSTOMER VALUE

CHAPTER 15
Integrated Marketing Communications

CHAPTER 16
Mass Communications

CHAPTER 17
Digital Marketing

CHAPTER 18
Directing and Managing the Field Sales Effort

PART C: DELIVERING CUSTOMER VALUE

CHAPTER 19
Distribution Decisions

CHAPTER 20
Retailing and Wholesaling

PART D: GETTING PAID FOR CUSTOMER VALUE

CHAPTER 21
Critical Underpinnings of Pricing Decisions

CHAPTER 22
Setting Prices

IMPERATIVE 5
Secure Support from Other Functions

CHAPTER 23
Ensuring the Firm Implements the Market Offer as Planned: Becoming an Externally Oriented Firm

IMPERATIVE 6
Monitor and Control Execution and Performance

CHAPTER 24
Monitoring and Controlling Firm Performance and Functioning

SECTION V: SPECIAL MARKETING TOPICS

CHAPTER 25
International, Regional, and Global Marketing

CHAPTER 26
Ethical, Legal, and Socially Responsible Decisions in Marketing

....

TABLE OF CONTENTS IN BRIEF

....

TABLE OF CONTENTS IN DETAIL

PREFACE

In *Managing Marketing in the 21st Century* you will learn about marketing language, logic, strategy, and implementation. To get us off to a good start, we'll begin by providing you the book's positioning.

POSITIONING

As you will learn in Chapter 9, positioning comprises four elements — customer targets, competitor targets, value proposition, and reasons to believe. The positioning for *Managing Marketing in the 21st Century* is:

- **Customer targets.** Marketing instructors who specify texts for graduate and senior undergraduate marketing courses, and the students who will learn to practice marketing in these courses.

- **Competitor targets.** All textbooks titled *Marketing Management*, or some close approximation, for use in graduate and senior undergraduate marketing courses.

- **Value proposition.** *Managing Marketing in the 21st Century* supports instructors in their quest to enhance students' grasp of marketing. Students learn how to successfully address simple and complex marketing problems. They learn *what to do* and *how to do it*, and how to infuse the organizations in which they work with a customer-focused view of business. And they pay a fraction of the price of traditional textbooks.

- **Reason to believe.** Professor Capon is among the world's most experienced marketing educators, from one of the world's leading business schools. The author has extensive experience educating students at all levels of business degree programs, as well as senior and midlevel executives in major corporations globally.

PURPOSE

Managing Marketing in the 21st Century is about understanding how to develop market strategy, implement market offers, and manage the marketing process. This is not a book that attempts to describe all there is to know about marketing, but focuses on what the prospective manager needs to know. *Managing Marketing in the 21st Century* differs from other senior undergraduate and introductory graduate marketing texts. The author takes a position on what he believes is a better or worse course of action for marketers. Marketing is an applied field; the author believes he should provide guidance for good marketing practice.

Furthermore, *Managing Marketing in the 21st Century* focuses on the manager, not just the marketer. For readers committed to a career in marketing (and we hope there are many), this book forms a solid foundation as you study marketing further and deeper. But the vast majority of you will not work in marketing departments, but will instead become senior executives, general managers, CFOs, and CEOs. This book is also for you because an understanding and appreciation of marketing is central to virtually every important decision that senior managers make. This may be the only marketing course many of you will take, so *Managing Marketing in the 21st Century* provides what every general manager and senior executive *must know* about marketing.

Marketing activity lies at the core of leading and managing a business by providing the focus for interfacing with customers. Marketing is also the source of insight about the market, customers, competitors, and complementers, and the business environment in general. Marketing is concerned with the firm's long-run relationships with customers as well as short-run sales activity. Marketing must be a major organizational thrust, not just a responsibility assigned to a single functional department. For this reason, *Managing Marketing in the 21st Century* emphasizes the role of marketing in creating value for customers — this leads to the creation of value for other firm stakeholders, including shareholders and employees.

CUSTOMERS: STUDENTS

To better understand how marketing fits into the broader challenge of leading and managing a corporation, we address marketing at the firm/business-unit level, as well as in the marketing function. *Managing Marketing in the 21st Century* provides you with a set of concepts and ideas for approaching marketing decisions. The book also gives you a common language for thinking about marketing issues. You will learn to structure and analyze managerial problems in marketing. *Managing Marketing in the 21st Century* prepares you to deal with core marketing issues that future marketers, senior executives, general managers, and CEOs will have to face. The book will also help you think strategically about your firm's markets, products, and services so that you can:

- Develop frameworks for approaching simple and complex marketing problems.

- Analyze markets, customers, competitors, your company, and complementers.

- Identify and assess market opportunities and develop market strategy.

- Prepare strategic marketing plans.

- Design implementation programs comprising product, promotion, distribution, and price, aka the marketing mix.
- Understand the importance of working across organizational boundaries to align firm capabilities and strengths.
- Assess the success of your marketing initiatives.
- Gain practical experience in addressing marketing issues in a variety of contexts — domestic and international, entrepreneurial startups and established corporations, business (B2B) and consumer (B2C) markets, products and services, and private and public and not-for-profit sectors.

As you work your way through *Managing Marketing in the 21st Century* you will develop a high tolerance for ambiguity — a quality of all successful senior executives, general managers, and CEOs. You will learn that there are no right or wrong answers to marketing problems, just some answers that are better than others. There are no simple — or even complex — formulae in which to plug a set of numbers and find the *right* answer. Rather, you must learn to approach complex and unstructured marketing problems in a creative and measured way. Throughout the book, and at the end of each chapter, are questions and exercises that can help you dig deeper. When appropriate, we urge you to use secondary sources, especially the Internet, to address these issues.

CUSTOMERS: MARKETING FACULTY

For marketing instructors, *Managing Marketing in the 21st Century* provides an opportunity to support your efforts in the classroom by presenting a contemporary perspective on how marketing works within the modern corporation. The book not only offers a firm basis on which to ground a first graduate or senior undergraduate marketing course, but will also challenge your students by including material and ideas not typically covered in marketing texts. Of course, *Managing Marketing in the 21st Century* focuses on how marketing should address customer needs, but also emphasizes marketing's *bottom line* — shareholder value. By understanding and acting upon the principles and frameworks in this book, students will avoid the many pitfalls of operating in an increasingly complex, competitive, and global environment.

In order to learn how to think appropriately about marketing problems, students must develop skills in marketing problem-solving and analysis. We recommend that your course also use marketing cases and/or simulations in context with this text.[1] Rather than write or include lengthy cases in the text, the Instructor's Manual and website <*www.wessexlearning.com*> provide numerous suggestions for course outlines, cases, and other activities linked to topics in the text. The website also shows ways to approach case analysis.

DIFFERENTIAL ADVANTAGE

As indicated in the foreword, many good marketing textbooks have been published over the years, but they can grow into comprehensive tomes or reference books. Further, they often contain excessive descriptive data and lots of pictures as they move from edition to edition. *Managing Marketing in the 21st Century* has a fresh look and feel for how marketing really works, and offers instructors and students many compelling benefits and values that clearly differentiate this book from others:

1. **More useful and less costly.** When students access *Managing Marketing in the 21st Century*, they pay a fraction of the price of traditional marketing textbooks. Students have three options: printed book, pdf e-book for downloading, and iTunes and Kindle. Quite simply, students who use this book will also be able to afford lunch.

2. **Improving shareholder value.** Business is ever more complex. Students learn the important link between success in delivering value to customers and success in improving shareholder value. This relationship is explicit and shows how world-class marketing decision-making must always consider the impact on shareholders.

3. **Normative focus.** *Managing Marketing in the 21st Century* takes a position on what are appropriate courses of action. Readers should know where the author stands and what he believes. Chapter 1 identifies a set of Marketing Imperatives and a set of Marketing Principles as guides for developing market strategy. The Marketing Imperatives form the basis for the book's macro-organization. Chapter 9 lays out core elements of a market strategy; a strategy that does not include these elements is incomplete.

4. **New ideas relevant to modern marketing environments.** *Managing Marketing in the 21st Century* introduces several genuinely new ideas drawn from personal research and writings, and helps students develop critical thinking and problem-solving skills to use them. A textbook should present established procedures, processes, and generalized norms, but such a narrow mandate would perform a disservice to readers. Changes taking place in marketing are dramatic and rapid. They require good problem-solving and analytic skills, as well as sound understanding of principles and practice.

5. **Applying the marketing mix** — as the means of *implementing the firm's market strategy*. For far too long, marketing students have completed their introductory marketing courses believing that marketing equals the marketing mix — product, promotion, distribution,

---

[1] We have had very good experience with Markstrat, www.stratxsimulations.com/.

price. Other critical questions must necessarily precede decisions about marketing mix elements. For example:

- What is the essential role of marketing?
- How does marketing increase shareholder value?
- What is a market strategy? How do you know if your market strategy is complete?
- Why are brands important? What are key issues for developing a branding strategy?

Only after these and other questions have been resolved should the firm make marketing-mix decisions.

6. **Balance between B2C and B2B marketing** is critically important. In chapter discussions, sometimes customers are consumers; other times they are organizations. *Managing Marketing in the 21st Century* favors neither one nor the other, but puts significant effort in both B2C and B2B marketing to address key developments in marketing practice today.

7. **Branding and marketing metrics** are increasingly important strategic issues for firms — the book devotes full chapters to each.

8. **International, regional, and global marketing.** The world is fast globalizing and firms increasingly seek opportunities outside their domestic markets. They face new and complex issues; hence this chapter focuses exclusively on international, regional, and global marketing.

9. **Public and not-for-profit marketing.** This book focuses squarely on marketing challenges facing managers in for-profit businesses. But it will also prove useful for those students interested in not-for-profit and public-sector marketing. First, the vast majority of concepts are readily transferable to these sectors — major differences concern organizational objectives. In the for-profit sector, objectives are unambiguously concerned with profit and shareholder value — in the not-for-profit and public sectors, setting objectives is often a complex undertaking. Second, experience shows that students who develop a firm grounding in for-profit marketing are better prepared for the challenges of not-for-profit and public-sector marketing.

10. **Ethical and legal issues.** We devote an entire chapter to discussing ethical and legal issues in marketing. We believe it is very important to provide students with a basic grounding in these critical areas.

A PEDAGOGICAL FRAMEWORK FOR STUDYING AND LEARNING

The book includes several features to enhance your learning experience:

- **Learning Outcomes.** These highlight the learning you will gain from diligently studying material in each chapter.

- **Opening Case.** To bring the book to life, each chapter opens with a real-life example of an organization that helps focus the upcoming material.

- **The Changing View.** The Old Way/New Way device shows the direction of change regarding the upcoming material.

- **Examples.** The book showcases examples to illustrate specific ideas in each chapter.

- **Key Ideas.** Key ideas are distributed throughout the book and highlighted in the margins for easy reference.

- **Marketing Questions.** To engage you with the text and deepen your understanding. Questions about the material are in the margins.

- **Special Topics.** Several chapters contain special-topic material highlighted in boxes.

- **Marketing Enrichment.** *Managing Marketing in the 21st Century* has no appendices. Rather, additional material is clearly noted and easily accessible (FREE) via Axcess Capon codes (p. xxv).

- **Key Messages.** This section concisely identifies the key learning points in the chapter

- **Videos, Audios, Documents.** Many chapters offer links to publicly available material on the Internet. They also provide links to video and audio interviews of the author with marketing leaders. Students may access these materials via PC, tablet, or smartphone at *www.axcessvids.com* (p. xxvi).

- **Questions for Study and Discussion.** Each chapter concludes with questions to help you reflect on the chapter material and gain deeper insight.

- **True/False Questions** and **Multiple Choice Questions.** You may test yourself on chapter material; you may access answers from the Internet using Axcess Capon codes (p. xxv).

- **Glossary.** At the end of the book, we gather together and provide an explanation of key marketing terms.

Managing Marketing in the 21st Century is pretty light on pictures, fluff, and entertainment value. This is deliberate; after all, marketing is a serious business.

ORGANIZATION OF THE BOOK

As laid out in the Table of Contents, *Managing Marketing in the 21st Century* addresses the challenge of *marketing in the Middle East* in five sections and 25 chapters. Briefly:

SECTION I   — MARKETING AND THE FIRM
SECTION II   — FUNDAMENTAL INSIGHTS FOR STRATEGIC MARKETING
SECTION III — STRATEGIC MARKETING

SECTION IV — IMPLEMENTING THE
              MARKET STRATEGY
SECTION V — SPECIAL MARKETING TOPICS

SECTION 1 — MARKETING AND THE FIRM. This section introduces fundamental concepts in marketing and emphasizes the importance of customers. The section comprises two chapters:

• Chapter 1, *Introduction to Managing Marketing*, provides an introduction to the book. This chapter makes the case for the critical importance of marketing in the modern corporation. The chapter describes two key meanings of marketing — *marketing as a philosophy* and *six marketing imperatives* that encompass the tasks of strategic marketing. Chapter 1 also introduces four principles that should form the basis for all marketing decision-making — they continue thematically throughout the book.

• Chapter 2, *The Value of Customers*, delves into the notion of customers as critical firm assets. This chapter introduces the concept of customer lifetime value (CLV) and emphasizes the importance of customer retention. The chapter also shows that, in addition to measuring product profitability, the firm should measure customer profitability. The second part of the chapter focuses on actions designed to bind customers closer to the firm, notably customer relationship management (CRM) and customer loyalty programs.

SECTION II — FUNDAMENTAL INSIGHTS FOR STRATEGIC MARKETING. The four chapters in this section focus on securing insight — situation analysis — that lays the foundation for developing market strategy.

• Chapter 3, *Market Insight*, focuses on understanding the market. The chapter framework embraces market structure, market and product evolution, industry forces, and environmental forces.

• Chapter 4, *Customer Insight*, focuses on customers — consumers and organizations. This chapter addresses three main questions: Who are the customers? What do customers need and want? How do customers buy?

• Chapter 5, *Insight about Competitors, Company, and Complementers*, focuses on those three areas with an extended section on competitors and a five-step process — identify, describe, evaluate, project, and manage.

• Chapter 6, *Marketing Research*, focuses on marketing research methodologies to gain insight relative to markets, customers, competitors, company, and complementers.

TRANSITION TO STRATEGIC MARKETING. This material shows how planning assumptions form the supporting pillars for strategic marketing and implementation.

SECTION III — STRATEGIC MARKETING. *Marketing Imperatives 1, 2, 3* are the *to-dos* of marketing: when and how to apply the four marketing principles. *Strategic marketing* embraces the first three of six imperatives; these imperatives address issues the firm must consider in building the strategic market plan from the foundation of fundamental insights in the situation analysis — Section II.

Marketing Imperative 1 — Determine and Recommend Which Markets to Address

• Chapter 7, *Identifying and Choosing Opportunities*, focuses on growth opportunities. The chapter develops growth strategy frameworks, introduces the venture portfolio, explores criteria to evaluate growth opportunities, and identifies implementation methods.

Marketing Imperative 2 — Identify and Target Market Segments

• Chapter 8, *Market Segmentation and Targeting*, covers two basic topics: methods of grouping customers into market segments, and targeting — the process of deciding which segments to address.

Both Imperatives 1 and 2 exemplify the *Principle of Selectivity and Concentration.*

Marketing Imperative 3 — Set Strategic Direction and Positioning

This imperative comprises three separate chapters and advances the concept of market strategy as a fundamental integrating force.

• Chapter 9, *Market Strategy — Integrating Firm Efforts for Marketing Success*, presents critical market strategy components in some depth and shows how they play an integrating role for the marketing mix and other functional programs. In particular, the chapter illustrates applying the *Principles of Differential Advantage, Customer Value, and Integration.*

• Chapter 10, *Managing through the Life Cycle*, uses the product life cycle to focus on the competitive aspects of market strategy. This chapter adopts a scenario approach for developing strategic options for different competitive and life-cycle situations.

• Chapter 11, *Managing Brands*, addresses the management of brands and the increasingly important brand equity concept. Specific issues addressed in this chapter are developing and sustaining a strong brand and managing brand architecture.

SECTION IV — IMPLEMENTING THE MARKET STRATEGY. *Marketing Imperatives 4, 5, and 6* focus on implementing the market strategy.

Marketing Imperative 4 — Design the Market Offer

Eleven chapters address Imperative 4; they describe the marketing mix and when and how to manage each component in a way that reinforces and implements the market strategy. Appropriately designing the firm's offer is a critical component of the marketing plan.

Each marketing mix element may bestow value on customers, but our fourfold framework focuses on the major role of each element. Part A — *Providing Customer Value*; Part B — *Communicating Customer Value*; Part C — *Delivering Customer Value*; and Part D — *Getting Paid for Customer Value*.

PART A. PROVIDING CUSTOMER VALUE

Four chapters focus on managing and developing product and services:

- Chapter 12, *Managing the Product Line*, concerns managing product line composition. This chapter leans heavily on strategic portfolio frameworks to complement traditional financial analysis methods. The chapter also addresses complementarity, product line breadth (including trade-offs between product proliferation and simplification), bundling, counterfeiting, evolving the product line, extending product life, product quality, product safety, secondary markets, packaging, and product and packaging disposal.

- Chapter 13, *Managing Services and Customer Service*. Services are important factors in all advanced economies yet they display important differences from physical products. Furthermore, as product quality has improved across the board, customer service has become an increasingly important competitive weapon.

- Chapter 14, *Developing New Products*, discusses success factors for innovative companies and different ways to approach the innovation challenge. This chapter also describes the evolving stage-gate new-product-development process and the new product development portfolio.

PART B. COMMUNICATING CUSTOMER VALUE

Four chapters focus on personal and impersonal communications:

- Chapter 15, *Integrated Marketing Communications*, presents an integrated communications framework for developing communications strategy in the context of external and internal challenges.

- Chapter 16, *Mass Communications*, focuses on impersonal communication, specifically advertising, direct marketing, publicity & public relations, and sales promotion.

- Chapter 17, *Digital Marketing*, addresses the exciting new world of digital communications. We show how to use e-mail; search, blogs, social media; display, classifieds, and video advertising; websites; and mobile marketing to enhance the firm's marketing efforts.

- Chapter 18, *Directing and Managing the Field Sales Effort*, deals with personal selling efforts and highlights critical issues in managing the field sales effort. This chapter presents six tasks for developing sales strategy and organization, and addresses contemporary challenges of managing key/strategic/global accounts.

PART C. DELIVERING CUSTOMER VALUE

- Chapter 19, *Distribution Decisions*, focuses on providing customers with products and services, when and where they want them. The chapter discusses choosing and managing channel relationships, an area of substantial innovation where the Internet is playing a critical role.

- Chapter 20, *Retailing and Wholesaling*, extends the distribution discussion from Chapter 19 to focus on retailing and wholesaling.

PART D. GETTING PAID FOR CUSTOMER VALUE

- Chapter 21, *Critical Underpinnings of Pricing Decisions*, highlights the tremendous revenue and profit implications of pricing decisions. The chapter focuses on critical factors in developing pricing strategy — customer value, costs, competition, and the firm's strategic objectives.

- Chapter 22, *Setting Prices*, shows how to both set actual prices and avoid price changes. The chapter highlights the pricing toolkit and price waterfall, and illustrates various pricing approaches.

Imperatives 3 and 4 draw heavily on the *Principles of Customer Value and Differential Advantage*.

Marketing Imperative 5 — Secure Support from Other Functions

- Chapter 23, *Ensuring the Firm Implements the Market Offer as Planned*, returns to the distinction between marketing as a philosophy and marketing as a function. The chapter highlights successful externally oriented firms and develops a system for making the firm externally oriented and customer-focused, so that the various functions support the marketing effort.

Marketing Imperative 6 — Monitor and Control Execution and Performance

- Chapter 24, *Monitoring and Controlling Firm Performance and Functioning*, discusses ways of ensuring the firm implements its planned marketing effort and achieves desired results.

Both Imperatives 5 and 6 rest on the *Principle of Integration*.

SECTION V — SPECIAL MARKETING TOPICS

- Chapter 25, *International, Regional, and Global Marketing*, focuses on marketing activity outside the firm's domestic market. This chapter addresses foreign-market entry — how to select countries and how to enter. The chapter also addresses alternative international marketing strategies and options for marketing organization.

- Chapter 26, *Ethical, Legal, and Socially Responsible Decisions in Marketing*, develops a framework for thinking about marketing decision-making. The chapter explores ethical and legal issues in a variety of implementation areas, and discusses approaches to corporate social responsibility.

SUPPLEMENTAL MATERIAL FOR TEACHING AND LEARNING

Managing Marketing in the 21st Century is a standalone book, but several additional materials can help instructors design courses and make the learning experience more meaningful for students. Instructors can access these materials in a protected area at *www.wessexlearning.com*.

- **Instructor's manual.** The manual employs a consistent format, chapter by chapter. Essentially, the manual summarizes critical learning points in each chapter and provides approaches to address *Marketing Questions* distributed throughout the text. For the *Questions for Study and Discussion* at the end of each chapter, the manual offers suggestions for managing class discussion.

- **Test item file.** Prepared by experienced test developer Andrew Yap this file contains well over 1,000 multiple choice and essay questions for use by instructors in setting tests and examinations. Organized by chapter, this material is available in Word, and for Blackboard and Respondus.

- **PowerPoint files.** Each chapter comes with a set of teaching materials in the form of PowerPoint files. Each slide has a *notes* page that suggests how the instructor may use that particular slide for teaching purposes.

- **Case studies.** Two sets of materials are available: a list and short descriptions of many traditional marketing case studies, and a large number of short case studies for FREE pdf download. In both cases, organization is by book chapter. This material also includes two approaches to studying marketing cases — a faculty perspective developed at Columbia Business School and an approach prepared by Mary Cunningham Agee, then a Harvard Business School student, to help fellow students.

Additional study aids for students are accessible from *www.wessexlearning.com*.

- **Student study guide.** The purpose of this publication is to help students in their marketing studies. The guide is structured in the same way as the textbook so that students can easily work back and forth between the two volumes. Available as a printed book and e-book.

- **Electronic flash cards.** Similar in concept to traditional flash cards, electronic flash cards are designed to improve students' marketing expertise.

- **Financial analysis for marketing decisions.** A good understanding of financial analysis is critical for sound marketing decision-making. Financial analysis comes in many shapes and forms; students should understand the specific issues that concern marketers. We discuss financial issue throughout *Managing Marketing in the 21st Century*, but do not have space to lay the groundwork. Hence, we have prepared the Marketing Enrichment FM.1 **[308p]** document that we hope you will find useful. Feel free to download the file and use it as a handy reference. See also Video Books (p. xxvi)

> **MARKETING ENRICHMENT FM.1**
>
> *Financial Analysis for Marketing Decisions* **308p**

Finally, students have access to three other learning sources via the Internet:

- **Marketing Enrichment.** A difficult problem for textbook authors is what material to put in the book and what to leave out. We have tried to alleviate this problem by adding a new *Marketing Enrichment* feature. From time to time, throughout *Managing Marketing in the 21st Century*, we have developed additional material. We note each Marketing Enrichment item in the text and in the margin; students can easily access this material via an Axcess Capon code (next section).

- **Videos.** Videos of the author interviewing marketing experts are at the end of each chapter. We note these files with a video icon 🎬 and an Axcess Capon code (next section). We also provide links to publicly available videos.

- **Audios.** The author speaks with Dave Basarab about *Marketing Mastery*. We list these files with an audio icon 🔊 at the end of appropriate chapters, noted by Axcess Capon codes.

AXCESS CAPON CODES

An innovative feature of the fourth edition of *Managing Marketing in the 21st Century* is Axcess Capon codes. The purpose of Axcess Capon codes is to link items in the text to additional material you may find interesting, in an easy way. Axcess Capon codes act as hot-links in the book's digital versions. Perhaps more importantly, Axcess Capon codes are simple links between the printed version and the Internet. With Axcess Capon codes, you enter a simple 4-digit alphanumeric code on your PC, tablet, or smartphone, at *www.axcessvids.com*. If you're reading the printed book, we suggest you bookmark *www.axcessvids.com*; then you'll be able to access the item you require with just four keystrokes.

CHAPTER TEXT. The chapter text contains four item types. Each item has an Axcess Capon code*:

- **Videos.** Videos appear throughout the book. Each Axcess Capon code comprises three figures, then ends with the letter *v*.
- **Audios.** Audios appear at the end of chapters. Each Axcess Capon code comprises three figures, then ends with the letter *a*.
- **Documents.** The text notes some additional documents. Each Axcess Capon code comprises three figures, then ends with the letter *p*.
- **Video Books.** The text refers to three items designed to support your learning:
  - *Capon's Marketing Video Book* — **264v**
  - *Financial Analysis for Marketing Decisions* — **325v**
  - *Managing Global Customers* — **314v**

THE VIRGIN MARKETER: CREATE YOUR MARKET PLAN

No matter how well-written a textbook, the only way to really learn marketing is by doing it. You simply have to take the ideas, concepts, and frameworks and put them into practice. *The Virgin Marketer: Create Your Market Plan* is a companion volume to *Managing Marketing in the 21st Century. The Virgin Marketer: Create Your Market Plan's* chapters correspond to chapters in the textbook. Each chapter contains a set of tried-and-true experiential exercises designed to help the user prepare a strategic marketing plan — analyze a marketing situation, develop a market strategy, and design a series of implementation programs.

The best approach is for you to select a product or service as your *marketing case*. Your instructor may assign the case — perhaps a local firm or an entrepreneurial startup. Alternatively, you may select your own product or service. The ideal way to *learn by doing* is to complete each chapter of *The Virgin Marketer: Create Your Market Plan* right after you have completed a chapter of this book. Then you use the ideas, concepts, and frameworks while they are fresh in your mind. If you work through your marketing case assiduously, you will finish the book with an operating marketing plan. Examples of strategic marketing plans using *The Virgin Marketer: Create Your Market Plan* in Marketing Enrichment FM.2 **[665p]**.

> **MARKETING ENRICHMENT FM.2**
>
> *Sample Marketing Plans using* The Virgin Marketer: Create Your Market Plan **665p**

ACKNOWLEDGMENTS

Many individuals contributed to *Managing Marketing in the 21st Century* in this and earlier editions. I thank them for their continued support. Here I want to recognize several special groups of people for their roles in bringing this third edition to fruition. Current colleagues include Eva Ascarza, Asim Ansari, Silvia Bellezza, Mark Cohen, Jacob Goldenberg, Kamel Jedidi, Kinshuk Jerath, Gita Johar, Eric Johnson, Ran Kivetz, Rajeev Kohli, Don Lehmann, Oded Netzer, Michel Pham, Miklos Sarvary, Bernd Schmitt, Scott Shriver, Olivier Toubia, Hitendra Wadhwa, Elizabeth Webb, and Keith Wilcox. Former colleagues include Dan Bartels, Rajeev Batra, Jim Bettman, Bill Brandt (deceased), Lee Cooper, John Farley, Andy Gershoff, Rashi Glazer, Brett Gordon, Sunil Gupta, Dominique Hanssens, Morris Holbrook, John Howard (deceased), Morgan Jones, Oded Koenesberg, Aradhna Krishna, Leonard Lee, Rich Lutz, Natalie Mizik, Bill Moore, Mike Ryan, Abe Shuchman (deceased), Russ Winer, and Dave Wooten. Former students are too numerous to mention but include include George Belch, Hubert Gatignon, Steve Hoch, and Itamar Simonsen. Thanks also to marketing instructors at other business schools including the many adopters of my textbooks; my MBA and EMBA students; and participants in my various educational and consulting engagements with corporations around the world. In various ways, all of you have stimulated and challenged my thinking: I thank you for that. I also thank all members of Wessex Press' production team. I specially recognize my longtime co-author, Mac Hulbert, now Emeritus Professor at Columbia Business School. Mac contributed to previous editions of *Managing Marketing in the 21st Century* and has been a friend and collaborator for more than 45 years: Mac, many thanks.

We acknowledge contributions of the business press. To keep *Managing Marketing in the 21st Century* as relevant as possible, we gleaned many examples, news, and trends from respected online and print business sources like *Bloomberg Businessweek*, *The Economist*, *Financial Times*, *Fortune*, *The New York Times*, and *The Wall Street Journal*, and Wikipedia. We thank these publications for their contributions. Chapter endnotes contain citations to specific quotations. We also thank the many corporations whose experiences and images we have included to help fulfill the educational objective of *Managing Marketing in the 21st Century* in a socially responsible — affordable price — manner.

---

* Codes for some publicly available material may become inactive by the time you read this book; other public sites show advertisements before the identified content. We regret any inconvenience.

CONCLUDING STATEMENT

The extensive experience the author brings to *Managing Marketing in the 21st Century* has infused the book with the very real marketing challenges that face corporations daily around the world. The author writes from the standpoint of a marketing academic with a deep commitment to helping corporations improve their marketing practice, and imparting his knowledge and expertise to students at the dawn of their careers.

The material in *Managing Marketing in the 21st Century* will help you to learn about marketing. It will equip you to survive and prosper in your careers as marketers, senior executives, general managers, and CEOs. All those who have helped bring this book to fruition wish you well as you develop your careers.

Managing Marketing in the 21st Century is also a reference for future use. If you become an entrepreneur, this book will help you launch and manage your new business. If you join a firm's marketing department, you will never have enough books on the subject; hopefully this will be one of your favorite reference guides. And, if you find yourself in another function where you work with marketing, you will be equipped to ask your marketing colleagues the right questions.

Good luck!

Noel Capon
R. C. Kopf Professor of International Marketing
Graduate School of Business
Columbia University, New York, New York

ABBREVIATIONS GLOSSARY

To improve readability we avoid spelling out the full names of organizations in examples. Rather, we use the shortened versions or mnemonics by which they are typically known.

Corporations

Advanced Micro Devices	AMD
American Express	AmEx
Barnes & Noble	B&N
Bausch & Lomb	B&L
Black & Decker	B&D
Boston Consulting Group	BCG
Bristol-Myers Squibb	BMS
British Airways	BA
General Electric	GE
General Motors	GM
GlaxoSmithKline	GSK
Hewlett Packard	HP*
Home Box Office	HBO
International Business Machines	IBM
International Paper	IP
Johnson & Johnson	J&J
Procter & Gamble	P&G
Texas Instruments	TI
Volkswagen	VW

General Business Terms

Chief executive officer	CEO
Chief financial officer	CFO
Chief marketing officer	CMO
Customer relationship management	CRM
Fast moving consumer goods	FMCG
Personal computer	PC
Public relations	PR
Research and development	R&D
Senior vice president	SVP
Standard & Poor's	S&P

U.S. Government Departments

Consumer Product Safety Commission	CPSC
Environmental Protection Agency	EPA
Federal Communications Commission	FCC
Federal Drug Administration	FDA
Federal Trade Commission	FTC
National Transportation Safety Board	NTSB
Securities and Exchange Commission	SEC

International Organizations

European Union	EU
International Monetary Fund	IMF
United Nations	UN
United Nations Educational, Scientific and Cultural Organization	UNESCO
United States	U.S.
World Trade Organization	WTO

---

* In 2015, Hewlett-Packard (HP) split into two firms — Hewlett Packard Enterprise and HP Inc.

SECTION I

MARKETING AND THE FIRM

For complimentary material, see Axcess Capon codes at www.axcessvids.com

MARKETING AND THE FIRM comprises two chapters: Introduction to Managing Marketing — Chapter 1, and The Value of Customers — Chapter 2.

Chapter 1 introduces two marketing concepts that form the basis for *Managing Marketing in the 21st Century* — marketing as a *philosophy*, and marketing as *six imperatives* — the *must-do* activities the firm performs in marketing. Chapter 1 also presents four marketing principles and shows the relationship between customer value and shareholder value.

Chapter 2 focuses on the value of customers to the firm and introduces the customer-lifetime-value (CLV) concept. The chapter discusses various ways to enhance CLV, paying special attention to customer retention. The chapter concludes with the role of customer relationship management (CRM) in driving customer loyalty.

Managing Marketing in the 21st Century

SECTION I: MARKETING AND THE FIRM

> **CHAPTER 1**
> **Introduction to Managing Marketing**

> **CHAPTER 2**
> **The Value of Customers**

SECTION II: FUNDAMENTAL INSIGHTS FOR STRATEGIC MARKETING

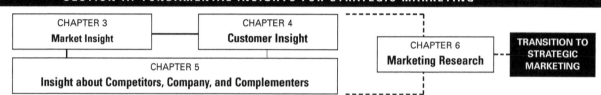

> **CHAPTER 3**
> **Market Insight**

> **CHAPTER 4**
> **Customer Insight**

> **CHAPTER 5**
> **Insight about Competitors, Company, and Complementers**

> **CHAPTER 6**
> **Marketing Research**

> **TRANSITION TO STRATEGIC MARKETING**

SECTION III: STRATEGIC MARKETING

IMPERATIVE 1
Determine and Recommend Which Markets to Address

> **CHAPTER 7**
> **Identifying and Choosing Opportunities**

IMPERATIVE 2
Identify and Target Market Segments

> **CHAPTER 8**
> **Market Segmentation and Targeting**

IMPERATIVE 3
Set Strategic Direction and Positioning

> **CHAPTER 9**
> **Market Strategy – Integrating Firm Efforts for Marketing Success**

> **CHAPTER 10**
> **Managing through the Life Cycle**

> **CHAPTER 11**
> **Managing Brands**

SECTION IV: IMPLEMENTING THE MARKET STRATEGY

IMPERATIVE 4
Design the Market Offer

PART A: PROVIDING CUSTOMER VALUE

> **CHAPTER 12**
> **Managing the Product Line**

> **CHAPTER 13**
> **Managing Services and Customer Service**

> **CHAPTER 14**
> **Developing New Products**

PART B: COMMUNICATING CUSTOMER VALUE

> **CHAPTER 15**
> **Integrated Marketing Communications**

> **CHAPTER 16**
> **Mass Communications**

> **CHAPTER 17**
> **Digital Marketing**

> **CHAPTER 18**
> **Directing and Managing the Field Sales Effort**

PART C: DELIVERING CUSTOMER VALUE

> **CHAPTER 19**
> **Distribution Decisions**

> **CHAPTER 20**
> **Retailing and Wholesaling**

PART D: GETTING PAID FOR CUSTOMER VALUE

> **CHAPTER 21**
> **Critical Underpinnings of Pricing Decisions**

> **CHAPTER 22**
> **Setting Prices**

IMPERATIVE 5
Secure Support from Other Functions

> **CHAPTER 23**
> **Ensuring the Firm Implements the Market Offer as Planned: Becoming an Externally Oriented Firm**

IMPERATIVE 6
Monitor and Control Execution and Performance

> **CHAPTER 24**
> **Monitoring and Controlling Firm Performance and Functioning**

SECTION V: SPECIAL MARKETING TOPICS

> **CHAPTER 25**
> **International, Regional, and Global Marketing**

> **CHAPTER 26**
> **Ethical, Legal, and Socially Responsible Decisions in Marketing**

CHAPTER I

INTRODUCTION TO MANAGING MARKETING

For complimentary material, see Axcess Capon codes at www.axcessvids.com

LEARNING OUTCOMES

When you have completed this chapter, you will be able to:

- Define the term *marketing*.
- Explain the fundamental business model.
- Articulate why marketing is so important for business organizations.
- Explain how success in attracting, retaining, and growing customers improves shareholder value.
- Articulate how marketing as a philosophy embraces an external orientation.
- Understand how an external orientation differs from various internal orientations.
- Be ready to act on the six marketing imperatives.
- Identify the four marketing principles.
- Understand the book's structure and additional features to enhance learning.

OPENING CASE: STARBUCKS

By 2016, Starbucks operated 21,000 stores in more than 60 countries. It all started in 1982, when 28-year-old Howard Schultz joined Seattle's specialty coffee emporium, Starbucks Coffee, Tea & Spice (formed 1971), as director of retail operations and marketing — selling coffee beans to coffee aficionados. In 1983, while on a buying trip to Milan, Schultz became fascinated by Italy's espresso bars — people gathered to read newspapers, converse, and socialize while drinking coffee. Schultz persuaded Starbucks' owners to transplant the concept to downtown Seattle; it was wildly successful. Schultz left Starbucks to form his own firm but, in 1987, together with local investors, purchased Starbucks and renamed the firm Starbucks Coffee Company. Starbucks began a major store expansion: In 1992, when Starbucks went public, it had 140 stores in the northwest and Chicago. By 2006, Starbucks was the world's leading retailer, roaster, and brand of specialty coffee with 7,950 stores in the U.S. and over 11,000 globally.

To fulfill its primary goal of providing high-quality coffee to customers, Starbucks purchases coffee direct from growers, roasts all its coffee, and distributes to its stores. Howard Schultz commented: "We own and operate almost all our own stores — the only exceptions are in foreign countries, where we have partnership and licensing agreements with local businesspeople, and in licensed locations in the U.S., such as campus bookstores and airports, where we cannot own and operate the store outright. All people in company-owned stores work for Starbucks."[1]

Schultz continued: "Starbucks is one of the world's great experience brands … . All the stores are similar, yet they're also all different. A Starbucks on Wall Street in downtown Manhattan doesn't look exactly like one in Berkeley, or in Barcelona, but they all have the same spirit." He added, "In 1989, when we had only 50 stores, we decided to bring all of our architecture and design work in-house. We have over 200 architects … and more people in our own design studio."

Schultz talked about the meaning of the Starbucks brand: "We decided early on that the equity of the brand is linked to all of the cues of the brand experience, from the overall look of the store and subtle visual cues, to the senses of aroma and the sound of the music that we have playing … . [They are] a very significant component of the customer's experience. And that became a very, very large competitive advantage, because there wasn't a competitor around that was willing or able to spend the amount of money that we spent on these things and that we continue to spend."

For Schultz, Starbucks should be its customers' third place — after home and work. "As a customer, I walk into the store and I'm swept away for a minute, even if I get a coffee to go, because I'm part of this experience that makes me feel better. A missing part of our lives as consumers is that we don't feel valued. So we really take notice when someone touches us and says, 'I appreciate you, I respect you, and I can help you.' … We have to ensure that there's incredible consistency without having every location seem like a fast-food franchise. That is part of the genius of Starbucks."

Starbucks enhances customer value by focusing on its employees — partners. Schultz observed: "The keys are the culture and values of our company that allow our people to feel the way they do about Starbucks, so that they genuinely want to convey the attributes, the characteristics, the aspirational qualities of what we offer the customer … . We've made a very large investment over the last 20 years in training. We've spent more money every year on training than we do on advertising." Early on, Starbucks did no advertising, preferring to let its clusters of stores fulfill the communications function. Schultz went on: "Starbucks has the lowest attrition of any retail restaurant in North America. We do a cultural, internal audit every year where we go to our people, and we ask them to evaluate our behavior and practices and their trust and confidence in management. And we share those scores with the company.

"The training is twofold. One path is on the fundamentals of what we do — how to make great coffee; how to explain the differences in features and benefits between different coffee makers, different coffees, all that stuff. The other piece is who we are, what we expect, how customers experience the store … . [We work on] hiring the right kind of people and not just filling shifts. A colleague said it best: 'We're not in the coffee business; we're in the people business serving coffee.' … People recognize when they get in the company that this is a special place and they want to protect it, so … good people are hired and developed." Starbucks offers comprehensive healthcare and stock options to all employees, including part-timers. Said Schultz, "That was the transformational event, where everyone then had a stake in the company." In 2014 Schultz launched its Starbucks College Achievement Plan; *eligible employees could complete a bachelor's degree online at Arizona State University, with full tuition reimbursement. This initiative and other benefits continue to bring all employees into one company-wide conversation about serving customers better.*

Starbucks continues to look for new market segments. Schultz explained: "Several years ago we were in the morning day-part business. And we had no business to speak of in the afternoon. Our stores closed at seven at night, and we were done for the day. Customers started driving a new business for us by using our stores in multiple day-parts … We had to create an afternoon beverage business and an after-dinner dessert business." Product innovation is also very important to Starbucks — it has introduced many new products, some not related to coffee. A major success is Frappuccino, sold

Case Question

What other firms have grown as successfully as Starbucks? What accounts for Starbucks' success? How have Schultz's more recent actions and competition affected the Starbucks brand?

widely in supermarkets under an agreement with PepsiCo. Starbucks also added recorded music and occasional events to the store experience.

Starbucks works hard to transfer best practice. Said Schultz: "At our first global conference, it was like the United Nations at Starbucks — 30 countries … we had a mini Starbucks trade show with booths for every country to show their best practices. The people from Japan showed us how to utilize small spaces. The people from the Philippines, our best food market, shared how they achieve such high-quality food."

Seeking fast growth, by the mid-2000s Starbucks made a series of decisions that harmed the brand. Starbucks relaxed location criteria and overexpanded, introduced drive-through windows, added breakfast sandwiches, put in automated espresso machines, ceased coffee grinding, and made the stores less comfy. Strong competitors emerged — Dunkin' Donuts and McDonalds. As its stock price plunged in the 2008 recession, Starbucks fired its CEO and Howard Schultz returned. Schultz took several actions — gave stores more local-ness; closed underperforming stores; refocused on the customer experience; introduced Via instant coffee in Starbucks outlets, supermarkets, and mass merchandisers; undertook disciplined expansion in Asia; slimmed the supply chain; and reinvigorated a second brand, Seattle's Best.

More than 40 million customers monthly frequent Starbucks locations around the world. The most loyal customers visit Starbucks an average of 18 times per month. Starbucks customer loyalty has brought significant financial success. 2014 revenues were $16.4 billion; net income exceeded $2 billion; share price had increased twelvefold from its 2009 low.

WHAT DOES MARKETING MEAN TODAY?

Marketing plays a critical role in modern business practice, where maximizing *shareholder value* is an increasingly important goal. The essence of marketing focuses on how firms attract, retain, and grow customers by enhancing relationships with them. Success in delivering *customer value* leads directly to improving shareholder value and long-run firm prosperity. In *Managing Marketing in the 21st Century*, we explore both the strategic aspects of marketing and the tactical implementation decisions marketers make every day. But first, we investigate two quite different but related meanings of marketing.

KEY IDEA

Marketing is a guiding philosophy for the firm as a whole.

MARKETING AS A PHILOSOPHY embraces the view that marketing is the guiding force or orientation for the entire organization. Firms with a marketing philosophy operate with an external orientation. Such firms focus their attention and resources *outside* the corporation — to acquire, retain, and grow customers — but take careful account of competitors and the broader external environment. By contrast, internally oriented firms focus largely on internal issues like products, services, and processes.[2] *Managing Marketing in the 21st Century* embraces the *marketing-as-philosophy* perspective. The author believes, and has seen in his own career, how powerful and effective a business can be when the entire organization is attuned to the external world. Such agile firms not only sense critical environmental factors but also adapt and change to address them.

In addition to the philosophical perspective, marketers must possess the tools and decision-making skills to get the marketing job done. Effective marketers focus attention on six marketing imperatives.

MARKETING IMPERATIVES describe the specifics of the marketing job. For executives with marketing and product-management titles, these marketing imperatives are the *must-dos* of marketing. We identify two groups:

---

1 STRATEGIC MARKETING

- *Imperative 1:* Determine and recommend which markets to address.
- *Imperative 2:* Identify and target market segments.
- *Imperative 3:* Set strategic direction and positioning.

---

2 IMPLEMENTING THE MARKET STRATEGY

- *Imperative 4:* Design the market offer.
- *Imperative 5:* Secure support from other functions.
- *Imperative 6:* Monitor and control execution and performance.

As a broader framework when thinking about markets and marketing, marketers must also consider the *four principles* of marketing. These principles should form the basis for marketing decision-making. They act as guidelines for executing the six imperatives. The four principles are:

- **Principle 1:** Selectivity and Concentration
- **Principle 2:** Customer Value
- **Principle 3:** Differential Advantage
- **Principle 4:** Integration

Chapter 1's discussion of these issues sets the stage for the entire book.

KEY IDEA

Marketing embraces six imperatives — the *must-dos* of marketing.

Four marketing principles guide execution of the six imperatives.

THE CHANGING VIEW

OLD WAY	NEW WAY
Accounting profit most important	Shareholder value critical
Core marketing job is the marketing mix	The marketing job encompasses six marketing imperatives
Customers a necessary evil	Customers are the firm's core assets
Firm must manage the status quo	Firm must manage change
Firm operates to suit managerial goals	Firm operates to deliver value to customers
Internal orientations acceptable	External orientation critical for success
Marketing department does the marketing	All firm employees have a marketing orientation
Marketing is one of the firm's functions	Marketing is a philosophy as well as a function
Organizational survival a major firm objective	Shareholder value the major firm objective
Seller power dominates	Customer power dominates
Shareholder value an issue for finance	Shareholder value an issue for marketing
Suppliers choose options	Customers choose options

MARKETING QUESTION

Choose two familiar firms, one that exemplifies the *old way* and one the *new way*. What criteria led you to identify these firms? Why?

THE MARKETING JOB

William Rosenberg, Dunkin' Donuts (DD) pioneering entrepreneur, had a very simple philosophy: "The boss is the customer." To find out how to make his customer "the boss," Rosenberg and his wife drove all around the country visiting every donut shop they could find. By implementing Rosenberg's philosophy, DD's franchise operates more than 10,000 outlets in over 30 countries and sells four million donuts and three million cups of coffee daily. Echoing Rosenberg, P&G CEO A.G. Lafley commented: "Everywhere I go, I try to hammer home the simple message that the consumer is boss."[3]

Target and Kmart are two of America's largest retailers. But while Target has grown successfully for many years, Kmart has struggled. Target understands and addresses customer needs in a compelling manner — Target has a cool brand, the right product mix, and excellent service. Target illustrates the essence of effective marketing.

MARKETING QUESTION

What marketing question would you like to ask your favorite CEO? How do you think the CEO would answer?

The popular press seems to confuse *marketing* with *advertising* and *sales*. Even many executives are unclear about marketing.[4] It seems so intuitive. Can't anybody be a marketer? Real people at real companies told us:

- "Marketing is just advertising."
- "Marketing is giving away T-shirts, products, and concert tickets to potential clients."
- "Marketing's job is to support our sales force."
- "Marketing is what consumers do at the supermarket on a Saturday morning."

These activities relate to the two broader meanings of marketing we just discussed — *marketing as a philosophy*, and *marketing as six imperatives* — but none really captures the true essence of marketing that we highlight in Figure 1.1.

FIGURE 1.1
The Fundamental Business Model

Because of its focus on customers, marketing is the firm's fundamental activity.[5] When marketing delivers *customer value* to satisfy customer needs, the firm *attracts, retains, and grows customers.*[6] If costs are in line, *profits* follow. Profits help the firm *survive* as an independent entity and secure resources to *grow*. Of course, if the firm does not earn profits consistently, it will go bankrupt. Survival and growth are the critical links between earning profits and enhancing *shareholder value* by increasing stock price.[7] Enhanced shareholder value makes funds available for renewed investment.[8] Apple delivers great customer value; Apple also delivers great shareholder value. **[770v]**

Marketing's role includes identifying opportunities, figuring out customer needs, understanding competition, developing appealing products/services, and communicating value to potential customers. When the firm does a good job of completing these tasks, shareholder value

MARKETING QUESTION

Pluto Inc. (fictional electronics firm) spends $100 million annually on research and development (R&D). Pluto management believes that eliminating all R&D will increase profits by $80 million in the current year. What would happen to Pluto's stock price? Why?

increases. Reread the Opening Case to see how Howard Schultz accomplished these tasks at Starbucks and the success he achieved. Well-known authors Michael Tracy and Fred Wiersema stated, "Creating shareholder wealth is not the purpose of the business; it is the reward for creating customer value."[9] And China's e-commerce leader's Alibaba CEO Jack Ma emphasized that customers come first and owners come last.[10]

Figure 1.1 also demonstrates the process for achieving the firm's goal of enhancing shareholder value, both for private firms with few shareholders and public firms with many. Growth and long-run profits are the means. Increasing profits in the short run is easy: Just reduce R&D, cut advertising, and fire half of the sales force — but such decisions typically lead to long-run problems. For forward-looking businesses seeking long-run profits, customers are the core assets. Of course, *competitors* seek these same customers. The competitive battle to attract, retain, and grow customers is central to all business activity.

The critical weapon in the battle for customers is straightforward in concept, but may be complex and difficult in execution. Quite simply, the firm must deliver to customers greater value than competitors. Customers reward firms that deliver greater value by purchasing their products/services, today and tomorrow. This *exchange* is the basis of all markets. Customers prefer the value inherent in the firm's products/services to their own money or other resources; conversely, the firm prefers customers' money or other resources to its own products/services.

In sum, when the firm delivers greater customer value than competitors, good things happen. But if customers perceive that competitors deliver greater value, ultimately the firm will perish. Just ask one of the more than 100,000 business that fail each year in the U.S. And don't just take the author's word for the power of this framework. Lou Gerstner, who led IBM's rejuvenation from a near-death experience, stated, "Everything starts with the customer."[11]

The late Peter Drucker, preeminent management theorist, is generally credited with developing the customer orientation and modern marketing perspective.[12] Drucker stated, "If we want to know what a business is, we have to start with its purpose. There is only one valid definition of business purpose — *to create a customer*. It is the customer who determines what a business is. For it is the customer, and he alone, who through being willing to pay for a good or service, converts economic resources into wealth, things into goods." Drucker added, "What the business thinks it produces is not of first importance — especially not to the future of the business and its success. What the customer thinks he is buying, what he considers *value* is decisive ... . Because it is [the purpose of a business] to create a customer, [the] business enterprise has two — and only these two — basic functions: marketing and innovation."

Furthermore, today's customers are the firm's core assets — attracting, retaining, and growing customers is critical to firm health.[13] But this task is ever more difficult. Competition is growing in depth and scope as the firm's environment becomes increasingly more complex and changes more quickly. Globalization, the rise of BRICI (Brazil, Russia, India, China, Indonesia) and other national economies, Internet-based and mobile solutions, and deep structural changes in the world economy are driving increased competition.[14] Many countries and industries are shifting from *scarcity of supply* to *scarcity of demand*. When supply is scarce, the firm's critical skill is production; when demand is scarce, the firm's critical skill is marketing.

Notwithstanding increased competition, today's customers are more aware and knowledgeable about competitive offers and prices, in part because of the Internet. Airline travelers can easily compare prices on Expedia, Travelocity, Orbitz, Kayak, and airline websites. Consumers in advanced affluent societies have ever-increasing options for discretionary products/services, like expensive clothes, iPhones, and European vacations. And intelligent agents — *bots* — may make buying decisions and shop for us.

Marketing encompasses a wide variety of activities the firm undertakes to attract, retain, and grow customers — of course, competitors are trying to do the same thing. If the firm is more successful than competitors in creating customer value, it will make profits, survive and grow, and enhance shareholder value.[15]

KEY IDEA

The firm's major task is to attract, retain, and grow customers by developing and delivering valued offers.

The firm enhances shareholder value by successfully attracting, retaining, and growing customers.

KEY IDEA

The firm has two basic functions:
• Marketing
• Innovation

KEY IDEA

Marketing is critical for firm success in today's increasingly complex and fast-changing environment.

MARKETING AND SHAREHOLDER VALUE

Electronic Accounting Systems (EAS) successfully sold payroll services to firms with 50 to 100 employees; customers filled in payroll sheets and EAS arranged courier pickup. But EAS could not serve smaller customers profitably. Former EAS employee Tom Golisano founded Paychex to target smaller businesses. Paychex prices were lower than EAS — partly because customers phoned in payroll information. Paychex also provided a payroll tax return service. Golisano became a billionaire and created significant value for Paychex shareholders.

Progressive identified a relationship between people's credit history and driving record, then used this insight to profitably insure customers rejected by mainstream insurers — mainly young drivers and those with poor driving records. Progressive is now a leading U.S. insurer; it has considerably enhanced shareholder value.

KEY IDEA

The shareholder-value perspective is increasingly widespread around the world.

The central focus on shareholder value is deeply rooted in many capitalist countries — particularly the U.S. The *shareholder-value perspective* defines management's job as maximizing returns for firm owners — its shareholders.[16] When this perspective dominates, government regulations tend to favor owners. Active shareholder opposition, CEO departures, and unfriendly takeover bids tend to occur when the firm underperforms in shareholder value.

The firm also has other *stakeholders*, like management, labor, and the public at large. In some countries, these stakeholders are more favored than shareholders. Regulations in these countries generally favor managers and protect them from unwelcome mergers and acquisitions. The stakeholder view is particularly popular in Asia, where many firms and politicians are ardent advocates of managerial power.

MARKETING QUESTION

Can you identify some firms that work especially hard to enhance shareholder value by focusing on creating customer value? Specifically, what do they do?

In recent years, developing global capital markets have favored the shareholder-value perspective. Conservative Japanese electronics giant Panasonic has share-repurchase plans, provides stock options for senior executives, and links manager salaries to stock market performance. In China, stock markets are now firmly established. The shareholder-value perspective is also having a significant impact on public companies in France, Italy, the Netherlands, and Germany. Restrictions on corporate acquisitions have diminished, and when new owners take control, significant corporate restructuring often occurs. Increased globalization will inevitably spread the shareholder-value perspective. Enhanced share ownership will give shareholders greater political power — both directly as individual investors, and indirectly via third-party investment vehicles like mutual funds.

Rheinmetall (RM), a family-controlled, Düsseldorf-based industrial conglomerate, had $4 billion revenues; but stock market value was only $300 million! A New York investment group purchased 7.8 percent ownership and demanded improved profits. Management took strategic action by shedding many peripheral businesses and making several global alliances for its three main divisions. Shareholder value increased significantly.

KEY IDEA

Customers are the sole source of firm revenues; relatedly, all firm activities are costs.

Customers are the firm's core assets, yet they do not appear on the balance sheet.

Some balance-sheet assets act as strategic liabilities.

Earlier, we asserted that customers are the firm's core assets. Traditionally, we find assets on the firm's balance sheet. Balance-sheet assets (current and fixed) include cash, accounts receivable, inventory, land, and plant and equipment — they do not include customers! Balance-sheet assets may be important, but none is absolutely crucial! The only critical asset the firm must secure is paying customers. Customers are the sole source of firm revenues; all firm activities are costs. Balance-sheet assets are assets only because they contribute to attracting, retaining, and growing customers.

But what if balance-sheet assets are not *assets*? What if they are really *strategic liabilities*? Consider the following: Firm A builds a factory to meet market demand for its *swish* product. Later, customers shift their preferences to *twish*. Firm A focuses efforts on trying to persuade customers that they really need *swish*. By contrast, competitors B and C each develop their own versions of *twish*. Firm A's factory investment constrains its actions — it fails to invest to meet customer needs for *twish*. The *swish* factory was not a real asset — it was a *strategic liability*. The retail book industry provides a good illustration. In the 1980s, Barnes & Noble (B&N) became the dominant U.S. bookseller using a bricks-and-mortar strategy. But as the Internet grew, B&N was slow to embrace purchasing books online. Seeing an opportunity, Jeff Bezos launched Amazon.com. Amazon is the premier online bookseller and has developed online businesses far beyond books. B&N eventually reacted, but its online book business is a distant second to Amazon.

The firm increases shareholder value only if incoming cash flows earn a return on investment at least equal to its *cost of capital* (the weighted average of the firm's cost of equity and debt).[17] When the firm fails to earn its cost of capital, it destroys shareholder value. Unfortunately, managers sometimes forget that the only source of firm cash flows (except new debt and equity) comes from attracting, retaining, and growing customers. Customers provide revenues and cash flow when they believe the firm's products/services offer better value than competitive alternatives.

KEY IDEA

Customers are the critical source of cash inflows.

Of course, the firm's strategy and operations must conform to a business model that allows it to earn its cost of capital.[18] Many Internet organizations do a good job of securing large numbers of customers but do not have such models.

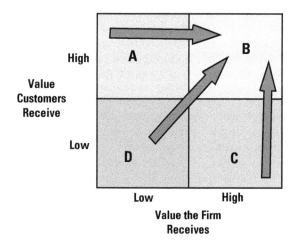

FIGURE 1.2
Value Customers Receive;
Value the Firm Receives

MARKETING QUESTION

LinkedIn is a publicly traded social networking firm. Who are LinkedIn's customers? What value does LinkedIn provide its customers? What value do customers provide LinkedIn's shareholders?

Figure 1.2 shows the relationship between the *value customers receive* from firm products/services, and the *value the firm receives* as revenues and profits. Cells B and D represent stable situations:

CELL B. Customers receive high value. The firm attracts, retains, and grows these customers — it also receives high value. The firm should continue to deliver significant customer value by innovating new products/services and enhancing its offers.

CELL D. Both customers and the firm receive low value. Perhaps firm resources are poorly matched to customer needs. Better alignment may shift the position to Cell B, but the firm may decide to focus attention on other customers.

The other two cells are essentially unstable positions:

CELL C. Customers receive low value but the firm receives high value, perhaps because of long-term relationships. Ultimately, competitors will offer greater value and customers will switch suppliers.

CELL A. Customers receive high value, but the firm receives low value. Perhaps prices are too low — the firm should convince customers of its value or possibly reduce service.

If customers believe competitors offer greater value they will simply take their business elsewhere. If the firm fails to deliver superior value, the firm will go out of business — by bankrupt-

KEY IDEA

Value has two sides:

• When the firm delivers high customer value, it attracts, retains, and grows customers.

• When the firm attracts, retains, and grows customers, it earns high value for shareholders.

cy, merger, or acquisition. Today, more than ever, customer value and shareholder value are closely intertwined. Increased acceptance of the shareholder-value perspective has raised the stakes considerably. Quite simply, if marketing does not perform consistently well, the firm should anticipate a bleak future.

MARKETING AS A PHILOSOPHY: EXTERNAL AND INTERNAL ORIENTATIONS

You just learned that the firm enhances shareholder value by attracting, retaining, and growing customers. At a *philosophical* level, then, each employee has some responsibility and marketing is *everybody's* business. At a personal level, because customers are the firm's only revenue source, they also pay everyone's salary! To quote Drucker again, "Marketing is so basic that it cannot be considered a separate function (i.e., a separate skill or work) within the business ... it is, first, a central dimension of the entire business. It is the whole business ... seen from the customer's point of view. Concern and responsibility for marketing must, therefore, permeate all areas of the enterprise."[19] More recently, David Haines, former brand czar of Vodafone (world's largest cell phone service provider) said: "Marketing is too important to be left to the marketers. It's the obligation of every single individual in the company, whether you're a phone operator, the CEO, or anyone else in the company."[20]

Marketing as a philosophy concerns the firm's entire *orientation*. A firm embracing marketing as a philosophy has an *external orientation*. Other firms focusing on internal business drivers have one of several *internal orientations*.

THE EXTERNAL ORIENTATION

Lou Gerstner described the IBM he inherited as CEO: "[IBM had a] ... general disinterest in customer needs, accompanied by a preoccupation with internal politics ... a bureaucratic infrastructure that defended turf instead of promoting collaboration, and a management class that presided rather than acted."[21] Gerstner described one of his key strategic decisions: "Drive all we did from the customer back, and turn IBM into a market-driven rather than an internally focused, process-driven enterprise"[22]

The externally oriented firm looks outward to the environment and knows that customers are central to its future — Gerstner really understood this aspect of marketing. Marketing is the *point person*[23] — and marketing must gain insight into customers, competitors, and broader environmental factors. The externally oriented firm knows that its current products, services, and processes are the reasons for past and present success. This firm also knows that as the external environment changes, its products, services, and processes must also change. The externally oriented firm does not fear change — it knows that change is inevitable and that new opportunities are its *lifeblood*. The externally oriented firm invests in new capabilities and competencies to exploit opportunities and create and serve customers. (Marketing Enrichment 1.1 [168p] for a measurement approach.)

In difficult economic times, when profits are under pressure, many firms cut spending and investment; the externally oriented firm invests. It may invest in human capital, increase the marketing budget, acquire weaker rivals, and/or cut prices. In recent recessions, several firms invested in customers and markets and swept past more internally oriented competitors[24]:

- Cisco invested in Asia as competitors were contracting. Within one year, Cisco had lead market share in many countries.

KEY IDEA

External and *internal* orientations are core concepts for examining the firm's basic philosophy.

KEY IDEA

An externally oriented firm goes beyond a customer focus. It works hard to understand competitors, markets, and environmental forces in general.

MARKETING ENRICHMENT 1.1

The C4I: Capon's Customer-Centric CEO Index **168p**

- Coca-Cola CEO Muhtar Kent said: "We don't cut marketing in this crisis around the world. We make sure our brands stay healthy and that we exit this tunnel with more market share than when we went in."[25]

- Intel maintained R&D and production spending. Said then Intel CEO Craig Barrett: "You never save your way out of a recession. The only way to get out of a recession stronger than when you went in is to have great new products."[26] Mobile phone chip maker Qualcomm similarly increased R&D spending, sometimes substantially.

- During the recession, Tata Consulting Services (India's largest IT services firm) restructured to develop a customer-centric organization, invested in customer relationships. and came out ahead.

- Said then Xerox CEO Anne Mulcahy, "Everywhere I went, lenders and investors were demanding I cut R&D spending. But Xerox innovation is sacred … investing in innovation was the best decision I ever made."[27]

Spending on Marketing — Investment or Expense?

A graduating Columbia MBA joined an FMCG firm. Her first job was to shepherd a new product from development to launch. The firm believed it had one year's lead time over competitors. As she developed her launch plan, the MBA realized the sales force was working at capacity. The new product would get insufficient attention and would not secure adequate retail distribution. Her innovative solution was to hire a temporary sales force. These salespeople would gain distribution; the regular sales force would later perform maintenance. Her financials showed a first-year loss, but then forecast profits rose steadily. She presented her launch plan to senior management.

Senior managers were unhappy about the first-year loss. But, by eliminating the temporary sales force and using the regular sales force, the financials worked. The firm launched on this basis. Unexpectedly, the first competitor entered after six months, and within one year, the firm had three competitors. Two years after launch, the firm exited the market.

MARKETING QUESTION

How did senior managers view the temporary sales force? Did they view these expenditures as an investment — returns expected in the future? Or, did they think of them as expenses — returns expected in the short term?

CEOs and top managers are generally responsible for establishing an external orientation as the overarching corporate thrust. Leaders of firms like Amazon, Google, P&G, and Starbucks understand; they really *get it*. Only a CEO like former Wachovia (now Wells Fargo) banker John Medlin can dismiss the *tyranny of the quarterly earnings statement* and say: "You've got to expect a down quarter from time to time."[28] Only a CEO like James Burke at Johnson & Johnson (J&J) can make customer concerns central to the firm. In the 1982 Tylenol cyanide-lacing crisis, J&J immediately withdrew Tylenol capsules until it developed fail-safe packaging. J&J's $250 million write-off demonstrated a long-term investment in customers, and Tylenol quickly returned to market leadership. [442v]

KEY IDEA

The firm should view marketing expenditures as *investments*, NOT as *expenses*.

Some of the world's most successful companies practice marketing as a philosophy. P&G spends $400 million annually seeking customer and market insight. A senior Pfizer executive asserted: "Our strong belief at Pfizer is that marketing is really an investment, not an expense. Our former CEO believed it was important to invest in R&D. He also believed it was equally important to invest in marketing. He said if you are best at both, there's no way you can be beat! We invest billions and billions of dollars in R&D to have better science and develop innovative products. But we have always had the leading industry investment in marketing. We parallel our R&D spending with a similar investment in research about markets and customers. What separates us from competitors is an assiduous pursuit of information, knowledge, and understanding of our customer."[29]

Table 1.1 (p. 13) shows general characteristics of internal and external orientations.[30]

TABLE 1.1
*General Characteristics of
Internal and External
Orientations*[31]

Dimension	Internal	External
Customer perspective	Transactional	Relational
Focus	Products	Customers and markets
Know-how	Inherent in patents, machinery	Inherent in people, processes
Measurement	Profit, margin, volume	Customer value, satisfaction, retention
Organizational philosophy	Bureaucracy	Adhocracy
Priorities	Efficiency and productivity	Flexibility and responsiveness
Process	Mass production	Mass customization

INTERNAL ORIENTATIONS

> Johnson & Johnson (J&J) pioneered the stent — a metal scaffold that holds open human arteries to allow blood flow. After two years, J&J enjoyed more than 90 percent market share and $1 billion revenues. Five years after entry, J&J's market share was 8 percent! What happened? Competitors responded to physicians' newfound needs for different sizes and materials; J&J ignored these concerns. J&J's internal orientation had a direct and negative impact on profits and shareholder value.

In a small and simply organized firm, the entrepreneur/sole proprietor (SP)/owner conducts most activities. The SP seeks and serves customers, arranges financing, performs operational functions, and manages payroll. At a visceral level, the SP knows that customers are critical assets and operates with an external orientation almost by instinct. Can you recall an occasion when your local garage, dry cleaner, hardware store, or other small business treated you personally as an important and valuable asset?

As firms grow, they seek efficiency through specialization and differentiation — operations, sales, product design, finance, legal, technology, and other functions have specific responsibilities. Typically, these functions develop their own missions, objectives, systems and processes, and business philosophies. Rather than working together to deliver customer value, they may pursue their own agendas, spurred by local cultural norms, and management systems that measure, motivate, and reward securing departmental objectives. Nonproductive differentiation that history and internal political rivalries exacerbate may trump customer focus.

Frequently, internal functions act in mutually inconsistent ways. The sales department tries to increase sales, but operations, working to produce acceptable-quality products at low cost, cuts down on product varieties; and R&D sees no reason to hurry the new product development process. Marketing wants to increase advertising spending, but finance reduces budgets to meet financial targets. These individual functions are often important strengths for the firm, but some, like accounting and R&D, are organizationally distant from customers. Focusing too heavily on one function versus another often leads to problems. The common denominator when firms operate in silos (stovepipes) is that delivering customer value often takes a back seat. These firms follow an *internal orientation*.

> A former Microsoft vice president described difficulties in securing in-house acceptance of ClearType, a broadly applicable, innovative way to display text on a screen that received much public praise, internal promotions, and patents. "It annoyed other Microsoft groups that felt threatened by our success. Engineers in the Windows group falsely claimed it made the display go haywire when certain colors were used. The head of Office Products said it was fuzzy and gave him headaches. The vice president for Pocket Devices was blunter: He'd support ClearType and use it, but only if I transferred the program and the programmers to his control."[32]

At internally oriented firms, you often hear the statement: "That's the way we do things around here." Regardless of changes in customer needs, competitor actions, and/or the external environment in general, the firm continues on its current course. Let's look at several internal orientations — operations, sales, finance, or technology.

Wholly owned by its growers, Zespri is New Zealand's sole kiwifruit exporter. Many Zespri customers requested fruit with higher proportions of pulp to liquid. But growers were highly reluctant to change agricultural practices to produce these products.

OPERATIONS ORIENTATION. The firm with an *operations orientation* typically focuses on reducing unit costs. There is nothing wrong with cutting costs — indeed, low costs allow firms to reduce prices and/or earn higher profit margins. Cutting costs is particularly important when customers are price sensitive, and/or competitors compete on price. But cost-cutting should not be a priority when the firm introduces new products or when product varieties, promotional effort, and/or short delivery times are crucial for attracting, retaining, and growing customers.

Problems occur when the firm fails to think through its cost-cutting program. Pruning the product line, taking design shortcuts, reducing customer service, curbing promotional spending, and/or lengthening delivery times typically reduce costs. But they do not deliver greater customer value — they may create dissatisfaction. Union Pacific Railroad employees met operating budgets by canceling cargo pickups and sending out trains with insufficient locomotive power! The plant manager at a leading cell phone supplier replaced a crucial part with a cheaper alternative; the phone failed.

KEY IDEA

Achieving long-run success can be difficult for internally oriented firms.

Internal orientations often focus on operations, sales, finance, and/or technology.

Nabisco developed a new corporate policy. Regardless of where Nabisco made and sold products, recipes, raw materials, process control, and quality standards were identical to the U.S. But in China, market conditions were very different. Nabisco did not focus on customer needs, made overly optimistic forecasts, had significant excess capacity, and suffered major losses. Said a spokesperson for competitor Danone: "I'm grateful to Nabisco. Their actions have strengthened our position!"[33]

SALES ORIENTATION. Increasing sales is a worthy objective. After all, sales revenues and cash flow are critical for enhancing shareholder value. The problem: Firms with a *sales orientation* focus on short-term sales. They are less concerned with profits and long-run customer relationships. They set prices too low and offer excessive discounts and/or too-favorable credit terms — and may create a perception of low quality. They spend little on marketing research and planning, target customers indiscriminately, offer too many products, and overinvest in finished-goods inventories. Taiwan-based Chi Mei was this sort of firm — but became very profitable by abandoning its sales orientation:

Chi Mei's Chairman Wu made a plant visit. In the warehouse, he found many acrylic sheets cut to various sizes — *excessive* attention to customer needs. Wu ordered the plant to refocus on four types of sheets, accounting for 70 percent of sales — and set premium prices for special sheet sizes. As production and inventory costs dropped, Chi Mei reduced prices. Market share and profits increased dramatically. Chi Mei is now one of the world's largest plastics producers.

MARKETING QUESTION

Interview an executive. Identify examples where functional silos hurt performance — and where different functions worked well together. Why did these different behaviors occur?

The sales-oriented firm places excessive effort on *getting customers to buy what the firm has to offer*; the externally oriented firm focuses on *getting the firm to offer what customers want to buy*.

FINANCE ORIENTATION. The firm with a *finance orientation* focuses too heavily on short-term profits. When a firm *manages by the numbers*, it tends to avoid expenditures with long-term payoff. The finance-oriented firm mortgages its future by indiscriminately cutting back on R&D, capital investment, marketing research, and/or advertising. Pricing focuses on short-term profits, and planning processes are weak or nonexistent. Sometimes a single-minded focus on short-term profits and cash flow is the right approach — if the firm consistently loses money or makes marginal profits. In other cases, the finance-oriented firm makes insufficient long-term invest-

Name some firms you believe are internally oriented; name some firms you believe are externally oriented. Why did you select these firms?

ments and is vulnerable to competitors. J&J's stents (p. 13) exemplifies a firm that focused on short-term profits and paid a heavy long-term price. Al Dunlap is another example:

> Scott Paper CEO "Chainsaw" Al Dunlap laid off 35,000 employees (11 percent of the workforce) and sold $3.5 billion assets. Return on investment and shareholder value increased. Kimberly-Clark purchased Scott Paper and Dunlap became CEO of small-appliance-manufacturer Sunbeam. Dunlap applied the same approach but major problems soon emerged. As Sunbeam's share price dropped precipitously, the board of directors fired Dunlap.[34]

TECHNOLOGY ORIENTATION. Sun Microsystems cofounder Bill Joy, often called the *Edison of the Internet*, said: "My own biggest mistake in the last 20 years was that sometimes I designed solutions for problems that people didn't yet know they had. That's why some of the things that could've made a difference couldn't find a market." A firm with a *technology orientation* focuses on R&D and pays little attention to customer value. Engineering and manufacturing make new product and facility decisions; marketing has little role in product development, and product planning is inadequate. The firm's products are often over-engineered; customers will not pay for unneeded features. First-class products are critical for attracting, retaining, and growing customers, but the firm's product development efforts must center on customer requirements. Panasonic learned this lesson:

> Panasonic engineers believed that lots of buttons and technical gadgets would add value to camcorders and increase market share. Sales stagnated; customers wanted easy-to-use products and manuals in everyday language. Philips had a similar orientation but conducted more than 200,000 customer interviews and refocused on what they wanted — sense and simplicity.

THE SIX MARKETING IMPERATIVES

The job of putting the marketing philosophy into practice normally falls to professionals with marketing and/or product-management titles. These people tend to engage in many marketing activities, like securing data on customers and competitors, developing advertising campaigns, designing direct-mail brochures, meeting with R&D on new products, devising online and mobile strategies, setting prices, and/or preparing persuasive messages for the sales force. Certainly these activities often enhance the firm's market position, but deciding how to allocate marketers' time and/or other resources requires answers to several questions:

- Which of these activities is critical?
- Do these activities represent the core elements of marketing?
- What critical tasks must the firm perform to truly accomplish its marketing agenda?
- In what order should the firm perform these tasks?

We now discuss the six marketing imperatives — the firm's *must-dos* — the core elements for *managing marketing in the 21st century*. The first three imperatives focus on *strategic marketing*; the remaining three imperatives zero in on *implementing the market strategy*.

The Six Marketing Imperatives

Strategic Marketing
- Imperative 1: Determine and recommend which markets to address.
- Imperative 2: Identify and target market segments.
- Imperative 3: Set strategic direction and positioning.

Implementing the Market Strategy
- Imperative 4: Design the market offer.
- Imperative 5: Secure support from other functions.
- Imperative 6: Monitor and control execution and performance.

STRATEGIC MARKETING — IMPERATIVE 1: DETERMINE AND RECOMMEND WHICH MARKETS TO ADDRESS

Until the start of the 21st century, the Japanese antidepressant market was untapped. To the Japanese, *depression (utsubyo)* was a bad word — a social stigma. Other pharmaceutical firms avoided Japan, but GlaxoSmithKline (GSK) saw a market opportunity. Using a consistent message, GSK changed the way Japanese thought about depression — "Does your soul have a cold *(Kokoro no Kaze)* ... depression is a disease that anyone can get. It can be cured by medicine. Early detection is important." For four years, 1,300 GSK salespeople visited selected doctors twice a week with this message. In three years, GSK's Paxil sales tripled — from \$108 million to \$298 million. GSK's message hit home — online bulletin boards had many conversations about depression.

KEY IDEA

Imperative 1: Marketing should identify market opportunities and advise top management on potential strategic actions.

Simply put, the firm must choose those markets in which to compete — as GSK chose the Japanese antidepressant market. To help make these choices, the firm should ask: What business(es) are we in? What business(es) do we want to be in? Market-choice decisions are typically strategic for the firm, or at least for individual business units. Choosing markets is often more important than choosing technologies and/or products. Given the choice of owning a market or owning a factory, most senior executives would prefer owning a market.

The firm must continually make market-choice decisions. Rapid environmental change opens up new market opportunities, but may also lead the firm to exit current markets. IBM has been successful in the information-technology services market — but exited PCs by divesting to China's Lenovo. Market-choice decisions can totally transform a corporation. Nokia exited its traditional paper-making, rubber-goods, and electric-cable markets as it evolved from a diversified conglomerate to global leadership in wireless communication, but failed in smartphones and sold its handset business to Microsoft.

The firm must decide where to invest — to compete or not — in various markets, and decide how much to invest. The firm must answer critical questions about its business and market portfolio:

- In which new businesses and markets shall we invest — people, time, dollars?
- In which current businesses and markets shall we continue to invest?
- How much investment shall we make in these various businesses and markets?
- From which businesses and markets shall we disinvest or withdraw?

Typically, marketing does not *make* these decisions. Top management has this responsibility but marketing must *provide good advice*. For Imperative 1, marketing plays two key roles:

- **Identify opportunities.** Marketing is the only function with explicit responsibility to focus attention externally on the market, customers, and competitors — outside the firm. Marketing personnel should research the environment to identify potential opportunities and bring these to top management's attention. They should also collect and analyze data that bear on entry decisions. Marketing should be intimately involved with the firm's current markets and businesses and advise on investment, disinvestment, and exit decisions. Incoming Philips' Healthcare CEO Deborah DiSantano said: "Our markets are going through dynamic change. Who should lead our transformation? It must be marketing. Marketers must know where their markets are going and where their customers are going, and then lead the rest of the organization."[35]

MARKETING QUESTION

In recent years P&G has divested many businesses and acquired several others. How do you assess P&G's choices regarding Marketing Imperative 1?

- **Advise on proposed strategic actions.** Many firm functions develop strategic initiatives. Finance may suggest acquisitions and divestitures; R&D may propose strategic alliances; and the sales force may champion a new distribution system. Marketing has the responsibility to insert itself into these decisions. The firm should fully explore the marketing ramifications of its decisions or disaster may ensue. Most observers believe the AOL/TimeWarner and Quaker/Snapple acquisitions were failures. Perhaps the acquirers would have made superior decisions with better marketing advice!

KEY IDEA

Imperative 2:

- Marketing must identify market segments — groups of customers with similar needs that value similar benefits, with similar levels of priority.

- The firm should target those market segments where it can best use its strengths and exploit competitor weaknesses.

STRATEGIC MARKETING — IMPERATIVE 2: IDENTIFY AND TARGET MARKET SEGMENTS

> Boeing purchased de Havilland Canada (DHC) to address the market segment for smaller, regional aircraft (under 20 to 90 seats). Boeing believed DHC's family of Dash 8 turbo-prop planes satisfied customer needs. During the following six years, Boeing lost nearly $1 billion on the DHC acquisition, then sold DHC to Bombardier. Potential customers for Dash 8 planes were new to Boeing, but Bombardier already operated in this segment. Bombardier tripled the Dash 8 family's turbo-prop market share to 35 percent — Dash 8 then accounted for two-thirds of regional planes sold worldwide.

In any *B2B* or *B2C* market, customers have a diverse set of needs. A single offer directed at the overall market may satisfy some customers, but typically many customers are dissatisfied. Imperative 2 states that marketing must identify *market segments* — groups of customers with similar needs that value similar benefits, with similar levels of priority.

When the firm does *market segmentation* well, the priority order of needs, benefits, and values that define one segment are quite different from the needs, benefits, and values that define other segments. Once the firm has identified market segments, it must decide which to target.

Note the two elements of Imperative 2: A *creative and analytic* part — identifying market segments; and a *decision-making* part — choosing which segments to target, based on the firm's ability to deliver customer value. The Dash 8 example demonstrates both elements quite clearly. Both Boeing and Bombardier did a good job of identifying the small, regional segment of the overall aircraft market. Bombardier had the appropriate skills and resources to target this market segment; Boeing did not. This lesson is important — a market segment may be attractive to one firm but unattractive to another.

Figure 1.3 illustrates segmentation and targeting by noting several segments, then showing a firm targeting a subset of those segments. Once top management has decided which markets to address — Imperative 1 — market segmentation and targeting is arguably the most critical marketing imperative. Effective segmentation and targeting drive profits.

FIGURE 1.3
Market Segmentation and Targeting

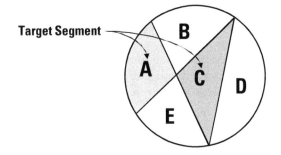

Target Segment

Note: The entire *pie* represents the population of existing and potential customers. Each *slice* or segment — A,B,C,D,E — reflects specific needs and required benefits of customers in that segment. Note that each segment may contain *subsegments*.

STRATEGIC MARKETING — IMPERATIVE 3: SET STRATEGIC DIRECTION AND POSITIONING

KEY IDEA

Imperative 3: Marketing should fix the firm's strategic direction and positioning. These decisions set the stage for designing the market offer.

> P&G's Gillette brand is the global leader in both men's and women's shaving markets. Gillette continually introduces higher-value products in advanced countries. In the U.S., Gillette offers Trac II, Atra, and Sensor brands (two blades), Mach3 and battery-operated M3Power (three blades), and Fusion and Fusion Power (five blades). In less-developed countries, Gillette offers double-edge blades, twin- and four-blade shaving systems, and disposable razors. **[296v]**

In Imperative 3, the firm decides how to compete in those market segments it has targeted. For each target segment, marketing must formulate performance objectives. These objectives guide the firm's strategic decisions in the target segments. Second, the firm must decide on its positioning for each segment. It must identify target customers and target competitors, design a more persuasive value proposition than competitors, and provide reasons for customers to believe the firm can deliver that value. Together with Imperative 2, positioning completes the critical STP triumvirate — **s**egmentation, **t**argeting, **p**ositioning.

Typically, individual market segments are at different developmental stages and hence require different approaches. The appropriate way to address a growing market segment is quite different from a mature or declining segment. Furthermore, decisions about strategic direction also include questions of branding — how the firm wants customers to view the corporate entity and its products. Top management increasingly views firm brands as major corporate assets; hence, *branding* issues are among its most important strategic decisions.

Of course, the firm does not make these decisions only once. It faces an ever-changing environmental landscape: Customer needs evolve and competitors enter, exit, and adopt different strategies. The firm's products also evolve as target segments grow, mature, and decline. The firm must continually assess its strategic direction and make necessary course corrections.

IMPLEMENTING THE MARKET STRATEGY — IMPERATIVE 4: DESIGN THE MARKET OFFER

KEY IDEA

As the 20th century wound down, Indian watch firm Titan introduced the Fastrack watch brand to appeal to youthful consumers. Success with watches led Titan to develop Fastrack into a youth fashion brand comprising many product lines — bags, belts, helmets, sunglasses, wallets, watches. Fastrack product designs, advertising, retail channels, and pricing are carefully chosen to appeal to the youth market. Indeed, Fastrack has opened more than 150 exclusive stores in major cities. Realizing that target consumers were active on social media, Fastrack was an early Indian user of Facebook and Twitter; Fastrack has a six-million-strong fan base. Youth icons like cricketer Virat Kohli and Bollywood actress Genelia D'Souza promote Fastrack products. Promotional campaigns appeal to Indian youth; they are provocative and designed to shock. Fastrack is Titan's fastest growing business: Revenues 2004–5 — ₹0.20 crore (approx. US$40,000); 2011–12 — ₹600 crore (approx. US$120 million). In 2013, Brand Equity ranked Fastrack as India's fourth *Most Exciting Brand*.

Imperative 4: The firm designs the market offer using the tools of the marketing mix:

- Product
- Promotion
- Distribution (Place)
- Price

Imperative 4 focuses on design of the *market offer*. The market offer is the total benefit package the firm provides customers. Tools for designing the offer are the best known part of marketing. If you took a previous marketing course, the professor probably spent significant time talking about the *marketing mix* — aka *4Ps*. The marketing mix is an important part of marketing, but note: The marketing mix represents just *one* out of *six* marketing imperatives. Marketing-mix elements comprise the basic building blocks of the firm's market offer:

- **Product.** In general, the product embodies the major benefits the firm offers to satisfy customer needs — these benefits provide value to customers. If the firm provides greater value than its competitors, customer purchases increase. Here we use the term *product* to embrace both physical products and intangible services — like airline travel, entertainment, and additional customer service. Hence, FedEx's core offering is overnight package delivery — but special handling, insurance, tracking, and other customer services are important competitive weapons.

- **Promotion.** Promotion embraces various ways the firm communicates with customers — informing and persuading them to purchase its products. Promotion includes *mass communications* like advertising, and sales promotions; *digital communications* like e-mail, blogs, search, advertising, social media, websites, and mobile marketing; and *personal communications* like the sales force. In addition to informing and persuading, communications may add customer value directly by providing imagery, status, and reassurance.[36]

MARKETING QUESTION

- **Distribution.** Distribution focuses on how and where customers secure the product. To conform to the 4Ps nomenclature, marketers sometimes refer to *distribution* as *place*.

- **Price.** Price is what customers pay. The firm establishes the feasible price by the equivalent amount of value it offers through its product, promotion, and distribution.

Identify three examples each of well-integrated and poorly-integrated market offers.

The Fastrack example shows interrelationships among marketing's design elements. When the firm offers significant benefits and high customer value from its product, communications, and distribution, it can set a high price. But if customer benefits and value are low, price must also be low. When the firm designs good market offers, customers purchase its products.

When the firm targets multiple market segments, it should design multiple offers. Toyota offers the Camry for one segment and the Lexus for a quite different segment. These cars have different physical designs and customers have different buying experiences. Even the type and location of dealerships is different. Customers receive different values and, accordingly, pay different prices. When targeting a market segment, the firm can combine marketing-mix elements in an infinite number of ways. Creativity, imagination, innovation, and capability are core ingredients.

Marketing and Other Functions: The Architect and the Builder

A useful metaphor for capturing functional roles in organizations is *architect* and *builder*. Marketing is the architect — designs the house. The other functions represent the builder — builds the house. Certainly, builders could build houses on their own but the architect provides significant design value. Similarly, in the firm, marketing *designs* the offer; other functions *implement* the offer.

IMPLEMENTING THE MARKET STRATEGY — IMPERATIVE 5: SECURE SUPPORT FROM OTHER FUNCTIONS

Integrating across firm functions is a critical organizational competence at Valeo, a major French car-parts manufacturer. Said a senior executive, "Customers expect seamless delivery, and they don't care how we're organized. We have to work as a team and forget our internal battles." Valeo bases its organization on seven principal *domains* — broad product areas that have separate functions inside a car.[37]

KEY IDEA

Imperative 5:
- Marketing must keep the firm focused on customer needs, regardless of current feasibility.
- Marketing must exercise leadership to encourage cooperation across multiple functions.

Imperatives 1, 2, 3, and 4 concern *where* and *how* questions. Imperatives 1, 2, and 3 focus on *where* the firm will place its resources. Imperative 4 concerns *how* the firm will use its resources to design the market offer. Imperative 5 focuses on how firm functions work together to ensure the firm executes the market offer as designed. **[292v]** Marketing requires two very different types of support:

- **Support for design** — relates to technical, operational, and economic feasibility.
- **Support for implementation** — assumes the design is agreed upon and fixed.

SUPPORT FOR DESIGN. Imperative 4 focuses on designing the market offer that best meets customer needs in a target segment. The firm's ability to deliver the market offer depends on its capabilities and resources. The *best* design for customers may require a product feature the firm cannot make. When the best design is not feasible, marketing must develop extraordinary strength to keep the firm focused on satisfying customer needs — and push specific functions to evolve their capabilities.[38] In the face of short-run pressures for a less demanding route, marketing must commit to this long-run task.

Pete Swenson, new product head at leading industrial floor cleaner Tennant, developed a new carpet scrubber using innovative cleaning technology. A major customer and four senior executives including Swenson's boss told him to kill the project. Swenson persevered and ReadySpace became Tennant's best-selling carpet cleaner.

SUPPORT FOR IMPLEMENTATION. We often call this support *internal marketing*, or getting *buy-in*. In many firms, marketing designs the offer — but has little authority to implement the design. Marketers must possess the leadership and interpersonal skills to encourage and stimulate cooperation across multiple functions. After all, *the chain is only as strong as its weakest link*. If a key function does not perform, other functions may waste their efforts.

We should not underestimate the importance of Imperative 5. Many firms suffer from inter-departmental strife and rivalry driven by *silo thinking*. Destructive internal conflicts siphon off precious management time the firm could spend addressing external opportunities and threats. Some firms address the *silo* problem head-on by forming cross-functional teams — like marketing, operations, and R&D. Others redesign their organizations. At GE, CEO Jack Welch introduced the *boundaryless* organization, and *boundarylessness* became a core value.[39] Most approaches use some form of team-based evaluation to encourage cooperation.

IMPLEMENTING THE MARKET STRATEGY — IMPERATIVE 6: MONITOR AND CONTROL EXECUTION AND PERFORMANCE

> Pfizer has a strong reputation for optimizing spending on the marketing mix. Pfizer continually tests different budgets for selling effort and advertising and promotion. Said a senior Pfizer executive: "We're measurement-intense. So *metrics are us*. We believe in it. We measure everything. That is the root of our business."[40]

KEY IDEA

Imperative 6: Marketing must monitor and control firm actions and performance to keep on track.

It's one thing to plan and implement, but figuring out firm performance is quite another. Imperative 6 focuses on *monitor and control* of marketing programs. Is the firm achieving its desired results? All things equal, if the firm is successful, it should keep on truckin'; otherwise, it should make changes.

Essentially, marketing should continually secure answers to three questions and act accordingly:
- Are the firm's various functions and departments *implementing* the market offer?
- Are the firm's market and financial *performance* reaching planned objectives?
- Based on the current *environment*, are firm objectives, strategies, and implementation plans on track, or should it make changes?

IMPLEMENTATION. The firm may have many implementation problems, like lack of buy-in — Imperative 5. But even with excellent buy-in, antiquated or inappropriate management systems create implementation difficulties. For example, if the firm sets unrealistic sales force objectives, salespeople may be unmotivated and lack effort. Ratchet-based compensation systems — success in one year leads automatically to higher sales targets for the following year — are a prime example. In mature and declining markets, ratchet-based systems generate significant dissatisfaction, low motivation, and employee resignations.

MARKETING QUESTION

How well has Google implemented the six marketing imperatives?

POOR PERFORMANCE. If the firm is not achieving market and/or financial performance objectives, marketing may require more data and further analysis. If environmental change is low, marketing should focus on course corrections by fine-tuning its strategy and/or modifying implementation plans.

ENVIRONMENTAL CHANGE. The firm bases objectives, strategy, and implementation on its best insight into customer needs, competitive offers, and the external environment. A good strategy should accommodate evolutionary changes — more significant change may require new objectives and strategies.

THE FOUR PRINCIPLES OF MARKETING

You just learned that six imperatives are the *must-dos* of marketing. Four marketing principles serve as guidelines for implementing these imperatives:

The Four Principles of Marketing
- Principle 1: Selectivity and Concentration
- Principle 2: Customer Value
- Principle 3: Differential Advantage
- Principle 4: Integration

KEY IDEA

Principle 1: Selectivity and Concentration

- *Selectivity.* Marketing must carefully choose targets for firm efforts.
- *Concentration.* The firm should concentrate resources against those targets.

PRINCIPLE 1: SELECTIVITY AND CONCENTRATION

Retail stockbroker Edward D. Jones consistently earns among the highest financial returns in its industry. Jones has successfully expanded its geographic focus from rural and small-town America to most major U.S., Canadian, and British cities. Jones' approach remains consistent — a focus on customers who want personal service. Jones has expanded, while being *selective and concentrating* its resources.

Providing advice on market selection — Imperative 1 — and deciding which market segments to target — Imperative 2 — are among marketing's primary responsibilities. The basic principle underlying these imperatives is the *Principle of Selectivity and Concentration.*[41]

Two aspects comprise the Selectivity and Concentration principle:

- **Selectivity.** Marketing must carefully choose targets for firm efforts.
- **Concentration.** The firm should concentrate resources against those targets.

This principle is about choosing the firm's battles. It is dangerous to dissipate limited resources over too many alternatives by trying to do too much. No organization, no matter how large or how successful, has infinite resources. Each must make timely choices. The selectivity element comes into play when marketing recommends which markets to target — Imperative 1, but the best-known manifestation is identifying and targeting market segments — Imperative 2. Market segmentation is a fundamental topic in marketing, but we repeat the distinction between two related, but quite different, issues:

- **Market segmentation process.** The firm divides the market into groups of customers — segments. In each segment, customers have similar needs and value similar benefits with similar levels of priority.
- **Targeting market segments.** Good segmentation only *allows* for better strategic decisions; it does not guarantee them — *selectivity* is crucial. Which segment(s) should the firm select for effort? Which should it *target?*[42] The firm that skillfully implements this principle probes selected segment(s) in greater depth and uncovers hidden opportunities.

Small firms that concentrate their slender resources on specific market segments often gain leverage over larger competitors, like eBay and Google did in their early years. Small firms concentrate their limited resources by default. Large firms have greater resources but often spread themselves too thin because they have difficulty concentrating.

Of course, concentration involves risk. When the firm concentrates resources on some opportunities, it forgoes others.[43] The firm will fail with some chosen options — and options it does not choose will be successful for others. Get used to it: As a marketer, you are a gambler. You make bets on markets and segments — your reward is market share and profits. Gamblers in Atlantic City, Macau, Monte Carlo, and Las Vegas play against an impersonal house and win only by chance. You play against living, breathing, unpredictable competitors and shift the odds in your favor by practicing your marketing craft well.

As markets become increasingly competitive, hedging bets by allocating small amounts of resources to a broad set of options will certainly fail. For this reason, some experts relabel this principle *Concentration and Concession.* Not only must the firm concentrate its resources in chosen segments, it should affirmatively concede other segments to competitors:

Samsung is a highly successful electronics firm — it ruthlessly practices selectivity and concentration. Said a senior marketing executive: "We had an explicit strategy to get out of low-end commodity-oriented channels. We actually withdrew from places like Walmart and Kmart, even though these were a big source of revenues. Instead, we focused on channels like Best Buy, Sears, and several regional electronics specialists. We establish deep relationships with our true value-added channel partners. This focus provides us direct benefits from our marketing."[44]

PRINCIPLE 2: CUSTOMER VALUE

KEY IDEA

In its ongoing battles with HP (now HP Inc.) and Lenovo, Dell focuses on delivering high levels of customer value. Said a senior marketing executive, "We're very centered on truly understanding customer behavior and having a deep level of customer insights. We use those insights and customer access to align the entire organization. We're really the only major player with a totally seamless link from the customer back to the component manufacturer, so we're the best placed to really deliver customer value. We have a knowledge base that enables us to meet customer needs better than anyone else. At the highest level, we understand what customers want. We tailor our product offerings and our suppliers' product offerings to what customers want. We have a pretty tight set of feedback loops. Our account executives talk to customers regularly and feed that back. Our Platinum Council (Customer Advisory Board) of our best customers meets periodically and looks at our forward-looking product roadmaps. The members give us feedback on whether these product development plans are geared to their needs. In a very real sense, the Council is part of a virtual product development organization — they really shape our priorities at a fairly early stage and enable us to ratchet up our ability to deliver customer value."[45] **[629v]**

Principle 2: Customer Value

- The firms earns success by providing value to customers.
- The firm develops, produces, and delivers products/services, but customers perceive value only in the benefits these products/services provide.

According to the *Principle of Customer Value*, marketplace success depends on providing value to customers. This principle is central to marketing's job. Customer insight should drive the design and implementation of market offers. Customer value should drive the firm's product and investment decisions — and performance evaluations. The firm develops, produces, and delivers products/services, but customers perceive value only in the benefits these products/services provide. To be very clear: Customers *do not want* the firm's products; they only want *the value* those products deliver. Repeat: Customers do not want the firm's products; they only want the value those products deliver.

Customer value is a moving target. As the environment changes, customers accumulate experience; their needs and the values they seek evolve also. World-class companies continuously invest in marketing research to probe deeply into customer needs, priorities, expectations, and experiences. They feed these results into the product development process to produce greater value for customers.

Cisco continues to be the market-share leader and a major force in technology and networking. Said an important Wall Street analyst: "They [Cisco] don't have the best technology, but they do have the best [customer] relationships."[46] Firms that take their eye off the *customer ball* can get into serious trouble. Sears and Kmart (U.S.) and Sainsbury's and Marks & Spencer (Great Britain) were once powerful and successful retailers. In recent years, each has been in crisis.

We reinforce the point by adapting from U.S. presidential politics: "It's the customer, stupid!"[47]

PRINCIPLE 3: DIFFERENTIAL ADVANTAGE

KEY IDEA

A senior executive explained ExxonMobil's efforts to secure differential advantage. "We woke up and realized that people didn't care about our product. The government wrote standards for fuel specification, so the consumer said 'hey, fuel is fuel.' We started to think, not about the product, but about people's experience. All of our research around the world confirmed the same thing. It's a mobile society, everybody's in a rush. We moved from being auto-centric — we're here to serve the car, tires, batteries, and fan belts — to driver-centric — we'll give you gas and fuel, but also clean restrooms, telephones, the things you need to enhance your life on the move. Our convenience stores were the same as competitors', nice designs and colors — everything inside is great, but it's a box. The stuff we sell is the same. What we bring to the party is location — we make it convenient and give you the right experience. If you just want gasoline and are in a hurry, use your speed pass, pay at the pump, get in, and get out. If you want to get out of traffic for a minute, or feel like a cup of coffee, need a restroom, then we welcome you inside. We will take as good care of you inside the store as when you are outside."[48]

Principle 3: Differential Advantage

For the firm to secure differential advantage, customers must perceive greater value in the firm's offer than in competitor offers.

The *Principle of Differential Advantage* is closely related to the Principle of Customer Value. **[164v]** Differential advantage is similar to having *competitive advantage, unique selling proposition*, or *edge*. Differential advantage lies at the heart of every successful market strategy. The Principle of Differential Advantage asserts that the firm should offer customers something they value but cannot get elsewhere.

More formally, *a differential advantage is a net benefit or cluster of benefits, offered to a sizable group of customers, which they value and are willing to pay for but cannot get, or believe they cannot get, elsewhere.* To implement this principle, the firm must develop well-designed market offers based on the marketing-mix elements we discussed earlier. This principle leads to several implications:

MARKETING QUESTION

Groupon and OpenTable each target restaurants. Suppose you were able to invest $5,000 in either Groupon or OpenTable. Which would you choose? Why?

- **Competition.** The principle emphasizes competition. Offering customer value is not enough. To avoid competitive parity, the firm must offer greater value than competitors. The firm must create and re-create its differential advantage to beat competitors. As former GE CEO Jack Welch said: "If you don't have a competitive advantage, don't compete."

- **Superiority of differential advantages.** Some differential advantages are better than others. A differential advantage based on proprietary intellectual property (IP), unique product design, or product availability may be more sustainable than one based on communications. A differential advantage based on an organizational process like parts delivery or qualified technicians may be even more sustainable.[49] But in an increasingly complex, competitive, and changing world, the firm's true differential advantage may belong in a meta-level adaptive ability to create a series of differential advantages over time.[50]

- **Eroding differential advantages.** Competition will eventually erode away even the apparently most sustainable differential advantage.[51] Motorola had a 2004 hit with the superthin RAZR phone but lost market share when it failed to produce a follow-up advantage. (Later, Google, then Lenovo, acquired Motorola.) Maintaining differential advantage is marketing's most fundamental challenge; the search for differential advantage must be continuous and ongoing. Ideally, the firm should have a hidden differential advantage, ready to trump the competitor's ace!

- **Cannibalizing a differential advantage.** To stay ahead of competition, the firm must be willing to cannibalize its own offers. Many firms will not do so, in part because of strong political constituencies for the status quo, and in part because profit margins may be lower. Adhering to the sentiment *If it ain't broke, don't fix it* runs the risk of missing opportunities and passing market initiative to a competitor.[52]

- **Differential advantage and difference.** A *differential advantage* is not the same as a *difference*. To develop a different market offer may not be difficult. But the firm's differences must create benefits that customers recognize, value, and are willing to pay for.[53]

PRINCIPLE 4: INTEGRATION

KEY IDEA

Principle 4: Integration
- The firm must carefully integrate all elements in the design and execution of its market offer.
- To achieve integration at the customer, the firm must coordinate and integrate internal functional activities.

Integration is critical to Target's success. "Every one of us, in every functional group, from Stores to Merchandising, from Logistics to Support, identifies with the role as marketing. We're all attempting to build better relationships with our guest (Target's term for customer). And every decision starts with the guest, so everyone becomes a marketer. We instill that attitude with evangelical passion and great consistency — the evangelizing starts at the top with our Chairman and CEO. Our core brand promise since 1962 has been *Expect more, pay less.* We live it — every single function of this company lives it. We search the globe for the best products to serve our guest needs and everyone in the store is hard-wired to meet guest expectations at all times."[54]

The *Principle of Integration* — critical for all marketing efforts — has two dimensions:

- **At the customer.** The firm must carefully integrate and coordinate all design and execution elements it offers customers. Poor advertising can ruin an excellent product; delayed promotional materials can doom a product launch; and improper pricing can cause havoc with sales forecasts. *New York Magazine* designed a new-subscriber promotion — offer free magazines for six weeks and then follow with a subscription request. Unfortunately, the subscription request arrived before the first free magazine!

- **In the firm.** To achieve integration at the customer, the firm must carefully integrate and co-ordinate all internal functional activities — this can be difficult. Different functions and/or departments may squabble over priorities or senior management may send ambiguous messages. A senior executive at a well-known multinational described the situation to his incoming superior: "There have been too many years of business units versus corporate; too many years of control versus trust; too many years of operating in silos; too many years of manipulating the facts to serve personal interests; and too many years of defending internal turf at the expense of market share and position."[55]

Examples of insufficient integration are legion. Consider the following dialogue, involving the author, at an in-house seminar for a major U.S. computer firm. During the presentation, a participant asked several questions about sales forecasting. The following exchange occurred:

AUTHOR: "How come you're so interested in sales forecasting?"

PARTICIPANT: "Well, I have a sales forecasting department, and since you were here, I thought I might learn something."

AUTHOR: "That's fine, but tell me, what's your position in the firm?"

PARTICIPANT: I'm the production director."

AUTHOR: "Oh! That's a little unusual. I'd have thought the sales forecasting department might have been in marketing, or in sales."

PARTICIPANT: "Sure, they have one too. But we can't believe a word they say, so we have to have our own."

Or consider this scenario in a major electronics firm: Business unit (A) shared salespeople with sister business unit (B). But senior managers in business unit (B) would not allow these salespeople or their managers to attend business unit (A)'s annual strategy conference!

Firms with an external orientation are more likely to achieve integration because the shared value of serving customers promotes a common purpose. Sharing responsibility for designing and implementing market offers drives agreement on priorities, together with close and cooperative working relationships.

MARKETING QUESTION

Apple's success has made it one of the world's most admired and most valuable firms. How do you assess Apple's adherence to the four marketing principles?

KEY MESSAGES

- Firms that deliver greater customer value than competitors are more successful in attracting, retaining, and growing customers.
- Firms that successfully attract, retain, and grow customers earn profits. They are more likely to survive and grow, and enhance shareholder value.
- Value has two sides. When firms deliver customer value, they attract, retain, and grow customers. When firms attract, retain, and grow customers, they create shareholder value.
- Marketing as a philosophy embraces an external orientation — all organizational members have a responsibility for delivering customer value.
- Six marketing imperatives are *must-dos* for the firm.
- Four marketing principles provide the guiding framework within which the firm implements the six marketing imperatives.

MARKETING QUESTION

What other messages did you glean from this chapter?

VIDEOS AND AUDIOS
For complimentary material, see Axcess Capon codes at www.axcessvids.com

Marketing Careers	**402v**	Ellen	Columbia Business School
Pharmaceutical Marketing	**588v**	Robert Essner	Wyeth; Columbia Business School
The Role of Marketing	**771a**	Noel Capon	Columbia Business School
The Externally Oriented Firm	**263a**	Noel Capon	Columbia Business School
Four Marketing Principles	**971a**	Noel Capon	Columbia Business School

QUESTIONS FOR STUDY AND DISCUSSION

Can you answer the questions implied by this chapter's learning outcomes? Check!

1. Select a well-known FMCG firm. From its financial statements, identify the book value of its assets. Identify the firm's market value based on its stock price. Is there a difference? What accounts for this difference? Do these findings change the way you think about marketing's role in delivering value?

2. The chapter describes how Barnes & Noble's balance-sheet assets became strategic liabilities. Describe another example. What was the outcome? What would you have done differently? Would it have been easy to implement your decisions? Why or why not? How would your decisions have affected firm employees? Can you identify firms facing similar challenges?

3. Does your school approach the market for new students in a systematic way? How could it use the six marketing imperatives to improve performance?

4. Identify a successful local merchant. Use the six marketing imperatives to explain its success.

5. Why did Kmart decline? Which marketing principle(s) did it neglect? What would you have done differently? How do you assess Kmart's merger with Sears? Compare Kmart's performance with Target's — what accounts for the performance differences?

6. How has the Internet and mobile marketing affected marketing practice?

7. Describe the challenges and opportunities that marketing faces in your school or firm.

TRUE/FALSE QUESTIONS
Answers on page A1 and at www.axcessvids.com — 509p

1. The firm only increases shareholder value if its incoming cash flows earn a return on investment at least equal to its cost of capital. ❑ **TRUE** ❑ **FALSE**

2. Firms with a sales orientation focus on short-term sales volume and are less concerned with profits and long-run customer relationships. ❑ **TRUE** ❑ **FALSE**

3. A firm with a finance orientation focuses on research, development, and engineering. ❑ **TRUE** ❑ **FALSE**

4. The market offer is the total benefit package the firm provides to its customers. ❑ **TRUE** ❑ **FALSE**

5. Firms with an internal orientation are more likely to achieve integration because the shared value of serving customers promotes a common purpose. ❑ **TRUE** ❑ **FALSE**

MULTIPLE CHOICE QUESTIONS

Answers on page A1 and at www.axcessvids.com — 947p

1. All of the following represent critical questions required to be answered about a firm's business and market portfolio for Imperative 1 EXCEPT:

   a. In which businesses and markets shall we invest?
   b. From which businesses and markets shall we withdraw?
   c. Is the firm's market and financial performance reaching planned objectives?
   d. In which current businesses and markets shall we continue to invest?

2. The firm with a(n) _____ is typically less concerned with profits and long-run customer relationships.

   a. sales orientation
   b. operations orientation
   c. finance orientation
   d. technology orientation

3. Which of the following is NOT one of the marketing-mix elements that comprise the basic building blocks of a firm's offer?

   a. product
   b. promotion
   c. position
   d. price

4. Which of the following four Principles of Marketing emphasizes competition?

   a. The Principle of Selectivity and Concentration
   b. The Principle of Customer Value
   c. The Principle of Differential Advantage
   d. The Principle of Integration

CHAPTER 2

THE VALUE OF CUSTOMERS

For complimentary material, see Axcess Capon codes at www.axcessvids.com

Success is getting the right customers ... and keeping them.

— Charles Cawley, founder of credit card giant MBNA

LEARNING OUTCOMES

When you have completed this chapter, you will be able to:

- Identify the critical elements that define customer lifetime value.
- Calculate customer profitability and customer lifetime value.
- Recognize the importance of investing in, and retaining, the *right* customers.
- Relate delivering customer value to generating long-term customer loyalty.
- Explain the importance of measuring customer profitability.
- Make tough decisions on dealing with unprofitable current customers.
- Make tough decisions about accepting/rejecting potential customers.
- Establish a customer relationship management program.
- Design customer loyalty programs.

OPENING CASE: ROYAL BANK OF CANADA

Toronto-based Royal Bank of Canada (RBC) has 78,000 employees, and serves more than 18 million personal, business, and public-sector customers via offices in North America and 38 other countries. RBC is Canada's leading bank. What sets RBC apart from competitors is its focus on customer profitability. In RBC's retail business, 17 percent of customers account for 93 percent of profits — an extreme version of the 80/20 rule — 93/17. RBC concentrates on this 17 percent and discourages, or even discards, its least profitable and loss-making customers.

RBC calculates economic profit by customer.[1] Identifying revenues, product profit margins (spreads), and invested capital is easy. RBC tracks labor costs via activity-based costing. RBC monitors costs for back office processing, call centers, serving customers through various channels, and other activities. RBC calculates labor costs per customer, based on product portfolios and monthly transactions.

Because RBC knows which customers earn it economic profit (loss), it can take actions other firms cannot. RBC determines the shareholder value each individual customer or segment creates. RBC also calculates an intrinsic price/earnings (P/E) multiple and compares this P/E ratio to the market average. Golden *customer segments — higher than average P/E ratios — are profitable investment opportunities. RBC rationalizes, closes, or sells off customer segments with low P/E ratios.*

RBC's retail bank has nine customer segment managers and many product managers. Each segment and product manager has individual and primary responsibility for strategy and profit and loss (P&L) for their segment/product. They compete with functional managers — marketing, human resources, facilities — for bank resources. This matrix organization encourages collaboration; it works because RBC's culture is customer-centric and consensus driven. Also, senior management has clearly signaled that managing for team success is important for career advancement.

RBC'S NEW APPROACH. *RBC traditionally ran mortgage promotions in the spring home-buying season, emphasizing RBC's rates. Competitor banks operated similarly. But RBC's builders and borrowers segment leader pursued a different approach — RBC targeted the* life event *of a first home purchase. RBC created a value proposition to serve the total needs of first-time home buyers, and add significant value for shareholders:*

- *First-time home buyers have most of their financial lives ahead of them. Attracting these customers promises long-term banking relationships, with significant growth prospects.*

- *On average, first-time home buyers borrow larger amounts for longer terms than other buyers and are less sensitive to rates. They promise larger investment opportunities, longer-term relationships, and higher returns on invested capital than other customers.*

RBC distributed (direct mail and e-mail) a freestanding newspaper insert — First Time Home Buyers' Guide *— full of information and expert advice. RBC's offer included the mortgage, a $500 savings deposit, and a free financial review (annually for the first five years). Customers also received six months free online banking, one year free Internet service, and a no-fee Visa card.*

RBC's product-centric organization could not have executed this promotion; the promotion required coordination among managers responsible for mortgages, savings accounts, financial advice, and marketing. The segment leader was a powerful catalyst, stating: "Looking through the customer lens," the promotional ideas "jump right out at you."

RBC's customer-focused strategy delivered impressive results: First-time-mortgage share grew significantly, particularly in the longest, most profitable (for RBC) terms. By 2014, RBC revenues were $37 billion; net income was $8 billion; stock price reached $70. Each result represented at least a fivefold increase in the prior two decades.

Case Question

What challenges do firms face in securing customer-focused data and implementing customer-focused strategies like RBC?

KEY IDEA

When the firm creates value for customers, it successfully attracts, retains, and grows those customers.

By being attracted, retained, and grown, customers create value for the firm and its shareholders.

KEY IDEA

Customer lifetime value (CLV) is the crucial link between:

- Delivering value to customers
- Creating value for shareholders

Chapter 1 discusses the critical role customers play for firm well-being. By attracting, retaining, and growing customers, the firm makes profits today and promises profits tomorrow. Profits allow the firm to survive and grow, and enhance shareholder value. Because of these relationships, customers are the firm's core assets. More precisely, customers are core assets because of two sides of the value concept. When the firm creates value for customers, it successfully attracts, retains, and grows those customers. By being attracted, retained, and grown, customers create value for the firm and its shareholders.[2]

A retained customer returns to buy more products/services. If your local coffee shop provides good value, like a tasty cup of coffee and a fresh snack for a reasonable price, you will keep going back, morning after morning, and you will probably tell your friends. The value you bring to the coffee shop is more than just one morning's purchases. You make a stream of purchases because the coffee shop gives you value. By delivering customer value, the firm generates customer loyalty, either from positive attitudes or from habit. This relationship applies to all customers regardless of product — automobiles, credit cards, haircuts, jet engines, or TVs.

The first part of this chapter moves beyond the customers-as-assets concept to *measure* the value customers bring to the firm. The critical concept is *customer lifetime value* (CLV) — what the customer is worth. CLV is the discounted future stream of profits the customer will generate over the life of its relationship with the firm. CLV is the crucial link between the value the firm delivers to customers and the value customers deliver to the firm. Increasing CLV enhances shareholder value. This chapter shows how to use CLV to increase the value customers bring to the firm — both current customers and potential new customers. This chapter also identifies the right customers and shows that some customers are undesirable.

Specifically, we address two questions:

- How can we put a monetary value on the firm's current customers, and on potential customers it may acquire? This monetary value is CLV.
- How can we use the CLV concept to help the firm enhance shareholder value?

In the second part of this chapter, we examine practical ways of using CLV to bind customers closer to the firm. Specifically, we address customer relationship management (CRM) and customer loyalty.

THE CHANGING VIEW

OLD WAY	NEW WAY
Accept that some customers are difficult to address	Strive to give customers consistently good experiences
Acquiring customers is critical	Retaining and growing profitable customers and acquiring new customers are critical
Customer databases nonexistent	Customer databases pivotal
The firm manages products	The firm manages customers
The firm should attract, retain, and grow all customers	The firm should *fire* some current customers and be selective in acquiring new customers
Fragmented information on customers	Sophisticated CRM systems and data mining
Measure product profitability	Measure customer profitability and customer lifetime value
Plant and equipment are the firm's core assets	Customers are the firm's core assets
Product profitability drives incentive systems	Customer profitability drives incentive systems
Product and sales territory considerations dominate resource allocation	Customer and customer segment considerations dominate resource allocation
Products at the heart of firm decision-making	Customers at the heart of firm decision-making
Zero or negative reward for customer loyalty	Customer loyalty incentives very common

Why Customers Are So Important for the Firm

CUSTOMER LIFETIME VALUE (CLV)

> Several local, regional, and national electronics retail chains have suffered, giving manufacturers like Sony serious problems — a long-term customer could go out of business. Sony uses CLV to decide whether, and how much, to invest in a troubled retailer. Said a senior Sony executive: "We sometimes invest in these customers to try to help them stay healthy. We actually hire outside consultants to work with them on process reengineering. We're working on advertising productivity. We're working on supply-chain management. If we invest and that customer somehow turns, we're not going to take credit for it, but we certainly didn't help them go down."[3]

When customers purchase firm products/services, the firm earns sales revenues; it also accrues costs. If sales revenues are greater than costs, the firm earns profits. The profit earned from an individual customer during a single time period (year) is the *profit margin* — the annual value the customer brings to the firm.[4]

Of course, many customers — consumers (B2C), partners, distributors, resellers (B2B) — purchase the firm's products for several successive years. Each year, the firm receives sales revenues, accrues costs, and earns a profit margin. CLV takes into account profit margins the firm earns in each of these years by using a *discount rate*.[5] Pharmaceutical firms traditionally focused sales efforts on mature, high-prescribing physicians; some firms now place more effort on young physicians (currently low prescribers), using new digital resources to secure adoption — these physicians have many more prescribing years ahead of them.

Some firm customers this year will not be customers next year. They may defect to competitors, or stop buying the types of products the firm offers. In calculating CLV, we must consider customer *defection* and customer *retention*. *Retention rate* is simply the number of customers at the end of the year (who were customers at the start of the year), divided by the number of customers at the start of the year. If the firm starts the year with 100 customers and ends the year with 80 of these same customers, retention rate = 80 percent. Retention is the inverse of defection/churn. In this illustration, the *defection rate* = 20 percent (100 percent minus 80 percent). Understanding CLV allows the firm to better manage its customer base.

CALCULATING CLV

In each year, the firm earns a portion of its CLV. In the first year, it earns CLV (1):

$$\text{CLV (1)} = m \times r/(1 + d)$$

Restating this simple expression in words, CLV (1) is:

- The *profit margin (m)* the firm earns in year 1,[6]
- Multiplied by the *retention rate (r)* — the probability that a customer at the start of the year will still be a customer at the end of the year,
- *Discounted* back to the start of the year, using the term *1/(1+d)*. The *discount rate (d)* is the firm's *cost of capital* — typically provided by the chief financial officer (CFO).

To calculate a customer's total CLV, we simply add up the CLV contributions for each successive year.[7] This is complicated mathematically. We simplify the calculation by assuming that each term — profit margin (m), discount rate (d), retention rate (r) — is constant year to year.

With these assumptions, CLV equals the profit margin (m) multiplied by the *margin multiple*. (For interested readers, Marketing Enrichment 2.1 [283p] derives the margin multiple formula.)

The margin multiple = r/(1 + d – r), so that:

$$\text{CLV} = m \times r/(1 + d - r)$$

KEY IDEA

CLV depends on three factors:
- Profit margin
- Retention rate
- Discount rate

MARKETING QUESTION

What question about firm customers would you like to ask your favorite CEO? How do you think the CEO would answer?

KEY IDEA

The margin multiple is a handy way to estimate customer lifetime value.

MARKETING ENRICHMENT 2.1
Derivation of Customer Lifetime Value (CLV) Formula **283p**

Estimating CLV is quite straightforward using this formula. Table 2.1 makes it easier by providing margin multiple values for different retention rates (r) and discount rates (d).

TABLE 2.1
Margin Multiple =
r/(1 + d – r)

Retention Rate (r)	Discount Rate (d)			
	8%	12%	16%	20%
60%	1.25	1.15	1.07	1.00
70%	1.84	1.67	1.52	1.40
80%	2.86	2.50	2.22	2.00
90%	5.00	4.09	3.46	3.00
95%	7.31	5.59	4.52	3.80

KEY IDEA

Increasing customer retention rate has greater leverage on CLV than reducing the discount rate.

Suppose the firm's annual profit margin = $500,000, customer retention rate = 70 percent, and the discount rate = 12 percent. From Table 2.1, margin multiple = 1.67. Hence, CLV = **$500,000 × 1.67 = $835,000**. Of course, we lose some precision with these assumptions but, in most cases, being in the right ballpark is sufficient.

Note several items about Table 2.1:

1. The ranges of values for discount rate (d) (8 percent to 20 percent) and retention rate (r) (60 percent to 95 percent) are quite large. They cover most cases for most firms — the margin multiple value spans 1.00 to 7.31.

2. The median value for the margin multiple is around 2.5.

3. Improving retention rate (r) has a greater impact on the margin multiple than reducing discount rate (d):
   a. When retention rate (r) = 90 percent, reducing discount rate (d) from 20 percent to 8 percent improves the margin multiple from 3.00 to 5.00 — 67 percent.
   b. When discount rate (d) = 12 percent, increasing retention rate (r) from 60 percent to 90 percent increases the margin multiple from 1.15 to 4.09 — well over three times! It follows that:

4. All things equal, the firm is better off increasing retention rate (r) than reducing discount rate (d) — cost of capital — by financial engineering. Finance students, please note!

5. Customer retention is a big deal. More on this later.

MARKETING QUESTION

How do you assess CLV for the following firms' customers — Apple, Facebook. Google, Hershey, Pfizer, United Airlines, and Walmart? If CLV is high — why? If CLV is low — why?

MARKETING QUESTION

If you were FedEx's CMO, what options would you consider to increase CLV? Why?

Here's how we use the margin multiple to calculate CLV for a FedEx customer:

Example: Lifetime Value of a FedEx Customer

FedEx has identified a market segment — these data apply to FedEx customers in that segment:

Assumptions
- Total FedEx letters shipped per month = 2,285
- Number of FedEx customers = 140
- FedEx profit margin per letter (m) = $8.25
- Discount rate (cost of capital) (d) = 12%
- Annual retention rate (r) = 90%

We assume these numbers remain constant year to year.

Customer lifetime value calculation
Number of FedEx letters per customer per annum = 2,285 × 12/140 = 195.8
FedEx profit margin per customer per annum = $8.25 × 195.8 = $1,616
Discount rate (d) = 12%
Retention rate (r) = 90%
From Table 2.1, the **margin multiple** = 4.09

CLV = FedEx profit margin per customer per annum × margin multiple = $1,616 × 4.09 = **$6,609**

Marketing Enrichment 2.2 [345p] shows an alternate way to calculate CLV for FedEx. (We may also use CLV to calculate shareholder value — Marketing Enrichment 2.3 [329p].)

MARKETING ENRICHMENT 2.2
Alternate Way to Calculate CLV for a FedEx Customer **345p**

MARKETING ENRICHMENT 2.3
Customer Lifetime Value (CLV) and Shareholder Value **329p**

INCREASING CUSTOMER LIFETIME VALUE

We now explore ways to increase CLV. Restating the CLV formula:

$$CLV = \frac{m \times r}{(1 + d - r)}$$

→ Increase profit margin, m

→ Increase customer retention rate, r

→ Reduce discount rate, d

Quite simply, the firm has three, and only three, ways to increase CLV:

- Increase the profit margin (m) the firm earns from customers.
- Increase customer retention rate (r) (reduce customer defection rate).
- Reduce discount rate (d). This is a matter for finance, not for marketing.

If the firm spends resources to increase customer retention (r), it reduces profit margin (m). Or the firm may increase profit margin (m) by raising prices — but customer retention (r) may fall. Nonetheless, we consider these approaches separately. The third item, discount rate (d), is the firm's cost of capital — the CFO's responsibility. As marketers, we encourage CFOs to reduce the firm's cost of capital, but marketing can do little to help. Hence, we drop further discussion of discount rate and focus on increasing profit margin and customer retention.[8]

INCREASE THE PROFIT MARGIN THE FIRM EARNS FROM CUSTOMERS

The firm has several options for increasing CLV by raising profit margins from current customers:

- **Customer selection.** Well-selected current customers provide a base level of profit margin.
- **Customer satisfaction and loyalty.** Well-served customers increase purchases over time. Hence, revenues and profit margins increase.[9]
- **Customization.** Targeted offers to defined segments provide greater customer value.
- **Pricing.** If customer satisfaction is high, the firm may be able to set higher prices.
- **Operating costs.** As the firm becomes more proficient in serving customers, it reduces operating costs, and may reap scale economies with individual customers.

In addition, satisfied customers may help the firm secure revenues from other customers:

- **Learning.** The firm learns by working closely with customers and becomes better able to attract new customers.
- **Network externalities.** In some markets, customers bring value to other customers. Consider auction sites: When eBay attracts more *buyers*, it becomes more valuable to *sellers*; when eBay attracts more *sellers*, it becomes more valuable to *buyers*. Television, some printed media, and websites are free, yet their customer traffic has value to advertisers. Deciding what marketing resources to allocate for securing *free* customers is often a crucial firm decision.[10]
- **Positive word of mouth and referrals.** Satisfied customers generate positive word of mouth and provide referrals to potential customers. Lexus secures more new customers from referrals than any other source.[11]
- **Referral programs.** Successful referral programs secure new customers, but may also increase CLV from referring customers.[12]
- **Signals.** Securing a high-profile customer may provide the firm with credibility among potential customers.

KEY IDEA

The firm has several ways to increase revenues and profit margins from customers.

Do you tend to increase purchases from firms that treat you well? Have you told others about these experiences?

Figure 2.1 shows results from a classic study of annual profit margin per customer in the U.S. credit card industry. In year 1, the average credit card issuer loses $80 (from customer acquisition and startup costs); in year 2, the customer earns the firm $40. Profit margin per customer increases steadily with customer longevity.[13]

FIGURE 2.1

Profit Margin in the U.S. Credit Card Industry by Length of Customer Relationship

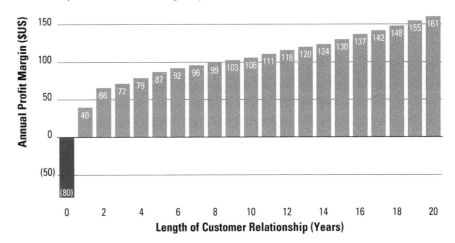

Figure 2.2 shows similar results from other industries in the same study.[14]

FIGURE 2.2

Profit Margins in Several Industries by Length of Customer Relationship

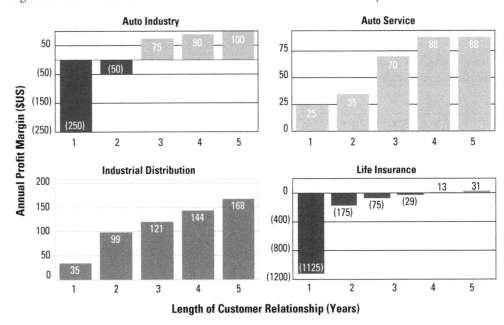

Increasing customer profit margin has an important impact on CLV.[15] Recall, CLV is simply *profit margin* multiplied by the *margin multiple*:

$$CLV = m \times r/(1 + d - r)$$

If profit margin grows at a constant rate (g), then:

$$CLV = m \times r/(1 + d - r[1 + g])$$

As g increases, $r[1 + g]$ also increases, but the entire denominator $(1 + d - r [1 + g])$ decreases; hence CLV increases. Table 2.2 (p. 34) shows the margin multiples for different profit margin growth rates, assuming a 12 percent discount rate (*d*). (Marketing Enrichment 2.4 **[178p]** shows the formula derivation.)

MARKETING ENRICHMENT 2.4

Derivation of Customer Lifetime Value (CLV) Formula with Constant Annual Profit Margin Growth **178p**

Retention Rate (r)	Profit Margin Growth (g)				
	0%	2%	4%	6%	8%
60%	1.15	1.18	1.21	1.24	1.27
70%	1.67	1.72	1.79	1.85	1.92
80%	2.50	2.63	2.78	2.94	3.13
90%	4.09	4.46	4.89	5.42	6.08
95%	5.59	6.33	7.31	8.64	10.56

TABLE 2.2
Margin Multiple with Profit Margin Growth and 12 Percent Discount Rate = $r/(1 + d - r[1 + g])$

Because we selected a 12 percent discount rate, the first column of Table 2.2 is identical to the *12%* column in Table 2.1. Note two items from Table 2.2:

- Regardless of retention rate, higher profit margin growth leads to higher margin multiples. For example, when retention rate is 80 percent:
  - At 0 percent profit margin growth, margin multiple = 2.50
  - At 6 percent profit margin growth, margin multiple = 2.94
- As retention rate increases, higher profit margin growth has greater impact:
  - At 70 percent retention rate:
    - Profit margin growth rate = 0 percent: margin multiple = 1.67
    - Profit margin growth rate = 8 percent: margin multiple = 1.92 — 15 percent increase
  - At 90 percent retention rate:
    - Profit margin growth rate = 0 percent: margin multiple = 4.09
    - Profit margin growth rate = 8 percent: margin multiple = 6.08 — 50 percent increase

KEY IDEA

The profit margin the firm earns from a customer tends to increase over time.

Of course, this last result is not surprising. Customers with higher retention rates have longer time periods to provide the firm with higher profit margins.[16]

INCREASE CUSTOMER RETENTION RATE — REDUCE CUSTOMER DEFECTION RATE

Medco Health Solutions (MHS) provides pharmacy services to 60 million Americans. In 2003, MHS secured independence from Merck with a $12 share price (adjusted). By 2010, MHS's retention rate among corporate customers leveled off at 98 percent; in 2014, the share price was $70.

We just showed that increased profit margin (m) leads to CLV increase. Of course, profit margin is only relevant if the customer continues to be a customer! Figure 2.3 (p. 35) shows retention/defection patterns based on customer tenure — 90 percent and 80 percent retention rates. Defection is greater at 80 percent retention rate than at 90 percent. Regardless, the number of customers defecting is greatest in the first year — as time goes on, fewer customers defect. Assume the firm acquires 1,000 new customers at the beginning of year 1:

Suppose you were advising a local restaurant located on a busy street. The owner tells you she receives plenty of walk-in traffic but has few returning customers. What options can you suggest?

Year Start	90% retention	80% retention
	1,000 customers	1,000 customers
Year 1	900 remain; 100 customers lost	800 remain; 200 customers lost
Year 2	810 remain; 90 customers lost	640 remain; 160 customers lost
Year 3	729 remain; 81 customers lost	512 remain; 128 customers lost

These data tell us that customer retention rate has an important impact on CLV. Figure 2.4 (p. 35) shows that a 5 percent increase in customer retention rate enhances CLV by over 50 percent in several industries.[17] Figures differ by industry because of different profit patterns — and different retention/defection rates. We discuss customer relationship management and specific programs to encourage customer loyalty later in the chapter.

FIGURE 2.3
Retention/Defection Patterns — Percent of Starting Customers Remaining by Length of Customer Relationship — 80% and 90% Retention Rates

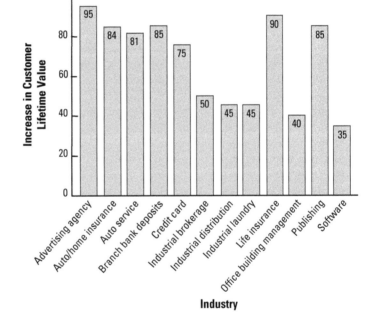

FIGURE 2.4
Increase in Customer Lifetime Value by Improving Customer Retention 5% in Selected Industries

KEY IDEA

Small increases in customer retention can dramatically improve CLV.

MARKETING QUESTION

In 2014, GM faced serious ignition-switch-related quality problems. Assume GM's retention and acquisition rates fell: retention rate — 60 percent to 50 percent; acquisition rate — 15 percent to 10 percent. What would be the effect on GM's long-run market share? What actions did GM take? How effective were they?

HOW CUSTOMER RETENTION WORKS

We just saw that customer retention rate is an important CLV driver. We now show how small differences in customer retention lead, over time, to major differences in sales and market share. Figure 2.5 (p. 36) shows three hypothetical scenarios — A, B, C — each with two firms, Jane's Makeup Emporium and Joe's Beauty Aids, and two time periods, year 1 and year 2. Each scenario shows customer acquisition and retention (defection) patterns. To keep things simple, we assume 1,000 customers in total and that Jane and Joe each start with 500. Our task is to figure out the number of customers Jane and Joe eventually secure in each scenario, and their steady-state market shares.

FIGURE 2.5
Illustrative Long-Run Market Share Scenarios

Scenario A. In year 2, Jane retains 80 percent of her year 1 customers and acquires 20 percent of Joe's. Joe's pattern is identical. This scenario is trivial, but it provides a useful baseline. Jane and Joe essentially swap equal numbers of customers back and forth. In year 2, Jane's 80 percent retention yields her 400 customers — 500 × 80% = 400 — and she acquires 100 customers from Joe — 500 × 20% = 100. Jane ends up with 500 customers (400 + 100), the same number she had originally. Joe's situation is identical. Jane and Joe each earn 50 percent long-run market share.

Scenario B. Jane does better. In year 2, she retains 90 percent of her year 1 customers — versus 80 percent in Scenario A — but again, Jane acquires 20 percent of Joe's customers. Joe's retention pattern is identical to Scenario A — 80 percent — but he acquires only 10 percent of Jane's customers. Jane retains 450 of her original 500 customers — 500 × 90% = 450 — and acquires 100 customers from Joe — 500 × 20% = 100. Jane now ends up with 550 customers (450 + 100); Joe has 450 customers.

In year 3, Jane's starting customer base is higher — 550 versus 500 — so she retains 495 customers — 550 × 90% = 495. Joe's starting base is lower — 450 versus 500 — so Jane only acquires 90 of his customers — 450 × 20% = 90. But the combination of acquisition and retention increases Jane's customers from 550 to 585 (495 + 90). Joe has 415 customers. These numbers converge to a steady state where Jane and Joe have 670 and 330 customers, respectively — 67 percent and 33 percent market shares.

Scenario C. Jane does even better. In year 2, she retains 95 percent of her year 1 customers and again acquires 20 percent of Joe's. Joe's retention pattern is the same as previously — 80 percent — but he acquires only 5 percent of Jane's customers. Using the same process as before, the steady-state customer numbers are 800 for Jane and 200 for Joe — 80 percent and 20 percent market shares, respectively — Table 2.3. (You may want to confirm this result for yourself. The formula to calculate steady-state market share is in Marketing Enrichment 2.5 **[846p]**.)

Suppose a firm's annual revenue growth goal were 15 percent. Consider two situations:

- Customer retention rate = 80 percent
- Customer retention rate = 95 percent

What customer acquisition rate would be required in each case? What implications would the firm face?

TABLE 2.3
Illustrative Steady-State Market Shares[18]

Jane's Retention Rate	Steady-State Market Shares	
	Jane	Joe
80%	50%	50%
90%	67%	33%
95%	80%	20%

In sum:

- As retention rate increases, steady-state market share increases.
- The higher the retention rate, the greater the impact on market share for a given retention rate increase. For example:
  - When Jane's retention rate is 80 percent, a 10 percent increase — to 90 percent — increases her market share by 17 points — from 50 percent to 67 percent; but,
  - When Jane's retention rate is 90 percent, a 5 percent increase — to 95 percent — increases her market share by 13 points — from 67 percent to 80 percent.

Of course, it may be more expensive to improve retention rate from 90 percent to 95 percent than from 80 percent to 90 percent!

This simple exercise demonstrates an important truth — customer retention is a big deal! Relatively small differences in customer retention lead to large differences in long-run market shares. Table 2.4 shows steady-state market shares for various retention and acquisition rates.

TABLE 2.4

Steady-State Market Shares for Various Acquisition Rates and Retention Rates

Retention Rate (r)	Acquisition Rate (a)					
	5	10	15	20	25	30
60	11.1	20.0	27.3	33.3	38.5	42.9
70	14.2	25.0	33.3	40.0	45.5	50.0
80	20.0	33.3	42.9	50.0	55.6	60.0
90	33.3	50.0	60.0	66.7	71.4	75.0
95	50.0	66.7	75.0	80.0	83.3	85.7

The key implication of increased retention rate is longer customer tenure — individual customers provide sales revenues and profit margins for longer periods.[19] Table 2.5 shows this *duration effect*. Note: At high retention rates, small retention rate increases have a disproportionate impact on average customer tenure:

- When customer retention rate is 50 percent, a 30-point increase in retention rate — to 80 percent — increases average customer tenure by 3 years — from 2 years to 5 years; but,

- When customer retention rate is 90 percent, a 5-point increase in retention rate — to 95 percent — increases average customer tenure by 10 years — from 10 years to 20 years.

Boeing's relationship with Southwest Airlines (SWA) is a good example. In the early 1970s, SWA was a startup airline serving Dallas, Houston, and San Antonio, but later became the U.S.'s largest domestic airline. Boeing supplied SWA's original planes — SWA has never purchased planes from any other supplier!

TABLE 2.5

The Duration Effect: Retention Rate and Average Customer Tenure

Customer Retention Rate	Average Customer Tenure
50%	2 years
75%	4 years
80%	5 years
90%	10 years
95%	20 years

PROFIT MARGINS AND CUSTOMER RETENTION

Table 2.6 combines credit card profit margin data — Figure 2.1, with customer retention data — Figure 2.3; we assume 10 percent discount rate. We see the effect of increased profit margin over the length of the customer relationship, based on two different retention rates. Table 2.6 (p. 38) shows:

- When retention rate is 90 percent, total annual profit peaks at $53,460 (year 2), then declines annually. Ten-year discounted profits = **$205,721**.

- When retention rate is 80 percent, total annual profit also peaks in year 2, but at a lower figure — $42,240. Ten-year discounted profits = **$93,475**.

The 90 percent to 80 percent retention rate difference leads to a **$112,246** CLV difference ($205,721 − $93,475).

Age of Account	Annual Profit Margin per Customer by Age of Account	90% Retention Rate			80% Retention Rate		
		Number of Customers Remaining	Total Annual Customer Profit Margin by Age of Account	Total Discounted Annual Customer Profit Margin by Age of Account	Number of Customers Remaining	Total Annual Customer Profit Margin by Age of Account	Total Discounted Annual Customer Profit Margin by Age of Account
0	−$80	1,000	−$80,000	−$80,000	1000	−$80,000	−$80,000
1	$40	900	$36,000	$32,727	800	$32,000	$29,091
2	$66	810	$53,460	$44,182	640	$42,240	$34,910
3	$72	729	$52,488	$39,435	512	$36,864	$27,696
4	$79	656	$51,824	$35,396	410	$32,390	$22,123
5	$87	590	$51,330	$31,872	328	$28,536	$17,719
6	$92	531	$48,852	$27,576	262	$24,104	$13,606
7	$96	478	$45,888	$23,548	210	$20,160	$10,345
8	$99	430	$42,570	$19,859	168	$16,632	$ 7,759
9	$103	387	$39,861	$16,905	134	$13,802	$ 5,853
10	$106	348	$36,888	$14,221	107	$11,342	$ 4,373
			Total CLV	**$205,721**		**Total CLV**	**$93,475**

TABLE 2.6
Profits in the U.S. Credit Card Industry at Different Customer Retention Rates

MARKETING QUESTION

Suppose a firm can sustain a 15 percent customer acquisition rate; its goal is to double the customer base. Consider two situations:

• Customer retention rate = 90 percent
• Customer retention rate = 95 percent

In each case, how many years will it take for the firm to reach its goal?

MARKETING QUESTION

What is the source of CLV for: Capital One, Domino's Pizza, Potemkin automobile dealership, and Rolls-Royce aero engines?

ACQUIRING NEW CUSTOMERS

So far, we used CLV to focus on the firm's current customers. We showed that increasing both profit margin and customer retention rate raises CLV. But what about potential future customers? How valuable are they? We can use the same approach to consider potential customers. The main difference is that, right now, the firm earns no revenues from these potential customers and, to attract them, it must incur an *acquisition cost* (AC). Using the same approach as before, we include the cost to acquire these new customers:

$$CLV = m \times r/(1 + d - r) - AC$$

We now have a useful way to think about new customers. All things equal, the firm should acquire a customer if the first term in the CLV expression, $m \times r/(1 + d - r)$, is greater than the AC. If the AC is greater, the firm will lose money.

The actual cost to acquire new customers varies widely by company and industry. Table 2.7 (p. 39) shows public data on company experience in acquiring customers.

Per-customer acquisition costs in a petroleum industry study varied by acquisition method: personal selling — $500; direct mail — $115; telesales — $95; and e-mail and websites — $30.[20] The firm should assess acquisition costs for the various ways it secures new customers and redesign its processes accordingly. One firm found the typical sales rep's time allocation was direct selling — 45 percent; lead qualification — 40 percent; and administration — 15 percent. Adding telesales to supplement personal selling lowered the small-customer-acquisition cost.[21]

KEY IDEA

The firm should try to acquire customers whose expected CLV is greater than the acquisition cost — AC.

	Industry	Firm	Acquisition Cost per Customer
TABLE 2.7 *Selected Data on Customer Acquisition Costs*[22]	Financial	Ameritrade	$202
		Credit card	$ 25 – $ 35 (subprime)
		Credit card	$ 75 – $150 (platinum)
		E-Trade	$475
		Lending Tree	$ 28
		Mortgage	$300 – $700
	Satellite/Cable	Cable companies	$150
		Direct satellite broadcasting companies	$400
		DirecTV	$550
			$670
			$758
			$894
		XM Satellite Radio	$123
	Telecom	Nextel	$430
		Sprint	$315
	Travel	Priceline.com	$ 8.66

OPTIONS FOR ADDRESSING CUSTOMERS

Much of *Managing Marketing in the 21st Century* focuses on increasing CLV from current customers and approaches for acquiring profitable new customers. From Chapter 7 onwards, we elaborate on the six marketing imperatives that encapsulate approaches for achieving these goals. Here, we identify a broad set of options for addressing current and potential customers — Figure 2.6.[23]

FIGURE 2.6

Approaches to Improving Customer Lifetime Value

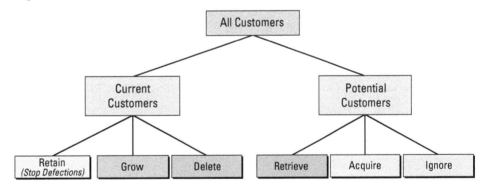

When asked to divide promotional expenses into two buckets — one for retaining current customers and one for attracting new customers — most executives report a focus on attracting new customers. Of course, new customers are critical for firm growth, but the issue is one of balance. Far too often, the firm takes current customers for granted and spends too little on customer retention. Furthermore, retaining current customers is generally less costly than acquiring new customers. We do not suggest that current customers are more important than new customers. After all, new customers may have greater growth potential. But we do believe the firm should make customer investment decisions carefully and deliberately.[24]

British mobile phone operator O2 outperformed its peers, and reduced customer churn (defection) by half, in part by encouraging renewals and placing equal effort on retention and acquisition.

CURRENT CUSTOMERS

MARKETING QUESTION

Suppose your research for the local restaurant (Marketing Question, p. 34) reveals that customer retention is suffering because the restaurant is too crowded. What options would you suggest to reduce the number of walk-in customers?

Figure 2.6 shows three firm options for addressing current customers and improving CLV — retain, grow, delete.

RETAIN. The firm's customer base is like a leaky bucket; the firm should plug its holes. Astute customer relationship management, updating products/services to meet evolving customer needs, and taking other actions binds customers more closely. The firm enhances customer satisfaction, reduces defections, and increases loyalty.[25] Satisfied and delighted customers are more likely to continue buying than dissatisfied customers. Some firms — especially in services — believe employee satisfaction drives customer satisfaction. [Southwest Airlines: **939v** (long); **376v** (short)] For its most loyal fans, The Grateful Dead's telephone hotline provided its touring schedule before any public announcement, reserved some of the best seats, and distributed tickets through a proprietary mail-order house. Today, Pearl Jam Ten Club hosts the most loyal fan base in the music industry.

Wachovia Bank's (now Wells Fargo) customer satisfaction scores improved from 5.5 to 6.5 (1 to 7 scale — Gallup) over a five-year period; annual customer defection declined from 20 percent to 11 percent.[26] In the insurance and mutual fund industries, firms use sophisticated applications to match preferences and try to sell extra products to existing single-product customers. This increased reliance on the firm creates *lock-in*.[27]

Table 2.8 shows that monthly churn for cable firm Cox Communications is less for multiple-product customers. Some firms conduct lost-customer research to identify and repair the reasons for defection. Others implement early warning systems to identify potential defectors:

> OfficeMax has a *defection detector*. Said a senior executive: "We have automatic warning signs that apply to all major customers, and also customer-specific special warning signs we enter manually. Has the customer gone more than 12 weeks without placing an order? Are orders becoming less frequent? Has the purchasing manager changed? Has the content or size of the average order decreased? Has the sales rep changed? There may be eight warning signs for a customer, and if five of them go off that's when our CEO gets on the plane and pays a call to see what's going on and make sure we don't lose a valuable account."[28]

Number of Services per Customer	Services Purchased	Monthly Churn Rate
1	TV only	3.0%
2	TV plus high-speed Internet	2.3%
	TV plus phone	2.2%
	High-speed Internet plus phone	1.9%
3	TV plus high-speed Internet plus phone	1.4%

TABLE 2.8
Churn Rates for Cox Communications

Some firms budget *maintenance expenses* as a retention strategy by offering current customers extra services. Maintenance expenses are not trivial; they reduce the firm's profit margin from current customers. But they are often more cost-effective than having customers defect.

GROW. Satisfied customers may be willing to increase current purchases. By providing good information and employee training, the firm may also increase revenues by *cross-selling*— selling additional products/services to current customers. Your cable company provides basic channels for a standard fee, but offers *higher-value* channels like HBO and special sports events for extra fees. Amazon increases revenues via cross-selling. Initially, Amazon offered books, then CDs, but now sells a vast array of different products, enabling and personalizing one-stop shopping, encouraged by its *Prime* service. Actually, Amazon has two types of marketing effort: Type 1 attracts customers to its website through targeted offerings; type 2 encourages visitors to explore the site for new items, driving multiple purchases, membership, and enhanced customer satisfaction.[29]

KEY IDEA

The firm's options for addressing current customers are:
• retain
• grow
• delete

DELETE. Generally, the firm tries to retain and grow current customers to increase profit margins and CLV. But some customers are not worth having. Sprint Nextel disconnected 1,000 subscribers who called customer service excessively; Marsh & McLennan (insurance brokers) terminated thousands of clients; and many local newspapers, like the *Atlanta Journal-Constitution*, reduced geographic delivery footprints. Most firms have unprofitable customers; they should evaluate ending these relationships, taking care to avoid potentially negative word of mouth. We address customer deletion later in the chapter.

POTENTIAL CUSTOMERS

Potential customers offer an excellent way for the firm to grow. But as we learned earlier, not all customers are alike. Returning to Figure 2.6, we evaluate three broad options for addressing potential customers — retrieve, acquire, ignore.

KEY IDEA

The firm's options for addressing potential customers are:
• retrieve
• acquire
• ignore

RETRIEVE. All firms have customers that defect; the prior relationship makes them *winback* opportunities. These customers are a special category because the firm often has more information about them than about other potential customers. The firm knows (or can find out) what they purchased; what they spent; how they make decisions; why they left; and other data that can help the firm serve them better in the future. Netflix has a targeted *winback* program. If the firm understands why customers defect, winbacks can increase.

ACQUIRE. To reach sales and profit goals, most firms must acquire profitable new customers. Sometimes the firm seeks customers with similar characteristics to current customers; in other situations, it wants to acquire very different customers. Regardless, the firm should be selective in acquiring only the *right* customers — those whose CLV exceeds AC.[30]

Some firms have well-developed systems for accepting/rejecting customers. In the credit card and insurance industries, firms leverage extensive databases to analyze customer demographics and past behavior to make accept/reject decisions.[31] Most venture capital firms conduct extensive analyses of potential investment opportunities, accepting only a small fraction. Flextronics (leading electronics contract manufacturer) conducts similarly detailed analyses to select the few customers it believes will be successful and it will supply.

Four major approaches for acquiring customers are:

MARKETING QUESTION

Think of a local business. What approaches does it use to acquire customers? What alternative approaches could it implement?

• **Direct marketing activities.** Most firms use communications to reach potential customers and persuade them to buy products/services. AT&T, GM, P&G, Time Warner, and others spend immense sums on advertising; life insurance firms like AXA and New York Life place major resources into personal selling. So do FedEx, Xerox, and many other firms. We discuss these and other approaches later in the book.

• **Affiliations.** The firm makes formal or informal relationships with individuals or other organizations to feed it customers. Informal relationships are very common in the service sector. General medical practitioners *refer* patients to specialist physicians; specialist consulting firms *refer* clients to consultants with different specialties. Some firms formalize this process by paying directly for delivered customers. On the Internet, websites and blogs play this role; Amazon has more than one million *affiliate* relationships that send customers to its website.

• **Channel strategies.** Rather than approach potential customers directly, the firm works through third parties like agents, brokers, and distributors. Historically, Cisco made 85 percent of sales direct to customers; today, it makes more than 85 percent of sales though distributors and value-added resellers (Opening Case Chapter 18).

• **Firm and business-unit acquisitions.** Regardless of purpose, whenever the firm completes a merger or acquisition, it acquires customers. But firms make some acquisitions — like cable TV franchises and credit card portfolios for this specific purpose.

IGNORE. The firm must decide on desirable customer characteristics and make investments in potential customers that conform to its market strategy and bring positive CLV. By the same token, it should ignore customers that do not possess these favorable characteristics. Bottom line: The firm must be selective in making investments to secure new customers.

BEING SELECTIVE ABOUT CUSTOMERS

Most customers bring value to the firm, but some do not. Quantifying customer value is important in understanding how to identify customers the firm wants to serve, and develop options for addressing unwelcome customers.[32]

CUSTOMER PROFITABILITY

Most firms understand and measure product profitability — revenues minus costs for individual products. Product profit is a key metric for most product managers. Many firms invest heavily in sophisticated accounting systems and data analysis tools that help answer questions like:

- Are our current products profitable?
- Shall we discontinue this old product and, if so, when?
- Shall we introduce a new product?[33]

KEY IDEA

Measuring product profitability is insufficient; the firm should also develop systems for measuring customer profitability.

By contrast, few firms can answer equivalent questions about customers. This failure is especially critical in large global firms with multiple business units. Profitability data typically reside in individual businesses and geographies whose systems may not always interface with one another. Hence, without major system upgrades, it is difficult to extract and integrate sales and profit data for individual customers across businesses and geographies.

Indeed, several different businesses and/or geographies may have the same customer, but not know it! In many multibusiness firms, each business acts independently regarding customers and does not share data with sister businesses. Consider the following: A business executive regularly entertained clients at a top-level restaurant in his home city. He called the restaurant's catering division to arrange for his daughter's wedding. Catering did not know who he was and gave him no special consideration. Unsurprisingly, he started taking clients elsewhere!

The firm's difficulty in measuring *customer profitability* stands in sharp contrast to treating customers as assets and understanding CLV. Product profitability is important, but products/services are only a means to attract, retain, and grow customers. To paraphrase an old management saying: "If you can't measure it, you can't manage it!"

At Bharat Paper (disguised) the top ten customers generated 70 percent of revenues. Detailed analysis showed that three of these customers were unprofitable. At contract renewal time, Bharat offered sales incentives to *lose* contracts with these customers. Six months later, senior management said: "Revenues are down, but profits are way up."[34]

When customers purchase products/services, the firm earns sales revenues; unfortunately, most firms have some unprofitable customers. The firm must examine the relevant metrics across products to assess whether or not customers are profitable. In other words, are revenues greater than costs?

Firms use a variety of methods to gather and assess data relevant to customer activity and profitability, notably via customer relationship management (CRM) systems. We explore CRM later in the chapter. When firms examine revenues, costs, and profits by customer, they often find an *80:20 rule* — 80 percent of revenues derive from 20 percent of customers. Of course, this rule is not absolute, but is a better working hypothesis than assuming all customers have similar revenue/profit relationships.

Some firms have even more skewed distributions. A major magazine publisher found a 90:10 pattern: 90 percent of revenues from 10 percent of customers! We have even seen 95:5 ratios. The firm's strategic (key) accounts can be very profitable and many firms have installed account management systems to serve them — Chapter 18. Losing a strategic account to a competitor or from bankruptcy can be serious. When $9.5 billion hedge fund Amaranth Advisors closed, it voided contracts on 221 Bloomberg terminals, an expensive loss for Bloomberg.

Demonstrating Customer Profitability

Table 2.9 shows how to convert product profits into customer profits. Suppose the firm's three businesses, each with its own sales and service operation, sell three products (X, Y, Z) to a large customer:

- *Sales revenues.* Sales revenues for products X, Y, Z are respectively $4 million, $5 million, $6 million — total sales revenues = $15 million.

- *Gross margin.* The firm makes a positive gross margin of $1.5 million on each product — total gross margin = $4.5 million.

- *Profits.* The firm makes profits of $125,000 and $50,000 respectively on products Y and Z — it loses $500,000 on product X. Overall, the firm loses $325,000 on this customer, despite $15 million sales revenues.[35]

TABLE 2.9
From Product Profits to Customer Profits ($000s)

	Product X	Product Y	Product Z	Total
Sales revenues	4,000	5,000	6,000	15,000
Cost of goods sold	2,500	3,500	4,500	10,500
Gross margin	1,500	1,500	1,500	4,500
Selling expenses	750	275	150	1,175
Service expenses	500	600	700	1,800
Additional expenses	750	500	600	1,850
Profit	(500)	125	50	(325)

Note: These same products may be more profitable with other customers: Production lot sizes may be larger, prices may be higher, and selling, service, and/or additional expenses may be lower.

Illinois Tool Works (ITW) acquired more than 200 firms. ITW developed and successfully implemented an 80:20 process — each business-unit manager focused exclusively on the 20 percent of customers providing 80 percent of revenues. ITW increased the average operating margin of acquired firms from 9 percent to 19 percent; revenue per employee increased 50 percent, and net income doubled.

BrainQUICKEN (BQ) (online sports-nutrition supplements) sold products through 120 wholesalers. Founder Tim Ferriss discovered that five wholesalers produced more than 90 percent of profits, yet BQ spent 90 percent of effort on the other 115. Ferriss switched effort to BQ's profitable five wholesalers and added several more with similar profitability profiles.

Returning to the 80:20 rule, the converse analogue is the *20:80 rule*: 20 percent of revenues from 80 percent of customers. This rule raises two critical and related questions:

- What does it cost to serve these customers?
- Is it profitable to serve these customers? If not, what action(s) should the firm take?

KEY IDEA

At many firms, 20% of customers provide 80% of revenues.

At these same firms, 80% of customers provide 20% of revenues.

Frequently, firms find these costs are very high and many customers are unprofitable. Some firms use extended rules:

- **80:20:120** — 80 percent of revenues from 20 percent of customers; these customers provide 120 percent of profits.
- **20:80:20** — 20 percent of revenues from 80 percent of customers; these customers reduce profits by 20 percent.

Examples of skewed profit distributions are legion. In the Opening Case, we noted that 17 percent of RBC's customers accounted for 93 percent of profits.[36] At Starwood Hotels, 2 percent of travelers bring in 30 percent of profits; at a major media company, 17 of 1,017 advertisers accounted for *all* profits. A major software company found only seven of 307 customers were profitable. Marsh & McLennan's insurance brokerage unit lost money on about a quarter of its clients. One study found similar CLV distributions for B2B and B2C firms — Figure 2.7 (p. 44).[37]

....
FIGURE 2.7
Customer Lifetime Value Distributions for B2B and B2C Firms by Customer Decile

We should not forget that unprofitable customers may be small or large. Unprofitable small customers typically provide insufficient revenues to offset the costs to serve. By contrast, high-revenue customers may require expensive customization and/or service support. They may also bargain down prices below sustainable levels.

The firm has two broad options for addressing low-profit or unprofitable customers:

- **Invest for the future.** Two types of customer may have significant potential: small organizations that may grow — think Google in the late 20th century; and large organizations where the firm is underperforming. Citigroup consistently targets a few large firms like these; each receives a structured two-year program as Citigroup attempts conversion into a profitable customer.

- **Reduce resource commitment.** Essentially, the firm has two options:

  - **New communications strategy.** The firm may switch an on-the-road sales force to telesales. In Scandinavia, Reebok made this change to address *mom-and-pop* shoe retailers. Regular contact became weekly (versus monthly); the telesalesperson was always available to answer questions; customer satisfaction improved; and Reebok cut costs. Internet and e-mail approaches also reduce costs, and combination Internet/telesales systems that direct website visitors to salespeople can be especially effective.

  - **Hand-off to third parties.** In many industries, third parties like agents, brokers, contract sales forces, distributors, and value-added resellers conduct selling efforts. They often have lower operating costs: Unprofitable customers for the firm become profitable for third parties. But,

    - Customers that object to losing field salespeople may shift purchases to competitors.

    - Over time, a third-party organization may grow customer revenues. The now-successful customer wants a direct relationship with the firm. Yet this switch would cut out the third party and negatively affect its relationships.

- **Fire customers.** The firm stops selling to loss-making customers with little potential. Profitability may increase, but firing customers may generate negative word of mouth.

A critical firm challenge is to correctly identify the *right* customers. After all, today's unprofitable customers could be tomorrow's big winners. Also, unprofitable large customers may carry significant overhead allocations; eliminating them lowers overall profits because the overhead remains.[38]

Deciding how to deal with today's unprofitable and least profitable customers is a tricky matter. Creative approaches may increase current profits and/or generate profitable future customers. The following boxed insert and Figure 2.8 (p. 45) show how changes in customer classification helped a financial services firm better isolate customer profitability and improve overall profits.[39]

MARKETING QUESTION

You learn from an internal report that 20 percent of customers provide 80 percent of profits, but customer retention is slipping. Develop a list of potential actions to halt the defections.

A Financial Services Firm Classifies Customers by Profitability

Simpson Inc. (disguised financial services firm) traditionally classified customers by account balances and demographic characteristics. Simpson developed four different customer groups: *upscale* — age over 45 years, balances more than $60K; *prime* — age over 45 years; *emergent* — balances less than $60K, age under 45 years; and *small business*. Simpson based marketing efforts on these groups.

Incoming marketing director Charlotte Ward believed this classification provided few insights into customer buying behavior. Figure 2.8 shows each group was profitable, but Ward believed some customers were unprofitable.

Ward developed a new classification also containing four groups: *heavy hitters* — long-term customers with high balances and high activity; *comfortables* — long-term customers with high balances and low activity; *growers* — newer customers with low activity; and *movers* — newer customers with high activity. Figure 2.8 shows a markedly different profitability pattern. In particular, *movers* were unprofitable.

Simpson implemented two key decisions. First, it raised prices for products purchased largely by *movers*. This action reduced the number of high-activity customers — the remaining movers were profitable. Second, Simpson developed a targeting scheme to acquire more *heavy hitters*.

FIGURE 2.8
Customer Classification by a Financial Services Firm

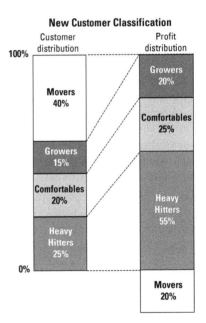

KEY IDEA

In general, customers are critical firm assets, but some customers may be liabilities and should be fired.

The firm may have to reject some potential customers because of predicted unprofitability.

CUSTOMER SUITABILITY

Best Buy (BB) implemented a strategy to avoid several types of undesirable customers. According to the CEO, BB's worst customers "can wreak enormous economic havoc." These customers follow various strategies. They buy products, apply for rebates, return purchases, and then buy back products at returned-merchandise discounts. They purchase large quantities of loss leaders and clearance items, then resell them on eBay. They also secure the lowest price quotes from websites, then demand that Best Buy honor its lowest-price pledge.[40]

Unprofitable customers do not deliver value to the firm. But the firm may cease doing business with a current customer or forgo a potential customer for other reasons:

- **Capacity constraints.** The firm may have insufficient ability — expertise, financial resources, physical capacity — to serve all its customers. When the Sarbanes-Oxley Act vastly increased compliance requirements for large public companies, some accounting firms dropped many smaller clients.[41] Failure to match firm resources to customer needs can lead to dissatisfaction, monetary losses, and harmful word of mouth.[42] EDS (now part of Hewlett Packard Enterprise) had great difficulty performing on an $8.8 billion computer modernization contract with the U.S. Navy, resulting in significant losses.

- **Competition.** The customer is a current or potential competitor that could reverse engineer firm products, then launch its own. Hi-tech firms often refuse to sell to competitors; they also stop customers from reselling their products.

- **Evolving strategy.** When the firm shifts direction, drops products, or divests a business, it sheds customers as a byproduct of strategic change.

- **Foreclosing options.** The customer prohibits the firm from serving other customers. A P&G advertising agency is unlikely to work for Colgate or Unilever![43]

- **Impact on the firm's reputation.** A firm/customer relationship negatively affects the firm's brand image: Can you find Gucci in Kmart? Or the customer may use firm products inappropriately, leading to aggravation and negative word of mouth, and/or financial loss.

- **Impact on the offer.** In many service businesses, fellow customers are integral to the offer. Bad behavior by some customers reduces value for all customers and can negatively affect employee morale. Rowdy sports fans negatively affect the ambiance in expensive restaurants; college admissions departments screen out many applicants. Specific customer profiles the firm should avoid include: *cheats* — like Best Buy faces (boxed insert); *thieves* — like pickpockets and shoplifters who rob other customers or the firm; *belligerents* — like diners who display insufficient patience in waiting for their meals and verbally abuse waiters; *family feuders* — a subcategory of *belligerents* who fight among themselves; *vandals* — who destroy equipment; and *rule breakers* — like unruly airline passengers who pose a physical danger to other customers and affect the service experience. Customers who behave badly also raise firm costs.[44]

- **Instability.** The customer may be profitable but too unstable. People-intensive service businesses like advertising or PR agencies often add employees to serve new customers. When those customers leave, necessary staff reductions are often very difficult.

- **Nonpayer.** This customer would be profitable if it paid, but it doesn't! Or it eventually pays, but the collection costs — money, human resources, aggravation — are too high.

- **Potential costs.** The future costs of doing business are too high. The customer may require costly customization, or the firm believes future servicing costs will be prohibitive.

MARKETING QUESTION

Which companies do you believe affirmatively seek to fire and/or reject customers? Are they successful in pursuing these activities? What firms inadvertently fire and/or reject *good* customers?

KEY IDEA

Poor profitability is not the only reason to fire current customers or reject potential customers.

MARKETING QUESTION

What economic value do you offer your educational institution? How could the institution enhance the value you provide?

How to Bind Customers Closer to the Firm

CUSTOMER RELATIONSHIP MANAGEMENT

A customer relationship comprises the series of over-time interactions/*touch points* between the customer and the firm. *Customer relationship management* (CRM) is a synthesis of relationship marketing, customer insight, customer service, and quality management that helps firms manage these touch points. More precisely, CRM is *the ongoing process of identifying and creating new value with individual customers and sharing these benefits over a lifetime of association with them.*[45] CRM helps the firm *know* its customers better. In B2C, mom-and-pop stores often form personal relationships with customers; CRM helps large firms build and foster relationships with their customers in a systematic way by leveraging both qualitative and quantitative data to synchronize marketing activities. Strong relationships should drive customer purchases over a long time period. (What is CRM? **[407v]**)

Tesco, the leading British supermarket (revenues — £70 billion [$105 billion]), has a very successful CRM program:

Tesco has more than 3,000 stores and in excess of 30 percent market share of retail food sales, and 15 percent market share of all retail sales. Tesco lives its catch phrase — *every little helps* — by removing irritants in the shopping experience. Tesco tackled queues, improved product availability, introduced a *Value* product line, and refurbished stores. A critical element in Tesco's success is *Clubcard*: Tesco collects data on customer purchases, then makes highly segmented offers based on customer needs. Said Tesco's CEO, "The customers get what they want, not what some *bod* in head office wants."[46]

The underlying value of a CRM system is understanding and improving CLV. Forming *mutually beneficial relationships* with the firm's most critical assets is crucial, but CRM systems are only really successful in firms committed to a true external orientation.[47] Unfortunately, many firms invest millions of dollars in CRM programs but do not realize the promised benefits. Three issues are crucial for success:

- **Objectives.** The firm must be clear about its objectives. Without good direction, the firm cannot select from myriad CRM initiatives. Costs can easily spiral out of control and the firm does not meet its objectives.[48]

- **Customer benefits.** The CRM system must provide benefits/values to customers — delightful new products/services, attractive offers, high customer service levels. Many firms focus on value to the firm first, often by cutting costs and giving short shrift to customer value. The CRM system must drive *mutually* beneficial relationships with customers.

- **Technology.** Many people think that databases, analytics engines, and other technology are the only components of an effective CRM system. Of course, technology, databases, and data-mining tools often play an important role in gaining customer insight by gathering and analyzing data. But CRM is not only about technology. To repeat, CRM is the holistic approach firms use when forming mutually beneficial relationships with customers.

KEY IDEA

CRM helps the firm form *mutually beneficial relationships* with customers.

Technology has an important role in CRM, but CRM is not about technology.

DEVELOPING A CRM SYSTEM

Customer databases for effective CRM systems must be accessible, accurate, complete, consistent, current, relevant, secure, and structured. According to one expert, "To implement CRM, a firm must have an integrated database available at every customer touch point and analyze that data well. ... [CRM] allows companies to automate the way they interact with their customers and to communicate with relevant, timely messages."[49] A large B2C firm's database contains longitudinal (over time) data, including responses to promotional campaigns, on millions of customers — even prospective customers. Royal Bank of Canada maintains data on rejected loan applicants, periodically reviews credit status, and offers credit when improvement is significant.

Adding state-of-the-art *data-mining* technology in the context of a *test-and-learn* culture secures and manipulates these data to yield market insight. Capital One's expertise has shaken up the credit card industry, and Harrah's (casinos and hotels) has achieved marked success with timely and relevant multichannel customer communications. Communication with customers is more personal, and the firm can mass-customize its offers. U.S. direct marketer Fingerhut maintains 100 pages of data per customer, mostly about buying habits.[50] Customer data is equally important for firms with few customers, like your local dry cleaner or garage — paper and pencil may be adequate technology.

The firm must identify each customer. In some service industries, customer databases are fundamental to formal relationships, like bank accounts, insurance policies, and telephone service. But these firms often collect and store data by account or policy number, rather than by customer. Hence, the best customers — those who buy multiple services — escape firm attention. Unfortunately, many firms neither collect a full set of customer data nor use it for building long-term relationships. At other firms, marketing data resides in the transactional sales/invoice system, not in a longitudinal and relationship-based form. Many retailers do not know who buys their products — hence, the introduction of customer value cards:

Shoppers Stop (SS) started as a single fashion and lifestyle store in Mumbai, selling only menswear. SS has earned tremendous brand recognition via high-quality products and efficient service provided by friendly staff. SS has 27 stores in 12 Indian cities. SS's *First Citizen* loyalty program comprises three levels — Classic Moments, Silver Edge, Golden Glow — based on purchase volume. Members earn reward points convertible to gifts and discounts. *First Citizen* has 1.5 million active members contributing 50 percent of SS's annual sales. SS's growth confirms the high level of customer value it offers.

Identifying customers that purchase from intermediaries like distributors or retailers can be difficult for suppliers. Indirect methods of gathering these data include customer-get-customer campaigns, customer value cards, factory warranties, loyalty cards, mail inserts, social media, special events, syndicated questionnaires, telephone help lines, third-party lifestyle databases, and websites — supplemented by data from marketing information firms. Many firms invest heavily in customer databases. Table 2.10 identifies the sorts of data required[51]:

- **Customer characteristics.** Demographic data independent of the firm: B2C — name, gender, age, family size (birth dates), address; B2B — sales revenues, number of employees, organization age, industry, decision-makers, influencers.

- **Customer contact history.** B2C — phone calls for product information, customer service requests; B2B — deliveries, sales calls, technical service.

- **Customer purchase history.** What was purchased — by sku; when; by what method — cash or credit; through what intermediary (if any); at what price and/or discounts; how and when delivered. Data should include firm profit margins per purchase.

- **Customer responses to firm decisions.** Purchases following sales promotions, direct marketing offers, price changes — also perceptions and preferences (from research).

- **Customer value received.** Value delivered over and above purchased items — especially in B2B (organizational and individual).

- **Customer value to the firm.** Data for assessing CLV, like purchase history, cost to serve.

Customer Identifier	Customer Characteristics	Customer Contact History	Customer Purchase History	Customer Responses to Firm Decisions	Customer Value Received	Customer Value to the Firm
Jane Doe						
John Smith						
Name						
Name						
Name						
XYZ Inc.						
XYZ influencers and decision-makers						
Company						
Company						
Company						

TABLE 2.10
The Customer Database

MARKETING QUESTION

CVS/Caremart (CC) is the U.S.'s largest single buyer and dispenser of prescription drugs. What actions could CC take to help reduce national healthcare costs?

The database should be sufficiently flexible to follow individuals and track life changes. In B2C, consumers move houses and cities, and change jobs, marital status, names, and family size;

needs also change.[52] In B2B, employees change jobs within firms, change firms, and have changing business and individual needs.

Every customer response, contact, and purchase deserves an entry. But the firm should not limit itself to data on its own customer relationships; it should also seek data on its customer relationships with competitors. An equipment provider should know the age and equipment types installed at the customer by *all* providers. A financial services firm should collect data on its customers' relationships with other suppliers. These data may be available direct from customers or from third-party data providers.

FinSer Inc. (FI) (disguised) became market leader in cross-selling. FI developed new lead-identification guidelines for service reps (SR). SRs entered leads into a lead-tracking system that routed them to the appropriate sales reps.

Cell Inc.'s (CI) (disguised) website received five million unique visitors monthly; 10,000 purchased cell phones, but 27,000 started a purchase process, then quit. By collecting and passing these data to sales teams, CI secured 8,000 additional subscribers per month. CI also followed up on the 20 percent of visitors who left contact information; CI added an additional 35,000 new subscribers monthly.

CONTROL OF, AND ACCESS TO, THE CUSTOMER DATABASE

Control of, and access to, the customer database are critical issues. Consider a firm with several businesses — each business (or product group) may have its own customer database. When there is little customer overlap across businesses, independent databases work fine. But when customer overlap is considerable, a corporate-level database that integrates all customer information makes more sense. Regardless, individual businesses may not be pleased. They may fear competition from sister businesses and/or be concerned how other businesses may use their valuable data: Internecine territorial disputes often impede cross-selling initiatives. Top managers should strongly support enterprise-level data systems and repositories; they should also gain agreement on use — sales, customer service, collections; control; and access to individual business and aggregated data.[53] If building a corporate-level database is infeasible, the firm should at least implement processes that cross organizational boundaries.

A well-developed customer database is valuable to the firm and others. Many B2C firms earn significant revenues by selling customer data to noncompetitors. But privacy is a serious concern: American Airlines, jetBlue, and Northwest provided passenger records to firms with U.S. government contracts, causing an outcry of negative publicity. Personal data theft — *hacking* — is also an issue: Home Depot, Sony's PlayStation, and Target each suffered *unauthorized and illegal intrusions*, potentially affecting millions of customers.

The firm must carefully think through its privacy policy. Some firms like Amazon and UPS absolutely refuse to sell customer data. Said an Amazon spokesperson, "We don't want to create an enormous database that becomes a public relations risk or something that offends our customers. We believe that we have done well because of the trust customers have for Amazon and their belief that our privacy policies are taken very seriously. It's partly a moral point of view, but it's also a sensible business decision."[54]

19th-Century National Politics

Klemens Furst Von Metternich, Foreign Affairs Minister, Austro-Hungarian Empire: "I don't care who the King is as long as I control the purse strings."

21st-Century IBM Politics

Senior IBM Executive: "I don't care who the CEO is, as long as I control the customer databases."

KEY IDEA

Superior customer databases are accessible, accurate, complete, consistent, current, relevant, secure, and structured.

The customer database should distinguish among customers on behavioral measures and value to the firm.

Customer databases are more valuable when they also contain data about relationships with competitors.

ASSESSING THE VALUE OF CUSTOMERS AND DESIGNING FIRM ACTIONS

The firm implementing CRM well acts with significantly greater focus. The firm estimates profitability and CLV by customer, anticipates key customer events, and initiates action. A B2C firm may send consumers vacation ideas; a B2B firm may alert customers that ordering seasonal stock can add value. The more comprehensive the customer database, and the more creative the firm, the more valuable will be its initiatives. The firm can offer new products/services, and give greater customer service to its more valuable and loyal customers. In making offers, the firm should be concerned about the *communications tipping point* — the level after which communications create customer resentment. Amazon spends significant effort to identify its tipping point. Figure 2.9 suggests firm objectives and actions, based on customer value and loyalty.

		Low Customer Loyalty	**High** Customer Loyalty
Customer Value	High	**Objective:** Switch customers from competitors to high-value/high-loyalty group **Action:** Sampling and targeted sales promotion to gain trial, then loyalty/reward programs	**Objective:** Customer retention **Action:** Targeted customer loyalty/reward programs
	Low	**Objective:** No special objective **Action:** No special effort	**Objective:** Increase purchases **Action:** Cross-sell other products

FIGURE 2.9
Customer Value and Loyalty

High-value, high-loyalty customers are very important, yet some firms offer better service to low-value customers. Express checkout lanes in supermarkets reward customers who make few purchases. The Fairway supermarket on New York's Upper West Side and Central Market stores in Texas strive to cut waiting time for all customers.

EVENT-DRIVEN MARKETING[55]

Firms experienced in CRM identify events in customer lives that provide communications opportunities to enhance the relationship and/or make sales. A simple classification comprises three types of significant events[56]:

- **Triggers.** Do not require a customer decision but are often valuable for activating straight-forward business processes — credit card expiry (send a new card) or reaching a predetermined inventory level (reorder).
- **Scheduled events.** Examples include the end of a contract (offer/negotiate new contract), birthdays and anniversaries (congratulatory communications), and graduation. They provide sales opportunities for some firms — Hallmark develops/maintains birthday/anniversary data for offering customers greeting cards and e-cards.
- **Significant events.** Represent significant changes in customer life stage, like marriage, divorce, first child, first job, first apartment, and relocation. Customers are often responsive to receiving communications when these events occur, but firms may have difficulty identifying them.

Evite is the leading digital invitation and social event planning service — more than 32 million registered users.

Austra Bank (disguised) uses high-powered CRM systems to identify indicators of significant events. Twice daily, Austra examines its five-million-consumer database against a set of predefined criteria like exceptionally large deposits, salary cessation, and criteria combinations. A four-person call center makes telephone calls to identified customers. Austra claims that over 50 percent of calls lead to sales and that all customers value the personal contact.[57] For Bunca Bank (disguised), many middle-market firms are potential customers, but they are reluctant to switch banks because of administrative hassle. Bunca identified three events that increase the probability of a firm switching banks: The current bank merges and the firm anticipates painful bank integration; the firm has rapid growth and requires new and better services; and a new leadership team wants to make its mark.[58]

Centura Banks (Raleigh, NC) rates two million customers on a 1-to-5 profitability scale. High-value customers receive several service calls annually, plus a *happy holidays* call from the CEO. In four years, customer attrition dropped 50 percent. Less-valued customers receive less service — unprofitable customers dropped from 27 to 21 percent.

CUSTOMER LOYALTY PROGRAMS

KEY IDEA

Loyalty programs measure and reward sustained customer commitment to the firm.

Loyalty is a customer's sustained commitment to the firm demonstrated by repeat purchase and positive word of mouth. *Loyalty programs* are central to many CRM systems. **[884v]** Their goal may be to retain current customers, increase wallet share, secure new custoers, or save money. All loyalty programs have a similar structure: Customers earn rewards by purchasing goods and services (examples below). Some programs are simple, like JCPenney's *baker's dozen: Buy 12 panties, get the 13th free.* Other programs, like those from airlines, credit cards, and hotels, drive loyalty through complex, multitiered incentives;[59] higher tiers earn greater rewards, but customer demotion to lower tiers may jeopardize loyalty.[60] Complex programs use currencies such as *points* that customers exchange for various rewards. Some programs, like AmEx's Membership Rewards, are well designed; others fail, or are too generous.[61] Program designers should keep their programs fresh, and make sure they are working by delivering value both for customers and the firm.[62]

Loyalty Program Examples

King Soopers — Consumers automatically earn members-only discounts when they pay with the 1-2-3 Rewards Visa card. They also earn points toward free groceries.

Nestlé — Family Nestlé. Members earn bonus points for various activities — registering an account, referring friends, and reading articles. Members can check account status online and redeem points for Nestlé products.

Saks Fifth Avenue's — SaksFirst. Members earn points for each $1 charged on Saks Fifth Avenue MasterCard at Saks stores, Folio catalog, and *www.saksfifthavenue.com.* Customers earn double points for dining and essentials like groceries and gasoline, and triple points for purchases at salons and spas.

Tesco — Club Card Loyalty Program. All Internet customers and 90 percent of store customers belong. Tesco uses 13 market segments to tailor store inventory and creates up to eight million coupon variations for Club Card mailings.

United Airlines — MileagePlus Program. Members earn award miles by flying on United and companion airlines, and by purchasing products/services from partners worldwide. Members use award miles for travel, hotels, and car rental, plus a wide variety of everyday purchases and activities.

VALUE OF REWARDS PROGRAMS: CUSTOMERS

Designing a customer loyalty program can be complicated. Design considerations include:

- **Rate of earning.** Should the reward design comprise *equal* or *accelerated* earning? For a vacation package reward, should the customer earn the same *points* for each dollar spent? Or should she earn more points per dollar as she nears the goal? Some smartphone apps used by restaurants provide patrons with prizes *on the spot*.

- **Aspirational value of the reward.** Two rewards can have the same cash value but different psychological value — like groceries versus vacation travel. Consumers engage in *mental accounting* by placing funds and resources in different mental accounts **[649p]**. AmEx Membership Rewards program offers airline travel, cruises, hotel stays, and many luxury products.

- **Cash value of the reward.** The reward should offer real economic value. Some programs, like the Discover card, pay cash; airline frequent-flier programs provide free travel.

- **Deterministic or probabilistic rewards.** Many reward programs are *deterministic* — the customer accumulates *points*, then collects the reward. In *probabilistic* programs, the customer wins a large reward, or nothing. Internet portal *iWon* used sweepstakes entries. *McDonald's monopoly game* had both reward types. Customers won sweepstakes prizes but could also exchange *Collect & Win Game Stamps* for certain rewards.

- **Ease of collecting the reward.** The customer must be able to redeem the reward. Airlines face criticism for blocking rewards on some routes. On other routes they offer so few reward seats that large families cannot travel together.

- **Length of time to earn the reward.** Many consumers engage in *hyperbolic discounting* —the tendency to increasingly choose a smaller-sooner reward versus a larger-later reward as the delay occurs sooner rather than later **[649p]**. The design question for reward programs is: Should the program have smaller rewards earned frequently or larger, delayed rewards? Many airlines and AmEx Membership Rewards program alleviate the problem by providing data on progress to the reward goal. The firm may also use reminders, or periodically provide small rewards to keep customers engaged.

- **Rewards based on the firm's products/services, or a broad variety.** Some programs reward customers with their own products/services. *Buy X, get one free* programs, like at BestBuy and Subway, are ubiquitous. Many small firms use these programs, often by punching out a card (or digitally accruing points) with each purchase. The alternative is to partner and offer many different rewards, like AmEx Membership Rewards program.

- **Soft versus hard rewards.** *Hard rewards* are denominated in dollars and cents or points. *Soft rewards* include toll-free information numbers, restaurant seating, theater ticket availability, and hotel room and airline seat upgrades.

- **Type of reward.** Should the reward be *cash* or *products/services*? The Discover program, historically cash back, now includes frequent-flier miles and goods and services. Should entry into the reward program be free? A fee may discourage entry, but encourage commitment.

MARKETING QUESTION

Go to *www.colloquy.com* to learn more about loyalty programs. You have to register, but it's free. Which loyalty programs are especially good deals for customers? Why?

MARKETING QUESTION

Many students have low incomes. But your educational investment may lead to high future income. Which firms understand that and actively seek your business with an eye to your future? How do they do so? Which firms seem oblivious?

VALUE OF THE REWARDS PROGRAM: THE FIRM

A well-designed loyalty program increases customer retention (decreases defection), and enhances share of wallet. Specific firm benefits include:

- Creates barriers for competitors.
- Gains insight into customer behavior.
- Lowers costs to serve loyal customers.
- Makes loyal customers less price sensitive.
- Encourages loyal customers to spend more.

KEY IDEA

The firm should examine its privacy policy for the impact on customer relationships.

Customer loyalty programs have many design parameters.

- Stimulates loyal customers to spread positive word of mouth.
- Increases sales via purchase acceleration as customers approach the goal.[63]

The firm should assess loyalty programs via hard-nosed financial analysis, but this can be difficult. First, assessing potential revenues is not simple. Second, some costs — like launching, creating, and maintaining the database; issuing status reports on earned rewards; and the cost of rewards — are highly visible. But managerial opportunity costs versus other activities are less easy to identify. Furthermore, the firm should consider both purchase quantity and loyalty: A totally loyal customer who buys infrequently may not be very valuable. The firm should evaluate loyalty programs against alternative spending like increased advertising, better customer service, and/or lower prices. Loyalty programs have value, but are just one of many revenue-generating tools at the firm's disposal.[64]

An important evolution in loyalty programs is linking CRM systems with social media. Social media informs which groups customers join and where they gather information. By combining CRM systems like salesforce.com with marketing automation applications like marketo.com, the firm can track, manage, and build customer preference profiles at a granular level. These profiles enable the firm to design loyalty programs that deliver personalized rewards.

What other messages did you glean from this chapter?

KEY MESSAGES

- Customer lifetime value (CLV) is the critical link between delivering value to customers and creating value for the firm and its shareholders.
- The firm improves CLV by increasing profit margin (m) and customer retention rate (r), and decreasing discount rate (d).
- Increasing customer retention rate (r) has greater leverage on CLV than decreasing discount rate (d).
- The firm has three broad options for addressing current customers — retain, grow, delete.
- The firm has three broad options for addressing potential customers — retrieve, acquire, ignore.
- The firm should strive to understand the reasons for customer retention and defection and act accordingly.
- Some of the firm's current customers are probably unprofitable — but a fraction of these may present future opportunities.
- The firm may forgo a customer relationship for reasons other than poor profitability.
- A well-designed customer relationship management (CRM) system deepens firm knowledge about customers.
- Understanding customer value to the firm and customer loyalty allows the firm to design effective loyalty programs.

VIDEOS AND AUDIOS

For complimentary material, see Axcess Capon codes at www.axcessvids.com

Loyalty Programs   **199v** 🔊   Ran Kivetz   Columbia Business School

QUESTIONS FOR STUDY AND DISCUSSION

Can you answer the questions implied by this chapter's learning outcomes? Check!

1. A cable company spends on average $600 to acquire a customer. Annual maintenance costs per customer — $45; record-keeping and billing costs — $30 per customer per annum. Price of a basic service package — $30 per month. Typically, 40 percent of customers buy a premium package — $50 per month; 10 percent buy the superpremium package — $80 per month. Over time, 80 percent of customers remain with the company from one year to the next.
   • What is the average CLV for all customers?
   • What is the CLV of a superpremium customer?

2. Chapter 11 introduces *brand equity*. Skip forward and read the brand equity section. What is the relationship between CLV and brand equity?

3. Which firms do a good job of retaining and growing current customers, while simultaneously acquiring new customers? What has made these firms successful?

4. Sonik CD (disguised) was a wholesale buying club for classical, jazz, and blues enthusiasts — annual membership fee $40. Sonik scoured distributors and independent retailers for hard-to-get and out-of-print releases. Sonik's price of $10.95 per CD was lower than average retail price; average Sonik cost — $10.50 per CD. Shipping and handling price — $4.00 per package; average cost — $0.50. Subscribers purchased 19.9 CDs annually, mostly at Sonik's website; annual retention rate — 90 percent. Sonik fulfilled all orders — annual fixed cost, $400,000; shipments averaged 3.7 CDs per package. Annual marketing expenses — $230,000; 90 percent for new subscribers, 5 percent for retention. Sonik's cost of capital — 12 percent. Three growth options were:

   a. *Continue niche strategy.* Sonik anticipated acquiring 20,000 to 30,000 new customers annually for several years without major new investment. Spending $0.5 million annually would increase customer retention to 95 percent.

   b. *Mass-market strategy.* Abandon the subscription model; add many music genres; build a mass-market brand. An initial $1 million to $2 million investment would build brand awareness; distribution and warehousing would require $0.5 million annually. Sonik estimated adding 40,000 to 50,000 new subscribers per quarter for $12.50 acquisition cost on average; annual profit margin — $15; retention rate — 60 percent.

   c. *Distribution strategy.* Sonik also distributed products for other online retailers. AmeriNet Radio (ANR) operated 43 radio stations (southeast U.S., 25 million listeners); ANR sold CDs through station websites. ANR asked Sonik for an exclusive arrangement: Sonik would close retail operations; it would become sole distributor for all ANR CD sales, charging its normal handling fee. Sonik's CD price — $13.25; Sonik would pay ANR $1.50 per CD. Research suggested: 5 percent ANR listeners bought CDs online; 10 percent would buy from Sonik; a typical customer would buy twice a year, averaging two CDs per order. Sonik's additional fixed costs — $0.5 million annually.

   Which option should Sonik choose?[65]

5. Develop a loyalty program for your favorite restaurant. Justify the variables — used/omitted.

6. Select a firm and one of its products. Alternatively, consider *Managing Marketing in the 21st Century*. Who are the customers? Use the Figure 2.6 framework to suggest how you would address customers. Then, design a CRM program.

TRUE/FALSE QUESTIONS
Answers on page A1 and at www.axcessvids.com — 148p

1. Retention is the inverse of defection or churn. ❑ **TRUE** ❑ **FALSE**

2. As retention rate increases, the firm's steady-state market share decreases. ❑ **TRUE** ❑ **FALSE**

3. The higher the retention rate, the greater the impact on market share for a given increase in retention rate. ❑ **TRUE** ❑ **FALSE**

4. The 80:20 rule means that 80 percent of the firm's revenues come from 20 percent of its customers. ❑ **TRUE** ❑ **FALSE**

5. The firm should continue selling to all customers since revenue generation and profitability are synonymous. ❑ **TRUE** ❑ **FALSE**

6. Many customer loyalty programs are probabilistic in nature. In these programs, customers accumulate points, then collect the reward. ❑ **TRUE** ❑ **FALSE**

MULTIPLE CHOICE QUESTIONS
Answers on page A1 and at www.axcessvids.com — 742p

1. Which of the following is the correct formula for customer lifetime value?
   a. $CLV = m \times r / (1 + d - r)$
   b. $CLV = m - r / (1 \times d)$
   c. $CLV = m / r (1 - d)$
   d. $CLV = m + r / (1 + d + r)$

2. Which of the following is NOT one of the three options for current customers in enhancing customer lifetime value?
   a. increasing retention rate
   b. increasing profit margins
   c. decreasing discount rate
   d. increasing churn rate

3. All of the following are options for potential customers in enhancing customer lifetime value EXCEPT:
   a. retrieving customers
   b. acquiring customers
   c. ignoring customers
   d. growing customers

4. Which of the following is NOT one of the three major options for addressing low-profit or unprofitable customers?
   a. devising a new business model for low-profit or unprofitable customers
   b. investing in customer's future potential
   c. reducing resource investment
   d. firing customers

5. All of the following are reasons a firm may cease doing business with a current customer or forgo a relationship with the potential customer EXCEPT:
   a. customer standardization requirements
   b. nonpayer
   c. foreclosing options
   d. impact on firm's reputation

6. Which of the following is NOT a critical issue for success in customer relationship management programs?

   a. objectives
   b. just-in-time inventory
   c. customer benefits
   d. technology

SECTION II

FUNDAMENTAL INSIGHTS FOR STRATEGIC MARKETING

For complimentary material, see Axcess Capon codes at www.axcessvids.com

FUNDAMENTAL INSIGHTS FOR STRATEGIC MARKETING comprises four chapters, Chapter 3 through Chapter 6. These chapters focus on the data, knowledge, and insights the firm must secure to make effective marketing decisions. Data are facts about a particular topic, like customer demographic characteristics and purchase data. Knowledge is the meaning the firm gains from combining data as in a customer profile. Insight results from further knowledge combinations that provide ideas for action, like linking a customer profile to an R&D project. The firm needs data and knowledge, but should strive for insight.

To build a strong foundation for developing market strategy, the firm must secure insight in several core areas — market, customers, competitors, company, complementers — the M4Cs. This insight comprises the *situation analysis* for the market plan.

- **Market.** Good market insight helps the firm decide what parts of the market to address. The firm must understand market demand, today's participants and the pressures they face, and how each may evolve over time — Chapter 3.

- **Customers.** The firm tries to satisfy customer needs through market offers. The firm must identify customers, and gain insight into their needs and the processes they use to make purchase decisions — Chapter 4.

- **Competitors, company, and complementers.** Both the firm and competitors seek to attract, retain, and grow customers. As the firm secures *competitive* insight, it also learns about its own *company* capabilities and how to win in the market. We also discuss firm *complementers* — organizations that can help the firm achieve its objectives — Chapter 5.

Chapter 6 addresses approaches to securing insight via *marketing research*. Following Chapter 6, we show how to use insight from the situation analysis to construct assumptions that form the foundation of the market plan.

KEY IDEA

The firm must secure insight in three broad areas:

- Market
- Customers
- Competitors, the company, and complementers

— the M4Cs.

Managing Marketing in the 21st Century

SECTION I: MARKETING AND THE FIRM

CHAPTER 1
Introduction to Managing Marketing

CHAPTER 2
The Value of Customers

SECTION II: FUNDAMENTAL INSIGHTS FOR STRATEGIC MARKETING

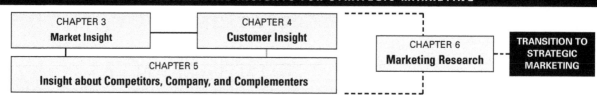

CHAPTER 3
Market Insight

CHAPTER 4
Customer Insight

CHAPTER 5
Insight about Competitors, Company, and Complementers

CHAPTER 6
Marketing Research

TRANSITION TO STRATEGIC MARKETING

SECTION III: STRATEGIC MARKETING

IMPERATIVE 1
Determine and Recommend Which Markets to Address

CHAPTER 7
Identifying and Choosing Opportunities

IMPERATIVE 2
Identify and Target Market Segments

CHAPTER 8
Market Segmentation and Targeting

IMPERATIVE 3
Set Strategic Direction and Positioning

CHAPTER 9
Market Strategy – Integrating Firm Efforts for Marketing Success

CHAPTER 10
Managing through the Life Cycle

CHAPTER 11
Managing Brands

SECTION IV: IMPLEMENTING THE MARKET STRATEGY

IMPERATIVE 4
Design the Market Offer

PART A: PROVIDING CUSTOMER VALUE

CHAPTER 12
Managing the Product Line

CHAPTER 13
Managing Services and Customer Service

CHAPTER 14
Developing New Products

PART B: COMMUNICATING CUSTOMER VALUE

CHAPTER 15
Integrated Marketing Communications

CHAPTER 16
Mass Communications

CHAPTER 17
Digital Marketing

CHAPTER 18
Directing and Managing the Field Sales Effort

PART C: DELIVERING CUSTOMER VALUE

CHAPTER 19
Distribution Decisions

CHAPTER 20
Retailing and Wholesaling

PART D: GETTING PAID FOR CUSTOMER VALUE

CHAPTER 21
Critical Underpinnings of Pricing Decisions

CHAPTER 22
Setting Prices

IMPERATIVE 5
Secure Support from Other Functions

CHAPTER 23
Ensuring the Firm Implements the Market Offer as Planned: Becoming an Externally Oriented Firm

IMPERATIVE 6
Monitor and Control Execution and Performance

CHAPTER 24
Monitoring and Controlling Firm Performance and Functioning

SECTION V: SPECIAL MARKETING TOPICS

CHAPTER 25
International, Regional, and Global Marketing

CHAPTER 26
Ethical, Legal, and Socially Responsible Decisions in Marketing

CHAPTER 3

MARKET INSIGHT

For complimentary material, see Axcess Capon codes at www.axcessvids.com

Why am I a great player? Because I go to where the puck will be.

— Wayne Gretzky, ice hockey legend

LEARNING OUTCOMES

When you have completed this chapter, you will be able to:
- Analyze and understand market structure.
- Understand alternative ways of thinking about products that firms offer.
- Distinguish among product class, product form, product line, and product item.
- Forecast market and product evolution using a life-cycle framework.
- Summarize industry forces exerting pressure on the firm.
- Recognize major environmental forces affecting the firm and industry.
- Show how industry and environmental forces interact.

OPENING CASE: NETFLIX

By 2016, Netflix's original business model, based on mailing DVDs directly to subscribers, was in severe decline — little more than five million subscribers, down from a peak of 20 million (2010). By contrast, Netflix's streaming video service (introduced 2007) had more than 65 million subscribers in more than 50 countries. By 2017, Netflix expected its streaming service to be fully global.

Netflix's business-model transition is just one more evolutionary step in the history of home video. Since the mid-1970s, when Sony introduced Betamax technology, watching videos at home has become a major sociocultural trend. VHS eclipsed Betamax, and consumers used videotape machines to record and play back TV programs, and play movies secured from retailers. Initially, most retailers were small local stores, but many went out of business in the 1990s as Blockbuster became dominant, in part because of larger inventories.

When DVDs replaced VHS cassettes, California entrepreneur Reed Hastings founded Netflix, an online DVD-rental service. Netflix subscribers created lists of videos they wanted to rent, selecting from tens of thousands of movies and TV programs. DVDs arrived by U.S. Mail in distinctive red envelopes. Netflix analyzed subscriber choices and recommendations; subscribers searched by actor, critic, customer recommendation, decade, director, genre, new releases, studio, and title. Subscribers could request movies not yet released on DVD; Netflix sent them out as available. Initially, Netflix competed mainly against Blockbuster (filed for bankruptcy — 2010). More recently, Netflix's DVD model faced competition from Redbox — 35,000 standalone kiosks containing relatively few popular DVDs in supermarkets, drugstores, and fast-food restaurants.

Netflix's video-streaming model incorporates many features of the DVD model but offers movies and TV episodes for viewing on various devices: personal computers; TVs; Xbox 360 (Microsoft), PS3 (Sony), and Wii (Nintendo) game consoles; Blu-ray disc players (Samsung, LG, Insignia); smart (Internet-connected) TVs (LG, Sony, Vizio); digital video players (Roku [Netflix has minority stake]), and digital video recorders. Netflix faces current and potential competition from Apple, Amazon, Google, Hulu, Roku, and Vudu.

A critical competitive area for Netflix is securing rights to recently released movies from movie studios, and length of the movie-house-only window (traditionally averaging 120 days). Netflix has also diversified into content production. In 2014, Netflix received its first-ever Academy Award, for The Square (2013). Netflix's investment in original programming exceeds $5 billion annually.

Notwithstanding the success of its video-streaming service, Netflix shows no sign of abandoning its U.S.-centric DVD-by-mail model. In some cases, Netflix secures rights to new video content for DVDs months before streaming is possible; also, U.S. Internet service is patchy, leading to low-quality (or none) video streaming in some areas. Perhaps more importantly, technological advances in handling DVDs have helped make DVD rental highly profitable. Because of the differing demands and ambitions of DVD rental and video streaming, Netflix maintains organizational separation between the two product lines.

What environmental changes enabled Netflix to successfully innovate in the home video market? How do you assess Netflix's decision to maintain DVD rental in the face of its successful video-streaming service? Do you agree with this decision? Why or why not?

Netflix 2014 revenues exceeded $5.5 billion; net income — $267 million. Originally priced at around $15, in 2015 Netflix's share price briefly exceeded $690. **[696v]**

In 2010, Nokia was global market-share leader in cell phones — 450 million sold. But Nokia faced fierce price competition from Asian producers for basic cell phones; also, Nokia's market share of smartphones dropped considerably as Apple's iPhone and Android phones (Google software) gained strength. In 2011, Nokia's share price dropped 80 percent from a 2008 high. More recently, Google purchased Motorola Mobility, then sold it to Lenovo. Nokia abandoned its smartphone operating system in favor of Microsoft's Windows Phone 7, then sold its handset business to Microsoft.

Defining the market is a fundamental but tricky marketing challenge. If the firm defines the market too narrowly, it risks being blindsided by competitors. If the firm defines the market too broadly, it will not allocate resources effectively. The firm must also understand the market's evolutionary patterns and the forces that drive this process. Because most forces are external in nature, the firm that embraces an external orientation, with customers and competitors in mind, generally understands markets better than firms with internal orientations.

Figure 3.1 shows the four aspects of *market insight* this chapter covers, each equally important. Each aspect provides a different window on the market and lays a foundation for developing the market strategy. Together they help the firm anticipate market change, and identify and size new opportunities:

- **Market structure.** We define the market and show that effective market partitioning helps the firm identify opportunities and gain differential advantage. The chapter shows how different product classes and product forms serve customer needs, and explores factors affecting market size. We defer discussion of market and sales potential, and market and sales forecasts until Chapter 6.

- **Market and product evolution.** Markets evolve. Sometimes evolutionary patterns are predictable, like the market for geriatric healthcare — secured from age-distribution demographics. Other markets are unpredictable, like demand for home-rebuilding products in hurricane-prone areas. Products also evolve as customers refine their needs and competitor firms compete for sales. Technological evolution can also drive market evolution. We use a life-cycle framework to show how markets and products evolve.

- **Industry forces.** Industry forces include various competitive and supply-chain pressures. The *five forces* we identify impinge directly on the firm.

- **Environmental forces.** These broad-scale environmental forces impact both the firm and other industry participants. We use the PESTLE framework — political, economic, sociocultural, technological, legal/regulatory, environmental (physical) — to gain insight.

KEY IDEA

Market insight comprises four separate aspects:
- Market structure
- Market and product evolution
- Industry forces
- Environmental forces

....
FIGURE 3.1
Critical Building Blocks for Securing Market Insight

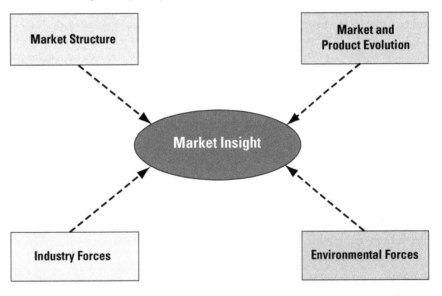

The firm must keep two things squarely in mind when seeking insight into these four aspects:

- **State of nature.** The firm must understand the current state of nature. For example: What competitors does the firm face today? How many baby boomers are in its target market?

- **Trends.** The firm must also identify trends. For example: What additional direct competitors will the firm face in two years? How will demographic changes affect the market?

Good market insight can put the firm ahead and provide the basis for securing differential advantage. Post-September 11, 2001, Alcoa predicted significant demand for secure cockpit doors on passenger aircraft; it won a commanding share of the retrofit market.

KEY IDEA

When firms secure good market insight, they do a better job of identifying and sizing opportunities and gaining differential advantage.

THE CHANGING VIEW

OLD WAY	NEW WAY
Change is evolutionary	Change is revolutionary
Change is a problem	Change is an opportunity
Competitive advantages long-lasting	Competitive advantages quickly dissipated
Firms operate independently	Firms are networked
Focus on national and regional economies	Understand the integrated global economy
Future predictable — all that's needed is good forecasting	Future not completely predictable — need to be flexible and able to move quickly
Imitation common	Innovation essential
Life cycles fixed and constrained	Life cycles dynamic and subject to firm influence
Reacting to environmental change is sufficient	Proactively influencing environmental change is a reasonable goal
The firm has ample time to recoup front-end investment	Peak profit-margin periods arrive sooner, and disappear earlier

MARKET STRUCTURE

> Attendance at Dallas Mavericks' (Mavs) games was half stadium capacity. In 2000, Mark Cuban bought the Mavs and transitioned the offering from *sports team* to *entertainment*. The Mavs then competed with movies and restaurants — customer service was crucial. By 2002–3, the Mavs sold out every game, and by 2005, revenues more than doubled — to $124 million. Franchise value increased from $167 million (1999) to $765 million (2014). The Mavs have only been in the playoffs once since 2000, and won the NBA championship in 2011.

We use three separate concepts to describe *market structure*: the market; products/services serving the market; and the firm's products. We also discuss factors affecting market size.

....

THE MARKET

Markets comprise customers — people and organizations — who require products/services to satisfy their needs. Basic customer needs like food, clothing, and shelter are enduring; many offerings satisfy these needs. Other needs, like entertainment, tend to be more transitory. Of course, to be in the market, customers must also possess sufficient purchasing power, and interest, to buy what firms are offering.[1]

The concept of a *market* is slippery because we can identify a market at several different levels. The transportation market is the basic need to move people and things from point A to point B. In turn, the passenger transportation market comprises several more narrowly defined markets — ground, air, water. Even more narrowly, we can define the automobile market and, more narrowly still, the market for particular types of automobiles like SUVs and hybrids. Good market definition drove the Dallas Mavericks' market success.

We can partition all broadly defined markets. Figure 3.2 (p. 63) shows market partitions for endovascular products that treat aneurysms (expansions in the walls of blood vessels like arteries).

KEY IDEA

Markets comprise people and organizations requiring goods and services to satisfy their needs that are willing and able to pay.

FIGURE 3.2
*Example of Market
Structure for Treating
Aneurysms*

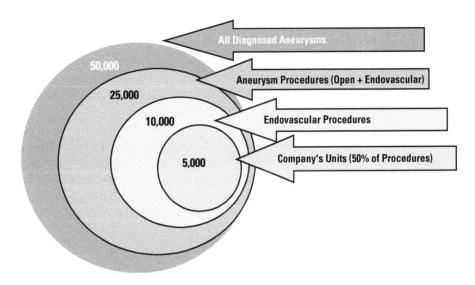

**MARKETING
QUESTION**

Select a firm/product with which you are familiar. Define the market at different levels. How much more broadly could you go (as Mark Cuban with the Mavs) and still maintain focus? Illustrate your answer similarly to Figure 3.2.

When defining a market, it's best to start broad, then focus as necessary. A broad approach ensures against *marketing myopia*[2] — missing opportunities by defining a market too narrowly — Chapter 7.[3] Hence, in the aneurysm illustration, the firm's 50 percent share of endovascular procedures (5,000/10,000) suggests limited opportunity. But viewed as 20 percent share of all procedures (5,000/25,000), 10 percent share (5,000/50,000) of all diagnosed aneurysms, or an unknown share of all aneurysms (diagnosed and undiagnosed), the opportunity is much greater.

Unfortunately, biases, insufficient data, and/or defective measurement systems can narrow market definitions. At GE, Jack Welch's (CEO) initial approach was to retain GE businesses whose market share was #1 or #2; GE sold other businesses. After early success, managers began to define markets narrowly to ensure high market share. To spur opportunity search, Welch told managers in each business that actual market share was less than 10 percent; managers had to redefine their businesses to seek growth opportunities.

**MARKETING
QUESTION**

Kodak was once the world's leading producer of photographic film. **[784v]** What happened to Kodak? Why? If you had been a senior Kodak executive in the 1990s, what action might you have taken?

For more than 90 years Smith-Corona (SC) was market leader in typewriters. In the 1970s and 1980s, SC continued to define its market as typewriters. Because of this narrow definition, SC was late entering word-processing, computer hardware and software, and document processing. SC now serves only a very small part of a redefined market.

More generally, a market definition that focuses on customer needs reinforces an external orientation and offsets tendencies toward internal orientations. But working with a broad market definition is not easy. Broader market definitions — especially regional (multicountry) or global — imply greater complexity and greater data-gathering challenges.

PRODUCTS SERVING THE MARKET

Both the firm and competitors provide products/services to the market. A useful categorization of product offerings is *product class*, *product form*, *product line*, and *product item*.[4] These distinctions help the firm identify opportunities and emerging competitors. When P&G launched Whitestrips for teeth whitening, consumer options included toothpaste, bleaches, gels, and professional dental procedures. Because P&G focused on customer needs for convenience, ease of use, economy, and safety, sales quickly reached $50 million annually with this new product form, in a seemingly mature market. (Here, we use *product* for anything a firm offers for sale, both physical products and intangible services.) Figure 3.3 shows a hierarchical decomposition of the entertainment market, illustrating relationships among market, product class, product form, and product item, based on established customer preferences.

- **Product class.** A group of products offered by competing firms that serve a subset of customer needs in a roughly similar manner. Figure 3.3 shows theater, live music, television, home video and DVDs, and theatrical movies each serving consumer entertainment needs. Each product class provides distinct customer benefits.

- **Product form.** Several *product forms* comprise each *product class*. Figure 3.3 shows that comedy, science fiction, romance, action/adventure, and horror are each product forms in the theatrical movies product class. In general, product items within a product form are more similar to each other than to product items in other product forms — comedy and science-fiction movies versus live theater. Hence, competition is typically more intense among product forms than among product classes. Several firms typically offer products in each product form.

Product classes and product forms provide a useful framework for thinking about markets, but things are not always straightforward. Competitive changes and technological evolution often blur product-class/product-form boundaries. In the entertainment market, Netflix changed movie-rental dynamics by introducing online ordering and home delivery; streaming video is causing another market change. Several years ago, many consumers purchased cash management, life insurance, property and casualty insurance, and investments from different firms. Deregulation led to a single *financial services* market offering *one-stop* shopping. Similarly, engineering plastics compete with metal in many applications. Previously, your automobile's oil pan and fuel tank were made of metal; today, they are probably made of plastic. (The PAM, TAM, SAM framework, Marketing Enrichment 3.1 **[137p]**, offers useful insight for market opportunities.)

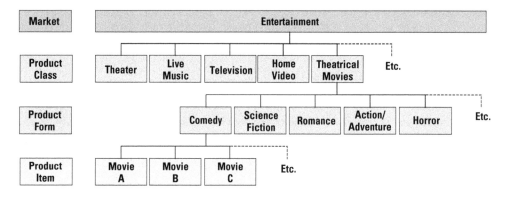

> **KEY IDEA**
>
> We can view any market as comprising several different areas.
>
> The firm avoids *marketing myopia* by using a broad market definition.

> **MARKETING ENRICHMENT 3.1**
>
> *PAM, TAM, and SAM* **137p**

FIGURE 3.3
Hierarchical Decomposition of the Entertainment Market

THE FIRM'S PRODUCTS

Product classes and product forms embrace products from all competitors. Some firms offer products in multiple product classes; other firms specialize in just one or two product forms. IBM offers products in many (but not all) product forms in the information systems product class. By contrast, Acer offers only PCs (IBM no longer offers PCs). When we consider individual firms, we speak of product lines and product items.

- **Product line.** A group of related products that a single firm offers. Lenovo offers a product line of desktop PCs and a product line of laptop PCs.

- **Product item.** A subset of the product line. A product item is uniquely identified, like having a specific size and color. The firm offers various product items to meet different customer needs. Lenovo offers several desktops, each with a unique item (model) number; laptops (notebooks and netbooks) are available as separate product items with different capabilities and in various colors.

> **KEY IDEA**
>
> A useful way of categorizing products in a market is:
>
> *Market level*
> - Product class
> - Product form
>
> *Firm level*
> - Product line
> - Product item

KEY IDEA

Critical variables affecting market size include:

• Population size
• Population mix
• Geographic population shifts
• Income and income distribution
• Age distribution

FACTORS AFFECTING MARKET SIZE

Current and potential market sizes are important data for evaluating opportunities. Before entering a market, the firm should know the numbers of current and potential customers and their purchasing power. For B2C markets, the firm should consider factors like population size, population mix, geographic population shifts, income and income distribution, and age distribution.[5] (Of course, underlying consumer demand typically drives B2B market size: Demand for automobiles [B2C] drives demand for steering wheels by automobile firms [B2B]; demand for medical procedures [B2C] drives demand for sutures by hospitals [B2B]).

POPULATION SIZE. World population exceeds 7 billion (versus 1960 — 3 billion). Increasing by 200,000 daily, by 2030, population will exceed 8 billion.[6] Population is unevenly distributed across nations: highs — China, 1.3 billion; India, 1.2 billion: lows — Nauru, 9,000; Tuvalu, 10,000. See Table 3.1 for 2010 and 2020-predicted populations in selected countries.

Population growth rates also differ markedly across nations and are falling globally. In many developed nations, annual growth rates are less than 1 percent, and some are negative, leading to domestic population declines.[7] Important drivers are social norms promoting education, work opportunities for women, and greater access to birth control. Conversely, in many less-developed countries, particularly in Latin America, population growth is well over 2 percent. Population control programs are successful in some countries like Bangladesh; China enforces a one-child policy. In some African countries, birth rates are high, but AIDS, Ebola, and other viruses are taking a heavy toll.

TABLE 3.1
Population Size in Selected Countries (millions)[8]

Country	2010 Population	2020 Population (est.)	Country	2010 Population	2020 Population (est.)
Argentina	41	45	Malaysia	28	33
Australia	22	24	Mexico	112	125
Bangladesh	156	183	Nigeria	162	208
Brazil	201	222	Paraguay	6	7
Colombia	44	49	Pakistan	184	214
Chile	17	18	Poland	38	38
China	1,330	1,385	Russia	139	132
Egypt	80	96	Saudi Arabia	26	30
France	65	68	Singapore	5	6
Germany	82	80	South Africa	49	49
Great Britain	62	66	South Korea	49	49
Greece	11	11	Spain	47	50
India	1,173	1,326	Sweden	9	9
Indonesia	243	268	Thailand	66	70
Iran	77	87	Turkey	78	87
Israel	7	9	Ukraine	45	43
Italy	61	62	U.S.	308	337
Japan	128	126	Venezuela	27	31
Kenya	41	50	Vietnam	90	99

MARKETING QUESTION

Consider Tables 3.1, 3.2, 3.3 and other data you can secure. What are the pros and cons of entering either the Brazilian (GDP/capita = $16,000) or Japanese markets with a new line of bicycles?

POPULATION MIX. In many developed countries, immigration drives population-mix changes. Of the world's 200 million immigrants (foreign-born residents), the U.S. leads with 35 million. Other countries with large immigrant populations are Russia (13 million); Germany and Ukraine (7 million each); France, India, and Canada (6 million each); and Saudi Arabia (5 million). Most labor migration — legal and illegal — is from less-developed countries to more-developed countries. Armed conflicts — like the Syrian civil war — also drive immigration. Frequently, provider and receiver countries are geographically proximate, like Mexico and the

U.S., and Turkey and Germany. Reduced mobility barriers as in the European Union (EU) increase population shifts; the long-standing pattern of Asian workers in Middle Eastern countries continues apace.[9] Foreign workers have a major impact on home-country economies via remittances; they send back well over $300 billion annually (more than twice the official aid received by OECD members):

> Goya Foods, the largest Hispanic family-owned U.S. food firm (fourth-largest Hispanic firm overall) has revenues exceeding $1 billion. In many grocery stores, Goya has its own shop within a shop. Goya offers a broad range of imported products including Spanish olive oil, seasonings like Mexican chiles, and Caribbean fruit juices.

In some ethnic and/or language groups, immigrants and offspring represent significant market opportunities — Goya example. In the U.S., more than 10 percent of Americans speak Spanish at home, versus 3.8 and 2.7 percent, respectively, for European and Asian languages. More than 100 U.S. television stations broadcast Spanish-language programs, and growth in Hispanic advertising outpaces overall advertising growth.[10] Some firms target subsegments of the Hispanic market based on national origin — Dominican Republic, Guatemala, Mexico, Puerto Rico; others focus on purchasing tendencies, cultural influences, and affordability.

DOMESTIC POPULATION SHIFTS. Generally, as national income grows, people leave rural areas for urban areas. Then urban areas become overcrowded: Mumbai (India) — 14 million; Sao Paulo (Brazil) — 11 million. China predicts 500 million people will move from rural to urban areas by 2050. In developed countries, a more recent trend is *exurban* growth — return to rural communities. Desire for less crowding, a slower life pace, and advances in information technology enable this trend. Conversely, some affluent empty-nester baby boomers are returning to regenerate city centers.

Population shifts often follow the sun. In the U.S., the Northeast is losing population to the Southeast and Southwest. In the first decade of the 21st century, U.S. population grew by 9.7 percent, but several states grew much faster — Nevada (35 percent), Arizona (25 percent), Utah (24 percent), Idaho (21 percent), Texas (21 percent). States growing less than half the national average were North Dakota (4.7 percent), New Jersey (4.5 percent), Mississippi (4.3 percent), Maine (4.2 percent), Iowa (4.1 percent), Vermont (3.8 percent), West Virginia (3.5 percent), Pennsylvania (3.4 percent), Illinois (3.3 percent), Massachusetts (3.1 percent), Vermont (2.8 percent), West Virginia (2.5 percent), New York (2.1 percent), Ohio (1.6 percent), Louisiana (1.4 percent), Rhode Island (0.4 percent), Michigan (0.6 percent decline). Similarly, in Europe, many Northern Europeans move to Croatia, southern France, Italy's Tuscan region, Portugal, and Spain.

INCOME AND INCOME DISTRIBUTION. Table 3.2 shows the world's richest countries. Several countries now surpass the U.S. in per capita income. Most countries are far less wealthy than those in Table 3.2. Forty-four countries have GDP per capita between $10,000 and $20,000; 49 countries have GDP per capita less than $5,000; the largest group of countries has GDP per capita less than $2,000 per annum.

Cold Stone Creamery (CSC) offers freshly made ice cream, Italian sorbet, and yogurt. CSC blends products to order on a frozen granite stone with the consumer's choice of mix-ins. CSC (formed 1988) has well over 1,400 stores in the U.S., Japan, and Korea. If you were advising CSC, how might U.S. population shifts affect your recommendations for seeking new franchisees?

Country	GDP/Capita	Country	GDP/Capita	Country	GDP/Capita
Qatar	137	Australia	47	France	41
Luxembourg	98	Austria	47	Great Britain	40
Switzerland	98	Germany	46	Ireland	39
Singapore	83	Sweden	46	Italy	35
Kuwait	71	Canada	45	South Korea	35
Norway	67	Denmark	45	Spain	34
UAE	66	Japan	38	Israel	33
Hong Kong	55	Iceland	44	Cyprus	31
U.S.	54	Belgium	43	Slovenia	30
Netherlands	48	Finland	41	Greece	26

TABLE 3.2

Gross Domestic Product per Capita (GDP) Purchasing Power Parity (PPP) for Selected Wealthy Countries (2014) ($000s)[11]

MARKETING
QUESTION

How would an analysis of population, income, and income distribution help PepsiCo defeat Coca-Cola in developing countries?

In many poor countries, small elite minorities enjoy most national wealth. The elite-population-income ratio (EPIR) (top 20 percent income divided by bottom 20 percent income) is frequently very high. EPIR exceeds 25 in Botswana, Central African Republic, Colombia, Ethiopia, Guatemala, Lesotho, Namibia, Nicaragua, Paraguay, Sierra Leone, and South Africa. By contrast, ratios for wealthy countries like Great Britain, Japan, and Sweden are well under 10.[12] Increasing EPIR in the U.S. has become a political issue.

Population, income, and income distribution influence the size of many markets. Economic development and demographic changes are shifting opportunities from traditional markets to emerging markets. Especially important growing markets are BRICI countries — Brazil, Russia, India, China, and Indonesia. Western firms like Citigroup, ExxonMobil, GE, Nestlé, and P&G continue to develop their global organizations to tap this potential. Additionally, emerging-market countries are generating their own multinationals: Brazil — Embraer; China — Haier, Huawei, Lenovo; India — Tata Motors, Wipro.

AGE DISTRIBUTION. Table 3.3 shows increasing median ages in selected developed and developing countries. Major drivers are decreasing birth rates and family size, and increasing life expectancy. In developed countries, relative decreases in the *productive* age group — 15–64 years — versus *unproductive* — 0–14 and 65+ years — will cause economic strains, changed immigration patterns, and shifting markets. These shifts have enormous implications for B2C marketers. For example, large numbers of retirement-age consumers (baby boomers) are active, have significant discretionary income, and are sophisticated buyers; cruises and assisted-living facilities are growth markets. By contrast, countries with median ages in the mid-20s and lower — Brazil, Indonesia, Mexico — offer opportunities for Coke, Pepsi, KFC, McDonald's, and other marketers whose products appeal to a younger demographic.

TABLE 3.3
Median Ages in Selected Countries[13]

Country	Median Age, 2014/15	Projected Median Age, 2040
Japan	46.1	54.2
Spain	40.2	52.3
Australia	37.3	43.3
U.S.	37.0	39.0
Indonesia	29.6	37.4
Mexico	27.6	38.7
Brazil	23.1	38.8
Niger	15.1	17.8

MARKETING
QUESTION

Think about the firm/product you selected earlier (p. 63). What factors help determine current market size — population (size, mix, geographic shift), income distribution, and/or age distribution? What other factors help determine market size in three to five years?

Other important market-size drivers include marriage, marrying age, divorce and remarriage, same-sex marriage, infant and adult mortality, and workforce composition. These variables often help the firm make good market-size predictions — birth rates and infant mortality influence demand for products like diapers and car seats.

For approaches to assessing market and sales potential, and forecasting market size and firm sales — Chapter 6.

MARKET AND PRODUCT EVOLUTION

Canon, Fuji, Kodak, Minolta, and Nikon together invested around $1 billion to develop the Advanced Photo System (APS). Several firms introduced APS cameras, but sales lagged expectations. Question: Why isn't APS widely used today? Answer: The APS life cycle was cut unexpectedly short by the introduction of digital photography.

Life cycles are the most common ways to describe the evolution of markets and products — product class, product form, product line, product item.[662v][14] Figure 3.4 (p. 68) shows a classic

S-shaped curve depicting the sales trajectory. Understanding life cycles helps the firm predict future market conditions and develop robust market strategies.[15] Typically, we partition life cycles into five stages (phases) — introduction, early growth, late growth, maturity, decline.

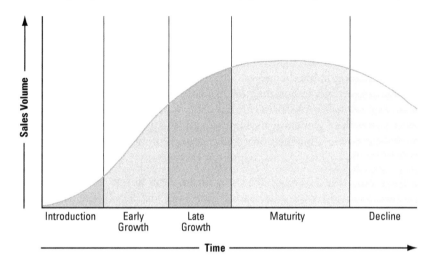

FIGURE 3.4
The Classic Life Cycles

THE FAMILY OF LIFE CYCLES

The several life cycles fall into a simple hierarchy based on longevity and demand. *Market life cycles* last longest — generally, the firm has little impact on market life cycles. *Product-class* and *product-form* life cycles are each shorter than the market life cycle — understanding these two life cycles is helpful in developing market strategy. Several product-class life cycles typically comprise the market life cycle. Figure 3.5 shows several product-form life cycles, each starting at a different time, coexisting within a single product-class life cycle. Typically, newly launched product forms compete with previously introduced product forms but also secure sales from new customers — e-cigarettes and Greek yogurt are contemporary examples. By developing and launching new products, the firm and its competitors affect the trajectories of these life cycles.[16]

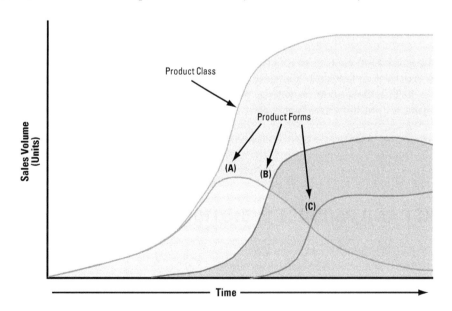

FIGURE 3.5
*Product-Class and
Product-Form Life Cycles*

Product line and *product item* life cycles are critical for product and brand managers — they significantly influence product line and product item performance. Firm actions greatly impact these life cycles; they are shorter than product-class and product-form life cycles and come in many different shapes. But because they provide little insight into competitor activity, they are not very helpful for drawing strategic implications.

PRODUCT-FORM LIFE CYCLES

The firm gains the greatest insight into market and product evolution by examining product forms. Although product classes compete with one another, competition within and across product forms is typically more intense. For example, although desktop PCs compete with laptops and netbooks, the various brands of laptop PCs compete more fiercely with one another. Although actual life-cycle curves often depart from the idealized shape in Figure 3.4, across product forms, life-cycle stages follow one another in a remarkably consistent fashion. Hence, product-form life cycles can provide important strategic insights.

As Figure 3.4 shows, we typically categorize product-form life cycles into five stages:

- **Introduction**. Sales volume is initially low.
- **Early growth.** Sales volume grows at an increasing rate.
- **Late growth**. Sales volume grows, but at a decreasing rate.
- **Maturity**. Sales volume grows at about the same rate as GNP.
- **Decline**. Sales volume eventually declines.

STAGE 1: INTRODUCTION. Product introduction frequently follows many years of R&D and reflects the first market entry/entries by leading firms. Honda launched the first gasoline/electric hybrid car in 1999, but modern-day research started in the mid-1970s.[17] Uncertainty characterizes introduction. The firm explores questions like: Will the product perform adequately? What is the best technology? What segment(s) should we target? What is the optimal market strategy? Will customer demand be sufficient? What specific benefits do customers require? Which competitors will enter? When? What resources will be necessary? What are our chances of success? Products currently in introduction include implantable ID chips for humans and RFID (radio frequency identification) chips for tracking products.

In the introduction stage, firms struggle to build profitable volume. Typically, the firm offers a single product design, but prices may not cover total costs. Managers expect unit costs to fall as sales increase, and the firm ultimately earns profits. Introduction requires significant educational effort. Firms use advertising and/or personal selling to show product value to customers and distributors. But production problems, product failures, and/or an inability to expand capacity may cause delays.[18] Sometimes the first product version has low quality and performs poorly, yet may possess the seeds of an important breakthrough.[19] Smartphones, iPads, and other handheld electronic devices are now widely popular, but they owe their success, in part, to the Apple Newton, the failed pioneer (launched 1993/withdrawn 1998). The introduction stage may last many years, but fierce competition, increased innovation, and customer willingness to try new products are shortening this stage.

STAGE 2: EARLY GROWTH. Many products do not reach early growth, but survivor sales revenues grow at an increasing rate. Hybrid cars and car service apps — Uber, Lyft — are in early growth; smartphones have moved to late growth. Increasing sales and high profit margins attract other new entrants. These players often bring capacity, resources, and a loyal customer base to fuel market growth. As competitors struggle for market position, new distribution channels open up, and promotional effort remains high. Previously, advertising and promotion emphasized generating primary demand — *buy a hybrid car*. Now the focus shifts to differentiation and selective demand based on customer perceptions, features, and functionality — *buy a Ford Fusion hybrid*. Firms secure production and marketing efficiencies, and price becomes a competitive weapon. Many firms increase sales revenues and work at managing costs. Caution: Firm sales may increase, but market share *decreases* if competitors grow faster!

KEY IDEA

The product life cycle comprises several stages:
- Introduction
- Early growth
- Late growth
- Maturity
- Decline

MARKETING QUESTION

Select automobiles, recorded music, smartphones, or a product class of your choice. Using the product life-cycle framework, project product-class and product-form life cycles for the next three to five years.

STAGE 3: LATE GROWTH. By late growth, the many uncertainties from introduction and early growth are largely resolved. Sales continue to increase, but the growth rate slows. Strong competitors initiate tough actions to maintain historic growth patterns, and force weaker entrants to withdraw — aka competitive turbulence. Customer product experiences reveal more specific needs and market segmentation opportunities. Firms differentiate products by introducing and promoting design and packaging variations. The distribution infrastructure is usually well developed, but outlets are more selective about brands and product items. Price is a major competitive weapon, squeezing distributor margins. Purchase terms like credit, customer service, and warranties become more favorable to purchasers.

STAGE 4: MATURITY. Slow growth or flat year-to-year sales characterize maturity. Most sales are to repeat and loyal users. Examples include everyday products like detergents and kitchen appliances. Because competitive situations vary widely, the firm must secure deep market insight. Some markets are concentrated, others are fragmented:

- **Concentrated markets.** For economists, a concentrated market is an *oligopoly*. A few major players enjoy most sales; niche firms make up the rest. Market leaders often enjoy *entry barriers* like economies of scale, brand preference, and/or distribution-channel dominance. Firms that become market leaders by early maturity often survive for many years, like IBM — mainframe computers; GE — steam turbine generators; and Gillette — shaving products.

  Many firms pursue product differentiation approaches, but competitors may quickly offer *me-too* products. Increasingly, firms focus on value-added services, packaging, distribution, and branding and promotion. They streamline operations and distribution to reduce costs, then price competitively. Leaders get in trouble when they fail to innovate new products and processes and do not reduce costs. Xerox's experience is a strong caution:

  > Xerox, the pioneer and market leader in dry copying, was slower than Canon and Savin to introduce small copiers. Xerox has almost failed several times and narrowly avoided bankruptcy. At one point, Japanese producers had a 40 to 50 percent cost advantage; U.S. prices approximated Xerox's manufacturing costs![20]

- **Fragmented markets.** No firm has large market share. Fragmentation generally occurs because of some combination of low entry barriers, high exit barriers, regulation,[21] diverse market needs, and high transportation costs. Examples include personal services like dentistry, education, home plumbing, and electrical contracting.[22]

STAGE 5: DECLINE. Maturity may last many years, but eventually sales turn downward. Products in decline include carbon paper, chemical-film cameras, and videotapes. Sometimes decline is slow — payphones; but may also be precipitous — chemical-film cameras. When decline is swift, overcapacity often leads to fierce price competition. Managing costs is a high priority — firms prune product lines and reduce inventory and marketing expenses. Strong firms may increase sales as weaker competitors exit. Firms often raise prices to cover costs as sales drop, but sales decline further in a vicious cycle. Marketing efforts should target remaining customers. Firms with good cost management and a core of loyal price-insensitive buyers can be quite profitable.

Sometimes products in decline enjoy resurgence. In the U.S., creative marketing led to growth in cigar smoking, and vinyl records are surging. Improved technology has made yo-yo tricks easier; yo-yos are now more attractive to young consumers and sales have increased.

SUMMARY. The product-form life cycle is a useful framework, but two points are important:

- **Life-cycle shape.** A product form's sales trajectory depends on several factors — underlying customer demand, product quality and consistency, and overall resource commitment by participating firms. In general, life cycles are shortening.[23]
- **Profit curves.** Profit curves do not mirror sales curves. Figure 3.6 (p. 71) shows that, on average, profit margins are greatest in early growth — then drop in late growth and matu-

KEY IDEA

Markets and products generally evolve in a consistent manner.

The life-cycle framework is useful for describing market and product evolution.

KEY IDEA

Product-form life-cycle stages have consistent characteristics across products/services.

Profit-margin life cycles do *not* mirror sales life cycles.

MARKETING QUESTION

Think about the firm/product you selected earlier (p. 63). In what life-cycle stage is the product form? How did you make this assessment? What are the implications for the firm's product strategy in the next three to five years?

rity. But do not confuse profit margin with gross profit. Gross profit may be greater later in the cycle — lower profit margins, but higher volume.

FIGURE 3.6
Profit Margin over the Product Life Cycle

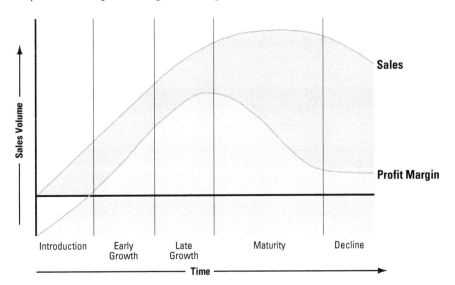

FIGURE 3.6
Profit Margin over the Product Life Cycle

INDUSTRY FORCES

United Airlines (UA) battles daily with peer carriers like American Airlines and Delta. But Southwest Airlines and newer entrants like jetBlue are also strong competitors. On short-haul U.S. routes, customers may drive or take the train. UA must also contend with rising fuel prices and corporate travel offices pushing hard for lower prices.

The *five-forces model* — solid arrows Figure 3.7 — identifies several industry forces firms face — current direct competitors, new direct entrants, indirect competitors, suppliers, buyers.**[756v]**[24] To these original and well-known five forces, we add a sixth force — complementers (dotted arrow). Some forces affect the firm specifically; others may impact the entire industry, like fuel prices for airlines. Strong industry forces may drive profitability downward, as in the worldwide paper industry.[25] The firm must develop a good understanding of these forces and their implications.

FIGURE 3.7
Industry Forces — The Five-Forces Model

CURRENT DIRECT COMPETITORS

The firm's *current direct competitors* offer customers similar benefits with similar products, technology, and/or business models. Current direct competitors are the competitive status quo, the traditional rivalry between established players. In the automobile industry, Ford, GM, and Toyota have been direct rivals for decades; U.S. domestic banking rivals include Bank of America, Citigroup, and JPMorgan Chase; Panasonic, Philips, Samsung, and Sony compete in consumer electronics; and Airbus and Boeing in large commercial jet aircraft. Typically, managers in rival firms know their traditional competitors well. They observe their actions and performance, their successes and failures. They have good insight into strengths and weaknesses and likely strategic moves. They may even have worked for them!

Current direct competitors may be traditional or may have been created via acquisitions and divestitures, mergers, and/or private equity buyouts that continually change the competitive landscape.

- **Traditional direct competitors.** These competitors fight according to *established rules of the game.* In mature markets, one firm rarely gains advantage quickly; rather, an improved position typically results from long-run sustained effort. Establishing differential advantage is difficult. Firms sometimes *cross the line* by working with competitors: Hoffman-La Roche and BASF paid $725 million to settle U.S. Justice Department charges of collusion in maintaining high global prices for vitamins. Sometimes competitors declare bankruptcy, restructure, and improve their capabilities — GM (automobiles) and American, Delta, and United (airlines). Or employees bolster competitors — most employees of failed investment bank Lehman Brothers joined either Barclays or Nomura.

  Globalization and industry concentration affect direct competition in many markets. Consolidation leads to global oligopoly — a few firms share the global market.[26] In large commercial jet aircraft, only Airbus and Boeing remain. In passenger tires, Bridgestone, Continental, Goodyear, and Michelin together enjoy more than 80 percent global market share.

- **Acquisitions and divestitures.** Suppose a direct competitor or an outside firm acquires a second competitor — independent firm or via a divestiture. Your competitor has changed: Objectives, strategy, action programs, and resources will most likely all be different.

  > Miller Brewing was No. 2 to Anheuser-Busch (AB) among U.S. brewers. South African Breweries acquired Miller to create SABMiller (SABM), the No. 2 brewer worldwide. Among SABM's strategic changes at Miller were packaging redesign; importing Chinese, Polish, and Czech Republic brands into the U.S.; and exporting Miller overseas.[27]

- **Mergers.** In a *merger,* two entities combine as *equal* partners to create a stronger firm. By pooling strengths and mitigating weaknesses, the new entity is often a tougher competitor with capabilities that outstrip either former firm. Mergers between Chase Manhattan and J.P. Morgan, then between JPMorgan Chase and Bank One, created JPMorgan Chase — a much tougher competitor for Citigroup and Bank of America. Other examples include Grand Metropolitan/Guinness — Diageo; Disney/ABC; Exxon/Mobil creating ExxonMobil; and the New York Yankees/New Jersey Nets. Of course, many mergers do not succeed — Sears/ Kmart, and Quaker/Snapple.

- **Private equity buyouts.** Sometimes firms rationalize their portfolios and *spin off* business units; typically, these private equity buyouts incur heavy debt as the price for independence.[28] Lacking corporate resources, the now-independent unit may struggle. But it may also focus on debt reduction and become a more nimble and tough competitor. Firestone spun off its Accuride division — rims and wheels for truck manufacturers. Free from Firestone's budget constraints, neglect, and low status, Accuride preemptively increased production capacity, lowered prices, and offered better financing. In less than two years, Accuride doubled market share and increased profits by two thirds.[29] Other spinoffs

KEY IDEA

The firm faces many industry forces:

- Current direct competitors
- New direct entrants
- Indirect competitors
- Suppliers
- Buyers
- Complementers

These forces can frustrate the firm's ability to earn profits and seize new opportunities.

KEY IDEA

The firm's current direct competitors can change via:

- Acquisitions and divestitures
- Mergers
- Private equity buyouts

MARKETING QUESTION

Suppose you were advising Heineken. How do you react to the acquisition of SABMiller by Anheuser-Busch InBev (ABI)?

include Ciba Specialty Chemicals from Ciba Geigy; Cytec from American Cyanamid; Praxair from Union Carbide; Clariant from Sandoz; Rhodia from Rhone Poulenc; Solutia from Monsanto; and Quest Diagnostics from Corning. Sometimes the new firm, freed from corporate restraints, outperforms its former parent!

NEW DIRECT ENTRANTS

We define *new direct entrants* as companies offering products/services similar to the firm, but previously they did not compete. Historically, Nintendo and Sega dominated electronic games; the Sony PlayStation and Microsoft Xbox were new direct entrants. Entry barriers significantly affect market entry by new firms, but new entrants may emerge from many sources:

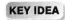

The firm may face competition from new direct entrants:

- Firm employees
- Geographic expansion
- Networks
- New sales and distribution channels
- Startup entry
- Strategic alliances

- **Firm employees.** In some industries, firm employees pose a significant competitive threat. They may develop new business ideas and/or technologies the firm will not fund, then leave to pursue them. Frequently, they set up shop locally; hence, Silicon Valley for Hi Tech and Warsaw, Ind. for orthopedic devices. Several former Fairchild Semiconductor employees founded Intel. Potential competition from employees is greatest when the firm's core asset is intellectual capital as in advertising, consulting, and financial services. Credit Suisse First Boston hired Deutsche Bank's entire 132-person technology group. When *the firm's major assets arrive at 9 a.m. and leave at 5 p.m.*, retaining them is crucial.

- **Geographic expansion.** New direct entrants are often profitable, well-capitalized firms from a different geography. They have solid strengths and cost advantages but may lack market knowledge and customer relationships. They may use superior cost positions to support low price strategies and aggressively seek market share. Many Asian firms entered U.S. and European markets to devastating effect: consumer electronics — Panasonic, Samsung, Sony; high-speed copying — Canon; automobiles — Nissan, Toyota; cell phones — LG, Samsung.[30]

- **Networks.** A network is a group of firms and/or individuals that collaborate using their combined talents and resources. Networks are very flexible and change composition as requirements evolve.[31] *Managing Marketing in the 21st Century* competes with traditional textbooks, but a network made it possible. Critical components were an author; reviewers; developmental, copy, and permissions editors; book, cover, and website designers; test-bank, caselet, and instructor manual developers; video technicians; credit card processors; and for the printed version, a prepublication service provider, printer, fulfillment house, wholesaler, bricks-and-mortar and online retailers, and package delivery services.

- **New sales and distribution channels.** Firms that develop new distribution channels can pose significant challenges to traditional players. Direct marketers L.L. Bean and Lands' End are tough competitors for department stores. Amazon competes with traditional distribution via the Internet. And pyramid sales forces like Amway (consumer goods) and Primerica (life insurance) are tough competitors.[32] Strong firms that add channels also heighten competition. Avon became more competitive with cosmetics firms by adding department store distribution to traditional door-to-door Avon Ladies.

- **Startup entry.** A startup is unencumbered by the status quo; flexibility and talent can make startups potent competitors. By contrast, the incumbent firm may have old facilities, old technology, old processes, and/or an established organization and personnel set in their ways. Successful airline startups include jetBlue (U.S.) and easyJet and Ryanair (Europe).

- **Strategic alliances.** Some firms will not assume the risks and costs of new market entry. They may lack critical assets like capital, skills, technology, or market access. When two firms pool resources, the *strategic alliance* may be stronger than either firm separately. Many U.S. and European firms enter Asian markets with local partners. Of course, many partnerships fail — partner objectives diverge, and/or one partner fails to provide agreed resources.

INDIRECT COMPETITORS

Indirect competitors and the firm offer customers similar *benefits/values*, but provide them in significantly different ways. These *functional substitutes* often appear as different product forms or product classes. Xerox copiers convey information — they compete with computers, fax machines, video conferencing, and the Internet; e-books compete with physical books from bricks-and-mortar and Internet booksellers. Indirect competitors may redefine the industry by using different distribution methods, suppliers, technologies, and/or business models. Netflix customers pay monthly subscription fees; they receive their selections by mail and/or streaming video (Opening Case); Redbox offers vastly fewer DVDs from vending machines in supermarkets, drug stores, and fast-food restaurants — $1 overnight. More broadly, cruise lines compete with automobile and clothing manufacturers — each seeks discretionary consumer income. Movie theaters compete with cable TV, online video, restaurants, sporting events, and other entertainment.

> The New York Knicks is a professional basketball team. The Knicks competes for spectators and TV viewers against many other sports teams like New York Rangers (professional ice hockey), New York Jets (football), New York Yankees (baseball), and other entertainment.

Indirect competitors often attack from different industry sectors; incumbents sometimes ignore them. International Paper's market share in paper cups increased, but sales declined as plastic replaced paper. Sometimes regulations prohibit responding to indirect competitors. For many years, U.S. commercial banks could not offer money-market and mutual funds to compete with Fidelity and Vanguard. Changes in the law removed this restriction.[33]

SUPPLIERS

Suppliers provide firm inputs. Typically, pressure on the firm increases as supplier importance increases — like providing a critical input or a large percentage of purchases. Periodically, Apple faces pressure from music labels unhappy with iTunes' sales terms. Extreme pressure can send firms into bankruptcy: Business-class-only airlines Eos, MAXjet, and Silverjet each failed when fuel prices rose.[34] Pressure may also arise if the supplier brand is attractive to firm customers: PC buyers value the Intel brand; PC manufacturers feel pressure from Intel and Intel earns high profit margins. Pressure is strongest when the supplier is a monopoly like local telephone firms, government services, and railroads; the firm may also have to accept poor service and/or delivery. Sometimes multiple suppliers form *cartels*, like oil (OPEC) and diamonds (De Beers), to manage production volumes and hence prices.

A supplier's most important job is to supply! Supplier failure to honor commitments can play havoc with firm operations. Nissan cut its steel supplier base from five to two — Nippon Steel and JFE. When these firms could not meet its needs, Nissan had to close plants and slash automobile output by tens of thousands. To produce the Dreamliner, Boeing modified its traditional production system to rely more heavily on suppliers; supplier-management problems (including suppliers' suppliers) caused significant delays. GM and Ford acquired plants from Delphi and Visteon, respectively, to assure parts supplies for automobile production. Sometimes firms seek supply guarantees; hence, Toyota invested in lithium extraction so as to control supply of a critical raw material for car batteries. Many firms form supplier partnerships to ensure security of supply: The firm and its supplier set joint long-term goals, engage in equitable value-sharing, and cooperate in investment decisions and technological development. As firms increasingly outsource activities to third parties, the potential for supplier issues grows. Of course, supplier products must fulfill their functions: The global automobile industry suffered grievously (and customers died) due to faulty ignition switches and airbags purchased from suppliers.

MARKETING QUESTION

Think about the firm/product you selected earlier (p. 63). Identify:

- Current direct competitors
- Potential new direct entrants
- Indirect competitors
- Suppliers
- Buyers

In the next few years:

- What changes do you expect in current direct competitors?
- What positive and negative implications for the firm may occur from acquisitions, mergers, and private equity buyouts?
- How should relationships with the firm's suppliers and buyers affect its strategy?

The most severe supplier threat is *forward integration* — the supplier becomes a direct competitor by conducting operations the firm currently performs.[35] Boeing suppliers gained expertise that could benefit Boeing's competitors. Many firms in less-developed countries are outsourced manufacturers for U.S. and European firms; but they also develop the skills for future forward integration. Indian diamond jewelry makers now sell branded products that compete with former customers. Some firms work hard to inhibit such forward integration: One firm relabeled and repainted supplier components to disguise their origin; another designed products to be incompatible with component suppliers.[36]

KEY IDEA

The most significant threats from suppliers and buyers are, respectively:

• Forward integration
• Backward integration

BUYERS

Buyers purchase firm products/services. A firm with many small customers faces little buyer pressure, but a small number of large customers can exert tremendous pressure. Parts suppliers for popular automobile models or electronics products like the iPhone may be severely damaged if not chosen for the next model. Buyer pressure typically increases as market share increases. Firm profit margins shrink when powerful customers demand price discounts and expensive services. One year, Cablevision blacked out ABC channels less than 24 hours before the Academy Awards over a fee dispute. De Beers sets the price for diamonds; suppliers can take it or leave it! Walmart demands, and receives, many supplier concessions; leading automobile firms secure large concessions from parts suppliers. Buyer pressure may ease if some suppliers go out of business and the remainder refuse to submit.

The most severe buyer threat is *backward integration* — the buyer becomes a new direct competitor by conducting operations the firm currently performs. Competition from backward-integrating buyers is especially difficult to address as they often enjoy better relationships with end customers. The fertilizer example illustrates the supplier's dilemma:

FD (fertilizer distributor) (disguised) purchased fertilizer bags from the manufacturer,then resold them to farmers. FD believed it could increase profits by buying fertilizer in bulk, then bagging itself; FD planned to erect a small bagging plant in its parking lot. FD asked the manufacturer to supply fertilizer in bulk rather than in bags. The supplier was unwilling to give up profit margin on bagging and refused. FD secured bulk fertilizer elsewhere and entered the bagging business.

THE SIXTH FORCE

The five-forces model is a powerful means of understanding market dynamics, but we make an extension. We add a sixth force omitted from the five-forces model — complementer.

Complementers may play a critical role in firm success or failure. A complementer is any organization whose actions affect firm sales. Consider a simple example — automobiles and oil companies. Cars powered by internal combustion engines don't work without gasoline; oil firms would not sell gasoline unless there were automobiles powered by internal combustion engines. Furthermore, the price of gasoline directly affect purchases of such automobiles: When gasoline prices are high, automobile sales decline and buyers switch to smaller cars. Intel and Microsoft are another good illustration:

Microsoft and Intel — aka *Wintel* — have an exceptionally strong complementary relationship. PC sales depend jointly on Intel's advances in chip design and Microsoft's improved software. Each firm commits large employee teams to optimize their complementary strategies. Intel's share of PC processors is over 80 percent; Microsoft's share of PC operating software is around 90 percent.

Sometimes complementers are five-force entities behaving in nontraditional manners — Chapter 5.

MULTIPLE INDUSTRY FORCES

In certain situations, businesses face multiple sets of industry forces. Also, some businesses exert multiple forces.

- **Businesses facing multiple sets of forces — two-sided markets.** Multibusiness firms face multiple industry forces, but individual businesses may also face multiple industry forces. In *two-sided markets*, the firm faces two distinct buyer groups. The firm's ability to attract, retain, and grow customers in one buyer group depends directly on its success in attracting, retaining, and growing customers in a second buyer group. Examples include: TV stations — viewers and advertisers; recruitment agencies — job seekers and employers; video game hardware supplier — players and developers; HMOs — patients and doctors; taxi service — drivers and passengers.[37] The firm faces a separate set of industry forces in each of the two markets.

- **Businesses exerting multiple forces.** In the five-forces model, we generally consider individual entities exerting each force — some entities are direct competitors, others are indirect competitors, new direct entrants, suppliers, *or* buyers. As environmental complexity grows, individual entities increasingly play multiple roles in relation to other organizations. IBM (supplier) sells information technology products to Citigroup (buyer); but Citigroup (supplier) sells financial products to IBM (customer). Samsung makes and sells consumer products like cameras, computers, printers, smartphones, TVs; Samsung also makes and sells product components. Samsung is both supplier and direct competitor to other electronics firms. Indeed, in some industries like chemicals and financial services, the relationship of one firm to another may be supplier/buyer, buyer/supplier, partner, and competitor (direct, indirect, new).

ENVIRONMENTAL FORCES[38]

Environmental forces affect the firm and other industry participants. Figure 3.8 shows how these **PESTLE** forces — *political, economic, sociocultural, technological, legal/regulatory* and *environmental (physical)* — and industry forces relate to one another. Some PESTLE forces affect individual businesses. Other PESTLE forces like the World Trade Organization (WTO) (political), exchange rate movements (economic), and the Internet (technological) impact the entire firm. Most observers believe that environmental change overall is much greater than at any previous time. Current businesses may face greater threats but, correspondingly, entrepreneurial thinking identifies new opportunities.

> **KEY IDEA**
>
> The firm faces a broad set of environmental forces — PESTLE:
>
> - Political
> - Economic
> - Sociocultural
> - Technological
> - Legal/regulatory
> - Environmental (physical)

FIGURE 3.8
The PESTLE Model — Environmental Forces Acting on the Industry

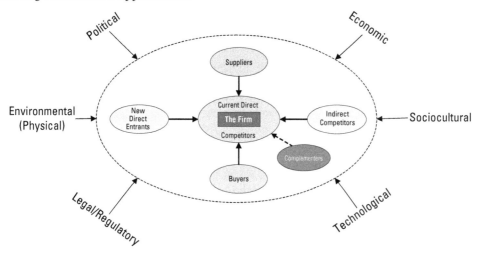

Forward-thinking firms seek leading indicators of environmental trends: Many firms now develop *green* products that appeal to environmentally concerned customers. Germany leads in environmental legislation and related political activism; California spawns many youth-oriented trends; African-American male teenagers are a leading fashion influence; and research at universities like Cambridge, Columbia, MIT, and Stanford often leads the way in biotechnology, computers, medicine, and telecommunications. Siemens has identified and organized around four megatrends — climate change, demographic change, globalization, and urbanization.

POLITICAL

Governments set the frameworks for regulators to develop the rules for business. Table 3.4 identifies several policy variables and their general goals. Separate government departments at different levels (federal, state, local) are also often large purchasers, in part to make investments for the public good; and sometimes are sellers — like the U.S. Postal Service.

TABLE 3.4
Selected Political Variables

Policy Variable	General Goal
Competition policy	Enhance competition
Employment law	Protect employees
Exchange rates	Enhance exports
Government spending	Implement government policy
Multinational agreements	Enhance trade and investment
Political stability	Enhance investment
Privatization	Enhance competition
Regulation of financial markets	Protect investors
Taxation policy	Redistribute income, encourage investment

MARKETING QUESTION

Google took several actions related to disagreements with the Chinese government over censorship. Research these. Do you agree with Google's actions? Why or why not?

Typically governments intervene in economies via fiscal and monetary policy to pursue political ends, encourage investment, and enhance consumer welfare by creating a *level playing field*. But they may also intervene to assist preferred local firms, like the U.S. favoring (allegedly) Boeing over EADS (Europe) for next-generation aerial-refueling planes. In recent years, many national governments realized that regulations designed to protect consumers actually lock-in competitive structures, restrict competitive entry, and stifle innovation, contrary to intended results. Many governments have cut back regulations and placed greater reliance on the market. Regardless, some countries continue to regulate acquisitions and divestitures, consumer protection, competitive entry, imports (tariffs and quotas) and exports, product performance, price-setting, distribution, and advertising. India and Japan no longer focus so heavily on import substitution and increasing exports; some countries have privatized state-owned enterprises but they remain well-entrenched in Brazil, China, and Russia. In a reversal of this trend in the 2008–9 financial crisis, the U.S. government took significant ownership in AIG and GM; the British government took ownership in the Royal Bank of Scotland.

MARKETING QUESTION

Several U.S. states have legalized (or effectively legalized) the recreational use of marijuana. Some observers believe the federal prohibition may be repealed, and marijuana will be treated like alcohol. How would you advise a potential entrant to the marijuana industry?

Governments sometimes intervene directly in the market. During the early 21st century anthrax scare, the Canadian government pressured Bayer to supply one million anthrax-fighting Cipro tablets — at a *special price* — by threatening to invalidate Bayer's patent. Brazil and India sometimes threaten compulsory licenses unless drug prices fall, or they ignore patents. As a result, in Brazil, Roche priced Viracept (AIDS drug) at 30 percent of the U.S. price. Although the Indian government generally encourages foreign direct investment, it strictly controls entry into sectors like agriculture, education, and retail, because of the potential impact on lower-income citizens — the largest voter group.

Firms try to influence political actions by contributing to political campaigns. They also hire lobbyists to influence legislation and the rule-making process. Sometimes trade associations undertake these actions. Four U.S. insurance firms — Chubb, Hartford, Kemper, Liberty Mutual — lobbied the U.S. Congress (unsuccessfully) to close an income-tax loophole they believed disadvantaged U.S. firms. Political action committees (PACs) and special-interest groups, like environmentalists, consumerists, and disease-related advocacy groups (breast cancer, obesity), also try to influence the political process. Some special-interest groups focus directly on firms: PETA (People for the Ethical Treatment of Animals) has caused over 30 firms to ban wool from mulesed merino sheep.

ECONOMIC

The country's economic well-being influences market demand. Of course, governments may also impose sanctions, as on Iran and Russia. High inflation, high and rising interest rates, falling share prices, and a depreciating currency point to an unhealthy economy. But some measures can be ambiguous. High inflation rates are generally a negative indicator, but very low and below zero inflation rates are also negative. High savings rates are generally positive, but too high rates lower consumption. Because *expectations* influence spending patterns, evaluating direction and rate of change are critical. China's GDP is quite low, but GDP growth has been generally high; China is now a major market. Table 3.5 shows several economic variables and their general impact on economic well-being.

In difficult economic times many firms suffer, but others prosper. Name some firms that prosper. Why are they successful?

TABLE 3.5
Selected Economic Variables

Economic Variable	Impact on Economic Well-Being
Balance of payments	Negative balance of payments means government must borrow — increased pressure for higher taxes.
Exchange rates	Value of national currencies. Low exchange rates help exports; high exchange rates are better for purchasing foreign goods.
Disposable income	An individual's income after paying taxes — available for spending and saving. Higher is better.
GDP or GDP per capita	The measure of a nation's output, or output per person. Higher is better.
Inflation	Rate of price increases. Lower is better, but too low means deflation.
Interest rates	Affect customer spending — especially for durables and business investment. Lower is better, but too low may fuel deflation.
Savings rate	Affects interest rates and consumer spending. Higher is better, but too high means insufficient consumption.
Unemployment	Population out of work. Lower is better, but too low and labor costs increase.

Per capita GDP and disposable income are generally good indicators of market demand, but the firm must also consider distribution across the population and population size. Average incomes in India and China are low, but India's middle class exceeds 200 million. Residents of Beijing, Shanghai, and other Chinese cities have significant incomes, and SUVs are popular among middle-class Chinese!

Of course, most firms suffer in poor economies but some may prosper. Campbell's soup and private-label sales increase significantly during recessions, and firms like Dollar General (25 percent of products sell for $1 or less) and Walmart perform well. Conversely, bankruptcy specialists and turnaround consultants that thrive in recessions perform poorly in good economies.

Increased globalization has led to more closely integrated individual country economies. Indeed, many countries have entered into bilateral trade agreements, free-trade areas, and/or political unions — Chapter 25. An economic downturn in one country may affect many others. In the early 21st century, no country escaped the U.S.-led recession. Furthermore, global firms must be concerned about exchange rate movements — they often incur costs in currency A but earn revenues in currency B. The euro introduction has eased this problem for many European firms.

SOCIOCULTURAL

Culture is *the distinctive customs, achievements, products, outlook, etc., of a society or group; the way of life of a society or group.* People learn culture early in life, largely influenced by family, school, and religious institutions. Cultural norms are resistant to change but do evolve; example — the switch from traditional burial to cremation in western cultures. Generally, people do not notice culture in their everyday lives, but recognize cultural values by comparison with different cultures.

Hispanics in the southeastern U.S. suffer from different diseases and make healthcare decisions differently from other cultural groups. Community and family are central to the buying process. Pfizer created market managers for Hispanics. The challenge: Determining how Pfizer's drugs could best meet Hispanics' specific cultural needs.

What is considered normal to one culture may seem odd to another. Most cultures make gifts, but meanings can differ widely. Chinese associate white, blue, and black gifts with funerals; sharp objects like knives, scissors, and letter-openers symbolize cutting off a friendship. In Germany, an even number of flowers is bad luck, but red roses suggest a strong romantic interest![39] For cleaning products, Americans value labor-saving convenience, but Italians want tough cleaners, not timesavers. Placing condoms in workplace bathrooms is fine in France and Scandinavia, and on-the-job flirting is normal. In the U.S., flirting may lead to termination of employment. Acquiring pirated products is acceptable in some cultures but viewed as stealing in others.

CULTURAL GROUPS. A cultural group may inhabit a nation-state, like Brazil or Iran; a geographic region within a nation, like the South or Midwest in the U.S.[40]; or a multinational region, like Latin America or Southeast Asia. A cultural group may also comprise a people, regardless of geographic location, like the Armenian, Jewish, and Kurdish diasporas. A person may belong to several cultural groups, like Turkish immigrants in Germany. Table 3.6 outlines cultural variables.

MARKETING QUESTION

Suppose your firm transfers you to a marketing position in Brazil (France, Japan, Saudi Arabia, or your choice). What issues will you focus on to avoid professional and personal missteps?

TABLE 3.6
Selected Sociocultural Variables[41]

Cultural Dimension	Elements of Cultural Dimensions
Aesthetics	Beauty, good taste, color, music, brand names, architecture
Education	Formal, vocational, primary, secondary, higher, literacy, human resources planning
Language	Spoken, written, official, linguistic pluralism, hierarchy, international, mass media
Law	Common, code, foreign, home country antitrust policy, international, regulation
Politics	Nationalism, sovereignty, imperialism, power, national interests, ideologies, political risk
Religion	Sacred objects, philosophical systems, beliefs and norms, prayer, taboos, holidays, rituals
Social organization	Kinship, institutions, authority structures, interest groups, mobility, stratification, status systems
Technical and material	Transportation, energy systems, tools and objects, communications, urbanization, science, invention
Values and attitudes	Time, achievement, work, wealth, change, scientific method, risk-taking, community involvement

A cultural group may comprise different subcultures, each reflecting both group-culture and subcultural elements. Important U.S. subcultures are baby boomers, generation X, and millennials; each represents a different market opportunity.[42] Consider music: baby boomers — Simon and Garfunkel; generation X — Nirvana; millennials — Bruno Mars. Of course, subcultures evolve; perhaps, in 20 years, today's millennials will appreciate Simon and Garfunkel? Religious and social-issue groups may also play a critical role by pressuring firms to behave in ways they view as appropriate: Several groups target Walmart for various reasons, and religious and family groups boycotted Ford for sponsoring gay rights parades.

Intel's ethnographers made home visits focusing on people's lives and computer needs. Chinese parents worried that computers would distract children from schoolwork. Intel changed its design to include several education applications and a lock. Chinese parents could help children with schoolwork and stop them *wasting time* on the Web.

LOCALIZATION AND GLOBALIZATION. An important contemporary cultural issue is the tension between localization and globalization. Some groups seek identities based on religion: Middle East and North Africa — Muslim fundamentalism; India — Hindu fundamentalism. Other groups focus on ethnicity: Kurds — Iraq, Iran, Turkey; Basques — France, Spain; Welsh — Wales. By contrast, organizations like the UN, WTO, and UNESCO promote globalism.[43] Enhanced travel, improved communications and transportation, the Internet, and globally available television and movies are ready lubricants. Indeed, Levi's jeans and Marlboro cigarettes benefited from scores of cowboy movies distributed around the world. And Pokémon (Japanese media franchise) has captured a large global audience.

But many individuals and groups resist globalization in general, and U.S. and Western influence in particular. Protesters routinely disrupt WTO meetings; the Iraq war spurred global boycotts of U.S. products; and U.S. consumers boycotted French products. European countries banned genetically altered foods; Muslims boycotted Danish products after a Danish newspaper published unflattering cartoons of the Prophet Muhammad; and Saudi Arabia banned Barbie dolls — symbol of *Western decadence*. Global and local trends have a profound impact on firms and their products. For the 1.4 billion Muslims worldwide, Dubai-based Ilkone Mobile Telecommunications designed a mobile phone, loaded with the Koran, that alerts owners to prayer times; the phone incorporates a compass that points toward Mecca. Relatedly, major western banks offer Islamic banking products (no interest charges) like Islamic loans, Islamic bonds, Islamic credit cards, and even Islamic derivatives!

TECHNOLOGICAL

Since World War II, technological innovation has produced many products/services we now take for granted. A partial list: color television, dry copiers, synthetic and optical fibers, cell phones, computers, integrated circuits, microwave ovens, passenger jet aircraft, communication satellites, ATMs, virtually all plastics, antibiotic drugs. These innovations changed individual, household, and organizational life; restructured industries; and drove economic growth.

Today, the pace of technological change continues to accelerate. In the 20 years between 1970 and 1990, six product classes in consumer electronics achieved mass acceptance — video recorders, video cameras, videogame consoles, CD players, telephone answering machines, and cordless telephones. Since the mid-1990s, widely adopted products include personal computers (desktop, laptop, tablet), personal digital assistants (PDAs), digital cameras, DVD players, MP3 players, and digital video recorders (DVRs). Digitization and the Internet (boxed insert p. 81) has changed the way entire industries compete and offers previously unimaginable customer benefits. Organizations like Khan Academy and TutorVista.com provide low-cost online tutorial services by connecting tutors in many countries with students around the world. eBay affects the way many people buy and sell products — half a million U.S. residents make their living selling products on eBay. In South Korea, many households are connected to the Internet at one gigabit per second, *200 times faster* than the average U.S. connection.

Some technological innovations are industry-specific; others, like the shift in payment methods — cash to checks to credit/debit cards to smartphones — affect the entire economy. Moore's law states that transistor density on computer chips and microprocessor speed double every 18 to 24 months; improving price/performance ratios — Table 3.7 (p. 81) — are transforming industry and commerce. Access to computers and smartphones continues to increase, and computing power infuses increasing numbers of products. Automobiles, aircraft, surgical equipment, and elevators already use computer technology to operate more efficiently, predictably,

---

MARKETING QUESTION

Nestlé Prepared Foods (NPF) identified several trends — increasing time pressure on dual-income households, sharpening decline in culinary skills, growth of empty-nester households, increasing belief that good food equals good health, and growing concern with obesity. How would you advise NPF?

MARKETING QUESTION

Many technological changes have affected the recorded music industry — wax cylinders, vinyl, cassettes, CDs, MP3s, streaming. Assess the various approaches to streaming music. Which business model do you believe will be most successful? Why?

and safely. Experts believe genetic engineering and nanotechnology will have similarly broad impact.

TABLE 3.7

Implications of Moore's Law[44]

Year	Cost	Power
1967	$10,000,000	1
2002	$7.0	1,500,000
2007	$0.7	11,000,000
2017 (forecast)	$0.01	67,000,000

Technological change can be either sustaining or disruptive[45]:

- **Sustaining technologies** are often incremental. They improve performance for *current* products on dimensions that *existing* customers value. Examples include *cordless* vacuum cleaners, and *power* drills.

THE DIGITAL WORLD

Perhaps the most significant technological evolution of recent years is digitization and growth of the Internet. Like movable type, the telephone, and the automobile, the Internet has changed the way society works and functions. The automobile changed the way people live, shop, work, and spend leisure time — the Internet is doing the same. The Internet has enormous implications for marketers by reducing costs and facilitating several interrelated behaviors. Columbia colleague David Rogers identifies access, engagement, customization, connection, and collaboration.

Access *Access* refers to the ability of organizations and individuals to connect with each other continuously — 24/7/365. In the digital world, opening and closing hours are a thing of the past; the firm's website is always open to provide and receive information, and to execute transactions. Similarly, individuals can connect with each other instantaneously.

Engagement *Engagement* refers to the ability of both organizations and individuals to offer information content that has value to others. *Access* represents potential; by offering value via websites, blogs, and social media, organizations and individuals secure *engagement.*

Customization *Customization* refers to the ability of firms to provide the specific values that customers require in products, services, and communications. Firms can easily deliver specialized information-based services like books, movies, and music. They can also combine well-designed customer interfaces with flexible manufacturing and low-cost storage to offer customized physical products.

Connection *Connection* is a further step beyond *engagement* in building a relationship. Rather than the customer *receiving* value (engagement), s/he is part of the conversation. Such conversations may occur on open forums like Facebook and Twitter, or on private forums on firm websites where individuals provide feedback, offer advice, and comment on communications from others.

Collaboration *Collaboration* takes *connection* relationships to a higher level. The firm forms some type of partnership with individuals or other organizations to develop new products/services. Partnerships range from formal agreements to competitions for ideas, product features, or even entire products.

Cost Many communication-related activities are much less costly on the Internet — Table 3.8 shows a banking example. But the Internet commerce may also be less expensive inasmuch as physical goods can be inventoried in low-cost locations.

TABLE 3.8

Average Cost per Transaction in Retail Banking[46]

Mode	Cost / Transaction
Branch teller	$2.50
Telephone	$1.00
ATM	$0.40
Voice response	$0.24
Internet	$0.10

Each of these behaviors impacts various aspects of the marketing job. As we shall see in later chapters, digitization impacts both market strategy and implementation. Some behaviors impact firm decisions regarding products; others focus on promotion, distribution, and price. Initially focused on static personal computers, smartphone mobility has opened up a completely new digitization domain.

- **Disruptive technologies** bring new and very different value propositions. They change customer behavior by finding new applications and initially a few new-to-the-market customers. Included are PCs versus typewriters; digital music streaming and downloads to iPods and other devices versus store-bought CDs; and voice-over-Internet protocol (VOIP) versus long-distance telephone. Disruptive technologies spawn products that threaten and change entire industries. For existing customers, early product versions are often inferior — the first digital cameras were more expensive and complicated than chemical-film cameras. But as cost-benefit ratios improve, the disruptive technology surpasses the old technology. When disruptive technology becomes mainstream, it threatens old technology firms that do not adapt. Examples: Digital cameras significantly affected market leaders Fujifilm and Kodak, and changed the industry; similarly discount brokerages impacted full-service brokers like Merrill Lynch.[47]

Generally, current suppliers develop sustaining technologies to serve the needs of current customers; new entrants introduce disruptive technologies that initially satisfy new and different customers. In the disk-drive industry, current disk-drive suppliers pioneered 14-inch Winchester and 2.5-inch drives — sustaining innovations for mainframe and laptop computers, respectively. By contrast, 8.5-, 5.25-, 3.5-, and 1.8-inch drives were disruptive technologies. Initially, each innovation satisfied the needs of different customers, respectively, manufacturers of minicomputers, desktop PCs, laptops, and portable heart-monitoring devices.[48]

Current suppliers tend to ignore disruptive technologies, or at least underfund them. Two factors seem crucial:

- **Inferior performance.** Early on, the disruptive technology has inferior performance versus current technology; products lack critical attributes current customers require.
- **Firm rewards.** Initial expectations of sales and profit in the disruptive technology are less attractive than continued investment to serve current customers.

To escape this trap, the firm should manage sustaining and disruptive technologies in separate organizations, like Netflix (Opening Case). For a disruptive technology, some firms set up independent units or take equity stakes in a specially formed organization for developing the new technology.

Much new technology emerges from corporate R&D. But individual entrepreneurs are very influential; consider the births of Acer, Apple, HP Inc., Intel, Microsoft, TI, Sony, and Xerox. Some inventors are very prolific. Jerome Murray held 75 patents on a diverse range of new products — electric carving knife, audible pressure cooker, passenger aircraft-boarding ramp, and a pump for open-heart surgery. Leading firms do not always appreciate independent inventors' discoveries: 3M, A.B. Dick, IBM, Kodak, and RCA each rejected Chester Carlson's xerography invention.[49] When all major appliance manufacturers declined James Dyson's vacuum cleaner, he launched independently; Dyson's net worth is now close to $1 billion.[50] Trevor Baylis, inventor of the Freeplay wind-up radio, had a similar experience.[51]

> Steve Jobs reflected on his and Steve Wozniak's experience with the personal computer: "So we went to Atari and said, 'Hey, we've got this amazing thing, even built it with some of your parts, and what do you think about funding us? Or we'll give it to you. We just want to do it. Pay our salary, we'll come work for you.' And they said 'No.' So, then we went to Hewlett-Packard, and they said 'Hey, we don't need you. You haven't gone through college yet.'"

LEGAL/REGULATORY

The legal framework (LF) establishes the rules for business. LF aims to protect societal interests, regulate market power, hinder collusion, and stop deceptive practices. LFs differ across countries, but generally govern mergers and acquisitions, capital movements, consumer protection,

KEY IDEA

Technological innovation can be:
- Sustaining — improving performance of established products
- Disruptive — offering new value propositions

and employment conditions. In the aftermath of the 2008–2009 economic crisis, the U.S. placed heavy restriction on the financial sector via Dodd-Frank legislation.

The U.S. and Britain have well-developed systems based on statute and case law; the Napoleonic Code generally forms the LF in continental Europe. By contrast, poorly developed and/or implemented systems of commercial law in China, India, and Russia cause major problems for foreign firms. In China, product copying and illegal use of brand names is rampant, despite China's WTO membership and government efforts.

Individuals, firms, and governments use LFs to advance their interests. Individuals file lawsuits about poorly designed/manufactured products. Firms sue suppliers, customers, and competitors, and governments bring lawsuits. Regulation operates at various governmental levels. Several New York attorneys general sued financial service firms and their senior executives. And local regulations have often stopped Walmart from opening new stores.

Typically, legislation drives regulation. Powerful regulatory bodies like the EPA, FCC, FDA, FTC, and NTSB — U.S. — and their equivalents in other countries enact rules embodying legislation. The FDA decides what drugs pharmaceutical firms can make and sell, what diseases they can treat, and what data they must provide, and to whom. After Enron's collapse, the SEC acted to reduce conflicts of interest: Investment banks made greater separations between research and investment banking; some accounting firms exited consulting by divestiture (but have since reentered — Ernst & Young [E&Y], PricewaterhouseCoopers [PwC]).

International agreements developed via supranational organizations like the EU, IMF, UN, and WTO also lead to regulation. China's WTO entry may someday ameliorate the copying problem. Early this century, the U.S. government signed a *consent decree* with Microsoft for antitrust violations; a few years later, Microsoft suffered a major defeat by losing a related EU lawsuit.

ENVIRONMENTAL (PHYSICAL)

MARKETING QUESTION

Many specific environmental forces seem to take firms by surprise. How would you prepare your firm to deal with unexpected environmental shocks?

Natural and man-made forces coexist in an uneasy equilibrium. Humans have little or no control over natural phenomena like asteroids hitting the earth, earthquakes, erupting volcanoes, hurricanes and tornadoes, monsoons, tsunamis, and everyday weather patterns. In recent years, volcanic ash from Iceland and Chile, respectively, upset European air travel for several days and devastated the Bariloche, Argentina, tourist industry. Recent forces like Hurricane Sandy in the U.S., Japan's tsunami, and Thailand's floods highlight the fragility of increasingly decentralized yet tightly integrated global supply chains — production of many products and commerce suffered from these events in many parts of the world.

By contrast, human action is driving global warming and climate change,[52] pollution, rainforest and wetland destruction, raw material shortages, retreating coastlines, and the shrinking ozone layer. Such changes to the natural environment has spawned demand for pollution control and renewable energy products. Furthermore, global warming influences demand for beer, soft drinks, umbrellas, and pantyhose.

KEY IDEA

Environmental forces are constantly in flux; they also interact with each other.

Man-made modifications to the physical environment, typically involving large government investment, often have an important impact on commerce. The openings of the Suez (mid-19th century) and Panama (early 20th century) Canals cut costs and transit time for much international trade; the new Panama Canal widening will permit much larger ships. The planned Central Bioceanic Corridor (rail) across the Andes — Argentina to Chile — will have a similar impact in southern South America. Water diversion and other irrigation projects create and/or sustain farmland, and river modification allows electricity production via hydroelectricity.

Firms face increasing pressure from governments, environmentalists, single-issue advocacy groups, and the public at large to provide increased transparency and assume greater environmental responsibility for products, packaging, and production systems. In Germany, disposable packaging use has decreased substantially.[53] European automakers will soon have to reuse 80 percent of a car's weight, or pay for recycling.[54] Some firms are aggressively enacting *green* strategies. HP Inc. recycles 70,000 tons annually (about 10 percent of sales); Best Buy accepts virtually any junk electronic product from customers and directs its own recycling program; Walmart sells environmentally friendly products like concentrated laundry detergent and fluorescent bulbs; and Philips is investing heavily in LED (light-emitting diodes) — 98 percent more efficient than some incandescent bulbs.

Natural resource availability is a significant environmental issue. Oil is the basic raw material for energy, plastics, synthetic fibers, transportation, and other industries, yet new supplies are increasingly scarce. New industries like fuel cells, solar power, and wind power are starting to address this problem. Hybrid car sales are fast increasing, and Tesla and others are introducing electric cars. U.S. paper companies plant trees in the southern U.S., where they mature faster. Bamboo flooring use is also expanding; bamboo matures faster than trees.

INTERACTIONS AMONG PESTLE FORCES

Figure 3.9 shows the PESTLE forces acting on the industry as interconnected; examples are legion. The Internet (technological) has major implications for sociocultural and political forces, especially in countries with little political freedom, and has major implications for industry forces. In South Korea, huge government investment in broadband infrastructure (political) is spurring domestic innovation (technological).[55] In Germany, recycling has vital economic, environmental (physical), and political dimensions. As environmental change and turbulence grow, interconnectedness among PESTLE forces will surely increase.

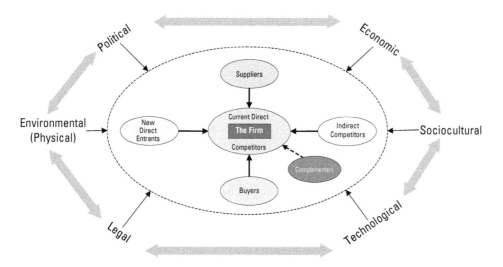

THE MANAGERIAL PROCESS ENVIRONMENT

Executives use *intellectual capital* (IC) — concepts, frameworks, ideas, and tools — to lead and manage firms. IC evolves via research efforts at business schools, culling of consulting experience, and learning by practicing managers.

Consider how the dominant view on corporate strategy has changed over the years. In the 1960s and 1970s, *conglomeration* was the received wisdom. The cojoining of many disparate businesses formed major firms like ITT, Gulf & Western, and Litton Industries — U.S. — and Slater Walker and the Hanson Trust — Great Britain. The underlying rationale was risk diversification. In today's dominant view, investors can diversify more efficiently by investing in multiple single, or related, business firms, or by buying diversified mutual funds.[56] The watchword for

---

MARKETING QUESTION

Think about the firm/ product you selected earlier (p. 63). How does each PESTLE force — political, economic, sociocultural, technological, legal/regulatory, environmental (physical) — affect the product or market? What changes do you expect in the next three to five years? Will these be positive or negative for the firm? Why or why not?

FIGURE 3.9
The Augmented Industry Environment

KEY IDEA

The managerial process environment comprises the intellectual capital for leading and managing a business.

Examine evolution of P&G's business portfolio since 2000. What did you learn?

How has your personal intellectual capital grown so far in this course? Identify three specific items. (Revisit this question at the end of the course.)

executives is *focus*. Firms should *stick to their knitting*, base strategies on core competence, and divest businesses unrelated to a common strength or purpose. PepsiCo divested Kentucky Fried Chicken, Taco Bell, and Pizza Hut; food and drinks giant Diageo divested Häagen-Dazs and Pillsbury; and British conglomerate, Unigate, sold its dairy, logistics, and bacon manufacturing to focus on fresh convenience foods — Uniq Foods.[57] By these means, firms avoid the *conglomerate discount* — reduced stock price related to investors' inability to discern the firm's future.

IC spreads through the business environment much like other innovations, and enters the modern manager's *kit bag*.[58] In recent years, firms have adopted benchmarking, best practice sharing, branding, customer relationship management (CRM), experience curves, market share/profitability relationships, outsourcing, policy matrices, portfolio models, positioning, strategic objectives, reengineering, shareholder value, and total quality management (TQM).[59] We discuss some of these in this book.

We do not suggest that each new *buzzword* has value. Rather, your challenge is to distinguish fads from new concepts that add to your personal IC. In *Managing Marketing in the 21st Century*, we offer the latest thinking on marketing, but marketing will continue to evolve during your careers. Learning is a lifelong commitment. We hope you will invest the effort to stay current with the evolving managerial process environment.[60]

PULLING IT ALL TOGETHER

The previous sections present four different facets for understanding the firm's current and/or anticipated markets — market structure, market and product evolution, industry forces, and environmental forces; the managerial task is making sense of the variety of disparate data and turning them into information and insight. The critical problem firms face is increasing change and turbulence, and hence uncertainty and surprises regarding the various factors we discussed, and their growing interdependence. Many experts converge on several broad-scale trends — evolving market structures, continuing technological advances, growth in emerging markets, aging in developed countries, globalization, spikes and spot shortages in commodities, and continuing pressure on prices and costs. Simple extrapolation of the past is increasingly likely to lead to false conclusions. Managers must simply become much smarter in seeking market insight; the preferred approach is *scenario planning*.

Select a firm and product that interests you. Use the material in this chapter to construct two alternative scenarios and related assumptions for a three-to-five-year time horizon.

Traditional uni-dimensional planning prepared the firm for a single future; scenario planning (SP) prepares the firm for multiple potential futures. SP comprises three essential elements:

- **Construct scenarios.** Reflect on trends and distinguish between certain and uncertain trends. Analyze the development of uncertain trends and prepare several internally consistent and mutually exclusive scenarios.
- **Form assumptions.** For each scenario, develop a series of external and internal assumptions that form building blocks for strategy in each scenario.
- **Prepare strategy.** Test the current strategy in each scenario and develop more appropriate strategies as necessary.[61] (Chapter 5 shows how to develop competitive scenarios.)

For any market where the firm competes or could compete, management must develop workable estimates of current and potential market size. The factors Chapter 3 discusses are critical influences on market size, and form the intellectual raw material for market-size forecasts. Chapter 6 discusses specific methodologies for making *good* forecasts.

KEY MESSAGES

What other messages did you glean from this chapter?

To gain market insight, the firm should focus on four broad areas — market structure, market and product evolution, industry forces, and environmental forces:

Market Structure:

- The *market* comprises customers willing to pay for goods and services to satisfy their needs.
- The firm should define the market at several levels.
- *Product class* and *product form* refer to products that all competitors offer. Product class is a broader level of aggregation than product form.
- Firms offer *product items* to the market — a *product line* comprises multiple product items.
- Fundamental drivers of market size are population and purchasing power.

Market and Product Evolution:

- The life-cycle framework is a good way to think about market and product evolution.
- The length of life cycles is in order: market > product class > product form.
- Life cycles have several stages — *introduction, early growth, late growth, maturity, decline* — each with distinguishing characteristics.
- Profit-margin life cycles do not mirror sales life cycles.

Industry Forces:

- The *five-forces model* is a useful way of examining pressures on the firm.
- The five forces are *current direct competitors, new direct entrants, indirect competitors, suppliers,* and *buyers.* Each force affects the firm in a different way.
- Complementers may be a potent sixth industry force.
- The firm may play multiple roles in relation to other organizations.

Environmental Forces:

- Environmental forces impact the firm and other industry players.
- Environmental forces — *political, economic, sociocultural, technological, legal/regulatory, environmental (physical)* — PESTLE.
- PESTLE forces are in a continuous state of flux, and are increasingly interconnected.
- The *managerial process* environment comprises intellectual capital for leading and managing firms.

Scenario planning is a useful approach for pulling together the various market-insight elements and predicting the future. To forecast market size — Chapter 6.

VIDEOS AND AUDIOS

For complimentary material, see Axcess Capon codes at www.axcessvids.com

Market Insight   **826a** 🔘   Noel Capon   Columbia Business School

QUESTIONS FOR STUDY AND DISCUSSION

Can you answer the questions implied by this chapter's learning outcomes? Check!

1. In the early 2000s, Krispy Kreme Doughnuts (KKD) was a fast-growing U.S. firm. Then, the widely publicized Atkins low-carb diet changed consumer attitudes toward food. Some food firms quickly offered low-carb options; others repositioned their products. KKD did not

address the low-carb trend. Rather, KKD manipulated financial results, and shareholder value collapsed. If you had been KKD's marketing director, how would you have addressed the low-carb trend?

2. Interpersonal communication is fundamental to the human condition. Develop life cycles for this market and the various product classes and product forms that satisfy this need.

3. For many years, Kodak was a leading U.S. firm. Use the five-forces model to assess the reasons for Kodak's failure and bankruptcy today.

4. American Airlines (AA) is a major U.S. carrier. Use the five-forces and PESTLE models to scope out the various external challenges AA faces.

5. Identify and classify environmental pressures that Walmart faces. Why does Walmart face these pressures? How do you assess Walmart's performance in addressing them?

6. Select a product in which you are interested. Alternatively, consider *Managing Marketing in the 21st Century*. What are the direct and indirect competitors? What competitors do you expect tomorrow? How would you compete against direct competitors? Indirect competitors? How would you prepare for tomorrow's competition?

TRUE/FALSE QUESTIONS

Answers on page A1 and at www.axcessvids.com — 983p

1. Market life cycles are the longest in the family of life cycles. ❏ **TRUE** ❏ **FALSE**

2. Most new products reach early growth and level off in the maturity stage of the product life cycle. ❏ **TRUE** ❏ **FALSE**

3. Indirect competitors often attack from different industry sectors, and incumbents sometimes ignore them. ❏ **TRUE** ❏ **FALSE**

4. The most severe supplier threat is backward integration. ❏ **TRUE** ❏ **FALSE**

5. Disruptive technologies spawn products that threaten and change entire industries.
 ❏ **TRUE** ❏ **FALSE**

MULTIPLE CHOICE QUESTIONS

Answers on page A1 and at www.axcessvids.com — 791p

1. A firm has the least amount of impact on which of the following families of life cycle?
   a. product form
   b. market
   c. product class
   d. product item

2. Which of the following stages of the product life cycle is most characterized by uncertainty?
   a. introduction
   b. early growth
   c. maturity
   d. decline

3. In which of the following stages of the product life cycle are sales mostly to repeat and loyal customers?
   a. introduction
   b. early growth
   c. maturity
   d. decline

4. In a(n) _____, two entities combine as equal partners to create a stronger firm.

   a. acquisition
   b. merger
   c. leveraged buyout
   d. backward integration

5. Which of the following is NOT one of the PESTLE forces?

   a. political
   b. sociocultural
   c. technological
   d. economic
   e. localization

CHAPTER 4

CUSTOMER INSIGHT

For complimentary material, see Axcess Capon codes at www.axcessvids.com

LEARNING OUTCOMES

When you have completed this chapter, you will be able to:

- Define and describe customer insight.
- Distinguish between macro and micro customers.
- Distinguish between direct and indirect customers.
- Identify various roles people play in the purchase-decision process.
- Use several frameworks to understand customer value.
- Analyze critical stages in the purchase-decision process.
- Highlight how customers choose among purchase alternatives.
- Classify customer purchasing processes to help develop market strategies.
- Understand key influences on consumer (B2C) and organizational (B2B) purchases.

OPENING CASE: IKEA

IKEA is the world's most successful global retailer. All IKEA stores operate under a franchise from IKEA Systems B.V. The first IKEA store opened in Almhult, Sweden, in 1958. IKEA's vision is to create a better everyday life for many people. IKEA is not just another furniture retailer; franchising supports IKEA's vision by easing market expansion. IKEA provides designers with customer insight for fashioning many different types of value.

In 2013, revenues for the 315 IKEA stores in 27 countries exceeded €28 billion. In 2015, IKEA was 27 in Interbrand's global brand ranking. Targeting middle-class customers, IKEA offers a broad range of affordable, IKEA-designed, contemporary home-furnishing products. IKEA's immense product line spans 20 different categories with 9,500 products including bathroom, beds and mattresses, bookcases and storage, pet products, lighting, TV and media solutions, tables and chairs, and work areas. Many IKEA stores also offer food products.

What makes IKEA such a different firm is the IKEA Concept, an obsessive drive for low costs via focus on design and function. For each product, IKEA designers start with a functional need and a price. They avoid nonvalue features like expensive finishes on shelf-backs or table undersides. Rather, design expertise and low-cost manufacturing lets IKEA develop products that suppliers can produce at the lowest possible cost.

Low costs and high volumes push prices down even further. To reduce transportation costs, IKEA designs and ships most products in flat packs. *Customers purchase products in the store, pick them up at the warehouse, then drive them home. Customers do simple assembly, with an IKEA-provided wrench and instructions. IKEA's mantra —* You do your part; we do our part; together we save money *— supports its low-price approach.*

By close attention to customer needs, IKEA has become a home furnishings icon. IKEA distributes millions of catalogs, printed in multiple languages, free to households in its primary market areas around the world. The catalog, also available online, offers solutions, inspiration, and low-price products. Prices are valid for 12 months.

Case Question

Each IKEA store is a large blue and yellow building averaging 300,000 square feet. IKEA wants customers to become comfortable with its home-furnishing solutions. Hence, IKEA displays products in realistic room settings and encourages customers to sit, lie down, open and close drawers, compare styles, compare prices, and imagine the possibilities.

A typical IKEA store displays up to 10,000 individual items. IKEA makes life easy for shoppers by laying out a unidirectional marked path through the store's many showrooms. Each store has a play-room at the entrance where parents can drop off children for more leisurely shopping, and a restaurant for shopping breaks. In 2015, IKEA stores globally had 800 million visitors. **[734v, 797v]**

What benefits and values does IKEA deliver to customers? How do you assess the introduction of food products in IKEA stores?

IKEA strives to deliver great customer value; customers are the firm's core assets. When the firm does a good job of delivering value, it attracts, retains, and grows customers, makes profits today and tomorrow, survives and grows, and enhances shareholder value. To succeed in the customer-value challenge, the firm must develop good *customer insight*, based on deep customer understanding. This chapter focuses on how successful firms secure customer insight.

To deliver customer value, the firm must answer the three core questions in Figure 4.1 (p. 91):

- **Who are the customers?** So far, we have used the term *customer* fairly loosely. Now we sharpen focus by considering direct and indirect customers, and current and potential customers. The firm must know who is involved in the purchase decision, and the various roles individuals play in the *decision-making unit* (DMU).

- **What do customers need and want?** Understanding customer needs is critical for delivering benefits and values. Securing customer insight may require in-depth customer research and a deep understanding of customer value.
- **How do customers buy?** The firm must know the intricacies of the customer *decision-making process* (DMP), and the various influencing factors. We consider consumer (B2C) and organizational (B2B) purchase decisions separately.

FIGURE 4.1
Customer Insight

Customer insight requires deep customer understanding.

Good customer insight requires answers to three questions:

- Who are the customers?
- What do customers need and want?
- How do customers buy?

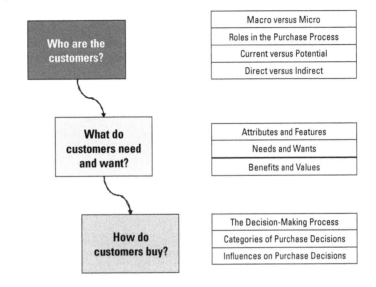

THE CHANGING VIEW

OLD WAY	NEW WAY
Basic customer understanding is sufficient	Sophisticated and timely customer insight is critical
Cognitive bias regarding customer insight	Broader view of customer behavior
Customer insight mainly applied in FMCG	Customer insight applied in many domains: product and service, public and nonprofit, nation states, politics, and personal careers
Customers passive	Customers proactive and interactive; want to be informed and engaged
Customers uninformed and accepting	Customers well-informed and demanding
Domestic view of customers is sufficient	Global view of customers essential
Focus on customers only	Focus also on organizational stakeholders and other influencers
Marketing concepts apply to consumers as buyers	Marketing concepts apply both to consumers and organizations as buyers
Narrow view of customers — like direct customers only, or consumers only	Multitiered, more complex view of customers
Supplier power dominates	Customer power dominates

WHO ARE THE CUSTOMERS?

A contact lens salesperson waited to see an eye doctor. The receptionist asked how his products compared with the doctor's current purchases. The salesperson patiently answered all her questions and left with an order. What he did not initially understand: The receptionist was the doctor's wife and made most purchasing decisions.

A man entered the largest Chevrolet dealership in West Texas, looking like he'd just left an oil rig. The experienced salespeople passed him to the rookie, who treated the customer well. The man was president of the region's largest oil-drilling firm; he purchased two pickups and three Corvettes — $8,000 commission.[1] Relatedly, a man walked into a GM dealership in Shanghai and bought 24 Hummers as gifts for friends and relatives!

A major New York investment bank sought the lead underwriter position for a firm's initial public offering (IPO). The bank lavished attention on the CFO and CEO but it did not win the business. Why? It neglected the person with decision-making authority — the major shareholder!

Identifying customers is the crucial first step in securing *customer insight*. The boxed examples highlight that customer identification is not a trivial matter. The customer pays for goods and services. Right? This answer is often wrong and is almost always inadequate. Figure 4.2 shows the firm must cast a wide net for customers. We prefer this definition:

> *A customer is any person or organization, in the channel of distribution or decision (excluding competitors), whose actions can affect the purchase of firm products/services.*[2]

This definition is purposely broad because identifying customers is often like a detective's job. Decisions for purchasing firm products/services may involve many individuals. The definition reflects the fact that:

- Both organizations — *macro level* — and individuals — *micro level* — are customers.
- Customer roles in purchase decisions include influencers and decision-makers.
- The firm should consider both *current* customers and *potential* customers.
- *Direct* customers pay the firm for products/services. *Indirect* customers — customers of direct customers (and of other indirect customers) — frequently influence purchase decisions.[3]
- Some *two-sided markets* comprise customers who *pay* for products, and customers who receive *free* products. Examples: Sellers pay auction houses, buyers receive services free; advertisers pay TV stations, consumers watch TV programs free; companies pay employment agencies, job seekers use services free.[4]

KEY IDEA

To secure good customer insight, the firm must correctly *identify* customers.

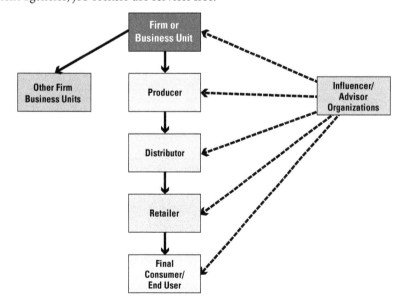

FIGURE 4.2
Identifying Customers

MARKETING QUESTION

UPS makes offers to mailroom personnel; shipping, customer service, and logistics managers; CFOs; and CEOs. If you were developing a message for the CFO, what needs would you highlight? If you focused on the shipping manager, how might your message differ?

MACRO-LEVEL CUSTOMERS AND MICRO-LEVEL CUSTOMERS

To gain customer insight, the firm must understand how various customer types fit into the buying process. *Macro-level* customers are the organizational units — producers, wholesalers, retailers, government entities (B2B)[5] and families (B2C) that purchase products/services. *Micro-level* customers are individuals within the macro-level customer who influence purchases or have decision-making authority. Let's be very clear: Organizations do not make purchase decisions; people in organizations make purchase decisions. When micro-level customers jointly make a purchase decision, they act as a *decision-making unit* (DMU).[6] Consider two situations — the purchase of a single product and purchases of multiple products.

- **Purchasing a single product.** Individual micro-level customers have specific needs and typically focus on different elements of supplier offers. Suppose Intel is buying nitrogen gas for making computer chips. Design engineers want product purity; operations personnel focus on delivery and establishing nitrogen plants on-site; and procurement managers are concerned about price. DMU members want offers that meet their individual needs but typically also want the purchase to satisfy their colleagues. AT&T won a global deal with Monsanto by meeting face-to-face with Monsanto's geographic regional heads around the world.

- **Purchasing multiple products.** The broad needs of a macro-level customer provide opportunities to sell multiple (often complementary) products to a single customer. An IBM macro-level customer may purchase several hardware products, software, and consulting services.

Individual micro-level customers often make purchase decisions as members of several macro-level customers — most commonly as an executive (B2B) or as a family member (B2C). The executive may be a micro-level B2B customer for car rental, airline flight, personal computer, and smartphone, and similarly partake in many B2C household decisions.

ROLES IN THE PURCHASE DECISION

Both macro-level and micro-level customers may play several different roles in purchase decisions. Macro-level customers like distributors and retailers *purchase* firm products; they also *sell*, *deliver*, *store*, and/or *service* them. Customers like governments, standards bodies, and consulting firms may *influence* other macro-level customers to buy firm products.

Micro-level customers play similar roles in both B2C and B2B purchase decisions:

- **Initiator.** Recognizes a problem and sets the purchase process in motion.
- **Gatekeeper.** Has the power to impede access to decision-makers and influencers. Secretaries, administrative assistants, and purchasing agents often play this role.
- **Information provider.** Provides the firm with important information about the customer.
- **Coach.** Helps the firm navigate the customer organization and advises how to address influencers and decision-makers.
- **Specifier.** Exercises influence indirectly by providing expertise like setting specifications. Examples include an architect for a family house purchase or an organization's design engineer.
- **Influencer.** The decision-maker values the influencer's opinion. B2C — influencer may be a friend, colleague, spouse, child, or grandparent; B2B — influencers include operations, engineering, marketing, and/or general management personnel. Two special types of influencer are:
  - **Champions/Sponsors** promote the firm's interests — may have previous positive experiences and/or personal relationships.
  - **Spoilers** try to prevent purchase of firm products — may be disgruntled former employees or have relationships with other suppliers.

Sidebar (left margin)

MARKETING QUESTION

Who participates in your family's summer vacation decision?

KEY IDEA

Macro-level customers are organizations.

Micro-level customers are individuals.

KEY IDEA

Organizations do not make decisions; people in organizations make decisions.

KEY IDEA

Purchase decisions involve many customer roles:

- Initiator
- Gatekeeper
- Information provider
- Coach
- Specifier
- Influencer:
  - Champion/Sponsor
  - Spoiler
- Decision-maker
- Buyer
- User

- **Decision-maker.** Has the formal power to make the purchase decision.
- **Buyer.** Has formal power to execute the purchase, like a company purchasing agent.
- **User.** Has little direct role in the purchase decision but may have veto power. Young children often have strong opinions about breakfast cereal, and the factory worker who says, "I'm not working with that red stuff," can be very influential.

Table 4.1 illustrates these various roles in B2C and B2B purchase decisions.

Purchase Decision	Organizational – B2B *Multinational firm seeks supplier for marketing training programs*	Consumer – B2C *Family is deciding whether to take a cruise for the family vacation*
Roles		
Initiator	Head of human resources (HR)	Family physician — advises family to take vacation for mother's health
Gatekeeper	Senior HR personnel	Live-in housekeeper
Information provider	Bricker's — good source on executive education	Travel agent
Coach	Consultant to firm; previously Columbia faculty member	Neighbor — takes three cruises annually
Specifier	Junior HR personnel who develop the program	Grandmother (has basic requirements that must be met)
Influencer	Senior line executives	Children
Champion/sponsor	Senior executives committed to Columbia Business School	Second cousin (works for cruise line)
Spoiler	Two senior line executives with MBAs from Harvard and Wharton	Daughter's boyfriend — has summer job at a Caribbean resort
Decision-maker	CEO	Mother
Buyer	Purchasing officer	Father
User	Middle managers	Mother, father, children, grandparents

TABLE 4.1
Illustration of Roles in B2B and B2C Purchase Decisions[7]

MARKETING QUESTION

Think of when you were selling something — product, idea, or yourself for a job. Who played what roles in the decision? Hint: Don't underestimate gatekeepers, influencers, spoilers, or champions who may have worked in the background.

The Importance of Users

Venice (disguised), a large industrial manufacturer, worked directly with Baltimore Plastics (BP) on product development. Venice purchased large quantities of BP's tapes on annual contracts from Gary Ludlow's brokerage firm. Ludlow had sold BP products since Venice was a small customer, and had many close, first-name relationships with Venice personnel — factory managers and shop-floor workers. Ludlow was well known for arriving at Venice factories with boxes of donuts that he distributed widely.

Venice's new owners replaced top management. Venice's new procurement strategy required cutting out middlemen like Ludlow and dealing directly with manufacturing suppliers. Venice put its BP-Ludlow tape business out to competitive bid. BP refused to bid, citing its long-standing Ludlow relationship. Washington, a tough BP competitor, won the contract to replace BP-Ludlow.

Washington made several sample tape deliveries to Venice; the tapes comfortably met Venice's rigorous testing standards. But the Washington tapes failed in production. Venice managers worked hard with shop-floor personnel, but the tapes would just not work! Shop-floor workers provided many reasons. Ultimately, Venice canceled the Washington contract and ordered BP products from Ludlow. Venice had no further problems!

VARIETY AND EVOLUTION OF PURCHASE-DECISION ROLES. Because macro-level customers make many different types of purchases, DMU composition may vary markedly across decisions.

KEY IDEA

In B2B and B2C, the roles individuals play vary from purchase decision to purchase decision.

- **B2C**. Roles for two typical household decisions may be:
  - Home purchase: decision-maker — wife; influencers — many family members; buyer — husband
  - Family movie trip: decision-makers — children; influencer — father; buyer — mother

Generally speaking, in traditional U.S. families, influence by mothers and children is increasing and by fathers is declining: Women are decision-makers for more than 80 percent of discretionary purchases. These dynamics are driving marketing changes for many products — from automobiles to breakfast cereal. Of course, significant family events, like divorce, remarriage, and death, change family purchasing patterns. Furthermore, an increasing percentage of the U.S. population lives in nontraditional family settings.

- **B2B**. Organizations use many different DMU constellations for their various purchases. DMUs evolve; suppliers should anticipate that before, during, or after the purchase process, individual customer employees may:
  - Change roles and responsibilities.
  - Enter/leave the DMU.
  - Resign from the customer and join a different organization (maybe another customer).

In difficult economic times, purchasing decisions may escalate to the CFO, senior management committee, or even the board of directors for large dollar purchases. The firm may also drive change in customer DMUs by modifying the offer. High-end supplier Hilti shifted focus from *selling power tools* to *providing a tool management program*; customer decision-making evolved from construction-site crew leaders and purchasing managers to CFOs and CEOs. Roles also change as customer organizations evolve from low-status *purchasing* to high-status *procurement*, or even more broadly to managing the entire *supply chain*. Corporate events like mergers and acquisitions frequently drive changes in the purchasing process. Finally, B2B purchase decisions may influence B2C purchases and vice versa. Executives whose firms make advantageous hotel contracts (B2B) stay at those same hotels when on family vacations (B2C). And the widespread popularity of the iPhone with consumers (B2C) led many organizations also to standardize on the iPhone (B2B). The firm should anticipate change.

CURRENT CUSTOMERS AND POTENTIAL CUSTOMERS

KEY IDEA

The firm must pay attention to both:
- Current customers
- Potential customers

Current customers provide revenues and profits today; Chapter 2 highlights the role of customer retention for future revenues and profits. But the firm must also identify *potential* customers. Alcoa and McKinsey devote major efforts to identifying and creating *tomorrow* customers:

"In our aerospace system, senior Alcoa executives spend extensive time creating an environment to make customers open to innovation. We interact with the top universities that train aerospace and aeronautical engineers.[8] We help design curricula, teach classes, have design contests, and offer internships and jobs. We show students and faculty the latest and greatest in metals. These kids are going to be designing airplanes over the next 20 years — they know Alcoa, they know metals, and they feel pretty good about it. We also do opinion work with other influential groups — airline executives, pilots, mechanics, and frequent travelers. We are creating a very favorable climate for demanding metallics in airplanes, particularly Alcoa metallics."[9]

McKinsey is a world-leading consulting firm; many business students aspire to work for McKinsey. McKinsey expects new hires to stay about six to ten years. McKinsey is quite willing to lose consultants to high-level jobs at client companies, but it works hard to maintain contact, in part via an alumni magazine. When the former employee's new employer wants advice, which consulting firm will it call?

DIRECT CUSTOMERS AND INDIRECT CUSTOMERS

Typically, the firm's *direct* customers exchange money for products/services. Many *indirect* customers buy the firm's products from these direct customers or from other indirect customers. Sometimes direct customers are distributors or retailers, or end users that buy and use the firm's finished products. In other cases, direct customers transform the firm's product before their own product reaches their customers:

A sales team from packaging firm Mead Westvaco (MW) found that a potential direct customer's food products spoiled in the freezers of potential indirect customers — supermarkets. The direct customer accepted MV's redesigned package; sales and profits increased for MW and its direct customer.

A small German producer sold sheet zinc to fabricators for the building trade — direct customers. The fabricators sold roofing sheets and drainpipes to builders and roofers — indirect customers. Research with builders, roofers, and consumers led the zinc producer to develop a new alloy with better durability and color fastness. Sales soared.

The distinction between direct and indirect customers is critically important. The firm has a business relationship with direct customers. But the firm *may not know* its indirect customers, and hence have little insight into the benefits and values they seek. Until *customer relationship management* (CRM) technology became widely available, FMCG firms like P&G typically could not identify their indirect customers — consumers purchasing their products. Today, FMCG firms learn via contests, promotions, and websites. Stouffer's (Nestlé) encourages consumers to register at its website to learn about recipes and menu items; correspondingly, Stouffer's gains better insight into consumer needs.

Two examples emphasize the importance of a broad customer view and indirect customers:

Intel traditionally focused efforts on direct customers — computer manufacturers. But much Intel success resulted from the *intel inside* campaign that placed emphasis on indirect customers — consumers, distributors, and retailers.[10]

Monsanto (U.S.) spent heavily to develop genetically modified seeds that improved yields for direct customers — farmers. But Monsanto offered no visible benefit for indirect customers — consumers. Monsanto faced enormous criticism and product boycotts from European consumers.

To reinforce the importance of indirect customers, consider what a senior UPS executive told us: "As a company we are very focused, not just on our customers and what we do that helps them, but on what we do that helps their customer. We're always looking through our customer to their customer. We continually ask ourselves ... how does our technology, our products/services and opportunities transcend our customer's relationship with their customers. If they provide better customer service, and achieve lower costs, and really achieve their business vision, and help their customer be successful ... we have a stronger relationship than if we just focus on our relationship with our customer."[11]

WHAT DO CUSTOMERS NEED AND WANT?

The firm attracts, retains, and grows customers by delivering value to satisfy their needs. *Customer value* equates to the value in the firm's offer less the customer's monetary, time, effort, and emotional costs.[12] Two firm actions are crucial:

- Make offers of value to satisfy customer needs.
- Communicate the value of those offers to customers.[13]

The Opening Case shows how IKEA provides customer value and communicates customer value. If the firm offers value, but customers don't know about it, they will not purchase. If the

---

MARKETING QUESTION

Banks are persistent in soliciting students for credit cards. Why? How could solicitations be more effective?

KEY IDEA

Indirect customers may be more important than *direct* customers — they are often final users and ultimately drive market demand.

MARKETING QUESTION

What product did a firm target to you that did not satisfy your needs? What needs did the product not satisfy? Why do you think this occurred?

KEY IDEA

To *attract*, *retain*, and *grow* customers, the firm must:

• Develop offers of value to satisfy customer needs

• Communicate the value of those offers to customers

KEY IDEA

Customer needs are *recognized* or *latent*. Recognized needs are *expressed* or *nonexpressed*.

firm communicates its offer extensively, but customers don't perceive value (like GM advertising the Hummer as gasoline prices rise), they will not purchase. We discuss customer needs, how they relate to product attributes/features, and the benefits and values customers receive.

RECOGNIZED NEEDS VERSUS LATENT NEEDS

Sometimes customers understand their needs — *recognized* needs; sometimes they don't — *latent* needs. Recognized needs are *expressed* or *nonexpressed*:

• **Expressed needs.** Customers often ask for advice on how to satisfy their needs.

• **Nonexpressed needs.** Customers sometimes do not express their needs, like teenage girls contemplating condom purchases.

Customers may have a recognized need but do not associate the firm with satisfying that need. Henry Ford famously said: "If I'd asked my customers what they wanted, they'd have said a faster horse!" (Apple's Steve Jobs had a similar perspective. **[903v]**) Indeed, one of marketing's core tasks is to identify value that customers are not expecting. In the 2008–9 recession, Hyundai successfully offered unexpected value; car buyers could return vehicles at no cost nor credit-rating impact if they lost jobs/income within one year of purchase. When a Wipro (Indian outsourcing firm) salesperson asked a *Fortune 500* IT decision-maker how Wipro could earn outsourcing business, the executive replied: "Surprise me!" In other words, "Show how you can deliver value I'm not expecting."

Customers are not consciously aware of latent needs. These needs may surface as technological innovation raises awareness and customers require benefits/values they could not previously articulate. Some people suggest that marketing *creates* customer needs; surfacing and satisfying latent needs is a more parsimonious explanation for customer behavior. A few years ago, few consumers could have articulated a need for cell phones. But widespread availability surfaced a latent need of wanting to stay in constant contact.

Watermelons are a traditional fruit. Technological advances address recognized needs and latent needs. Figure 4.3A shows watermelons that address recognized needs for display and refrigerator storage. Figure 4.3B shows a *personal* watermelon that satisfies the latent need for a one- or two-person product.[14]

FIGURE 4.3A (LEFT)
Satisfying a Recognized Need: Cubic Watermelons

FIGURE 4.3B (RIGHT)
Satisfying a Latent Need:
Personal *Watermelons*

ATTRIBUTES AND FEATURES VERSUS BENEFITS AND VALUES

Many firms define their products/services in terms of *attributes* and *features*. Think about television advertising touting *new and improved*. Now read very carefully: Customers *do not care about your products/services* — they are not interested in the attributes and features. Customers *do care* about satisfying *their needs* and the *benefits and values* your products/services provide. You must communicate these well. Let's be very clear about these terms:

- **Attributes and features.** Design elements or functions the firm builds into its products/services — typically of great concern to design engineers.
- **Benefits.** Something the product/service delivers that satisfies customer needs.
- **Values.** Something the product/service provides that has broader scope than a benefit.

The Black & Decker (B&D) example exemplifies attributes/features, benefits, and values:

B&D makes hand-held electric drills. *Attributes/features* include color, drill speed and weight, bit gauge and hardness, presence/absence of battery, battery life, and the ability to use other tools like sanders. The statement "Last year we sold 40 million drill bits that nobody wanted"[15] captures the irrelevance of attributes/features to customers. B&D drills provide *benefits* to customers; they make holes easily. *Values* that B&D drills enable include improving a living room by hanging pictures and ornaments, or building a tree house and having fun with children.

Marty Homlish — former CEO of SAP Global Marketing — explained the transformation from attributes/features to benefits and values he directed. "We used to talk about successful implementation like this: 'Customer XYZ implemented SAP Supply-Chain Management. They had to do it in 100 days, but they went live in 99 days and only had one critical crisis.' But that was not the issue. The real story was, 'Customer XYZ implemented SAP Supply-Chain Management. As a result, it reduced its on-hand inventory from 2.8 months' supply to 2.1 months' and its on-the-water inventory from one month to two weeks. And XYZ saved $500 million.'"[16]

The firm should relate product attributes/features to customer benefits and values, then identify strong ties, weak ties, and orphans:

- **Strong ties.** The attribute/feature is strongly related to a value — in fact and in the customer's mind. Generally, the firm should strive to enhance strong ties.
- **Weak ties.** Customers perceive the attribute/feature as weakly related to the value. Options: improve the attribute/feature; or, if the attribute/feature is sufficiently strong, improve communications.
- **Orphan attributes/features.** The attribute/feature is unrelated to a customer value. Product redesign to remove the attribute/feature may reduce costs.
- **Orphan values.** The firm does not provide an attribute/feature to deliver required customer value. Product redesign should add the required attribute/feature.

Select a product. What are its *strong ties* and *weak ties*? Can you identify *orphan attributes* and/or *orphan values*?

Most firms sell products/services that provide benefits and values. Some firms sell benefits and values directly to customers. The *cloud* provides storage capacity; firms do not have to purchase computer hardware. Some airlines pay for airplane engines per hour of operating life; and Spotify *streams* music directly — consumers do not purchase.

HIERARCHIES OF NEEDS, FEATURES, BENEFITS, AND VALUES

Psychologists have studied individual needs extensively. We explore the popular need framework developed by psychologist Abraham Maslow that marketers often use. Maslow's ideas form the basis of the feature/benefit/value ladder. (For simplicity, we omit the term *attributes* when stating the ladder.)

KEY IDEA

MASLOW'S HIERARCHY OF NEEDS. Maslow's classic framework identifies five major groups of needs — *physiological, safety and security, social, ego, self-actualization* — ordered low to high.[17] Generally, we expect individuals to satisfy lower-level *physiological* and *safety and security* needs before higher-level needs like *ego* and *self-actualization*.

Maslow's approach places a person's needs in an ordered hierarchy.

Products like groceries, clothing, and housing satisfy lower-level *physiological* needs; sports equipment and educational services satisfy higher-level *social, ego*, and *self-actualization* needs. But firms can design market offers (products, promotion, distribution, price) for groceries, clothing, and housing that also satisfy higher-level *social* and *ego* needs. Examples, respectively: organic food, designer fashions, and neighborhood location. Satisfying both *higher-level* needs and *lower-level* needs should provide greater customer value than satisfying only *lower-level* needs. A woman is more likely to buy a shampoo she believes will make her attractive (*ego* need) than one that just cleans her hair (*physiological* need). Table 4.2 applies Maslow's framework to two purchasing decisions.

....
TABLE 4.2
*Using Maslow's Hierarchy
of Needs to Gain Insight
into Two Consumer
Purchases*

Need	Product – Folgers Coffee	Product – Krispy Kreme Donuts
Self-Actualization (self-fulfillment)	Savoring	Be part of a cultural phenomenon
Ego (prestige, success, self-respect)	Confidence, achievement	Be in vogue (especially among Gen-Xers)
Social (love, affection, friendship, belonging)	Togetherness, freshness, taste	Eating donuts is a group experience that creates a sense of *togetherness*
Safety & Security (protection, order, security)	Easy on the stomach, no jitters	Safe, easy for kids to eat — and no mess
Physiological (food, drink, air, shelter, sex)	Satisfies thirst, keeps you alert, keeps you warm	Satisfies hunger and the sweet tooth

Develop a feature/benefit/value ladder for the marketing course you are taking right now.

LADDERING FEATURES, BENEFITS, AND VALUES. Many marketers meld Maslow's hierarchical approach to individual needs with the feature/benefit/value distinctions to form a *feature/benefit/value ladder*.[18] Figure 4.4 demonstrates the ladder's three main characteristics:

- **Focuses attention on providing benefits and values.** Firms typically design attributes/features into their products/services. The feature/benefit/value ladder forces a translation into benefits and values for customers. B&D's drills deliver many benefits and values.

- **Provides communications options.** The variety of benefits and values broadens firm options for communicating with customers. The best communications depend on factors like stage of market development and competitive threats. Potential B&D communications like *drill speed and bit hardness, makes holes easily*, and *supports do-it-yourself activity* are quite different from each other.

- **Broadens the view of competition.** When the firm focuses on attributes/features, competition is direct competitors. Focus on customer benefits and values broadens this scope to indirect competitors. With an attributes/features focus, B&D's competitors are other electric drill manufacturers. Focusing on Benefit A — makes holes easily — introduces competitors like explosives, lasers, nails, water drills, and woodpeckers(!). Higher-level benefits broaden competitive scope even further.[19]

KEY IDEA

The feature/benefit/value ladder ensures the firm:

- Focuses on providing benefits and values
- Provides communications options
- Broadens the view of competition

....
FIGURE 4.4
*Feature/Benefit/Value
Ladders for Black &
Decker Drills and
Nivea Skin Cream*

Excedrin contains aspirin, caffeine, and acetaminophen. Sales of a companion product, advertised as *aspirin-free* Excedrin, were declining. A new advertising message focused on *treating tension headaches*. The messaging switch from attributes/features — *aspirin-free*, to benefits — *treating tension headaches*, drove a significant sales increase.

Xerox supplied about 10 percent of AT&T's more than 60,000 copiers (mostly black and white). Traditionally, copier suppliers competed on *feeds* and *speeds*, but Xerox knew AT&T liked its 5,000 color machines. Xerox provided additional service value by conducting a multimonth study of AT&T's copier use and proposed a replacement program requiring 40,000 color copiers. AT&T agreed and Xerox became AT&T's sole supplier.

In general, customers using firm products/services focus on the benefits and values they provide. By contrast, resellers like distributors, retailers, and wholesalers are more interested in economic benefits like profit margins, net profit, and return on investment. Different customer types seek different benefits and values, so the firm should develop several feature/benefit/value ladders.[20] In practice, the firm may identify multiple feature/benefit value ladders for a single offer. Figure 4.5 shows how three Volvo attributes/features provide one major benefit — *safe car* — that in turn delivers three higher-level values.[21]

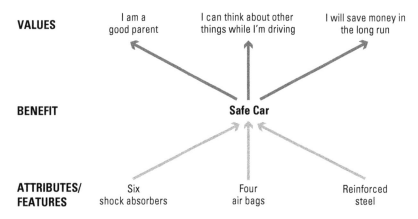

FIGURE 4.5
Feature/Benefit/Value Ladder for Volvo

FUNCTIONAL, PSYCHOLOGICAL, AND ECONOMIC BENEFITS AND VALUES

Customers base their purchase decisions on a need hierarchy. The firm must translate the attributes/ features of its offer into a hierarchy of benefits and values that aligns with these needs. But we must go one step further to explore three types of benefits and values.[22]

FUNCTIONAL BENEFITS AND VALUES. Firms design products/services to provide functional benefits and values that satisfy customer needs. Food products satisfy hunger needs; disc brakes stop automobiles. Typically, products offer multiple functional benefits: an electric car may have fast acceleration, save fuel, stop quickly, and be quiet. Some attributes/features may provide both benefits and detriments: An electric car's quietness is a benefit to drivers/passengers, but may be a detriment to pedestrians if they cannot hear it coming. Sometimes customers and firms discover functional benefits serendipitously: Customers found Avon's *Skin So Soft* moisturizer was effective as a mosquito repellent; Pfizer developed Viagra to address heart disease but discovered it could treat erectile dysfunction.

PSYCHOLOGICAL BENEFITS AND VALUES. Psychological benefits and values typically satisfy status, affiliation, reassurance, and security needs. Customers receive benefits and values after purchase, but brands may provide risk-reduction benefits before purchase. Firms often offer psychological and functional benefits together. Fine-dining restaurants provide high-quality food and ambience (functional) but also prestige (psychological). An automobile may provide

MARKETING QUESTION

The three major overnight shipping firms offer various benefits and values. Do you agree with these category assignments, based on their slogans?

Functional Provider:
UPS — *Moving at the speed of business* and *See what Brown can do for you.*

Psychological Provider:
FedEx — *Be absolutely sure* (that is, don't get fired).

Economic Provider:
United States Postal Service (USPS) — *We deliver.* USPS's prices are lower than UPS and FedEx.

MARKETING QUESTION

Think about one of your favorite products. What *functional* benefits does it provide? What *psychological* benefits does it provide? Be creative!

KEY IDEA

In B2B, the firm delivers economic value by:
- Reducing customer costs and/or investment
- Increasing customer revenues

KEY IDEA

EVC is the maximum price customers should pay.

fast acceleration, efficiency, and comfort (functional), but also status (psychological) — many consumers purchase Ford Fusion and Toyota Prius hybrids to make an environmental statement (psychological). Laundry detergents clean clothes, and make them soft and nice smelling (functional); they also provide self-confidence and reinforce caring for the family (psychological). Generally, psychological values transcend functional benefits, like female self-esteem for Dove's *Real Beauty* campaign [883p], and appear higher up the feature/benefit/value ladder.[23]

ECONOMIC BENEFITS AND VALUES. Economic benefits and values concern financial aspects like price and credit terms. Price is often the primary purchase driver, especially in tough economies when customers trade off functional and psychological benefits for low price. Walmart, purchasing clubs, dollar stores, discount airlines, and generic drug producers provide economic benefits via lower prices. Similarly, many FMCG firms offer *everyday low pricing*. In B2B, price is often critical, but sometimes firms deliver cost-cutting economic benefits and *lower total cost of ownership* at higher prices by providing greater functional benefits.

U.S. furniture manufacturer Haworth competes successfully in China against fierce local price competition. Teams of Haworth designers and psychologists develop complete workplace environments for multinational and Chinese firms anxious to retain talent. The design service is free, but Haworth's furniture prices are 30 to 50 percent above local suppliers.

Traditionally, lumber firms used wood waste at zero cost to heat drying kilns. Jackson (natural gas supplier) identified several sources of savings from switching to natural gas — labor costs to fuel and maintain the kilns, production losses from closing kilns to clean out ash residue, and EPA compliance problems. When a firm switched to natural gas, Jackson helped identify revenue-producing markets for its wood waste.[24]

GE strengthens customer relationships by helping customers improve operational effectiveness.[25] The firm may also provide economic value by reducing customer maintenance, ownership, transactions, usage, and disposal costs, and investment.[26] The Jackson example shows the importance of assessing customer economic benefits. We calculate *economic value for the customer* (EVC) from the competitive product price, plus the net added value — positive differentiation value less negative differentiation value — from using the firm's product. The boxed insert shows the EVC calculation for a new polyester product for making conveyor belts.[27]

Illustration of Economic Value for the Customer (EVC)

Industrial-strength conveyor belts comprise a textile fabric core covered with rubber. Textile fiber strength is crucial for conveyor belt life. Traditionally, *sevens** cotton yarn was the core; 750 denier polyester yarn was a potential replacement. Critical data for calculating the economic value of polyester fiber in conveyor belts are:

- Price of sevens cotton — 90 cents per lb.
- 750 denier polyester yarn is four times stronger than cotton — 8 versus 2 grams per denier (g.p.d.)
- Extra cost of processing polyester versus cotton — 30 cents per lb.

EVC answers the following question: What is the maximum price a conveyor belt manufacturer will pay for polyester yarn? (We assume that conveyor belt life does not change when polyester replaces cotton.) Since polyester is four times stronger than cotton, customers can use four pounds of cotton or one pound of polyester — Figure 4.6 (p. 102):

- Reference value — sevens cotton yarn @ 90 cents per lb.
- Polyester equivalence — 1 lb. of 750 denier polyester yarn or 4 lbs. of sevens cotton = 90 cents × 4 = $3.60 — reference value plus positive differentiation value
- Extra cost to process polyester yarn — 30 cents per lb. — negative differentiation value
- Net polyester equivalence — $3.60 less $0.30 = $3.30 — EVC[28]

*Sevens cotton is the standard type of cotton yarn used in industrial applications.

continues

In sum, based on economic value analysis, conveyor belt manufacturers should be indifferent between:

a. Sevens cotton @ 90 cents per lb., and

b. 750 denier polyester @ $3.30 per lb.

Hence, the maximum polyester price is $3.30 per lb. At any price above $3.30 per lb., conveyor belt manufacturers would be better off sticking with cotton.

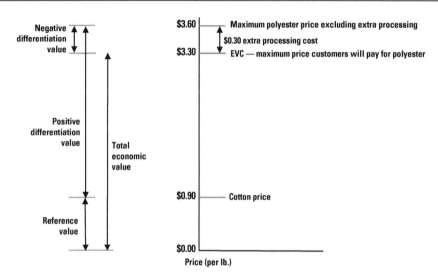

FIGURE 4.6
Illustration of Economic Value to the Customer

Many EVC calculations are more complex than this simple illustration.[29] Factors for inclusion are customer financing, maintenance, and operating costs plus revenue changes. International Paper (IP) developed new packaging for fresh fruit that reduced costs for its customers (supermarkets); by enhancing display, IP also increased customer revenues.

MARKETING QUESTION

What type(s) of value did Kodak offer? **[484v]** Why did Kodak declare bankruptcy?

The firm's challenge is to deliver the *right* combination of functional, psychological, and economic benefits and values to those customers it wants to attract, retain, and grow. Figure 4.7 shows the mix of benefits and values a pharmaceutical firm might deliver to physicians.

Psychological
- Enhanced status
- Sense of belonging
- Sense of assurance
- Reduced risk

FIGURE 4.7
Functional, Psychological, and Economic Benefits for a Physician

Functional
- Improved efficacy
- Less side effects
- Lower drug interactions

Economic
- Reduced input costs
- Increased reimbursements

KEY IDEA

For customers the firm wants to attract, retain, and grow, it must deliver the *right* combination of three types of benefits and values:

- Functional
- Psychological
- Economic

MARKETING QUESTION

How do decision-makers evaluate the success/failure of their purchases?

CHARACTERISTICS OF BENEFITS AND VALUES

In many cases, firm attributes/features provide customers with benefits and values at (or soon after) purchase in a straightforward manner. We enjoy a Starbucks latte; the taxi delivers us to our destination; the refrigerator preserves our food; and the retailer makes a profit margin. But sometimes the benefits and values are not so clear cut. We examine several situations.

DEFERRED BENEFITS AND VALUES. Customers may receive benefits and values in the future:

- **Defined value if and when required.** The critical value the firm offers may not lie in the product itself. Rather, the core value may be the ability to secure additional value if and when needed. The AmEx Platinum Card Concierge program locates hard-to-find items, delivers gifts, provides secretarial services in remote areas, and offers secure reservations in upscale restaurants: Most cardholders rarely use these services but their availability has high value.[30] Insurance companies offer Mayo Clinic as a policy benefit, but relatively few patients assume the extra travel, hotel, and other out-of-pocket expenses to visit Mayo.

- **Potential but uncertain value.** The core purchase driver may be the expectation of as-yet-unknown potential future benefits and values. When a B2B customer purchases from a technology firm, the key factor may be benefits inherent in the supplier relationship — like preferential access to *beta* (prerelease) versions of future technology. Dell buys most of its computer chips from Intel (versus AMD), in part because Intel gives Dell early insight into new technologies.

PRESENCE VALUE. The firm may provide considerable customer value just by being a supplier, so long as its products are acceptable and prices are reasonable. When a customer has one strong and one weak supplier, the weak supplier's presence keeps the strong supplier *honest* and inhibits the exercise of monopoly power. For many years, Airbus played this role versus Boeing in passenger aircraft; AMD acts similarly versus Intel in computer chips.

MARKETING QUESTION

What products offer *potential value*, *future value*, *presence value*, and/or *scarcity value*?

SCARCITY VALUE. Customers realize value from the limited availability of the product/service. Fashion retailer Zara deliberately make small product volumes to provide scarcity value. Beanie Babies notoriously limited production runs, then ruthlessly retired prized stuffed animals. Many Harley-Davidson models have long wait times.[31] Nike Air Force 1 sneakers have been a market leader for a quarter-century; Nike launches new versions every couple of months, but deliberately keeps supplies tight to develop scarcity value and create pent-up demand.

On a warm and sunny Saturday afternoon in August, a New York-based Uber car took Ellen and her month-old twin daughters to visit a friend — $20. To return home in the evening, Ellen again engaged Uber. By now it was dark and raining — Uber's scarcity *surge pricing* kicked in — $80!

WHEN CUSTOMERS RECOGNIZE VALUE. Sometimes customers have good data about the benefits and values a product/service provides; other times they are uncertain and cannot assess value until long after purchase. *Search*, *use*, and *credence* benefits capture this uncertainty and may offer important insight:

- **Search benefits.** Significant product/service data is available from the firm and/or independent sources like *Consumer Reports*. Customers may even inspect and try products — like test-driving a car.

- **Use benefits.** Relatively little actual data is available on customer value before purchase — like many services. Customers recognize value when they *consume* the product/service — like a concert performance, or an expensive restaurant meal.

MARKETING QUESTION

Choose one product each that offers mainly *search*, *use*, and *credence* benefits. How would your communications to potential customers differ?

- **Credence benefits.** It is impossible for customers to assess value until long after purchase. Examples: economic benefits from investments, and health benefits from some medical procedures.

VALUE FOR WHOM. Consumers (B2C) typically make purchases for themselves, family members, friends, colleagues, or a group like a club. B2B purchases may satisfy either organizational or individual needs. For the customer organization's well-being, the purchase value should be for the organization, but this is not always the case:

> A large British mail-order firm was deciding which new computer system to purchase. Head of management services steered the purchase to his favored supplier. "[By sitting] ... at the junction of the communication channels between his subordinates, the manufacturers, and the board [of directors] ... he was able to exert biases in favor of his own demands and at the same time feed the board negative information about the demands of his opponents."[32]

KEY IDEA

To gain greater customer insight, the firm should ask: "What motivates people in customer roles to behave the way they do?"

Some suppliers have large budgets for entertaining customer employees and providing personal items to those with significant influence and/or decision-making power — like hospital physicians and radio disc jockeys. Individual benefits may be ethically questionable and even illegal — like *facilitation payments* (*kickbacks*). U.S. and European authorities fined German engineering giant Siemens a record $1.6 billion to settle allegations that it won lucrative overseas power and telecom contracts via bribery.

Some firms work hard to ensure their employees do not benefit personally from suppliers. Walmart prohibits employees from accepting gifts, meals, trips, or other items of value. Sometimes suppliers take advantage of customer processes to provide individual value. Suppose a customer firm pays purchasing agents (PA) bonuses based on the difference between the final negotiated price and the initial offering price. Suppliers that initially price high, then offer large discounts, may enhance their chances of winning by helping PAs earn bonuses.

BEYOND CUSTOMER BENEFITS AND VALUES – CUSTOMER EXPERIENCES

As competition grows, firms increasingly focus on providing customer *experiences* — conditions, events, states — that consciously affect buying behavior. Table 4.3 categorizes these experiences as *real* (experienced directly), *anticipatory* (looking forward to), or *vicarious* (experienced through someone else). Experiences are an important factor in gaining insight into customer behavior and how and why customers value market offers.[33] Using a TV remote is a superior experience to dialing controls on the TV set; changing channels by simple hand gestures will be even better. Consider the value customers receive from Napa Valley Reserve:

Napa Valley Reserve

Most wineries offer value based on wine quality, but not Napa Valley Reserve (NVR). NVR offers the Napa Valley experience *by invitation only* for a $145,000 membership fee. The NVR experience includes using facilities for dinner, hosting guest receptions, making wine — supervised by an experienced wine maker — and bottling five barrels; members can buy the wine — $55 per bottle. NVR has several hundred members.[34]

Type of Experience	Example
Real	Go to see a movie
Anticipatory	See an advertisement for the movie
Vicarious	Send daughter to the movie

TABLE 4.3
Types of Customer Experiences

A single event may create many different experiences. New York City ballet aficionados experience a touring Bolshoi performance differently from those seeing their first ballet. Also, the experience may have more value than the product. Consider coffee: Many cafes sell coffee for around $1 per cup: Starbucks coffee is several dollars per cup but it also offers a personal and memorable experience — the language of the *baristas*, the noise of the grinders and espresso machines, the sight of scores of coffee varieties and products, the feel of hot coffee in the hand, and an atmosphere permeated by coffee aroma.[35] Many Starbucks customers continually return because of the experience.

MARKETING QUESTION

Think about your favorite entertainment — concert, restaurant, sports event, theater. Which mode(s) — sense, feel, think, act, relate — best describes your experience? Did the provider consciously create this experience? How?

Five modes of customer experience are[36]:

- **Sense.** Creates sensory experiences through sight, smell, sound, taste, and touch.
- **Feel.** Appeals to inner feelings and emotions. Attempts to create affective experiences, ranging from mildly positive to strong emotions of joy and pride.
- **Think.** Appeals to the intellect. Creates problem-solving experiences that engage creatively.
- **Act.** Enriches by showing alternative ways of doing things, different lifestyles and interactions.
- **Relate.** Contains aspects of sense, feel, think, and act, but reaches beyond individual personal, private feelings to something outside his/her private state.

This framework offers a methodical way of determining those experiences the firm wants customers to associate with its products. Are you familiar with any of the examples in Table 4.4?

TABLE 4.4
Customer Experience Examples

Experience Mode	Company/Brand	Example
Sense	P&G	*Tide Mountain Fresh*
Feel	Campbell's Soup	*Mmm, Mmm! Good for the body, good for the soul*
Think	Apple Computer	*Think Different*
Act	Nike	*Just do it*
Relate	Harley-Davidson	*Harley is a way of life*

KEY IDEA

Sense, feel, think, act, and *relate* are experience modes through which customers receive value from their experiences.

By 2030, the U.S. population aged 65 and older will exceed 70 million. Kimberly-Clark (KC) educates retail executives about senior citizen shopping experiences. KC simulates common vision impairments like cataracts, eye lens yellowing, glaucoma, and macular degeneration via cardboard glasses; and limited manual dexterity from arthritis via large rubber gloves. CVS, Rite Aid, and Walgreens are also investing to improve the elderly's shopping experience.

HOW DO CUSTOMERS BUY?

KEY IDEA

The firm must identify the customer's decision-making process (DMP).

Diesel makes high-priced denim jeans — $150 to $350 per pair. Diesel deliberately designs stores to *intimidate* shoppers, frequently inexperienced young men. Diesel salespeople *rescue* shoppers and *shepherd* them through the buying process.

The purchase *decision-making process* (DMP) ranges from the relatively simple — buying a midmorning snack — to highly complex — U.S. government purchasing a new fighter jet. The DMP can be as quick as an impulse purchase or take months or even years.[37] Marketers must understand how customers move through the process, then identify options for influence.

PURCHASE-DECISION STAGES

Figure 4.8 shows the DMP as a robust purchase model with six stages.[38] Each DMP may involve multiple feedback loops both within and among stages. The customer may identify a need/problem early on, and then elaborate that need/problem as she secures information and evaluates alternatives. Some purchases are *planned*, like the Table 4.5 (p. 106) example; others are *unplanned* — made spontaneously during a shopping trip — or in response to an online offer.

FIGURE 4.8
The Purchase Decision Process

Decision Process Stage	Customer Action and Cognitions
1. Recognizing problems	Sees advertisement: "That looks cool and I don't have one."
2. Acquiring information	Demonstration in store: "What is this thing?" "What does it do?" "What does multiformat mean?" "What is the price?"
3. Evaluating alternatives	Examine various options: "Is Sony better than Toshiba and Philips?"
4. Making a choice	"I am going to buy Sony."
5. Purchasing and securing the product	"Where can I buy it?" "When will it arrive?"
6. Postpurchase processes	"How do I hook this up?" "Where do I get service?"

TABLE 4.5

An Individual's Purchase Decision Process for a DVD Player

STAGE 1 – RECOGNIZING PROBLEMS. Some customer needs are critical to system functioning: food and drink for individuals; raw materials and capital equipment for firms. Indeed, the firm should keep good records of customer contract-expiry and capital equipment replacement dates for its own and competitor products so as to recognize problems early. Some needs are (or may become) habitual, as for air fresheners, chewing gum, healthy snacks, smoking, and toothpaste. Other needs are discretionary: "Should I buy a vacation package?" "Should the firm lease a corporate jet?" The customer may recognize a need independently, or a potential supplier may point it out.

> In Ghana, only 4 percent of the population washed hands with soap and water after using the restroom; by comparison 50 percent washed hands when they believed they were dirty. Advertising messages associated bathroom visits with feelings of disgust; post-bathroom hand-washing increased sharply.
>
> P&G introduced Febreze for removing bad smells from smelly clothes but was initially unsuccessful. Advertising that associated Febreze with the finishing touch of cleaning the kitchen, living room, and laundry created a habit and generated significant revenues.

KEY IDEA

The critical purchase decision stages are:
1. Recognizing problems
2. Acquiring information
3. Evaluating alternatives
4. Making a choice
5. Purchasing and securing the product
6. Postpurchase processes

STAGE 2 – ACQUIRING INFORMATION. After recognizing a problem, customers generally seek information to help identify:

- The *feature* set — attributes/features that may satisfy the need.
- Criteria for evaluating satisfactory performance by the attributes/features.
- The *awareness* set — alternatives that may satisfy the need.
- The degree to which each alternative meets the attribute/feature criteria.

Customers may acquire information *externally* and/or *internally*. *External* information: from *personal* sources like colleagues, family, friends, social media, and salespeople; and from *impersonal* sources like advertising, the press, blogs, or online reviews. The degree of external search relates to current knowledge, involvement in the purchase, and perceived risk. Both B2C and B2B customers increasingly search the Internet for information. *Internal* information: from the customer's perceptual information store, including memory. Of course, distinguishing between fact and opinion is critical for the evaluation stage.

STAGES 3 AND 4 – EVALUATING ALTERNATIVES AND MAKING A CHOICE. Customers evaluate alternatives based on information they acquire in Stage 2.[39] Frequently, customers exclude several alternatives in the *awareness set* with little evaluation by forming a short list — *consideration* set — based on purchase criteria — Table 4.6. Membership in the consideration set is crucial as customers choose among this restricted number of alternatives.

KEY IDEA

Membership in the customer's *consideration* set is crucial for the firm.

Awareness Set		Consideration Set	
Mountain Dew	Hi-C	Cherry Coke	Snapple
Coke	Snapple	Cherry 7-Up	7-Up
Pepsi	Sprite	Dr Pepper	Diet Pepsi
Diet Pepsi	7-Up	Diet Dr Pepper	Root Beer
Root Beer	Diet 7-Up	Mr. Pibb	Dr Pepper
Ginger Ale	Orange Slice	Caffeine-free Coke	
Diet Ginger Ale	Fanta		

TABLE 4.6

Awareness and Consideration Sets for a Teenager's Choice of Soft Drink[40]

Customer choices from the consideration set may be rational, or may deviate from rationality. By understanding the customer evaluation process, the firm can influence the purchase decision in its favor. We examine one rational approach, and others that deviate from rationality:

A. Rational approach. In Table 4.7 a business traveler is choosing an airline to fly to London. We assume the customer:

- Identifies attributes/features that deliver required benefits and values — *attributes/features*.
- Decides on the relative importance of these benefits and values — *column A (sum to 100)*.
- Forms a belief about how well the attributes/features of each alternative deliver these benefits and values — *three B columns (1–10 scale)*.

KEY IDEA

The firm should try to understand customers' evaluation processes.

The *linear-compensatory* model is the most studied approach to evaluation and choice. An alternative's overall value comprises contributions from each attribute/feature — good performance on one attribute/feature balances poor performance on another.[41] We consider each alternative separately. For each attribute/feature, we multiply the relative importance **A** by the belief **B**; we then sum the resulting **A × B** product terms. Table 4.7 totals are: British Airways — 670; American Airlines — 450; United Airlines — 730. The traveler chooses United Airlines.

TABLE 4.7

A Business Traveler's Evaluation of Airlines for a London – New York Trip

Attributes/Features Benefits/Values	Relative Importance	British Airways		American Airlines		United Airlines	
		Belief		*Belief*		*Belief*	
	A *(1–100)*	**B** *(1–10)*	**A × B**	**B** *(1–10)*	**A × B**	**B** *(1–10)*	**A × B**
Frequent-flier program	30	9	270	2	60	8	240
Price	20	6	120	6	120	6	120
Schedule	20	8	160	5	100	6	120
Service level	20	5	100	7	140	9	180
Upgrade probability	10	2	20	3	30	7	70
Total	100		670		450		730

KEY IDEA

The *linear-compensatory* approach to evaluation and choice balances firm performance on relevant attributes/features.

The firm can take several actions to enhance the value it offers customers:

- Improve perceived performance on important attributes/features.
- Add new valued attributes/features, especially important ones.
- Show customers that it performs better than competitors on important attributes/features.
- Show that the attributes/features where it performs really well are highly important.

MARKETING ENRICHMENT 4.1

Rational Evaluation and Choice Processes **806p**

Some attributes/features may be baseline requirements — *antes*; only alternatives scoring sufficiently well enter the consideration set. Safety is often an *ante* for airline travel; customers do not trade off schedule or frequent-flier miles for safety.[42,43] For other rational evaluation and choice processes based on *cognitive algebra*, see Marketing Enrichment 4.1 **[806p]**.

Sometimes customer effort is an important decision factor. When the customer makes a choice, the firm may present several alternatives, or provide a default. Customers often select the default since *opting in* takes effort. Organ donation research shows much higher donation rates in countries with *opt-out* versus *opt-in* systems. Also, the U.S. government seeks to increase worker savings by automatic enrollment unless individuals opt out.[44]

B. Deviations from rationality. *Behavioral decision theory* and *behavioral economics* researchers have identified many purchase processes that seem *irrational* in both B2C and B2B markets. Customers seem to base their choices on irrelevant factors. Consider the following scenario: Many consumers would travel for the book, but not for the home entertainment system, yet they would save the same amount in each case!

MARKETING QUESTION

Do you always act rationally in your purchase decisions? Identify situations where you behaved less than rationally.

MARKETING
QUESTION

You are in a store about to buy a $25 book. Your friend walks by and says you can buy the same book a couple of blocks away for $10. Would you walk two blocks to save $15 ($25–$10)? Now, suppose you are in a store about to buy a home entertainment system for $765. Your friend appears. He says you can buy the same system a couple of blocks away for $750. Would you walk two blocks to save $15 ($765–$750)?[45]

Based on your deviations from rationality (previous question), suggest marketing actions a firm could take with one of the products you purchased.

Other deviations from rationality in purchasing decisions include[46]:

- ***Compromise* effect.** Customers tend to avoid extreme price/value options in favor of intermediates. Given the choice between two microwave ovens, low price — $109.99 and medium price — $179.99, 43 percent chose the medium-price oven. When customers chose among three ovens, the original two ovens plus a high-price oven — $199.99, they chose the $179.99 more than 60 percent of the time.[47] How many drink-size choices are at McDonald's/Starbucks?

- ***Decoy (asymmetric dominance)* effect.** Adding another option — acting as a decoy — affects customer choice among alternatives. Suppose options A and B have two attributes — quality and price — option A (high quality, $50); option B (low quality, $35). Some customers prefer option A — high quality better than low quality; others prefer option B — $35 better than $50. Suppose a third option C (medium quality, $55) becomes available. Option A dominates C (*decoy*) on both quality and price: Customer preference shifts toward option A.[48]

KEY IDEA

Customers often deviate from rationality in making purchase decisions.

- **Describing alternatives.** Researchers asked customers to choose between ground beef — *75 percent lean*, or *25 percent fat*. After tasting the *identical* products, customers preferred the *75 percent lean* ground beef![49]

- **How customers evaluate alternatives.** Many factors affect how people evaluate alternatives, even just focusing attention on an alternative. Suppose a waiter offers the diner a choice between yogurt and fruit salad, then says, "How much more or less attractive to you is yogurt?" The probability of choosing yogurt increases![50] Even store organization has an impact:
  - *Display A*. Each display has several brands of a similar model.
  - *Display B*. Each display has several models of a single brand.

  With Display A, customers are less likely to choose the lower-priced alternative.[51]

- **When customers evaluate alternatives.** Time of purchase may be rational — we buy Coke and Pepsi when it's hot and we are thirsty. But researchers found eBay prices for weekend purchases were 2 percent higher than during the week. (For more deviations from rationality, see Marketing Enrichment 4.2 **[649p]**.)

MARKETING ENRICHMENT 4.2
More Deviations from Rationality **649p**

STAGE 5 – PURCHASING AND SECURING THE PRODUCT. Purchasing and securing products in a supermarket shopping trip — from a list or by impulse — is straightforward. But for many customer needs, product choice is insufficient; the customer must decide where to purchase — offline or online — and which supplier. Purchasing may still not be easy; the product may be unavailable or there may be a queue.

After the customer makes the purchase, still more time may elapse. The supplier may have to design and manufacture the product. Even if the product is available, delivery takes time. Time delay may lead to reevaluation and a different purchase decision.

STAGE 6 – POSTPURCHASE PROCESSES. Customers typically engage in several postpurchase processes. These can affect future purchases — for customers and others they influence[52]:

MARKETING
QUESTION

- **Use.** For some products the firm may only be concerned with sales; for others, like credit cards, use is important. Use is particularly critical in pharmaceuticals; *compliance* failure — not filling prescriptions and not taking medicine — causes 125,000 U.S. deaths annually. Hospital/nursing home costs and lost pharmaceutical revenues amount to tens of billions of dollars annually.

Describe your DMP for choosing the educational institution you currently attend. Identify the various stages. How did you approach each stage?

- **Use experience.** The customer may be satisfied/dissatisfied with the product/service, and hence develop/diminish the firm/brand-customer relationship.

- **Dissonance reduction.** If the product/service does not meet expectations, customers may reduce dissonance by seeking information and/or recalibrating product performance.[53] Most dissonance reduction occurs when customers expend significant time and/or money to acquire the product.

- **Communications with customers/potential customers.** Word of mouth (WOM) has always been an important postpurchase process; many firms hire people to stimulate customer-to-customer communication. Social media has increased WOM importance. Antifirm websites like *chase-sucks.com* and *walmart-blows.com*, blogs, and *tweets* can be significant issues for brand owners. Entrepreneurial startups are helping firms address these problems.[54]

- **Comparison with others.** Consumers modify consumption when they learn that neighbors' behavior is more socially acceptable. Electricity consumption decreases when utilities tell customers that neighbors with similar-size homes are more frugal.

- **Product and packaging disposal.** Environmental advocates are paying increasing attention to disposal. Many jurisdictions require customers to separate garbage into different categories. In France and Germany, firms must recover packaging and used products! HP Inc. encourages returning used printer cartridges.

- **Repurchase.** Repurchase drives customer lifetime value. All things equal, high customer satisfaction increases customer loyalty and repurchase.

By mapping the customer DMP for B2C and/or B2B decisions, the firm learns how and when to influence the purchase process. At the DMP front end — stages 1 and 2 — the firm may help customers identify needs and understand options. At the back end — stages 5 and 6 — the firm may make it easy for customers to pay, store, move, use, return and exchange, repair and service, and dispose of the product.[55] **[391v]**

PURCHASE-DECISION CATEGORIES

> Madden Graphics (MG) earned thin margins selling printing services to purchasing departments. At a supermarket customer it served with printed displays and sales promotion materials, MG identified large inefficiencies and waste. Madden developed a direct-to-store printing and shipping program, integrating construction design, manufacturing, assembly, and distribution of point-of-sale materials. MG also developed direct relationships with the supermarket's sales, marketing, and product-promotion executives. In seven years, MG increased revenues from the supermarket twelvefold.[56]

We can usefully distinguish three *purchase-decision categories*: *routinized-response behavior*, *limited problem-solving*, and *extended problem-solving.*[57]

ROUTINIZED-RESPONSE BEHAVIOR (RRB). The customer has well-defined purchase criteria and frequently makes similar purchases. The customer must choose among several familiar suppliers; the offers are well known and very similar. The customer makes choices rapidly with little effort, often based on brand loyalty, like B2C purchases of FMCG products and B2B purchases of raw materials and supplies. Frequently, a single individual makes RRB decisions. Established behavior patterns are typically resistant to change. The supplier must demonstrate superiority by promoting its *net competitive advantage*.

LIMITED PROBLEM-SOLVING (LPS). The customer has well-defined purchase criteria but one (or more) purchase alternatives is novel, and performance is uncertain. The customer may have to test the new alternative and/or gather new data. Examples include evaluating a potential new supplier or replacing traditional purchases with a new material — like substituting plastics for metal, or replacing traditional seeds with genetically altered varieties. Typically, LPS decisions

KEY IDEA

Customers may engage in several types of post-purchase activity.

MARKETING QUESTION

What type of purchase decision did Madden Graphics' (MG) customers make previously? What type of decision did customers make with MG's new approach?

KEY IDEA

Three categories of purchase decisions are:
- Routinized-response behavior
- Limited problem-solving
- Extended problem-solving

involve several influencers/decision-makers. The supplier must make the customer comfortable and reduce uncertainty by addressing specific concerns.

EXTENDED PROBLEM-SOLVING (EPS). The purchase is novel and the alternative(s) and potential supplier(s) are often new to the customer. Purchase criteria are not well developed and the customer expends time and effort resolving uncertainty and reducing risk. If the customer purchases, other behaviors will probably also change. Examples: B2C — first purchase of a house; B2B — purchase of video-conferencing facilities; first outsourcing of work previously done internally. In B2B, EPS purchases often affect several departments and/or management systems. Because of their broad impact, many people are involved in EPS decisions. The supplier must help the customer decide and reduce its perceived risk.

Morgan Stanley (MS) successfully won a lucrative contract to broker the sale of Hughes Aircraft. Observers believed Hughes trustees selected MS because of Robert Greenhill's presentation. Greenhill focused on the problems of being a trustee, developed a vision of how trustees should decide, then laid out their goals and alternatives.

These three purchase categories have important implications:

- **DMU varies by type of purchase.** EPS typically involves more individuals and more senior individuals. Extended-family members often guide newlyweds buying their first home. Middle managers may work on an EPS purchase, but senior managers make the final decision. Firms often program RRB decisions as a set of rules that mid- and low-level purchasing executives implement — in households, children may make these sorts of purchases.

- **Purchase categories depend on the customer, not on the product.** Different customers use different purchase criteria and purchase processes for identical products. A new-home purchase for young newlyweds is probably EPS; for a family that moves frequently, it's LPS; and for buyers/sellers of foreclosed homes, it's RRB. Purchasing video conferencing is EPS for a first-time buyer, but may approach RRB for an experienced firm. In purchasing complex products, customers gain experience; one-time EPS purchases shift to LPS and may reach RRB.

- **Potential suppliers should consider shifting decision making from simple to complex.** This is the message from Madden Graphics. RRB often favors established suppliers. For LPS and EPS, customers must reframe the decision. Reframing typically shifts the decision from purchasing agents to a broader decision-making unit. The challenger's job is motivating the customer to reframe the decision, and so enter the consideration set.

KEY IDEA

The firm should identify its customers' purchase decision categories.

INFLUENCES ON CONSUMER PURCHASE DECISIONS

We explore several influences on consumer purchase decisions (B2C).[58] Deep understanding of *environmental* and *individual* factors can help the firm be proactive in developing strategy.

ENVIRONMENTAL FACTORS

Figure 4.9 (p. 111) shows *environmental influences* ranging from broad to narrow: culture, social class, other people, family, and the situation.

KEY IDEA

By identifying sources of influence in the consumer decision-making process, firms formulate better market strategies.

....
FIGURE 4.9
*Environmental Influences
on Consumer Purchase
Processes (B2C)*

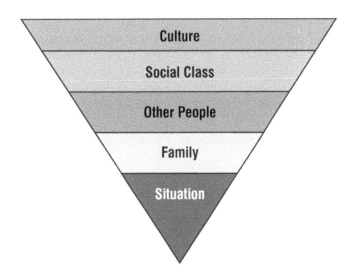

KEY IDEA

A variety of environmental
factors affect consumer
purchasing decisions:

• Culture
• Social class
• Other people
• Family
• Situation

CULTURE. Cultural and subcultural norms condition consumer purchasing behavior and product preferences. The firm must be careful not to violate these norms, especially abroad.[59] In the West, the female head of household traditionally does the weekly shopping; in rural Bangladesh, men do the shopping. Indonesians smoke more than 200 billion cigarettes annually, but only 10 percent are the standard *white variety*; 90 percent are kreteks — clove/tobacco cigarettes flavored with chocolate, cinnamon, coffee, licorice, and pineapple.[60] In the U.S., business-casual dress policies have affected detergent, fiber, garment, and washing machine manufacturers. Increasing life spans focus baby boomer attention on saving for old age with important implications for life insurance and mutual funds. Because cultural influences are so deeply seated, many firms develop separate marketing programs for cultural groups — like Asian-Americans and Hispanics in the U.S. Some consumers purchase to emulate cultural and subcultural norms: White middle-class teenagers adopt dress styles from inner-city African-Americans; most Japanese eat raw fish, but Japan is also an attractive market for Levi's, Marlboro, McDonald's and Starbucks. The Internet has spawned a global tech-savvy youth culture addressed by brands like Unilever's Axe deodorant (Bom Chika Wah Wah). In some subcultures, for some products, consumers are shifting from purchasing to renting/leasing.

Cosmopolitan (sex-oriented women's magazine) appears in 50 countries. Local editions consider cultural sensitivities and legal realities. Indian editions do not publish articles on sexual positions; sex is rarely explicitly mentioned in China; and Swedish society is so open that sex receives little attention. In Hong Kong, most models are local Asian celebrities, but in China most models are Western.

Cemex (Mexican cement producer) tapped into *tandas* — traditional community savings scheme. In Cemex's *Patrimonio Hoy* program, groups of 70 persons contribute about 120 pesos per week for 70 weeks. Each week, the program selects a *winner* who receives sufficient cement and other materials to build an extra room onto his/her home. Cemex also provides technical building assistance. Cemex's cement consumption by do-it-yourself homebuilders tripled.[61]

SOCIAL CLASS. All societies have hierarchically ordered groupings — social classes. Wealth and income are key discriminators, but education, occupation, and residential location also matter. Sometimes individuals migrate across classes. Interests, values, and purchases — like clothing and leisure activities — are often similar within a social class. Table 4.8 (p. 112) shows a U.S. scheme.

Broad Category	Narrower Category	Description	
Upper Class	Upper-upper (0.3%)	Inherited wealth, aristocratic names	**TABLE 4.8**
	Lower-upper (1.2%)	Newer social elite, corporate leadership	*Social Classes in America*[62]
	Upper-middle (12.5%)	Managers and professionals	
Middle Class	Middle class (32%)	Average pay white-collar workers	
	Working class (38%)	Average pay blue-collar workers	
Lower Class	Lower (9%)	Working, living standards just above poverty	
	Real lower-lower (7%)	On public assistance, poverty-stricken, often without work	

OTHER PEOPLE. Other people and groups influence consumers. Individuals have frequent face-to-face contact with *primary* reference groups like family members and organizational work groups. *Secondary* reference groups include club and church members and professional organizations. *Aspirational* groups are those a person would like to join for prestige and other reasons.[63] People with expertise are particularly influential if they belong to attractive reference groups. Soccer player Lionel Messi (Barcelona) is influential with many teenagers: He has significant expertise and belongs to an aspirational reference group — professional soccer players. Sometimes individuals join groups for influence and purchases: Medical advocacy groups pressure drug companies and the FDA for speedier trials of promising drugs. In China, *tuangou* groups, formed on the Internet, bargain en masse with retailers for special deals.

FAMILY. The *nuclear* family (father, mother, children) and/or *extended* family (grandparents, aunts, uncles, cousins, in-laws) may exert considerable influence. The relative nuclear family versus extended family influence is culturally determined. *Nuclear* family influence predominates in the West; *extended* family influence is very important in many Asian countries. In nuclear families, the wife and/or husband typically make family purchase decisions, often based on product type — but children may be important influencers. In the U.S., husbands generally make major financial decisions; wives make most shopping decisions, including 60 percent of auto buying. Decision making in *nuclear* families is changing in many societies:

- High divorce rates lead to increased numbers of single-parent and reconstructed families.
- Technological advances in medicine allow middle-aged women to become single-parent *mothers by choice.*
- Young people delay marriage, wait longer for children, and limit family size.
- Same-sex partnerships redefine the nature of couples and marriage.
- Women's roles change as they increasingly demand, and receive, equality.

SITUATION. Consumers face situational influences daily — presentations and displays (real and virtual), and time constraints. *Purchase location aesthetics* are also important. People purchase real estate on vacation while enjoying free meals and other perks. U.S. college students purchase and consume more alcohol at football games, parties, and spring break than other times.

A Korean firm was considering Britain for a new European factory. When its delegation visited a potential supplier, the Korean flag was flying. This thoughtfulness and attention to detail was a key factor in the decision to build in Great Britain.

INDIVIDUAL FACTORS

Several individual factors also influence purchase decisions. We commence with resources:

COGNITIVE. Consumers need *cognitive resources* to process information. The firm must secure *direction of attention* to break through the *clutter* of thousands of messages per day people

MARKETING QUESTION

The last time you purchased a ticket for long-distance air travel, what critical resource most influenced your decision?

Individual factors that affect
purchase decisions include
several resource types:

- Cognitive
- Economic
- Technological competence
- Time

Other factors include:

- Physical and mental health
- Should/want conflicts
- Life-cycle stage
- Lifestyle

receive. *Intensity of attention* affects the ability to process received information. Consumers often minimize cognitive effort and require reminders, like brand name cues, to access stored associations. Better education, government action, and increased competition are making consumers more sophisticated buyers.

ECONOMIC. Economic resources are necessary for purchase. When people have fewer resources — at the end of the month (versus beginning) and in recessions — purchasing behavior changes. Developed countries have most global resources, but purchasing power is increasing in emerging economies. Malaysia, Singapore, and South Korea grew rapidly in the late 20th century; in this century, Chinese and Indian middle classes are growing fast. Access to credit increases purchasing ability; the U.S. has highly sophisticated credit systems, but other countries less so.

TECHNOLOGICAL COMPETENCE. Internet websites offer consumers immediate access to many options — and are changing shopping patterns. Amazon and other websites feature wide varieties of product categories. Online supermarkets, like FreshDirect (U.S.) and Tesco (Britain), are quite successful. Using eBay and other sites, people transact commerce worldwide.[64] These trends will increase as young, technologically literate consumers age.

TIME. In many societies, time is an increasingly scarce resource — hence, fast-food restaurants, prepared meals, in-home medical test kits, and robotic vacuum cleaners. Less time to search for information, evaluate alternatives, and make purchases fueled the growth of direct marketing and Internet shopping. Time-saving requirements also led to service innovations like express checkout in hotels, single queue/multiple checkouts in supermarkets like Whole Foods, and speedy car rental at airports.

Other individual factors include:

PHYSICAL AND MENTAL HEALTH. The ability of individuals to present themselves and function as desired has a major impact on many purchasing decisions — prescription pharmaceuticals, health and beauty products, and health services. These factors also drive decisions like sports and exercise equipment, and related services.

SHOULD/WANT CONFLICTS. Individuals often face should/want conflicts. A long-term-best-interest option like saving money is a *should*; going to a drinking party is a *want*. Other conflicts include: restaurant choice — pepperoni pizza or healthy salad; movie choice — action-adventure or Holocaust documentary.[65]

LIFE-CYCLE STAGE. Age, family size, and marital status are critical elements in the consumer life cycle. Life-cycle stage often influences purchasing behavior; Table 4.9 shows one version:

TABLE 4.9
*Stages in the
Human Life Cycle*

Infant and preschool — parents make all purchase decisions
School age — may influence parents making purchase decisions
Teenager, living at home — purchases from allowance, gifts, part-time jobs
Young, single, head of household, no children
Married, no children
Married, young children
Married, teenage children
Married, second family, young children
Married, no children, empty-nesters
Single, widow/widower

LIFESTYLE. Lifestyle embraces how people live their lives and spend their time. The **VALS** lifestyle framework integrates several foregoing factors and is the most influential approach to categorizing lifestyles. **[377p]** VALS recognizes two major lifestyle dimensions — *self-orientation* and *resources*:

- **Self-orientation** comprises three ways that consumers pursue and acquire products/ services and experiences to give their identities *shape, substance, and character*.

  - **Action orientation** — guided by a desire for social/physical activity and risk-taking. These people purchase fast cars and take physically exacting vacations.

  - **Principle orientation** — guided by abstract idealized criteria. Environmental advocates purchase hybrid automobiles to reduce pollution; educational advocates support school-related causes and products.

  - **Status orientation** — guided by a desire for approval and opinions of others. Brand name products are important to these people.

- **Resources** encompass the full range of demographic, material, physical, and psychological assets, including eagerness to buy, education, energy, health, and income. Resources both allow and constrain purchases and range from minimal to abundant.

Table 4.10 shows how these dimensions form the eight lifestyles[66]:

MARKETING QUESTION

Take the VALS survey. What VALS type are you? Do you agree with this assessment? How does your VALS type compare with the VALS types for your friends and family members? Can you identify a person for each of VALS' eight lifestyles? Can the VALS types explain differential preferences for breakfast cereal, cars, leisure activities, or vacation preferences? How?

TABLE 4.10
VALS Lifestyle Framework

High Resources

1. Innovators	Successful, active, sophisticated, take-charge — high self-esteem and abundant resources; seek to develop, explore, and express themselves in a variety of ways. Eager to try new products.

Moderately High Resources

2. Thinkers (principle-oriented)	Mature, satisfied, comfortable, well-educated, reflective — value order, knowledge, and responsibility; tend to base decisions on strongly held principles; seem calm and self-assured; focus leisure activities on the home.
3. Achievers (status-oriented)	Successful career and work-oriented — feel in control of their lives; value structure, predictability, and stability; are deeply committed to work and family. Social life is structured around family, church, and business.
4. Experiencers (action-oriented)	Young, vital, enthusiastic, impulsive, and rebellious — seek variety and excitement; quickly become enthusiastic about new possibilities, but are equally quick to cool; energy finds an outlet in exercise, outdoor recreation, sports, and social activities.

Moderately Low Resources

5. Believers (principle-oriented)	Conservative and conventional — concrete beliefs based on traditional established codes such as family, church, community, and nation; follow established routines largely structured around homes, families, social, and religious organizations.
6. Strivers (status-oriented)	Seek motivation, self-definition, and approval from their world — unsure of themselves and low on economic, social, and psychological resources; deeply concerned with the opinions and approval of others.
7. Makers (action-oriented)	Practical with constructive skills; value self-sufficiency — live in traditional contexts of family, practical work, and physical recreation; unimpressed by material possessions, except with a practical purpose.

Low Resources

8. Survivors	Have limited economic, social, and emotional resources — the world is pressing and difficult; focus on the needs of the moment.

INFLUENCES ON ORGANIZATIONAL PURCHASE DECISIONS

Organizational buying generally concerns larger sums of money than consumer purchases, is often more protracted and complex, engages more people, and may involve company politics.[67] Processes and/or rules often govern organizational purchasing or *procurement* and interfacing with suppliers.[68] **[202v]**

CHANGES IN THE PROCUREMENT PROCESS

Important changes include:

BROADER SCOPE OF PROCUREMENT RESPONSIBILITIES. Historically, purchasing departments focused on buying factory inputs. Today, procurement is often also responsible for spending categories like auto rental, consulting services, and travel.

CENTRALIZATION. Technological advances in telecommunications, computers, and the Internet provide corporate buyers with greater leverage. They secure complete, accurate, and timely purchasing data on individual suppliers from the firm's decentralized units and track purchasing performance against benchmark databases. Home Depot centralized purchasing and cut costs significantly. Some customers demand a single supplier interface to avoid dealing with multiple salespeople. Previously, many P&G salespeople, each responsible for a product group like laundry detergent, toothpaste, or deodorants, visited Walmart. Today P&G's Walmart account executive directs a dedicated team of more than 400 employees, including specialists in finance, logistics, various products, and transportation.

> A hardware-products salesperson described his experience with a large customer. "They asked us to arrive in the late afternoon to negotiate next year's contract. They gave us a room, then called us to make our proposal. When we went back to our room, they called in our major competitor — from a similar room. A couple of hours later, they called us back and told us where the competitor had lower prices. They asked us to go to our room and return with a better offer. After we rebid, they did the same to the competitor. We left at 10 a.m. the next morning. It was brutal; we were in prison and just couldn't leave."[69]

GLOBALIZATION. The centralizing trend just discussed is expanding globally as multinational firms broaden supplier searches. These firms want global contracts; they are increasingly ready to switch suppliers as price differentials appear and disappear.

INTERNET. Using *reverse auctions*, Internet-based B2B exchanges significantly affect the purchase of standard products. Buyers have better (and cheaper) access to information to drive out market inefficiencies and price differentials.

PROCUREMENT EXPERTISE.[70] Skilled procurement staffs introduce new strategies like *strategic sourcing* to reduce costs, improve quality, and increase efficiency. To become a *preferred supplier*, the firm must complete an extensive *request for information* (RFI); only then can it respond to a detailed *request for proposal* (RFP). Long-standing relationships mean little as procurement personnel gain deep insight into supplier cost structures and aggressively negotiate prices.[71] Some buyers, like Honda, assign efficiency consultants to supplier plants; others go to great lengths to get secure low prices.

EVOLUTION IN BUYER-SELLER RELATIONSHIPS

Some firms evolve relationships with selected customers from vendor to quality supplier, and even to partner.

VENDOR. Customer and supplier operate at *arm's length* in this traditional adversarial relationship. Contracts are typically short term with frequent rebidding. Price is critical; buyers switch

KEY IDEA

Important considerations for organizational purchase processes are:

- Changes in the procurement process
- Evolution in buyer-seller relationships
- Increased corporate attention to procurement
- Reducing the number of suppliers

suppliers for small price differentials and/or better delivery. Salespeople meet with purchasing agents who restrict information they provide suppliers to maintain negotiating positions.

QUALITY SUPPLIER. Both supplier and customer believe they receive value — like acceptable profit margins/high-quality products — from a close long-term relationship. Each firm plans for continuous quality improvement. The supplier secures advantage by providing greater value than competitors.

PARTNER. Both firms share (or jointly develop) resources, strategies, and technologies, and focus on the entire value chain. The customer bases critical buying decisions on value versus price. Each firm is deeply involved in the other's product-development cycles. Routine and sensitive information flows freely, as the supplier learns about/solves important customer problems. Partnerships involve multifunctional, multilevel interactions, joint quality control, and joint project teams. The supplier helps the customer achieve its objectives and undertakes many activities a *quality supplier* or *vendor* would not contemplate.[72] Armstrong World Industries runs a management development program for partners. When a supplier realized its distributor-partner often requested rush orders, yet later *discovered* lost inventory, Armstrong installed an inventory control system.

INCREASED CORPORATE ATTENTION TO PROCUREMENT

At many firms, the *procurement-spend/company-revenue ratio* has increased dramatically. Traditional *purchasing* is evolving from an unimportant managerial backwater into highly strategic *procurement*. High-quality, fast-track managers reduce procurement costs — by $1.5 billion at a $10 billion pharma firm! Several factors are responsible:

BRANDING. The rising importance of branding allows many firms to resell products made by others. The author is writing this book on a MacBook Pro; Apple did not manufacture the computer, carrying case, or power cord — but the complete package arrived ready to use.

ORGANIZATIONAL DOWNSIZING. Many firms are downsizing by replacing labor with capital. Equipment, raw material, and supply expenses have increased, relative to other costs.

OUTSOURCING. Outsourcing allows firms to reduce balance-sheet assets and fixed costs while increasing flexibility, functional expertise, and productivity. Many major firms outsource data centers and other business processes to Accenture, Hewlett Packard Enterprise, and IBM. Others outsource call centers, human resource and accounting functions, and software development to Brazil, India, Malaysia, and Poland.

REDUCING THE NUMBER OF SUPPLIERS

Traditional purchasing departments sent specifications to many potential suppliers, then chose on criteria like price and delivery. Because streamlined supply-chain systems improve efficiency and effectiveness in converting raw materials to finished products, many firms are forging closer relationships with fewer suppliers. Table 4.11 (p. 117) shows several examples. Factors driving this trend include attempts to:

- Address increased purchase complexity involving multiple technologies.
- Improve product quality by securing tighter control over raw materials and other inputs.
- Move closer to suppliers and enjoy better communications, greater transparency, improved operational excellence like just-in-time (JIT) inventory systems, and greater control.
- Reduce input costs via:
  - Increased procurement effectiveness.[73]
  - Purchase assemblies versus parts.
  - Secure lower prices by letting selected suppliers gain economies of scale.
- Secure better and more consistent service in multiple geographies.

	Company	Previous Number of Suppliers	New Number of Suppliers	Reduction (%) in Number of Suppliers
TABLE 4.11 *Reducing the Number of Suppliers*	Airbus	3,000	500	83%
	BAA Airports	11,500	3,000	74%
	Barclay's Bank	2,000	180	91%
	Boeing	30,000	10,000	67%
	Motorola	10,000	3,000	70%
	Texas Instruments	22,000	14,000	36%
	Volkswagen	2,000	200	90%
	Xerox	5,000	500	90%

MARKETING QUESTION

What other messages did you glean from this chapter?

KEY MESSAGES

To attract, retain, and grow customers, the firm gains deep customer insight by answering three critical questions:

Who are the customers? The firm should explore several issues:

- Macro-level customers — organizations; micro-level customers — individuals.
- Direct customers — exchange money for firm products/services; indirect customers — receive value from firm products/services through intermediaries.
- Current customers and potential customers.
- Roles in the purchase decision.

What do customers need and want? The firm satisfies customer needs by making value offers. The firm should gain customer insight into:

- Recognized needs — expressed and nonexpressed, versus latent needs.
- Who receives the firm's value — the customer organization or an individual in the organization.
- Attributes and features versus benefits and values.
- Hierarchies of needs, attributes/features, benefits, and values.
- Different types of value — functional, psychological, economic characteristics of benefits and values.
- Customer experiences — sense, feel, think, act, relate.

How do customers buy? The firm gains insight from the customer's purchase-decision process:

- The process comprises six stages — recognizing problems, acquiring information, evaluating alternatives, making a choice, purchasing and securing the product, engaging in post-purchase processes.
- The dominant way customers evaluate alternatives is the linear-compensatory approach.
- Customers may deviate from rationality in their purchase decisions.
- We can usefully categorize purchase decisions into three types — routinized-response behavior, limited problem-solving, extended problem-solving.
- Environmental factors influence consumer purchase decisions — culture, social class, other people, family, the situation.
- Important individual factors influence consumer purchase decisions — various types of resources, physical and mental health, should/want conflicts, life-cycle stage, lifestyle.
- Key factors influence organizational purchase decisions — changes in the procurement process, evolution in buyer-seller relationships, increased corporate attention to procurement, reducing the number of suppliers.

VIDEOS AND AUDIOS

For complimentary material, see Axcess Capon codes at www.axcessvids.com

Procurement at Merck	**747v**	Howard Richman	Merck
Behavioral Economics	**216v**	Itamar Simonson	Stanford Business School
Behavioral Economics	**154v**	Dan Ariely	Fuqua School of Business, Duke University
Investment in Customer Insight	**508v**	Walmart	
Customer Insight	**360v**	Mohan Sawhney	Kellogg School of Management, Northwestern University
Customer Insight	**615a**	Noel Capon	Columbia Business School

QUESTIONS FOR STUDY AND DISCUSSION

Can you answer the questions implied by this chapter's learning outcomes? Check!

1. a. Airbus developed the A380, a jet aircraft with more than 500 seats. Other than the airlines, what organizations should Airbus consider as macro-customers? Why did you select them?

   b. Suppose your job was to sell a fleet of A380s to Singapore Airlines. Who would you target for effort? What issues would you focus on for each of these targets?

2. Many teenagers have smartphones. Use the feature/benefit/value ladder to identify the benefits and values smartphones deliver. Suppose you were advising Apple on new products — what benefits and values could smartphones offer teenagers that they do not currently receive? How would these benefits and values differ for adults?

3. All credit cards provide transaction value. What benefits and values differentiate one card from another?

4. Motorco (fictional) is launching a new synthetic motor oil. The primary benefit is less-frequent oil changes — once every two years, regardless of mileage. Assume a car owner changes oil every 6,000 miles and keeps the car at least two years. Current oil-change cost = $50 (5 quarts @ $5/quart = $25; labor = $20; used oil disposal = $5). What is the new oil's EVC for a car owner who drives 15,000 miles annually?

5. a. Suppose you are planning a two-week vacation when you graduate. How will you decide on your destination? Use the six-stage purchase-decision process to structure your answer.

   b. Based on your answer to 5a, what marketing program would you suggest for a vacation company targeting graduating students like yourself?

6. Select a product in which you are interested. Alternatively, consider *Managing Marketing in the 21st Century*. Identify customers. What are their needs? What are their DMPs?

TRUE/FALSE QUESTIONS

Answers on page A1 and at www.axcessvids.com — 812p

1. Identifying customers is the crucial first step in securing customer insight. ❏ **TRUE** ❏ **FALSE**

2. Users of a product/service often have a direct role in the purchase decision process.
   ❏ **TRUE** ❏ **FALSE**

3. Typically, the firm's direct customers buy the firm's products from intermediaries like manufacturers or distributors. ❏ **TRUE** ❏ **FALSE**

4. Economic value for the customer (EVC) is the competitive product's price, plus the net added value from the firm's product. ❑ **TRUE** ❑ **FALSE**

5. Membership in the awareness set is more important than membership in the consideration set as customers choose among the alternatives in the awareness set. ❑ **TRUE** ❑ **FALSE**

MULTIPLE CHOICE QUESTIONS

Answers on page A1 and at www.axcessvids.com — 265p

1. Which of the following is NOT a major group of needs according to Maslow's Hierarchy of Needs?

   a. psychological
   b. safety
   c. ego
   d. self-actualization

2. Which of the following best describes customer benefits/values that are NOT known until long after purchase?

   a. search benefits
   b. use benefits
   c. credence benefits
   d. virtual benefits

3. All of the following are modes of customer experiences EXCEPT:

   a. sense
   b. feel
   c. think
   d. All of the selections represent a mode of customer experience.

4. Which of the following types of problem solving is described as a novel purchase where the alternative(s) and potential supplier(s) are often new to the customer?

   a. routinized-response behavior
   b. limited problem-solving
   c. extended problem-solving
   d. perceptual problem-solving

5. According to the VALS framework, which of the following orientations comprises three ways that consumers pursue and acquire products/services and experiences to give their identities "shape, substance, and character"?

   a. self-orientation
   b. principle orientation
   c. status orientation
   d. action orientation

CHAPTER 5

INSIGHT ABOUT COMPETITORS, COMPANY, AND COMPLEMENTERS

For complimentary material, see Axcess Capon codes at www.axcessvids.com

The ability to learn faster than your competitors may be the only sustainable competitive advantage.

— Arie de Gues, former head Strategic Planning Group, Shell

LEARNING OUTCOMES

When you have completed this chapter you will be able to:

- Articulate the importance of gaining *competitor* insight.
- Identify the firm's current (today) competitors and potential (tomorrow) competitors.
- Identify the firm's direct and indirect competitors.
- Describe competitor capabilities and difficulties.
- Evaluate competitors by identifying their strategic options.
- Project competitor objectives and future actions.
- Manage competitor behavior.
- Assess the firm's competitive position.
- Understand the various sources and types of complementarity.

OPENING CASE: BOEING AND AIRBUS

Boeing and Airbus — headquartered in Chicago and Toulouse, France, respectively — compete intensely in the large passenger jet aircraft market.[1] *Boeing (founded 1916) launched modern jet aircraft in 1958 and has 25,000 in service; Airbus started in 1972 and has more than 5,000 planes flying. Boeing has been market leader since the 1930s but Airbus has challenged its position. In 2003, for the first time, Airbus delivered more aircraft than Boeing; Airbus also secured more aircraft orders.*

Year	Airbus Orders	Boeing Orders	Year	Airbus Orders	Boeing Orders
2002	300	251	2009	271	142
2003	284	239	2010	574	530
2004	370	272	2011	1,419	805
2005	1,055	1,002	2012	833	1,203
2006	790	1,044	2013	1,503	1,355
2007	1,341	1,413	2014	1,456	1,432
2008	777	662			

By 2016, Airbus and Boeing roughly split the market for annual plane sales and on aircraft value. Boeing's 747 dominates the wide-body market, but Airbus' high-passenger capacity A380 threatens Boeing's position. The Boeing 737 and Airbus 320 account for about 80 percent of aircraft sold, but Boeing's 787 fuel-efficient Dreamliner *competes strongly in shorter-haul markets.*

There is no love lost between Boeing and Airbus. Rival executives commonly denigrate each other's products, and the firms have a long-standing dispute over government subsidies. The World Trade Organization (WTO) supported Boeing's claims that Airbus received illegal subsidies from European governments for developing the A380 and other planes. The WTO supported Airbus claims that Boeing received illegal subsidies via U.S. government tax breaks, and defense and research contracts. The European Union (EU) also claims Boeing receives investment subsidies from Japanese airlines related to its close relationships with Japanese consortia, notably for 787 wing production.

A consortium of European aviation firms formed Airbus (1960s) to compete with the U.S. In 2001, this loose alliance evolved into the European Aeronautic Defence and Space Company (EADS). EADS (80 percent) and BAE Systems (formerly British Aerospace) (20 percent) owned the new Airbus. From the start, conflicts between French and German shareholders troubled EADS. In 2006, BAE Systems sold its 20 percent ownership; in 2014, EADS became the Airbus Group. Airbus has manufacturing facilities in France, Germany, and China; and, since 2015, in the U.S.

Boeing (2014 revenues $1 billion; 70,000 employees) offers the following models:

- *Boeing 737 (first flight 1966): twin-engine narrow-body, 85–215 passengers, short-medium range*
- *Boeing 747 (1969): quad-engine large wide-body, 85–524 passengers, long haul*
- *Boeing 767 (1981): twin-engine small narrow-body, 180–375 passengers, short-medium range*
- *Boeing 777 (1996): twin-engine medium wide-body, 330–550 passengers, long haul*

Boeing's newest aircraft is the twin-engine medium wide-body 787 — Dreamliner — seating 210–330 passengers. Boeing claims the Dreamliner is 20 percent more fuel efficient than comparable planes. Fuel savings come from engine (GE and Rolls-Royce) and aerodynamic improvements, greater use of lighter-weight composites, and advanced systems. Supply-chain problems delayed the Dreamliner's introduction by several years, and battery problems later stalled deliveries.[2] Regardless, in 2015, Boeing had more than 800 firm orders.

Airbus (2014 revenues € 61 billion, 63,000 employees) offers several passenger models:

- *Airbus A320 (1987): twin-engine single aisle, 180 passengers, short-medium range*
- *Airbus A318 (shortened A320) (2002): twin-engine twin aisle, 107 passengers*
- *Airbus A319 (shortened A320) (1995): twin-engine single aisle, 145 passengers*
- *Airbus A321 (stretched A320) (1993): twin-engine single aisle, 220 passengers, long haul*
- *Airbus A330 (1992): twin-engine twin aisle, 253–440 passengers*
- *Airbus A340 (1991): quad-engine twin aisle, 261–440 passengers, long haul*

Airbus' newest aircraft is the A380, a quad-engine twin-aisle plane seating 555–840 passengers, the world's largest passenger aircraft. Airbus also planned the A350, derived from the A330, a twin-engine twin-aisle plane seating 250–350 passengers designed to compete with Boeing's Dreamliner.

Notwithstanding their fierce rivalry, Airbus and Boeing must both carefully watch potential competitors: Bombardier — Canada; Comac — China; Embraer — Brazil; and Sukhoi — Russia. [298v]

Case Question

If you were responsible for competitor research at Boeing (Airbus), what insight would you want to secure on Airbus (Boeing)? How would you go about securing it?

How does activity in the passenger airline market affect Boeing and Airbus? [529v]

Chapter 5 builds on the five-forces model from Chapter 3 to discuss the firm's competitive challenges. We *identify* specific competitors and present a process for gaining competitor *insight*. The firm secures *competitive insight* from deep understanding of competitors, and gains a unique strategic perspective.

Ultimately, we would like to know:

- What competitors *cannot do.*
- What competitors *will not do.*
- What will *put competitors at a disadvantage if they do.*

Specifically, we develop a competitive insight framework by exploring how to:

- *Identify* competitors.
- *Describe* competitors — capabilities and difficulties (strengths and weaknesses).
- *Evaluate* competitors — strategic options.
- *Project* competitor actions — figure out what they will do.
- *Manage* competitors — influence their behavior to benefit the firm.

As the firm gains insight into competitors, it also gains insight into itself — *company insight.* We also explore the sixth force — complementers: these organizations can help the firm achieve its objectives — *complementer insight.*

THE CHANGING VIEW

OLD WAY	NEW WAY
Competitive analysis concerns sales and marketing	Multifunctional involvement
Competitive consolidation nationally	Competitive consolidation globally
Competitive focus local/regional/national	Competitive focus regional/multinational/global
Competitive strategy a low priority	Competitive strategy a high priority
Competitor description only	Competitor evaluation and projection widespread
Conflict-based views of competition	Collaborative arrangements more common
Customers purchase firm products	Customers as potential competitors — backward integration
Ethical considerations often ignored	Ethical considerations becoming more salient
Examine competition at the firm level	Examine competition by brand and market segment
Focus only on direct competitors	Focus on a broad competitor set — direct, indirect, supply chain; current and potential; and competitor networks
Industry structure fixed	Industry structure evolving
Limited attention to gaining competitor insight	Increased emphasis on gaining competitor insight
Passive and reactive competitive strategy	Active and proactive competitive strategy
Suppliers supply raw materials	Suppliers as potential competitors — forward integration
The firm operates independently	The firm operates interdependently

Competitors

DEVELOPING COMPETITIVE INSIGHT

"It is my business to know what other people don't know." — Sherlock Holmes

Dell's chief marketing officer said: "We have a wonderful healthy paranoia. At one level, we watch the competition like a hawk and we watch everything they do. And we watch the global competition, 'cause we fully recognize that tomorrow's fight may be with the guy that's today a small local, low-cost player in some remote region."[3] Dell knows the value of competitive insight.[928v]

Competitive intensity is increasing across the board in virtually all industries. Any executive will tell you that increased competition is a global phenomenon. Competition is especially tough where: industries are deregulating, rapid changes are occurring in product and/or process technology, state-owned enterprises are privatizing, and governments are reducing/removing tariffs, quotas, and other competitive barriers. Competition is also challenging in industries where regulatory restrictions are increasing, like financial services and pharmaceuticals. The firm must work harder and smarter to attain in-depth competitive insight and build that insight into strategic marketing decision-making. Only then will the firm develop the differential advantage it requires to attract, retain, and grow customers. Failure to gain good competitor insight can be serious, as Jaguar discovered:

Ford acquired then divested Jaguar. Discussing Jaguar's failure to meet the goals that Ford established, Joe Greenwell, Jaguar's new chairman, said, "We were overoptimistic, and we under-estimated the amount of competitive activity, which is a typical and dangerous assumption to make when you are in management."[4]

Prior to its bankruptcy, things were no better at GM. Indeed, car czar Steven Rattner noted: *Charts of selling prices showed no comparative data as if there were no such thing as Ford, Honda, or Toyota ... It seemed incredible that no board member or senior executive had ever demanded such basic rigor to inform their decisions.*[5] Many firms put too little emphasis on gaining competitive insight. They may claim lack of time or other resources, or simply be myopic, perhaps paralyzed by *groupthink*,[6] and not understand the competitive threat. Good competitor insight reduces decision-making uncertainty. The fundamental marketing job is to attract, retain, and grow customers, but other guys are trying to do the same thing! The firm should always know who competitors are today and who they will be tomorrow; what they are doing now and what they may do in the future. This chapter shows that developing good competitive insight has major firm value.

Gaining sound competitive insight is not easy, but most leading firms like Citibank, IBM, Shell, and Volkswagen deploy significant effort. Firms often face internal challenges in securing and acting on competitive insight. The firm gets into trouble when it:

- Bases insight on out-of-date data from tired sources.
- Claims the cost of securing good competitive data is too high.
- Does not commit necessary resources.
- Fails to go beyond basic competitor description.
- Focuses on current competitors but ignores potential competitors.
- Gains good insight but does not take action:

A competitive intelligence professional presented the following data to top management[7]:

- A Japanese competitor is building a U.S. plant.
- The Japanese firm intends to penetrate the U.S. market via low price, high advertising, and a large sales force.
- The Japanese firm has a history of sacrificing short-term profits for long-term gain.
- The Japanese firm hired salespeople from our firm and our domestic competitors.
- We have just lost one of our largest customers to the Japanese firm.

Top managers did not accept the analysis and ignored these warning signs!

MARKETING QUESTION

As a Starbucks competitive analyst, what information would help you complete the competitive insight framework — Figure 5.1?

Good competitive insight can be invaluable. By the turn of the century, Google had the best search engine and had raised $25 million venture capital; but Google did not have a financially viable business model. Sergey Brin and Larry Page studied competitors including GoTo.com (renamed Overture). GoTo made money selling advertisements to accompany search results. Google introduced Adwords — the rest is history.[8] **[421v]**

Figure 5.1 shows a five-step framework for gaining competitor insight. Steps 1 and 2, *identifying* and *describing* competitors, are critical but insufficient; unfortunately, many firms stop right here. Identifying and describing competitors are the foundation for *evaluating* — step 3; *projecting* — step 4; and *managing* — step 5. To gain superior competitor insight, the firm must excel at each step and be very clear about what it does and does not know.[9]

FIGURE 5.1
Framework for Gaining Competitive Insight

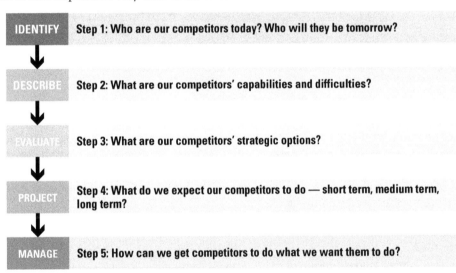

IDENTIFY — **Step 1: Who are our competitors today? Who will they be tomorrow?**

DESCRIBE — **Step 2: What are our competitors' capabilities and difficulties?**

EVALUATE — **Step 3: What are our competitors' strategic options?**

PROJECT — **Step 4: What do we expect our competitors to do — short term, medium term, long term?**

MANAGE — **Step 5: How can we get competitors to do what we want them to do?**

KEY IDEA

Competitive insight is securing a sufficiently deep understanding of competitors to provide a unique perspective.

Competitive insight is crucial for attracting, retaining, and growing customers.

The firm must act on competitive insight in its own decision making.

IDENTIFY COMPETITORS

A *competitor* is any organization whose products/services provide similar or superior benefits and values to the same customers the firm seeks to attract, retain, and grow. Of course, by making purchases, customers decide who competes with whom. Today the firm faces *current* competitors; tomorrow it may face today's *potential* competitors. Chapter 5 argues for a broad view of competitors, just as Chapter 4 argues for a broad view of customers. Many firms view competition too narrowly, focusing only on firms like themselves. For years, Hollywood did not realize television was a competitor; paper cup manufacturers did not address competition from plastic cups, only from other paper goods suppliers.[10] When the firm views competition too narrowly, it fails to identify many medium- and long-term threats. The firm should consider three key areas:

- Structure of competition
- Competitive dynamics
- The firm as competitor

KEY IDEA

Critical elements for gaining competitive insight are:
- **Identify**
- Describe
- Evaluate
- Project
- Manage

STRUCTURE OF COMPETITION

Figure 5.2 reprises the *five-forces model* — Chapter 3. Three of the five forces represent competition: *current direct competitors*, *new direct entrants*, and *indirect competitors*. The two other forces are *suppliers* and *buyers*. We learned earlier that extreme forms of supplier and buyer pressure are, respectively, *forward* and *backward integration*. By undertaking operations the firm currently conducts, they become *direct competitors*. We simplify the five-forces approach and develop two identifying dimensions that help evaluate competitors and gain deep insight.

FIGURE 5.2
Structure of Competition:
The Five-Forces Model

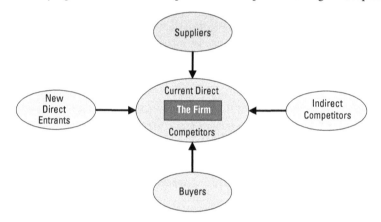

DIRECT VERSUS INDIRECT COMPETITORS. *Direct competitors* target similar customers to the firm by offering similar benefits and values with similar products, technology, and/or business models. *Indirect competitors* target the same customers with similar benefits and values, but have *different* products, technology, and/or business models. Table 5.1 shows examples of direct and indirect competitors leading firms face.

Firm	Customer Benefits and Values	Direct Competitors	Indirect Competitors
BusinessWeek	Business information	*Fortune, Forbes*	MSNBC, Yahoo! News
Citibank (retail)	Financial deposits	JPMorgan Chase, Bank of America	Vanguard, Merrill Lynch, T. Rowe Price
Disney World	Family fun	Universal Studios, Busch Gardens	Beach or ski vacation; home entertainment system (for disposable income)
ESPN	Men (to advertisers as customers)	CBS, Fox, NBC, Fox SportsNet	Comedy Central, Discovery Channel
Monster	Employee recruiting	CareerBuilder, Yahoo!, Hot Jobs	LinkedIn, Facebook, Twitter
Home builders	New homes	Other builders	Foreclosed homes
Metropolitan Museum of Art	Spending leisure time	Museum of Modern Art, Whitney Museum	Broadway plays, movies, Central Park
Professional sports	Live sports entertainment	Other professional sports	Movie theaters, restaurants, TV

TABLE 5.1
Examples of Direct and Indirect Competitors

MARKETING QUESTION

Use the five-forces model to chart out McDonald's competitors.

KEY IDEA

The firm's most serious competitive threats may be the least obvious.

CURRENT VERSUS POTENTIAL COMPETITORS. Today the firm faces *current competitors*; tomorrow it may face today's *potential competitors* — some may not even be around today. Potential competitors may even be firm employees who take intellectual capital developed at the firm and set up business on their own.

Robert Noyce and Gordon Moore left Fairchild Semiconductor to form Intel. Fairchild alumni formed many other Silicon Valley firms.

HP executive Karl Lamb formed a flat-panel TV firm while working on a flat-panel TV project for HP.

As Bear Stearns was collapsing, star broker Douglas Sharon joined Morgan Stanley; almost all his 90 customers and $1 billion investment moved also.

Star lawyer David Boies resigned from Cravath, Swaine & Moore; within a few days his new firm had four former Cravath clients including DuPont and Georgia-Pacific.

MARKETING QUESTION

Consider your most common mode of transportation — bicycle, automobile, train. What firms are:

- Current direct competitors?
- Current indirect competitors?
- Potential direct competitors?
- Potential indirect competitors?

The Figure 5.3 framework identifies four types of competitive threat. The framework helps the firm decide which threats are most serious and where it should deploy resources:

- **Current direct competitors — cell A.** The competitive status quo — traditional rivalry between established firms.
- **Current indirect competitors — cell B.** More difficult to identify than cell A competitors — act differently and develop customer benefits and values differently.
- **Potential direct competitors — cell C.** Behave like Cell A competitors, but may emerge from different industries and/or geographies.
- **Potential indirect competitors — cell D.** The most difficult competitors to identify — do not compete today; unclear when and from where they will emerge.

FIGURE 5.3
Framework for Identifying Competitive Threats

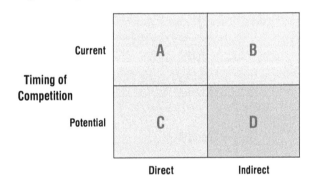

MARKETING QUESTION

Sony Music Entertainment (SME) is a world leader in recorded music. Use a direct/indirect competition spectrum like Figure 5.4 to identify SME's competitors.

Sometimes the distinction between direct and indirect competitors is not very clear. Figure 5.4 shows a spectrum of direct versus indirect competitors. For United Airlines, Amtrak rail is a very different indirect competitor from video conferencing.

FIGURE 5.4
Spectrum of Direct/ Indirect Competition: United Airlines Example[11]

In mature, low-profit industries, entry of new direct competitors may be unlikely. Consequently, firms in such industries should focus on identifying current and potential indirect competitors. Few firms enter the paper industry to compete with International Paper and Boise

Cascade, but plastics and imaging solutions are replacing paper in some markets. By contrast, new firms have significant incentive to enter profitable and growing industries like digital documents and knowledge management solutions; hence, new direct competitors are more likely.

COMPETITIVE DYNAMICS

We extend Figure 5.3 to show competitive evolution. Dramatic changes may occur: New competitors may enter or local/regional competitors may become national/multinational/global. Figure 5.5 shows various paths competitors can take. These paths help the firm forecast competitive threat transitions. We identify eight transitions:

- **Transition I.** From *potential direct* competitor (C) to *current* direct competitor (A).
- **Transition II.** From *potential indirect* competitor (D) to *current* indirect competitor (B).
- **Transition III.** From *potential direct* competitor (C) to *withdrawal* — no longer a threat.
- **Transition IV.** From *potential indirect* competitor (D) to *withdrawal* — no longer a threat.
- **Transition V.** From *current direct* competitor (A) to *withdrawal* — no longer a threat.
- **Transition VI.** From *current indirect* competitor (B) to *withdrawal* — no longer a threat.
- **Transition VII.** From *current direct* competitor (A) to *current indirect* competitor (B) — the direct competitor has developed some new approach to satisfy customer needs.
- **Transition VIII.** From *current indirect* competitor (B) to *current direct* competitor (A) — the indirect competitor has decided to compete on an *apples-to-apples* basis.

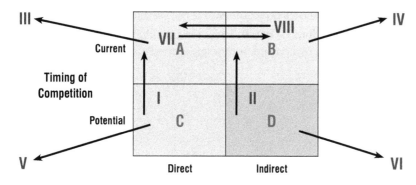

FIGURE 5.5
Framework for Tracking Competitive Threats

THE FIRM AS COMPETITOR

Our unstated assumption is that all competitors are other firms. But for product and brand managers, the toughest competition may be internal. Different businesses always compete for financial, human, and system resources, and perhaps for sales force time — but they may also compete for customers. The firm may encourage *intrafirm* competition, or it may occur by happenstance.

DELIBERATELY INDUCED INTERNAL COMPETITION. Employees at one major corporation refer to its business units as *warring tribes*. Some firms foster Darwinian *internal* competition to improve effectiveness against *external* competitors. These firms believe increased competitiveness more than compensates for resource duplication, especially if customers tend to switch products and/or brands. P&G regularly mounts parallel product-development efforts to innovate better products and get to market faster.

> Citibank undertook several parallel initiatives to develop electronic letters of credit for foreign trade. At one point, the successful Asia Pacific Group was selling its new system to customers of its sister North America Group. Simultaneously, Citibank North America was developing its own system![12]

KEY IDEA

Be aware of potential competition from within your own firm.

When product technology changes, the firm may place responsibility for old and new products in different businesses, as at Netflix (Chapter 3 Opening Case).[13] At Microsoft, one business unit supports Office, a different unit supports Windows; Microsoft also separates new Office versions from older versions.

INTERNAL COMPETITION BY HAPPENSTANCE. Internal competition often evolves. Suppose the firm targets two market segments: segment A — product I; segment B — product II. Over time, these segments may merge, and/or firm products/services become more similar. Two originally independent approaches now become competitive:

Australian resource firm BHP's steel division found that compared to other industrialized countries, Australian high-rise buildings used more reinforced concrete than structural steel. Three BHP product groups funded the structural steel development group (SSDG) to increase use of structural steel; SSDG was quite successful. Later, one group discovered that structural steel used less of its products than reinforced concrete. The group withdrew from SSDG and helped form an industry group to support Australian reinforced concrete technology.

In competitive insight framework step 1, the firm probably identifies several external competitors. In steps 2 through 5, the firm should focus on the most serious competitive threats and develop deep competitive insight about them.

DESCRIBE COMPETITORS

KEY IDEA

Critical elements for gaining competitive insight are:
- Identify
- **Describe**
- Evaluate
- Project
- Manage

Jackson and Walker (disguised) are strategically important chemical subsidiaries of major U.S. multinationals operating in Asia Pacific. Jackson has 60 percent market share and is highly profitable; Walker has 20 percent market share and is barely breaking even.

Jackson learns that Walker's president is retiring. Available information on the new president — male; early 40s; chemical engineer by training; 20+ years with Walker's parent; joined Walker's parent after graduate school; known as a turnaround manager; has just successfully completed a smaller turnaround; known as a *margin-raiser.*

Jackson's analysis and action: Jackson decided that, within reason, it wanted Walker to be successful — a successful competitor would take predictable actions; an unsuccessful competitor could be a *wild card.* Jackson knew that Walker would not leave the market; it focused on the new president's *margin-raiser* reputation.

Jackson raised prices modestly. Because of its 60 percent market share, Jackson management knew it would significantly increase profits if Walker followed suit. When Walker's new president arrived, he also raised prices. Walker became moderately profitable. Jackson invested some of its increased profits in additional services to strengthen its position.

Jackson based its action on good competitor insight. By learning about Walker's new president, Jackson developed an innovative strategy that allowed it to *win.*

Describing competitors requires four key questions:[14]
- What *competitor data* should the firm collect?
- What *sources* of competitor data are available?
- What *processes* should the firm use for competitive data-gathering?
- What *frameworks* can the firm use to describe competitors?

COLLECTING COMPETITOR DATA

To describe competitors effectively, the firm must decide what it wants to know, based on the sorts of decisions it has to make. We hear a lot about *big data*, but to secure good competitor insight we must get the *right* data. We focus on *level of data* and *type of data*.

LEVEL OF DATA. The firm should consider several organizational levels like corporate, business unit, market, and market segment. A *competitive data* profile on GE by a home appliance firm might include answers to several types of question. To illustrate:

- **Corporate.** How does GE allocate resources across major businesses like healthcare, home appliances, and jet engines? What are its acquisition and divestiture plans? What effort is GE placing on innovation versus increasing efficiency?

- **Business unit.** How does GE allocate resources across its home appliance portfolio — dishwashers, ranges, refrigerators, washers and driers?

- **Market.** What is GE's strategy in the refrigerator market? How does GE segment the market? Where is GE focusing efforts by segment? What is GE's R&D in refrigerators? What is GE's capacity and capacity utilization for refrigerator production?

- **Market segment.** For segments where the firm competes with GE: What brand(s) does GE offer? How does GE position these brands? What are GE's models? What are GE's prices? What are GE's credit terms? How do retailers display GE products? What is GE's promotional emphasis — advertising, direct mail, sales force, social media? What is GE's core message? How do target customers evaluate GE offers? What is GE's refrigerator profitability by segment?

Responsibility for competitor data-gathering typically varies by organizational level and data type. At corporate and the business units, a competitive intelligence group often has direct access to industry analysts and consulting firms. Product and/or market managers are generally responsible for market and market-segment data; they use these data to *reverse engineer* competitor market and market segment strategies. Responsible persons should develop their own data networks. Because the types of data vary by level, appropriate data-gathering approaches and methodologies vary widely.

TYPE OF DATA. The firm should collect both quantitative and qualitative data. *Quantitative* data include measures like market share and profitability: SEC filings often provide these data for public companies; business data services supply profiles for private firms. *Qualitative* data include competitor manager expertise, commitment to various businesses, and anticipated strategic moves. The Internet offers many ways to secure qualitative data. The data Jackson compiled on Walker's new president are in the qualitative category.

Competitive data-gathering should not focus solely on marketing issues. Information about products/services is crucial, but the firm should also seek data on costing systems, financial strength, logistics, operations, R&D, speed of action, and business philosophy (including willingness to innovate and take risks). In his early days in oil and gas, T. Boone Pickens learned about a rival's drilling activity by having a spotter watch the drilling floor with binoculars from half a mile away. By counting the number of joints connecting 30-foot lengths of drill pipe, Pickens knew the depth of competitor wells.[15] Xerox purchases competitive products from dealers and assesses customer value and manufacturing costs. Under severe price pressure from Schott Glass (Germany), Corning's competitive intelligence discovered Schott was implementing a deliberate strategy of taking losses in a specific product class to drive Corning from the market.[16] The firm should always be on the lookout for illegally acting competitors. Misleading advertising, patent and trademark violations, predatory pricing, and price fixing should be matters of concern.

Cisco suspected that low-cost Chinese competitor Huawei Technologies was illegally using Cisco's copyrighted software in its routers. Cisco secured a Huawei router from a customer and confirmed copyright infringement; Huawei's routers even had the same software bugs! Cisco filed charges. Huawei's subsequent legal problems compromised its ability to compete against Cisco.

MARKETING QUESTION

Suppose you were brand manager for leading U.S. bottled-water firm Poland Spring. Identify a direct or indirect competitor. On a single sheet of paper, sketch out a data-gathering plan. For each data item, note why you want to collect it.

KEY IDEA

The firm should seek competitive data at several levels:

- Corporate
- Business
- Market
- Market segment

These data may be:

- Primary
- Secondary

SOURCES OF COMPETITIVE DATA

The firm probably already has some competitive data internally; it needs a process to make these data available to its competitor analysts. The firm should also seek competitor data externally. Two approaches are available for both internal and external data:

- *Secondary data* — located in various reports, publications, and the Internet; the firm must collect, sort, and give these data meaning, based on the questions it wants answered. According to McKinsey, the major sources of competitive secondary data are news reports, industry groups/conferences, annual reports, and CEO speeches.[17]
- *Primary data* — require a focused acquisition effort like customer interviews and surveys. For important data, the analyst should seek multiple sources, filter for reliability, and cross-validate. Table 5.2 lists data sources for various competitive issues.

TABLE 5.2
Sample Internal and External Data Sources[18]

Generic Modes of Competition	Sample Internal Sources	Sample External Sources
Availability	Distribution and logistics personnel Sales force reports	Customer satisfaction surveys Third-party (industry analysts) studies Distributor access
Features	Sales, marketing, engineering personnel Internal analyses and trials	Trade publication product reviews Competitor literature, consultants Competitor websites
Functionality	Competitor supplier analysis Product comparison studies Reverse engineering	Customer reports Specialist trade reports/industry observers

General information	Senior firm executives	The Internet, including
		  • Competitor websites
		  • Rumor sites, e.g., www.gawker.com
		  • Complaint sites, e.g., www.PayPalsucks.com
		  • Blogs and forums
		Investment bankers/industry analysts
		Media (local, national)
		Regulatory filings like annual reports, 10Ks,
		   offering memoranda, asset disclosures
		Suppliers

Image and reputation	Marketing, sales, and advertising
	   personnel
	Tracking studies
		Customer perceptions, third-party studies
		Competitor advertising, promotion, and
		   public relations

Product line	Sales, marketing, engineering personnel Industry studies	Competitor product catalogs Trade shows Trade associations, press, consultants Regulatory and patent filings
Price	Marketing, sales, and service personnel Sales force reports	Competitor price lists Interviews with end customers
Selling and relationships	Sales force reports Managerial assessments	Interviews with customers and channel members
Service	Service personnel comparisons Comparative studies	Customer, third-party assessments Mystery shopper reports

MARKETING QUESTION

Returning from an industry conference, the attractive young woman took her seat on the plane. The middle-age man in the next seat glanced at her reading material, noting they had both attended the same conference. He introduced himself as marketing VP of a major pharmaceutical firm. She introduced herself as a product manager for its chief competitor. Trying to impress, the VP discussed, at length, his firm's market plans. The young woman listened attentively!

Did the young woman behave ethically? Would your answer change if she had not indicated her employment status? What do you think of the VP's behavior?

....
INTERNAL PROCESSES FOR SECURING COMPETITIVE DATA

Many competitive data-gathering efforts fail because of poor processes — too few sources, failure to cross-validate, and/or short-term focused when the firm needs a longer-term view. Competitive data-gathering options differ by focus and required resources:

- **Competing.** Sometimes the best way to learn about competitors is just to observe them. By operating in the marketplace day-by-day, an observant firm can gain significant competitive insight. Many automobile firms compete vigorously in Chile — where import duties are low or zero; opportunities for competitive learning are enormous.

- **Competitive intelligence department (CID).** The CID is responsible for collecting, analyzing, and distributing competitive information. The CID can be highly focused, but is expensive.

- **Competitive intelligence system.** The firm builds a culture where all employees are responsible for competitive intelligence. They come across competitive data daily; the critical step is to share these data with a competitor intelligence group. Group members check, sort, and digest data they receive, then redirect as appropriate. This approach is inexpensive, but is relatively unfocused.

- **Formal development of strategic plans.** When the firm has few major competitors, it can develop strategic plans as though it were the competitor. This highly focused approach is usually only practical for one or two competitors. Boeing may use it (and the following approach) for Airbus, AMD for Intel, and vice versa.

- **Gaming with multifunctional teams.** In these *war games*, executive teams play one of two roles — firm or competitor. Each team develops and presents its strategies and action plans. *Firm* and *competitor* then develop counterstrategies and action plans. Conducted at one- or two-day offsite meetings, this process often generates important insights.[19]

- **Review of business lost and business gained.** When the firm wins or loses a sale, it should find out why it won or lost. In well-managed firms, this process is standard operating procedure. Typically, customers are willing to share these data.

- **Shadow system.** Individual executives or teams *shadow* specific competitors, either as a full- or part-time job. When shadowing is an extra responsibility, it can be an effective way of focusing attention on specific competitors, at relatively low cost.

Hospitals throughout the U.S. used Surgical (disguised) products; Surgical enjoyed more than 60 percent market share. Hove was Surgical's largest competitor. Hove grew by acquiring several small players and became a significant threat to Surgical. Surgical executives were unclear about Hove's objectives and strategy. During a two-day offsite, teams of Surgical executives role-played Hove and Surgical. Surgical gained significant insight about Hove's potential actions.

Students and executives are often concerned about the ethics and legality of competitor data-gathering. Our position is clear: There are many ethical and legal approaches to securing competitor data. The firm *should not use* unethical or illegal methods like bribery, covert recording, knowingly jeopardizing someone's job, misrepresentation (including pretexting [gaining phone records]), placing *moles* at competitors, setting up fake job interviews to trawl for competitive data when no jobs are available, or theft (including hiring employees who steal data from former employers). Some firms have specific policies: HP prohibited examining *information about competitive proposals or products that was submitted to customers, channel partners, suppliers, other business partners, or anyone else with the understanding they would treat it as confidential.*[20] The firm must ensure it enforces data-gathering policies, especially if agents are responsible; P&G's experience is instructive[21]:

P&G hired agents to secure competitive data about Unilever. The agents collected 80 documents from trash bins, on public property, outside Unilever's Chicago offices. The documents laid out Unilever's long-term hair-care strategy. P&G's possession of these documents was not illegal, but the data-gathering process breached its ethics policy. P&G agreed to a third-party audit and paid Unilever $10 million compensation. P&G fired three executives.

KEY IDEA

The firm can secure timely and relevant competitive information from many internal and external sources.

MARKETING QUESTION

Which data-gathering process did Surgical use? Considering Surgical's strategic position, was this a wise decision? Why or why not?

KEY IDEA

The firm should develop formal processes to secure timely and relevant competitive data.

A widespread perception of industrial espionage by foreign governments led the U.S. Congress to pass the Economic Espionage Act, making the theft or misappropriation of trade secrets a federal crime.

Firms can secure good competitive data without breaking any rules — most organizations are *leaky*. When the firm's competitive data-gathering efforts fail, the reason is usually insufficient resources and/or unfocused efforts. But if competitors are leaky, your firm may also be leaky! Counterintelligence is vital. The firm should take affirmative steps to protect its data:

MARKETING QUESTION

Select a firm; identify its major competitor. Use the Internet and other resources to complete the competitive analysis framework for the firm you chose.

- Classify information according to the degree of secrecy warranted.

- Execute employee *noncompete agreements* to prohibit former employees from working for competitors for a defined time period.

- Train employees on the danger of loose tongues, especially when attending industry meetings and social events. Teach them to be good listeners — ears open, mouths shut!

- Use *nondisclosure agreements* (NDAs) to prohibit revealing information to third parties. NDAs are standard for consultants and others working on contract.

FRAMEWORKS TO DESCRIBE COMPETITORS

To gain competitor insight, the firm must organize competitive data into a useful framework. Good competitive insight often results from a *differential diagnosis* of the firm versus competitors. We use four basic building blocks — *competitor organization, strengths and vulnerabilities, firm in the environment, mind-set*. These analytic guidelines help the firm understand the fifth building block — *current strategy and performance*. The firm also gains insight into the competitor's future strategy.[22] The firm should adapt the framework for the level of competitive insight it seeks — corporate, business unit, market, market segment.

KEY IDEA

The firm should not use unethical or illegal processes to collect competitor data.

When a competitor organization is leaky, the firm can more easily secure competitor data.

Good counterintelligence procedures prevent proprietary data from leaking to competitors.

ORGANIZATION. How the competitor organization functions:

- **Culture.** The behaviors, norms, beliefs, and values that together describe what the competitor stands for and how its members operate and behave.

- **Infrastructure.** The line organization — basic responsibilities and reporting relationships.

- **Processes.** Accounting, information, monitor and control, and reward systems and processes.

STRENGTHS AND VULNERABILITIES. Assets, capabilities, competences (and failings). This part of the framework comprises the strengths and weakness elements of a SWOT (strengths, weaknesses, opportunities, threats) analysis:

- **Assets.** Financial, human, knowledge, organizational, perceptual, physical, and political assets that embrace the competitor's brand equity and customer loyalty — proprietary and nonproprietary. The firm should also evaluate competitor liabilities, emotional commitments or *blind spots* that sometimes compromise hard-headed business judgments.

- **Capabilities and competences.** Activities the competitor does well, including *local* expertise and broad-scale abilities, and areas where it does poorly. Specific product-related abilities — conceive and design, finance, produce, manage, and market. The competitor's approach to risk and speed of action may also be a competence — or not!

FIRM IN THE ENVIRONMENT. Embraces relationships with other organizations:

- **Value chain.** Major work activities the competitor conducts and how they connect to external entities like suppliers and customers — Figure 5.6 (p. 134).[23] The firm asks four core questions:
  - Where does the competitor have a cost advantage?
  - Where is the competitor at a cost disadvantage?
  - Where does the competitor have a value advantage?
  - Where is the competitor at a value disadvantage?

FIGURE 5.6
The Value Chain

KEY IDEA

The firm should use a rigorous framework to organize competitor data-gathering.

- **Alliances and special relationships.** *Alliances* are formal economic relationships between the competitor and other entities (partners) — customers, distributors, suppliers. *Special relationships* are informal and may embrace government agencies, political parties, and public interest groups — as well as customers and suppliers.

- **Networks.** Interconnected sets of alliances and relationships, each fulfilling a unique role. Rather than compete with a single competitor, the firm may compete with a network.

MIND-SET. How the competitor thinks and the bases for its decisions. What are its *assumptions*? What does the competitor take for granted, or as a *given*? Assumptions are the outcomes of analyst judgments, inferred from competitive data.

CURRENT STRATEGY AND PERFORMANCE. How the competitor behaves and its results:

- **Market strategy.** The firm observes competitor actions and infers its objectives, segment choices, and strategies.[24]

- **Other major resource commitments.** The competitor may build new factories, expand existing plants, and/or spend extensively on a particular type of R&D. The competitor may also display different levels of commitment to various businesses.

- **Performance.** Most performance measures are market-oriented or financially based. Market measures include market share and customer satisfaction. Financial measures range from product line profitability and operating margin, to share price.

Won't the firm using this framework collect a tremendous amount of data, and won't it be overwhelming? Right! Describing competitors is not for the faint-hearted. When the task seems too great, remember that competitors are trying to attract, retain, and grow the same customers as your firm. If they are successful, they will survive and grow, and your firm will not. And you will be out of a job. The best way to appreciate this framework is to use it. We suggest you answer the Marketing Question, p. 133.

PUTTING IT ALL TOGETHER

Sometimes the firm gains competitive insight directly from the data it collects; other times, it must integrate several data items. The firm may secure data on competitor products/services, promotion, distribution, price, and other factors — but does not *see* what was behind these actions. The firm must make inferences from these data. Table 5.3 illustrates making inferences from *indicator* data.

Indicators	Inferences
Hired new customer service manager	Competitor is going to upgrade service quality
Reorganized customer support and service (CSS)	Initial confirmation of alerting signal
CSS now reports to VP of marketing (versus sales)	Signals increased importance of service
Initiating new training programs for sales force	Enhancing service for all key customer segments
Emphasizes customer service in advertising	Service seen as a valuable to attract, retain, and grow customers
CEO comments: "Customers expect quality in services as well as in the product."	Service is becoming part of the competitor's mind-set — will be institutionalized
Customer to our salesperson: "ABC is now doing things for us they never did before."	Confirms competitor is institutionalizing and leveraging service

TABLE 5.3
Drawing Inferences from Competitor Data[25]

MARKETING ENRICHMENT 5.1

More on Competitor Analysis Frameworks **254p**

KEY IDEA

Organizations do not make decisions — *people* in organizations make decisions.

Finally, competitors *do not make* decisions: People working for competitors make decisions. The firm should identify competitor decision-makers and influencers. The Jackson example (p. 129) shows that career backgrounds, successes, and failures provide good competitor insight. (More on competitive analysis frameworks in Marketing Enrichment 5.1 **[254p]**.)

EVALUATE COMPETITORS

The reason for *evaluating* competitors is to generate their strategic options. Knowing these options allows the firm to *project* competitor actions. Identifying competitors (step 1) and describing competitors (step 2) are fine, but these are just the building blocks of competitive insight. The firm can only justify competitive intelligence efforts if those efforts provide insight into competitors' future actions. *Competitor assessment analysis* and *game theory* help answer three competitive evaluation questions:

- What options does the competitor have to be successful?
- What would the competitor have to do to pursue each option?
- Is the competitor capable? (Does it have the resources to implement a particular option?)

COMPETITOR ASSESSMENT ANALYSIS

Competitor assessment analysis (CAA) is a powerful tool. CAA focuses on an individual competitor or group of similar competitors in a market or market segment. CAA maps customer perspectives into required resources. The firm and competitors satisfy customer needs by delivering benefits and values. But they must possess resources to deliver these benefits and values. CAA allows the firm to identify where it possesses a *differential advantage* and where competitors have *differential advantages*. Recall from Chapter 1: *A differential advantage is a net benefit or cluster of benefits, offered to a sizable group of customers, which they value and are willing to pay for but cannot get, or believe they cannot get, elsewhere.* Identifying differential advantage has five stages. Table 5.4 illustrates CAA for a single competitor in a market segment.

TABLE 5.4
Illustration: Competitor Assessment Analysis

Customer Requirements: Needs, Benefits, Values **A**	Customer Importance Rank **B**	Necessary Capabilities / Resources **C**				
		Efficient Manufacturing	Good Distribution	Just-in-Time Delivery	Well-Funded R&D	Access to Low-Cost Materials
Easy product availability	1	* YN	* YYY			
Low prices	2	* YN				* YYN
Low inventories	3			* N		
Access to cutting-edge technology	4				* YYN	
Etc.						

KEY IDEA

Critical elements for gaining competitive insight are:
- Identify
- Describe
- **Evaluate**
- Project
- Manage

- **Stage 1 – Identify customer requirements in terms of needs, benefits, values.** Brainstorm and/or use marketing research.
- **Stage 2 – Rank in order of importance.** Reduce Stage 1 items to a manageable number, typically six to 10. Rank items in order of importance to customers — columns A and B.
- **Stage 3 – Determine necessary capabilities/resources.** Any firm would require these capabilities/resources to satisfy customer requirements in column A. Needs/benefits or values map directly into capabilities/resources. To satisfy the most important item, *easy product availability*, requires *efficient manufacturing* and *good distribution*. To offer *low prices* requires *efficient manufacturing* and *access to low-cost materials*. Enter capabilities/resources in row C.

- **Stage 4 – Identify the matches.** Place an asterisk (*) in each matrix cell where a customer need/benefit/value — column A — intersects with a firm capability/resource — row C. Typically, the result is a sparse matrix; for any particular customer need/benefit/value, some capabilities/resources are irrelevant. For customer requirement *easy product availability* — *just-in-time delivery, well-funded R&D*, and *access to low-cost materials* are not decisive. Of course, sometimes a capability/resource addresses more than one customer need/benefit/ value.

- **Stage 5 – Examine the matches.** Ask *up to three* questions of each asterisked matrix cell. Whether or not to ask a subsequent question depends on the answer to a previous question:

    a. *Relevance.* Does the firm have the capabilities/resources necessary to address the customer need/benefit/value? If yes, enter **Y**; if no, enter **N**, and stop.

    b. *Superiority.* For each cell where you entered **Y**: Are firm capabilities/resources superior to the competitor? If yes, enter **Y**; if no, enter **N**, and stop.

    c. *Sustainability.* For each cell where you entered **YY**: Would it be difficult for the competitor to match/exceed firm capabilities/resources? If yes, enter **Y**; if no, enter **N**.

The meaning of the entries is:

- **YYY.** The firm has a sustainable *differential advantage*. Firm capabilities/resources match customer needs/benefits, values; they are superior to the competitor; it would be difficult for the competitor to catch up.

- **YYN.** Firm capabilities/resources match customer needs/benefits, values; the firm has an advantage, but the competitor could match the firm relatively easily.

- **YN.** Firm capabilities/resources match customer needs/benefits, values, but are no better than the competitor.

- **N.** The firm has a significant weakness/gap. The competitor completing a similar analysis would likely show a **YYY** and have its own differential advantage.

Returning to Table 5.4, we explore competitor options by examining several cells:

- **YYY** — *easy product availability/good distribution.* The firm has a differential advantage in the customers' most important requirement. If the competitor is serious about this market segment, it would expend significant resources to improve distribution.

- **YYN** — *low prices/access to low-cost materials; access to cutting-edge technology/well-funded R&D.* The firm leads the competitor in customers' second and fourth most important areas. The competitor may invest in procurement and/or increase R&D.

- **YN** — *easy product availability/efficient manufacturing; low prices/efficient manufacturing.* The firm and competitor perform equally well in the customers' most and second most important areas. The competitor may work on improving manufacturing efficiency.

- **N** — *low inventories/just-in-time delivery.* The competitor dominates; it will probably focus customer communications on *low inventories* to make sure it stays ahead.

Now that the firm views the market segment from the competitor perspective, it can project those options the competitor will likely pursue. The firm should repeat the analysis for another competitor.

GAME THEORY

Game theory is a structured way of identifying options and evaluating consequences. Game theory helps marketers think through the impact of firm actions on competitors, and vice versa. Game theory helps assess consequences for the firm and competitor of pursuing each option.[26] In Figure 5.7 (p. 137), both firm and competitor must make a pricing decision.

MARKETING QUESTION

Huawei is a major Chinese technology firm that frequently competes with Cisco. Write a short memorandum identifying the type and level of threat that Huawei poses for Cisco.

KEY IDEA

Competitor assessment analysis (CAA) is a powerful tool for marketers. CAA maps customer requirements — needs/benefits or values — directly into necessary supplier capabilities/ resources.

KEY IDEA

Game theory is a structured way of identifying options and evaluating consequences.

Columbia and Wharton (disguised) are major players in a steel-pipe market segment. Each competitor sends a quarterly price list to customers on the last day of the preceding quarter: December 31 — quarter I, March 31 — quarter II, and so forth. These prices are effective for the quarter. In previous quarters, prices have been either $6 or $7 per yard. Sometimes Columbia is higher; sometimes Wharton is higher. Based on historic purchasing patterns, Columbia predicts sales volumes — for itself and Wharton — for each of the four possible price configurations. Columbia uses its own costs and competitive cost data about Wharton to predict each firm's profits.[27]

FIGURE 5.7
Game Theory Approach to Evaluating Competitors: Projected Profits from Combinations of Price Actions

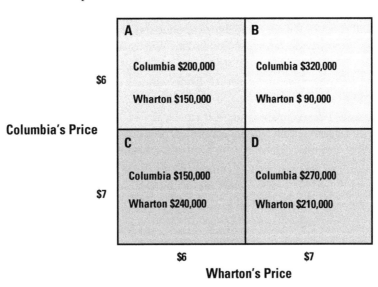

Cells D and A — Columbia and Wharton each set the same price:
- **Columbia $7, Wharton $7 – Cell D.** Profits — Columbia $270,000, Wharton $210,000.
- **Columbia $6, Wharton $6 – Cell A.** Profits — Columbia $200,000, Wharton $150,000.

Cells C and B — Columbia and Wharton each set different prices:
- **Columbia $7, Wharton $6 – Cell C.** Profits — Columbia $150,000, Wharton $240,000.
- **Columbia $6, Wharton $7 – Cell B.** Profits — Columbia $320,000, Wharton $90,000.

We draw several conclusions:
- When the firms set identical prices, Columbia is more profitable than Wharton.
- When the firms set identical prices, $7 prices earn greater profits than $6 prices.
- When the firms set different prices, the firm with the $6 price fares better.
- Columbia makes greatest profit with a $6 price, but only if Wharton's price is $7.
- Wharton makes greatest profit with a $6 price, but only if Columbia's price is $7.
- Columbia makes least profits when its price is $7 and Wharton is $6.
- Wharton makes least profits when its price is $7 and Columbia is $6.

The pricing decision is not trivial. Columbia should base its price on the best prediction of Wharton's price. Wharton should base its price on the best prediction of Columbia's price. One firm may try to signal an intended price of $7, but price-fixing allegations could ensue. (airline example **[127v]**)

PROJECT COMPETITOR ACTIONS

KEY IDEA

> J&J's Tylenol was the leading over-the-counter analgesic. Bayer planned to launch Aleve as an indirect competitor, but J&J did not know when Bayer would receive final FDA approval. The Tylenol brand team monitored raw material shipments to Bayer's Aleve plant in Puerto Rico. J&J predicted the Aleve launch to within one week. Shortly before launch, J&J flooded the market with *two-for-one* coupons and took other competitive actions.[28]

Critical elements for gaining competitive insight are:
- Identify
- Describe
- Evaluate
- **Project**
- Manage

The evaluation step generates a set of options for the competitor; the firm must assess which option the competitor will choose. Will the competitor continue its current strategy? Or make a strategic change — short term, medium term, or long term? What specific change(s) will the competitor make? To start: what is the competitor trying to achieve? Specific questions include:

- What are the competitor's objectives in the market? Understanding objectives can help predict resource allocations.
- What market segments will the competitor address? How will the competitor try to achieve its objectives — price leadership, operational excellence, product leadership, distribution strength, or what? What customer behavior is the competitor seeking to address?
- What is the competitor's staying power? Is it committed for the long run, or will it withdraw if the going gets tough? Of course, sometimes withdrawal is not in the firm's best interest, inasmuch as a competitor's divested unit may become a stronger and more difficult competitor.

MARKETING QUESTION

Abu Dhabi, Dubai, and Qatar are investing substantially in new airports. Flagship carriers — respectively, Etihad Airways, Emirates, and Qatar Airways — are each growing at double-digit rates. As an airline industry analyst, identify three likely scenarios and implications for Lufthansa.

Scenarios are a particularly effective way of evaluating competitor options; they help the firm understand and predict competitor actions.[29] The scenario for a plausible option is a descriptive narrative of how the future may evolve; the firm should develop a scenario for each option. Based on various conditions and assumptions, the firm can compare and contrast the scenarios to gain insight into possible competitor actions. The firm projects competitor behavior by selecting the most probable action from the set of alternative scenarios. Three major scenario types are:

- **Emergent scenarios.** Start with the current strategy and consider what may emerge.
- **Unconstrained scenarios.** Based on open-ended *what-if* questions that suggest possible end states.
- **Constrained scenarios.** *What-if* scenarios that ask how the competitor may act under different market and/or industry conditions.

Effective scenarios have several important attributes:

- **Articulated plot and logic.** The *story* comprises a set of events and a coherent logic.
- **Internally consistent logic.** The *story* hangs together.
- **Specific time frame.** The *story* specifies a time element for key actions, events, and results.
- **Decision/action-oriented.** The firm can derive and demonstrate implications for its current and future decisions.

As the firm builds scenarios, it must incorporate:

- **An end state.** An outcome at some specific future point.
- **A plot.** What the competitor must do to get to the end state.
- **Driving forces.** The circumstances, conditions, events, and trends that shape or drive the story described in a particular plot.
- **Logics.** The evidence and rationale for the end state and plot.

KEY IDEA

The firm projects future competitor actions by identifying the most likely scenario from a set of alternative scenarios.

This description of scenarios and their attributes is fairly abstract, so we show an illustration. Our fictional firm is a yogurt manufacturer — Sunshine. Sunshine's major competitor — Moonglow — is contemplating a low-price market entry. We start by elaborating Moonglow's

A good approach to project-ing future competitor actions is developing a set of robust scenarios that examine the competitor's strategic options.

projected strategy alternative — low-price entry. This option, together with *supporting logics for Moonglow* and *supporting logics for Moonglow's environment*, allows us to *identify consequences for Moonglow*. These *consequences* lead directly to *implications for Sunshine*.

MOONGLOW'S PROJECTED STRATEGY ALTERNATIVE. Key elements in the strategy are:

- Add a low-price product line aimed at customers for generic products.
- Use a different brand name.
- Maintain a high service level and use the same superior national distribution.
- Price similarly to low-end competitors and position against rivals' low-end products.
- Gain financial breakeven in one year and 10 percent low-end market share in three years.

SUPPORTING LOGICS FOR MOONGLOW.

- Moonglow must extend its product line to gain scope economies and preempt competition.
- Moonglow can acquire product supply from well-established vendors.
- Moonglow has demonstrated a capacity for building the required alliances.
- The entry fits Moonglow's apparent core assumptions that distinct market segments exist.
- The entry would leverage Moonglow's extensive marketing and sales capabilities.
- Moonglow's organizational culture — to be *the best in the industry* — supports the entry.

SUPPORTING LOGICS FOR MOONGLOW'S ENVIRONMENT.

- Growth rates in Moonglow's current segments do not support announced revenue targets.
- Low-end segments have higher growth rates.
- Channels are demanding broad product coverage from suppliers.
- Successful competitors at the low end may contemplate adding higher-end products.
- New vendors are specializing in providing products to branded competitors.
- The projected strategy could succeed if Moonglow can quickly establish a superior brand image at a comparatively low price, with strong channel support.

CONSEQUENCES FOR MOONGLOW. Moonglow will have to:

- Determine product content.
- Secure vendors.
- Create marketing programs.
- Develop products.
- Establish its own manufacturing.
- Build trade relationships for the new product line.
- Organize its sales force.

In addition:

- Moonglow could gain significant early market penetration.
- Moonglow will face significant issues on how best to differentiate its product line, build brand image, and leverage distribution channels.
- Moonglow will need to monitor each execution step.

IMPLICATIONS FOR SUNSHINE. Moonglow's new market entry:

- Would pose a direct threat to Sunshine's current market strategy.
- Would radically change current market assumptions.
- May eliminate potential sources of supply.
- May jeopardize potential alliance partners.
- Similar products would address the same customers through the same channels.
- Sunshine's existing capabilities may be insufficient to sustain sales growth.
- Sunshine will need to introduce new options.
- Sunshine may need to introduce a new product line more quickly than planned.

Note how this scenario fulfills the conditions we outlined. The scenario has an *articulated plot and logic*, an *internally consistent logic*, and a *specific time frame*, and is *decision/action-oriented*. Of course, this is just one possible scenario Sunshine might develop for Moonglow. To predict what Moonglow will actually do, Sunshine must develop a scenario for each of Moonglow's plausible options. Sunshine then selects from the various scenarios what it believes is Moonglow's most likely course of action, and acts accordingly.

MANAGE COMPETITORS

Multinational electronics firm Colorado's (disguised) corporate objective was to be the dominant producer in each product/market it entered. Colorado developed a four-part strategy to accomplish its objective — aggressive pricing to follow planned cost reductions, continued efforts to improve products and reduce costs, use experience with one product to improve performance in other products, and keep capacity growing ahead of demand. Colorado published its objectives and strategy in a letter to shareholders. The message to potential competitors was very clear: Enter our markets if you want. But the game will be tough. And we shall set the rules!

KEY IDEA

Critical elements for gaining competitive insight are:
- Identify
- Describe
- Evaluate
- Project
- **Manage**

Identifying competitor options and projecting competitor strategies put the firm in good position. But shaping (managing) competitor actions is even better! Before trying to get competitors to behave in beneficial ways, the firm must answer two questions:

- What actions does the firm want its competitor(s) to take?
- What actions does the firm prefer that its competitor(s) not take?

Ecolab and Diversey (disguised) were leading suppliers of cleaning chemicals to U.S. hospitals, office buildings, restaurants, and schools. Ecolab *encouraged* Diversey to focus on smaller independent customers by raising prices modestly; Diversey *took the bait* and gross margins improved. By contrast, Ecolab targeted large chain customers and won business with aggressive pricing. But Ecolab had thrown Diversey a *curveball*; higher gross margins did not offset increased costs-to-serve and Diversey lost money. By focusing on large customers, Ecolab reduced its costs-to-serve and profits improved.

SIGNALING[30]

Sometimes firms send *signals* to competitors, hoping they will process the information and take appropriate actions. The firm should ensure its signals are clear, believable, and have time to take effect; and do not violate antitrust laws.

PREEMPTIVE SIGNALS. The firm sends *preemptive* signals so that competitors will make decisions favorable to the firm. In mature industries, market share often approximates production-capacity share. Hence, to hold market share, the firm tries to maintain capacity share by discouraging competitors from adding capacity; it also announces its own capacity additions. AMD's vice president of manufacturing stated: "Within two years, we shall be fully positioned to service one-third of the market. We will manage, as we always do, these capacity additions. We aren't going to build too much; we aren't going to build too little."[31] The Colorado example above is another excellent illustration of preemptive signaling.

Sometimes the firm must decide whether, and how, to *respond* to competitors. Many competitor moves do not require direct action, but the responding firm must make several decisions:

- Where should we respond? In the same market or in a different market?
- How fast should we respond — immediately or wait to assess market reaction?[32]
- How large should our response be? Match or outdo the competitor?

Two types of response signal are:

TIT-FOR-TAT SIGNALS. The firm designs signals to bring competitors into line and to impede unilateral gains. The firm encourages the competitor to behave by matching (but not overreacting to) competitor actions. Sagebrush shows a tit-for-tat signal:

> Sagebrush (disguised) was U.S. market-share leader. A new Japanese entrant sharply undercut Sagebrush prices. Sagebrush did not respond directly. Sagebrush's U.S. managers instructed its Japanese subsidiary to drastically cut prices in Japan immediately. The Japanese firm raised U.S. prices! The U.S. firm followed by raising prices in Japan.

WARNING SIGNALS. Warning signals alert competitors that the firm will take serious steps if the competitor exceeds certain thresholds. The firm makes sure competitors can predict its responses. Example: A senior executive from a toothpaste market leader stated: "We believe there is a place in the market for natural toothpaste. But if market share exceeded 3 percent, that could be a real problem. We would necessarily have to protect our market position!" The warning: "Don't let your market share exceed 3 percent."

MISINFORMATION

The firm designs *misinformation* to mislead competitors. Relating to the capacity discussion above, capacity-increase announcements are relatively common in the chemical and other industries, but frequently new capacity is never added! Misinformation may buy time for a developing strategy, but overuse can cause credibility problems. EIX (disguised) shows misinformation in practice:

> Electrical component supplier EIX discovered customers would pay price premiums for faster delivery. EIX sought distributors to implement a new system for order-taking, product design, and assembly; but it needed time to make the change. EIX leaked a fictitious story to an industry trade journal: EIX planned to shrink delivery time for circuit boards and other customized components from 10–12 weeks to one week. EIX would maintain large inventories and have employees work overtime. EIX's competitors knew the industry demanded customization and skilled labor and believed EIX's proposed actions were stupid. The report convinced them that EIX was headed in the wrong direction. EIX gained the head start it needed.

The Company

The starting point for developing good firm insight has three components:

- *intended* strategy — what the firm planned to do;
- *revealed* strategy — what the firm actually did; and
- *results* — what the firm achieved. (Chapter 24 discusses monitor-and-control procedures.)

Understanding firm ability to implement planned actions, and the results of its actions, provides excellent insight into firm competencies. The firm can secure additional insight by using two approaches previously discussed for gaining competitor insight — *company description* and *company assessment analysis*.

COMPANY DESCRIPTION

We previously discussed the five building blocks when describing competitors (pp. 133–134) — *organization, strengths and vulnerabilities, firm in the environment, mind-set,* and *strategy and performance.* These elements help show how the firm settled on its *current strategy* and achieved *current performance.* To apply this framework, simply substitute *firm* wherever *competitor* appears.

KEY IDEA

The firm may be able to *manage* competitors by sending signals.

Major signals available to the firm are:

- Preemptive
- Tit-for-tat
- Warning

The firm may also send competitors misleading information.

MARKETING QUESTION

What lessons does the video **[278v]** offer for addressing competitors?

COMPANY ASSESSMENT ANALYSIS

Competitor assessment analysis (CAA) (pp. 135–136) identifies where the firm *possesses* a differential advantage, and where it might place resources to *secure* future differential advantage. We reproduce the analytic findings but now interpret them from the firm's perspective. Table 5.4 is the starting point:

- **YYY** — *easy product availability/good distribution.* The firm has a differential advantage in the customers' most important requirement. The firm should maintain its position by making deliberate investments to continually enhance its distribution system.

- **YYN** — *low prices/access to low-cost materials; access to cutting-edge technology/well-funded R&D.* The firm leads the competitor in the customers' second and fourth most important areas. The firm should keep a close eye on the competitor and make the necessary investments to maintain leadership.

- **YN** — *easy product availability/efficient manufacturing; low prices/efficient manufacturing.* The firm has a significant vulnerability in the customers' most important and second most important areas. The firm and its competitor perform equally well, but effective investment would put the competitor ahead. The firm cannot afford to allow this to happen.

- **N** — *low inventories/just-in-time delivery.* The competitor dominates; no doubt it emphasizes its good performance with customers. The firm may find it difficult to achieve parity, but this is the customers' third most important need/benefit/value!

Company description and company assessment analysis give the firm invaluable insight into its own position versus competitors. For *company description*, the firm must gather significant amounts of data. For *company assessment analysis*, it simply reinterprets CAA from the firm's perspective.

KEY IDEA

Competitor assessment analysis (CAA) is a valuable tool for gaining company insight.

Complementers

We introduced complementers in Chapter 3. We find the most obvious examples of complementary products in economics texts — bread and butter, coffee and cream. More modern examples are laboratory equipment and chemicals; printers and toners; and hardware and software (computers and video games).

Recall, a *complementer* — sixth force — is any organization whose actions affect firm sales[33]; we exclude the *five forces* — three competitor types, suppliers, and buyers — Chapter 3. Independent organizations and competitors can be complementers; the firm may also act as its own complementer — Chapter 12.

INDEPENDENT ORGANIZATIONS AS COMPLEMENTERS

When independent organizations develop mutually beneficial strategies, they frustrate competitors and help each other generate sales. IBM has a complementer relationship with software firm SAP. IBM and SAP cross-license and develop software to integrate each other's products; SAP also trains IBM service engineers on SAP products. SAP generates 25 percent of sales from its IBM relationship; SAP helps IBM sell several million dollars' worth of hardware annually.

Microsoft, Nintendo, and Sony successfully persuade complementers to develop games for their consoles. Likewise, Apple's iPhone has well over one million complementary applications and accessories produced by thousands of developers; but the iPhone (and iPad) put tremendous pressure on wireless complementers like AT&T and Verizon. In home laundry, design changes in washers and driers have major implications for detergent manufacturers; fabric designs have important implications for both appliance and detergent manufacturers. P&G and major appliance manufacturers work together to address new customer needs and align innovations across

KEY IDEA

Independent organizations, including customers and suppliers, can be complementers for the firm.

various industry sectors. Complementary relationships often drive major industry changes — rising oil prices have major implications for automobiles; indeed, electric utilities may switch to electric car fleets to spur market development.

CUSTOMERS AS COMPLEMENTERS. Customers act as complementers when they enhance firm offers. Comfort (disguised) specializes in fraud detection systems based on statistical models. Customers supply data to Comfort's data consortium; Comfort uses these data to improve its detection systems. Similarly, Google's advantage over Bing and Yahoo! in search relates in part to its greater market share — more data to test hypotheses, leading to increased advertising effectiveness.

SUPPLIERS AS COMPLEMENTERS. Suppliers often complement firm actions to increase sales. Car makers expect suppliers to conduct R&D to improve automobile performance. McDonald's expects suppliers to contribute ideas and concepts to help grow McDonald's business — to become *McPartners*, suppliers must do more than just deliver products.

COMPETITORS AS COMPLEMENTERS

As a general rule, competitors are the firm's nemesis. They try to attract, retain, and grow the same customers as the firm. But competitors can also act as complementers without getting into antitrust problems. We distinguish among strong, weak, and unwelcome complementarity.

STRONG COMPLEMENTARITY. We distinguish between front-office (marketplace) and back-office complementarity.

- **Front-office (marketplace).** Sometimes competitors work together to better satisfy customer needs, like agreeing on technological standards. Verizon and other telephone firms agreed on standards for ultrafast fiber optic lines that reduced costs, sped introduction, and helped each firm compete with cable companies. Without this type of cooperation, customers are often uncertain about which technology will succeed; they may withhold purchases, and the market fails to develop, or develops more slowly.

The innovative firm with new technology making a direct market entry often has two choices — go it alone or offer its technology to competitors. If the firm acts alone, it must shoulder the entire market development effort. When the innovator decides on *cooperation*, the market develops faster, but the firm must accept a diminished position. This decision involves difficult trade-offs.

For many years, Citibank successfully operated a proprietary ATM system, but when national and international networks like Cirrus, Maestro, and Star grew, Citibank eventually joined. By contrast, Intel gave competitors AMD and Cyrix access to MMX technology for graphics and video chips. Faced with *cloud* competition from Amazon and IBM, long-time rivals Microsoft and Oracle agreed to work together: Oracle would ensure its software ran on Microsoft's cloud platform; Microsoft would promote Oracle's database software. At different times, Sony has used *go-it-alone* and *marketplace-cooperation*:

Sony was first to enter consumer videotape with Betamax. Sony failed, in part because JVC provided its VHS format to competitors. JVC's licensees helped expand acceptance and Sony ultimately withdrew. By contrast, all major electronic firms adopted the DVD-replacing Blu-ray format championed by Sony.

- **Back-office.** Competitors may *compete* fiercely in the market, but their back offices *collaborate* extensively. *Back-office cooperation* in non-customer-facing activities reduces costs and improves efficiency for all firms. Examples:
  - General Mills, Colombo yogurt, and Land O'Lakes butter share delivery trucks.[34]
  - Italian tile manufacturers jointly purchase freight to reduce international shipping costs.
  - Major airlines collaborate in interline arrangements to move luggage.[35]

- Retail brokerage houses work closely with competitors to clear trades.
- U.S. paper makers routinely swap products at list price to save freight costs.

WEAK COMPLEMENTARITY. Marketplace and back-office complementarity generally require formal agreements. Other types of complementarity are weaker but may contribute positively:

- **Cost reduction.** When several competitors have common suppliers, one competitor's actions may affect the others. Dell and HP Inc. compete in PCs, but if either firm's sales expand total volume, joint purchases of computer chips increase. Chip suppliers achieve scale economies that reduce costs — ultimately, chip prices decline for all producers.
- **Greater customer value.** The firm may provide greater customer value when customers combine its product with a rival's product. Complementary drug regimens — *drug cocktails* — are an increasing trend; they dominate AIDS treatment. BMS initially introduced blood-thinner Plavix as a competitor to aspirin; today BMS positions Plavix and aspirin as complementary products.
- **Increasing demand.** Competitors engage in joint advertising and other promotions so all firms benefit. Many shopping malls draw consumers from large distances; all stores gain.[36]
- **Keeping the firm sharp.** Tough competition keeps the firm on its toes. Some firms deliberately seek out tough competitors. One German engineering firm always launches new products in Japan.
- **Market development.** Competitor market development actions may assist the firm. Apple's iPhone opened up the smartphone market; several other firms benefited, like Samsung. Monsanto's success with genetically modified seeds has helped competitor DuPont.
- **Political action.** Competitors join trade associations to lobby governments for favorable decisions.

UNWELCOME COMPLEMENTARITY. Sometimes firms do not want their products associated with other firms — *unwelcome* complementers. Automobile and aircraft manufacturers fight fiercely against unauthorized parts manufacturers; they believe these parts degrade their products. Callaway Golf was very successful with oversized Big Bertha golf clubs. Spalding advertised that its Top-Flite/Club System C balls improved play with Big Bertha clubs. Callaway sued Spalding for trademark infringement, false advertising, and unfair competition; the case was settled out of court. Callaway later launched Callaway Rule 35 premium golf balls!

KEY IDEA

Competitors may provide front-office (marketplace) or back-office complementarity.

Competitors may be *strong* or *weak* complementers.

MARKETING QUESTION

What organizations are complementers for NBC (U.S. television network)?

KEY IDEA

Competitors may not welcome the firm's complementary product activities.

KEY MESSAGES

- In pursuit of differential advantage, the firm must gain deep competitor insight.
- A structured competitor insight process asks several questions:
  - *Identify.* Who are our competitors:
    - Current competitors — today?
    - Direct competitors?
    - Potential competitors — tomorrow?
    - Indirect competitors?
  - *Describe.* What are our competitors' capabilities and difficulties?
  - *Evaluate.* What are our competitors' strategic options?
  - *Project.* What do we expect our competitors to do — short term, medium term, long term?
  - *Manage.* How can we get our competitors to do what we want them to do?
- Answering these questions is not simple but, for each question, several approaches help improve competitor insight.
- The firm must know itself.
- The firm must understand its complementary relationships. Complementers can help the firm achieve its objectives.
- Both independent organizations and competitors can be complementers, each in different ways.

MARKETING QUESTION

What other messages did you glean from this chapter?

VIDEOS AND AUDIOS

For complimentary material, see Axcess Capon codes at www.axcessvids.com

Competitor Insight   **393a** ◎   Noel Capon   Columbia Business School

QUESTIONS FOR STUDY AND DISCUSSION

Can you answer the questions implied by this chapter's learning outcomes? Check!

1. Evidence suggests large companies sometimes dismiss competitive threats. Do you believe this is true? Why or why not? How could you ensure a successful large company retains a competitive outlook?

2. Many observers believe competition between Microsoft and Google will increase. Microsoft has a large lead in operating systems, office suites, and browsers; Google leads in search. Identify one or two colleagues to act as Google top managers; identify one or two colleagues to act as Microsoft top managers. First, the Google team develops a market strategy for Google; the Microsoft team develops a market strategy for Microsoft. The two teams exchange strategies. Second, the Google team develops a market strategy to counteract Microsoft's strategy, and vice versa. How did you define the field of competition? What did you learn from this competitive-gaming exercise? (Feel free to substitute Facebook for Microsoft.)

3. In the hair-coloring market, L'Oreal competes with Clairol; in men's shaving, Gillette competes with Schick. Suppose you work for Clairol — use the competitor assessment analysis to evaluate L'Oreal and identify its strategic options. Or suppose you work for Gillette — use the competitor assessment analysis to evaluate Schick and identify its strategic options.

4. Southwest Airlines (SWA) carries more domestic passengers than any other U.S. airline. Early in its history, SWA faced a difficult competitive situation with Braniff Airlines — a large domestic and international carrier. SWA operated three routes — Dallas–Houston, Houston–San Antonio, Dallas–San Antonio. Overall, SWA was unprofitable. To increase volume on the Houston–San Antonio and Dallas–San Antonio routes, SWA reduced prices from $26 to $13 for a one-way trip. Braniff offered a sale on the Dallas–Houston route — $13. Dallas–Houston was the only profitable route for SWA. How would you have advised SWA?

5. Slovak Inc. (disguised) hired Peter Fry for a summer internship. Peter arrived at Slovak's Budapest headquarters in late June. The CEO directed Peter to visit competitors in different European countries. Peter was to pose as a student seeking data for a term paper — Slovak would pay Peter's travel and accommodation expenses. Peter was troubled by the required misrepresentation but was relying on income from Slovak to pay his fall MBA tuition. It was too late to secure another summer job. What would you have done in Peter's place? Why?

6. Explain the impact of oil prices on product design decisions for car manufacturers. Compare and contrast GM and Toyota.

7. Printers and ink account for a high percentage of HP Inc.'s profits. Fast-growing retailers like Cartridge World sell refills at one-half HP Inc.'s prices. How should HP Inc. respond? Use scenario analysis to develop options for HP Inc.

8. How would you define 7-Up's competitive landscape?

9. Select a product in which you are interested. Alternatively, consider *Managing Marketing in the 21st Century*. From the competitors you identified in Chapter 3: What are their capabilities and difficulties? What are their strategic options? What do you expect them to do?

TRUE/FALSE QUESTIONS
Answers on page A1 and at www.axcessvids.com — 158p

1. Direct competitors target the same customers as the firm with similar benefits but have different products, technology, and/or business models. ❏ **TRUE** ❏ **FALSE**

2. Quantitative data include measures like market share and profitability. ❏ **TRUE** ❏ **FALSE**

3. Secondary data are available in various publications and on the Internet. ❏ **TRUE** ❏ **FALSE**

4. Game theory helps marketers think through the impact of the firm's actions on competitors — and of the competitors' actions on the firm. ❏ **TRUE** ❏ **FALSE**

5. Tit-for-tat signals tell competitors that if their actions reach certain thresholds, the firm will take serious steps to create a disadvantage for them. ❏ **TRUE** ❏ **FALSE**

MULTIPLE CHOICE QUESTIONS
Answers on page A1 and at www.axcessvids.com — 477p

1. Which of the following types of competitive threats is the competitive status quo?

   a. current direct competitors
   b. current indirect competitors
   c. potential direct competitors
   d. potential indirect competitors

2. Which of the following is NOT one of the key areas for describing competitors?

   a. type of competitor data the firm should collect
   b. available sources of competitive data
   c. processes the firm should use for gathering competitive data
   d. All selections represent key areas for describing competitors.

3. Which of the following describes the internal process for securing competitive data where executive teams play one of two roles: the firm or the competitor?

   a. shadow system
   b. competitive intelligence system
   c. formal development of strategic plans
   d. gaming with multifunctional teams

4. A _____ prohibits former employees from working for competitors for a defined time period.

   a. nondisclosure agreement
   b. noncompete agreement
   c. value chain
   d. shadow system

5. As a firm builds scenarios, it must incorporate all of the following EXCEPT:

   a. an end state
   b. a plot
   c. a beginning state
   d. logics

CHAPTER 6

MARKETING RESEARCH

For complimentary material, see Axcess Capon codes at www.axcessvids.com

LEARNING OUTCOMES

When you have completed this chapter, you will be able to:

- Translate marketing problems and issues into actionable research questions.
- Think systematically about the marketing research process.
- Become familiar with the language and terminology of marketing research.
- Interact productively with specialist marketing researchers.
- Appreciate the importance of big data.
- Use marketing research data to secure greater customer insight.[1]
- Identify new marketing research techniques to help secure differential advantage.
- Assess market and sales potential, and make market and sales forecasts.
- Understand the category development index (CDI) and brand development index (BDI).
- Become a sophisticated user (and client) of marketing research.
- Recognize the limitations and drawbacks of marketing research.

OPENING CASE: THOMSON FINANCIAL

Thomson Financial (TF) provides information and decision analysis tools for the financial market and has evolved steadily in recent years via organic development and acquisition.[2] TF continually redefines offerings to keep pace with evolving market needs. TF focuses on helping organizations inform and build front-end customer strategy by developing unique ways to gather, interpret, and disseminate customer insight. TF has a large customer base and many competitors; insight gleaned from customer experiences play a key role in differentiation and strategy development.

Warren Breakstone, TF COO for global sales, marketing, and services, realized the importance of measuring overall customer experience at all service touch points — sales, account management, training, and help-desk support. Breakstone launched an annual global benchmarking satisfaction study, together with intermittent check-ups of clients that recently used training or help-desk services. Breakstone said, "The most important result was a deeper understanding of customer satisfaction drivers; that helped priority-setting and framed resource allocation decisions. We began to understand the complex interplay between product satisfaction and customer services."

Breakstone said customers might be very satisfied with a particular aspect of help-desk support. But that might not be a strong driver of customer satisfaction or increase the likelihood of referrals (an important customer-loyalty measure). Teasing out key customer-satisfaction drivers allowed TF to focus on actions generating the greatest impact. Breakstone said, "As the result of our studies, we have more discipline in resource allocation — dollars, personnel, and management focus." One high-end customer subgroup greatly valued TF's financial-modeling consulting service. TF doubled its modeling investment, and consulting services became more successful.

For Breakstone, gaining customer insight is more than executing quantitative benchmarking studies. "The key is to incorporate an understanding of how the data impact ongoing decisions. Customer satisfaction measures have allowed us to challenge assumptions and make more fact-based decisions. We introduce more data into our discussions of what we should do differently going forward. We are dedicated to linking customer research to our day-to-day decisions. Many firms do not have this discipline; research reports lie dormant and they never explore their customer insights. The amount of unused or poorly used marketing research is astounding."

Kim Collins, marketing SVP for TF's Corporate Services, builds client insight via structured monthly pulse *surveys measuring customer satisfaction with TF training and support functions. Collins said, "I believe that true* insight *is gleaned from comprehensive, detailed, and continual measurement of customer experiences with products/services at every touch point with customers. Insight is the intelligence we gather when we stop to listen to clients. Only then do we begin to understand the impact, positive or negative, we're having on customer workflow."*

Collins' online surveys are briefer than the annual benchmarking studies — only five to 10 questions — but they deliver important data for trend analysis. They also alert Corporate Services to potential problems with customer experiences. TF's rapid response mitigates dissatisfaction, but also reminds customers that TF is listening to their concerns and cares about their experiences. By involving cross-functional teams in the pulse initiative, customer insight infiltrates important functional areas.

Collins said, "When product developers understand first-hand the frustrations or work-arounds that customers encounter with TF products, they prioritize development efforts to address key issues affecting customer satisfaction. When marketers understand how diverse customers use the same product for different purposes, they can more closely target key messages and product benefits."

Gaining customer insight is crucial for Thomson Financial. TF gains short-term and long-term insight, then applies this insight to its decision-making processes.

Case Question

What insight about marketing research can you draw from Thomson Financial's experience?

© Mauritius/Superstock

I think one of the big dangers in today's marketing is that you get these big volumes of stuff — data — which mean nothing. In fact, I hate marketing research, but I love actionable customer insight. You have to work a bit harder. You have to apply your brain to really think through what questions you want to ask people. I think the issue is really thinking through what action you're going to take as a result of your study, rather than just producing a 150-page report that isn't actionable. What's important is research to take action, rather than research just to prove a point. We're not into that.

—David Haines, former Director of Global Branding, Vodafone[3]

MARKETING QUESTION

What marketing research challenges does the video [621v] illustrate?

Marketing research is any process of data collection, analysis, and interpretation the firm adopts to improve the quality of its marketing efforts.[507v] The firm may conduct marketing research on actual and potential customers and their decision-making units, but also on external influencers like legislators and regulators. Sometimes marketing research focuses on behavior. Other times it concerns mental states like awareness, perceptions, attitudes, and intentions — at any and all stages in the customer experience. Marketing research also subsumes activities like gathering competitive intelligence — Chapter 5 — and measuring marketing effectiveness. The related term *market research* has a narrower focus — specifically gathering data about current and potential markets.

We did not design Chapter 6 to make you a marketing research expert. There are many fine books and courses to guide you toward that goal. But we do believe that astute marketers must become *intelligent customers* of marketing research. You need to know where marketing research can be helpful and where it cannot.[903v] You must learn what sorts of questions to ask your marketing research suppliers and how to interpret their answers. Marketing research also encompasses the increasingly important field of *big data*. Finally, this chapter addresses specific and very important topics for marketers: assessing market and sales potential and making sound marketing and sales forecasts.

THE CHANGING VIEW

OLD WAY	NEW WAY
Basic analysis — tabs, X-tabs, regression	Sophisticated analysis — complex methods, choice models, big data
Customer market focus only	Research on multiple constituencies
Data are scarce	Data are plentiful, even overwhelming — big data
Descriptive orientation	Causal orientation
Direct elicitation techniques	Projective techniques
Focus groups and one-on-one interviews	Eclectic methodologies
Identify trends	Build trends into market strategy
Loose measurement technology	Careful measurement technology
Market research is unfamiliar to much of the public	Market research is familiar to much of the public but many people are unhappy with intrusive phone calls
Observational methods rare	Observational methods often employed
One major market research approach	Combination of multiple research methodologies
Pencil and paper surveys	Web panels and online surveys
Quantitative results	Actionable results
Sometimes cavalier attitude to confidentiality	Much stricter observance of privacy rights
Strive to increase sample sizes	Strive to improve management of large databases
Typically instrumental	Purely investigative is more common

THE MARKETING RESEARCH PROCESS

Bristol-Myers Squibb's (BMS) marketing research mission is *to ensure the superior use of information and analysis to objectively identify opportunities, frame and validate strategic options, monitor results, provide insight, and build cumulative knowledge.*[4] BMS believes superior customer understanding provides critical insights for integrating into the decision-making processes. By championing industry-leading techniques, BMS understands and anticipates market evolution, providing critical insight into strategic issues. Insight from marketing research allows BMS to create leading programs, earn superior marketing and financial results, and develop and retain top business leaders. These lofty goals provide a window into the importance of timely and effective marketing research in developing the firm's future.

The purpose of marketing research is simple: to help the firm make better marketing decisions. The *marketing research process* should follow a basic problem-solving approach. After all, without problems marketing research would be unnecessary. A critical element of success rests on the relationship between the manager and the researcher. Marketing research is a support function helping the firm make better decisions, but *never forget*: The manager is ultimately responsible for interpretation, making decisions, and the outcomes. We know many cases where the manager, in effect, tossed the problem *over the wall* to marketing research with little guidance or direction, and then expected an answer. This is an especial problem when the firm outsources marketing research to a marketing research supplier. Failure to define the research problem is abdication of managerial responsibility, often leading to dissatisfaction and frustration for all involved. Absence of a clear problem statement does not lead to actionable marketing research.

Sometimes the marketing research department conducts studies for marketing managers. Other times, marketing research helps frame individual studies, but specialist research suppliers provide data and/or conduct analyses. Indeed, marketing research is a major industry with many players; Nielsen has $6 billion annual revenues. IMRB International, Hansa Research, and Majestic MRSS are large Indian marketing research firms.

Responsibility for marketing research often extends beyond the marketing research department, single manager, or business unit. At B2B firms, various individuals with customer relationship responsibilities may meet periodically to discuss customer needs. Medical equipment firm Hill-Rom (HM) has various hospital contacts — maintenance, nurses, purchasing, senior administrators, and ward orderlies. Pooled insight led HM to redesign its beds to reduce nurse injuries, save time on nonnursing tasks, and cut hospital costs. When the firm has a few major customers, strategic (key) account managers may orchestrate the search for insight — Chapter 18.

B2C firms have similar processes. A former senior Target executive shared the retailer's approach to securing significant growth: "We identify trends with a dedicated trend group that travels the world to find new trends in everything from apparel to home décor to food, and we use a tool called the *trend curve* to segment trend life cycles. This approach helps us determine when it will be hot, so we can get it into our stores at the right time for our guests. But we also involve the rest of the company. When anyone is traveling abroad, the expectation is that they will carve out time to go and understand what is happening in Antwerp, Berlin, London, Prague, Tokyo, or wherever they were. We want to know what's emerging? What is the cool restaurant? What are the teenagers wearing? What are the young artists showing? Target has an excellent trend department, but we also have people in every area of the company who have carved out the niche of being trend czars, because everyone has that role to play. We expect everyone to cultivate an eye."[5]

To ensure marketing research is tightly aligned with marketing decision-making, the marketing research process must follow a consistent methodology — Figure 6.1 (p. 151).

KEY IDEA

The purpose of marketing research is to help the firm make better marketing decisions.

KEY IDEA

The marketing research process comprises several sequential steps:
- Define the business issue
- Identify a researchable problem
- Formulate objectives and hypotheses
- Conduct a preliminary investigation
- Develop the research plan
- Collect and analyze data
- Prepare the report

MARKETING QUESTION

Suppose you were General Motors' Marketing VP. For what top 5 marketing research questions would you like answers?

DEFINE THE BUSINESS ISSUE

As a marketing manager, you have primary responsibility for defining the business issue. Of course, marketing researchers (internal department or outsourced supplier) may encourage you to think more deeply about your concerns. Sometimes the *presenting* (immediate) problem may actually be a symptom. You may believe that poor sales performance is due to lazy salespeople, but marketing research may suggest other potential causes — untrained first-line sales managers or unsatisfactory products. A total quality management (TQM) methodology — Table 6.1 — asks *five whys* as it seeks the root cause of an issue. Of course, you may already have sufficient data to solve the problem. If not, you should state the issue as clearly, completely, and simply as possible, then call in the marketing researchers.

FIGURE 6.1
The Marketing Research Process

TABLE 6.1
Illustration: Defining the Business Issue

Round	Apparent Business Issue (Symptom)	Question (Cause)
1	Our sales performance isn't up to par.	Why?
2	Salespeople aren't putting in enough effort.	Why?
3	It's hard to persuade customers to buy our products.	Why?
4	Our products don't really satisfy customer needs.	Why?
5	Our product design process is deficient on customer insight.	Why?

IDENTIFY A RESEARCHABLE PROBLEM

Marketing research will not solve all your problems, but a good marketing researcher will help you frame the issues so research can be useful. (Sometimes exploratory research is necessary to frame the problem; outside perspectives from a consultant may also be useful.) Good marketing research can highlight the facts, point you in the right direction, and help reduce uncertainty. But there is always a time cost of executing marketing research — forgone revenues and/or competitor action. You should always weigh the value of reducing uncertainty against these costs, and collaborate with your researchers to define a researchable problem.

FORMULATE OBJECTIVES AND HYPOTHESES

Together with marketing researchers, you should agree on the research objectives and hypotheses you will test. (You may revise the hypotheses after exploratory research.) Objectives and hypotheses are usually related, but hypotheses are always more specific. Suppose your objective is to identify market opportunities for a new product. Specific hypotheses may relate to positioning alternatives, price points, and brand name. You should be very clear about what insight you are seeking. Examples include:

- **What:**
  - What do consumers think about our product versus competitor products?
  - What specifically do they think are key benefits and values we offer?
  - What benefits and values should we highlight in our communications?

- **Why:**
  - Why do some consumers switch brands?
  - Why are some consumers fiercely brand loyal?

- **How and how much:**
  - How frequently do consumers purchase our product?
  - How do consumers prefer to buy?
  - How much do consumers purchase on each purchase occasion?
  - How much do consumers consume on each use occasion?

- **Who:**
  - Who makes the purchase decision for these types of products?
  - Who influences the purchase decision?
  - Who consumes these products?

- **When:**
  - When do consumers make the decision to purchase these products?
  - When do consumers purchase these products?
  - When do consumers consume these products?

Different research questions may require different methodologies like exploratory or causal research for *why* questions, and qualitative research for *what, how, how much, who,* and *when* questions.

> **KEY IDEA**
>
> Marketing research typically answers questions commencing with:
> - What
> - Why
> - How and how much
> - Who
> - When

CONDUCT A PRELIMINARY INVESTIGATION

Before conducting primary research directly with respondents, you should always evaluate secondary data. Secondary data (existing sources) may be inside the firm, but are often outside. (We discuss distinctions between primary and secondary data, and qualitative and quantitative data, later in the chapter.) Secondary data may provide partial (or even complete) answers to your research questions more quickly and less expensively than primary data. In other cases, you may commence primary research by talking informally to colleagues — someone may have previously addressed a problem like yours in a former job or company. You may also conduct an exploratory qualitative study to secure preliminary insight. These means may allow you to narrow the scope of enquiry by identifying gaps between the data you need to meet your research objectives and data you already possess. Typically, this information gap is the basis for larger-scale and more quantitative research, where costs really mount. Skipping the preliminary stage can lead to heavy expenditures without commensurate insight.

DEVELOP THE RESEARCH PLAN

As your marketing research blueprint, the more detailed research plan should include data-collection methodologies, embracing data collection instruments like questionnaires. The research plan should also comprise a sampling plan identifying who will provide data. You must specify the:

- target group for your study;
- sample size for securing statistically significant results;
- sampling method — how to choose your respondents.

Typically, you want to project study results to your universe; hence, you must ensure the sample you select is random and unbiased. You have two options: Each universe member has an equal chance of being selected; or you divide the universe into mutually exclusive groups before random selection.[6] You should avoid nonrandomly selected (biased) samples like *convenience samples* or allowing respondents to self-select. You must also rule out *nonresponse bias* — when responders are different from nonresponders. The researcher's job is to make sure you get the right data from the right people at the right time.

You should also specify the analytic methods you anticipate using. This can be intellectually challenging, but you should never collect data and then scratch your head wondering how to analyze. Your research plan should also include time and cost estimates, both for management approval and negotiating contracts with outside suppliers. Experienced firms apply a similar discipline to internal research projects and suppliers.

**MARKETING
QUESTION**

Your firm collects confidential consumer data via face-to-face interviews. You suspect one of your interviewers is lazy and is faking the data, yet he denies your accusations. How would you proceed?

COLLECT AND ANALYZE DATA

With a research plan in place, you are now ready to begin your research. Make sure you use the *right* method, not just one that's easy.[7] If you plan to collect survey data:

- Make sure your subjects are representative of the target population.
- Pay careful attention to response rates.
- Implement procedures for dealing with nonresponders.
- Be concerned with data integrity.
- Make sure data collectors act honestly.

No matter how carefully you plan your analysis, additional follow-up analyses may seem appropriate, but they add time and expense. Carefully weigh anticipated value versus the scope of your research plan.

Dishonesty in Marketing Research

Early this century, Coca-Cola rigged a market test in several Burger King outlets. A Coke employee supposedly manipulated the popularity of Frozen Coke (FC) (a slushy drink), by hiring a consultant to buy value meals including FC for children. Coke paid $540,000 to a former auditor who claimed wrongful dismissal for exposing the scheme, and $21 million to Burger King.

The marketing manager and marketing researcher should collaborate in interpreting research results. Marketing researchers should serve as experts on questionnaire design, sampling methods, analytic techniques, and interpreting statistically significant results. But marketing managers are responsible for restricting researcher interpretations to these issues; marketing researchers may lack insight into the problem context. Marketing managers have ultimate decision-making responsibility and should not encourage researchers to make recommendations beyond their expertise.

PREPARE THE REPORT

As a marketing manager, you will often review marketing research reports others prepare. They present research findings, but your goal and responsibility is always to seek insight.

Figure 6.2 illustrates distinctions among *data and information, knowledge,* and *insight.* Many firms are rich in *data* and *information,* but lack *knowledge* and may have little *insight.* Take seriously David Haines' comments, p. 149.

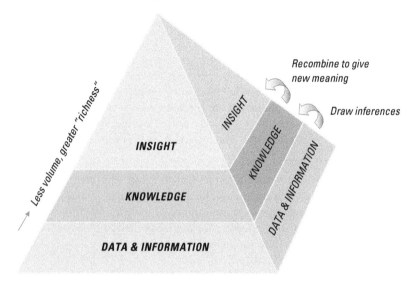

Reproduced by permission of Impact Planning Group

FIGURE 6.2
Data and Information, Knowledge, and Insight

Accurate inferences drawn from raw data or processed information constitute knowledge. Many firms devote considerable effort to codifying knowledge and making it widely available (often with varying access); some firms even appoint *knowledge czars* (chief knowledge officers). Insight is different from knowledge. You develop insight by combining different knowledge elements, or using knowledge to create new meaning. Fred Smith's (FedEx) classic insight was that freight forwarders using passenger airlines could not provide reliable overnight package delivery. Other key insights leading to innovation and significant success include: Jeff Bezos — Amazon; Steve Jobs and Steve Wozniak — Apple and the PC industry; Mark Zuckerberg — Facebook; Sergey Brin and Larry Page — Google; Andrew Mason — Groupon; Reed Hastings — Netflix; Howard Schultz — Starbucks; Jack Dorsey — Square, and with Evan Williams — Twitter.

Good reports make assumptions transparent so they can be challenged and defended, clearly present the findings, and develop managerial implications. You may propose further research to clarify incompletely answered questions, but marketing research can only reduce uncertainty, never eliminate it entirely. A good report proposes alternative courses of action and makes specific recommendations; after all, the goal of any research project should be some change in practice. Changes may range from minor course corrections to major innovations. If the report recommends no changes, at best you validated a current direction; at worst, you asked the wrong questions! Beware research that is mere ritual; managers who ignore results, perhaps because they offend a comfortable status quo.

MARKETING QUESTION

It's the first day at your new job and your boss calls you into her office. "I want you to design a marketing research study to determine the reasons for customer loyalty." Prepare a response for your boss.

BIG DATA

In recent years, driven largely by growth in the Internet and social media, the availability and quantity of digital data has mushroomed; hence, the term we hear so much about — *big data.*[8]

From a marketing perspective, the firm's challenge is to secure meaning and insight from big data to make better decisions. The firm succeeds by identifying relevant data and applying appropriate analytic methods to gain insight.

Three trends (3Vs) are driving marketers to use big data[9]:

- **Volume.** Data quantity is fast growing — 2.5 exabytes* of data are created daily, doubling every 40 months.
- **Velocity.** Data are increasingly available very quickly; hence, the firm can take action in real time.
- **Variety.** Data sources and data types continue to multiply.

A simple example concerning book retailers illustrates the opportunities that big data and *predictive analytics* offer marketers:

> Traditional retail booksellers typically have little data on individual customers. At best, an effective loyalty program provides data on member purchases and facilitates generalized promotional offers. By contrast, today's online booksellers have individual-level data on books purchased. These retailers also have data on books viewed, samples downloaded, and website navigation. And they can assess the influence of promotions, reviews, and page layouts on purchase decisions. Online retailers can make and automate informed recommendations to individuals, personalize promotional offers, and even enhance the service experience. By examining similarities across individuals and groups, online retailers can more accurately forecast future sales, and continually update customer insight.[10]

A critical driver for increased use of big data is declining costs for data storage, memory, data processing, and bandwidth. Marketers can now access many data sources that previously were either very expensive or did not exist. These sources include alerts (customer/competitor actions); clickstreams from web browsing; eye tracking; GPS signals from mobile devices (smartphones, tablet computers); messages, updates, and social connections from social networking sites (Facebook, Instagram, Twitter); product sensor data; purchase transactions; and user-generated content from forums, blogs, and product reviews. Data may be text based, or visual as in video, pictures, emotions, eye movements, facial tracking, and body and brain responses.[11] Of course, the firm must always address privacy and intellectual property concerns.

The good news for marketers is the increased 3Vs of data. The bad news is that many data sources are unstructured and unwieldy, and originate and/or are stored in multiple locations. Indeed, data scientists routinely spend 50 percent of their time in *data munging/data wrangling/data janitorial work*, cleaning up databases for analysis. Note, this data characterization may be equally true for firm-level data — spread across various functions, businesses, and geographies — as for external data.

KEY IDEA

The firm should design and implement processes to mine big data and secure insight.

To take advantage of big data and address these difficulties, marketing research groups must develop new skill sets; data analysts (data scientists) require advanced capabilities in handling cleaning, and organizing large datasets. Marketing research groups must become experts in current and newly developing data analytic tools, techniques, and modeling.[12] Furthermore, marketing researchers must learn to work with firm engineering teams; these teams may be more interested in building and scaling the firm's website than in making changes to enhance the customer experience based on new insights. Marketing research groups will also require developers of visualization tools and techniques for communicating results to managers. GE spent $2 billion on a center for excellence in software and plans on a 400-data-scientist staff; IBM spent $14 billion in acquisitions to boost data analytics capabilities. But many firms will have difficulty in securing their desired data-scientist headcount. Big data is a new field and data scientists are in short supply; conversely, career opportunities are very attractive.

The payoff for creating value from big data analytics is huge, and particularly so if the firm can *connect the dots* among multiple data sources. For example, using location data from mobile devices, and purchase data from clickstreams, the firm can identify and contact the *right* customers, at the *right* time, in the *right* place. Traditionally, Sears housed data for its Sears Craftsman and Lands' End brands in different databases and data warehouses. As a result, comprehensive

---

*1 exabyte = 1 billion gigabytes

cross-brand promotions were difficult, time-consuming, and costly to prepare. By synchronizing these data and viewing them in one place, Sears was able to identify opportunities and design better promotions (more timely, granular, and personalized). Sears also reduced development time for a comprehensive set of promotions from eight weeks to less than one week.

Marketing researchers seek meaning from data via *data mining*. Data mining uses powerful statistical methods and algorithms to search databases for patterns. One increasingly popular data-mining approach for brand managers is *social-listening tools*, in particular *sentiment analysis*. By *mining* vast amounts of user-generated content on social media, the firm learns how current and potential customers perceive its brands. The firm can track changes and develop new approaches to improve emotional connections with customers.

In essence, data mining is an inductive approach, following the core principle to *let the data speak*.[13] This approach may lead to a shift in decision-making power in organizations. Decisions based on advanced analytics applied to large datasets may outperform human judgment. Hence, rather than base decisions on the HiPPO (highest-paid person's opinion) principle, big data and analytics may drive decision making. Hence, actual customer behavior becomes a more important factor, leading to major cultural shifts within organizations.

Using big data and advanced analytics, the marketing research goal is to isolate the *signal* in the vast amount of *noise* in the data so as to make *predictive* (forward-looking) judgments. Simple systems predict a person's future purchases based on his/her past purchases, and purchases by other customers who bought the same item. More advanced systems layer in data from many other databases to secure deeper insight. The *holy grail* is to *surprise* customers: to offer products they weren't really looking for, yet satisfied a latent need and led to a purchase. Of course, the firm must ensure the relationships it finds are meaningful and replicable, and must clearly distinguish between *correlational* and *causal* relationships. To avoid potential errors, it is a good idea to separate data into three types:

- Training data — to identify relationships
- Test data — to evaluate various candidate relationships
- Validation data — to confirm selected relationships

Perhaps the best metaphor for understanding big data is a river (data) fed by many tributaries (data types); the surrounding topography allows new tributaries to form from time to time (new data types).[14] The marketing researcher and data scientist fish in the river, trying to hook a tasty fish (insight) that lives out of sight. Only fishing skill (good methodology), focus on desired types of fish (insights sought), and perseverance can ensure catching a tasty fish (insight) rather than an old boot![332p][15]

CRITICAL DISTINCTIONS IN MARKETING RESEARCH

As a marketing manager, you will be responsible for directing marketing researchers and the marketing research process. Here we make some critical distinctions that can help you devise marketing research plans.

PRIMARY AND SECONDARY RESEARCH

Best practice dictates assessing available secondary data, then filling information gaps with primary data.[503v]

SECONDARY RESEARCH. Some person or organization has already collected secondary data for another purpose or for sale to corporations. Three basic types of secondary data are:

- **Company data.** Comprises routinely generated data from transactions with customers and suppliers; information from internal databases — capacity, costs, production; customer

KEY IDEA

Secondary marketing research uses data relevant to your research that some person or organization has already collected for another purpose.

Primary marketing research requires you to collect new data.

MARKETING QUESTION

Select a product class or product form. Suppose you require sales data. What secondary sources will provide these data?

KEY IDEA

Key types of secondary data are:

• Company data
• Public data
• Technical analysis

lists; customer purchases (what, when, how many, prices), complaints, information requests, payment history, and service calls; delivery, maintenance, and servicing reports; salesperson call reports; and previously completed marketing research reports. Company data also includes data collected by customers or partners, like bar code *scanner data* and RFID tracking data.

• **Public data.** Includes information about competitors, customers, and suppliers; industry trends; and technologies. Sources include competitor annual reports; competitor and public domain websites; general business and industry-specific media and books; government and trade associations; government and published academic research; websites (like dnb.com, Dialog.com, LexisNexis.com); legal and government filings; supplier white papers; trade show literature; and presentations. Public data also include semipublic data like syndicated research reports from firms like Nielsen and IRI, and reports from industry and financial analysts. Locating data is often a challenge, but subscription databases and Internet search engines have eased this task.

• **Technical analysis.** Includes objective, repeatable descriptions of products/services and/or production capacity collected by internal engineers or developers. Examples include benchmarking product design and reverse engineering competitor products to estimate manufacturing costs and supply-chain processes.

PRIMARY RESEARCH. As noted earlier, primary research is typically more expensive than secondary research. The firm usually collects primary data for a specific purpose, often to close gaps between data required to make decisions and secondary research data. Primary data sources depend on the research problem but may include previous, current, and/or potential customers, especially people in various purchase and consumption roles; industry experts and trade association personnel; and distribution channel members like agents, brokers, distributors, retailers, and wholesalers. Sometimes the firm lowers primary data costs by joining a syndicate/consortium whose members seek data from similar respondents.

All primary research requires a stimulus, frequently a question the researcher wants answered. Sometimes the firm provides specific stimuli like advertising or positioning concepts, attribute lists or product profiles, advertising or sales messages, or competitive materials/products.

QUALITATIVE AND QUANTITATIVE RESEARCH

> "We used to position Lean Cuisine as 'calorie control,' competing with Healthy Choice and Weight Watchers, then as *great taste but low fat/low sodium*. Then we gained a key insight from qualitative marketing research with customers — one-on-ones and focus groups. Our new positioning is, *it's easy to do something good for yourself because it tastes so good*. Now Lean Cuisine competes with all the junk in people's refrigerators, and we have double-digit growth."[16]

Two major approaches to marketing research are qualitative and quantitative:

QUALITATIVE RESEARCH. *Qualitative research* (QualR) is typically not concerned with numbers. QualR is generally flexible and versatile, but is rarely conclusive and does not project to a larger population. Firms often conduct QualR to pursue interesting questions, uncover customer needs, identify buyer behavior, gain better understanding of business issues and the *language* people use, develop ideas, and help define and prioritize marketing research problems. QualR can help assess how customers *feel* about products and suppliers. Small-scale exploratory primary QualR often precedes large-scale quantitative data collection.

KEY IDEA

Qualitative research (QualR) is not concerned with numbers.

Quantitative research (QuanR) focuses on quantitative analysis.

A particular issue in QualR is the difference between self-reported responses and data on actual behavior. Both can be valuable, but the researcher should always be skeptical about self-reports. Just because a respondent says, "I did X" or "I will do X" does not mean the respondent actually did, or will do, X. Respondents may purposely mislead researchers, but mismatches between self-reports and actual behavior are often due to bias, poor memory, and/or unclear questions. Researchers should seek convergence; the Kimberly-Clark example is instructive:

> Focus groups provided Kimberly-Clark (KC) with little insight into why Huggies baby wipes were losing sales. KC introduced a new observational technique, a camera mounted on a pair of glasses that consumers wore at home. In focus groups, mothers talked about changing babies on a diaper table. From the cameras, researchers saw that mothers changed babies on many surfaces, often in awkward positions, and struggled with containers requiring two hands. KC redesigned packages for wipes, shampoo, and lotions so mothers could easily dispense them with one hand.

QUANTITATIVE RESEARCH. *Quantitative research* (QuanR) uses numerical data and mathematical analyses, often from large representative samples. Marketing researchers use QuanR to test hypotheses formulated earlier in the research process. Some analyses are quite simple; other analyses are highly complex. The researcher should ask three types of question:

- **Internal validity.** Do these data measure what I want to measure?
- **Reliability.** If I repeat data collection, will I get the same results?
- **External validity.** Will the results I secure generalize to other populations?

Sometimes drawing the line between QualR and QuanR is difficult. Some forms of qualitative data are amenable to quantitative analysis. Researchers are always pursuing new forms of quantitative analysis, but qualitative data gathering is also evolving. Firms striving for increased customer insight are driving these innovations.

Figure 6.3 shows how primary and secondary research can be either qualitative or quantitative. Generally, quantitative approaches to primary research data yield more insight than qualitative approaches. But with secondary research, the firm can often gain significant insight from the large amounts of qualitative data that are often available.

KEY IDEA

Critical concerns in quantitative research are:

- Internal validity
- Reliability
- External validity

	Primary	**Secondary**
Qualitative	Small-group discussions with customers about product alternatives	Review of advertising campaigns from various product suppliers
Quantitative	Large-scale sample survey of customers about product alternatives; test hypotheses by quantitative methods	Secure independent research reports on customers' views of product alternatives; conduct quantitative analyses

FIGURE 6.3
Illustration: Research Types

SECURING QUALITATIVE RESEARCH DATA

The simplest form of QualR is informal — a marketing executive talks to a few customers, scans competitor advertisements, buys competitive products and/or calls competitor employees and service centers, and/or visits distributors to see how they display products. Nine West (shoes) founder Vince Camuto said: "Listen to the consumer. I'm out every week in the stores, talking to women and salespeople. What do people want? Where is their lifestyle going? Trends don't come from designers. They come from consumers."[17] While chatting to a call-center phone operator, J. Crew's CEO Mickey Drexler learned that women were placing multiple orders for a popular beach dress in different sizes. Within a few weeks, J. Crew was successfully offering bridesmaid's dresses. The firm may also invest in more formal qualitative data-gathering approaches for securing insight.

FOCUS GROUPS

MARKETING QUESTION

Hundreds of consumer complaints corroborate allegations that Internet, telephone, and television service providers make it difficult to leave at the end of a contract. Develop a focus group facilitator guide for investigating this practice at a service provider of your choice?

Single-location *focus groups* are one of the most popular qualitative data-collection methods. Typically, focus groups comprise eight to 12 members (often paid for participation and selected for their interest, knowledge, and/or experience with the topic) moderated by a skilled facilitator. The facilitator asks carefully scripted probing questions, maintains good participant interaction, and tries to ensure comparable contributions per member. Focus groups have the advantage that one member's ideas can spark responses in another. Potential problems include strong individuals dominating the discussion, less than honest responses, psychologically defensive behavior, yea-saying (unreflective agreement), and a conservative bias in favor of the known versus the unknown. The requirement of a central location may also limit participation and skew results if the firm takes insufficient care with member selection. Managers and researchers often receive immediate feedback by watching focus group discussions through one-way glass. Typically, researchers record and transcribe focus group discussions. To conduct an effective focus group requires significant skill; indeed, Whirlpool gained differential advantage by developing a specific competency in running focus groups for trade partners. Brainstorming — Chapter 14 — is a variant of traditional focus groups. Telephone and video-conference focus groups are newer alternatives. These approaches reduce problems of dominating participants and travel costs, but limit degree of participant interaction.

ONE-ON-ONE INTERVIEWS (OOOs)

One-on-one interviews (OOOs) combine direct and indirect questions to probe an individual's needs and underlying purchase motivations. Mostly, researchers conduct OOOs in person — in the respondent's home or office, in a public place like a shopping mall, or on the telephone. OOOs avoid the various biases sometimes found in focus groups and can address more sensitive topics. OOOs can also dig more deeply into issues by asking several *why* questions, but are generally more expensive and time-consuming. OOOs cannot build on ideas from others, but dialog can be more open and skilled interviewers secure significant insight.

A market researcher for Zachys (Zs) (disguised) fast-food restaurant discovered that Zs sold 40 percent of daily milk shakes in the early morning; purchasers were mostly alone and bought nothing else. When she interviewed purchasers individually, most told her they bought milk shakes to make long boring commutes more palatable and stave off hunger until noon. Zs took several actions: made thicker shakes (last longer); added tiny fruit chunks (unpredictability to offset monotony); put in countertop dispensers; and introduced prepaid swipe cards (save time).[18]

INTERNET: BLOGS AND SOCIAL MEDIA

Securing customer data by traditional means frequently requires significant firm effort and expense. The Internet has substantially changed the data dynamic and data acquisition is no longer such a significant impediment to securing insight. Using *cookies*, firms gain direct insight into customer *travel* patterns on the web. In this new world of big data, researchers are developing new methods to analyze the substantial quantities of customer data that are becoming available.

One specific feature of the online world is that customers are increasingly willing to post complimentary and/or critical comments about brands, firms, and products. By offering its own forum, the firm may receive valuable customer feedback. Del Monte maintains a 400-member *I Love My Dog* online network that responds to new product ideas for dog food. But the firm must be vigilant about independent online postings; many bloggers develop significant followings and become very influential. Data-mining services capture consumer ratings on independent sites, and count and analyze web conversations for specific phrases about brands, firms, and products; hence, they quantify essentially qualitative data — *sentiment analysis*. Firms learn about performance perceptions, where to improve, and ideas for new product features and services. Dell's 40-person team engages with communities on Facebook, Twitter, and other social media to capture responses to Dell's actions. Of course, because posters are often anonymous, marketing researchers must carefully weigh the validity of these types of qualitative data.

KEY IDEA

Approaches to securing qualitative data are:

• Focus groups
• One-on-one interviews
• Internet
• Projective techniques
• Planned observation
• Unplanned observation

PROJECTIVE TECHNIQUES

Researchers use projective techniques (aka motivation research) mainly to uncover latent customer needs. Developed by psychologists, projective techniques have a long history in marketing:

- **Constructing a collage.** The respondent collects pictures from newspapers and magazines that express his feeling about the topic:

> Researchers asked diabetes sufferers to make a collage expressing how they felt about diabetes. One respondent collage showed images of doctors with patients, pills, fast-food logos, several cheeseburgers, and glasses of thick liquid. She explained: "It represents the foods I can't have anymore because they got me into trouble, trips to the doctor, testing, pills, and new foods I must learn to like." Key insights: The patient focused on inconvenience and medication more than its consequences; she blamed the disease on poor eating habits.[19]

- **Imagery.** The respondent draws a picture showing her interacting with the product, then interprets the picture.[20]
- **Role-playing.** Respondents pretend they are a brand's friend and write it a letter, or they explain why a neighbor/work colleague may like/dislike a particular product. Role-playing and storytelling (below) avoid arousing the respondent's subconscious defenses.
- **Sentence completion.** The respondent completes an incomplete sentence.
- **Storytelling.** The respondent receives a stimulus — picture/description — of a situation relevant to the topic. The respondent makes up a story about one or more characters in the stimulus.[21]
- **Word associations.** The researcher supplies a stimulus word. The respondent offers the first word that comes to mind. Applications include image studies and branding research.

PLANNED OBSERVATION

"You can see a lot just by looking." — Yogi Berra[22]

The firm gains insight just by observing; it does not ask questions, but secures insight by watching (sometimes using one-way mirrors) and recording behavior (often by video) in naturalistic settings. The researcher assesses subjects' behavior, including body language, emotional responses, and person-to-person interactions. General Mills observed children playing in school yards; it developed Yoplait Go-Gurt — yogurt in a squeezable tube for kids on the go. Many FMCG firms use observational techniques in supermarkets to gain insight into consumer shopping behavior. P&G observes consumers in specially designed innovation laboratories like its Baby Discovery Center, typical middle-class homes, and grocery and drug stores. Observation is a reliable technique provided the researcher uses correct methods. Although difficult to code, observational data are accurate, objective, and unbiased by researcher intervention[23]:

Ritz-Carlton's *Mystique* system catalogs and shares employee observations about guests among its 60 hotels. When a guest checks in to a Ritz-Carlton hotel, employees act on these observations to provide extra service.

Observational data may be more accurate than other data types.[24] When PepsiCo surveyed owners/managers at 7,000 restaurants serving Pepsi, respondents said price was the critical decision variable in choosing between Coke and Pepsi. An observational study of 800 restaurant *switchers* (Coke to/from Pepsi) showed four highly correlated service variables: poor delivery, unreliable equipment, emergency shipments, and poor equipment maintenance.[25]

ETHNOGRAPHIC RESEARCH. Derived from anthropology, *ethnographic research* is an observational method where researchers spend *a day in the life of (DILO)* their customers,[26] corresponding to the anthropologist *living with the tribe*. Observers gain insight into culture and belief systems, uncover needs, and understand how customers integrate products into their daily lives. Intel cultural anthropologists examine the interface of technology and humanity; when Tom Katzen was responsible for marketing Levi's jeans to teenagers, he spent Saturday mornings in ticket lines at San Francisco's Fillmore Auditorium, observing the way teenagers customized their blue jeans.[27] Many firms employ *cool hunters* to observe people's behavior and clothing in natural settings like inner-city basketball courts and fashionable nightclubs. Cool hunters also hang out on social networking sites like Facebook and Twitter. Relatedly, defense contractor employees embed with U.S. military forces in global hotspots to identify unmet needs.

Before Toyota designed the Lexus LS 400 specifically for the U.S., the chief engineer and his team lived for several months in Southern California's upscale Laguna Hills. They visited many upscale metropolitan areas around the U.S. — Coral Gables, Miami; north Lake Shore Drive, Chicago; and Westchester County, New York. They learned how luxury car owners drive, treat their cars, and deal with valet parking. They learned the role cars played in these people's lives, and their product and service expectations. The Lexus has been an unqualified success.

In the *Living It* program, P&G employees live with consumers for several days, following them shopping, running errands, and talking with peers. After one study, New Tide advertising differed sharply from the traditional cleaning power message — women could focus on their lives, because Tide was taking care of the laundry. In *Working It*, employees work behind the counters of small shops to gain insight about consumer purchasing behavior.[28]

MARKETING QUESTION

Go to your local supermarket and observe consumer behavior in the cereal aisle. What can you learn? What hypotheses can you develop that you could test by quantitative methods?

UNPLANNED OBSERVATION

Individuals may gain significant insight about markets, customers, and/or competitors without planning to do so. Simple observation may trigger an idea with tremendous payoff:

- On an Italian coffee-buying trip, Howard Schultz saw Italians at expresso bars, reading newspapers and meeting friends. He believed the U.S. was ready for coffee houses — Starbucks.
- On a Mumbai street, Ratan Tata saw scores of motor scooters precariously carrying entire families. Tata now offers a safer inexpensive alternative — the $2,500 Tata Nano mini-car.
- Former Virginia governor Gerald Baliles said: "When I was in China, I was struck by how often I encountered chicken feet in the soups, foods, and markets. When I got back, my people called our poultry industry to find out what they do with chicken feet. They were chopped off on the assembly lines and discarded. Today Virginia ships 40 tons a month of chicken feet to the Far East."
- Ralph Lauren observed mothers and daughters leaving a Lauren store in Connecticut — mothers with shopping bags, daughters without. Lauren developed Rugby to address the 14-to-29-year-old demographic.

SECURING QUANTITATIVE RESEARCH DATA

Alternative ways of securing data for quantitative analysis are:

SURVEYS

Sample *surveys* of the target population are the most common way to secure primary data for quantitative analysis. Selecting a sample reflecting the underlying population is critical. So is assessing the required sample size for estimating parameters of interest at the desired accuracy level. Detailed discussion of both topics is beyond the scope of this chapter, but as a rule, there are critical trade-offs between cost, flexibility, and time.[29] Table 6.2 identifies advantages and disadvantages of alternative ways to collect survey data.

TABLE 6.2
Techniques for Collecting Survey Data

Technique	Advantages and Disadvantages
Face-to-face personal interviews (home, office, mall intercepts)	*Advantages:* High completion rates; high level of control; researcher knows who was present at the interview; missing data minimized; researcher can show exhibits and samples and probe more deeply with follow-up and branching questions.
	Disadvantages: Most expensive; time-consuming; difficult to supervise; interviewers can bias results; interviewers may cheat — fill in questionnaires without interviews.
Telephone interviewing	*Advantages:* Fairly quick completion; better response rates than mail surveys, significantly less costly than face-to-face interviews; less interviewer bias; likely better for sensitive questions; ability to clarify and follow up; easier supervision of interviewers; useful for existing customer relationships.
	Disadvantages: Refusal rates generally higher than personal interviews (U.S. households with *no call* restrictions are increasing); growing population without landlines; limited to short interviews; cannot use complex questions; cannot show exhibits or samples; lack of control over the respondent's environment.
	Despite disadvantages, telephone interviewing will continue to be useful for existing consumer relationships and in B2B settings. (Some researchers collect simple survey data by text messaging [especially about TV programs]).
Mail surveys (paper and pencil, disk/CD)	*Advantages:* Inexpensive; no interviewer bias; okay for simple branching questions.
	Disadvantages: Response rates generally low; responses delayed (follow-ups often needed); others may influence respondent; respondent can look forward and back on questionnaire to inflate consistency; questionnaire must be short; cannot use probes or complex branching questions; missing data and confused responses frequently pose analytic problems.
Internet surveys	*Advantages:* Fast and easy to implement; can show exhibits; lower cost due to no printing or postage (or interviewers); software programming reduces incomplete answers; data fed directly into analysis programs and reviewed almost in real time.
	Disadvantages: May not be appropriate for some products/topics; possible non-representative samples because of limited computer use; low respondent patience for anything but very short questionnaires; limited attention to the task[30]; low response rates from questionnaires viewed as *spam* or lying dormant in an e-mail inbox. (Using a website survey tool may mitigate these problems.)

KEY IDEA

When designing a process to collect survey data, the firm must make several important trade-offs among:

- Cost
- Flexibility
- Time

Questionnaire design is critical to survey success and should involve marketing researcher and marketing manager. Development can be relatively unstructured and qualitative, but producing the final questionnaire requires much thought. The questionnaire should avoid biases from yea-saying and question order. Questions should not be vague, ambiguous, complex, difficult to answer, easily misinterpreted, or contain jargon. In good questionnaire design, some questions require *closed-ended* responses — all possible answers specified[31]; other responses should be *open-ended* — respondents answer in their own words. The simplest types of question are dichotomous (e.g., yes/no) and multiple choice (select one or more from several options). Table 6.3 identifies several standard, yet more complex, approaches to asking questions. The firm should always pretest the questionnaire.

When conducting survey research, Xerox always asks: Does the question tie into survey objectives? Will data from the question be actionable? If either response is No, Xerox deletes the question.

TABLE 6.3

Selected Standard Approaches to Asking Questions

Approach	Example	Comments
Rank ordering	Put "1" for the brand you would most likely buy; "2" for the next most likely brand, etc., until you have ordered all brands: Dell, HP, Lenovo, Macintosh, VAIO	Rotate brand order. Secures ordinal measures.[32]
Constant sum	Allocate 100 points among these benefits so more important benefits receive most points.	Secures ratio measures.[33]
Paired comparison	Circle the brand in each pair that you would most likely buy: Dell or HP Dell or Macintosh Lenovo or VAIO	Comparisons limited by respondent fatigue.[34] Secures interval measures.
Likert-type scales	Agree or disagree: Dell computers are easy to maintain: 1 — Strongly agree 2 — Agree 3 — Neutral 4 — Disagree 5 — Strongly disagree	Be careful of positivity bias. Use positively/negatively worded items. Use multiple items for reliability.
Semantic differential scales	Rate (focal object) on these scales by circling the number that best reflects your opinion. Dumb 1 2 3 4 5 6 7 8 9 10 Smart Weak 1 2 3 4 5 6 7 8 9 10 Strong Bad 1 2 3 4 5 6 7 8 9 10 Good Soft 1 2 3 4 5 6 7 8 9 10 Hard Easy 1 2 3 4 5 6 7 8 9 10 Difficult Fast 1 2 3 4 5 6 7 8 9 10 Slow	Use 7–12 sets of bipolar adjectives. Factor analyze to secure the underlying meaning.

PANELS

For many marketing research projects, securing survey data from different respondent samples is fine. But sometimes the firm wants to follow up on individual responses. In a *tracking (longitudinal)* study, the firm forms a *panel* of individuals who agree to provide responses periodically. Maintaining a panel is challenging because members drop out, but judicious replacement can keep a panel going almost indefinitely.[35] Panel data allow the firm to *keep its pulse* on customers, conduct more sophisticated analyses, and better identify causal relationships.[36] Because panels are expensive to maintain and administer, firms like Nielsen and IRI form and manage panels. These panels provide a sense of data independence and several user firms share the costs. Online marketing research firms like Greenfield Online and Harris Interactive maintain large panels from which firms can select subpopulations for specific surveys.

Panels provide data with varying degrees of intrusiveness. Panelists may commit to write down purchases, answer questionnaires, or accept a simple installation to monitor TV viewing. Panelists may use supermarket value cards providing scanner data (p. 164) on purchases. Combining self-reported panel data with actual use data may provide significant insight.

OBJECTIVE SALES DATA

The firm's sales reporting system can provide valuable quantitative data. But sales data to end-user customers may be difficult to secure when products move through distribution channels. In supermarkets, the widespread use of barcodes and retail scanners makes it easy to collect and store sales data by *stock-keeping unit* (SKU). IRI and Nielsen each secure scanner data from several thousand supermarkets in many urban markets; they aggregate and sell these data to manufacturers.[37] Availability of automatically collected sales data is likely to increase. By remotely monitoring vending machine sales, the firm can better schedule deliveries, adjust product mix, price dynamically, and make personalized offers to consumers for purchasing by smartphone. EZ Pass systems automatically measure use of road services.

Sales data organized by customer can provide significant insight. Supermarket loyalty cards allow consumer profiling for making targeted offers. Internet firms combine sales data directly from individuals and search data from *cookies* to develop buyer profiles for making purchase recommendations.

BEHAVIORAL MEASUREMENT

Increasingly, firms use technology for marketing research. *Infrared sensors, video cameras,* and *digital voice recorders* monitor supermarket aisle-traffic patterns; *checkout scanners* measure consumer purchases. Electronic metering systems capture radio listenership and TV viewing by channel; GPS-enabled *smartphones* identify consumer locations. Some researchers provide subjects with *digital cameras,* like Burger King — several dozen *SuperFans* recorded and photographed everything they ate for two weeks. Others use *galvanometers* to measure consumer physiological changes to stimuli like advertising, displays, products, and questions. *Tachisto-scopes* (now mainly computer controlled) measure recognition speed by projecting images like package designs for short time periods.

Advertising researchers often use *eye-movement* devices: A TiVo study found consumers focused attention on the center of the screen when fast-forwarding through commercials[38]; IBM and Cisco use *heatmapping* to track attention to elements of e-mail messages. Using *brain-scans,* Coke and Pepsi each activated brain reward systems in blind taste tests.[39]

PRIVACY. Although technological advances allow firms to secure increasing amounts of customer data, they raise serious privacy issues because of their potentially intrusive nature. Video cameras in stores are a privacy concern, but are quite legal when used on private property. Regardless, the firm should protect itself against misuse and serious PR problems by developing and implementing clear privacy policies. Privacy is an especially important issue on the Internet — Facebook and Google have run afoul of government watchdogs.

EXPERIMENTS

Experiments allow researchers to definitively establish causal relationships like A → B. The researcher manipulates independent variables like advertising and price, and measures results (dependent variables) like awareness and sales. Because many nonmanipulated and unmeasured variables can affect results, researchers typically use random assignment for experimental and control groups. Experiments range between limited-scale laboratory studies and large field experiments.[40] The critical trade-off is typically between cost and the researcher's ability to draw conclusions.

Relatively few firms conduct experiments; and these are mostly laboratory studies. FMCG firms often use field experiments for test marketing new products and assessing alternative promotional programs. Experiments are a serious business at Pfizer; Pfizer spends millions of dollars to test different promotional strategies and ways of allocating selling effort. Amazon continuously tests different e-mail messages.

KEY IDEA

Approaches to securing quantitative research data include:

- Surveys
- Panels
- Objective sales data
- Behavioral measurement
- Experiments
- Prediction markets

How would you design an experiment to measure the impact of advertising spending and price on sales? Choose your own product.

What most firms fail to realize is that day-to-day business life can function as a *natural experiment*. Rather than manipulate independent variables, the firm can use the *natural* variability in its actions to seek relationships with results. Costs of data storage and analysis are fast reducing and some firms evolve their actions in real time. Leading firms are becoming *learning organizations* by treating their entire set of marketing actions as data in natural experiments.[41]

PREDICTION MARKETS

In prediction markets, buyers and sellers trade assets whose cash value is tied to a particular event. Public prediction markets have successfully predicted Oscar nominations and various economic events. Some firms like GE and Microsoft use employee prediction markets to improve decision making; Lloyds TSB assesses new product ideas. In its *TagTrade* market, Best Buy employees trade imaginary stocks for new service packages and sales forecasts. In many cases, prediction markets outperform experts.[42]

ANALYZING QUANTITATIVE RESEARCH DATA

Quantitative research data are amenable to a broad variety of statistical analyses. If the underlying assumptions are valid, quantitative methods can have significant predictive power and be very helpful to the firm in making marketing decisions. But quantitative data analysis is a huge topic that we do not address in this chapter. Rather, we provide material on types of variables, and simple and complex quantitative analysis techniques as Marketing Enrichment 6.1 **[710p]**.[43] Furthermore, many fine marketing research courses and textbooks are available for interested students.

MARKETING ENRICHMENT 6.1

Analyzing Quantitative Research Data **710p**

MARKETING QUESTION

In 1999, Airbus predicted demand for its superjumbo A380 jet aircraft (launched 2007) at 1,440 planes and forecast that 10 U.S. airlines would buy 281. By end 2014, Airbus had received orders from 18 airlines for 317 planes and delivered 152; none of these airlines were U.S.-based. How do you explain the discrepancies?

KEY IDEA

In assessing the market, the firm should project:

- Market potential
- Market forecast

In assessing firm possibilities, the firm should project:

- Sales potential
- Sales forecast

MARKET AND SALES POTENTIALS; MARKET AND SALES FORECASTS

"It's tough to make predictions, especially about the future." — Yogi Berra[44]

Chapters 3, 4, 5, and now Chapter 6 have armed you with many approaches, concepts, ideas, and options for designing and conducting marketing research studies. You now have a solid base of knowledge for securing greater insight into markets, customers, competitors, and complementers. These insights will enable you to build more powerful market strategies and implementation plans, as you prepare to deliver customer value and secure differential advantage.

One topic we deferred from Chapter 3 — Securing Market Insight — is forecasting market size and firm sales. These predictions are critical for many reasons — identifying attractive market opportunities; production planning; and budgeting financial, human, and other resources.

Two related concepts — *potentials* and *forecasts* — are important for understanding market demand and firm sales. Unfortunately, many managers are confused about these terms. *Potentials* and *forecasts* are quite different, but each has important quantitative aspects. *Potential* embraces having a *capability or future state*:

- **Market potential** — what market sales could become.
- **Sales potential** — what firm sales could become.

By contrast, *forecast* concerns *expectations*:

- **Forecast market size** — expected market sales in a given time period.
- **Sales forecast** — expected firm sales in a given time period.

We explore ways to assess potentials and forecasts; we conclude Chapter 6 by discussing *category development index* (CDI) and *brand development index* (BDI).

ASSESSING MARKET POTENTIAL

Market potential is the *maximum market-level sales*, from all suppliers, that the firm believes could occur in a future time period. Since all markets go through life cycles, the firm requires some idea of market sales at various life-cycle stages. Market potential is an upper bound to actual sales, based on a set of assumptions about future market conditions. Market potential is especially important when contemplating entry in new markets.

To assess market potential, the firm should estimate the number of likely customers and the quantities they are likely to buy. These estimates are based in part on market prices and the potential aggregate marketing effort from the firm and its competitors. Of course, the identity of likely customers may change as the life cycle evolves; propensity to buy evolves also. Three steps for assessing market potential are:

- **Identify likely market segments.** Most markets comprise several segments. The firm should predict how these segments may evolve. Of course, customers in some segments will not buy at each time period.

- **Estimate numbers of customers in each segment.** The firm estimates the number of customers likely to buy in the time period for which it seeks market potential.

- **Estimate the number of products customers will purchase.** The firm estimates the number of products customers in each segment are likely to buy for the relevant time period.

Table 6.4 shows typical market potential calculations for a new consumer product — for three years, six years, and 10 years after launch. In this illustration, we assume three market segments.

Time Period	Market Segments	Total Number of Customers in Each Segment (millions) A	Percent Likely to Buy (%) B	Expected Number of Customers Likely to Buy C = A × B (millions)	Number of Units Each Purchaser Is Likely to Buy D	Segment Potential Calculation E = C × D (million units)	Market Potential (million units): Sum of Es
3 years after launch	Seg. 1	10	50%	5	5	25	
	Seg. 2	6	20%	1.2	2	2.4	**27.4**
	Seg. 3	8	0%	0	0	0	
6 years after launch	Seg. 1	11	70%	7.7	6	46.2	
	Seg. 2	6	40%	2.4	4	9.6	**58.6**
	Seg. 3	7	10%	0.7	4	2.8	
10 years after launch	Seg. 1	12	70%	8.4	7	58.8	
	Seg. 2	6	50%	3.0	6	18	**93**
	Seg. 3	6	30%	1.8	9	16.2	

Several interesting points within this table are:

- The firm believes the numbers of customers in each segment will change over time — segment 1 increases; segment 2 stays the same; segment 3 decreases.

- The percentage of customers likely to buy also evolves — segment 1 increases, then stays constant; segment 2 increases continuously; segment 3 is zero initially, then increases.

- For each segment, the firm predicts only a fraction of customers will purchase.

- The amount purchased increases for each segment, quite dramatically for segment 3.

- For each time period, market potential is the sum of individual segment potentials.

- To assess dollar potential in each time period, the firm simply multiplies market potential in units by the expected market price.

The firm can estimate *market potential revenues* by multiplying *potential units* by estimated prices in each time period.

MARKETING QUESTION

Dietrich Mateschitz ignored marketing research data showing weak market potential for his new product in the highly competitive beverage market. Red Bull has been a spectacular global success. Does Mateschitz's experience imply that marketing research is irrelevant?

TABLE 6.4
Market Potential Calculations

KEY IDEA

Market potential is the maximum sales the firm expects in the market in a given time period from all suppliers.

Sales potential is the maximum sales the firm could achieve in a given time period.

Market forecast is the expected market size.

Sales forecast is the firm's expected sales.

ASSESSING SALES POTENTIAL

Sales potential is the maximum sales the firm could achieve in a given time period. Of course, sales potential is conditioned on assumptions about market potential, expected firm prices, likely firm efforts, and future market conditions like number and strength of competitors.

The firm can calculate sales potential directly from market potential by assessing potential market share. The firm's potential market share depends both on its prices, the resources it could commit to the market, and on actions it believes competitors will take. If the firm contemplates increasing resource commitment (and/or believes competitors will reduce commitments) estimated potential market share should increase. Table 6.5 shows illustrative sales potential calculations based on market potential estimates from Table 6.4.

TABLE 6.5
*Sales Potential
Calculations*[45]

Time Period	Market Potential (million units) A	Potential Firm Market Share (%) B	Sales Potential (million units) C = A × B
3 years after launch	27.4	10%	2.74
6 years after launch	58.6	20%	11.72
10 years after launch	93	30%	27.9

FORECASTING MARKET SIZE

Market forecasts often focus on the short run, like the upcoming year, where the firm can assess market conditions with a fair degree of accuracy. To forecast market size, the firm may focus either on the overall market or on individual segments it later aggregates. Generally, a segmented approach provides better forecasts (if data are available). Three broad approaches to assessing market size are:

KEY IDEA

Two judgmental methods for market-size forecasting are:

• Executive judgment
• Delphi method

Time-based methods for market-size forecasting are:

• Judgmental extrapolation
• Linear extrapolation
• Moving average
• Exponential smoothing

JUDGMENTAL METHODS. These are the simplest methods for forecasting market size:

- **Executive judgment.** The responsible manager has deep familiarity with the product class/ form, competitive offers, customer needs and satisfaction levels, current market size, and many environmental factors. She makes her own intuitive judgments.

- **Delphi method.** A valuable approach when several people have opinions about the market. Each person makes a market forecast and specifies the rationale. Each person then receives all forecasts and rationales, and revises their forecasts. Forecasts often converge after a couple of rounds, but may require several rounds.

TIME-BASED METHODS. These methods use past sales to predict future sales directly:

- **Judgmental extrapolation.** A special case of executive judgment using history to predict the percentage change from the previous year. The basis could be the most recent year-to-year change, a simple average of the previous two (three, four, five) years' changes, or a weighted average of previous changes, with greater weight to more recent years.

MARKETING ENRICHMENT 6.1

Analyzing Quantitative Research Data **710p**

- **Linear extrapolation.** Two-variable regression analysis (Marketing Enrichment 6.1 **[710p]**) estimates year-by-year change in market size. Forecast market size for next year is market size last year plus an increment (or decrement) based on prior years. The forecaster calculates the extrapolation increment mathematically, but must decide how many prior years to include.

- **Moving average.** The manager uses market-size data from previous years to calculate an average; this average is the forecast. For each successive year, the manager drops the earliest market-size datum and adds in the most recent datum. Hence, data from several years ago do not weigh too heavily in the forecast. Once again, the manager must judge how many years to include.

- **Exponential smoothing (ES).** This method uses previous sales data in a slightly unusual way. Rather than making the forecast based only on actual market size (AMS) data from previous years, exponential smoothing uses both AMS from last year together with last year's forecast market size (FMS). ES calculates a smoothing parameter — a — from previous market size (MS) data:

$$FMS_{t+1} = a \times AMS_t + (1 - a) \times FMS_t$$

The value of "a" depends on the relative weight given to prior year AMS versus prior year FMS; "a" ranges from zero to one. If historic AMS was fairly constant, FMS weighs quite heavily, and "a" is on the low side. If AMS changes substantially year by year, as in growth markets, "a" may be close to 1.

Table 6.6 shows how to use these methods to forecast global market size for consumer durable A. Column 2 shows AMS; columns to the right show FMS using judgmental extrapolation, linear extrapolation, moving average, and exponential smoothing. Forecasts by judgmental extrapolation are based on the percentage change in AMS for the most recent year. For other methods, forecasts are based on AMS for the previous five years. For example, the forecasts for year 6 are based on data for years 1, 2, 3, 4, 5; forecasts for year 9 are based on years 4, 5, 6, 7, 8. We can make several inferences:

- AMS increases markedly in year 9 and subsequent years; deviations are mostly greater for later years for all forecasting methods.

- Because AMS growth is high in later years, simple judgmental extrapolation does best. Other methods are handicapped, to a greater or lesser extent, by AMS from earlier years. This finding is especially marked for the five-year moving average. (Moving-average forecasts with fewer years [not reported] do better.)

- For all years, the exponential smoothing forecast is the previous year's AMS. AMS increased significantly and the smoothing constant a=1.

MARKETING QUESTION

Form a group of five or six students. Each person in the group forecasts the Dow Jones average (or some other event) for the last day of class and provides a rationale. Team members exchange forecasts and rationales and repeat the process one or more times. On the last day of class, compare the forecast with the actual Dow Jones average.

TABLE 6.6
Predicting Global Market Size for Consumer Durable A (000s)

Year	Actual Market Size	Judgmental Extrapolation Forecast Market Size	Judgmental Extrapolation Deviation from Actual Market Size	Linear Extrapolation Forecast Market Size	Linear Extrapolation Deviation from Actual Market Size	Moving Average Forecast Market Size	Moving Average Deviation from Actual Market Size	Exponential Smoothing Forecast Market Size	Exponential Smoothing Deviation from Actual Market Size
1	8,791	—	—	—	—	—	—	—	—
2	11,148	—	—	—	—	—	—	—	—
3	14,043	—	—	—	—	—	—	—	—
4	15,482	—	—	—	—	—	—	—	—
5	19,858	—	—	—	—	—	—	—	—
6	26,352	25,470	(882)	21,805	(4,547)	13,864	(12,488)	19,858	(6,494)
7	27,968	34,970	7,002	28,224	256	17,377	(10,591)	26,352	(1,616)
8	30,799	29,683	(1,116)	32,357	1,558	20,741	(10,058)	27,968	(2,831)
9	39,365	33,917	(5,448)	35,715	(3,650)	24,092	(15,273)	30,799	(8,566)
10	48,926	50,313	1,387	41,907	(7,019)	28,868	(20,058)	39,365	(9,561)
11	65,271	60,809	(4,462)	51,646	(13,625)	34,682	(30,589)	48,926	(16,345)
12	82,314	87,076	4,762	70,286	(12,028)	42,466	(39,848)	65,271	(17,043)

CAUSAL-FACTOR METHODS. The most common causal-factor method for forecasting market size is *multiple regression analysis*. The researcher selects several independent (predictor) variables that she believes could be related to market size, the dependent (criterion) variable. She uses historical data to determine the relationships, if any, between these predictor variables and market size. She then uses these relationships to forecast future market size. (We discuss this process in somewhat more detail in Marketing Enrichment 6.1 **[710p, pp. 9–10]**.)

MAKING THE SALES FORECAST

The sales forecast is expected firm sales in a future time period, often the upcoming year. The sales forecast is central to many day-by-day operating processes like financial budgeting and production planning. Of course, *actual* factors can cause *actual* firm sales to be quite different from *forecast* sales. The following dialog — Chapter 1 — reinforces the importance of sales forecasting and the difficulty many firms face in making sales forecasts. The dialog is part of a real conversation when the author gave an in-house seminar at a major U.S. computer firm. One participant asked several questions about sales forecasting, leading to the following exchange:

Author: "How come you're so interested in sales forecasting?"

Participant: "Well, I have a sales forecasting department, and since you were here, I thought I might learn something."

Author: "That's fine, but tell me, what's your position in the firm?"

Participant: "I'm the production director."

Author: "Oh! That's a little unusual. I'd have thought the sales forecasting department might have been in marketing, or in sales."

Participant: "Sure, they have one too. But we can't believe a word they say, so we have to have our own."

Many firms use three broad approaches to sales forecasting: *top-down*, *bottom-up*, and *synthetic*.

TOP-DOWN SALES FORECASTING. Top-down sales forecasts follow directly from analyses of market potential, market-size (or individual market segment) forecasts, and the firm's market-share estimates — typically contained in the market plan. Calculations are relatively simple but the marketer should consider market subtleties and nuances:

Sales forecast = Forecast market size × Forecast market share

Table 6.7 illustrates a market-segment approach using market-segment size and market-share forecasts:

TABLE 6.7
Top-Down Sales Forecasts

Market Segment	Forecast Segment Size (million units) A	Forecast Segment Share (%) B	Sales Forecast by Segment (million units) C = A × B	Sales Forecast (million units) Sum of the Cs
Segment 1	120	10%	12	
Segment 2	70	20%	14	53
Segment 3	90	30%	27	

BOTTOM-UP SALES FORECASTING. Bottom-up forecasts embrace the granularity (and reality) of sales by customer, absent from top-down forecasts — salespeople can personally discuss customer requirements. The firm aggregates forecasts from individual salespeople to develop the bottom-up sales forecast. (In some firms, the sales forecast derives from a sales pipeline system — Chapter 18.) A serious downside of bottom-up forecasting is salespeople *lowballing* estimates when forecasts drive sales quotas; in turn, these quotas affect take-home pay!

SYNTHETIC SALES FORECASTS. Synthetic sales forecasts combine the best features of top-down and bottom-up forecasting. The top-down forecast derives from the market planning process; the sales department independently prepares the bottom-up forecast. If these numbers are similar, the task is over. In most cases, the top-down sales forecast is higher; sales managers and individual salespeople must reexamine their forecasts customer by customer to see where increases are possible. These reworked forecasts are building blocks for a revised bottom-up sales forecast. Simultaneously, marketing reworks the top-down forecast. Hopefully, the revised forecasts agree. If not, senior management typically decides the forecast by executive decision, and sales managers apportions increases to individual salespeople.[46]

KEY IDEA

Many firms develop synthetic sales forecasts by combining *top-down* and *bottom-up* approaches.

CATEGORY AND BRAND DEVELOPMENT INDICES

The *category development index* (CDI) and *brand development index* (BDI) are useful devices for assessing market and sales, potentials and forecasts. Each index relies on dividing the market into separate areas; CDI and BDI measure category (product class/form) and brand strengths in those areas. FMCG firms typically base CDIs and BDIs on geography:

- CDI — percentage of category sales divided by percentage of U.S. population, converted to a percentage.
- BDI — percentage of brand sales divided by percentage of U.S. population, converted to a percentage.

KEY IDEA

Important practical approaches for assessing market and sales potentials are:
- Category development index (CDI)
- Brand development index (BDI)

Table 6.8 illustrates CDI and BDI calculations for Brand X in Denver. The 90 percent CDI shows that the product category is less developed in Denver than in the U.S. overall. By contrast, the 120 percent BDI shows that Brand X performed better than average in Denver. The firm can use market-area distributions of CDI and BDI (and over-time trends) to assess market and sales, potentials and forecasts, and hence decide where to place marketing effort.

Market Data	Brand Data	Population Data
Sales = $250 million	Sales = $50 million	U.S. = 320 million
Sales in Denver = $4.5 million	Sales in Denver = $1.2 million	Denver = 650,000
Denver percent of sales = 4.5/250 = **1.8 percent**	Denver percent of sales = 1.2/50 = **2.4 percent**	Denver population percent = 650,000/320 million = **2 percent**

Category development index (CDI) = Percent market sales/Percent population: Denver = 1.8/2 = **90 percent**
Brand development index (BDI) = Percent firm sales/Percent population: Denver = 2.4/2 = **120 percent**

TABLE 6.8
Illustration: CDI and BDI Calculations

We covered a lot of ground in this chapter, but in many ways we have only scratched the surface of marketing research. We hope your key take-away is: Marketing research can be very helpful in securing insight the firm requires to successfully execute the six marketing imperatives. But you should also realize that marketing research is no panacea. The manager and researcher must make many decisions before investing in a particular study. We have given you a glimpse of some of the available options.

KEY MESSAGES

MARKETING QUESTION

What other messages did you glean from this chapter?

- Marketing research results should be actionable.
- Good marketing research can form the basis of securing differential advantage.
- Marketing researchers should provide analysis and insight; marketing managers make decisions.
- Marketing research studies should follow a rigorous process.
- Marketing researchers make critical distinctions between primary and secondary research, and qualitative and quantitative research.
- Both qualitative and quantitative research use several methodologies. Qualitative research is increasingly popular.
- Various techniques for collecting survey data have advantages and disadvantages.
- Quantitative analysis methods range from simple to highly complex.
- Several methods are available for assessing market and sales potentials, and making market and sales forecasts.

VIDEOS AND AUDIOS

For complimentary material, see Axcess Capon codes at www.axcessvids.com

The Future of Marketing Research	**926v** 🔵	Oded Netzer	Columbia Business School
Securing Insight	**802v** 🔵	Spencer Pingel	Colgate-Palmolive
Pitfalls of Marketing Research	**523v** 🔵	Malcolm Gladwell	
Marketing Research Careers	**426v** 🔵	AMAmarketing	

QUESTIONS FOR STUDY AND DISCUSSION

Can you answer the questions implied by this chapter's learning outcomes? Check!

1. Suppose you are product manager for a pharmaceutical firm hoping to launch a new drug to treat schizophrenia. Identify the types of people from whom you would secure marketing-research data and the sorts of data you would seek.

2. Suppose you are marketing director for a hotel chain, responsible for an observational technique to learn about customer needs and to provide data to individual hotels. You receive the following report from your San Francisco property. "Last night, one of our regular customers, Mr. Jackson, arrived to check in with a female companion. The desk clerk used the information system to greet the couple: 'Welcome back, Mr. and Mrs. Jackson, it's good to see you at the hotel again.' Apparently, the woman was not Mrs. Jackson, and Mr. Jackson had not told his companion he was married. The woman was furious with Mr. Jackson; Mr. Jackson was furious with us; they both stormed out of the hotel." How would this incident affect your observational program?

3. The table below provides global market-size data for consumer durable B. Select two forecasting methods that use past sales. Predict sales annually for years 6 through 12 using pre-year 6 data. How do the methods compare? Is one better than another? Why? How do your forecasts compare with consumer durable A predictions in Table 6.6? Are you more accurate? Why or why not?

Year	Actual Sales (000s)	Year	Actual Sales (000s)	Year	Actual Sales (000s)
1	50,003	5	98,5414	9	111,570
2	59,461	6	111,163	10	124,608
3	68,496	7	104,366	11	136,104
4	79,577	8	104,101	12	138,528

4. What secondary sources (including websites) would you use to find out how best to engage undergraduate college students for an innovative news website?

5. Suppose you are consulting for a local restaurant with strong brand recognition and loyalty that has many weekend customers; yet from Monday through Thursday, business is slow. Design a questionnaire to understand consumer behavior, lifestyle, and eating habits on weekdays. Your objective is to identify and address marketing opportunities during the week.

TRUE/FALSE QUESTIONS

Answers on page A1 and at www.axcessvids.com — 781p 🔘

1. Before conducting secondary research, a marketing researcher should always check on available primary data. ❏ **TRUE** ❏ **FALSE**

2. Qualitative research is generally flexible and versatile, but is rarely conclusive and does not project to larger populations. ❏ **TRUE** ❏ **FALSE**

3. Marketing researchers conduct most focus groups on the telephone. ❑ **TRUE** ❑ **FALSE**

4. Sales potential is conditioned on assumptions about the firm's likely efforts and future market conditions, like the number and strength of competitors. ❑ **TRUE** ❑ **FALSE**

5. Synthetic sales forecasts combine the best features of top-down and bottom-up forecasting. ❑ **TRUE** ❑ **FALSE**

MULTIPLE CHOICE QUESTIONS

Answers on page A1 and at www.axcessvids.com — 133p

1. Which of the following is NOT one of the three types of questions a researcher should ask when collecting and evaluating quantitative data?

   a. internal validity
   b. reliability
   c. flexibility
   d. external validity

2. In which of the following projective techniques does the research ask the respondent to draw a picture that shows the respondent interacting with the product, and then asked the respondent to interpret the picture?

   a. word association
   b. storytelling
   c. role-playing
   d. imagery

3. Which of the following techniques for collecting marketing research data is the most common way to secure primary data for quantitative analysis?

   a. surveys
   b. focus groups
   c. objective sales force data
   d. experiments

4. Rather than forecasting based only on actual sales data from previous years, _____ uses both last year's actual sales and last year's forecasted sales.

   a. judgmental extrapolation
   b. exponential smoothing
   c. linear extrapolation
   d. moving average

5. The most common causal-factor method for predicting market size is _____.

   a. exponential smoothing
   b. moving average
   c. linear extrapolation
   d. multiple regression analysis

TRANSITION TO
STRATEGIC MARKETING

KEY IDEA

Insight developed from the situation analysis forms the foundation for developing planning assumptions.

Planning assumptions are the critical supporting elements for developing market strategy and implementation plans.

CHAPTERS 3 THROUGH 6 FOCUS ON SECURING market, customer, competitor, company, and complementer insight. Some insight is fairly broad — like factors driving market growth or anticipated technological change; other insight is much narrower — like identifying new competitor entry or a specific competence the firm may secure. Regardless, the material in these chapters forms the basis for the *situation analysis* — the foundation for the market plan. We address market planning issues in *Strategic Marketing* — Section III, and *Implementing the Market Strategy* — Section IV. An *effective* market plan provides the firm with a well-developed direction forward; an *ineffective* market plan, with a weak situation analysis, is prone to collapse.

The best way to build a solid superstructure for market strategy and implementation is to transition from *insight* gained in the situation analysis to *assumptions* about the future. *Planning assumptions* help the firm anticipate the future, identify forces for change, and outline expected business conditions. *Planning assumptions* are critical supporting elements in the market plan — both three-year strategic market plans and one-year operational market plans. Drawing from the various insight elements — market, customer, competitor, company, and complementer — marketers should identify candidate *planning assumptions* on which to build market strategy and implementation. Table T.1 illustrates *planning assumptions*.

TABLE T.1
Illustration:
Planning Assumptions

1. The government will impose high import tariffs within the next two years.

2. Competitors will make a technological breakthrough that adds significant customer value.

3. The textile market will grow in excess of 3.5 percent annually.

4. By 20XY, Asian brands will gain at least 10 percent market share.

5. Consumers will not accept price increases greater than 1 percent annually.

6. E-commerce will capture greater than 15 percent of revenues for textile chemicals by 20XY.

7. New textile fibers will gain greater than 10 percent market share by 20XY+1.

8. Environmental regulations will significantly increase costs and/or cause the removal of major chemicals.

9. Our new plant will come on stream in summer 20XY.

10. The R&D department will successfully reduce our processing costs 15 percent by early 20XY.

11. At least two major competitors will forward integrate to secure greater access to the industry value chain.

12. New local chemical suppliers will gain at least 8 percent market share.

Of course, planning assumptions vary on several dimensions; two of the most important are *magnitude of effect* and *probability of occurrence*. Figure T.1 plots the Table 1 planning assumptions on these two dimensions. Core assumptions for market plans are those with *high* magnitude of effect and *high* probability of occurrence — assumptions 3 through 9. Assumption 11 (low magnitude of effect, low probability of occurrence) is not worth worrying about. Neither is assumption 10; even though probability of occurrence is high, magnitude of effect is low. Assumption 12 falls outside the critical region but the firm should probably keep its eye on this issue. Assumptions 1 and 2 are unlikely to occur but the effect would be high if they did; these assumptions are good candidates for *contingency plans*.

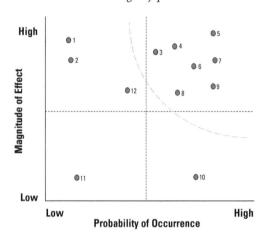

FIGURE T.1
Planning Assumptions

To complete the process, marketers should identify implications for the firm of each high-magnitude-of-effect and high-probability-of-occurrence assumption — 3 through 9 — then turn these assumptions into "We believe…" statements. Drawing from Table T.1, examples are:

- We believe consumers will not accept price increases greater than 1 percent annually.
- We believe new textile fibers will gain greater than 10 percent market share by 20XY+1.

These assumptions are the pillars on which the firm builds market strategy and implementation.

A useful metaphor for illustrating the role of planning assumptions in the market plan is the *bridge* — Figure T.2. The bridge represents market strategy and implementation, taking the firm from *today* toward *tomorrow*. The bridge is built on pillars — the pillars represent *planning assumptions*, supported by a foundation — *situation analysis*. If the pillars are weak and/or the foundation is insecure, when the water becomes turbulent and rises the bridge will collapse. Correspondingly, if the situation analysis is weak and/or planning assumptions are ill developed, the market strategy and implementation will collapse. But if the situation analysis and planning assumptions are strong, the market strategy will be robust, and form a strong bridge. **[112v]** Section II teaches how to develop insight to construct a solid foundation of situation analysis; *planning assumptions* transition from that foundation into critical support for market strategy and implementation.

KEY IDEA

The firm should assess each planning assumption on:

- Probability of occurrence
- Magnitude of effect

The firm constructs "We believe…" statements for *high probability of occurrence* and *high magnitude of effect* planning assumptions.

The firm should develop market strategy and implementation plans on high probability of occurrence and high magnitude of effect assumptions.

The firm should develop contingency plans for high magnitude of effect/low probability of occurrence assumptions.

FIGURE T.2
Planning Assumptions — The Bridge Metaphor

SECTION III

STRATEGIC MARKETING

For complimentary material, see Axcess Capon codes at www.axcessvids.com

STRATEGIC MARKETING comprises five chapters, Chapter 7 through Chapter 11. These chapters focus on the firm's critical strategic marketing decisions. The section embraces the first three Marketing Imperatives: Imperative 1 — Determine and Recommend Which Markets to Address; Imperative 2 — Identify and Target Market Segments; Imperative 3 — Set Strategic Direction and Positioning.

Chapter 7 — Identifying and Choosing Opportunities — addresses Imperative 1. This chapter develops approaches for making market-choice decisions — what markets to address; what markets not to address; what markets to avoid. Chapter 7 also offers various approaches for implementing market choices.

Chapter 8 — Market Segmentation and Targeting — addresses Imperative 2. This chapter follows logically from market-choice decisions. Having selected markets, the firm must decide what parts of those markets to address and what to avoid. We shall see that the firm must engage in two processes — form market segments, then decide which of those segments to target for effort.

Chapters 9, 10, and 11 together address Imperative 3. Chapter 9 — Market Strategy: Integrating Firm Efforts for Marketing Success — lays out the critical components of a market strategy; market strategies that omit any of these components are incomplete. The purpose of Chapter 10 — Managing through the Life Cycle — is to help firms develop preemptive strategies by examining alternative scenarios based on life-cycle stage and competitive position. Finally, Chapter 11 — Managing Brands — discusses the value of brands, key branding concepts, and approaches to building and maintaining strong brands.

Managing Marketing in the 21st Century

SECTION I: MARKETING AND THE FIRM

CHAPTER 1
Introduction to Managing Marketing

CHAPTER 2
The Value of Customers

SECTION II: FUNDAMENTAL INSIGHTS FOR STRATEGIC MARKETING

CHAPTER 3
Market Insight

CHAPTER 4
Customer Insight

CHAPTER 5
Insight about Competitors, Company, and Complementers

CHAPTER 6
Marketing Research

TRANSITION TO STRATEGIC MARKETING

SECTION III: STRATEGIC MARKETING

IMPERATIVE 1
Determine and Recommend Which Markets to Address

CHAPTER 7
Identifying and Choosing Opportunities

IMPERATIVE 2
Identify and Target Market Segments

CHAPTER 8
Market Segmentation and Targeting

IMPERATIVE 3
Set Strategic Direction and Positioning

CHAPTER 9
Market Strategy – Integrating Firm Efforts for Marketing Success

CHAPTER 10
Managing through the Life Cycle

CHAPTER 11
Managing Brands

SECTION IV: IMPLEMENTING THE MARKET STRATEGY

IMPERATIVE 4
Design the Market Offer

PART A: PROVIDING CUSTOMER VALUE

CHAPTER 12
Managing the Product Line

CHAPTER 13
Managing Services and Customer Service

CHAPTER 14
Developing New Products

PART B: COMMUNICATING CUSTOMER VALUE

CHAPTER 15
Integrated Marketing Communications

CHAPTER 16
Mass Communications

CHAPTER 17
Digital Marketing

CHAPTER 18
Directing and Managing the Field Sales Effort

PART C: DELIVERING CUSTOMER VALUE

CHAPTER 19
Distribution Decisions

CHAPTER 20
Retailing and Wholesaling

PART D: GETTING PAID FOR CUSTOMER VALUE

CHAPTER 21
Critical Underpinnings of Pricing Decisions

CHAPTER 22
Setting Prices

IMPERATIVE 5
Secure Support from Other Functions

CHAPTER 23
Ensuring the Firm Implements the Market Offer as Planned: Becoming an Externally Oriented Firm

IMPERATIVE 6
Monitor and Control Execution and Performance

CHAPTER 24
Monitoring and Controlling Firm Performance and Functioning

SECTION V: SPECIAL MARKETING TOPICS

CHAPTER 25
International, Regional, and Global Marketing

CHAPTER 26
Ethical, Legal, and Socially Responsible Decisions in Marketing

*Determine and Recommend
Which Markets to Address*

CHAPTER 7

IDENTIFYING
AND CHOOSING
OPPORTUNITIES

For complimentary material, see Axcess Capon codes at www.axcessvids.com

Progress occurs when courageous, skillful leaders seize the opportunity to change things for the better.

— Harry S. Truman, U.S. President

I am going to wait for the next big thing.

— Steve Jobs, Founder and CEO, Apple[1]

LEARNING OUTCOMES

When you have completed this chapter, you will be able to:

- Understand marketing's role in identifying new opportunities.
- Ensure the firm makes its strategic decisions with marketing input.
- Determine the fundamental elements that comprise a strategy for growth.
- Develop criteria for evaluating individual opportunities.
- Assess alternative ways to implement a strategy for growth.

OPENING CASE: ZIPCAR

Established nationwide car-rental firms include Advantage, Alamo, Avis, Budget, Dollar, Enterprise, Hertz, National, and Thrifty. Hertz, Avis, and National mainly compete on location and service, especially at airports. Advantage, Alamo, Budget, Dollar, and Thrifty compete on price. Enterprise became the leading car-rental firm overall by offering replacement cars for owners whose cars were being repaired.

Car sharing started in Germany, but Zipcar was first in the U.S.[2] Car-rental firms traditionally offered minimum one-day rentals to customers with good driving and credit records who met age requirements. By contrast, Zipcar is a membership organization — customers pay an annual $50 membership fee and rent by the hour. The more than 50 cities with car-sharing service include Atlanta, Baltimore, Boston, Chicago, Gainesville, Los Angeles, New York, Philadelphia, Pittsburgh, Portland, San Diego, San Francisco, Seattle, Washington D.C., and Vancouver. In 2010, Zipcar entered Europe by acquiring London-based Streetcar.

Zipcar members share cars; each Zipcar has a home address in a pay garage, street, or other designated location. Members can book 30 makes and models, including hybrids, Smart cars, sedans, pickup trucks, SUVs, minivans, and sports cars online or by phone. They open the car with an access card (similar to a credit card), return the car to the same location, and check out with the card. Fees are around $10 per hour including gas and insurance; Zipcar also offers monthly arrangements for specified hours (like 6 p.m. to midnight, Monday through Friday), and daily commuting. Zipcar's small staff monitors cars via wireless and computer technologies. Some cities, hoping to ease congestion, provide free or subsidized parking.

City dwellers use Zipcars evenings and weekends; important customer groups for daily use are business and government. Portland uses car sharing for its motor pool fleet, aiming to reduce annual operating, maintenance, and fuel costs by 25 percent, and cut capital outlays. Discussing its business membership, mainly for hybrids, Starbucks spokespeople said, "We need our partners [employees] to be able to take short trips to meetings and for other business purposes." And, "The Zipcar program and hybrid offering is a win-win for the environment and Starbucks. We reduce the number of vehicles ... and offer environmentally friendly, hassle-free, mobility for our partners."

Zipcar also partners with university parking and transportation departments to offer car sharing to students, faculty, and staff. Because many students are aged 18–20 years and ineligible for car rentals, Zipcar has an under–21 program that offers special deals. In 2011, Zipcar agreed to use Ford cars at campus locations; Ford subsidizes student Zipcar membership and rental fees. Hertz with Connect by Hertz, Enterprise, and U-Haul also offer car sharing in some urban locations.[3]

Zipcar was marketing success but consistently unprofitable. In 2013, Avis Budget Group acquired Zipcar for $500 million. By 2016, Zipcar had 900,000 members globally.

Do you think Zipcar will be successful in the long run? Why or why not? Do you think *Connect by Hertz* or Enterprise's *WeCar* will be successful? Why or why not? How should these market changes affect Zipcar's long-run strategy?

In Chapters 3 through 6, we learned to develop *insight* into the M4Cs — markets, customers, competitors, company, and complementers; and then made the transition to form *planning assumptions*. Now we shift direction to make *decisions* and focus on the six marketing imperatives. Marketing's first, and arguably most important, imperative is to influence firm decisions about what markets to address. *Market-choice decisions* are typically strategic for the firm or business unit. CEOs/general managers usually decide which opportunities are the most attractive, but marketing should play a critical role.

Growth is critical for injecting vigor into the firm, providing resources and rewards, keeping management on its toes, and retaining talent. Marketing should identify growth opportunities by systematically screening many alternatives. These opportunities may be in the firm's core

Can you identify examples of firms that have successfully entered *white spaces*?

business areas, in *adjacencies* close to the core, or further afield.[4] In consumer truck rental, U-Haul was barely breaking even with an older truck fleet, higher maintenance costs, and lower prices than competition. But when No. 2 Ryder exited, U-Haul prospered by tapping an adjacent *profit pool* — accessories like boxes, insurance, trailer rental, and storage space.[5] Examples of successfully identifying opportunities in unrelated areas — *white spaces* — where customer needs were unsatisfied include Airbnb — lodging rental; Cirque du Soleil — neither traditional circus nor theater; NetJets — partial ownership of corporate jets; Uber — transportation network; Viagra — erectile dysfunction; Zipcar — automobile rental.[6]

Marketing should play a key role in developing screening criteria for individual opportunities and helping make the business case for firm investments. Marketing should assess market potential, validate market size and growth, evaluate likely competitive challenges, and examine individual opportunity alignment with strategic initiatives. Marketing may also act as internal entrepreneur, mobilizing resources like market development, R&D, strategic alliances, and acquisitions for pursuing opportunities.

Some opportunities may be unprofitable in the short run but offer significant long-run potential. Some opportunities surface in good times; others result directly from adverse economic circumstances.[7] Regardless, opportunities may originate in many places. R&D develops new technologies and/or product ideas it believes have market viability. Sales and engineering may propose strategic alliances or buying, selling, or licensing technology. When opportunities have marketing implications, marketing should be part of the discussion. The firm should make go/no-go decisions with the best available market insight — including voice-of-the-customer input. Unfortunately, in many firms, finance drives acquisition and divestiture decisions with little or no marketing input.

Figure 7.1 presents a systematic three-stage approach for identifying, generating, selecting, and implementing opportunities:

1. **Strategy for growth** — provides guidance and analysis to generate opportunities;
2. **Screening criteria** — used to evaluate and select individual opportunities;
3. **Implementation** — specific actions the firm may take to achieve objectives.

FIGURE 7.1
Comprehensive Approach for Securing Higher Growth

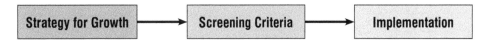

THE CHANGING VIEW

OLD WAY	NEW WAY
Competencies are fixed	Competencies are variable
Conglomeration is good	Conglomeration is bad
Firm goes it alone	Firm considers strategic alliances and other interorganizational relationships
Growth always desirable	Right and timely growth desirable
Insourcing is a growth strategy	Insourcing and outsourcing are growth strategies
Organic growth by developing new products internally	Organic growth by expanding into global markets
Reinvest in historically profitable businesses	Prudent selection of appropriate growth ventures
Swift implementation of new opportunities is desirable	Swift implementation of new opportunities is critical

STRATEGY FOR GROWTH

KEY IDEA

Exiting the memory chip market was an agonizing decision for Andy Grove, Intel founder and CEO. Facing intense competition, Intel changed its mission and stopped selling the products on which it had been founded — memory chips. Intel pursued growth in the microprocessor market and now has a commanding leadership position.[8] Many observers believe Andy Grove merits a place among great business leaders of the 20th century. [560v]

Texas Instruments (TI) was a technology leader that lost out to Intel. In the 1980s, TI diversified widely but later divested from many markets, including chemicals, defense electronics, inspection equipment, memory chips, mold manufacturing, notebook computers, and software. TI is now market leader in chips for wireless phones, large-screen television processors, and many new electronic devices like the Slingbox (transfers TV programs from user's home to a PC anywhere in the world), as it focuses on mobile TV service, cell phones, and other devices. For the past several years TI has outgrown the semiconductor market. [536v]

A comprehensive approach for securing higher growth comprises:

- **Strategy for growth**
- Screening criteria
- Implementation

KEY IDEA

Some pizza restaurant chains are highly profitable, but IBM does not make pizzas. Smartphones are fast growing and profitable, but Walmart does not produce them. Streaming music from the Internet is a growing business, but Carnival Cruise Lines does not offer this service. Each opportunity seems attractive, but these firms did not invest. Why not?

The reason is simple. Each of these firms has a *strategy for growth*; their strategy generating processes did not surface these options. A strategy for growth uses a set of frameworks to help the firm evaluate current businesses, decide which businesses *to be in*, and which businesses *not to be in*. Figure 7.2 shows that firms can generate attractive opportunities using four components: *vision, mission, growth path,* and *timing of entry*.

A strategy for growth has four components:

- Vision
- Mission
- Growth path
- Timing of entry

FIGURE 7.2
Components of a Strategy for Growth

VISION

Vision is a description of the firm's ideal future state — an impressionistic picture of what the future should be.[9] *Corporate vision* concerns the firm as a whole; *business-unit vision* focuses on an individual business. Good visions set a broad direction — they should inspire employees for the long run. A good vision is not too broad, nor too specific, nor easily achieved.[10]

KEY IDEA

Vision is the description of an ideal future state for a firm or business unit. Vision sets a broad direction for the firm. When developed with employee participation, a vision can inspire the entire organization for the long run.

Visions

Amazon – *To be the world's most customer-centric company*

Disney – *To make people happy*

Ford Motor Company – circa 1920s – *A car in every garage*

Google – *To organize the world's information and make it universally accessible and useful*[11]

Instagram – *Capture and share the world's moments*

Salesforce.com – *The end of software*

These examples show the power of a good vision. Ford's vision led to the Model T, the production-line system, and continual price reductions. Ford's share of the U.S. automobile market reached over 50 percent by the mid-1920s. Disney has been highly successful with a very clear vision.

How do you evaluate the
following visions? Are they
too broad? Are they too
narrow? Are they inspiring?

• IBM (1990s) – *To lead big
companies into the brave
new networked world, IBM
will devise their technology
strategies, build and run
their systems, and ultimately become the architect and
repository for corporate
computing, tying together
not just companies, but
entire industries.*

• Merck – *We are in the
business of preserving and
improving human life.*

• Pinterest — *To discover
and save creative ideas*

Marketing should make sure the vision is outward-looking. Without marketing input, vision can easily be too inwardly focused on what the firm does well. Of course, firm actions must support the vision — simply stating a goal doesn't mean you will achieve it. One CEO publicly announced his firm's vision: *to become our customers' most preferred supplier across all purchasing categories.* This statement raised customer expectations far beyond the firm's ability to deliver, ultimately creating customer dissatisfaction. A former British Airways (BA) CEO made a similar mistake, publicly committing to *excellent customer service.* He then single-mindedly pursued cost-cutting and outsourcing that alienated BA staff. The ensuing strike stranded tens of thousands very unhappy customers.

Developing a vision is one thing; having employees actively embrace the vision is another. When senior executives and consultants construct the firm's vision in isolation, employee buy-in may be minimal. Consider Oracle's experience:

With little discussion, CEO Larry Ellison developed Oracle's new vision as an Internet-based firm. He mandated that Oracle should convert all enterprise software to work as Web-based applications. Development would cease on client-server products, and the sales force would tell customers that Oracle was phasing them out. Several months later, Ellison discovered his product development directive being ignored and the sales force was assuring customers that Oracle would not withdraw client-server products. Clearly, Ellison did not get employee buy-in!

When the firm involves employees, vision takes longer to develop. But broad participation and input lead to better visions. At Aramark (Philadelphia-based services firm), more than 8,500 employees participated directly in developing the new vision. Apple visionary CEO Steve Jobs coupled his quest for perfection with mobilizing ideas from the *top 100* employees he believed were the smartest (not always highest ranked). Consider also Howard Schultz's (Starbucks founder and CEO) perspective, "People want to be part of something larger than themselves. They want to be part of something they're really proud of, that they'll fight for, sacrifice for, that they trust."[12] Successful entrepreneurs have very clear visions and succeed by surrounding themselves with others who buy into their perspectives. Recent examples:

• Airbnb — to connect people who need a place/space to stay with people who have surplus space to host people.

• Facebook — to give people the power to share and make the world more open and connected.

• Uber — to connect passengers with drivers of vehicles for hire and ride-sharing services.

In each case, the founders' clear visions made their firms very successful and themselves very wealthy.

MISSION

The firm creates a vision to provide a lofty aspirational view of its overall direction. *Mission* guides the firm's search for opportunities more directly.[13] A well-developed mission keeps the firm focused in a limited arena where success is likely. Mission avoids dispersing firm energy and resources in multiple directions. An ideal mission codifies opportunity areas where the firm does well or aspires to do well.[14] A firm with several business units should develop missions at both the corporate and business-unit levels; of course, the corporate mission should encompass individual business missions.

ARTICULATING THE MISSION. Mission states what the firm/business unit *will do*; by what it omits, mission also states what the firm/business unit *will not do*! (What business shall we be in? What business shall we *not* be in?) Three internal resource (IR) dimensions and two externally focused (EF) dimensions are critical:

• **IR — Core ingredient or natural resource.** The firm maximizes value from a core ingredient or natural resource. *We are a forest products company* implies the firm could make and sell products for many technologies to many markets, but they must be wood-based.

- **IR — Product/service.** This firm's mission focuses on a product/service. *We are an automobile firm* directs management to make cars that may use various fuels — alcohol, diesel, ethanol, gasoline, hydrogen, or natural gas based on several technologies — electro-mechanical, fuel cell, gas-turbine, internal-combustion, hybrid, or steam.

- **IR — Technology.** The firm focuses on a core technology. *We are an electronics firm* directs the search for opportunities to electronics, using any raw material and selling products into any market. China's BYD, a world leader in cell phone batteries, entered the automobile industry with the long-run goal of producing electric cars.[15]

- **EF — Customer needs.** This mission directs the firm to serve customers having a specific set of needs, with any product, using any technology. *We satisfy people's transportation needs* could embrace making bicycles, automobiles, trucks, helicopters, or airplanes.[16] Otis Elevator has a transportation-based mission — *to provide any customer a means of moving people and things up, down, and sideways over short distances with higher reliability than any similar enterprise in the world.*

- **EF — Market/market segment.** A firm with this type of mission could make many products, using various raw materials and technologies targeted at a single segment. *Our markets are families with young children* is the mission for many FMCG firms like P&G and Unilever that offer household and personal-care products to consumers.

The firm/business unit can choose among these dimensions to develop missions, or may combine dimensions. Courtyard by Marriott's mission — *To provide economy and quality-minded frequent business travelers with a premier lodging facility, which is consistently perceived as clean, comfortable, well maintained, and attractive, staffed by friendly, attentive, and efficient people* — combines product/service and market/market segment.

To reiterate, every mission answers the question "What business are we in?" Mission states what the firm/business unit *will do* — externally focused missions also specify *for whom*. But by what it omits, a well-crafted mission also states what the firm/business unit *will not do*!

EVOLVING THE MISSION. "Change everything except your wife and children." — Lee Kun-hee, CEO Samsung. Typically, successful firms evolve their missions. If opportunities are scarce with the current mission, or a target of opportunity appears, the firm should consider *broadening* the mission, but be cautious about the modified direction. Cannondale successfully expanded its mission from high-end bicycles to embrace dirt bikes and all-terrain vehicles, but Cisco's B2C Flip video camera was a failure. Successful mission broadenings include:

Amazon. Amazon's initial mission was product-based — Internet book selling. As Amazon grew, it added many other products, broadening its mission to become an Internet retailer. Today, Amazon has morphed into a firm that grows based on technology: *Amazon Web Services* delivers a set of services that together form a reliable, scalable, and inexpensive utility computing platform *in the cloud.*

Apple. For many years Apple's mission focused on personal computers, reliant on continuous Macintosh upgrades. More recently, Apple's mission expanded to embrace and manage digital music — iPod and iTunes; smartphones — iPhone; tablet computers — iPad; the Apple watch; Apple Pay.

Dell, HP, IBM, and Xerox each broadened their missions to embrace services, in part through acquisition; these firms acquired, respectively, Perot Systems, Electronic Data Systems (EDS) (now Hewlett Packard Enterprise), PricewaterhouseCoopers, and Affiliated Computer Services. By contrast, Oracle broadened into hardware by acquiring Sun Microsystems.

Google significantly broadened its original *search* mission by extending its software-led participation in smartphones — Android, maps, and other domains — and changing the corporate name to Alphabet.

continues

KEY IDEA

Mission guides the firm's search for opportunity.

Five approaches to developing mission are:

Internally focused:
- Core ingredient or natural resource
- Product or service
- Technology

Externally focused:
- Customer needs
- Market or market segment

KEY IDEA

The firm's mission can use a single approach or combine several approaches.

The firm should proactively revise its mission.

MARKETING QUESTION

Based on your knowledge and/or online research, write one-sentence missions for AXA, Citigroup, Comcast, Disney, ExxonMobil, Facebook, Ford, GE, Groupon, Hitachi, Morgan Stanley, Novartis, Siemens, Toyota, Twitter, Verizon, Yahoo!, and/or Xerox.

MARKETING QUESTION

In recent years, Google acquired YouTube, Double Click (online advertising network), Motorola Mobility, and Zagat (restaurant reviews) and renamed the firm, *Alphabet*. Write a mission for Alphabet. As Larry Page, Alphabet's CEO, where will you seek future growth?

Pampers. P&G evolved its baby business mission from *we want the driest diapers* to *helping moms with all facets of baby's healthy development*. This evolution led to new products like Easy Ups training pants and Kandoo baby wipes.

ServiceMaster. For many years, ServiceMaster's (SM) compound annual growth rate and shareholder returns consistently exceeded 20 percent. Originally a mothproofing business, SM expanded into carpet cleaning, general household and commercial cleaning, and grounds management.

Firms faced with resources stretched too thin, poor financial performance, new/evolving competition, looming takeover threat, activist shareholders, and/or better opportunities to deploy capital often *narrow* their missions. These firms drop products and/or divest businesses. DuPont exited oil and textile fibers; Corning divested healthcare services and consumer products; GE is exiting financial services. Other firms simply *return to the core business* (*stick to the knitting*): Under CEO A.J. Laffley, P&G grew from its core — laundry products, baby diapers, feminine care, hair care — and built on its strengths to enter new beauty and personal-care categories. P&G expanded in developing markets but divested less-strategic food and beverage brands (Crisco, Jif, Folgers), and weak household (Comet) and beauty (Clairol, CoverGirl, Noxzema, Wella) brands, and exited pharmaceuticals. Some firms *narrow* product scope but place major effort on *expanding* geographic scope.

Guinness. Post-WWII, the Irish brewer launched a major diversification program, adding 250 businesses. As profitability declined, Guinness *aggressively divested* most of these businesses, rebuilt the Guinness brand, and *expanded internationally*. Guinness share price increased nearly 10,000 times.

Knorr-Bremse. Munich-based Knorr-Bremse (KB) offered a diversified product line, mainly to German customers. After a management buyout, KB *narrowed its product line* to braking systems for trains and trucks, and *expanded geographic scope* globally. KB made 28 acquisitions and has 40 percent global market share.

Other firms seek opportunity by totally changing their missions:

American Can. American Can (AC) was the U.S. No. 2 canning company in the post-WWII decades. AC divested its entire canning operations and morphed, via acquisition, into Primerica, a financial services firm.

Westinghouse Electric. Westinghouse acquired CBS, divested its electricity businesses, changed its name, and focused exclusively on media. CBS subsequently merged with media conglomerate Viacom.

Some firms narrow their missions by breaking up into two or more parts — aka *starburst*. Each new firm has a narrower, more focused mission than the original company. Frequently, the motivation for splitting the firm is the perceived *conglomerate discount*. Activist investors and/or private equity firms believe separate more focused firms secure greater shareholder value. Tyco split into three firms — Covidien (healthcare), TE Connectivity (electronics), Tyco International (security, fire protection, flow control); Kraft split into two firms — grocery, snacks; McGraw-Hill split into McGraw-Hill Markets (business information), McGraw-Hill Education; Bayer, HP, and Motorola acted similarly. Notwithstanding the general sentiment in favor of focus, some successful firms are active in multiple unrelated businesses — *conglomerates*. Over the years, U.S. firms have largely rejected the conglomerate model but some remain — Berkshire Hathaway and GE are good examples. Conglomerates are more popular outside the U.S.: Tata (India), Samsung (Korea), and Toyota (Japan) are exemplars for their countries. The argument in favor is efficient internal capital markets, the ability to tap human and information resources from across the organization, and the power to deter competitive entry into markets where they are active.[17]

GROWTH PATH

Mission provides a broad approach to identifying potential opportunities; *growth path* is more focused. (Gap Analysis, Marketing Enrichment 7.1 **[718p]**, is a useful conceptual device for framing the growth-path challenge.) Growth path is specifically concerned with the trade-off between expected financial return and risk.[18] The firm should consider three factors in evaluating opportunities:

MARKETING ENRICHMENT 7.1

Gap Analysis **718p**

- revenue and profit potential relative to required investment;
- core competencies from its portfolio of businesses, technologies, products, and markets;
- risk assessment.

The firm's expected financial returns, competencies, and risks from opportunities it pursues coexist in a dynamic relationship. By investing in one opportunity, the firm may develop new competencies. These enhanced competencies may, in turn, make previously unattractive opportunities attractive. Expected financial returns and risks also change.

Figure 7.3 shows the growth-path matrix's two dimensions — *market* and *product/technology* — to analyze opportunities. We trisect each dimension — *existing, related, new* — to develop nine matrix cells — A through I. Each cell represents a different type of opportunity. For ease of exposition, we combine individual cells to develop four broad approaches to growth: *market penetration, product growth, market growth,* and *product and market diversification.*[19]

	Existing	**Related**	**New (to firm)**
New	**Market Growth 2:** Market Expansion (G)	**Business Expansion:** Concentric Products (H)	**Conglomeration** (I)
Related	**Market Growth 1:** Market Extension (D)	**Business Extension** (E)	**Business Expansion:** Concentric Markets (F)
Existing	**Market Penetration** (A)	**Product Growth 1:** Product Extension (B)	**Product Growth 2:** Product Expansion (C)

Market ↑ / Product/Technology →

FIGURE 7.3
Growth-Path Matrix

MARKETING QUESTION

Use the growth-path matrix to identify the growth trajectory of your favorite firm, or a firm for which you would like to work.

MARKET PENETRATION (CELL A). Most firms spend significant resources pursuing market-penetration strategies. The firm focuses effort on existing (or slightly modified) products in existing markets, but may also improve profits by increasing operational effectiveness. The firm bases growth on core competencies, and has relatively low *knowledge* risk. Of course, the firm may face significant risk from competitors and generally heightened environmental turbulence.

PRODUCT GROWTH (CELLS B AND C). The firm brings new products to existing markets. A ski resort that adds ice-skating, downhill sledding, snowmobiling, and tubing pursues a product-growth strategy. VF Corporation acquired Timberland (boots) to add to its outdoor and action sports business brands like North Face and Eastpak. *Product growth 1 (product extension — cell B)* and *product growth 2 (product expansion — cell C)* differ in the degree of product newness. Product extensions relate to current products; product expansions are unrelated and hence more risky. For a bank skilled in making corporate loans, lock-box services are a product extension. Complex derivatives, requiring significant new technical expertise, are a product expansion.

MARKET GROWTH (CELLS D AND G). The firm sells existing products to new markets via market development. *Market growth 1 (market extension — cell D)* and *market growth 2 (market expansion — cell G)* differ in degree of market newness. For the bank skilled in corporate loans,

ADJACENCIES

Adjacencies are special cases of product and market growth. Product and market growth 1 (extensions) (Cells B and D) are close to the firm's core competencies. Related technology products are less risky than new products. From a market perspective, a U.S. firm's geographic expansion to an English-speaking country with similar cultural values and legal system, like Australia, Britain, Canada, or South Africa, is much closer to the core than entry into China or Japan that have very different languages and cultures.

Sometimes the firm bases *adjacent* growth on *hidden assets* — underutilized competencies, resources, or skills. De Beers shifted from a production focus to market focus by strengthening its brand and leveraging consumer, jeweler, and distributor relationships into new products. Marvel's comic-book franchise could not stave off bankruptcy but its 5,000-strong stable of characters (Green Goblin, Incredible Hulk, Spiderman, Wolverine) drove the turnaround via movies and merchandising. Internal functions may provide the basis for adjacent growth. American Airlines secured revenue from its Sabre reservation system (later spun off as a public company and developed as Travelocity); Disney Institute offers seminars based on Disney's brand building and service excellence; Zappos offers seminars and insight-videos about its unique culture; and IBM formed its highly successful Global Services from a subunit of the sales force.[20]

KEY IDEA

The four fundamental *growth-path* directions are:

• Market penetration
• Product growth
• Market growth
• Product and market diversification

These four growth directions comprise nine individual growth paths.

loans to public and/or nonprofit enterprises is a market extension. Loans to individuals is a market expansion. Generally, market expansions are more risky than market extensions.

Porsche makes and sells automobiles — market penetration — but also pursues market growth. Porsche operates a highly profitable *rent-an-engineer* business to customers like Airbus, Harley-Davidson, Linde forklifts, Opel Zafira, and Smart microcar. As a result, Porsche keeps its engineering team intact and also earns significant revenues.

Geographic expansion is a popular market growth option. Increasingly, firms are expanding to new countries.**[389v]** Readers will recognize that many large firms, headquartered in various countries, operate globally, including Cemex (Mexico), IBM (U.S.), Pechiney (France), Sony (Japan), Samsung (Korea), South African Breweries, and British Airways.

PRODUCT AND MARKET DIVERSIFICATION (CELLS E, F, H, I). A critical characteristic of *market penetration*, *product growth*, and *market growth* is that at least one of the two growth dimensions is *existing*, and just one changes. For product and market diversification, both *market and product/technology* change to either *related* or *new*. Opportunities are more risky, and the business as a whole shifts direction.

Business extension (cell E) requires moderate change for both *market* and *product/technology*. Nike made a product extension when it added athletic apparel to its core footwear line. By contrast, adding sporty street apparel was a business extension — *related* product to *related* market. *Business expansion* requires new products and related markets *(concentric markets — cell F)*, or new markets and related products *(concentric products — cell H)*.[21] Risk is greatest in *conglomeration (cell I)* — new products and new markets. Conglomeration by internal development is generally more risky than by acquisition, but many conglomerate acquisitions also fail. Quaker purchased Snapple from Triarc for $1.7 billion but made significant errors in distribution and promotion. Three years later, Triarc repurchased Snapple for $300 million.[22] **[706v]** Another conglomeration failure:

MARKETING QUESTION

Pick a country other than your own. Which firms from that country earn revenues from countries in more than three continents? What other diversification directions have these firms taken?

Under CEO Jean Paul Messier, a French water utility firm renamed itself Vivendi and began acquiring entertainment, media, and communications firms. Vivendi purchased Seagram to secure Universal Studios and bought USA Networks' entertainment assets — it also began divesting water companies. When Vivendi faced bankruptcy, the board fired Messier and started selling assets. Vivendi exited water, and now focuses on media and telecommunications.

CHOOSING THE *RIGHT* GROWTH PATH. To identify and separate worthwhile opportunities from others typically requires significant marketing research and analysis. The firm should identify the scope of the opportunity, competition, and assess its ability to deliver the necessary customer value to secure differential advantage. More generally, the firm should evaluate its ability to be successful in various growth paths. For example, the firm may perform well with *market growth* but poorly with *product and market diversification*. If so, the firm should probably favor *market-growth* opportunities and set a higher bar for *product and market diversifications*.

Firms with technical expertise tend to choose product-focused growth; firms with market-development expertise select market-focused growth. By trial and error, the firm may discover it has greater competence in one growth area than another. Yet even firms with technical expertise need marketing expertise. Observers have often lauded Philips and Alcatel-Lucent (acquired by Nokia) for great technology but criticized them for not capitalizing on these strengths in their chosen markets. By contrast, Cisco has successfully acquired many technology firms, then introduced marketable products that customers value highly.

As a starting point for developing decision rules about new opportunities, the firm should conduct a retrospective growth-path analysis. The firm could go back, say, five years and classify each pursued opportunity into one of the nine cells, then assess success or failure. The firm may discover some areas where it generally performs well and others where it performs poorly. Sunstar (Japan) secured great insight using this procedure.

TIMING OF ENTRY

Along with identifying the *right* growth path, when to seize an opportunity — *timing of entry* — is also crucial. Chapter 3 discusses five product life-cycle stages — *introduction, early growth, late growth, maturity, decline*. Early stages have high uncertainty in both products and markets, but uncertainty decreases as the life cycle evolves. Correspondingly, competitive pressures typically increase. Figure 7.4 explores links between the first four life-cycle stages and specific strategic options for timing of market entry — *pioneer, follow-the-leader, segmenter, me-too*.[23]

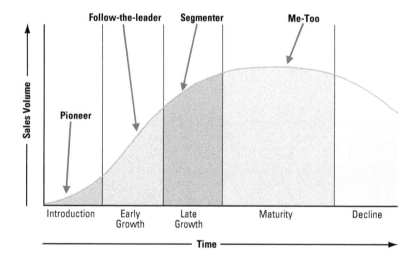

....

FIGURE 7.4
Timing of Market Entry

For the firm you chose on p. 184, identify the timing-of-entry strategy for various growth initiatives.

PIONEER. *Pioneers* blaze trails and create new markets via consistent and extensive R&D. Pioneers accept risk and understand that failure often accompanies success. Pioneers possess the R&D skills and internal processes to consistently develop new products/services, and the marketing capabilities to open up new markets. Pioneers have sufficient resources to support heavy R&D expenditures and fund market development; sometimes market-entry costs exceed R&D spending. Firms that commonly pioneer new products include Apple, DuPont, IBM, Intel, 3M, Sony, major pharmaceutical firms (like GSK, Novartis, Pfizer), and biotech firms.

Of course, pioneers are not always successful, even when they bring products to market. Apple's experience illustrates the benefits and risks of pioneering:

> Founded by entrepreneurs Steve Jobs and Steve Wozniak, Apple pioneered personal computers, but the IBM PC and clones overtook it. Apple pioneered personal digital assistants (PDAs) with the Newton, but lost out to Palm. Apple pioneered paid-music downloading — iTunes and iPod; smartphones — iPhone; and tablet computers — iPad. Has Apple sustained these early leads?

Successful pioneers often enjoy patent monopolies for limited time periods and related high margins. Pioneers protect intellectual property ferociously; they may also gain first-mover advantages and raise entry costs for followers. Some first-mover advantages are short-lived, but others can last for many years and pose difficult challenges for later entrants.

FOLLOW-THE-LEADER. *Follow-the-leader* firms enter rapidly growing markets on the heels of pioneers. Pioneers make large research investments to develop innovative new products/ services; follow-the-leader firms focus on development. In what is sometimes called the *bad-apple* policy, the *follower* lets the pioneer take the first bite. If the apple is fine, the follower enters; if not, it passes.[24] Follow-the-leader firms are happy for pioneers to invest heavily in R&D and market development — followers pursue the pioneer quickly with developmental R&D. Market insight is critical; followers should enter as soon as possible after a successful pioneer. Successful follow-the-leaders should have:

- Vision of serving a mass market;
- Good competitive intelligence to develop products/services as soon as possible;
- Good developmental engineers to leverage/enhance the pioneer's successful research;
- Good insight about evolving customer needs;
- Proactive patent lawyers to identify weak spots in pioneer patents;
- Financial strength and commitment to outspend the pioneer;
- Ability to differentiate offers and deliver superior customer value;
- Will and persistence to succeed.[25]

Samsung is a follower to Apple in smartphones. Many industry leaders like FedEx (air package delivery), Gillette (razors), Google (search), Intel (microprocessors), Microsoft (operating system software, browsers, search), Pampers (P&G) (disposable diapers), and Xerox (copiers) entered their markets as follow-the-leader firms.[26] Ethicon (J&J) consistently follows medical-device innovations from Covidien, typically 18 months later with improved products at lower prices. Ford and Nissan both introduced hybrid cars many years after Toyota.

SEGMENTER. *Segmenters* enter established markets in late growth by adding value for specific market segments. Segmenter strategies can be very effective in maturing markets. As customers gain knowledge and experience, their preferences typically become more specific. Using insightful marketing research, segmenters identify unique needs of specific customer groups, then offer specially designed products/services.

Segmenter skill sets and competencies differ markedly from pioneers and follow-the-leaders. Technological expertise and innovation are no longer the driving forces. Segmenters require marketing research skills to identify unsatisfied customer needs, but also the flexibility to address narrow market niches. Segmenters often target several segments simultaneously, at low cost — perhaps using modular-design or platform-engineering processes — combined with flexible operating systems.

Medical-device-maker Medtronic used successful segmentation and platform engineering to capture market share in cardiac pacemakers and implantable defibrillators.[27] Airbus and Boeing use modular design to produce commercial aircraft families — Boeing designed the 707, 727, 737, and 757 aircraft on the same fuselage platform. The automobile industry is a heavy user of

KEY IDEA

Four *timing-of-entry* options are:

- Pioneer
- Follow-the-leader
- Segmenter
- Me-too

These options correspond to entry in various stages of the product life cycle, respectively:

- Introduction
- Early growth
- Late growth
- Maturity

The firm must match capabilities to timing-of-entry strategy. Capabilities must evolve as markets develop.

DISCOVERY-DRIVEN GROWTH

Discovery-driven growth addresses problems of unfocused growth in many firms. To begin, the firm should develop challenging yet realistic goals. Management examines current growth initiatives to assess whether they can meet these goals; if not, what are the gaps? Using vision, mission, growth path, and timing of entry, the firm identifies the kinds of projects that can close the gaps.

An important tool is the *reverse income statement* — starting with the bottom line, then working backward to figure out what the firm must accomplish. Consider profit goals: Return on sales (ROS) assumptions lead to revenue targets — lead to volume and price targets — lead to market-share targets (via market size and growth assumptions) — lead to resource requirements like product development, sales force, advertising. At each stage, the firm should test assumptions for realism.[28]

these design and engineering approaches. In Asia and elsewhere, Toyota builds many different pickups, light trucks, SUVs, and minivans on the same Hilux platform.

Automobile companies, especially smaller firms, use segmentation to launch specialist vehicles that may be key to their survival. Chrysler minivans transformed its financial performance; failing Mazda revived sports cars with the Miata (MX5). Daimler AG's Smart microcar is similarly aimed at a narrow urbanite group.

ME-TOO. *Me-too-ers* enter mature markets with limited product lines. They base low-price/low-cost strategies on value engineering, efficient high-volume production (often in low-cost countries), low overhead, aggressive procurement, and great attention to detail. They spend little on R&D, have similar products to market leaders, are often leaders in process innovation, and have very focused marketing. Generic-drug producers, notably Teva (Israel), are *poster children* for this strategy, although technological copying difficulties may cause problems. Me-too-ers can wreak havoc in segmented markets where firms compete with value-added offers; many Chinese firms pursue this approach. Norwegian Air Shuttle is a me-too-er in the trans-atlantic passenger airline market.

Dell became global PC market leader by continually reducing costs and putting enormous price pressure on competitors. Dell minimizes inventory, receives payment before production, and has negative working capital. Dell lost ground to HP and Lenovo, but Taiwan's Acer places huge price pressure on the leaders.[29]

CHOOSING THE *RIGHT* TIMING-OF-ENTRY STRATEGY. Similar to growth-path decisions, the firm should identify which *timing-of-entry* strategy best fits its capabilities, then match this strategy to market opportunities. Of course, as markets evolve, the firm must also evolve its capabilities.[30]

SCREENING CRITERIA: EVALUATING OPPORTUNITIES

We showed how growth strategy helps the firm identify opportunities; but which specific opportunities should the firm pursue? Figure 7.5 (p. 189) shows five *screening criteria — objectives, compatibility (fit), core competence, synergy, contribution to the venture portfolio* — that help the firm evaluate opportunities and decide where to invest.

KEY IDEA

A comprehensive approach for securing higher growth comprises:

- Strategy for growth
- **Screening criteria**
- Implementation

FIGURE 7.5
Screening Criteria

KEY IDEA

The firm should consider five perspectives when evaluating opportunities:

• Objectives
• Compatibility (fit)
• Core competence
• Synergy
• Contribution to the venture portfolio

KEY IDEA

In setting *objectives*, the firm should strike a balance between:

• Revenue and profit growth
• Risk
• Timing
• Stability
• Flexibility

OBJECTIVES

The crucial first criterion for an investment opportunity is to satisfy objectives. Revenue and profit growth are critical for creating shareholder value, but unmitigated growth can be a real problem. The firm must temper growth ambitions with concern for risk, timing, stability, and flexibility.

REVENUE AND PROFIT GROWTH. To assess revenue and profit potential, the firm should consider both financial and nonfinancial measures. Standard financial measures include timing of cash flows, payback, return on investment (ROI), profit margin, net present value (NPV), and internal rate of return (IRR). Leading indicators of profit performance include market size, expected market growth, market potential, forces driving market growth, number/strength of competitors, and market-share forecasts. These factors influence revenue, cost, and profit forecasts.

Sometimes firms reject opportunities because *forecast* performance is inferior to *historic* performance of an existing product(s). This comparison is incorrect. The firm should compare forecast market share, revenues, and profits from the *new* opportunity versus forecast market share, revenues, and profits *without* it. Example: Despite a significant lead in expensive laser printers, HP added inexpensive inkjet printers (lower margins) to avoid losing market share.

RISK. The firm must weigh forecast revenues and profits against the risk and required investment. Risks the firm should consider include:

• **Demand risk.** Fundamental for every cell in the growth-path matrix: Is there an opportunity? Is there market demand?
• **Product/technology risk and market risk.** Generally, opportunities farther from *market penetration* (cell A) of the growth-path matrix are more risky. The firm lacks experience with either product/technology (cells B and C) or market (cells D and G). Product and market diversification (cell I) is the most risky — opportunities are very different from firm experience. Also, early life-cycle entries like *pioneer* and *follow-the-leader* may be more risky than later *segmenter* and *me-too* strategies. Critical questions: Will the technology work? Does (will) our product(s) satisfy customer needs?
• **Competitor risk.** In general, the lower product/technology and market risk, the tougher the competition; hence, competitor risk is typically high for market penetration. By contrast, direct competition may be minimal for pioneers.

Other risks the firm should evaluate for each opportunity are:

• **Financial risk.** Is the opportunity sufficiently sustainable to justify the investment?
• **Firm risk.** Does the firm have the competencies, resources, and will to succeed?
• **Physical environment risk.** Are natural disasters likely to affect the opportunity?
• **Political risk.** How stable is the local government? Will it (or successors) take actions to make the market less attractive? Is there expropriation risk?

Opportunities differ in degree and type of risk; hence, the firm should set different profitability cut-offs. Generally, more-risky opportunities should offer higher potential returns than less-risky opportunities.[31,32]

TIMING. The firm must consider the timing of contribution to profits. A moderate return opportunity that delivers profits in the medium term may be more attractive than a higher return opportunity promising profits much later.

STABILITY. Suppose the firm must choose between two opportunities: high growth, significant profit variability versus lower growth, low profit variability. The firm may prefer the lower growth, low variability — higher *stability* — option. Schneider Electric Mexico focuses on markets it can serve through existing distributors. Schneider believes these revenues are more stable than revenues from potentially more profitable large electricity generation projects requiring major investments. Similarly:

> A well-known ski resort had two investment options: develop ski trails on a neighboring hill or invest in mountain slides and outdoor concerts to attract summer visitors. The ski resort elected to develop summer facilities so as to even out annual revenue and profit streams.

FLEXIBILITY. All firms face increasing environmental change, complexity, and turbulence. No matter how good its forecasting, the firm may be blindsided by unexpected events. *Insurance policies* give the firm *flexibility* to deal with changed circumstances:

- **Acquisition.** Intel, Microsoft, and Cisco acquire firms with positions in adjacent markets.
- **Joint technology agreements.** Oil companies often form partnerships for oil-drilling platforms and operations — like Texaco and Shell in the Gulf of Mexico.
- **Partial ownership.** Major drug companies frequently take this approach with biotechnology firms. BMS purchased shares in cancer-drug developer ImClone.
- **Research and development (R&D).** The firm hedges its bets by investing in competing fields. Car companies invest in hybrid, electric, and fuel cell technologies.
- **Venture capital.** The firm provides venture capital to startup companies but retains options to increase ownership. Cisco is a leader in this approach. Microsoft invests in firms that conduct *spam* marketing; it also invests in firms that develop *antispam* software.

Originally a textile power-loom producer, Toyota morphed into automobiles. Today, Toyota investments include advertising agency, airport management, consulting, golf course operations, helicopter operations and surveying, horticulture, prefabricated houses, a professional soccer team, and resort development. Some, but not all, have synergies with its automobile business.

COMPATIBILITY (FIT)

Can the firm be successful in the opportunity? The firm should examine three core types of compatibility (fit):

PRODUCT-MARKET FIT. Is the product appropriate for the market? Restated: Does the product satisfy customer needs in target market segments better than competitors? Firms most often assess *product-market fit* through ongoing marketing research and market-testing. Timing is particularly important in assessing product-market fit as the firm and environment evolve.

MARKETING QUESTION

Can you identify three examples of successful product-market fit? Can you identify three examples of failed product-market fit? What are the risks of unsuccessful product-market fit?

PRODUCT-COMPANY FIT. Does the firm possess the financial, human, and other capabilities/resources to succeed? Can the firm successfully upgrade efforts as the market evolves? British-based EMI's experience with the CAT scanner is a classic example of insufficient *product-company fit*. Best known for recorded music (particularly the Beatles), EMI successfully pioneered the first CAT scanner in the U.S. EMI retained market leadership for several years, but

The three important types of *compatibility (fit)* are:
- Product-market fit
- Product-company fit
- Company-market fit

continued pressure from major players in medical imaging — GE, Hitachi, Technicare — eventually forced its withdrawal.[33]

Sometimes the firm has great product-market fit but lacks distribution strength to reach customers. Independent inventors and startups often have this problem — product-market fit is great, but product-company fit is poor. Un-du's experience is classic:

> Charles Foley developed Un-du (manufactured by Doumar Products) for removing oil-based stickers. The Business Product Industry Association gave Un-du its best-new-product award, but getting distribution was a major problem. Magic American introduced Sticker Lifter through established distribution and gained dominant market share.

COMPANY-MARKET FIT. Can the firm compete effectively in the market? Does the firm have sufficient customer insight, reputation, resources, and skills to defeat competitors? Product-market fit and product-company fit may both be fine, but poor *company-market fit* may lead to a reject decision. Geographic expansion offers many examples. Suppose a foreign market is attractive for the firm's product — good product-market fit — and the firm is skilled at producing, promoting, and distributing the product in its home market — good company-product fit. Little experience in the foreign market — poor company-market fit — may lead to rejection. Consider the different perspectives of Citibank and Capital One concerning credit cards in Asia:

> Citibank launched credit cards in several Asian countries. Because Citibank had operated in Asia for many years, credit cards in Asia were a good company-market fit. By contrast, Capital One was a strong U.S. competitor but did not have operations in Asia. Regarding an Asian entry, Capital One had poor company-market fit.

RELATIONSHIPS AMONG THE THREE FORMS OF FIT. All three compatibility criteria are important for evaluating individual opportunities, but product-market fit differs from the others. If product-market fit is poor — product does not satisfy customer needs — the firm should dismiss the opportunity regardless of the other fits. If product-market fit is good, and either product-company fit or company-market fit is poor, the firm should consider options:

- **Poor product-company fit.** Divest the product/technology to a firm better suited to make and sell the product.[34] Many biotechnology firms make these arrangements with major pharmaceutical companies because they possess greater marketing expertise and resources.
- **Poor company-market fit.** Form a strategic alliance with a better-positioned firm. General Mills — cereal expertise — and Nestlé — brand equity and distribution — formed Cereal Partners Worldwide (CPW) to produce and market cereals outside the U.S. Kellogg previously dominated the global market, but CPW now offers more than 50 brands in 130 markets worldwide. CPW international market share in cold cereal now exceeds 20 percent.

CORE COMPETENCE

Core competence comprises capabilities, knowledge, skills, and resources.

Core competencies are capabilities, knowledge, skills, and resources the firm possesses.[35] The *core-competence* criterion is straightforward: Does the firm *bring anything to the party*? Can the firm *take anything from the party*? More formally: Does this opportunity leverage firm core competencies or allow it to develop new ones? If the answer is *no* to both questions, the firm should probably reject the opportunity. But one *yes* may be sufficient to continue.

Generally, the firm is better off pursuing opportunities that use its core competencies. The firm can more easily gain differential advantage, like Coca-Cola introducing a new sports drink or Toyota launching a new automobile. Two Boston entrepreneurs developed a competence in buying common Internet domain names — beer.com, creditcards.com, chocolate.com — then developing and selling websites.

Of course, an opportunity may be attractive *even if the firm has little competence* — if it can *secure* the required competence. Intel abandoned its core competence in memory chips, but gained competence in microprocessor technology and manufacturing. When Jeff Bezos left New York for Seattle in his secondhand car, he had little competence for building Amazon, but it became the leading online retailer.[36] Apple was a PC manufacturer that successively introduced the iPod, iTunes, iPad, and iPhone. Samsung shifted from low-cost manufacturing to become a leading global electronics brand; today Samsung's market value is several times Sony's. Together, these illustrations exemplify a focus on opportunity. Also:

> Sir Richard Branson addressed Virgin's anticipated $300 million–$400 million investment in ethanol plants: "There were skeptics in the record business, but we built the biggest independent record company. With the airline, we've seen 13 competitors go bankrupt, and we've survived. We've built a successful mobile phone business. We're a slightly unusual company in that *we go into industries we know nothing about and immerse ourselves*" (emphasis added).[37]

SYNERGY

Synergy explores how an opportunity relates to existing firm capabilities/resources.[38] *Positive synergy* reflects the notion that 2+2 can be greater than 4! Synergy kicks in when the firm uses existing resources to develop an opportunity. When the firm sells a new product through existing distributors — like P&G or Unilever adding new products for supermarkets — it gains distribution synergy. When the firm makes a new product in existing facilities, it gains manufacturing synergy. The firm should not decline an opportunity for lack of positive synergy — but positive synergy can enhance profits.

KEY IDEA

Synergy expresses the idea that 2 + 2 = 5.

Sometimes the firm enjoys *positive synergy* by embarking on a new growth path. Disney teaches firms to deliver top-notch customer service; Alcoa helps customers install and implement safety systems; New York's Metro-North Railroad rents space in train stations for restaurants/cafés.

When 2+2 is less than 4, *negative synergy* is at work; pursuing an opportunity may erode revenues and profits from existing products. Allergy-relief prescription drug Claritin was a major profit-maker for Schering Plough (SP); SP launched an over-the-counter version to reach the larger market for nonprescription allergy-relief medicines. Prescription Claritin sales dropped more than 40 percent.

CONTRIBUTION TO THE VENTURE PORTFOLIO

In addition to considering opportunities individually, the firm should assess all opportunities as elements in its *venture portfolio*. A firm with good cash flow but few growth businesses may invest heavily on longer-term, higher-risk options. A firm with little cash may focus on short-term, low/moderate-risk opportunities. Generally, conservatively managed firms invest in low-risk opportunities that pay off quickly. Aggressive firms accept greater risk for potentially higher returns that pay off in the long term. Novartis shifted R&D focus from drugs designed for major diseases where the underlying science was deficient (long term/high risk), to drugs backed by strong science even if potential markets were small (moderate term/moderate risk). Potential return and risk are typically correlated, but some opportunities may offer good returns at low risk.

INDEPENDENCE AND INTERDEPENDENCE. Suppose the firm is considering two opportunities, A and B. The firm may invest in A, in B, or in A plus B. The A plus B option has four potentially important interdependencies:

- **Costs.** Development and manufacturing costs are lower.
- **Marketing.** Sales of A may enhance or diminish sales of B.

- **Resources.** Uses fewer resources than A and B independently.
- **Technical.** Development success for A affects development success for B.

Interdependencies complicate opportunity selection, but are critical for developing the venture portfolio. Hence, in the semiconductor and consumer electronics industries, firms often invest in multiple related opportunities.[39] The firm should consider the opportunity's return-risk profile and the impact each opportunity has on the entire venture portfolio.[40]

IMPLEMENTING GROWTH STRATEGIES

KEY IDEA

A comprehensive approach for securing higher growth comprises:
- Strategy for growth
- Screening criteria
- **Implementation**

P&G funded Corporate New Ventures with $250 million seed money. Using *My Idea*, a corporate collaboration network, P&G employees funnel ideas to an innovation panel. Accepted projects tap into P&G's entire global resource base. Within two years, P&G launched 58 new products; Swiffer, the successful cleaning product, reached the market in 10 months — half the normal time.

Figure 7.6 shows several options for implementing the firm's growth strategy.[41] Until recently, many firms would not have entertained several of these approaches. P&G's successful Crest SpinBrush introduction was atypical for P&G; rather than an internal development, P&G purchased SpinBrush technology from an entrepreneur.

FIGURE 7.6
Implementing Growth Strategies

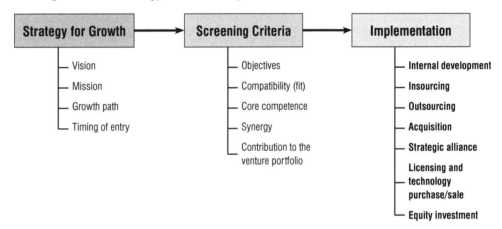

INTERNAL DEVELOPMENT

Many firms put significant effort into *internal development* of new products/services. Internal development is appropriate in all cells of the growth-path matrix and for all timing-of-entry options. Some evidence suggests a strong positive correlation between R&D spending and corporate profitability.[42]

Many firms place internal development in business units (versus corporate) so as to get closer to the market. Business-unit location clarifies responsibility for R&D, but can *silo* development and minimize synergies among businesses. Properly harnessed, interbusiness synergies can be extensive. P&G developed several products: Crest Whitestrips (teeth whitener); Dawn Power Dissolver (pot and dish cleaner); Mr. Clean AutoDry (car-wash sprayer); Olay Daily Facials (cleansing cloths).

Internal development is not just for technologists and engineers; marketing can play a major role in directing R&D efforts by infusing external insight at all developmental stages. Said a senior Pfizer executive, "We always have marketing people on our early product development teams. They interact with researchers from the first preclinical experiments in the laboratory.

Before that, we have marketing people and researchers looking together at the drug market and asking, 'Where is the most potential to help a lot of people and sell a lot of medicine?'"[43]

Advantages of internal development over alternative growth modes are:

- **Control.** The firm has control over the entire development process. The firm secures required resources and makes all decisions about suppliers and distributors. The firm solves human-resource shortfalls by hiring and acculturating newcomers.

- **Cost.** Internal development is typically less expensive than obtaining new products by acquisition and other means.

Disadvantages of internal development are:

- **Expertise.** The firm must successfully direct R&D efforts, or the resulting products may require commercialization skills the firm does not possess.

- **Resources.** Some resources may be unavailable, or too expensive to develop/acquire.

- **Time.** Market windows are increasingly short; internal development takes time.

To address these disadvantages, some firms modify internal development processes by streamlining bureaucracies and tapping employees' creative potential. They may reward employees based on the success of products their ideas generate — like P&G's *My Idea.*[44]

KEY IDEA

Options for implementing growth strategy include:
- Internal development
- Insourcing
- Outsourcing
- Acquisition
- Strategic alliance
- Licensing and technology purchase/sale
- Equity investment

INSOURCING

The firm captures more added value in the supply chain by undertaking additional activities in developing, producing, marketing, distributing, and promoting. The firm can expand upstream by conducting supplier activities — *backward integration*, or downstream by conducting customer activities — *forward integration.*

Adjacencies (activities closely related to core competencies) are prime insourcing candidates and may help develop new core competencies. Prudential fired its advertising agencies and now develops all advertising in-house; Amazon launched several imprints like Montlake Romance to publish digital, physical, and audio books; Netflix produces original content. Opportunities for insourcing evolve as profit pools in the supply chain migrate. Managers should evaluate where to invest in building new competencies.[45] Coca-Cola and Merck, respectively, demonstrate successful and unsuccessful insourcing:

> Historically, Coca-Cola focused on syrup manufacture and brand building. More recently, Coca-Cola acquired bottlers. Forward integration provided increased flexibility and enabled closer relationships with major customers.
>
> Merck insourced pharmaceutical distribution by acquiring Medco, the largest U.S. drug-benefits manager. Merck-Medco (MM) became a lightning rod for accusations that Medco favored Merck products over lower-priced competitor drugs. Ten years after acquisition, Merck dissolved MM.

OUTSOURCING

Outsourcing is the opposite of insourcing — the firm engages other firms to undertake activities it previously conducted in-house. With outsourcing, the firm can better focus resources on delivering customer value and securing differential advantage. Firms outsource a wide range of activities like managing information systems and technology infrastructure, accounts payable, benefits management and payroll, and procurement.

A common contemporary outsourcing aspect is *offshoring* — contracting with non-U.S-based firms. A common area is customer service operations. We're sure many readers have called a help desk and spoken with someone in India, Malaysia, or the Philippines. Cost reduction typically drives offshoring, but partners in different time zones can also provide scalable, flexible staffing. Quality control is important, especially when customer care is involved; Capital One dropped Wipro's outbound telemarketing service for quality reasons.[46]

Some home electronics firms like Apple focus major internal efforts on R&D, design, and marketing, but outsource manufacturing. Boeing mainly assembles aircraft; contractors (often foreign) produce airplane parts like the fuselage and wings. Downsides include:

- **Manufacturing.** Outsourced suppliers may also outsource. The supply chain becomes fragmented and difficult to manage; quality can be a serious issue. Delivery delays for Boeing's Dreamliner were largely due to excessive supplier outsourcing.

- **Marketing.** The outsourced supplier absorbs the firm's technological expertise. The supplier could supply a competitor, or itself become a strong competitor. Taiwan's Acer and Asustek (PCs) and HTC (cell phones) grew in this manner.[47]

MARKETING QUESTION

Why did Facebook pay so much for WhatsApp — $21.8 billion?

ACQUISITION

Facebook Acquired WhatsApp for $19 billion.

We learned earlier that the firm can use *acquisitions* — individual business units or entire firms — to gain competencies that provide customer value and secure differential advantage. Generally, growth by acquisition has a speed advantage — the firm gains immediate access to new products and/or markets. The firm also gains supporting infrastructure — human resources, operational capabilities, and systems and processes.[48] Firms that grow extensively by acquisition include Cisco, GE, J&J, Microsoft, and Oracle. Former IBM CEO Lou Gerstner said:

> *IBM made 90 acquisitions during my tenure. The most successful were those that fit neatly into an organic growth plan. IBM's purchase of Informix is a great example. We were neck-and-neck with Oracle in the database business; Informix, another database company, had lost its momentum and market leadership. We didn't need to buy Informix to get into the database business or to shore up a weak position. However, we did acquire a set of customers more quickly and more efficiently than we could have following a go-it-alone strategy.[49]*

To broaden its product line, eBay made more than $6 billion of acquisitions — Baazee.com, Bill Me Later, Brands4Friends, EachNet, GSI, Half.com, iBazar, Kurant (Prostores), Marktplaats.nl, PayPal (since divested), Rent.com, Shopping.com, Skype (acquired by Microsoft), StubHub, StumbleUpon, Tradera.[50] Pfizer acquired Warner-Lambert and its cholesterol-lowering drug Lipitor, taken daily by more than 10 million people in the U.S.[51]

But acquisitions are no panacea. Acquiring successful firms/business units can be expensive; marrying the cultures of acquired and acquiring firms/businesses may also be difficult, especially when the acquirer is well established and the acquiree is younger and entrepreneurial. Uncertainty and delays can also diminish an acquisition's value:

> General Mills (GenM) took 18 months to complete its Pillsbury acquisition from Diageo. During this period, Diageo cut back marketing efforts; retailers complained about service reductions. Many Pillsbury salespeople resigned, unsure of their futures. By the time GenM completed the merger, rivals had cut severely into Pillsbury's market positions. While GenM was distracted, Kellogg launched many new cereal products and increased market share.

MARKETING QUESTION

Many U.S. car-rental firms have changed ownership in recent years. Trace this evolution; why did it occur?

Acquisitions may improve margins via employee layoffs and other economies when integrating corporate staffs, purchasing, R&D, sales forces, warehousing, and other functions; Pfizer reduced costs by $1 billion following the Wyeth acquisition. But losing employees at an acquired firm can be a significant issue. Credit Suisse First Boston acquired DLJ from AXA for $13 billion; rival Swiss bank UBS quickly hired away 20 percent of DLJ's Los Angeles-based investment bankers. Cisco believes employees are the most significant asset it acquires and works especially hard to retain human resources by offering opportunity and freedom for creativity.

Some acquisitions add value; some do not. Value creation depends on the specific acquisition, but we can usefully distinguish between two very different types:

MAJOR ACQUISITIONS. These multibillion-dollar acquisitions often make the headlines: Alcan's acquisition of Pechiney and BHP Billiton's subsequent acquisition of Alcan (aluminum); AT&T/DirecTV; Comcast/Time Warner Cable; Delta Airlines/Northwest; GE/Alstom; United Airlines/Continental. But bigger is not always better; many business leaders and scholars have spoken out against these types of acquisition. They assert CEO hubris often drives $100 million-plus acquisitions.[52] Academic studies suggest that 70 percent of acquisitions are dilutive for the acquiring firm's shareholders, and that *in the heat of the chase* acquirers typically overpay.[53] Sir George Bull (former Diageo CEO) asserted that *organic growth* (internal development) created greater value for shareholders, and that acquisitions often destroy value. Eli Lilly (pharmaceuticals) reduced the accounting (book) value of its distribution arm (McKesson) by $2.4 billion; given the $4.1 billion acquisition price, this was a stark admission that Lilly overpaid. Even worse, HP wrote down $9 billion of its $12 billion Autonomy acquisition!

Government oversight on large acquisitions can cause major realignments of products and markets. Glaxo Wellcome and SmithKline Beecham (SKB) completed a $68 billion merger to form GlaxoSmithKline (GSK), the world's second-largest pharmaceutical firm. To pass *regulatory muster*, SKB sold rights to Kytril (chemotherapy) and Famvir (herpes). GSK also had to resolve its dominant market position for antismoking drugs — Nicorette gum, NicoDerm patches, and prescription drug Zyban.

SMALL *FILL-IN* ACQUISITIONS. Small *fill-in* acquisitions complement an existing strategy. Amazon was unsuccessful in selling footwear online, so it acquired Zappos.com (leading online footwear retailer). IBM's experience (previous page) exemplifies this type of acquisition; Cisco and Oracle are other good examples of firms making many small acquisitions. Research suggests that modest acquisitions are the most successful — they are easier to implement and acquirers may get good deals.[54] A firm making many small acquisitions gains experience and does a better job of identifying candidates, managing bids, and integrating acquired entities.

STRATEGIC ALLIANCE

Generally, *strategic alliances* address poor product-company fit and/or poor company-market fit without the capital investment and risks inherent in acquisitions.[147v] A good alliance partner complements firm strengths and/or compensates for weakness; the combined entity is stronger than either firm acting alone. IBM has a strategic alliance with Apple to bring IBM services to the iPhone's iOS platform. Other popular alliances are between small, innovative firms and well-established firms with strong marketing, good customer reputations, and deep pockets. BMS has several successful alliances: Other firms make basic drug discoveries; BMS conducts final development and marketing. IBM and P&G also have successful alliances:

> IBM's software group has many strategic alliances with application software specialists like Siebel Systems (owned by Oracle) and SAP. Alliances add billions of dollars in incremental revenues from hardware, services, database programs, and middleware.[55]

> P&G has successfully launched several new products developed by strategic alliances and from buying/licensing technology. Included are Glad Press'n Seal (supersticky food wrap), Mr. Clean Magic Eraser (spot remover), Olay Regenerist (antiaging cream), and Swiffer Duster (microfiber picker-upper).

Some alliances embrace many firms. Airline industry alliances allow travelers one-stop shopping for international trips; correspondingly, alliance members secure customers. Star Alliance comprises almost 30 airlines including Air Canada, Lufthansa, Singapore, and United; the somewhat smaller SkyTeam includes Aeroflot, Air France, Delta, and KLM; OneWorld members include American, British Airways, Cathay Pacific, Japan Airlines, and Qantas.

MARKETING QUESTION

Startup biotech firm Clinuvel developed Scenesse. Scenesse promises to provide significant relief to patients suffering from ultraviolet-light diseases. How would you advise Clinuvel **[628p]** to proceed in drug development, regulatory approval, marketing and sales?

Strategic alliances can be an attractive way to secure needed resources. But like acquisitions, strategic alliances are no panacea; many fail due to changed objectives by one or more partners, incompatible organizational cultures, insufficient resources, lack of planning, and/or managerial attention.[56] Ericsson and STMicroelectronics ended the ST-Ericsson joint venture because of commercial failure. What appears attractive in theory can be difficult to execute in practice.

Wessex Press (WP) formed a strategic alliance with major textbook publisher CPM. CPM has many textbook titles that sell insufficient copies to meet profit targets. But WP can make profits on small volumes. CPM finds a home for authors it would otherwise orphan. WP makes profits. Both CPM and WP gain.

LICENSING AND TECHNOLOGY PURCHASE/SALE

Licensing and technology purchase are alternative ways to access technology developed by others. Firms seeking technologies should execute a rigorous search process. In licensing, the licensor owns the technology; the licensee typically pays a minimum royalty (fixed payment regardless of use) plus an earned royalty rate based on volume (units/dollars) or profits. Technology purchasers typically pay a fixed price to own the technology. In both cases, the acquiring firm avoids R&D risks and expenses, but may pay a high price to access successful new technology. Forest Laboratories employs a licensing strategy that enhances its product portfolio and market presence[57]:

Forest Laboratories (FL) licenses, develops, and sells drugs that small pharmaceutical firms develop. FL's drug portfolio includes Aerobid (asthma), Celexa (depression), Infasurf (respiratory distress syndrome in premature babies), and Tiazac (angina and hypertension).

Conversely, the firm may grow revenues and profits by selling or licensing technology. Sometimes firms sell products directly in favored markets but license technology to gain market access for other uses, or for the same use in different geographies. Monsanto employs this approach for genetically modified seeds. Firms owning unexploited technologies can earn significant revenues from these unused assets. Nokia's Alcatel-Lucent patent portfolio earns hundreds of millions of dollars annually; IBM earns billions.

EQUITY INVESTMENT

Many firms augment internal development efforts by making *equity investments* — taking partial ownership in startups. Sometimes firms form or *incubate* startups by spinning off their own successful product development efforts. Typically, the firm retains the ability to increase its equity position later. Xerox's program was highly successful:

Classically, in the 1970s and 1980s, Xerox's Palo Alto Research Center (PARC) developed many new technologies that Xerox failed to commercialize.[58] Xerox Technology Ventures (XTV) (now closed) invested in firms focusing on Xerox-related technologies — electronic publishing, document processing, electronic imaging, workstation and computer peripherals, software, and office automation. XTV earned a net internal rate of return greater than 50 percent.[59]

KEY IDEA

Increasingly, firms employ multiple approaches for securing growth.

IMPLEMENTING GROWTH STRATEGIES IN THE MODERN CORPORATION

We learned the components of a strategy for growth — *vision, mission, growth path, timing of entry*. Together, these elements form a set of lenses the firm can use to approach markets and identify, generate, and decide to invest (or not) in opportunities. Each entry strategy demands quite different capabilities for success. Maintaining contrasting growth strategies in a single business unit is very difficult.[60] Many full-service airlines have failed with low-cost carrier entries — Song (Delta) and Ted (United). Discount broker Schwab stumbled badly when trying to serve both discount clients and high-net-worth clients via its U.S. Trust acquisition.

MARKETING QUESTION

Develop a table for assessing pros and cons of each way to implement a strategy for growth.

Today, leading firms use multiple approaches to implement growth strategies, often built on *repeatability*. These firms leverage skills in internal development, in/outsourcing, acquisitions, strategic alliances, and/or equity investment. Hence, they are better able to address challenges and results are more predictable. P&G and J&J are good examples. J&J invests significantly in internal R&D and regularly introduces several hundred new products annually, developed in its laboratories. Yet, J&J purchased Cougar Biotechnology ($1 billion) and Pfizer's consumer health business ($16 billion). J&J acquired brands like Bengay, Listerine, Rolaids, Sudafed. J&J also paid well over $1 billion for research alliances with Elan Pharmaceuticals (Ireland) and Crucel (The Netherlands).

KEY MESSAGES

MARKETING QUESTION

What other messages did you glean from this chapter?

Marketing's first imperative is to determine and recommend which markets to address. A marketing perspective should infuse critical strategic decisions — marketing should focus on two areas:

• Identify potential opportunities.
• Provide marketing input for other strategic actions the firm is contemplating.

A systematic approach to developing, selecting, and implementing opportunities has three elements:

• Strategy for growth — frameworks to help decide which businesses to be in/not in:
  • Vision — description of an ideal future state for the firm/business unit
  • Mission — directly guides search for opportunity
  • Growth path — a focused approach to identifying opportunities; trades off return and risk
  • Timing of entry — market-entry options related to product life cycle stage
• Screening criteria — ways of evaluating individual opportunities:
  • Objectives — growth, risk, timing, stability, flexibility
  • Compatibility (fit) — product-market fit, product-company fit, company-market fit
  • Core competence — capabilities to achieve differential advantage
  • Synergy — 2 + 2 = 5
  • Contribution to the venture portfolio
• Implementation — specific actions to implement growth strategy:
  • Internal development — new products/services developed via firm efforts
  • Insourcing — capturing greater value-added, upstream or downstream
  • Outsourcing — engaging other firms to conduct needed activities
  • Acquisition — purchasing a firm/business unit
  • Strategic alliance — agreement with a partner firm to jointly exploit an opportunity
  • Licensing and technology purchase/sale — accessing technology developed by others/earn revenues
  • Equity investment — taking ownership positions in startups

VIDEOS AND AUDIOS

For complimentary material, see Axcess Capon codes at www.axcessvids.com

Being Entrepreneurs	**281v**	Steve Jobs, Bill Gates	Apple, Microsoft
Lessons from Entrepreneurs	**839v**	Harvard iLab	
Marketing Imperative 1	**723a**	Noel Capon	Columbia Business School

QUESTIONS FOR STUDY AND DISCUSSION

Can you answer the questions implied by this chapter's learning outcomes? Check!

1. Develop a *strategy for growth* for Alphabet including vision, mission, growth path, and timing of entry. Identify growth options for Alphabet. Define and set standards for measuring Alphabet's success.

2. From your knowledge of business, identify current-day examples of pioneer, follow-the-leader, segmenter, and me-too entry strategies.

3. In the early 2000s, MySpace was by far and away the leading social networking website. Yet MySpace declined and Facebook became market leader. Use the concepts in this chapter to discern why MySpace declined and Facebook rose so dramatically.

4. American, British Airways, Delta, United, and Virgin Atlantic compete on North Atlantic routes. Round-trip, business-class fares list for $8,000 to $9,000, but major corporate buyers may pay as little as $3,000. In 2005, Eos and MAXJet started offering low-price, all-business-class, New York-to-London (Stansted) flights. MAXJet priced flights from $4,000 to $1,500 for bulk purchases; Eos prices were somewhat higher, but less than the majors. In 2008, both Eos and MAXJet filed for bankruptcy. Did Eos and MAXJet identify a market opportunity? How do you assess Eos' and MAXJet's strategies?

5. Is Twitter successful? Why or why not?

6. What is the marketing significance of the question, "What business are we in?" How does the answer help decide what markets to address?

7. Select a product in which you are interested. Alternatively, consider *Managing Marketing in the 21st Century*. Lay out a strategy for growth — vision, mission, growth path, timing of entry.

TRUE/FALSE QUESTIONS

Answers on page A1 and at www.axcessvids.com — 547p 📖

1. Typically, successful firms evolve their missions over time. ❏ TRUE ❏ FALSE

2. Segmenter firms enter rapidly growing markets on the heels of pioneers. ❏ TRUE ❏ FALSE

3. Me-too-ers enter mature markets with limited product lines. They base their low-price/low-cost strategies on value engineering, efficient high-volume production, low overhead, aggressive procurement, and great attention to detail. ❏ TRUE ❏ FALSE

4. Core competencies are capabilities, knowledge, skills, and resources the firm possesses.
   ❏ TRUE ❏ FALSE

5. Positive synergy reflects the notion that 2 + 2 is equal to 4. ❏ TRUE ❏ FALSE

MULTIPLE CHOICE QUESTIONS

Answers on page A1 and at www.axcessvids.com — 746p 📖

1. A successful follow-the-leader strategy must have all of the following criteria EXCEPT:
   a. a vision of serving a narrow market segment
   b. the ability to differentiate its offer by delivering superior customer value
   c. the will and persistence to succeed
   d. financial strength and commitment to outspend the pioneer

2. _____ enter established markets in late growth by adding value for specific segments.

    a. Pioneers
    b. Follow-the-leaders
    c. Segmenters
    d. Me-too-ers

3. With _____, the firm captures more value-added in the supply chain by undertaking additional activities in developing, producing, marketing, distributing, and promoting.

    a. insourcing
    b. offshoring
    c. outsourcing
    d. downsizing

4. Which of the following is NOT a disadvantage of internal development as an option for implementing a firm's growth strategy?

    a. control
    b. expertise
    c. resources
    d. time

CHAPTER 8

MARKET SEGMENTATION AND TARGETING

For complimentary material, see Axcess Capon codes at www.axcessvids.com

LEARNING OUTCOMES

When you have completed this chapter, you will be able to:

- Deconstruct a market into readily distinguishable customer groups.
- Recognize differences between market segments and customer segments.
- Select a market-segmentation scheme to better understand market opportunities.
- Understand needs and preferences common to customers in a market segment.
- Develop criteria for constructing *good* market segments.
- Assess identifying characteristics for market segments.
- Address several complex issues in developing and engaging market segments.
- Know where *standardized market segments* can be useful.
- Decide which segments to target for marketing effort.
- Appreciate the value of perceptual maps.
- Understand how different size firms should approach market segmentation.

OPENING CASE: MARRIOTT HOTELS, RESORTS, AND SUITES

In 1985, Marriott Hotels, Resorts, and Suites was a domestic (U.S.) mid- to large-size hotel chain, managing 67,034 rooms at 160 properties. Marriott decided to enhance traveler value by segmenting the market, then targeting selected segments each with a different hospitality brand. Then, as now, Marriott was the flagship brand. Each new brand supports Marriott's overall brand identity — individually distinctive, collectively powerful, a commitment to superior customer service — and trains employees to have a passion for service. Employees:

- *Do whatever it takes to take care of customers.*
- *Pay extraordinary attention to detail.*
- *Take pride in their physical surroundings.*
- *Use their creativity to find new ways to meet the needs of customers.*

Marriott believes all customers require a base service level, but that customers differ in their willingness to pay for different levels of comfort and luxury. Management also knows that many customers stay a few nights, but a growing number, like businesspeople on assignment, require accommodations for several weeks. Recognizing the varying needs of hotel customers, Marriott was the first major hotel chain to base its strategy on market segmentation. Marriott grew new brands organically, but implemented its strategy in part by acquisition.

Marriott's flagship brand continues to target customers needing fine restaurants, meeting rooms, athletic facilities, and other upscale amenities.[1] But Marriott added several additional brands addressing different segments:

- **AC Hotels** — *upper-moderate-tier lifestyle hotel brand for cosmopolitan, design-conscious, younger travelers in great city locations*
- **Autograph** — *high-personality independent hotel*
- **Courtyard** — *moderately priced hotel for business travelers, providing amenities like business services, exercise room, and a stylish but casual bistro restaurant for breakfast*
- **Edition Hotels** — *personal, intimate, individualized, and unique lodging experience*
- **ExecuStay** — *furnished apartments for stays of 30 days or more*
- **Fairfield Inn & Suites** — *inexpensively priced, high-quality hotel easily accessible by car, on or near the U.S. main interstate highway system*
- **Renaissance Hotels** — *international hotel with upscale amenities*
- **Residence Inn** — *extended-stay hotel for job relocation, job assignment, and government contracting*
- **Ritz-Carlton** — *the ultimate in luxury hotels in urban centers*
- **SpringHill Suites** — *all-suites hotel at an upper-moderate price*
- **TownePlace Suites** — *similar to Residence Inn, but lower priced*

Case Question

Each Marriott brand has a distinct personality and style. Marriott works hard to communicate the essence and strength of each brand so that target customers know what to expect. There is some customer crossover, but each brand focuses on a defined market segment. Internal competition is small.

How do you assess Marriott's approach to segmenting the hotel market? Can you think of alternative approaches that may present market opportunities?

Marriott has achieved extraordinary results from its segmentation and targeting strategy. The Courtyard brand manages more rooms than the entire firm managed in 1985. In 2015, Marriott managed 700,000 rooms at 4,000 properties in 80 countries. Twenty percent of Marriott's rooms are outside the U.S. In 2014, Marriott revenues were well in excess of $13 billion; net income — $750 million.

Market segments and market segmentation are fundamental marketing concepts. Customers in a market either have a variety of different needs, or have similar needs with different priorities. A *market segment* is a subset of the total market that comprises a group of actual and potential customers with similar (homogeneous) need profiles, seeking similar sets of benefits/values, with similar levels of priority. *Market segmentation* is the process of grouping together customers in a market for the purpose of forming market segments.

A specifically designed market offer satisfies customers in one market segment; a different market segment requires a different market offer. To design and produce effective market offers, the firm must understand each segment's need profile. A firm intent on serving a large market like snack foods must make several market offers, targeted at various market segments, to meet different customer preferences. Typically, a single offer — like potato chips — fails to satisfy the many diverse customers who purchase *snack foods*.

Because customers have different need profiles, marketers must complete three separate, but related, strategic marketing tasks:

1. **Identify market segments.** Figure out the best way to group customers based on market, customer, competitor, and complementer insight — Chapters 3, 4 — using approaches from Chapter 6.
2. **Target market segments.** Resources are always scarce. The firm must decide which segments to target for effort; rarely can a firm address all market segments.

Note an important distinction between these tasks. *Identifying* market segments is creative and analytic. *Targeting* market segments requires a strategic decision. The firm applies resources to some market segments and ignores others. Identifying and targeting the *right* market segment(s) is a crucial strategic marketing task.

3. **Develop market-segment strategy.** The firm develops a market-segment strategy, including a positioning statement, for each target segment — Chapter 9. Typically, the firm's *market strategy* combines several *market-segment strategies*.

Section IV — Chapters 12 through 24 — focuses on implementing market and market-segment strategies.

KEY IDEA

Critical strategic marketing decisions are:
• Identify market segments
• Target market segments
• Develop market-segment strategy

THE CHANGING VIEW

OLD WAY	NEW WAY
Crude market segmentation	Precise market segmentation
Databases poorly developed	Databases central to segmentation
Few large segments	Many small segments — tend to segments-of-one
Intuition-driven segmentation	Analytically driven segmentation
Low levels of analytic expertise	Increasingly sophisticated analyses
Market segments based mainly on demographics	Market segments based on many variable types
Segmentation applied mainly in FMCG	Segmentation in B2B and B2C, public and non-profit, nation-states, politics, personal careers
Segmentation focuses primarily on consumers	Segmentation extends to multiple customer levels and other firm stakeholders

Two couples visit an electrical appliance superstore — each couple wants a kitchen range. Presumably they have similar needs, but let's look more closely. Couple A's new house will be built in six months — they are evaluating appliances to install in a high-tech kitchen. Couple B just received a call from the babysitter. A broken water pipe flooded the kitchen and ruined the range; what should she do about the children's dinner? These couples have different requirements and priorities. Each couple needs a range, but there's a big difference between a dream home and an emergency replacement!

THE MARKET-SEGMENTATION PROCESS

Most National car-rental customers are corporate executives; most Alamo customers are leisure travelers. National and Alamo's parent company combined their operations — airport counters, buses, rental agents, automobiles — and displayed dual Alamo/National logos widely. Customers had difficulty distinguishing the brands. Complaints doubled, especially from National customers, who paid 10 to 20 percent more than Alamo customers.[2]

KEY IDEA

Market segmentation is a conceptual and analytic process. Market segmentation is critical for developing and implementing an effective market strategy.

Market segmentation is a conceptual and analytic process critical for developing and implementing effective market strategies. In the market-segmentation process, the firm groups actual and potential customers in a market into various *market segments*. The firm then chooses which segments to *target* for effort. Then, the firm must *position* itself in each target segment — segmentation, targeting, positioning (STP) — and develop a *market-segment strategy*. When the segment strategy is set, the firm designs, then implements, a suitable market offer.

Figure 8.1 describes the process of designing and implementing market offers for each target segment. By executing the process well, the firm:

- Secures better insight into the market, customers, competitors, company, and complementers — particularly, customer needs — and forms stronger planning *assumptions* — Transition to Strategic Marketing.
- Develops a clearer focus on market strategy by targeting specific market segments.
- Identifies opportunities to customize offers for target segments.
- Designs better offers comprising product, promotion, distribution, and price.
- Secures superior differential advantage, and greater customer satisfaction and loyalty.
- Uses resources more efficiently and earns higher profits.

FIGURE 8.1
Segmentation, Targeting, and Positioning — STP

The fundamental premise underlying market segmentation is this: In any broadly defined market, customer need profiles are heterogeneous (different). Customers have different needs and/or different priorities of needs. They seek different benefits/values based on these differing need profiles. The segmentation task is to divide the market into several discrete groups of customers, each with relatively homogeneous (similar) need profiles. These customer need profiles differ from segment to segment, so an individual customer falls into one, but only one, segment.[3] Customers requiring the rugged strength of a Panasonic Toughbook are quite differ-

KEY IDEA

The market-segmentation process identifies groups of customers. When segmentation is done well, customers within a segment have similar need profiles. Customers in different segments have different need profiles.

ent from those attracted to mini-laptops like Asustek's Eee PC! But Alamo/National's parent (previous boxed insert) does not seem to understand that the market comprises two distinctly different segments.[4]

Market segmentation is often a compromise. At one extreme, the firm develops one strategy, one positioning, and one offer for the entire market — *mass marketing*. This one-size-fits-all approach is the most efficient, lowest-cost way to address a broad market. But customer need profiles are typically heterogeneous, so many customers would be unsatisfied. At the other extreme, the firm develops a unique/specialized offer for each customer. Such customization ensures a good match between customer needs and firm offers. But firms rarely earn sufficient revenues to offset development and implementation costs. Market segmentation operates between these extremes. The firm identifies homogeneous groups of customers — *market segments* — with similar need profiles: The firm targets one or more of these segments, and develops specific strategies, positionings, and offers to satisfy the needs of customers in those segments.

MARKETING QUESTION

Why would a startup like LMM create customer segments? Do its market-segmentation and customer-segmentation approaches provide valuable insight?

LEVELS OF SEGMENTATION

Are you a *Kinda, Sorta,* or *Alota*? San Francisco sock firm LittleMissMatched (LMM) identified a unique customer need in *tweens* (around 11 years old) — desire to resist fashion orthodoxy. LMM offers this segment color-drenched, mismatched socks in packs of three.

Within the tweens market segment, LMM identified and advises three finer-grained customer segments. *Kinda* customers are conservative — pick socks from the same color wave, creating a slightly off-kilter look. The *Alota* segment is wildest — mix and match colors, patterns, and styles. *Sortas* are in between. LMM's promotional book — *My MissMatched Life* — celebrates the joys of nonconformity.

Segmentation forms smaller, more discrete groups out of a whole. The firm chooses a broad market to address — Marketing Imperative 1 — then identifies several market segments. Within any single market segment, the firm may segment further, forming *customer segments*. Some practitioners define the first-level grouping as market segmentation, and the finer-grained, second-level segmentation as customer segmentation.

LMM identified the *tweens* market segment — the core need was a desire to resist fashion orthodoxy. LMM also identified three customer segments, defined by level of resistance — *Kinda, Sorta, Alota*. The important idea: Segmentation can operate at different levels as the firm decides where to place its marketing efforts.

We reinforce this idea with a simple example. Suppose half of the students in your class prefer *hot tea* and half prefer *iced tea*. Figure 8.2 (p. 206) (left) shows a tea supplier that *does not understand* this segmentation and so offers the best *average* product — *warm tea*. Without alternatives, students wanting tea will purchase warm tea. They may desire hot tea or iced tea, but at least warm tea is tea!

Suppose a new supplier understands the segmentation. This supplier offers hot tea — the hot-tea students switch from warm tea to hot tea. If a third supplier enters with iced tea, the iced-tea students also switch. The warm-tea supplier quickly loses customers because its competitors are more insightful about market segmentation.

How should the original supplier respond? The hot-tea and iced-tea suppliers focus on different segments and are doing just fine. One response is to segment at an even deeper level. Some students may like sweetened tea; others like unsweetened tea. Figure 8.2 (right) shows how to deconstruct the market into four segments — *hot sweetened tea, hot unsweetened tea, iced sweetened tea, iced unsweetened tea*. A focus on one or more of these segments better satisfies customer needs. The firm may have to creatively segment the market at increasingly finer levels to beat competitors.

....
FIGURE 8.2
*Benefits of Finer-
Grained Segmentation:
Tea Market Example*

MARKETING
QUESTION

What firms demonstrate
the *warm-tea* syndrome —
address markets generally,
even though customer groups
have different need profiles?

DEVELOPING MARKET SEGMENTS

The firm can approach the market-segmentation process from two directions: *customer needs* first or *candidate descriptor (segmentation) variables* first. The firm can also use *qualitative* or *quantitative* approaches.

CUSTOMER NEEDS FIRST. The firm identifies differing customer need profiles, then uses these profiles to form groups. Customers within each group have relatively homogeneous (similar) need profiles, but the various groups have heterogeneous (different) profiles. The second task is to select descriptor (segmentation) variables that identify these groups.

KEY IDEA

The best approach for form-ing market segments is to group customers based on need profiles. The firm should then use descriptor (segmentation) variables to identify different segments.

AT&T's data system organization identified three market segments based on complexity of customer communications needs:

• Tier 1 segment — needs satisfied by common *off-the-shelf* products.

• Tier 2 segment — needs satisfied by *off-the-shelf* products plus some options.

• Tier 3 segment — requires tailored solutions.

These segments seem sensible — each segment's needs differ from the other segments. AT&T's challenge is to identify distinguishing customer characteristics for each segment. Illustration — Tier 1: What characteristics define customers wanting *off-the-shelf* products? Are these small companies or large companies? Do they compete in specific industries? Are they located in specific geographic areas?

Sometimes the link between customer needs and distinguishing characteristics is straight-forward. Table 8.1 shows that the benefits/values consumers want from skin-care products depend on age.

Customer Need/Required Benefits and Values	Age-Based Market Segments					
	14–18	19–29	30–39	40–49	50–64	65 and over
Beauty	5	4	**1**	2	2	3
Confidence	2	2	3	3	3	4
Economy	4	5	7	7	6	5
Health	6	6	4	4	4	2
Sexual Allure	3	**1**	2	5	5	6
Status	**1**	3	6	6	7	7
Youthfulness	7	7	5	**1**	**1**	**1**

....
TABLE 8.1
*Market Segments in the
Female Skin-Care Market:
Importance Rank Order of
Customer Needs/Required
Benefits/Values by Age-
Based Market Segments*

MARKETING
QUESTION

CANDIDATE DESCRIPTOR (SEGMENTATION) VARIABLES FIRST. The firm uses candidate descriptor (segmentation) variables to construct customer groups. Then it searches for homo-geneous (similar) need profiles within each group and heterogeneous (different) need profiles across groups. If the firm cannot find *good* need profiles — similarity within groups and differ-ences across groups — it tries again with different descriptors. Table 8.2 (p. 207) shows *candi-date descriptor (segmentation) variables* in four categories — geographic, demographic, behavioral, sociopsychological.

Review the data in Table 8.1. Suppose your firm decides to target the 14–18 and 40–49 age groups. How would you attract customers in each seg-ment? How would your offers differ? How are the three over-40 segments similar?

<table>
<tr><td>**TABLE 8.2**
Examples of Candidate Descriptor (Segmentation) Variables</td><td colspan="2">

Variable Type	Examples of Descriptor Variables
Geographic	Country, region, county size, city or Standard Metropolitan Statistical Area (SMSA)[5] size, population density, climate
Demographic	B2C — age, education, family life-cycle stage, family size, gender, income, language, national origin, occupation, race, religion, social class, wealth. B2B — balance sheet items, firm size, growth, industry, profitability, legal entity, length of time at location, number of years in business
Behavioral	Composition/type of purchase decision, decision-making practice, decision-making unit, new or existing user, use occasion,[6] user situation. B2B — procurement organization — centralized/decentralized, and power structure — like engineering dominated, financially dominated.
Sociopsychological	B2C — attitudes; life stage; lifestyle characteristics like activities, interests, and opinions; personality (ambitiousness, authoritarianism, autonomy, compulsiveness, conservatism, gregariousness, leadership); sexual orientation. B2B — inward/outward orientation, organizational climate and culture.
</td></tr>
</table>

KEY IDEA

Four categories of candidate descriptor (segmentation) variables may define market segments:

- Geographic
- Demographic
- Behavioral
- Sociopsychological

Table 8.3 shows examples of customer groups formed with these descriptor (segmentation) variables.

TABLE 8.3
Examples of Descriptor (Segmentation) Variables and Groups

Variable Type	Variable	Examples of Groups
Demographic (B2C)	Education	Grade school or less, some high school, high school graduate, some college, college graduate
Demographic (B2B)	Firm size	*Fortune* 500, *Fortune* 501 to 1000, sales > $100 million, sales $50 to $100 million, sales < $50 million
Sociopsychological (B2C)	Life stage	Single, just married, married with children, divorced with children, empty-nester couple, empty-nesters with grandchildren, widow/widower[7]

MARKETING QUESTION

How do *Millennials* differ from other age-based market segments? In partnership with ABC, Univision (Spanish-language network) launched a new bilingual TV channel — *Fusion* — to address Millennials. How do you assess Univision's market entry? (How hospitality firms address Millennials [654p].)

Geography and demography are popular categories of descriptor (segmentation) variables.[8] Many retailers like Macy's cater to local tastes. MTV frequently uses country or geography when tailoring customer offers: MTV operates 38 separate nationally focused channels like MTV Romania and MTV Indonesia. In the Philippines, local hamburger chain Jollibee significantly outsells McDonald's by using national origin and demographics to better meet Filipino needs. Jollibee's stores in Asia and California target customers of Filipino descent. Successful uses of geography, ethnic origin, and/or religion as descriptor (segmentation) variables include:

Geography, Ethnic Origin, and Religion as Descriptor (Segmentation) Variables

- **Automobile distributor ACLN developed a $200 million business shipping used cars to North and West Africa.**

- **65 percent of 54 million U.S. Hispanics are of Mexican descent. Banamex (Mexican bank) allows these customers to charge household appliances to U.S. credit cards for delivery in Mexico.**

- **P&G grew Gain to a $1 billion laundry detergent brand by recognizing the importance of fragrance to Hispanics.**

- **Pollo Campero is a Guatemalan fast-food franchise. At the Guatemala City airport, Guatemalan expatriates stock up before flying home, often buying hundreds of chicken pieces, sometimes for resale. Campero also has more than 300 stores in 13 countries (Latin America, Europe, India, Middle East, China) and 15 U.S. states.**

- **SABMiller targets ethnic minorities by importing foreign brands to the U.S. In Chicago and other cities with large Polish communities, SABMiller offers the popular Polish beer, Tyskie.**

- **Samara Produce (SP) (southern California) grows high-quality okra, chilies, opo squash, and daikon radishes. SP targets Indians, Pakistanis, and Bangladeshis in North America. SP ships vegetables to Chicago, New York, Toronto, Vancouver, and London.**

- **U.S. Muslims cluster in relatively few geographic areas. American Halal Meat (East Newark, NJ) slaughters animals according to Islamic teachings for butchers and restaurants serving Muslim customers.**

Forming groups using geographic and demographic variables is relatively easy, but the resulting groups may not be *good* market segments. Behavioral and sociopsychological variables are often more effective. Suppose a sneaker firm has four customers: male – 20 years, male – 40 years, female – 20 years, female – 40 years. How should the sneaker firm segment? By gender or by age? Neither may be effective. Suppose the 20-year-old male and the 40-year-old female exercise every day, but the 40-year-old male and the 20-year-old female exercise rarely. Grouping customers into two *lifestyle* segments — high exercise and low exercise — may be far more effective. Figure 8.3 shows a pharmaceutical firm's attempt to segment the physician market using two variables. Each variable has two levels: *approach to treatment* — aggressive or conservative; *type of data* — relies on scientific evidence or on clinical experience. The firm formed four segments: *risk taker, hard headed, path finder, tortoise.* The firm could easily identify physicians characterizing each segment; this approach was far more effective than classifying by geography or demography.

The main problem of starting with candidate descriptor (segmentation) variables is that customer groups may not have distinct need profiles — descriptor variables do not produce segments at all! The marketer must repeat the process with other descriptor variable(s). The physician example shows that behavioral and/or sociopsychological variables may be more effective than geographic and demographic variables in forming *good* market segments. But assigning customers to market segments formed from behavioral and/or sociopsychological variables may be difficult. Generally, segmentation approaches that start with customer needs are preferable.

FIGURE 8.3
Example of Two-Variable Segmentation of Physicians

MARKETING QUESTION

How would you segment the market for dog food? Two possible approaches are:

1. Descriptors of dogs.
2. Need profiles of dog owners.

Which approach is easier? Which approach provides greater insight into the dog food market?

FORMING MARKET SEGMENTS: METHODOLOGICAL APPROACHES

Methodological approaches to forming market segments fall into two main categories:

QUALITATIVE. The segmentation task is highly judgmental, requiring significant conceptual skill. Raw material is creative insight — Chapters 3, 4, 5 — typically gained from marketing research — Chapter 6 — and/or customer relationship management (CRM) systems — Chapter 2. Table 8.1 (p. 206) shows a typical segmentation matrix formed in this manner.

QUANTITATIVE (DATA CRUNCHING). Large-scale market-segmentation studies use extensive customer survey data and sophisticated multivariate statistical techniques. Cluster analysis approaches include the following steps — Marketing Enrichment 6.1 [710p, pp. 8–9]:

• Develop many statements (variables) about customer needs.
• Develop a set of questions (variables) for identifying customers.

MARKETING ENRICHMENT 6.1
Analyzing Quantitative Research Data **710p**

Many observers believe electric vehicles will gain significant share in the automobile market. How would you segment the market for electric vehicles? What are the implications of your segmentation scheme for product design?

- Administer statements and questions to a random sample of current and potential customers.
- Analyze customer need responses by cluster analysis. Choose the number of clusters (segments) that form the *best* groupings of customer needs.
- Examine each customer cluster (segment) for identifying characteristics.

Mobil used a similar process to segment the gasoline market (p. 212).[9]

The fundamental segmentation task is to link each segment's need profile to appropriate descriptor (segmentation) variables. If segmentation is done well, each segment has a well-defined need profile and is easily described by descriptor variables. Frequently, the firm makes several successive attempts to segment a market. As Figure 8.4 shows, each attempt uses customer need profiles and candidate descriptor (segmentation) variables; they converge somewhere in the middle.

FIGURE 8.4
Forming Market Segments

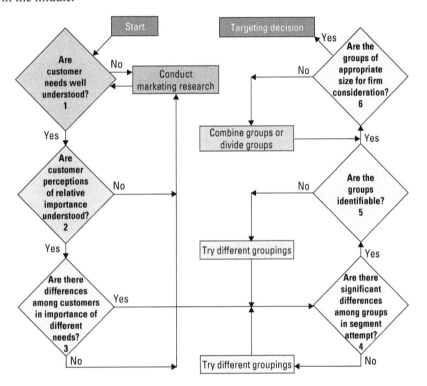

Market segmentation is a critical step in developing market strategy. Regardless, some firms approach the process as ritual, without a clear conviction of its strategic importance.

HOW *NOT* TO APPROACH MARKET SEGMENTATION

That's the way we've always done it — Ignores market, customer, competitor, company, and complementer evolution. Segments that worked in the past may be obsolete.

That's the way data are available — Firms use secondary data from governments/trade associations and the Internet. This approach implicitly assumes the firm's segmentation method drove datagathering: It did not. Also, because all competitors have access to the same data, the firm may not gain advantage through segmentation.

That's the way we're organized — Organization design often drives strategy for internally oriented firms. Externally oriented firms respond to environmental imperatives. Structure should follow strategy, not vice versa.

That's the way competitors do it — The firm accepts equivalence with competitors. Innovative segmentation can help achieve differential advantage. If competitor segmentation fits its capabilities, the firm is disadvantaged.

Segmentation at Thomson Financial

Traditionally, Thomson Financial (TF) segmented the information products market by sales channel — Figure 8.5A. A new end-user resegmentation, based on deeper customer insight, provided TF with a more actionable framework — Figure 8.5B. Figures 8.5A and 8.5B highlight TF's estimated competitive position by segment.[10]

FIGURE 8.5A

Thomson Financial: Traditional Segmentation

MARKETING QUESTION

How do you assess Thomson Financial's change in segmentation approach?

FIGURE 8.5B

Thomson Financial: New End-User Segmentation

MARKETING QUESTION

When the magazine *Mirabella* ceased publication, *The New York Times* noted that *Mirabella* was aimed at *women who are no longer 24 years old, who care passionately about literary criticism and serious articles about, say, contemporary philosophers — and equally as passionately about where to buy those just adorable hot-pink leather pants.*[11] Where did *Mirabella* fail in its segment criteria?

KEY IDEA

Criteria for *good* segments:
• Differentiated
• Identifiable
• Accessible
• Appropriate size
• Measurable
• Stable

KEY IDEA

The market-segmentation process may combine creativity and sophisticated data analysis.

MARKET SEGMENTS

We just discussed developing market segments, but was the market-segmentation process successful? *Good* segments are those the firm could target for marketing effort with a reasonable chance of success. So far, we focused on two important segmentation criteria:

• **Differentiated.** Customers in different segments have different need profiles. Accordingly, they should respond differently to market offers.
• **Identifiable.** The firm can identify customers by using descriptor (segmentation) variables and hence reach them with market offers.

Good market segments satisfy four additional criteria:

• **Accessible.** The firm can reach the segment via communications and distribution channels using appropriate and cost-effective approaches.
• **Appropriate size.** Different firms like different size segments. Generally, large firms prefer large segments to justify their efforts and costs. By contrast, small firms tend to prefer small segments so they can avoid large and powerful competitors.
• **Measurable.** The firm can measure important characteristics like size and growth.
• **Stable.** Customers stay in the segment for a reasonable time period.

But marketers must be clear: Market segments are not *real, correct, incorrect,* or *unchanging.* Customers do not have market-segment membership stamped on their foreheads! Market segments derive from appropriate data collection, analysis, and creative insight. Market segments help the firm direct resources to those parts of the market where success is likely.

MARKET-SEGMENTATION EXAMPLES

Segmentation schemes and targeting decisions developed by major U.S. firms include[12]:

 Best Buy (BB) is the leading U.S. consumer electronics retailer — revenues exceed $40 billion, market share — 20 percent. Market segmentation drives BB's approach to the market. BB identifies its most valuable customers, then uses sophisticated marketing research techniques to form market segments. BB's most valued segments, described by archetypes, are:

• **Barry** — affluent tech enthusiast
• **Mr. Storefront** — owns a small business
• **Buzz** — young gadget fiend
• **Ray** — price-conscious family guy
• **Jill** — busy suburban mom

BB is also interested in *Carrie* — young single woman; and empty-nesters *Helen* and *Charlie.* To address the five core segments, BB *centrizes* and remodels stores. *Barry* stores have expert salespeople and a separate department for home-theater systems; *Jill* stores have personal shopping assistants; *Buzz* stores have many video games. Some stores target more than one segment. BB trains employees to identify customers by segment and make product/service offers that research shows they value.[13]

Mobil Before the Exxon merger, Mobil profits were under severe pressure — gasoline prices were low and Mobil was not the low-cost producer.[14] Mobil's large-scale segmentation study identified five segments of gasoline buyers — Table 8.4 (p. 212).

Segment	Size (% of all buyers)	Description
Generation F3 — Food, Fuel, Fast	27	Upwardly mobile men and women; half under 25; constantly on the go; drive a lot and snack heavily from the convenience store.
Homebodies	21	Usually housewives shuttling children around during the day; use whatever gasoline station is in town or along their travel routes.
Price Shoppers	20	Generally neither loyal to a brand nor a gas station; rarely buy premium; frequently on tight budgets; historically Mobil's target customers.
Road Warriors	16	Generally higher-income, middle-aged men; drive 25,000 to 50,000 miles per year; buy premium gas with a credit card; purchase sandwiches and drinks from the convenience store, sometimes use the car wash.
True Blues	16	Usually men and women with moderate to high incomes; brand loyal and sometimes gas station loyal; frequently buy premium gasoline and pay cash.

TABLE 8.4
Market Segments of Gasoline Buyers Identified by Mobil

MARKETING QUESTION

What lessons can you learn from segmentation of the fertilizer market? **[650v]**

These five segments satisfied criteria for *good* segments. Mobil targeted three segments — Road Warriors, True Blues, Generation F3. Mobil actions were:

• Upgrade convenience stores so they would become *destination* convenience stores.

• Speed up refueling by introducing the Mobil Speed Pass, based on new technology.

• Introduce widespread customer service training for employees.

• Develop a direct marketing program to recognize and encourage customer loyalty.

Mobil improved market share and profits in a highly competitive mature market. When Exxon and Mobil merged, ExxonMobil adopted Mobil's pioneering approach.

 Ford uses birth year to form six truck-market segments — Table 8.5. Ford targeted baby boomers with the F-150 pickup, narrowing and lengthening the cab to make it more comfortable to drive. The F-150 was a best seller.

Segment	Born Between	Description
Depression Kids	1920-1934	Attitudes formed during the Depression and World War II — plan for a rainy day, status-seekers.
Quiet Generation	1935-1945	Childhood of peace and prosperity made for an extended period of innocence; little parental pressure and lots of free time — prefer movies with humble heroes.
Baby Boomers	1946-1964	The first TV generation; indulged by parents and pushed to win — seek instant gratification; want an image of being smart purchasers.
Lost Generation	1965-1969	Disenfranchised; grew up in the boomers' shadow; hurt more by parental divorce — wait for life to get better; not affluent.
Birth Dearth	1970-1977	Grew up in the rich 1980s and acquired a taste for excellence, but jobs don't support it — practical, focused, future-oriented.
Baby Boomlet	1978-present	Children of boomers — strong desire for the affluence of their parents' generation; unlikely to have as much money.

TABLE 8.5
Market Segments: Ford Motor Company

MARKETING QUESTION

Think about your grandparents, parents, peers, and other friends and acquaintances. Do Ford's segments describe them well? If not, how could Ford have segmented differently?

STANDARDIZED MARKET SEGMENTS

In the previous examples, individual firms identified and developed market segments. By contrast, some B2C firms competing in mature markets use *standardized segments* based on established buying trends, habits, and customer needs. The best-known approach is *Prizm* (U.S.) (Nielsen Claritas).

The Prizm scheme — based largely on income, urbanity, and life stage — comprises 66 clusters organized as 14 social groups: Affluentials, City Centers, Country Comfort, Elite Suburbs, Inner Suburbs, Landed Gentry, Micro-City Blues, Middle America, Middleburbs, Midtown Mix, Rustic Living, Second City Society, Urban Uptown, Urban Cores.[15]

We illustrate Prizm's clusters by showing the Rustic Living social group — six mostly white clusters (some ethnic diversity), predominantly owners of single-family homes:

- **Back Country Folks.** Poor, over 55 years old, living in older, modest-sized homes and manufactured housing on remote farm communities.

- **Bedrock America.** Young, economically challenged, modestly educated, sprawling families with blue-collar jobs in small, isolated towns. One quarter live in mobile homes; one third haven't finished high school. Spend time fishing, hunting, hiking, and camping.

- **Crossroads Villagers.** Middle-aged, blue-collar couples and families with rural lifestyles. High-school-educated, with lower-middle incomes and modest housing; one quarter live in mobile homes. Somewhat self-reliant; spend time fishing, gardening, and hunting.

- **Golden Ponds.** High-school-educated seniors, singles, and couples, living in small apartments in small towns on less than $25,000 per annum; one in five resides in a nursing home. Daily life is often a succession of sedentary activities like reading, watching TV, playing bingo, and doing craft projects.

- **Old Milltowns.** Retired singles and couples from once-thriving mining and manufacturing towns living on downscale incomes in pre-1960 homes and apartments. Enjoy gardening, sewing, socializing at veterans clubs, or eating out at casual restaurants.

- **Young & Rustic.** Young, restless, lower-income, high-school-educated singles living in tiny apartments in exurban towns. Service industry jobs and modest incomes; fast-paced lifestyles center on sports, cars, and dating.

KEY IDEA

The firm may identify opportunities at the *base of the pyramid*.

MARKETING QUESTION

In difficult economic times, most advanced Western countries have their own base-of-the-pyramid consumers. What opportunities can you identify for addressing them?

THE BASE OF THE PYRAMID

Around the world, four billion people live in poverty; many more have minimal economic resources, even in developed countries. But people at the base of the economic pyramid may represent attractive market opportunities.[16] Pfizer sells discounted brand-name prescription drugs to clinics in Latin American's dangerous shanty towns. In rural India, Hindustan Unilever successfully offers cold-water shampoo sachets and water-purification systems via a 45,000-women — Shakti Ammas — network.[17] Smartphone sales are rising fast, and banks are following Grameen Bank's (Bangladesh) example and making microloans to entrepreneurs (often women).[18]

In Kenya, PeePoople AB (Sweden) introduced the peepoo, a self-sanitizing biodegradable single-use toilet sold by locals. Peepoo replaces *flying toilets* (plastic bags containing human waste) for the extremely poor residents of informal settlements. Kenyattaa Light World leases and sells solar-powered LED systems to replace paraffin lamps. And because many rural herdsmen face potential catastrophic drought-related losses when livestock (camels, cows, goats) die, innovative weather-based index insurance pays out when real-time satellite images of grass and other vegetation show significant risk of animal death.

Two issues are critical for base-of-the-pyramid success:

- **Changing consumer behavior.** Many behaviors are deeply ingrained, especially in rural areas. Investment, time, and creative approaches may be necessary.
- **Changing firm operations and distribution.** Prices must be low, so the firm must innovate to develop low-cost models.[19,20]

Using Standardized Segments

Ace Hardware launched the *Helpful Hardware Club* customer loyalty program by assigning a Prizm cluster code to each of seven million members. Twelve clusters generated most Ace revenues. Ace targeted female shoppers in those household clusters to buy Valentine's Day gifts for their husbands.

Hyundai identified high-potential clusters for purchasing automobiles. Hyundai selects zip codes with high cluster membership, then sends test-drive offers. Results show more test drives, increased sales, and significantly lower marketing costs per vehicle sold.

KEY QUESTIONS ABOUT MARKET SEGMENTS

Managers often raise questions regarding their own approaches to market segments and the market-segmentation process. Here are the most common[21]:

HOW MANY MARKET SEGMENTS ARE ENOUGH? How should the firm trade off enhancing customer satisfaction by defining large numbers of market segments, and seeking cost efficiency via few segments? Walmart faces this problem: Walmart's low-cost, low-price business model has brought great success; a key current challenge is addressing segments defined by local needs without incurring significant cost penalties.[22] Core options are:

- **Large number of segments.** As the firm identifies large numbers of segments; the similarity of customer need profiles within each segment increases. The firm can earn high customer satisfaction by targeting specialized groups. But product development, marketing costs, and other resource requirements are high and economies of scale are few. Also, managing many segments is a complex challenge.
- **Small number of segments.** When the firm develops fewer segments, customer needs in any segment are less granular and more diffuse. Customer satisfaction from addressing individual segments is necessarily lower, but costs are also lower and segment management is less difficult.

Firms experienced in market segmentation typically opt for relatively few segments, often between five and eight. They may develop more discrete segments during the segmentation process, but include a rationalizing step to a smaller number.

In some industries, firms target several fine-grained segments via *modularity. Modularity* speaks to product design, using individual components in multiple products to serve multiple segments. Chapter 7 notes how Boeing and Airbus each use modular design, parts standardization, and advanced information technology in airplane manufacture. The Boeing 727, 737, and 757 serve different customer needs, yet some fuselage sections are identical, inherited from the 707.

Technological advances increase design and production flexibility. Computer-aided design (CAD) speeds development; computer-aided manufacturing (CAM) reduces set-up times. CAD/CAM innovations make product variations less expensive and allow customer personalization without the typical cost of making *one-offs*. Amazon offers an excellent example of using information technology to personalize the user experience and reduce the cost of variety. Amazon uses *recommendation systems*, based on historic purchasing patterns, to advise customers about products meeting their needs.

CAN AN INDIVIDUAL CUSTOMER BE A MARKET SEGMENT? Firms that address B2B markets, or sell consumer goods through large retail chains, often focus efforts on individual customers — *segments-of-one*. The firm treats an individual *strategic (key) account* as a market segment in its own right.

Historically, in B2C markets, individual artisans like custom tailors offered personally designed *bespoke* products to individuals, typically at high prices. Today, many firms integrate personally

KEY IDEA

B2B firms often treat major customers as individual market segments. In B2C markets, many firms practice mass customization.

designed products with flexible mass production techniques — *mass customization* — and gain two advantages.[23] More precisely tailored products enhance customer satisfaction and loyalty; the firm reduces finished-goods inventory throughout production and distribution, and has fewer products to discard at *fire-sale* prices.

Panasonic retailers measure consumers for bicycles, just as tailors measure for suits. Retailers transmit measurements to the factory; custom-made bicycles are available in a few days. Similarly, Levi Strauss and Lands' End offer custom-made pants through Internet-based systems. Optical retailers like LensCrafters and Warby Parker deliver individually fashioned spectacles within a few hours. At Callaway and Golfsmith *performance centers*, golfers receive computer analyses of golf swings; they place orders for clubs cut to a precise length and bent to a specific angle.**[949v]** Renault's goal is to build and deliver cars within 15 days of receiving customer orders.

Many Internet firms personalize products using *choiceboard* models.[24] Dell customers design PCs; Mattel customers design Barbie dolls. Hallmark sends personal e-mail reminders for birthdays and other anniversaries so customers can send cards that arrive on time.

DO MARKET SEGMENTS EVOLVE? We emphasize that market segmentation is critical to developing market strategy. If two firms are equally accomplished in designing market offers, the firm with better market segmentation will win; its offers will be more precisely tailored to customer needs than competitive offers.

KEY IDEA

As customer need profiles evolve, the firm must continually evolve its segmentation.

But customer need profiles are constantly evolving. Firm segmentation must also evolve, based on good market, customer, competitor, and complementer insight. When markets are young, early entrants are often successful providing basic functional benefits. Then, as the product life cycle evolves, competitors enter and basic functional benefits become the *cost of entry*. The firm achieves differential advantage by identifying customers with finer-grained needs and delivering appropriate benefits/values. Cell phones are a good example: Early in the product life cycle, the most important benefit was telephone portability and connectivity. Later, these benefits became less important in customer decision-making, and need profiles of some market segments focused on additional functional benefits like e-mail, text messaging, and taking photos. Other segments focused on design and fashion statements.

Regardless, we should remember that many mature markets have segments requiring only basic functional benefits. easyHotels offers tiny rooms (cabins) at extremely low nightly rates; and discount airlines, netbooks, and many private-label supermarket products serve these segments. Conversely, many markets have super-luxury segments: automobiles — Ferrari, Lamborghini (> \$1 million); designer dresses; smartphones — Vertu (> \$10,000).

HOW DO CUSTOMER LIFE CYCLES AFFECT MARKET SEGMENTS? Generally, promoting and selling products to current customers is less expensive than focusing on new customers. Firms increasingly recognize the lifetime value of current customers (CLV) and continually refocus efforts to increase long-term customer loyalty — Chapter 2. B2B customers may continue indefinitely, but individual human consumers follow a predictable life cycle. B2C firms have two polar options:

MARKETING QUESTION

Digg Inn, LYFE Kitchens, SweetGreen, TenderGreens, and Veggie Grill are restaurant chains, each with fewer than 50 outlets. What segment(s) does each target? Should McDonald's be concerned?

- **Focus on a fixed age group.** The firm targets an age-defined segment, continually adding new consumers as current customers age and leave the market. Magazines often favor this approach — *Time for Kids*, *Sports Illustrated for Kids*, and *Seventeen*.
- **Retain consumers as they age.** The firm evolves its offer/adds new offers to match changing customer need profiles, and reaps customer loyalty benefits. But eventually, consumers stop buying. Ford and GM abandoned Mercury and Oldsmobile respectively.

The Old Spice (OS) brand (aftershave and cologne) has followed both strategies. When Richardson Vicks owned OS, it was relatively successful targeting 18- to 25-year-old men as they aged but product use declined and sales stagnated. When P&G acquired OS, it retargeted the 18- to 25-year-old segment, now populated by new consumers. OS is the U.S. market leader.

DOES A *SEGMENT* OF CUSTOMERS DIFFER FROM A *GROUP* OF CUSTOMERS? We take a hard line on the definition of market segments. Within a segment, customers have similar need profiles; these profiles differ from customers in other segments. By contrast, the firm can form groups in many ways: by degree of use, propensity to buy innovative products, and customer loyalty. Groups may be very important for understanding buyer behavior, but they may not be segments.

To illustrate, many firms group customers by level of use — heavy, medium, light. This grouping is often very useful for allocating marketing effort; generally, firms place more effort on heavy users than light users. But the heavy-user group is *not* a segment; customers may be heavy users for very different reasons. Consider frequent users of car rental: Two very different segments are traveling businesspeople — want cars during the week; and city dwellers — want to leave town on the weekends. Each segment has different needs. McDonald's has a heavy-user group, but those customers fall into quite separate segments: families with young children, and single males in blue-collar jobs.[25] In general, the firm should develop groups *before* segments.

CAN WE DEVELOP SEGMENTS BASED ON JUST OUR CURRENT CUSTOMERS? Most firms segment the entire market, both current and potential customers. But when the firm has many current customers, it may use customer relationship management (CRM) approaches — Chapter 2 — to place purchase transactions in a *data warehouse*. The firm can then use *data-mining* techniques to identify groups based on purchasing patterns and tailor offers to individual customers based on those patterns.[26]

Tesco (British supermarket) provides an excellent example of data mining in action. Tesco's loyalty card pays quarterly rebates based on cumulative purchases. Tesco has more than 16 million card users; 10 million consumers use their cards weekly. Tesco analyzes data from more than 600 million shopping baskets annually and places customers into roughly 40,000 groups. Tesco tailors rewards and incentives to consumers in these groups via 36 million personalized mailings annually.[27]

TARGETING MARKET SEGMENTS

Chicago-based Seigle's operated many home centers in and around Chicago — 60 percent of sales to builders, 40 percent to consumers. Seigle's anticipated tough competition from Home Depot. Seigle's closed stores, reduced the product line from 7,000 to 1,500 items, and focused its 33 on-the-road salespeople on the builder segment.

The firm never has sufficient resources and/or capabilities to address all segments in a market; it must decide where to place its efforts. Some segments receive greater effort and resources; some segments receive little or no effort. By effective targeting, the firm better addresses customer needs and minimizes competition. When making targeting decisions, the firm should be conscious of the Principle of Selectivity and Concentration — Chapter 1.

KEY IDEA

For each target market segment, the firm should develop a unique offer precisely tailored to the needs of customers in that segment.

- Marketing must carefully choose targets for firm efforts.
- The firm should concentrate resources against those targets.

The Principle of Selectivity and Concentration governs both Marketing Imperative 1 and Marketing Imperative 2, but there is a difference. For Marketing Imperative 1 — Determine and Recommend Which Markets to Address — marketing's role is *advisory*, helping the firm decide. For Marketing Imperative 2 — Identify and Target Market Segments — marketing has a *decision-making* role. When the firm has chosen its markets, marketing has the explicit responsibility to identify and target segments.

Whole Foods (WF) is a good example of successful segmentation and targeting in the competitive supermarket industry. WF targets the health-conscious segment with supermarket-style

MARKETING QUESTION

How do you assess Nike's targeting decisions? **[997v]**

natural food stores, offering one-stop shopping and educational materials on its environmental practices. WF has grown from a single store (1980) to a $14 billion, 400-store chain with 80,000 employees; average sales per square foot are close to twice that of regular supermarkets. Monsanto offers a second example. Faced with mounting criticism of its genetically modified seeds, it abandoned efforts on edible products like bananas, potatoes, tomatoes, and wheat. Monsanto successfully focused on four commodity crops — corn, soybean, cotton, canola. Precise targeting illustrations:

Koss (headphones), Keefe (MP3 players, music downloads), and JPay (PP3 players, money transfers, e-mail communications) target the U.S.'s 2.3 million prison-inmate population. Physical products have special features: transparency — to prevent hiding contraband; plastic parts — cannot be made into knives or other sharp objects; weaker-than-normal cords (music systems) — cannot strangle or restrain.

International document and package delivery firm DHL used successive approaches to targeting. Initially, DHL formed three segments based on customer needs:

- **Ad hoc** — small irregular shippers or occasional buyers
- **Regular** — high-volume shippers not requiring supply-chain solutions
- **Advantage** — shippers that need and want a supply-chain solution

The *advantage* segment was attractive because it required DHL supply-chain solutions; it offered high revenue and profit potential, and good partnership candidates. DHL selected 10 industry segments where it could offer industry-specific knowledge and solutions. Finally, DHL focused on specific firms in those industries for selling effort.

MARKETING QUESTION

Newsstand sales and subscriptions declined for many news magazines — *Bloomberg Businessweek, Fortune, Time. Newsweek* and *U.S. News & World Report* have ceased print production. By contrast, *The Economist* has enjoyed significant circulation increases. Why? What market segment(s) does *The Economist* target? Why is *The Economist* successful?

Sometimes, the most successful firms target market segments other firms ignore. Consider Allegiant and Redbox:

Allegiant is the U.S.'s most profitable airline — pretax profit margins in excess of 15 percent, versus airline majors in the low single digits (or negative). Operating a low-cost model, Allegiant flies from small cities to holiday destinations or for connections. Since other airlines abandoned many cities, Allegiant faces airline competitors on less than 10 percent of its routes.

Netflix (Chapter 3 Opening Case) offers more than 100,000 titles via DVD and streaming video. By contrast, Redbox targets a different segment via 40,000 kiosks in supermarkets, drugstores, and fast-food restaurants; each kiosk contains 200 titles, for $1 per day rental.

Two separate approaches can help the firm decide which segments to target.

MULTIFACTOR MATRIX APPROACH TO TARGETING (STRATEGIC POSITION ANALYSIS)

The *multifactor matrix* (*strategic position analysis*) helps the firm decide which market segments to target.[28] For each candidate segment, the firm must answer two questions:

- How attractive is this segment? (Later, we discuss what makes a segment attractive.)
- Does the firm have the business strengths to *win* in this segment?

Figure 8.6 (p. 218) shows the analysis conclusion — *market-segment attractiveness* versus *business strengths* matrix. We trisect each axis — *high, medium, low* — and label the nine cells A through I. We illustrate by considering three cells:

- Cell C — high market attractiveness, high business strengths: A segment with these characteristics is a no-brainer; the firm should target this segment.
- Cell G — low market attractiveness, low business strengths: A segment with these characteristics is also a no-brainer, but the decision is very different; do not waste resources.

- Cell E — medium market attractiveness, medium business strengths: This decision is more difficult; the segment is somewhat attractive and the firm has some strengths.

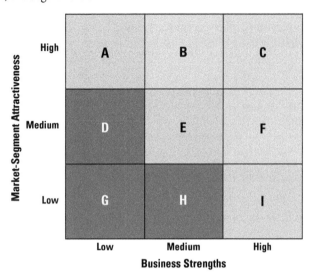

FIGURE 8.6
Multifactor Matrix (Strategic Position Analysis) — Market-Segment Attractiveness versus Business Strengths

More generally, the firm should seriously consider targeting market segments that fall in the top right corner — B, C, F — but avoid the bottom left corner — D, G, H. Segments in diagonal cells — A, E, I — are more questionable; each has both positive and negative features.

We just discussed the conclusion of the analysis — the multifactor matrix. Now, we show how to develop the matrix, and how to make the most effective market-segment-targeting decisions. First, we identify two sets of criteria:

- **Market-segment attractiveness.** Factors that make a market segment attractive to the firm.
- **Business strengths.** What any competitor would need to be successful in the segment.

Factors that make market segments attractive differ from firm to firm; business strengths needed to win differ from market segment to market segment. Table 8.6 identifies general factors to start an evaluation; actual factors are specific to the firm and candidate segments.

Market-Segment Attractiveness	Business Strengths
Ability to use available resources	Brand value
Barriers to entry	Distribution facilities
Barriers to exit	Financial leverage
Customer service valued	Government relations
Degree of vertical integration	Liquidity
Likely competitor actions	Market-segment share
Market-segment growth rate	Marketing skills
Market-segment potential	Plant and equipment modernity
Market-segment size	Production capacity
Potential profit margins	Profitability record
Regulatory constraints	Raw materials position
Social factors	Sales force
Technological change	Service levels
	Technological expertise

TABLE 8.6
Targeting Market Segments: Typical Criteria for Assessing Segment Attractiveness and Business Strengths Needed to Win

KEY IDEA

In deciding which segments to target, the firm should ask two questions:

- How attractive is this segment?
- Do we have the business strengths to win?

MARKET-SEGMENT ATTRACTIVENESS. The firm should identify useful factors for evaluating many segments. Sometimes the firm considers corporate-level attractiveness factors; other times it focuses on an individual business. A business with growth and market-share objectives typically has different attractiveness factors than a business focused on improving cash flow.

For each attractiveness factor, the firm should also consider *direction*. Market-segment size is a factor for many analysts. A large firm may prefer large segments; a smaller firm may prefer small segments. Michael Steinbeis, CEO of Steinbeis Holding (global leader in battery labels), said: "We want to be big in small markets. We may even pull out if a market becomes too large and, due to our size and resources, we can only be a small player."[29] Also, many firms view excessive government regulation as a negative factor. But for a firm with experience in dealing with regulatory bureaucracies, extensive regulation may be positive — as an entry barrier for potential competitors. Table 8.7 lays out a five-step process to score market-segment attractiveness.

....
TABLE 8:7

Scoring Market-Segment Attractiveness

Step Number	Step	Description
1	Identify factors	The firm seeks several factors (typically five to eight) according to the statement: *Given our history, objectives, culture, management style, successes, and failures, we like to be in market segments that offer ...*
2	Weight factors	Weight each factor by allocating 100 points based on its importance to the firm. Factor weights sum to 100.
3	Rate market segments	Rate each candidate market segment according to how well it performs on each factor (1 = poor; 10 = excellent).
4	Develop factor scores	For each candidate segment, form individual factor scores by multiplying the results of Step 2 and Step 3 for each factor. Factor score = Weighting × Rating.
5	Develop market-segment-attractiveness score	Sum individual factor scores.

MARKETING QUESTION

Choose a firm and an appropriate market segment. Complete the market-segment-attractiveness analysis.

The firm completes Steps 1 and 2 once. These results are constant for all segments the firm is evaluating, for which it has similar objectives. At Step 3, the analysis shifts to individual market segments. At Step 5, the firm develops a market-segment-attractiveness score — from 100 to 1,000. More attractive segments earn higher scores.[30] Table 8.8 shows how Robinson (fictional plastics firm) evaluated the plastic accessories segment — 595.

....
TABLE 8.8

Assessing Plastic Accessories Market-Segment Attractiveness to Robinson

Factor	Robinson's Weighting	Plastic Accessories Segment Rating (1 to 10 scale)	Factor Score (weighting × rating)
Ability to build new strengths	10	6	60
Easy customer access	15	9	135
High market growth	20	7	140
Large potential size	20	5	100
Little regulation	10	8	80
Use excess resources	10	2	20
Weak competition	15	4	60
Total	100	**Market-Segment-Attractiveness Score 595**	

BUSINESS STRENGTHS. Required business strengths are specific to each market segment. First, the firm must identify those strengths/capabilities/resources *any* competitor would require to be successful. Second, the firm must assess its possession of those strengths. Table 8.9 lays out a five-step process to score the firm's business strengths for a market segment.

....
TABLE 8.9

Scoring Business Strengths

Step Number	Step	Description
1	Identify factors	For each segment, the firm selects several factors (typically five to eight) according to the statement: *To be successful in this market segment, any competitor must possess the following strengths ...*
2	Weight factors	Weight each factor by allocating 100 points based on its importance for being successful in the segment. Factor weights sum to 100.

continues

Step Number	Step	Description
3	Rate firm	Rate the firm according to its possession of these strengths (1 = poor; 10 = excellent)
4	Develop factor scores	For each factor, form individual factor scores by multiplying the results of Step 2 and Step 3 for each factor. Factor score = Weighting × Rating.
5	Develop business strengths score	Sum individual factor scores.

....
TABLE 8.9
continued

For the firm and market segment you selected on p. 219, conduct a business-strengths analysis.

Steps 1 and 2 focus on the necessary strengths for being successful in the particular market segment. At Step 3, the analysis shifts to evaluating the degree to which the firm possesses these strengths. At Step 5, the firm develops a business-strengths score — from 100 to 1,000. Higher scores demonstrate greater strengths for competing in the segment. Table 8.10 shows how Robinson assessed its strengths in the plastic accessories segment — 645.

Factor	Plastic Accessories Segment Weighting	Robinson's Rating (1 to 10 scale)	Factor Score (weighting × rating)
Deep pockets	10	9	90
Fast-moving organization	5	3	15
Good R&D	25	7	175
High-quality service	15	6	90
In-place distribution	20	5	100
Low-cost operations	10	4	40
Well-trained sales force	15	9	135
Total	100	**Business-Strengths Score 645**	

....
TABLE 8.10
Assessing Robinson's Business Strengths in the Plastic Accessories Market Segment

Review the Robinson example — Table 8.10. How could Robinson secure a better business-strengths score?

The market-segment attractiveness/business-strengths analysis is a one-time snapshot; both market segments and firm strengths evolve. Segment attractiveness factors, importance weightings, and/or individual segment assessment will change. Similarly, business-strength factors, importance weightings, and firm assessment will also change. This analysis is not a *one-time deal*; the firm should update periodically.

WHICH MARKET SEGMENTS TO TARGET? The multifactor matrix produces two index numbers per market segment: *attractiveness* and *business strengths*. In the Robinson example, index numbers are 595 and 645 respectively — the "X" point in Figure 8.7. The *cut points* — 400 and 700 — discriminate low, medium, and high.[31]

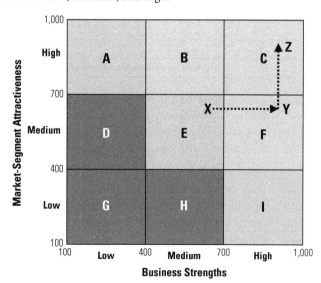

....
FIGURE 8.7
Robinson's Assessment of the Plastic Accessories Market Segment

MARKETING QUESTION

For the firm and market segment you worked with on p. 219 and p. 220, plot its position on a market-segment attractiveness/ business-strengths matrix.

The "X" position is not immutably fixed; we must assess whether the plastics accessories segment can shift from cell E to cells B, F, or C. Robinson has two movement options — horizontal and vertical:

- **Horizontal:** To move from X to Y, Robinson must improve business strengths. Returning to Table 8.10, *Good R&D* (25) and *In-place distribution* (20) are most important; Robinson scored 7 and 5 respectively. Astute investment, acquisition, or forming an alliance may improve business strengths. Columbia Business School has alliances with London Business School and University of Hong Kong to address separate Executive MBA segments.

- **Vertical:** To move vertically — from Y to Z — is more subtle. This shift depends upon the plastic accessories segment being more attractive. Robinson should secure deeper market insight and refine its segment definition. The Medicines Company was successful with Angiomax (anti-blood-clotting/thrombosis drug) in part by refining its segmentation scheme to focus on *very high risk* (versus high risk) patients.[32]

Of course, whether or not Robinson targets the plastic accessories segment depends on other alternatives and firm strengths/capabilities/resources.

PERCEPTUAL MAP APPROACH TO TARGETING

KEY IDEA

The firm can improve market-segment position in two ways:

1. Invest in those business strengths that are most important for success.
2. Identify more attractive market segments by refining its segmentation approach.

The *perceptual map* complements the multifactor matrix approach. The firm may use conventional marketing research techniques to develop perceptual maps or may analyze social media using advanced methods.[33] The targeting process has four stages:

- **Stage 1 — Customer need dimensions.** Identify two key customer need dimensions.
- **Stage 2 — Product perceptions.** Plot customer product perceptions on the map.
- **Stage 3 — Market segments.** Plot market segment ideal points and size on the map.
- **Stage 4 — Targeting decisions.** Use product data (stage 2) and segment data (stage 3) to target market segments.

We illustrate perceptual mapping using over-the-counter pain relievers and toy animals. Pain relievers show the basic perceptual map; toy animals show how to use the perceptual map for targeting decisions.

THE BASIC PERCEPTUAL MAP. Figure 8.8 (p. 222) illustrates Stages 1 and 2 for over-the-counter pain relievers.

- **Stage 1 – Customer need dimensions**[34] — *effectiveness*: low to high/left to right; *gentleness*: low to high/bottom to top
- **Stage 2 – Product perceptions.** The map shows eight products.
  - *Effectiveness* — Advil and Nuprin dominate aspirin; Tylenol and Bufferin are intermediate.
  - *Gentleness* — Tylenol dominates all other products; Bufferin is the most gentle of the others.

The perceptual map provides additional interesting insight. Advil, Nuprin, and Excedrin compete closely with one another; Bayer aspirin, private-label aspirin, and Anacin are also closely competitive. Tylenol has no direct competitors. The map also shows unserved market areas. No product combines *high gentleness* and *high effectiveness*. This observation suggests a market opportunity. But the even more empty *high gentleness/low effectiveness* area is probably not attractive. Regardless, to explore and confirm opportunities requires more information. We illustrate with toy animals.

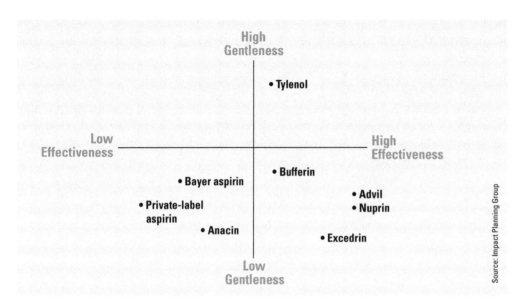

Source: Impact Planning Group

FIGURE 8.8
*Perceptual Map —
Pain Relievers*

USING THE PERCEPTUAL MAP FOR TARGETING DECISIONS. Figure 8.9 (p. 223) uses the toy animal market to illustrate all four stages of the targeting process:

- **Stage 1 – Customer need dimensions** — *realism*: low to high/left to right; *cuddliness*: low to high/bottom to top.[35]

- **Stage 2 – Product perceptions.** The four products are: Lankester, McLean, Johnson, and Tellis — 1, 2, 3, 4, respectively.

- **Stage 3 – Market segments.** We have significant information:

  - There are five segments — *perfectionists, searchers, accepters, dreamers, realists* — A, B, C, D, E, respectively.

  - Specifically, A, B, C, D, E represent market segment *ideal points* — need profiles of customers in the segments.[36] Hence, *realists* (E) want *highly* realistic, noncuddly toys.

  - Circle size around ideal points are proportional to market-segment size — revenues, units, or numbers of customers. *Dreamers* (D) is the largest segment; *searchers* (B) is the smallest segment.

  - Some segments are/are not well served by products. Product 3 — Johnson — satisfies the needs of *dreamers* (D), but no product serves *realists* (E) very well.

- **Stage 4 – Targeting decisions.** Segment opportunities by enhancing product and/or communications include:

  - *Perfectionists* (A). Lankester (1) has highest segment share. Lankester modifies customer perceptions to appear less realistic — follows the arrow.

  - *Searchers* (B). McLean (2) is closest to the segment ideal point, but does not serve it well. McLean modifies customer perceptions — follows the arrow to appear more cuddly and less realistic.

  - *Accepters* (C). McLean (2) probably captures some sales from this segment, but less than Tellis (4). Tellis follows the arrow to appear more cuddly and less realistic (but less so than McLean).

  Options for new entries include:

  - *Dreamers* (D). Johnson (3) seems secure, but this large segment may support another entrant, from Johnson or a competitor.

  - *Realists* (E) represent an opportunity; no product serves this segment.[37]

KEY IDEA

Perceptual maps show how various products serve market-segment needs. For each segment, perceptual maps show segment size and customer ideal point. These data help make targeting decisions.

Source: Impact Planning Group

FIGURE 8.9
Perceptual Map —
Toy Animals

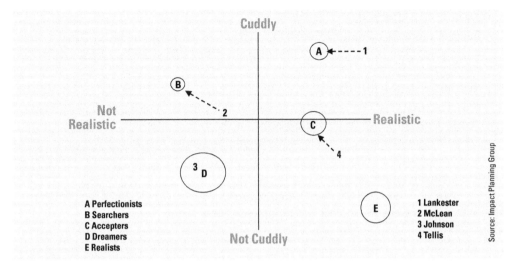

A Perfectionists
B Searchers
C Accepters
D Dreamers
E Realists

1 Lankester
2 McLean
3 Johnson
4 Tellis

Perceptual maps can be helpful in targeting decisions, but have limitations:

- Maps show segment size, but not other characteristics like growth and profitability.
- Maps suggest unserved market areas but do not address required business strengths.

TARGETING MARKET SEGMENTS AND COMPANY SIZE

Large firms generally have greater resources than small firms, so a large firm that segments and targets well is difficult to beat. The Opening Case showed how hotel-industry leader Marriott targets several market segments with various brands; Marriott's performance is exemplary. Whirlpool is another large firm that targets multiple segments — in both developed and less-developed countries (LDCs). In LDCs, Whirlpool targets low-income customers with its Ideale washing machine, making minor design changes to appeal to local tastes. In Brazil, Ideale is white, has a transparent acrylic lid, and sits on four legs. In China, Ideale is light blue and gray, has a foldable top, and a heavy-duty cycle for *grease removal*. In India, Ideale is green, blue, and white; has casters for easy rolling; and includes a delicate *sari* cycle.[38]

Market segmentation and targeting can even the odds for smaller firms. Many large firms cannot achieve specialized focus on market segments — internal constituencies disagree about segment targets and decision making is often protracted. Large firms may also spread resources too thin over many segments; smaller, more-focused competitors are able to gain advantage. Southwest Airlines and jetBlue pressure airline majors like American, Delta, and United; and easyJet and Ryanair are winning in Europe.

Sometimes small firms win when larger firms ignore, reduce service to, or withdraw from less attractive (for them) market segments. In passenger aircraft, Bombardier Aerospace (Canada) and Embraer (Brazil) profitably produce *short-hop* planes designed to travel between main hubs and smaller regional airports. They avoid stiff competition from large plane builders Airbus and Boeing.

Small firms with limited resources enjoy focus advantages by targeting few segments and building strong customer relationships, almost by default. They don't *choose* to target fewer segments: they just don't have the resources to target more.[39] But successful small firms must understand their success is due to focus. When a small firm does not understand this reality it may expand into segments dominated by resource-rich competitors, and fail:

Virtual bookstore *www.Positively-You.com* focused on self-help and motivational books and became profitable in six months! *New York Times* columnist Thomas Friedman wrote a highly complimentary op-ed piece, and website traffic increased dramatically. Positively-You expanded to compete more directly with Amazon.com — disaster! Within one year Positively-You was out of business. Said owner Lyle Bowlin: "We were doing well as a small niche player, but when we decided to go after Amazon, we lost our way."[40]

MARKETING QUESTION

Think of a small firm that failed. What role did segmentation and targeting play in its failure? Which pitfall(s) contributed to its failure? What could the firm have done better to understand the limitations of its market strategy?

KEY IDEA

Large firms and small firms each have advantages in targeting market segments. Missteps can cause each to lose a strong position.

Smaller firms face three additional problems:

- **Demand shortage.** Of necessity, small firms target few market segments. If demand drops in these segments, other segments cannot cushion the impact. Industry-wide recessions wreak havoc with specialized firms.
- **High costs.** Narrow focus implies high costs that may not be offset by high prices.
- **Too successful.** The small firm is *too* successful and attracts attention from major players. Startup Guiltless Gourmet (GG) grew baked low-fat tortilla chips into a $23 million enterprise. When snacks giant Frito-Lay entered, GG revenues fell precipitously.[41]

Alternatively, success in a small segment may lead a large firm to acquire the small firm. Such acquisitions significantly enrich the small firm's shareholders. Examples are legion: Amazon acquired Zappos — $1.2 billion; Google acquired YouTube — $1.7 billion and DoubleClick — $3.1 billion: and Facebook acquired What'sApp — $21.8 billion.

SEGMENT INTERRELATIONSHIPS IN TARGETING

Generally, the firm targets segments individually but sometimes it must target segment A to reach segment B. In many markets, like pharmaceuticals and medical diagnostics, the firm must successfully target a segment of influentials before addressing segments that make purchases.

Are marketing instructors *the plumbers* of the marketing textbook market? How do you suggest Wessex segment and target the textbook market?

In the British plumbing market, consumers typically rely on plumbers to advise on shower choice. Aquilisa developed the revolutionary, easy-to-install, electronic Quartz shower, providing significant consumer value via consistent water pressure and temperature. But plumbers distrusted electronics and were very conservative; hence they did not recommend Quartz to consumers. Aquilisa achieved success by targeting showrooms where consumers selected showers and *forced* plumbers to install their choices. Plumbers learned Quartz's value and started recommending it to customers.[42] Similarly, target customers for *Managing Marketing in the 21st Century* are students in marketing courses, yet Wessex directs marketing effort at instructors — the decision makers.

KEY MESSAGES

What other messages did you glean from this chapter?

- Market segmentation is fundamental to developing the market strategy. The firm has three separate, but related, strategic tasks:
  - Conduct a market-segmentation process to identify market segments.
  - Decide which of the identified market segments to target for effort.
  - Develop a market-segment strategy and positioning for each target segment.

  We discuss the first two items in this chapter; we take up the third item in Chapter 9.

- Segmentation is a process for deconstructing the market into customer groups defined by need profiles.

- Customers in each market segment have homogeneous (similar) need profiles. Customer need profiles differ from market segment to market segment.

- The firm can approach the segmentation process in two different ways:
  - Identify groups of customers with different need profiles.
  - Use candidate descriptor (segmentation) variables to form groups, then see if need profiles differ across groups.

- The firm should avoid ineffective ways of segmenting markets.

- *Good* market segments satisfy six separate criteria — differentiated, identifiable, accessible, appropriate size, measurable, stable.
- The segmentation process is creative and analytic — requires good market, customer, competitor, and complementer insight. Targeting requires decision making.
- Commercially available standardized segmentation schemes may be useful for some firms.
- The *multifactor matrix* and *perceptual maps* are alternative approaches for making targeting decisions.
- Large firms generally succeed by targeting multiple segments; small firms succeed by targeting few segments.

VIDEOS AND AUDIOS

For complimentary material, see Axcess Capon codes at www.axcessvids.com

Market Segmentation and Targeting	**350v** 🌐	Ron Boire	Toys R Us
Marketing Imperative 2	**498a** 🌐	Noel Capon	Columbia Business School

QUESTIONS FOR STUDY AND DISCUSSION

Can you answer the questions implied by this chapter's learning outcomes? Check!

1. Suppose your firm decides to address the human pain-relief market. How would you segment this market? What market segments can you identify? Can you identify both coarse- and fine-grained segments — market segments and customer segments?

2. Select a product/market with which you are familiar. Develop a segmentation matrix identifying the importance order of benefits/values for the various segments.

3. Assume you are marketing manager at a firm competing in the product/market you identified in Question 2. Select one or more segments to target by completing a multifactor matrix analysis.

4. Do politicians employ segmentation? Describe an example.

5. Describe a segment of the higher education market that includes you. Appraise this segment in terms of criteria for *good* segments — differentiated, identifiable, accessible, appropriate size, measurable, stable.

6. Visit retail outlets for Banana Republic, The Gap, and Old Navy. Observe customers and products. What do you infer about owner Gap's segmentation and targeting decisions?

7. Select a product in which you are interested. Alternatively, consider *Managing Marketing in the 21st Century*. How would you segment the market? Describe the segments.

8. Select a market with which you are familiar. Develop a perceptual map by identifying two dimensions, product offerings, and your best guess at market segments.

9. What are the risks and limitations of a strategy based on market segmentation? How can you measure the effectiveness of a market-segmentation approach?

10. Market segmentation raises serious ethical issues. Do you agree? Why or why not?

TRUE/FALSE QUESTIONS

Answers on page A1 and at www.axcessvids.com — 448p ⬤

1. Candidate descriptor (segmentation) variables include geographic, demographic, behavioral, and sociopsychological. ❏ **TRUE** ❏ **FALSE**

2. Large-scale market-segmentation studies use extensive customer survey data and sophisticated multivariate statistical techniques. ❏ **TRUE** ❏ **FALSE**

3. *Good* market segments should always be large in size. ❏ **TRUE** ❏ **FALSE**

4. If two firms are equally accomplished in designing market offers, the firm with better market segmentation will win. ❏ **TRUE** ❏ **FALSE**

5. The multifactor matrix produces two index numbers for each market segment: market-segment attractiveness, business strengths. ❏ **TRUE** ❏ **FALSE**

MULTIPLE CHOICE QUESTIONS

Answers on page A1 and at www.axcessvids.com — 656p ⬤

1. Attitudes, life stage, personality, and lifestyle characteristics are examples of which of the following categories of candidate descriptor variables?

    a. geographic
    b. demographic
    c. behavioral
    d. sociopsychological

2. *Good* market segments should satisfy all of the following criteria EXCEPT:

    a. stable
    b. measurable
    c. undifferentiated
    d. accessible

3. Firms that address B2B markets, or sell to consumer goods through large retail chains, often focus efforts on individual customers, aka _____.

    a. segments-of-one
    b. the modularity approach
    c. data mining
    d. factor analysis

4. When a firm has many current customers, it can use _____ approaches to place purchase transactions in a data warehouse. The firm can then use data mining techniques to identify groups based on purchasing patterns, then tailor offers to individual customers based on those patterns.

    a. perceptual mapping
    b. factor analysis
    c. linear extrapolation
    d. customer relationship management

5. All of the following are problems smaller firms face regarding targeting market segments EXCEPT:

    a. demand shortage
    b. being too successful
    c. high costs
    d. backward integration

IMPERATIVE 3

Set Strategic Direction and Positioning

CHAPTER 9

MARKET STRATEGY – INTEGRATING FIRM EFFORTS FOR MARKETING SUCCESS

For complimentary material, see Axcess Capon codes at www.axcessvids.com

LEARNING OUTCOMES

When you have completed this chapter, you will be able to:

- Articulate the purpose and functions of market and market-segment strategies.
- Provide direction to the firm and/or business unit.
- Know how to achieve differential advantage.
- Guide effective allocation of scarce resources.
- Achieve cross-functional integration.
- Lay out the elements of a market-segment strategy.
- Select strategic focus and design positioning statements.
- Identify effective and ineffective market and market-segment strategies.
- Develop and manage market strategies targeted at multiple segments.

OPENING CASE: MAYO CLINIC

Mayo Clinic is the best-known and most powerful healthcare brand in the world. Since the late 1880s, Mayo Clinic has delivered superb medical care to patients, provided value to many constituencies, and wielded differential advantage over competitors. Mayo Clinic's history continues to define its market strategy even as every major hospital and medical institution has added professional marketing and public relations staffs.

Mayo Clinic's market strategy has two core operating principles. First: The best interest of the patient is the only interest to be considered. Second: Two heads are better than one, and three are even better. Focused on these principles, Mayo Clinic has more than 50,000 employees (more than 3,000 physicians) serving more than one million patients annually — from the U.S. and around the world — at three clinic and hospital centers in Rochester, Minnesota; Jacksonville, Florida; and Scottsdale and Phoenix, Arizona. Mayo Clinic also maintains offices in Canada,

Mexico, and the United Arab Emirates (UAE) to facilitate appointments, and provide hotel and visa assistance. Mayo Clinic's annual research budget exceeds $500 million annually.

Mayo Clinic's brand awareness is extraordinary. The chair of Mayo Clinic's marketing division said: "Our research shows that in the U.S. we register over 1.8 billion consumer impressions a year — 90 percent of the population is aware of Mayo Clinic; 33 percent know someone who has been a Mayo Clinic patient; and 18 percent would make us their first choice for a serious health need if there were no financial barriers. Patients from all 50 U.S. states as well as from 150 countries typically visit each of our three clinics every year."[1]

Mayo Clinic is a multispecialty clinic based on a collaborative practice model inaugurated by the Clinic's founders. In most large healthcare institutions, physicians, nurses, and researchers are relatively isolated within their departments, laboratories, specialties, and subspecialties. Not at Mayo Clinic; all caregivers serve as consultants to one another and as members of multiple-patient care teams led by the patient's primary physician. Mayo Clinic extends this collaboration to physicians and administrators. Said one administrator, "Mayo Clinic is run by physician leaders who implicitly and respectfully value the counsel and skills of the administrators they are paired with. The mutual respect flows both ways."

Mayo Clinic's model is difficult to maintain and even harder to duplicate. Despite several attempts, no other clinic has been able to fully copy its approach or success, and no competitor looks like Mayo Clinic. Part of Mayo Clinic's success results from its alignment of mission and organization. Hence, all employees receive salary checks from the same account, signed by the same person.

Mayo Clinic's collaborative model extends to patients' referring physicians. Mayo Clinic views other healthcare providers as potential collaborators. Mayo Clinic's chief marketer said: "Both the patients and Mayo Clinic need them to have a doctor back home, and our doctors will collaborate with their doctors in the best interests of the patient. When a physician or patient needs our specialty services, we're here for them. But because Mayo's market share is extremely small, it is rarely seen as a competitive threat."

Mayo Clinic has world-class facilities, staffed with the best and brightest, and the right organizational design, systems and processes for its collaborative model. Mayo Clinic also communicates broadly to physicians, other healthcare professionals, and the general public. Clinicians and researchers publish several thousand articles, chapters, textbooks, and abstracts annually; and its peer-reviewed journal — Mayo Clinic Proceedings *— has 150,000 physician subscribers. Mayo Clinic publishes a widely read newsletter —* Clinical Update *— for healthcare professionals. For the general public, Mayo Clinic offers* Mayo Clinic Health Letter, *published in four languages — 800,000 subscribers for the English-language edition — and the similarly successful* Mayo Clinic Women's Health Source, *both monthly newsletters.* Mayo Clinic Family Health Book *has sold over one million copies, and www.Mayoclinic.org is one of the most heavily visited health information sites on the Internet.*

Mayo Clinic receives extensive public relations coverage when celebrities like entertainers, professional athletes, and government and business leaders visit for care. In small U.S. towns, word of mouth about someone's good experience at Mayo Clinic often leads to a local feature story in the newspaper, TV, or radio, and is frequently picked up by regional and national news services.

Communications about Mayo Clinic bring patient referrals from doctors and other healthcare providers. Word of mouth from active and former patients is also very strong. Ninety-five percent of patients are very positive about Mayo Clinic; on average, each patient urges 20 others to go to Mayo, and seven become new patients. In Rochester, Mayo Clinic cares for patients from nearly 40 percent of all U.S. residential zip codes, but few zip codes send ten or more patients. Demand typically outpaces available appointments, creating a significant patient-scheduling challenge.

Mayo Clinic's tiny share of a huge market makes it attractive to many insurers. Research shows the greatest benefit from the Mayo brand is peace of mind — knowing it's there if you need it. Midwest U.S. consumers, in particular, find great value in insurance products that include Mayo Clinic.

Case Question

What are the critical elements in Mayo Clinic's market strategy?

Mayo Clinic grounds its market strategy in delivering customer value and securing differential advantage. Although a nonprofit organization, Mayo Clinic's enormous financial success funds leading-edge research and hospital facilities, a medical school, a high staff-patient ratio, and a roster of world-class physicians and researchers. All these constituents count on customer willingness to pay and to face the inconvenience of traveling to a Mayo Clinic for treatment.[2]

KEY IDEA

The goal of market and market-segment strategies is very simple — *to attract, retain, and grow customers in the face of competitors trying to do the same thing.*

The market strategy is the firm's game plan for addressing the market. The market strategy states:

• What the firm is trying to achieve
• What the firm *will do*
• What the firm *will not do*

MARKETING ENRICHMENT 9.1

Levels of Strategy **373p**

In earlier chapters, we discussed Imperative 1 — Determine and Recommend Which Markets to Address, and Imperative 2 — Identify and Target Market Segments. Imperative 2 addressed two separate, but related, strategic-level tasks: how to conduct the *market-segmentation process* and identify *market segments*, and how to decide which segments to *target* for marketing effort.

Chapter 9 is the first of three chapters that explore separate aspects of Imperative 3 — Set Strategic Direction and Positioning. Here we focus on developing *market strategy*, arguably marketing's most important role and responsibility. As we learned in earlier chapters, the market-strategy goal is very simple — *to attract, retain, and grow customers, in the face of competitors trying to do the same thing.* The market strategy declares what the firm *will do* and what it *will not do*. Externally, a well-developed strategy reflects the common theme and emphasis of the firm's approach to the market. Internally, the firm coordinates the actions of many departments, functions, and people. An effective market strategy is crucial for success.[3]

The firm partitions each chosen market into several market segments; then decides which segment(s) to target for effort. If the firm's segmentation is effective, customers in each segment have homogeneous (similar) need profiles. But across segments, these profiles are heterogeneous (different). The extent and type of competition also varies by segment. Because of these differences, the firm must develop a separate strategy for each target segment; positioning is the heart of the *market-segment* strategy. The *market strategy* comprises one or more *market-segment* strategies. (For discussion of different levels of strategy, Marketing Enrichment 9.1 **[373p]**.)

THE CHANGING VIEW

OLD WAY	NEW WAY
Market strategy developed by marketing and general management	Cross-functional teamwork is crucial in market strategy development
Competitor considerations ignored or demeaned	Competitor considerations play a major role
Compromise is common — fuzzy value propositions	Clarity is critical — value propositions are clear and differentiated
Internal and budgetary focus to market strategy	External and strategic focus to market strategy
Marketers focus on volume and market share	Marketers concerned with creating shareholder value
Objectives uniform across products and markets	Objectives differ across products and markets
Positioning is poorly understood	Positioning is a crucial strategic element
Market strategy is the marketing mix	Market strategy drives the marketing mix
Integration limited to the marketing mix	Integration spans all functions
Functional programs are poorly coordinated	Market strategy links together functional programs

THE PURPOSE OF MARKET AND MARKET-SEGMENT STRATEGIES

Imagine an NFL team going through the football season without a strategy. What are its chances of reaching the Super Bowl? Very slim — luck only goes so far. The team would lack direction and focus, and be unable to leverage its strengths. The team would not deploy players effectively, and they would not coordinate with one another. In short, the team would not develop a differential advantage against opponents. *The same is true in business. To be successful, the firm must have a clear market strategy to win in the marketplace.*

Strategy is one of the most abused and most misunderstood terms in business, yet is important in the managerial vocabulary. The market strategy builds on planning assumptions formed from market, customer, competitor, company, and complementer insight — Transition to Strategic Marketing, pp. 173–174. Market strategy is the firm's game plan for the market, pointing the way to firm actions. The firm must make three types of decisions:

- **Results.** What the firm wants to achieve.
- **Resources.** Broadly, how the firm will deploy resources to achieve these results.
- **Actions.** What specific actions the firm intends to take.[4]

Well-developed market segment and market strategies fulfill four purposes: Provide strategic direction in the market; show how to secure differential advantage; guide the effective allocation of scarce resources; and achieve cross-functional and cross-business integration.

PROVIDE STRATEGIC DIRECTION IN THE MARKET

Market and market-segment strategies provide strategic direction on how to attract, retain, and grow customers in the face of competitors trying to do the same thing. We expect markets, customer needs, and competitive challenges to evolve and become more complex. The market strategy must guide the firm in this changing environment. Providing direction is more difficult, yet more essential, the greater the complexity and change the firm faces.[5]

MARKETING QUESTION

What is *your* career strategy? What will you do when you graduate? Describe:

- your objectives
- the job market segment you intend to enter
- your strategy for managing your career and achieving your goals

---

MARKETING QUESTION

How do you assess Steve Jobs approach to developing market strategy? [420v]

KEY IDEA

The market strategy requires decisions about:

- Results
- Resources
- Actions

KEY IDEA

Well-developed market and market-segment strategies fulfill four purposes:

- *Provide* strategic direction in the market
- *Secure* differential advantage
- *Guide* effective allocation of scarce resources
- *Achieve* cross-functional integration

SECURE DIFFERENTIAL ADVANTAGE

> In January 2006, Chipotle Mexican Grill went public at $22 per share; in 2015, Chipotle's share price reached $750. Chipotle behaves differently from most fast-food competitors — no TV advertising, no franchising, highest industry ingredient costs. (Notwithstanding its stellar performance, Chipotle's stock price dropped abruptly when it suffered an E. coli outbreak.)

Well-developed market-segment and market strategies must clarify why customers should buy from the firm rather than competitors. They also show how the firm will gain differential advantage. Recall from earlier chapters — *a differential advantage is a net benefit or cluster of benefits, offered to a sizable group of customers, which they value and are willing to pay for, but cannot get, or believe they cannot get, elsewhere.* Table 9.1 describes criteria for evaluating *good* market-segment and market strategies, and shows how Semic (fictional electronics firm) may attempt to secure differential advantage.[6]

TABLE 9.1
Securing Differential Advantage

Criteria	Strategy Description	Example
Competitors cannot do	The firm takes actions competitors cannot duplicate — typically they lack key resources or competence.	Semic secures patent protection on a new discovery — competitors cannot copy.
Competitors will not do	Competitors could match the strategy, but are unlikely to do so. The firm requires significant competitive insight to make this judgment.	Semic enters a new distribution channel. The competitor CEO tells an industry audience it will maintain its existing distribution strategy.
Competitors will be relatively disadvantaged if they do	The firm believes competitors will copy its actions but the firm will receive a disproportionate advantage.	Semic launches a major advertising campaign aiming for market growth and larger market share. Semic expects competitor sales to increase, but believes Semic will improve market share in a larger market.
Competitors and the firm will benefit	The firm believes its actions will benefit both the firm and competitors.	Semic joins with competitors to launch a major PR campaign to ward off adverse legislation, by showing the value all firms deliver to customers.

MARKETING QUESTION

As marketing VP for a global medical-device supplier, how would you approach developing market strategy? Would you have each region supply you with individual strategies (bottom-up)? Or would you develop a broader global strategy, then have each country and/or region incorporate local market strategies (top-down)? Why?

The firm should reject any market-segment or market strategy that cannot withstand probable competitor responses.[7] The firm should also develop contingency plans — *what if* responses — to possible competitor actions. Contingency planning leads to strategies that secure differential advantage, and helps the firm act preemptively — before competitors. (World-class chess players compete by identifying potential opponent moves and thinking several moves ahead!)

GUIDE EFFECTIVE ALLOCATION OF SCARCE RESOURCES

All firms have limited resources like capital, plant capacity, sales force time, and technological capability. These limitations apply at each organizational level and functional area — typically, some resources are more limited than others. Faced with these constraints, the firm must allocate these scarce resources to secure differential advantage. A *good* market strategy considers resource limitations and defines, generally yet clearly, effective allocations to support the firm's strategic direction.

The firm must make two types of allocations. *Externally*, the firm allocates resources among target market segments and customers, selecting the resources for securing differential advantage by segment. *Internally*, the firm allocates resources among activities like product development, advertising, and selling.

ACHIEVE CROSS-FUNCTIONAL INTEGRATION

Achieving integration across different parts of the firm and/or business unit is critical, yet is often elusive. Sometimes critical integration is among different firm functions; other times different business units within the firm must work together.[8] The market strategy must coordinate the actions of various parts of the firm, so they all pull together to secure differential advantage. Without effective integration, significant internal conflict can arise.

Market-strategy owners must develop support throughout the firm. The various functions and/or business units likely have different opinions about the market strategy: The sales department wants to increase sales and operations wants to reduce costs, in part because they are paid to do so. But actions that seem reasonable from a specific functional perspective may be inappropriate when market considerations are paramount. Well-managed contention is healthy; it surfaces different perspectives on key issues.[9] But all parties must focus on external issues and take an holistic view on how the firm can win.

ELEMENTS OF THE MARKET-SEGMENT STRATEGY

Samsung refocused semiconductor efforts from the mass PC market to niche segments with higher prices and fatter margins — camcorders, flash memory for handheld computers, game consoles. Samsung has also been successful in many consumer electronics products, and shown impressive growth in sales and profits — the results of a successful market strategy.

We can best view a market as a set of market segments. To be successful, the firm should target specific segments with strategies that create differential advantage. Generally, firms perform well when they focus on individual segments versus the market as a whole. Hertz, Alamo, and Enterprise are major players in car rental, but each focuses major effort on a specific segment: Hertz — business travelers who want speed and convenience; Alamo — vacation travelers seeking low prices; Enterprise — insurance companies and local convenience for drivers whose cars are being repaired.

Because of market-segment differences, the basic market-strategy unit is the market-segment strategy. A market strategy frequently combines several interrelated market-segment strategies. The four pillars of a market-segment strategy — Figure 9.1 (p. 233) — are:

- **Performance objectives.** Stated as results the firm seeks; include strategic objectives and operational objectives.
- **Strategic focus.** The broad direction of the strategy.
- **Positioning.** How the firm wants customers to view its offer; comprises *customer targets, competitor targets, value proposition, reasons to believe*.
- **Implementation programs.** How the firm should implement the strategy; includes the marketing mix and supporting functional programs.

Performance objectives, strategic focus, and *positioning* are conceptual devices requiring creativity. Product and brand managers or marketing and business directors typically develop these elements based on planning assumptions formed from market, customer, competitor, company, and complementer insight. *Implementation programs* are more tangible. The firm secures integrated implementation by clearly articulating and gaining commitment to performance objectives, strategic focus, and positioning. Key executives must build relationships, manage group processes, and coordinate many activities. By securing widespread cross-functional support early on, marketing sets the stage for successful design and implementation of the market-segment strategy.

KEY IDEA

An effective market strategy helps the firm allocate resources:

- *Externally* — the firm makes allocations to target market segments and customers to secure differential advantage
- *Internally* — the firm makes allocations across internal activities

KEY IDEA

Interfunctional conflict is endemic. Formulating the market strategy should resolve these conflicts and achieve cross-functional integration.

MARKETING QUESTION

Your firm is launching a new product. You anticipate high short-run market growth and six months' competitive lead-time. How will these factors affect your marketing, sales, finance, human resources, operations and R&D decisions?

MARKETING QUESTION

In rural areas of emerging countries, the farmer uses a yoke on his team of oxen. Is *yoke* a good metaphor for the market strategy?

FIGURE 9.1
Elements of the Market-Segment Strategy

MARKETING QUESTION

The market strategy is not visible, but we can *reverse engineer* a strategy by observing firm actions. Suppose you compete with McDonald's. What implementation programs can you identify? Then ask these questions: What core segment does McDonald's address? How do you assess McDonald's performance objectives?

- What is McDonald's strategic focus?
- What is McDonald's positioning?
- How do you assess McDonald's positioning?

KEY IDEA

The market-segment strategy:
- **Performance objectives**
- Strategic focus
- Positioning
- Implementation programs

PERFORMANCE OBJECTIVES

If you don't know where you're going, any road will get you there.

— Lewis Carroll, *Alice in Wonderland*

Before the firm figures out what it will do, it must know where it's headed. *Performance objectives* articulate the firm's goals for the market segment. Two components state clearly and simply what the firm is trying to achieve — strategic objectives and operational objectives.

STRATEGIC OBJECTIVES

Strategic objectives establish the types of results the firm requires; they are qualitative and directional. Strategic objectives are not concerned with numbers, but declare, in general terms, how the firm will measure success. Many people confuse strategic objectives with mission statements — Chapter 7. The difference is clear: Mission states where the firm will seek market opportunities; strategic objectives state the types of results the firm seeks.

The three broad categories of strategic objectives are *growth and market share, profitability,* and *cash flow.* Each strategic objective is attractive, but they often conflict. Many firms set growth and market share as key strategic objectives, but must invest in fixed assets, working capital, and marketing activities. These expenditures negatively affect short-term cash flow and profitability.[10]

Because these strategic objective categories typically conflict, the firm must make trade-offs. The firm must set explicit priorities — primary and secondary — for various stages of the market or product life cycle. The firm must resist the tendency to demand increased growth, market share, profit, *and* cash flow, all at the same time. The conditions for achieving on all dimensions simultaneously are very rare. Wheatcorn (fictional) strategic objectives trade off profits for market share. Wheatcorn wants both, but can't have them in the short term; Wheatcorn focuses first on increasing profits:

Wheatcorn targeted the *young family with children* segment of the cold-cereal market. Wheatcorn stated its strategic objectives: Our *primary objective* is *to* increase profits *from our* Cold Chunks *brand.* Our *secondary objective* is *to* maintain market share.

Reaching internal agreement on strategic objectives may not be easy. Spending to develop new products or exploit growth opportunities versus pressure for short-term profits is a common tension that often pits marketing (and other functions) against finance. Marketing must seek out and optimize opportunities, but must also recognize that profits are necessary to maintain a healthy share price, secure low-cost funding, and pay our salaries![11]

GUIDELINES FOR CHOOSING AMONG STRATEGIC OBJECTIVES. Figure 9.2 is a classic illustration of how strategic objectives evolve in a product life-cycle framework. In the introduction and early-growth stages, firms often set priorities on growth and/or market share. These objectives shift to profit in late growth and for much of the maturity stage. Late in the maturity stage, especially if decline is imminent, cash flow predominates; hence the term *cash cow*.[12] Table 9.2 shows quantitative results from a PIMS (Profit Impact of Market Strategy) study supporting this pattern.[13] Sales growth is high in early life-cycle stages, but is lower late in the life cycle. Return on investment and cash flow are often negative for startups but turn positive later.

KEY IDEA

The firm must make trade-offs among the three categories of strategic objectives:
• Growth and market share
• Profitability
• Cash flow

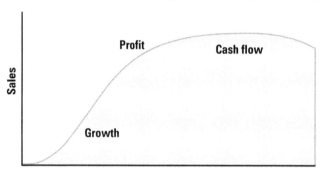

FIGURE 9.2
Evolution of Strategic Objectives

Category	Measure	Life Cycle Stage			
		Startup	*Growth*	*Early Maturity*	*Late Maturity*
Market Performance	Sales Growth (%)	74	23	11	6
	Market Share (%)	8	25	24	24
Budget Levels	R&D/Sales (%)	10	3	2	1
	Marketing/Sales (%)	26	11	9	8
Financial Performance	ROI (%)	−19	25	22	17
	Net Income Growth (%)	7	20	15	11
	Investment Growth (%)	38	19	9	3
	Cash Flow/Investment (%)	−46	1	6	9

TABLE 9.2
*Operating Results of PIMS Businesses**

* Data are four-year average percentages, except growth rates; these are annual rates (current dollars); data in the *startup* column are medians. Figures (except net income growth) secured from Strategic Planning Institute, Cambridge, MA.

These guidelines are not cast-iron prescriptions for selecting primary strategic objectives, but simply show many firms' behavior, assuming results reflect original objectives (on average).

Examples of Setting Strategic Objectives

Growth: When economies enter recession, leading firms sometimes cut prices in attempts to increase growth and market share.

Profit: When Howard Schultz returned as Starbucks' CEO, strategic objectives shifted from growth to profit.

Cash flow: When patents protect products, major pharmaceutical firms generally earn high operating profits. When patent protection ends and generics enter, leading firms often cut expenses to sustain positive cash flow.

KEY IDEA

Priorities for strategic objectives evolve during product life-cycle stages.

OPERATIONAL OBJECTIVES

Strategic objectives are qualitative and directional; *operational objectives* are quantitative and time-bound. Operational objectives provide the numbers and time frame to attach to strategic objectives. What types of numbers? Operational objectives answer the following questions: *How much is required*, and *by when?* Operational objectives should specify how much growth, market share, profit, and/or cash flow the firm should earn during a specific time frame.[14] Table 9.3 returns to Wheatcorn, showing operational objectives in context with each strategic objective.

TABLE 9.3

Strategic and Operational Objectives

* Typically, the firm sets operational objectives by year in the strategic market plan. In the annual market plan, the firm calendarizes these annual objectives by quarter or by month.

	Strategy Objectives	Operational Objectives*	
Primary	*Increase profits* from our *Cold Chunks* brand	from:	\$12 million in 20XY
		to:	\$15 million in 20XY+1
			\$20 million in 20XY+2
			\$25 million in 20XY+3
Secondary	Maintain market share	at:	25% from 20XY through 20XY+3

KEY IDEA

Operational objectives provide numbers to attach to strategic objectives. Operational objectives specify *how much* and *by when*.

The firm uses operational objectives to evaluate performance. Operational objectives should be **SMART** — **s**pecific, **m**easurable, **a**chievable, **r**ealistic, **t**imely. Operational objectives should also be challenging, but not out of reach and demotivating. A particular problem is pursuing growth too aggressively. Starbucks (Chapter 1 Opening Case) had problems because it allowed growth objectives to override its rigorous location policies. The UBS and Volkswagen examples are cautionary:

> Zurich-based UBS's investment-banking arm lagged competition in fixed-income products. UBS expanded quickly in structured credit and commodities, but emphasized revenue growth at the expense of risk. UBS focused on high-fee, but riskier (*mezzanine*) collateralized debt obligations of U.S. mortgage-backed securities, with minimal hedging. In the 2008–9 financial crisis, UBS lost \$38 billion, significantly reducing core capital and share price.

> In 2008, Volkswagen set a goal of surpassing Toyota as global automobile leader and tripling U.S. sales of diesel-powered cars. In 2015, Volkswagen admitted installing software that faked emission test results — share price fell more than 30 percent. Volkswagen's CEO resigned and many senior executives were fired.

KEY IDEA

Managers should explicitly discuss trade-offs and expectations among strategic objectives before setting operational objectives.

The firm should establish tentative short-term and long-term operational objectives early in the strategy development process. As the firm develops market-segment and market-strategy and implementation programs, it should continually assess budgetary implications. The firm should also revisit operational objectives, ultimately freezing as finite expectations and targets.

SETTING PERFORMANCE OBJECTIVES

Sometimes managers fail to distinguish between strategic objectives and operational objectives. Far too often, they state objectives in terms of profits — *Our profit target for 20XY is \$45 million*. In principle, setting a \$45 million target is not wrong, but the problem is in not asking (let alone answering) two basic questions: *How will achieving this profit objective affect the firm's overall objectives?* and *How shall we get there?*

Improving short-term profits is not that difficult. Just cut spending on new products, advertising, sales promotion, and salaries; raise prices; and tighten credit terms. The firm will quickly increase profits, but in time will lose market share and profitability. To avoid such results, the firm must articulate the trade-offs among the various strategic objectives and secure agreement from all functional areas. Only then should the firm insert numbers to form operational objectives.

Generally, strategic and operational objectives should not change during the operating period. But if significant environmental change occurs, adjusting performance objectives may be crucial. If planning assumptions underlying market evolution change substantially, then forecasts and performance objectives should change also. Some firms fail to modify market forecasts and objectives in the face of significant environmental change:

Environmental Change and Performance Objectives

In recessions, many capital goods firms do not act on data that predict lower future sales. Examples:

• Sales take longer to close.

• The economy slows — sales for one-time infrastructure development are likely to drop.

• Venture capital funding dries up — customers are likely to cancel purchases based on venture capital.

Upwardly biased sales projections also occur when customers order difficult-to-find products from several distributors and direct from the manufacturer.

Of course, the firm may have specific marketing objectives like brand awareness and customer satisfaction that affect strategic and operational objectives; we discuss these later.

MARKETING QUESTION

BlackBerry was once a corporate badge of honor, but has been significantly diminished by severe competitive pressure. Develop a viable market strategy for BlackBerry.

STRATEGIC FOCUS

Once the firm has established performance objectives for a target market segment, it must decide where to allocate resources. The *strategic focus* does exactly that. Figure 9.3 illustrates firm options using a *means/ends tree* to outline, assess, and choose among various alternatives for improving profits and return on investment (ROI).[15] The tree has two main branches: Branch A — *increase unit sales*; Branch B — *improve margins and investment returns*. The firm must select among these branches and subbranches to create a focus that best helps achieve strategic and operational objectives.

FIGURE 9.3
*Strategic Focus –
A Tree of Alternatives*

KEY IDEA

The market-segment strategy:
• Performance objectives
• **Strategic focus**
• Positioning
• Implementation programs

INCREASE UNIT SALES — BRANCH A

Branch A has two subbranches — C and D — for increasing unit sales. Each subbranch provides two alternatives. In subbranch C, the firm enhances current revenues by *increasing customer*

KEY IDEA

The four ways to increase unit sales are:
- Increase customer retention
- Increase customer use
- Attract customers from competitors
- Secure new business

MARKETING QUESTION

How does Amazon use purchase patterns to increase sales to current customers?

MARKETING QUESTION

Your firm wants to gain customers from competitors. How will you approach *win-back*? How will win-back differ from gaining new customers by *switching*?

retention — C1, and *increasing customer use* — C2. In subbranch D, the firm secures new revenues by *attracting customers from competitors* — D3, and *securing new business* — D4.

CURRENT REVENUE BASE: INCREASE CUSTOMER RETENTION — SUBBRANCH C1. The firm's customer base is like a leaky bucket. Some customers defect to competitors; others stop buying altogether. Chapter 2 shows that *plugging holes* by deploying approaches to reduce customer defection helps the firm retain customers longer and grow faster. This thinking also underpins customer relationship management (CRM). The New York Stock Exchange (NYSE) tries to persuade successful NASDAQ firms to join its exchange; NASDAQ retention managers reduce defection and enhance loyalty via extensive contact with *at-risk* firms. Many firms have loyalty programs that reward customers for repeat purchases — we're all familiar with airline *frequent-flyer* programs, retail clubs, and supermarket loyalty cards. But many small retailers like your local dry cleaner or car wash also use loyalty programs, often via simple physical cards they *chop/nick* with each purchase.

CURRENT REVENUE BASE: INCREASE CUSTOMER USE — SUBBRANCH C2. The firm encourages customers to increase repeat purchases and/or buy other products. In B2C, the firm sells products in larger containers[16]; speeds up obsolescence by introducing new versions — like cars and software; finds new product uses — like Arm & Hammer baking soda for cat litter, cleaning agent, deodorizer, toothpaste, and even cattle feed; provides price incentives for purchasing large quantities — like grocery store coupons[17]; and offers bundling opportunities like shampoo and conditioner, and durable goods with maintenance packages.

In B2B, many firms work with customers to engineer new product applications. Alcoa helps auto manufacturers reduce weight and increase gas mileage by replacing steel with aluminum. Helping customers grow their revenues is a powerful alternative. Xerox redesigned Citibank's monthly customer account statement to be more customer friendly (easier to read/understand); Citibank gained banking clients.[18] Other approaches include distributor training, joint promotions, advertising and promotion allowances, guarantees and warranties, and *spiffs* — cash incentives for retailer and distributor salespeople.

Many firms incorporate their brands into other firms' products, then advertise directly to consumers. The *intel inside* advertising campaign increased sales of personal computers — and Intel chips. Other firms focus on cross-selling — additional products to existing customers. Vanguard and Fidelity mutual fund customers can easily transfer deposits from fund to fund — and buy additional products like life insurance and annuities. This focus is easier to implement if the firm organizes around customers, rather than products or brands — Chapter 23.

NEW REVENUES: ATTRACT CUSTOMERS FROM COMPETITORS — SUBBRANCH D3. This category comprises two customer types:
- Previous customers that defected to competitors.
- Customers that purchase exclusively from competitors.

These customer types are quite different. Type 1 customers previously had a relationship with the firm — the challenge is *win-back*. Type 2 customers have never had a relationship — the challenge is *switch* from competitors. In either case, the firm must offer significant customer value to be successful. Winning back and switching customers are especially important in mature markets like credit cards because there are fewer *new* customers. How many credit card offers did you receive last month? If you have a decent credit history, probably quite a few.

In many cases, like credit cards and other financial services, customers split purchases among several suppliers; the firm's task is to increase *share of wallet*. Failed competitors offer good opportunities for attracting customers: Macy's focused on fallen rivals like Fortunoff, Gottschalks, and Mervyn's; Westchester County's (New York) Phoenix gym made special offers when a neighboring gym closed.

NEW REVENUES: SECURE NEW BUSINESS — SUBBRANCH D4. *Nonusers* have never purchased this type of product — from the firm *or* competitors. In subbranches C1, C2, D3, customers already have product experience; the firm's challenge was to beat competitors. In subbranch D4, the firm has a double selling task. First, the firm must convince nonusers to buy this type of product. Second, the firm must convince nonusers to purchase from the firm. Right now, firms making flat-screen plasma televisions must sell both product value and their brand.

INCREASE UNIT SALES — BRANCH A — REPRISE. The firm has four alternatives to increase unit sales — *increase customer retention* — C1; *increase customer use* — C2; *attract customers from competitors* — D3; *secure new business* — D4. Examples are in the boxed insert. How should the firm decide which alternative(s) to pursue? Two important factors are product life-cycle stage and the firm's competitive position. Early in the life cycle, few customers have tried the product; nonusers make most purchases — the firm spends heavily on market development. Moving toward maturity, the proportion of nonusers decreases, and focus shifts to retaining current customers and attracting competitor customers. Late in maturity when there are fewer nonusers, competitive position is particularly important. High-market-share leaders typically focus on retaining current customers and increasing their purchases — these customers are most of the market. Low-share firms focus on attracting competitor customers.

Examples of Increasing Unit Sales — keyed to Figure 9.3

C1. *Increase customer retention* — To consumers who financed a new GM automobile, GM offered identical financing for a second new car purchased within the financing period.

C2. *Increase customer use* — Verizon cross-sells long distance, Internet access, and television services. Similarly, cable TV firms sell telephone service and Internet access. Often these firms make bundled offers.

D3. *Attract customers from competitors* – DirecTV explicitly targets customers of cable TV firms; natural gas retailers target heating oil customers.

D4. *Secure new business* — Drug companies make *ask-your-physician* appeals, targeting *nonusers* to generate interest, leading to trial. Examples include Plavix — blood thinner; Viagra — erectile dysfunction; Wellbutrin — anxiety disorder.

IMPROVE MARGINS AND INVESTMENT RETURNS — BRANCH B

Branch B has two subbranches — E and F — for improving margins and investment returns, holding unit sales constant. Each subbranch provides two alternatives. In subbranch E, the firm increases revenues by *raising prices* — E5 and *improving the sales mix* — E6. In subbranch F, the firm lowers costs and assets by *reducing operating costs* — F7 and *improving asset utilization* — F8.

INCREASE REVENUES: RAISE PRICES — SUBBRANCH E5. This option is straightforward: The firm increases revenues by raising prices. Chapter 22 shows many options like increasing list price, cutting discounts, and reducing trade allowances.

INCREASE REVENUES: IMPROVE THE SALES MIX — SUBBRANCH E6. The firm sells more higher-profit products and fewer lower-profit products. Gillette pursued this strategy for many years by introducing successively more expensive two-blade shaving systems like Trac II, Atra, and Sensor. Then Gillette introduced the three-blade Mach3, followed by the battery-operated M3Power priced 67 percent higher than Mach3. Later, Gillette introduced the first five-blade razors — Fusion and Fusion Power — with refill prices one third greater than Mach3 Turbo, and the Fusion ProGlide at a 15 percent price premium. The firm can also de-emphasize less-profitable customers and place more effort on higher-profit customers.

KEY IDEA

The four ways to improve margins and investment returns are:

- Raise prices
- Improve the sales mix
- Reduce operating costs
- Improve asset utilization

REDUCE COSTS AND ASSETS: REDUCE OPERATING COSTS — SUBBRANCH F7. The firm has many options for reducing operating costs — related and/or unrelated to marketing. Marketing-related cost reductions include the sales force, promotion and advertising, administration and training, and new product development. The firm may also reduce operating costs by outsourcing, insourcing, and reengineering work processes.

REDUCE COSTS AND ASSETS: IMPROVE ASSET UTILIZATION — SUBBRANCH F8. Generally speaking, the firm has little asset investment in marketing — the closest items are accounts receivable and finished-goods inventory. Marketing can reduce accounts receivable by implementing stiffer credit terms and insisting on faster payments. Supply-chain improvements can reduce inventory investment. In the Walmart and P&G relationship, marketing plays a major role getting retail store transaction data into the P&G system. These data help reduce inventory throughout the supply chain and benefit not only P&G, but also its suppliers and Walmart.

IMPROVE MARGINS AND INVESTMENT RETURNS — BRANCH B — REPRISE. The firm has four alternatives to improve margins and investment returns — *raise prices* — E5, *improve the sales mix* — E6, *reduce operating costs* — F7, *improve asset utilization* — F8. Examples are in the boxed insert. The choice among these alternatives has a less sharp focus than Branch A. The firm should pursue alternatives providing the best financial returns.

Examples of Improving Margins and Investment Returns — keyed to Figure 9.3

E5. *Raise prices* — Firms with monopoly-like positions often use this approach — cable TV firms and suppliers like ESPN and Disney; also, seasonal products like amusement parks and airline travel.

E6. *Improve the sales mix* — Many B2B firms add services or offer additional features, trying to persuade customers to trade up to more expensive offers with higher profit margins.

F7. *Reduce operating costs* — Many firms reduce costs by downsizing (firing workers), reengineering work processes, and outsourcing internal operations. Other approaches include cutting back on advertising, and other promotional and selling expenses.

F8. *Improve asset utilization* — Dell's make-to-order manufacturing system minimizes inventory investment. Also, by receiving payment before making the product, Dell operates with *negative working capital.*[19]

CHOOSING A STRATEGIC FOCUS: INCREASE UNIT SALES OR IMPROVE MARGINS AND INVESTMENT RETURNS?

Question: How should the firm trade off alternatives in Branch A with alternatives in Branch B? After all, many are in conflict. Targeting competitor customers — D3 — may be a viable option for increasing unit sales, but it won't be successful if the firm simultaneously cuts advertising and selling expenses — F7!

Answer: The firm's choice of alternative(s) should closely parallel its primary strategic objective. For growth objectives, the firm should focus on Branch A alternatives; for increasing cash flow, the firm should focus on Branch B. If the primary strategic objective is improving profits, the firm should mix and match — select alternatives from both Branches A and B. One item is very clear: Pursuing too many alternatives simultaneously violates the Principle of Selectivity and Concentration, and causes the firm to lose focus.

POSITIONING

For many marketers and marketing faculty, *positioning* is the heart of the market-segment strategy. The firm seeks to create a unique and favorable image in customers' minds. Clarity is key; confusion is positioning's enemy.

We emphasize the critical distinction between *targeting* a market segment and *positioning* in a market segment. Chapter 8 discusses targeting market segments; Chapter 9 assumes the firm has made the targeting decision. Now we focus on developing a strategy to compete successfully in the target segment. Positioning requires four key decisions *within* the segment:

- Select customer targets.
- Frame competitor targets.
- Design the value proposition.
- Articulate reasons to believe.

KEY IDEA

The market-segment strategy:
- Performance objectives
- Strategic focus
- **Positioning**
- Implementation programs

We discuss these decisions sequentially but they are highly interrelated. Typically, the firm goes back and forth among these decisions until they form a coherent whole. Figure 9.4 breaks down the process by identifying considerations in selecting customer targets, framing competitor targets, and designing the value proposition.

FIGURE 9.4
Positioning Elements

SELECT CUSTOMER TARGETS

Customer targets are where the firm places the bulk of its marketing efforts. To have a good chance of being successful, the firm must target the *right* customers. Three issues are important:

- **Choosing the distribution system.** The firm must identify the appropriate distribution system — possibly comprising multiple levels — so its products reach consumers/end users.
- **Targeting levels within the distribution system.** The firm must decide which level(s) in the distribution system should receive the most marketing effort.
- **Targeting specific person types/roles.** The firm must identify what specific person types/roles it should target for effort at the chosen distribution level(s).

CHOOSING THE DISTRIBUTION SYSTEM. The firm's products/services may reach consumers/end users in many different ways — direct or via third-party organizations.[20] Examples for tangible products include:

- A component manufacturer sells products to finished-goods manufacturers.

KEY IDEA

Positioning elements are:
- Select customer targets
- Frame competitor targets
- Design the value proposition
- Articulate reasons to believe

KEY IDEA

Critical issues in selecting customer targets are:
- Choosing the distribution system
- Targeting levels within the distribution system
- Targeting specific person types/roles

MARKETING
QUESTION

Pret A Manger (PAM) (*ready to eat*) (British-based sandwich chain) entered the U.S. by opening stores in New York, Chicago, and Washington, DC. Conduct research to identify PAM's positioning. How do you assess PAM's chances for success in the U.S.?

- A component manufacturer sells products to subassembly manufacturers; in turn, subassembly manufacturers sell their products to finished-goods manufacturers.

- Products produced by finished-goods manufacturers pass through distributors, wholesalers, and/or retailers before reaching consumers/end users.

Many industries have well-established distribution systems whereby products travel *downstream* from level to level, ultimately reaching consumers/end users. But the firm may develop innovative channels to gain differential advantage. Today, many firms avoid distributors, wholesalers, and retailers (and their margins) by targeting consumers directly via the Internet.

TARGETING LEVELS WITHIN THE DISTRIBUTION SYSTEM. With limited resources, the firm must decide which distribution levels to target for effort. Broad options are *push* and *pull*:

- **Push strategy.** The firm places most marketing effort *upstream* on direct customers . A firm selling finished consumer products focuses on retailers; a raw material/component producer focuses on finished-goods producers like original equipment manufacturers (OEMs). The firm expects these customers (and/or their customers) to undertake promotional efforts at consumers/end users.

- **Pull strategy.** The firm places most marketing effort *downstream* on indirect customers — consumers/end users. FMCG firms focus on consumers; raw material/component manufacturers focus on consumers/end users — like the *intel inside* campaign.

Typically, the firm cannot apply equal effort at all potential customer targets. The firm should designate primary and secondary targets. Mattel shows the importance of customer targeting:

Mattel introduced *Barbie* at the 1959 Toy Fair — retail buyer response was negative. Essentially, they told Ruth Handler, Mattel founder and Barbie's originator: "Little girls want baby dolls; they want to pretend to be mommies." Motivational researcher Ernest Dichter advised Handler to launch Barbie with TV advertising. When girls saw TV ads for Barbie, they — and their mothers — stampeded the stores.[21] By targeting the final consumer, Mattel achieved global market leadership in the toy industry.

Japan's Okidata makes office products like fax machines and printers. Its U.S. subsidiary exclusively targeted a small number of geographically focused distributors. These distributors sell products to dealers, who in turn sell to corporate customers. To speed sales, Okidata reduced focus on distributors, and targeted dealers and corporate customers.

TARGETING SPECIFIC PERSON TYPES/ROLES. Once the firm has selected distribution level, it must decide which specific influencers and/or decision makers to target. Typically the firm wants to change or reinforce behavior and/or mental states like knowledge, attitudes, and purchase intentions. Recall: Organizations do not make purchase decisions — people in organizations make purchase decisions! For a firm targeting traditional households, potential individual targets include husband, wife, children, grandparents, uncles, and aunts.

College Savings Bank (CSB) offers certificates of deposit (CDs) indexed to college-cost inflation. CSB guarantees sufficient funds to pay college tuition at a specified future date. CSB targets parents and grandparents.[22]

China's one-child policy leads toy firms to target doting grandparents; in the U.S., firms target children directly. Tweens (8 to 12 years) are an increasingly important segment; they spend $15 billion annually and *heavily* influence $30 billion of parental spending. Popular products include privacy doorbells for their rooms, chairs shaped like baseball catcher's mitts, fanciful bed headboards, and fake-fur computer covers.

B2B firms also make individual-level targeting decisions. A firm selling raw materials to manufacturers may target operations managers, design engineers, marketing and sales executives, purchasing agents, and/or general managers. Relatedly, a well-known floor-covering firm reaches consumers via distributors and retailers. The firm markets heavily to retailers, but focuses on retail salespeople by providing spiffs (defined earlier).

Creativity is important in customer targeting. The firm should consider:

- **Reachability.** Target customers should be easy to reach, but gaining access may be difficult. In B2B, individual customers like designers, engineers, operations personnel, sales and marketing managers, and senior executives often want customized value. But the procurement system places barriers for sellers, forcing them to deal with purchasing professionals who often focus on short-term cost minimization and lower prices, rather than value. The creative CEO of one major telecommunications firm took a sales training course, then pitched the value of his firm's services directly to potential customer CEOs, bypassing procurement.

- **Obvious versus creative targets.** Some customers are easy to identify and reach, but targeting them can be ineffective because they are obvious — they may also be competitor customer targets! Deep customer insight, creativity, and a contrarian position can pay great dividends.[23] FedEx's early success came from targeting executives and their secretaries rather than shipping managers, the traditional decision makers. Much of Michelin's initial U.S. success in passenger tires was due to focusing on parents, primarily mothers, with young children.

- **Influentials.** Customer targets may not be decision makers, but they should influence the buying decision, like retail sales people for passenger tires and home appliances. Neglecting important influentials can be fatal. In B2B, overeager sellers often neglect subordinates, who may:
  - Identify specific criteria for supplier selection.
  - Determine which suppliers enter the customer's consideration set.
  - Have *nay* power, even if they don't have *yea* power.
  - Eventually replace their bosses. Firms that treat *the little guy* poorly may later encounter significant obstacles, especially if competitors have been more solicitous.

- **Personally benefits but does not pay.** The ideal customer target has significant influence and personally benefits from the purchase, but does not pay. Examples include:
  - Accountants, financial advisors, and lawyers for customers with investable funds.
  - Architects, interior designers, and product designers.[24]
  - Children influencing parental decisions.
  - Doctors writing prescriptions.
  - Executives whose firms pay travel expenses.
  - Politicians and regulators serving their constituents — they spend taxpayers' money.

Targeting these customers can raise ethical issues. Many people object to children's advertising; others object to targeting by government lobbyists.

FRAME COMPETITOR TARGETS

The firm decides which competitors to compete against. *Competitor targets* may be current and/or potential competitors, direct and/or indirect competitors, and/or supply-chain competitors. Choice of competitor target depends on firm strength in the market segment. For small competitors, choosing the right targets is vital — large and strong firms can be less delicate; Dr. Pepper has less leeway than Coca-Cola. Key issues are:

COMPETITOR CATEGORIES. Competitors fall into one of two categories — competitors to avoid, and competitors the firm is quite happy (and chooses) to face. This partition helps the firm design the value proposition.[25]

CUSTOMER PERCEPTIONS. Competitive targeting shapes customer perceptions of the firm's offer and helps refine its claims. Table 9.4 (p. 243) positioning alternatives suggest four competitor framings for 7-Up. Choosing among these options has important implications for 7-Up's market opportunities.

MARKETING QUESTION

State-owned Russian airplane manufacturer Sukhoi is expanding beyond Russia, Cuba, Iran, and a few African countries with its 75–95 seat, short-haul, single-aisle Superjet 100. Developed in partnership with French and Italian firms, Sukhoi has made Superjet sales to Armavia (Armenia) and Interjet (Mexico) airlines. Prepare a strategy for entering the U.S. and/or Western European markets.

KEY IDEA

The firm competes for customer targets — decision makers and/or influencers.

·················
TABLE 9.4
Positioning Options for Different Competitor Targets — 7-Up Illustration

Claim	Claim Type	Market Opportunity	Customer Implications
"7-Up tastes better than Sprite"[26]	Comparison with direct competitor	One lemon-lime soda substitutes for another	Compare us
"7-Up, the best-tasting lemon-lime soda"	Product-form superiority	The whole lemon-lime product form	The best choice when drinking lemon-lime
"7-Up, the Uncola"	Out of product form	The cola product form	The alternative to cola. "We're different"
"7-Up, the real thing, the only one," etc.	Implied or claimed uniqueness	All beverages	There's no other drink quite like it

KEY IDEA

The firm's competitive target can be:

- Current or potential
- Direct or indirect
- Supply chain

Sometimes the target competitor is not immediately obvious.

SUBTLETY IN COMPETITOR TARGETING. The most effective competitor targeting may not be obvious. Who benefits from designating major accounting firms as the Big 3? — Number 3! The Big 3's competitor target is number 4. When Avis *tries harder*, what is the competitor target? Maybe Hertz, but more likely smaller players like National and Budget. Visa advertises that many restaurants globally accept its card, but relatively few accept AmEx. Visa wants customers to believe AmEx is a direct competitor. But Visa's real competitor target is MasterCard.

·················
DESIGN THE VALUE PROPOSITION

A well-designed *value proposition* provides a convincing answer to a deceptively simple question: *Why should target customers prefer the firm's offer to those of competitors? Positioning* is *the heart of the market-segment strategy* — the *value proposition* is the heart of positioning. The firm bases the value proposition on functional, psychological, and economic value and related benefits it offers customers. The value proposition defines how the firm wins customers and defeats competitors. Related terms are *key buying incentive, differentiated core benefit, core strategy,* and *unique selling proposition,* but *value proposition* best captures the concept.[27]

KEY IDEA

The value proposition is the firm's major competitive weapon for *attracting, retaining,* and *growing* customers; it also defines the firm's implementation focus.

The firm must develop a value proposition for each target customer type.

Examples of Clear and Effective Value Propositions

- Apple's Macintosh computers — high quality, excellent user experience
- *Cosmopolitan* — fun, fearless, female
- FedEx — delivers on time — *When it absolutely, positively has to get there overnight*
- HSBC — global reach, local understanding
- iPod — take your music with you
- Kate Spade — curious, charming, clever
- Telephone calls made with Sprint are very clear — *You can hear a pin drop*
- Victoria's Secret — sexy, sophisticated, glamorous, feminine, forever young
- Walmart — always low prices, *always*

The firm should base its value proposition on the Principles of Customer Value and Differential Advantage — Chapter 1:

- focus on satisfying important customer needs;
- meet these needs better than competitors and, where possible;
- offer customer benefits/values that competitors find difficult to imitate.

MARKETING QUESTION

Google is the market leader in Internet search; Microsoft's search entry is Bing. How would you advise Microsoft to increase market share? How would you advise Google to resist Microsoft's efforts?

In particular, the value proposition should follow the **BUSCH** system — **b**elievable, **u**nique, **s**ustainable, **c**ompelling, **h**onest.[28] The value proposition plays two separate but related roles:

- **Externally** — is the firm's major competitive weapon to attract, retain, and grow customers. *Value proposition* defines why the firm's benefits/values — functional, psychological, economic — are superior to competition.

- **Internally** — defines the firm's implementation task; provides the organizing framework for firm activities.

The firm must develop a value proposition for each target customer type. FMCG firms often target both consumers/end users and retailers. They must develop two value propositions:

- **Consumers.** The value proposition typically focuses on specific consumer benefits/values. Detergent manufacturers Unilever and P&G offer functional benefits like *clean clothes, stain removal, whiter whites*. They also offer psychological benefits/values like *caring for the family* and the ability to demonstrate *being a good parent*.

- **Retailers.** The value proposition typically focuses on economic benefits like *potential profits* and *promotional support*, or functional benefits like *ease of doing business, one-stop shopping, expertise*, and *product delivery*.

Value propositions for separate customer targets are not independent. Suppose the firm communicates its value proposition for consumers with heavy advertising and promotion. High advertising spending weakens the economic value proposition the firm can offer retailers. By contrast, private-label manufacturers offer retailers a strong economic value proposition based on low prices by avoiding heavy advertising and promotion expenditures.

MARKETING QUESTION

Club Med's slogan — *The antidote for civilization* — suggests a somewhat rebellious holiday destination. What is Club Med's positioning — customer target, competitor target, value proposition, reasons to believe?

ARTICULATE REASONS TO BELIEVE

Declaring the firm's intentions in the value proposition is one thing; convincing target customers that the firm will deliver on its promises is quite another. The *reasons-to-believe* statement is an essential component of positioning; it supports the value proposition with compelling facts to make its claims believable — like scientific evidence, independent testing data, testimonials, proven competencies, prior performance, and/or factual information on product attributes. Examples include:

- Cisco — technical expertise in routers and many successful installations worldwide
- Citibank — vast network of branches around the world
- CommerceOne — a convenience bank: hours 7 a.m. to 7 p.m., 7 days a week
- J&J — Tylenol: clinical evidence of superior pain relief
- P&G — detergents: long experience in detergents and huge R&D commitment

DEVELOPING POSITIONING STATEMENTS

Positioning is not what you do to a product — positioning is what you do to the mind of the prospect.[29]

The capstone of the positioning process is a compelling positioning statement: Positioning is vital for guiding and coordinating the firm's marketing efforts. But developing the positioning statement is complex, difficult, and time-consuming. Many people may be involved. A senior Unilever marketing executive alleged that it often takes longer to develop product positioning than to develop the product! When P&G introduced *Whitestrips* (teeth whitener), it delayed expensive TV ads and store testing. Rather, P&G refined Whitestrips positioning and assessed consumer interest while undertaking a six-month online advertising and sales campaign.

Positioning must clearly distinguish the firm's offer from competitor offers.[30] Positioning should:

Convince	customer target
In the context of alternatives	competitor target
That they will receive these benefits and values	value proposition
Because we have these capabilities/features	reasons to believe

Table 9.5 shows a positioning statement for Cemex (Mexican multinational cement producer). Note the value proposition differs by customer target.

....
TABLE 9.5
*Example: Positioning
Statement for Cemex*[31]

Task	Focus	Positioning Item
Convince	Builders and contractors; site managers and project investors	Customer Target
In the context of other alternatives	Traditional cement producers	Competitor Target
That they will receive these benefits and values	Site managers: Consistent delivery within 30 minutes of Cemex receiving an order — versus the three-hour standard Project investors: Additional revenues from early project completion	Value Proposition
Because we have these capabilities and resources	A global positioning satellite system on each truck. Computer software that combines truck positions with plant output and customer orders to calculate optimal destinations. Ability to redirect trucks en route.[32]	Reasons to Believe

Positioning statements should be **d**istinct, **c**ompelling, **a**uthentic, **p**ersuasive, and **s**ustainable (DCAPS). Creativity can be crucial. Guinness Stout traditionally served a limited market of older men and women.[33] Guinness repositioned Guinness Stout as a friendly beverage for younger consumers. Guinness also leveraged brand heritage by offering the Guinness experience at more than 2,000 Irish pubs worldwide. Sales increased dramatically.

Positioning is especially important for new products. Unilever and P&G *get it*, but many firms launch new products with ineffective positioning. Philips (Dutch electronics firm) has a stellar product innovation record but does not market innovations well. Some of Philips' technical successes were marketing failures due to ineffective positioning. Many firms waste millions of advertising dollars because of poorly developed positioning. Positioning statements are not advertising messages, but DCAPS positioning provides excellent guidance for creative personnel at advertising agencies.

IMPLEMENTATION PROGRAMS

Strategic focus and positioning specify the firm's approach to achieve performance objectives. *Implementation programs* describe specific actions the firm must take to execute its approach. Any good market or market-segment strategy must seriously address both the marketing mix and other functional programs. Marketing and associated functions like the sales force are responsible for implementing the marketing mix. Personnel from functions like finance and manufacturing implement other functional programs. Integrating the marketing mix and other functional programs is critical for optimizing firm efforts — Figure 9.5. Top executive support is crucial for superb implementation.

....
IMPLEMENTING THE MARKETING MIX

Two issues are important for implementing the marketing mix:

SUPPORT THE VALUE PROPOSITION AND EACH OTHER. Chapters 12 through 22 focus on individual marketing-mix elements. These elements must support the value proposition, and must also support other marketing-mix elements. Table 9.6 (p. 246) shows how Steubenware marketing-mix elements support one another for high-quality glass crystal in the gift segment. We assume that the value proposition revolves around psychological value, assurance that recipients will love Steubenware gifts for their high quality, scarcity, and image.

MARKETING QUESTION

Select your favorite (or least favorite) politician. In his/her most recent political campaign, what segment(s) did s/he target? How did the positioning — customer target, competitive target, value proposition, reasons to believe — differ from segment to segment? How did multiple segment strategies mutually interface?

MARKETING QUESTION

Sales of erectile dysfunction drugs — Viagra, Levitra, Cialis — approximate $4 billion annually. Viagra and Cialis each have about 40 percent market share. How are the three drugs positioned? How, if at all, have their positionings evolved? What recommendations would you make for each drug? How does patent expiration factor into your recommendations?

KEY IDEA

The market-segment strategy:
• Performance objectives
• Strategic focus
• Positioning
• **Implementation programs**

Marketing-Mix Element	Steubenware Implementation
Product	Extremely high quality — Steuben destroys imperfect products
Service	High-quality pre- and postsale service
Advertising	High-quality shelter magazines like *Good Housekeeping*
Sales promotion	High-quality brochure material and display racks
Selling strategy	Focuses on product quality
Distribution	Few retail outlets, but high quality — specialty stores and upscale department stores
Price	High price — reflecting high-quality image

....
TABLE 9.6
Marketing Mix for Steubenware in the Gift Segment

KEY IDEA

The firm implements market-segment strategy via:

• Marketing mix
• Other functional programs

BUDGET SIZE AND ALLOCATION. Budgetary issues are critical in designing the marketing mix. The firm must set an overall budget but be prepared for modifications based on corporate priorities, competitor actions, and/or difficult economic times. The firm must allocate the budget across different marketing-mix areas. In some areas the firm's budget exceeds competitors; in other areas, competitors spend more. The firm must be sure its efforts are superior in areas supporting the value proposition, and should continually test budget allocations:

Hamfirm (HF) (disguised) believed product improvement was the only way to grow sales and profits. Interviews at retail stores carrying HF products revealed it should moderate product improvement efforts and allocate greater resources to advertising, in-store promotions, promotional giveaways, and salesperson spiffs.

Amazon's 16-month test in two cities showed advertising was not working — Amazon transferred resources to free shipping.

Heinz improved financial performance by reducing incentive payments to retailers and investing in advertising.

MARKETING QUESTION

What is the iPhone's value proposition? What is its marketing mix? Do the marketing-mix elements support the value proposition and each other?

....
ALIGNING CROSS-FUNCTIONAL SUPPORT

Marketing *owns* the market-segment and market strategies. Regardless, competition is so intense, the entire firm must work together as a competitive weapon. In particular, the firm must align all functional areas — like finance, human resources, legal, operations, and R&D — to support the value proposition — Figure 9.5 (p. 247). Key factors in successful alignment include open and clear leadership, early involvement of key personnel, team-based planning, and interpersonal sensitivity. A leading U.S. business magazine was in crisis when competition challenged its 50-year market dominance. The firm pulled together a cross-functional team to develop and implement a new market strategy. This approach successfully reinforced the magazine's leadership and produced its best-ever financial result!

Domino's Pizza provides functional support for its value proposition — delivering hot pizza quickly. Domino's selects locations with easy access to many homes; the customer database saves time taking orders and making deliveries; and R&D produced new technology to cook pizza en route to the customer. On weekends, Hertz city locations sold out while cars sat idle at airports; Hertz hired *transporters* to move cars back and forth on Thursday and Sunday nights. Disney designs theme parks to implement its value proposition — *the fantasy*; a lot happens behind the scenes: Customers never see Mickey in the bathroom or two Dumbos at the same time; even street-sweepers are *scripted*. Disney simplified ticket books to *one price* and installed an *easy pass* system to minimize queuing hassles.

KEY IDEA

Implementation:

• Marketing-mix programs should support the value proposition
• All elements should support each other

If one or more functional areas cannot provide support, the firm must revisit the value proposition. This analysis is critical. Going forward without full support commits the cardinal marketing sin — making promises to customers the firm cannot keep. Customers do not care which individual or department is at fault. They want, and expect, the benefits/values the firm promised. They rightly believe the firm should fix the problem.

FIGURE 9.5
*Integrating Functional
Programs*

KEY IDEA

Functional areas must
support the market-segment
strategy.

Sometimes required support extends beyond various functions in a single business unit to collaboration across several businesses. Cross-business support is increasingly critical in strategic (key) account management; strategic account managers must design offers that integrate products/services from multiple businesses. The critical barrier to cross-business collaboration is often perceived impact on individual business profitability. Top management support and modifying of managerial measurement and incentive systems are ways to address this problem.

Wheelwright (disguised medical-products firm) comprised several businesses making products for hospital operating rooms. Wheelwright's corporate marketing group designed a *one-stop-shop* offer including products from several businesses. Customers were enthusiastic, but some individual businesses refused to make necessary distribution and service changes and price concessions. The initiative failed.

TEST YOUR FIRM'S MARKET STRATEGY ON A BAKER'S DOZEN ITEMS[34]

1. *Clarity* — Is it clear what we *are* going to do and what we *are not* going to do?

2. *External consistency* — Are our offers consistent with best insight about the market, customers, competitors, and complementers?

3. *Value* — Do our offers deliver significant benefits/values to customers?

4. *Advantage* — Do our offers promise greater customer value than competitors'?

5. *Flexibility* — Do our choices allow us to address expected evolution in the market, customers, competitors, and complementers, and the environment in general?

6. *Financial consistency* — Are our choices consistent with our financial goals?

7. *Focus* — Are our offers consistent with our capabilities/resources?

8. *Internal consistency* — Are our choices internally consistent?

9. *Focus* — Are our employees able to prioritize their work to deliver our offers?

10. *Learning* — Does the strategy development process build our intellectual capital?

11. *Functionally integrated* — Is the market strategy well integrated with other functional strategies?

12. *Cross-market integrated* — Is the market-segment strategy well integrated with our other market-segment strategies?

13. *Robustness* — Are our choices able to withstand external shocks?

Rate your firm's market strategy on each item: 1 = strongly disagree; 10 = strongly agree.

MANAGING MULTISEGMENT STRATEGIES

This chapter shows how to construct a strategy — performance objectives, strategic focus, positioning, implementation programs — for addressing a target market segment. But the firm often targets several segments simultaneously; hence it must develop several market-segment strategies. Each segment strategy requires its own performance objectives, strategic focus, positioning, and implementation programs. The firm must ensure that each segment strategy is distinct. Pottery Barn Kids' positioning is distinct from Pottery Barn — but Pottery Barn is not well distinguished from its down-market chain — West Elm. Banana Republic is distinct from Gap and Old Navy, but Gap and Old Navy are less distinct from each other.

When the firm targets multiple segments, it faces three possible implementation situations:

- **Independence.** Individual segment strategies and implementation programs are unrelated.
- **Positive synergies.** The firm enjoys positive *synergies* from implementation programs across segments. The firm may secure cost efficiencies from using the same sales force, distribution channels, and/or sharing brand equity. The GE brand is so well known and widely respected that new product entries gain enormously.
- **Negative synergies.** The firm suffers negative synergy from implementation programs across segments. Multiple products confuse the sales force; brand extensions confuse customers. Almaden is a strong brand of popularly priced wine, but a $100 Almaden bottle would probably not do well!!

KEY IDEA

Together, individual market-segment strategies must form a coherent market strategy.

Market-segment strategies must be individually distinct, yet the firm should seek positive synergies in implementation programs.

The firm's individual market-segment strategies and implementation programs must together form a coherent market strategy. Because of increasing complexity in customer need profiles and related implications for internal coordination, multiple-segment issues are especially intriguing and challenging. Sometimes the firm is unable to address two segments simultaneously: In general, *big pharma* firms seem unable to address low-price segments when drugs come off patent, and no major airline has successfully operated a low-cost carrier. Table 9.7 identifies the sorts of problems that may arise and potential solutions.

Marketing-Mix Element	Potential Problem	Possible Solution
Product	Increased production costs, increased inventory costs, delivery delays	Modular design, just-in-time (JIT) assembly
Service	Alienate customers not receiving premium service package	Try to ensure perceived equity; maintain physical separation where possible
Advertising	Exposure to different appeals	Ensure appeals do not conflict and messages across segments are consistent; use specialized media
Sales force	Salespeople ineffective with multiple products and/or in multiple segments	Extra training or develop specialized sales forces
Distribution	Alienate intermediaries	Secure financial-service package for selected intermediaries; consider different brands and packages
Pricing	Transshipment — diversion from one segment to another	Manage price differentials; differentiate elements like brand and package

TABLE 9.7
Issues in Targeting Multiple Market Segments

What other messages did you glean from this chapter?

KEY MESSAGES

The market strategy has four key purposes:
- Provide strategic direction in the market.
- Secure differential advantage.
- Guide the effective allocation of scarce resources.
- Achieve cross-functional integration.

The market-segment strategy comprises four key elements; each element has several constituent parts:

- *Performance objectives:* Results the firm hopes to achieve:
  - *Strategic objectives* — qualitative and directional. Strategic objectives typically fall into one of three categories — growth and market share, profitability, cash flow.
  - *Operational objectives* — quantitative and time-bound. How much and by when.

- *Strategic focus:* The broad direction of the strategy. Has two main branches — *increase unit sales* and *improve margins and investment returns.*
  - *Increase unit sales* has two subbranches:
    - *Current revenue base — increase customer retention; increase customer use.*
    - *New revenues — attract customers from competitors; secure new business.*
  - *Improve margins and investment returns* also has two subbranches:
    - *Increase revenues — raise prices; improve the sales mix.*
    - *Reduce costs and assets — reduce operating costs; improve asset utilization.*

- *Positioning:* How target customers should view the firm's offer. Requires four key decisions:
  - *Select customer targets* — choose the distribution system, level(s) to target, and the specific person types/roles.
  - *Frame competitor targets* — competitors the firm decides to go up against.
  - *Design the value proposition* — why customers should prefer the firm's offer.
  - *Articulate reasons to believe* — supporting evidence for the value proposition.

- *Implementation programs:* Actions the firm must take to execute the strategy. Two types:
  - *Marketing mix: Externally* — product, service, promotion, distribution, price.
  - *Supporting functional programs: Internally* — integrate functional areas to work together.

If the firm targets multiple market segments, each segment strategy must be distinct. The firm should seek positive synergy among implementation programs.

VIDEOS AND AUDIOS

For complimentary material, see Axcess Capon codes at www.axcessvids.com

Segmentation, Targeting, Positioning	406v	Wayne DeSarbo	Smeal College of Business, Pennsylvania State University
Why Strategies Fail?	590v	Mark Chussil	Advanced Competitive Strategies
Marketing Imperative 3 — Market Strategy	602a	Noel Capon	Columbia Business School
Marketing Imperative 4	173a	Noel Capon	Columbia Business School

QUESTIONS FOR STUDY AND DISCUSSION

Can you answer the questions implied by this chapter's learning outcomes? Check!

1. Apple's iPod is one of the 21st century's most successful consumer products. Using the frameworks in this chapter, describe Apple's market strategy for the iPod.

2. Better Place (BP) signed agreements with national and local governments — Australia, Canada, Denmark, Israel, California, and Hawaii — to build recharging networks for electric cars. What are BP's strategic marketing challenges? How would you address them?

3. P&G's Tide has led the household detergent market for more than a half-century. Why? What lessons can you draw from Tide's success?

4. The National Basketball Association (NBA) has slumped, whereas the National Football League (NFL) is very successful. Why? How would you turn around the NBA?

5. Quidel manufactures home-pregnancy-test kits. What segments can you identify in the home-pregnancy-test market? How should Quidel position its products in these segments? What implementation programs do you suggest? Hint: Check out your local supermarket.

6. Historically, several competitive battles stand out: Adidas vs. Nike; Bloomberg vs. Thomson-Reuters; Boeing vs. Airbus; Coke vs. Pepsi; GM vs. Ford; Google+ vs. Facebook; Intel vs. AMD; Microsoft vs. Google; Oracle vs. SAP; Sears vs. Montgomery Ward. Compare and contrast two or more rivalries that interest you. What can you learn about market strategy?

7. What are the challenges of designing an effective market strategy? Use two current examples to explain. Use the Baker's Dozen items to assess the effectiveness of these strategies.

8. Select a product in which you are interested. Alternatively, consider *Managing Marketing in the 21st Century*. Refer to Chapter 8, question 7. Lay out a strategy for a market segment you identified.

TRUE/FALSE QUESTIONS

Answers on page A2 and at www.axcessvids.com — 962p

1. The basic market-strategy unit is the market-segment strategy. ❏ **TRUE** ❏ **FALSE**

2. The three broad categories of strategic objectives are growth and market share, profitability, and cash flow. ❏ **TRUE** ❏ **FALSE**

3. A firm implementing a pull strategy places most marketing effort upstream on direct customers. ❏ **TRUE** ❏ **FALSE**

4. A compelling positioning statement is vital for guiding and coordinating the firm's marketing efforts. ❏ **TRUE** ❏ **FALSE**

5. The firm enjoys positive synergies by targeting an additional segment, although new products may confuse the sales force. ❏ **TRUE** ❏ **FALSE**

MULTIPLE CHOICE QUESTIONS

Answers on page A2 and at www.axcessvids.com — 651p

1. The firm must make all of the following types of decisions when determining which segments it will target for effort and how it will position itself in those market segments EXCEPT:

   a. results
   b. resources
   c. actions
   d. retraction

2. Which of the following is NOT one of the four pillars of a market-segment strategy?

   a. performance objectives
   b. cultural identity
   c. strategic focus
   d. positioning

3. Positioning requires the firm to take each of the following actions within segments EXCEPT:

   a. Screen new product ideas.
   b. Frame competitor targets.
   c. Design the value proposition.
   d. Articulate the reasons to believe.

4. Which of the following is NOT one of the three important issues when targeting customers?

   a. Identify the appropriate distribution system for its products/services to reach consumers/end users.
   b. Select the distributor that uses a focus strategy to target its customers.
   c. Decide at which level(s) in its distribution system organizations should receive the most marketing effort.
   d. Identify what specific persons or types of person at the chosen distribution levels it should target for effort.

5. The firm _____ from implementation programs for individual segments. The firm may gain cost efficiencies from using the same sales force and similar distribution channels and/or sharing brand equity.

   a. experiences independence
   b. suffers negative synergy
   c. experiences interdependence
   d. enjoys positive synergy

Set Strategic Direction and Positioning

CHAPTER 10

MANAGING THROUGH THE LIFE CYCLE

For complimentary material, see Axcess Capon codes at www.axcessvids.com

There are risks and costs to a program of action. But they are far less than the long-range risks and costs of inaction.

— John F. Kennedy, U.S. President

LEARNING OUTCOMES

When you have completed this chapter, you will be able to:

- Appreciate the critical importance of preemption in developing market strategy.
- Use the product life-cycle framework to generate several plausible scenarios.
- Identify and assess business characteristics and strategic considerations for each scenario.
- Generate strategic options for each scenario.
- Recognize effective life-cycle strategies.

OPENING CASE: RYANAIR

Ryanair upset the life cycle for European air travel when it entered the Ireland-England market in 1985 with flights from Waterford (southeast Ireland) to London's Gatwick Airport. In 1986, Ryanair challenged the government-owned British Airways and Aer Lingus duopoly on the Dublin-London route with flights to London's Luton Airport. Ryanair's initial £99 round-trip price was less than half the £209 duopoly price. In 1986, Ryanair alone carried 82,000 passengers versus route totals of 500,000 annually for the previous several years. Observers believed Ryanair passengers came from three sources: British Airways and Aer Lingus passengers; new air travel passengers from the 750,000 annually who made the nine-hour trip by rail and ferry for fares as low as £55; and passengers who previously didn't travel because of high airline prices and/or the inconvenience of ferry travel on the often-stormy Irish Sea and British Rail.

In the late 1980s, Ryanair added jet aircraft and rapidly expanded its route network to 15 destinations: from Dublin to other British cities and continental Europe, and from London (Luton) to different parts of Ireland. Ryanair offered conventional airline services including business-class travel and a frequent-flier club. But intense price competition and new capacity from British Airways and

Aer Lingus led to significant accumulated losses and a forced restructuring. Ryanair then adopted Southwest Airlines' model to become Europe's first low-fare airline, offering a single class of service, using a single type of aircraft configured with the maximum number of seats, and high-frequency schedules. Ryanair switched from London (Luton) to Stansted Airport — its new terminal had a direct rail link to London's Liverpool Street station. Dublin Airport became the origin of most Irish flights. Ryanair was profitable by 1991.

To support its low-price strategy, Ryanair obsessively cut costs: Ryanair eliminated free drinks and meals; high-capacity utilization pushed down overhead costs. Airport destinations were a significant distance from the advertised cities; Ryanair promised economic growth and employment benefits to negotiate lower landing fees and other costs, and secure local marketing support. Ryanair revamped its route structure so that typical flights were one hour or less, and organized its hubs to reduce maintenance costs and turnaround times.

Ryanair's major continental European expansion occurred post-1996, following the European Union's Open Skies agreement. Ryanair addressed new markets with its successful low-fares model. Other airline startups used similar models, but none was as successful as Ryanair. British Airways and KLM formed Go Fly and Buzz, respectively, but sold out to easyJet and Ryanair. Ryanair's most significant competitor was easyJet.

Ryanair's conduct differed from traditional airlines in several ways:

- *Around 20 percent of Ryanair's revenues derived from ancillary activities: Flight attendants used in-flight time to sell snacks, beverages, and duty-free items. Ryanair sold advertising space on seat backs, aircraft exteriors, and in-flight magazines, and earned commissions from hotel bookings and car rental.*

- *Ryanair's advertisements were often racy: one advertisement with the headline* Expensive Bastards! *compared Ryanair with British Airways; another featured a model dressed as a schoolgirl, with the words* Hottest back-to-school fares. *Ryanair's advertising frequently led to lawsuits, some won, some lost; regardless, Ryanair secured significant publicity.*

- *Ryanair earned publicity from CEO Michael O'Leary's frequent tirades against Ireland's government ministers, Aer Rianta (Ireland's state-owned airport authority), the European Union, and any person/organization that O'Leary believed interfered with Ryanair's low-air-fare strategy.*

- *Passenger convenience was not a high priority: New aircraft did not have reclining seats nor seatback pockets; Ryanair did not refund passengers for missed flights; passengers paid for all checked bags and airport check-in. Other proposed (but not implemented) measures included eliminating some toilets to add more seats, charging for toilet use, redesigning aircraft to allow standing passengers, charging extra for overweight passengers, and asking passengers to carry checked-in luggage to the plane.*[865v]

By 2005, Ryanair was Europe's largest airline, carrying 31 million passengers mostly via online booking. To celebrate its 20th birthday, and continuing its practice of airline-seat sales, Ryanair offered 100,000 seats at 99 pence. In 2006 and 2008, Ryanair made unsuccessful hostile takeover bids for the recently privatized Aer Lingus, but retained a significant ownership stake. By end 2013, Ryanair was flying 1,600 flights daily, from 70 bases, on 1,600 routes, connecting almost 200 destinations in 30 countries, including three destinations in North Africa. In 2014, Ryanair carried 85 million passengers, earned more than $7 billion revenues; net income — $700 million. By 2016, Ryanair's share price had increased more than 10 times since its 1996 IPO.[666v][1]

Case Question

The Ireland-Britain market seemed to be in maturity when Ryanair entered. Ryanair's actions shifted the life cycle into a period of dynamic growth. How do you explain this transformation? How do you assess criticisms of Mr. O'Leary, and his responses? **[885v]**

NEW AIRPORT SECURITY PROCEDURES

PUT FUN BACK INTO FLYING

Ryanair and easyJet have been highly successful in Europe with low-price strategies. Norwegian Air Shuttle (NAS) has entered the highly competitive north-Atlantic route with a similar model. Do you think NAS will be successful? Why or why not?

Firms failing to act preemptively may face significant opportunity costs.

Chapter 10 is the second of three chapters discussing separate facets of Imperative 3: Set Strategic Direction and Positioning. Chapter 9 shows how to develop market-segment strategy and market strategy. Earlier in the book, Chapter 3 shows how the *life-cycle framework* can help the firm generate useful market insights. In this chapter, we revisit the life-cycle framework to help the firm make more effective decisions in competitive markets.

By anticipating competitor actions — and sometimes their timing — the firm can develop *preemptive* strategies. A preemptive strategy means acting before your competitors, perhaps targeting an emerging segment or introducing a new product. Ryanair is a good example of preemptive action. Acting preemptively often involves risks, and failure may be visible and costly. But the costs of not acting may be significant, particularly for established players. These *opportunity costs* are the market-share gains and increased profits the firm did not earn. Opportunity costs are insidious; they do not appear on the firm's income statement, but they may be much higher than costs that do.

Consider Apple and the iPod — many observers counseled caution. They said to Apple: "You are a computer company; you have no experience in digital music. Napster has closed, and downloading music via the Internet faces immense uncertainty. Sony owns portable music players with the Walkman; this is their turf, and they will fight you fiercely." Many executives would have heeded these arguments, but not Steve Jobs. The iPod launch was an enormous success and even helped Apple sell more Macintosh computers. Think of the opportunity costs Apple would have incurred by not launching the iPod, iPhone, or iPad — *what did Apple know about recorded music or mobile communications?*

By not acting, the firm opens up potential entry windows for competitors. Firms often fail to address competitor threats because they view competition differently or misunderstand competitive strategy — *we don't really compete* or *we have different strategies*. Or firms hesitate because *going out on a limb* is visible and risky. Consider the impact on BlackBerry of not taking the risks that Apple took. Once the symbol of corporate and political power, BlackBerry is now a shadow of its former self; many observers predict its imminent demise. Microsoft also missed this opportunity. Said former CEO Steve Ballmer, "I regret that there was a period in the early

2000s when we were so focused on what we had to do around Windows that we weren't able to redeploy talent to the new device called the phone." Neither Aer Lingus nor British Airways acted effectively in the face of Ryanair's disruptive change in air travel. Market-leading firms should view preemption as an insurance policy — when change is swift, the costs of inaction escalate rapidly. Firms that will not pay *insurance premiums* should prepare to lose market position.

The life-cycle framework offers a good way to design *insurance policies*. Understanding how life cycles and market strategies evolve is valuable for forecasting and anticipating likely scenarios. With these scenarios, the firm is better equipped to generate good competitive strategic options.

The Value of Preemptive Strategy

Meyer Feldberg, then Columbia Business School dean, realized that several leading U.S. schools were developing strong international presence. He knew London Business School would be a desirable partner for many U.S. schools, particularly Wharton. Feldberg also knew that a London-Philadelphia axis could marginalize Columbia and would be a PR coup for Wharton. He flew to London, met with London Business School dean John Quelch, and created a strategic alliance for the now highly successful EMBA Global program.

THE CHANGING VIEW

OLD WAY	NEW WAY
Accept low returns and cross-subsidize products	Apply rigorous shareholder value discipline
Commoditization viewed as inevitable	Innovation is a major strategic weapon
Competition to the death	Merger and consolidation viewed as legitimate strategies in shareholder interest
Evolutionary change of management approach	Proactively planned change of management approach
Firms cut costs when times are bad	Firms monitor efficiency and continually cut costs
Firms hide behind regulatory barriers, often supported by government	Governments work aggressively to increase competition
Firms maximize cash flow by minimizing investment in mature markets	Innovation rejuvenates market growth
Industry structure viewed as fixed	Industry structure viewed as variable
Preemptive strategies rare	Preemptive strategies commonplace
Sequential product development	Concurrent product development
Slow market development with sequential product introductions worldwide	Rapid market development with simultaneous new product launches in multiple countries
Tied to traditional distribution systems and business models	New business models, distribution methods, and technologies to increase efficiencies and add value
Uninformed entry strategies	Entry strategies driven by sophisticated understanding of market development

DEVELOPING COMPETITIVE STRATEGIC OPTIONS

The firm generates *strategic options* by developing scenarios that let it anticipate future competitor actions. The main building block is the classic life cycle — introduction, early growth, late growth, maturity, decline — typically at the product-form level. The *life-cycle approach* is very powerful because market conditions tend to be similar at the same life-cycle stage across many products/technologies. Each scenario generates a limited number of strategic options. These options are valuable input into formulating firm strategy, but creativity is always important. The firm should avoid becoming too predictable, even when it is market leader. This chapter discusses how to generate strategic options from nine scenarios — Figure 10.1.

FIGURE 10.1
Life-Cycle Scenarios

Can you identify firms and products corresponding to each scenario — Figure 10.1?

John Deere took advantage of market disarray created when farm-implement firm Case merged with New Holland to create CNH Global. Deere offered loyal Case and New Holland customers steep discounts, low interest rates, and $5,000 in cash to swap their products for new Deere products. Deere also slashed trade-in prices, undercutting sales of new CNH products and creating nervousness about trade-in values!

Although the scenarios and strategic options are valid for many product life cycles, generally life cycles are shortening — Figure 10.2 (p. 258).[2] Implications are:

- When life cycles were longer, firms could enter a market, fail, redevelop products, and reenter with a reasonable chance of success. Today, reentry windows are closing.

- Shortening product life cycles reduce the time — in early growth — to earn the highest unit margins.

- Good strategic thinking early in the life cycle is more important than ever.

- Faster cycles require proactive management of strategy over the life cycle; evolutionary approaches may be too slow.

Identifying scenarios and developing strategic options is more important than ever. We designed this chapter specifically to improve student abilities to formulate strategic options and design market strategies to defeat competitors.[3]

KEY IDEA

Nine scenarios based on:

- Product life cycle
- Competitive position

are basic building blocks for developing competitive strategic options.

Life cycles are shortening for many products.

Source Data: W. Michael Cox, Federal Reserve Bank of Dallas (2007)

FIGURE 10.2
Shortening Product Life Cycles

KEY IDEA

Scenarios help the firm generate competitive strategic options.

Successful strategies should have a strong creative element.

Building Product Life-Cycle Scenarios

Let's walk through the nine product life-cycle-based scenarios in Figure 10.1. Each scenario description begins with a brief introduction; then we focus on creating and analyzing alternative objectives and strategies. But we must be very clear about one important issue: We cannot tell you what strategy to follow for a given scenario — your best strategy depends in part on competitor actions. Rather, we provide some strategic options for you to build into your decision process. (Marketing Enrichment 10.1 **[836p]** summaries the strategic options.)

SCENARIO 1: INTRODUCTION STAGE — PIONEERS

Gillette spent $1 billion on developing and initially marketing the Mach3 razor. First-year marketing spending was $300 million for simultaneous launch in 19 countries. Gillette corporate profits dropped in the launch year due to Mach3 startup expenses.

Most products do not generate profits in the introduction stage. Pioneering firms typically incur significant R&D and market launch expenditures; they must also invest in plant, equipment, and systems and processes, before launch. Marketing expenses are high, and revenues may not cover ongoing operating costs, much less fixed costs. Early on, cash flows are often neg-

KEY IDEA

Pioneers must be prepared to tap multiple sources to fund early life-cycle losses.

ative. Kevin Plank, founder of *Under Armour*, lived in his grandmother's basement for several years before earning profits from launching new athletic wear. Under Armour went public 10 years after founding and now pursues a mission of clothing athletes head to toe, including running shoes. Many other firms like Apple and HP famously started life in garages.

Some firms are better able to sustain new product losses and negative cash flows than others. Large firms typically cross-subsidize new product launches with cash earned from more established products at later life-cycle stages, as part of a long-term product strategy. Tide laundry detergent funds many new ventures for P&G; other examples include operating system software and Windows for Microsoft; Google AdWords funds Alphabet/Google initiatives.

Of course, pioneering firms must have vision and be willing to take risks. Pioneers generally make many mistakes; the key is *productive* failure so the firm learns and continually moves forward. Pioneers must be willing to introduce less than perfect product versions for later upgrade and, if necessary, cannibalize current products. Despite huge resources, Microsoft initially failed in search. Microsoft shut down its rudimentary *Keywords* system for fear of cannibalization and later rejected the opportunity to buy Overture, the pioneer in combining search with advertising. Google became the dominant search leader.

KEY IDEA

Barriers to competitive entry:
• Government-imposed
• Product-specific
• Firm-driven

Small firms typically have fewer resources and often require outside financing. In the very early stages, wealthy individuals — aka *angel investors* — often provide startup funding for new ventures. Later, *venture capitalists* may provide financial backing when the opportunity starts to show promise. If the value proposition is sufficiently compelling, the firm may raise funds from an IPO.[4] Internet firms like Amazon, eBay, Facebook, Groupon, Priceline, and Yahoo! all got off the ground with venture capital and/or IPOs.

The introduction stage has few *pioneer* firms, often only one. The pioneer should lay the foundation for achieving market leadership and profitability, at least in the short and medium run. The pioneer must develop an appropriate strategy as the life cycle moves toward early growth. The pioneer must demonstrate value to target customers and reduce any market uncertainty that the product is just a *short-term wonder* — the firm may even work with competitors to agree on technological standards — Chapter 5 discussion of VHS and Blu-ray.[5,6] The pioneer must also build a marketing organization and distribution infrastructure.

A critical pioneering task is to keep ahead of competitors by slowing their progress. Some years after introduction, Apple's pioneering iPod achieved iconic status and held competitors to small market shares. Apple's iTunes breakthrough in commercial music downloading was critical, but Apple now faces competition from Spotify, pioneer in music streaming. Sometimes partnerships and alliances can buttress the firm's position. Apple formed a (short-lived) partnership with HP for the iPod, and with Motorola and Cingular (now AT&T) for smartphone distribution. A particularly effective way of slowing/forestalling competitive entry is to create (or exploit) *entry barriers* — government-imposed, product-specific, firm-driven.[7]

GOVERNMENT-IMPOSED BARRIERS

KEY IDEA

The most common government-imposed barriers are patents.

Firms sometimes lobby governments to impose regulations on competitors.

Patents are the most common government-imposed barrier. Patents provide owners with legal monopolies for several years. Firms can petition the courts to enforce these patent monopolies via patent infringement lawsuits, effectively creating long-term entry barriers for competitors, like Apple's successful lawsuit against Samsung in smartphones. Even filing patents that are not ultimately approved can act as short-term barriers. Pharmaceutical firms are especially frequent users of patent barriers. Other government impediments include trade barriers, preferential tax treatment, and outright subsidies. Sometimes the pioneer benefits from a barrier or barrier structure already in place; other times, it may lobby the government for a specific benefit. In the early days of the Internet, Sun, Netscape, and Novell encouraged the U.S. government to take action against Microsoft, slowing its entry into various markets. Conversely, the Norwegian government offers tax breaks and other incentives to spur sales of electric cars.

PRODUCT-SPECIFIC BARRIERS

Product-specific barriers relate directly to the product — access to capital, raw materials, human resources, minimum scale of operations. Sometimes these barriers relate to the product itself so the firm can exploit them; other times, the firm can actively raise barriers. Corning secured differential advantage over Nextel and Lucent in optical-fiber technology by aggressively hiring most of the few optics Ph.D.s graduating each year. Of course, product and/or process innovations cause product-specific barriers to diminish over time. In previous decades, consumers sent film rolls to central laboratories for processing; then storefront minilabs made the process much more convenient; today, consumers take photos on smartphones and share via the Internet.

FIRM-DRIVEN BARRIERS

The firm can build *low-cost* barriers via *penetration pricing*. The firm may also develop and exploit *first-mover advantages*:

LOW-COST BARRIERS AND PENETRATION PRICING. With penetration pricing (PP), the firm plans on low profit margins for a substantial time period, aka *buying market share*. PP is risky and takes significant resolve in the face of large prelaunch and postlaunch expenditures and market uncertainty. PP requires substantial resources as the firm continually reduces costs and prices, builds capacity, and grows quickly. If successful, low prices — built on low costs and experience curve advantages — pose significant entry barriers. Figure 10.3 shows the relationship between price and unit cost for a PP strategy.[8]

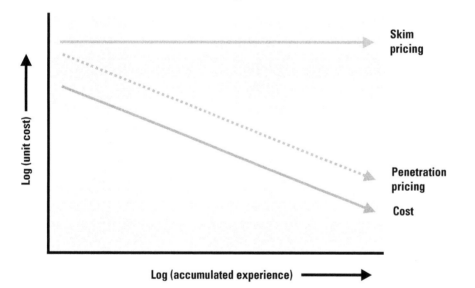

FIGURE 10.3
Price and Unit Cost Trajectories for Penetration Pricing and Skim Pricing

The most advantageous conditions for PP are price-sensitive markets with few government- or product-specific entry barriers.[9] The classic example was Henry Ford's goal to put a Model T in every American garage. Ford invented the assembly line, dramatically lowering production costs; reduced prices continuously; and by the mid-1920s, exceeded 50 percent market share.

PP is particularly attractive if customer *switching costs* are high and the after-market for complementary products is significant. Software service providers are good examples. These firms often set initial prices low to generate an *embedded* base of loyal users, but set high prices for upgrades and/or peripherals. Firms selling durable goods and consumables — razors and razor blades, printers and toner — frequently price durables low and consumables high.

MARKETING QUESTION

Do you have an idea for a revolutionary new product? Suppose development is successful and you are about to launch. What steps would you take to keep ahead of anticipated competitive threats?

KEY IDEA

When the firm executes a low-price penetration strategy, it must accept low profit margins for a substantial time period. Continual cost reductions are essential for sustaining low prices.

THE EXPERIENCE CURVE

The cost curve in Figure 10.3 is a classic *experience curve* (EC). As accumulated volume (experience) in making, promoting, and distributing a product increases, costs can be made to decline in a predictable manner. The EC is a straight-line relationship when we plot log (unit cost) against log (accumulated experience). Cost reductions result from preferred access to raw materials, and enlightened cost management that makes tough decisions to take advantage of organizational learning, economies of scale, advances in process technology, and product redesign. The EC has an important influence on many marketing decisions, especially pricing. (More on the Experience Curve in Marketing Enrichment 10.2 [554p].)

**MARKETING
ENRICHMENT 10.2**

The Experience Curve 554p

KEY IDEA

A *pioneer* can sustain first-mover advantages by producing high-quality products. The firm earns a leading reputation and sets the stage for creating a strong brand.

PP works only if demand for the basic product remains strong; PP fails when customers demand variation. To continue the Ford illustration, in the late 1920s, GM identified several market segments where customers wanted additional benefits/values. While Chevrolet competed with Ford's Model T for price buyers, GM offered Buick, Cadillac, Oldsmobile, and Pontiac to other segments. GM swept past Ford in the late 1920s and early 1930s. Amazon provides a great contemporary example of both a low-cost/low-price strategy and first-mover advantage.

FIRST-MOVER ADVANTAGE. The pioneer may earn advantages because it was first. The pioneer may be able to sustain technological advantage by improving products and/or developing new applications. Classic examples include DuPont's successes with nylon, polyester, and aramid fibers; Citibank's leadership in ATMs; Duracell with alkaline batteries; 7-Eleven with convenience stores (especially in Japan).[10] More recent examples include Airbnb — residential rental; Netflix — video rental/streaming; Open Table — restaurant reservations; Rent the Runway — clothes rental; Uber — taxi service.

If products are high-quality, the pioneer may earn a leading reputation among consumers and distributors. Early market entry also gives the pioneer superior market knowledge.[11] But the pioneer must judiciously turn these advantages into buyer switching costs, or be surpassed by a fast follower. The key for sustaining first-mover advantage is to build a strong brand, establishing the *standard* against which customers judge subsequent entries.[12] Examples include Jeep (in the U.S.) — four-wheel-drive vehicles; Xerox — high-speed dry copying; Kleenex — paper tissue; Hoover — vacuum cleaners; Cadillac — luxury automobiles; Apple's iPod, iPhone, and iPad.

Coca-Cola departed India in 1977 rather than comply with government regulations forcing it to share the secret formula with an Indian partner. Rival PepsiCo took advantage of Coke's 16-year absence (until 1993). *Pepsi* is now a common synonym for cola drinks in the fast-growing Indian soft-drink market, and outsells Coke by 2:1.

Whereas a successful penetration strategy implies continual price reductions, a firm with first-mover advantages may maintain high prices — *price skimming* (PS).[13] As Figure 10.3 shows, PS keeps prices high, even as the firm reduces costs and earns high profits.[14] PS works if government and/or product-specific entry barriers are high; customer willingness to try is strong; and customers are relatively price insensitive. The pharmaceutical industry is the poster-child for PS strategies; patents protect firms from competition, and products deliver significant healthcare benefits. PS strategies fail when entry barriers are low and/or customers are price sensitive. PS also fails if the firm ignores customer needs and potential competition:

Many heart patients undergo balloon-angioplasty procedures. The surgeon inflates a balloon inserted to widen the artery, then implants a wire-mesh device — a *stent* — to stop the artery closing. Three years after entry, J&J stent revenues were $1 billion, profit margins were 80 percent, and market share was 90 percent. But J&J angered cardiologists by not improving stents significantly and refusing price discounts for large purchases.

Guidant entered three years after J&J. Within 45 days, Guidant gained 70 percent market share; one year later, J&J's share was under 10 percent. J&J introduced new products and recovered some market share, but not its early dominance. J&J tried to acquire Guidant but lost out to Boston Scientific. J&J later exited the stent business.

Generally, new entrants erode first-mover advantages: As product life cycles shorten, advantages erode more quickly. Firms executing PS strategies must be able to shift direction when advantages disappear. Pioneers face an environment full of risk, but several strategic options can lay the foundation for achieving long-run market leadership and profitability.

SCENARIO 2: EARLY-GROWTH LEADERS

KEY IDEA

By the early-growth stage — Figure 10.4 — customers have accepted the product form and market demand is growing rapidly. Generally, the market leader has a strong position. The leader has worked out market-entry problems and unit costs are under control. As Figure 10.3 shows, unit costs should reduce as volume builds and the EC takes effect. The firm should be profitable, but cash flows may be negative as it invests to grow the market and adds capacity.

By the early-growth stage, customers accept the product; the market leader should be profitable.

FIGURE 10.4
Early-Growth-Stage Scenarios

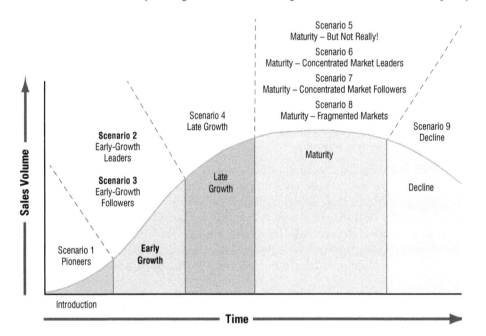

MARKETING QUESTION

The iPod and iTunes have gained large shares of the digital music market. What barriers did Apple erect for potential followers? How successful were these barriers in deterring Spotify?

The leader has four strategic options — two each based on *continuing* and *surrendering* leadership:

- Continue to be leader — enhance position.
- Continue to be leader — maintain position.
- Surrender leadership — retreat to a market segment(s).
- Surrender leadership — exit the market.

CONTINUE TO BE LEADER — ENHANCE POSITION

The firm leverages its success to seek market dominance. The firm grows and broadens the market by continuously investing in R&D to produce new products, extensive advertising, and personal selling. The firm increases production capacity ahead of market demand and aggressively reduces costs. In India's cell phone market, leader Bharti Airtel reversed the traditional model by outsourcing network and information technology to European and U.S. providers, so it could concentrate on marketing. In Russia, VimpelCom focused corporate efforts on sales, as cell phone penetration accelerated from 20 percent to 80 percent in two and one half years.

As competitors enter, firm communications shift from market development to emphasizing firm superiority over competitors. Leaders may also block competitors by entering emerging

MARKETING QUESTION

Uber has successfully navigated introduction and now faces the early-growth stage. Using the framework in this chapter, and whatever data you can secure, suggest a growth strategy for Uber.

market segments, new distribution channels, and new geographies — like eBay, Microsoft, Netflix. Starbucks, Walmart, Tylenol:

> Tylenol achieved acetaminophen leadership by offering a huge number of product varieties. For adults: Tylenol Regular and Extra Strength, Tylenol Extra Strength Cool Caplets, Tylenol 8 Hour, Tylenol Arthritis Pain Extended Relief, Tylenol PM, Simply Sleep, Women's Tylenol, Tylenol Sore Throat, Tylenol Cold, Tylenol Flu, Tylenol Sinus, and Tylenol Allergy. For children: Children's Tylenol, Children's Tylenol Meltaways, Children's Tylenol Flu, Children's Tylenol plus Cold Daytime, Children's Tylenol Cold, Children's Tylenol Cold and Allergy, Simply Stuffy, and Simply Cough. Tylenol packages products in various forms — tablets, capsules, caplets, and liquid.

CONTINUE TO BE LEADER — MAINTAIN POSITION

The firm may prefer a more conservative approach and merely try to maintain market position. The firm may enjoy monopoly-like status and be concerned about potential political, legal, and regulatory difficulties, like Microsoft and Google have faced. Alternatively, customers may demand additional sources of supply, and/or strong competitors may enter, making it clear they intend to stay.

Sometimes technological standards drive this option. Multiple standards cause uncertainty, prospective customers postpone purchases, and the market develops more slowly. The firm may elect to work with competitors on a single standard rather than go it alone. The early consumer-video, HDTV, and wireless technology markets are all good examples. In consumer video, Sony's early Betamax entry had limited success but VHS quickly surpassed Beta when several producers settled on a single standard and shared market development efforts. Had Sony brought other firms into the *Betamax family,* VHS might have been the also-ran.[161v] Apple's early refusal to license the Macintosh operating system undoubtedly stimulated Microsoft to develop the *Windows* graphical user interface.

KEY IDEA

Early-growth leaders have four quite different options:
- Continue to be leader — enhance position
- Continue to be leader — maintain position
- Surrender leadership — retreat to a market segment(s)
- Surrender leadership — exit the market

Maintaining a leading market position may be more difficult than striving for market dominance. The firm requires good up-to-date competitive intelligence, and must carefully select customer and competitor targets. The firm must have a clear strategy, sufficient resolve to stick to the strategy despite temporary hiccups, and thoughtful contingency and/or scenario planning. Historically, U.S. firms in the automobile, steel, and aluminum industries pursued this approach to mitigate antitrust action and possible breakup.

CONTINUE TO BE LEADER — CONCLUSION

Whether the firm undertakes to *enhance* or *maintain* market position, the broad thrust is the same: Ride the leadership position through the life cycle to maturity. Along the way, the firm shifts focus from selling to first-time users, to selling to repeat users and acquiring competitor customers. To be successful, the firm must broaden and refresh the product line, add services, and build the brand by enhancing communications. Amazon is a textbook example: Amazon began by selling books, then added recorded music, electronics, and many other product category *stores*. Amazon also places major effort on personalizing the customer shopping experience. In marked contrast, some leaders become complacent; blinded by early success, they may treat customers arrogantly (like J&J with stents). As customer needs evolve and they become comfortable with the product form, followers may be more adept at listening.

SURRENDER LEADERSHIP — RETREAT TO A MARKET SEGMENT(S)

Unlike market-share loss from competitive pressure, the firm makes a deliberate choice to surrender leadership. The firm may lack resources to fully develop the market and/or fund an ongoing stream of new products. Or a financially stronger competitor sets a market-leadership goal, and the firm knows it cannot win a head-to-head battle. The firm decides to target one or more market segments as a specialized competitor, believing that *discretion is the better part of valor.*

Sometimes, followers initiate penetration strategies by building economies of scale and cutting prices. The firm must identify less-price-sensitive segments where it can add value and overcome its cost disadvantage. The firm requires good market research capabilities to identify market segments and the organizational flexibility to address them. Both Apple and IBM have all felt this sort of pressure at various times. Apple's Macintosh survived because of strengths in the education and graphic arts segments, new product creativity, and enhanced user experience, but both Compaq and IBM exited the PC business.

SURRENDER LEADERSHIP — EXIT THE MARKET

Leaving a market after being the pioneering leader may seem defeatist, but can be prudent. Throughout the life cycle, as customer needs and markets evolve, the firm should continually assess the value of its market position, based on the projected stream of discounted profits. If this projected value is less than the current price, the firm should consider exiting, especially if the product is not central to its mission.[15]

The firm's products may be strategically significant for a potential acquirer, fit well with its current products, and hence be of immense value. The acquirer may also have sufficient resources to invest and drive product growth, like Facebook's WhatsApp and Oculus VR acquisitions. Biotech and other technology firms often face the *sell* decision by inventing products they are ill-equipped to commercialize. Britain's Sinclair Research produced many innovations — amplifiers, calculators, high fidelity, personal computers and peripherals, radios, television, and transportation vehicles — but has an almost legendary inability to commercialize them. Successful innovators are often better off selling to firms with strong marketing expertise. Colgate's liquid soap and P&G's Crest SpinBrush were both secured from small firms that elected to sell.

MARKETING QUESTION

Suppose you have the following information about a market:

- Market growth rate — 15 percent annually
- Leader's market share — 40 percent
- Follower's market share — 10 percent
- Leader's growth rate — 15 percent annually.

Question: How fast must the follower grow annually to overtake the leader in six years?

Answer: 47 percent.

SCENARIO 3: EARLY-GROWTH FOLLOWERS

KEY IDEA

Generally, followers in growth markets are unprofitable and may also have negative cash flows.

The follower's objective should be to learn from others and minimize cost and risk.

Some firms prefer to be *followers*; they enter markets in the early-growth stage. By pursuing a *wait-and-see* strategy, they can better assess market potential, and *free ride* on the pioneer's efforts in market development. Followers leverage past successes and learn from the leader's mistakes. But early on, the follower trails the market leader. The follower has lower sales, higher unit costs, and less experience than the leader. Unless the leader is price skimming, followers are often unprofitable; cash flow may also be negative.

Followers in early growth have similar strategic options to the leader. But because they start from inferior positions, choosing among them has a different cadence. Options are:

- Seek market leadership.
- Settle for second place.
- Focus on gaining leadership in a market segment(s).
- Exit the market.

MARKETING QUESTION

Because of Coca-Cola's 16-year absence from the Indian market (p. 261), *Pepsi* became synonymous with cola drinks. Pepsi now outsells Coke by 2:1. What actions should Coke take to regain market leadership?

SEEK MARKET LEADERSHIP

The follower can pursue leadership by *imitating* or *leapfrogging* the market leader. In each case, the follower requires good competitive insight and should enter as soon as possible:

IMITATION. Imitation means what it says. The follower copies the leader but executes more effectively. Successful imitators spend heavily to play *catch-up* on product development and outspend the leader in promotion. If possible, the follower leverages an existing marketing or distribution infrastructure, and clearly highlights its differentiated value. The follower should not confuse imitation with price cutting. Early in the PC life cycle, suppliers offered many designs that earned price premiums, but price competition accelerated as the industry standardized. In search, follower Google eclipsed Overture with a well-executed imitation strategy, and Facebook raced ahead of MySpace in social media. Low price was not a factor in either case.

KEY IDEA

Imitation means copying the leader but being more effective in execution.

Leapfrogging goes one better than the leader by developing innovative and superior products and/or targeting emerging market segments.

LEAPFROG. The follower improves on the leader. The follower offers enhanced value by developing innovative and superior products, and/or it enters emerging market segments before the leader. Generally, the leapfrogger avoids head-to-head price competition; it may spend more heavily on R&D than the leader; marketing spending is also high. In video games, Nintendo and Sega leapfrogged first-mover Atari's original video game. Later, Sony PlayStation leapfrogged both Nintendo and Sega by offering 3D graphics and enhanced digital soundtracks. PlayStation 3 and Microsoft's Xbox target a different segment — late teens and early 20-somethings — than Nintendo's young teenager target. But Nintendo leapfrogged both Sony and Microsoft by introducing the Wii, featuring active games for many age groups.

Effective leapfroggers often do an excellent job of anticipating emerging customer needs. They spot segment opportunities before leaders, quickly offering new values and securing differential advantage. The most successful followers *change the rules*.[16] Netflix took advantage of the VHS-to-DVD switch to develop a rent-by-mail option that devastated bricks-and-mortar leader Blockbuster, and ultimately drove its bankruptcy. More recently, Netflix has been a leader in streaming video (Chapter 3 Opening Case). Apple leapfrogged BlackBerry and other smartphones by introducing the iPhone **[564v]**.

For either *imitation* or *leapfrog*, followers must make long-run commitments. Because they must play catch-up, resource requirements can be enormous. Sometimes pioneers make it easy for followers by neither improving products nor investing sufficiently in promotion and distribution, and by keeping prices high. As noted, J&J's actions in the *stent* market helped follower Guidant.

SETTLE FOR SECOND PLACE

Former GE CEO Jack Welch famously mandated that GE be number *one* or *two* in each market it addressed.[17] A follower needs substantial resources to become market leader, so settling for second place may be a reasonable and profitable option. Several situations argue for this alternative. Perhaps the leader is content with current market share and does not seek increases; customers may demand a second supplier; multiple competitors may help simplify product standards; and/or the political/legal/regulatory environment may be favorable. Smorgon Industries is a good example of a follower with limited ambition:

> Smorgon set out to become Australia's second domestic steel producer. Smorgon did not challenge market leader BHP, but hoped to operate under BHP's price umbrella. Smorgon believed BHP would rather accept its presence than battle for market share. Smorgon was successful in settling for second place and achieving acceptable market position.

FOCUS ON A MARKET SEGMENT(S)

This option may be attractive if the follower has fewer resources than the leader and other followers, and if the segment (or segments) is attractive.[18] When drugs go off patent, pharmaceutical firms often withdraw marketing support, but add services for a narrow physician segment. In Britain, BMS earns sales and profits from anticancer-drug Taxol, long after patent expiration. BMS provides kits to prepare the drug for patients and replaces these free of charge if patients miss appointments.[19]

EXIT THE MARKET

If the business sale value is greater than the projected discounted profit stream, the firm should consider exiting. Because the product is in early growth, it may have high value for a potential acquirer eager to enter the market (market segment).

SCENARIO 4: LATE GROWTH

> Early on, most cell phones offered the same set of basic functions. Later, major players added features like text messaging, music, and color user-interface displays. Some producers offered features like rubberized phones, hybrid phone/PDA organizers, and still- and video-camera phones. Samsung's *Ladyphone* had a biorhythm calculator, a fatness function to calculate height-to-weight ratios, a calorie counter, and a calendar to track menstrual cycles. Nokia offered a platinum-cased handset with a sapphire crystal screen — for only $21,000! Later, of course, the iPhone and Android smartphones raised customer benefits/values to an entirely new level.

By late growth — Figure 10.5 (p. 267) — the firm receives minimal value from early market leadership or being a fast follower. Although customer benefits/values that drove purchases in introduction and early growth are still important, they may not enter customer choice decisions. More likely, these elements have become *qualifiers* or *antes*, rather than *determining*. The firm must focus on identifying and offering customers *determining* benefits/values. Early in the passenger air travel market, safety was critical. Today, most travelers believe major airlines, flying similar airplanes, are equally safe: Safety is an *ante*. *Determining* benefits/values include frequent-flier miles, time convenience, and availability of direct flights.

KEY IDEA

Early-growth followers have four quite different strategic options:
- Seek market leadership
- Settle for second place
- Focus on gaining leadership in a market segment(s)
- Exit the market

KEY IDEA

By late growth, basic customer benefits/values are still important but may not enter into customer choice decisions. Customers are more likely to base purchase decisions on additional benefits/values.

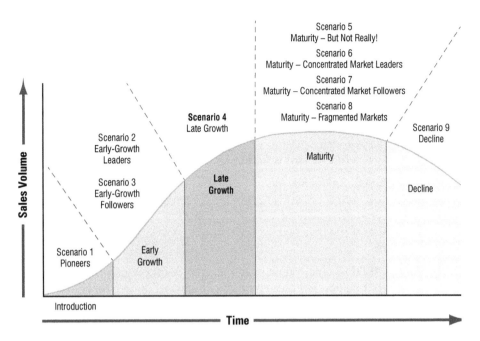

FIGURE 10.5
*Late-Growth-Stage
Scenario*

The firm requires considerable marketing research skills to conduct market-segmentation studies; determine which segment(s) to target; decide how to satisfy customer needs in the target segment(s); and monitor evolving segments for new opportunities. Successful firms address target segments with focused *rifle-shot* marketing, then build defensible positions against competitors.

Even small segments may offer good profit potential. Many local and regional retailers successfully compete against national chains. Think about your own town: What examples can you identify? In the New York area, P.C. Richard is a successful electrical goods retailer; Stew Leonard's — *Disneyland of Dairy Stores* — has the greatest sales per square foot of any U.S. food store. More broadly, many U.S. supermarket chains are suffering, but Whole Foods successfully targets a market segment prepared to pay more for higher-quality groceries.

KEY IDEA

In late growth, the firm must decide whether to target *many* segments or just a *few*.

The critical success factor for both leaders and followers boils down to commitment. There are really two broad strategic options — target many segments, or settle for a more limited position by targeting just a few. The firm should base its decision on clear insight about markets and market segments, and rigorously assess its ability to serve them successfully in the face of competition.

SCENARIO 5: MATURITY — BUT NOT REALLY

Former Coke CEO Roberto C. Goizueta used to quote fondly from a 1937 *Fortune* article opining that a typical investor concluded it was too late to make money on Coke stock because the market for its product was saturated!

Before the firm examines strategic options in maturity — Figure 10.6 (p. 268) — it must affirm that the life cycle really is in *maturity*. Perhaps there are possibilities for market growth. To make the point succinctly, some authors assert, "There is no such thing as a mature business, there are only mature managers!"[20] When assessing if the life cycle is in maturity, the firm should analyze barriers to growth:

BEHAVIORAL BARRIERS. Requiring significant behavioral change by customers is often a barrier. *Techies* were early users of PCs and their difficult-to-use operating systems like CP/M and MS-DOS. The mass market developed only when Apple, and then Microsoft, launched *easy-to-use* intuitive options. Customer behavior changes can also rejuvenate markets. Bicycles were old-fashioned, but sales increased dramatically when exercising became fashionable. Coffee consumption outside the home skyrocketed as consumers embraced new and trendier establishments like Starbucks.

ECONOMIC BARRIERS. Economic barriers are often linked to technology. When Roundup herbicide lost patent protection in the Philippines, Monsanto cut prices to compete with cheaper generics. Monsanto discovered it had vastly underestimated price elasticity[21]; sales grew dramatically when many farmers could afford Roundup.

GOVERNMENT-IMPOSED BARRIERS. When governments remove regulations, competitors often enter and growth explodes. The U.S. government opened bandwidths to commercial use and wireless-based products expanded rapidly. Deregulation of air transportation spawned rapid growth in airfreight and passenger air travel as new competitors entered with low prices and other innovations.

TECHNOLOGICAL BARRIERS. Innovation may obliterate technological barriers to growth. AT&T's transistor technology rejuvenated radios. Improved microprocessors made PCs portable and much cheaper. Inline skates revived the almost-dead roller-skating industry, and Trevor Baylis' new clockwork technology led to the *Freeplay* wind-up radio, flashlights, global positioning handsets, cellular phone chargers, and landmine detectors. Airbnb, Uber, and Spotify have each used Internet-based platforms to challenge traditional models.

Generally, if the market is not *really* mature, the key strategic objective should be growth. The most serious barrier to growth may be lack of creativity.[22] Creatively generating and analyzing opportunities and approaching seemingly mature markets can spur growth in several ways.

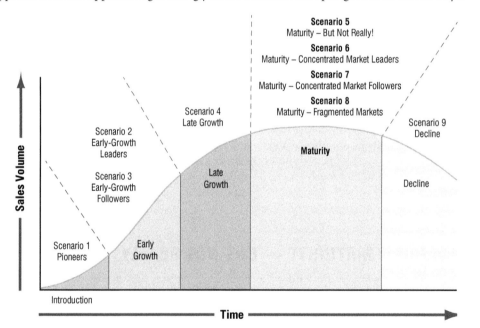

FIGURE 10.6
Maturity-Stage Scenarios

MARKETING QUESTION

Assume you work for Ford or GM. What barriers to growth exist in the automobile market? Are these barriers different for foreign manufacturers?

INCREASE PRODUCT USE

The firm may increase product use via reminder and reinforcement communications; promoting different use applications, occasions, or locations; providing incentives and bundling opportunities; and reducing undesirable consequences of frequency. Specific techniques include:

• **Change the model.** Fashion firms make frequent changes in clothing styles; automobile firms change models annually; and software companies continually introduce new and improved versions.

- **Design the product to expire.** Incorporate devices to indicate product discard dates and encourage repurchase. Read this book quickly ... it was printed with disappearing ink to defeat the secondary market — *just kidding!* Firms use expiration and *best-if-used-by* dates on beer and soft drinks, and physical indicators on razors, batteries, toothbrushes, and water filters.
- **Develop new product uses.** New product forms replaced baking soda for baking and antacids, leaving Arm & Hammer as the sole surviving brand. Arm & Hammer developed many new uses — removing refrigerator and sink odors, treating swimming pools, eliminating perspiration odor, and sanitizing laundry.
- **Improve packaging for better ease of use.** Examples include single-serving cereals, storage-friendly packages, individual laundry and dishwasher tablets, easy-to-pour condiments, and storage-friendly bulk items like Coke and Pepsi 12-packs for refrigerators.
- **Increase quantity per use occasion.** Options include increasing package size, like 20- versus 12-ounce Pepsi[23]; and/or designing packaging for dispensing ease, like adding a larger-size opening for Tabasco hot sauce.
- **Make the product easier to use.** Consumers do not have to clean or disinfect disposable contact lenses. Pharmaceutical firms often redesign injectable drugs as tablets, time-release capsules, and/or long-lived patches to ease patient burdens and encourage use.

KEY IDEA

Creative ways to drive growth in the maturity stage are:
- Increase product use
- Improve the product/service
- Improve physical distribution
- Reduce price
- Reposition the brand
- Enter new markets

IMPROVE THE PRODUCT/SERVICE

Firms should expect sales to slow if products do not satisfy customer needs. The remedy is simple: *Improve the offer!* Before Steve Jobs returned as CEO, many analysts believed Apple would not survive its quality problems. But Apple returned to growth and profitability and became the world's most valuable firm.

Sometimes even apparently minor changes can increase sales significantly. Clorox introduced a lemon-fresh version of Pine-Sol household floor and wall cleaner — sales grew by 25 percent. Clorox added a squirt of floral scent or a twist of lemon to Clorox bleach and gained 1 percent market share. Clorox also slightly modified Formula 409, a popular countertop cleaner, and increased market share from 17 to 20 percent. Changes in clothing include availability of wrinkle-free and EKG-monitoring shirts, expandable collars, and products containing odor-absorbing micro-granules.

Because product quality has improved significantly in many industries, and gaining product-based advantage is difficult, many firms use services to rejuvenate their brands. IBM based its recent success on a shift from hardware and software to providing services. Today, IBM operates information technology systems and platforms for thousands of major firms like DuPont and Merck.[24]

IMPROVE PHYSICAL DISTRIBUTION

KEY IDEA

Seemingly mature markets may have growth potential waiting to be unlocked via creative approaches.

Sophisticated package delivery and tracking systems helped grow electronic commerce. But Coca-Cola uses whatever distribution works in a given geography — motorcycles, pack mules, camels — to get Coke to rural backwaters. Traditionally, upscale New York City restaurants secured fish from the local Fulton Fish Market several days after the catch landed in Maine. Today, buyers in Maine inspect fish at 6 a.m., purchase at 11:15 a.m., pack at 12:15 p.m., and send to New York. Unpacked at 9 a.m. the next day, ready for lunch, the fresher cod earns twice the price. Off the Alaskan coast, Bill Webber e-mails pictures of caught salmon to chefs, packs chosen items in insulated bubble-wrap liners for shipping boxes, then ships by FedEx. The premium-priced fish arrive at restaurants 48 hours after leaving the water.

REDUCE PRICE

This chapter's Opening Case shows how Ryanair transformed a seemingly mature airline market into growth with a low-price strategy. Southwest Airlines previously had similar success in the U.S. The author is trying to transform the marketing textbook market via Wessex Press — *Southwest Airlines of college textbooks.* Of course, low prices demand low-cost operations.

REPOSITION THE BRAND

The firm offers the same product but with new benefits/values for new customers; fine-grained segmentation may reveal growth segments.[25] In a classic example, Honda repositioned motorcycles from a product made for *long-haired guys* and *the police officers chasing them* to *a family activity.* The new mantra — *You meet the nicest people on a Honda* — revolutionized the industry. Swiss mechanical watches, fountain pens, and vinyl LPs have similarly enjoyed a resurgence. Sears and Cadillac have tried to reposition their brands, but with mixed results.

ENTER NEW MARKETS

When fax capability threatened overnight document delivery, FedEx refocused efforts on shipping physical goods for direct marketers. Customers receive products more quickly, and direct marketers gain advantage over brick-and-mortar stores. The changed focus has positioned FedEx as an essential part of the e-commerce industry; UPS quickly followed. Furthermore, both FedEx and UPS secured retail presence by acquiring Kinko's and Mail Boxes Etc., respectively.

Many firms define new markets by geography, in particular, emerging markets like BRICI countries — Brazil, Russia, India, China, Indonesia — with millions of low-income customers. To supply sufficiently low-priced products, firms must modify traditional practices. In India, Cummins gained 40 percent share in the low-horsepower power generator market. Cummins created a series of smaller, lower-powered modularized engines with add-ons — ready-to-assemble *gensets* (generation sets) for different segments like farmers and small retailers. Cummins also gained significant new capabilities.[26]

SCENARIO 6: MATURITY — CONCENTRATED MARKET LEADERS

Historically, Kirin enjoyed 60 percent share of the Japanese beer market; Asahi maintained less than 10 percent. Over time, positions shifted and Asahi's share reached about 50 percent. What happened? Kirin's market dominance led to overconfidence and failure to act on industry trends. Distribution shifted from small local stores, where Kirin was strong, to supermarkets and discounters; Kirin responded slowly as cans replaced bottles; and Kirin overemphasized new, small-volume beers rather than supporting core brands. By contrast, Asahi offered convenience, quality, and value.

KEY IDEA

Market leaders in concentrated mature markets should have:
• Low costs
• Decent profits
• Positive cash flows

Generally, *concentrated markets* support a few substantial competitors whose aggregate market share often exceeds 60 percent[27]; several small players may target market niches. The market leader should have an incumbent's advantage — deeper understanding of customer needs and profitability metrics than followers — and hence be more effective.[28] Profit margins should be high for low-cost leaders; investment should be relatively low (because growth is low); and cash flow should be strongly positive.

The market leader has two strategic options:

- Maintain leadership over the long run.
- Harvest the business.[29]

MAINTAIN LEADERSHIP OVER THE LONG RUN

The core decision for maintaining market leadership is choosing the *right* investment level. Generally, we advocate *cautious* investment. With the *right* investment, in the *right* areas, the firm may reap profits for many years. *Overinvestment* to gain market share from entrenched competitors often wastes resources. Pressures for overinvestment include:

- **Few alternative opportunities.** The firm fails to develop other growth opportunities like new products or strategic alliances. Success depends on a few products so the firm continues to invest aggressively when it should invest modestly.

- **Internally focused funding criteria.** The firm bases funding on current financial performance. The firm underfunds in new products that are not yet profitable and overinvests in mature products.

- **Political power of mature-product champions.** Senior executives directing large product lines are typically powerful — their products are today's profit-makers. They lobby successfully for large budgets.

Conversely, *underinvestment* can leave the firm vulnerable to aggressive competitors. The firm may set overly ambitious profit targets and lose market share. Profit Inc. (PI) (disguised) increased revenues for its major product 2 percent annually for five years. Simultaneously, by slashing investment and other costs, PI's annual profit growth increased to 12 percent! Good news? No! Sales imploded due to underinvestment. Increasing short-run profits is not difficult; the trick is finding the *right* investment level to sustain profits in the medium and long run. Reasons for underinvestment include:

- **Fear of cannibalization.** The firm could maintain leadership by introducing a lower-profit version(s). The firm fails to act because it fears losing sales of higher-profit product(s).

- **Inertia.** Performance is acceptable; the firm sees no reason to change.

- **Limited view of competition.** The firm takes a too-narrow view: International Paper took little action as disposable plastic cups replaced its market-leading paper cups.

- **Misunderstanding the challenger's strategy.** Competitive data-gathering and analysis is weak; the firm fails to gain good competitive insight.

Suppose you managed the Gillette brand for P&G. What actions would you take to secure long-run profits?

Of course, complacency and arrogance can accentuate any or all of these errors, and past success can blind the firm to evolving market realities. To maintain leadership, the firm should be ready to react to follower actions, like Whirlpool's Maytag acquisition to frustrate Haier. Generally, the firm can maintain leadership via incremental product improvements; it should also invest in marketing activities that build and sustain brand equity and demonstrate competitive superiority. When a clinical trial showed that Lipitor (cholesterol-lowering drug) reduced heart attack risk by 16 percent, Pfizer widely advertised the result; Lipitor achieved over 40 percent market share.

The firm should speed up product development and invest in process technology for more efficient lower-cost operations. Process technology change can severely affect market leaders that do not adapt. Traditional integrated steel firms like U.S. Steel and Bethlehem Steel were competitively disadvantaged versus Nucor and others with electric arc minimills. The firm should also consider *variating* fixed costs — reducing fixed costs and increasing variable costs. Then, if sales slip, costs also reduce. The firm should tightly manage working capital by reducing accounts receivable and inventory, and lengthening accounts payable. Dell strives for the lowest possible costs and continually adjusts prices to reflect supplier cost data. Dell only makes-to-order, has minimal inventory, and gets paid before manufacture — hence, *negative working capital.*

New product innovation should also concern market leaders. Products based on new technology can destroy leadership positions — music downloads versus compact discs versus vinyl records; e-mail versus fax. Kodak could not make the transition from chemical film to digital imaging successfully and filed for bankruptcy. An external orientation is the best protection against this sort of market erosion.[30]

Distribution can also be challenging. Early in the life cycle, a B2B firm may have developed a distribution system to reach end users. But as some end users grow in size and expertise, they demand direct distribution to secure lower prices by cutting out distributor margins. The firm faces a difficult *catch-22* situation. If the firm remains loyal to distributors, it risks losing sales to powerful end users. If the firm goes direct to end users, it upsets long-standing distributor relationships.[31] Many B2C firms face related problems with electronic commerce. Sony sells computers, cameras, camcorders, home audio and video products, and TVs in big-box *bricks-and-mortar* stores like Best Buy and Sears. But consumers can also purchase these products at Sony's website. Of course, presence in multiple distribution channels improves customer *share of mind.*

ADDRESSING LOW PRICE COMPETITORS[32]

Leaders in mature Western markets often face competition from low-price/low-cost competitors. Aldi (Germany — supermarkets), Huawei (China — telecommunications equipment), IKEA (Sweden — furniture), Ryanair (Ireland — air travel), and Teva (Israel — pharmaceuticals) have each made life difficult for traditional leaders. Follower low-cost models drive price competition, but price wars are generally not good responses. Strategic options include:

- **Do nothing.** *Wait-and-see* allows the market leader gain insight into the new entrant's strategy and performance, while it formulates a response.

- **Enhance value.** Use creative options from Scenario 5.

- **Develop a dual strategy.** Continue with current products but introduce low-cost/low-price offers to compete with the follower head-on. This strategy fails if insufficiently aggressive — Go (British Airways), Song (Delta), and Ted (United) are good examples — they all failed. The firm must set clear customer expectations — low price implies less service — and be prepared to cannibalize the original business. Under attack from low-cost entrants in silicones, global market leader Dow Corning set up Xiameter as a low-price (20 percent less) competitor. Several actions reduced costs: limited product range; website-only orders (extra fees for e-mail/phone); no technical service; shipping 7 to 20 days after order (extra charge for rush); and delivery only in full truck, tank, or pallet loads. Revenues and profits increased.

- **Switch to solutions.** The firm makes price less transparent by bundling products/services. Dell, IBM, and Xerox each adopted this strategy. Orica (Australia's leading explosives supplier to stone quarries) was in a price war with new entrants. Orica used technical expertise to provide greater flexibility at the blast site (mixing explosives on-site) and improved blasting efficiency by advising on drilling-hole placement. Orica now sets price based on broken-rock quantity — the fundamental customer value.

- **Become a low-cost/low-price competitor.** This option represents a huge change in business model and may be difficult to execute. Ryanair (Opening Case) started out as a traditional airline but transformed to a low-cost/low-price airline, with great success.

KEY IDEA

Market leaders in concentrated mature markets have two major options:
- Maintain leadership over the long run
- Harvest: May be *fast* or *slow*

HARVEST

The firm is market leader, but a *harvest* strategy may be more important than maintaining sales and market share. Reasons include:

- **Change in firm strategy.** The product becomes less central to the firm. BMS and Pfizer each redefined themselves as pharmaceutical firms and divested over-the-counter products. Financial markets may pressure the firm to focus — eliminate noncore products to avoid the *conglomerate discount*, and *get back to basics*.

- **Desire to avoid specific competitors.** If the firm forecasts tougher competition, harvesting may be the best option. Westinghouse exited traditional markets in electrical products where GE was frequently more successful.

- **Government regulations.** The government may restrict the industry or eliminate product use — many governments have placed severe restrictions on cigarette manufacturers; other governments have banned use of some pesticides.

- **Investment requirements are too high.** Necessary investment for continued competitiveness, like new product or new process technology, may be too high. British Aerospace (BA) launched the world's first jet aircraft — de Havilland Comet. But costs to develop and produce large commercial jet aircraft rose; BA withdrew, except as a part-owner and subcontractor for Airbus.

- **New technology.** The product will soon become obsolete. Classically, DuPont sold rayon operations as it developed nylon.

Once the firm decides to harvest, the critical question is *fast* or *slow*? *Fast* harvesting — divest the product and gain immediate cash. *Slow* harvesting — the firm should focus on three issues:

- **Cut costs.** Simplify the product line; streamline distribution; reduce advertising, promotion, and services; and eliminate small and unprofitable customers.

- **Minimize investment.** Make little or no further product investment.

- **Raise prices.** Raise prices or eliminate extras like free delivery or extended warranties.

The more aggressive the firm's actions, the more quickly it exits the market.

SCENARIO 7: MATURITY — CONCENTRATED MARKET FOLLOWERS

KEY IDEA

Followers in concentrated mature markets typically have higher costs, lower profits, and less financial strength than market leaders. But followers may rejuvenate to become major threats to leaders.

Followers have smaller market shares than leaders; they probably also have higher costs, lower profits, and are weaker financially. But leaders can lose position by poor decisions, and followers may attain leadership by inspired management. Airbus caught up with Boeing in large commercial jet aircraft (Chapter 5 Opening Case); Southwest Airlines is now the leading domestic U.S. airline; American, Delta, and United Airlines each emerged from bankruptcy to become solid competitors.

Most firms have products that fit scenario 7; hence, this scenario has broad applicability. The follower has three basic strategic options, each with several suboptions.

IMPROVE MARKET POSITION

Careful and creative market segmentation, kenneling, and direct attack are three primary alternatives to grow and, perhaps, ultimately dethrone the market leader:

MARKET SEGMENTATION. Options for segmentation typically appear in early growth and become numerous in late growth and maturity. Creative segmentation is the dominant option for counteracting market leader advantages.[33] The follower should conduct careful marketing research to identify and target emerging segments. Examples include:

BetterBags (BB) targets upscale and specialty food markets like D'Agostino, Schnucks, and Whole Foods. BB's plastic bags are 20 percent more expensive than traditional bags, but are thicker and can be printed with six colors. The bags feature fewer defects, a patented pull-down dispenser, and one-at-a-time automatic opening.

Enterprise is the U.S. market leader in automobile rental. Initially Enterprise identified and targeted the insurance and *car-under-repair* segment of the rental market.

Jakks Pacific has built a successful video-game business by targeting preteen boys and girls, and price-conscious adults.

MBNA (now part of Bank of America) has been very successful targeting affinity groups like universities, veterans, and fans of sports teams.

Red Bull competes successfully in the global soft-drink market by developing and dominating the energy drink segment.

Firms often identify and target market segments by adding benefits to satisfy customers' ever more fine-grained needs, often at higher prices. But maturity often includes one segment requiring just basic product benefits — *getting back to basics* — at low prices. Examples include: automobiles — Citroën 2CV, Mini, Smart cars, Volkswagen Beetle; passenger airlines — Southwest, Spirit, Sun Country Airlines (U.S.), and Air Berlin, easyJet, Ryanair (Europe); and cruises — easyCruise. Acer (Taiwan) gained significant market share with low-price netbooks. For a low-price strategy to be successful, the firm must have low-cost operations.

KENNELING. *Kenneling* is a metaphor for bringing several *dog* (seemingly worthless) products together. A follower may acquire several unprofitable (or marginally profitable) low-market-share products, and then execute a *roll-up* into a single offer. By rationalizing operations, distribution, and/or marketing, the follower may become a strong competitor. In commercial banking, JPMorgan Chase resulted from a roll-up of Chemical Bank, Manufacturers Hanover, Chase Manhattan, JPMorgan, and Bank One.[34] Fortress Investments is kenneling U.S. local small-town newspapers. Partnerships like the code-sharing Star Alliance including Air Canada, Air New Zealand, ANA, Asiana Airlines, Austrian Airlines, Lot, Lufthansa, Mexicana, SAS, Singapore Airlines, South African Airlines, Spanair, Swiss Airways, TAP, Thai Airlines, United, and Varig is another form of kenneling. Asea Brown Boveri (ABB) combined segmenting and kenneling globally:

ABB acquired many small, local, heavy-equipment manufacturers in different countries. Each acquired entity eliminated marginal and unprofitable products so as to specialize in producing a few products. Each national firm offers a full product line, in part by securing products from sister firms, and provides local customer service. ABB secured significant production economies and rates its kenneling strategy as very effective.[35]

DIRECT ATTACK. If the leader has been lazy, underinvested, set prices too high, and/or served customers poorly, direct attack may be the follower's best option. Good market insight helps identify the leader's weak spots, so the follower can invest to exploit them. In financial information, new-entrant Bloomberg went head-to-head against Dow Jones and Reuters; Bloomberg preinstalled software in custom-made terminals and let subscribers do their own financial analyses. Now Bloomberg and Thomson-Reuters share the terminal market. Similarly, Bratz dolls were the most successful direct attack on Mattel's Barbie.

In industries as diverse as credit cards and pharmaceuticals, market leaders have lost share to new entrants offering better products and/or lower prices. Firefox, offering greater virus security and faster interwebsite speed, has earned roughly 20 percent global market share of web browsers, mostly taken from market leader Internet Explorer.

KEY IDEA

Followers in concentrated mature markets have several options:

- Improve market position
  - Market segmentation
  - Kenneling
  - Direct attack
- Keep on truckin'
  - Maintain position
  - Rationalize position
- Exit
  - Divest
  - Liquidate

MARKETING QUESTION

Anheuser-Busch InBev's share of the U.S. beer market exceeds 50 percent; Pabst Blue Ribbon's market share is less than 2 percent. Develop a strategy for Pabst Blue Ribbon.

KEEP ON TRUCKIN'

This adage describes maintaining or rationalizing the firm's current position:

MAINTAIN POSITION. Holding market share roughly constant over the long run can be viable if the firm has a profitable market position and strengths in one or more segments. Harley-Davidson has a relatively small share of the motorcycle market, but design, performance, and community-building have provided a loyal user base.[36] The firm may also leverage its position to other markets and segments, like Harley-Davidson restaurants.

RATIONALIZE POSITION. If profits are marginal or negative, rationalizing operations may be the way to go. The firm should examine all aspects of operations, distribution, and sales with *a fine-tooth comb*, and make tough cost-cutting decisions. The firm may forestall exit, retain a skilled workforce, and have continued access to raw materials and/or technology — these may be useful in the future.

EXIT

Followers should choose *exit* if profitability is unlikely and/or the product's future is doubtful, perhaps due to negative brand image or slowing market demand. Choices are twofold:

DIVEST. By finding a buyer for which the product is a good fit, the firm may secure cash quickly. BMS divested Clairol to P&G, and Excedrin to Novartis; Pfizer divested over-the-counter products to J&J. Each divestiture was a good fit for the acquirer. When the firm divests, it should avoid strengthening a potential competitor. Boeing divested its commuter aircraft operation — De Havilland Canada — to Bombardier. Bombardier upgraded the product line by emphasizing jets and introducing larger aircraft. Boeing later stopped producing its smallest 717 jet.

LIQUIDATE. If no buyers appear, the only reasonable action may be liquidation — closing down and selling assets.[37] British Aerospace (BAE) was producing 25 jet aircraft annually versus 370 for Bombardier (Canada) and 130 for Empresa Brasileira (Brazil); BA stopped production.

Sometimes the firm faces exit barriers and is unable (or unwilling) to leave the market, despite compelling strategic arguments. Delivery contracts, buyback guarantees, union contracts, and/or potential damage to brand equity may each make exit difficult. Community relations may be important if plant closing would devastate the local economy. Emotional commitments can also be an exit barrier. Ingersoll-Rand (IR) continued with rock drilling, despite losses, largely because it was IR's original business. U.S. liquor importer W. A. Taylor sold mostly up-market brands, like B&B liqueur. Old Smuggler scotch whisky did not fit. But most top managers had been brand managers for Old Smuggler; they couldn't bear to part with it![38]

SCENARIO 8: MATURITY — FRAGMENTED MARKETS

Fragmented markets have many players, but no firm is dominant. Hence, leader/follower distinctions have little relevance. An important objective is increasing market share. The firm has two strategic options for restructuring or repositioning.

ACQUISITION

Acquisition is similar to kenneling — p. 274; this approach can be very successful when geography drives fragmentation. A global firm may acquire many national companies to secure greater global market share. French insurance giant AXA built strong regional positions in the

MARKETING QUESTION

For decades, P&G and Unilever competed fiercely in U.S. laundry detergents, but P&G had been market leader for many years. A few years ago, Unilever divested its U.S. business to a private equity firm. Why? What five-year strategies would you suggest for P&G and the new private equity owner?

MARKETING QUESTION

Many service businesses like dentists, doctors, electricians, general contractors, and plumbers are very local. Pick one of these services or another of your choice. How would you increase market share for one of the players?

KEY IDEA

In mature fragmented markets, no firm has a large market share.

fragmented insurance industry by acquiring several European insurance firms and Equitable (U.S.). Copart executed a successful domestic roll-up:

> Copart auctions (including online bidding) totally wrecked vehicles to dismantlers, rebuilders, and used-car dealers. Copart offers insurance-company customers database access to track sales. Copart expanded to 35 percent market share by purchasing dozens of independent auto junkyards. Copart's net margins are 15 to 20 percent.

KEY IDEA

Major options in fragmented markets are:
- Acquisition
- Standardization and branding

STANDARDIZATION AND BRANDING

In fragmented industries, many players typically offer a wide range of products/services. Standardization is a way to reduce variation and improve consistency across various suppliers; branding assures customers that each provider supplies the same value. BASF and ADP both offer lesser-known products in many markets. By promoting the corporate brand, customers have confidence that individual products will deliver the promised value.

Sometimes firms use *franchising* to attract small, independently owned players — Chapter 19. Franchisees maintain independence, but take advantage of the franchisor's brand and other services. Examples include Century 21 — real estate; Holiday Inn — hospitality; Kampgrounds of America (KOA) — campsites. Alternatively, the firm enters a fragmented industry using wholly owned operations and/or franchising, like KFC, McDonald's, Pizza Hut, and Subway — fast food; ServiceMaster — cleaning services.

SCENARIO 9: DECLINE

Figure 10.7 identifies the decline scenario. "So now you've graduated; we're delighted that you've joined us. We're going to throw you in the deep end. You will be in charge of our *Franklin* product, where both our sales and product-form sales have been declining for the past few years." How would you like this assignment? Most new managers would not be happy, yet firms can make good profits from decline products. Table 10.1 (p. 277) shows the results of one study: 21 (8+13) percent of businesses made no profits or had losses. But 78 percent were profitable and almost 40 percent earned over 35 percent ROI.[39] Today the market for large traditional SUVs is declining, yet GM makes large profits from Tahoe, Suburban, Yukon, and Yukon XL. Furthermore, environmental change may turn decline into growth — retiring baby boomers have helped place Winnebago on *Fortune's* list of fastest-growing firms.

KEY IDEA

Firms can make considerable profits in declining markets.

FIGURE 10.7
Decline-Stage Scenario

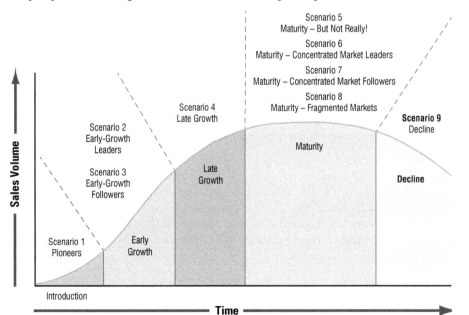

TABLE 10.1
*Profitability Distribution
for Decline Businesses**

* To be read as, for example,
38% of sample businesses
had an average ROI of 15%.

							Total
Percent of businesses	8%	13%	38%	25%	5%	9%	100%
Return on investment (ROI)	−10%	0%	15%	35%	55%	60%	

We learned earlier that pioneers face little competition early in the life cycle. But as the market grows, competitors typically enter. In the decline stage, the reverse occurs — new entry is unlikely and competitors exit. Good examples include carbon paper, many canned foods, full-service travel agents, public telephones, *sake* in Japan, and videotape recorders. Two dimensions are important in analyzing declining markets — market hospitality and firm business strengths.

MARKET HOSPITALITY. A declining market is *inhospitable* if:

- Decline is rapid and/or uncertain.
- The market is commodity-based — no price-insensitive segments.
- Competitors:
  - are viable and credible.
  - are evenly balanced and view the market as strategically important.
  - have high fixed costs and are very sensitive to unit sales declines.
- Customer switching costs are low.
- Bankruptcy laws allow failing competitors to return with lower costs — like U.S. airlines.
- Competitor exit barriers are high — for example, they cannot easily redeploy assets.
- Competitors are emotionally committed to their products.
- The product is part of a vertically integrated supply system.
- The government or the community pressures (or subsidizes) some firms to remain.

Characteristics of *hospitable* markets tend to be the opposite of these conditions.

BUSINESS STRENGTHS. Firms with good *business strengths* should have low costs, good raw material contracts, and/or be able to keep productive assets running without major investment.

Figure 10.8 shows the four-cell matrix formed by combining market hospitality and business strengths. Each matrix cell suggests a different strategic option.

KEY IDEA

In declining markets, options
depend on:

- Market hospitality
- Firm business strengths

FIGURE 10.8
*Strategic Options
in Decline*

LEADERSHIP

MARKETING
QUESTION

> Many newspapers have circulation declines because of television, the Internet, and other forms of communications. But several major U.S. newspapers are showing modest sales gains. These publications offer higher quality — like color pages and later press deadlines to accommodate late-breaking news, door-to-door sales, and earlier delivery. Distribution has improved: *USA Today* sells in corporate cafeterias, university dining halls, hospitals, hotel lobbies, and Starbucks.

Suppose you were a full-service travel agent. What actions would you take to ensure your survival?

Pursuing leadership (cell D) is a viable option when the market is hospitable and the firm has high business strengths. The firm should:

- Publicly recognize the decline — but also demonstrate commitment.

- Market aggressively, by adding new products, increasing advertising and promotion, and/ or cutting prices — the newspaper industry is a good example.

- Consider reducing production capacity, like International Paper and domestic airlines. White Consolidated (now part of Electrolux) purchased Frigidaire from GM and immediately closed the plant.

- Consider encouraging competitors to exit by offering long-term supply contracts for their customers. Buying competitors or their assets may also be an option.[40]

HARVEST, DIVEST, SEGMENT

Generally, firms in cells A, B, C should harvest or divest. But for a cell C firm — inhospitable market, high business strengths, well positioned in price-insensitive segments — medium-run viability may be an option. New entry may even be an alternative for attractive market segments: BoltBus and MegaBus each offer frequent, low-price bus service with curbside pickup in the Boston–New York–Washington corridor and other routes; new buses have wifi connectivity. We discussed harvesting options earlier.

LEVERAGE THE BRAND

Notwithstanding market decline, and in addition to the above options, the firm may be able to leverage a strong brand in other markets. By diversifying away from its original business, the firm may yet survive and grow. Faced with a decline in cigarette smoking, Zippo, makers of the iconic lighter, introduced lifestyle products like camping supplies, casual clothing, fragrances, and watches. But this path may be quite difficult; Zippo discontinued earlier entries into tape measures, key holders, and belt buckles.

KEY IDEA

The firm may be able to leverage a declining brand into new markets.

MANAGING MARKETING IN TOUGH ECONOMIC TIMES

"Great companies excel in tough times, and in tough times customers turn to great companies."

— Mark Hurd, co-CEO, Oracle

"The time to buy is when there is blood on the streets." — Baron Rothschild

"Never let a serious crisis go to waste … it's an opportunity to do things you couldn't do before."

— Rahm Emanuel, then Chief of Staff, President Obama

In tough times, the firm should focus special attention on three entities — the firm, customers, and competitors. We offer some ideas and options that guide many successful firms.

Firm. The firm faces new realities: External — demand weakness and high price sensitivity; internal — corporate demands for marketing and sales budget cuts. Marketing must develop a laser-like focus on unit sales, prices, and expenses. Marketing should figure out where demand problems are worst by examining revenue streams by customer, product, and market segment — then decide which deserve more effort, and which less. Mostly, the firm should invest in its core business, and focus efforts on retaining and growing profitable customers, in part via significant communications — good news and bad news. The firm should be ready to make changes as circumstances evolve, but consider several specific actions:

- Retain key employees and continue to make R&D investments for the recovery.
- Cut prices by offering short-term discounts — not permanent price reductions.
- Ensure incentive compensation drives the right behavior; use recognition as a reward.
- Explore new pricing models like bundling, unbundling, mixed bundling; or offer the product benefit rather than the product itself — aircraft engine *power by the hour* versus aircraft engines, and cloud computing versus servers.
- Identify inefficiencies: Drop poorly performing products and brands; eliminate marginal value services; withdraw from unproductive market segments; eliminate unproductive sales, service, and support personnel, and distributors; reduce advertising not leading to near-term sales.
- Introduce stripped-down products with minimal service at lower prices — Burger King introduced a $1 Whopper (2-ounce versus 2.2-ounce patties), and/or introduce products that focus on value — luxury-goods firm Coach introduced the Poppy accessory line.
- Renegotiate contracts with (or drop) service providers like advertising agencies and marketing researchers.
- Respond to requests for aggregate spending cuts carefully by using zero-base budgeting. Never be *fair* by making equal across-the-board cuts.
- When operations drives use of less expensive raw materials, be sure customers do not react negatively — Campbell's received negative publicity when it reduced meat quantity in chicken-noodle soup!

Customers. B2C and B2B customers face difficult environments. Challenges vary by type and scope but decision-making units, decision-making processes, and purchase requirements may change dramatically. Decision making takes longer and many B2B purchases receive increased scrutiny from higher-level executives. The firm must identify these changes, take appropriate actions, and be creative. GameStop is the market leader in selling used video games (accepted as trade-ins for new-game purchases); in the most recent recession, Hyundai customers could return purchased cars if they lost their jobs within one year. Other considerations:

- Customers can't afford firm products — Can the firm offer new pricing and/or provide leasing options?
- Customers need longer to pay — Can the firm offer attractive credit terms?

Competitors. Competitors behave in new and different ways; the firm should watch carefully for opportunities to make gains. Considerations:

- Competitors sharply cut advertising and sales budgets — Can the firm increase spending and gain market share?
- Competitors lay off marketing and sales executives (or declare bankruptcy) and remaining employees are nervous — Can the firm make attractive hires?
- Competitors may be willing to sell brands, intellectual property, or themselves — Can the firm secure valuable assets from wounded competitors?

The firm must manage through tough times but simultaneously plan for economic recovery.[41]

What other messages did you glean from this chapter?

KEY MESSAGES

Preemption is an important dimension of market strategy-making; acting before competitors can put the firm in good competitive position. Using the product life-cycle framework, we constructed nine scenarios for developing preemptive strategies:

- Introduction
- Early-Growth Leaders
- Early-Growth Followers
- Late Growth
- Maturity — But Not Really
- Maturity — Concentrated Market Leaders
- Maturity — Concentrated Market Followers
- Maturity — Fragmented Markets
- Decline

These scenarios can help the firm think through its strategy by anticipating, and striving to influence, change. For each scenario, we developed a family of strategic options. Notwithstanding the value of identifying these options, the best competitive strategies are often contrarian. When the firm surprises competitors, it can gain significantly.

VIDEOS AND AUDIOS

For complimentary material, see Axcess Capon codes at www.axcessvids.com

Managing through the Life Cycle   953v 🜨   Ron Boire   Toys R Us

QUESTIONS FOR STUDY AND DISCUSSION

Can you answer the questions implied by this chapter's learning outcomes? Check!

1. Identify the product life-cycle stage for each product. Why did you choose those stages?

Smartphones	Digital cameras	Music downloads	Index mutual funds
Netbooks	Music on compact discs	Vacation travel	Social media

2. Suppose you are the newly appointed marketing VP for the Segway Human Transporter.**[570v]** Identify feasible strategic options. Be prepared to support your choices.

3. How did Nokia rise to global leadership in cell phones? Why did Nokia fail? Why did Microsoft acquire Nokia's handset business? As Microsoft's global marketing VP for mobile devices, how would you approach the future?

4. Suppose you own several specialty coffee shops in a midsize U.S. urban center. Starbucks enters. What are your options? What action(s) will you take? Why?

5. On p. 278, we noted several ways in which U.S. newspapers are addressing flat or declining circulation. What options are available for your local newspaper? What action(s) do you recommend? Why?

6. Installations of U.S. payphones are declining by several percentage points annually — payphone calls are also decreasing. How would you advise an independent payphone firm?

7. Vonage offers low-price voice telecom services; what is the current life-cycle stage? Prepare for a job interview at Vonage by describing current challenges, objectives, strategies, and success measures.

8. As Sirius XM Radio's incoming marketing VP, lay out your strategy going forward.

9. Select a product in which you are interested. Alternatively, consider *Managing Marketing in the 21st Century*. What is its product life cycle stage? What strategic options does it have? Which do you recommend? Why?

TRUE/FALSE QUESTIONS
Answers on page A2 and at www.axcessvids.com — 574p

1. A firm generates strategic options by developing scenarios that let it anticipate future competitor actions. ❏ TRUE ❏ FALSE

2. The follower's strategic objective is to lay the foundation for achieving market leadership and profitability, at least in the short and medium run. ❏ TRUE ❏ FALSE

3. Patents are the most common government-imposed barriers that firms can exploit. ❏ TRUE ❏ FALSE

4. In a leapfrog situation, the follower improves on the leader and offers enhanced value by developing innovative and superior products, and/or enters emerging market segments before the leader. ❏ TRUE ❏ FALSE

5. During the late growth stage, the value to the firm from early market leadership, or being a fast follower, is still growing rapidly. ❏ TRUE ❏ FALSE

MULTIPLE CHOICE QUESTIONS
Answers on page A2 and at www.axcessvids.com — 998p

1. The options for a follower in the early growth stage of the product life cycle include all of the following EXCEPT:
   a. seeking market leadership
   b. exiting the market
   c. settling for third place
   d. focusing on gaining leadership in a particular market segment or segments

2. Which of the following is NOT a method of generating growth in a mature market?
   a. increasing product use
   b. increasing price
   c. repositioning the brand
   d. improving physical distribution

3. All of the following are reasons that firms underinvest in mature products EXCEPT:
   a. limited view of the competition
   b. internally focused funding criteria
   c. fear of cannibalization
   d. inertia

4. Which of the following is NOT a matter of focus for a firm considering harvesting its product line slowly?
   a. cutting costs
   b. minimizing investment
   c. raising prices
   d. decreasing prices

5. Which of the following is NOT a broad strategic option for followers in concentrated mature markets?

   a. improving market position by growing sales
   b. keep on truckin'
   c. exiting
   d. developing a new product

IMPERATIVE 3

Set Strategic Direction and Positioning

CHAPTER 11

MANAGING BRANDS

For complimentary material, see Axcess Capon codes at www.axcessvids.com

If this business were to be split up, I would be glad to take the brands, trademarks, and goodwill, and you could have all the bricks and mortar and I would fare better than you.

— John Stuart, then Chairman of Quaker Oats[1]

LEARNING OUTCOMES

When you have completed this chapter, you will be able to:

- Understand the nature of brands and the values they provide for buyers and sellers.
- Comprehend the changing role of brands and branding.
- Distinguish between customer brand equity and firm brand equity.
- Measure the monetary value of customer brand equity and firm brand equity.
- Build and sustain a strong brand.
- Construct brand architecture.
- Make decisions about multibranding versus umbrella branding, brand broadening, and brand migration.
- Address branding issues for strategic alliances.
- Revitalize struggling brands.

OPENING CASE: SAP

In the first decade of the 21st century, SAP doubled the value of the SAP brand and moved significantly up the global rankings — 26 in 2015. How did SAP achieve such success?

At the turn of the century, SAP was the world's largest enterprise systems software firm and third-largest independent software supplier overall.[2] SAP had 12,500 customers and 25,000 software installations in more than 50 countries, mainly with large global firms. SAP's culture was technologically driven; innovative product development drove success — marketing and branding were not significant. SAP decentralized marketing at the national level; multiple advertising agencies produced local campaigns. In the previous decade, SAP's advertising tagline changed frequently: We Can Change Your Business Perspective; A Better Return on Information; The City of "e"; The

Time of New Management; *and* You Can, It Does. *SAP had one global website, 30 local country sites, many subsidiary sites, and more than 9,000 web pages — without a common theme. SAP's brand vision was weak and unclear; CEO Hasso Plattner concluded SAP messaging was sprawling, inconsistent, and confusing.*

Plattner broke several taboos by bringing in Martin Homlish from Sony Electronics as SAP's new Global Chief Marketing Officer — hiring from outside SAP, outside the software industry, and outside Germany. Homlish's challenge was to transform SAP's marketing and to reposition the SAP brand to have broader, sustainable appeal. Said Homlish, "I saw SAP as a marketer's dream ... great products, strong history of innovation, and a loyal customer base. All we had to do was transform marketing." Homlish faced three core challenges: Communicate the SAP brand consistently, align the organization, and create a brand flexible enough to support challenging business objectives in a dynamic industry. Homlish's first decision was to base SAP Global Marketing in New York City, center of media and marketing, rather than at SAP's headquarters in Waldorf, Germany.

Homlish sought a brand vision that could evolve over time. Meeting with customers, Homlish said, "I found a common theme. SAP was considered a mission-critical part of almost every great company." SAP brand vision became: SAP turns businesses into best-run businesses. *The tagline to convey the new identity was,* The Best-Run Businesses Run SAP.

Homlish redesigned SAP's brand architecture: SAP became the masterbrand; product brands like my SAP *were subbrands. SAP cut its web pages by two thirds and aligned national websites with the global site, often by direct translation. Global site changes then triggered changes to local sites using state-of-the-art web content management applications. SAP placed all global advertising with Ogilvy & Mather, and reinforced its new brand vision with simple headlines that complemented the tagline:* Lufthansa Runs SAP *and* Adidas Runs SAP. *Large posters in airports around the world helped globalize the SAP brand.*

Homlish fended off potential internal challenges to global integration by developing a series of tools to align regional marketing. Regions received incentives for adopting Global Marketing's rules and syndicated tools. Said Homlish, "We drove change through alignment ... working with stakeholders across SAP. [It] takes more time versus strict 'command and control,' but ultimately it results in wider acceptance."

One Voice *was an online resource available to every SAP employee.* One Voice *included information on approved names and trademarks, key messages, and positioning for all SAP solutions and products, in customer-friendly language. An SAP Global Marketing team set policy, updated tools, and edited every piece of global collateral and web content before publication. The Sales and Marketing Asset Repository Toolset (SMART) delivered sales and marketing content and assets to field offices, and helped employees search for content, adaptable to local needs. The Sales and Marketing Intranet enhanced SAP Global Marketing efforts by including* One Voice *and* SMART, *together with branding standards, image library, customer brochures, industry reports, BlackBerry tools, and online customer demos.*

Homlish developed a branding culture by involving local field offices as co-developers of global messaging. Homlish addressed kick-off meetings to field organizations in the North America, Europe, Middle East, and Africa (EMEA) regions. SAP Global Marketing created country champions *to roll out each campaign and gain internal support. Said Homlish, "When I arrived at SAP and would ask questions about our company and our products, I would get a lot of jargon ... SAP-anese — it confused me and our customers." SAP Global Marketing distributed pocket-sized brand cards, stating core positioning, attributes, and personality of brands to all employees worldwide. SAP Global Marketing also selected brand ambassadors to champion the brand locally. "Today if you ask an SAP employee about the company and its products ... they can tell you, 'We help every customer become a best-run business.'"*

To attain growth objectives, SAP targeted small and medium-sized enterprises (SME) with less complex, easy-to-install new enterprise software. This thrust posed challenges for Homlish's branding strategy as SAP had always supplied large firms. SAP addressed the low awareness of SME

What core approaches did Marty Homlish use in developing SAP's new brand vision?

products with bold brand-building ads that announced, Finally, powerful software for the Fortune 500,000. *Then, the ads addressed challenges head-on with headlines like,* Companies that thought they couldn't afford SAP run SAP. *SAP also incorporated midmarket customers:* Oakley Runs SAP *and* The North Face Runs SAP.

Homlish's actions led SAP — 240,000 customers in 180 countries — to powerful results. According to Interbrand's *annual brand rankings, from 2000 to 2014, SAP's brand value more than doubled, to $17 billion. In 2015,* SAP *ranked 26, above established brands like Ford, Sony, Volkswagen, and Xerox. SAP's revenues and net income grew from $5.1 billion and $796 million, respectively, in 1999, to $23 billion and $4.6 billion in 2014 (but dropped slightly in 2015).*

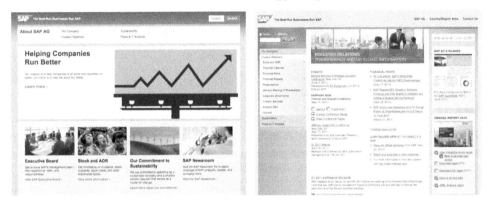

Chapter 11 is the third of three chapters discussing separate facets of Imperative 3 — Set Strategic Direction and Positioning. Chapter 9 discusses developing strategy for market segments and markets; Chapter 10 focuses on preemption, using the life-cycle framework to develop scenarios for generating competitive strategic options. In this chapter, we focus on branding and managing brands. As with previous topics, deep insight into markets, customers, competitors, company, and complementers is critical for making good branding decisions.

In recent years, branding has shifted from being a relatively low-level tactical issue concerned with naming products/services, to becoming a critical driver of contemporary marketing practice. Today, the combined value of many firm brands far outstrips the value of their tangible assets. Accountants and financiers are reexamining the nature of brands as they rethink basic assumptions about the value of the firm. Indeed, branding is now a major decision area for both senior managers and marketing executives alike. And, of course, brands also have significant value for customers.

THE CHANGING VIEW

OLD WAY	NEW WAY
Brand management is a junior executive responsibility	Brand management is an important senior management responsibility
Brand owners desire total control over their brands — co-branding is rare	Brand owners are willing to engage in cooperative strategies — co-branding is increasing
Brand proliferation common	Brand rationalization common
Branding is a name	Branding is a multisensory memorable experience
Brands help customers reduce purchase risk	Brands provide customers with many values
Brands tied to products and stock-keeping units (skus)	Brands are assets to be managed in their own right
Firms add brands haphazardly	Firms carefully consider brand architecture
Local and regional brands are dominant	Global brands are increasingly preeminent
Only brand owners use brands	Brand licensing is increasingly common

WHERE WOULD WE
BE WITHOUT THEM?

WHAT IS A BRAND?

Brands are different from products. A leading marketer once said, "A product is something that is made in a factory; a brand is something that is bought by a customer. A competitor can copy a product; a brand is unique. A product can be quickly outdated; a successful brand is timeless."[3]

Throughout history, sellers have branded their goods and services. Medieval goldsmiths and silversmiths branded their products. The branding iron was an essential tool for U.S. ranchers (*Brand* is an Old Norse word meaning *to burn*); if a rancher had a reputation for high-quality cattle, his brand secured higher prices at market. The traditional definition follows logically: A brand is a *name, term, sign, symbol* or *design* (letter, number, character), or a combination of them intended to identify the goods and services of one seller or group of sellers and to differentiate them from the competition.[4] Brands are a part of everyday life for firms and customers — logos, names, package designs, symbols, trademarks are on virtually everything we eat, drink, drive, and wear.[5]

The most often used *signifier* is brand name, but other *signifiers* can be as (or more) important. We associate Target stores with the color red, and UPS with brown; the *Financial Times* and fiberglass insulation from Dow Corning (U.S.) and ACI (Australia) are pink. We all recognize other brands via *visual* signifiers: Absolut and Coca-Cola — bottles;[6] Gerber — baby; Merrill Lynch — bull; Nike — Swoosh; Pillsbury — doughboy; Volkswagen — *Beetle*. *Sound* signifies Harley-Davidson — motorcycles; and a distinctive perfume — *smell* — denotes Shanghai Tang (ST) (Shanghai-based designer-wear retail chain).[7]

Today, brands have meaning far beyond these outward manifestations. By offering customers value via its brands, the firm secures value for shareholders. The brand has become a symbol around which the firm and customers construct a relationship. We define a *brand* as: *A collection of perceptions and associations that customers hold about a product, service, or company. This collection embodies values that create meaning for customers, and represent a promise of the experience customers expect when they have contact with the brand.*[8] Important implications of this definition are:

- The primary meaning of any brand exists in customer minds. Great brands are really owned by customers, not by firms — hence Coca-Cola's spectacular failure with New Coke. Brand meaning may stay relatively unchanged, but the products/product lines may evolve substantially in attributes, features, underlying technologies, and customer benefits/values.

- Brands make implicit or explicit promises of customer experiences.[9] These promises provide value to customers over and above products/services. By providing additional value, the firm earns value for shareholders.

MARKETING QUESTION

What is your favorite brand? What promise does this brand offer over and above the generic product/service?

KEY IDEA

The brand is a symbol around which the firm and customers construct a relationship.

KEY IDEA

The firm may brand products at different levels of aggregation.

- Figure 11.1 shows the term *brand* applies widely to individual products, product lines, or groups of product lines:
  - **Individual product** — Aveo (Chevrolet), Camry (Toyota), Fiesta (Ford), Leaf (Nissan), Town & Country (Chrysler), MX-5 Miata (Mazda).
  - **Product line** — a group of closely related products serving a similar function. The Ragu *family* or *masterbrand* embraces several types of sauces — Cheese, Chunky Garden Style, Light, Old World Style, Pizza, Robust Blend Hearty.
  - **Group of product lines** — a group of product lines fulfilling many different functions. Such *monolithic* brands are often *corporate brands* — Carrefour, Citigroup, GE, IBM, Marks & Spencer, Microsoft, Nike, Yamaha.

FIGURE 11.1
Branding Levels

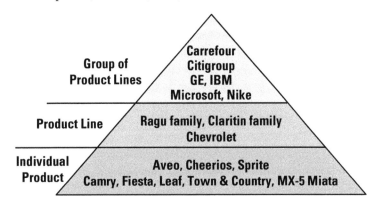

Sometimes brand meaning evolves. Honda's original U.S. association was motorcycles — today, Honda's associations include automobiles and lawnmowers. Some brands — like Virgin — move away from their origins and become quite abstract:

MARKETING QUESTION

Does the video **[504v]** reflect Virgin's brand vision?

Virgin — Evolution of a Brand

Virgin's original brand associations were tied to publishing rock-and-roll records. Expansion into record stores broadened Virgin's brand associations, but Virgin sold its record business and diversified into many product classes — Virgin Atlantic, Virgin America (airlines), Virgin Books, Virgin Bridal Shops, Virgin Cars (retail distribution), Virgin Direct (financial services), Virgin Electronics, Virgin Galactic (space travel), Virgin Limousines, Virgin Megastores (retail distribution), Virgin Mobile (cellular phone service), Virgin Sound and Vision (educational computer software), Virgin Vacations, Radio Free Virgin.

The Virgin brand is now uncoupled from its origins, yet still articulates its original abstract values. Brand vision is a higher-order sense of fun-loving, hip, irreverent, antiestablishment *underdogness*. Virgin's ongoing battles with British Airways and CEO Sir Richard Branson's personal activities — including attempts at around-the-world balloon flights — strongly support the brand vision. Some observers criticize Virgin extensions as random and capricious but Branson's response is direct: "Branding is everything. I think it's also wise to diversify; this enables you to have a contingency plan when the economy is going through a rough patch."

MARKETING QUESTION

Find a working friend or relative, and give the *Brand Coffee Machine Test*. Stand at the coffee machine and ask, "What does your product or company brand stand for?" Then press the *fill* button or lever. If the person cannot give a good answer by the time your cup fills, the brand fails. The organization cannot expect customers to understand brand meaning if employees do not.[12]

Firms often combine brand names, like Toyota Corolla or the American Express Personal Card. The firm earns value from the monolithic brand — Toyota, American Express — and additional value from individual product brands. Large retailers also develop brands: Sam's Choice — Walmart, and Michael Graves — Target; even cell phone service providers like Vodafone offer private-label phones.[10] Other brand features include:

- Anything can be branded — product; service; town, city, country; even yourself![11] Early PC buyers were indifferent to microprocessors; *intel inside* changed that. Water is the world's most common substance: Compare prices of Evian, Perrier, and Poland Spring with Budweiser, Coca-Cola, and milk; they demonstrate brand power.

- Brands can provide psychological value: safety and security — ADT, Volvo; caring/nurturing — Gerber, J&J; self-indulgence/reward — Dove, Häagen-Dazs; winning attitude — Nike, Wheaties.

- Brands may become generic — synonymous with the product class. U.S. examples include Aspirin, Band-Aid, eBay, Google, Kleenex, Lego, Rollerblade, Vaseline, Xerox; Britain — Biro, Hoover; Austria — Walkman.[13]

- Customer judgments and expectations about brands drive purchase decisions.

- Customers often form communities to demonstrate brand commitment — Harley-Davidson riders (HOGs), Macintosh users.[14]

The firm must construct a *brand vision (identity)* for each brand — associations like personal, lifestyle, or type of customer it *wants* people to hold. When the firm offers multiple brands, it must also decide how the various brand visions should relate to each other. By contrast, *brand image* comprises the actual associations customers hold about the brand. Much firm branding effort — *brand positioning* — focuses on bringing brand image and brand vision into alignment. Hence, the firm should audit brand image on a regular basis.

BRAND ASSOCIATIONS

The firm should strive for *brand associations* that reinforce the desired brand vision, and align these associations with brand image.[15] Brand associations are thoughts the customer generates when faced with a stimulus like brand name, logo, message, or spokesperson. *Brand personality* captures the idea of enduring and distinct human or emotional characteristics associated with a brand — Table 11.1.

Dimensions	Descriptors	Examples
Competence	Intelligent — technical, corporate, serious	*The Wall Street Journal*
	Reliable — hardworking, secure, efficient, trustworthy, careful, credible	
	Successful — leader, confident, influential	
Excitement	Daring — trendy, exciting, off-beat, flashy, provocative	MTV, Mountain Dew
	Imaginative — unique, humorous, surprising, artistic, fun	
	Spirited — cool, young, lively, outgoing, adventurous	
	Up-to-date — independent, contemporary, innovative, aggressive	
Ruggedness	Outdoors — masculine, Western, active, athletic	L.L. Bean
	Tough — rugged, strong, no-nonsense	
Sincerity	Cheerful — sentimental, friendly, warm, happy	Hallmark, Skippy peanut butter
	Down-to-earth — family-oriented, small-town, conventional, blue-collar, all-American	
	Honest — sincere, real, ethical, thoughtful, caring	
	Wholesome — original, genuine, ageless, classic, old-fashioned	
Sophistication	Charming — feminine, smooth, sexy, gentle	Chanel, Dior
	Upper class — glamorous, good-looking, pretentious, sophisticated	

Effective brand associations are:

- **Strong** — personally relevant for customers and presented consistently over time.

- **Favorable** — desired by customers and successfully delivered by the brand.

- **Unique** — perceived by customers as unique, different from other brands.

Generally, the firm uses implementation tools like communications, distribution outlet, and product design and quality to achieve alignment between brand vision and brand image. Sometimes brand associations — positive and negative — are outside firm control. Many people

KEY IDEA

Brand vision — associations the firm *wants* people to hold.

Brand image — associations people *actually* hold.

TABLE 11.1
Brand Personality[16]

KEY IDEA

Brand personality comprises five important dimensions:

- Competence
- Excitement
- Ruggedness
- Sincerity
- Sophistication

MARKETING QUESTION

Select a brand. How did you learn about it? Write down all your associations. For each brand association, assess the extent to which it is:

- *strong* versus *weak*
- *favorable* versus *unfavorable*
- *unique* versus *common*

**MARKETING
QUESTION**

To some people, the name iPad recalls a feminine hygiene product. Do you think that has affected iPad sales? Why or why not?

associate Levi's (jeans) and Marlboro (cigarettes) with U.S. cowboy movies. These associations are generally positive; in contrast, widespread opposition to U.S. policies (Iraq war) affected some brands negatively, notably Coca-Cola and McDonald's in Persian Gulf countries. To avoid negative associations, McDonald's focuses on local ownership, local suppliers, distinct store designs, and unique menu items — like the *McArabia* — a chicken sandwich on Arabian-style bread.[17] Evian emphasized youthfulness associations with its inner baby TV commercials.**[245v]**

BRANDING IS NOT JUST FOR CONSUMERS ...

Many people assume that branding is just for B2C marketing. Not so! Branding is also very important in B2B markets, especially for firms with many customers like SAP (Opening Case). Specific industries include banking, capital goods, computing, consulting, office equipment, and shipping. Individual firms for which branding is critical are Brother, Canon, Caterpillar, DuPont, FedEx, GE, IBM, Intel, Microsoft, Oracle, Staples, Xerox — Figure 11.2.

FIGURE 11.2
*Branding Is Not
Just for Consumers!*

B2C and B2B branding use different languages: B2C firms focus on brand image or associations; B2B firms talk about building relationships and customer confidence. B2B firms want customers to view them as experienced, risk-free, and trustworthy suppliers, preferably with solid track records and stellar market reputations. B2B branding is increasingly important as firms in many industries shift buying decisions from technologists to employees with less technical expertise. Oftentimes, branding is more important than technology — a well-managed brand outlasts many technology changes.

... AND IS NOT JUST ABOUT ADVERTISING

Another common misunderstanding is that branding should focus only on consumers/end users and that advertising is the only approach. Not so! Reaching a broad audience with communications is as important for corporate brands as for many product brands. Communications targets extend far beyond current and potential customers and include:

• Alliance partners	• Intermediaries	• Government bodies	• Regulators
• Bondholders	• Investment analysts	• Owners/shareholders	• Suppliers
• Current employees	• Media	• Prospective employees	

In addition to traditional advertising, the firm can build and reinforce brand vision via other communication forms — brochures, direct mail; managerial actions like speeches and broadcasts; products/packaging, promotions, publicity & public relations, physical facilities, stationery, telephone interactions; and the panoply of new alternatives made possible by digital marketing — Chapter 17. The CEO can have a major impact on firm branding by becoming the *face and feel* of the company — Richard Branson — Virgin; Tim Cook — Apple; Mark Cuban — Dallas Mavericks; Warren Buffett — Berkshire Hathaway.

FIGURE 11.3
The CEO as Brand[18]

Figure 11.3 contains pictures of some well-known current and former CEOs. How many do you recognize? Can you name their firms? How does your view of the CEO affect your associations of the firm and its product brands? For answers, Endnote 18, p. E16.

Firm employees are an increasingly important branding audience and communications channel. Eli Lilly (pharmaceuticals), Verizon (telecommunications), and many other leading firms conduct extensive branding programs to ensure employees internalize and represent firm brand vision properly. Regularly and periodically, these firms measure how employees perceive company brands, then act on the findings. Internal branding is especially important for business services and consulting firms, and B2C firms like retailers, where employees regularly interface with customers. Corrado Passera, CEO of struggling Italian Banca Intesa, even wrote a small book for the 60,000 employees detailing bank goals and planned actions.[19] Many firms carefully select employees to *evangelize* and represent firm brands on social media — chat rooms, forums, other online communities, and *tweets*. The firm should also conduct branding audits of constituencies like affiliates and suppliers, then take appropriate steps to enhance *brand commitment*.

THE BASIS FOR BRANDING

Historically, brander and producer were synonymous — firms made products and branded them. Today, there is no necessary relationship between *brand owner* and *branded-product producer*. Most readers know that retailers do not manufacture private-label products. But, as Figure 11.4 shows, many traditional manufacturers do not make their branded products either. The brand/production relationship may take many forms:

- **Totally integrated production operations.** Ford's production of the Model T is the prototypical example. Ford received iron ore and coal at one end of the production line; Model Ts rolled off at the other end. Integrated aluminum and oil producers fall into this category.

- **Subcomponent assembly.** The brand owner assembles components produced by other firms. Examples include contemporary automobile manufacturing and Boeing's *Dreamliner*.

- **No production responsibility.** The brand owner may design the product, set quality control standards, then distribute and market branded products. The firm does not manufacture, but rather *owns* the customer experience. Examples include Apple — consumer electronics; Nike — sports shoes; Nintendo — game cartridges; Perdue — chicken; Ralph Lauren and Tommy Hilfiger — designer products; Xerox — copiers.

KEY IDEA

The brand/production relationship may take several different forms.

Totally Integrated Production	Subcomponent Assembly	No Production Responsibility
Model T Ford; integrated aluminum firm	Many contemporary auto firms; aircraft manufacturers	*Nike*; designer products
Firm branding the product responsible for most production operations	Firm mainly assembles components from other firms	Firm branding the product undertakes little or no production operations

FIGURE 11.4
Alternative Production and Branding Relationships

You, the reader, are a brand! What is your *brand vision*?

1. What *brand image* and *brand associations* do people hold about you?

2. Do these associations conform to your desired brand vision?

3. Are the image and associations consistent, or do they differ across people — friends, parents, professors, prospective employers?

4. Are you satisfied with these associations? If so, how will you sustain and enhance them? If not, how will you change them?

5. How do your postings on Facebook, LinkedIn, and other social media sites support your brand vision?

In industries like electronic consumer goods, contract manufacturing is a fast-growing trend. Many brand owners focus resources on customer service, design, marketing, and R&D; they view manufacturing almost as a service function. If the brand does not identify the producing organization, we must ask: What value does a brand deliver?

BRAND EQUITY AND THE VALUE OF BRANDS

By effectively developing and implementing market strategy, the firm creates brand value. The firm may also use brand value to develop and implement market strategy. Excellent branding operates as a virtuous circle, continually employing and enhancing firm equity in its brands.

Brand equity captures the idea that brands deliver value, over and above actual products/ services. The most widely accepted definition of brand equity is *a set of brand assets and liabilities linked to a brand, its name, and symbol that add to (or subtract from) the value provided by a product or service to a firm and/or that firm's customers.*[20] From this definition we see that brand value accrues to both the *firm* and its *customers*. It follows that there are two types of brand equity: *customer brand equity (CBE)* — the value customers receive; and *firm brand equity (FBE)* — the value the firm receives.

CUSTOMER BRAND EQUITY

Products/brands provide customers three types of value — Chapter 4:

- **Functional** — doing the job they were designed to do — *FedEx packages arrive on time*
- **Psychological** — prestige, security, status — American Express Platinum card; Air Jordan and Air Max sneakers; fashion items from Armani, Dior, Prada, Versace
- **Economic** — low price, low cost of ownership — jetBlue, Southwest Airlines (U.S.); easyJet, Ryanair (Europe)

Related to these values, customers receive two types of brand equity — *prepurchase* and *postpurchase*:

PREPURCHASE EQUITY — what customers believe *before* purchase that they will receive *after* purchase. In particular, *prepurchase* brand equity reduces customer search costs and purchase risk. The classic prepurchase CBE example focuses on what will *not* occur: *You never get fired for buying IBM.*

POSTPURCHASE EQUITY enhances the customer consumption experience. After purchase, customers actually receive some combination of functional, psychological, and economic values.

KEY IDEA

Customers may secure significant value from a brand — *before* and *after* — purchase.

Coke versus Pepsi

On a blind taste test, Pepsi — 51 percent — scored better than Coke — 44 percent. But in an open test, Coke — 65 percent — exceeded Pepsi — 23 percent, attesting to Coca-Cola's brand value.[21]

Sometimes high CBE focuses on a specific product class. Tide *detergent* typically engenders positive functional and psychological benefits/values. But how would you react to Tide *toothpaste* or Tide *cookies*? Other brands provide customer value across several product classes — corporate brands like *Virgin*. Movie brands like *Star Wars* and *Harry Potter* earning significant revenues from a wide variety of accessory products.[22] Pre- and/or postpurchase CBE is generally greater when:

- comparing alternative products is difficult;
- customers do not realize value until some time after purchase;
- customers are inexperienced or unfamiliar with the product form/class;

- product quality from some suppliers is variable;
- the product is socially visible;
- there is mental flexibility in portraying the brand.

Table 11.2 shows brands can deliver significant CBE for many years.

Product	Leading Brand 1925	Position 2016	Product	Leading Brand 1925	Position 2016
Batteries	Eveready	Leader	Razors	Gillette	Leader
Breakfast cereal	Kellogg	Leader	Shortening	Crisco	Leader
Canned fruit	Del Monte	Leader	Soap	Ivory	Leader
Chewing gum	Wrigley	Leader	Soft drink	Coca-Cola	Leader
Chocolates	Hershey	Leader	Soup	Campbell's	Leader
Cookies	Nabisco	Leader	Tea	Lipton	Leader
Flour	Gold Medal	Leader	Tires	Goodyear	Leader
Paint	Sherwin-Williams	Leader	Toothpaste	Colgate	Leader

TABLE 11.2
Leading U.S. Brands —
1925 and 2015[23]

FIRM BRAND EQUITY

FBE results from customer responses to firm actions and links directly to CBE. High brand awareness, positive attitudes, high perceived quality, positive word of mouth, intention to purchase, purchase, brand loyalty, positive brand image and associations, and high customer satisfaction all enhance FBE.[24,25] CBE and FBE reflect the trust between brand and customers. Former American Express, RJR Nabisco, and IBM CEO Lou Gerstner took a strong position on branding:

> Shelly Lazarus, then CEO of Ogilvy & Mather Worldwide, said: "I learned a big lesson from Lou. Once you've set a strategy, you never ever violate it. Nobody ever got a free card, a discounted card, or bundled pricing. Lou would say, 'This is a violation of the brand, and we're not doing it.'"[26]

KEY IDEA

FBE reflects the trust established between brand owner and customers.

High FBE has many positive features. Firms with high FBE can:

- set higher prices and earn better profit margins;
- more easily introduce similarly branded items in different product forms/classes and markets;
- use cross-selling to encourage existing customers to purchase in different product forms/ classes;
- generate leverage in distribution channels by securing more and better shelf space, and more favorable transaction terms. Foot Locker reduced orders from Nike to protest price and selection terms; Nike significantly cut Foot Locker's allocation. Consumers shopped elsewhere for Nike products and eventually Foot Locker accepted Nike terms.
- raise entry barriers for competitors;
- exploit licensing opportunities.

KEY IDEA

FBE generally builds up slowly over time.

> Disney acquired Marvel Entertainment, owner of superheroes like Spiderman, the Incredible Hulk, and X-Men. Disney uses Marvel characters for creative activities, but also earns substantial revenues from product licensing.

KEY IDEA

Generally, CBE and FBE build slowly, but new brands sometimes gain strength relatively quickly — Airbnb, eBay, Facebook, Google, Leapfrog, Red Bull, Ryanair, Uber, Yahoo! Nonetheless, CBE, and hence FBE, are fragile and may dissipate quickly if the firm missteps. Many firms unwittingly cause brand equity declines by product proliferation, price cutting, offering discounts and promotions, using inferior components, squeezing suppliers or channel partners, and simple neglect.[27] Tommy Hilfiger sales went from red hot to stalled when product prolifer-

A brand can quickly lose value if not managed properly.

ation and out-of-control distribution (more than 10,000 department stores/discount outlets) diluted brand value. Quaker Oats experience with Snapple is a salutary lesson:

Quaker Oats purchased Snapple (fruit and tea soft drinks) from Triarc for $1.7 billion; much of the acquisition price reflected Snapple's brand value. Barely two years later, Triarc repurchased Snapple for $300 million. During the two years, Quaker had $160 million in operating losses — overall, Snapple cost Quaker $2 million per day of ownership. One of Quaker's several strategic errors was believing it could distribute Snapple in supermarkets and drug stores, even though more than half Snapple's sales were impulse purchases in convenience stores, gasoline stations, and similar outlets. Quaker also stopped Snapple's quirky, yet memorable, advertising featuring Wendy Kaufman (Snapple employee), and spokespersons Howard Stern and Rush Limbaugh. Snapple lost significant brand equity.[28]

Managerial mishaps can also wreak havoc with FBE: Product recalls include Dow Corning — breast implants; Merck — *Vioxx* [990v]; Perrier — water; product failures include Firestone — *Ford Explorer* tires; Toyota — unplanned acceleration; Volkswagen — faked emission tests; impure products include Schlitz (beer).

In the early 1970s, Schlitz was a strong second to Anheuser-Busch (AB) in the U.S. beer market. From 1974 to 1976, Schlitz took several actions to reduce costs: Schlitz substituted cheaper corn syrup for barley malt, and introduced *accelerated batch fermentation* — shortened the fermentation process from 12 days to 4 days. These changes caused a slightly lighter taste and spawned a rumor that Schlitz beer was green. AB publicly committed to more expensive ingredients. Schlitz aggressively used discounts and promotions — inconsistent with Schlitz' longtime premium positioning. In 1976, Schlitz changed a stabilizer to avoid adding an ingredient required by a new labeling law. The production process supposedly filtered out the new stabilizer, but reaction with other ingredients formed tiny flakes in the beer. One fix removed the stabilizer but the beer went flat; Schlitz *secretly* recalled and destroyed 10 million bottles and cans. In 1974, Schlitz sold 17.8 million barrels; in 1986, it sold less than one million — a stunning destruction of brand equity.[29]

MARKETING QUESTION

Some individuals build brands; others reap the fruits of successful brand building; still others attempt to recover brand equity following well-publicized missteps. What can you learn about branding from Bill Clinton, Hillary Clinton, Paris Hilton, Michael Jordan, Kim Kardashian, Sarah Palin, Martha Stewart, Maria Sharapova, Donald Trump, Tiger Woods? Feel free to substitute your own selections.

Notwithstanding brand equity's fragility, some brands have greater *brand resilience* than others. In 1982, J&J withdrew Tylenol capsules in the face of a cyanide-poisoning scare (six people died; unsolved); sales plummeted to zero. J&J's timely and caring response led to a quick Tylenol rebound when it introduced more secure packaging and ramped up distribution and promotion. By contrast, *Perrier* never really recovered from a recall caused by product impurities. Unhappy customers, disgruntled employees, and aggressive competitors aided by blogs, Facebook, Twitter, YouTube, and third-party websites, can also sabotage FBE; planning for damage control and crisis management is increasingly important.[30]

MONETIZING BRAND EQUITY

We just explored the value the brand brings to customers — customer brand equity (CBE); and to the firm — firm brand equity (FBE). Now we focus on the monetary value of brands.

CUSTOMER BRAND EQUITY

Customers receive value from a *generic* product; typically, they receive greater value from a *branded* product. The difference in value — brand less generic — equals CBE. The *dollarmetric* method — Chapter 21 — assesses CBE's monetary value. The firm asks customers how much extra they would pay for the branded product versus an unbranded product; this amount is CBE's monetary value. More specifically, this figure is *prepurchase* CBE — the customer only receives *postpurchase* CBE after purchase. If the branded price is higher than customers are willing to pay, there is no *postpurchase* CBE. The firm can also assess the *marginal* CBE of one brand versus another — the extra price customers will pay for their favored brand. Conjoint analysis — Chapter 6 Marketing Enrichment6.1 **[710p, pp. 3–7]** — is a valuable methodology for *indirectly* assessing CBE's monetary value.

MARKETING ENRICHMENT 6.1

Analyzing Quantitative Research Data **710p**

FIRM BRAND EQUITY

FBE relates directly to the brand's current and future ability to attract paying customers and increase shareholder value — about 30 percent of S&P stock market value. We assess FBE's monetary value at the firm level.[31] Valuation components are:

- **Revenues.** The price difference between the branded product and an identical generic product, multiplied by forecast excess unit sales volume.
- **Cost.** The costs of supporting the brand.

Various approaches are available to calculate FBE.

BASIC APPROACH. FBE's monetary value is the sum of the year-by-year differences between revenues and costs, discounted to the present.[32] Unfortunately, this straightforward approach has two inherent problems:

- An unbranded equivalent to the branded product may not exist.
- Ignores potential for brand broadening (leveraging) — using the brand to enter a new product form/class. Brand value is unconstrained by current products, product lines, or customers. Many brands have customer-attracting properties over and above the products/product lines to which they are currently attached. The brand *Pan Am*, unattached to an aircraft or airline, sold for several million dollars.

MARKET VALUE METHOD. The market provides the best FBE measure; this approach works well for publicly traded corporate brands. FBE equals market value less book value, plus nonbrand intangibles like human resources, know-how, and patents. When Ford purchased Jaguar for $2.5 billion, book value was $0.4 billion. Observers viewed the $2.1 billion difference (2.5 less 0.4) as Jaguar's brand equity. When market value does not exist — most product brands — the firm must use internal methods.

INTERNAL METHODS. Two internal methods for assessing FBE are:

- **Replacement cost.** The firm multiplies the anticipated brand-replacement cost by the probability of success.[33]
- **Cash flow.** This approach is intuitively more appealing, but estimating future cash flows is difficult. Interbrand (brand consultant) uses a proprietary method to estimate FBE based on future cash flows. Marketing Enrichment 11.1 **[668p]** illustrates the method and presents 2015 results.

MARKETING ENRICHMENT 11.1

Interbrand Method for Calculating Brand Equity and 2015 Results **668p**

Calculating the *marginal* FBE of one brand versus another is probably easier than calculating an absolute value. New United Motor Manufacturing Inc. (NUMMI) (GM/Toyota joint venture) manufactured two virtually identical cars — Geo Prizm (GM) and Corolla (Toyota). Corolla sold at a premium price and depreciated more slowly. After five years, Corolla's secondhand value was 18 percent more than Prizm. Figure 11.5 (p. 295) shows Corolla annual sales were 200,000 @ $11,100; Prizm annual sales were 80,000 @ $10,700. Clearly, Toyota has greater FBE; operating profit exceeded GM by $128 million, and Toyota dealers earned $107 million more than GM dealers.[34,35]

KEY IDEA

Internal approaches for calculating firm brand equity are:

- Replacement cost
- Cash flow methods

FIGURE 11.5
*Monetary Value of
Firm Brand Equity —
Automobile Example*

RELATIONSHIP BETWEEN CUSTOMER BRAND EQUITY AND FIRM BRAND EQUITY

We just showed how to assess individual CBE and FBE. We now develop a brand typology based on the relationship between CBE and FBE.

CBE AND FBE. For two hypothetical brands — A and B — Figure 11.6 shows price and willingness to pay for an individual customer:

- **Brand A.** The customer is willing to pay $8 versus the generic product's $2 price. Since brand A's price is $7, she would purchase and gain $6 CBE (8–2=6). (Actually, the customer has a good deal; she receives $6 CBE for $5 additional price over the generic value [7–2=5].) The firm earns revenues and positive FBE profit contribution.

- **Brand B.** The customer is willing to pay $5 versus the generic product's $2 price. Hence, CBE appears to be $3 (5–2 = 3). But the brand B price is $6, so the customer will not purchase. CBE is zero. The firm earns zero revenues, and zero FBE profit contribution.

Although potential CBE and FBE are positive for both brands, actual CBE and FBE only occurs when customer willingness to pay exceeds price (and price exceeds cost for FBE).

FIGURE 11.6
Monetary Value of FBE

KEY IDEA

The firm earns a contribution to FBE only when a customer purchases the brand.

CBE, FBE AND A BRAND TYPOLOGY. CBE and FBE allow us to develop a brand typology — Figure 11.7 (p. 296). CBE is either high or low; FBE is also high or low, depending on unit sales volume.

- **CBE-low, FBE-low: Commodity brand.** Like store-brand canned goods.

- **CBE-low, FBE-high: Mass-market brand.** High-volume, low-price brands like Almaden wine and Lenovo PCs.

- **CBE-high, FBE-low: Specialty brand.** Low-volume, high-price brands like Lafite-Rothschild wine, Steubenware glassware, and Rolex watches.
- **CBE-high, FBE-high: Iconic brand.** Customers enjoy high brand equity; the firm sells high volume at high prices. Includes brands like Apple and Nike.

Monetary Value of Firm Brand Equity

	Low	High
High	Specialty	Iconic
Low	Commodity	Mass Market

Monetary Value of Customer Brand Equity

FIGURE 11.7
A Brand Typology[36]

BUILDING AND SUSTAINING A STRONG BRAND

An important goal of developing and implementing market strategy is to build and sustain strong brands. Strong brands induce positive responses from customers. In turn, positive customer responses enhance brand strength and are a powerful influence on market strategy.

BUILDING A STRONG BRAND

Strong brands have value for both the firm and its customers. The firm builds a strong brand by making good decisions during the branding process — Figure 11.8.

Brand Vision
↓
Brand Awareness
↓
Brand Associations and Brand Image
↓
Brand Quality and
Value Perceptions
↓
Brand Loyalty
↓
Brand Broadening

BRAND VISION. Brand vision (identity, purpose) is aspirational — what the firm wants the brand to mean.**[464v]** Said Eli Lilly CEO Sidney Taurel, "Our brand is our identity (vision). It is who we are in the eyes of our customers ... shareholders, prospective employees, suppliers, and the communities where we operate."[38] Vodafone has a clear vision, a related *brand promise*, and core values:

> "Vodafone's vision is to be the leader of mobile communications in the world, and our brand promise is to go around the world. We back that with five core values — dependability, *can do* (we can solve your problem), practical innovation (we deliver on our promises), empathy, and *joie de vivre.*"[39]

Barcelona and Manchester United are the world's leading soccer clubs. How would you suggest they monetize their brand equities? (Or substitute your favorite sports team.)

FIGURE 11.8
Building a Strong Brand[37]

Why do you think Gap is in trouble? Do you believe store closings are the answer? **[394v, 578v]** What actions would you take?

MARKETING QUESTION

1. Write down 10 or more associations for each of the brands noted below.

2. For each brand, use the associations to write a one-sentence statement of brand image.

3. Compare your associations and brand image with a fellow student.

4. Write a one-sentence statement of what you believe to be the brand vision.

5. If brand vision and brand image are different, what actions would you take to bring them into alignment?

List of brands: Apple, Facebook, Goldman Sachs, Microsoft, Snapchat, Toyota, Uber.

Brand vision is the blueprint for many marketing decisions; indeed, brand vision defines the limits on product quality, service, promotion, distribution, and price. Executing on brand vision is critical to customers forming the desired associations and brand image (below).

BRAND AWARENESS. The firm must decide how customers should recognize the brand, including brand name and visual appearance. Choosing a brand name may involve extensive research with considerations of associations, legal availability, length, memorability, and pronounceability. The firm should be especially careful if it plans to use the brand in different countries and cultures with different language systems. Visual appearance requires careful choice of colors, materials, shapes, styles, themes, and related visuals for advertising and packaging.

Typically, the firm must invest significantly to achieve *brand awareness* at target customers. When the brand is first entrant in a new product form, the pioneer must educate potential customers about the product form, as well as about the brand. Gojo educated consumers, medical professionals, and retailers about a new type of hand-washing liquid — Purell. Launching a new corporate brand is also very costly. Lucent spent $50 million to create corporate brand awareness. But a brand may stay in memory for many years — Datsun, Esso, Master Charge — even after retirement by brand owners.

BRAND ASSOCIATIONS AND BRAND IMAGE. Brand associations are the meanings the brand has for individual customers — *brand image* is the overall sum of brand associations. Each and every marketing implementation decision the firm takes has a role in developing customer brand associations and hence brand image — product design, service, communications, distribution outlet, and price. Consistency is critical: Walmart developed guidelines and processes to ensure uniformity among circulars, in-store signage, and TV advertising. Other elements requiring consistency include packaging, stationery, uniforms, vehicles, websites; and symbols like pictures and graphic illustrations, slogans and jingles, and taglines. A critical firm task is to secure congruence between brand image and brand vision. Brand equity always suffers when brand vision and brand image are mismatched. Suppose the basis for brand vision is high prestige — yet customers form brand image from inferior product and service quality, poor advertising execution, downscale distribution, and/or low price. Customer response would most likely be negative, and FBE would suffer:

> For many years under Ford ownership, Jaguar (since acquired by Tata Motors) did not deliver on its luxury brand vision, nor make profits. Jaguar's entry-level X-type compact car had stale styling, one-size-fits-all marketing, and several thousand dollars in rebates — for a luxury car! Furthermore, Jaguar's slogan, *Born to Perform,* was a mismatch with U.S. owners, who purchased mostly for style.

BRAND QUALITY AND VALUE PERCEPTIONS. Consistency in communications and customer *brand experiences* are crucial for developing positive brand quality and value perceptions.

KEY IDEA

A well-structured process for building a strong brand embraces:

• Brand vision (identity)
• Brand awareness
• Brand associations and brand image
• Brand quality and value perceptions
• Brand loyalty
• Brand broadening

A specific problem for value perceptions is cutting prices and/or offering short-term price promotions. Sales may spike in the short run, but cause long-term brand damage as customers defer purchases until the next promotion. Vlasic discounted pickle prices so far that, despite volume increases, margin declines eventually forced bankruptcy. Clorox faced a similar problem, but reduced discounting and increased television advertising led to higher long-run revenues and profits.[40]

Many global 100 firms have *brand police* (or *brand czar*) to oversee brand consistency. These executives make sure brand names, logos, symbols, and all messaging — including advertising, brochures, social media, websites — remain consistent. Brand czars provide specific guidance on colors, font size, graphics, signs, stationery, uniforms, vehicles, and words; they also ensure conformity to consistent standards. We saw this consistency in the SAP Opening Case.

Achieving consistency is always difficult, but organizational practices can make it impossible. To explain: Many firms frequently rotate brand managers. New brand managers wanting to make their marks on a product (product line) reformulate brand vision. Each reformulation sacrifices consistency, brand quality, and *customer value* perceptions. This problem may diminish as branding becomes more important, and responsibility moves up the managerial hierarchy, the traditional brand manager role diminishes. The firm should also be wary of advertising agencies, communications specialists, consultants, and design and identity firms. By striving for creativity, these organizations may sacrifice brand vision consistency, and confuse customers. It's no accident that market leader L'Oreal has maintained the same tagline — *Because you're worth it* — for more than a quarter-century.

BRAND LOYALTY. Consistency in brand quality and value perceptions leads to *brand loyalty*. Brand loyalty inspires repeat purchase, referrals, and positive word of mouth.[41] Firms like Starbucks and Zappos cultivate *brand advocates* — loyal/*diehard* customers — as promoters and problem solvers, by providing communication options and and rewards for their support. Vertical marketers (own retail outlets) like Starbucks and Ben & Jerry's know the importance of consistency. They build *brand coherence* through personnel and the design and decor of retail facilities. By contrast, most automobile firms have difficulty providing brand-enhancing experiences in independently owned dealerships. A serious problem for hotel management firms like Hilton, Holiday Inn, and Sheraton is *off-message* execution by individual franchised hotels; inconsistency in the customer experience affects loyalty to the entire chain.

The firm earns high brand loyalty by:

- Selecting the *right* brand vision for target customers and consistently executing on that identity.
- Motivating firm employees and third-party organizations (like advertising agencies) to deliver on the brand vision.
- Continuously measuring customer satisfaction with the brand and making the necessary course corrections. (Following section: Sustaining a Strong Brand.)

BRAND BROADENING. Brand loyalty, repeat purchase, referrals, and favorable word of mouth should follow successful brand vision development and execution. The firm may broaden (leverage) a strong brand to other product forms/classes. Apple evolved its brand — PCs (desktop/laptop), iPod, iTunes, iPhone, iPad, Apple Pay, Apple Watch.

SUSTAINING A STRONG BRAND

The key to sustaining a strong brand for the long run is continual assessment of *brand health*. Many firms measure brand managers on short-term revenues, profits, and/or market share; these metrics often lead to cutting prices or reducing promotional expenditures for short-term results. Focusing exclusively on such measures is rather like examining the income statement but neglecting the balance sheet. FBE is really the brand balance sheet. *Brand health checks* use metrics indicating FBE changes.

Typical brand health checks use a *balanced-scorecard* approach — Chapter 24. Four popular types of measures — Table 11.3 (p. 299) — and sources are:

- **Purchasing and sales** — firm accounting and CRM systems; industry-focused research suppliers
- **Perceptual** — survey research
- **Marketing support** — firm accounting and business intelligence systems; industry-focused suppliers
- **Profitability** — firm accounting system

MARKETING QUESTION

In 2014, Coca-Cola was dethroned as the world's most valuable brand by Apple and Google. Coke is under fire from the antiobesity lobby. Sales have stagnated, and share price is well below the November 2014 high. How would you propel Coca-Cola back to the Number 1 position?

KEY IDEA

Carefully chosen brand vision and consistent execution are critical for developing brand loyalty.

MARKETING QUESTION

Major retailers like 7-Eleven, Costco, Supervalu (Albertsons, Jewell-Osco), and Walgreens introduced private-label beer. Do you think they will be successful? Why or why not?

KEY IDEA

FBE represents the brand balance sheet.

Brand health checks compare the brand versus historic trends and benchmark competing brands.

Brand health checks are not one-time events. Brand health checks should occur regularly — quarterly or biannually. The firm should compare current brand health versus historic trends and benchmark competing brands.[42] Results from brand health checks should lead to appropriate changes in market strategy and/or execution.

TABLE 11.3
Representative Selection of Brand Health Check Measures

Type of Measure	Measure	Description of Measure
Purchasing and sales	Market breadth	Number and type of customers purchasing the brand
	Market depth	Extent of repeat purchase
	Market share	Brand sales as a percentage of total market sales (units and/or dollars)
Perceptual	Awareness	Degree of brand awareness
	Brand image	Brand associations, congruence with brand vision
	Quality	Perception of brand quality (from blind tests)
	Uniqueness	Extent of differentiation from competition
	Value	Extent to which the brand provides good value for money
Marketing support	Advertising	Market share/advertising share
		Advertising/total marketing spend
	Distribution	Extent of distribution coverage in target outlets
		For retail goods, quality of display, especially key/strategic accounts
	Relative price	Price compared to competitive brands
Profitability	Profit	Gross margin earned from the brand
		Economic value added (EVA) of the brand — Marketing Enrichment FM.1 [308p, pp. 16–17]

MARKETING ENRICHMENT FM.1

Financial Analysis for Marketing Decisions **308p**

KEY IDEA

The firm should carefully manage evolution of the brand portfolio.

Firms adjust brand portfolios in response to:
- shifting customer trends,
- competitor action,
- mergers and acquisitions.

MARKETING QUESTION

How do you assess the branding strategy for your college, school, or university? Does your institution pursue a multibrand strategy or an umbrella branding strategy? How could your college, school, or university improve its branding?

MANAGING BRAND ARCHITECTURE

Many firms maintain *brand portfolios* — multiple brands, each with their own brand visions. The LVMH (global luxury-goods leader) corporate brand offers *Louis Vuitton* tan and brown monogrammed bags for several hundred dollars, *Murakami* bags at $1,000, and *Suhali* goatskin bags averaging $2,000. *Brand architecture* — the organizing structure for multiple brands — is an important decision area for the firm.

Because brands have a major impact on shareholder value, branding decisions should have high priority. The firm should carefully consider what to brand; decide on brand visions; desired brand associations to avoid negative effects on shareholder value; carefully plan brand additions (internally developed and/or secured by acquisition); and brand deletions. The firm should also consider interrelationships among the corporate brand, product-class brands, and individual product brands.

Firm brand portfolios should evolve as markets evolve. Anheuser-Busch changed its portfolio as customers switched to different beers — from low-end to higher-end, and from fuller to lighter. The firm should avoid drastic action like P&G's phasing out 1,000 brands in five years, and Unilever's Path-to-Growth program that dramatically cut its 1,600-brand portfolio.[43] We now discuss several brand architecture decisions, but defer global branding to Chapter 25.

MULTIBRANDING VERSUS UMBRELLA BRANDING

In *multibranding* — aka *House of Brands* strategy — the firm uses multiple brands for its various products.[44] The firm seeks target-customer loyalty to individual brands, but not necessarily to the parent-company brand. Do you know the corporate owner of Aguila, Coors, Cristal,

Foster's, Hamm's, Henry Weinhard, Icehouse, Keystone, Leinenkugel, Miller, Milwaukee's Best, Mickey's, Molson, Olde English 800, and Tyskie?* More consumers know of Procter & Gamble than SABMiller, but many would not associate P&G with all the following brands — Always, Ariel, Bounty, Braun, Charmin, Crest, Dawn, Downy/Lenor, Duracell, Fusion, Gain, Gillette, Head & Shoulders, Iams, Mach3, Olay, Oral-B, Pampers, Pantene, Tide, and Wella.**

KEY IDEA

Both *multibranding* and *umbrella branding* enjoy pros and cons.

By contrast, a firm using *umbrella branding* emphasizes a monolithic brand for several products/product lines. Consumers know Yamaha for electronic musical instruments (keyboards, guitars), traditional musical instruments (pianos), home audio products, computer peripherals, motorcycles, and even Grand Prix engines. The *One Ford* strategy led Ford to drop Aston Martin, Jaguar, Land Rover, and Volvo. A single firm may have several monolithic (master) brands: Toyota — Toyota, Lexus, Scion; Chrysler — Chrysler, Dodge, Jeep. Each masterbrand may offer finer-level subbrands: Dodge — Caravan, Dakota, Dodge Neon, Durango, Magnum, SRT-4, Stratus, Viper. Some factors favor multibranding; other factors favor umbrella branding — Table 11.4.

In Favor of Umbrella Branding	In Favor of Multibranding
Company culture. Enhances the firm's ability to deliver a consistent message.	*Transfer of negative associations from an umbrella brand.* Customers may transfer negative associations across products. In the 1980s, several women contracted toxic shock syndrome (and some died) after using P&G's ultra-high-absorbent tampon — *Rely*. P&G withdrew *Rely* and suffered financially. But suppose the product had been P&G tampons? In 2010, Lexus largely avoided the negative impact from Toyota's quality problems.
Intrafirm competition. Reduces the likelihood of intrafirm competition.	*Intrafirm competition.* Some firms favor enhanced intrafirm competition, particularly FMCG and pharmaceuticals.
Scale economies. By promoting a single brand, the firm secures economies in advertising, labeling, logos, and other communications efforts.	*Targeting and positioning.* The firm can better target and position products in multiple market segments. Stanley Black & Decker offers power tools under the company name — do-it-yourselfers; DeWalt — construction; Porter-Cable — woodworking.
Transfer of positive customer experiences across products. A positive customer experience with one product benefits similarly branded products in a different product form/class. Apple's success with iPod and iPhone helped Macintosh; Yamaha pianos help sales of electric guitars, and vice versa.[45]	*Inability to transfer positive customer experiences across products in umbrella branding.* Customers may not transfer positive brand associations across product forms/classes. A Yamaha piano experience may transfer to electric guitars, but to motorcycles? An umbrella brand can even cause problems within the same product form/class. Gallo's association with inexpensive wines led it to a multibrand approach for higher price points.

TABLE 11.4
Factors Favoring Multibranding and Umbrella Branding

MARKETING QUESTION

In the mid-2000s, Starbucks acquired Seattle's Best Coffee (SBC). As SBC's incoming brand manager, how would you position SBC? Would you relate SBC to the Starbucks brand? Why or why not? What marketing decisions would you make to support the new positioning?

A more recent trend is for some multibrand firms like P&G and Unilever to emphasize corporate ownership. In this way, the firm communicates overarching corporate values supporting its brands.**[527v]**

BRAND BROADENING (LEVERAGING)

Brand broadening (*leveraging*) occurs when the firm undertakes a *brand extension* — attaching an existing brand to a different product form/class to address a new opportunity. For several approaches to brand broadening — Table 11.5.[46]

Brand Extension	Examples
A. Common benefit or attribute	Deodorizing: Lysol for the air, toilet bowl, tile Mildness: Ivory in soap and shampoo

continues

TABLE 11.5
Approaches to Brand Broadening (Leveraging)

---

* SABMiller
** P&G's billion-dollar brands

TABLE 11.5
continued

Brand Extension	Examples
B. Companion product	Coffee: Starbucks coffee mugs
	Pancake mix: Aunt Jemima pancake syrup
C. Customer franchise	Harley-Davidson: restaurants, armchairs
	Coca-Cola: clothing, fishing lures
D. Designer/ethnic image	Ralph Lauren: clothing, sunglasses
	Ferrari: automobile, watches
E. Distinctive component/ingredient	Baking soda: Arm & Hammer cat litter
	Cream cheese: Philadelphia cream cheese salad dressing
F. Expertise	Electronics: Sony Walkman and Discman
	Low-cost manufacturing: Bic disposable razors, pens
G. Same raw material, different product form	Cranberries: Ocean Spray cranberries to cranberry juice cocktail
	Pineapples: Dole pineapples to pineapple sauce

MARKETING QUESTION

Using well-known brands, suggest some brand extensions. Why do you think they would succeed? Suggest brand extensions you think would not succeed. Why?

MARKETING QUESTION

In 1984, Bulgari sold Bulgari brand luxury products in five Bulgari stores. By the early 2000s, Bulgari had 180 stores; 600 outlets also sold Bulgari watches; 14,000 outlets sold Bulgari perfumes. Bulgari formed Bulgari Hotels and Resorts in a joint venture with Marriott. Do you think Bulgari hotels will succeed? Why or why not? Where did Bulgari open its first group of hotels? How do you assess these choices?

For approaches A, B, E, F, G, the brand owner generally retains control of the marketing effort. In C and D, the brand owner typically makes *brand licensing* agreements with third parties — the licensee has primary marketing responsibility, subject to the brand owner's guidelines.[47] A single brand may cross scores of product classes. Harley-Davidson has more than 100 licensing agreements include — armchairs, restaurants, and toys; Coke — baby clothes, beach towels, boxer shorts, earrings, fishing lures; Radio City Music Hall (New York) — coloring books, costumes, DVDs, high-end dolls, holiday ornaments, jewelry, wallpaper.[48]

Brand broadening reduces launch costs and/or increases profits for small investments.[49] A new product with a leveraged brand gains automatic brand awareness.[50] Before leveraging, the firm must consider potential opportunities and obstacles, and several branding issues.

OPPORTUNITIES AND OBSTACLES. The firm must address the following sorts of questions:

- Is there sufficient demand for the new opportunity?
- Is the firm sufficiently strong to succeed in the face of competition?
- Can the firm access the new market through current distribution channels?
- Is the firm capable of satisfying potential demand?
- Does the firm have access to raw materials and other production inputs?
- Does the firm possess other competencies necessary for success?

BRANDING ISSUES. These concern brand associations held by customers, and their fit with the extension[51]:

- Do customers perceive a fit between the original product form/class and the new product form/class in terms of product features and concepts?
- What are customer brand image and associations for the core product? Will these associations *transfer* to the new product?
- What is the reverse relationship? How will customer associations for the new product *back transfer* to associations for the core product?
- How does the corporate and/or monolithic brand relate to these associations?

Once the firm has addressed opportunities, obstacles, and several issues, the brand must meet two baseline conditions for a viable extension:

- The brand must have strong positive associations.
- Brand associations and the product extension should not be incongruous. How do you rate the likely success for *Apple* candies? *Mercedes-Benz* orange juice? *Microsoft* floor cleaner? *Calvin Klein* mutual funds? *Victoria's Secret* soup?

Brand extensions tend to fail when:

- associations between the brand and the extension are not obvious;
- the brand has a unique image and associations that do not transfer;
- the new product form/class has a dominant competitor;
- positioning is confusing and/or inconsistent;
- extension quality does not match customer expectations for the brand.[52]

Brand dilution is a potentially serious issue: The brand extension fails, FBE reduces, and overall sales fall. Trouble![53]

HOW BRAND BROADENING (LEVERAGING) FITS IN. Brand leveraging is one option in a family of strategies relating brands and product forms/classes — Figure 11.9. The other options are:

- **Line extension** — new but similar product to the product line, using the same brand name. Jell-O comes in various colors and flavors, all under the Jell-O brand; J&J offers Tylenol in several sizes, shapes, and physical forms — capsules, caplets, liquid, tablets; *Sports Illustrated* added *Sports Illustrated for Kids.*[54]
- **Flanker brand** — new yet similar product, but develops a new brand, or a distinguishing subbrand.
- **New product** — new product form/class and develops a new brand.

KEY IDEA

Firms that leverage brands secure automatic brand awareness for the new product. These firms avoid new brand introduction costs and may increase profits for little additional investment.

KEY IDEA

For an extension to be viable, the brand must have strong positive associations. The difference between these brand associations and the product extension should not be incongruous.

FIGURE 11.9
Branding Choices

Product Form/Class

	Existing	New
Existing	Line Extension	Brand Broadening (Leveraging)
New	Flanker Brand	New Product

(Brand)

BRAND MIGRATION

Firms sometimes retire individual brands. Perhaps the target market/market segment has contracted; competition may be severe, and/or brand vision may no longer fit with evolving customer needs. Sometimes brand support is expensive, and/or a brand may have lost value because of managerial neglect, a lost internal battle for resources, and/or harvesting for profits and cash.[55] Other times, the firm may decide to refocus efforts on fewer, stronger brands and/or seek economies of scale in marketing. Federated Department Stores retired Abraham & Strauss, L.S. Ayers, Bon Marché, Bullocks, Burdines, Famous-Barr, Filene's, Foley's, Goldsmith's, Hecht's, Jordan Marsh, Kaufmann's, Lazarus, I. Magnin, Marshall Field's, Meier & Frank, Rich's, Robinsons-May, Stern's, Strawbridge's, and The Jones Store in favor of Macy's.

KEY IDEA

Brand migration transfers equity in one brand to another brand.

FIGHTER (AKA FIGHTING) BRANDS

Firms often introduce *fighter* brands (lower-price *flanker* brands) when existing brands face strong price competition. The fighter brand's job is to *protect* the core brand and secure sales and profits from customers who would otherwise purchase from competitors. Celeron successfully protected Intel's Pentium brand against AMD's K6; P&G's Luvs protected Pampers from private-label diapers. Many fighter brands fail, like Ted — United Airlines, Song — Delta Airlines, Saturn — GM. Some pharmaceutical firms introduce fighter drug brands — branded generics — when patent protection ends. When introducing a fighter brand, the firm must set clear customer and competitor targets, minimize premium-brand cannibalization, keep management focused on the core business, and be profitable.[56]

Sometimes the firm secures brands via acquisition and then retires them. Citigroup retired Schroder Salomon Smith Barney; Morgan Stanley retired Dean Witter. Also, the firm may be contractually obligated to stop using the brand: B&D acquired GE's small appliance (housewares) business but could use the GE brand for only five years. In such cases, the challenge is to retain the brand equity by transfer to another brand — *brand migration*. Most approaches have two main stages:

- Associate the retiring brand with the surviving brand;
- Drop the retired brand.

KEY IDEA

The firm conserves brand equity by effective brand migration.

Vodafone previously comprised many strong domestic brands. Vodafone migrated these brands to *Vodafone* (Vo - voice, da - data, fone - phone). Said Vodafone's global-branding director, "Vodafone uses a dual branding strategy designed to give all constituents — employees, customers, trade partners — a period of time so people can intellectually *get it*. In Germany we did *D2/Vodafone*, then *Vodafone/D2*, and then we just dropped the *D2* to become *Vodafone*. In various markets, we've done it in one month, nine months, and 15 months. It all depends on the local market situation."[57]

STRATEGIC ALLIANCES

KEY IDEA

The firm can enhance brand equity with effective strategic alliances.

Strategic alliances can extend firm brands into new market segments. Alliances can range from informal or contractual working relationships to new entities structured as legal joint ventures. Most alliances focus on competency — one firm's strengths compensate for the other firm's weaknesses. Strategic alliances have important *co-branding* implications when partners can transfer positive customer attitudes. Co-branding between customers and suppliers is increasingly common. Two major steel companies — OneSteel and Corus — successfully co-branded with customers,[58] and many PC manufacturers co-brand with Intel. Ruth Owades, founder of Calyx and Corolla (C&C) (direct marketer — fresh flowers), believed the FedEx brand was essential to establish C&C's credibility for service excellence. She asserted she would not have founded C&C without the alliance. But co-branding is no panacea; if the firm does not manage the process well, customers become confused and brand equity suffers.

When firms co-brand with themselves, they must ensure that brand associations are appropriate for the product and target market segment(s). In Asia, Holiday Inn closely associates its parent brand with Crowne Plaza hotels — *endorsed brand*. By contrast, in the U.S., Crowne Plaza is a *standalone brand*; Holiday Inn associations negatively affect the Crowne Plaza brand image.

AGING AND DEFUNCT BRANDS

MARKETING QUESTION

Founded during the California Gold Rush, Levi Strauss' denim (de Nîmes) jeans became an American icon. In 1996, Levi's sales were $7.1 billion, mostly in midmarket outlets like JCPenney and Sears. Annual sales are now less than $5 billion; most manufacturing is offshore. What advice would you give Levi Strauss' top management?

Some aging brands — Table 11.2 (p. 292) — have loyal customers and survive for many years. But these are exceptions. The marketing landscape is littered with the corpses of once-valuable and famous brands. As markets evolve, brands may develop negative reputations and/or be weakly positioned. They are economically unviable, despite enjoying high brand awareness. Rebranding may be an option, like GMAC's name change to Ally Financial; Chapter 10 identifies a second option for improving sales in mature markets — *repositioning the brand*.

Brand reintroduction and/or *revitalization* is the key objective for repositioning. Key options are:

- **Target new market segment(s).** Colgate-Palmolive, Avon, and *Reader's Digest* each increased sales by targeting new geographic segments outside the U.S. To its surprise, Sears found that core U.S. customers were *not* male hardware buyers, but 25-to-50-year-old women with children. Sears successfully repositioned by refocusing promotion and expanding clothing and cosmetics products. When P&G acquired Old Spice (OS), OS was mainly known for aftershave and cologne, and a graying customer base — OS deodorant was tenth in market share. P&G focused on first-time deodorant users, aged 18 to 34. OS is now the top-selling deodorant and antiperspirant among male teenagers — Chapter 8.

Sales of Memorex (audio cassettes), TDK (stereo products), and Imation (floppy discs) fell substantially but each brand now targets new market segments with new products.

- **Change brand associations.** Successful examples are Honda's classic motorcycling repositioning from *long-haired guys and the police officers chasing them* to a family activity — *you meet the nicest people on a Honda* — Chapter 10. Britain's Labour government changed the country's associations from backward-looking and tradition-based to future-oriented youthfulness, excitement, and opportunity. Lean Cuisine is attempting a shift from *weight loss* to *healthy food*. Some firms develop nostalgic (retro) associations for the *good old days* — Ovaltine powdered drink mix, Burma-Shave shaving cream, and British motor racing at Goodwood.
  - **Alter the competitive target.** Bacardi successfully repositioned its light rum to compete against vodka and scotch whisky, rather than other rums.

The firm can avoid the necessity for revitalization by continually innovating, adding new products, and keeping the brand vital and relevant.[59] Intel continually introduces new products for its corporate brand — *Intel*, and for subbrands — *Celeron, Pentium, Core*.

Sometimes firms rediscover brands they dropped years earlier or inherited in acquisitions. If such a brand has high awareness and nostalgic appeal, straightforward reintroduction may be an option — Eagle Snacks, Metrecal, Silkience.

Florida's Himmel Group acquires defunct brands, then reintroduces them. Successes include Ovaltine; Topol — tooth polish; Lavoris — mouthwash.

KEY IDEA

Three ways to reposition a brand are:
- Target new market segment(s)
- Change brand associations
- Alter the competitive target

Continuous innovation preempts the need to revitalize a brand.

MARKETING QUESTION

CNN (Time Warner subsidiary) total daily ratings dropped 30 percent; prime-time ratings dropped 35 percent. How should CNN revive its brand image?

MARKETING QUESTION

What other messages did you glean from this chapter?

KEY MESSAGES

- The nature of brands has changed from signifiers of goods and services to symbols for constructing relationships between the firm and customers.
- Positive relationships between brands and customers can significantly enhance shareholder value.
- The firm can brand individual products, product lines, and/or product groups.
- The firm should choose a brand vision and supporting associations.
- Brand image represents the associations customers hold about the brand. The firm should strive to achieve alignment between brand image and brand vision.
- Some important items about brands and branding are:
  - branding is important in both B2C and B2B;
  - branding is much more than advertising;
  - customers are only one of several targets for brand messages;
  - for product brands, we cannot assume that the brand owner is also the manufacturer.
- Customer brand equity (CBE) and firm brand equity (FBE) are two distinct constructs.
- To build a strong brand, the firm must execute a process to establish brand vision; create brand awareness; form brand associations and brand image; develop consistent brand quality and value perceptions; build brand loyalty and, possibly, broaden (leverage) brand strength to new products/services.
- To sustain a strong brand, the firm should regularly measure brand health and act on the results.
- To secure the best results from branding efforts, the firm should make serious decisions about various facets of brand architecture.

VIDEOS AND AUDIOS

For complimentary material, see Axcess Capon codes at www.axcessvids.com

Branding	**241v**	Schmitt	Columbia Business School
Brand Management	**630v**	Barton Warner	Bayer HealthCare
Branding in Action	**882v**	Dr. Bez	Aston Martin
Building Brands	**447v**	Sasha Strauss	
Branding Stories	**146v**	David Aaker (skip 7 mins.)	University of California, Berkeley
Marketing Imperative 3 – Branding	**226a**	Noel Capon	Columbia Business School

QUESTIONS FOR STUDY AND DISCUSSION

Can you answer the questions implied by this chapter's learning outcomes? Check!

1. Bring to class an example of a B2C brand advertising campaign. Using the positioning statement format — Chapter 9, identify what you believe is the advertisers' desired positioning. How well does the advertising reflect this positioning?

2. Bring to class an example of a B2B branding campaign. Think hard about who is the target of the advertising.

3. Your text quotes a leading advertising executive as saying: "A successful brand is timeless." Do you agree? Should the statement be modified in the context of young consumers valuing change, innovation, and unique choice? Support your answer with current examples.

4. Select a well-known brand and track its brand history. How have brand vision and brand image evolved? Did the brand owner attempt to change brand vision to keep the brand contemporary? Or was the brand owner trying to broaden market scope?

5. Identify a firm that provided you with a good customer experience. Call the central number and ask for the CEO by name to offer your congratulations on performance. Keep a written record of the interactions. What impact does this experience have on your feelings about the corporate brand? If you reach the CEO — highly unlikely — pass on your reactions on how you were treated.

6. The American Red Cross comprises many local chapters that develop local market strategies and communications. As marketing director for the national organization, how would you go about developing a consistent brand vision and brand image for the American Red Cross overall?

7. Contact a firm you know and determine if it measures brand health. Ask about the metrics the firm uses and be prepared to report them in class. If there is no system, ask how the firm ensures that striving for short-term performance does not damage long-run brand health.

8. Identify an example of poor brand architecture; be prepared to explain your assessment. The example could include multibranding versus umbrella branding, unwise brand extensions or attempts at broadening (leveraging), brand migration, strategic alliances, and aging brands.

9. Select a product in which you are interested. Alternatively, consider *Managing Marketing in the 21st Century*. Using the concepts and ideas in this chapter, recommend an approach to branding.

TRUE/FALSE QUESTIONS

Answers on page A2 and at www.axcessvids.com — 889p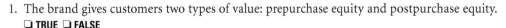

1. The brand gives customers two types of value: prepurchase equity and postpurchase equity.
   ❏ **TRUE** ❏ **FALSE**

2. In the dollarmetric method of monetizing brand equity, the firm asks customers how much extra they would pay for the branded product versus an unbranded product. This extra amount is the CBE monetary value. ❏ **TRUE** ❏ **FALSE**

3. Firm brand equity equals market value times book value and nonbrand intangibles like patents, know-how, and human resources. ❏ **TRUE** ❏ **FALSE**

4. In multibranding, a firm emphasizes a monolithic brand for several products.
   ❏ **TRUE** ❏ **FALSE**

5. Brand leveraging occurs when the firm undertakes a brand extension. The firm uses an existing brand to address a new opportunity, typically in a different product form/class.
   ❏ **TRUE** ❏ **FALSE**

MULTIPLE CHOICE QUESTIONS

Answers on page A2 and at www.axcessvids.com — 269p

1. All of the following are characteristics of effective brand associations EXCEPT:
   a. strong
   b. favorable
   c. unique
   d. common

2. Which of the following is NOT a form in which the brand/production relationship may take?
   a. totally integrated production operations
   b. subcomponent assembly
   c. no production responsibility
   d. All selections represent viable forms the relationship may take.

3. _____ reduces customer search costs and purchase risks because of what customers believe before purchase.
   a. Prepurchase equity
   b. Postpurchase equity
   c. Cross-sectional purchase equity
   d. Virtual equity

4. Which of the following brand typologies best describes a commodity brand like store-brand canned goods?
   a. low consumer brand equity, low firm brand equity
   b. low consumer brand equity, high firm brand equity
   c. high consumer brand equity, low firm brand equity
   d. high consumer brand equity, high firm brand equity

5. Which of the following measures is NOT part of a balanced scorecard?
   a. purchasing and sales data
   b. perceptual data
   c. profitability
   d. depreciation data

SECTION IV

IMPLEMENTING THE MARKET STRATEGY

For complimentary material, see Axcess Capon codes at www.axcessvids.com

IMPLEMENTING THE MARKET STRATEGY comprises 13 chapters, Chapter 12 through Chapter 24.**[912v]** The section embraces the second three Marketing Imperatives: Imperative 4 — Design the Market Offer; Imperative 5 — Secure Support from Other Functions; and Imperative 6 — Monitor and Control.

The largest group of chapters — Chapters 12 through 22 — address Imperative 4. We organize the material on designing the market offer into four parts.

Part A, *Providing Customer Value*, comprises three chapters. Chapter 12 — Managing the Product Line — considers firm products as elements in a product portfolio, each with specific roles, together with several product-related issues. Chapter 13 — Managing Services and Customer Service — focuses on product/service differences and highlights the importance of customer service. Chapter 14 — Developing New Products — introduces the stage/gate process for developing new products.

Part B, *Communicating Customer Value*, comprises four chapters. Chapter 15 — Integrated Marketing Communications — frames an integrated communications strategy. Chapter 16 — Mass Communications — focuses on advertising and other nonpersonal communications approaches; Chapter 17 addresses the fast-growing field of digital marketing. Chapter 18 — Directing and Managing the Field Sales Effort — discusses six core tasks for developing and implementing the sales strategy.

Part C, *Delivering Customer Value*, comprises two chapters. Chapter 19 — Distribution Decisions — focuses on how firm products reach consumers/end users. Chapter 20 — Retailing and Wholesaling — delves more deeply into especially important channel intermediaries.

Part D, *Getting Paid for Customer Value*, also comprises two chapters: Chapter 21 — Critical Underpinnings of Pricing Decisions — and Chapter 22 — Setting Prices.

Imperatives 5 and 6 each merit a single chapter. Chapter 23 — Ensuring the Firm Implements the Market Offer as Planned — addresses Imperative 5 and focuses on building an externally oriented firm. Chapter 24 — Monitoring and Controlling Firm Functioning and Performance — considers Imperative 6 and shows how to maintain the firm's planned trajectory.

Managing Marketing in the 21st Century

SECTION I: MARKETING AND THE FIRM

CHAPTER 1
Introduction to Managing Marketing

CHAPTER 2
The Value of Customers

SECTION II: FUNDAMENTAL INSIGHTS FOR STRATEGIC MARKETING

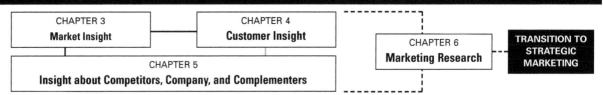

CHAPTER 3
Market Insight

CHAPTER 4
Customer Insight

CHAPTER 5
Insight about Competitors, Company, and Complementers

CHAPTER 6
Marketing Research

TRANSITION TO STRATEGIC MARKETING

SECTION III: STRATEGIC MARKETING

IMPERATIVE 1
Determine and Recommend Which Markets to Address

CHAPTER 7
Identifying and Choosing Opportunities

IMPERATIVE 2
Identify and Target Market Segments

CHAPTER 8
Market Segmentation and Targeting

IMPERATIVE 3
Set Strategic Direction and Positioning

CHAPTER 9
Market Strategy – Integrating Firm Efforts for Marketing Success

CHAPTER 10
Managing through the Life Cycle

CHAPTER 11
Managing Brands

SECTION IV: IMPLEMENTING THE MARKET STRATEGY

IMPERATIVE 4
Design the Market Offer

PART A: PROVIDING CUSTOMER VALUE

CHAPTER 12
Managing the Product Line

CHAPTER 13
Managing Services and Customer Service

CHAPTER 14
Developing New Products

PART B: COMMUNICATING CUSTOMER VALUE

CHAPTER 15
Integrated Marketing Communications

CHAPTER 16
Mass Communications

CHAPTER 17
Digital Marketing

CHAPTER 18
Directing and Managing the Field Sales Effort

PART C: DELIVERING CUSTOMER VALUE

CHAPTER 19
Distribution Decisions

CHAPTER 20
Retailing and Wholesaling

PART D: GETTING PAID FOR CUSTOMER VALUE

CHAPTER 21
Critical Underpinnings of Pricing Decisions

CHAPTER 22
Setting Prices

IMPERATIVE 5
Secure Support from Other Functions

CHAPTER 23
Ensuring the Firm Implements the Market Offer as Planned: Becoming an Externally Oriented Firm

IMPERATIVE 6
Monitor and Control Execution and Performance

CHAPTER 24
Monitoring and Controlling Firm Performance and Functioning

SECTION V: SPECIAL MARKETING TOPICS

CHAPTER 25
International, Regional, and Global Marketing

CHAPTER 26
Ethical, Legal, and Socially Responsible Decisions in Marketing

IMPERATIVE 4

Design the Market Offer

....

PART A – PROVIDING CUSTOMER VALUE

CHAPTER 12

MANAGING THE PRODUCT LINE

For complimentary material, see Axcess Capon codes at www.axcessvids.com

LEARNING OUTCOMES

When you have completed this chapter, you will be able to:

- Understand the importance of managing the product line as a portfolio.
- Apply alternative approaches to managing product portfolios.
- Manage key interrelationships among products.
- Address pressures for product proliferation and product line simplification.
- Manage both diverse and complementary product lines.
- Deal with important product issues like bundling, counterfeiting, evolving the product line, extending product life, product quality, and secondary market products.
- Anticipate concerns about product safety, packaging, and disposal of products and packaging.

OPENING CASE: SWIFFER

P&G's Swiffer Sweeper (SS) was not just a new product; Swiffer was first in a new product class — products for cleaning surfaces. The Swiffer product line now comprises several different cleaning products for various surfaces. The Swiffer design includes both hardware and disposables. Hardware is a pole and attachment that grips the disposable, typically a dry or wet cloth. Choice of disposable depends on the surface being cleaned; regardless, the consumer discards the cloth after cleaning. P&G provides refills in various scents: SS dry cloths — 16-count refills, in unscented, Original Lavender Vanilla & Comfort, or Sweet Citrus & Zest; wet cloths — 12-count refills, in Open Window Fresh, Lavender Vanilla & Comfort, or Sweet Citrus & Zest. Some products are available as starter kits.

Swiffer comprises the following products:

- **Swiffer Sweeper.** *Cleans hard-surface floors. Dry cloths compete with brooms and dustpans; wet cloths compete with mops and pails of water.*

- **Swiffer Sweeper + Vac.** *Combines SS dry cloth with a vacuum cleaner. The dry cloth picks up fine debris; the vacuum picks up larger objects.*
- **Swiffer Dusters.** *Reach into nooks and crannies. One version — lockable pivoting head and telescoping handle — extends up to three feet.*
- **Swiffer Dust & Shine** *furniture polish. Sold in Original, Citrus & Light, Hawaiian Aloha, and Lavendar Vanilla & Comfort scents.*
- **Swiffer Sweeper X-Large.** *Similar to SS but with a larger head; cloths are about one and a half times the size of two regular SS cloths.*
- **Swiffer WetJet.** *Replaces mops for difficult-to-clean floors. Premixed cleaning solutions are available in various scents.*

Most Swiffer products have differently designed hardware and disposables, but P&G has a consistent business model. Hardware has a low price and generates little profit; P&G makes its money on refills. The premium-priced Swiffer line is part of P&G's Fabric and Home Care sector.

P&G has 23 billion-dollar brands. Swiffer is one of 14 brands with revenues between $500 million and $1 billion with the potential to become a billion-dollar brand.

How do you assess P&G's development of the Swiffer product line? What are the critical elements in Swiffer's success?

Chapter 12 is the first of three chapters in Part A of Imperative 4 — *Design the Market Offer.* Part A focuses on *Providing Customer Value.* Chapter 12 addresses *Managing the Product Line.*

Products/services are central to the marketing mix. Since decisions about products/services cross functional lines, they have a broader impact on firm operations than other marketing-mix variables like promotion, distribution, customer service, and pricing. Firms also face difficult issues allocating limited resources across product portfolios. Optimal product line breadth is a critical issue; product proliferation and product line simplification can each have dramatic effects on shareholder value. Introducing new products — Chapter 14 — is critical. Bundling, counterfeiting, evolving the product line, extending product life, packaging, product quality, and secondary market products are important related issues. Product safety can embroil the firm in legal and ethical problems; increased societal expectations regarding health (fast food, sugary soft drinks, obesity), and environmental concerns (pesticides, packaging, product disposal), highlight the importance of product decisions.

THE CHANGING VIEW

OLD WAY	NEW WAY
Caveat emptor (buyer beware)	*Caveat venditor* (seller beware)
Ethical considerations relatively rare	Ethical considerations recognized as vital
Focus on profits	Focus on shareholder value
Judgments made exclusively with financial criteria	Judgments based on market and financial criteria
Product managers on pedestals	Product managers subject to executive control
Product profitability data are rare	Product profitability data are becoming ubiquitous
Product proliferation is common, rationalization rare	Product line breadth is carefully managed, rationalization is common
Products and brands often treated similarly	Products and brands carefully discriminated
Products viewed independently	Products managed as a portfolio
Quality variable	Focus on total quality management (TQM)
Reluctance to cannibalize products	Cannibalization an element in product line renewal
Uniform business objectives by product	Business objectives tailored by product and segment
Waste products and packaging ignored	Environmental concerns important

THE PRODUCT PORTFOLIO CONCEPT

GE's business-unit portfolio includes Appliances, Aviation, Healthcare, Industrial Systems, Lighting, and Transportation. The product portfolio for GE's Appliances (GEA) business unit includes air conditioners, dehumidifiers and air purifiers, dishwashers, disposers and compactors, microwave ovens, ranges, refrigerators and freezers, wall ovens, washers and dryers, and water systems. GEA must allocate resources among these products and decide which, if any, to add and/or drop.

KEY IDEA

Firm products have important resource-related interrelationships.

The firm does not optimize its overall profits by maximizing profits from individual products. The firm must consider the entire product portfolio.

Firms with *imbalanced* portfolios are vulnerable to acquisition.

The firm's *product portfolio* is a collection of products.[1] Large firms offer thousands of products/ product lines, often grouped by business unit (GE example). Corporate leaders allocate resources among business units. Business-unit heads make resource allocations among products/product lines based on their assessments of potential growth and profitability. (In this section, we use the term *product* to embrace individual products and product lines.)

The firm does *not* optimize overall profits by maximizing short-run profits from each individual product. Rather, the firm should use a *portfolio* approach to product management, balancing objectives and resource allocations across all products. Hence, new products typically require investment in R&D, plant and equipment, and promotional activities; these products consume cash. Frequently, the firm believes securing market position is more important than earning profits, at least in the short run when the market is growing. By contrast, when growth slows and investment requirements diminish, established products become cash generators. The firm uses this cash to develop and support new and younger products. The cycle continues.

The firm optimizes shareholder value when the *product portfolio* is *balanced*; *imbalanced* portfolios put shareholder interests at risk. Imbalances occur when the firm funds too many new products and creates shortages of cash and other resources. Imbalances also occur when the firm has too many old products; good short-term financial results may mask a failure to invest sufficiently in the future. Securing the *right* balance of successful new products and profitable established products is important for enhancing shareholder value. Firms with seriously imbalanced product portfolios may become acquisition candidate for firms seeking either growth or cash flow.

The key to successful product strategy is setting objectives and allocating resources based on each product's role in the portfolio. The firm should manage some products to achieve growth objectives, and other products to maximize profits or cash flow. The core challenge is to allocate the *right* financial and human resources such that each product achieves its objectives. Of course, within the firm, the various products compete for scarce resources.[2]

This chapter shows portfolio analysis methods used by many firms to make these difficult resource allocation decisions. But first we describe traditional financial analysis methods, then discuss their advantages and disadvantages.

FINANCIAL ANALYSIS METHODS

Superior financial performance is critical for delivering increased shareholder value. Hence, a *financial analysis perspective* for assessing forecast financial return from products is both important and proper.[3] Approaches include[4]:

- **Return on investment (ROI).** ROI calculations project future accounting data. They compare the product's forecast rate of return with a target — *hurdle rate*. If the forecast rate exceeds the target rate and resources are available, the firm invests.[5]

- **Payback.** Payback is the forecast time to pay back the investment. In general, shorter paybacks are better than longer paybacks. Payback's problem is ignoring profits earned after the payback period.

Neither *ROI* nor *payback* distinguishes among time periods. Each method treats financial flows similarly regardless of when they occur. Because of this defect, most firms use approaches that account for the time value of money:

- **Net present value (NPV)** and **internal rate of return (IRR).** NPV and IRR are the most common financial analysis methods for assessing investment opportunities. Discount factors account for the time value of money. Both methods use actual cash flows rather than financial and cost accounting data. They assess cash inflows (like sales revenues) when earned and cash outflows (like costs and investments) when paid out.
  - *NPV* uses a predetermined discount factor, typically the firm's cost of capital. The firm calculates NPV for various opportunities, then ranks by monetary value.
  - For *IRR*, the firm calculates the discount rate that equalizes cash inflows and cash outflows. IRR typically ranks opportunities whose IRR exceeds the hurdle rate.

More recently, firms use *economic profit* or *economic value added (EVA)*. EVA equals annual profit less an explicit charge for capital.[6] To summarize:

MARKETING QUESTION

How would you convince a skeptical finance vice president that she should enhance her investment assessments by using portfolio analysis?

KEY IDEA

Financial analysis methods rely on forecasts — can be highly uncertain.

Financial analysis does not consider strategic issues; ignores marketing considerations.

Too much reliance on financial analysis can lead to misallocation of resources across products and markets.

FINANCIAL ANALYSIS APPROACHES

1. *Forecast Return on Investment* (%) (ROI) — (Sales Revenues less Costs)/Investment = Profits/Investment (based on forecast accounting data).
2. *Payback* (years, months) — time to pay back initial investment.
3. *Net Present Value* (NPV) — dollar value of an opportunity. Discounts all cash outflows and inflows by a predetermined factor, typically the firm's cost of capital.
4. *Internal Rate of Return* (IRR) — discount rate that equalizes cash inflows and cash outflows.
5. *Economic Profit* — the opportunity's annual profit less an explicit charge for capital.

ADVANTAGES OF FINANCIAL ANALYSIS (FA). Pluses for FA are:

- **Clarity.** Decisions flow clearly from FA. So long as opportunities exceed a target number, the firm makes selections in attractiveness order.
- **Conceptual simplicity.** Calculations may be complex, but each approach is conceptually simple. The inputs — costs, investments, revenues — are generally readily available.
- **Comparable results.** Each approach ultimately produces a single figure — the firm can easily compare several opportunities to each other, and to a standard.

DISADVANTAGES OF FINANCIAL ANALYSIS. Problems with FA are:

- **Internal political dynamics.** FA can lead to organizational game-playing. Figure 12.1 shows how opportunity-champions may *hockey-stick* sales revenue forecasts up, and cost and investment forecasts down — marginal opportunities become spectacular performers! Of course, hardnosed financial managers make *realistic adjustments* — forecast sales revenues down, forecast cost and investment estimates up! Because managers can change projected financial performance with *the stroke of a pen*, choosing opportunities often reflects political power, rather than intrinsic value.

....
FIGURE 12.1
Hockey-Stick Adjustments to Sales Revenue, Costs, and Investment Forecasts

Suppose products in your business unit span the range from introduction to decline. Corporate has sent a finance VP to assess your business unit and to *help you*! What would you be most concerned about?

- **Potential misallocation of investment funds.** FA leads some firms to allocate investment funds based on historic profitability. These firms invest in mature, low-growth products but starve potential high-growth products — current profits are low (or negative) and uncertainty is high. Also, some firms use larger discount factors for new products — forecasting errors are typically greater. Insufficient investment in new products helps competitors, especially when environmental change requires major shifts in products and markets.[7]
- **Silence on strategic issues.** FA ranks opportunities by forecast financial performance but generally does not consider strategic imperatives. Suppose projected IRR for two opportunities are 22 percent and 18 percent; the hurdle rate is 12 percent, so both opportunities are viable. Using IRR, 22 percent is always more attractive than 18 percent. But suppose the 18 percent opportunity is central to firm strategy and the 22 percent option is peripheral. Strategically, the 18 percent opportunity makes more sense, but IRR concludes differently. Also, FA does not consider marketing issues like brand building.

Suppose you were GE's marketing manager for refrigerators. How would you address assumptions underlying your financial analysis — target market share, technological change, future competitive structure, competitor strategies, and the role of government?

- **Uncertainty in the estimates.** FA relies on estimates of sales units, prices, costs, and investments. Estimating short-term investment requirements for even well-defined opportunities is difficult; predicting sales units and prices several years in the future is daunting.

Today, many firms modify/augment financial analysis by examining the assumptions underlying financial projections, and requiring managers to think more deeply about them. Typically, precise answers are not possible, but the process leads to more externally oriented approaches — like portfolio analysis — for allocating resources. Critical questions include:

- What is the expected future market growth rate?
- What is target market share?

- What is the likely future market structure?
- In what ways is the market changing?
- Against which companies will the firm compete?
- How is technology expected to evolve?
- What will be the government's role?
- Are there legal/regulatory issues to consider?

PORTFOLIO ANALYSIS

Portfolio analysis (PA) is central to many firms' strategic planning processes. PA is best viewed as an *additional* tool for allocating resources, not as an *alternative* to FA. PA is a systematic, organized, and easily communicable way of assembling, assessing, and integrating important information about products and markets with the goal of constructing a *balanced* portfolio. PA helps the firm set strategic direction, establish investment priorities, and allocate resources. The firm can use portfolio analysis to evaluate both businesses and products.

PA has dramatically affected many firms' resource allocation processes; PA includes factors traditional financial analysis ignores. Table 12.1 illustrates several differences between FA and PA.[8] Using FA and PA together leads to better investment decisions than either approach alone.

KEY IDEA

Portfolio analysis is a systematic, organized, and easily communicated way of assembling, assessing, and integrating important information about product/market opportunities.

Variable	Financial Analysis	Portfolio Analysis
General approach	Financial- and budget-oriented	Market- and competitive-oriented
Investment decision focus	Technologies/facilities	Products/markets/customers/applications
Key concerns	Derived profit and cash flow numbers	Market and competitive factors underlying financial numbers
Tools	Capital budgeting	Growth-share and multifactor matrices
Typical measures	ROI, payback, NPV, IRR, EVA	Market — size, growth, competitive strength

TABLE 12.1
Financial and Portfolio Analysis — Investment Decisions and Strategic Directions

KEY IDEA

Portfolio analysis addresses many problems with financial analysis.

Two important PA methods are the *growth-share matrix* and the *multifactor matrix*.

GROWTH-SHARE MATRIX. The Boston Consulting Group (BCG) developed the original PA.**[522v]** As the name implies, core dimensions are growth and share: *forecast long-run market growth* and *relative market share.*[9] Figure 12.2 shows each dimension bisected to produce BCG's four-cell classification. Matrix entries represent products (or businesses). Typically, each circle's size is proportional to sales revenues or invested assets.

FIGURE 12.2
Illustrative Growth-Share Matrix

KEY IDEA

Key dimensions defining the growth-share matrix are:
- Long-run market growth
- Relative market share

The growth-share matrix can be overused and misinterpreted

Growth-Share Matrix Dimensions

Long-run market growth. Estimated future market growth over a three-to-five-year time horizon. Typically, forecasts are for sales units — meters, pounds, tons. If price competition is severe, using revenues may be appropriate. All things equal, high-growth opportunities are more attractive than low-growth opportunities.

Relative market share (RMS). Firm market share divided by market share of its largest competitor. RMS indicates the dominant player directly — RMS > 1. RMS focuses directly on firm competitive strength. Consider two situations, I and II. In each case, the market leader has 40 percent market share:

I. *Few competitors* — No. 2 firm has 30 percent market share: RMS = 40/30 = 1.33

II. *Many competitors* — No. 2 firm has 15 percent market share: RMS = 40/15 = 2.67

A focus on market share alone does not distinguish between situations I and II; in each case the leader has 40 percent market share! RMS shows the leader's position is much more favorable in II — RMS = 2.67, than in I — RMS = 1.33.[10] In general, firms with high RMS have lower costs, stronger positions in customers' minds, and other marketing advantages.

KEY IDEA

Portfolio analysis is best viewed as an additional tool for setting investment priorities — not as an alternative to financial analysis.

A practical question concerns placing the dividing line — cut-point — between high- and low-growth markets. Placement is arbitrary, but many firms find a choice rule helpful. An *external* benchmark like growth in *gross domestic product* (GDP) is far superior than an *internal* standard, like current firm growth rate. To explain: If annual firm growth rate were 1 percent, an aggressive internal cut-point might be 4 percent. Any opportunity with growth greater than 4 percent would appear attractive. But if annual GDP growth were 8 percent, a 4 percent standard would imply the firm is willing to shrink relatively. Based on 8 percent GDP growth, a better cut-point would be 10 percent, or even 12 percent. A good rule of thumb is forecast GDP growth plus a few additional percentage points based on firm goals. The RMS cut-point is typically 1.0; market-leading products to the left, all others to the right.

BCG's growth-share matrix places heavy emphasis on the financial characteristics by cell. High-share products are typically more profitable than low-share products. Growth products typically require significant investment in fixed assets, working capital, and market development. The boxed insert (p. 316) describes conventional labels and classic strategic recommendations for products in each cell.

The experience curve — Chapter 10 — and PIMS research — Chapter 9 — generally support characteristics in the boxed insert (p. 316). Table 12.2 shows the positive relationship between market share and profitability. ROI for products with less than 10 percent market share is 14 percent; by contrast, ROI for products with over 40 percent market share is 33 percent.

....
TABLE 12.2
Market Share and Profitability Relationships from the PIMS Study

Market Share	< 10%	10–20%	20–30%	30–40%	> 40%
ROI	14%	18%	23%	24%	33%

Table 12.3 shows a related analysis for a diversified *Fortune* 500 firm. Low-market-share products (MS < 10%) are 46.5 percent of all products; 27.5 percent of revenues; and 34.2 percent of assets; but they generate just 4 percent of profits. Conversely, high-market-share products (MS > 40%) are 21.1 percent of products; 17.6 percent of revenues; and 26.7 percent of assets; but they generate fully 56.7 percent of profits. Market share matters!

....
TABLE 12.3
Individual Firm Example: Distribution of Number of Products, Sales Revenues, Assets, and Profitability by Market Share

Market Share	< 10%	10–20%	20–30%	30%–40%	> 40%
Number of Products (%)*	46.5	14.8	10.6	7.0	21.1
Sales Revenues (%)**	27.5	15.8	7.9	31.2	17.6
Assets (%)	34.2	16.1	7.4	15.6	26.7
Profits (%)	4.0	8.1	9.1	22.3	56.5

*To be read as: 46.5% of products are in markets where the firm has < 10% market share.

**To be read as: 31.2% of sales revenues are in markets where the firm has 30% – 40% market share.

PRODUCT CHARACTERISTICS IN THE GROWTH-SHARE MATRIX[11]

Cash Cows. Low Market Growth/High Market Share (Cell A)
Classic characteristics are:
- Low costs. From experience curve effects — Chapter 10.
- Premium prices. As market leader, cash cows may command premium prices.
- Low reinvestment. Low-growth, mature products require relatively low investment.

Cash cows should be highly profitable; they are often the firm's primary internal cash source. Examples include Google AdWords, Microsoft Office, and P&G Tide detergent. If the firm successfully holds market share, it can *milk* a cash cow and generate cash for many years. Environmental changes like currency devaluations, innovative competitors, new technology, and/or regulatory shifts threaten cash cows by changing demand patterns. Then the firm may *harvest* the product to increase short-term cash flow — raise prices, reduce or eliminate services, cut promotional support.

Firms with cash cows are subject to two types of errors. First, they *overmilk* cash cows — cash flow *dries up*. Starved of investment, products trail in technology, and lose cost leadership and market position.[12] U.S. and European car and steel firms are good examples. Second, the firm overinvests, reducing financial return and leaving little cash for other opportunities.

Stars. High Market Growth, High Market Share (Cell B)
Stars are relatively rare; few products enjoy dominant positions in high-growth markets. Stars are often profitable in accounting terms, but use significant cash because their growth requires substantial investment.[13] Groupon and Twitter are good examples. Despite firm actions, market growth eventually slows. If the firm invests appropriately and retains good market share, profits and cash flow improve; the star transforms into a *cash cow*. The major error firms make with stars is to cut back investment too early. The star loses dominance and transforms into a *dog* — cell C.[14]

Dogs. Low Market Growth, Low Market Share (Cell C)
Dogs is a pejorative term for products with unfavorable characteristics:
- High costs relative to the leader; dogs do not enjoy the same economy-of-scale or experience curve advantages.
- Prices may be lower than the market leader.

Dogs are often unprofitable or earn only low profits; they are often the focus of top management attention. Better-positioned dogs generate positive cash flow but may still be a drag on firm resources. Dogs are the most numerous of all products in any economy. Examples include Lenovo personal computers and CBS and Fox in U.S. broadcast television.[15] Firms with dogs should consider:
- Developing new segmentation approaches that strengthen their positions.
- Refreshing products with additional value from new features.
- Maximizing short-run cash flows by liquidating or divesting. IBM sold its *barely profitable* PC business to Lenovo.
- Implement a *kennel* strategy — Chapter 10 — by acquiring similar products to achieve viable scale.

Problem Children (aka Lottery Tickets, Question Marks, Wildcats).
High Market Growth, Low Market Share (Cell D)
Problem children combine the uncertainties of high-growth markets with nondominant market shares. Examples include iRiver, RCA, and M-Pio MP3 players; each has less than 10 percent market share versus well over 50 percent for Apple's iPod. Problem children that grow with the market consume substantial investment capital. Such investment may be risky, as growth does not guarantee future profits. Growing with the market moves the problem child from cell D to cell C. Hence the key choice for problem children is often *double or quit*!
- *Double.* Large strategic investments can move the product to market leadership. Sony's Playstation successfully overtook Nintendo in video games with high spending in product development and promotion. By contrast, Philips' CD-Interactive (CDI), a user-friendly interactive CD system launched when CD-ROM was in its infancy, was quickly overtaken. A less risky approach seeks dominance in a defensible market segment(s).
- *Quit.* Exit, immediately or gradually. The product may command a good price from an aggressive follower. Small biotech firms often sell their new drugs to big pharma; major players often acquire hi-tech startups.

KEY IDEA

Product labels derived from the growth-share matrix are:
- Cash cows
- Stars
- Dogs
- Problem children

MARKETING QUESTION

Identify all Disney businesses — amusement parks, movies, retail stores, character licensing — and place them in a growth-share matrix. (You may have to guess a bit.) Which businesses are Cash cows? Dogs? Stars? Problem children? How do you think Disney should allocate resources? What additional factors should Disney consider in examining new wholly owned or alliance opportunities?

MARKETING QUESTION

Suppose 20 percent of all products are in *high-growth* markets and 80 percent are in *low-growth* markets. Suppose also that 10 percent of all products are market leaders. What percentage of products are Cash cows? Dogs? Stars? Problem children? What does your result imply for the challenges you will face as an executive?

The firm should consider the generalized recommendations from the boxed insert (page 316) carefully, because they are widely advocated and applied. Firms typically view high-growth markets as attractive. Yet, if many firms enter and build excess capacity, and prices drop sharply, all competitors may lose. The best way to view the growth-share matrix is as a device for raising and discussing *what-if* or contingency questions. Like any decision-making aid, the matrix has value only if its assumptions are valid. Issues include:

- **Long-run market growth** is the exclusive measure for market attractiveness. Problems may arise because the framework ignores other factors.

- **Relative market share** captures the firm's competitive strength. The firm can usually validate RMS in mature markets, but this is more difficult in growth markets.[16]

- **Market-share/profitability relationship.** Tables 12.2 and 12.3 show a strong relationship between market share and profitability. But this relationship may not be universal, in part because market boundaries may not be clear-cut.[17] Also, market definition affects measures of long-run market growth and RMS, and hence placing products in the matrix.

- **Downward-sloping experience curves** imply an inverse relationship between RMS and unit costs. The growth-share matrix assumes comparable cost curves across competitors, but small focused firms often have lower costs than relatively well-managed major players.

THE MULTIFACTOR MATRIX. The growth-share matrix spawned many other portfolio approaches — some public, some proprietary.[18] The most popular is the *multifactor matrix*, aka GE/McKinsey screen. The multifactor matrix redefines the growth-share axes: *Long-run market growth* becomes *market attractiveness*; *relative market share* becomes *business strengths*. The user identifies several factors to measure each dimension. (To see how to develop this matrix — Chapter 8, pp. 217–221 — where we use a similar approach to assess market segments.)

Figure 12.3 illustrates the multifactor matrix.[19] The most attractive cell — C — is empty, but the firm has some small entries in two other attractive cells — B and F; the firm should probably invest in these products. The large entries in cells A and E are questionable; the firm should examine them carefully. Finally, the firm should make the tough decision — retain or remove — about the poorly positioned large cell G product:

FIGURE 12.3
Illustrative
Multifactor Matrix

Siemens classifies products as green, amber, or red. Green — invest and grow; amber — consider; red — target for improvement. Classification is fluid. In the last recession, Siemens reclassified several amber products as red.

GROWTH-SHARE AND MULTIFACTOR MATRICES. Each method helps the firm make resource allocations, in part by visual display. Table 12.4 shows advantages and disadvantages of each approach.

The *growth-share matrix* has only two criteria — long-run market growth and RMS. Once managers agree on market definition, the firm can measure these criteria objectively. Reasonable people may disagree about forecast market growth, but RMS is relatively simple to measure. Hence, managers have limited ability to manipulate entries for their *favorite* products. But having just two criteria can also be a weakness; forecast long-run market growth and RMS may not capture all relevant issues. By contrast, the *multifactor matrix* addresses the realism issue by using several criteria, and so embraces many factors that the growth-share matrix omits. But reasonable managers may disagree about the criteria, and weightings and ratings are often highly subjective. Hence, political and organizational power issues can enter the analysis.

In sum, it is generally easier to evaluate and communicate about a firm's diverse products using the growth-share matrix than the multifactor matrix. Also, refinements to the growth-share matrix can analyze product trajectories and test results from various resource allocations. But the multifactor matrix can assess both current products *and* potential new products. The growth-share matrix is really useful only for current products; by definition, all new products have zero RMS and are points on the matrix's right side.[20] The multifactor matrix can address risk by choice of criteria — the growth-share matrix cannot. And because market definition is often difficult, the growth-share matrix does not deal well with fragmented markets; this issue is no problem for the multifactor matrix. Neither approach assesses the cost to change matrix positions, but the multifactor matrix does address business strengths directly.

Comparison Criteria	Growth-Share Matrix	Multifactor Matrix
Ability to manipulate entries	Difficult	Easy
Accommodates new businesses	Not well	Yes
Application across firm	Single set of criteria	Multiple sets of criteria
Appropriate for fragmented markets	No	Yes
Communicability	Easy	More difficult
Criteria	Limited but unambiguous	Unlimited but disputable
Explicit consideration of risk	No	Yes, if required
Grouping tendency of entries	Low market growth/low market share (bottom right)	High/high, high/medium, medium/high, medium/medium (top right)
Implementability	Easy	More difficult
Measures	Basically objective	Highly subjective
Realism	May be limited	May have more
Sensitivity to basic assumptions	Yes	Yes
Sensitivity to market definition	Yes	Yes
Underlying focus	Cash flow	ROI

Many firms use these matrices to examine their various products, communicate options, and even select managers skilled in specific strategic situations. But, we repeat: Each method is an aid for strategy development, not a substitute. Executives gain insight *in the process* of developing the matrices, particularly the criteria and weightings for the multifactor matrix. Some portfolio matrices link market performance and financial performance. Figure 12.4 (p. 319) shows the product portfolio for a healthcare business specializing in chemicals and laboratory equipment, and how it links business-unit position and pretax return on assets (ROA). Firms have also used equipment age, human resource spending, investment requirements, and advertising and promotion in portfolio models.[21]

KEY IDEA

The firm can use the multifactor matrix for resource allocation among products.

The growth-share and multifactor matrices have advantages and disadvantages that impact the viability of strategic recommendations they generate.

TABLE 12.4
Comparison of the Portfolio Approaches

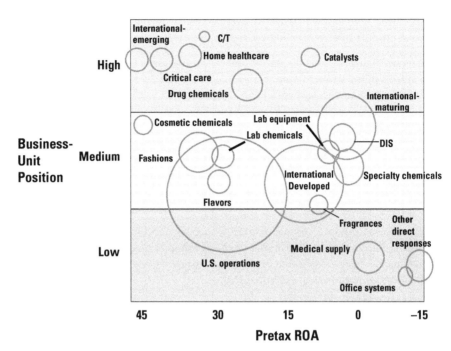

FIGURE 12.4
Portfolio Example

OTHER IMPORTANT PRODUCT INTERRELATIONSHIPS

KEY IDEA

Firm products may have important interrelationships both with *customers* and within the *firm*.

Products compete for resources; they may also be interrelated in other strategic ways.

INTERRELATIONSHIPS AT THE CUSTOMER

Some products are directly complementary — razors and razor blades, printers and toner, satellite dishes and program content, hardware and disposables (Swiffer Opening Case). When each product *needs* the other, the firm can be successful by placing either or both in its portfolio. When the firm offers both products, like HP Inc. printers and toner, pricing becomes particularly crucial. Product interrelationships at the customer may be positive, as in the Bloomberg example; they may also be negative.

> Bloomberg terminals support the investment community. A Bloomberg executive said: "We surround people with information. They watch TV [Bloomberg channel] when they're having breakfast. They drive into the city and listen to the [Bloomberg] radio station. Then they work on their Bloomberg terminals. Our products complement each other. We always have something for our customer."[22]

MARKETING QUESTION

Movie theaters offer popcorn and soft drinks as complements. How would you design a new movie house to enhance service and offer a broader variety of complementary products/services?

POSITIVE COMPLEMENTARITY. In many markets, customers who buy one type of product are more likely to buy a related product — *positive complementarity*.[23] The *Michelin Guide* encourages car travel; when travel increases, tire wear is greater and tire sales rise. Michelin believes that positive attributes associated with the *Michelin Guide* carry over to Michelin tires, and vice versa. Verizon knows that traditional local wire-based telephone service is declining (but not dead yet!), so it offers customers long-distance, DSL, and wireless services. Satisfied customers for Apple's iPod are favorably disposed to buy Macintosh computers; Lou Gerstner drove IBM's turnaround by integrating customer hardware, software, and services. Motion pictures and derivative products are positive complements; sales of accessory products, like Harry Potter toys and DVDs, often eclipse box office revenues. And at movie houses, popcorn and soft drinks are complementary with movies. Conversely, when Toys "R" Us formed Babies "R" Us, Toys "R" Us traffic dropped sharply as it no longer stocked products like pacifiers and bibs. Sometimes firms increase sales of one product directly by adding a complement:

> HMS Host, the largest U.S. airport bar and restaurant concessionaire, carried six bottled beers. To accept Heineken Lite, Host would have to drop another brand. Heineken worked with a signature chef to design a calamari dish to complement Heineken Lite, and developed a major promotion for Host locations. Host's margins on Heineken Lite plus the calamari dish were greater than margins on Michelob Lite: Michelob Lite was out and Heineken Lite was in.

KEY IDEA

Sometimes one product helps another — *positive complementarity.*

Sometimes one product hurts another — *negative complementarity.*

Sometimes a complementary product is closely related to an initial purchase. Positive complementarity occurs when customers trade up to higher-quality, higher-profit products. GM's historic strategy traded customers up from Chevrolet to Pontiac, Buick, Oldsmobile, and Cadillac. Similarly, many software customers buy successive product versions.

Parts are a special case of product complementarity. Durable products break down, suffer damage, and require replacement parts. Parts sales often bring higher revenues and greater profits than the original part.[24] But products that break down frequently and need many parts earn a poor reputation and may negatively affect initial sales.

NEGATIVE COMPLEMENTARITY. Customer dissatisfaction with one product may negatively affect sales of another. PepsiCo's expansion was a *negative complement* to its core business:

> PepsiCo acquired Pizza Hut, Taco Bell, and Kentucky Fried Chicken for growth and guaranteed sales of Pepsi products. Coca-Cola convinced McDonald's, Burger King, Wendy's, and other fast-food chains that selling Pepsi helped competitors (Pepsi subsidiaries) — these chains agreed to sell Coke products exclusively. PepsiCo spun off its restaurant businesses.

Before passage of the Sarbanes-Oxley Act, investment banks knew that critical equity research reports negatively affected their ability to sell investment banking services. Professional services and accounting firms knew that company audits exposing financial problems might cut off lucrative consulting contracts. Arthur Andersen failed to acknowledge and address Enron's irregular accounting because it feared such negative complementarity, with disastrous consequences. More generally, spreading attention over multiple products may leave the firm vulnerable to highly focused competitors. Further, negative complementarity at one customer may negatively affect relationships with other customers:

> Tradebank (disguised) offered leasing products for capital equipment. When customer York (disguised) had financial problems and missed a lease payment, Tradebank placed a lien on its assets. Several other Tradebank customers did business with York; the lien caused significant problems. Some severed relationships with Tradebank.

INTERRELATIONSHIPS AT THE FIRM

Sometimes firm products have important internal interrelationships with each other.

STRATEGIC ROLES. Different products may have separate yet mutually reinforcing strategic roles. The Swatch Group (TSG) markets watch brands in five price ranges:
- Prestige and Luxury range — Breguet, Blancpain, Glashütte Original, Jaquet Droz, Léon Hatot, Omega
- High range — Longines, Rado, Union Glashütte
- Middle range — Tissot, Calvin Klein, Balmain, Certina, Mido, Hamilton
- Basic range — Swatch, Flik Flak
- Private label — Endura

Each range targets a different market segment and has a different strategic role for TSG. TSG earns most profit from products in the top two ranges and less from the middle range. Basic range and private-label products are profitable, but act as *firewalls — fighter brands.* They drive down costs and stop competitors offering low-price watches, thus protecting TSG's middle-, high-, and prestige- and luxury-range products.[25] Similarly, many supermarkets offer private-label products to attract price-sensitive shoppers; Best Buy sells private-label electronic cases and accessories, flash drives, GPS, radios, televisions, and video cables.[26]

In many industries, leading U.S. firms made critical strategic errors in abandoning low-price segments to competitors. They retreated upmarket, unwilling to accept low profits from potential firewall products. Xerox and auto firms allowed Japanese companies to gain footholds in the U.S. Similarly, Nucor and others entered steelmaking with electric-arc minimills and dethroned once-powerful integrated steel firms. Once established, these competitors eventually added higher-profit products.[27]

MULTIPLE BUSINESS UNITS. Interrelationship issues occur with products from different business units when they address (or could address) the same market (segment). The firm has three options:

- **Develop separate missions.** Products from different business units have different missions — Chapter 7. The firm does not *squander* resources by having multiple business units address a single market opportunity.
- **Intrafirm collaboration.** The firm develops processes for separate business units to work together. At J&J, corporate account managers integrated products from several units to form a single offer for operating rooms: Ethicon — sutures and topical products to stop bleeding; Ethicon Endo Surgery — cutters, staplers, and electro-surgery devices; Codman — surgical instruments and shunts to relieve pressure on the brain; Dupuy — orthopedic implants. When business units do not work together, the firm may miss significant opportunities. Sony was late to follow Apple into digital music, in part because it could not resolve conflicts between its electronics and content divisions. Bertelsmann had a joint venture with AOL. Yet *Stern*, Bertelsmann's biggest magazine, placed a CD-ROM on its cover offering access to T-Online, Deutsche Telekom's Internet service and AOL's principal competitor!
- **Intrafirm competition.** This Darwinian approach allows products from different business units to pursue overlapping missions. As long as one business unit seizes the opportunity, the firm accepts efficiency losses in product development and promotion. Chapter 5 shows Citibank undertook parallel initiatives to develop electronic letters of credit for foreign trade. At one point, Citibank Asia Pacific was selling its system to U.S. customers; simultaneously, Citibank North America was developing its own system!

PRODUCT LINE BREADTH: PROLIFERATION VERSUS SIMPLIFICATION

Firms often face conflicting pressures for product line size: pressures for *broadening* and pressures for *narrowing.* The firm must trade off these pressures. Since return on investment (ROI) is the operating financial goal for most firms, decomposing ROI can provide insight:

ROI = Profit/Investment

By adding *sales* as both a numerator and divisor:

ROI = Profit/Sales × Sales/Investment
ROI = Return on Sales (ROS) × Investment Turnover

MARKETING QUESTION

Which of the following approaches best captures P&G's product line management philosophy?

- Separate mission
- Intrafirm competition
- Intrafirm collaboration

Answer the same question for Marriott. Describe possible conflicts for each firm.

KEY IDEA

When making product decisions, the firm should carefully consider current and potential interactions with its other products.

KEY IDEA

Firms face conflicting pressures for broad versus narrow product lines.

ROS and ROI measure very different things.

Competition often shrinks *ROS*, and only high-volume products generate sufficient *investment turnover* to meet ROI targets. Many firms avoid (or withdraw from) low-ROS products, believing volumes will be too low to compensate for slim profit margins. But firms can lower the costs of product variety by integrating information technology into product design, systems, and manufacturing. Investment turnover can also be critical:

Relating ROS and ROI

FMCG firm PGA (disguised) faced price pressure from supermarket customer SMC (disguised). SMC complained its profit margin — ROS — on PGA products was only 1 percent; SMC pressed PGA for price reductions. PGA confirmed that SMC's key performance measure was ROI and that most SMC investment was in inventory. PGA implemented a new logistics system that cut SMC's average inventory holding period from two weeks to one week. SMC data were:

Current — Profit Margin = ROS = 1%; Average Inventory Holding Period = 2 weeks
    — Investment turnover = 52 weeks/2 weeks = 26
    — ROI = Profit/Investment = ROS × investment turnover = 1% × 26 = **26%**

New   — Average Inventory Holding Period = 1 week
    — Investment turnover = 52 weeks/1 week = 52
    — ROI = Profit/Investment = ROS × investment turnover = 1% × 52 = **52%**

SMC was very pleased with these results!

PRODUCT PROLIFERATION

Variety in customer needs often drives *product proliferation* as firms add products to fill product line gaps. Time Inc. traditionally published male-oriented magazines, like *Time*, *Fortune*, *Money*, and *Sports Illustrated*. Time sought growth by targeting new audiences like children, minorities, teenagers, and women, and broadened its product line to include *Baby Talk*, *Entertainment Weekly*, *In Style*, *Martha Stewart Living*, *Parenting*, *People*, *People en Español*, *Sports Illustrated for Kids*, *Sunset*, and *Teen People*.

Sometimes firms tap different customer needs by offering products in different versions or variations. Common version differentiators are[28]:

- **Access and functionality.** Some firms offer differing versions of information/media products for different audiences based on user interface — simple for casual users, complex for serious users — and/or speed of operation — slow for casual users, fast for professional users. The firm may also vary access to features/functionality, like limiting types or time of use, or the ability to copy or download products/information.

- **Product performance.** Some firms, like plastics producers, make high-quality products for high prices and *degrade* those same products for price-sensitive customers — *versioning*. Production economics makes this approach more viable than manufacturing lower-value versions directly.[29] The IBM LaserPrinter Series E was identical to the standard LaserPrinter, but contained a chip that slowed printer speed from 10 to five pages per minute.[30] Mathematica offers software as a professional version and as a degraded student version.

- **Time availability.** Package delivery firms like FedEx and UPS offer next-day delivery before 10 A.M., after 10 A.M., and second-day delivery. Publishers initially offer hardcover books and sell paperback copies later. Hollywood launches movies in theaters, then releases them later on DVDs or for streaming. Airlines make multiple ticket offers for the same flight; prices differ based on booking time and available capacity.

Firms seeking market dominance in FMCG frequently offer multiple products to maximize display space. They also offer *firewall products* to defend profitable products and deter competitive entry. P&G maintains market leadership in laundry detergents by offering six brands,

MARKETING QUESTION

Visit the toiletries aisle at your local supermarket or drugstore. How many toothpaste skus can you identify? Do you think Colgate and/or Crest should reduce the number of product items?

KEY IDEA

Firms often differentiate individual products by:

- Access and functionality
- Product performance
- Time availability

Implementing a firewall strategy can lead to product proliferation.

embracing more than 50 versions and 100 skus — Table 12.5; Coca-Cola offers Coke in 7.5-, 16-, 20-ounce, and 2-liter sizes; many firms package individual products, like batteries, razors, and ballpoint pens in multiple-unit packs. Packs may contain a single product type or multiple types; regardless, the firm provides consumers with the perception of greater value.

Brand	**Powder**	**Liquid**
Tide	Tide Powder (4)	Tide Liquid (6) Tide Clean Breeze (scented) (2)
	Tide Clean Breeze (scented) (2)	
	Tide Mountain Spring (scented) (4)	Tide Mountain Spring (scented) (5)
	Tide Powder with Bleach (5)	Tide with Bleach Alternative (6)
	Tide Clean Breeze with Bleach (scented) (3)	Tide Clean Breeze with Bleach Alternative (scented) (4)
	Tide Mountain Spring with Bleach (scented) (1)	Tide Mountain Spring with Bleach Alternative (scented) (2)
	Tide Free (unscented) (1)	
	Tide High Efficiency (2)	Tide Free (unscented) (3)
	Tide Lavender (scented) (2)	Tide High Efficiency (3)
	Tide with Febreze (scented) (2)	Tide High Efficiency Clean Breeze (scented) (1)
	Tide with Dawn Stain-Scrubbers (1)	Tide High Efficiency Free (unscented) (2)
	Tide with a Touch of Downy (3)	Tide Loads of Hope (1)
	Tide Cold Water (1)	
Cheer	Cheer (5)	Cheer with Colorguard (5)
	Cheer for Darks (1)	Cheer for Darks (1)
	Cheer Free & Gentle (1)	Cheer Free & Gentle (3)
	Cheer Fresh Linen (scented) (1)	Cheer Fresh Linen (scented) (1)
Dreft	Dreft (1)	Dreft (6); Dreft High Efficiency (3)
Gain	Gain Original Fresh (2)	Gain Original Fresh (2)
	Gain (four scented versions) (6)	Gain (four scented versions) (6)
	Gain with baking soda (1)	Gain with baking soda (1)
Ivory Snow	Ivory Snow Powder (1)	Ivory Snow Liquid (1)
Era	NO PRODUCT ENTRY	Era Liquid (5); Era Crystal Springs (scented) (2)
		Era with Oxi Booster (3); Era Free (2)
		Era High Efficiency (2)

TABLE 12.5
Procter & Gamble's U.S. Offerings of Laundry Detergent (Number of Package Sizes)

When product proliferation is excessive, costs spiral out of control and the firm loses market position. Motorola lost global leadership in cell phones in part because of a large product line. Fifteen teams of 20 people each supported 128 separate phone types, often with little parts commonality. Purchasing, manufacturing, administrative, and marketing costs were very high.

Product proliferation looks different on the Internet. Shelf space constraints virtually disappear and inventory costs are much lower than for physical stores. Variable production costs are zero for digital products. Hence, sellers can offer very long product lines. Walmart.com offers 1.2 million skus versus 132,000 in a typical store; Amazon has 4 million book titles versus 100,000 for a typical Barnes & Noble bookstore; online music sites offer several million music tracks versus 55,000 for Walmart. Correspondingly, these firms earn significant revenues from the *long tail* of products not offered in regular stores.[31]

PRODUCT PROLIFERATION AND MARKET SEGMENTATION. The difference between product proliferation and market segmentation confuses many people. *Product proliferation* refers to product variety. *Market segmentation* explores differences in customer needs that may be satisfied with different products — Chapter 8. But the firm may not require a broad product line to target multiple segments. The firm may generate multiple *offers* from a single product by vary-

KEY IDEA

Product proliferation and *market segmentation* are quite different constructs. Product proliferation refers to product variety. Market segmentation explores differences in customer needs.

The firm may develop multiple offers based on a single product, each targeted at a different segment.

ing brand name, packaging, distribution, and price. Relatedly, the firm secures R&D, manufacturing, and service economies:

- Merck sells *finasteride* as Propecia for hair loss and as Proscar for enlarged prostate. GSK sells *bupropion hydrochloride* as Wellbutrin for depression and as Zyban for smoking cessation.
- Monsanto sells Roundup herbicide to hobby gardeners and commercial farmers. The active ingredient (glyphosate) is identical, but Monsanto uses different packaging, distribution, and promotion, and sets different prices for each segment.
- Ricoh developed its copier portfolio by purchasing Savin, Gestetner, Lanier, and other brands. Each brand targets market segments where it is strong: Savin — government and education; Gestetner — hospitals. But the products are identical.
- Some private-label FMCG brands are identical to manufacturer brands, often made on the same production lines.

Generally, product variations do not target different market segments; they just offer variety.[32] Customers for cereals, fasteners, jams and jellies, salad dressings, spices, and even water (flavors, vitamins) demand wide choice assortments. Sometimes firms provide variety through packaging, like Tylenol — caplet, cool caplet, EZ tab, geltab, liquid.

SIMPLIFYING THE PRODUCT LINE

The late Peter Drucker famously posed the question, "If you weren't already in your business, would you enter it today?" If the answer is no, the firm must answer a second question: "What are you going to do about it?" One answer is to slim down its brand and product portfolios.[33] Under pressure from Samsung, Sony decided its TV offerings were confusing and slimmed its product line by 40 percent. Unilever reduced brand portfolio to 400 global and regional brands (from 1,600) — approximately 90 percent of revenues — and exited the U.S. detergent market. Unilever then sold, reduced support for, and/or consolidated its remaining national and local brands into stronger brands. Firms typically streamline product lines due to pressure from increased competition. In B2C, distribution-channel consolidation and store brand growth are important factors.

Pressures for product line simplification also result from supply-chain initiatives. *Efficient consumer response*, developed by food manufacturers and distributors, drives out excess inventory by focusing on consumer demand-pull, rather than supplier-push. *Direct product profitability* uses direct costing to identify products' true net margins. These initiatives mean less shelf space for many brands and lead firms to streamline offerings.

Many global B2B firms rationalize product lines. Historically, these firms' foreign subsidiaries would develop tailored products to meet local needs for multinational customers. These customers now want standard products to execute global contracts. BetzDearborn (U.S.-based global manufacturer of chemicals for treating wastewater) standardized specifications and cut product lines by over 50 percent. Customers for information technology products want standard hardware and software so they can better control processes and data around the world. UPS has a central tracking system for global shipments requiring identical scanning and sorting processes. Many global customers ask IBM to send products to a central location, load and test software, then *shrink wrap* the configuration for shipment to any location, ready to work. Both EMI and Warner Music Group dropped large numbers of artists to refocus efforts on high potentials.

The firm may reap significant benefits from simplifying the product line, but should make product-deletion decisions carefully. Firms often use a single criterion for dropping products — *bottom-line* profits. This procedure is not always wise. When firms eliminate high-volume *loss-making* products, they often discover these products were carrying a large share of overhead.

MARKETING QUESTION

What was Unilever's marketing objective? How has Unilever performed since brand consolidation? Did Unilever's approach work? Why or why not? With hindsight, would you have taken similar actions had you been leading Unilever's marketing efforts?

KEY IDEA

A simplified product line can make the firm more competitive. But the firm should use appropriate criteria for deletion decisions.

KEY IDEA

Beware deleting products without considering all relevant issues.

The remaining products must assume this overhead; their costs increase and overall profits fall! Note the Gillette example and the product-deletion illustration (below), and Table 12.6:

Gillette's Brazilian subsidiary concluded that the personal-care product line was unprofitable, and divested. Gillette later realized that it still had to assume many fixed costs previously allocated to personal care. Furthermore, without those allocated costs, personal care had been quite profitable.

Illustration of a Poor Product-Deletion Decision

Delco (fictional) has two products — A and B. Table 12.6 rearranges Delco's traditional cost breakdown — cost of goods sold (COGS); selling, and general and administrative costs (SG&A) — into three categories:

- *Variable costs.* Vary directly with number of units sold — include raw materials, direct labor, and transportation costs associated with producing and selling individual products.

- *Direct fixed costs.* Do not vary directly with number of units sold, but are associated with individual products; include salaries for product managers, supervisors, and technicians.

- *Indirect fixed costs.* Not directly related to individual products; include corporate functions like R&D and legal. Delco allocates costs between products A and B, based on percentage of sales revenues.

TABLE 12.6
Illustration of a Poor Product Deletion Decision ($millions)

	1 Overall Firm	2 Product A	3 Product B	4 Firm less Product A
Sales Revenues	$35	$15	$20	$20
Variable Costs	$19.5	$ 8.5	$11	$11
Contribution Margin	$15.5	$ 6.5	$ 9	$ 9
Direct Fixed Costs	$ 8	$ 4.5	$ 3.5	$ 3.5
Indirect Fixed Costs	$ 7	$ 3	$ 4	$ 7
Profit	$ 0.5	($ 1)	$ 1.5	($ 1.5)

MARKETING QUESTION

Think about firms where you have worked or those you have read about. Can you identify examples of ill-advised product eliminations?

We make several observations:

- Delco's profit is $0.5 million (column 1): ROS is poor; $0.5 million/$35 million = 1.4 percent.
- Delco's $0.5 million profit derives from Product A — $1 million loss (column 2), and Product B — $1.5 million profit (column 3).
- Suppose Delco eliminates loss-making Product A. Delco's bottom line goes from $0.5 million profit (column 1), to $1.5 million loss (column 4).
- Previously, Product A carried $3 million of indirect fixed costs (column 2). With Product A eliminated, Product B must now absorb these costs.

Firms that simplify product lines should make product-deletion decisions using a well-developed set of elimination criteria. Table 12.7 lists candidate criteria.

TABLE 12.7
Evaluation Criteria for Product-Deletion Decisions[34]

• Availability of new product	• Product elimination effect (PEE) on capacity utilization
• Component interchangeability	• PEE on customers/distributors
• Contribution to profit center	• PEE on firm image
• Likely competitive reaction	• PEE on firm sales volume
• Market potential	• PEE on fixed capital
• Reallocation of executive and salesperson time	• PEE on full-line policy
	• PEE on other products (sales/profits)
• Reallocation of resources	• PEE on overhead recovery
• Substitute available	• PEE on working capital

Sometimes the firm can reverse a product elimination decision, as at Avon. "We have a partial issue when we replace products consumers are used to. Particularly for foundations and lipsticks, and where people have a favorite color. Sometimes we get a lot of noise from customers saying, 'I miss this certain product.' Then we will bring it back and say in the brochure, 'Back by popular demand.'"[35]

KEY IDEA

Sometimes the firm can successfully resurrect deleted products.

Other times firms reduce product lines by divesting, but this approach can lead to problems:

- **Competition.** Divestiture helps the firm refocus, but sale to a potential competitor may upset its plans.
- **Insufficient investment.** The firm starves the product of marketing support and earns good short-run profits. But investment to rebuild the brand may be too high for potential acquirers.

OTHER PRODUCT LINE ISSUES

Now we examine several other issues for managing the product line:

BUNDLING

The firm can sell products as single *unbundled* items; but it may also combine products or products/services as *bundled* offers. Typical types of *bundled offers* include:

- Alternative products/services.
- Complementary products.
- Product plus after-sales service.
- Product plus parts or consumables.

Sometimes firms bundle attractive products with less-attractive products to increase overall sales and profits. Viacom bundles popular channels like MTV and Nickelodeon with lesser-known channels like Tr3s and Palladia; performing arts organizations often sell series subscriptions combining popular and less-popular events. B2B firms often bundle products with service support. In *mixed bundling*, the firm sells products both unbundled and bundled. Rooms to Go designs and packages complete rooms, but also sells individual furniture items. Microsoft bundles Word, Excel, Outlook, and PowerPoint into Microsoft Office, but also sells these products individually.[36]

Bundling and unbundling decisions are difficult. If the firm shifts from bundling to unbundling, customers may reject less-attractive items. But continued bundling risks losing sales to more focused competitors. Major airlines emphasize round-trips — bundled; but often lose sales to discounters offering low-price one-way fares — unbundled. Weak competition is more conducive to bundling than strong competition, but the firm should develop contingency plans for unbundling.

Bundling to Unbundling — Changing Wall Street

Traditionally, Wall Street firms bundled research and trading. Customers paid an *all-included* price based on trading volume. Giant mutual fund Fidelity, a major customer for brokerage firms, told suppliers it was unbundling purchases — Fidelity would pay for trading and research separately.

COUNTERFEITING

Prototype theft, illegal product copying, and brand piracy are increasingly prevalent globally.[37] Intellectual property loss via prototype theft is a serious matter for R&D-intensive firms. Counterfeiters and pirates offer a broad range of products including automobiles, ballpoint pens, cigarettes, car parts, deodorant, fashion items, medicines, mobile phones, movies, printer

KEY IDEA

The firm should be vigilant about organizations counterfeiting its products.

ink cartridges, recorded music, soap, shoe polish, software, pharmaceuticals, and toothbrushes. U.S. Customs and Border Protection seizes and destroys about one million electrical items displaying fake safety labels like Underwriters Laboratories annually. In Shanghai, Starbucks competes with *Xing Ba Ke* — *Shanghai Starbucks* — upscale coffee shops with waiters and higher prices![38] Also in China, Hyatt hotels must deal with Hajyatt hotels. In the U.S., consumers can buy equipment for pirating satellite TV signals.

Customer desires for branded products and increasing sales on eBay and other websites fuel *counterfeiting*. British police arrested counterfeiters shipping inexpensive table wine disguised as expensive Rioja Spanish wine. Hard-to-copy features like holograms, special inks, watermarks, and invisible features help authenticate products. Spanish winemakers now attach metallic refractive labels to their bottles, guaranteeing Spanish provenance. The best protection is continual vigilance regarding copyright, design patents, and trademarks. The firm should keep tight control over suppliers and distributors, and work with local law enforcement. Regardless, problems multiply when counterfeiters operate internationally.[39]

In rare cases, counterfeiting and piracy may provide firm benefits like market awareness and trial. Brazil banned Monsanto's genetically modified soybean seeds, so local farmers secured pirated seeds from Argentina. When Brazilian restrictions ended, Monsanto entered a well-developed market. For many years, most copies of Microsoft products sold in China were counterfeit; Microsoft *market share* was high but revenues were low. Microsoft revenues and *real* market share improved when China's antipiracy enforcement strengthened and Microsoft cut prices by more than 90 percent, invested in local R&D, and worked with the Chinese government on software security. **[460v]**[40]

....
EVOLVING THE PRODUCT LINE

The firm should address several key issues in evolving the product line:

EXTEND PRODUCT LIFE. Firms often try to extend product life. We illustrate with typical practice by pharmaceutical firms when patents expire. Firms in other industries apply variations of these approaches:

- Add additional services to support customers.
- Combine the drug with another drug for a complementary effect.
- Develop new dosage formulations.
- Devise a different method of drug delivery — like patch versus pill.
- Secure FDA approval for other *indications* — additional disease states.
- Persuade more physicians to prescribe the product and educate pharmacists.
- Switch the drug from prescription to over-the-counter.

IMPROVE THE PRODUCT MIX. Firms can increase profits by introducing higher-margin products, possibly by replacing lower-margin products. Gillette pursued this strategy for many years with successively more expensive razor systems. Nissan and Toyota entered the U.S. market with low-price cars and then moved upmarket, eventually introducing the Infiniti and Lexus, respectively. Monsanto introduced genetically modified soybean seed — Roundup Ready 2 — offering higher crop yields than highly popular Roundup Ready 1.

LIMITATIONS ON PRODUCT AVAILABILITY. Some firms deliberately underproduce so as to create customer value via scarcity. This practice is common in sneakers — Adidas, Converse, Diesel, Nike, and Vans each offer limited editions; Harley Davidson and others offer limited-edition eyeglass frames. Limited editions can also help generate interest in a brand. In Japan, PepsiCo significantly increased market share, in part by offering limited quantities of soft drinks like Ice Cucumber soda; similarly, Nestlé produces special KitKat flavors like Cantaloupe Melon and Koshian Maccha (green tea with red-bean filling).

PRODUCT CANNIBALIZATION. To preempt (or stave off) competitive threats and/or address new market segments, firms often introduce relatively low-profit products. These products may *cannibalize* sales of higher-margin products. FedEx complemented air package delivery by purchasing several ground package firms to form FedEx Ground. FedEx risked cannibalizing air package delivery, but believed FedEx Ground would compete strongly with UPS and USPS. When contemplating cannibalization, the firm should consider three important issues:

- **Balancing effects.** New product entry may cannibalize existing product sales and cause an immediate profit reduction. But the firm should enjoy incremental value from improved market share and brand presence.

- **Fear of lower profits.** When the firm introduces a new lower-price (lower-profit) product, customers may switch from the original higher-price (higher-profit) product to the new entry, reducing overall profits. Fear of this scenario frequently generates internal pressures against new entry and immobilizes the firm. Before J&J introduced Tylenol, Bayer Aspirin was so central to Sterling Drug that it refused to introduce its leading European non-aspirin pain reliever — Panadol — in the U.S. This cannibalization fear ultimately led to Sterling Drug's acquisition by Kodak.[41]

- **How to decide.** Many firms make product entry decisions by comparing their most recent results with forecast results after introducing the new product. This practice is incorrect. The firm should always compare forecast profits *with* the new product versus forecast profits *without* the new product. In many markets, some customers want low-price products. If they cannot buy from the firm, they will buy from competitors. The firm is generally better off accepting limited cannibalization and selling lower-profit products, than losing sales to competitors. Intel's Pentium chips faced growing price competition from AMD — Intel introduced lower-price Celeron as a *fighter* brand to stem market-share loss.

KEY IDEA

Product managers should address several issues related to evolving the product line:

- Extend product life
- Improve the product mix
- Limitations on product availability
- Product cannibalization
- Product replacement
- Product shrinking

Failure to Cannibalize in the U.S. Automobile Industry

Datsun (Nissan), Toyota, Volkswagen, and other foreign firms entered the U.S. with small cars. Because of low profit margins on small cars, U.S. firms did not respond aggressively. Essentially, U.S. firms ceded the small-car market segment, frequently entry-level buyers, to foreign entrants.

In the 1980s, lobbying by U.S. carmakers forced Japanese automakers to accept *voluntary* import quotas. Japanese firms behaved logically; they introduced higher-value, higher-price models, with greater profit margins. They also started producing cars in the U.S.!

If U.S. firms had successfully addressed the small-car segment, foreign entrants would have been less successful, and expansion would have been more difficult. Today, GM, Ford, and Chrysler would likely have higher market shares and better financial results.

Ivan Seidenberg, Verizon CEO, transformed and grew Nynex/Verizon from $13 billion (1995) to $127 billion (2014). Said Blair Levin, former FCC Chief of Staff, "One of Ivan's greatest strengths is he is not afraid to cannibalize his own business."[42]

PRODUCT REPLACEMENT. When the firm secures differential advantage with a better product, competitors often imitate and reduce price. The best approach is to replace the older product with an innovative successor. Ideally, the firm introduces a higher-value replacement shortly before competitive launch. Successful preemption weakens competitor resolve to attack the incumbent. Good competitive intelligence and appropriate timing is critical for managing the replacement cycle.

With patent expiry approaching, AstraZeneca (AZ) protected $6 billion revenues from stomach-drug Prilosec. AZ launched Prilosec derivative Nexium containing a separately patented compound. Eli Lilly protected revenues from antidepressant Prozac by introducing newly patent-protected Prozac derivatives — once-a-week and premenstrual disorder versions.[43]

PRODUCT SHRINKING. Faced with margin pressure from tough price competition and rising raw material costs, many firms shrink product offerings. Products like Snickers and Tropicana have taken *weight out* (about 10 percent); toilet tissue producers like Kimberly-Clark and P&G have similarly *desheeted*.

PRODUCT QUALITY

It goes without saying: Product quality is very important to customers and is necessary for any serious competitor. In recent years, quality has improved in many industries. Table 12.8 shows PIMS results demonstrating that higher quality is closely related to higher profitability. *BusinessWeek* showed that the share price of Baldridge winners (U.S. quality award) consistently outperformed the S&P 500 index by 3:1.[44]

TABLE 12.8
Relationship between Quality and Profitability Demonstrated by PIMS[45]

Market-Perceived Quality Ratio	less than 0.76	0.76 to 0.92	0.92 to 1.08	1.08 to 1.24	more than 1.24
Return on Sales (%)	4%	7.2%	8.3%	10.3%	12.5%

Leading firms work hard to produce high-quality products. They avoid problems from poor design by working simultaneously on new products and manufacturing processes. Poor design can lead to customer dissatisfaction and ultimately product withdrawal — *The New York Times* reported that expensive U-shaped bicycle locks could be picked in a few seconds with a simple ballpoint pen. Maintaining high quality is an ongoing challenge for even the best companies. Mercedes, historically a symbol for quality cars, had to postpone delivery of 30,000 cars for faulty diesel pumps; Mercedes also recalled 1.3 million cars for braking problems.

MARKETING QUESTION

What does the video **[231v]** say about the importance of product quality?

Sometimes even well-designed products are poorly made. Until relatively recently, received wisdom believed product quality and unit costs were positively correlated — high quality, high costs. The quality movement demonstrated a negative correlation. Poor quality embracing waste, rework, servicing and repairs, and loss of customers lead to higher costs. Figure 12.5 outlines four key steps in total quality management.

FIGURE 12.5
Total Quality Chart[46]

Unfortunately, some firms falsify product quality. Meat Hope (Japan) mixed ground pork and chicken with ground beef — sold as 100 percent ground beef. Other food-product mislabeling involves sell-by dates.[47] Product quality declines may lead to product safety issues:

Product Quality at Toyota

Toyota Motors emphasizes product quality, revolutionized manufacturing, and grew consistently to become the world's largest automobile firm. In 2010, a major scandal arose over reports that Toyota cars sometimes accelerated unintentionally, causing more than 30 fatalities. The U.S. National Highway Transportation Safety Administration (NHTSA) opened eight separate investigations. Toyota recalled millions of its eight most popular automobiles including Camry, Lexus, and Prius globally. Toyota even received complaints from owners of *repaired* vehicles.

Toyota was severely criticized for responding slowly to NHTSA information requests, issuing false statements, being late with apologies, misdiagnosing the problem as relating solely to floor mats (accelerator pedals [and possibly the electronic control system] were also involved), and issuing conflicting statements. Some observers believed Toyota's ambitious growth goals and pressure on suppliers to reduce costs and weight for each generation of parts by 10 percent ($10 billion over six years) led to quality declines. Ultimately, the U.S. government fined Toyota $1.2 billion. [976v]

Product Quality at Otis Elevator

Otis had 16,700 elevator installations in the region affected by Japan's 2011 earthquake/tsunami. Most elevators were equipped with seismic detectors — returned elevators to the ground floor so passengers could exit — and stayed switched off until checked. Despite the enormous devastation, no elevator passengers were injured or trapped.

MARKETING QUESTION

As Toyota's U.S. CEO, what action would you take? As marketing VP for Ford or GM, what action would you take?

PRODUCT SAFETY

In many jurisdictions, regulatory bodies like the FDA and CPSC (U.S.) enforce laws protecting consumers from product hazards. (Safety at Virgin America **[304v]**) Regardless, producers have a special responsibility to ensure their products do not harm customers. Unfortunately, some firms do not behave properly. Chinese firms added toxic melamine (protein powder) to animal feed so as to mimic protein in laboratory tests. Several children died, thousands were hospitalized, and tens of thousands sickened from ingesting tainted milk/milk products. China executed two producers and jailed 15 others. In the U.S. and other countries, *whistle-blowers* increasingly highlight safety concerns. Related examples are:

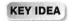

KEY IDEA

Product quality and product safety have critical marketing implications.

- American Airlines continued to fly a Boeing 767 aircraft after finding a mouse infestation.
- Bayer's Cutter Biological (CB) unit sold blood-clotting medicine with high risk of transmitting AIDS to Asia and Latin America. Simultaneously, CB sold a new, safer product in western countries. GSK paid $750 million to settle U.S. criminal and civil charges for knowingly selling contaminated and ineffective medical products.
- Guidant allegedly sold heart defibrillators it knew might short-circuit and cause death.
- Hallmark/Westland Meat slaughtered sick cows: Tainted beef entered the human food chain; the USDA recalled 143 million lbs.
- Maclaren USA recalled one million strollers after a side hinge amputated fingertips from 12 children.
- Mattel withdrew one million China-made lead-painted toys; Mattel also recalled 10 million Power Wheels ride-on cars and trucks for electrical problems and children's burn injuries.
- McNeil Consumer Healthcare (J&J subsidiary) suffered eight recalls — including 136 million bottles of Benadryl, Motrin, and St. Joseph's children's Tylenol — produced at its Fort Washington, Pa., factory. Management had replaced experienced quality control officers with lower-cost inexperienced employees, and reduced performance standards to enhance production efficiency.
- Merck withdrew top-selling arthritis drug Vioxx because of heart attack and stroke risks. Merck allegedly knew about Vioxx's safety problems, but bullied outside researchers and taught salespeople to *dodge* tricky questions from physicians.

- Mister Donut shops sold 13 million dumplings containing a banned additive.
- Peanut Corporation supplied peanut butter that caused salmonella poisoning in hundreds of people; many peanut brands suffered recalls.
- Snow Brand — Japan — recycled milk and poisoned 15,000 people.
- Universal Studios (US) — U.S. and Japan — falsified labels and served beef, caviar, and salami nine months after the sell-by date. US also supplied untreated wastewater to a drinking fountain.

Poor product and/or service design can harm or kill customers. Many motorists died when Ford Explorer SUVs fitted with Firestone tires overturned. Takata recalled 34 million airbags due to unpredictable explosions that cause death and serious injury. Barriers collapse at sporting events, and in many subways passengers can fall or be pushed onto the tracks. How firms respond to product safety issues affects customer perceptions and buying behavior — and product survival. GM and J&J behaved very differently in situations involving death. Restoring faith, trust, and credibility in a damaged brand can take years, if at all:

GM. In *Unsafe at Any Speed*, Ralph Nader alleged GM's first rear-engine car — Corvair — was unsafe.[48] Nader alleged several people died when their Corvairs went out of control. GM denied the problem and hired private detectives to investigate Nader's private life. Nader won a defamation suit against GM — GM withdrew the Corvair. [958v] More recently, GM was severely criticized for failing to address known ignition-switch issues that caused several deaths.

J&J. Several people died when Tylenol capsules were laced with cyanide. J&J withdrew Tylenol capsules throughout the U.S. Reintroduced several months later, with triple packaging, Tylenol quickly regained market leadership. [537v, 501v]

MARKETING QUESTION

How do you assess Nike's role in the secondary market for sneakers? [466v]

SECONDARY MARKET PRODUCTS

Owners of durable products like automobiles often resell in the *secondary market*. For customers purchasing new cars, forecast resale price is often an important product attribute. In the U.S., Toyota gains because resale prices are typically relatively high. Toyota and other automobile firms enhance resale prices by certifying previously owned vehicles. Most financial markets are secondary markets; share price is important for raising capital and measuring shareholder value. Secondary markets in sports tickets — *scalping* — were traditionally illegal, but Internet ticket exchanges like StubHub have driven the shift to legality.

PACKAGING

Packaging is important for guaranteeing product integrity in storage and distribution. But packaging can also communicate information, represent a significant brand statement (like the hourglass Coke bottle), and/or provide convenience benefits. Chobani grew the Greek yogurt product form in part by using innovative packaging — a shorter, fatter cup, quite different from tall, thin traditional yogurt cups; relatedly, Yoplait is successful with Go-Gurt in-a-tube yogurt for on-the-go kids. Riverwood's 12-can Fridgepack improved soft drink sales by increasing consumers' cold-can inventories. In India, Hindustan Lever achieved success by selling many products in single-use packages for cash-strapped customers, especially in rural areas. J&J invests in a special design unit that devises new packaging (and displays) for products launched many years previously.

DISPOSAL: PRODUCTS AND PACKAGING

Most packaging is worthless when the product reaches the end customer. Traditionally, customers were responsible for disposing of packaging and used products — these issues did not concern producers. But governments, particularly in Europe, have passed environmentally friendly laws focused on disposal. In Germany, federal authorities can restrict or ban materials with problematic toxicity or waste volume. Municipalities charge volume-based garbage fees; using large trash bins carries a social stigma in some communities.[49] A California law mandates safe disposal of toxic materials in PC monitors and circuit boards.

To address disposal issues, cost concerns, and the potential impact on brand image, many firms promote recycling. Mainetti (garment hangers), Van Leer (oil drums), and others recycle products. Because their products contain expensive (and often dangerous) components, electronics firms like Dell, HP Inc., and Sony manage recycling programs as profit centers. Some firms make new products with parts from discarded products. Good examples include auto parts, car batteries, computers, and toner cartridges. *Remanufacturing* is a $50 billion industry — firms can achieve 40 to 65 percent cost savings and also please customers. Some firms build remanufacturing into product-development processes. Packaging and product disposal are not pressing issues for all firms, but they should be aware of growing environmental concerns and potential government action.

MARKETING QUESTION

KEY MESSAGES

Managing the firm's product line is a major challenge. The firm must make decisions in four areas:

What other messages did you glean from this chapter?

- *Product portfolio.*
  - The firm should construct a *balanced* portfolio where some products generate growth and market share, some products earn profits, and some deliver cash flow.
  - The firm's key challenge is allocating resources across the portfolio. Financial analysis methods have advantages and disadvantages. The firm should supplement financial analysis with portfolio analysis, using the growth-share and/or multifactor matrices.
- *Other product interrelationships.* Firm products may be interrelated at the customer — the firm should seek positive complementarity and avoid negative complementarity. Products may also be interrelated at the firm, playing different strategic roles.
- *Product line breadth: proliferation versus simplification.* The firm faces conflicting pressures for *product proliferation* and *product simplification.* Variety in customer needs drives proliferation; many firms offer similar versions of the same product. The reader should not confuse product proliferation with market segmentation. Industry consolidation often drives product simplification, but the firm should make product-deletion decisions carefully, using well-thought-through criteria.
- *Other product line issues.* The firm should address many other product-management issues, including bundling; counterfeiting; evolving the product line; product quality; product safety; secondary market products; packaging; and disposal of products and packaging.

VIDEOS AND AUDIOS

For complimentary material, see Axcess Capon codes at www.axcessvids.com

Luxury Goods   **927v** 🔊   Ketty Maisonrouge Columbia Business School
Best-in-Class Product Management   **485v** 🔊   Steven Haines

QUESTIONS FOR STUDY AND DISCUSSION

Can you answer the questions implied by this chapter's learning outcomes? Check!

1. Table 12.9 shows market research data for PortCo (fictional). Develop a growth-share matrix. How do you assess PortCo's product portfolio? What do you recommend?

Product	Long-run (5-year) Market Growth Rate (%)	PortCo Market Share (%)	Leading Competitor Market Share (%)*	PortCo Sales Revenues ($ millions)
A	5%	15%	30%	$100
B	7%	30%	12%	$150
C	15%	40%	15%	$ 20
D	1%	50%	10%	$200
E	15%	10%	40%	$ 30
F	20%	20%	20%	$ 40

If the firm has leading market share, this is the competitor with second-highest market share.

2. The World Health Organization (WHO) estimates 5.4 million people annually die prematurely of tobacco-related causes like lung cancer, mainly in low- and middle-income countries. Suppose you were offered product manager jobs, with opportunities for extensive overseas travel, at leading cigarette manufacturers Altria and R.J. Reynolds. Starting salaries are 20 percent higher than other offers. Which, if either, will you accept? Why or why not? What challenges would you face if you did accept?

3. Review cereal product lines at your local supermarket. How do you assess General Mills, Kellogg's, and Quaker? What are their strategies? What recommendations can you offer them?

4. The president of Sony Electronics Sales put the problem this way: "If we're selling a $200 DVD player, we may want to give away Sony DVD software. But that's not in the best interest of Sony Pictures. And Sony Music may want to sell a Springsteen box set for $80 with a coupon that says, 'Get $20 off your Sony CD Player.' Why would Sony Electronics want to do that?" How would you advise the president of Sony Electronics? How would you advise the president of Sony Corporation?[50]

5. Some service providers bundle services — products and service packages. Others unbundle services — restaurants with a la carte menus. Prepare guidelines for a service provider making bundling/unbundling decisions.

6. Your electronic components firm contemplates offering a new high-quality device — *Super Great* — to its current product, *Super*. Market research and internal cost data reveal:
   - *Super.* Average price — $25; variable cost — $15; fixed costs — $850,000; expected next-year sales — 250,000.
   - *Super Great.* Fixed costs — $1.6 million; variable cost — $20; *Super* fixed costs reduce to $750,000 due to resource sharing. Expected sales at two price points:
     - Price — $30: sales — 200,000. Sources: 30% from new customers; 30% from competitors; 40% from Super customers.
     - Price — $35: sales — 150,000. Sources: 20% from Super customers; 80% from elsewhere.

   Should you introduce Super Great? If so, at what price?

7. AT&T, Sprint, and Verizon offer many usage plans to address target segment needs. How would you determine the *right* number of plans? What are the marketing challenges of offering many plans?

8. Select a product line in which you are interested. Alternatively, consider Wessex Press. How do the various individual products relate to each other?

TRUE/FALSE QUESTIONS

Answers on page A2 and at www.axcessvids.com — 679p 🔊

1. The firm's product portfolio is a collection of products. ❏ **TRUE** ❏ **FALSE**

2. The growth-share matrix has only two criteria: market growth rate and firm growth rate.
❏ **TRUE** ❏ **FALSE**

3. It is generally easier to evaluate and communicate about a firm's diverse products using the multifactor matrix than the growth-share matrix. ❏ **TRUE** ❏ **FALSE**

4. Positive complementarity takes place when customers who buy one type of product are more likely to buy related firm products. ❏ **TRUE** ❏ **FALSE**

5. Product proliferation refers to product variety; market segmentation explores differences in customer needs and developing strategies for market segments. ❏ **TRUE** ❏ **FALSE**

MULTIPLE CHOICE QUESTIONS

Answers on page A2 and at www.axcessvids.com — 419p 🔊

1. Which of the following financial analysis approaches focuses on the opportunity's annual profit less an explicit charge for capital?
   a. payback
   b. net present value
   c. internal rate of return
   d. economic profit

2. Advantages of using financial analysis for product management include all of the following EXCEPT:
   a. having a single figure
   b. comparable markets
   c. conceptual simplicity
   d. clarity

3. Which of the following Boston Consulting Group Matrix labels apply to products that have high market growth and high market share?
   a. cash cow
   b. star
   c. dog
   d. problem children, question mark, lottery ticket, wildcat

4. All of the following are options for effectively managing multiple business units EXCEPT:
   a. developing separate missions
   b. intrafirm competition
   c. intrafirm collaboration
   d. competitor strategic alliance

5. Which of the following is NOT one of the common differentiators for a firm offering a product in different versions or different variations?
   a. time availability
   b. product performance
   c. limitations on access and functionality
   d. market penetration pricing

Design the Market Offer

PART A – PROVIDING CUSTOMER VALUE

CHAPTER 13

MANAGING SERVICES AND CUSTOMER SERVICE

For complimentary material, see Axcess Capon codes at www.axcessvids.com

LEARNING OUTCOMES

When you have completed this chapter, you will be able to:

- Distinguish among products, services, and customer service.
- Understand why services are becoming increasingly important to firms and customers.
- Identify critical dimensions across which products differ from services.
- Discriminate among different types of services.
- Diagnose quality-related problems and opportunities in service delivery.
- Specify key dimensions of customer service.
- Appreciate the strategic role of customer service.

OPENING CASE: CELEBRITY CRUISES

Celebrity Cruises (11 ships) is a subsidiary of Royal Caribbean Cruises Ltd., positioned upscale of Holland America and Carnival Cruise lines. At 91,000 tons, Celebrity Constellation *is a member of the Millennium class with a 940-person crew and capacity for 2,450 passengers. Serving mostly U.S. guests,* Celebrity Constellation *and sister ships cruise Alaska, Bermuda, the Caribbean, Canada/New England, the Mexican Riviera, Hawaii, Transcanal (Panama), Northern Europe, the Mediterranean, and South America.* Celebrity Constellation *typically spends November to April in the Caribbean, summers in Europe, and late spring and early fall in Canada and New England. Celebrity fleet itineraries minimize downtime — each ship has a two- to three-week complete dry dock overhaul every five years.*

Key officers are Chief Engineer, Staff Captain, and Hotel Director. The Hotel Director is responsible for the entire guest experience, from embarkation to disembarkation. He described how Celebrity optimizes every guest's experience: "Celebrity has made sure that the ship's design and craftsman-ship are first rate — from guest staterooms to all public areas like Celebrity Theater, San Marco restaurant, and pools. We maintain that excellence by systematic maintenance on each of our 12 floors. For example, we shampoo carpets every two weeks. If there is a stateroom issue, we can do a complete overhaul when the ship is not completely full. Constellation *spends little time in port, so maintenance in public areas can be challenging, but we keep them at 100 percent with minimal or no guest inconvenience.*

"*We make an important distinction between port-intensive and non-port-intensive cruises. Generally, port-intensive cruises take seven to ten days — we travel at night, and most guests spend a lot of time off the ship. The routing for this seven-day cruise is San Juan (Puerto Rico), St. Maarten, Dominica, St. Lucia, Margarita Island, Aruba, and San Juan. We offer various land-based tour packages but guests can explore on their own. For 14-day cruises, transatlantic crossings, and some other cruises, we spend more time at sea. We change the on-board activity mix and give guests more options.*

"*Many guest options are continuously available. We have over a dozen restaurants, cafés, and bars. There's a show every night in the Celebrity Theater — our own Celebrity Singers and Dancers do four shows a week, but we also have comedians and a capella singers. There's a library, casino, Internet café, swimming pools, whirlpools, a shopping arcade, and a fully equipped gym and schedule of classes. On the day at sea from Aruba to San Juan, we have an art auction, bingo, karaoke, shuffleboard, bridge, ping-pong, and many other activities. Then there are special children's programs. We provide guests with many options — they can partake of them or not — and we change them from time to time, based on feedback. All guests have a card that acts as identification, room key, and credit card.*

"*The crew is the most important factor in delivering the guest experience; we call them Celebrity Family Members (CFMs). We think of ourselves as a family and believe very strongly that happy employees lead to happy guests. We carefully select the entire staff. Agents in many countries around the world source CFMs from the many applications they receive for positions we need filled.* Celebrity Constellation *has CFMs from 58 different countries. That makes for a more interesting guest experience. We encourage guests to get to know the CFMs they interact with most closely — like waiters and stateroom attendants — but CFMs must not cross the line and become too familiar.*

"*All CFMs are on contracts — ranging from eight months for waiters to four months for officers — with two months off. Fleet-wide, staff retention is 60 to 70 percent. Our on-board training and development manager puts a lot of effort into training, especially the first week of a contract, to set clear expectations. Many CFMs don't interact with guests regularly, but we want to make sure they behave appropriately when they do. We continue training throughout the person's contract — some about the current job, but also for different jobs. Inevitably we lose people — for health reasons, home emergencies, and sometimes we just let people go — then we need CFMs to pick up different jobs. They can also advance, so we train for the next position.*

"*There's a lot of management by walking around and a systematic staff-appraisal system. The CFMs work hard for long hours — that's partly the reason for the two-month break between contracts. Each month we give the* Shining Star *award for outstanding service. We select five CFMs from a host of nominations — the winners earn cash and other prizes. We also make things pretty comfortable; mostly CFMs live two to a room, and they have TVs and Internet access. There are smoking and nonsmoking bars, a game room, and exercise facilities. Sometimes our entertainers put on special shows for the staff.*

"*If we provide a great guest experience, we get customer loyalty. On this cruise, about 800 of our 2,000 guests are repeaters from Celebrity cruises. On European cruises, the loyalty rate is often more than 50 percent. We have three levels of the Captain's Club customer loyalty program: Classic — 1 to 5 cruises; Select — 6 to 10 cruises; Elite — 11 + cruises. Each level offers rewards like stateroom upgrades, interaction with the captain and senior officers, preferential treatment for embarkation and disembarkation, and restaurant seating. Guests can book future cruises on board, and we keep in touch after the cruise.*

Case Question

What special human resource issues do cruise line management face? How do these issues differ from managing a passenger airline?

"*We use a comprehensive formal system for guest evaluations, including CFM performance — both scaled and open-ended responses — at the end of each cruise. They go to the head office in Miami, and we get the results in a couple of days. These are very important — they are the raw material for appraising our crew and making changes in the guest experience.*"

Chapter 13 is the second of three chapters in Part A of Imperative 4 — *Design the Market Offer*. Part A focuses on *Providing Customer Value*. Chapter 13 addresses *Managing Services and Customer Service*.

Some firms produce and sell *tangible* products like cars, computers, kitchen equipment, and TVs. Much of *Managing Marketing in the 21st Century* focuses on these firms and their approaches to markets. Many other firms produce and sell *intangible* services like beauty treatments, information technology, retail distribution, tax preparation, and transportation. Unfortunately, the product/service distinction is often fuzzy, as many products also have service components. Car companies offer financing, insurance, and warranties; Sony provides delivery, extended warranties, and installation. Further, technology advances allow some products to morph into services as customers purchase the benefits/values the product delivers as a service, rather than the product itself. B2C customers may lease (service), rather than buy, an automobile (product); B2B customers may hire IBM or Hewlett Packard Enterprise to support and manage their information systems (service), rather than buy hardware and software (product) directly. Services account for more than 70 percent of employment and GDP in developed countries. Walmart, the world's largest firm, is a service organization that sells products.

Because they are intangible, services can pose a real managerial challenge. Yet well-designed and well-delivered services create customer satisfaction and loyalty, differential advantage, positive word of mouth, high profits. *Customer service* is a special type of service — a key way for the firm to augment its *core product* or *core service* by providing experiences to earn differential advantage. Samsung and many other firms sell electronic *products*, but offer *customer service* in the form of online and telephone support.

THE CHANGING VIEW

OLD WAY	NEW WAY
Customer expectations ignored	Customer expectations crucial to satisfaction
Customer service is an afterthought	Customer service is a key competitive weapon
Customer service separate from marketing	Customer service crucial to customer retention
Low tech	High tech
Management of peak demand rare	Management of peak demand ubiquitous
Mass services, common to all customers	Customized/personalized services
Most services provided internally	Many services provided via outsourcing
Narrow view of service	Broad view of service
Products important — services relatively unimportant	Services critical sources of revenues and profits
Relatively narrow range of services offered	Explosive growth in service variety
Service performance is unmeasured	Service performance is carefully tracked
Services and customer service are blurred	Services and customer service are distinct parts of the market offer
Services are distinct from products	Products are morphing into services

PRODUCTS, SERVICES, AND CUSTOMER SERVICE

KEY IDEA

> GE is a leader in patient diagnostic products like X-rays and CAT scanners. Traditionally, GE provided after-sales customer service to hospitals and clinics to ensure products performed well. Today, GE services *any* diagnostic machine, even competitor machines. GE service provides real value — single source for all equipment servicing. For some customers, GE manages all diagnostic operations — including maintaining, upgrading, and replacing existing equipment. Some hospitals and clinics no longer purchase equipment outright — they pay GE on a per-image basis.

A service: Any act or performance that one party offers another that is essentially *intangible* and does not result in the ownership of anything.

Customer service: Enhances benefits/values inherent in the product or service.

The distinction between *products* and *services* remains one of marketing's great confusions. Some people use the term *product* to describe any core offering — including both *physical products* and *services.* We use this convenient shorthand throughout much of the book. Regardless, in Chapter 13, we separate a tangible *physical product* — that can be touched and perhaps kicked or sat upon — from a service. A *service* is *any act or performance that one party can offer another that is essentially intangible and does not result in the ownership of anything.* Or, "*anything that cannot be dropped on your foot!*"[1] Most services concern *people* — education, medical treatment, restaurants, theater, transportation[2]; *products* — car repair, house cleaning, real estate, and retail distribution; or *information* — business, financial, and legal services, marketing research, tax preparation.

KEY IDEA

As we discuss in Chapter 4, fundamental to marketing is a core underlying notion: *Customers do not want your products or services; they want the benefits and values your products and services provide!* Sometimes customers receive benefits and values from physical products like a car, clothing, food, house, or washing machine. Other times, they receive benefits and values from services like a haircut, Internet provider, medical procedure, sporting event, or travel. Regardless, to *attract, retain,* and *grow* customers, the firm must develop offers of value to satisfy customer needs. Relatedly, increasing numbers of firms promote the benefits/values their products provide as services (GE boxed insert above), rather than the products themselves. GE and Rolls-Royce sell jet engines, but traditionally made significant profits from spare parts and maintenance agreements. As engine quality and performance have improved, customer needs for spare parts and maintenance have decreased. Rolls-Royce offers *TotalCare* (now more than 50 percent of revenues) — customers pay a fee *per hour of flight* — a service. Today, firms offer many products like automobiles, computers, copiers, furniture, light bulbs, locomotives, railroad cars, and software as services. Customers lease, rent, or subscribe to products — they avoid capital outlays.

Customers buy *offers* — promises of benefits and values; the key element may be a product or a service.

MARKETING QUESTION

The firm can enhance the benefits/values inherent in its products/services by adding customer service — delivery, information, repair, sales support, technical support, warranties. Honda offers the Accord as a core physical product, but also provides customer service before, during, and after purchase. FedEx core service is overnight package delivery, but it surrounds the core with billing statements, documentation, information, logistical advice, order-taking, package-tracking, pickup, and supplies. Finally, a core service for one firm can be customer service for another. Delivery may be *customer service* for your local pizza parlor, but for a chain that only delivers pizza, delivery is part of its *core service.*

Next time you call a customer-service department, ask the representative where they are located. It may be South Dakota, but most likely another country where English-speaking skills are well developed. Ask how they like their jobs, and their biggest challenges. What are the implications for firms outsourcing customer service?

GROWTH IN THE SERVICE SECTOR

The service sector in advanced economies has grown dramatically in recent years; hence, product, service, and customer-service distinctions are increasingly important. Services account for upward of 70 percent of total employment and GDP in developed countries.[3] Many service firms now populate the *Fortune* 500,[4] and social enterprises like government and nonprofit organizations (NGOs) almost exclusively offer services. Prime examples are education, garbage collection, health and human services, and policing. Rising incomes and age-related demographic shifts are each driving services growth (for China). Other important private-sector growth factors are:

- **Customer behavior changes.** Customer preference for purchasing is decreasing. Many consumers prefer to avoid ownership responsibilities; firms want to remove investments from balance sheets to increase return on investment (ROI). Correspondingly, financial services like credit, leasing, and rental are growing.[5]
- **Deregulation.** Deregulation in service industries like electricity, financial services, natural gas, telecommunications, and transportation eases market entry; entrants with innovative strategies fuel growth.
- **Franchising.** *Franchising* is the backbone of the hospitality, restaurant, and tax preparation industries; leading brands include Hilton, McDonald's, and H&R Block respectively. But businesses like closet installation, commercial property restoration, onsite computer and electronics repairs, and window-cleaning are also growing via franchising.[6]
- **Globalization.** Innovations in technology and communications make products/services accessible to global markets. Firms conduct business across the world using many derivative service strategies to meet the diverse needs of new customers.
- **Leveraging core competence.** Some firms find in-house activities valuable to other firms, so they repackage and sell them as services. Florida Light and Power — winner of Japan's prestigious Deming quality award — offers quality workshops; Xerox consults on quality management and document services systems. Disney offers executive programs in leadership and customer service. Shell provides information technology and other support services to firms outside the oil and gas industry; Amazon's Web Services' offerings use spare computing capacity (cloud computing) from retail operations. SAS trains flight crews from other airlines, maintains planes, and helps Swedish firms prepare employees for relocation.[7]
- **Outsourcing.** Many firms narrow missions and downsize to focus on core competencies. They *outsource* activities and processes previously performed internally, and often secure better value/cost ratios. Examples include call-center customer-service support, financial transactions, human resource (HR) functions (benefits, payroll), legal advice, security, technology, telephony, manufacturing. Outsourcing provides suppliers with service opportunities and potentially higher profit margins than physical products. IBM, Hewlett Packard Enterprise, and Unisys design, install, and operate customer computer and information systems; firms like Accenture manage various transactional and transformational business process outsourcing relationships.[8]
- **Technology.** Technological advances allow firms to connect with customers on increasingly individualized bases, and deliver ongoing and complementary services.[9]

MARKETING QUESTION

Identify franchises that appeal to you. **[582p]** Select the most attractive franchise. What are the pros and cons of becoming a franchisee?

KEY IDEA

Services represent over 70 percent of employment and GDP in developed countries.

Factors driving services growth include:

- Rising incomes
- Age-related demographic shifts
- Customer behavior changes
- Deregulation
- Franchising
- Globalization
- Leveraging core competence
- Outsourcing
- Technology

CHARACTERISTICS OF SERVICES

Physical products differ from services in several important ways:

INTANGIBILITY

Services are not physical in nature; they are intangible. Services are concerned with people, products, and information. Services focusing on *people* generally require the customer's physical presence or interactivity; services focusing on *products and information* generally do not. Locations for services like factory maintenance, gardening, and house cleaning are generally fixed. Customers consume other services in various places like seeing a movie in a theater, at home, or on smartphones; and receive medical services at a doctor's office, hospital, at home, or perhaps virtually.

Although some services like restaurant meals and in-store product purchases are more tangible than others, the core experience is still intangible. In general, *intangibility* makes customer evaluation of services more subjective than for physical goods. Hence, tangible service elements

KEY IDEA

Key service characteristics are:

- **Intangibility**
- Inseparability
- Variability
- Perishability
- Divisibility
- Lack of acquisition
- Role of customers

often play an important role in forming customer expectations and evaluations of the service experience. Service tangibles include equipment, facilities, and personnel.[10] Some firms provide additional tangibility via service guarantees.

SERVICE EQUIPMENT. Generally, services require tangible physical products: air travel — airplane; iTunes — iPod/iPhone; haircut — scissors and mirror. *Service equipment* quality often influences the service experience. Many passengers choose airlines with new planes (Singapore Airlines, jetBlue) versus those with older fleets.

SERVICE FACILITIES. Consideration for where the firm delivers the service:

- **Exterior.** Includes the location, outside view, and signage. These tangible elements provide information about the interior where the firm provides the service; the exterior either attracts customers to, or detracts from, the service experience. Delta Air Lines spent $1.2 billion to renovate and expand its JFK (New York) terminal to reflect its approach to customer service.
- **Interior.** Has two dimensions:
  - *Offstage.* Out of customer sight.
  - *Onstage.* Where customers experience deeds, efforts, and performance.[11]

The type and quality of onstage facilities significantly affects the service experience — a small intimate theater versus New York's Radio City Music Hall — or servicing your car in a clean versus dirty and messy facility. The firm can redefine a service by moving an offstage activity to onstage (or vice versa). To enhance the customer experience, some restaurants shift cooking from offstage to onstage. Although generally out of sight, offstage facilities may provide important clues to service quality.

KEY IDEA

Customers often focus on tangible aspects of intangible services:
- Service equipment
- Service facilities
- Service personnel
- Service guarantees

SERVICE PERSONNEL. Some personnel work offstage; others work onstage. Airline mechanics and baggage handlers generally work offstage; ticket agents and flight attendants are onstage. The customer experience depends on how well all *service personnel* perform their functions. Because appearance, demeanor, and manner of onstage personnel offer important quality cues, many service personnel wear uniforms. Bringing offstage personnel onstage can enhance the customer experience. Jimmy Fallon frequently brings crew members onstage for his late-night TV talk show. Airline pilots make frequent announcements and often converse with deplaning passengers.

Customers have many interactions with onstage service personnel. Jan Carlzon (former SAS airline president) used the phrase *moment of truth* to emphasize their importance. At each *moment of truth*, customers can be satisfied or dissatisfied.[12] Customers make judgments based on their own interactions, and the interactions of service personnel with other customers. Managing customer/service personnel interactions across all engagement channels is a major firm challenge. Disney's elaborate training and management program carefully controls employee response behavior so each customer has a *magical* and consistent experience. Even more difficult is managing customer interactions with distributor and franchisee employees.

KEY IDEA

Moments of truth are opportunities for customer satisfaction or dissatisfaction.

Another serious concern for service firms like advertising agencies, beauty salons, and those offering business and professional services is the relative strength of employee versus firm relationships with customers. When the service person-to-customer relationship is strong, employees may resign and take customers with them — Chapter 5. Better company communications can strengthen firm-customer bonds. The firm can also bind critical employees more closely by enlightened contractual provisions that make employees happy but also place barriers to working for (or as) competitors.

MARKETING QUESTION

Think about the last time you purchased a smartphone. During the purchase, how important to you was the product? How important was the associated service?

SERVICE GUARANTEES. Guarantees about the service experience provide tangible value should the firm fail to keep its promises. Good *service guarantees* are unconditional, painless to invoke, and easy and quick to collect.[13] Cort Furniture Rental guarantees on-time delivery and pickup, showroom-quality products, upgraded replacement if substitution is necessary, exchange of any item within two days, and a total refund if any problem cannot be fixed. The service agreement should be simple to understand and communicate, and meaningfully related to the service it

MARKETING QUESTION

Again, think about your most recent purchase of smartphone service. Was there a service guarantee? Did the guarantee meet the noted criteria? Did the provider communicate the guarantee well? What could the provider have done better? Have you received guarantees for other purchases? How do you evaluate these guarantees?

guarantees. Good guarantees work because customers have positive experiences with the guarantee. They should also motivate employees to improve service quality by working hard to avoid customers invoking the guarantee. Guarantees are most appropriate when:

- customer ego is involved;
- customers have little experience with the service;
- customers make frequent purchases;
- firm and customer do not trust each other;
- industry image for service quality is poor;
- sales are strongly affected by word of mouth;
- service failure has significant negative consequences;
- service price is high.

INSEPARABILITY

 KEY IDEA

For services, production and consumption are inseparable.

Many firms manufacture, sell, ship, and store physical goods. These firms deal with demand and supply fluctuations and imperfect forecasting via inventory controls. For service businesses, provider and customer are inexorably linked, making production and consumption innately *inseparable*. Because firms cannot inventory services, demand forecasting is critical; hence, data mining and predictive analytics are becoming important tools. Crowded restaurants, long ski-lift lines, and standing-room-only on public transportation all result from excess demand. To address supply/demand imbalances the firm must modify supply and/or demand.

KEY IDEA

The firm cannot inventory services; it must address excess supply (demand) by decreasing (increasing) supply or increasing (decreasing) demand.

MODIFY SUPPLY. The firm can address short-run demand fluctuations by *increasing* (stretching) capacity like working longer hours, outsourcing, renting or sharing extra facilities and equipment, and/or adding full-time or part-time workers. The critical challenge is maintaining service quality: An upscale hair salon should not hire temporary stylists unless their skills meet salon standards. The firm can *decrease* supply by scheduling employee training, maintenance, renovations, and/or vacations.

MODIFY DEMAND. The firm should analyze demand patterns, answering questions like:

- Does service demand follow a regular, predictable cycle? If so, is the cycle length daily, weekly, monthly, or annual? Or does demand follow some other pattern?
- What causes these fluctuations — climate, paydays, school vacations, work schedules?
- Are there random demand fluctuations — births, crime, economic conditions, weather?
- Can we disaggregate use patterns by market segment or profitability?

KEY IDEA

Key service characteristics are:
- Intangibility
- **Inseparability**
- Variability
- Perishability
- Divisibility
- Lack of acquisition
- Role of customers

Based on the answers, the firm must decide which segments to target — then increase/decrease demand as necessary. To *increase* demand, the firm may improve service offerings, provide better time and place convenience, communicate more effectively with potential customers, and/or reduce prices. To *decrease* demand — *demarketing* — the firm can offer customers incentives to switch purchases to lower demand periods, or reduce marketing activities like advertising/promotion spending and service availability, or increase prices.[14] To discourage certain types of visitors, some tourist destinations advertise capacity limitations; others emphasize banned activities and inappropriate tourist behavior.

The annual demand pattern for many resort hotels has *peak*, *shoulder*, and *low* seasons. In *peak* season, demand often outstrips supply at standard prices. Traditional actions included minimizing vacancies via effective scheduling, raising prices, and switching customers to *shoulder* seasons. In *low* season, supply outstrips demand: Hotels often run promotions targeting nontraditional segments with discounts for conventions and/or other events. In *shoulder* seasons, effective marketing and sales promotions evened out supply and demand.[15] Today, big data and analytics help hotel revenue managers price dynamically to maximize revenues. InterContinental Hotels, Marriott, and others have significantly increased average revenues per room.[16]

VARIABILITY

In general, *variability* in service delivery implies reduced customer satisfaction. Lack of consistency follows directly from human involvement in service delivery. Firms address variability in product manufacturing using quality tools, but these are more difficult to implement for services. Nonetheless, approaches like *six sigma*, a data-driven methodology that eliminates defects in any process, can be effective for securing consistency in service systems.[17]

HUMAN CAPITAL. Employee selection and training are critical for improving employee performance and reducing service variability. Treating employees appropriately is also important. Virgin puts employees ahead of customers under the philosophy that *happy employees mean happy customers.*[18] Virgin believes that poorly treated employees will not deliver high customer satisfaction.

Sometimes service variability is positive; service providers enhance satisfaction by tailoring actions to individual customers and responding to their personal needs in real time. To secure such behavior, reward systems and empowerment should encourage employees *to go the extra mile* to serve customers, not penalize them for innovating or for breaking rules to provide a better customer experience. Ritz Carlton allows every employee up to $2,000 to remedy customer-service issues on the spot — no questions asked. **[387v]** Many firms identify and applaud company heroes who deliver exceptional service.

> "We seek a highly motivated and skilled group of people. Our corporate culture encourages entrepreneurial thinking, as well as the ability to react quickly and creatively in light of market developments. Recruitment, training, and job evaluation and promotion procedures are designed to ensure we select and treat individuals on the basis of their merits and abilities." — Virgin Mobile
>
> Bob Catell, chairman and CEO of KeySpan (gas utility) regularly delivers appreciation messages to employees whose managers identify their contributions. KeySpan is widely recognized for valuing human capital: No. 1 in Brand Keys *Energy Provider* category for several straight years; top gas utility in the American Customer Satisfaction Index; and winner of *Brandweek's* Customer Loyalty Award.[19]

SUBSTITUTE CAPITAL FOR LABOR. The firm can remove human variability via automation like using dispensing machines for cash, drinks, sandwiches, and subway cards. Cost reduction objectives often drive these innovations, but they reduce variability nonetheless. The downside: Machines break down and customers may desire human contact. Some bank customers prefer human tellers to ATMs, and many people object to quasi-personal communication (voice-recognition systems) in call centers; they want human interaction. Do you?

PERISHABILITY

Perishability is tightly linked to inseparability and the inability to inventory services, but focuses on situations where supply is committed but demand is not. Two cases are important:

- **Demand apparently sufficient but unpaid.** Customers agree to purchase the service but default on their obligations. When patients miss doctor appointments or restaurant patrons are no-shows for reservations, expected revenues are lost forever. Reminder systems (and blacklists) attempt to address this problem.
- **Demand insufficient.** The firm has several options for increasing demand; lower prices is a favorite approach. New York and London theaters sell full-price tickets at the theater and via ticket-ordering services; they also sell discount tickets shortly before the performance at last-minute ticket booths in theater districts. StubHub is a similar service for sporting events.

KEY IDEA

Key service characteristics are:
- Intangibility
- Inseparability
- **Variability**
- Perishability
- Divisibility
- Lack of acquisition
- Role of customers

KEY IDEA

Reducing variability is more difficult for services than for products.

KEY IDEA

Service variability can be positive when service providers tailor behavior for individual customers.

The firm can reduce human variability via automation.

KEY IDEA

Because they cannot be inventoried, services are perishable.

KEY IDEA

Key service characteristics are:

- Intangibility
- Inseparability
- Variability
- **Perishability**
- **Divisibility**
- Lack of acquisition
- Role of customers

Many services like airlines, hotels, telecommunications, and theaters have high fixed costs but low variable costs. Hence, profit contribution per customer is very high. Coach fares on trans-Atlantic flights are $700–$1,500, but the marginal cost per passenger is minimal — a little fuel, meals, and sundries. Hence, airlines often steeply discount some tickets.[20] But they must be careful that customers willing to pay a higher price do not switch to discount tickets.[21] Many airlines optimize profitability via complex computer-based yield management systems.

DIVISIBILITY

Shouldice Hospital (near Toronto) has a long waiting list of prospective U.S. and Canadian patients with uncomplicated hernias requiring repair. Shouldice does not advertise and receives few physician referrals, but prices are one third lower than U.S. hospitals. Shouldice has a highly focused strategy and service design with ample customer participation. Patients fill out preregistration forms, shave their groins and abdomens, and conduct physical therapy by walking and climbing stairs. Assigned roommates have similar background and interests; frequent social activities include interactions with post- and preoperative patients to minimize anxiety. Many former patients attend Shouldice alumni events![22]

KEY IDEA

Services are divisible — the *service blueprint* is the sequence of activities comprising the service.

We view most products as single entities: An automobile is a single unit, not a collection of components like an engine, seats, transmission, and wheels. *Divisibility* is a key service characteristic; many core and surrounding services comprise a sequence of activities conducted over time, like those at Shouldice. Figure 13.1 illustrates an activity sequence for an evening adult education course.[23]

The activity sequence functions as a service *blueprint* for identifying and addressing service issues. The service blueprint can help redesign service delivery by adding, subtracting, or reorganizing service elements. Many airlines redesigned ticket counters by adding machines for issuing boarding passes — ticket-counter agents deal only with passengers needing luggage check-in or other assistance.[24]

FIGURE 13.1
Service Blueprint for an Evening Adult Education Course

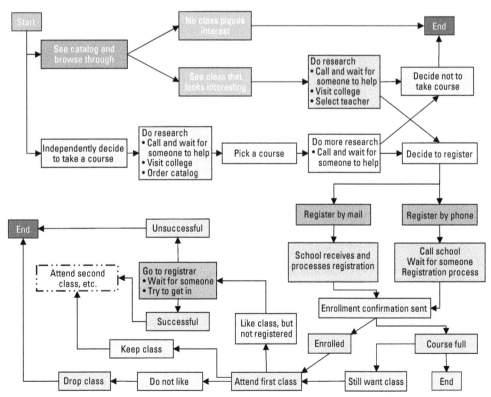

MARKETING QUESTION

Think about a recent positive service experience. Did you buy the service again? Did you post your experience online? How? Did you tell friends, family, and colleagues? Did they buy the service?

Think about a recent negative service experience. Did you buy the service again? Did you post your experience online? How? Did you tell friends, family, and colleagues? Did they buy the service?

LACK OF ACQUISITION

People acquire and frequently own products, but not services. They *experience* the physical manifestation of services like a smoother-running car, a dashing haircut, or an auction *win* on eBay. But typically the service is, at best, a set of associations in memory. Yet a service experience can be highly salient, and related associations very influential. Positive associations drive repurchase and positive word of mouth. Negative associations lead customers to avoid the service provider and dissuade others.

ROLE OF CUSTOMERS

Firms rarely refuse to sell products to customers because of the effect on other customers. But customers experience many services in group settings, so customer-customer and customer-service provider interactions are critical issues for many service firms. The drunken airline passenger, the sleeping student in a finance class, and the baseball fan behind home plate shouting out pitches — each affects other customers' experiences. The firm must not unthinkingly believe *the customer is always right.* Some organizations have systems for rejecting customers — like college admission departments; nightclub bouncers and restaurant maitre d's also eject unwanted customers.

KEY IDEA

Key service characteristics are:

- Intangibility
- Inseparability
- Variability
- Perishability
- Divisibility
- **Lack of acquisition**
- **Role of customers**

SERVICE QUALITY

In general, high customer satisfaction drives customer loyalty, repurchase, and positive word of mouth, and enhances shareholder value.[25] The converse is also true. Figure 13.2 (p. 345) shows the *SERVQUAL* model: Customer satisfaction relates to service quality via *expectations disconfirmation* — Gap 5 is the *difference* between perceived quality and expected quality[26]:

- **Customer satisfaction.** Perceived service is *better* than expected service.
- **Customer dissatisfaction.** Perceived service is *worse* than expected service:

> Two computer hardware firms competed fiercely. Firm A promised service visits within four hours of a request; firm B promised eight hours. Firm A averaged five and a half hours; firm B averaged seven hours. Firm A's service performance was better, but firm B's satisfaction ratings were higher!

Gap 5 depends on four other gaps:

- **Gap 1.** The firm does not understand customer service expectations.
- **Gap 2.** Service quality specifications do not reflect firm beliefs about customers' service expectations.
- **Gap 3.** Service delivery performance does not meet service specifications.
- **Gap 4.** External communications about service quality do not reflect service performance.

SERVQUAL identifies a dilemma. The firm may increase short-run sales by advertising high service quality. But if *perceived* quality is lower than *expected* quality, customers will be dissatisfied. Yet, if the firm underpromises on service quality, sales may be low. Also, rising customer expectations make it increasingly difficult to deliver greater-than-expected service.

KEY IDEA

Expectations disconfirmation is perceived quality less expected quality.

SERVQUAL identifies five gaps for diagnosing service quality.

KEY IDEA

SERVQUAL's subscale scores —

- Tangibles
- Reliability
- Responsiveness
- Assurance
- Empathy

— provide actionable items for improving service performance.

FIGURE 13.2
*SERVQUAL Model for
Diagnosing Service Quality*

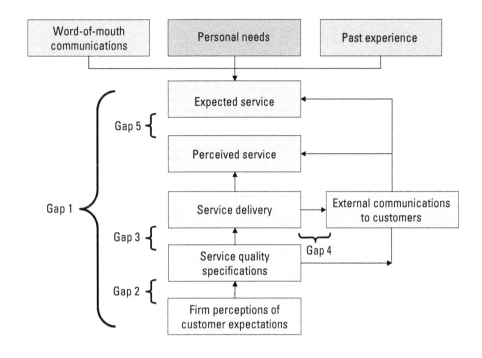

FIGURE 13.2
*SERVQUAL Model for
Diagnosing Service Quality*

MEASURING AND MANAGING SERVICE QUALITY

In SERVQUAL, five key variables influence perceived service quality[27]:

- **Tangibles.** Appearance of communication materials, equipment, personnel, and physical facilities.
- **Reliability.** Ability to perform promised service accurately and dependably.
- **Responsiveness.** Willingness to help customers and provide prompt service.
- **Assurance.** Employee courtesy, knowledge, and ability to convey confidence and trust.
- **Empathy.** Provision of caring, individualized attention to customers.[28]

Table 13.1 (p. 346) shows the 22-item SERVQUAL scale. Respondents provide service quality expectations data — QE[29]; and service perceptions data for providers — QP. The provider's total SERVQUAL score comprises QP minus QE differences, summed over all 22 items. Subscale scores for tangibles, reliability, responsiveness, assurance, and empathy provide more granular data and offer action recommendations. Figure 13.3 (p. 347) plots hypothetical scores for one provider: *Reliability* and *empathy* are fine, but the firm may be overemphasizing *empathy*. The firm should focus on *assurance* — high expectations but low perceived performance — and *tangibles*, and keep an eye on *responsiveness*.

**MARKETING
QUESTION**

Think about your favorite coffee shop. How do you perceive service quality? Evaluate tangibles, reliability, responsiveness, assurance, and empathy.

Scott's (disguised) expensive capital goods were integral to customer production lines; many customers ran factories 24/7/365. But Scott was only marginally profitable. The CEO reduced costs by cutting the field-service force in half. The following year, Scott's service performance rated worst in the industry. The CEO believed the survey results would be bad for morale, so he kept the findings confidential!

Dimensions	Expectations Item — QE	Perception Item — QP
Tangibles	1. Excellent_____companies will have modern-looking equipment.	XYZ has modern-looking equipment.
	2. The physical facilities at excellent _____ companies will be visually appealing.	XYZ's physical facilities are visually appealing.
	3. Employees at excellent _____ companies will be neat-appearing.	XYZ's employees are neat-appearing.
	4. Material associated with the service (such as pamphlets or statements) will be visually appealing in an excellent _____ company.	Material associated with the service (such as pamphlets or statements) are visually appealing at XYZ.
Reliability	5. When excellent _____ companies promise to do something by a certain time, they will do so.	When XYZ promises to do something by a certain time, it does so.
	6. When a customer has a problem, excellent _____ companies will show a sincere interest in solving it.	When you have a problem, XYZ shows a sincere interest in solving it.
	7. Excellent _____ companies will perform the service right the first time.	XYZ performs the service right the first time.
	8. Excellent _____ companies will provide their services at the time they promise to do so.	XYZ provides its services at the time it promises to do so.
	9. Excellent _____ companies will insist on error-free records.	XYZ insists on error-free records.
Responsiveness	10. Employees in excellent _____ companies will tell customers exactly when services will be performed.	Employees in XYZ tell you exactly when services will be performed.
	11. Employees in excellent _____ companies will give prompt service to customers.	Employees in XYZ give you prompt service.
	12. Employees in excellent _____ companies will always be willing to help customers.	Employees in XYZ are always willing to help you.
	13. Employees in excellent _____ companies will never be too busy to respond to customers' requests.	Employees in XYZ are never too busy to respond to your requests.
Assurance	14. The behavior of employees in excellent _____ companies will instill confidence in customers.	The behavior of employees in XYZ instills confidence in you.
	15. Customers of excellent _____ companies will feel safe in their transactions.	You feel safe in your transactions with XYZ.
	16. Employees in excellent _____ companies will be consistently courteous with customers.	Employees in XYZ are consistently courteous with you.
	17. Employees in excellent _____ companies will have the knowledge to answer customers' questions.	Employees in XYZ have the knowledge to answer your questions.
Empathy	18. Excellent _____ companies will give customers individual attention.	XYZ gives you individual attention.
	19. Excellent _____ companies will have operating hours convenient to all their customers.	XYZ has operating hours convenient to all its customers.
	20. Excellent _____ companies will have employees who give customers personal attention.	XYZ has employees who give you personal attention.
	21. Excellent _____ companies will have the customer's best interests at heart.	XYZ has your best interests at heart.
	22. The employees of excellent _____ companies will understand the specific needs of their customers.	Employees of XYZ understand your specific needs.

a. All questions answered on a 1-to-7 scale: 1 = Strongly disagree, 7 = Strongly agree.
b. The blank line in the Expectations items is for the particular industry, subindustry, or department being studied.
c. XYZ in the Perception items stands for the company being studied.

FIGURE 13.3
*Customer Expectations
and Performance
Perception on Five
Service Dimensions*

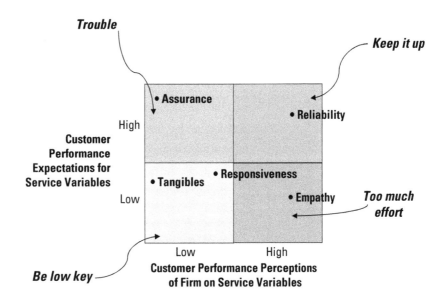

LIMITATIONS OF CUSTOMER SATISFACTION

KEY IDEA

High satisfaction no longer
guarantees high customer
retention. The firm must
delight customers.

Achieving high customer satisfaction is critical for most firms. But increasing competition implies that high satisfaction no longer guarantees high customer retention; defecting customers may be highly satisfied![30] Figure 13.4 depicts two types of market: uncompetitive — **AA'A"** and competitive — **BB'B"**.[31] Starting from the low/low position:

- **Uncompetitive.** Along **AA'A"** satisfaction is low, but customer loyalty rises quickly. Customers are loyal because they have few, if any, alternatives.

- **Competitive.** Along **BB'B"** satisfaction increases, but loyalty stays low! Customers have many alternatives and switch suppliers, even though currently satisfied. Moderate satisfaction is insufficient. The firm should strive for high satisfaction by delighting customers with exceptional, and possibly, unexpected but great service.[32]

FIGURE 13.4
*Customer Satisfaction/
Loyalty Chart*

KEY IDEA

All firms experience service
failures; how the firm
addresses them is key.

Most insurance firms believe stable policyholders are better risks — *time at current address* is a popular stability metric. Military officers move frequently, hence securing insurance was difficult and expensive. USAA believed *time at current address* made no sense for military officers; they have stable careers. USAA introduced policies designed for military careers, and developed a nationwide distribution system — mail, telephone, Internet. Military officers are very satisfied and highly loyal — less than 2 percent defect voluntarily each year.[33]

Of course, customers sometimes trade off satisfaction for low price. Discount carriers Ryanair (Europe) and Spirit Airlines (U.S.) receive low customer satisfaction ratings but fill their planes via low prices.

ISSUES IN IMPROVING SERVICE QUALITY

To improve service quality, the firm should consider several issues:

- **Customer co-production.** Some firms improve service quality via customer participation in service delivery. Examples include self-service restaurants, self-checkout supermarkets, and self-check-in at airports. Previously, FedEx customers tracked packages by phoning customer-service representatives; today they track packages via the Internet. Customers enjoy better service and FedEx cuts costs — Nirvana! Some firms promote co-production via differential pricing, like airlines — online prices are often lower than telephone reservations.

- **Improving the offer.** The firm enhances service quality by adding customer service. FMCG firms provide retailers with *plan-o-grams* (layouts) for arranging shelf space. Private banks offer money management seminars for children of high-net-worth clients. Additional customer service is particularly important in mature markets:

> Bandag sells truck tire retreads to more than 500 U.S. dealer/installers. Bandag products have no price/quality advantage over competitors, so Bandag offers additional services:
>
> - Helps dealers file/collect on warranty claims from tire manufacturers.[34]
>
> - Offers comprehensive fleet management services to its largest national accounts.
>
> - Embeds computer chips in newly retreaded tires — measures pressure and temperature and counts revolutions.
>
> - Advises the optimal time to retread — reduces downtime caused by blowouts.

Sometimes firms improve quality by removing services! Popular and profitable Southwest Airlines (SWA) uses secondary airfields, on-board ticketing, and nonassigned seats; and has no interline baggage transfer with other airlines. By reducing costs, SWA continues to offer low fares, high-frequency flights, good on-time performance, and a fun experience; customers rate service quality high.[35]

KEY IDEA

Few aggrieved customers *complain* — they just *defect*. The firm should make complaining easier, then follow up swiftly and aggressively.

- **Maintaining the service environment.** The output from some services negatively affects the physical environment: dirty plates and glasses in restaurants, dirty towels in health clubs, and hair on the barber's floor. Quickly restoring the environment improves service quality.

- **Service performance and information.** Customers want high service quality, but they also want to know when they will receive the service. London's Heathrow Express provides passengers with accurate estimates of train arrivals and departures — on the platform and on the train: New York City's subway has a similar system for train arrivals. In many cities, clocks advise pedestrians when traffic lights will change. And when customers line up for services, some firms provide queue-time expectations.[36]

- **Service quality failures and service recovery.** Service failure has several potential customer-focused costs — allowances, complaints, liability, loss of goodwill, product recall, returned materials, servicing and repair, and warranty claims. Despite the firm's best efforts, service errors do occur. Some may be *critical incidents* (CI) — extraordinary events that customers perceive and recall as unusually negative.[37] "Our wagons were loaded, but we didn't get a locomotive. When the locomotive finally arrived, we didn't get a locomotive driver. Our transport was delayed for 12 hours."[38] (Of course, some CIs may be positive.) Service failures also happen when the firm's drive for efficiency leads to inflexible systems that cannot deal with idiosyncratic customer behavior:

KEY IDEA

A drive for service efficiency can lead to inflexible systems that cannot deal with idiosyncratic customer behavior.

Jack parked in a lot next to Townbank (disguised); the sign read *Free Parking for Townbank Customers*. Jack cashed a check and asked the teller to validate his parking ticket. The teller refused, saying that Jack had not made a deposit. Jack explained that he had a longtime relationship at another Townbank branch, including several million dollars in deposits. Neither teller nor bank manager would budge. Jack drove 40 blocks to his regular branch. He told the manager he would close all accounts unless he received a phoned apology by the end of the day. No phone call was made. Jack closed all his accounts![39]

To minimize customer defection, the firm should deal swiftly with service failure and aggressively manage service recovery. Done well, the firm may benefit from the *recovery paradox* — formerly unhappy customers become loyal, even advocates. The firm should also address the underlying cause by upgrading products, services, and/or customer service, as necessary. Failure to fix the cause leads to enhanced customer dissatisfaction on the next occasion and morale loss among front-line employees. Overall, few aggrieved customers complain — they just defect. But complaints are an opportunity to learn customer *pain points* and enhance service delivery overall.[40] The firm should make complaining easier but should follow up swiftly and aggressively:

IBM receives around 100,000 complaints annually, ranging from "My computer won't work" to "Did you think about adding an XXX to your software?" IBM assigns a complaint owner for each complaint, and completely addresses 95 percent in five to seven business days.

Some firms dig deeply to address customer complaints:

Ben & Jerry's (B&J) noticed increased customer complaints about Cherry Garcia ice cream — too few cherries. B&J matched complaints against shipments — the problem was not regional. Manufacturing analysis showed the recipe and ingredients were normal and also ruled out other causes. Finally, B&J identified the problem. The picture on the container was not ice cream but frozen yogurt. Frozen yogurt had more cherries. B&J changed the picture; customer complaints ceased.

Increasingly, customers complain in public, especially on the Internet. They post stories on bulletin boards, Twitter, and YouTube, or set up attack websites: AOL, The Gap, JPMorgan Chase, McDonald's, Microsoft, and United Airlines [303v] have all been targets.[41] How the firm manages its reputation within the digital realm is an increasingly critical issue. Some firms employ web watchers to monitor complaints and answer questions; other firms use *sentiment analysis (opinion mining)* to assess text polarity, then act appropriately. Sears tested a web answer line and received *a couple of hundred* questions per day. Sears abandoned the effort — too many questions to answer! Many firms sponsor *user groups* on Facebook or LinkedIn; or host YouTube channels to help manage perceptions.

A severe ice storm hit New York City, jetBlue's home base. Over six days, jetBlue canceled 1,000 flights and stranded many passengers on runways for hours — a service quality and public relations disaster. jetBlue took several service recovery actions: Quickly apologized and introduced a passenger Bill of Rights, including a service guarantee; proactively made personal apologies to all inconvenienced passengers, seeking opinions on problem causes and fix-it ideas. jetBlue implemented many operational changes. The CEO made a YouTube video addressed to customers and gave many high-profile interviews including *BusinessWeek* and *David Letterman*. [575v, 102v] Relatedly, after any delay or other flight problem, Southwest Airlines e-mails passengers an apology, short explanation, and gift.

CUSTOMER SERVICE

It's 6:30 p.m.; Joe is leaving his office. He remembers it's his turn to prepare dinner. He accesses the Pillsbury website; it recognizes Joe's address and queries the corporate database. Joe was here six days ago, and two weeks before that. Both times he wanted data on meals he could prepare with a minimum of fuss. Bet he's back for the same thing.

The computer accesses another database — it identifies popular meals with time-sensitive professional males (research-based). What's on the menu? — Garlic Pasta Chicken Salad? No! He had that last time — on a Saturday. Joe picked it the last three times. Something else in poultry? Ah! Fiesta Chicken. Quick, simple to prepare, spicy — Joe picks spicy meals every time he downloads a recipe. They're popular with males in his age range.

By the time Joe has finished clicking on *What's new in main dishes*, an entire meal has been planned — including recipes, suggested side dishes, and even the wine. Joe looks at the Fiesta Chicken page and sees a lovely picture of the dish, recipe beside it.

Now, where is Joe located? Last time he requested data on stores carrying the Green Giant brand along Route 128 near the Mainfair intersection. A quick check of the MapInfo business-oriented geographic information system shows light industry populated by R&D startups. Joe is probably at work — he's going to pick up his dinner items on the way home. A map flashes on the screen, identifying stores where he can most easily pick up Green Giant products for Fiesta Chicken and Pillsbury baked goods for dessert![42]

MARKETING QUESTION

Joe's scenario with Pillsbury is feasible with today's technology. Do you regard it favorably or unfavorably? Why or why not?

At the start of this chapter, we showed that core services differ from customer services. Core services like an airline trip or a theater production are central to the offer; all other services are *customer service*. Customer service is any act, performance, or information that enhances the firm's core product/service. Customer service is critical for *customer relationship management* (CRM) — Chapter 2 — and can be as important as the core product. IBM did not dominate mainframes because of superior technology or lower prices. IBM's differential advantage was customer service: *You never get fired for buying IBM*.[43]

KEY IDEA

Customer service can be more central to customer decision-making than the core product/service.

GE Power Systems (GEPS) focused on improving customer service when electric utility deregulation spawned severe price pressure. GEPS reduced replacement time for old or damaged parts from 12 to 6 weeks, and advised U.S. customers on doing business in Europe and Asia. GEPS provided maintenance staff for equipment upgrades and moved one third of its engineers from new product development to new service development.

Positive word of mouth follows from great customer service. [889v] Financial terminal provider Bloomberg is very clear: "One of the reasons for our heavy customer-service emphasis is referrals. The person who's really going to sell you a terminal is the guy sitting next to you, not necessarily our salesperson."[44] Negative word of mouth can be devastating. Customers receiving bad customer service tell more people than recipients of good customer service.[45] Company-sponsored clubs, like Mac User and Harley Owners Group (HOG), are increasingly important for positive word of mouth. Clubs create strong product affinity, provide positive group experiences, and validate purchase decisions. Sometimes members share experiences on sponsored websites — like physicians reporting experiences with J&J products — and help with more effective product use.[46]

TYPES OF CUSTOMER SERVICE

Figure 13.5 shows the *flower of customer service*, embracing eight dimensions for augmenting the core product/service.[47] We illustrate the information dimension:

CIS, a leading U.S. computer-based information supplier to professional firms, faced tough pressure. CIS' major competitor, seeking increased market share, offered a more comprehensive and easier-to-access database, and annual contracts at 30 percent of CIS' prices! CIS leveraged corporate contacts to provide clients with insight into current and potential customers, and maintained prices. Customer information value far exceeded the 70 percent price differential; CIS retained market share.

FIGURE 13.5
*The Flower of
Customer Service*

**MARKETING
QUESTION**

Recall when you last purchased an expensive product/service online or from a bricks & mortar store. Where did the provider do well — billing, consultation, exceptions, hospitality, information, order-taking, payment, or safekeeping? Where could the provider improve?

KEY IDEA

Customer service has eight *flower-of-service* dimensions:

- Billing
- Consultation
- Exceptions
- Hospitality
- Information
- Order-taking
- Payment
- Safekeeping

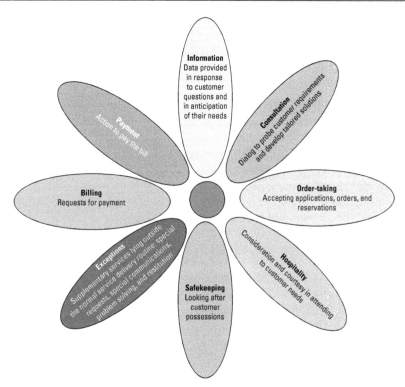

We can also classify customer service by phase of the purchase process. Each phase has different customer requirements where different customer services are appropriate.[48] Of course, first-time versus repeat purchasers typically have different requirements:

- **Prepurchase.** Assist customers preparing for purchase, including help identifying needs. Also, promotional activities providing information about products and purchase locations.

- **During purchase.** Includes help with selection, customization agreements, financing, personal selling, product assortments, product trial, and quality assurance.

At The Musician's Planet, customers can try out a guitar and make a demo tape. At REI (Seattle), consumers can attempt a 64-foot climbing wall, examine a water pump in an indoor river, or test a Gore-Tex jacket in a rainstorm. Some clothing stores use advanced imaging technology to portray dresses with different styles and fabrics. Levi Strauss imaging machines take precise customer measurements for custom jeans.

- **Postpurchase.** Most marketing activity occurs pre- and during purchase; most customer service occurs after purchase. Postpurchase service (PPS) helps customers pay for, transport, receive, install, use, return and exchange, repair, service, and dispose of products.[49] PPS addresses problems and complaints and includes remanufacturing, spare parts availability, technical service, toll-free service telephone numbers, training, and warranties. The firm may provide some PPS (for some customers) at no charge, but with astute segmentation and pricing, PPS can be very profitable.[50] PPS can also act as an early-warning system for detecting quality problems; hence, PPS raises repurchase rates, enhances cross-selling, and increases customer retention. By tracking buyers after purchase, customer-service leader Pulte Homes doubled repeat and referral business.

KEY IDEA

In relationship to purchase, the firm may offer customer service:

• Before
• During
• After

The GE Answer Service handles over four million calls annually for GE's entire product range — from dishwashers to jet engines. Bloomberg provides extensive training on using its terminals — experienced users find it very difficult to switch.[51] Caterpillar has built a profitable business disassembling and rebuilding used customer engines — Caterpillar also sells rebuilt engines at a discount in the aftermarket.

DELIVERING EXCEPTIONAL CUSTOMER SERVICE[52]

The firm has several levers for delivering outstanding customer service:

KEY IDEA

Customers requiring *similar* products/services may have *different* customer-service needs, and vice versa.

TOP MANAGEMENT SUPPORT AND INVOLVEMENT. Top managers should overcommunicate that serving customers well is crucial — they should build a culture where all employees emphasize customer service. It's one thing to *talk the talk*, but top managers should also *walk the walk* by *getting their hands dirty* interacting with customers. In B2C firms, they might spend a day or so a month in customer service, like senior Toyota executives when introducing the Lexus. They should identify and reward customer-service *heroes* and publicly acknowledge their successes. In B2B firms, top managers should support strategic account managers by serving as *Executive Sponsors* for strategic customers — Chapter 18. CEO Larry Ellison is Oracle's executive sponsor for GE.

Nordstrom is well known for exemplary customer service. Nordstrom accepts returned merchandise, no questions asked; employees perform above reasonable expectations to serve customers. Top managers and the reward system foster this culture — Chapter 23. Quik Trip (QT) convenience store chain (700 stores, 11 U.S. states) trains employees to acknowledge customer presence, no matter how busy they are.[53]

ExxonMobil works hard on customer service. "An elderly woman was parked in the lot next to one of our stations. She had no family in the area, had locked her keys in her car, and didn't know what to do. The store manager had her come in, gave her a cup of coffee, flipped through the yellow pages to find a locksmith, and just paid the guy off on the side because the woman didn't look like she was very well-to-do."[54]

CUSTOMER-SERVICE STRATEGY. In developing its market strategy, the firm identifies customer *product/service-based needs*, then develops a value proposition to satisfy those needs — Chapter 9. In formulating a *customer-service strategy*, the firm focuses on customer *needs for customer service*. Customers with similar product/service-based needs may have very different customer-service needs, and vice versa.[55] Wells Fargo did not understand this basic issue:

San Francisco-based Wells Fargo (WF) acquired First Interstate Bancorp (FIB) in a hostile takeover. FIB offered traditional handholding and personal service. WF focused on lowering customer transaction costs, closing branches, and firing employees. Customer service degraded — competitors took advantage. One handed out business cards to customers queuing at former FIB branches. Another advertised for former FIB customers to call 1-800-FED-UP. They heard: "We have just bought your old bank. For a summary of the ways we will be jerking you around, press one. For a list of employees you like who have been fired, press two." Customers outside California defected at 1 percent per month.

Standard marketing research techniques provide insight about customer-service needs. At retail, mystery shopping programs examine customer experiences with the firm and competitors. Generally, the firm should strive to surpass competitor service levels. Setting customer expectations slightly below the firm's ability to deliver leads to positive expectations disconfirmations. Because it can be expensive to provide, some firms offer customer service at varying levels. All customers receive a basic customer-service backbone; additional service depends on customer importance.[56]

HUMAN RESOURCE MANAGEMENT (HRM). Human resource (HR) planning — especially for onstage personnel — is integral to superior customer service.[57] Many *front-line* positions, particularly in retail and hospitality, are low skill and low pay. The firm should develop good HR policies that may include improving work conditions to enhance employee attitudes, and apply them rigorously. Said AmEx CEO Ken Chenault, "Great service starts with the people who deliver it."[58][519v] Relatedly, Starbucks funds employee (work 20 hours per week) tuition costs for online degree education at Arizona State University.

When the firm is under cost pressure, indiscriminately cutting customer-service personnel reduces service quality; a better approach is cross-training employees for multiple tasks.[59] Traditional recruiting, selecting, training and development, appraisal, recognition, reward, and retention tools are important to ensure good employee/firm fit. The firm may recruit well-trained customer-service personnel (low training costs); or the firm may prefer to hire candidates that meet recruitment criteria, but need extensive training. In Hong Kong, major hairdressing salons Le Salon Orient and Rever operate their own schools, carefully selecting the most promising graduates for their salons.

> Australian chemical firm Orica has a stellar reputation for high-quality telephone-based B2B customer service. Orica uses HRM tools imaginatively. Customer-service reps rarely meet customers face-to-face, but they work hard to develop personal relationships. Each Christmas they send greeting cards, photos attached, and a personal note.

High personnel costs lead many firms to outsource customer-service call centers to India, Kenya, Malaysia, and the Philippines. Although well-educated and English-speaking, candidates typically require training in products/services and speaking with a U.S. accent. Costs often drive outsourcing decisions, but the firm must balance cost reductions with cultural fit and service quality.[60]

Customer-service needs frame the knowledge, skills, and abilities (KSAs) customer-service personnel require. KSAs vary by specific customer service, but a general list includes competence, courtesy, credibility, responsiveness, and commitment. Of course, required competence varies widely: Compare the average Service-Master employee with the GE Answer Service employee who advises on maintaining jet engines.

> $6 billion Service-Master's (SM) 50,000-person workforce specializes in low-skill, low-pay services that few people like doing — shampooing carpets, spraying pesticides, and stripping hotel beds. SM's training program ranges from enhancing *social graces* to remedial reading. Annual turnover is 30 percent versus 40 percent at competitors.
>
> ExxonMobil (EM) trains gas station personnel at company-owned and franchised dealerships. EM's area personnel make frequent visits to ensure gas stations operate to company standards and deliver good customer service.

The firm must ensure that customer-service personnel do their jobs effectively and consistently — a single poorly executed interaction may lose a customer. Significant investment in ongoing coaching and best-practice sharing enhances organizational performance.[61] And individual performance feedback tied to creative and well-designed reward programs can encourage employees to go the extra mile.[62]

KEY IDEA

Human resource planning for customer-service employees requires special attention to:

- Recruiting
- Selecting
- Training and development
- Appraisal
- Recognition
- Reward
- Retention

BankCo's (leading U.S. bank) Personal Service Feedback (PSF) process measures customer satisfaction for interactions with bank employees. Weekly reports allow managers to coach and counsel employees on well-performed and underperformed areas. Customer satisfaction scores increased, customer attrition decreased, and shareholder returns increased.

At Vinataxi in Ho Chi Minh City, founder Alan Ho installed a rigorous driver selection program — only 3 percent of applicants passed. Failed yet determined applicants could take a two-week driving course and retake the test. All Vinataxi drivers take a personal grooming course. On-duty drivers wear Vinataxi-provided uniforms — white T-shirt, yellow cap with Vinataxi logo, dark trousers, and shoes.[63] Ho placed drivers in teams — high-revenue teams earn bonuses. In Ho's motivational system, each driver is awarded 20 points — Vinataxi awards and subtracts points for on-the-job behavior. *Good deeds* like returning passengers' wallets or personal belongings, and for customer testimonials to excellent service, earn extra points. Ho deducts points for customer complaints and damage that results from driver carelessness. When a driver's score falls below 10 points, he is fired; high point levels earn drivers bonuses.[64]

Madrid's TelPizza (TP) had 185 stores and 40 percent market share (double Pizza Hut's) five years after launch. TP focused on managing and rewarding 4,000-plus delivery men. Each *ambassador* has a small geographic area, so he can get to know customers. Ambassadors spend up to 20 percent of time on presales customer service — handing out coupons and menus. TP rewards ambassadors when territory revenues increase.

SERVICE INFRASTRUCTURE. The firm must design the appropriate infrastructure, including technology and human resources, to support the customer-service strategy. Some customer services, like repairs, depend heavily on people; others, like web-based reservation systems, depend on technology. Paradoxically, many highly people-intensive service systems, like airline passenger and baggage check-in, require the most sophisticated technology investments.

KEY IDEA

Critical elements in delivering exceptional customer service are:
• Top management support and involvement
• Customer-service strategy
• Human resource management
• Service infrastructure
• Measuring customer-service quality

France's Supervox (SV) distributes electrical, gardening, and sanitary products to 10,000 mom-and-pop stores in Europe. SV enhanced customer-service infrastructure by purchasing cheap PCs — *too primitive for schools*. SV placed PCs at customer locations, complete with web browsers and basic software. Retailers access SV's catalog on the web and place orders. SV confirms orders by fax or e-mail, and cut order-fill time by more than 20 percent.

Customer interfaces are crucial. Most customers want simple interfaces and a single customer-service representative; customers dislike being passed around. Many firms generate customer dissatisfaction by creating specialists (for cost reasons) and making one-stop calls impossible. Other firms outsource customer service to third-party providers, but create serious problems. The author purchased an HDTV and related accessories from Best Buy. The store experience was excellent and an automated phone call provided installation information. But then the customer-service experience fell apart: a half-hour spent on the telephone waiting to speak to a human — a third-party installer. And of course, we're sharing the experience with *you*.

Many firms use web-based technological solutions to reduce personnel costs. Well-designed systems — like some airline and hotel reservations — guide customers seamlessly; they improve customer service, provide intimacy and connectivity to the firm, *and* reduce costs. Poorly designed systems can be intensely annoying and highly dissatisfying. Automated telephone systems are some of the worst offenders. How often have you been transferred to out-of-service extensions, trapped in voice-mail hell, or tormented by inadequate voice recognition systems? Consider the message from a $5 billion New Jersey-based firm one weekday at 4:35 p.m. "This is the World Headquarters of XYZ Company. Our switchboard is open from 9:30 a.m. to 4:30 p.m. Eastern Standard Time. In an emergency, please contact security at [telephone number]." This approach contrasts sharply with Fidelity Investments' 24/7/365 service to buy, sell, and transfer mutual funds.

KEY IDEA

Customer-service infrastructure combines technological and human resources necessary to deliver high-level customer service.

Reporting relationships and customer-service interfaces with other firm functions are important infrastructure issues. At global delivery firm TNT, a driver running behind schedule called the control center, which called customer service, which called the customer. By this time, the driver had made the delivery; the call annoyed the customer and embarrassed the driver. TNT solved the problem by allowing drivers to call customers directly. Xerox customers interfaced with sales, service, and business operations. Commissioned salespeople strove to place machines, but were difficult to find when customers required information or wanted to switch to better-suited products. (Salespeople were seeking more commission opportunities.) Customer service had to clean up many problems created by the sales force. Xerox eventually teamed up sales, service, and business operations to share responsibility in sales districts and regions. Districts were responsible for resolving customer problems, exploiting business opportunities, and advertising locally. Xerox harmonized reward systems.[65]

MEASURING CUSTOMER-SERVICE QUALITY. *If you can't measure it, you can't manage it.* Customer satisfaction is a good measure of service quality, but across-the-board quality improvements have made it less useful. Customer defection rate is better.[66] Identifying defectors is easy when customers must terminate a formal relationship like banking, insurance, and telephone service, but difficult when individual customer records do not exist. Regardless, the firm should be careful not to rely exclusively on easy-to-collect hard/quantitative measures, while ignoring difficult-to-collect soft/qualitative measures that capture customer perceptions.

Analyzing causes of defection provides valuable information for improving service delivery. The firm should identify and regularly measure critical customer-service elements against performance standards. Differences between standards and actual performance should form the basis for modifying customer service. The firm should also design employee-reward programs based on performance against standards.

KEY IDEA

Customer defection rate is a more valuable performance measure than customer satisfaction. The firm should identify and measure critical elements driving customer satisfaction.

Amazon periodically measures customer satisfaction by randomly sampling customers contacting the customer-service department. Performance measures include total contacts, cost per contact, and response time by e-mail and telephone. Amazon measures representative performance by customer contacts per day and average turnaround time per contact. Amazon also captures all interaction details about unhappy customers.

AmEx believes *length of time to answer the phone* is an important customer-service measure. AmEx monitors this measure assiduously. Waiting time is prominently and continuously displayed for all customer-service operators. Supervisors monitor employee behavior by listening to customer-employee conversations. Other measures focus on time to replace lost cards and speed in customers receiving bills.

Xerox's *sense-and-respond* Sentinel Satisfaction Assurance System regularly e-mails 130,000 registered customer contacts at 300 major customers, in 12 countries (multiple languages). Customers may reply with a comment, suggestion, or problem. Sentinel enables Xerox to detect, appropriately route, and visibly track all unresolved reported problems.[67]

MARKETING QUESTION

What other messages did you glean from this chapter?

KEY MESSAGES

- Sometimes the firm's core offering is a service — sometimes a physical product.
- Customer service complements either a core product or a core service.
- Some products are transitioning to services as customers purchase the benefits/values physical products deliver, rather than purchase products.
- Several characteristics distinguish services — core services and customer service — from physical products. Each has important marketing implications:
  - Intangibility
  - Variability
  - Divisibility
  - Role of customers
  - Inseparability
  - Perishability
  - Lack of acquisition

- SERVQUAL is an important diagnostic tool for understanding and improving services.
- High service quality generally leads to greater customer satisfaction, but greater competition and increased quality are weakening the customer satisfaction/loyalty relationship.
- The firm can deliver customer service pre-, during, and post-purchase.
- Well-designed and well-delivered customer service allow the firm to reap significant benefits from repurchase and positive word of mouth.

VIDEOS AND AUDIOS

For complimentary material, see Axcess Capon codes at www.axcessvids.com

Customer Service   **463v** 🖨   Joseph Michelli

QUESTIONS FOR STUDY AND DISCUSSION

Can you answer the questions implied by this chapter's learning outcomes? Check!

1. Use the SERVQUAL scale to assess service quality for some aspect of your school, college, or univeristy — like the admission process or a finance class. How does your institution rate on tangibles, reliability, responsiveness, assurance, empathy?

2. The human interface is critical for many service firms. Sometimes customer loyalty to employees is greater than loyalty to the firm. How would you minimize customer defections to departing employees?

3. A midsize U.S. city wants to address rush-hour problems. Streets are clogged with traffic and public transportation — bus, rail, subway — is heavily overcrowded. What actions would you suggest the city consider?

4. Select a local restaurant or bar. How could this business improve customer service and enhance customer loyalty? What advice would you give the proprietor?

5. Many airlines are roundly criticized for poor customer service. Chart out your interactions with the airline on your most recent trip — from the time you decided to take the flight until you exited your destination airport. Identify the various touch-points. At each touch-point where service was poor, develop a system to improve customer service.

6. Select a product/service that you purchased recently, or *Managing Marketing in the 21st Century*. What types of customer service surrounded the product/service? How do you assess customer-service quality? How would you improve customer service — pre-, during, and post-purchase?

TRUE/FALSE QUESTIONS
Answers on page A2 and at www.axcessvids.com — 764p

1. A service is any act or performance that one party can offer another that is essentially intangible and does not result in the ownership of anything. ❏ **TRUE** ❏ **FALSE**

2. The variability concept in services marketing is tightly linked to inseparability and the inability to inventory services. ❏ **TRUE** ❏ **FALSE**

3. The SERVQUAL model relates customers satisfaction to service quality via expectations disconfirmation. ❏ **TRUE** ❏ **FALSE**

4. Most marketing activity occurs postpurchase and most customer service occurs before and during purchase. ❏ **TRUE** ❏ **FALSE**

MULTIPLE CHOICE QUESTIONS

Answers on page A2 and at www.axcessvids.com — 989p

1. Which of the following is NOT a factor related to the delivery at a service facility?

    a. exterior
    b. interior
    c. offstage
    d. indivisible

2. Service guarantees are most appropriate for each of the following EXCEPT when:

    a. the service price is low.
    b. the customer's ego is involved.
    c. sales are strongly affected by word of mouth.
    d. there are high negative consequences of service failure.

3. Which of the following does NOT represent one of the key variables influencing perceived service quality?

    a. responsiveness
    b. reliability
    c. variability
    d. assurance

4. During which of the following phases of the purchase process should the firm assist customers by helping them identify needs and by providing promotional information about products and purchase locations?

    a. prepurchase
    b. during purchase
    c. postpurchase
    d. cross-purchase

IMPERATIVE 4

Design the Market Offer

PART A – PROVIDING CUSTOMER VALUE

CHAPTER 14

DEVELOPING NEW PRODUCTS

For complimentary material, see Axcess Capon codes at www.axcessvids.com

The best way to predict the future is to invent it.

— Alan Kay, Xerox PARC scientist, 1971

LEARNING OUTCOMES

When you have completed this chapter, you will be able to:

- Distinguish among different types of innovation for developing and marketing new products.
- Identify critical success factors for consistent innovation.
- Understand and explain the relationship between marketing and innovation.
- Contrast the different ways firms approach the innovation challenge.
- Explain how innovative firms develop successful new products.
- Understand the marketing significance of being an innovative firm.
- Implement the stage-gate, new-product-development process.
- Understand factors driving successful new product adoption.
- Classify product adopters into various categories by speed of adoption.

OPENING CASE: THOMSON FINANCIAL — BOARDLINK

Thomson Financial (TF) provides information and decision tools for the financial market. TF successfully launched BoardLink, a product that facilitates information flow between firms and their boards of directors.[1] BoardLink's launch was consistent with TF's focus on informing and building front-end customer strategy throughout the organization. The Corporate Communications Broadcast Network Inc. (CCBN), a Boston-based provider of web-based corporate and investment solutions with 3,000 customers, generated the idea that became BoardLink. TF acquired CCBN, formed Thomson Corporate Executive Services, and supported BoardLink's continued development and launch.

Prior to the Thomson acquisition, Greg Radner, CCBN's marketing head, was responsible for identifying CCBN's next generation products. Radner leveraged CCBN's traditional customer touchpoints like sales and service calls to understand the challenges clients were facing. These informal customer discussions, many with corporate secretaries, identified a common pain point — providing board members with information they needed for board meetings in a timely manner.

With this customer need in mind, Radner and CCBN's sales and support teams conducted in-depth informal customer discussions. They sought a deeper understanding of the difficulties firms faced in executing timely and effective board communications. They generated solution ideas and tested them with potential customers. Radner believed anecdotal findings from informal customer discussions typically had limited value — they often raised more questions than they answered. Radner's new-product-development team took detailed notes of every customer conversation and shared these data with every team member. This circulation process demonstrated a broad consensus among customers about the problem — it also increased team member convictions about the new product ideas they were developing.

Radner asserted the core underpinning of his new-product-development effort was securing a deep understanding of customer needs. "Because this was a new space for us, we couldn't make the assumption that we knew what our customers wanted," he said. Radner's group found many corporate secretaries were frustrated with preparing information for board meetings, sometimes held monthly. To produce a board book was a time-consuming process involving multiple revisions, often with last-minute changes. Board books had to be professional-looking, but corporate secretaries also had to ensure that board members received them in adequate time for preparation. Said Radner, "We knew from anecdotal evidence that there was significant pain; our question was, 'Can we alleviate that pain?' Because of our strong customer focus, we let the client drive product development, its features and functionalities, rather than letting our idea of the product guide decision-making."

Business school graduate Jeron Paul joined Radner and CCBN's clients in developing the concept. Paul leveraged his personal contacts, CCBN clients, and attendees at corporate secretary conferences. Concept development quickly morphed into concept validation as potential customers became excited at the prospect of solving a significant problem. By this time, CCBN had joined Thomson — BoardLink also generated significant internal excitement because of the potential for organic growth. Senior TF management gave BoardLink the green light, allowing Radner to leverage Thomson resources to execute the product concept and move into development.

Radner quickly built a 15-person product-development team spanning technology, sales, quality assurance, and product developers in the U.S. and Bangalore, India. Radner and Paul also worked with market research professionals from Client Insight LLC (CI), a market research firm specializing in financial markets. CI implemented a three-phase marketing research plan that included: (1) a real-time concept test with a small sample of board members in several industries, (2) a more quantitative, concept test with a large sample of potential customers; and, once the prototype was developed, (3) a usability study to understand potential users' ability to execute common tasks. Throughout development, Radner ensured that each team member heard every potential customer voice as they gave feedback and interacted with the evolving prototype. Hence, internal pushback to design and user interface changes was minimal. Because the prototype continually reflected feedback from potential users, TF minimized time to launch and optimized development time spent with hard-to-reach board members.

CI made three particularly important findings in developing and launching BoardLink: (1) the sales cycle is long and complex, (2) the original price point was too high, and (3) the product had to be very easy to use. TF successfully launched BoardLink with significant efforts by its small sales force and advertisements in Corporate Secretary *magazine and on the corporate secretary organization website. Within a few months, BoardLink was the solution of choice for board members in 12 organizations. Between 75 percent and 85 percent of the 100-plus board members who signed up to access BoardLink were regular users.*

Radner said BoardLink's success was due to two key factors: First, the strong focus on product usability throughout the development process ensured that customers could easily make BoardLink part of their workflow. "This was especially important because board members have a wide disparity in abilities and willingness to try the product. Indeed, some board members don't have access to a PC. Regardless, we could market our product as Director-tested; *by working with customer organizations and their board members, we can drive and track usage of BoardLink." Second, Thomson launched BoardLink at an acceptable price.*

Case Question

How do you assess Greg Radner's process for developing BoardLink?

In 2015, BoardLink was a customizable portal that supports sophisticated corporate governance. Personalized tools deliver relevant information aligned to individual needs, like secure messaging, surveys, and voting. BoardLink has 1,500 customers. In October 2015, Thomson-Reuters sold Boardlink to Diligent Corporation.

Chapter 14 is the third of three chapters in Part A of Imperative 4 — *Design the Market Offer.* Part A focuses on *Providing Customer Value.* Chapter 14 addresses *Developing New Products.*

New products are crucial for delivering customer value, earning profits, and enhancing shareholder wealth. As globalization pressures drive increasing competition, innovation success is ever more important. Whether developed internally, acquired, or generated from a strategic alliance, successful new products beat competitors and drive growth. Winning firms in the 21st century will have much greater expertise than competitors in *innovation,* developing and launching new products, and providing customers with new and improved product choices. Today, many firms are dissecting and improving internal systems and processes and culture to increase innovation capabilities, and sharpening external searches for new products. New technologies and development processes improve new product success rates and help firms reduce time to market. Both business and academia now pay great attention to managing innovation and developing new products as a critical way to achieve differential advantage.[2] Notwithstanding the critical role of innovation in securing new products, many firms are successful by *copying.* These firms identify successful new product introductions, then introduce their own versions in the same and/or different markets.

KEY IDEA

Successful new products enhance shareholder value.

THE CHANGING VIEW

OLD WAY	NEW WAY
Bureaucratic and slow	Entrepreneurial and fast
Financial criteria only	Market and financial criteria
Functional orientation	Cross-functional teams
Ideas generated internally	Ideas encouraged from many sources; copying prevalent
Innovation seen as risky	Managing innovation and risk are critical to success
Innovation strategy unfocused	Innovation strategy clearly focused
Innovation viewed as secondary importance	Innovation seen as primary importance
Not-invented-here syndrome	Best-in-class benchmarking
Poor risk assessment	Risk profiles assessed
Poor support tools	Advanced support tools — quality function deployment (QFD), computer-aided design (CAD), rapid prototyping processes (RPS)
Sequential processing	Parallel processing

WHERE AND HOW INNOVATION OCCURS

If we are to achieve results never before accomplished, we must employ methods never before attempted.

— Sir Francis Bacon, English author, philosopher, scientist, and statesman (1561–1626)

The late Peter Drucker asserted that marketing was one of two basic firm functions, but:

... Marketing alone does not make a business enterprise. The second function of a business, therefore, is innovation. In the organization of the business enterprise, innovation can no more be considered a separate function than marketing. It is not confined to engineering or research, but extends across all parts of the business. Innovation can be defined as the task of endowing human and material resources with new and greater wealth-producing capacity.[3]

> In 2015, *Fast Company's* top-20 leading innovators were Warby Parker, Apple, Alibaba, Google, Instagram, Color of Change, HBO, Virgin America, IndiGo, Slack, Houzz, Catapult, Inventure, Line, WeWork, Gilead Sciences, Tesla, Toyota, Cree, Stripe. **[438v]**

Chapter 14 focuses on product innovation and its impact on developing, launching, and managing new products. In general, successful innovation provides better, cheaper, and/or faster benefits/values to customers.

Some innovation requires significant R&D effort by highly trained scientists in expensive facilities for long time periods. But much innovation consists of bringing together, in a different way, ideas that are already known.[4] Consider the perspectives of several leaders:

Drucker: "[The best opportunities] are visible, but not seen."

Thomas Edison: "Genius is one percent inspiration and 99 percent perspiration."[5]

Steve Jobs: "Creativity is just connecting things. When you ask creative people how they did something,they feel a little guilty because they didn't really do it, they just saw something. It seemed obvious to them after a while. That's because they were able to connect experiences they've had and synthesize new things."[6]

Two good examples are Microsoft and Apple:

> At a Harvard Square (Cambridge, MA) newsstand, Bill Gates and Paul Allen saw the cover of *Popular Electronics* showing the Altair, a new $400 desktop computer. They related the Altair and its Intel 8080 chip with their experience programming a PDP-8 minicomputer (DEC) in BASIC. Gates and Allen secured the Altair software contract; later they won contracts for IBM and other PCs. Microsoft has dominated the PC operating system market ever since.

> Steve Jobs visited Xerox's Palo Alto Research Center (PARC); he saw a graphical user interface (GUI) with a *mouse* on a refrigerator-size computer. Jobs realized he could use GUI on a PC — Macintosh.

Chapter 3 introduces the ideas of *sustaining* and *disruptive* technologies. *Sustaining* technologies spawn innovations that improve established products on performance dimensions valued by major customers. Innovations driven by *disruptive* technologies offer new and very different value propositions. Initially, these innovations may underperform existing products or processes, but a few *explorer* customers recognize value. Later, as cost-benefit ratios improve, disruptive technologies surpass the old technology and broaden their appeal.[7] Researchers believe leading firms often miss disruptive innovations because they are committed to an existing way of doing business via *cultural lock-in.*[8] Some observers believe that, for several years,

MARKETING QUESTION

Select two modern-day successful entrepreneurs. Use the Internet and your analytic skills to assess why each has been successful.

KEY IDEA

Innovation embraces new products, but also new processes and technologies.

KEY IDEA

Sustaining innovations improve products and processes on existing performance dimensions.

Disruptive innovations offer new and very different value propositions.

Leading firms often invest in *sustaining* versus *disruptive* innovations.

KEY IDEA

The firm should serve current, especially loyal, customers — the firm must also *create* new customers.

Microsoft was so focused on upgrading the Windows operating system — sustaining technology — that it failed to identify disruptive technologies. One well-respected researcher asserts:

> *[G]ood management was the most powerful reason they [leading firms] failed to stay atop their industries. Precisely because these firms listened to their customers, invested aggressively in new technologies [to] provide their customers more and better products of the sort they wanted, and because they carefully studied market trends and systematically allocated investment capital to innovations that promised the best returns, they lost their positions of leadership.[9]*

Is this heresy? Not at all! Listening to customers can actually lead to failure? Yes! Firms typically design marketing efforts to satisfy existing customer needs. Yet, in a world where change is constant, marketing must also *create* customers, especially for really new products where currently there are only *prospective* customers. Serving existing customers is an important objective, but creating new customers is essential. Many firms focus on existing customers by investing in sustaining innovations, but they ignore disruptive innovations where entrenched interests may place roadblocks.[10] Because sustaining and disruptive innovations are so different, when firms pursue both, they should do so in separate organizational units.[11] Relatedly, firms that focus too heavily on operational excellence may have difficulty with their innovation programs. As Sam Walton (Walmart founder) said, "Incrementalism is innovation's worst enemy! We don't want continuous improvement. We want radical change."[12]

WHAT FOSTERS PRODUCT INNOVATION

MARKETING QUESTION

Your CEO has asked why General Mills and P&G are successful innovators. What will you tell her? Use your competitive insight skills.

> Dalsey, Hilbloom, and Lynn learned that ships anchored outside Hawaii harbor were waiting for bills of lading to clear U.S. Customs. They formed document courier DHL; DHL delivered shipping documents before ships arrived, and other time-sensitive material. DHL is now a major global package delivery and logistics firm (owned by Deutsche Post) (Chapter 25 Opening Case).

Firms vary widely in their abilities to develop innovative new products. A Columbia Business School study classified less than one third of a *Fortune* 500 sample as *product innovators*, but these firms earned the best returns on capital. Three factors were most important for success:

- **Market selection** — high-growth markets to stimulate innovation
- **Organization** — formal structures to foster R&D efforts; supportive cultures
- **R&D** — significant and consistent R&D spending, especially applied versus fundamental

Supportive factors are in Table 14.1[13,14]:

TABLE 14.1
Factors That Encourage Innovation

Appropriate personnel	Idea generators, coaches, mentors, sponsors
	Boundary spanners for internal/external boundaries
	Product champions/internal entrepreneurs
Right type of support	Top management commitment
	Selective top management involvement
Well-designed system	Multiple new-product-development efforts
	Continuous project evaluation
	High importance to cross-functional communications
	Measurement system rewards creativity and innovation

KEY IDEA

Critical factors for successful new product development are:

- Market selection
- Organization
- R&D

Supportive factors are:

- Appropriate personnel
- Right type of support
- Well-designed system

Funding and business objectives are always critical innovation issues. Some firms worry that business units focus too narrowly on short-term profits; hence investments to create *disruptive* innovations and/or new businesses are insufficient. P&G's Corporate Innovation Fund and HP Inc.'s Innovation Program Office are alternative devices for funding innovation teams. Team members from different businesses search widely for technologies to focus on specific opportunities. Innovation occurs in structures like DuPont Ventures or P&G's Future Works. Increasingly, major firms seek innovation both inside and outside corporate structures. Over 50 percent of P&G's initiatives involve at least one external partner.

Google's Innovation Principles [323p]

1. Innovation comes from anywhere
2. Focus on the user
3. Aim to be ten times better
4. Bet on technical insights
5. Ship and iterate

6. Give employees 20 percent time
7. Default to open processes (to secure improvements)
8. Fail well (without shame)
9. Have a mission that matters

MARKETING QUESTION

How do you assess the potential for *footgolf* — using feet, soccer ball, 21-inch holes?

NEW PRODUCT DEVELOPMENT

Approaches to innovation and new product development are deeply embedded in firm cultures. If innovation performance is unsatisfactory, the firm's culture may have to change:

> Whirlpool had limited competitive advantages and faced declining appliance prices. Whirlpool evolved the culture by trial and error. First, consultants trained select employee groups in innovation techniques, but most new product ideas were useless and unrelated to Whirlpool's business. Second, top managers urged all Whirlpool's 60,000 employees to innovate. Ideas poured in, but had poor fit with Whirlpool's business. Then Whirlpool added discipline: Ideas had to enhance Whirlpool products and brands, and go through a formal evaluation and funding process. Promising ideas were thoroughly vetted; businesses had annual revenue and pipeline targets. Whirlpool's culture changed, and innovation revenues quadrupled annually.[15]

New product success is critical for the many firms that introduce thousands of new products annually.[16] These firms often set aggressive product-development targets — like 30 percent annual revenues from products launched in the previous four years. HP earned over 50 percent revenues from products introduced in the previous two years; Reckitt Benckiser earns 35–40 percent revenues from products launched in the previous three years. There are many approaches:

- *Benchmarking.* Identify global best practice in new product development, then make appropriate changes.
- Reengineer existing systems and processes.
- Encourage broad employee experimentation by allowing unapproved *skunkworks* projects.

> Google encourages employees to spend up to 20 percent of work time on their own ideas.[17]
> W.L. Gore (Gore-Tex) nurtures many small projects, often started by employees who convince peers their ideas have merit.

MARKETING QUESTION

Have you participated in a Massively Open Online Course (MOOC)? Are MOOCs a valuable educational innovation? Why or why not? How do you assess Capon's Marketing Video Book?[264v]

MARKETING ENRICHMENT 6.1
Analyzing Quantitative Research Data **710p**

- Adopt new technologies for development processes — *computer-aided design/computer-aided manufacturing* (CAD/CAM); *rapid prototyping systems* (RPS); cross-functional teamwork; *quality function deployment* (QFD); and conjoint analysis — Chapter 6 Marketing Enrichment 6.1 **[710p, pp. 3–7]**.[18] Conferences, executive training, job-changing employees, trade associations, and trade publications all help diffuse new methodologies. Social media strategies involving forums like LinkedIn, Twitter, and Vine encourage community members to inject innovation ideas.

By appropriate actions, the firm may improve innovation processes, but standards of excellence have risen and sustaining differential advantage is difficult.[19] One widespread problem is that product developers are sometimes indifferent to the potential marketability of their discoveries.

The New York Times reviewed the new Chevy Silverado Hybrid pickup. The Hybrid delivered significantly better fuel economy than the equivalent gas-only model but had a much higher price and towed two tons less. When asked who would buy the product, John Turzewski, lead development engineer, said, "That is a good question."[20]

KEY IDEA

Product-development trade-offs include:
- Time
- Risk
- Financial return

The firm can address this issue by using market-oriented criteria in the development process. At BASF, scientists write marketing plans for products they expect to develop. At GE, scientists regularly meet with marketing and business-unit executives to ensure their projects are linked to the businesses. At Philips, research is no longer funded solely at the corporate level; product divisions pay two thirds of budgets for research projects.

Traditionally, BMS researchers secured FDA approval for pharmaceuticals, then turned them over to brand teams to develop market strategies. Today, marketers work with researchers early in the drug development process and lend expertise to development decisions.

KEY IDEA

Four new product development approaches are:
- Basic technology research
- Applied technology research
- Market-focused development
- Market tinkering

Four approaches to new product development, each with its own financial return, risk, and time characteristics, are:

- **Basic technology research.** Typically aimed at disruptive innovations rather than immediate new products. Examples: DNA mapping, finding new chemical entities for pharmaceuticals, advanced analytics, and electrical superconductivity.
- **Applied technology research.** Uses basic technology to develop new products. Examples: pharmaceutical research adapting new chemical entities to treat specific medical conditions; electrical superconductivity researchers seeking easy-to-make and easy-to-use materials.
- **Market-focused development.** Focuses on marketable products, often by improving ease of use or developing complementary products. Example: pharmaceutical firms developing new delivery methods like pills and patches to replace injections. Electrical superconductivity has not progressed this far.
- **Market tinkering.** Makes minor modifications to current products. Examples: new dessert flavors or different scents for a floor cleaner.[21]

MARKETING QUESTION

Using the four approaches to new product development, how would you classify Airbnb, Apple's iPod, Coke Zero, Lyft, Spotify, *The Apprentice*, *The Apprentice: Martha Stewart*, Uber? Why?

Basic technology research generally takes a long time, can generate profitable new products for many applications, but is risky. Indeed, risk-taking is a given in new product development. When a Google vice president made a several-million-dollar error, cofounder Larry Page said, "I'm so glad you made this mistake, because I want to run a company where we are moving too quickly and doing too much, not being too cautious and doing too little. If we don't have any of these mistakes, we're just not taking enough risk."[22] But note also comments by Talleyrand and George Santayana, respectively: "Any man may make a mistake once, but only a fool makes the same mistake twice," and "Those who cannot remember the past are doomed to repeat it."

By contrast, *market tinkering* is relatively quick, much less risky, but generally less profitable. Regardless, speeding the process and reducing risk typically improve financial returns for all approaches. From the firm's perspective, these four approaches lead to five new product types

— *new-to-the-world products*, *new product lines*, *additions to existing product lines*, *improvements/revisions of existing products*, and *repositioning existing products to new segments*.[23]

The way the firm incurs costs strongly influences the approach to new products. For many FMCG firms, distribution and promotion (for commercialization) may consume up to one half of product-development budgets — hence, much market tinkering and market-focused development. By contrast, many B2B products like commercial airplanes and other durable goods incur most costs in actual product development — hence, greater focus on basic and applied technology research. When approaching new product development, marketers should think carefully about several areas:

- **Problem focus.** New product development should address important customer needs. Customers trying to solve problems provide tangible evidence of real needs. Furthermore, supply-chain entities like distributors, resellers, and wholesalers may provide insightful *voice-of-the-customer* perspectives. The firm should also be aware of the costs to customers of switching from current products.

- **Market knowledge.** Market knowledge is always valuable. Sometimes innovative firms ignore market information and overestimate the value of technological novelty. Regardless, the firm should treat market data cautiously. Although customers typically provide data to be helpful, sometimes their contributions have little value — especially for *really new products*. As Henry Ford and Steve Jobs said, respectively, "If I had asked people what they wanted, they would have said faster horses!" and "A lot of times people don't know what they want until you show it to them."[24]

- **Firm competence.** A new product must be made, distributed, sold, and serviced. The firm must possess (or acquire) the appropriate competencies.[25]

- **Complementer products.** During product development, the firm should consider complementer products — Chapter 5. When initially launched, Microsoft's Vista lacked drivers for many printers, scanners, and other peripherals; hence these devices did not work.

- **Effectiveness measures.** The firm should measure the effectiveness of its new-product-development process. Three types of measure are relevant (with examples):

  - *Inputs* — R&D spending, number of projects in active development

  - *Intermediates* — percent of idea/concepts commercialized; time/cost budgets versus actuals

  - *Outputs* — revenue growth; percent of sales from new products — also Chapter 24.

  Specifically, the firm should isolate where it performs well in new product development and where it performs poorly. Intuit CEO Steve Bennett identified great idea generation but poor ability in choosing ideas to pursue. P&G CEO Art Laffley evolved a not-invented-here organization into one that actively and successfully sources ideas outside the firm.[26]

- **Stage-gate process (next section).** Successful new product development requires tough go/no-go decisions at several stages in the process. The firm requires product champions that bring enthusiasm to projects, but should beware a collective belief in ultimate success that blinds it to setbacks. The firm may need *exit champions* to stop failing projects from consuming excessive resources.[27]

The Stage-Gate Process for New Product Development

The *stage-gate process* is a systematic way of generating, then pruning, a large number of new product ideas into a small number of products the firm successfully launches.**[899v]** Figure 14.1 (p. 367) shows a *gate* after each *stage* where the firm must make a go/no-go decision.[28] At each gate, two errors are possible:

KEY IDEA

The firm should rigorously implement a stage-gate process for new product development.

KEY IDEA

In new product development, the firm must manage two error types:
• Type I
• Type II

TYPE I ERROR. Investing in a project that ultimately fails; these errors occur when the firm allows such a project to move from one stage to the next. All firms make Type I errors. Type I errors at the commercialization stage include a host of dotcom failures like Pets.com and Webvan; and business-class-only airlines like Eos, Maxjet, and Silverjet.[405v]

TYPE II ERROR. Rejecting a project that would have succeeded. These errors are difficult to isolate as, typically, the firm cannot know the results from investments that didn't happen! Sometimes we gain insight from *independent inventors*. Examples include:

- Beatles — rejected by Decca Recording Company
- Cellular telephony — not exploited by AT&T
- Personal computers — initially rejected by Atari, HP
- Telephone — rejected by Western Union
- Xerography — rejected by IBM, GE, Eastman Kodak

FIGURE 14.1
The Stage-Gate New-Product-Development Process

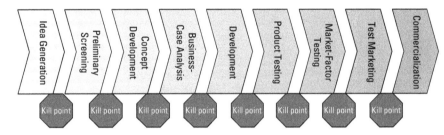

Firms that minimize Type I errors accept only the safest alternatives. Failure is low, but developing products with significant financial returns is unlikely. Firms that minimize Type II errors develop many products that fail, but some may succeed. The firm must balance these two error types in setting criteria for passing through each gate. Type I errors are ultimately highly visible and measurable. Type II errors are more difficult to identify, but are no less real!

KEY IDEA

The firm should develop clear criteria for projects to pass through each gate and advance to the next stage.

Figure 14.2 shows that resource commitments increase dramatically as a project moves from idea to new product launch. Dismissing an idea is inexpensive, but the costs of a failed launch are substantial. Each gate is a place to stop — *kill point*. The firm should clearly specify criteria for each gate; only projects that meet the criteria pass through the gate and enter the following stage — Table 14.2 (p. 368). Since each subsequent stage typically involves greater investment and risk, projects should not pass kill points lightly.[29]

FIGURE 14.2
Cost of Failure in New Product Development

KEY IDEA

In new product development, the cost of failure increases from stage to stage.

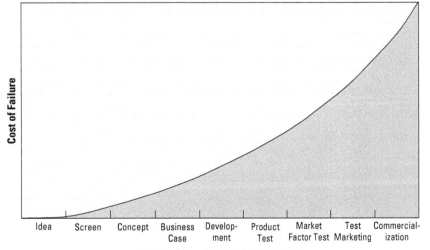

Stage in the Process	Typical Criteria
Idea generation	Provides incremental customer value; makes sense as a potential product
Preliminary screening	Technologically feasible; likely market need; fits with firm strategy
Concept development	Well-defined product concept; continues to meet previous criteria
Business-case analysis	Fits firm strategy; coherent business plan; forecasts meet market and financial goals
Development	Fulfills concept definition
Product testing	Performs as planned in business-case analysis
Market-factor testing	Customer attitudes and purchasing as anticipated in business-case analysis
Test marketing	Positive customer response; revenues, market position, and profitability as anticipated
Commercialization	Revenues, market position, and profitability as anticipated

TABLE 14.2
Types of Criteria for Moving from One Stage to Another in the Stage-Gate Process

IDEA GENERATION

"No one can resist an idea whose time has come." — Victor Hugo

The firm requires a large number of high-quality ideas to create a new-product-development portfolio that drives long-term growth. Customers are often a good source of new product ideas, but the firm should use any possible idea source — Hyatt example (below).[30] The firm should document and assess the most promising ideas. Typically, the firm quickly discards many ideas, but discarded ideas may help generate new ideas with greater promise.

> Jay Pritzker waited for a flight at Los Angeles International Airport. He noticed that Fat Eddie's coffee shop, in Hyatt Von Dehn's hotel, was unusually busy and the hotel had no vacancies. Pritzker bet that executives would want to stay in quality hotels near large airports. He wrote out a $2.2 million offer for the hotel on a napkin. In 2016, Global Hyatt Corporation owned, operated, managed, or franchised 550 hotels and resorts in 50 countries.

KEY IDEA

New-product-development stages are:

- **Idea generation**
- Preliminary screening
- Concept development
- Business-case analysis
- Development
- Product testing
- Market-factor testing
- Test marketing
- Commercialization

NUMBER OF IDEAS

Firms that generate only a few marginal-quality ideas have few new product successes. Successful firms eliminate many ideas during the development process. Hence, they must identify a large number of ideas to find the one idea that produces a successful product. In many studies, the average ratio of new product ideas to successful products is about 100:1; in agricultural chemicals the ratio is 10,000:1. Figure 14.3 shows *universal* success data for substantially new products.

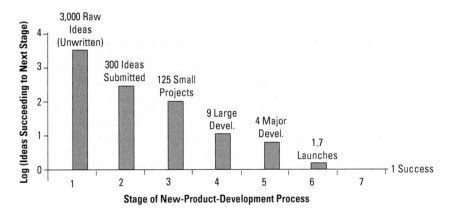

FIGURE 14.3
Universal Industrial Success Data for Substantially New Products[31]

MARKETING QUESTION

Many sports are trying new approaches — some major, some minor: Basketball — 11-minute quarters/44-minute game (versus 12/48); cricket — Twenty20 (match completed in several hours versus several days); golf — 15-inch-diameter hole (versus 4 inches); soccer — vanishing spray (to enforce ball placement and player positions in free kicks); tennis — Fast4 (minimum four games to win a set versus six); volleyball — ability to win points on every serve (versus only when serving). Select your favorite sport. What improvement ideas do you have? What are the implementation barriers?

SCOPE OF SEARCH

Focused search within the firm's mission — Chapter 7 — typically generates better ideas than unfocused search (Whirlpool boxed insert, p. 364).[32] As the firm's mission evolves, so should the scope of search.

> Most ski resorts focus resources on ski hills. But skiers and snowboarders spend only 20 percent of time on the slopes; they spend the rest in restaurants, après-ski bars, and shops. Vail Resorts (Colorado) understands; Vail manages six hotels, 72 restaurants, 40 shops, and more than 13,000 condominiums, in addition to ski slopes.

NEW IDEA SOURCES[33]

The firm should secure ideas from many sources, both inside and outside the organization. The firm must resist the *not-invented-here* syndrome that denigrates ideas from outside sources. P&G embraces a *reapplied-with-pride* approach via its successful *Connect and Develop* program. P&G deploys 70 *technology entrepreneurs* globally to participate in external networks, seek ideas, and generate innovations from outside the firm.[34] Sources include:

INTERNAL GENERATION. R&D is often a major idea source. Success rates depend on factors like budget, type of people hired, and their motivations. Kellogg's Institute for Food and Nutrition Research invests heavily in food laboratories and restaurant-quality kitchens. Researchers are diverse in education and training (from 22 countries). They are also very productive; in one month they generated 65 new product concepts and 94 new packaging ideas — more than 15 percent of revenues derive from center projects.

The sales force, customer service, and manufacturing and operations also generate new product ideas. Many firms conduct employee competitions[35]; in one competition, Cisco received 1,100 submissions from 104 countries. Some firms form employee brainstorming groups; Best Buy Studio (web design consulting for small business) resulted from putting four groups of salespeople into an apartment complex for 10 weeks. Starbucks developed 15th Ave. Coffee & Tea when CEO Howard Schultz challenged an employee group to open a store to compete with Starbucks. Urban Decay (UD) created a Pinterest contest — *Get Electric with UD* — to secure clothes and cosmetic design ideas; UD gained 50,000 Pinterest followers — winners earned tickets to the *Coachella* music festival. Some firms even offer employees seed capital to pursue their own ideas. The *GameChanger* panel at Shell's Exploration and Production division can allocate $20 million to unconventional business ideas. In three years, the process generated 300 ideas, some for entirely new businesses; most did not surface in the conventional management system.[36]

Multinational firms may take successful ideas from one country and implement them in others: Häagen-Dazs Argentina added a new flavor — *dulce de leche* — in its single Buenos Aires store. *Dulce de leche* became the store's leading seller; Häagen-Dazs rolled it out globally.

CUSTOMERS. Many innovations start with customers. Kraft used insight from customer focus groups to launch new variations of Oreo cookies; Starbucks improved the in-store experience by switching to quieter blenders, and introduced more healthy breakfast items. Sometimes firm employees spend time with customers to observe their likes, dislikes, difficulties, and *pain points* with current products and processes. Lego works with 44 Lego ambassadors from 27 countries seeking advice on new products. (Over one million people annually attend Lego conventions.) Lego also secures feedback from its social media community — *Mindstorm* — early in the development process. Cisco, GE, PepsiCo, and others conduct customer-idea competitions: Staples generated 8,300 ideas in one contest[37]; BMW prototyped several suggestions from more than 1,000 customers who used its idea tool-kit during one year.

> A longtime customer complained that L.L. Bean's traditional outerwear was useful only for weekends: "I need something to wear the rest of the time." L.L. Bean introduced *Freeport Studio*, offering affordability, low maintenance, and style.

COMPETITORS. Some firms just copy competitor products[38] — Cialis, Levitra, Staxyn, Stendra all essentially copied Viagra. Other firms identify improvement options; and still others seek opportunities via gaps in competitor product lines. Nottingham-Spirk conducts Walmart reconnaissance trips looking for product-class omissions. One such trip led to development of P&G's highly successful Crest SpinBrush.

INDEPENDENT INVENTORS. These persons can be a vital source of ideas. Inventors and outside firms now provide 35 percent of P&G's new product ideas. Table 14.3 shows some *independent inventors* and the ideas they successfully developed and marketed. Of course, independent inventors founded Airbnb, Apple, Facebook, Google, HP, Nike, Spotify, Uber, and many other well-known successful firms.

Product Innovation	Circumstances of Creative Recognition
Kitty Litter	Kaye Draper's cat sandbox froze. Neighbor Edward Lowe gave her kiln-dried, highly absorbent, granulated clay his father sold to mop up grease spills. Draper returned for more. Then Lowe marked five-pound bags as *Kitty Litter* and sold them through a local pet shop at 65 cents per bag (versus sand @ 1 cent per pound).
Velcro	Swiss engineer George de Mestral saw a connection between burrs sticking on clothing and a new way of fastening.
Zebco	Fisherman R.D. Hull knew the *backlash* problem — the spool turned faster than the fishing line. A grocery clerk pulling string from a spool to wrap meat gave him the idea for an improved fishing reel. Zebco has sold over 300 million reels based on Hull's prototype.
Matchbox Toys	Jack Odell of Lesney (small London die-casters) made a small brass road roller for his daughter — friends were envious. The following year, Lesney sold one million miniature versions of Queen Elizabeth II's coronation coach. Lesney expanded into cars, and within 10 years was making 50 million annually — 1/64th size. Mattel now makes Matchbox Toys.
Gang-Nail Plate (GNP)	John Calvin Jureit imagined the Gang-Nail plate (GNP) in church while meditating; he named it in the shower. The GNP, made of galvanized steel, is machine-pressed into two adjoining pieces of wood, typically in a roof truss. The GNP transformed home building.
Dental implants	Swedish researcher Dr. Per-Ingvar Branemark discovered, serendipitously, that titanium fused to bone. This discovery led to modern-day dental implants.
Gatorade	A University of Florida football coach asked why players didn't urinate after games. J Robert Cade developed a drink to rehydrate athletes, replenish carbohydrates, and was drinkable.
Cuisinart	At a French cookery show, Carl Sontheimer saw an ungainly but versatile machine for processing food in restaurants. This idea led to his Cuisinart invention for the home.
Nike	University of Oregon track coach Bill Bowerman developed a running-shoe outsole by pouring rubber compound into his wife's waffle iron. From this experiment, Bowerman and athlete Phil Knight formed Nike.
SuperSoaker water gun	Aerospace engineer Lonnie G. Johnson conceived the SuperSoaker water gun at home while working on a different project. When he compressed air into a separate chamber, water squirted at far greater velocities than traditional water guns.
PowerBar	World-ranked marathoner Brian Maxwell had a stomach ailment near the end of a race. Maxwell mixed low-fat, easily digestible potions in his kitchen, then worked with a biochemist and food scientist to produce PowerBar. Maxwell sold PowerBar to Nestlé for $375 million.
Nature Boy & Girl diapers	Swedish mother and lawyer Marlene Sandberg quit her job to launch environment-friendly diapers — 70 percent biodegradable (versus 20–30 percent for regular diapers). *Nature Boy & Girl* diapers distributes products to many countries.

TABLE 14.3
Examples of Ideas Turned into Products by Independent Inventors

Four Wharton graduates founded Warby Parker (WP), an online eyewear retailer. WP operates through a mail-order, home-trial program. Get together with a few classmates; can you generate some new product ideas on which to found a business?

In addition to employee and customer contests (p. 369), some firms harness the power of independent innovators to generate new product ideas. Using a sharing approach, Cisco received 1,200 distinct ideas from 2,500 innovators in 104 countries.[39]

> Netflix awarded a $1 million prize for improving its movie-recommendation system. Thousands of teams (more than 50,000 people) from 186 nations took part. Toward the contest conclusion, many teams merged in an attempt to improve performance. Netflix CEO Reed Hastings termed the contest a great success.[40]

3M is well known for its systematic approach to idea generation. 3M identifies *lead users* — individuals and organizations who think up (and may even prototype) products before producers. 3M secures these inventions, completes development, and markets the products[41]:

> 3M focused development effort on surgical drapes — thin adhesive-backed film that sticks to patient skin at the incision site prior to surgery. 3M lead users were surgeons in developing countries, specialists at leading veterinary hospitals, and Hollywood makeup artists. Lead users generated concepts for six new product lines and a radical new approach to infection control.[42]

DIFFERENT ENVIRONMENTS. Many successful business activities in one country/culture may be transferable to another country/culture. Ideas from England's textile industry led the U.S. industrial revolution. Two hundred years later, Howard Schultz secured the idea that became Starbucks while on a coffee-buying trip to Milan, Italy (Chapter 1 Opening Case). Ryanair, easyJet, and many other European and Asian discount airlines copied Southwest Airlines' business model; Britain's Asda copied Walmart. More recently, German Samwer brothers copied many successful U.S. e-commerce startups — Airbnb, eBay, eHarmony, Pinterest — and introduced them around the world, to great effect.[43]

DISRUPTIVE INNOVATIONS. Increasingly, innovative products/services disrupt existing markets — Airbnb, smartphones, Uber. Typically, disrupting products/services (and copycats) secure significant attention and revenues, but their successes often create new product ideas. Examples include: carrying cases for iPads; selfie-sticks for smartphones; automobile leasing packages for Lyft and Uber drivers; property management services for Airbnb renters.

REGULATIONS. Regulations often cause market inefficiencies that stimulate ideas to build businesses. Leased lines, satellites, and voice-over-Internet protocol (VOIP) each helped circumvent local monopolies for international telephone calls. Government regulations concerning global warming, healthy lifestyles, and product safety are good recent examples. In response to calorie-labeling required in New York City stores, Starbucks introduced smaller, lower-calorie pastries.

> Strong German shopping laws mandated store closing times: weekdays — 6 p.m., Saturdays – 2 p.m., Sundays — all day; but gas stations were exempt. BP developed an electronic shopping kiosk. Consumers enthusiastically use screens to view short videos, secure advice, and select merchandise for next-day collection/delivery.[44]

Regulatory removal can also stimulate ideas. When the U.S. Supreme Court abolished resale price maintenance (price setting by manufacturers), Alex Grass started a discount drug store that became Rite Aid — now more than 4,500 stores and $26 billion revenues.

SERENDIPITY. New product ideas sometimes arise unexpectedly. Pfizer was testing sildenafil citrate for angina when it discovered the unexpected side effect of treating erectile dysfunction. Pfizer developed Viagra, also useful for pulmonary hypertension, a rare disease mainly affecting women. (Also dental implants — Table 14.3 — for another serendipity example.)

> An Orthovita scientist left for lunch with his work on modified calcium drying in the sun. Upon return, he found a spongelike substance, riddled with microscopic holes, allowing passage of nutrients and bone-building cells. Orthovita markets *Vitoss* for helping broken bones in the spine, extremities, and pelvis to reknit faster. Twelve weeks after doctors insert *Vitoss* in a fracture, they cannot distinguish broken bone from healthy bone.

IDEA LIBRARIES. Ideas have their right time. The environment changes and ideas with no value at time A may have great value at time B. AT&T's video telephone failed, but reappeared many years later as video conferencing and Skype. Whirlpool has a library of more than 700 shelved ideas; the 2011 Ford Explorer incorporates previously discarded ideas like lightweight steel body parts, direct injection engine technology, stop-start (engine switches off at traffic lights/in traffic), and turbocharging. Firms should develop *idea libraries* and search them periodically and systematically.[45]

NEW IDEA PROCESSES

The two main approaches for generating new product ideas are[46]:

- **Structured thinking.** Uses logical methods to generate new product ideas — can be very effective for improving current products.
- **Unstructured thinking.** Comprises a family of approaches that attempt to *break the mold* and develop totally new ideas by thinking *outside the box*.

Structured Thinking for Generating New Product Ideas[47]

- *Attribute listing.* Write down all product attributes. For a ballpoint pen, these may include casing material and color, ink quality and color, point width, weight, price. Construct a table with attributes as column heads. Identify attribute variations, focusing on ways to improve.
- *Idea generator.*[48] Use innovation templates; the two stages are:
  1. List essential elements of a current product, like physical characteristics and attributes like color and expected useful life. Repeat for the product's environment, like ambient temperature and user type.
  2. Manipulate these elements to identify something new, using one or more of five innovation templates — subtraction, multiplication, division, task unification, and attribute dependency change — Table 14.4 (p. 373).

  Select one or more templates to generate virtual products and explore potential customer value. Most products will not *make the cut*, but several repeats can lead to breakthroughs.

- *Morphological analysis.* Builds on attribute listing. Combine items in each column to develop new and interesting new product ideas.

Unstructured Thinking for Generating New Product Ideas

- *Brainstorming.* Focus on a problem and seek radical solutions.[49] Brainstorming helps participants break everyday patterns and find new ways to look for solutions. Ideas should be as broad and odd as possible. Because judgment and analysis stunt idea generation, brainstorming prohibits discussion and/or evaluation until idea flow is exhausted — evaluation occurs in a second stage. Because it avoids production blocking (inability to articulate in a group setting), evaluation, and free-riding, individual brainstorming tends to produce a wider range of ideas; group brainstorming tends to be more effective because of the experience and creativity of all members. Incentives can improve idea generation. In *reverse brainstorming,* participants seek ideas on how to cause or enhance the problem, then reverse the process to solve the original problem.[50]

- *Mind mapping.* Write the problem in the center of a page and draw a circle around it. Write associations with the problem in circles elsewhere on the page and draw links to the problem. Each *association* is the focus for another linked set of associations. Seek a solution by examining local clusters of associations.

- *Provocation.* Uses a stupid untrue statement to shock participants from established patterns. A *provocation* in the ballpoint pen example might be: "Ballpoint pens cannot write."[51]

Select one of the *unstructured thinking* processes. Work with some fellow students to generate ideas to keep people cool in summer.

continues

- *Random input.* Used to regenerate brainstorming sessions. The facilitator selects a random noun from book titles, a prepared word list, or a random picture to help generate ideas. In the ballpoint pen example, random words might be cars, trees, factories, carpets.
- *Six Thinking Hats.* Each of six different-colored real or imaginary *hats* represents a different nature of thought. *Green* — creative ideas; *red* — emotions, by expressing feelings about an idea or process; *white* — analytic; *black* — pessimistic; *yellow* — optimistic; *blue* — procedural.[52] Participants think according to the hat they are *wearing*.

....
TABLE 14.4
Examples Using the Idea Generator

Innovation Template	Definition	Example	Action	Result
Subtraction	Remove components that are particularly desirable or even indispensable	Child's high chair	Remove legs	Seat that attaches to table
		DVD player	Remove control buttons	Philips (award-winning) Slimline Q-series
Multiplication	Make one or more copies of an existing component	Builders' level — vial filled with liquid and air bubble	Vials set at different angles like one or two degrees	Levels for builders laying floors with small slopes — for draining water
		Conventional Gillette razor	Add extra blades at different angles	Razor cutting action improved
Division	Divide an existing product into its component parts	Typewriter	Forming letters; printing letters	Word processor
		Musical instruments	Making notes; creating sound	Yamaha's Silent Series — piano, violin, cello, trumpet, tuba, drums — do not produce sound. Electronic sensors make sounds via headsets.
Task unification	Assign new task to an existing element	Radio reception in automobiles	Use defrosting element as radio receptor	No longer need separate radio antenna
		Separate instruction sheet for product assembly	Print instructions on packaging	Saves costly booklet, simplifies packaging, reduces chances of lost instructions
Attribute dependency change	Involves dependent relationships among product attributes and attributes of immediate environment	Eyeglasses and external lighting conditions	Eyeglass lenses that change color when exposed to sunlight	No need for two pairs of glasses
		Identical razors for men and women	Women's line of razors	Product better suited to women

MARKETING QUESTION

A standard portable oscillating fan has three speeds. Use the Innovation Templates to *subtract* something — what actions and results do you secure? Try *multiplication, division, task unification,* and *attribute dependency change.* What were the actions and results? How will you decide which ideas to pursue?

KEY IDEA

The firm should tap multiple sources for new ideas.

"The best way to get a good idea is to get *a lot* of ideas."[53]

KEY IDEA

Preliminary screening seeks a balanced portfolio of new product ideas. Screening criteria differ across idea types.

PRELIMINARY SCREENING

The goal of *preliminary screening* is to create a balanced portfolio of high-potential new product ideas. For most firms, a balanced portfolio includes ideas ranging from low return, low risk to high return, high risk. Revenue generation spans short run and long run.[54] Screening decisions for high-risk, high-return, long-time-to-revenue ideas are quite difficult. Figure 14.4 shows a portfolio balanced on return and risk. (Also New-Product-Development Portfolio, p. 382.)

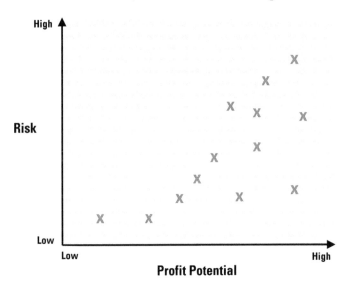

FIGURE 14.4
Risk and Return in New Product Ideas — A Balanced Portfolio

KEY IDEA

New-product-development stages are:

• Idea generation
• **Preliminary screening**
• Concept development
• Business-case analysis
• Development
• Product testing
• Market-factor testing
• Test marketing
• Commercialization

Preliminary screening typically involves securing opinions from knowledgeable marketing and/or technical personnel, customers, and even suppliers.[55] The exact mix depends on the idea. Preliminary screening is the first stage for eliminating new product ideas. Typical criteria for preliminary screening include:

• Fits with business-unit strategy
• Complements existing products
• Seems to meet customer needs

• Uses firm core competencies
• Likely to meet/exceed growth targets
• Likely to meet/exceed profitability targets

Because return and risk profiles differ markedly among ideas, the firm should use several sets of criteria. For example, criteria for ideas leading to new-to-the-world products should differ from those for additions to existing product lines. A useful way to assess new product ideas is the *spiderweb* diagram — Figure 14.5. Each 10-point-scale spoke represents a screening criterion; poor scores are near the center, good scores are near the periphery. The firm has assessed an idea on eight criteria; it scores relatively well on several criteria, but poorly on two.[56]

MARKETING QUESTION

What does Seinfeld tell us about customer service in a market where the firm has strong differential advantage in product quality?[549v]

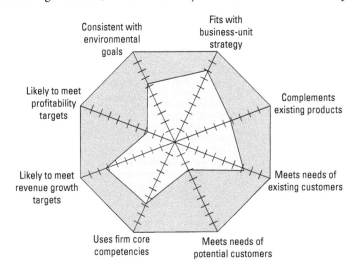

FIGURE 14.5
Assessing New Product Ideas

MARKETING QUESTION

Collect the ideas you developed for Marketing Questions in this chapter. Develop a set of screening criteria and select the most promising idea.

CONCEPT DEVELOPMENT

KEY IDEA

New-product-development
stages are:

* Idea generation
* Preliminary screening
* **Concept development**
* Business-case analysis
* Development
* Product testing
* Market-factor testing
* Test marketing
* Commercialization

The *product concept* (*concept definition*) describes the product idea. Good concepts detail deliverable customer benefits/values. FMCG firms take pains to express new product ideas as robust product concepts. The process is highly iterative. Some examples (status) include:

* Breath fresheners for dogs — successful new product
* Inexpensive four-passenger business jet — under development at Honda and GE
* Diet baby foods — not under development
* GPS locator for children — launched and doing well
* Rechargeable laptop using energy from typing on the keyboard — not under development
* SUV Smart car — under development by Smart for the U.S. market
* Self-driving car — Google prototype being tested
* Ultrasound touchless gesturing technology allows control of smartphones and tablet computers with simple touchless gestures — under development

**MARKETING
ENRICHMENT 6.1**

*Analyzing Quantitative
Research Data* **710p**

Criteria for product concept approval should be similar to preliminary screening criteria. Understanding customer needs, particularly unmet needs, is very helpful in crafting and testing product concepts. Market research tools like conjoint analysis may also be helpful — Chapter 6 Marketing Enrichment 6.1 **[710p]**:

Developing a Product Concept Using Conjoint Analysis

NBV successfully screened its idea for a narrow-band video telephone. The four critical design attributes were *accessibility, hard copy, resolution,* and *transmission time*. NBV used conjoint analysis to assess relative attribute importance to customers, and to develop a product concept. Figure 14.6 shows customer utility (y-axis) for the four design attributes. Interpretations are:

* *Accessibility* — very important: Increasing accessibility from 30 minutes to every office raises customer utility significantly — 0.42.

* *Hard copy* — quite important: Hard copy availability has reasonable customer utility — 0.27.

* *Resolution* — unimportant: Increasing from home TV to 4x home TV raises customer utility only marginally — 0.09.

* *Transmission time* — can be very important: Reduction from 30 to 20 seconds adds only 0.04. Reduction from 20 to 10 seconds adds significant utility — 0.38 (0.42 – 0.04).

FIGURE 14.6
*Results from Conjoint
Analysis Study for a
Narrow-Band Video
Telephone*

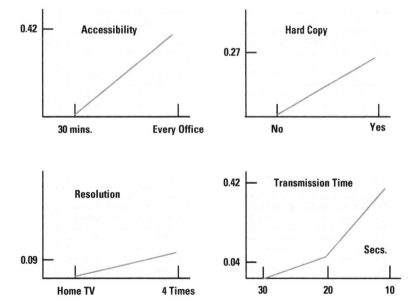

MARKETING
QUESTION

Develop a product concept
for a successfully screened
idea from the Marketing
Question, p. 374.

Product concepts must appeal to customers and guide development teams. Indeed, many pharmaceutical firms test and retest product concepts via Facebook, Twitter, patient forums, and physician networks. Firms get in trouble when concepts *drift* during development. Pontiac's concept for the Aztek was a small, youth-oriented sport utility. But to launch the car quickly and economically, Pontiac used GM's minivan frame. Aztek's appearance received mixed reviews. The $22,000–$27,000 price was too high for the youth market; Aztek sold poorly. New market data may force firms to rethink product concepts during development, and may lead to midstream changes. But serious design compromises may result in products that customers will not buy. Product concepts that led to failed products are legion — New Coke, Ford Edsel, McDonald's Arch Deluxe, Corfam (artificial leather), bottled water for pets.

KEY IDEA

The product concept should appeal to customers and guide development.

BUSINESS-CASE ANALYSIS

Business-case analysis (BCA) sits between *concept approval* and *development*. BCA assesses the concept's financial viability and considers various risk factors. Xerox carries out incremental BCA — worldwide with the new product *versus* worldwide without the new product. Projects must meet minimum financial targets to move forward. The heart of BCA is a draft marketing plan; the firm lays out its market strategy, given successful development. The firm must think through market segmentation, choose target segments, and prepare positioning — including a value proposition for securing differential advantage — Chapters 8, 9, 10. The firm faces significant uncertainty but should base the market strategy on best available market, customer, competitor, and complementer insight. Of course, financial and human resource commitments jump significantly in development.

Forecast financial performance depends on estimates of sales revenues, costs, and investment. Typically, revenue estimates (unit volumes × prices) are the most uncertain, especially for new-to-the-world products. *BASES* is a popular yet sophisticated way to forecast unit sales. The firm makes premarket forecasts via simulated test markets; forecasting repeat purchase is critical.[57] For FMCG and durables, BASES *improves* premarket sales forecasts using a databank based on past experience[58]:

KEY IDEA

New-product-development stages are:

- Idea generation
- Preliminary screening
- Concept development
- **Business-case analysis**
- Development
- Product testing
- Market-factor testing
- Test marketing
- Commercialization

The BASES Approach

Sales Forecasting Questions. The firm secures data from a survey instrument:

- *Generating awareness.* How many people will seek information about the product? How many people will know about the product? (Based on advertising quantity and quality.)

- *Estimating distribution.* Can interested customers find the product? (Based on number of outlets and placement in stores [end-aisle displays, number of facings, height].)

- *Calculating trial appeal.* How many people are interested in the product?

- *Calculating repeat purchasing.* Are triers satisfied enough to become repeaters? (Based on product quality.)

- *Estimating transaction size.* How many product units will triers and repeaters purchase?

- *Estimating the purchase period.* When is the customer likely to purchase the product — first month, first year?

- *Incorporating promotions.* How effective will the deals be?

Constructing the Sales Forecast (per period)

Total Volume = Trial volume (1st purchase) + repeat volume (2nd and later purchases)

Trial Volume = No. of households × trial rate × quantity purchased

Repeat Volume = (No. of triers = [trial rate × no. of households]) × repeat rate × no. of
repeat purchases × quantity purchased

continues

Sales Forecast Example

No. of households = 30 million; trial rate = 15%; trial units = 1.5

Trial Volume = 30 million × 0.15 × 1.5 = **6.75 million** units

Repeat Triers = repeat rate = 30%; repeat units = 1.8; repeat purchases = 4.0

Repeat Volume = (30 million × 0.15 = 4.5 million) × 0.30 × 1.8 × 4.0 = **9.72 million** units

Total Volume = 6.75 + 9.72 = **16.47 million** units

Four considerations underlie forecast financial performance:

- **Sales revenues.** These forecasts can be highly uncertain (p. 376).

- **Cost of goods sold (COGS).** All ongoing costs to make, distribute, and sell the product. *Gross profit* equals sales revenues less COGS. The firm may incur losses in the launch phase.

- **Investment costs.** Include all costs to develop the product, plus fixed investment for factories and equipment. The firm incurs many of these costs before revenues accrue.

- **Discounting.** The firm must discount all future cash flows to the present.

The firm may combine these figures in several ways to forecast financial results — IRR, NPV, EVA — Chapter 12. If forecast results exceed financial thresholds, the concept enters development; if not, the firm shelves the concept, at least temporarily. Some firms use varying discount rates to adjust for risk.

Regardless, BCA is a critical step requiring thoughtful analysis and tough decision-making. Regrettably, far too many firms conduct less than thorough BCAs and end up with their own versions of the Ford Edsel!

DEVELOPMENT

Successful business-case analysis sets the stage for *development*. Development typically occurs deep in the firm and consumes significant resources. Design, engineering, and R&D focus initially on product design and functional performance, but the firm must also involve other groups.[59] Sourcing decisions are critical for determining product performance and cost. Furthermore, when suppliers share the development effort, the firm must ensure they are fully capable. Boeing ran into considerable trouble with its technologically advanced 787 — *Dreamliner* — because it outsourced design and construction of the wings, one of the most exacting aircraft elements. Development delays are always expensive (lost revenues and increased costs); Dreamliner delays resulted from the inability of a few suppliers to produce sufficient quantities of parts, ranging from small metal fasteners to entire sections of the aft fuselage. Input from manufacturing and service helps ensure the product can be made and serviced efficiently.[60] Development also benefits from customer involvement. Earlier, when Boeing designed the 777, it worked closely with major airlines to address design trade-offs promptly and thoroughly.[61] The firm should also consider complementers; the 777 refueling orifice was 18 inches higher than on other aircraft, and airports had to rerig equipment. Avoiding complementers may be beneficial: Apple has greater flexibility with Macintosh because it designs both hardware and software; most other PC makers use Microsoft software.

Sometimes concerns about trade secrets deter firms from involving customers in designing functional characteristics. But the firm should always seek customer input for aesthetic, ergonomic, and use characteristics. The emergency brake on one American sports car was between the driver's seat and the door; a woman wearing a skirt could neither enter nor exit gracefully. Table 14.5 (p. 378) highlights other poor designs.

KEY IDEA

Business-case analysis assesses the financial viability of a product concept.

Forecasting sales revenues is the most difficult step.

KEY IDEA

New-product-development stages are:

- Idea generation
- Preliminary screening
- Concept development
- Business-case analysis
- **Development**
- Product testing
- Market-factor testing
- Test marketing
- Commercialization

Product	Type of Customer Dissatisfaction
Audio and video systems	Controls (remote or others) labeled in gold on a black casing — virtually impossible to read in low-lighting conditions.
Controls for electronic products	Markings wear off when used normally.
Horn button on American-made car with airbags	Button initially on the steering wheel perimeter but moved to the center; then required greater force. Moving controls around is a hazard.
Building plans for New York school prepared in Indonesia	Plans prepared in metric units — considerable construction delays and increased costs.

TABLE 14.5

Products That Went Wrong

To route 350 miles of bundled electric wiring in each 500-plus seat Airbus 380 took several weeks. But the wires came up short when connecting aircraft sections. The reason: Airbus Hamburg (Germany) engineers used a two-dimensional computer program; Toulouse (France) engineers worked in 3D!

Many drivers use cars as on-the-road offices. Show how you would design any midsize model for office use. Would this change if the car were also the family vehicle?

Development by multifunctional teams, including *voice of the customer*, helps avoid time-consuming back-and-forth interactions that slow linear, sequential processes. Achieving consensus may be difficult, but teams often produce better products. Caution: Using teams may lead to loss of specialist expertise. Functional experts — designers, developers, manufacturing experts, service personnel — can become organizationally disconnected from their specialties. Development by autonomous project teams also inhibits standardization across the firm. Requiring clear written reports, intensive problem-solving meetings, good direct supervision, and standard work procedures can mitigate these problems.[62] New project management software and communications technologies can also help, especially when team members work in different locations.

Sometimes, new product development proceeds best by *breaking the rules*. Apple CEO Steve Jobs echoed this sentiment when he said, "Remember that *Think Different* ad campaign that we ran? It was certainly for customers, but it was even more for Apple." **[592v]**

PRODUCT DESIGN

As product quality improves, design becomes increasingly important for customer satisfaction:

- **Sony Electronics, President Consumer Sales.** "I think one of the true powers of Sony is great design. We think about the human interface, not just from a 'how do things work' standpoint, but 'how do they fit and feel in human contact.' This is a human strategic advantage. It's something we've invested in for decades, in our design centers, R&D, and product planners, and we're very good at it."[63]

- **Samsung, Chief Marketing Officer.** "We have invested very, very heavily in design for several years. Right now, we're the second most awarded design company in our category. Our products are not simply consumer products, but lifestyle products. We put a very strong emphasis on understanding our consumers and their lifestyles."[64]

Many firms use design as a competitive weapon — Converse and Nike (sneakers), Oakley (sunglasses), Steve Madden (shoes). Several firms employ choiceboard approaches where customers design their own products. Design is also important for packaging: IKEA designs furniture to minimize packaging costs. *Frustration-free packaging* and eye-catching displays are especially important in B2C. Figure 14.7 (p. 379) shows examples of superb design.[65]

Product Design at Sony

A senior Sony Electronics executive said: "The most exciting thing about Sony to me is when you're in a lineup review and they're showing you a product and you get this 28-year-old product planner and this 30-year-old designer and they walk into a room and they pull back a piece of cloth and they show you a product that you've been working together on for a year and you go 'Oh my God, it's perfect.' And when you get into those moments, you know, it's about the passion that Sony has for great products. This is a passionate organization that really believes in creating the best possible product that you can create, and the designers, product planners and senior marketers just love what they're doing.

"There's this one designer in Tokyo. He's in his 30s now, but when you see this guy! He's going to walk into the room and you're going to think, 'Oh my God, a street person has escaped and he's loose in the building.' And his pants are four sizes too big and his clothes just hang on and he looks like he hasn't slept in a week ... Most products you'll look at and you'll say, 'OK, I could give you 20 comments on how to improve the design.' But when he pulls back the drape, you're not going to have anything to say. On this one occasion I was in Tokyo and he showed us a CD player, and the stuff was perfect. It was just perfect. That line of CD players sold six million units in the U.S. alone. And we didn't have to touch it. So that's the strength of Sony, people like that ... somebody with passion designed that thing."

FIGURE 14.7
Superb Design Has Always Been a Part of Product Development

MARKETING QUESTION

Identify three examples of superb design. Bring visuals or the actual product to class.

KEY IDEA

Many firms make very large investments in product development.

Multifunctional teams and customer involvement aid the development process.

Design is increasingly important in the development process.

During development, the firm must make performance trade-offs among product attributes, but should always keep the value proposition squarely in mind. The firm must also address negative side effects, possibly with creative design approaches. Clozapine is an effective anti-schizophrenic drug for a small subset of patients who are unresponsive to other medications. Unfortunately, 1 percent of clozapine users suffer a potentially fatal drop in white blood cell counts. Novartis, clozapine's manufacturer, designed a revolutionary solution by offering clozapine users a 24-hour service for blood testing at home.[66]

Many pharmaceutical firms spend 15–20 percent of sales on R&D. *Research* seeks out new chemical entities to meet patient needs. *Development* tests promising entities for patient benefits and drug delivery methods. Pharmaceuticals are a good example of synthesizing *research-based discovery* and *customer-sensitive development*.

QUALITY FUNCTION DEPLOYMENT

Quality function deployment (QFD) brings producers and users together. QFD maps customer needs into design, development, engineering, manufacturing, and service functions. QFD helps firms identify spoken and unspoken needs and makes the translation into actions and designs. QFD also helps various business functions to communicate and focus on achieving a common goal.[67] Figure 14.8 (p. 381) shows QFD's basic design tool — the *House of Quality*.[68] Process steps include:

KEY IDEA

The House of Quality maps *customer needs* into *product design*.

1. **Collect customer requirements as customer attributes — CAs.**[69] Organize CAs into bundles of higher-level requirements — primary, secondary, tertiary. Example for a car door:

   • **Primary CAs** — *good operation and use*[70]

   • **Secondary CAs** — for *good operation and use* include: *easy to open and close the door*; *isolation* — inside the car from outside the car.

   • **Tertiary CAs** — for *good operation and use* are secondary CAs for *easy to open and close the door.* Included are: *easy to close from outside*; *stays open on a hill*; *easy to open from outside*; *doesn't kick back.*

2. **Measure each tertiary CA:**

   • **2A Relative importance.** Importance weights sum to 100 across all CAs.

   • **2B Firm performance.** Customer perceptions versus competing suppliers on 5-point scale — worst = 1; 5 = best.

3. **Translate CAs to engineering characteristics — ECs.** The firm uses ECs to design and modify products. The firm may identify more CAs and/or redundant ECs. Positive and negative signs show direction. The negative sign on *energy to close door* implies a hoped-for reduction of energy.

4. **Identify CA/EC relationships and their strengths.** Complete the sparse matrix — an EC may affect more than one CA; several ECs may affect a single CA.

5. **Assess objective performance measures for ECs.** Relate to current performance of firm and competitor products. Act as the basis for eventually establishing target levels.

6. **Identify interrelationships among ECs.** The sparse matrix in the *roof* identifies engineering trade-offs. *Energy to close door* is negatively related to *door seal resistance, acoustic transmission-window,* and *road noise reduction.* If the firm makes the door easier to close, road noise may be worse. The firm would require creative engineering solutions.

7. **Design conclusions.** The *basement* identifies technical difficulty, importance to customers, estimated costs, EC targets.

The firm may link design specifications developed in the House of Quality to parts deployment, process planning, and production planning. Some design elements are more fundamental than others; they form *platforms* for designing other elements. The firm must make platform decisions early in development. Other elements are more flexible; the firm can redesign these elements as it collects market data.[71]

Development is typically the most time-consuming stage in new product development. Faster development helps gain first-mover advantage and enhances revenues. Approaches include:

   • **Continuous development.** Working on a 24/7 cycle, Bechtel and other firms place development teams in London, U.S., and Japan. Teams take over from each other as the day ends/begins.

FIGURE 14.8
The House of Quality

- **Parallel development.** GE, Toyota, and others form competitive teams that work in parallel toward the same goal. At some point in the development process, the firm selects one approach for completion.

- **Successive development.** Some firms use multiple teams to develop separate successor products. At Intel, different development teams work simultaneously on successive chip developments.

Firms may also secure significant economies by integrating development across products rather than focus on one product at a time. Traditionally, Lego used 90 percent of new bricks/elements just once; new toys comprised on average 13,000 bricks! Designers now reuse parts; new toys have less than 7,000 elements. Relatedly, the firm should ensure that pursuing multiple projects does not create bottlenecks and slow the development process.

Quality Is Not Just for Products

Safeway was *stuck in the middle* between price-oriented Walmart and specialty retailers like Whole Foods. Safeway's first annual loss spurred a remodeling of all 1,775 stores — the largest by a U.S. supermarket chain. Safeway continued offering low-price popular food brands but upgraded perishables by adding products like more tender beef, sweeter grapes, fresher bread. Same-space sales increased by 90 percent; Safeway returned to profitability.

CO-CREATION

Some firms form collaborative relationships with customers and independent individuals/organizations to increase the number of projects in, and broaden the scope of, new product development. Lego and others extend customer collaboration beyond idea generation into co-creating and co-design, even providing product design toolkits.[72] Wikipedia, Linux, and Firefox are other good collaboration examples. Open collaboration (OC) requires tight rules for community involvement but volunteer control may be significant. OC generates lots of ideas but screening and selecting may be cumbersome. Threadless (T-shirts) operates a 600,000-member innovation mall that submits (and evaluates) proposals for about 800 new designs weekly. Threadless pays for selected and launched designs; other OC rewards are social/psychological — altruism, fame, fun, sense of achievement. By contrast, closed collaboration (CC) relies on selected collaborators whose ideas are generally more focused. IBM chose Freescale, Infineon, Samsung, Siemens, and STMicroelectronics as CC partners for a Microelectronics Consortium to develop semiconductor technologies.[73] Sometimes two firms with complementary technology and/or market access co-create — like Nike and Apple to develop FuelBand.

NEW-PRODUCT-DEVELOPMENT PORTFOLIO

For most firms, the new-product-development portfolio is a critical element in the entire venture portfolio, along with insourcing, outsourcing, acquisition, strategic alliance, licensing and technology purchase, and equity investment — Chapter 7. Regardless, the new-product-development portfolio is especially critical because of ongoing and large resource commitments involved. Further, environmental change; strategy evolution; development successes, failures, advances, and retreats; and new entries from successful business-case analyses require updating the portfolio periodically. Successful new product firms display top management commitment, selective top management involvement, and multiple efforts. Specifically, four goals are important:

- **Portfolio value.** The firm should consider forecast profits, risk, timing, and required resources.
- **Portfolio balance.** Ensure projects are appropriately dispersed among high/low risk, short/long term; across various product forms, markets, and technologies; and across types of development efforts — basic technology research, applied technology research, market-focused development, market tinkering.[74]
- **Strategic alignment.** The product innovation strategy should be directly linked to the business strategy via resource allocation into *strategic buckets*.
- **Right number of projects.** Resources are limited. Excessive numbers of projects slows the entire product development process. The result: Missed deadlines including product launches. The firm should rank projects and make the tough decisions to cull those that don't make the cut.[75]

PRODUCT TESTING

The firm should test new products for aesthetic, ergonomic, functional, and use characteristics. There is no single test or type of test. Rather, development follows a series of *develop* → *test* → *develop* feedback loops until the product is ready for market-factor testing.

The two major types of product test are:

- **Alpha tests — in-company.** For most new products, firm employees provide critical feedback. Several *alpha tests* may run simultaneously; alpha tests often lead to further development. Automakers test new cars on northern Sweden's frozen lakes **[831v]**; Google tests its driverless car in many environments. **[493v]** New Otis elevator models complete several alpha tests, including drops, electrical sabotage, fire and flooding, and simulated earthquakes.

KEY IDEA

The firm should conduct *in-company alpha* tests throughout development. The firm should conduct *customer beta* tests in later phases.

Failure to test products sufficiently can have serious marketing and financial consequences.

KEY IDEA

New-product-development stages are:

- Idea generation
- Preliminary screening
- Concept development
- Business-case analysis
- Development
- **Product testing**
- **Market-factor testing**
- Test marketing
- Commercialization

KEY IDEA

Product testing is insufficient — the firm should test the entire market offer.

MARKETING ENRICHMENT 14.1

The Bass Model **143p**

- **Beta tests — with customers.** *Beta tests* typically follow successful alpha tests. But firms sometimes conduct beta tests on product features before they finish development.[76] The firm may also conduct several beta tests as development is concluding. Beta tests give customers an early look at developing/soon-to-be-introduced new products. Microsoft's eight-million-user beta test for Windows 7 was the largest ever, and helped avoid problems that plagued Vista. Beta tests also generate word of mouth about the new product. Relative geographic isolation and favorable demographics lead many firms to beta test digital products in New Zealand.

Speedy testing has many advantages,[77] but inadequate testing can cause major problems. During a moose-avoidance test in a sharp turn at 38 mph, a Swedish journalist tipped over Daimler-Benz's (DB) first subcompact car (Mercedes A-Class). DB had invested $1.5 billion in the car; DB spent $171 million to solve the problem. Virgin Galactic's SpaceShipTwo crashed in the Mojave desert. Executives responsible for choosing coffee for the merged United/Continental Airlines did not test their selection in everyday use; they did not realize coffee pot designs differed across airlines, leading to many customer complaints. P&G's Gillette successfully tested a razor designed for Indian men on Indian students at MIT, but the razor failed in India: Problem — differential access to running water.

MARKET-FACTOR TESTING

The product is just one element in the market offer. First-rate products fail if the firm poorly designs and/or implements other factors in the marketing mix. Conversely, the firm may be successful with marginal products if other marketing-mix elements are superior. The firm should evaluate implementation elements like advertising and distribution via *market-factor testing*. Generally, the firm tests these factors when product development is complete, but sometimes market-factor and product testing occur in parallel. The firm can test using simulated environments or virtually on the Internet.

SIMULATED ENVIRONMENTS

In B2C, the firm can test advertising messages via split-cable TV or in movie houses — Chapter 16. The firm can test packaging, pricing, and shelf placement in mock-up store displays in trailers adjacent to shopping malls. Consumers selecting the test product receive a trial sample; later they report experiences, repurchase intentions, and/or usage rates. Alternatively, consumers may select products from mock-up brochures and magazines when researchers visit them at home. Coach offers bags, wallets, and other fashion accessories in a wide variety of colors, materials, shapes, and styles, then focuses on those that sell best and discontinues others.

In many tests, critical measures are *trial* and *repeat*. These variables are input into analytic procedures that predict sales volume and market share. BASES (p. 376) is one approach; ASSESSOR is a second.[78] Many practitioners use the Bass model and extensions for new product forecasts — Marketing Enrichment 14.1 **[143p]**.[79])

ASSESSOR

The **ASSESSOR** approach has the important feature of incorporating a *preference* model and a *trial-and-repeat* model. Each model predicts market share and sales volume. If the results converge, the researcher has greater confidence in the predictions. Divergent results act as a diagnostic; they suggest further analyses to identify sources of discrepancies and reconcile findings. For new products entering *established product classes/forms*, market share from the preference model multiplied by total product class/form sales provides the sales volume estimate. The firm compares this estimate to the long-term sales volume estimate derived from the trial-and-repeat model. For a *new product class/form*, the preference model is not useable, so the trial-and-repeat model alone provides sales estimates.

VIRTUAL TESTING

Virtual testing is a new approach to customer testing. The firm creates an online shopping display; customers shop as in a real store, with all the distracting clutter. An important benefit of virtual testing is the ability to modify displays quickly and analyze results instantaneously:

> In a Goodyear study, 1,000 recent and potential passenger-tire purchasers shopped in virtual tire stores; several brands and models had various prices and warranties. Goodyear identified strong and weak competitors, gained insight into brand equity, and developed repricing ideas.[80]

Both virtual testing and simulated testing are artificial. Test marketing provides greater realism.

KEY IDEA

Market-factor testing includes simulated environments and virtual testing.

TEST MARKETING

Test marketing simulates actual market conditions. Typically, the firm selects two geographic areas with similar market and customer profiles, considering issues like seasonality. The firm implements the full market launch program in one geography; the other geography acts as a control to isolate product launch results. Global firms often speed time to commercialization by test marketing simultaneously in several countries. P&G test marketed Swiffer in France and the U.S.; Swiffer reached global distribution within 18 months versus the typical five years. For any test market, measurement is crucial and includes:

- **Input measures** — advertising, training, sales effort
- **Intermediate measures** — customer awareness, interest
- **Output measures** — sales, profits, customer satisfaction

FMCG firms collect point-of-sales data from supermarket scanners; *value shopping* cards measure repeat purchase. Consumer panels and/or independent surveys provide intermediate measures and customer satisfaction.

Test marketing has pros and cons.[81] *Pros* include:

- **Fine-tunes launch.** Test marketing provides invaluable data for fine-tuning actual launch.
- **Provides unexpected insight.** Test market failures may provide unexpected data.

> Febreze, P&G's laundry product for removing cigarette and other noxious odors from dry-clean-only fabrics, failed in test market — only 10 percent of consumers were *extremely pleased*. But test consumers found additional uses like odor removal from sofas, carpets, car interiors, and other household furnishings. In a second test market, Febreze had a broader *odor neutralizer* positioning. This test was a huge success; initial demand exceeded forecast tenfold.

- **Saves launch costs.** The firm can withdraw products that perform poorly in test market and avoid spending resources on new products that would have failed.

Cons for test marketing include:

- **Alert competitors.** The test market may show firm intentions and reduce time-to-market advantages.
- **Competitor actions.** Competitors may interfere with the test market by increasing promotion and/or offering cut-price deals. These actions reduce the test's predictive power.
- **Excessive attention.** The firm may put in special effort and make the test market successful. If the firm cannot duplicate this effort at launch, product introduction may fail.

> Coca-Cola encouraged Burger King to invest in *Frozen Coke*. When a legitimate test market was going poorly, fountain-division employees paid a Virginia man $10,000 to take hundreds of children to Burger King to buy value meals and Frozen Coke. Several Coke executives lost their jobs, and Coke paid Burger King $21 million to settle lawsuits.

- **Expense and time.** Test marketing is expensive and takes time. The firm forgoes revenues from an otherwise successful launch.

KEY IDEA

New-product-development stages are:
- Idea generation
- Preliminary screening
- Concept development
- Business-case analysis
- Development
- Product testing
- Market-factor testing
- **Test marketing**
- Commercialization

MARKETING QUESTION

Have you ever been part of a test market in your local grocery store or other retail outlet? Did you try the product? Did the firm launch the product? If yes, was the launch successful?

KEY IDEA

In deciding whether or not to test market, the firm should consider several pros and cons.

KEY IDEA

New-product-development
stages are:

* Idea generation
* Preliminary screening
* Concept development
* Business-case analysis
* Development
* Product testing
* Market-factor testing
* Test marketing
* **Commercialization**

**MARKETING
QUESTION**

Segway is a battery-driven
personal transportation
vehicle developed by Dean
Kamen. **[570v]** Segway has
been less successful than its
inventor predicted. What barriers to adoption did Segway
face? Could Segway have
done a better job in addressing these barriers? Where is
Segway successful?

KEY IDEA

Firms make their biggest bets
at the commercialization
stage.

**MARKETING
ENRICHMENT 14.2**

Product introductions by
Apple:
* Macintosh **867v, 361v**
* iPod **151v**
* iPhone **344v** (first), **920v**
* Apple Watch **841v**
* Apple Pay **530v**

KEY IDEA

A useful classification for
timing of new product
adoption is:

* Innovators
* Early adopters
* Early majority
* Late majority
* Laggards

COMMERCIALIZATION

Successful completion of previous stages in the stage-gate process results in a product ready for launch and *commercialization*.[82] The firm assigns resources to construct facilities and expend marketing effort. The launch strategy must consider issues like forecast sales, time to bring facilities on line, production and inventory requirements, adherence to planned launch date,[83] competitive lead time, expected competitive response, patent or trade secret protection, and available resources. Launch delays can be very costly; furthermore, the firm should synchronize communications and distribution to avoid the sort of problem Under Armour encountered with cross-training shoes — Super Bowl advertising ran months before shoes reached the stores. Early launch announcements may also inhibit customers from buying the firm's current products.

All marketing-mix elements are important for launch. Pricing and distribution decisions are critical, but are more difficult the newer the product. Regarding communications, B2C firms often use celebrity spokespersons and advertising to promote new products. They also use *product placement*, working with directors and producers so that actors use products in movies and TV shows. B2B firms focus on good distribution and support programs, including persuading key opinion leaders (KOLs) to use new products — medical device and pharmaceutical firms target leading specialists at university teaching hospitals. *Word of mouth* is often critical for adoption; prospective buyers reduce purchase risk by learning from trusted sources. In its early days, Starbucks rarely advertised, but gained enormously from positive word of mouth. Today, firms try to manage word of mouth and social media communications, rather than just leaving the task to customers.

Traditionally, firms launched new products domestically, then addressed foreign markets later. Today, many firms launch in multiple national markets simultaneously; Mattel introduced Rapunzel Barbie in 59 countries. Information products, where copying is a problem, are a special concern; 20th Century Fox launched *X2: X-Men United* in 93 territories within 48 hours.

The firm should not confuse completing product development (or even satisfactory test market-ing) with commercial success. Extensive testing is no guarantee against commercial failure. After 10 years development, S.C. Johnson (SCJ) introduced Allercare to remove dust mites (leading cause of childhood asthma) from carpets/upholstery. SCJ tested Allercare in tens of thousands of homes and launched with a $10 million national TV campaign. But consumers with severe allergies and asthma reported negative reactions; SCJ withdrew Allercare after one year.[84]

The best companies learn from commercialization mistakes.[85] Corning failed with a DNA chip designed to print all 28,000 human genes onto slides for research purposes, but identified the drug-discovery market and now sells *Epic* for testing potential drugs. British Airways' flat beds upstaged Virgin's reclined sleeper seats, but Virgin used its learning to develop a *leapfrog* inno-vation — *upper-class suite* — that helped improve business-class market share. For successful product launches by Apple — Marketing Enrichment 14.2.

PRODUCT ADOPTION

The goal of commercialization efforts is customer product adoption. But not all customers adopt at the same time. As part of product planning, the firm should anticipate five categories of customer adoption behavior[86]:

* **Innovators** (2.5 percent) — *Explorers*.[87] The first to adopt the innovation but are only a small part of the population. Take pride in being first, are considered *experts*, and pro-actively seek opportunities to try new things. Typically, other customers do not emulate these *venturesome* risk-takers.

* **Early adopters** (13.5 percent) — *Visionaries*. Follow the innovators. Seek understanding of future possibilities and are willing to take risks and break with the past. Are more *respected* in their communities and are opinion leaders for others.

- **Early majority** (34 percent) — *Pragmatists.* Motivated by current problems and make decisions *deliberately*, based in part on the experience of early adopters. Look for proven track records; prefer to buy recognized brands from market leaders.

- **Late majority** (34 percent) — *Conservatives.* A *skeptical* group that adopts only when half the population has adopted. Tend to be price sensitive.

- **Laggards** (16 percent) — *Critics.* These *traditionalists* gain utility by sticking to the old, are suspicious of change, averse to novelty, and adopt only when adoption and use are widespread.

Identifying potential customers by *adoption category* for a new product innovation is a critical marketing challenge. In B2C, early adopters tend to be better educated, socioeconomically advantaged, and younger. Avon maintains a database on innovators and early adopters for cosmetics, and targets them for new product launches. But innovators and early adopters for one product may be early or late majority for another. Figure 14.9 shows that product innovations must cross the *chasm* from early adopters to early majority and enter the mainstream market to be successful.[88] Many new products fail to cross the chasm; for others, it takes a long time.

**MARKETING
QUESTION**

Talk to an executive about her firm's new-product-development process. How does it compare with the process described in this chapter? Where is it better? Worse?

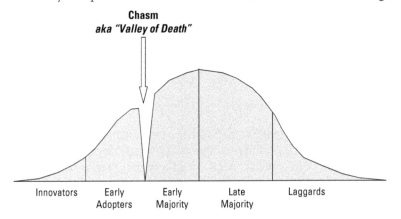

**Chasm
aka "Valley of Death"**

Innovators   Early Adopters   Early Majority   Late Majority   Laggards

FIGURE 14.9
*The Adoption
Curve and Chasm*

**MARKETING
QUESTION**

What products can you identify that did not *cross the chasm*? What products took a long time to cross the chasm?

TABLE 14.6
*Factors Affecting the Speed
of Adoption (ACCORD)*

Factor (direction of effect)	Meaning
Advantage (increase)	Extent of benefits offered compared to existing alternatives
Compatibility (increase)	Relationship with past experience and current lifestyle
Complexity (decrease)	Implies greater learning requirements
Observability/Communicability (increase)	Extent to which the relative advantage is easily observed and communicated
Risk (decrease)	Financial, physical, and psychological/social risk
Divisibility/Reversibility (increase)	Ability to try on a limited basis and revert to previous product

The *ACCORD* acronym summarizes several factors affecting speed of adoption and commercial success — Table 14.6.[89] Consider the successful introduction of EZ Pass on toll roads and bridges. The EZ Pass device attaches to a vehicle windshield. An electronic signal at the tollbooth recognizes the device, allows passage, and deducts payment from an account linked to a credit card. The account automatically replenishes when the balance falls to a preset level:

- **Advantage.** Saves time at tollbooth; automatic bill payment more convenient than cash (but raises privacy concerns).

- **Compatibility.** Driver behavior largely unchanged; initiating the credit card account is trivial.

- **Complexity.** Learning minimal: driver attaches the device; drives through the tollbooth.

- **Observability** (Communicability). Benefits easy to understand and communicate.

- **Risk.** Little risk to trying the EZ Pass system — no upfront payment.

- **Divisibility** (Reversibility). Driver can easily switch back to cash.

KEY IDEA

ACCORD is a useful acronym for factors influencing the speed of new product adoption:

- Advantage (+)
- Compatibility (+)
- Complexity (−)
- Observability (+)
- Risk (−)
- Divisibility (+)

What other messages did you glean from this chapter?

KEY MESSAGES

- Successful new products are a major factor in creating shareholder wealth.
- Innovations can be either *sustaining* or *disruptive.*
- The most important factors for innovation success are market selection, R&D spending, organization.
- Four approaches to new product development are basic technology research, applied technology research, market-focused development, market tinkering.
- The stage-gate process is a systematic approach to new-product-development. Key stages are:

1. Idea generation
2. Preliminary screening
3. Concept development
4. Business-case analysis
5. Development
6. Product testing
7. Market-factor testing
8. Test marketing
9. Commercialization

- At each stage, the firm should be concerned about two types of error: Type I — investing in a project that eventually fails; Type II — rejecting a project that would have succeeded.
- The cost of failure increases as a project moves through the new product development process. Hence, each *gate* in the stage-gate process should be a *kill point.*
- New product success depends on *crossing the chasm* from early adopters to early majority.
- The speed of adoption for a successful project depends on the ACCORD factors. (Do you know what they are?)

VIDEOS AND AUDIOS

For complimentary material, see Axcess Capon codes at www.axcessvids.com

Innovation	**687v**	William Duggan	Columbia Business School
Service Innovation	**648v**	Dean Crutchfield	
Disruptive Innovation	**996v**	Clayton Christensen	Harvard Business School
Creativity	**925v**	Jacob Goldenberg	Hebrew University/ Columbia Business School

QUESTIONS FOR STUDY AND DISCUSSION

Can you answer the questions implied by this chapter's learning outcomes? Check!

1. Customer dissatisfaction is an opportunity for firms to learn. When were you dissatisfied with a purchase experience? Why? What new product/service ideas would you suggest?

2. Consider a common product you use frequently — like a newspaper, fast food outlet, computer, or smartphone. Work with two or three friends to develop new product ideas using the five innovation templates — subtraction, multiplication, division, task unification, attribute dependency change.

3. Take the product you selected for Question 2 and develop a House of Quality.

4. Suppose that, on graduation, you accept a position as new product director for a medium-size firm with a poor new-product-development record. The CEO has set a three-year goal for 20 percent of sales to derive from new products. What actions will you take in your first 100 days?

5. Apple has been successful with Macintosh computers, iPod, iTunes, iPhone, and iPad. But Apple withdrew the Newton and G4 Cube computer (now in New York's Museum of Modern Art). How do you assess Apple's new product performance? How does your assessment reconcile with Apple's profit performance?

6. Describe the marketing significance of new product innovation. What challenges and opportunities face firms that introduce new products in competitive markets?

7. Select a product in which you are interested. Alternatively, consider *Managing Marketing in the 21st Century*. What related new product ideas do you have?

TRUE/FALSE QUESTIONS

Answers on page A2 and at www.axcessvids.com — 445p

1. Sustaining innovations offer different value propositions. Initially, these innovations may underperform existing products or processes, but a few fringe customers recognize value.
   ❏ TRUE ❏ FALSE

2. Type II errors are more difficult to identify than Type I errors. ❏ TRUE ❏ FALSE

3. Firms that minimize Type II errors accept only the safest alternatives. Failure is low, but these firms are unlikely to develop products with significant financial return.
   ❏ TRUE ❏ FALSE

4. Early adopters are the first to adopt an innovation, but represent only a small part of the population. ❏ TRUE ❏ FALSE

5. Product innovation must cross the chasm from early adopters to early majority and the mainstream market to be successful. ❏ TRUE ❏ FALSE

MULTIPLE CHOICE QUESTIONS

Answers on page A2 and at www.axcessvids.com — 440p

1. Which of the following is NOT one of the four approaches to new product development?
   a. physiological profile research
   b. applied research technology
   c. market-focused development
   d. market tinkering

2. All of the following are considerations that underlie the forecast of firm financial performance EXCEPT:
   a. sales revenues
   b. investment costs
   c. cost of goods sold
   d. market tinkering

3. Which of the following is an advantage for test marketing a new product?
   a. Test marketing may alert competitors.
   b. Competitors may interfere with the test market.
   c. Test market failures may provide the firm with unexpected insight.
   d. The firm may invest extra effort to make the test market successful.

4. Which of the following categories of consumer behavior is a skeptical group that adopts only when half the population has adopted?
   a. early adopters
   b. early majority
   c. late majority
   d. laggards

Design the Market Offer

CHAPTER 15

INTEGRATED MARKETING COMMUNICATIONS

For complimentary material, see Axcess Capon codes at www.axcessvids.com

LEARNING OUTCOMES

When you have completed this chapter, you will be able to:

- Understand communications challenges and opportunities firms face.
- Articulate causes of miscommunication problems.
- Enumerate communications tools available to the firm.
- Integrate communications tools in a communications strategy.
- Distinguish between *push*, *pull*, and combination *push/pull* communication strategies.
- Set communications objectives.

OPENING CASE: CALIFORNIA CHEESE

California's dairy industry faced a significant problem that would likely become more severe — milk surpluses caused by increasing milk productivity. The California Milk Advisory Board (CMAB) evaluated several options and selected cheese as its flagship product, in part because 1 pound of cheese required 10 pounds of milk.

Californians annually consumed 23.3 pounds of cheese per capita (national average — 19.7 pounds). Demographic growth in the heavy-cheese-using Hispanic population would increase demand. But California's cheese-making reputation paled beside Wisconsin and Vermont. Hence, California was a net cheese importer: 80 percent of natural U.S.-produced cheese, and nearly all processed cheese, came from out of state. For California to become a preeminent cheese producer, CMAB had to design and implement an effective communications strategy.

To meet its challenge, CMAB implemented a three-part strategy:

- **Certification mark.** *The* mark (seal) *showed California with a rising sun and rolling plains on a golden, cheese-colored background:* Real California Cheese *was at the periphery. CMAB had this mark placed on as many cheese packages as possible; in all advertising, coupons, and promotional literature; and on restaurant menus and table tents.*

- **Advertising campaign.** *CMAB implemented the* Real California Cheese *campaign,* California cheese is great cheese, *in newspapers, magazines, outdoors, and on radio and TV. The primary target was women aged 25-54, married with children, income slightly above the national average. The copy strategy avoided more traditional, rational, tangible claims of cheese superiority. Rather, the tone and manner tried to create an emotional bond of fondness and affection for California cheese.*[538v] *The advertising used human, intelligent, and humorous messages; but no superiority claim.*

- **Promotional campaign.** *CMAB used in-store cross-promotions with instantly redeemable coupons, product sampling, and self-liquidating offers, like high-quality coffee table books about cheese, that reinforced the advertising campaign. Cross-promotional partners were products frequently consumed with cheese, like bread, crackers, pizza crust, tortillas, poultry, champagne, and wine. CMAB also placed cross-brand coupons on Real California Cheese-identified cheeses.*

After 10 years, CMAB introduced It's the cheese — *making the exaggerated claim that people came to California for the cheese. The tagline appeared adjacent to the Real California Cheese seal on TV spots, retail, print, outdoor executions, coupons, and all other promotional materials.*

Several years later, CMAB introduced Happy Cows *with the tagline* Great cheese comes from Happy Cows. Happy Cows come from California. *The advertisements showed cows talking, enjoying, and thinking like people about California's best-known features — sunny skies, lack of snow (versus the Midwest), earthquakes (portrayed positively), and beautiful scenery.*[999v, 481v] *More recently, the loquacious cows implored consumers to make California milk and cheese part of their family.*

CMAB used spot TV advertising in markets outside California where Real California Cheese had a major presence, supplemented by outdoor, bus and bus-shelter, and radio advertising. Later, when Real California Cheese was sold in many major U.S. markets, CMAB introduced national advertising, including during the Super Bowl. CMAB continued its emotional appeals by launching the Family Farms *campaign featuring website documentaries and shorter versions for television advertising.*

Case Question

California cheese achieved spectacular awareness levels. Three out of four Californians reported seeing the Real California Cheese seal where they shopped; 95 percent purchased Real California Cheese. Sales increased 600 percent over a 20-year period. Cheese production increased dramatically: Before the first campaign, 17 percent of California's milk produced 280 million pounds of cheese; 20 years later, 45 percent of California's milk produced 1,990 billion pounds.

What factors account for CMAB's success?

Chapter 15 is the first of four chapters in Part B of Imperative 4 — *Design the Market Offer.* Part B focuses on *Communicating Customer Value.* Chapter 15 addresses *Integrated Marketing Communications.*

We've all heard the popular saying: *If we build a better mousetrap, customers will come.* Rubbish! Customers will not *come* unless they know about the mousetrap; that's the purpose of communication. To be successful, the firm must communicate benefits and value to target customers. Also, good communication by itself has value in its impact on customers. Many communications tools and techniques are available. In this chapter, we consider several broad categories:

- **Personal communications** — face-to-face personal selling, telemarketing/telesales, service
- **Traditional mass communications** — advertising, direct marketing, packaging, publicity & public relations, sales promotion (including product placement and trade shows)
- **Digital communications** — e-mail; search, blogs, social media; advertising — display, classifieds, video; websites; mobile marketing

Traditionally, firms also plan some *word-of-mouth* communications to enhance the value of their messages. Social media has changed the paradigm, creating greater communications options between and among customers. For marketing professionals, the vast array of communications options is both a blessing and a curse. *Blessing:* The firm has many more communications alternatives. *Curse:* Coordinating multiple messages to multiple targets, yet producing a coherent, consistent, and integrated whole can be very difficult.

Integrated marketing communications captures the idea of coordinating various communications messages with the *right* communication tools and techniques, delivered to the *right* audience at the *right* time.**[936v]** This chapter reviews communications strategies and tactics for reaching target audiences and achieving firm communications objectives.

THE CHANGING VIEW

OLD WAY	NEW WAY
Broad appeal	Targeted messaging
Customers are sole communications target	Multiple communications targets — complementers, customers, employees, governments, influencers, shareholders, suppliers
Limited media/vehicle choices	Proliferating media/vehicle choices
Mass communication	Interactive communication
Siloed communications effort	Integrated communications effort
The firm communicates with customers	The firm communicates with customers; customers communicate with customers; customers communicate with the firm
Word of mouth may provide relevant communications	Managing social media is a critical managerial challenge

COMMUNICATIONS CHALLENGES

In the first 10 years, Starbucks spent less than $10 million on advertising yet gained high brand awareness. Starbucks clustered retail outlets in highly visible urban locations, was zealous about good coffee, visibly branded all products and materials, had consistent brand positioning, invested smartly in public relations, used the emerging Internet to advantage, and enjoyed strong word of mouth.[1]

An integrated communications program is critical for successfully implementing market strategy and achieving firm objectives. But it's not easy. The firm must address many challenges from both outside and inside the organization.

··

EXTERNAL CHALLENGES

As the firm tries to determine the right mix of tools and techniques for communicating with various audiences, it must address several external challenges:

- **Competitive communications.** Competitors have similar communications targets to the firm. Competitors use varied communications approaches to promote their products and disadvantage the firm. Airbus tried to slow advance orders for Boeing's *Dreamliner* by suggesting Airbus might revamp the A330. By attacking government loans to Airbus for aircraft development, Boeing questioned future Airbus products. Some firms suffer attacks by third-party interest groups like Greenpeace and animal-rights activists.

- **Evolving communications technologies.** Communications choices are expanding rapidly. Growth in digital media allows firms to personalize messages, modify product placement and promotions for different audiences through different communications channels, even inserting virtual products into movies and TV shows. But digital video recorders allow consumers to opt out of traditional advertising.

- **Multiple information sources.** Customers receive information about the firm and its products/brands from many sources — advocacy groups, competitors, customers, governments, intermediaries, testing and other third-party organizations, and the media. Communications may be negative, neutral, or helpful; they can also be very powerful.[2] Reports that Nike used child labor in Indonesia, and that PepsiCo India used excessive amounts of scarce groundwater and sold contaminated products, were negative. Media coverage of AFL-CIO asking Verizon customers to switch carriers during angry union negotiations were equally problematic. Conversely, many positive press and analyst reports have helped firms like Apple and Google.

Examples of Public Communications

Positive. Ben and Jerry's and The Body Shop generally receive favorable press coverage, in part because they endorse social causes.

Positive. Pharmaceutical firms gain positive public perceptions when the press reports FDA approval of new drugs.

Negative. Accounting firm Arthur Andersen received such negative press coverage for negligent business practices related to the Enron scandal that it collapsed.

Negative. U.S. firms like Accenture, Stanley Works, and Tyco received negative publicity when they attempted to reincorporate abroad. Many believe these actions exploit loopholes in U.S. tax laws and are unethical. Stanley Works remained in the U.S., but Accenture and Tyco shifted incorporations to Ireland and Switzerland respectively.

- **Noise.** Customers and other audiences live in information-rich environments. Myriad messages — *clutter* — bombard them daily; few messages are relevant to customer needs or firm products. Effective communications must *cut through* the clutter so firm messages resonate with intended targets.

- **Public perception.** Sometimes firms face public criticism for communications activities and feel compelled to change. NBC accepted liquor advertising on a trial basis, then ended the three-month experiment. NBC received such criticism from the American Medical Association, members of Congress, federal regulators, and public advocacy groups that it voluntarily reinstituted its ban.[4]

- **Regulators.** Firms are biased information providers; hence, government agencies review communications to ensure fairness and accuracy. Many countries have *truth-in-advertising* laws.[5] Some countries (not the U.S.) ban comparative advertising. The U.S. main regulator is the Federal Trade Commission (FTC); entities like the National Advertising Review Board serve as self-regulating industry bodies.[6] Because self-regulators have no enforcement power,

MARKETING QUESTION

The FDA approves drugs for specific indications — medical conditions. Physicians can *use* an approved drug for different indications, but drug firms cannot *promote* such *off-label use* without FDA approval. The FDA approved Natrecor (J&J) for *short-term* treatment of heart-failure patients with breathing problems. Nurse practitioner Regina Massaro worked closely with Dr. Altschul, the physician who pioneered Natrecor for *longer-term* heart-failure treatment — off-label use. J&J paid Massaro to make nationwide trips to discuss heart-failure management with physicians. Massaro couldn't promote Natrecor for off-label use, but she could answer questions about her experiences with *longer-term* Natrecor treatment.[3] How do you assess J&J's actions in arranging and funding Massaro's trips?

KEY IDEA

Critical external communications challenges include:

- Competitive communications
- Evolving communications technologies
- Multiple information sources
- Noise
- Public perception
- Regulators
- Social media

KEY IDEA

In formulating an integrated communications program, the firm faces significant *external* and *internal* challenges.

MARKETING QUESTION

Compare and contrast *external* communications challenges firms face when introducing a new product/brand versus sustaining a mature product/brand.

some advertisers ignore them. Ryanair routinely ignores the British Advertising Standards Authority.

> A U.S. federal district court ordered Philip Morris (PM) to pay $10 billion damages. PM did not tell customers that *light* cigarettes were as harmful as *full-tar* cigarettes.
>
> H&R Block faced lawsuits over *rapid refunds* of taxes. Block hid the fact that rapid refunds were actually high-interest-rate loans — over 500 percent annually.

- **Social media.** The explosion of social media has vastly increased the volume of unmanaged communications about the firm and its brands. Positive communications can help the firm, but negative communications may severely damage firm/brand reputations.

INTERNAL CHALLENGES

Communication challenges also occur inside the firm. Often-heard internal opinions about communications are:

- **We don't need it.** Many technically oriented firms assume the *best* product, as defined by their engineers, will *win*. "Our product will sell itself." But customers must believe the *entire offer* (including the product) provides the best value. Communications play a major role in forming these beliefs.
- **We've already done that.** Executives believe the firm has already communicated sufficiently. Perhaps the firm published technical papers or gave literature to the sales force. The firm may underestimate both the communications effort required to get the message across to customers, and competitor efforts. Hence, the firm underfunds communications, then wonders why customers don't know about its products.
- **It's an unnecessary expense.** Many firms prefer to spend resources for tangible assets like land and plant and equipment. Communications provide difficult-to-measure intangible benefits, so firms minimize communications expenses. As we shall see, measuring the impact of communications initiatives can be very challenging.
- **We need different messages for different audiences.** The firm has multiple communications targets like current and potential customers, complementers, employees, suppliers, and shareholders — sometimes even competitors. When different groups inside the firm have responsibility for communicating with these varied audiences, achieving communications consistency can be very difficult.

THE COMMUNICATIONS PROCESS

KEY IDEA

In the communications process, senders *send* information; receivers *receive* information.

Miscommunication arises from three messaging problems:
- Encoding
- Distortion
- Decoding

Before we get into the marketing aspects of integrated communication, let's revisit communications principles. In any *communication process*, the *sender* sends a *message* to a *receiver*; the *receiver* receives the message — Figure 15.1 (p. 394). The dotted line shows that, in some communication processes, the *receiver* also communicates with the *sender*. Ideally, the receiver receives the message the sender *intended* to send. If this does not happen, *miscommunication* occurs — typically not a good outcome, particularly for marketers. Three main sources of miscommunication are:

- **Encoding.** Typically, some person or organizational entity decides on the intended message, but this message is not sent properly. Perhaps the advertising agency misinterprets product positioning. Or sales force training is ineffective, and salespeople do not communicate the *right* message.
- **Distortion.** The firm sends the intended message, but communication is distorted; hence, the receiver does not receive the sent message. Consumers may receive similar print and TV

advertisements differently — TV advertising on *The Daily Show* versus an identical message on *60 Minutes*. Or the salesperson's accent affects the received message.

- **Decoding.** Communications targets may receive the same message differently — selective attention, perception, and/or retention — related to individual perception, memory, and/or belief systems. Hence, the message is misperceived and/or misunderstood.

A critical marketing challenge is understanding and minimizing causes of miscommunication.

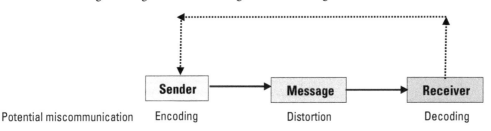

FIGURE 15.1
The Communications Process

COMMUNICATIONS TOOLS

Communications tools are the ways marketers interface with target audiences. Traditional categories are *personal communication* and *mass communication*. In this chapter, we embrace two additional categories — *digital communication* and *word-of-mouth* (WOM) *communication*, and their impact on today's integrated communications strategies — Figure 15.2.

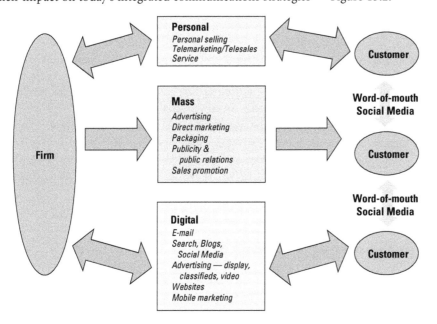

FIGURE 15.2
Communications Tools and the Communications Process

PERSONAL COMMUNICATION. Most personal communication in marketing occurs when salespeople and other firm representatives — technical and customer-service personnel — interact with customers individually or as team members. In B2B marketing, salespeople typically visit customer locations; much face-to-face B2C communication occurs in fixed locations like retail stores. In many firms, *telemarketing/telesales* forces supplement/replace field salespeople. Some firms script personal communications, but most often personal communication evolves spontaneously during the interaction.[7]

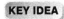

KEY IDEA

Personal communication occurs among individuals and/or groups.

MASS COMMUNICATIONS. The most pervasive marketing communication occurs without interpersonal interaction between sender and receiver, particularly in B2C marketing.[8] Typically, the firm has greater control over message content in mass communications than in personal

KEY IDEA

Mass communication occurs without interpersonal contact between sender and receiver.

MARKETING QUESTION

When you last contemplated acquiring smartphone service, how did potential suppliers communicate with you? What personal communication methods did they use? What mass communications methods? Was any digital communication involved? Did any supplier encourage social media or conventional WOM? Which communication method(s) were credible and engaging? Which methods had the greatest impact on your selection? Did communication methods change during your buying process?

KEY IDEA

WOM communication occurs among customers and potential customers.

communications. Various types of mass communications include:

- **Advertising.** In its traditional form, the firm pays for communications directed at a mass audience. Advertising embraces different modes, typically visual and audio, deployed via many types of media.[9] *Visual-static media* refers to printed matter, including billboards, brochures, magazines, newspapers, point-of-purchase displays, signage, and trade journals. *Visual-dynamic media* includes television, movies, and online advertising. *Audio* includes radio and newer communications types like podcasts.[10]

- **Direct marketing.** Includes all paid and company-sponsored communications directed at individuals. Most direct marketing is printed *direct* mail, but modern versions include targeted audio/video messages and direct e-mail.

- **Packaging.** Packaging's main value is to protect the product. But packaging is also a communications vehicle, delivering information and visual appeal.

- **Publicity & public relations (P&PR).** Publicity is communication for which the firm does not pay directly. Typically, the firm provides or *places* information like a photograph, press release, story, or video with a third-party transmitter. The transmitter, like an industry analyst, magazine, or news organization, incorporates the material in its own communications. Public relations (PR) embraces publicity but is broader; PR includes other ways of gaining favorable responses. Typical PR activities include donating money to charity, giving speeches, participating in community activities, sponsoring events, and other public-facing activities.

- **Sales promotion (SP).** Provides extra value for customers; firms often design SP to induce immediate sales. Consumer promotions include contests, coupons, games, point-of-purchase materials, premiums, rebates, and samples. Distributor (reseller) promotions include contests, merchandising allowances, special price deals, rebates, and volume buying. Special forms of SP are:

  - **Product placement.** The firm places products in movies and TV shows. Placement can be real, or virtual via electronic insertion of products, logos, and signs.[11] Three major types of placement are:
    - Product used by actors
    - Product integrated into the plot
    - Product associated with a character[12]

  - **Trade shows.** In many industries, suppliers (vendors) display and/or demonstrate products to large numbers of current and potential customers, at one time, in one convenient location. In turn, customers can communicate with large numbers of suppliers offering similar products/services.[13]

WORD-OF-MOUTH (WOM) COMMUNICATIONS. Communication among customers and potential customers can impact many purchase elements like brand choice, distribution channel, and timing. Communications about a firm/product/brand can be positive or negative, depending on customer experience. Because customers typically have no commercial interest, they often have higher credibility than paid communicators.[14] Generally, firms have little control over WOM, but increasingly they orchestrate *buzz-marketing*, *guerrilla-marketing*, and *viral-marketing* campaigns. In the digital domain, firms may pay bloggers to encourage positive communications.[15] Philips gave 33,000 samples of its new Sonicare Essence power toothbrush plus $10 rebates to U.S. consumers. Microsoft gave Halo 2 (new version of popular video game) to an inner circle of committed players 18 months before launch; first-day sales, largely from pre-orders, were over $100 million.

WOM Communications

- Ford supplied 155,000 of 400,000 workers with home PCs and Internet connections to encourage them to join chat groups and be ambassadors for Ford products.[16]

- Half.com launched its website by persuading citizens of Halfway, a small Oregon town, to rename itself *Half.com.*[17]

- Pharmaceutical firms identify KOLs in the medical community. They map physicians' social networks, focusing on individual physicians who link separate subnetworks.[18]

- P&G enrolled 600,000 moms — *connectors* — with extensive social networks, in its *Tremor* program. Screened on the Internet, each mom receives a handful of coupons and carefully crafted messages for specific P&G products.

- Salesforce.com CEO Marc Benioff, said: "We don't have a couple of hundred salespeople, we have a couple hundred thousand salespeople. They're called our customers. And it would be really cool if they were out there chatting it up, telling their friends, because it takes a really long time to go out and visit all the customers."[19]

- *The Big Tease* producers invited hundreds of hairdressers to previews in New York, Los Angeles, San Francisco, and London, hoping for WOM with customers.[20]

- Toyota used a multimillion-dollar *ride-and-drive* guerrilla-marketing campaign to introduce the Scion in California. Scion team members, positioned on busy San Francisco street corners frequented by millenials, encouraged passersby to take a test drive.

- Zappos success is largely driven by repeat customers and WOM. 75 percent of orders are from repeat customers; one third of 1,400 employees are on Twitter, engaging with current and potential customers.

Some firms tap into established groups to take advantage of *social networking*. Cheerleaders are often popular students in high school: Both P&G and PepsiCo provide information and samples to organizations promoting high school cheerleading camps and competitions. *Bunco* is a three-dice game increasingly popular among suburban women: P&G sponsored the Prilosec (heartburn medicine) OTC Bunco World Tour to encourage WOM for Prilosec. Marketers are increasingly using social media for WOM advertising — Chapter 17.[795v]

DIGITAL COMMUNICATIONS. The Internet provides firms with many additional options for customer communications. Some methods are electronic analogues of traditional communication tools like direct marketing via *outbound* e-mail.

Other methods are specific to the medium. Search, blogs, and social media help customers find the firm; advertising options include display, classifieds, video. Social media vastly enhances traditional word of mouth, and mobile marketing has introduced an entirely new medium for interfacing with customers. Technologies like *Bitly* and *Quick Response* (QR) codes link print media with digital content via URLs, Facebook pages, and Twitter hashtags. At firm websites and social media destinations, customers frequently self-select the communications they receive. Firms use web analytics to track what customers see and do online; hence, digital communications are increasingly personalized. Amazon's repeat customers receive recommendations based on prior purchases; Netflix subscribers receive movie tips; individuals receive advertisements based on their web behavior.

Furthermore, the Internet is shifting quickly from a personal computer medium to TV sets (and TV programs onto computers); and to smartphones and tablet computers — mobile marketing.

MARKETING QUESTION

How can firms encourage positive social media or conventional WOM communication about their products? How would you use social media or conventional WOM to increase viewership for a new movie?

MARKETING QUESTION

In the past month, have you recommended a product/brand to someone — or did someone give you a recommendation? Did the firm take any action to encourage social media or conventional WOM?

KEY IDEA

Digital communication embraces all forms of communication enabled by the Internet.

DEVELOPING COMMUNICATIONS STRATEGY

Stainmaster advertises carpets directly to consumers. Stainmaster does not manufacture carpets, just the fiber, but successfully convinces consumers that Stainmaster carpets are stain-resistant. Stainmaster's effective communications drive high consumer awareness and demand for Stainmaster carpets — and for its fibers.

Table 15.1 depicts critical questions for developing communications strategy.[21]

TABLE 15.1
Critical Questions for Developing Communications Strategy

Basic Questions	Subsidiary Questions
1. Who are our communications targets?	Specifically, with what people/entities shall we communicate?
2. What are our communications objectives?	How do communications objectives vary by communications target?
3. What key message(s) do we want to get across?	How should our message(s) vary across communications targets?
4. What communications tools shall we use?	What combination of personal, mass, digital, and WOM communications is appropriate?
5. What communications budget shall we set?	How shall we apportion the budget among different communications targets and communications tools?
6. When is the *right* time to communicate?	What is the appropriate timing for the various targeted messages, considering seasonality and other factors?

COMMUNICATIONS TARGETS

The firm has two major types of communication targets: *directly related* and *not directly related* to firm offers. We focus mainly on directly related targets, but briefly consider not directly related targets. Some directly related targets are decision makers; others are influencers.

DIRECTLY RELATED COMMUNICATIONS TARGETS. The firm should be most concerned with reaching customers specified in the positioning statement of the market strategy — Chapter 9. These include current and potential customers, direct and indirect customers, and third-party specifiers and advisors — Figure 15.3 for a subcomponent manufacturer.

FIGURE 15.3
Potential Communications Targets for a Subcomponent Manufacturer

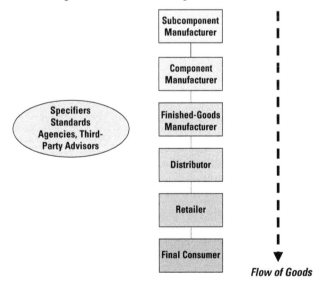

Broadly speaking, communications strategies are either *push* or *pull* — Figure 15.4:

- **Push strategy.** Communications focus on *direct* customers — Figure 15.4 (left). The sub-component manufacturer (SM) places efforts on component manufacturers (CMs). The SM expects CMs to communicate with finished-goods manufacturers and other indirect customers further down the channel. Many B2B firms use *push* communications strategies, most effectively delivered by the sales force.

> Diamond Foods (DM) developed a *push* strategy to encourage retailers to carry its full snack food product line, and secure better shelf placement and in-store marketing support. DM advertised in *Supermarket News* and e-newsletters distributed by the Grocery Manufacturers Association and Food Retailing Institute. DM's message conveyed profitability and brand growth. Sales increased 70 percent.

- **Pull strategy.** Communications focus on *indirect* customers further down the channel, like final consumers or other end users — Figure 15.4 (right). By encouraging these customers to request and purchase finished goods, the firm generates *pull* and drives its own sales. Consumers/end users demand impacts each channel entity, back to CMs and the SM.

This process can be *resultant* — the firm generates strong consumer demand, leading inter-mediaries to purchase products. But the process may also be *anticipatory* — the firm plans a high-spending promotional campaign, and convinces indirect customers to purchase sufficient product volume to satisfy anticipated demand.

Most firms use *either* push or pull strategies, but resource-rich firms often use push/pull combinations. FMCG firms like P&G and Unilever rely heavily on *pull*-based advertising directed at consumers — *indirect* customers. But they also execute major *push* efforts targeted at retailers — *direct* customers. Indeed, P&G's budget for push is roughly the same as for pull. Figure 15.5 (p. 399) illustrates Intel's communications.

KEY IDEA

Two major types of communications targets are:

- *Directly related* to firm products
- *Not directly related* to firm products

FIGURE 15.4
Communications Targets: Push and Pull Strategies

KEY IDEA

Major communications strategies:

- Push
- Pull

Resource-rich firms often use combination *push/pull* strategies.

MARKETING QUESTION

What are the benefits and challenges of using a *pull* strategy?

FIGURE 15.5
Illustration: Push and Pull Strategies Working Together

Regulations influence communications targets in some industries. The FDA previously banned direct-to-consumer prescription-drug advertising but has relaxed this prohibition in recent years (many countries still ban the practice); pull strategies now encourage patients to *ask your doctor*. Firms may also be successful by breaking with traditional practice, like the Stainmaster carpet and *intel inside* campaigns. Both product-ingredient campaigns achieved success selecting innovative communications targets.

Competitors can be important communications targets. Frequently, formal communication with competitors is illegal, so some firms *signal* preferred competitor behavior — Chapter 5. When American Airlines (AA) introduced *value pricing*, it aimed full-page advertisements in *The Wall Street Journal* at Delta, United Airlines, and other major carriers. AA wanted competitors to follow its lead; most did so within a couple of days. Of course, firms also send messages to confuse competitors. Suppliers and complementers may also be communications targets.

Marketing may also have various internal communications targets. Marketing must ensure salespeople *buy in* and use the *right* communications when addressing customers. Marketing may also communicate with all employees so they internalize the brand vision — Chapter 11.

NOT DIRECTLY RELATED COMMUNICATIONS TARGETS. Many firms have communications targets *not directly related* to products. Capital markets are a special case; firms (or agents — like investment banks) target investors to secure debt and equity financing. Firms may also target specific investor types — like long-term investors — to influence shareholder composition.[22] Many firms also *lobby* legislators and special-interest groups.

Although *not directly related* to firm products, communications to such targets can have a serious customer impact. Help-wanted advertisements for highly trained personnel may indicate technological leadership. Lobbying against environmentally friendly legislation may lose sales to *green* consumers.

COMMUNICATIONS OBJECTIVES

Typically, long-run communications objectives focus on increasing sales units, revenues, and/or repeat purchase of firm products. Major considerations in setting short-run objectives for *directly related* communications targets are the specific target and the firm's market strategy.

KEY IDEA

Firms have many communications targets other than customers.

MARKETING QUESTION

Develop a communications plan for your favorite local restaurant. How does your plan improve on the restaurant's current actions?

COMMUNICATIONS TARGET. The firm typically has different objectives for direct and indirect customers, competitors, and complementers.

- **Direct and indirect customers.** Figure 15.3 (p. 397) highlights several direct and indirect customers for a subcomponent manufacturer. Table 15.2 shows that communications objectives for each customer type would likely be quite different.

Type of Customer	Communications Objectives for Customers
Component manufacturer	– Learn how to assemble firm subcomponents into customer components – Purchase subcomponents for use in components – Inventory sufficient components to satisfy finished-goods manufacturers
Third-party advisor	– Recommend firm subcomponents to component manufacturers
Finished-goods manufacturer	– Agree to purchase components for finished products – Agree to place subcomponent brand logo on finished product
Distributor	– Train salespeople to communicate benefits and sell finished products to retailers
Retailer	– Agree to budget co-op advertising funds for finished products
Consumer	– Become aware, understand, like, try, and continue to purchase finished products

TABLE 15.2
Illustrative Communications Objectives for a Subcomponent Manufacturer

MARKETING QUESTION

Use the Table 15.2 framework. Identify target customers and short-term and long-term communications objectives for a firm making global position satellite (GPS) systems for pleasure boats.

- **Competitors and complementers.** Communications objectives are very different from firm objectives for customers. Typically, the firm tries to influence competitor and complementer actions so customers perceive firm offers more favorably.

MARKET STRATEGY. The firm identifies customer targets in the positioning statement of the market strategy — Chapter 9. These targets are also the firm's communication targets. The firm must align communications objectives with selected alternatives in the *strategic focus* to increase unit sales volume:

- Increase customer retention (reduce defection).
- Increase customer use.
- Attract customers from competitors.
- Secure new business.

Table 15.3 shows how market objectives and corresponding customer targets translate into specific communications objectives.

Market Objective	Customer Target for Increasing Unit Sales Volume	Communications Objective
Increase customer retention (reduce defection)	Current customers	– Reinforce customer beliefs that they made the best decision
Increase customer use	Current customers	– Persuade customers to purchase and use in larger quantities
Attract customers from competitors	Competitor customers	– Establish head-to-head trial against the competitor product
Secure new business	Nonusers	– Secure new sales leads – Qualify potential customers – Increase awareness, knowledge, interest, liking, or trial as appropriate

TABLE 15.3
Illustrative Communications Objectives by Customer Target

MARKETING QUESTION

Identify a firm relying heavily on a *pull* strategy. Is the firm successful? If so, why? If not, why not?

Communications objectives depend on market conditions and the firm's market position. In new markets, the firm most likely focuses on identifying, qualifying, communicating, and selling to *nonusers*. Conversely, in mature markets, objectives focus on retaining *current customers* and/or attracting *competitor customers*.

COMMUNICATIONS MESSAGES

Constructing the appropriate message for a customer target is central to developing the communications strategy. The core underlying principle: Message design should reflect the value proposition (positioning element) in the market strategy. If the firm has multiple customer targets, each with different value propositions, then the firm must design multiple messages. Firms spend heavily to develop messages, especially advertising messages; we defer discussion of message design to Chapter 16.

SELECTING COMMUNICATIONS TOOLS

Design a social media strategy for the Chevy Volt.

Communications objectives and messages drive choice of communication tools. Selecting the *right* tool(s) is critical in developing effective communications to reach target audiences. Suppose the communications objective were to build awareness for a new product among a broad consumer group; common sense tells us that advertising is probably more effective than sending salespeople door-to-door. But if the objective were selling sophisticated capital goods to large industrial companies, personal selling would likely be more productive in delivering messages and answering queries. Table 15.4 helps match communication tools to communications objectives and target customers. In the illustration, a wholesaler is trying to distribute and sell a new product. The wholesaler decides to:

- *Identify* potential retailers via direct marketing.
- *Qualify* retailers by telemarketing/telesales.
- *Sell* to qualified retailers via personal selling and the firm's website.
- *Provide* retailers with ongoing sales and service via a sales and service team.

TABLE 15.4

Matching Communications Targets, Objectives, and Tools

Communication Tools	Communications Targets and Objectives			
	Identify potential retailers	Qualify retailers	Sell to qualified retailers	Provide retailers with ongoing sales and service
Personal selling			****	
Telemarketing/telesales		****		
Individual service personnel				
Sales and service teams				****
Advertising				
Direct marketing	****			
Packaging				
Publicity & public relations				
Sales promotion				
E-mail				
Search, blogs, social media			****	
Online display advertising				
Website			****	
Mobile marketing				

Communications objectives and timelines drive choice of communication tools.

The wholesaler chooses *not* to use advertising, publicity & public relations, sales promotion, individual service personnel, or digital approaches other than its website. The wholesaler should develop a similar chart for each customer target.

BUDGETING AND TIMING

Budgeting and timing of communications efforts are critical for designing an effective communications strategy. Both budgeting and timing relate directly to communications objectives and selected communication tools.

A critical budgeting issue concerns choice of push versus pull communication strategies; cost parameters are very different:

- **Pull strategies.** Firms generally spend heavily on advertising to generate pull. These *fixed-cost* expenditures require large cash outflows for uncertain revenues. Hence, pull strategies are generally more popular with well-financed large firms than with small firms.

- **Push strategies.** Firms generally incur high *variable costs* from margins, discounts, and sales commissions earned by intermediaries like wholesalers and retailers. Payments directly relate to firm sales, limiting upfront cash outflows. Smaller firms generally favor push strategies.

Chapter 16 discusses budgeting in greater detail in an advertising context. Timing issues are especially critical in developing and executing *multipoint* integrated communications campaigns using communications tools combinations.

KEY IDEA

Core considerations for the communications strategy are:

- Communications targets
- Communications objectives
- Communications messages
- Communications tools
- Budgeting and timing

INTEGRATING MARKETING COMMUNICATIONS

By now, you should have a good understanding of the communications process, know the key questions for developing communications strategy, and be familiar with communications tools. The core challenge is developing an effective *integrated marketing communications* program to maximize the impact of firm strategy and achieve objectives.[907v, 159v] The firm should strive for four integration types — Figure 15.6:

A. Communications for all targets in a single market segment.

B. Communications with other marketing implementation variables — product, service, distribution, price.

C. Communications for all targets in several market segments.

D. Communications for all targets — market segments, markets, businesses, corporate.

FIGURE 15.6
Coordinating and Integrating Communications

EC (disguised) (electrical components supplier) had marginal success with radio advertising; EC also had little success with its website. When EC advertised the website on drive-time radio, the results were spectacular — a real synergistic result.

Glidden's interior paint market share was declining and the brand was losing relevance. Glidden relaunched its website so visitors could paint virtual rooms — walls, ceiling, trim, share creations via social media, and make shopping lists. Newspaper and TV ads offered the first 300,000 website registrants a free quart of paint; later registrants received coupons. Social media accelerated the promotion and Glidden increased market share by 1.5 percent.

A — INTEGRATE COMMUNICATIONS FOR ALL TARGETS, IN A SINGLE MARKET-SEGMENT STRATEGY.

This integration is fundamental. The firm should blend various communications campaigns (using different tools) to be mutually reinforcing and, if possible, synergistic. The core message, from a well-known B2B advertising execution (featuring a procurement professional), emphasized the importance of integrating advertising with personal selling — Figure 15.7. The critical pitfall is sending discrepant messages; message inconsistency damages firm credibility.

FIGURE 15.7
Advertising Message Highlighting the Importance of Integrating Print Advertising with Personal Selling

I don't know who you are.	**I don't know your company's customers.**
I don't know your company.	**I don't know your company's record.**
I don't know your company's product.	**I don't know your company's reputation.**
I don't know what your company stands for.	**Now, what was it you wanted to sell me?**

Sales starts before you call — with business-to-business advertising

MARKETING QUESTION

Can you identify a firm that confused customers by sending discrepant messages?

As digital media becomes more important, many firms are spending significant effort to effectively integrate various digital communication options, as well as integrating digital communications with conventional mass and personal communications.

B, C, D — REFLECT HIGHER INTEGRATION LEVELS.

In each case, messages must be consistent, even *synergistic*. Corporate-level advertising like GE's *Imagination at Work* (and IBM's *Watson*) may be a helpful door-opener for salespeople. But to achieve good corporate-to-market integration with GE jet engines (for example), GE must coordinate content and timing of product and corporate communications.[23]

KEY IDEA

Communications integration occurs at several levels.

Integration ensures maximum communications impact to achieve firm objectives.

Of course, communications to different groups — customers, competitors, complementers, shareholders, government entities — typically have different purposes. But a single individual may belong to multiple groups and be a target for multiple communications. At a minimum, these communications should not be inconsistent.

Increasingly sophisticated segmentation and *mass customization* practices, along with proliferation of communication tools, are creating more opportunities for marketers to deliver targeted and relevant messages in a granular way. But as 21st-century customers move easily among many communication channels, they expect ever more timely, relevant, and compelling (even entertaining) marketing communications. The firm must construct a clearly defined communications strategy that seamlessly integrates all its communications.

KEY MESSAGES

What other messages did you glean from this chapter?

The communications program is critical for implementing market strategy. To develop a successful program, the firm must address many external and internal challenges.

Three sources of miscommunication are:

- *Encoding* — the firm does not send the *intended* message.
- *Distortion* — the communication process distorts the *sent* message.
- *Decoding* — the receiver misperceives and/or misunderstands the *received* message.

The firm has four categories of communications options:

- *Personal* — mainly salespeople, telemarketing/telesales, service personnel
- *Traditional mass* — advertising, direct marketing, packaging, publicity & public relations, sales promotion
- *Word of mouth* — among customers/potential customers, traditional/digital social media
- *Digital* — e-mail; search, blogs, social media; advertising — display, classifieds, video; websites; mobile marketing

To develop a communications strategy, the firm must answer six critical questions:

- Who are our communications targets — *directly related* to firm offers; *not directly related*?
- What are our communications objectives — vary by communications target and market strategy?
- What key messages do we want to get across — vary by communications target?
- What communications tools shall we use — examine effectiveness of many options?
- What communications budget shall we set?
- When is the *right* time to communicate — consider seasonality and other factors?

The firm's core challenge is to integrate various elements of the communications strategy to form a coherent whole. Four types of integration are:

A. Communications tools for all targets in a single market segment;

B. Communications with other marketing implementation variables — product/service, distribution, price;

C. Communications for all targets in several market segments;

D. Communication tools for all targets — market segments, markets, businesses, corporate.

QUESTIONS FOR STUDY AND DISCUSSION

Can you answer the questions implied by this chapter's learning outcomes? Check!

1. Identify a personal communication that you sent but the receiver did not receive as intended. Was this an encoding, distortion, or decoding problem? How could you improve the communication?

2. Suppose you were marketing VP for Rolls-Royce Aero Engines. What are your communications targets? What are your communications objectives for each target?

3. For many years, U.S. commercial banks could issue only MasterCard and Visa cards. That changed, and banks can now also distribute both AmEx and Discover cards. Use the framework in Table 15.3 to identify new target customers and communications objectives for AmEx and Discover. Explain how and why target customers and communications objectives differ between AmEx and Discover.

4. Many firms have shareholder-relations departments. What do these departments do? Compare and contrast their activities to the advertising department in a business unit.

5. Sketch out an integrated communications program for Samsung's newest smartphone, for a product that interests you, or *Managing Marketing in the 21st Century*.

6. Repositioning by a regional bank involves longer weekday hours, weekend opening, and extensive online banking services. What steps would you take to develop an effective communications strategy for the *new* bank?

TRUE/FALSE QUESTIONS
Answers on page A2 and at www.axcessvids.com — 572p

1. Publicity is usually defined as communication for which the firm does not pay directly.
   ❏ TRUE ❏ FALSE

2. Advertisers generally view digital marketing as a subset of mass communications.
   ❏ TRUE ❏ FALSE

3. Typically, firms have little control over word-of-mouth communication, but are increasingly orchestrating buzz-marketing and guerrilla-marketing campaigns to encourage positive word of mouth. ❏ TRUE ❏ FALSE

4. The firm has two major types of communications targets: early adopters and late adopters.
   ❏ TRUE ❏ FALSE

5. Increasingly sophisticated segmentation and mass customization practices, along with the proliferation of communication tools, are creating more opportunities for marketers to deliver targeted and relevant messages in a granular way to customers. ❏ TRUE ❏ FALSE

MULTIPLE CHOICE QUESTIONS
Answers on page A2 and at www.axcessvids.com — 153p

1. Which of the following is NOT one of the three causes of miscommunication?
   a. encoding
   b. distortion
   c. decoding
   d. feedback

2. Which of the following types of mass communication is usually defined as communication for which the firm does not pay directly?
   a. direct marketing
   b. advertising
   c. publicity
   d. public relations

3. Which of the following is NOT a basic question for developing communications strategy?
   a. Which advertising/communications agency shall we use?
   b. What are the communications objectives?
   c. What communications tools shall we use?
   d. What communications budget shall we set?

4. Which of the following is NOT one of the four types of integration a firm should strive to attain to maximize impact of its strategy and achieve objectives?

   a. Integrate communications with other marketing implementation variables like product/service, distribution, price.
   b. Integrate communication for all targets in a single market.
   c. Integrate communication for all targets in several markets.
   d. Integrate communications, in parallel with competitor actions, mirror market-share growth.

IMPERATIVE 4

Design the Market Offer

CHAPTER 16

MASS COMMUNICATIONS

For complimentary material, see Axcess Capon codes at www.axcessvids.com

LEARNING OUTCOMES

When you have completed this chapter, you will be able to:

- Articulate how advertising works.
- Define and measure advertising objectives.
- Design an advertising campaign.
- Know when to use mass communications — traditional advertising, direct marketing, packaging, publicity & public relations, sales promotion.

OPENING CASE: MASTERCARD INTERNATIONAL

In the late 1990s, MasterCard (MC), a credit card company owned by member banks, was in trouble. Market share had declined for 10 straight years and competitive pressures from Visa, AmEx, and Discover were intensifying. MC enjoyed similar retail acceptance to Visa, but top-of-mind awareness was 10 percentage points inferior. MC was also losing support from member banks, both domestic and international: In the U.S., MC's share of direct-mail solicitations trailed Visa significantly.

MC conducted an extensive advertising agency review and selected McCann-Erickson (ME). ME concluded this once-dominant brand had lost emotional relevance with consumers. MC had also lost credibility with critical member banks, and the power to make independent decisions. Worse, not only did the MC brand have different campaigns in almost every international market, Visa and AmEx consistently outspent MC.

ME research in the U.S. and key international markets indicated consumers viewed MC as a stodgy, functional, everyday brand, with little aspirational relevance. AmEx was professional, worldly, responsible; Visa was sociable, stylish, on the go. By contrast, MC was unassuming, unpretentious, and practical. ME saw its task as shifting MasterCard from an emotionally neutral generic card to a card that consumers felt good about using.

ME's secondary data analysis revealed a shift away from the materialistic and outer-directed consumer culture of the 1980s/early 1990s. Success symbols like wearing designer clothes, shopping at prestigious stores, staying at luxury hotels, owning expensive cars, and using a prestigious credit card had been replaced. The new success symbols were being in control of, and satisfied with, one's life; having a good home and family; and being able to afford what was really important. The vast majority of consumers believed an unpaid credit card balance was necessary and justified. ME dubbed this emerging mind-set as good revolving *and set out to target* good revolvers, *by helping them lead* rich lives. *ME's selling idea was: MasterCard is* The Better Way to Pay for Everything That Matters.

Armed with this insight and direction, ME's three-person creative team — Joyce King Thomas, Jeroen Bours, and Jonathan Cranin — brainstormed extensively for one month. Cranin generated the tag line Some things money can't buy *in the shower. A couple of weeks later, over Sunday morning coffee and bagels, Thomas and Bours conceived the first advertisement — set at a baseball game featuring some ordinary transactions. In the ad, voice-over actor Billy Crudup intoned, "Two tickets, $28; hot dogs, popcorn and soda, $18; autographed baseball, $45; real conversation with 11-year-old-son, priceless ... there are some things money can't buy. For everything else, there's MasterCard."* **[457v]**

ME crafted more than 300 TV commercials, in 53 languages, shown in 112 countries. Globally, ME's work for MasterCard is the largest single campaign ever and won well over 100 creative awards. In the ultimate accolade, numerous comics and satirists parodied the Priceless *campaign, incorporating Bill Clinton,* **[991v]** *George W. Bush,* **[620v]** *and other parodies.* **[711v]**

More importantly, the Priceless *campaign delivered impressive results for MasterCard. MC's gross dollar volume increased by well over 250 percent; banks issued more than one billion cards; brand awareness rose significantly; and the gap with Visa narrowed.*[1] *MC carried forward the* Priceless *campaign by training its 8,000 employees to be* Social Brand Ambassadors. *Today, more than 3,000 regularly share MC content with friends on social media on internal and external MasterCard platforms.*

In 2006, MC's initial public offering (IPO) changed its status from a partnership of member banks to a public company. By 2015, MC's share price reached ten times higher than its IPO price.

> **Case Question**
>
> How do you account for MasterCard's success? What other advertising campaigns do you consider memorable? Why?

Chapter 16 is the second of four chapters in Part B of Imperative 4 — *Design the Market Offer.* Part B focuses on *Communicating Customer Value*; Chapter 16 addresses *Mass Communications.*

Advertising continues to be the most visible form of mass communications. Advertising consumes the largest percentage of many FMCG firms marketing budgets and is increasingly important for B2B firms. We focus on how advertising works, but also address other mass communications options — direct marketing, packaging, publicity & public relations (P&PR), sales promotion. We defer discussion of digital communications to Chapter 17.

Although we necessarily discuss various mass communications options individually, we must emphasize the importance of the focus in Chapter 15 — *Integrated Marketing Communications.* Without question, each communication option we discuss has value, but the power of the firm's communications program is integrating selected options into a coherent whole, versus putting forward a set of uncoordinated efforts.

Communications Effectiveness

P&G reinvigorated Old Spice with a series of cool *Spice Man* advertisements and YouTube videos — 40 million views; sales doubled within 30 days. [240v]

Beats by Dre *Before the Game* 2014 advertising campaign generated more than 22 million views.

Amex launched *Small Business Saturday* to gain awareness. By year 3, more than 6,000 small businesses participated — 100 million Americans *shopped small* on that day.

THE CHANGING VIEW

OLD WAY	NEW WAY
Creativity desirable in messaging	Creativity essential in everything
Direct response methods are rare	Direct response methods are ubiquitous
Direct media sales	Programmatic media
Exposure-driven	Impact-driven
Intermediaries are usually involved	Movement to direct marketing
Intuition	Measurement/tracking
Local/national advertising strategies	Regional/global advertising strategies
Media scheduling is pedestrian	Media scheduling creativity is essential
Passive audience	Active/interactive audience
Payments based on advertising spend	Payments based on revenue performance
Short-term promotions common	Long-term brand equity a key concern

Half the money I spend on advertising is wasted; the trouble is I don't know which half.

— John Wanamaker, marketing pioneer[2]

ADVERTISING FOUNDATIONS

At its essence, advertising is a service. When you pay attention to an advertising message, you receive the functional value of information and sometimes even find it entertaining. Indeed, many of us look forward to Super Bowl advertisements. You may also receive psychological and economic value, but you rarely ever pay for advertisements! From the customer perspective, TV advertising (and TV) is mostly free, and advertising subsidizes the price you pay for newspapers and magazines.[3]

Figure 16.1 (p. 410) explains how this system works. Mostly, you (as a customer) receive advertising messages together with some content you desire, like a TV show, newspaper article, or magazine story. The advertiser pays the media firm to *bundle* together advertising and content — but the advertiser receives nothing *directly* in return. The advertiser receives value *indirectly*, from the attention you give its messages with your eyes, ears, and hopefully switched-on brain. This attention has immense value for advertisers. Indeed, Google's high market valuation derives from substantial website traffic, and subsequent click-through from Google AdWords/Google+ to advertiser websites.

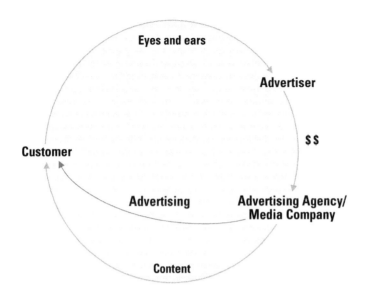

FIGURE 16.1
The Advertising Process

In many industries, particularly FMCG, advertising is central to implementing market and communications strategies. (MasterCard Opening Case) Table 16.1 shows critical questions for developing *advertising strategy* and relevant links to market and communications strategies. Similar questions are instrumental in developing strategy for other mass and digital communications (Chapter 17) options.

KEY IDEA

Advertising is critical for both market and communications strategies.

Element	Question	Link to Market and Communications Strategies
Communications target	Who are we trying to influence?	Customers in target segments (market strategy)
Advertising objectives	What are we trying to achieve?	Directly related to strategic and operational objectives (market strategy)
Messaging	What message(s) should communications targets receive?	Related to the value proposition (market strategy)
Execution	How shall we communicate the message?	The most effective way to reach communications targets
Media selection and timing	Where and when shall we place our advertising?	Select media to reach communications targets at the appropriate time
Advertising budget	How much shall we spend on advertising?	Advertising budget is one element of the entire communications budget
Evaluation	How shall we test our advertising and measure its effectiveness?	Choose from a variety of measurement methodologies

TABLE 16.1
Elements of Advertising Strategy

The firm should consider advertising as an *investment*. Today's advertising should achieve short-term results, but may also have long-run impact. Advertising may contribute to building the brand and lead to future customer purchases. Unfortunately, advertising is an expense on the income statement and counts against current revenues. Hence, many firms underfund advertising. But advertising may fail for other reasons — Table 16.2.

MARKETING QUESTION

Table 16.2 shows reasons that advertising can fail. Identify some *ineffective* advertising. Why did this advertising fail?

Unclear or nonspecific target	Weak creative content
Does not create a unique, ownable space	Creative does not support the message
Mismatched message and advertising vehicle	No way to measure effectiveness
Too much information (TMI)	Too many people involved in creative development
Inconsistent messages to multiple communications targets	Short-lived campaigns

TABLE 16.2
Why Advertising May Fail

Over and above these issues, the firm must address a fast-evolving set of advertising options. For many years, television, radio, newspapers, and magazines pretty much defined the communications landscape. Today, there is also digital media, embracing a whole set of new options — Chapter 17 — making the integration task ever more complex.

KEY IDEA

The advertising program comprises:

*   **Communications targets**
*   Advertising objectives
*   Messaging
*   Execution
*   Media selection and timing
*   Advertising budget
*   Evaluation

The Advertising Program

COMMUNICATIONS TARGETS

WHO ARE WE TRYING TO INFLUENCE?

As we learned earlier, a key element in formulating market strategy is deciding which segments to target. For each target segment, the positioning statement identifies customer targets with whom the firm wishes to communicate. For a *push* strategy, the firm focuses on direct customers; for a *pull* strategy, the firm focuses on indirect customers. The firm must also decide which decision makers, influencers, and other entities to reach during the purchase decision process. Because advertising funding is limited, the firm must carefully select *communications targets* before making budget allocations.

HOW ADVERTISING *WORKS*

Advertising effectiveness is perhaps the most-studied marketing topic.[4] *Hierarchy-of-effects* models are central to understanding how advertising works. Figure 16.2 shows models for *high-involvement* and *low-involvement* products.[5] Typically, the ultimate goal is to reinforce the brand and encourage *purchase* and *repeat purchase*. Note particularly the intermediate steps between *awareness* and *repeat purchase* in each model. High-involvement processes typically take longer.[6,7,8]

KEY IDEA

Hierarchy-of-effects models for high-involvement and low-involvement products are central to understanding how advertising works.

FIGURE 16.2
Hierarchy-of-Effects Advertising Models

MARKETING QUESTION

Apply a hierarchy-of-effects model to your purchase of a HDTV set.

High involvement. The customer believes the purchase, like a new automobile, is risky — functional, psychological, economic, financial risk. The customer engages in a staged learning process[9]:
*   *Awareness.* Learning the product is available for purchase
*   *Knowledge.* Understanding product attributes/features, benefits/values
*   *Liking/preference.* Developing favorable/positive feelings about the product
*   *Trial.* Testing the product before purchase and use
*   *Purchase.* Exchange money or other resources for the product
*   *Repeat purchase.* Purchasing the product again. Advertising can reinforce beliefs leading to repeat purchase

Low involvement. Customers see little risk and require little prepurchase knowledge — FMCG categories like soda or cereal. Hence, the hierarchical process is quite different. Advertising's role is creating high *awareness* and motivating customers to *trial*.[10] If customers like the product, they purchase and repurchase.[11]

ADVERTISING OBJECTIVES

WHAT ARE WE TRYING TO ACHIEVE?

Once the firm has validated advertising as the appropriate communications vehicle, it should formulate *advertising objectives*. Key considerations are:

- **Output objectives** — what the firm ultimately wants to achieve — sales, market share, brand loyalty — secured via purchase and repeat purchase.

- **Intermediate objectives** — relate to hierarchy-of-effects models; include awareness, knowledge, liking/preference, trial, and/or emotional commitment (to a brand). For new product launch, the firm may initially focus on *awareness* as the crucial objective. The importance of other intermediate objectives depends on the particular hierarchy-of-effects model — high involvement/low involvement — governing purchase.

To achieve output objectives, the firm may take many actions, like delivering and servicing products, in addition to advertising. Hence, failure to achieve an output objective like sales may not directly relate to success/failure of an advertising program. By contrast, monitoring well-chosen *intermediate objectives* provides excellent feedback on advertising effectiveness. The firm must choose specific output and/or intermediate advertising objectives for its strategic situation, then decide numerical performance targets and when to measure actual performance.[12] (For extensive focus on monitor and control — Chapter 24.)

Illustrative Advertising Objectives

- To secure *90 percent awareness* of antioxidant toothpaste Wiz-klene among dentists within *one month of launch.*

- To increase *repeat purchase* of Munchee candy bars *from 30 percent to 50 percent* among 10- to 16-year-old boys *by end June.*

MESSAGING

WHAT MESSAGE(S) SHOULD COMMUNICATIONS TARGETS RECEIVE?

The advertising message derives directly from the market strategy — Chapter 9. Look back at that chapter and revisit the four positioning elements:

Convince	[customer target]
In the context of other alternatives	[competitor targets]
That they will receive these benefits	[value proposition]
Because we have these capabilities/features	[reasons to believe]

Most importantly, the advertising message should closely align with the value proposition. The message should always focus upon core benefits/values, and reflect unique claims where the firm has differential advantage.**[446v]** Clear positioning statements provide excellent guidance for advertising agency creative personnel to help them develop effective messages. By contrast, poor positioning often leads to unsatisfactory and/or confusing messages. Messaging must also consider the amount of time communications targets may be exposed to advertisements. The life span for television advertisements is a few seconds; for newspapers — part of a day; for magazines — maybe one week. Messages must evolve and resonate with communications targets, but support consistent positioning (MasterCard Opening Case). Table 16.3 (p. 413) shows how FedEx's objectives and core messages evolved.[13]

KEY IDEA

The advertising program comprises:

- Communications targets
- **Advertising objectives**
- Messaging
- Execution
- Media selection and timing
- Advertising budget
- Evaluation

KEY IDEA

The firm should set two types of advertising objectives — output and intermediate.

Output objectives like sales and market share are what the firm ultimately wants to achieve, secured via:

- Purchase
- Repeat purchase

Intermediate objectives relate to hierarchy-of-effects models and include:

- Awareness
- Knowledge
- Liking/preference
- Trial

KEY IDEA

The advertising program comprises:

- Communications targets
- Advertising objectives
- **Messaging**
- Execution
- Media selection and timing
- Advertising budget
- Evaluation

MARKETING QUESTION

How do you assess Nike's messaging? **[888v]**

TABLE 16.3
*Advertising Objectives
and Messaging —
FedEx (Federal Express)*

Time Period	Objectives	Core Messages	Slogan
1972	Awareness	Who are we? How do we work?	*Take away our planes and we'd be just like anybody else.*
1978	Knowledge	How do we compare?	*When it absolutely, positively has to be there overnight.*
1980–1987	Trial and repeat purchase	Try us! Don't switch	*Why fool around with anybody else?*
1995–2003	Repeat purchase	Don't switch	*Don't be a dope.*
2004–2009	Supply-chain ownership	Convenience	*Relax It's FedEx*
2009–present	Awareness	Better technology, better service	*The World on Time*

**MARKETING
QUESTION**

How do you assess Federal Express/FedEx TV advertisements? Which advertisement do you think is most effective? **[424v, 876v, 569v, 287v, 225v, 932v]**

**MARKETING
QUESTION**

What advertising messages/slogans would/would not work globally?

Firms active in multiple countries must decide whether, and to what extent, they should *standardize* messages globally or *localize* for national/regional markets. National markets differ — cultural norms, living patterns, income distributions — hence, these variables provide useful *hooks* for developing localized messages. But standardization can provide cost and efficiency advantages and brand power. Samsung rose from a lesser-known electronics firm to the seventh most valuable global brand (2015) by deploying a consolidated, consistent, consumer-focused global advertising approach. Also, by exerting quality control centrally, the firm can avoid problems like Coke experienced. Regardless, standardization requires local input to avoid translation problems.[14]

> As part of a decentralization initiative, Coke gave advertising responsibility to regional marketers who previously relied on corporate expertise. Some advertising was un-Coke-like. In one U.S. advertisement, a grandmother is angry that Coke is not served in a restaurant — she knocks over a table with her wheelchair. In Germany, a scantily clad couple is shown groping while enjoying a Coke.[15]

KEY IDEA

The advertising program comprises:
- Communications targets
- Advertising objectives
- Messaging
- **Execution**
- Media selection and timing
- Advertising budget
- Evaluation

Standardization has also become easier as advertising agencies have *gone global*. Large firms increasingly rely on single agencies for communications around the world. HSBC placed all global advertising and marketing with WPP; a 600-person WPP team from 21 local agencies manages the $600 million account. Exxon shot commercials for the advertising campaign, *We're drivers too*, in two locations, but used more than 20 different casts for local airing. Mentos — *Stay Fresh* — approaches global advertising similarly. Of course, the *right* degree of standardization depends on the product form, target customers, and competition. Some messages may not work well in different countries.

EXECUTION

HOW SHALL WE COMMUNICATE THE MESSAGE?

KEY IDEA

Creating advertising is an enigma, more art than science, mysterious, and unexplainable.

Execution focuses on the method (style) firms use to turn core messages into effective — *priceless* — advertising. This task is daunting and challenging. **[799v]** Branding guru Schmitt explains: "Creative output [is] the most visible part of advertising. Although judging creative output may be easy, the creative process is an enigma, more art than science, mysterious and unexplainable. The essence of creativity seems to be a willingness to alternate between divergent and convergent thinking, between brainstorming and analytic reasoning, between pushing the limits and being reasonable and practical. [The result, ideally,] culminates in an illumination — the Big Idea."[16]

In the Opening Case, we saw how a *Big Idea* drove MasterCard's highly successful — *Priceless* — advertising campaign. Another creative success is Absolut vodka's print campaign. Absolut's share of imported vodka increased from 1 percent to over 60 percent. Figure 16.3 shows typical Absolut advertisements. Each advertisement has a two-word headline (*tag line*) starting with *Absolut*, then adding carefully chosen words to reinforce the imagery — Absolut Perfection, Absolut Appeal, Absolut Original — always highlighting the bottle shape. Absolut's campaign, featuring several hundred executions on a single theme, won many awards for elegance, simplicity, and effectiveness that set it apart from competition.[17] In 2015, Absolut reintroduced its bottle-focused campaign — new art, new tag lines — spending more than 50 percent of budget in digital media.

FIGURE 16.3
Absolut Advertisements: Examples

HSBC also ran a print campaign based on a similar premise — core message with multiple executions. HSBC's value proposition was global reach but also local knowledge. The advertising headline, *Never underestimate the importance of local knowledge*, appeared two thirds of the way down the page. Six short paragraphs then elaborated the local knowledge claim. The top part of the page showed two or three objects identified by country — Figure 16.4.

HSBC used two execution types:

- Type 1: *Identical* objects labeled *differently* in different countries. Figure 16.4 (left) shows the *grasshopper* advertisement (top part). Similar executions were: *hand position*: Egypt — *Be patient*; Italy — *What exactly do you mean?*; Greece — *That's just perfect*; and *foot position*: USA — relaxed; Thailand — rude.
- Type 2: *Different* objects labeled *similarly* — Figure 16.4 (right).

HSBC reinforced its *glocal* message by placing advertisements at major international airports — jet bridges, baggage claim.

Sometimes audience characteristics drive executional variety. A Unilever brand manager remarked that Sony avoided boring its target audience by using multiple executions for PlayStation. "They influenced us: Three years ago we ran three Lynx (deodorant for boys) executions a year; we raised this to 10, with more to come."[18]

FIGURE 16.4 (LEFT)
HSBC Advertisement:
Identical Objects: Example

FIGURE 16.4 (RIGHT)
HSBC Advertisement:
Different Objects: Example

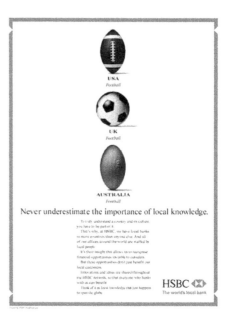

Advertising executions come in two major forms — *rational* and *emotional*.

RATIONAL APPEALS

By definition, rational appeals focus on people's sense of logic. Five main styles are:

- **Comparative (attack).** Successful comparative advertising demonstrates superiority over competition. Small-market-share firms often compare products versus the leader, so as to enter customer consideration sets. Examples include *We try harder* — Avis, **[792v, 163v]** Duracell versus Energizer batteries **[403v]**; Mac versus PC. **[353v]**[19]

  > Virgin Atlantic Airways chairman Sir Richard Branson makes a habit of exploiting gaffes by arch-rival British Airways (BA). BA's CEO referred to Hollywood stars as "gutless cowards" for refusing to fly after 9/11. Virgin advertised in *Variety* and the *Hollywood Reporter* featuring the "gutless cowards" remark and providing Virgin Atlantic's reservations phone number.

- **Demonstration.** Shows the product in use and focuses on performance, like many automobile advertisements. Many B2B communications use *demonstration ads*; they are also common in sales force materials.[20]

- **One-sided versus two-sided.** *One-sided* advertising focuses only on positive product attributes; *two-sided* advertising presents both positive and negative information. One-sided appeals are most effective when communications targets are less educated and feel positively toward the product. Two-sided appeals are more effective when the communications target has an initial opinion that is not necessarily positive; is educated; and/or is skeptical. By presenting opposing viewpoints, two-sided appeals enhance advertiser credibility; they may also inoculate targets against competitor communications by enhancing resistance to counterclaims.[21]

- **Primacy versus recency.** Research shows that items at the beginning of a message — *primacy* — and at the end — *recency* — are more effective than those in the middle.[22] When the audience is less interested in a product, or has an unfavorable prior impression, primacy is generally more effective in gaining attention and/or minimizing objections. When the audience is initially favorable, disinterested, and/or objections need not be overcome, recency generally works better.

Use available resources like print media and YouTube to identify advertisements using each of the rational and emotional appeals discussed. Bring to class.

Rational-style advertising includes:

- Comparative (attack)
- Demonstration
- One-sided versus two-sided appeals
- Primacy versus recency
- Refutational

• **Refutational.** A special case of two-sided advertising explicitly mentioning competitor claims, but then directly refuting them — beef advertisements note unhealthiness claims for red meat, then refutes them. Refutational appeals may also succeed by inoculation.[23]

Firms often use high-credibility sources to enhance rational appeals. When battling Oracle's takeover bid, PeopleSoft placed full-page advertisements in the *Wall Street Journal, Washington Post*, and other major papers. These ads quoted major U.S. newspapers and analysts, suggesting an Oracle-PeopleSoft merger would harm PeopleSoft customers and should be defeated (Oracle prevailed). Firms also use employees — CEOs and shop-floor workers **[118v, 631v]** — as credible sources; and encourage posting success stories on Instagram and Twitter.

EMOTIONAL APPEALS

These approaches appeal to emotions. Four main styles are:

• **Celebrity endorsement.** Advertisers often use well-known people to endorse products/brands, especially on TV. A good celebrity/product match creates product awareness and brand credibility. Coty offered a Jennifer Lopez fragrance; Elizabeth Arden countered with Britney Spears. **[809v]**[24] Beyoncé reportedly has a $50 million deal with PepsiCo. Celebrity endorsements reached a new level when former heavyweight champion George Foreman sold his name and image to grill manufacturer Salton for $137.5 million[25]; Papa John's Pizza spent more than $130 million on its Peyton Manning campaign.

But celebrity endorsement is not a *slam dunk*. To be effective, the audience must bond with the product, not just the celebrity! A celebrity may lose credibility by endorsing too many products. Former basketball star Michael Jordan endorsed AMF Bowling, Ball Park Franks, Bijan, CBS Sportsline, Chicagoland Chevrolet Dealer Association, Gatorade, Hanes, Nike, Oakley, Rayovac, Wheaties, and Wilson Sporting Goods! Furthermore, negative publicity for the celebrity may flow to the product. O.J. Simpson's murder trials hurt Hertz; Coca-Cola, McDonald's, and Spalding dropped Kobe Bryant (sexual assault accusations); Haynes dropped Charlie Sheen (felony assault and menacing charges); Nike dropped sprinter Justin Gatlin and seven-time *Tour de France* winner Lance Armstrong (performance-enhancing drugs) and football player Michael Vick (illegal dogfighting); Accenture, AT&T, Gillette, and PepsiCo dropped Tiger Woods (extramarital affairs).[26] Sometimes CEOs become celebrities by endorsing firm brands — Charles Schwab (investments) and Frank Perdue (chicken), but problems may occur: Pete Coors (Coors Chairman) strongly promoted responsible drinking, yet was arrested for DUI (driving under the influence).

• **Fear.** Fear appeals create anxiety; behaving as the advertising suggests removes anxiety. *Physical danger* is common in insurance advertising; *social disapproval* is typical for personal hygiene products; *monetary loss* for security products and credit cards; *aging insecurities* for cosmetic creams. A famous fear appeal series from Michelin focused on babies with the tag line — *because so much is riding on your tires.* **[916v, 369v, 731v]** Developing effective fear appeals is not easy: Too mild and they lack impact; too strong and audience defense mechanisms may block/reject them.[27]

• **Humor.** Humor is widespread in advertising but firms should use it carefully. Humor helps create awareness, sets a positive tone, and enhances memory; but improperly crafted humor may distract from the core message. The result: The audience remembers the ad but not the product/brand; finds the humor *unfunny*; or worse, may *mis-index* — link the humor to a competitor product/brand. Many people found GoDaddy's 2005 Super Bowl advertisement very funny — a well-endowed dancer struggled with her top while explaining a commercial to a stuffy Congressional committee.[28] Fox ran the ad early in the game, but canceled a planned second airing.[29] **[833v]**

• **Storytelling.** Storytelling can be a very effective way of appealing to emotions. MasterCard's *Priceless* campaign (Opening Case) and Nike's *Just Do It* are great storytelling examples. Budweiser advertisements with *Clydesdale* horses often tell stories evoking emotional responses.

MARKETING QUESTION

Select three of your favorite advertisements. Describe their message styles. Were they *rational* — comparative, demonstration, one-sided or two-sided, primacy or recency, refutational? Or *emotional* — celebrity endorsement, fear, humor, storytelling? Or a combination of styles?

KEY IDEA

Emotional-style advertising includes:

• Celebrity endorsement
• Fear
• Humor
• Storytelling

MARKETING QUESTION

Identify an advertisement using a fear appeal. What is the objective? Do you think the advertisement works?

MARKETING QUESTION

View Go Daddy's *Censorship Hearing* advertisement.**[611v]** Do you think the ad is funny? Why or why not? Bring your favorite humorous advertisement to class.

In practice, many firms combine/blend pure-form approaches. Regardless of appeal type, advertisers must understand the context, culture, and language of target customers to gain resonance. In *native* advertising — used in many traditional and online media — the firm employs the same form as the surrounding medium, like an article seemingly written by editorial staff.

MEDIA SELECTION AND TIMING

WHERE AND WHEN SHALL WE PLACE OUR ADVERTISING?

In 2014, U.S. advertising spending was $180 billion, led by television, followed by digital[30] — Figure 16.5. Media choices are expanding; digital is growing fastest.

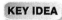

KEY IDEA

The advertising program comprises:

- Communications targets
- Advertising objectives
- Messaging
- Execution
- **Media selection and timing**
- Advertising budget
- Evaluation

FIGURE 16.5
U.S. Advertising Spending by Major Media Class 2014 ($ Billions)[31]

MARKETING QUESTION

Redraw Figure 16.5 with your forecast of advertising spending 10 years in the future.

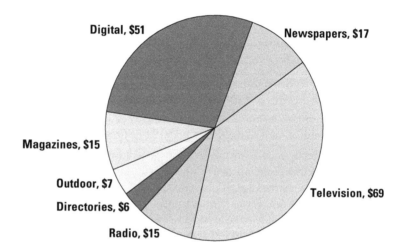

To evaluate and select appropriate media, the firm must answer five related questions:

- **Media objectives.** What should our media strategy accomplish?
- **Media classes.** What types of media shall we use — print, broadcast, digital, outdoor?
- **Media vehicles.** What specific media shall we use — *Vanity Fair*, *The Voice*, *Google*, bus stops?
- **Timing.** When should our advertising appear?
- **Media schedule.** Specifically, where and when shall we place our ads?

MEDIA OBJECTIVES

KEY IDEA

Critical media selection and timing decisions:

Media objectives
↓
Media classes
↓
Media vehicles
↓
Timing
↓
Media schedule

WHAT SHOULD OUR MEDIA STRATEGY ACCOMPLISH? Key concerns are *reach, frequency,* and *impact*:

- **Reach.** Number of target individuals exposed to advertising at least once — *impressions, eyeballs.*
- **Frequency.** Average number of times a target individual is exposed to advertising.
- **Reach and frequency.** Reach and frequency calculate *gross rating points* (GRPs).

    Gross rating points (GRPs) = Reach × Frequency

Generally, advertisers trade off reach and frequency. GRP objectives are popular, but may cause problems. For example, to secure 250 GRPs:

- 100 percent of the communications targets receives, on average, 2.5 exposures.
- 10 percent of the communications targets receives, on average, 25 exposures.

Many advertisers require a minimum number of exposures; hence, they set GRP objectives subject to minimum required frequency. For complex messages, messages in competition with others, and/or messages for new products, advertisers typically require high frequency, but they should also be concerned about diminishing returns. Of course, media objectives should relate directly to advertising objectives.

KEY IDEA

Important media objectives include:
- Reach
- Frequency
- Impact

Media Objectives: Illustration

- *Reach* 50 percent of communications targets five times in the next six months — *frequency*.
- Deliver 250 *GRPs* subject to minimum 70 percent *reach*.

Advertising Objectives and Media Objectives: Illustration

Advertising objectives: Increase repeat purchase of Munchee candy bars from 30 percent to 50 percent among 10- to 16-year-old boys by end of June.

Media objectives: Deliver 1,500 GRPs, subject to minimum 60 percent reach.

When the firm uses different media types, duplication can be an issue. Suppose the firm decides to advertise on both radio and TV; two relevant measures are:

- **Duplicated reach:** Receive a message from *both* radio and TV.
- **Unduplicated reach:** Receive a single message from *either* radio or TV, but not both.

Sometimes the firm wants to maximize *duplicated reach* by exposure to several media types. Alternatively, the firm may want to maximize *unduplicated reach* regardless of media type.

- **Impact.** Impact is directly related to creativity in generating advertisements — indeed, many *creatives* view the media department's job as boring and routine. But mass media has fragmented, many digital marketing options have emerged, and consumer media habits are more varied; hence, media decisions are increasingly challenging. Thirty years ago, FMCG firms could reach 70 percent of women aged 25 to 54 with less than 10 advertising spots on network TV; today it takes more than 100 spots. The best media executives are highly creative, deploying innovative strategies across several media classes. Some firms achieve media objectives with fewer GRPs and/or lower expenditures by placing a single basic advertisement across several media classes, like using varying length videos for TV, movie theaters, and digital. Branded content (BC) is a new form of communications, typically funded by advertisers, that fuses together entertainment and advertising. Example: IBM partnered with CNBC to produce a TV program, *The Business of Innovation*. BC addresses the *time-shifting* digital video recorder (DVR) problem of fast-forwarding through advertisements. Creative media strategies spawned advertising-supported bus shelters in New York and colorful buses and taxis in many cities.[32]

MARKETING QUESTION

Advances in DVR technology allow viewers to skip commercials automatically. What are the implications for television advertising? As a heavy TV advertiser, what if any action would you take?

Häagen-Dazs successfully launched superpremium ice cream in Britain, using only black-and-white newspaper advertisements, for just £375,000. This unexpected copy gained significant publicity — the creatives won a major advertising award.

Volvo truck's multivideo YouTube campaign featuring martial arts actor Jean Claude Van Damme doing a split between two Volvo trucks earned 66 million views in two months.[552v]

MEDIA CLASSES

WHAT TYPES OF MEDIA SHALL WE USE? A *media class* is a group of closely related media vehicles. Media classes differ from one another on dimensions like time availability and intrusiveness. A common category system embraces:

- **Broadcast** — television, radio. Exist for short time periods — significantly intrusive.
- **Digital** — Chapter 17. Read at leisure — more intrusive than print.

- **Outdoor** — billboards — increasingly dynamic — in-store. Long presence — relatively nonintrusive.
- **Print** — newspapers, magazines. Read at leisure — relatively nonintrusive.

Table 16.4 shows advantages and disadvantages of selected media classes for advertisers[33]:

TABLE 16.4
Selected Media Classes: Advantages and Disadvantages

Media Class	Advantages	Disadvantages
Television	Attention-getting	Clutter
	Favorable image	High absolute cost
	High prestige	High production costs
	High reach	Long production lead times
	Impact of sight, sound, motion	Low selectivity
	Low cost per exposure	Short message life
	Mass coverage	
Radio	Flexible	Audio only
	High frequency	Clutter
	Local coverage	Fleeting message
	Low cost	Low attention-getting
	Low production costs	Low remembering
	Well-segmented audiences	
Digital	Ability to optimize	Less understood than others
	Ability to remarket	Placement sensitivity
	Measurement by click-through	
	Multiple options	
	Growing audience	
	Personalized communications	
	Segmented audiences	
	Enhanced word of mouth via social media	
Outdoor	Easily noticed	Local restrictions
	High repetition	Poor environmental image
	Location specific	Short exposure time requires short advertisement
Newspapers	Ads can be placed in interest sections	Clutter
	Can be used for coupons	Low attention-getting capabilities
	High coverage	Poor reproduction quality
	Low cost	Selective reader exposure
	Reader controls exposure	Short life
	Short lead time for placement	
	Timely (current ads)	
Magazines	High information content	Lack of design flexibility
	Longevity	Long lead time for placing advertising
	Multiple readers (high pass-along)	Visual only
	Quality reproduction	
	Segmentation potential	

KEY IDEA

Critical media selection and timing decisions:

Media objectives
↓
Media classes
↓
Media vehicles
↓
Timing
↓
Media schedule

MARKETING QUESTION

You are launching an Internet security system for large and small businesses. Identify your communications targets. Identify media classes you would consider. Why these?

Figure 16.5 (p. 417) depicts the most widely used media classes — television, digital, newspapers, magazines — but many other options may be attractive. Some firms try to avoid clutter by using less-conventional approaches. Technological advances, low prices, and increased personal mobility make outdoor advertising attractive — airport signs, standard and dynamic billboards, blimps, buses, bus shelters, malls, racing cars, soccer jerseys, subways, street furniture, stadium displays. Ford purchased $50 million billboard advertising, gaining exposure on hundreds of U.S. billboards. Some firms base their success on outdoor advertising. Of course, mobile marketing offers a variety of new advertising options — Chapter 17 (pp. 448–449).

MARKETING
QUESTION

At the Taj Mahal, a sign reads, *Only 10,728 miles to Wall Drug.* Wall Drug (WD) (retail store in Wall, South Dakota [population 800]) has $10 million annual revenues. Initially, WD put signs on nearby Route 16, then on every South Dakota highway and in neighboring states, stating the distance to WD. WD spent $300K annually on a global outdoor campaign, including London buses and every train station in Kenya. WD gained publicity from newspaper and magazine articles and from U.S. GIs placing *xxx miles to Wall Drug* signs around the world.

Firms also use unusual outdoor advertising placements. Consider urinals: Brut placed print ads at eye level mostly in bars. Kentucky Fried Chicken paid to repair 350 Louisville potholes; *Refreshed by KFC* advertisements sprayed on the spots lasted about one month. In Beijing, groups of 15 teenagers, wearing identical Ai Jia (*love home*) neon-yellow warm-up jackets and matching baseball caps, ride bicycles in formation along set street routes.[34] In rural China, HP Inc. advertises by sending flashy buses with TVs to country schools and towns. Hotels.nl (Dutch online reservations firm) displayed its corporate logo on waterproof blankets worn by sheep. McDonald's placed *McDonald's* street signs in Bariloche, Argentina.

We should not forget that *packaging* is an important communications medium. Of course, packaging's major role is to protect product integrity — Chapter 12 (p. 331) — but the size, shape, colors, words and pictures on packages may play an important role in other communications, and during the purchase process at retail. Indeed, International Paper showed that fruit displayed in attractively designed boxes outsold fruit in generic boxes by 2 to 3 percent.

A *Sunny Day* was a full-length feature film sponsored by Starbucks and PepsiCo to introduce bottled frappuccino drinks to China. *A Sunny Day* played in Shanghai's modern subway system on 4,000 flat screens, in subway cars and at 95 stations, for a few minutes daily for 40 weekdays. What do you think of this communications initiative? Can you suggest other innovative communications approaches?

MEDIA VEHICLES

WHAT SPECIFIC MEDIA SHALL WE USE? A *media vehicle* is a specific entity in a media class. The *newspaper* media class includes *The New York Times, San Francisco Examiner, Wall Street Journal.* The *magazine* media class includes *Fast Company, Good Housekeeping, Time.* The *television* media class includes *60 Minutes, American Idol, The Daily Show,* Super Bowl **[759p]**; in-store (Walmart, Tesco). How do you select which vehicle is right for your product/service? Critical issues in choosing media vehicles are:

KEY IDEA

Critical media selection and timing decisions:

Media objectives
↓
Media classes
↓
Media vehicles
↓
Timing
↓
Media schedule

- **Audience size.** How many readers/viewers/listeners are there? Audited readership, listenership, or viewership statistics are available for most media vehicles; audited figures drive advertising costs.[35] Of course, the firm must assess the proportion of total audience with *target* audience characteristics. The firm must also consider behavioral attributes affecting audience size: multiple readerships from magazines in professional offices, and TV viewers leaving the room, changing channels, or using a DVR to avoid advertising. Listenership/ viewership in group settings like college dormitories, hospitals, and prisons is a difficult measurement issue.

- **Audience type.** Does the audience fit with the communications target? Specifically, does the audience have the right demographics — age, gender, lifestyle, marital status, product-use characteristics? If not, the media vehicle is inappropriate, regardless of audience size.

- **Cost.** Two costs are important:
  - **Absolute cost.** Total out-of-pocket cost — price for one half-page advertisement in *The New York Times* or a 30-second commercial on *60 Minutes.*
  - **Cost per audience member.** A breakdown cost for comparing media vehicles, based on audience size.[36] A popular measure for print media is:

    Cost per thousand (CPM) = Total cost of advertising space × 1000/Circulation[37]

- **Nature of the media vehicle.** Does the message have the right *fit* with the media vehicle? A *good* advertisement may be ineffective in a particular media vehicle, even with good audience fit and favorable costs — serious and fear-provoking in a TV comedy show. Said one influential media buyer, "I've got a number of advertisers who have told me: 'Don't put me next to negative coverage of the economy.'"[38]

KEY IDEA

Choice of media vehicle depends on:

- Audience size
- Audience type
- Cost
- Nature of the media vehicle

KEY IDEA
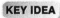

The advertising message must appear in the *right* place at the *right* time.

Major timing options are:
* Concentration
* Continuous
* Flighting
* Pulsing

TIMING

WHEN WILL OUR ADVERTISING APPEAR? Four main *timing patterns* are:

* **Concentration.** Commit all expenditures at one time.
* **Continuous.** A regular periodic pattern.
* **Flighting.** Repeated high advertising levels followed by low (or no) advertising.
* **Pulsing.** Combines continuous and flighting. Pulsing can occur within one media vehicle, within a media class, or across multiple media vehicles and classes.[39]

Generally, advertising experts believe *continuous patterns* are most effective for products purchased throughout the year. *Flighting* and *pulsing* are more effective when demand varies, as for seasonal products — air travel, cruises, holiday gifts.[40] Advertising carryover effects — advertising in one period has value in subsequent periods — may also be important.[41]

MEDIA SCHEDULE

SPECIFICALLY, WHERE AND WHEN SHALL WE PLACE OUR ADS? The firm tries to optimize media objectives — reach, frequency, GRPs — subject to a budget constraint. Securing the best media buy in one media class is a complex task; designing a campaign embracing multiple media classes is even more difficult. Major advertisers use computer models, modified by managerial judgment, to develop optimally effective *media schedules*. Table 16.5 shows a typical media plan.

TABLE 16.5
Media Plan for a Consumer Product: Illustration

a. Online comprises promotions, microsites, and rich media
b. Read "80/20" as 80% — 15-second slots, 20% — 30-second slots; 100% is all 15-second slots
c. Read 16 as gross rating points (GRPs) per week. The blocks indicate numbers of weeks.
d. All spot television is 30-second slots.
e. All spot radio is 60-second promotional spots.
f. Out-of-Home comprises aerial banners, king-size bus posters, 8-sheet posters, indoor billboards, and coasters.

ADVERTISING BUDGET

HOW MUCH SHALL WE SPEND ON ADVERTISING?

The *advertising response function* (ARF) helps marketers examine advertising spending relative to advertising objectives like sales. The ARF is crucial for setting the *advertising budget* but, typically, the firm does not know its shape. Two questions are important for deciding the advertising budget:

- **What shape is the ARF?** Figure 16.6 shows alternative ARFs — A and B. Each option has some intuitive appeal and research support.[42] Budget implications are different for low and moderate spending.

- **Where is the firm currently operating?** If the firm were at I on ARF **A**, it would probably increase spending modestly: at II, the firm would probably hold or reduce spending. At I' on ARF **B**, the firm should increase spending dramatically.

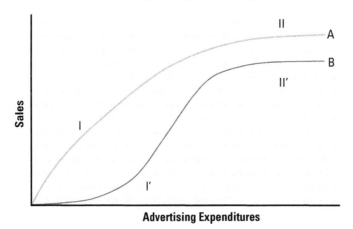

Advertising Expenditures

If the firm can answer these two questions, budgeting is simply a matter of marginal analysis: Set the budget where marginal revenue equals marginal cost. Marginal analysis underpins computer-based, decision-calculus models like ADBUDG.[43] Managers estimate sales at various advertising levels; the models calculate ARFs for different media vehicles, then determine optimal spending levels and media allocations. Because these determinations are difficult to make, in practice firms use several approaches:

OBJECTIVE AND TASK

This *bottom-up* approach focuses on securing advertising objectives like *achieving 80 percent awareness* by a specified time; then identifies the necessary tasks. The firm can use historical and/or experimental data to estimate the budget for each task, then sum the costs to calculate a total. Because linking advertising spending to advertising objectives is difficult, the objective and task method is not broadly popular. But as pressures grow to justify marketing and advertising expenditures, more firms will likely use this approach, if only to establish *ballpark* estimates.[44] Firms should invest in advertising research to gain better insights into advertising relationships.

OTHER BUDGETING METHODOLOGIES

The firm may also use *top-down* methods to calibrate budgets they develop by *objective and task*:

- **Percentage of sales.** The advertising budget is a *percentage of sales* (A/S); *sales* is current sales, anticipated next-year sales, or some combination.[45]

KEY IDEA

The advertising program comprises:

- Communications targets
- Advertising objectives
- Messaging
- Execution
- Media selection and timing
- **Advertising budget**
- Evaluation

FIGURE 16.6
Alternative Advertising Response Functions

KEY IDEA

The objective and task method should underpin the budgeting process. Rule-of-thumb methods can lead to unsatisfactory results.

Illustration of the Percentage of Sales Method for Setting the Advertising Budget

- Sales = $50 million
- Firm advertising to sales ratio = 5%
- Advertising budget = $50 million × 5% = $2.5 million

Percentage of sales is simple to implement but is logically inconsistent. The firm figures out *sales*, then calculates *advertising*. This logic implies that sales generate advertising! But the firm advertises because it believes *advertising leads* to sales! Practical problems using A/S include:

- **Advertising new products.** Because sales are low, advertising spending is also low; this makes no sense.
- **Basing the budget on anticipated sales.** The firm reduces advertising when it expects sales to dip, yet maintaining or increasing advertising may be the better strategic action. Example: Toy firms increase advertising in the fourth quarter.
- **Basing the budget on last year's sales.** Even if the firm believed sales would grow if it increased advertising, A/S ratios would not allow a budget increase.
- **Seduction.** The firm makes competitive comparisons based on **A/S** ratios; but these ratios do not specify actual advertising spending. Firm B — A/S ratio is twice Firm A — yet Firm B advertising is only $1 million, versus $5 million for Firm A.

Illustration of the Peril of Advertising to Sales (A/S) Ratios

	Firm A	Firm B
A/S ratio	5%	10%
Sales	$100 million	$10 million
Advertising	$5 million	$1 million

- **Competitive parity.** The firm bases advertising on competitor actions. The firm may decide to match the competitor dollar-for-dollar or use competitor spending as a benchmark. Some firms base their budgets on competitor spending per market-share point.[46] This method makes several implicit, and probably erroneous, assumptions:
  - The firm and competitors have similar communications objectives.
  - Competitors make good budgeting decisions.
  - Different advertising campaigns are equally effective at similar spending levels.

Illustration of the Competitive Parity Method

- Competitor advertising = $3 million
- Competitor's market share = 25%
- Firm market share = 15

Hence, firm advertising = $ 3 million × 15%/25% = $1.8 million

---

- **What the firm can afford.** There is no rational basis for this approach. Unfortunately, it is not uncommon.[47]

After several good years, Carter Inc. (CI) (disguised) suffered losses in a cyclical business downturn. Desperate for profits, the new CEO cut costs — starting with the entire advertising budget. Guess what happened to CI?

MARKETING QUESTION

The price of advertising during the U.S. Super Bowl is around $5 million for 30 seconds. Is it worth it?

EVALUATION

HOW SHALL WE TEST OUR ADVERTISING AND MEASURE ITS EFFECTIVENESS?

Now we have answered the who, what, how, where, when, and how much to spend advertising questions, we must evaluate advertising relative to objectives. The firm may test individual advertisements, different levels and types of spending, and/or evaluate the entire advertising program.

TESTING INDIVIDUAL ADVERTISEMENTS

The firm tests advertisements directed at communications targets — individually or in groups — in a laboratory or experimental field setting. Global advertisers typically test in multiple-cultures. Testing techniques include:

- **Laboratory/print.** Show subjects several advertisements or mock publications with advertising inserted — home, central location, virtual focus group.
- **Laboratory/broadcast.** Subjects watch a TV program — in a theater, shopping mall, or controlled online environment.
- **Field setting.** Similar to laboratory but with real publications and TV programs. A test may involve two or more publications or TV programs. Subjects typically see only one advertising vehicle. Firms often confine these tests to a limited geographic area.[48]

Laboratory testing allows researchers manipulate several advertising elements, exercise tight control over subject interaction with advertisements, and limit expenses — but at the cost of realism. Field settings reverse these pros and cons. *Advertising effectiveness measures* for field and laboratory tests include:

- **Recognition.** Widely used for print advertising. The researcher asks subjects which advertisements they recognize.
- **Unaided recall.** Widely used for broadcast advertising. The researcher asks subjects what advertising they remember, *without* prompting.[49]
- **Aided recall.** Widely used for broadcast advertising. The researcher asks subjects what advertising they remember, *with* prompting.
- **Purchase.** Used in field settings. Customer panel members present ID cards at grocery stores when they make purchases.[50]

Some observers argue these methods are too rational and verbal; they prefer nonverbal methods like galvanic skin response and pupil dilation. Significantly higher expenses limits use of these methods.[51]

TESTING DIFFERENT LEVELS AND TYPES OF SPENDING

The firm tests alternative spending patterns using experimental design procedures. The firm sets advertising objectives, then selects appropriate advertising effectiveness measures. Each of several different geographic test areas receives a different spending pattern. The firm compares results across test areas, using sophisticated analytic techniques to account for test-area differences.

EVALUATING THE ENTIRE ADVERTISING PROGRAM

Over and above testing individual advertisements and spending levels, the firm may wish to evaluate an entire advertising program. *Tracking studies* measure customer responses over time, using either a customer panel or randomly selected respondents. Suppose firm objectives

---

KEY IDEA

The advertising program comprises:
- Communications targets
- Advertising objectives
- Messaging
- Execution
- Media selection and timing
- Advertising budget
- **Evaluation**

KEY IDEA

The firm should test both individual advertisements and the entire advertising program.

Important advertising effectiveness measures are:
- Recognition
- Unaided recall
- Aided recall
- Purchase

KEY IDEA

Evaluating advertising effectiveness is a complex task. The firm must choose among various types of tests and measures.

mirror the high-involvement hierarchy-of-effects model: Awareness → liking/preference → trial → purchase → repeat purchase; the firm should base advertising objectives and actions on these stages. In a tracking study, the results from one period help define the advertising program for the following period.[52] Table 16.6 shows market research results, then firm actions, for four successive quarters. The boxed insert (below) shows an example.

TABLE 16.6
Advertising Program Evaluation — Percentage of Target Customers: Illustration

Time Period	Quarter I	Quarter II	Quarter III	Quarter IV
Awareness	25%	70%	70%	70%
Knowledge	20%	60%	60%	60%
Liking/preference	20%	20%	40%	40%
Trial	20%	20%	20%	30%
Purchase	18%	18%	18%	25%
Repeat purchase	15%	15%	15%	20%

- **QUARTER I.** The firm has problems: *awareness* — 25 percent — and *knowledge* — 20 percent. The firm aims to increase awareness and knowledge.

- **QUARTER II.** Advertising raised awareness and knowledge to 70 percent and 60 percent, respectively. But *liking/preference* and *trial* — 20 percent each — remain low. The firm focuses on liking/preference.

- **QUARTER III.** The *liking/preference* campaign was moderately successful — to 40 percent; but *trial* remained low — 20 percent. The firm initiates a new campaign focused on trial.

- **QUARTER IV.** The new campaign increased trial to 30 percent; purchase to 25 percent; and repeat purchase to 20 percent.

Example of a Tracking Study[53]

Campaign: *Pork — The Other White Meat.* A six-month TV campaign in 17 major metropolitan markets, supplemented by national magazine advertising.

Customer target: Primarily women (25–54) with children, purchasing for the family.

Test: Three different media exposures, each in two different cities:
- Cleveland and Sacramento — double TV exposure plus magazine
- Pittsburg and Denver — normal TV plus magazine
- Baltimore and San Diego — magazine only

Measurements:
- *Wave I. Benchmark.* Two months before the campaign — 1,200 men and women surveyed in the six test markets. Major findings:
  a. White meat preferred over red meat 42 percent versus 28 percent
  b. Most commonly recognized white meat — chicken
  c. Awareness of pork as white meat — 9 percent
- *Wave II. Post Campaign.* Phone survey — 1,800 consumers (25–54) in the six test cities:
  Goal A. Unaided association of pork and white meat
  - *Findings A.* Increases:
    - double TV markets — 10 percent to 35 percent
    - normal TV markets — 12 percent to 29 percent
  Goal B. Recall of advertising message
  - *Findings B.*
    - double TV — 72 percent
    - normal TV — 56 percent
    - no TV — 35 percent
  Goal C. Changed attitudes toward pork
  - *Finding C.* Preference for white meat over red meat increased from 42 percent to 50 percent

Revenue Result. Revenues increased $500 million

THE ADVERTISING AGENCY SYSTEM

KEY IDEA

The advertising agency system is in a continuous state of flux.

Most major U.S. advertisers outsource advertising program development to advertising agencies. But some firms, like The Prudential and Ryanair, run simple advertisements in print media and conduct advertising activities in-house.[54] Large in-house advertisers may secure superior access to low-price media deals. Regardless, by outsourcing, firms have better access to creative talent and greater flexibility. These firms demand refreshed creative teams; they may switch agencies on a few months' notice. The firm usually works with three agency groups:

- *Account/relationship managers* — the key agency interface; helps craft the advertising strategy;
- *Creative department* — develops messaging and executions;
- *Media department* — prepares the media schedule and provides supporting data.[55]

Traditionally, firms paid advertising agencies a fixed percentage (often 15 percent) of advertising spend or commitment. More recently, with better analytics available, firms and agencies negotiate fees, often making *value-based* arrangements. Coke and P&G cover agency costs and pay *gain-share* bonuses based on performance against agreed-upon metrics. Such arrangements more closely align firm and agency interests. Similarly, firms are starting to pay public relations agencies by metrics like number of press mentions. Firms like LG hire one agency for creative work, and a second larger agency for advertising placement. Other firms select separate agencies for traditional and digital marketing.

The core agency job is to translate market strategy into messaging, then execute the message. (P&G's perspective [378v]) Firm and agency personnel should jointly develop a *creative brief* (boxed insert) — a *contract* between firm and agency, particularly with *creatives*. Each messaging initiative should have a creative brief — for advertising, but also for visual aids like displays and sales force materials. Sometimes an advertising campaign requires two creative briefs: campaign idea, and idea execution.[56] When the firm's brand competes in multiple product forms/classes, like Dove — antiperspirant/deodorant, bar/body wash, face care, hair care, hair styling — the brand brief frames the creative briefs for individual products.

Core Elements of the Creative Brief

Marketing objective. What the firm wants to achieve — output and intermediate objectives.

Assignment. The type of campaign including media type, timing, and approval process.

Customer insight. Informs the creative process — critical insight into target market; identifies rational and emotional factors driving product purchase/use.

Competitive insight. Informs the creative process — includes barriers to achieving objectives.

Target audience. Whom the firm wishes to influence — customer types and segments; includes demographics, psychographics, and current products.

Key benefit. The most important benefit/value the firm wishes to emphasize.

Reasons to believe. Why the target customer should believe firm claims.

Brand vision. How the firm wants the target audience to feel about its product. Should be important to the audience, deliverable by the firm, unique to the brand.

Mandates. Elements outside the advertiser's control; must or must not be included — corporate and/or legal requirements advertising must meet.

Measurement. How the firm will know if the campaign has been successful.

MARKETING QUESTION

Suppose your school/college/university plans advertising to increase student applications. Develop a creative brief for developing a campaign idea.

Some important institutional changes are occurring in the *advertising agency* industry. These changes have major implications for advertisers:

- **Formation of large groups.** Many well-known individual agencies are now part of four major groups — Interpublic and Omnicom (U.S.), WPP (Britain), Publicis (France).
- **Globalization.** Advertising agencies have developed global scopes to serve clients globally.

- **Service broadening.** Advertising agencies are taking a more holistic view of communications by expanding services to include direct marketing, digital, P&PR, sales promotion, marketing research, and market-strategy development.

Regardless, creatives continue to leave large firms to form new agencies.

Other Mass Communications Options

DIRECT MARKETING

Direct marketing is a fast-growing communications tool embracing many ways of requesting customer response. Today, direct marketing includes traditional print and broadcast advertising, packaging, package inserts, warranty cards, and take-ones.[57] The direct-mail subcategory includes brochures, catalogs, and statement inserts. Firms like L.L. Bean, Lands' End, Lillian Vernon continually develop and refine demographic and product-preference customer databases to fine-tune product development, product assortment, and communications programs. Environmental changes like lower bulk postal rates, online shopping, and widespread credit card use have greatly impacted direct marketing. Other factors contributing to direct marketing growth include:

- **Data and analytics.** Big data and advanced analytics allow firms to develop, manage, and mine customer databases for more targeted efforts.
- **Delivery systems.** Package delivery firms like FedEx and UPS increasingly offer greater service variety.
- **Demographics and lifestyles.** Growth of dual-income families facing increasing time pressures, especially in developed countries, has reduced available shopping time. Direct marketing is attractive because consumers can shop from home.
- **Product quality.** The generalized increase in product quality has reduced customer risk when buying products remotely.
- **Professionalism.** Direct marketing firms are more professional and sophisticated, especially in segmenting, targeting, communicating.

Although direct marketing can be more expensive than advertising on a CPM basis, it offers several advantages:

- **Ability to identify prospects.** By relating customer profiles to purchase patterns, direct marketers can identify high-quality prospects.
- **Ability to tailor the offer.** Direct marketers know what customers purchase; hence, they can tailor messages and offers to individuals.
- **Action-oriented customer response.** Advertising programs typically work via an effects hierarchy; purchase often occurs after awareness, knowledge, and liking/preference. By contrast, direct marketing is more action-oriented and typically requests purchase.
- **Better customer knowledge.** Many direct marketing firms have extensive information on customers. But they must be sensitive to privacy concerns and act appropriately.
- **Better measurement.** The firm can test program elements like message, price, incentives, and/or type of direct marketing to assess impact on sales, and adjust accordingly.
- **Flexibility.** The firm can develop some direct marketing campaigns — like e-mail — much more quickly than mass advertising.
- **Predictability.** Because direct marketing typically requests purchase, sales forecasts for direct marketing programs can be fairly accurate. Budgeting for direct marketing is simpler than for advertising.

KEY IDEA

Direct marketing offers advantages over mass advertising:
- Ability to identify prospects
- Ability to tailor the offer
- Action-oriented customer response
- Better customer knowledge
- Better measurement
- Flexibility
- Predictability

PUBLICITY & PUBLIC RELATIONS

German condom manufacturer Condomi received significant press coverage in Europe and overseas for its plan to test condoms with British university students. Advertisements in college newspapers asking, *Want to get paid for having sex?* led respondents to a website asking questions like, *Who would you most like to do it with?*

KEY IDEA

Publicity & public relations relies on intermediaries — typically the press — to transmit messages to target audiences.

Publicity & public relations (P&PR) are closely related; publicity is really a subset of public relations. *Publicity* focuses on securing neutral or favorable short-term media coverage. *Public relations* (PR) is a formal communication process attempting to build favorable relationships between the firm and public audiences. PR embraces corporate reputation, crisis management, government relations (lobbying), internal relations, press relations, product publicity, shareholder relations. P&PR generally relies on intermediaries to transmit messages to target audiences. Advantage for P&PR: the audience may view the intermediary as impartial; the firm does not pay for media space and time!

The first modern PR example was the famous *Torches of Freedom* campaign. In 1929, a small group of women walked down New York's Fifth Avenue smoking cigarettes; newspapers nationwide carried the story. Subsequently, women in many cities smoked on the street. Figure 16.7 shows Edward L. Bernays' simple model of how PR could promote a product/cause.[58]

FIGURE 16.7
Bernays Model

Many firms focus communications efforts on P&PR.[59] Pharmaceutical firms use news releases to encourage patients to ask physicians about products. Mutual fund giant Vanguard does little advertising, but secures favorable press for low expense ratios. College Savings Bank launched the CollegeSure CD by focusing initial communication efforts on news releases and press conferences. Within one month, these efforts generated more than 300 news stories. Articles and editorials appeared in all major U.S. newspapers; weekly news magazines like *Time, Newsweek*, and *U.S. News and World Report*; major business magazines; and local newspapers.[60] The agency responsible for the Aflac talking duck commercial tried, unsuccessfully, to hire actor Ben Affleck. But on the *Tonight* show, Affleck said, "Everywhere I go, no matter what I do, there is always some drunk lady screaming, 'Aflac!'"[61] Firms also use P&PR and advertising synergistically. Victoria's Secret (VS) spends several million dollars advertising the annual fashion show; extensive publicity sends millions of visitors to the VS website.

For difficult situations in the public eye, P&PR can be positive or negative.

- **Positive.** J&J received considerable praise for its handling the mid-1980s Tylenol poisoning scare. CEO James Burke took charge and J&J focused concern on customers.[62] J&J temporarily withdrew Tylenol capsules, then relaunched in tamper-free packaging. J&J's actions and related P&PR campaign put senior executives, including Burke, on many U.S. talk shows; they explained J&J's actions and commitment to customers. J&J turned a major debacle into a major coup. **[442v]** More recently, jetBlue reacted quickly and extensively following a flight-cancellation crisis related to a severe ice storm at its New York hub — Chapter 13, p. 349 **[102v]**; Qantas received favorable publicity following a midair engine explosion on an Airbus A380; in the face of negative publicity over its role in the economic crisis, Goldman Sachs earned plaudits for its *10,000 Women* initiative. Walmart earned credibility with environmentalists for work on a sustainability index.

MARKETING QUESTION

BP (Gulf oil spill), Goldman Sachs (banking crisis), and Toyota (product quality) each received significant negative publicity. How do you assess their responses? What would you have done differently?

MARKETING QUESTION

Three African countries — Mozambique, Swaziland, South Africa — formed the *East3Route* initiative to attract European tourists. *East3Route* has issued an RFP (request for proposal) to develop a P&PR campaign to support the initiative. Prepare a proposal.

- **Negative.** When 200 Coke drinkers suffered nausea, headaches, and diarrhea, and several children were hospitalized, observers criticized Coke for *forget[ing] the cardinal rule of crisis management — to act fast, tell the whole truth, and look as if you have nothing to hide. The Economist* concluded that *Coca-Cola has made a big mess of what should have been a small public relations problem.*[63]

Regardless, P&PR has several drawbacks. The firm selects *friendly* intermediaries like editors, journalists, and media personalities but does not have direct control of audience choice. Also, despite the *pitch*, the intermediary may ignore, modify, or shorten the message — or worse, portray the firm inconsistently or even negatively.

SALES PROMOTION

MARKETING QUESTION

Identify a recent sales promotion. What were firm objectives? Was the firm successful? Why or why not?

Sales promotion (SP) is a complex blend of communications techniques providing extra customer value, typically for trial to stimulate immediate sales. Sometimes SP has longer-run objectives like increasing awareness. Three main SP types are:

- **Consumer promotion** — manufacturer to consumer
- **Trade promotion** — manufacturer to retailer
- **Retail promotion** — retailer to consumer

Consumer and retail promotions include cash refunds, contests, coupons, deals, games, rebates, point-of-purchase displays, premiums, prizes, samples, and sports sponsorships. *Trade promotions* include advertising and merchandising allowances; contests, deals and prizes; special price deals; *spiffs*; trade shows.[64] Firms are continually creating new SP techniques.

Like other communications methods, the firm should set clear objectives before selecting a SP device. Table 16.7 shows several SP techniques and related possible objectives. Cash refunds, *cents-off* coupons, and point-of-purchase displays may generate short-term sales. Sports sponsorships and naming educational facilities, sports stadiums, and theaters are options for long-term image building. A particular sales promotion technique may help achieve several objectives — Table 16.8 (p. 430) shows the ubiquitous *cents-off* coupon.

TABLE 16.7
Selected Sales Promotion Techniques and Objectives

Sales Promotion Technique	Possible Objectives
Cash refund	Purchase by reducing risk
Cents-off coupon	Table 16.8 (p. 430)
Custom publishing	Awareness, interest, knowledge by personalization
Deals	Increase use; preemptive inventory building
Events	Interest, knowledge, trial
Games	Trial, repeat purchase, increase use
Infomercials	Awareness, interest, knowledge
Point-of-purchase displays	Knowledge, trial, increase use, repurchase
Premiums	Trial, repeat purchase, increase use
Product literature	Interest, knowledge, increase use
Product placement	Awareness, interest, knowledge via association
Sampling	Trial (for new product)
Spiffs	Customer-salesperson effort, pull-through sales
Sports sponsorship	Corporate image building, awareness, community building
Building and stadium naming	Corporate image building, awareness
Trade shows	Awareness, interest, liking, intention to buy, trial, repurchase

Objective	Action
Encourage consumers to increase personal product inventories, create sense of urgency	Include expiration on coupon; publicize approaching expiration
Encourage repeat purchasing	Include coupon in product package
Induce trial among nonusers	Distribute coupon in a magazine

TABLE 16.8
Alternative Objectives and Actions for a Cents-off Coupon

Generally, SP is not a good standalone approach; the firm should tightly integrate SP with other communications. Firms often execute several sales promotions simultaneously, but these should all support (or be supported by) advertising and/or personal selling efforts. Rarely is SP the central element in communications strategy, but SP may account for a large portion of the communications budget. Examples are:

- **Product placement.** Increasingly popular in movies, music videos (and lyrics), TV shows, video games. The James Bond movie *Die Another Day* featured Aston Martin Vanquish (automobile), Ballantine (turtleneck sweaters), Brioni Roman Style (suits), British Airways (airline), Finlandia (vodka), Omega Seamaster (watch), Philips (mobile phone), Revlon (makeup), Samsonite (luggage).[65] *The Italian Job* (movie) vastly increased awareness for the Mini Cooper.[66]

- **Events, movies, skateboard parks.** Shoe manufacturer Vans operates 140 stores nationwide targeting skateboarding fanatics. Vans builds skateboard parks in malls, sponsors skateboarding events, and made a documentary film celebrating skateboarding.

- **Sports stadiums.** Philips Electronics paid $180 million to name home arenas for the Atlanta Hawks (baseball) and the Thrashers (ice hockey).[67] Goldman Sachs, Merrill Lynch, and Morgan Stanley funded *named* classrooms at Columbia Business School.

The firm should always track SP's long-term impact, particularly if SP involves short-term price reductions. Regular discounts may lead to competitive price escalation; or customers may accumulate inventory at promotional prices and never return to the *regular* (higher) price.[68,69] For trade promotions, manufacturers must ensure intermediaries pass on price savings to customers, and do not *divert* products — Chapter 19.[70] Pass-through price reductions at the trade level frequently depend on issues suppliers cannot control, like retailer profit margins, inventory turns, and retail competition.

Furthermore, volume fluctuations from frequent price changes may lead to mismatched production schedules, inventory build-up, and higher costs. Also, multiple SP programs are costly to manage. In the past, P&G conducted many special promotions and price changes; one in four orders from retailers contained errors. P&G's 150-person department corrected 27,000 orders per month, costing $35–$75 per order. These problems led P&G and many FMCG firms to switch to *everyday low pricing.*

The firm should always cost out the financial impact of SPs.

Hoover Britain (HB) launched a successful consumer sales promotion: £100 Hoover purchases — two free airline tickets to continental Europe. HB introduced a second airline promotion: £250 Hoover purchases — two free airline tickets to the U.S. Sales skyrocketed — more than 200,000 customers applied, but profits plunged. HB took an earnings charge of £48.8 million and fired many senior executives.[71] A word of advice for marketers: *Make sure your sales promotions make financial sense under all contingencies.*

MARKETING QUESTION

Why would Minute Maid sponsor a sports stadium? What are the benefits? What are drawbacks and risks?

KEY IDEA

Sales promotion comprises a potpourri of techniques, mostly for short-term objectives.

Poorly designed sales promotion programs hurt profits and brand image.

What other messages did you glean from this chapter?

KEY MESSAGES

- Advertising *works* via hierarchy-of-effects models incorporating awareness, knowledge, liking/preference, trial, purchase, repeat purchase.

- High-involvement and low-involvement products have different hierarchies.

- A well-developed advertising strategy requires answers to seven critical questions:

  - *Communications target.* Who are we trying to influence?
  - *Advertising objectives.* What are we trying to achieve?
  - *Messaging.* What message(s) should the communications target receive?
  - *Execution.* How shall we communicate the message?
  - *Media selection and timing.* Where and when shall we place our advertising?
  - *Advertising budget.* How much shall we spend on advertising?
  - *Evaluation.* How shall we test our advertising and measure its effectiveness?

- The core of the advertising message should reflect the positioning statement in the market-segment strategy.

- Advertising messages embrace many rational and emotional approaches.

- Key issues for media selection are reach, frequency, impact.

- The firm should approach the marketing budget from a marginal analysis perspective and limit rule-of-thumb approaches.

- The creative brief is the critical interface between the firm and advertising agency.

- Direct marketing (DM), publicity & public relations (P&PR), and sales promotion (SP) are mass communications approaches that supplement/replace advertising.

VIDEOS AND AUDIOS

For complimentary material, see Axcess Capon codes at www.axcessvids.com

Advertising	**546v**	Joseph T. Plummer	Columbia Business School
Buzz Marketing	**393v**	Mark Hughes	Buzz Marketing

QUESTIONS FOR STUDY AND DISCUSSION

Can you answer the questions implied by this chapter's learning outcomes? Check!

1. Many social critics attack advertising in general and specific advertising programs in particular. What are the major arguments against advertising? How would you respond? Why is it difficult to measure advertising effectiveness?

2. Suppose GM is about to launch a new car powered by fuel cells — suggested retail price about $30,000. Use the following table to develop a consumer advertising campaign.

Advertising Element	Question
Communications target	Who are we trying to influence?
Advertising objectives	What are we trying to achieve?
Messaging	What message(s) should communications targets receive?
Execution	How shall we communicate the message?
Media selection and timing	Where and when shall we place our advertising?
Advertising budget	How much shall we spend on advertising?
Program evaluation	How shall we test our advertising and measure its effectiveness?

3. Identify and bring to class examples of three recent advertising campaigns you believe were outstanding. Use the above table to analyze their success. What commonalities can you identify among these campaigns that will help you develop great advertising?

4. Identify and bring to class examples of three recent advertising campaigns you believe were ineffective. Use the above table to analyze why they failed. What commonalities can you identify among these campaigns that will help you avoid making truly bad advertising?

5. Identify a direct marketing campaign to which you responded. Why did you respond to that one yet ignore so many others?

6. Suppose your friend is planning to open a new retail seafood restaurant in your hometown but cannot afford to advertise. Develop a P&PR campaign. Alternatively, complete this task for *Managing Marketing in the 21st Century*.

7. Develop a creative new sales promotion device you will sell to a major national advertiser.

8. The following table shows firm sales by quarter. The firm ran a sales promotion in Q3 of 20XY+2. What is your estimate of baseline sales? What impact did the promotion have?

	20XY	20XY+1	20XY+2
Quarter 1	150	165	180
Quarter 2	190	207	165
Quarter 3	210	231	375
Quarter 4	120	132	135

9. Message execution includes rational styles — comparative, demonstration, one-sided and two-sided appeals, primacy, recency, refutational; emotional styles — celebrity endorsement, fear, humor, storytelling. Bring to class an example of each advertising style. Is the advertisement effective? Why or why not?

10. Identify the advertising campaign you believe is the most effective. Why did you choose this campaign? Annual prize — weekend in New York. Send your entry to *contactus@wessex21c. com*. Good luck!

TRUE/FALSE QUESTIONS

Answers on page A2 and at www.axcessvids.com — 193p

1. The two major forms of advertising executions are scientific and rational approaches.
   ❏ **TRUE** ❏ **FALSE**

2. Fear-based advertising is one style of rational advertising.   ❏ **TRUE** ❏ **FALSE**

3. Advertising frequency is the average number of times a targeted individual is exposed to an advertisement.   ❏ **TRUE** ❏ **FALSE**

4. Large advertising agencies are placing increasing effort on their domestic markets.
   ❏ **TRUE** ❏ **FALSE**

5. The advertising response function relates advertising spending to advertising objectives like sales.   ❏ **TRUE** ❏ **FALSE**

MULTIPLE CHOICE QUESTIONS

Answers on page A2 and at www.axcessvids.com — 258p

1. Which of the following is NOT a main style of rational advertising?

    a. demonstration advertising
    b. celebrity endorsement-based advertising
    c. comparative advertising
    d. primacy or recency advertising

2. All of the following represent main styles of emotional advertising EXCEPT:

    a. humor-based advertising
    b. fear-based advertising
    c. refutational advertising
    d. storytelling-based advertising

3. Which of the following represents the correct formula to calculate gross rating points (GRPs)?

    a. reach + frequency
    b. reach/frequency
    c. (reach + frequency) / 2
    d. reach x frequency

4. Which of the following advertising timing patterns has repeated high advertising levels followed by low (or no) advertising?

    a. concentration
    b. continuous
    c. flighting
    d. pulsing

5. Which of the following advertising classes secures most advertising investment in the U.S.?

    a. digital
    b. television
    c. newspapers
    d. radio

Design the Market Offer

....

CHAPTER 17

DIGITAL MARKETING[1]

For complimentary material, see Axcess Capon codes at www.axcessvids.com

LEARNING OUTCOMES

When you have completed this chapter, you will be able to:

- Understand how digital marketing differs from traditional mass communications.
- Be aware of variances in digital marketing objectives and strategies.
- Differentiate among various digital options — e-mail; search, blogs, and social media; display, classifieds, and video advertising; websites; mobile marketing.
- Relate various digital marketing activities to the purchase decision process.
- Learn how to take advantage of the enormous growth of social media.
- Be clear about the special characteristics of mobile marketing.

OPENING CASE: FACEBOOK

Mark Zuckerberg founded Facebook in 2004 as a sharing site for fellow students while a Harvard University sophomore. Facebook entered a fledgling social media market already served by Friendster, MySpace, and pioneer SixDegrees (founded 1997; shut down 2001); Friendster transitioned to a social gaming site and is now defunct. In the mid-2000s, MySpace (acquired by News Corporation — 2005) was the most visited website in the U.S. — 2008 revenues $800 million — but declined steadily thereafter.

Initially, Facebook grew rapidly in universities, colleges, and high schools but by 2006 was open to all. Angel investors and venture capitalists funded Facebook's growth. Recognizing the value of this new medium, in 2006 Zuckerberg rejected a $1 billion offer from Yahoo! By late 2007, Facebook had 100,000 pages that firms could use for advertising and promotion. When Microsoft purchased 1.6 percent of Facebook for $240 million (2007), Facebook's implied market value was $15 billion.

Facebook provides a platform for registered users to engage in social interaction. Users create personal profiles, and post updates, photos, videos on their Facebook pages. Users send messages to other users — friends — and provide them with access to their Facebook pages. Users can like, comment on, and/or forward posts they receive; Facebook forward likes to friends automatically. Friends also

435

receive notifications of profile changes and place each other into separate categories like close friends, family, and acquaintances. They can play games and join various types of interest groups. Firms can also develop Facebook pages and groups, build fans, post content, and send messages.

Many Internet startups have been highly successful at generating users, but less successful in securing revenues — but not Facebook. Over the years, Facebook has introduced many different products for advertisers. What continues to differentiate Facebook from others is the enormous traffic its website generates, plus the detailed information it possesses on users. Not only does Facebook have significant demographic data — secured when users register — Facebook also knows about individual preferences and creates stickiness *(keeps people returning) through deep user connectivity.*

Advertisers may use Facebook's demographic and preference data for targeting Facebook ads to highly selected individuals. Although initially developed for personal computers, Facebook has adapted to the growth of mobile devices by developing mobile-specific advertising options like mobile app installed ads — prompting the user to download an app.

Facebook enhances user data from its own site with web-browsing data secured from third parties. Hence, knowing a user's interests from Internet browsing behavior, Facebook auctions advertising spots when that user signs onto Facebook. Facebook also offers customer *audience targeting — an advertiser delivers a list to Facebook; Facebook shows an advertisement when that individual signs onto Facebook. The advertiser can also indicate which people it does not want to contact, like current customers when it engages in customer prospecting.*

Over the years, Facebook has evolved its policies for dealing with personal user information. Regardless, it is unsurprising that Facebook has had to address numerous privacy concerns. For example, in 2012, an FTC investigation concluded that Facebook's actions regarding photo sharing, and making user lists public, were unfair and deceptive. *The FTC mandated changes. Other problems for Facebook include false users; in 2012, Facebook removed more than 8 percent of registered users because they were fake. In addition, Facebook has had to address hate speech, including content promoting domestic and sexual violence against women.*

Since its founding, Facebook has made more than 50 acquisitions, both large and small. **[348p]** *Many acquisitions have allowed Facebook to improve/increase functionality and features it offers users. With other acquisitions, Facebook has entered new areas. In most cases, Facebook's focus has been acquiring human capital — teams pushing technological frontiers. Facebook's best-known acquisitions are Instagram — photo-sharing site — $1 billion (2012), and WhatsApp — messaging app — $19 billion (2014).*

By 2016, Facebook had 1.5 billion active monthly users globally. Facebook revenues (2014) exceeded $12 billion, net income more than $3 billion. Facebook's IPO (May 2012) was the third largest in U.S. history — $38 per share. In 2015, share price almost reached $100 and market value exceeded $300 billion. Just like Michael Dell before him, Mark Zuckerberg had built a global-leading company from humble beginnings in his college dorm.[2]

Case Question

Facebook has many ways of securing revenues from advertisers. Through research, identify Facebook's most effective approaches. What ideas do you have for increasing Facebook revenues and profits?

Chapter 17 is the third of four chapters in Part B of Imperative 4 — *Design the Market Offer*. Part B focuses on *Communicating Customer Value*; Chapter 17 addresses *Digital Marketing*. Chapter 16 discusses mass communications. In both chapters, we show that advertising continues to be the most visible form of customer communications, and consuming the largest portion of many firms' communications budgets.

Digital marketing is the fastest-growing approach for firms wishing to communicate and interact with customers. Digital marketing methods are very different from traditional mass communications options. Furthermore, digital marketing's unique characteristics provide marketers with many new ways of interfacing and engaging with customers.

THE CHANGING VIEW

OLD WAY	NEW WAY
Mass targeting by traditional mass media	Surgical targeting via data-driven digital approaches
Traditional media dominate promotional spending	Digital media increasingly important
Options for placing traditional advertising well developed	New digital advertising options being continually developed
Technology use in media selection well developed for traditional media	Technological approaches in ad placement fast developing
Advertising potential of social media is a mystery to advertisers	Social media is becoming increasingly important to advertisers
Many website visitors receive identical advertisements	Advertisements personalized based on data about individuals
Privacy is a modest issue on the Internet	Privacy concerns are becoming increasingly relevant
Ad blocking is not an issue for advertisers	Ad blocking is increasingly prevalent
Fraud in digital advertising is not an issue	Fraud in digital advertising is an increasingly serious problem

Compared to traditional media options, digital media is fast evolving, fast growing, and qualitatively different from traditional mass communications options — Figure 17.1. Digital marketing:

- makes it easy for customers to communicate with each other;
- makes it easy for customers to communicate with the firm;
- is not time based, communicating globally 24/7/365;
- allows firms to better target messages to potential customers;
- enables instant purchasing or other responses.

FIGURE 17.1
Digital Impact on Communication Options

Before you begin to consider which digital marketing approaches to use, you should be very clear about your objectives. People engage in digital marketing for many reasons, but two commercial reasons are paramount:

- Drive sales of firm products/services — in the short term, or in the long term via brand building. Over 50 percent of consumers explore digital channels prior to liking a brand or making a purchase.
- Earn revenues from advertising. Secure visibility by providing content where advertisers wish to associate their advertising. Many bloggers take this approach to attract the *right* audience.

Essentially, digital marketing provides a powerful alternative and enhancement to traditional communication methods — Chapter 16. Using digital approaches, the firm can capture data that follows customers as they search, visit websites, view advertisements, engage social media, and make purchases. The firm combines these data sets with bricks-and-mortar purchases, and other data to *predict* behavior, strengthen brand image, increase sales, and enhance customer satisfaction. Each approach uses similar tools, but the distinction in objectives is important.

Addressing Customers Online

In Chapters 15 and 16, we noted that the Internet offers many ways for marketers to communicate with customers and attract audiences. In Chapter 17, we focus exclusively on strategies involving digital communications. We explore various approaches — each with its own special characteristics. We commence with e-mail, a staple in outbound marketing communications, then turn our attention to the major ways customers may secure information about the firm and its products/brands — search, blogs, social media. We then turn to display, classifieds, and video advertising before addressing websites. We conclude with mobile marketing. Of course, a key firm challenge is to decide what portion of the promotional budget to spend on digital media.

We conclude with digital performance measures using analytics unique to digital marketing. We show various metrics the firm may use to assess performance, and hence better allocate resources among the various options.

Philips Norelco developed *Bodygroom* for male shaving below the neck. Develop a digital communications program for *Bodygroom*.

E-MAIL

Of the various forms of digital communication available to the firm, e-mail has the most direct relationship to traditional forms of communication. Indeed, e-mail is the *virtual* equivalent of direct marketing. E-mail is familiar, inexpensive, and measurable. *Outbound* e-mail communications fall into two broad categories for senders — prior relationship to the target audience and no prior relationship.

KEY IDEA

OUTBOUND E-MAIL

NO PRIOR RELATIONSHIP. The most common use of this type of e-mail is to acquire new customers. The firm may buy e-mail lists, or develop its own lists based on target segments. Wessex Press constructs marketing faculty lists comprising potential faculty adopters of its textbooks.

The CAN-SPAM Act (2003) and *spam* filters — designed to reject unsolicited e-mails — reduce the effectiveness of this promotional option. To minimize spam, many firms encourage prospective customers to provide e-mail addresses — *opt in* — then allow them to *opt out*. Regardless, the overall effectiveness of unsolicited e-mail is decreasing: 25 percent *open rate* — 2014;

Digital marketing embraces:
- E-mail
- Assessing customer information
  - Search
  - Blogs
  - Social media
- Advertising
- Websites
- Mobile marketing

versus 39 percent open rate — 2004.[3] Campaigns can achieve higher *open* rates by using specialty firms like Salesforce, Constant Contact, and MailChimp. The firm may also e-mail news releases and other publicity pieces for inclusion on news sites like CNN Digital Network and Yahoo! News, blogs, and nonfirm websites.

PRIOR RELATIONSHIP. E-mail is a popular way for firms to maintain contact with customers who have searched and/or purchased from its website. Internet retailers like CheapTickets and Netflix regularly send e-mails to maintain customer relationships and stimulate purchase. Such firms often include recommendations based on previous searches and/or purchases by individuals. Many community-oriented sites and content publishers regularly send e-mail news alerts to keep customers returning to their websites.

INBOUND E-MAIL

The main difference between traditional direct marketing and e-mail communications is the easy ability of customers to communicate with the firm. Unlike *snail mail*, e-mail is a two-way street! The firm must develop processes to address inbound communications candidly and promptly. Firms like Zappos (owned by Amazon) and many others encourage consumer contact.

Suppose you post a family photograph on Instagram. Then you discover your photo on a clothing manufacturer's website promoting its products. Has there been an invasion of your privacy? Why or why not?

Making Customer Information Available

In Chapter 4, we present a six-stage model depicting the customer decision process (pp. 105–109). We noted that for stage two — *acquire information* — potential customers increasingly turn to online sources. Whereas e-mail approaches *send* information to current and potential customers, the power of the Internet lies in the various ways that individuals can *access* information. Hence, the firm must ensure that information about its products/services is readily available, accurate, consistent, and relevant for current and potential customers, and easy to find. Creating such information — content marketing — is a critical component for firms engaged in digital marketing.

The firm has three broad approaches for making itself available to people — search, blogs, social media — Figure 17.2.

FIGURE 17.2
Securing Customer
Information Online

SEARCH

Individuals initiate close to 10 billion Internet searches daily, the vast majority on Google. By definition, searchers are looking for something. Smart digital marketers optimize their website content to capture the *right* searchers. Industry research indicates that leads firms secure from *search* are eight times more effective than those secured from *outbound* e-mail. The firm should strive to ensure that people looking for the sorts of products/services it offers can find them. Search engines like Google, Yahoo!, and Bing conduct searches using two related approaches — *organic* search and *paid* search. The firm must develop strategies for optimizing each approach.

ORGANIC (NATURAL) SEARCH

Search engines work using *web crawlers* (*spiders*) to periodically scan web pages, place them in the *search engine index*, and rank for relevance on important *keywords* — more correctly, key phrases. Simple keywords produce so many *hits*, the firm will never be highly ranked. Hence, a fashion retailer will secure better results for the keyword *brown men's belt* (119 hits) than for *belt* (450 million hits). Search engines employ complex algorithms to determine *relevance* — from analysis of website content — then factor relevance results by *authority* — number of incoming links to other web pages, factored by their *PageRank* — the number of links to those web pages. Quality of web page content drives the number and quality of links.

Search engine optimization (SEO) embraces a variety of strategies, tactics, and techniques for securing high rankings in search results. High search results increase the number of website visitors. High rankings are important. Research indicates that fewer than 90 percent of searchers go beyond the first search page; only 50 percent of searchers click beyond the first three links. Accordingly, firms allocate dedicated SEO resources to ensure their website and other digital content are optimized for best results.

Fashion blogger Nataly Antar took several actions to raise the ranking of her fashion blog — *www.insiderfashionreview.com.* [181v] First, Antar manually submitted her website to the major search engines, providing an XML site map. Second, she optimized the *<robots.txt>* file on her web server to help search engine crawlers find relevant (and exclude irrelevant) information. Third, Antar made sure her web pages — especially the home page and all headings and subheadings — comprised meaningful and interesting data. She titled one post *Why you should carefully consider ordering clothes from Chinese websites.* Antar constructed this intricate title to contain several key phrases she believed would interest people and for which they would search. Antar interacts with her readers, *likes* and *comments* on what they write, and responds to their comments. Within a few months, Antar's website rose to the top of the second page of organic Google searches — left-hand side — for several key phrases. To improve her ranking, Antar plans to link more articles and constantly update her website with interesting topics. She hopes this will allow her search ranking to rise organically.

MARKETING QUESTION

How do you assess Antar's approach to increasing traffic to her website? What additional actions would you advise Antar to take?

PAID SEARCH

Advertisers pay to appear next to, and be associated with, search results based on keywords. An electronics retailer using Google AdWords may pay to appear next to searches for HDTV or digital cameras. Typically, the advertiser pays only when a searcher clicks on the website — pay per click. Advertisers bid for position; higher bids, higher relevance, and higher click-through rates earn higher page listings.[4] Spending on paid search continues to grow each year — with mobile search leading the way.

To promote her fashion blog, Antar plans to buy *long tail* keywords like *runway clothes on real women, dressing on a budget,* and *the look for less.* When a person searches Google for one of these keywords, Antar's website will appear on the right-hand side of Google's page. The higher Antar's bid, the higher her website will appear. Antar believes her approach, plus linking with various social media sites like Facebook, Instagram, Pinterest, and Twitter will help grow readership, and lead to many future interesting opportunities and collaborations.

Both *organic search* and *paid search* are valuable for the firm but, in general, searchers are more likely to click on organic search results by a factor of 3:1.[5] As a general rule, search engines do not display results for social media sites like Facebook, Instagram, LinkedIn, and Twitter. Firms wishing to communicate with users of these sites must adopt alternative approaches.

BLOGS

MARKETING QUESTION

Firms increasingly use blogs for commercial purposes. Search the Internet. Which firm blog do you think is most effective? Why? What are the benefits and limitations of firm blogs?

KEY IDEA

The firm may make itself visible to customers via:
• Search
• Blogs
• Social media

Blogs are online platforms for audience communication; blog *posts* are discrete entries, typically displayed in reverse chronological order — most recent first.[6] Marketers usefully divide blogs into two categories — firm blogs for corporate communication, and blogs posted by independent *bloggers*:

- **Firm blogs.** Blogs offer the firm an effective way of communicating with interested parties: people who have signed up as *followers* and receive alerts to new blog posts as they occur. Some firms have millions of followers, due in part to followers forwarding or referencing blog posts to their contact networks, hence increasing the overall audience. A firm's blog tends to have two key purposes: to generate leads through *opt-in* subscription, and to build brand image. By continually posting interesting and compelling content, the firm gains reputation in a particular area. In addition, by providing interesting content and gaining followers, the firm scores higher on search engine rankings.

- **Independent bloggers** (like Nataly Antar) offer opinionated commentary on matters that interest them. They may blog for personal fulfillment, or for external rewards like becoming an *Internet celebrity*; earning advertising revenues, endorsement deals, collaborations; and/or securing a job. In most cases, bloggers allow readers to interact with them by posting comments on their blogs. Readers may also forward blog posts to their contacts. Blogs are often highly specialized — celebrities, politicians, food, travel, wine; some bloggers have enormous followings and are important opinion leaders. Because of the large numbers of *followers* independent bloggers may attract, they offer the firm two distinct opportunities:

  - The firm may feed content to bloggers for use in their blog posts. Technology firms often provide bloggers with advance versions of new products, hoping to generate favorable comments. This approach is similar to traditional public relations.

  - By attracting large followings for specialized topics, blog posts offer attractive options for placing online advertisements.

In constructing her blog (p. 440) Antar has developed a public persona. She explains: "I want readers to know I am a mother and love God; that I am smart, quirky, funny, sarcastic, and responsible. I neither post anything derogatory or defamatory, nor attack, hassle, or condescend. I want people to think of me as a leader and seek inspiration."

Brandweek reported, "Nike, Dr Pepper, Mazda, SBC, and others have ... found blogging an easy, cheap way to appear hipper and keep customers engaged with the brand."[7] Microsoft lets 1,000 developers set up personal blogs to build relationships, but not to release commercially sensitive information. Microsoft also hosts a site where developers talk with other community members — engaging around one million unique visitors per month.

But blogging can backfire. Dr Pepper/7-Up launched Raging Cow, a *milk-based product with an attitude*. 7-Up tried to reach a hip young audience turned off to traditional media by setting up a blog run by a cow. Some bloggers viewed the blog as too commercial — invading a non-commercial domain — and called for a product boycott. Whole Foods' cofounder/CEO John Mackey posted many comments to Internet bulletin boards anonymously; he was highly criticized when unmasked. A folksy couple known only as Laura and Jim drove an RV across the U.S., staying overnight in Walmart parking lots. Their trip blog pictured a host of happy Walmart employees, but when Laura was exposed as a freelance writer hired with company funds, Walmart's reputation suffered.

SOCIAL MEDIA

Social media (SM) comprises online tools and platforms that allow Internet users to send messages, share insights and experiences for business or pleasure,[8] and share content — words, pictures, audio, video.**[188v]** People also use SM to entertain, share reviews and opinions, and collaborate. SM communications can be very powerful. In the digital realm, customers often find strangers' opinions more credible than paid spokespeople![9]

KEY IDEA

Social media provides the firm with unique ways of gathering data about, and communicating with, large numbers of current and potential customers.

> **Nestlé builds highly targeted consumer communities. Nespresso is a several-million-person club whose members, like actress Penelope Cruz, *treasure quality coffee as part of the simple moments of pleasure in everyday life.* Club Buitoni members (Italian-culture lovers) click on favorite Italian recipes made with Buitoni pasta, and may win a trip to Buitoni's testing kitchens in Tuscany.**

SM sites collect significant demographic data on users; the firm combines these data with other browsing data, and purchasing behavior on the site and/or secured from third-party sites. This type of user data, combined with the high volume of SM users, offers the firm attractive options to communicate with large numbers of current and potential customers in many ways, including podcasts and webinars.[10]

Today, most firms create special pages for SM sites, then seek *friends* (*followers*) with whom to share information. Firms frequently post interesting new content — *feeds* — that *friends* and *followers* receive when they sign onto the SM site. When a *friend likes* (Facebook/Instagram), *retweets* (Twitter), or otherwise comments on a content item, that person's *friends/followers* also receive the content. The large number of SM users, together with the easy ability of peer-to-peer communications, offer enormous opportunities for word of mouth.

Many SM platforms are active on the Internet. Early sites like SixDegrees, Friendster, MySpace have disappeared or atrophied, while others have grown by capturing enormous participation. Some of the most popular sites are Facebook, Instagram, LinkedIn, and Twitter.[11] In general, each SM site has a specific focus and attracts a particular user type — Table 17.1.

Social Media Site	Number of Users	Vision/Mission
Facebook	1.4 billion	global sharing, connections, and openness
Google+	300 million	bringing the nuance and richness of real-life sharing to the web
Instagram	300 million	to allow you to experience moments in your friends' lives through pictures as they happen
LinkedIn	347 million	connect the world's professionals to make them more productive and successful
Pinterest	100 million	to help people discover the things they love, and inspire them to go do those things in their daily lives
Twitter	300 million	to give everyone the power to create and share ideas and information instantly, without barriers

TABLE 17.1
Social Media Users (2016)[12]

Of course, a specific SM option may not be relevant for your firm's digital marketing strategy. Each SM platform offers various options for firms to engage with its users. The firm may set up its own page on Facebook/Instagram/LinkedIn to post content, or implement a dedicated Twitter feed to highlight thought leadership. Frequently, firms assign different executives to manage content postings on different sites — typically minor variations of core content — to appeal to specific audiences. Increasingly, social media users add hashtags (#) to their posts/messages. Hashtags identify topics — even firms. Individuals may search on hashtags, and so broaden the scope of communications. Hashtags can pose a serious problem for firms receiving highly negative posts, especially when the poster has many followers. The firm may also advertise on SM sites.

MARKETING QUESTION

How do you assess Antar's approach to seeking success with her fashion blog? How would you advise her?

> **Antar's assessment of SM site followers drives her content variations:**
>
> Facebook — want to be your friend   Twitter — appreciate humor and sarcasm
> Instagram — want a glimpse into your life   LinkedIn — appreciate showcasing your achievements

Social media offers many opportunities for the firm. Many firms engage in community building by bringing together users, like Nespresso and Club Buitoni (p. 442), HOGs (Harley Owners Group), Cisco developers, and Mac users. These communities offer excellent opportunities to stimulate positive word of mouth, gain awareness, enhance brand image, expand product capabilities, build brand equity, and drive sales.[13] Microsoft formed offline partnerships with Burger King (Halo Whopper), Mountain Dew, Doritos, and Pontiac when it launched new video game Halo 3. Microsoft also built an event-planning website that invited journalists, bloggers, and fans to a prelaunch party. Party attendees uploaded photos to their blogs and discussed the anticipated launch; Internet users planned strategies to secure the game at online and offline retailers.[14] Sales and account management executives use social media to build customer relationships. Regional sales manager Jack Fitzroy encourages customer executives, together with his direct reports and firm executives on his team, to follow him on Twitter — then periodically tweets on matters of common interest. Fitzroy also uses LinkedIn to search for sales talent.

Bom-Chicka-Wah-Wah. To promote Axe deodorant, Unilever developed the bom-chicka-wah-wah campaign featuring TV ads, an all-female bom-chicka-wah-wah band, YouTube videos showing women chasing men using Axe, and online games where young men received fragrance recommendations for their chosen type of young woman. YouTube videos went viral as millions of people sent them to friends. Axe earned significant market share in many countries.

Many firms like EBags use customer feedback for product redesign; other firms engage customers in new product development — Chapter 14. Gardening retailer Burpee asks customers to post product reviews online; very positive reviews lead to immediate sales. Heinz's *Top This TV* contest, promoted on ketchup labels, challenged customers to design its advertising. Heinz received 6,000 YouTube submissions and 10 million views. During the contest, ketchup sales increased substantially.

Facebook (Opening Case), Instagram, LinkedIn, and Twitter are the best-known SM communities. Facebook and LinkedIn invite people to post personal information and automate connectivity with friends and professional associates. These sites also offer robust environments for marketers to establish branded communities where individuals can meet and connect with new people based on shared interests and experiences. Twitter allows users to follow others — people or brands — they find interesting.

Many other communities bring together like-minded users — TripAdvisor (hotel and vacation destinations), *Inthemotherhood.com* (mothers), and many disease-specific sites. Community members/followers are often attractive targets for coupons, online and offline conversations, product previews, and samples. Many of these sites discourage or ban traditional advertising. Firms must demonstrate commitment to that community by designing new strategies to build engagement, relationships, and interactive dialog. But communication fundamentals remain the same.

DARKER SIDE OF SOCIAL MEDIA

Much social media activity by firms aims to create favorable *buzz* — word of mouth — about the firm and brands among customers, potential customers, and third parties. But SM also enables customer-to-customer (C2C) communications; these can be negative. Defecting customers may encourage network members to defect also.[15] Disenchanted customers and/or Internet trolls (sowers of discord) can broadcast dissatisfactions widely using destinations like websites, blogs, and YouTube.[16]

Increasingly, firms deploy *sentiment analysis* and training for employees to monitor the Internet for negative communications, and implement ways to mitigate brand damage. Dell proactively looks for unhappy customers. By searching Twitter for *Comcast* (and *Comcrap*), Comcast can address customer problems before they become formal complaints. jetBlue, General Motors, Whole Foods, and many other firms also track Twitter and blogs.

continues

Former Pfizer marketing VP Peter Rost blogs about healthcare. **[139v]** Drug industry whistle-blowers provided information that led to Congressional investigations of AstraZeneca (Arimidex) and Pfizer marketing irregularities. Jeff Jarvis (unhappy Dell customer) blogged (BuzzMachine) about his negative experience with Dell customer service. Comments included: "The machine is a lemon and the service is a lie," and "DELL SUCKS. DELL LIES." BuzzMachine visits doubled to 10,000 daily and Dell's customer-service rankings dipped.

Firm response to negative communications should depend on the situation. Dell added more call centers and increased phone rep training. Some general options are:

- Correct misinformation;
- Do not respond, but allow loyal customers to address negative issues;
- Use customer comments as a form of marketing research;
- Fix the problem and advise the unhappy customer.

Sometimes the firm should bring in the lawyers but generally this is not a worthwhile option. Regardless, the firm should be ready to act quickly: Domino's Pizza suffered considerably when it waited over 48 hours to respond to a prank YouTube video by two employees. By the time Domino's acted, there had been one million views.

In general, the firm should develop creative approaches to enhance the positives and mitigate the negatives, both by acting directly and by engaging community members to implement its approaches.

SM can work in tandem with other communication vehicles. In 2015/6, Donald Trump secured significant publicity in national newspapers and TV shows for his political ambitions based on tweets and retweets. Kim Kardashian earned publicity for herself and the morning sickness pill — *Diclegis* — when the FDA sent her a warning letter regarding an Instagram posting. SM also works with sales promotion in distributing promotion codes for firm products/services. Burger King combined traditional P&PR with SM:

KEY IDEA

Social media offers the firm many opportunities to interface positively with current and potential customers. But the firm must also consider the dark side of social media.

In 2015, Floyd Mayweather defended his world heavyweight boxing title against Manny Pacquiao in Las Vegas — an advertising-free pay-per-view event attracting a record 4.4 million viewers globally. As Mayweather entered the MGM Grand Ballroom and made his way to the ring, Burger King's robed mascot — *the King* — followed right behind (along with Justin Bieber). Facebook and Twitter traffic was huge, and Burger King franchisees reported increased sales. Observers believe the $1 million payment to Mayweather was money well spent.

MARKETING QUESTION

As book publishers have embraced electronic publishing — iPad, Kindle, Nook — some are assessing the opportunity to secure additional revenues by placing advertising in both electronic and printed books. As a publishing marketing executive, how would you approach an assignment to investigate this opportunity?

Communicating in the Digital Age

ADVERTISING

So far in this chapter, we have discussed why the very large numbers of people using search, blogs, and social media make the *reach* of these audiences attractive for firm content. We discussed *search advertising*; here we take a deeper look at online advertising — display, classifieds, video.

The key benefit of digital advertising is the firm's ability to target segments of online users. With the advent of *big data*, the firm has significant information on individuals or groups of individuals — demographics, expressed interests, browsing behavior, and social network connectivity to other customers or brands. By knowing target audience characteristics, the firm is able to direct specific advertisements to select individuals. Clearly, this pinpointing ability infuses digital advertising with a very different character from traditional mass media approaches, where targeting is much blunter.

Sit next to a friend/colleague as each of you log on to Facebook. What advertisements do you see? What advertisements does your friend/colleague see? Are the advertisements the same or different? How do you explain the results?

DISPLAY

Display advertising, aka banner advertising, was originally based on a magazine model. Banner ads tend to come in standard sizes; hence, they are easy to develop, purchase, track, and measure. The basic banner advertisement has been standard for many years, but alternative sizes include tall skyscraper-like placements, medium-rectangle ads, and dynamic peel-away advertisements that cover web pages.[17] Advertisers serve the average person more than 1,700 banner ads per month. (Facebook is the largest source of online display advertising.)

Banner ads direct users to click to reach the advertiser's website. Advertisers attempt to match their advertising to stage in the customer purchase process.**[967v]** Hence, a consumer who explores a product form on Amazon will likely see advertisements for various purchase options the next time she logs in to Amazon; and may see similar ads when logged in to Facebook or Twitter — *remarketing/retargeting*. Firms measure banner advertising effectiveness by click rate or some other customer action like download, enquiry, registration, sign-up, sales lead, or sales (pp. 449–450). One or more of these measures typically forms the payment basis.

CLASSIFIEDS

Online classifieds are typically text listings for specific types of products/services like automobiles, jobs, real estate — similar to the yellow pages — and time-sensitive auctions. Migration of classifieds from *offline* to *online* has been swift and devastating for newspapers. The free Craigslist and Nextdoor networks of local community sites command huge audiences.

VIDEO

As bandwidth increases, so does Internet video. Firms place videos on their own and affiliate websites, and on branded *channels* in public sites like YouTube. Heineken Light reached 20 million people in just three days using video ads on Facebook. Videos can be advertising focused, humorous, or designed for PR purposes, like jetBlue's YouTube response to its winter-storm flight-cancellation crisis a few years ago. **[102v]** Increasingly, firms link video advertising directly to commercial websites to accelerate the consumer buying process. Furthermore, as more commercial TV-show episodes migrate to the Internet, video advertising choices will increase dramatically.

> Chevrolet identified people who had expressed an interest, or signed up to take a test drive, in a competitor's automobile, then sent advertisements to their Facebook pages and Twitter feeds.

PLACING ADVERTISEMENTS

Many firms have developed creative approaches using digital communications. What is your favorite example of a digital campaign? Was it successful? Why or why not?

Many firms automate their digital ad strategy by using *programmatic advertising* (box p. 446) to decide whether or not to show an advertisement to a specific customer, and which advertisement to show. Advertisers frequently construct multiple versions of a single advertisement based on consumer characteristics. Of course, creating multiple messages, each for a fine-grained group is expensive; advertisers must trade off potential additional value versus cost. Approaches to avoid overexposure include contextual targeting (advertising related to the site), rotation filters (based on customer profiles), frequency caps, and burn codes (stop exposures when the customer purchases).

Programmatic Advertising[18]

The following steps occur in milliseconds:

1. A consumer clicks on a link s/he finds on the web.

2. The publisher's content begins to load but with blank spaces for advertisements.

3. The publisher contacts an ad exchange, provides data on the consumer — Internet address, link's URL, browser and device types, browsing history, any other consumer data — and offers the blank spaces to advertisers.

4. The ad exchange contacts advertisers about the publisher's offer.

5. Potential advertisers decide whether and how much to bid for a blank space based on perceived probability of success. They may use simple decision rules — pay $X,Y,Z for a consumer clicking on links of type A,B,C. Alternatively (and increasingly), advertisers use complex algorithms that embrace data previously collected on the consumer — prior interactions, types of ads responded to/ignored — and data they secure from third parties.

6. Successful bidders' advertising loads with the publisher's content.

> **KEY IDEA**
>
> ---
>
> Programmatic advertising offers the firm cost-effective, automated ways to personalize digital advertising for current and prospective customers.
>
> ---

ADVERTISING CHALLENGES

Notwithstanding the many opportunities the Internet affords advertisers, challenges arise, specifically fraud and ad blocking.

FRAUD IN DIGITAL ADVERTISING. The advertising community is increasingly concerned about fraud in digital advertising.[19] The most pervasive form of fraud arises from *bots*, software that behaves like humans inasmuch as they mimic human Internet behavior. Bots click on display ads and video links, artificially raising click-through rates — 11 percent for display ads, 23 percent for video ads.[20] This behavior forces advertisers to overpay for digital advertising. *Bot* owners make money by constructing false websites; they direct their *bots* to legitimate websites and receive payment for false impressions and click-throughs. Fraud tends to be greater when web traffic arrives from traffic aggregators versus established social media sites.

AD BLOCKING. In recent years, traditional television advertising has come under attack from systems that block advertising messages. DVRs allow people to record shows; viewers fast-forward through advertisements. Newer systems automatically perform the skipping function. On the Internet, software packages perform similar functions when people visit websites. Although not widely distributed, their use is increasing. Relatedly, some digital product providers like Spotify offer two versions: paid — without advertising; free — with advertising.

WEBSITES

Most of us think about website design in terms of attractiveness and ease of navigation. For marketers, website design is critical for two very different reasons — *finding* the website, and offering an optimal website *experience*.

FINDING THE WEBSITE

Earlier in the chapter, we discussed the importance of search — *organic* and *paid* — in helping people find the firm's website. Because keyword selection is critical, the firm must design its website so that important keywords appear in the *right* places — title page, page names, headings, subheadings, text copy. Notwithstanding the importance of individuals finding its website, the firm may have to balance *finding* the website with *customer experience* on the website.

THE WEBSITE EXPERIENCE

**MARKETING
QUESTION**

Select your two favorite
websites; one you like for
navigation, the other you
like for the user experience.
Suppose you were designing
a firm's new website; what
features would you copy?
How would these features
help you reach and com-
municate with potential
customers?

At a minimum, the firm's website is a form of mass communications (brochureware), but it can also enable sales promotion by automating offers for discounts, free samples, and upgrades. Regardless, the website's true potential is its ability to function as an anchor for engaging customers, building brand equity, making sales. Websites allow firms to generate product awareness, provide product information aligned to user preferences, and explain and demonstrate products. Website design comprises words, pictures, and videos, but may also host blogs, webinars, podcasts; and offer branded games, free assessments, and mobile apps. Websites often allow customers to secure access, and/or register for information and premier content. These features encourage customers to interact with the firm by text message and telephone; posting responses; downloading content; uploading videos and photos; entering contests; posting reviews; and/or recommending products and distribution outlets. At Netflix, website customers order movies, rate movies, see movie ratings (from other customers), and discuss movie choices on bulletin boards.

Most commercial websites use *cookies* to track data on customer activity. Cookies are small text files installed on personal computers, tablets, and mobile devices; they are an important component in web-based marketing. Cookies and related identification technologies track user behavior, preferences, and time spent on particular websites. The data gathered allows marketers to target personalized messages to individuals who previously visited the firm's website.

Simple websites are inexpensive to establish and take down, but complex websites may ultimately be more cost-effective. Websites have become increasingly important for marketers. Websites help recognize customer needs; by gathering the *right* data, they help the firm develop/refine product specifications. Websites are often critical during evaluation and choice, like e-detailing events; or helping pharmaceutical reps make drug presentations and offer samples. Websites can also generate feedback on product performance. Some firms encourage customers to use the Internet for all routine tasks like searching for product information, posting frequently asked questions (FAQs), placing orders, and checking delivery status. Other firms use websites to replace traditional communication forms like telephone help desks and support for on-the-road salespeople, and/or integrate websites within different communication vehicles, like pop-up live chat using instant messaging.

Dell links its website and telephone sales reps by tracking customers who explore the website. Dell can take control of the search process to help customers find products faster than by searching alone. Dell's website can initiate telephone conversations between customer and sales reps. Also, customers can place innovative ideas for Dell to consider, view others' ideas, vote for favorites, and track the progress of ideas Dell selects. Dell has several blogs, sponsors online communities and owners' clubs, and has significant followings on Facebook, Twitter, and YouTube.

Many firms use the Internet to generate sales directly. (For potential conflicts with existing distributors — Chapter 19.) Included are most major traditional B2C retailers like Kmart, Macy's, Nordstrom, Target, Walmart; and catalog retailers like Brooks Brothers and Lands' End. Many merchants, like Amazon and Netflix, exist only on the Internet. (Amazon opened a physical store in Seattle.) The Internet also benefits many tiny specialty merchants like Germany-based Wurzburger — sheet music for accordion players; and Wessex Press — publisher of North American, Asia Pacific, Brazilian, Chinese, European, Latin American Spanish, Mideastern, and Russian editions of *Managing Marketing in the 21st Century*. Check out *www.wessexlearning.com.* [798v]

Whereas most traditional media targets domestic audiences, websites know no geographic boundaries. Websites for *The Times, Sunday Times, Guardian, Daily Mail, Independent,* and other British newspapers generate 50 percent or more Internet traffic from the U.S. Such shifts from conventional domestic media challenges advertisers that organize communications efforts geographically. Many services — like Google Analytics — are available for measuring sources of website traffic.

Some websites are morphing into quasi-personal communication (QPC), embracing interaction and feedback without human involvement, usually via artificial intelligence. *Siri*, the personal assistant available on iPhones and other Apple devices, is a prime example. Customers talk on the telephone to computer servers via voice recognition software. QPC allows firms and customers to communicate on a one-on-one basis[21] while reducing cost of service.

The New York Times reported positively on traveler responses to Julie: "Julie will remain unshakably courteous and tirelessly chipper. 'Hi, this is Amtrak. I'm Julie,' she says in a perky tone. 'O.K., let's get started.' She is casual: 'You'll want a pen and paper handy.' She is exacting: 'I think you said you want a 5 o'clock Acela to New York, am I right?' She is reassuring, interjecting 'Got it!' after each of the caller's answers. Occasionally, she is even apologetic: 'I'm sorry, I didn't get that.' Julie is not your normal telephone representative. Julie is more than an automated ticket agent. She offers a sympathetic ear and reassuring guidance."[22] Julie is Amtrak's computerized voice.**[433v]**

MOBILE MARKETING

Not long ago, if people used mobile devices at all, they made telephone calls. Nowadays, smartphones (iPhone, Android, Windows) and tablet computers (iPad) free web surfers from personal computers. Digital communication can now occur *on the go* 24/7/365. By some estimates, roughly half of all Internet traffic flows through mobile devices. Mobile marketing is the fastest-growing advertising channel and will increase considerably in importance as *mobile* device sales grow.

MOBILE DEVICE MESSAGES

Mobile devices offer several options for marketers, including messages:

- **Short message service (SMS).** Short text messages (up to 160 characters) remain stored until the user opens the mobile device.
- **Multimedia message service (MMS).** Similar to SMS but may include graphics, audio files, video clips.

Marketers must make good choices in order to gain customer engagement. They may send unsolicited messages — *spam* — but response rates are low. In developed countries, mobile carriers set guidelines, promote best practice, and police their networks to minimize/eliminate spam. Accordingly, most reputable firms tend to use *permission-based/opt-in* alternatives — users subscribe to a service — *Foursquare*; complete website registration — *Groupon*, *Shopkick*; or verify passwords or activity for sites like Facebook or consumer banking. Consumers can elect to receive advertisements, *coupons of the day*, loyalty points, promotions; and/or other benefits like feedback options, games, minidramas, music, polls, quizzes, ringtones, sports information, videos. Future mobile communications will only be limited by designer creativity.

MOBILE MARKETING FACTORS

Mobile marketing comprises several factors that differentiate it from digital marketing in general:

- **Apps and games.** As smartphone power increases and multiple screen sizes become available, consumers download apps and games. Marketers may embed advertising within apps and games, and even develop branded games.

- **Website marketing.** As the Internet developed, firms configured websites for personal computers. As smartphones and tablets have proliferated, specially designed websites now create superior user experiences, opening up many formerly static options for mobile consumers. Responsive website design is a crucial issue; leading firms design websites for optimum customer experience regardless of mobile device type or screen size.

- **QR (Quick Response) codes.** QR codes are two-dimensional images that consumers may scan with smartphones. The scan takes consumers directly to firm content.**[429v]** Check it out:

> In South Korea, Tesco reproduced its physical grocery store layouts virtually in subway stations. Instead of picking items from the shelf, consumers scanned QR codes to make purchases, then received deliveries at home. **[895v]**

KEY IDEA

Mobile marketing is differentiated from other digital marketing options:

- Apps and games
- Website marketing
- QR (Quick Response) codes
- Location-based services
- Mobile search

- **Location-based services.** Embedded GPS chips and other technologies identify smartphone locations. Hence, a bricks & mortar retailer with an *opt-in* system may communicate with, and/or make offers to, consumers close to its store to encourage them to visit. More generally, the best advertising message may vary by location — home, work, or at a ball game.

Some retailers use *Bluetooth*-enabled *beacons* to communicate with smartphones inside the store; retailers also secure shopping behavior data, analogous to website navigation.

- **Mobile search.** Mobile search is similar to regular search but differences exist. Most search engines deliver slightly different results depending upon the particular device type and screen size. Hence, the firm should test out how relevant searches appear on various devices.

MOBILE MARKETING CHALLENGES

Mobile marketing is fast growing, but faces similar fraud and ad blocking challenges as digital advertising in general. Indeed, the most recent version of Apple's operating system for the iPhone and iPad allows users to load ad blocking software. Widespread adoption of ad blocking could lead to retaliation by publishers blocking content to devices with such software installed.

KEY IDEA

Intermediate measures and output measures help the firm assess the results of digital marketing expenditures.

MEASUREMENT

The growth of digital media has spawned a host of new effectiveness measures — Table 17.2. Many measures relate to website traffic; some focus on more conventional advertisements in digital form; others focus on social media campaigns. Some measures concern *outputs* — related to sales and profits; other measures are *intermediate* — related to customer actions prior to purchase — Table 17.2, also Chapter 24. Payment approaches for digital media are in Table 17.3 (p. 450).

A particular feature of digital marketing is the prevalence of A/B testing. The firm offers two versions and measures their relative success. So long as statistical controls are appropriate, A/B testing enables firms to improve digital marketing performance.

TABLE 17.2
Selected Digital Media
Measures

Output Measures	
Average margin	Product affinity — products purchased together
Average order size (market basket)	Sales — by hour, day, week, month, quarter, year
Conversion rate (%)	Shopping cart abandonment rate (%)
New customer orders versus returning customer sales	

continues

Intermediate Measures		
Advertising	*Social Media*	*Websites*
Affiliate performance rates	Blog and microblog traffic	Chat sessions initiated
Brand or display advertising click-through rates	Facebook, Twitter, or Pinterest followers/fans	Daypart monitoring (when site visitors come)
Pay-per-click traffic volume	Number and quality of product reviews	Newsletter subscribers
	Texting subscribers	Page views per visit
		Search engine ranking (by keyword), click-through rate
		Time on site
		Traffic source
		Unique visitors versus returning visitors
		Website traffic — number of visitors

TABLE 17.2
continued

CPM — cost per thousand — advertisement shown 1,000 times

CPC — cost per click — on a banner advertisement

CPA — cost per action:

- CPR — cost per registration
- CPS — cost per sale (percentage or flat fee)

TABLE 17.3
Payment Approaches in Digital Media

KEY MESSAGES

MARKETING QUESTION

What other messages did you glean from this chapter?

- Digital marketing is the fastest-growing communications medium.
- E-mail advertising is a close cousin of direct marketing.
- Mass communication comprises mainly firm-to-customer communications. Digital communication also embraces customer-to-firm and customer-to-customer communications.
- Search, blogs, and social media offer opportunities for current and potential customers to find the firm and its products/services.
- In addition to search, the major forms of Internet advertising are display, classifieds, and video.
- The firm should design its website for both findability and the customer experience.
- Mobile marketing allows people to be online without geographic constraints.
- Mobile devices allow consumers to receive messages based on geographic location — outside the store and within the store.

VIDEOS AND AUDIOS

For complimentary material, see Axcess Capon codes at www.axcessvids.com

Internet Marketing	**472v** 🔊	Jeremy H. Kagan	Columbia Business School
Social Media	**677v** 🔊	Peter Propp	Consultant
Securing Social Media Followers	**321v** 🔊	BritMums	
Digital Marketing	**227v** 🔊	David Bain	

QUESTIONS FOR STUDY AND DISCUSSION

Can you answer the questions implied by this chapter's learning outcomes? Check!

1. What is your favorite commercial website? Why is it a good communications device?

2. In 2011, Facebook revenues were less than $5 billion, yet its IPO valued Facebook in excess of $100 billion. Today, Facebook's value is around $300 billion. Why? What actions should Facebook take to increase revenues and profits? (Or replace Facebook with LinkedIn.)

3. Amy's boutique fashion store earns on average $300 profit margin per dress. Amy knows: 10 percent of people receiving a banner advertisement click through to its website; 5 percent of website visitors purchase a dress. What is the maximum price Amy's should pay per banner advertisement shown?

TRUE/FALSE QUESTIONS

Answers on page A2 and at www.axcessvids.com — 979p

1. E-mail campaigns take full advantage of Internet characteristics. ❑ TRUE ❑ FALSE

2. The major value of online advertising is enhancing firm communications direct to customers. ❑ TRUE ❑ FALSE

3. In general, the firm can improve *organic* search results by increasing spending on *paid* search. ❑ TRUE ❑ FALSE

4. The major benefit of digital marketing is helping customers find the firm and its products/services. ❑ TRUE ❑ FALSE

5. Location-based services enhance the interaction between consumers and physical stores. ❑ TRUE ❑ FALSE

MULTIPLE CHOICE QUESTIONS

Answers on page A2 and at www.axcessvids.com — 700p

1. Which of the following digital marketing processes is most related to traditional word-of-mouth advertising?

   a. e-mail
   b. search
   c. blogs
   d. social media

2. Which of the following terms is commonly used to describe Internet searches for which neither the searcher, nor the entity found in a search, pays?

   a. organic search
   b. managerial search
   c. consumer search
   d. free search

3. Which of the following terms is NOT a major factor driving success in Google search rankings?

   a. superiority
   b. relevance
   c. accessibility
   d. authority

4. Which of the following is NOT a critical concern in website design?

   a. findability
   b. device compatibility
   c. customer experience
   d. erasability

5. Which of the following is NOT one of the main ways of addressing customers online?

   a. blogs
   b. display advertising
   c. e-mail
   d. radio advertising

Design the Market Offer

··

CHAPTER 18

DIRECTING AND MANAGING THE FIELD SALES EFFORT

For complimentary material, see Axcess Capon codes at www.axcessvids.com

LEARNING OUTCOMES

When you have completed this chapter, you will be able to:

- Understand marketing's role in the field sales effort.
- Lead a field sales force.
- Implement the six tasks of sales management.
- Develop a sales strategy: Set sales objectives, determine and allocate selling effort, and design sales approaches.
- Design and staff the sales organization.
- Manage critical organizational systems and processes to support sales strategy implementation.
- Integrate market strategy and sales strategy.
- Design a strategic/key account management program.

OPENING CASE: HONEYWELL BUILDING SOLUTIONS

Honeywell Building Solutions (HBS) provides building automation, security, and fire and life safety solutions and services to public- and private-sector facilities. HBS is also a global leader in energy services, helping organizations conserve energy, optimize building operations, and leverage renewable energy sources. HBS has a storied history as a Honeywell business unit. Chances are that when you adjust your heat or air conditioning at home or in the office, you are using a Honeywell product.

HBS addresses three market segments for commercial buildings:

- **Installation.** *Mostly for new buildings where the decision-making unit frequently includes owners, architects, and mechanical and electrical contractors.*
- **Service.** *Making sure that customer installations and equipment perform optimally.*
- **Energy.** *Retrofitting current buildings to improve energy efficiency. HBS acts as project designer and general contractor, but subcontracts most work to others.*

In 1999, Honeywell merged with AlliedSignal to form Honeywell International Inc. In 2000, United Technologies held merger talks with the new firm, but these broke down when GE attempted to buy Honeywell. The U.S. Justice Department approved the GE acquisition, but the European Commission refused; Honeywell continued as an independent firm.

Following months of turmoil — employees were preparing for the expected GE acquisition — HBS did not perform well: Sales declined 20 percent annually. To save the business, Honeywell CEO appointed a new leadership team for HBS — President and VPs of operations, marketing, and sales. Kevin Madden became worldwide VP of sales. The CEO gave the team 90 days to develop a turnaround plan, and to "get rid of their ancestors" — causes of poor performance.

Madden,* a 20-year Honeywell veteran, described the situation he inherited. "Not only were sales declining, internally a victim mentality was pervasive. Because of the turmoil, 35 to 40 percent of the intellectual capital had left and the business unit was in a tailspin. The entire organizational focus was on productivity and cost, and most sales were to current HBS customers; we were securing a minimal number of new customers. We had dismantled most of the sales teams that focused on installation of our systems. HBS had outsourced this activity to transaction-oriented partners who had little interest in building deep relationships or delivering complete solutions. Quite frankly, customers had lost confidence in HBS to do an installation and we no longer had any competitive advantage."

Madden said energy and many installation projects were make businesses. Sales reps had to be proactive in getting in front of customers and writing specifications. But that was not happening. Reasons were:

- *HBS had lost many good salespeople.*
- *Current salespeople were generalists; they sold in all three business lines. Yet the nature of the challenges and skills required tended to be quite different by market segment.*
- *The first-line sales leaders' spans of control averaged 25 to 1. Sales leaders were too preoccupied with administrative tasks; they gave little guidance and coaching to salespeople.*

Madden said the turnaround plan focused on five key areas:

- **Marketing and sales alignment.** *Marketing and sales became tightly integrated. The sales force not only agreed on all new marketing initiatives, but often stimulated new ideas.*
- **Customer coverage model.** *When Madden arrived, the Americas region had 192 generalist salespeople. Seven years later, the region had more than 400 salespeople, many hired from competitors. Madden challenged these salespeople to be part of the build, focused in individual market areas. Many new salespeople displaced outsourced partners as HBS returned to the installation marketplace.*
- **Sales planning.** *The five-stage sales process — HBS' playbook — was tightly linked:*
  - **First calls.** *The salesperson figures out the customer decision-making unit, what needs to be done, and secures agreement to develop a list of requirements.*
  - **Requirements definition.** *The salesperson prepares the list of requirements — technical, financial, legal — and gets the customer to agree.*
  - **Commitment.** *The salesperson identifies HBS resources meeting customer requirements, and gets agreement from the customer.*
  - **Solutions development.** *The salesperson brings in Honeywell engineers to design the installation.*
  - **Final negotiation.** *The customer and HBS sign the contract.*

  For all opportunities more than $750,000, HBS conducts an impact review with senior sales executives. The review team focuses on the customer's best competitive alternative and the team's next move. At these reviews, the team may telephone the customer to check its understanding and probe additional ways to add value. HBS also rigorously qualifies all sales opportunities; HBS only allocates expensive sales-support manpower where it believes it can win. HBS rigorously debriefs all wins and losses.

---

* Now VP and General Manager, Federal Systems Group

Can HBS sales force initiatives be applied to other sales forces? Why or why not?

MARKETING ENRICHMENT 18.1
Interviews with Kevin Madden **324v, 816a**

Honeywell

- **Roles and responsibilities.** *HBS reduced first-line sales manager spans of control — from 25 to 1 to an average 10 to 1 — to increase salesperson coaching.*
- **Performance management.** *HBS implemented a rigorous performance measurement system and pays for results. Base pay is comparable to competition, but HBS designs incentive compensation and rewards to be among the most lucrative in the industry.*

Madden said an important investment was in a sales force data system. The sales process also functions as a funnel and HBS knows, for example, that a certain number of agreements to prepare a list of requirements will lead to a certain number of contracts. HBS manages the funnel aggressively; salespeople must update their funnels continuously. If 10 days lapse without updating, Madden communicates with that salesperson.

The leadership team turned sales around; HBS is now a multibillion-dollar business and a strong member of the Honeywell portfolio. Sales growth rates have ranged from 6 percent to 30 percent, doubling the business. (Marketing Enrichment 18.1 [**324v, 816a**])

Permission by Honeywell Business Solutions

Chapter 18 is the fourth of four chapters in Part B of Imperative 4 — *Design the Market Offer.* Part B focuses on *Communicating Customer Value.* Chapter 18 addresses *Directing and Managing the Field Sales Effort.*

In many firms, the sales force is the only group specifically charged with, and compensated for, generating sales revenues. Field salespeople efforts are the firm's critical persuasive component. Some sales forces are huge. Several U.S. life insurance firms each employ more than 10,000 salespeople; GE, IBM, and Pfizer each employ tens of thousands of salespeople and sales managers around the world; Avon has close to one half million independent representatives in the U.S. alone.[1]

In B2B marketing, the field sales force has always been critical; salespeople typically introduce products/services directly to customers. Business customers increasingly want vendors to possess real expertise in their specific industries and/or functions. They expect salespeople to help solve business problems, not just sell widgets. In turn, many B2B vendors have expanded product lines and added solutions specialists to help knit together disparate products/services into integrated offers.

By contrast, in B2C marketing, mass communications and/or digital marketing are often the main communication channels for reaching consumers — the sales force plays a supporting role. But as the retail industry concentrates in many countries, and a few large retailers or distributors secure significant power, B2C field sales efforts are increasing. Some FMCG firms now spend more heavily on direct selling and *relationship management* to wholesalers and retailers than on advertising to consumers! At P&G, more than 400 persons work exclusively with Walmart.

Chapter 18 addresses four main topics: the marketing/sales interface, leading the selling effort, tasks of sales force management, and managing strategic/key accounts.

THE CHANGING VIEW

OLD WAY	NEW WAY
Evaluation based on sales volume	Evaluation increasingly based on profit contribution
Firms seek profits by cost reduction	Firms seek profits through revenue growth
Focus on making sales	Focus on building long-term, profitable customer relationships
Many low-powered sales personnel	Fewer high-powered sales personnel
Sales and marketing clearly separate	Sales and marketing increasingly intertwined
Sales efforts managed domestically	Sales efforts for global customers managed globally
Sales force organization, and systems and processes, are fixed for long periods of time	Sales force organization, and systems and processes, are modified to reflect environmental and strategic changes
Sales force/customer-service linkages are poor or loose	Sales force is closely linked to customer service
Salespeople act in ad hoc fashions	Salespeople developing planning skills
Salespeople individualism emphasized	Salespeople increasingly team players
Salespeople are undervalued in the firm	Salespeople are increasingly valued — the only firm function responsible for generating revenues
Salesperson as seller	Salesperson as educator and problem solver
Salesperson skill requirements are relatively low	Salesperson skill requirements are increasingly high
Salesperson is the sole interface with customers	Salesperson manages the organizational interface with many personnel
Transactions-based sales	Relationship-based partnerships
Salesperson customer-contact data are spotty	Powerful CRM tools enhance building customer relationships

MARKETING'S ROLE IN THE FIELD SALES EFFORT

This book's title is *Managing Marketing in the 21st Century*, so why do we include a chapter on directing and managing the field sales effort? Aren't there enough dedicated books on selling and sales management? Of course! But one in nine Americans works in sales.[2] Hence, understanding the sales role and aligning *selling efforts* with marketing is more crucial than ever. Indeed, many firms are evolving field sales efforts into strategic/key account management, so as to address their most important customers. Close marketing and sales relationships are paramount. Marketing also has an important role to play in helping decide which customers the firm should address with telesales and other alternatives — to secure efficiencies and lower costs. Marketers must be very clear that salespeople actions can *make* or *break* the market strategy:

At SalesCo (disguised), marketing's job was developing sales leads. Marketing worked hard but salespeople often did not follow up — sales leads languished in files. A new management team harvested 3,000 dormant leads and assigned a special sales group to work them. Within six months, 250 new customers were providing $5 million in new revenues.

Interview a senior marketing executive and ask two core questions:

- What works well in your relationship with the sales force? Why do these things work?
- What works poorly in your relationship with the sales force? Why do these things not work?

Interview a senior sales executive and ask two core questions:

- What works well in your relationship with marketing? Why do these things work well?
- What works poorly in your relationship with marketing? Why do these things not work?

KEY IDEA

Effectively managing the sales/marketing interface is critical for achieving sales excellence.

Old-fashioned stereotypes pose a serious problem in some firms: Marketing — *Salespeople don't understand the complexities involved in developing a market strategy*; Sales — *Marketing is full of ivory-tower types, removed from the market with limited understanding of customer needs and unwilling to* get *their hands dirty fighting competitors*. As in the SalesCo example, lead generation and qualification can also be fraught with conflict: Marketing complains about poor follow-up on sales leads; salespeople complain about poor lead quality.[3] As competition increases, these perceptions just don't cut it. Marketing and sales must be on the same team, each performing its own critical functions.

We do not pretend this is easy. Marketing and sales often have different perspectives on how to allocate budgets; marketing tends to have a more strategic long-term view; sales must deliver short-term performance. Regardless, creative tension may be beneficial to firm performance.[4] (Perceived compensation inequities can also cause problems.) The focus of market and sales strategies is also quite different. Marketing typically develops market strategy for various firm products — Chapter 9. A multiproduct firm has several product-market strategies; each product-market strategy comprises several market-segment strategies. The sales strategy must integrate these various market strategies into sales strategies reflecting a broad range of products sold to several market segments. Badly coordinated or ill-formed sales strategies can lead to distracting internal competition among product managers[5]:

Salespeople at FMAB (disguised) sold the entire product line to retail customers. Some brand managers devised incentive schemes to secure disproportionate sales force effort on their products. These actions caused considerable internal dissension.[6]

FMAB's practice is inexcusable in this day and age. Marketing and sales must work hand-in-hand; when they coordinate poorly, the sales force fights competitors *with one hand tied behind its back*. Many firms use a well-worked metaphor to capture the different responsibilities for marketing and sales: Marketing — *architect* — designs the overall approach to the market. Sales — *builder* — executes marketing's design. In construction, the architect/builder interface should be seamless; in business, the marketing/sales interface should also be seamless.

As leading firms increasingly adopt strategic/key account management programs, and customers have more access to data and information, the architect/builder metaphor is breaking down. The sales force has greater responsibility for securing deep understanding of customer needs, proposing actionable solutions, and accessing resources to solve customer problems. Leading sales organizations combine people, processes, and technology to optimize sales performance and stay ahead of competition. More recently, mobile, social media, cloud, and big data have all become technology enablers for sales leaders. When the sales person is in the driver's seat with a specific customer, marketing must play a supportive role.

In many firms and business units, marketing and sales have separate reporting lines. Although members of the same management team, their different approaches, backgrounds, objectives, and philosophies can create separate cultures; plans and execution are misaligned. Some firms pointedly address this issue by creating a combined position — Sales and Marketing VP (Chief Revenue Officer) — to whom both sales and marketing report. Other alignment processes include integrating marketing and sales metrics, or even sharing revenue and profit targets and reward systems.[7]

Well-managed firms implement processes that tightly coordinate marketing and sales efforts. They encourage disciplined reporting and communications (not just more), create joint assignments, rotate jobs, co-locate marketing and sales personnel, and improve sales force feedback. Marketing develops market plans in good time, with significant sales force input; work on the sales strategy should begin when market plans are well developed but not yet complete.[8] Senior marketing and sales managers meet frequently to hammer out realistic and coordinated marketing and sales objectives and priorities in a spirit of cooperation. Some firms even appoint sales/marketing coordinators whose job is to build effective senior marketing and sales manager relationships.[9]

LEADING THE SALES EFFORT[10]

Sales receives short shrift in many firms. "Most CEOs have financial, science, marketing, legal, or manufacturing backgrounds — but no sales experience. So they don't identify with the people who interact with customers."[11] These CEOs don't realize the firm will fail if the sales force generates insufficient revenues. This stark reality places a premium on leadership at each level in the sales organization. After all, the sales management job is to make salespeople successful. All sales managers, junior and senior, should *lead from the front*, spending time in the field with their salespeople — coaching, inspecting, observing, teaching, selling. They should empower salespeople to take initiative by fostering a culture of acting like "it's your own business." The most effective sales managers lead by example. They encourage two-way communication with customers, and emphasize teams and teamwork in collaborating with other organizational functions. These managers innovate new ways of delivering customer value, help drive entry into attractive markets, and spearhead evolution of new sales models and sales organizations.

To secure the best results, sales leaders treat human resource expenditures as investments; they view selling as a training ground for general management.[12] The sales force gets *tough love* — performance expectations are challenging and very clear, but sales managers provide plentiful support. Managers empower salespeople to succeed via day-by-day focus on their activities. Managers devote substantial effort and ingenuity to reward and recognition programs, and align individual salesperson financial incentives with required firm performance.

The most effective sales leaders *advance the science of sales* and *the art of the customer relationship*. They make fact-based decisions, like allocating sales resources — salespeople, strategic/key account managers, telesales — across customer segments and sales channels. They match sales models — like generalist versus specialist salespeople — to emerging customer needs, and leverage sophisticated intellectual capital by:

- supplementing firm products with advisory services to offer customer solutions;
- building specialist expertise by industry/market/product to fashion and develop customer solutions;
- working with specialists to install and implement customer solutions; and with customers to refine installed solutions, identify opportunities for additional solutions, and provide feedback to marketing.

Sales leaders understand viscerally that customer success drives firm success. They continually improve sales information, sales analytics, sales processes, and sales operations.

Sales leaders create a *risk-taking* culture where failed experiments for delivering customer value are *accepted* and *expected*. They celebrate and reward learning from honest mistakes, but penalize repeated mistakes. They hire and develop people willing to try, fail, and learn; and ensure cost-effective experimentation by coaching. Sales leaders' operating mantra is *fail quickly*, but aggressively transfer *lessons learned* from failed experiments and pilot programs to new efforts. By anticipating changes in market conditions and customer needs, sales leaders identify opportunities for new experiments with new sales models and sales processes. Sales leaders discover and develop best practice by following the *fail* or *scale* principle.

Perhaps the most critical leadership function is encouraging sales people to *live the mission* — providing a rationale for the sales job over and above financial rewards. Salespeople who internalize a greater purpose build credibility and trust with customers and develop a powerful differentiator for defeating competitors. A well-articulated sales purpose aids aligning resources with customer needs, attracts the best sales talent, and accelerates training and development. A sales purpose also motivates above and beyond the call-of-duty performance, and enhances innovation by cultivating openness to new opportunities for serving customers profitably.

KEY IDEA

Effective leadership is critical for developing a successful sales force.

Successful sales managers:

- Lead from the front
- Practice *tough love* with salespeople
- Advance the science of sales and the art of customer relationship
- Develop a risk-taking culture
- Encourage salespeople to *live the mission*

MARKETING QUESTION

How do you assess the sales manager's approach to motivation? **[950v]**

MARKETING QUESTION

Interview one or more senior sales executives. Ask how they do their jobs. Do they exhibit the leadership characteristics discussed in this section?

MARKETING QUESTION

Two truths:

- Car salesmen are the least trusted of all salespeople.
- Many people don't like haggling over car prices.

Your regional car dealership is making a strategic shift from haggling to fixed prices. As sales director, what challenges do you anticipate? How will you proceed?

The Tasks of Sales Force Management

To mount an effective selling effort, six sales force management tasks are critical. The first three tasks address *developing* sales strategy; the second three tasks deal with *implementing* sales strategy. We discuss the tasks sequentially but show how each relates to the others.[13]

Developing sales strategy	Implementing sales strategy
Task 1: Set and achieve sales objectives.	Task 4: Design the sales organization.
Task 2: Determine and allocate selling effort.	Task 5: Create critical organizational processes.
Task 3: Develop sales approaches.	Task 6: Staff the sales organization.

Developing Sales Strategy

TASK 1: SET AND ACHIEVE SALES OBJECTIVES

KEY IDEA

Sales objectives are desired results. Achieving sales objectives is the central sales force task. Sales objectives turned into specific performance requirements are *sales quotas*.

In 1973, Sidney Frank became U.S. distributor for Jägermeister, an odd-tasting golden German liqueur. Frank hired hundreds of provocatively dressed young women — Jagerettes — to offer bar patrons free shots. Their male counterparts — Jager Dudes — visit gay clubs. During the next 30 years, Jägermeister grew to dominate the on-premise *shot* occasion, reaching sales of 35 million bottles (2015). Jägermeister continues to dominate shots, but faced tough competition from *Fireball*.

Sales objectives are desired results. They derive from the strategic focus in the market-segment strategy — Chapter 9: Retain current sales, increase customer use, attract sales from competitors, secure new business.[14] Achieving sales objectives is the sales force central task. The firm makes profits, survives and grows, and enhances shareholder value only by selling products/services to customers. Achieving sales objectives takes precedence over all other activities some firms assign to salespeople — collecting payments, delivering goods, entertaining, gathering information. Sales objectives turned into specific performance requirements are *sales quotas*.

DEFINING SALES OBJECTIVES

KEY IDEA

Gross sales revenues are the traditional basis for sales objectives. Sometimes firms base sales objectives on profit contribution.

The firm may choose among several sales performance measures. Most firms set sales objectives in terms of volume measures like gross sales revenues (dollars) or gross sales units. But focusing solely on volume can short-change profits, so profitability objectives like *profit contribution* — gross profits less direct sales force costs — are also popular.[15] Well-set sales objectives specify *how much* and *by when* the sales force must meet targets. We illustrate sales objectives for Essex (fictional)[16]:

Essex: Overall Sales Objectives

In 20xy, sales revenue objective — $40 million.

In 20xy, gross profit contribution objective — $14.5 million.

RELATING SALES OBJECTIVES TO MARKETING OBJECTIVES

KEY IDEA

Sales objectives integrate firm market strategy and sales strategy.

Integrating market strategy with sales strategy is a difficult challenge for many firms. A useful way of driving integration is to rigorously translate marketing objectives into sales objectives.[17] Essex offers three products (I, II, III) to three market segments (A, B, C). Table 18.1 (p. 460) shows several ways to view Essex's sales revenue objectives:

- Overall objective — $40 million
- Objectives by market segment: A — $10 million, B — $20 million, C — $10 million

- Objectives by product: I — $26 million, II — $5 million, III — $9 million
- Individual cells show objectives by product/market segment. Essex sets revenue objectives for IA, IB, IC, IIB, IIC, IIIA, IIIB; but zero revenue objectives for IIA, IIIC.[18]

Although each approach to Essex's sales revenue objectives has value, only product/market-segment objectives really integrate market and sales strategy perspectives.

| | | Products | | | |
		I	II	III	Totals
Market Segment	A	$ 7	$0	$3	**$10**
	B	$13	$1	$6	**$20**
	C	$ 6	$4	$0	**$10**
	Totals	**$26**	**$5**	**$9**	**$40**

TABLE 18.1
Essex: Sales Objectives by Product and Market Segment ($ millions)

To illustrate objectives/performance relationships, Table 18.2 focuses on product I. Essex:

- exceeded overall objective by $2 million (28 minus 26 = 2);
- performed $6 million better than expected in segment B (19 minus 13 = 6), but
- fell short by $2 million in both segments A (5 minus 7 = –2) and C (4 minus 6 = –2).

Market Segment	Sales Objectives	Actual Sales Performance	Sales Performance versus Objectives
A	$7	$5	(2)
B	$13	$19	6
C	$6	$4	(2)
Totals	**$26**	**$28**	**2**

TABLE 18.2
Essex: Actual Sales Performance versus Sales Objectives — Product I by Market Segment ($ millions)

What does this analysis tell us about sales force performance for product I? Exceeding the overall objective for product I was great, and segment B performance was stellar. But Essex's sales force failed in segments A and C. If these were high-profit and/or high-growth segments, this sales force failure could be a severe problem and would outweigh the positive result in segment B. (Note: we only focus on revenue objectives.) Translating market-segment objectives into sales objectives by product is complex. (Marketing Enrichment 18.2 **[580p]** shows a simplification by partitioning products and customers into existing and new.)

MARKETING ENRICHMENT 18.2
Illustration of Setting Objectives and Allocating Selling Effort by Product and Customer Status — Old versus New **580p**

BREAKING DOWN SALES OBJECTIVES

Typically, the sales force breaks down overall sales objectives into *control units* like sales regions, sales districts, and individual sales territories. Senior sales managers gain significant insight by comparing actual sales performance versus sales objectives for individual control units; they see if a particular region, district, or territory is performing well or poorly.

Table 18.3 (p. 461) illustrates control-unit breakdowns for Essex in the San Francisco district (Western region). Essex set these objectives using a top-down/bottom-up process — Chapter 6.

- **Top-down.** Senior sales managers partitioned the overall $40 million revenue objective among sales regions. The Western region manager partitioned her objective among districts, including San Francisco.
- **Bottom-up.** The San Francisco district manager asked each salesperson to commit to certain sales levels by product and segment. Rolling up these figures across salespeople produced San Francisco's bottom-up objectives.
- **Integrating top-down and bottom-up.** Surprise! Top-down figures were higher than bottom-up figures. Discussions among Essex sales managers and salespeople ironed out differences. San Francisco's final overall revenue objective ended up at $5 million. Across

KEY IDEA

The firm should break down sales objectives by control unit — sales regions, sales districts, and individual sales territories. The firm should also calendarize sales objectives — quarterly, monthly, and possibly weekly.

the sales force, if each district met or exceeded its performance objectives, the entire firm would meet or exceed its targets.

		Products			
		I	II	III	Totals
Market Segment	A	$1,300	$ 0	$ 250	**$1,550**
	B	$1,420	$ 80	$ 500	**$2,000**
	C	$ 280	$1,170	$ 0	**$1,450**
	Totals	**$3,000**	**$1,250**	**$ 750**	**$5,000**

Firms also establish sales objectives in time units like quarterly, monthly, and weekly. *Calendarizing* allows the firm to monitor performance continuously and sets the stage for making course corrections when performance falls short of objectives — Chapter 24.[19] Table 18.4 shows the San Francisco district's overall sales revenue objectives by quarter.

Quarter 1	Quarter 2	Quarter 3	Quarter 4	Total
$1,100	$1,450	$950	$1,500	**$5,000**

ALTERNATIVE SALES PERFORMANCE MEASURES

Sales and profit-based objectives are the most popular sales performance measures, but the firm may consider several other metrics:

KEY IDEA

Alternative sales objective measures are:
- Close rate
- Customer retention
- Customer satisfaction
- Market share
- Price realization

- **Close rate** — proportion of sales attempts resulting in actual sales
- **Customer retention** — proportion of customers at start of year that were still customers at end of year — opposite of customer defection (churn) (This measure speaks to customer lifetime value issues — Chapter 2.)
- **Customer satisfaction** — specific metrics focusing on the customer experience
- **Market share** — performance versus competitors
- **Price realization** — extent to which the firm achieves planned price levels

The firm should choose sales objectives carefully, based on the nature of the business and its strategic situation.

ACHIEVING SALES OBJECTIVES

The remainder of this chapter focuses on *right* and *appropriate* actions for achieving sales objectives. Most salespeople are ethical and positively motivated to sell products/services to target customers. But some salespeople engage in unethical and/or illegal practices in pursuit of sales. Although relatively uncommon, sometimes firms pressure salespeople to make sales by any method — including giving customers improper payments (kickbacks) and/or all-expenses-paid trips. Ultimately, unethical and illegal behavior tends to come to light, damaging firm reputations and reducing shareholder value. A *win-at-all-costs* approach can be very expensive:

TAP Pharmaceuticals paid $885 million to settle U.S. government allegations that salespeople paid kickbacks and bribes to physicians for prescribing Lupron, and persuaded them to charge Medicare patients for free drug samples. AstraZeneca settled a similar free-sample suit for $355 million. J&J paid $70 million in civil and criminal fines for bribing Greek surgeons to use its products. Both AstraZeneca ($520 million) and J&J ($75 million) also paid fines for promoting pharmaceutical products for unapproved uses.[20]

TASK 2: DETERMINE AND ALLOCATE SELLING EFFORT

KEY IDEA

Key issues in determining and allocating selling effort are:

· Sales force size
· Sales force activities
· Selling effort allocation
· Telesales

The best way to determine and allocate *selling effort* is by examining four interrelated decisions:

- **Sales force size.** How much selling effort should the firm expend in total? In particular, how many salespeople should sell its products?

- **Sales force activities.** What activities should salespeople do? What proportion of total time should salespeople spend actually *selling*?

- **Selling effort allocation.** How should salespeople allocate selling time among products and market segments?

- **Telesales.** What proportion of overall selling effort should the firm allocate to telesales? What should telesales people do?

SALES FORCE SIZE

For effective selling effort, the firm must have the *right* number of well-trained, motivated salespeople. Managing *headcount* is typically a crucial HR function and sales managers often wage difficult internal battles to optimize sales force size. Figure 18.1 shows an underlying conceptual framework for determining sales force size — *sales response function.*[21] When selling effort is low, the firm makes few sales — A. As selling effort increases, sales increase — B. Ultimately, sales *top out* at a maximum level — C — even if the firm were to add extra salespeople — D. The firm should continue hiring until the marginal revenue from adding a salesperson equals that salesperson's marginal cost. Many sales managers find this curve intuitively reasonable, but do not know their sales force position. Approaches to the sizing decision are either experimental or analytic.

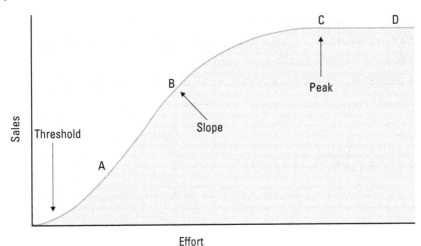

FIGURE 18.1
The Sales Response Function

EXPERIMENTAL METHOD. Sales managers change sales force size and see what happens. Two broad hypotheses follow from Figure 18.1:

1. The sales force is too small, perhaps at B.

2. The sales force is too large, perhaps at D.

Sales managers should decide what criteria would support/reject each hypothesis. Then they select one or more sales districts/regions for trial and comparable districts/regions as control. Sales managers increase/decrease sales force size in the trial geography for a predetermined period. If the experimental data supports hypothesis 1, the firm should add salespeople; if the data support hypothesis 2, the firm should reduce sales force size.

KEY IDEA

Sales managers should develop a hypothesis about the shape of, and their position on, the sales response function.

ANALYTIC METHOD. The analytic approach has three steps:

1. Total number of selling hours required to achieve sales objectives. Two broad approaches for calculating *required number of selling hours* are *single-factor* models and *portfolio* models:

- **Single-factor models.** Table 18.5 illustrates the single-factor model. The firm classifies current and potential customers into categories (I) — A, B, C, D — by a value measure like sales potential (II). Then:

  i. Identify number of customers in each category (III).
  ii. Estimate required selling hours annually for customers per category (IV).
  iii. Multiply III and IV to secure required selling hours annually per category (V).
  iv. Sum column V results across customer categories (VI).

TABLE 18.5

Illustration: Single-Factor Model for Calculating Required Selling Time

Customer category, **I**	Sales potential, **II**	Number of customers, **III**	Selling time per customer annually, **IV**	Required selling time annually, **III × IV = V**
A	>$2M	100 accounts	100 hours	10,000 hours
B	$250K to $2M	250 accounts	50 hours	12,500 hours
C	$10K to $250K	800 accounts	12 hours	9,600 hours
D	<$10K	3,000 accounts	4 hours	12,000 hours
Total				44,100 hours **(VI)**

Single-factor models are simple to use, but may not fully capture the complexity of selling to various customers. Portfolio models can do a better job.

- **Portfolio models.** The firm classifies customers on multiple dimensions. Figure 18.2 uses *customer potential* and firm share of customer business — *firm share*. The firm partitions each dimension into low, medium, and high. The firm then identifies the number of customers in each matrix cell (III); and the required selling time per customer (IV). The analysis proceeds as before.

FIGURE 18.2

Portfolio Model for Determining Required Selling Time

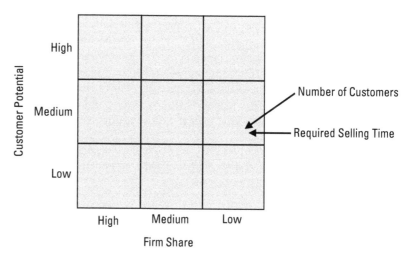

From this point on, calculations for single-factor and portfolio models are identical.

2. Available selling hours per salesperson. Salespeople conduct many activities (pp. 464–465). Sales managers must calculate the time available for selling. Suppose salespeople spend 30 percent of total time selling.

KEY IDEA

Salespeople conduct several activities. In many firms, salespeople spend less than 20 percent of time face-to-face with customers trying to make sales.

3. Required sales force size. Continuing the Table 18.5 illustration:

  i. Total available salesperson time per annum (hours)
    = (365 days less 104 [weekends] less 31 [holidays/vacations])
    = 230 × 10 hours per day = **2,300 hours**

ii. Actual selling time per salesperson
= Total available salesperson time × 30% (assumed)
= 2,300 × 30% = **690 hours**

iii. Number of salespeople required
= Total number of selling hours required/Actual selling time per salesperson
= 44,100/690 = **64 salespeople**

In practice, this calculation provides a *ballpark* estimate for sales force size. The firm should expect some variation from the actual size, but significant variation demands action.[22]

SALES FORCE ACTIVITIES

The main sales force job is making sales. But claims on salesperson time include checking credit and inventories, collections, customer service, delivering products, education and training, gathering market intelligence, internal communications, meetings, qualifying sales leads, receiving payments, record-keeping, report writing, sales planning, travel. In many firms, even the best salespeople spend less than 20 percent of time (equivalent of one day per week) face-to-face with customers trying to make sales. Many firms increase salesperson face time by using less-critical personnel for time-consuming sales-support activities; Xerox pairs on-the-road salespeople with inside sales resources (telesales) to increase selling time and tap expertise.[23] Other firms employ technological solutions:

MARKETING
QUESTION

If you or someone you know have worked in sales, what percentage of total time was *face time* with customers? What other activities did the firm require? Were time allocations good? Why or why not? What were the challenges of increasing face time?

Textile (disguised) sold products to department stores and specialty clothing stores. The stores continually called for order status reports. Salespeople spent many hours making phone calls to answer requests. Textile developed a barcode system to identify each order and posted status updates on a customer portal. Satisfaction improved and Textile's salespeople had more time for selling.

Firms regularly deploy technology to improve salesperson effectiveness. Most salespeople use e-mail, laptop and tablet computers, and smartphones; and standardized slide shows or interactive web-based demos in their presentations. Other devices and applications like *salesforce.com* **[126v]** enable advertising coordination, best practice and knowledge sharing, reseller training and virtual meetings, sales training, technical support, trade show participation, well-designed sales literature, and working models. Cisco's TelePresence reduces travel time by allowing remote face-to-face sales meetings.[24] Sales managers should develop guidelines specifying salesperson time commitment to various activities. A general classification like Table 18.6 can be very useful.

Hyundai provides all salespeople with iPads loaded with (and linked to) promotional material and product information. Marketing ensures all information is up-to-date. Customers are free to explore the iPads when visiting Hyundai showrooms.

Activity	Time Allocation	
Selling	Minimum	25%
Traveling	Maximum	30%
Servicing customers	Minimum	30%
Administration	Maximum	10%
Miscellaneous		5%
Total		100%

TABLE 18.6
Time Allocation Guidelines by Activity Focus

Time allocations differ from one sales territory to another. Salespeople in urban areas require less travel time than those in rural areas, hence greater face time. Salesperson activities also evolve. In growth markets, salespeople should make many sales calls to potential customers; they may also forecast product volumes, gather competitive intelligence, and train distributor

Sales managers should develop guidelines specifying how salespeople should spend their time.

salespeople. In declining markets, salespeople may consolidate distribution; dispose, liquidate, or reassign inventory; and collect unpaid invoices.

IBM had a face-time problem. Senior managers wanted data from the field; salespeople wanted advice, decisions, information, and resources from managers. Internal communications were sporadic, time-consuming, and frustrating. IBM developed guidelines for communications within various managerial levels in the sales organization — Table 18.7. Adherence to these guidelines was mandatory. Salesperson-customer face time increased considerably.

TABLE 18.7
Guidelines for Communications within IBM's Sales Force

Day	Time Allotted	Type of Communication
Monday	30 minutes	Salespeople and first-line sales managers
Tuesday	60 minutes	First-line sales managers and regional sales managers
Wednesday	60 minutes	Regional sales managers and zone sales managers
Thursday	60 minutes	Zone sales managers and sales vice presidents
Friday	2 hours	Sales vice presidents and executive management

SELLING EFFORT ALLOCATION

Selling effort (selling time allocation) should mirror the *structure* of sales objectives. For sales objectives by product, the firm should allocate selling effort by product. For sales objectives by product and market segment, the firm should allocate selling effort by product and market segment. Sales objectives by old versus new products requires similar selling effort allocations. Two important issues are:

- **Percentage allocations.** Although the *structure* of selling effort allocations and sales objectives should be identical, generally the *proportions* are different. Suppose sales revenue objectives required 70 percent of sales from existing products and 30 percent from new products. Most likely new product sales would require greater selling effort, maybe 60 percent versus 40 percent for existing products. After all, repeat sales are generally easier. Table 18.8 reproduces Table 18.1 (Essex's sales revenue objectives by product and market segment) but illustrates Essex's selling effort allocation for each product, market segment, product/market segment.[25]

  If Essex set sales objectives only by product: I — $26 million; II — $5 million; III — $9 million, it would allocate selling effort by product (not by segment). If Essex set sales objectives only by segment: A — $10 million; B — $20 million; C — $10 million, Essex would allocate selling effort by market segment (not by product). Since Essex sets sales objectives by product and market segment, it must similarly allocate selling effort by product and market segment.

TABLE 18.8
Essex: Sales Revenue Objectives ($ millions [Percent]), and Percentage Selling Effort by Product, by Market Segment, and by Product and Market Segment[26]

		Products I		II		III		Totals	
		Sales Objectives	Selling Effort	Sales Objectives	Selling Effort	Sales Objectives	Selling Effort	Sales Objectives	Selling Effort
Market Segments	A	$ 7 (18%)	20%	$0 (0%)	0%	$3 (8%)	15%	$10 (25%)	35%
	B	$13 (33%)	20%	$1 (3%)	15%	$6 (15%)	10%	$20 (50%)	45%
	C	$ 6 (15%)	10%	$4 (10%)	10%	$0 (0%)	0%	$10 (25%)	20%
Totals		$26 (65%)	50%	$5 (13%)	25%	$9 (23%)	25%	$40 (100%)	100%

- **Actual time allocations.** Suppose Essex believes the sales force can expend 50,000 hours selling effort annually. Table 18.9 (p. 466) translates Table 18.8's percentage allocations into selling time.

Product (% allocation)	Selling Time (hours)	Market Segment (% allocation)	Selling Time (hours)	Product/Market Segment (% allocation)	Selling Time (hours)
I (50%)	25,000 hours	A (35%)	17,500 hours	IA (20%)	10,000 hours
II (25%)	12,500 hours	B (45%)	22,500 hours	IB (20%)	10,000 hours
III (25%)	12,500 hours	C (20%)	10,000 hours	IC (10%)	5,000 hours
Total	**50,000** hours	*Total*	**50,000** hours	IIA (0%)	0 hours
				IIB (15%)	7,500 hours
				IIC (10%)	5,000 hours
				IIIA (15%)	7,500 hours
				IIIB (10%)	5,000 hours
				IIIC (0%)	0 hours
				Total	**50,000** hours

TABLE 18.9
Essex: Hourly Selling Effort Allocation by Product, by Market Segment, and by Product and Market Segment (hours)

Similarly to sales objectives, the firm should break down selling effort allocations by individual control units — sales regions, sales districts, sales territories. Table 18.5 shows how firms group customers into categories, based on required selling effort. Table 18.10 illustrates calling norms by customer category, based on Table 18.5 data.[27]

Customer Type	Selling Time per Customer (hours/years)	Calling Time per Call (hours)	Number of Calls per Year	Call Frequency
A	100 hours	2 hours	50	1 × per week
B	50 hours	1 hour	50	1 × per week
C	12 hours	0.5 hours	24	2 × per month
D	4 hours	0.33 hours	12	1 × per month

TABLE 18.10
Illustration: Calling Norms by Customer Class

Sales managers must make these selling effort allocations and ensure salespeople stick to guidelines. If managers do not lead, salespeople will set their own priorities. Individual salesperson decisions are unlikely to optimize firm performance:

- Product managers tasked with meeting sales objectives compete for salespeople time, perhaps by offering idiosyncratic rewards (boxed insert p. 457 — FMAB).
- Some sales tasks, like selling current products to current customers, are generally more *comfortable* than others. Without direction, salespeople gravitate to *comfort zones*.[28]

TELESALES

In recent years, many firms have reduced sales costs by adding telesales departments. Telesales functions differ markedly from firm to firm:

- **Lead generation.** Telesales makes cold calls, sets up appointments for on-the-road salespeople.
- **Potential customers.** Telesales may be more effective than impersonal communication methods for contacting potential customers. Xerox's 1,000-person telesales operation (Canada) calls on small/midsize organizations.
- **Current customers.** Reassign small current customers to telesales. In Scandinavia, Reebok stopped serving mom-and-pop shoe retailers with a field sales force and switched to telesales. Costs *reduced* and customer satisfaction *increased* — telesales people were always available to take customer calls.

KEY IDEA

Selling effort allocation guidelines must mirror the structure of sales objectives.

Typically, selling effort allocation is not proportional to sales objectives.

The firm must break down selling effort allocations by individual control units like sales regions, sales districts, and sales territories.

The firm should allocate selling effort by customer category.

- **Partner with field sales.** Both less-expensive telesales and field sales conduct customer-facing activities, hence increasing overall sales effectiveness.

> Pearson identified schools and school districts where sales were below threshold levels; they assigned these accounts to a new (typically female) U.S.-based telesales force. Benefits included positive group dynamics, no relocation for promotions, easy availability of temporary replacements, and training by listening to top reps. Sales performance improved substantially.

- **Combined with digital media.** Telesalespeople interact with prospects on firm websites by text message and/or voice communications.

TASK 3: DEVELOP SALES APPROACHES

The value proposition — Chapter 9 — anchors the *sales approach*, and is the central message the salesperson delivers to customers. Because customer needs differ by market segment, the firm should offer a different value proposition for each market segment. Hence, salespeople selling multiple products to multiple segments must have multiple sales approaches — one per market segment.[29] Aided by sales managers and product managers, salespeople should develop messages for specific customers and competitive threats. In particular, they should:

- Secure insight into specific needs and competitive threats at individual customers. Typically, salespeople must develop trusting relationships before customers will fully articulate problems.
- Understand various perspectives of customer decision makers and influencers.
- Develop sales approaches that provide solutions to critical customer needs, answer objections, counter competitor sales approaches.
- Ensure sales messages are consistent with other firm communications.
- Be sensitive to cultural imperatives, especially when selling in foreign countries.
- Secure support from sales managers and bring in senior executives as necessary to interface with customer executives.[30]

All sales aproaches are more effective when salespeople earn customer trust. The traditional sales approach has two major components:

- Tailor sales messages for different customer targets, and
- Design a process to explain benefits/values in the firm's offer.

TAILORING SALES MESSAGES FOR DIFFERENT CUSTOMER TARGETS

Customer needs and competitive offers drive the sales approach. Sometimes customers are clear about their needs; other times, individual decision-makers and influencers have different perspectives. Salespeople must decide whom to target and how to tailor sales messages for each person. Procurement personnel are typically interested in price; engineers focus on product design; and manufacturing personnel are concerned about production efficiency.[31] The salesperson must orchestrate the sales approach for each customer role (and individual), recognizing that customer needs may evolve as the buying process proceeds. Social media can help isolate response patterns that inform intra-organizational connections, and provide salespeople with useful clues.

> Enterprise remains the U.S.'s largest car rental firm. Starting in 1964, Enterprise provided temporary replacement cars for drivers whose cars were being repaired. One key customer target was garage mechanics — key influencers for drivers requiring a temporary car. Salespeople made morning calls and always carried donuts. This sales approach got garage mechanics' attention very quickly![32]

KEY IDEA

The value proposition
- anchors the sales approach
- informs the central message the salesperson delivers to customers

---

KEY IDEA

The firm should tailor sales messages for different customer targets and design a process for explaining benefits/values in the offer.

In designing the sales approach, salespeople should sharpen competitive focus. Table 18.11 shows firms I, II, III; each firm is trying to sell to a customer requiring four benefits — A, B, C, D. A consultant explored sales approaches for each firm.

Customer Benefits	Relative Importance	Firm I Benefit	Rank	Firm II Benefit	Rank	Firm III Benefit	Rank
A	1	A	1	A	2	A	3
B	2			B	1		
C	3			C	1	C	2
D	4	D	2			D	1

TABLE 18.11
Formulating Sales Approaches

Based on Table 18.11 and the boxed insert, what marketing research and product development would you suggest for Firm I? Firm II? Firm III?

When Xerox launches new products or product upgrades, it makes sure salespeople have in-depth knowledge of competitive products. Xerox provides easy-to-use charts and professional videos showing key strengths and weaknesses versus *face-off* products. Xerox laboratories create courses for salespeople including hands-on experience with competitive products, and techniques to combat competitive threats.

DESIGNING A PROCESS TO EXPLAIN BENEFITS/VALUES

Selling is a process that facilitates customer buying. We learned that a standardized process is undesirable, but sales managers should guide salespeople's approaches via coaching, counseling, and well-designed training programs. Good sales managers break the selling task into discrete easy-to-learn steps like:

- **Call objectives.** Know the desired results from each sales call at each stage in the buying process. Many salespeople use precall planning processes to set call objectives.
- **Sales interview tone.** Decide how strident or aggressive to be in different situations.

DEVELOPING THE SALES APPROACH: SHARPENING COMPETITIVE FOCUS

- The customer seeks four benefits in importance order — benefit A > B > C > D.
- The three firms — I, II, III — each offer different benefit packages.
- Each firm performs better on some benefits than on others:
  - Benefit A: All three firms offer — firm I > II > III
  - Benefit B: Only firm II offers
  - Benefit C: Firm II > III; firm I does not offer
  - Benefit D: Firm III > I; firm II does not offer
- *Firm I.* Should focus on the most important customer benefit — A. Firm I dominates on this benefit but is vulnerable on the other benefits.
- *Firm II.* Dominates firm III on benefits A, B; is inferior only on the least important benefit — D. Firm II's major challenge is from firm I. Firm II's major problem — firm I ranks best on the customer's most important benefit — A. Further insight and possible sales approaches for firm II are to persuade the customer that:
  - Competitive ranking on benefit A is incorrect; actually, firm II > I. Firm II should persuade the customer it offers the best benefit A. Firm II then dominates both competitors on the three most important benefits — A, B, C.
  - Customer benefits are incorrectly ordered; actually, B > A > C > D. By persuading the customer of its error, firm II dominates both competitors on the now most important benefit, B, and also on benefit C.
  - Customer should base its decision on the benefit set. Firm II's offer is superior; it provides all three of the most important benefits — A, B, C.
- *Firm III.* Has little hope of making the sale. Firm III's best sales approaches focus on benefit D and the combination — A, C, D. More importantly, why is firm III spending time with this customer when its benefits are so inferior?

No firm offers all of the desired benefits, so each is vulnerable to competition.

- **Need elicitation.** Develop procedures to elicit customer needs.[33] A more powerful approach is to previously identify customer needs from marketing research, then offer potential solutions (next item).

- **Presenting product benefits/customer solutions.** Present product benefits in the context of customer needs.[34]

- **Handling objections.** Anticipate customer objections and address them. Objections differ from product to product and from customer to customer.

- **Communications timing and closing the deal.** Communicate in a strategic sequence. For example, do not elicit customer needs after presenting product benefits. Learn how to close a sale and ask for the order. Learn when to accept rejection and move to another customer, and learn to better qualify prospects.

KEY IDEA

Selling is a system that facilitates customer buying.

Coaching, counseling, and training typically improves the selling process.

> In Bose retail stores and showcases, customers relax and enjoy exquisite sound from a large TV and huge speakers. When the show concludes, the salesperson executes *the reveal*. She removes the *fake* speakers to show baseball-sized Bose speakers.

A more recently developed but controversial approach — *The Challenger Model* — recommends that salespeople challenge customers.[35] Regardless, the salesperson's core job is to influence customers to purchase his/her products. Six universal principles of persuasion can help salespeople be more successful. Of course, behaving in an ethical manner is fundamental.

Influence Principles

Reciprocity. In general, people pay back what they receive. When someone receives a favor, gift, or invitation, they typically provide a favor, gift, or invitation in return. Reciprocity is most powerful if the *gift* is first, unconditional, personalized, and unexpected.

Scarcity. People tend to value more highly whatever is less available. This principle applies both to things and information. Salespeople increase their influence by providing customers with valuable and *scarce* information.

Authority. People tend to behave in ways conforming to the opinions of credible others. Salespeople earn credibility by gaining and displaying expertise in relevant content areas.

Consistency. People tend to act consistently with prior behaviors and/or statements. Salespeople can activate this principle by securing voluntary actions and public commitments, preferably in writing.

Liking. People prefer to act in ways requested by others they like. Familiarity and similarity tend to drive liking. For liking to be successful, it should be honestly developed, perhaps by joint working on common problems.

Social Proof. Before acting, people often look to the experience of relevant others. Salespeople should seek testimonials from customers to reinforce their messages.

MARKETING QUESTION

Baby food firm Gerber fired 250 salespeople and sold to grocery store chains via food brokers. By contrast, in the education market, Apple shifted from third-party sellers to an employee-based sales force. Why did these firms move in opposite directions? When is outsourcing the better decision?

Implementing Sales Strategy

TASK 4: DESIGN THE SALES ORGANIZATION

Tasks 1, 2, 3 address *developing* sales strategy. Tasks 4, 5, 6 focus on *implementing* sales strategy — ensuring the sales force delivers the planned levels and types of selling effort. Task 4 addresses sales organization design; firm choices should reflect strategic realities. For example, if the product line is complex and heterogeneous, perhaps the firm should have multiple sales forces. Three critical questions are:

- Should firm employees conduct the selling effort? Or should the firm outsource selling?
- How should the firm organize an employee-based sales force? Or reorganize?
- How should the firm design sales territories?

SHOULD FIRM EMPLOYEES CONDUCT SELLING EFFORT? OR SHOULD THE FIRM OUTSOURCE SELLING?[36]

Many firms outsource functions like call centers, computer systems, financial processes, legal, payroll, production operations, and security. Should the firm outsource selling effort? Three issues are critical to this decision:

- **Control.** Employee-based sales forces are more likely to follow managerial direction. Outsourced agents, brokers, and reps earn commissions; hence, the firm may exercise little control over time and effort, particularly if the outsourcer sells other firm (even competitor) products.

- **Cost.** Employee-based sales forces typically incur substantial fixed costs like salaries, travel and entertainment, sales management, and other overhead, regardless of sales volume. By contrast, third-party sellers on commission are a variable cost — no sales, no costs!

SALES OPERATIONS

A common feature of modern-day sales organizations is sales operations (SO). Historically, SO was a low-level function charged mainly with producing sales reports and ensuring salespeople were paid appropriately. Today, SO enhances the *science of sales*.[37] SO identifies and assesses sales potential via customer segmentation, and ensures alignment of sales resources to sales opportunities. SO also makes sales processes more fact-based, reliable, and predictable. Activities vary across firms, but mature SO departments form a flexible interface among marketing, field sales, in-house sales, and customer support processes. SO strives for both continuous improvement and transformational change.[38]

As a *front office*, SO drives top-line sales growth by improving sales productivity — *sales enablement*. SO works with marketing to ensure programs and events are effective. SO enhances the sales experience by developing and continually updating a central database of firm-wide sales knowledge. SO draws data from corporate marketing and R&D, product divisions, local competitive intelligence, sales force best practice, success stories. SO shapes and segments these data for specific sales roles and steps in the sales process. SO produces *playbooks* — specific customer solutions for individual salespeople. SO innovates with new sales tools, and becomes deeply involved when sales roles change, like developing strategic/key account managers.

As a *back office*, SO focuses on efficiency by handling repetitive, scaleable tasks like[39]:

- *Approval processes* — develops processes and guidelines to help salespeople navigate their own organizations.
- *Bids and contracts* — provides price information; drafts bid proposals and contracts.
- *Complaint management* — ensures the firm expeditiously addresses customer issues.
- *Executive sponsor program* — manages the executive sponsor program for high-value customers — recruits, selects, assesses, replaces.
- *Experiments* — conducts experimental pilots to push the envelope on selling effectiveness.
- *Lead generation and qualification* — interfaces with marketing to ensure sales leads have value to salespeople.
- *Low value activities* — develops alternative processes to minimize salesperson time.
- *Monitor and control* — develops metrics, creates standards, and designs dashboards to assess sales pipeline performance. Designs and manages customer and sales employee satisfaction surveys.
- *Pipeline management* — constructs a system and ensures consistent/complete data entry.
- *Reward and recognition* — designs salespeople and sales management compensation and recognition programs.
- *Role clarity* — constructs position descriptions for different selling roles; sets sales quotas; structures career paths.
- *Sales planning* — provides frameworks and templates for salespeople to prepare sales territory, account, and precall plans.
- *Sales-time management* — defines optimal sales-time profiles for various roles. Balances time among sales, service, administration; measures sales time against standards.
- *Training* — designs and implements training programs for salespeople and sales managers.

The firm must allocate resources between *front office* and *back office* activities. One major electronics firm operates 20:80 in mature markets but increases *front office* allocation in uncertain developing markets.

KEY IDEA

The employee-based/out-sourced sales force decision involves trade-offs among:

- Control
- Cost
- Flexibility

- **Flexibility.** To modify an employee-based sales force takes time in onboarding salespeople and equipment. Third-party sellers typically work with strict performance criteria and short-term contracts; hence, relatively easy termination.

> Direct sales costs were too high for software firm Altiris, so it fired the entire sales force. Altiris partnered with Dell, IBM, Microsoft, and others to sell its products. Altiris customized partner relationships, like making communications materials partner-specific. In less than 10 years, Altiris grew from $1 million sales to an acquisition value of $830 million (by Symantec).

Sometimes the balance favors employee-based selling; sometimes the balance favors outsourcing selling effort. There is no right or wrong answer. If the firm has insufficient salespeople for a new market entry, third-party sellers can take up the slack. Conversely, long lead times and/or high market share in mature markets with predictable sales may favor employee-based selling.

HOW SHOULD THE FIRM ORGANIZE AN EMPLOYEE-BASED SALES FORCE?

> Avon's sales organization comprises group vice president of sales, three regional vice presidents, seven regional sales directors, 85 division sales managers, and 2,500 district sales managers. In some geographies, district sales managers supervise several hundred representatives. Avon also aligns the sales force ethnically — language and culture.

KEY IDEA

Key sales organization design variables are:

- Degree of centralization/ decentralization
- Number of management levels
- Managerial span of control

Specialization may lead to higher sales but also higher costs. Specialization may also cause problems when several firm salespeople sell to the same customers.

Avon has a classic geographically organized sales force (boxed insert). Three interrelated variables for organizational design are:

- **Degree of centralization/decentralization.** Extent to which sales managers direct salespeople versus allow/encourage individual freedom and initiative.
- **Number of management levels.** Avon has five — group, regional (VP), regional (sales manager), division, district.
- **Managerial span of control.** Number of direct reports — the most critical is the first-line sales manager.

In general, as firms downsize, the sales force becomes more decentralized. There are fewer management levels and larger managerial spans of control — especially for first-line sales managers. Such *hollowing out* makes directing and coaching salespeople more difficult (Honeywell Building Solutions Opening Case).

Specialization is one of the most important design variables. Should the firm specialize its selling effort? If so, how?[40] Table 18.12 (p. 472) defines several *pure-form sales organizations*, shows conditions for use, and presents pros and cons.

- **Unspecialized.** We generally consider two organization forms as unspecialized. The firm:
  - does not place geographic bounds on salespeople's search for sales opportunities;
  - organizes territories by geography — salespeople sell all products, to all customers, for all applications, in specified geographic areas.
- **Specialized.** Specialization can take various forms — by product, maintenance/new business, distribution channel, market segment, and/or customer importance or size (strategic/key accounts). Generally, specialized selling effort leads to higher sales, but selling costs are also higher.

Specialization simplifies effort allocation; individual product and/or segment managers do not compete for salespeople time. The firm assigns salespeople consistent with planned selling effort. Referring to the Essex illustration — Table 18.8 — sales force specialized by product may assign salespeople to products I, II, III in the ratio 50:25:25. If Essex organized the sales force by market segment, it may assign salespeople to segments A, B, C in the ratio 35:45:20.[41]

Specialization can cause problems when two or more salespeople sell to the same customer. British Aerospace Regional Aircraft's (BARA) Asset Management Division (AMD) disposed of

TABLE 18.12
Sales Force Organization

Unspecialized

Organizational Form	Definition	Conditions	Pros	Cons
No Geographic Bounds	Salespeople free to make sales calls with no geographic constraints	• Difficult to identify customers • Relationships important (e.g., life insurance, stock brokerage)	• No artificial barriers to salesperson entrepreneurial drive	• Potential multiple calling on same customer • Little managerial control
Geographic	Salesperson has full responsibility in specific geographic area	• Customer requirements and applications similar, product complexity low • Sales force sometimes backed up by product specialists	• Maximizes selling time • Minimizes travel and admin. costs • Close supervision • Minimizes confusion for customer and salesperson	• Salesperson may be unable to understand full complexity of customer requirements and product line • Salesperson must be *jack of all trades*; may be *master of none*

Specialized

Organizational Form	Definition	Conditions	Pros	Cons
Product	Different salespeople responsible for different product lines	• Product line large and heterogeneous and/or at different life-cycle stages • Product sold to different market segments • Firm attempts to increase *face time* with critical customers	• Sales force deployment decisions for products made at policy level • Sales force becomes product experts through close relationships with product-oriented personnel • Customers value sales force knowledge	• Increased travel and admin. costs (vs. geographic sales force) • Multiple calling on individual customers
Maintenance/ New Business	Different salespeople responsible for: • Finding new business • Maintaining existing business	• Significant new business opportunities available, especially for new products	• Optimizes use of more-difficult-to-find new-business salespeople	• Increased travel and admin. costs (vs. geographic sales force) • Difficult handover from new business to maintenance sales force
Distribution Channel	Different salespeople responsible for different types of intermediaries and end users	• Products move through extended channel structure • Different selling activities required at each channel level	• Sales force deployment decisions for intermediaries made at policy level • Clarity of focus for salesperson	• Increased travel and admin. costs (vs. geographic sales force) • Potential for confusion among neighboring intermediaries
Market Segment	Different salespeople responsible for different market segments (e.g., by industry, buying center, customer application)	• Selling problems differ by market segment • Specific *types* of salesperson likely to be successful in different market segments	• Sales force deployment decisions for segments made at policy level • Greater flow of new product ideas from closer customer relationships • Customer offered *best* solution • Salespeople matched to market segments	• Increased travel and admin. costs (vs. geographic sales force) • Potential *feast or famine* with market segments • Some segments may be more lucrative than others
*Customer Importance (Strategic/ Key Account)**	Specific salespeople responsible for firm's most important customers	• Small number of customers (current and/or potential) responsible for a high proportion of revenues — 80/20 rule	• Focuses attention on customers most critical to firm future • Greater ability to identify opportunities	• Increased travel and admin. costs (vs. geographic sales force) • Difficulties interfacing with regular sales force

* Technically a form of market-segment organization.

secondhand planes recovered from bankruptcies. AMD competed vigorously with BARA's new plane sales division. Tough competition drove down prices![42]

Some firms combine different types of specialized organizations. Salespeople specialized by product are often effective in urban areas where travel times are low. In rural areas, customer density is low, travel times are high, and generalist (unspecialized) sales forces often work better. Product and/or market-segment specialists sometimes back up generalist sales forces. At WB (major regional bank), cash management, commercial finance, and leasing specialists supported account managers.[43] In a variant of the product-based organization, some pharmaceutical firms use *mirroring* organizations — multiple salespeople sell the same products to the same physicians.[44]

... OR REORGANIZE?

As the environment evolves, so also must the firm's market and sales strategies evolve. The sales organization must also evolve:

KEY IDEA

The firm should implement sales force reorganizations *very carefully*.

- **From a geographic-based sales force to a sales force with no geographic boundaries.** Manhattan-based Stuart Dean sells cleaning services to apartment and office buildings via a small, geographic-based sales force. Historically, building managers spent many years at a single building, but increasingly they move from building to building. Salesperson/building manager relationships are critical to capture and retain business. Stuart Dean abandoned its geographic structure. Each salesperson is free to seek business throughout the city.[45]

- **From a product-based sales force to strategic/key account managers.** Traditionally, P&G sold a wide variety of products — dental care, deodorants, detergents, floor-care items — via specialized sales forces. Supermarket chains complained about the interface costs of many different salespeople. P&G appointed strategic account managers (SAMs) for each supermarket chain. SAMs direct customer teams responsible for meeting strategic account needs.

- **From a geographic-based sales force to a product-based sales force.** Sales growth for Oracle's new application software was unacceptable. The product was very complex; salespeople found it difficult to demonstrate and sell. Oracle reorganized its global sales team into two separate product-based sales forces — applications and databases.

KEY IDEA

Important specialization dimensions for sales organization design are:

- Product
- Maintenance/new business
- Distribution channel
- Market segment
- Customer importance

- **From a geographic-based sales force to a distribution-level-based sales force.** Okidata's geographic-based sales force sold imported electronic goods to companies via regional distributors and local dealers. Okidata discovered that selling challenges for distributors, dealers, and creating customer pull were quite different. Okidata split the sales force into three: one each for distributors, dealers, end-user business customers.

- **From an undifferentiated account-based sales force to a strategic/key account-based sales force.** Merrill Lynch's (ML) U.S. retail brokerage provided the same costly service to clients with $100,000 to invest (67 percent of customers) as to multimillionaires. ML reorganized: Wealthy clients continued with their brokers, but ML served other customers through a call center. Regardless, each customer, however small, could talk to a broker by phone once per quarter.

Designing a new sales organization responsive to environmental and/or strategic change is one thing; implementing the new design is quite another. Reorganizations typically mean some salespeople have to do different jobs; others may have to relocate. Ill-planned changes can have serious consequences:

> In the early 2000s, Xerox fired its CEO after 13 months. The CEO shifted Xerox's sales organization from a product and geographic focus to an industry focus. The CEO viewed the salesperson job as analyzing an entire customer business and identifying the best way to manage complex flows of data, graphics, images. The CEO believed salespeople would develop intellectual capital by industry. But Xerox made the change before salespeople were trained, and did a poor job of switching accounts among salespeople. Xerox *orphaned* previously well-served customers. Many salespeople left rather than relocate. Competitors hired disgruntled Xerox salespeople.

Apple's shift to an employee-based sales force was also less than stellar:

> Apple CEO Steve Jobs said: "We were very straightforward and told these third-party salespeople that, 'Hey, in four months we're going to switch [the sales force organization] and you're going to be out of a job.' Obviously these folks did everything they could to sell as much as they could by June 30, when we let them go, and did absolutely nothing to build for sales in the July quarter. So when our folks got there, they found there was no pipeline work at all: They had to start from scratch. And, duh, this was during the *peak buying time for schools* [emphasis added]. It was just stupid on our part to do this then, and that was my decision. It was a train wreck, and it was totally my fault."[46]

HOW SHOULD THE FIRM DESIGN SALES TERRITORIES?

Within the sales organization structure, the firm must design (redesign) *sales territories*. Of course, frequent territory design changes are undesirable as they disrupt customer-salesperson relationships. The two key variables are *sales potential* — available sales; and *salesperson workload* — time to complete required activities. Four standard sales territory design steps are:

- **Design by sales potential.** The firm identifies geographically contiguous territories with roughly equal *sales potential*. Some trial territories are geographically larger than others. Equivalent potential territories for Xerox may be a few blocks of midtown Manhattan or several Western states.
- **Calculate workload.** Use sales-effort allocation decisions (Task 2) to determine *workload*. Based on the initial design, in some territories, salespeople may have time left over; in other territories, they may have insufficient time.
- **Adjust initial design for workload.** Make territory design adjustments to optimize sales potential and salesperson workload.
- **Continuous monitoring.** Sales managers must monitor salespeople and their territories and continually adjust. Some customers may grow faster or slower than expected; new customers may emerge; others may go out of business. Aggressive young salespeople may be frustrated with insufficient sales potential; experienced salespeople may *cherry-pick* (select) the best short-term accounts and avoid difficult sales. Sales management must continually optimize territory design:

> ConstructCo's (disguised) analysis showed that market share by territory ranged from 8 to 50 percent. Also, many high-revenue salespeople had low territory shares. ConstructCo redesigned sales territories to take advantage of untapped potential and added salespeople. Revenue decline turned into revenue growth.

KEY IDEA

Sales territory design should aim for roughly equal:
- Sales potential
- Workload

TASK 5: CREATE CRITICAL ORGANIZATIONAL PROCESSES

All sales organizations employ a variety of organizational processes to implement the sales strategy. We focus on sales planning, pipeline analysis and sales forecasting, evaluation methods, and reward systems to help implement planned selling effort. Today many firms enable these processes using powerful software tools like those available at *www.salesforce.com*.

SALES PLANNING

The firm should actively engage salespeople in a detailed sales planning process. As discussed earlier, senior sales managers work with regional and district sales managers to decompose overall firm sales objectives into individual control units like sales regions, districts, and territories. They also decide on broad selling effort allocations by product and market segment. In bottom-

KEY IDEA

The firm should actively engage salespeople in the sales planning process.

up planning, salespeople analyze their individual territories, work with district sales managers to agree on territory objectives, and develop sales action plans. Time is the salesperson's critical scarce resource — the sales action plan drives selling effort by specifying where the salesperson will place effort in the upcoming year, plus identify shorter-term action steps. Sales managers must ensure the firm implements planned selling effort at each control unit and achieves its sales objectives. Deviating from the sales strategy can cause problems:

> MD (startup medical device firm) specialized in hemodialysis treatments (blood cleansing for failed kidneys). MD decided to focus selling effort on major teaching hospitals. The sales approach required salespeople to provide customers with high service levels to ensure proper use. But in implementation, salespeople made sales to more hospitals than they could service. MD's product was widely misused and the firm suffered serious credibility problems.

MARKETING QUESTION

Talk to a salesperson about current and potential customers. Do IBM's six stages in the selling process —

• Discover
• Identify
• Validate
• Qualify
• Conditional agreement
• Business won

— work for them? Don't forget to check if customer expectations were met.

PIPELINE ANALYSIS AND SALES FORECASTING

The sales pipeline comprises stages in the selling process as customers move from prospects (potential customers) to buyers. *Pipeline analysis* tracks firm success as customers traverse these stages and is critical for sales forecasting. For example, IBM's pipeline — Figure 18.3 — comprises:

- **Discover.** The salesperson believes the customer is intending to buy.
- **Identify.** The customer is interested in working with IBM.
- **Validate.** The customer states a need and buying vision. The customer allows IBM access to project sponsors — customer personnel responsible for the purchase.
- **Qualify.** Project sponsors and an IBM team work on a preliminary solution.
- **Conditional agreement.** Project sponsors conditionally approve IBM's proposed solution.
- **Business won.** The customer and IBM team sign a contract.
- **Customer expectations met.** The customer is satisfied as purchase and installation move forward — and IBM receives payment as scheduled.

FIGURE 18.3
IBM Pipeline

IBM salespeople enter each potential opportunity into the pipeline and estimate potential sales revenues. Periodically, salespeople update each opportunity with a refined sales forecast. If plans change or the customer eliminates IBM as a potential supplier, the opportunity exits the pipeline. IBM aggregates pipeline data and constantly tracks opportunities by sales territory, district, and region. IBM also tracks percentage of opportunities moving from stage to stage, starting with *total sales leads.* Hence, IBM can project expected revenues by territory, district, and region, and identify where performance is on track and where it needs improvement. (Also Opening Case for Honeywell's system.)

KEY IDEA

A pipeline system continually tracks success at different stages in the selling process. Rigorous pipeline analysis leads to better sales forecasts.

To achieve organizational consistency, the firm should implement a single pipeline system across its many sales territories.[47] Many firms use software from SAP and others to track and manage sales pipelines, and decide where and when to apply additional selling resources — like securing leads or validating opportunities.[48] These applications have many tools: for salespeople to better analyze customer data; for sales managers to gain greater insight into sales force performance so they can make appropriate interventions. For various reasons, salespeople often resist entering pipeline data, but the firm must make this mandatory.[49] Table 18.13 illustrates typical pipeline data for a single sales territory.

	Total Sales Leads Discovered	Opportunities Identified	Opportunities Validated	Opportunities Qualified	Conditional Agreements Made with Customer	Business Won
Territory total	$76 million	$28 million	$17 million	$13 million	$10 million	$8 million
Percentage of total pipeline leads	100%	37%	22%	17%	13%	11%
Percentage success from previous stage	100%	37%	61%	76%	77%	80%

TABLE 18.13
Illustration:
Pipeline Analysis

We cannot overstate the importance of good sales forecasting. At a minimum, good forecasts are important for financial budgeting, production planning, and reporting future firm prospects to shareholders and financial analysts (public companies). Pipeline analysis is a fundamental tool for improving forecast accuracy. Poor forecasting can lead to significant problems:

To meet *explosive demand*, in the early 2000s, Canadian multinational telecom firm Nortel Networks (NN) added 9,600 jobs and spent $1.9 billion to boost production. One year later, NN lost $19 billion in a single quarter, eliminated 10,000 jobs, and later filed for bankruptcy (2009).

Cisco vastly overestimated demand by basing forecasts on orders. Cisco did not realize that end users, worried about product shortages, placed orders with several distributors. Cisco sales were less than expected, and inventory swelled.

EVALUATION METHODS

Chapter 24 provides a comprehensive view of monitor-and-control processes. For salespeople, the most critical evaluation measure is sales performance versus sales objectives. Sales managers should assess both the quantity and quality of selling effort. Are salespeople working hard? Are they working smart? Only by enhancing these *input* behaviors will salespeople improve *output* sales performance. Table 18.14 shows candidate input behavior measures and their limitations.

To assess selling effort, sales managers should use several measures — a single measure can be misleading. Suppose a salesperson has high sales per existing account; seems like great performance. Not so fast: The salesperson could have few existing accounts and overall territory sales may be low. Sales managers at every level — district, regional, national —should receive regular data on direct reports and *skip-level* access to select data as needed.

Measure	Value	Limitations
Calls per day	Identifies level of calling effort	Measures quantity of calls, not quality
Calls per account	Identifies level of calling effort	Measures quantity of calls, not quality
Calls per new account	Identifies where time is spent; links to sales strategy	Should be used together with calls per existing account
Calls per existing account	Identifies where time is spent; links to sales strategy	Should be used together with calls per new account

TABLE 18.14
Measures for Assessing a Salesperson's Effort

REWARD SYSTEMS

Reward systems are powerful motivators for salespeople. To establish a truly motivating system, salespeople should answer "yes" to the following questions[50]:

- Can I *achieve* my sales objectives?
- Do I *value* the rewards I will earn for meeting my sales objectives?
- Do I believe I will truly *receive* the rewards I earn?
- Is the reward system fair?

Pharma (disguised) paid sales representatives salary and incentive to sell to physicians. Pharma based the incentive portion on achieving sales goals and adhering to planned calling patterns. Pharma's marketing group discovered that, in some therapeutic areas, nurses and nurse practitioners influenced the medications patients received; sometimes they actually prescribed medications. Marketing devised a plan for salespeople to call on nurse practitioners, but Pharma did not change its compensation system. Salespeople were not paid for these calls and the initiative failed.

Sales reward systems can have several components:

KEY IDEA

The firm's reward system should motivate salesperson behavior. Primary components are:

- Financial incentives
- Recognition
- Promotions and work assignments

The primary ways to pay salespeople are:

- Salary
- Commission
- Bonus

- **Financial compensation.** The firm combines three financial rewards in various ways:
  - *Base salary.* Paid to the salesperson regardless of sales performance (in the short run).
  - *Bonus.* Reward paid for achieving quota — typically a target sales or profit level.
  - *Sales commission.* Variable compensation based on sales or profits. In some industries, like life insurance, salespeople earn no base salary and work strictly on commission.

- **Recognition.** This important reward is relatively inexpensive but can be a powerful motivator. Creative sales managers recognize salespeople for performance like highest revenues, best sales growth, most profitable sales, most new accounts, and/or most lost accounts retrieved. Many sales forces recognize high performers with membership in a President's Club, often associated with an annual trip (with spouse) to an exciting destination. Amica Mutual Insurance introduced a point-based system to motivate 900 sales and service reps to sell more policies. The online reward catalog, formed in part from salespeople suggestions, embraces products like airfares, gift cards, luggage, and PCs. To stimulate internal competition and provide recognition, Amica presents prizes in office ceremonies.[51]

- **Promotions and work assignments.** Promotions and more interesting and responsible job possibilities are highly motivating for some salespeople. Others may not value such advancement or change. They may prefer to be career salespeople and/or lack the necessary skills to move to other firm positions.

Generally, financial compensation is a salesperson's most important motivator. The firm should decide the take-home target pay range, then decide the particular combination of salary, commission, and/or bonus for reaching the target. Each component can have drawbacks:

- High salary — may not motivate salespeople to put in high selling effort
- High commissions and established customers — rewards historical rather than current efforts
- High bonuses — may lead to reduced effort after attaining quota and/or persuading customers to hold off placing orders until the next period, as salespeople try to beat the system.[52,53]

MARKETING QUESTION

Think about jobs you have had. How were you compensated? What types of incentives did the employer provide? What did you find demotivating?

The amount of incentive pay — commissions and bonus — should be proportionate to the role of selling effort in making sales.[54] A recent U.S. trend is to put more salespeople pay *at risk* by increasing the incentive portion.

By developing a fair and consistent compensation plan, the firm drives the behavior it desires. Commissions based on sales volume motivate sales but can ignore profits. LG's Kwang-Ro Kim says, "[We make] our salespeople responsible not just for sales but for profits too… [We make] the costs of the business readily available to them.... Our people know ... that they have to control their marketing expenses and other costs."[55] Previously, Computer Associates paid its 2,500 salespeople with upfront commissions; salespeople focused on renewing old contracts. A new compensation plan paid higher commissions for additional product sales; by paying over the contract's life, salespeople also focused on customer satisfaction.

Every six months, 400–500 customers provide Siebel Systems (Oracle division) with satisfaction data on its various departments and individual salespeople. These data drive bonuses and commissions. Salespeople do not receive full commissions until one year after a sale, and then only if customer satisfaction scores are up to par.

A well-designed compensation system can be highly motivating, but a poorly designed system can be highly demotivating. Firms should avoid systems where: Compensation and sales performance are not linked; the incentive portion is too low; and compensation is capped so that sales increases do not lead to higher compensation. Of course, the higher the incentive portion, the less predictable are the firm's selling costs. Whenever the firm contemplates a change in its sales compensation mix, it should simulate total sales force costs under various scenarios to avoid surprises for management and salespeople.

What are the challenges of consistently motivating a sales team? How would you address these challenges?

The firm should be especially concerned that the financial compensation system does not encourage aberrant behavior:

Dun & Bradstreet (D&B) paid credit-report salespeople salary and bonus. Base salary was low, and the bonus didn't take effect until sales exceeded the previous year plus 15 percent. In order to reach this difficult target, several salespeople sent to customers (and billed for) credit reports they hadn't ordered! When D&B unearthed this practice, it made substantial payments to customers including six-figure amounts to AT&T and IBM. Said a senior D&B executive, "We were a cesspool."[56]

Sears Auto Centers shifted the compensation system for 3,500 service advisors from salary to salary plus commission — based on product-specific sales quotas. Investigation by the California's Bureau of Automotive Repairs revealed that automobiles brought in for simple repairs typically received unnecessary expensive repairs. After many months negotiating and numerous lawsuits, Sears settled with California and 41 other states by distributing $46.6 million in coupons to dissatisfied customers; Sears also paid fines totaling $15 million.[57]

TASK 6: STAFF THE SALES ORGANIZATION

Salespeople are one of the firm's most important resources. Today, few sales professionals compare to Arthur Miller's classic Willy Loman stereotype in *Death of a Salesman* or David Mamet's manipulators in *Glengarry Glen Ross*.[58] But only salespeople can *bring home the bacon* by making sales. Sales managers must ensure the sales force is fully staffed and all territories are filled, at all times. To achieve this goal, sales managers must plan for natural attrition, dismissal, promotions, and/or transfers. Sales managers should *inventory* salespeople and have their own *pipeline* of candidates ready to move to a territory when one opens up.

Many firms have a policy of recruiting salespeople internally; they may create career paths in related departments like sales support or customer service. These employees are committed to customers, know firm products, and are ready to transfer into the sales force as needed. Other firms recruit externally; sales managers continually interview candidates, develop short lists, and are ready to bring in fresh perspectives and experience when needed. Staffing trade-offs include:

- **Availability.** If experienced competent salespeople are not available, as in new and growing industries, the firm must be ready to provide significant training.

KEY IDEA

Important trade-offs in populating the sales force include:
- Availability
- Hiring philosophy
- Time
- Tolerance for failure

- **Hiring philosophy.** The firm may require salespeople *uncontaminated* by *bad habits* from previous selling experiences.
- **Time.** If a new hire must perform effectively and immediately, there may be no time for a broad search and significant training.
- **Tolerance for failure.** Hiring only the best salespeople may be critical. In other cases, a *sink-or-swim* approach can be more effective.

KEY IDEA

The firm should develop rigorous systems for the sales force, including:

- Recruiting
- Selecting
- Training
- Coaching
- Retaining
- Replacing

The staffing process to hire and prepare effective salespeople involves several steps:

- **Recruiting.** Sizing and defining the pool from which the firm will select salespeople.
- **Selecting.** Using selection criteria to choose salespeople from the recruitment pool.
- **Training.** Ensuring salespeople have the knowledge, skills, and abilities (KSAs) to be effective.
- **Coaching.** Continuous efforts by first-line sales managers to improve selling effectiveness.
- **Retaining.** Maintaining high-performing salespeople.
- **Replacing.** Weeding out and replacing poorly performing salespeople.

RECRUITING

The recruitment pool reflects the firm's hiring philosophy. Two broad approaches are:

- **Experience.** Hire experienced sales professionals. Sales managers should monitor the job market for successful salespeople in their industries and/or geographies. A West Coast stock brokerage firm stated: "We'll recruit anyone with more than five years' experience at Merrill Lynch!"[59]
- **Inexperience.** Hire high-potential individuals with zero (or limited) sales experience. The firm may focus on recent college graduates or employees in telesales or nonsales functions.

In either case, the firm should continually monitor success with its current recruitment pool. If the firm seeks experienced salespeople, yet its yield of high performers is unsatisfactory, it should broaden the pool or shift to a new pool.[60] Many pharmaceutical firms believe their salespeople need two skills: selling skills and scientific skills. Historically big pharma recruited high-potential science majors direct from college, then focused training on selling skills. Today, many pharma firms recruit successful salespeople from any industry, then provide science training and backup support.[61]

Rubbermaid (NR) CEO hired 500 high-achieving recent college graduates. The special *Phoenix* sales force worked directly with major U.S. retailers like Home Depot, Lowe's, and Walmart. Phoenicians stocked shelves, demonstrated products, and organized in-store scavenger hunts; they also exchanged ideas online. Phoenicians generated double-digit year-over-year sales growth. NR promoted successful members to midlevel sales and marketing positions — more than 100 promotions in two years.

SELECTING

Selection criteria can be loose or tight. Loose criteria imply a *sink-or-swim* philosophy, prevalent in the life insurance industry. Of 100 salespeople hired, after five years only five are contributing performers (on average). For firms with an established customer base, criteria should be tight and salesperson selection rigorous. The firm should use previously developed selection criteria, including psychometric tests, but evolve these criteria as the environment and/or firm strategy changes.[62] Popular generalized criteria for salesperson selection are empathy, ego drive, and ego strength[63]; other important criteria are affability, credibility, sensitivity, and trustworthiness. In the selection process, several managers should interview each successful candidate. The firm must minimize two key selection errors:

- **Type I error** — Hiring a salesperson who eventually fails.
- **Type II error** — Not hiring a salesperson who would have succeeded had they been hired.

The firm soon learns about Type I errors. To detect Type II errors, sale managers should follow up on rejected candidates to assess their performance with other firms. By identifying and tracking hiring errors, the firm can sharpen its recruiting and selecting policies.

KEY IDEA

When making hiring decisions, the firm should consider two types of error:
- Type I
- Type II

TRAINING

Successful training turns newly hired salespeople into effective performers by making their KSAs congruent with the selling job. Training requirements depend on the firm's recruiting and selecting policies. If the firm hires inexperienced salespeople, training in selling skills is an absolute requirement. If the firm hires experienced salespeople, it should focus training on firm business practices, culture, products, and support services. Some training may be useful regardless of background — like advanced selling skills, negotiating, sales action planning, and time-management skills. Learning development groups may prepare individualized training programs but, more typically, firms offer standardized programs for all new hires. As firm strategy evolves, salesperson success requirements also evolve. Hence, sales training is not a one-time event; the firm should offer sales force development programs periodically. Even experienced salespeople need continuing education, but trainers should be sensitive to their experience.

> Rubbermaid (NR) has a well-developed training process for 1,500 salespeople in 90 countries. *Sales Excellence 101* for entry-level reps focuses on consumer-driven innovation and brand building; *Sales Excellence 201* for midcareer salespeople teaches how to be a value-added supplier; *Sales Excellence 301* for senior salespeople integrates sales and strategic planning. NR also administers online training and audiocasts.
>
> Sam Abdelnour, Whirlpool's VP U.S. Sales, described the *Real Whirled* program comprising several classes annually of fresh college graduates. "Each Real Whirled class has an average of eight people and has to be a minimum of 50 percent diverse. They live in a house together for eight weeks. They do their own cooking, their own cleaning, and they get their training there. They have to entertain Whirlpool people every night and cook them a meal. That's how they get to know people from different parts of the company. We change the appliances every week, so they not only use all of our appliances but they also use competitor products. At the end of the eight weeks, they know not only what products are available from the appliance industry but also how they all work."[64]

COACHING

Training typically occurs intermittently; coaching is ongoing. First-line sales managers should work with their salespeople to ensure they are as effective as possible.[65] Although sales results are critical, effective sales managers know that salespeople only achieve outstanding results by engaging in the right behaviors.[66] A particular concern in many sales forces is a tendency for salespeople to pick *low-hanging fruit* rather engage in deep customer penetration. Sales managers should coach all areas of the sales job, like territory analysis, call planning, identifying and gaining access to the *right* customers, and understanding customer behavior.[67] They make joint calls to provide feedback, help salespeople develop sales networks, and negotiate with customers and with their own organizations (to gain support).[68]

KEY IDEA

Coaching salespeople is perhaps the sales manager's most important job.

RETAINING

High-performing salespeople are valuable firm assets, and the relationships they forge with customers are often vital for long-term firm success. When a high-quality salesperson moves to new responsibilities or to a different company, firm/customer relationships become vulnerable. Succession planning and measured hand-overs mitigate these problems; unexpected vacancies and minimal succession planning can spell disaster.

Successful salespeople are vulnerable to *poaching* by competitors. They face switching costs and risks in moving to new employers, but firms that lag the market in reward systems will surely lose critical personnel. Sales force retention is an important measurement criterion for sales managers; they must ensure firm rewards are competitive. One useful device is a database for departing salespeople that tracks why they left and where they went.

REPLACING

The firm should plan for replacing high-performing salespeople who are promoted, transferred, or leave. The firm should also quickly replace underperforming salespeople. Sometimes the firm makes a hiring error; sometimes a previously high-performing salesperson cannot adjust to a new strategy, like being unable/unwilling to sell new products to new customers. When the *status quo* is unacceptable, sales managers must fire or reassign poor performers and secure better-equipped salespeople.

PrintCo's (PC) sales force analysis revealed that its top 15 (of 50) salespeople accounted for 71 percent of gross margin; the bottom few salespeople actually lost the firm money. PC implemented a three-fold plan: Top performers — focus on retention; worst performers — replace; midlevel performers — design and implement a new mandatory training program.

SALES MANAGEMENT

KEY IDEA

First-line sales managers may have the most important role in the sales force; securing effective first-line sales managers is crucial.

MARKETING QUESTION

How would you go about identifying potential candidates for first-line sales manager positions?

MARKETING ENRICHMENT 18.3

Improving Sales Performance at DHL **432p**

Securing effective salespeople is one thing; finding effective sales managers is quite another. First-line sales managers may have the most critical role in the entire sales force; they require very different KSAs than successful salespeople. Regrettably, many firms thoughtlessly promote their best salespeople to be sales managers. The firm may lose a great salesperson and gain a poor sales manager![69] The firm should implement a rigorous recruiting, selecting, and training process for sales managers by developing a clear set of job competencies. A particularly serious problem is the minimal training often given to new sales managers. At one leading life insurer, first-level sales managers often directed 50 or more salespeople. Said one newly appointed district manager: "The company brought us to New York for a two-day *dog-and-pony show*. That was it. Essentially no training for my new position."[70] The appropriate training mix varies by firm, industry, and management level but is too important to be haphazard.

To improve sales performance, sales managers must carry out the six tasks of sales management. Senior sales managers must be able to drive required change through the sales organization; they must also possess the skills to interface with marketing and other firm functions. Sales managers must be leaders; develop a sales culture; use heroes, rituals, symbols, and values that shape and reinforce appropriate salesperson behavior. (Marketing Enrichment 18.3 **[432p]** for sales performance actions at DHL.)

STRATEGIC/KEY ACCOUNT MANAGEMENT

Realizing that the 80:20 rule (or 80:20:120 — Chapter 2) applies to their revenue and profit distributions, many firms implement strategic/key account (SA) programs.[71] These firms identify the most important current and potential customers, then invest by providing additional resources and generally lavishing greater attention than on *regular* customers. Winning or losing a strategic account is a significant organizational event.[72]

KEY IDEA

SAMs are responsible for individual major customers.

In most SA programs, strategic account managers (SAMs) are responsible for building and sustaining relationships with individual strategic accounts.[73] Generally, SAMs have many fewer customers than regular salespeople. Traditionally, the average UPS salesperson managed 100 large accounts; when UPS introduced strategic account management, the average customer number dropped to about ten. For the firm's most important customers, individual SAMs may focus on single accounts and be responsible for many millions of revenue dollars annually.

> Vivek Gupta is a star IBM salesman. As SAM for wireless telco Bharti Mittal (BM), Gupta persuaded his fast-growing customer to outsource most back-office operations to IBM while BM focused on strategy, branding, operations. The $750 million, 10-year contract grew to $1 billion after five years. When Gupta became SAM for Vodafone, the managing director told Gupta: "I don't do any business with IBM, and I don't intend to." Gupta persuaded IBM to provide Vodafone employees with laptop computers; he secured his first server order one year later. After three years, Vodafone awarded IBM a $600 million contract to handle operations — from customer service to finances. Gupta's success relates to his ability to work both customer and IBM bureaucracies, deep client knowledge — specifically identifying *pain points* — deep knowledge of IBM capabilities, and forming personal and professional relationships.[74]

SAMs spend significant time working closely with customer corporate offices and typically locate in that vicinity. Walmart is a strategic account for many FMCG firms; P&G and others base team members in Bentonville, Arkansas, Walmart's head office location.[75] SAMs develop and execute plans to optimize firm revenues and profits at their account. SAMs direct teams that may include local sales and customer-service personnel, and others from product and brand management, finance, HR, logistics, market research, operations, and trade marketing. Firms often form partnerships with their most important accounts. These customers have input into product development and other key decisions, and may even embrace shared risk/return agreements for target cost savings.

MARKETING QUESTION

How does the SAM job differ from the salesperson's job?

Successful strategic account programs adopt the *congruence model*, requiring critical decisions in four areas:

KEY IDEA

Successful strategic account management requires critical decisions in:
• Strategy
• Organization structure
• Human resources
• Systems and processes

- **Strategy.** Includes deciding firm commitment to the strategic account program, overall resource allocation, number of SAs, revenue and profit targets, nominating and selecting criteria for SAs, and types of firm/SA relationships.
- **Organization structure.** Concerned with organizational placement of the SA program, reporting structure, and interfaces with other functions, notably the sales force.
- **Human resources.** Securing the appropriate personnel to be SAMs; includes other classic HR functions like training, retaining, compensation.
- **Systems and processes.** Methodologies for helping SAMs do their jobs — includes SA planning systems, customer profitability measurement, benchmarking, best-practice sharing.

In recent years, SA programs have evolved in two important ways:
- **Managing global accounts.** Increasingly, multinational firms are making their procurement decisions on a global (and/or multicountry regional) basis.[76] To better serve these customers, suppliers are adopting SA practices at a global level. As a senior 3M executive opined, "The fact that we are a multiproduct, multibusiness, multinational company should not be the customer's problem." *Global account managers* (GAMs) develop plans for

KEY IDEA

Global account managers are responsible for multinational customers that want to make global purchases.

KEY IDEA

Firms often group major customers into separate tiers, like:

- Tier I (platinum)
- Tier II (gold)
- Tier III (bronze)

Tier I customers typically provide the highest levels of sales and profits.

multinational accounts and manage global account teams that implement their strategies. IBM has about 150 global accounts, each with a GAM; for its top 40 customers, IBM GAMs are senior executives. GAMs function similarly to domestic SAMs but their job scope is much greater. GAMs must develop significant understanding of the global business environment, have comprehensive knowledge of global supply chains, and be sensitive to local cultural differences. Sometimes the firm's top executive acts as account manager or *point person* for the most global critical accounts: Oracle's Larry Ellison — GE; Nestlé's U.S. head — Walmart; and its French head — Carrefour. At Merck, IBM wrested an important contract from Accenture when CEO Sam Palmisano came calling. Former Cisco CEO John Chambers reviewed and summarized critical accounts around the world each night before going to bed.

- **Customer tiers.** Rather than classify major customers as either strategic accounts or regular accounts, leading firms partition SAs into several *customer tiers* based on current and potential revenues — like Tier I (platinum), Tier II (gold), Tier III (bronze) — and allocate resources accordingly. Microsoft uses a three-tier system for its most important customers — 40 *global* accounts, 250 *strategic* accounts, and 1,000 *corporate* accounts. Some firm tiering is more complex, based on profits and potential revenues, and more tiers. Whatever the basis, the firm has few Tier I, more Tier II, and many more Tier III customers, and addresses each tier differently.

Designing and implementing an SA program is not a simple matter. The firm improves its chances of success by focusing on nine critical success factors:

- Establish the scope — size and boundaries — of the SA program.
- Secure senior management commitment.
- Select the *right* strategic accounts.
- Design the line organization for managing SAs.
- Secure effective SAMs.
- Develop effective SA plans.
- Establish the supporting organizational infrastructure.
- Deliver and document the creation of incremental value.
- Put it all together — align the success factors in SA management.

Many salespeople are responsible for individual customers. They may also be local contacts for strategic accounts. Typically, such salespeople report to a first-line sales manager but also have dotted-line relationships to one or more SAMs (or GAMs).

MARKETING QUESTION

What other messages did you glean from this chapter?

KEY MESSAGES

- The marketing/sales interface should be seamless. Successful sales managers are true leaders.
- Effective sales managers must successfully complete six tasks.
- The first three sales management tasks address developing sales strategy:
  - *Task 1.* Set and achieve sales objectives.
  - *Task 2.* Determine and allocate selling effort.
  - *Task 3.* Develop sales approaches.
- The second three tasks focus on implementing sales strategy:
  - *Task 4.* Design the sales organization.
  - *Task 5.* Create critical organizational processes.
  - *Task 6.* Staff the sales organization.
- Many firms are developing strategic account and/or global programs for their most valuable customers.

VIDEOS AND AUDIOS

For complimentary material, see Axcess Capon codes at www.axcessvids.com

Consultative Selling	863v	Eric Baron	The Baron Group
Sales Force Compensation	183v	Dave Cichelli	The Alexander Group
Managing Strategic (Key) Accounts	268v	Hajo Rapp	Siemens AG
Becoming a Strategic Partner	175v	Gus Maikish	IBM

QUESTIONS FOR STUDY AND DISCUSSION

Can you answer the questions implied by this chapter's learning outcomes? Check!

1. A close friend has just become national sales manager for a small firm with 25 salespeople as direct reports. What advice can you offer for the first 100 days on the job?

2. Which of the six sales management tasks are the most important? Why? Interview a sales manager to develop your answer.

3. "Good salespeople are born, not made." Discuss! What are the most important skills and abilities for an effective salesperson?

4. Aco (disguised names) sells adhesives for a high-end printing application. Printfirm is a major customer, but its specifications are difficult to meet. Historically, Aco was Printfirm's sole supplier, but Bco has started to supply Printfirm with similar adhesives. Aco believes Bco is a low-cost producer that sometimes cuts corners. Last year, Aco's plant flooded and closed for one week. Aco halted all deliveries and Printfirm is adamant that it wants a second supplier. Aco's top management has set a goal of retaining 80 percent of Printfirm's business. How would you advise Aco's sales and marketing managers?

5. PrdCo's (fictional) recent sales growth mirrored the industry — the incoming CEO is demanding improved performance. She wants to implement forced ranking evaluation like Jack Welch introduced at GE. In the sales force, 20 percent would be rated superior, 70 percent average, and 10 percent inferior. Inferior salespeople would be fired. PrdCo's sales force comprises a national sales manager (NSM), three regional sales managers, 12 district managers, and 110 salespeople. Assume you are NSM; how do you respond to the CEO's ideas?

6. What are the most important changes occurring in sales force management? How will these changes affect firms' future market and sales strategies?

7. Select a product in which you are interested. Alternatively, consider *Managing Marketing in the 21st Century*. How would you complete the tasks for developing a sales strategy?

TRUE/FALSE QUESTIONS

Answers on page A2 and at www.axcessvids.com — 623p

1. Calendarizing allows the firm to monitor performance on a continuous basis and sets the stage for making course corrections if performance deviates negatively from objectives.
   ❏ TRUE ❏ FALSE

2. The firm's selling effort/selling time allocation should mirror the structure of its sales objectives. ❏ TRUE ❏ FALSE

3. For salespeople, the most critical measure is sales performance versus sales objectives.
   ❏ TRUE ❏ FALSE

4. An example of a Type I selection error is not hiring a salesperson who would have succeeded had they been hired. ❏ **TRUE** ❏ **FALSE**

5. Successful strategic account programs adopt the congruence model, requiring critical decisions in four areas — budgeting, manufacturing, innovation, social responsibility. ❏ **TRUE** ❏ **FALSE**

MULTIPLE CHOICE QUESTIONS

Answers on page A2 and at www.axcessvids.com — 276p

1. Sales objectives turned into specific performance requirements are called

   _____.

   a. sales quotas
   b. control units
   c. portfolio models
   d. spiffs

2. Which of the following is NOT one of the three interrelated decisions to examine when determining and allocating the selling effort?

   a. sales force size
   b. sales force activities
   c. sales force compensation
   d. selling effort allocation

3. In determining whether or not to outsource the selling effort, a firm must address each of the following critical issues EXCEPT:

   a. control
   b. cost
   c. flexibility in modification
   d. globalization

4. Which of the following is NOT one of the three basic financial rewards in determining financial compensation for a salesperson?

   a. base salary
   b. sales commission
   c. bonus
   d. spiff

5. Hiring a salesperson who eventually fails is an example of which of the following types of selection errors?

   a. Type I error
   b. Type II error
   c. Type III error
   d. Type IV error

Design the Market Offer

....

CHAPTER 19

DISTRIBUTION DECISIONS

For complimentary material, see Axcess Capon codes at www.axcessvids.com

LEARNING OUTCOMES

When you have completed this chapter, you will be able to:

- Understand the nature and function of distribution systems.
- Develop and implement effective distribution strategies.
- Trade off alternative forms of direct and indirect distribution.
- Identify challenges and opportunities in ongoing distribution channel management.
- Manage power and conflict in distribution systems.

OPENING CASE: CISCO

Cisco is the world's leading supplier of products to power the Internet. A small portion of Cisco's $50 billion annual revenues goes through direct channels, well over 85 percent through 28,000 channel partners in 160 countries.[1] Previously Cisco sold direct to end users, but in the late 1990s shifted its major efforts to three types of intermediaries:

- **Tier 1 partners.** *Systems integrators including global players like Accenture, Oracle, and SAP, but also well-established local partners. Tier 1 partners integrate Cisco products with technology products from other firms to provide end users with complete solutions.*

- **Tier 2 resellers.** *Intermediaries that sell to smaller end users than Tier 1 partners. Reseller sales range from a few thousand to several million dollars annually; they secure Cisco products from distributors. Distributors hold inventory and provide logistics value to Cisco. Cisco may have thousands of resellers in a particular geography, but only a few distributors.*

- **Service provider partners.** *Mainly telecommunications firms that supply Cisco equipment to their customers. These channel partners may also make customer-service agreements to relieve customers of the management burden of operating Cisco equipment.*

Cisco's sales force works hand-in-hand with channel partners to serve large end users. Salespeople develop end-user relationships and make joint sales calls with channel-partner salespeople. Channel partners are responsible for local relationships, developing business solutions, consultancy assistance, product delivery, after-sales support, and financing customer purchases. Cisco develops and monitors joint business plans with channel partners.

Channel partners provide significant value to Cisco. Most importantly, channel partners leverage Cisco salespeople's efforts, enabling much greater coverage and customer intimacy for Cisco products. Channel partners deliver and install Cisco products and provide significant after-sales service. Since Cisco insists on 30-day payment, channel partners supply their own working capital.

Cisco channel-partner relationships have evolved. An initial concern for partner growth developed into making money for partners, using measures like return on invested capital. Today, Cisco focuses on partner ability to grow and differentiate themselves in their markets. Cisco policy places all relevant business through partners; Cisco does not cherry-pick attractive business to serve directly.

Cisco classifies channel partners — Premier, Silver, Gold — based on partner investment in securing capabilities to provide value to end users. Higher value levels earn greater recognition from customers and greater resources and support from Cisco. This classification does not consider revenues, so some gold accounts are smaller than some premier accounts. Cisco's incentive system considers three performance categories:

- **VIP** — *Developing advanced technological expertise*
- **OIP** — *Seeking out new opportunities and/or new customers*
- **SIP** — *Developing new and innovative solutions*

Cisco encourages channel partners to earn VIP, OIP, and SIP incentives; an individual partner may earn incentives in more than one category.

In the mid-2000s, Cisco introduced an innovative organization structure, placing all emerging-market countries, regardless of geographic location, into an emerging-markets organization. Hence, a country like Saudi Arabia, formerly part of the Europe, Middle East, Africa (EMEA) region, no longer had to compete for resources with advanced western countries like France and Germany. The emerging-market organization comprised channel partners from 140 developing countries around the world. Cisco's tasks in these markets were:

- *Develop sufficient channel partners to have good coverage. Cisco hired country managers and salespeople, and identified partners in each country.*
- *Develop replicable channel-partner models by industry vertical to transfer across countries — like tourism, oil and gas. Partners could be nontraditional — like Schlumberger in oil and gas markets.*
- *Work with country-level policy makers to encourage investment in information technology infrastructure and spur economic growth.*

More than 95 percent of emerging-markets revenues go through channel partners (100 percent in many countries); annual growth rates exceed 40 percent. Cisco's challenge is to increase channel-partner capacity by adding channel partners and/or increasing existing partner capabilities. Having successfully established itself in many emerging markets, in 2011, Cisco folded emerging-market countries into a new global organization comprising three geographic regions. [709v]

How do you assess Cisco's distribution strategy? What are the drawbacks?

Chapter 19 is the first of two chapters in Part C of Imperative 4 — *Design the Market Offer.* Part C focuses on *Delivering Customer Value.* Chapter 19 addresses *Distribution Decisions.* Firm products reach customers through distribution channels. Distribution can be direct from supplier to customer, or can be highly complex involving many intermediaries. Intermediaries fulfill many different functions, and frequently enjoy mutually beneficial relationships with suppliers. But supplier and distributor goals rarely overlap completely; hence, distribution systems are riddled with conflict and power inequalities. FMCG firms like Colgate, Nabisco, and P&G work hard to secure good shelf positions in supermarkets. But they often compete with chains like Albertsons, Royal Ahold, and Walmart that put store brands in the best positions. Supermarkets also want suppliers to reduce prices and pay *slotting fees* for shelf space.[2]

Power inequalities may prevent firms from implementing distribution innovations. Yet no distribution system lasts forever; new approaches and technologies that add value and reduce costs can unseat market leaders. Consider video rental: Traditionally, consumers rented from retail outlets like Blockbuster or Hollywood Movies. But, as we see in Chapter 3 Opening Case, Netflix allows consumers to order movies directly online, initially DVDs delivered by mail but increasingly available via streaming (video on demand).

THE CHANGING VIEW

OLD WAY	NEW WAY
Conflict models dominate	Cooperative models ascendant
Customers are patient	Customers are impatient
Direct marketing is rare	Direct marketing is common
Distribution arrangements are fixed	Distribution arrangements are changeable
Distribution — local/regional	Distribution — regional/national/global
Fast delivery is rare	Delivery speed is highly valued
Information technology poorly used	Information technology essential
Manufacturer as channel captain	Retail power increasing
Overnight distribution unavailable	Overnight distribution increasing
Push inventory systems (loading intermediaries common)	Pull inventory — efficient consumer response (ECR) systems
Slow progression: exclusive → selective → intensive	Fast progression: exclusive → selective → intensive
Telecommunications infrequent	Telecommunications/Internet ubiquitous

FIGURE 19.1
Differing Views of Distribution

TWO VIEWS OF DISTRIBUTION — BROAD AND NARROW

Inputs like raw materials, subassemblies, and assemblies undergo changes in *state*, *physical location*, and/or *time* before the firm delivers a finished product to an end user.[3] The *broad view of distribution* includes all of these changes. Figure 19.1 (p. 489) shows changes for delivery of prefabricated steel beams to an Argentinean builder.

- *Raw materials.* Iron ore, coal, limestone — mined in Australia; separately shipped to integrated steel manufacturer in Korea.
- *Processing equipment.* Sourced in Germany for use in Korea.
- *Capital.* Bank loans to finance equipment purchase and working capital for manufacturer; based on Korean citizens' bank deposits.
- *Steel beams.* Manufactured in Korea.
- *Completed steel beams.* Shipped to distributor in Argentina.
- *Finishing.* The Argentine distributor does minor finishing operations; delivers steel beams to building site.

Major changes these activities embrace:

- *Change of state.* Iron ore, coal, and limestone into prefabricated steel beams.
- *Change of physical location.* Australian raw materials and German processing equipment shipped to Korea. Completed steel beams shipped to Argentina.
- *Change in time.* This process takes time to accomplish.[4]

Along with most marketers, we adopt a *narrow view of distribution.* We focus on changes in *physical location* and *time* of *finished* products. Marketing also addresses minor *state* changes like final processing and repackaging. Major state changes like turning iron ore, coal, and limestone into steel beams concern *manufacturing*; *procurement* secures raw material and capital equipment; *finance* secures capital.

Most executives understand firms create value by making *state* changes. Firms also create value by making *physical location* changes and in the *timing* of those changes. The Korean manufacturer creates value by forming steel beams from iron ore, limestone, and coal. But the Argentinean builder receives no value if the beams are in Korea or on a ship; they have value only at the building site. And unless they arrive on time, the entire construction project stops. Delays may cost millions of dollars.

DISTRIBUTION SYSTEMS AND THEIR EVOLUTION

Table 19.1 identifies and describes intermediaries that facilitate supplier goods and services reaching consumers and/or other end users. A *distribution channel* or *network* comprises a subset of these entities; the functions they perform and their interrelationships are continually in flux. Table 19.2 (p. 491) shows selected changes as customer needs, competitor actions, and environmental forces exert pressure. Leading indicators of impending change include unhappy consumers, end users, and/or suppliers; complacent intermediaries; deteriorating system economics; market coverage gaps; new technologies; outdated system interfaces; poor logistics; and unexplored channels.[5]

Distribution Entity	Distribution Entity Description
Agents, brokers, manufacturers' representatives	Have similar functions. Generally, these entities sell products; do not take title nor physically handle goods. They may work for supplier or customer, or be impartial between supplier and customer.
Banks and finance firms	Provide financing for customers to aid in purchasing products.
Distributors	Provide promotional support for suppliers, especially for selective or exclusive distribution. Often a synonym for wholesaler, conduct similar functions.
Retailers	Display and sell products to consumers. May operate at a fixed location — bricks & mortar stores, as traditional direct marketers, or on the Internet.
Shipping companies	Transport products.
Warehouse operators	Receive and inventory products, arrange product pickup, often break bulk.
Wholesalers	Primarily buy, take title, store, and physically handle goods in large quantities. Usually break bulk — resell to retailers or industrial businesses.

....
TABLE 19.1
Definitions of Selected Distribution Entities[*6]

* Developed in part from American Marketing Association Glossary of Terms

TABLE 19.2
Selected Changes Affecting Distribution Systems

Change Category	Change Type
Customers	Increasing expectation of multichannel access.
Direct marketing	Continuing growth.
Distributor concentration	Powerful intermediaries emerging.
Internet purchasing	B2C — accelerating as home access to broadband communication increases. B2B — growing popularity of reverse auctions. Spurring both disintermediation — direct-to-customer — and intermediation — intermediary placed between supplier and customer.
Production	Product-build times shortening, permitting widespread mass customization and inventory reductions throughout the supply chain.
Retailer sophistication	In B2C, industry concentration and better management shifts power to retailers.
Supplier focus	Greater attention to supply-chain management, working capital reduction.
Technology	Advances in capturing, transferring, and analyzing point-of-sale data drive supply-chain efficiencies. In B2C, purchasing behavior insights enhance retailer power.
Transportation	Speedy, reliable, inexpensive ways to transport goods globally increasingly available.

KEY IDEA

Distribution channels/networks comprise many entities like:

- Agents, brokers, manufacturers' representatives
- Banks and finance firms
- Distributors
- Retailers
- Shipping companies
- Warehouse operators
- Wholesalers

Ultimately, customer needs drive distribution arrangements. Early in the life cycle, products are often unreliable and service needs are high; customers require help to make choices, and support to use the new technology. These requirements diminish as customers become more self-sufficient, and may no longer require the benefits intermediaries provide. Early market leader distribution strategies may become increasingly outdated:

> When VHS technology launched home video, mom-and-pop stores initially dominated retail distribution; later, Blockbuster emerged as the leading national chain. As video technology shifted to DVD, Netflix became leader with a direct-to-home DVD distribution system via U.S. mail; Redbox grew but with an alternative distribution system via automatic dispensers in supermarkets and drug stores. Today, video streaming from content providers like Netflix, Amazon, and cable providers is direct-to-consumer distribution, bypassing intermediaries like retailers and USPS.

> In the 1890s, 70 percent of Americans lived on farms, miles from the nearest general store. Sears Roebuck (SR) revolutionized purchasing with a new distribution system — the catalog. SR offered practical hard goods — *Prairie-Breaking plows* and *Mark-Your-Poultry leg bands*, and luxuries — ladies' *kidskin-opera slippers* and *ostrich-plume hat trimmings*. Buyers no longer drove buggies for hours to reach the store; the store came to them, and everyone had access to the same goods at the same price. Across the U.S., people kept up with changing fashions and accessed the escalating product variety — the *money-back* guarantee reassured wary customers. In five years, SR's sales went from $750,000 (1895) to over $10 million (1900), as it surpassed retail leader Montgomery Ward.[7]

KEY IDEA

A distribution channel comprises many enterprises, their interrelationships, and the functions they perform.

Distribution system effectiveness evolves.

Distribution arrangements are longer lasting and more difficult to change than other marketing implementation elements.

The effectiveness of any distribution system changes over time as customer tastes and technology evolve, but suppliers often have difficulty making adjustments. Suppliers can revise prices overnight and, in the short run, develop new promotions or even add/delete products and services. By contrast, firm distribution arrangements often remain unchanged for many years, in part because of end-user loyalty to distributors. The average tenure of Caterpillar's nearly 200 dealer relationships worldwide exceeds 50 years!

Developing a Distribution Strategy

Hong Kong-based Li & Fung supplies garments to U.S. retailers like Abercrombie and Fitch, American Eagle, Ann Taylor, Disney, Guess, Kohl's, Laura Ashley, Levi Strauss, The Limited, and Reebok. Li & Fung's intranet-based, highly coordinated, and seamless global *supply chain* comprises hundreds of discrete links. For Guess jeans, yarn may be spun in Korea, fabric woven and dyed in China, and fastenings made in Hong Kong. The jeans are sewn in Guatemala, and finished goods delivered to the U.S.[8] **[763v]**

To develop distribution strategy, the firm must make several critical decisions[9]:

- **Distribution functions.** What actions must take place in the distribution channel?
- **Distribution channel: direct or indirect?** Should the firm deal directly with consumers/end users? Or should the firm use intermediaries; if so, which ones?
- **Distribution channel breadth.** How many intermediaries should there be at each distribution level? For example, how many wholesalers and/or retailers? Should there be selectivity or exclusivity?
- **Criteria for selecting and evaluating intermediaries.** How should the firm decide whether a particular intermediary is appropriate for handling its products?

We focus largely on physical goods but distribution is also important for services. Our focal concern is sometimes with manufacturers, sometimes with other entities. Consider Whirlpool and Nike: Whirlpool manufactures kitchen appliances but Nike outsources production.

DISTRIBUTION FUNCTIONS

By completing many functions, distribution closes gaps in physical location and time between factory-finished products and consumers/end users. Sometimes the supplier undertakes a particular function; other times intermediaries or end users do so. In a complex distribution channel, some functions, like physical movement, must happen several times. Table 19.3 shows various *distribution functions*.

Physical Product	Information	Ownership
Assortment[11]	Information-sharing[14]	Financing
Bulk-breaking	Marketing research	Impartiality[15]
Inventory	Order collection	Risk-shifting[16]
Physical movement[12]	Selling and promotion	Service
Physical-state changes[13]		Title Transfer
Quality assurance		

Increasingly, channel members, especially retailers, work at enhancing the customer buying experience. Product display is critical, but at Forum shops in Las Vegas, the visual experience of Atlantis rising and falling on the hour keeps customers in the store. The Mall of America (Minneapolis) attracts consumers to its 400 retail stores with Camp Snoopy (indoor amusement park) and Underwater World (walk-through aquarium). At Wizards stores (owned by toy manufacturer Hasbro), a game room occupies one third of retail space. Conversely, Costco and Sam's Club offer minimal services; they compete on price.

The firm should align incentives to motivate distribution channel entities to perform required functions. Actions that improve firm sales and profits should also benefit channel members. Unfortunately, distribution channels often contain significant inefficiencies and misaligned objectives.

MARKETING QUESTION

Which distribution entities do a good job of providing recorded music to consumers? Why did you select them?

KEY IDEA

Physical distribution closes gaps in *location* and *time* between finished products at the factory and consumers/end users.

TABLE 19.3
Distribution Channel Functions[10]

KEY IDEA

Critical distribution strategy decisions include:

- **Required functions**
- Direct versus indirect channels
- Distribution channel breadth
- Criteria for selecting intermediaries

For many years, Coca-Cola distributed 80 percent of U.S. products through independent firm Coca-Cola Enterprises (CCE); Coke had a significant minority interest. In the mid-2000s, CCE switched objectives from revenue growth to improving profit margins and raised prices sharply. CCE's action caused significant conflict with Coke, and Coke volume growth dropped. In 2010, Coke acquired CCE's North American assets for $15 billion!

KEY IDEA

Critical distribution strategy decisions include:
- Required functions
- **Direct versus indirect channels**
- Distribution channel breadth
- Criteria for selecting intermediaries

DISTRIBUTION CHANNELS: DIRECT OR INDIRECT?

The firm may select from several alternative channel designs for conducting distribution functions — Figure 19.2:

- **Direct channels.** Suppliers manage most contact with consumers/end users.
- **Indirect channels.** Intermediaries like distributors, wholesalers, retailers play a major role in transferring products to consumers/end users. Some indirect channels have a single intermediary; others have multiple intermediaries.

FIGURE 19.2
Reaching Consumers: Direct and Indirect Channels

MARKETING QUESTION

Fingood (disguised) distributed products to consumers via distributors and retailers. To spur consumer demand, Fingood cut prices to distributors by 20 percent, but Fingood's leading distributor held prices firm so as to increase profit margins. The price reduction failed. What were Fingood's mistakes? How should Fingood proceed?

REACHING CONSUMERS THROUGH DIRECT CHANNELS

Several forms of *direct distribution*, combined with CRM systems,[17] are serious alternatives to indirect distribution, particularly in B2C:

FACE-TO-FACE DIRECT SALES. Direct customer contact can provide suppliers intimate insight into customer needs. In advanced economies, direct selling and distribution costs are often too high for consumer goods. Regardless, Avon, Mary Kay, and Tupperware successfully sell and deliver products direct to consumers. In less-developed countries, lower incomes make personal selling more viable. In India, Citibank launched credit cards via face-to-face sales, and Hindustan Lever is successful with its 50,000-strong Shakti Ama program.[18]

KEY IDEA

Direct distribution methods, combined with CRM systems, are powerful alternatives to indirect distribution.

In Japan, salespeople sell automobiles by visiting consumers at home. In Britain, Malaysian-based automaker Proton supplements car showrooms with salespeople; they visit consumer homes with demonstration vehicles.

DIRECT SALES USING DIRECT MARKETING, MASS MEDIA, TELEMARKETING/TELESALES. The firm makes contact with individual consumers; they receive products directly by package delivery from remote locations.[19] The firm may initiate contact to target customer lists via *outbound* communications — firm-to-customer — or the customer may initiate via *inbound* communications — customer-to-firm. Regardless, message centralization gives the firm greater control and cost efficiencies in addressing customers. Face-to-face selling's high cost drives telemarketing/telesales; QVC (quality, value, convenience) and the Home Shopping Network (HSN) are effective means of selling some product forms/classes directly via television.

INTERNET. The Internet is the fastest-growing *inbound* communications method for many product forms/classes, even including luxury goods. Firms use various business models:

- **Consumers pick up products.** At Chronodrive (supermarket [France]), consumers order online, then pick up goods at easily accessible warehouses. At Best Buy, 30 percent of customers ordering online make in-store pickups.

- **Direct delivery.** Firms deliver many digital products like books, music, videos, financial services directly to customer smartphones, computers, tablets.

- **Integrate telesales and service.** When a Landsend.com visitor clicks on the *help* icon, a salesperson uses instant messaging to help the potential buyer navigate the site.

- **Package delivery.** Consumers receive products at locations they specify.

- **Link with visual displays.** Tesco covered Seoul subway station walls with images of supermarket shelves. Consumers assembled virtual shopping carts by scanning product codes with smartphones; home delivery occurred within a few hours.[20]

Some newspapers and magazines are abandoning traditional production and distribution for Internet-only distribution.[21] Digital distribution may offer lower prices on many products, reduce search costs, and often *disintermediate* wholesalers and bricks & mortar retailers. Hence, suppliers deal directly with consumers/end users.[22,23] Also, the *long-tail* effect enables very large inventories. (For digital communications approaches — Chapter 17)

SPECIALIZED RETAIL DISTRIBUTION. The supplier controls product display and the customer experience in retail outlets. Bulgari, Coach, Tiffany, and other luxury-goods firms operate their own upscale stores; Coach factory outlets offer a different experience for a separate market segment. International fashion firm Zara makes twice-weekly assortment changes to encourage frequent customer visits. Retail outlets are either *wholly owned* by the supplier — Apple, Gap, Body Shop, Starbucks (Chapter 1 Opening Case); or *franchised* to a third party — H&R Block (tax preparation), 7-Eleven (convenience stores). Toys "R" Us and other firms open *Pop-Up* (temporary) stores during holiday seasons.

The first Apple store opened in 2001, four years after Steve Jobs returned as CEO. Initial press reaction was negative: "What does Apple know about retail?" "Apple will upset its retail distributors." But Apple received little attention from retailers as market share was so small. Over the years, store design evolved but Apple maintained the *genius bar*. Apple's product line also evolved from Macintosh computers to include the iPod, iPhone, iPad. Apple has 450 stores in 16 countries, earning well over 10 percent of corporate revenues, and the highest sales per square foot of any retail chain — $4,500 — versus Murphy USA — $4,200 — and more than twice luxury retailer Tiffany (3rd — $3,040). [439v]

Many fast-food brands like KFC, McDonald's, Taco Bell use *franchising*. Typically the franchisor develops the business model and seeks entrepreneurs to invest capital. The franchisee agrees to implement the franchisor's strategy and pays an initiation fee and ongoing fees.[24] Franchisors often limit franchisees to a fixed number of outlets so as to retain control.[25] Sometimes firms use franchising to grow their brands, but later buy back successful franchises to secure wholly owned outlets. Luxury-goods supplier LVMH purchased its franchisees to gain greater control and cultivate a more upscale consumer experience.[26]

MARKETING QUESTION

Review websites for Hockey Monkey, Lands' End, or 1-800-Flowers. Order a product; in a couple of days, order another product. What data did the firm request on each occasion? Did the firm remember you from the first order to the second order?

KEY IDEA

Advantages for wholly owned retail distribution are greater operational control and earning the entire retail margin.

Disadvantages for wholly owned retailed distribution are capital required for growth, and operating risk.

KEY IDEA

Advantages for franchising are leveraging resources for faster growth and harnessing franchisees' entrepreneurial drive.

KEY IDEA

Disadvantages for franchising are loss of control and smaller profit margins.

Innovative Distribution Methods to Reach Consumers

- *Amazon, Barnes & Noble, Walmart.* Customers order online — receive *same-day delivery* in certain locations.

- *Amazon, UPS.* To address the problem of delivering products to unsecured locations like doorsteps, Amazon places lockers in 7-Elevens, and grocery or chain drugstores. Customers retrieve packages via an e-mailed code. Relatedly, UPS has 20,000 pickup locations in Europe and North America.

- *Banana Republic.* Sets up makeshift stores in corporate offices for several days at a time.

- *Banco Popular.* Serves Hispanic immigrant laborers with check-cashing vans. On Fridays, vans travel to factories, hospitals, nurseries, plants, and other locations where Hispanic immigrants (many illegal) congregate.[27]

- *DHL.* Delivers packages to hard-to-reach locations via drones.

- *Fifth Third Bank, Cincinnati, OH.* All employees are potential salespeople. They earn profit-sharing, bonuses, and stock options — up to 125 percent above base salary — for attracting new clients. Fifth Third Bank also places retail outlets in supermarkets. At a Kroger's branch, the manager makes frequent loudspeaker announcements about special loan rates and other services. She patrols grocery aisles, identifying prospective customers to discuss financial needs.

- *P&G.* In countries like Mexico and Venezuela, P&G faces serious cultural problems in marketing tampons. Religion and beliefs about health risks and loss of virginity from using tampons hamper sales. P&G focuses marketing efforts on *bonding* sessions in women's homes, much like *Tupperware* parties. Female hosts educate friends and neighbors about tampon benefits and provide free samples. Forty percent of attendees later become hosts.

- *Sogebank.* Aggressively markets to small, independent business owners in Haiti.[28] Loan officers sell from street-corner *offices*; they also make home visits to discuss client needs and assess collateral.

- *Walgreens.* Maintains several hundred health centers in corporate offices.

- *Walmart, Best Buy.* Customers may order goods online, then pick up from a local bricks & mortar store.

REACHING CONSUMERS THROUGH INDIRECT CHANNELS

Many B2C products reach consumers via *indirect distribution*: Distributors, wholesalers, and/or retailers provide *physical location* and *time* value. By constructing product assortments from many suppliers, indirect channels reduce customer search costs and provide an entire shopping experience. Indirect channels may also add brand value to supplier products, like Macy's (U.S.) and Harrods (Britain).[29] New technology products like Kindle, Nook, iPad offer distribution alternatives for digital products like books, magazines, newspapers.

KEY IDEA

Intermediaries offer value-added benefits like:

- Product assortments
- Shopping experience
- Market access

Intermediaries also reduce costs for various distribution functions.

Intermediaries may provide market access that would otherwise be very expensive (or impossible) for the firm to secure. By gaining U.S. distribution in Best Buy (more than 1,000 stores) and Home Depot (2,000 stores), Korean white-goods producer LG has earned more than 5 percent U.S. market share and is No. 3 globally behind Whirlpool and Electrolux. Individuals and organizations in Amazon's Associates program send millions of customers to Amazon's website. Market access is particularly important when venturing abroad. Many products fail because firms do not understand local cultures, customers, markets. Domestic partners can be invaluable. Efficiencies from using channel partners also reduce supplier costs:

- agents, manufacturers' representatives, brokers — selling economies
- banks and financial institutions — financing economies
- distributors, wholesalers, retailers — inventory, selling, transportation economies

- independent warehouses — inventory economies
- package delivery, transportation companies — transportation economies

---

The U.S. Postal Service (USPS) and FedEx are direct competitors in overnight and ground package delivery. Yet USPS allows 10,000 FedEx drop boxes at post offices nationwide, and delivers FedEx SmartPost and UPS SurePost; FedEx also ships Express, Priority, and First Class mail.

REACHING ORGANIZATIONAL CUSTOMERS

B2B firms also use both direct and indirect distribution to reach organizational customers:

- **Direct distribution.** Firms sell directly to end users through proprietary on-the-road sales forces, telemarketing/telesales, direct marketing, and/or the Internet. Suppliers use various transportation methods to deliver products to customers.
- **Indirect distribution.** Some suppliers reach customers, especially small businesses, through retail stores — like Staples for office supplies. Electrical, home-building, and plumbing suppliers reach customers via Home Depot and Lowe's. More generally, many firms reach customers via distributors and wholesalers.

Machine tool builder Okuma America requires each of 46 distributors to inventory a minimum number of machine tools and select repair parts. When customers order out-of-stock items, the distributor contacts Okumalink — a shared information-technology system. Okumalink keeps distributors informed about parts availability/location in Okuma warehouses. If a part is unavailable, the distributor contacts other distributors online and arranges delivery direct to the customer.[30]

Table 19.4 shows factors favoring, respectively, direct and indirect distribution.[31]

Direct Distribution	Indirect Distribution
Complex end-user purchasing decisions — multiple functions and high-level executives	Simple end-user purchasing decision — often by low-level purchasing agents
Custom-tailored products	Stockable items, manufactured in large quantities but sold in small quantities
Delivery speed not critical	Rapid delivery and service important
Large quantity sales	Small quantity sales
Small potential customer base	Large potential customer base

Distribution speed is increasingly important as firms use *just-in-time* (JIT) manufacturing and inventory systems, business process management, lean six sigma, and other techniques to increase operating efficiencies. Industrial distributors must provide customers with complex product assortments and associated distribution data in a timely manner. Typically, some requirements are predictable but others are not. Holding sufficient inventory to satisfy both predictable and unpredictable demand can be expensive. Okuma America (boxed insert above) has one approach for managing demand fluctuations; Volvo has another:

Volvo GM (VGM) Heavy Truck Corporation sells replacement parts via commercial truck dealers; VGM supplies dealers from regional warehouses. Parts inventories in Volvo warehouses were rising, but sometimes dealers could not secure needed parts because of stockouts! VGM worked with FedEx Logistics to set up a warehouse in Memphis (FedEx hub). Dealers with emergencies call a toll-free number; FedEx ships the required parts and delivers to dealer offices, holds for airport pickup, or drops off at the required site. VGM closed three warehouses, reduced total inventory by 15 percent, and regained much business previously lost to stockouts.[32]

KEY IDEA

Direct channels: Suppliers manage contact with consumers/end users.

Indirect channels: Intermediaries like distributors, wholesalers, retailers play a major role in transferring products from suppliers to consumers/end users.

TABLE 19.4
B2B Customers: Factors Favoring Direct and Indirect Distribution

DISTRIBUTION CHANNEL BREADTH

KEY IDEA

Distribution channel breadth refers to the number of channel members the firm uses at a particular distribution level — like wholesalers or retailers. The firm can increase/decrease channel breadth as circumstances dictate:

Critical distribution strategy decisions include:
• Required functions
• Direct versus indirect channels
• **Distribution channel breadth**
• Criteria for selecting intermediaries

In France, Norwegian furniture manufacturer J.E. Ekornes (JEE) distributed to consumers via 450 furniture dealers. JEE believed this was too many. Dealers put in little selling effort, in part because they carried small product selections. JEE dropped 300 dealers; the remaining 150 received exclusive territories. These dealers increased local advertising for JEE's furniture and dropped competing lines. JEE sales increased threefold.[33]

The firm should also consider different types of distributor. Adding a new distributor type can be important when customers have preferred outlets. In the Pacific Northwest, depending on their interests, consumers prefer to shop at *either* marine *or* forest-products distributors; each distributor type relates to specific problems and issues. Many suppliers sell products through both types of distributor.

KEY IDEA

For B2B suppliers, conditions typically favor either direct or indirect distribution. In each case, several options are available.

Adding new distributor types can be positive or negative. Tupperware halted a 15-year revenue slide by placing booths in shopping malls and selling on the Internet; later Tupperware added distribution in Target stores. With ready product availability, consumers no longer had a reason to go to Tupperware parties. Sales dropped 17 percent, profits fell 47 percent; Tupperware lost 25 percent of its sales force — many *good, solid performers* left. Tupperware stopped distributing at Target; profits doubled.

An average Staples store carries 8,000 office-supply items; an average shopper spends $600–$700 annually. Staples.com offers 200,000 items; an average store *and* catalog shopper spends $1,200–$1,400. Staples installed in-store computer kiosks linked to Staples.com; sales jumped to $2,500 per store *and* catalog shopper. Each of Staples' 1,500 retail outlets now has at least four computer kiosks.

MARKETING QUESTION

Best Buy discovered many customers were examining products in its stores, then searching the Internet for better prices and placing orders online. How would you advise Best Buy?

When the firm distributes through multiple channels, channel crossing becomes an issue — customers secure product information and/or try the product in one (or more) channels — *showrooming* — but purchase from a third channel. The first channel(s) provides free service — only the third channel earns revenues.[34] This problem is increasing for traditional channels as Internet commerce grows. The manufacturer/brand owner benefits from the sale, but some channel partners receive no revenues for their services. In the long run, showrooming may lead to channel breakdown.

Firms have three broad *distribution-channel-breadth* options:

INTENSIVE DISTRIBUTION. When customers limit search, products should be easily available. The firm maximizes the number/type of outlets where customers buy. Intensively distributed consumer products include convenience goods like snacks, soft drinks. In emerging markets, intensive distribution is a critical strategic thrust for firms like Coca-Cola and P&G.

WD-40, developed for the space industry as a rust-prevention solvent, is present in 80 percent of U.S. homes and has more than 2,000 uses. A major success factor is intensive retail distribution via well over 10,000 wholesalers.[35]

EXCLUSIVE DISTRIBUTION. When customers are willing to search and travel, the firm should select outlets carefully. When retailers provide brand equity and positive shopping experiences, a B2C firm may choose a few prestigious outlets. Fine china and crystal firms distribute products in high-class department stores like Saks Fifth Avenue and Macy's, or specialty stores like Tiffany. Relatedly, successful bands like AC/DC, the Eagles, Garth Brooks, and even Bruce Springsteen have made exclusive distribution arrangements with Walmart.

SELECTIVE DISTRIBUTION. Selective distribution is a compromise between intensive and exclusive distribution. Too many outlets can lead to excessive competition; too few outlets and firm products are difficult to find. Sony and Samsung distribute products selectively, making careful outlet decisions. Samsung repositioned its products upmarket and for a few years withdrew from Walmart and Kmart.

Distribution breadth is equally important in B2B and B2C marketing. Under competitive pressure from Dell, one PC manufacturer shifted distribution efforts from 40 distributors to four large wholesalers. Distribution breadth raises three related *distribution-exclusivity* issues:

- **Distributors — geographic exclusivity.** Should the supplier give distributors geographic exclusivity? (Within limits, most suppliers can enforce such restrictions.) Exclusivity eliminates *free riding* and intrabrand competition by providing geographic monopolies, but may breed complacency. Regardless, exclusivity motivates distributors to invest in promotion and improved service. When Canon's U.S. copier market share declined, Canon USA removed geographic restrictions so the strongest dealers could better compete with Xerox.

- **Distributors — product exclusivity.** Product exclusivity may reduce conflict, satisfy channel partners, and better meet end-user needs. Sometimes firms offer different product designs and/or brands to different distribution channels. Stanley Black & Decker sells *Black & Decker* brand products at Kmart and similar outlets, *Quantum* for serious enthusiasts at The Home Depot, and *DeWalt* for professional contractors/builders at trade dealers. Panasonic, Samsung, Sony produce separate models for major retail chains like Best Buy. Product exclusivity may also be important for market entry when suppliers require focused attention from intermediaries. Hence, Apple's iPhone was initially available only on AT&T's wireless network.

- **Supplier exclusivity.** Some suppliers require intermediaries to focus entirely on their products; others insist on exclusivity within a product form/class. Pepsi and Coke each have exclusive agreements with airlines, restaurants, retailers; Anheuser-Busch InBev has similar arrangements with beer distributors; Visa and MasterCard with some restaurants.[36] IBM's Authorized Assembly Program commits distributors to use only IBM original parts.

Suppliers seeking exclusivity should avoid the appearance of anticompetitive behavior. European Commission officials seized internal documents in dawn raids on Coca-Cola offices across Europe. Italy's competition authority alleged Coke designed a complex system of exclusivity bonuses and discounts to *oust . . . Pepsi from the market*. Regulators alleged Coke offered rebates and volume discounts only to retailers that regularly increased shelf space for Coke products and made in-store promotions and special offers.[37]

CRITERIA FOR SELECTING AND EVALUATING INTERMEDIARIES

Clear and unambiguous criteria for selecting channel partners favor *both* suppliers and distributors. The firm should clearly specify the functions and performance standards distributors must meet. Would-be distributors can then fairly assess their capabilities versus supplier requirements. IBM prevailed in a court case because it set and applied clear standards:

When IBM launched its personal computer, computer retailers who were denied the IBM franchise banded together to sue IBM. The courts ruled that IBM had not discriminated among retailers and that its selection criteria were clear and fairly applied.

KEY IDEA

Suppliers should select distribution channel(s) that are appropriate for their target segment(s) and perform required functions.

Providing customer benefits/values, not traditional industry practice, should guide supplier distribution choices.

KEY IDEA

Critical distribution strategy decisions include:
- Required functions
- Direct versus indirect channels
- Distribution channel breadth
- **Criteria for selecting intermediaries**

The firm and distributors should recognize their separate obligations before making an agreement. To improve success probabilities, the supplier should ask several questions of potential distributors[38]:

- Does the distributor have adequate market coverage?
- How competent is distributor management?
- How does the distributor rate on aggressiveness, enthusiasm, and taking initiative?
- Is the distributor the appropriate size to do business with us?
- What is the distributor's credit and financial condition?
- What is the distributor's general reputation among suppliers and customers?
- What is the distributor's selling capability? What is its historic sales performance?
- Will the distributor forgo competitive products? Does it welcome the supplier's products?

The answers drive supplier decisions to accept/reject potential distributors.

PUTTING IT ALL TOGETHER: THE DISTRIBUTION STRATEGY

Figure 19.3 shows an eight-step method for developing distribution strategy.[39] In the boxed insert (p. 500), a small candy supplier develops distribution strategy for three market segments. This illustration shows the complexity of distribution in a simple case; for large firms with many products targeting several segments, distribution can be very complex.

FIGURE 19.3
A Step-by-Step Approach to Developing and Implementing Distribution Strategy

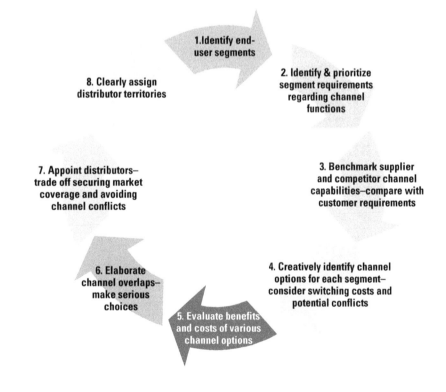

1. Identify end-user segments
2. Identify & prioritize segment requirements regarding channel functions
3. Benchmark supplier and competitor channel capabilities—compare with customer requirements
4. Creatively identify channel options for each segment—consider switching costs and potential conflicts
5. Evaluate benefits and costs of various channel options
6. Elaborate channel overlaps—make serious choices
7. Appoint distributors—trade off securing market coverage and avoiding channel conflicts
8. Clearly assign distributor territories

Distribution Strategy for a Small Candy Manufacturer

Buchan Inc. (BI) (fictional) is a small U.S. candy manufacturer. BI targets the domestic consumer midprice candy market for family consumption. BI distributes products through supermarkets and small retailers; these intermediaries add value by offering product assortments. BI does not sell direct to consumers; it believes that channel intermediaries can more efficiently finance, inventory, sell, and transport its products. BI evolved its market strategy by targeting two additional segments — domestic U.S. firms for employee consumption, and consumer markets in Latin America. BI now has several distribution arrangements:

- **Domestic consumer middle market**. Consumers purchase candy from supermarkets and small retailers:
  - *Major national and large regional chains.* BI's strategic account sales force sells direct to national and large regional chains. BI delivers to retailer warehouses direct from its factory warehouse via third-party truckers. Chains are slow payers, so BI discounts accounts receivable to a factor.[40]
  - *Small regional and local retail chains.* BI uses food brokers for selling effort. BI fills orders from geographically dispersed, independently owned warehouses. Third-party truckers, hired by BI, supply these warehouses from BI's factory warehouse; independent warehouses make store deliveries.
  - *Small stores.* BI sells to a national distributor, delivers to the distributor's main warehouse in its own trucks, and holds accounts receivable until payment. The distributor makes its own arrangements to ship products to the stores.
- **Domestic U.S. firms**: BI sales force sells direct to corporate purchasing groups and ships candy from independently owned warehouses.
- **Latin American consumer markets**: BI has an export agent with good Latin American contacts. Distributors in each country identify retail outlets and make all local arrangements. The export agent combines orders from distributors and makes all administrative arrangements in the U.S. BI receives payment by letter of credit; terms are FOB (free on board) BI's factory warehouse.[41]

KEY IDEA

Distribution strategies comprising multilevel channel systems for large organizations are often highly complex.

MANAGING DISTRIBUTION CHANNELS

Ensuring top performance from distributors day by day can be a significant challenge. We discuss intermediary compliance, power inequalities, conflict, and the emerging-partnership model.

INTERMEDIARY COMPLIANCE

The firm must ensure that channel intermediaries stick to their agreements and implement its market strategies. Table 19.5 (p. 501) lists problems that suppliers often experience with intermediaries when objectives become misaligned.

Honda had multiple retail dealers in major Pakistani cities: Lahore — 27; Karachi — 16. Despite agreements to adhere to Honda's suggested retail prices, some dealers cut prices. Dealers with significant showroom investments were very upset. Honda appointed committees comprising two dealers and one Honda executive to monitor price compliance in each major city. Honda fined noncompliant dealers.[42]

TABLE 19.5
Supplier Operating
Problems with Resellers

• Apply insufficient effort to consumers/end users the supplier has targeted
• Are inadequately financed
• Are overloaded with products from competing and noncompeting suppliers
• Can't or won't meet supplier goals
• Carry insufficient inventory
• Cherry-pick supplier product line
• Do an inadequate job of solving consumer/end-user problems
• Do not allow the supplier to contact its sales force
• Do not follow supplier suggested pricing
• Do not pass on promotional programs and rebates to consumers/end users
• Do not stress the supplier brand — in the extreme, push private-label and/or competitor brands
• Do not use supplier promotional materials
• Get very close to end users but will not provide customer data to the supplier
• Make ineffective use of supplier sales managers
• Primarily sell on price, not on value
• Require fixed payments to carry supplier products

MARKETING QUESTION

Have you or a friend or colleague been involved in distribution? Which issues in Table 19.5 posed problems? How did you solve them?

When suppliers compensate intermediaries with standard commissions for all products to all customers, they may encounter compliance problems. The supplier can better direct distributors by varying commissions by product and customer type. The supplier can also tie evaluation and compensation directly to contract requirements like maintaining inventory levels, providing customer service, and ensuring customer satisfaction.[43] Table 19.6 shows a partial list of performance measures for evaluating distributors.[44]

TABLE 19.6
Channel Member
Performance Evaluation[45]

Criterion	Frequently Used Operational Performance Measures	
Sales performance	Gross sales	Actual sales/sales quota
	Sales by product, market segment	Market share
	Sales growth over time	Realized prices
Inventory maintenance	Average inventory maintained	Inventory turnover
	Inventory/sales ratio	On-time delivery
Selling capabilities	Total number of salespeople	Salespeople assigned by geography
	Salespeople assigned to supplier products	Account managers assigned to strategic customers
Information provision	Sales data by customer[46]	Information on inventories and returns
	Information on end-user needs	

KEY IDEA

A well-designed compensation system can help the supplier direct distributor efforts.

The firm should continuously evaluate intermediary performance. But the firm must remember that intermediary relationships are a two-way street. Distributors also evaluate supplier performance. Are supplier products selling? Are consumers/end users complaining about supplier products? Are supplier deliveries prompt? Is the supplier easy to do business with?

A specific compliance problem occurs when the supplier sets different prices in different market segments. Distributors in low-price segments may arbitrage by reselling products in high-price segments — *diversion*.[47] Diversionary activity can play havoc with the supplier's market strategy.

POWER IN DISTRIBUTION SYSTEMS[48]

Amazon initially set $9.99 as the price for many Kindle books. Macmillan (publisher) objected to Kindle pricing; Amazon suspended sales of Macmillan books. One week later, Amazon backed down and allowed Macmillan to set its own Kindle prices.

Power and conflict are endemic in distribution systems. *Power* is one channel member's ability to get another member to act as it wants. Typically, some channel members have more power than others; they also have different objectives. When a supplier is more powerful, it can impose demands. Some suppliers pressure intermediaries to carry large inventories under the premise that *a loaded dealer is a loyal dealer*. Microsoft sets many conditions for PC manufacturers. Similarly, powerful intermediaries may exert power when they enjoy strong market positions. Walmart pressures suppliers for low prices, takes control of product delivery, and demands adherence to supply-chain guidelines and sustainability initiatives.

Over time, power tends to shift from one channel member to another. Sometimes firms seek greater control over supply chains by forward integration (FI) or backward integration (BI). Suppliers acquire customers (FI) — Coca-Cola and PepsiCo each purchased large bottlers; GM purchased parts supplier Delphi Automotive. Customers acquire suppliers (BI) — Boeing purchased a factory from aircraft fabricator Vought; steelmaker Nucor purchased a major scrap-metal processor. Table 19.7 identifies conditions for greater or lesser power for suppliers — *upstream* — and distributors/end users — *downstream*.

Upstream — Suppliers	Downstream — Distributors or End Users
Demand greater than supply	Supply greater than demand
Distributor has high switching costs	Distributor has few switching costs
Few substitute products available	Many firms can supply
Few substitute suppliers available	Few substitute distributors available
Individual distributors unimportant to supplier success	Distributor purchases are large percentage of supplier output
Proprietary technology	Products/services undifferentiated
Supplier enjoys monopoly-like position	Distributor enjoys monopsony-like position
Supplier has extensive end-customer contact	Supplier has little end-customer data
Supplier products important to distributor success	Supplier products unimportant to distributor success
Supplier poses credible threat of forward integration — to cut out distributors	Distributor poses credible threat of backward integration — to make supplier unnecessary

Figure 19.4 shows several entities in a distribution system. We explore power relationships among manufacturers/brand owners, distributors/wholesalers, retailers, and consumers/end users.

Raw Material Providers → Manufacturers, Brand Owners → Distributors, Wholesalers → Retailers → Consumers/End Users

MANUFACTURERS/BRAND OWNERS. In the early 20th century, manufacturers grew and increased power over distributors and wholesalers. Manufacturers researched customer needs, designed good products, and reduced costs and prices via mass production. Firms like Budweiser, Campbell's, Coca-Cola, Frito-Lay, Gillette, Kellogg's, Kodak, Levi's, and PepsiCo

---

KEY IDEA

Power is one channel member's ability to get another channel member to do what it wants it to do.

KEY IDEA

Power distribution among channel members is typically asymmetric.

TABLE 19.7
Conditions That Increase or Decrease Power Up and Down Distribution Channels

FIGURE 19.4
Power In Distribution Systems

MARKETING QUESTION

Many major FMCG firms like Anheuser-Busch InBev, Church & Dwight, Heinz, Kellogg, Mars, Procter & Gamble are extending payment terms for suppliers to 120 days. Why are they behaving in this manner? How should suppliers respond?

KEY IDEA

Over time, power shifts from one type of channel member to another.

KEY IDEA

Intermediaries occupy the nexus between suppliers and consumers/end users.

Intermediaries add value by reducing the number of relationships suppliers and consumers/end users must maintain.

MARKETING QUESTION

National retailers must balance the benefits and efficiencies of national purchasing with greater market responsiveness from decentralized buying. How would you advise Macy's?

used consumer advertising to build powerful brands and become *channel captains*. Not all brand owners are manufacturers: Calvin Klein, Nike, Polo outsource production but carefully manage distribution. Sometimes raw material/ingredient providers like NutraSweet (artificial sweetener) and Intel (chip maker) earn significant distribution power.

DISTRIBUTORS/WHOLESALERS. In the late 19th century, full-line, full-service wholesalers like Alexander T. Stewart and H.B. Claffin (long defunct) were channel captains. Wholesalers dominated U.S. consumer goods distribution, linking distant manufacturers with retailers and consumers.[49] Economic changes and growth in manufacturer and retailer power diminished these once-powerful intermediaries, but they still play a major role in many industries. As depicted in the movie *Blood Diamond*, De Beers buys nearly all of the world's raw diamonds and virtually sets diamond prices worldwide. *Value-added resellers* are a new type of intermediary, building software modules on other firms' platforms and modifying computer hardware for niche markets. *Systems integrators* like Accenture and Infosys add value by installing/servicing software and hardware from many vendors and making them work together.

These intermediaries often provide information value. Insurance brokers dominate business insurance by identifying and analyzing business risks and helping firms secure coverage from insurers. Intermediaries provide consumers/end users with product/brand choices and reduce the necessary number of supplier relationships. Consider the time you would spend to buy groceries from individual specialists: milk — farm; produce — various growers; meat — butcher. Dairies, grocers, and butchers were once valuable intermediaries, but today supermarkets provide their products in one convenient location.

As Internet commerce grows, many supplier websites offer customers greater product variety than traditional retail distribution. But intermediaries are also successful. Amazon's product assortment encompasses books, CDs, prescription drugs, and many other products from manufacturers *and* retailers.[50] eBay and Alibaba are also powerful intermediaries, using online auctions to link sellers and buyers. Expedia, Orbitz, Priceline, and Travelocity broker sales of airline tickets and hotel rooms online.

An investor diversified in several mutual funds has many interactions — multiple calls/website visits to purchase/sell individual funds and check fund balances, deposit/receive checks, receive multiple statements. By combining multiple funds (intermediation), Schwab's OneSource decreases the hassle and keeps funds continuously invested.[51]

Via intermediation, OpenTable (OT) allows consumers to make online reservations 24/7/365 at more than 30,000 restaurants in the U.S. and abroad. OT is free to diners; restaurants pay a one-time installation fee and one dollar per reservation (for diner reward points).

RETAILERS. Strong retail chains have evolved through industry consolidation. In the U.S., *category killers* like Best Buy, Home Depot, Toys "R" Us virtually dictate industry direction. ASDA, Sainsbury's, Tesco dominate British supermarkets; Walmart, Royal Ahold, Kroger, Safeway play a similar role in the U.S. National warehouse clubs like Costco and Sam's Club place significant pressure on grocery suppliers. Retailing has trailed many industries in globalization, but Carrefour (France), Walmart (U.S.), and vertically integrated Zara (Spain) have significant global operations. Online retailers like Amazon are placing increasing pressure on bricks & mortar retailers.

Major retailers are often price leaders. They use buying power and efficient logistics to drive down costs, but these large firms must trade off cost efficiencies from standardized product assortments against more customer-responsive local variations. More sophisticated chains study customer needs and use powerful CRM technology to tailor assortments and offer customized promotions. Organization is also important: Starbucks placed U.S. stores in time-zone-defined divisions; performance improved when Starbucks realized coffee-drinking habits varied by geography (Northeast, Pacific Northwest, Sun Belt) and reorganized on that basis.

Major retailers force suppliers to make direct payments to secure shelf space — *slotting fees.*[52] Data released a few years ago revealed that slotting fees for five major food companies — Campbell's, Coca-Cola, Kellogg's, Kraft, PepsiCo — were 14 percent of sales at retailers that sold their products. Coca-Cola — $2.6 billion, Kraft — $4.6 billion, PepsiCo — $3.4 billion spent large sums just to optimize product placement on retailer shelves.[53] Walmart has increased pressure on suppliers by also requiring fees for storing products at its distribution centers. An important trend is the introduction of smaller stores: Traditional Best Buy stores average 38,750 square feet; Best Buy Mobile stores average 1,420 square feet. Staples, Walmart, and Britain's Tesco also offer multiple store formats.

CONSUMERS/END USERS. In B2C markets, individual consumers seldom have significant power, but consumer groups can profoundly influence producers. European consumers boycotted genetically modified products like Roundup Ready corn, and local groups protesting McDonald's have vandalized its restaurants. In Germany, environmentally minded consumer coalitions encourage strict recycling laws. In B2B, mergers and acquisitions have left the remaining customers in several industries with significant power. The few global automobile firms and aircraft manufacturers Boeing and Airbus are good examples.

CONFLICT IN DISTRIBUTION SYSTEMS

Because distribution channel members have multiple organizational relationships, the potential for conflict is high. *Operational conflict* occurs daily due to late shipments, invoice errors, unfulfilled promises, unacceptable product quality, supplier attempts to *load* channels by *forcing* unwanted inventory on intermediaries, and/or price and margin disagreements. ESPN distributors (cable companies) continually complain about price increases but don't dare stop distributing ESPN. These conflicts are annoying, frustrating, and channel disrupting, so most members try to minimize them — real-time systems for tracking and viewing distribution data can alleviate some conflicts. Sometimes supplier and distributor are unable to work out their differences and the relationship stops, at least temporarily:

> When ABC's (supplier) largest cable distributor Cablevision balked at a requested price increase, ABC stopped transmitting its signal for the Academy Awards and other shows. Relatedly, Time Warner dropped CBS during a very public dispute over fees.
>
> Upset with Unilever price increases, major Belgian supermarket Delhaize removed 300 Unilever products from shelves in well over 700 stores.

Strategic conflict is more serious and may lead to significant change in channel relationships. Sometimes conflict emerges from *downstream* customers; other times from *upstream* suppliers. Sometimes strategic conflict develops slowly; other times, specific actions precipitate strategic conflict. Figure 19.5 shows a simple distribution channel we use for illustration.

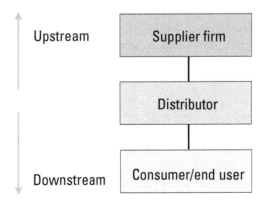

MARKETING QUESTION

Many local retailers make short-term offers at highly discounted prices via Internet firms like Groupon, Amazon Local, and LivingSocial that maintain e-mail subscriber lists. As consultant to a small retailer, would you advise signing up? Why or why not?

KEY IDEA

Distribution channel members have high conflict potential:
• Operating conflict
• Strategic conflict

FIGURE 19.5
Simple Distribution Channel

MARKETING QUESTION

In 2014, major publishers Hachette (France) and Bonnier (Sweden) disputed e-book pricing with Amazon. As the dispute dragged on, Amazon delayed shipping books, disallowed prepublication ordering, reduced price discounts, and removed books from its website. How do you assess Amazon's actions?

KEY IDEA

Both *upstream suppliers* and *downstream customers* have various options for initiating strategic conflict.

STRATEGIC CONFLICTS INITIATED BY DOWNSTREAM CUSTOMERS. Typically we see four types of conflict:

- **End users grow and desire direct-to-supplier relationships.** Many suppliers, especially small businesses, start out using distributors to reach end users. As these customers grow, they believe distributors provide insufficient value for the margins they receive. End users believe they can secure lower prices from direct supplier relationships.

> Jco (disguised) supplies disposable tableware for parties. Jco reaches retailers like Playstore through Disco, a major national distributor. Founded as a single store, Playstore now has more than 500 outlets. Playstore's new management team told Jco it wanted to cut out Disco and buy direct.

If the supplier agrees to such requests, it risks harming distributor relationships. After all, the distributor played an important role in growing the supplier's business. But if the supplier remains loyal to the distributor, it risks losing valuable end users.

> Norton was a large-scale producer of grinding wheels to U.S. industry. Norton became market leader by forging strong relationships with industrial distributors. Norton earned high market share with small business customers, like local machine shops. But market share dropped precipitously at large customers, like auto manufacturers. These customers bypassed industrial distributors and formed direct relationships with other grinding wheel suppliers.[54]

- **Distributors become large and change the power balance.** When small single-location retailers characterized U.S. automobile retailing, manufacturers like GM, Ford, and Chrysler were very powerful. But the emergence of multiple-location megadealers like AutoNation, CarMax, Potemkin selling huge volumes from several producers, has shifted the power balance from manufacturers to retailers.[55]

- **Distributors supply private-label products.** In B2C, many supermarkets, department stores, and other retail chains increasingly offer private-label products. In B2B, innovative distributors disrupt channel relationships by offering their own branded products in competition with (or instead of) supplier products. Distributors may secure products from other suppliers or backward integrate to make products they formerly only distributed. Nucor began as a steel distributor; dissatisfaction with suppliers led Nucor to manufacture steel. Nucor is now the most profitable U.S. steel producer.

- **New buying influences enter the distribution channel.** In some industries, independent buying groups amass buying power for members. The Independent Grocers Association (IGA) and TruValue have long served small grocery and hardware stores, respectively. In hospital supply, Novation and Premier purchase for many small and large hospitals.

STRATEGIC CONFLICTS INITIATED BY UPSTREAM SUPPLIERS. Here we see three types of conflict:

- **To reach end users more efficiently, the supplier goes direct.** Sometimes suppliers believe they can be more effective than distributors. Suppliers bypass distributors and sell direct to end users. Distributors typically resent these initiatives:

> British brewer Bass Ale piloted a home-delivery service. Cash-and-carry warehouses and convenience stores offering Bass Ale products feared they would lose business. Leading cash-and-carry firm Nurdin and Peacock stopped carrying several Bass beers and encouraged customers to avoid Bass products. Bass abandoned the pilot.[56]

The Internet has enhanced supplier ability to sell direct to end users and correspondingly increased the likelihood of conflict with intermediaries. Some firms place major efforts on Internet sales, but others restrict commercial Internet activity, directing website visitors to distributors so as to avoid conflict.

Sometimes suppliers go direct in a limited manner that minimizes conflict. Hershey, Mars, Nike (NikeTown) have their own retail stores. Wholesalers and retailers believe these stores enhance supplier brands, so there is little conflict. Mattel sells a wide range of toys and apparel at its website, but avoids conflict by never undercutting distributor retail prices, nor offering some popular items.

- **Supplier addresses a new market and competes with its distributor.** The supplier/distributor relationship may be fine, but the supplier introduces products that compete with the distributor, and strains the relationship. IBM (distributor) resells $3 billion of Cisco (supplier) products annually but Cisco server products compete directly with IBM in the data-center market.

- **For better market penetration, the supplier adds new distributors and/or distributor types.** Suppliers sometimes initiate *horizontal* conflict by adding additional distributors and/or new distribution channels. Current distributors are often unhappy with these initiatives and reduce efforts. Hill's Science Diet pet food experimented with a store-within-a-store pet-shop concept in grocery channels, but lost support from pet shops and feed stores.[57] By contrast, when Goodyear distributed through mass merchandisers like Walmart, it kept independent Goodyear dealers happy by working to increase market demand for replacement tires.[58]

PLANNING FOR POWER CHANGES

All things equal, the firm is better off having a stronger (versus weaker) power position relative to channel intermediaries. If the firm initiates strategic conflict, it must assess the likely impact on other channel members and anticipate how they may respond. A strong negative response may hurt the supplier. To continue the Norton illustration (boxed insert, p. 505): Norton eventually addressed market-share losses at large customers by going direct. Industrial distributors were upset, but remained loyal; there were no viable alternative suppliers. Similarly, major U.S. airlines eliminated travel-agent commissions and encouraged passengers to purchase flights at their websites. These disintermediated travel agents had few options and continued to sell airline seats. Tables 19.8 and 19.9 (p. 507) show possible actions for upstream suppliers and downstream customers, respectively, to improve power positions.

KEY IDEA

Suppliers and distributors each have various ways to improve power positions.

Type of Action	Examples
Become central to distributor success	• Develop joint marketing strategies with distributors. • Develop value-added services like sales training, field technical support, field selling support, inventory control systems, and product manuals — both directly and indirectly related to its own products.[59] • Hire a sales and marketing group to research end-user needs, then pass sales opportunities to distributors. • Innovate new products and (perhaps more importantly) develop expectations of continuous innovation. Strong supplier relationships assure the distributor of early access to these innovations. • Strongly support current products, especially in market downturns where such support may differentiate the supplier from competitors.
Broaden the scope of supplier options	• Broaden the distribution base by adding distributors. • Demonstrate the folly of backward integration by distributors. • Develop an information base on end users. Initiate direct communication, for example, by a technical support force or via e-mail. • Explore limited forward integration by adding a few wholly owned distributors.[60]
Improve bargaining power	• Integrate disparate product lines.[61]

TABLE 19.8
Illustrative Actions to Improve Supplier Power

KEY IDEA

When suppliers attempt to improve power positions, they should anticipate actions of other distribution channel members.

continues

TABLE 19.8 *continued*	Type of Action	Examples
	Raise distributor switching costs	• Develop customized products needing customized equipment and specialized training.
		• Develop dedicated online access for information and simplified order placing.
		• Improve supplier reputation by enhancing relationship quality.
		• Increase number of contact points within the distributor.
		• Offer benefits to concentrate purchases.[62]
		• Work to secure end-user/testing agency qualification by brand, rather than generic product.

TABLE 19.9 *Illustrative Actions to Improve Distributor Power*	Type of Action	Examples
	At end users	• Add value to end users.
		• Build loyalty with end users.
		• Consider branding service packages.
		• Introduce additional services.
	At suppliers	• Increase contact points with supplier.
		• Persuade supplier to outsource activities to the distributor.
		• Work to minimize supplier costs.
	Broaden the scope of distributor options	• Explore limited backward integration.
		• Secure additional suppliers.
		• Show disadvantages of forward integration by the supplier.
	Improve bargaining power	• Centralize purchasing operations.

THE PARTNERSHIP MODEL

KEY IDEA

The partnership model is an increasingly popular alternative to power/strategic conflict. Channel members jointly set goals and work together for greater efficiency and effectiveness.

MARKETING QUESTION

Walmart is well known for driving tough bargains with suppliers to secure low prices. Yet Walmart has a partnership agreement with P&G. Why? Why does P&G partner with Walmart?

When firms exercise power and generate strategic conflict, the underlying assumption is a *zero-sum game*. If the firm *wins*, another channel member *loses*, and vice versa. The *partnership model* assumes the possibility of a *positive-sum game*. By developing trust and working together, several channel members win; there are no losers.[63] Supplier-customer partnerships are at the heart of strategic account management — Chapter 18.

P&G sells billions of dollars of consumer products annually through Walmart; the two firms have developed have a highly effective strategic partnership. Walmart captures point-of-sale data for P&G products and transmits to P&G in real time using state-of-the-art information systems. By combining these data with seasonal purchasing trends, P&G improves forecast accuracy; gains purchasing, manufacturing, and packaging efficiencies; reduces inventory; and cuts costs. P&G codes products by store destination and places them directly on Walmart trucks at warehouse interchange points — *cross-docking*. Full trucks leave frequently for store-to-store delivery.[64] P&G and Walmart also use paperless systems for receiving goods and managing payables/receivables.[65] JCPenney has a similar relationship with Hong Kong shirt maker TAL Apparel. JCPenney sends TAL point-of-sale data from more than 1,000 North American stores; TAL forecasts JCPenney's requirements and replenishes each store, sometimes shipping by air.[66]

By developing partnerships, channel members can establish joint strategic goals like cutting costs, and reducing supply-chain inventory, while limiting stockouts.[67] Better forecasting allows retailers to offer more efficient product sets, conduct more effective promotions, and eliminate heavy discounts on unwanted merchandise. By working with retailers, suppliers can achieve lower production and distribution costs and better use promotional funds. Macy's used a re-engineering approach to cost-cutting[68]:

Macy's traditional garment-distribution practice involved several steps:

- *At the manufacturer.* Make the garment; add a hang tag; press the garment; place on a wire hanger and cover with polyethylene; put several garments in a box; ship the box to a Macy's facility.

- *At Macy's.* Remove the garment from the box; remove the polyethylene; throw out the wire hanger; put the garment on a floor-ready hanger; put the garment in new polyethylene; add a price tag; place the garment in a shipping container; ship to a Macy's store. This activity averaged 20 minutes per box.

Macy's gave garment producers floor-ready hangers and barcodes for each item. Macy's cut the average time to process new inventory from 4.5 days to 2.5 days and significantly reduced working capital.

KEY MESSAGES

MARKETING QUESTION

What other messages did you glean from this chapter?

- A broad view of distribution embraces *changes in state, physical location, time.* Marketing generally takes a narrow view — distribution includes *changes in physical location* and *time of finished products.*

- Distribution channels continuously evolve; the firm can gain differential advantage by innovating its distribution arrangements.

- In developing distribution strategy, the supplier must make crucial decisions in four areas:
  - *Distribution functions.* What exactly must be done in the distribution channel?
  - *Distribution channels: direct or indirect?* Should the firm deal directly with consumers/ end users? Or should the firm use intermediaries? If so, which ones?
  - *Distribution channel breadth.* How many intermediaries should the supplier select at each distribution level? For example, how many wholesalers and/or retailers? Should there be exclusivity?
  - *Criteria for selecting and evaluating intermediaries.* How should the firm decide whether a particular intermediary is appropriate for its products?

- Implementing strategy through distributors can be challenging. The supplier must clarify channel member responsibilities, understand potential distributor problems, and take steps to gain compliance.

- Typically some channel members have more power than others; each has options to improve its position. Distributors/wholesalers, manufacturers/brand owners, retailers, and consumers/ end users may each become *channel captains.* Many firms are moving to partnership models where each member gains.

- *Operating conflict* is endemic in distribution channels but most firms work at reductions. *Strategic conflict* is more serious and may lead to significant change in channel relationships.

- The Internet is driving many changes in distribution.

VIDEOS AND AUDIOS

For complimentary material, see Axcess Capon codes at www.axcessvids.com

The Future of Retailing   155v ☺   Mark Cohen   Columbia Business School

QUESTIONS FOR STUDY AND DISCUSSION

Can you answer the questions implied by this chapter's learning outcomes? Check!

1. Your friend operates a highly successful *loose-meat* sandwich restaurant (regional specialty) in his Iowa hometown. He wants to expand nationally. What are his options and the pros and cons? How would you advise him to proceed? Why? What pitfalls should he look out for?

2. Alasdair MacLean wanted a high-speed bicycle. He gathered information about several bicycles from a department store. He test-rode several models at a local bicycle store. Then he purchased his favorite model from the manufacturer's website. Several major department stores and a trade association of local bicycle stores have complained about this kind of customer behavior to BikeCo, a leading bicycle manufacturer. How would you advise BikeCo?

3. U.S.-based Detha (disguised) produces wire harnesses to protect electric wires in automobiles. Detha sells to a distributor; the distributor sells to CarSup, a Tier 1 supplier to U.S. auto firms. Detel, one of Detha's sister businesses, also sells significant quantities of electric wire direct to CarSup. Last year, Detha's sales to the distributor dropped by 20 percent. Detha discovered that auto firms were demanding local supply in various geographic areas globally. CarSup was enforcing compliance; 40 percent of requirements were now sourced in Asia, hence the drop in Detha's business. How should Detha proceed?

4. Refer to the Jco/Playstore/Disco example, p. 505. The retailer, Playstore, told Jco it would no longer purchase Jco products from the distributor — Disco. Playstore would *either* purchase direct from Jco *or* find a new supplier. Disco also distributes products for several Jco sister business units. Playstore owns roughly half its 500 outlets; the others are franchisees. Some franchisees are unhappy with Playstore's new management; one half have formed an independent federation. Jco expects the federation to assume greater control of shelf selection and purchasing. What should Jco do?

5. Select a product in which you are interested. Alternatively, consider *Managing Marketing in the 21st Century*. What are the key distribution decisions? What actions would you take?

TRUE/FALSE QUESTIONS
Answers on page A2 and at www.axcessvids.com — 727p

1. Distribution channel depth is the number of channel members the firm uses at a particular level. ❑ TRUE ❑ FALSE

2. Power is one channel member's ability to get another member to act as it wants. ❑ TRUE ❑ FALSE

3. Value-added resellers are a relatively new type of intermediary, building additional software modules on other firms' platforms, and modifying computer hardware for niche markets. ❑ TRUE ❑ FALSE

4. Strategic conflict occurs daily due to reasons like late shipments, invoice errors, and unfulfilled promises. ❑ TRUE ❑ FALSE

5. When firms exercise power and generate strategic conflict, they assume a positive-sum game, if the firm wins, another channel member loses, and vice versa. ❑ TRUE ❑ FALSE

MULTIPLE CHOICE QUESTIONS

Answers on page A2 and at www.axcessvids.com — 732p

1. Which of the following is NOT a critical decision that a firm must make to develop its distribution strategy?

   a. Determine distribution functions.
   b. Determine whether the distribution channel will be direct or indirect.
   c. Determine the distribution channel depth.
   d. Determine the criteria for selecting and evaluating intermediaries.

2. All of the following represent broad distribution-channel-breadth options EXCEPT:

   a. pulsing distribution
   b. intensive distribution
   c. exclusive distribution
   d. selective distribution

3. Which of the following does NOT represent an important question that the supplier should ask of potential distributors to improve the chances of success?

   a. What is the distributor's credit and financial condition?
   b. Does the distributor have adequate market coverage?
   c. How does the distributor rate on aggressiveness, enthusiasm, and taking initiative?
   d. All of the questions are important in improving the chances of success.

4. Which of the following is NOT a strategic conflict initiated by upstream suppliers?

   a. Supplier goes direct to end users.
   b. Supplier addresses a new market that competes with its distributor.
   c. Supplier adds new distribution types for better market penetration.
   d. All of the selections represent strategic conflicts initiated by upstream suppliers.

Design the Market Offer

CHAPTER 20

RETAILING AND WHOLESALING*

For complimentary material, see Axcess Capon codes at www.axcessvids.com

LEARNING OUTCOMES

When you have completed this chapter, you will be able to:

- Explain how the value producers offer consumers/end users differs from the value retailers offer their customers.
- Assess the value retailers offer consumers.
- Understand various types of retail operations.
- Assess retail performance.
- Explain three core sources of value retailers offer.
- Identify contemporary trends in retailing.
- Understand the values wholesalers offer suppliers and customers.
- Develop strategy and implementation for retailers and wholesalers.

OPENING CASE: UBER

Uber functions as a new type of retailer by managing the supply of transportation services to consumers. Uber's peer-to-peer (P2P) smartpone app provides an alternative system to traditional taxis by operating a two-sided market. On one side, Uber addresses consumers requiring transportation services; on the other side, Uber addresses drivers wishing to provide transportation services. **[208v]** *The Uber smartphone app brings the two sides together. Uber earns revenues by keeping a portion of each fare.*

Uber offers several services — Uber Black (luxury cars), Uber X (everyday cars), Uber XL (SUVs), UberPool (ride sharing). A key consumer benefit for using Uber is simplicity. Consumers install the Uber app on their smartphones and provide Uber with credit card information. To order an Uber car, consumers enter pickup and destination locations; Uber advises price and estimated wait time. If the customer accepts the ride, the car arrives and completes the journey. No money changes hands — Uber bills the credit card, and confirms by e-mail.

---

* Mark Cohen, Director of Retail Studies, Columbia Business School, participated in preparing this chapter.

Uber prices rides on distance, *but switches to* time *when traffic is heavy. In general, Uber X prices are 10 to15 percent below local taxi fares. When demand is high, Uber implements surge pricing — generally, from 20 percent to 100 percent more than regular prices* **[807v]**. *Uber justifies this practice to increase supply. Uber views its drivers as independent contractors — they receive on average 80 percent of the fare, paid weekly direct to bank accounts. Uber does little advertising but has launched several short-term promotional campaigns; most new customers — drivers and riders — come from word of mouth.*

Uber commenced operations in San Francisco (2010) and quickly expanded to many U.S. cities. In contrast to many other U.S.-based consumer-focused technology firms, Uber rapidly entered foreign markets. Observers estimate annual revenues in excess of $5 billion, doubling every several months. By 2015, Uber had entered more than 300 cities in around 60 countries.

Uber has faced and still faces considerable opposition from local taxi firms and local governments; these entities view Uber as operating unlicensed taxi services. In some cities, taxi drivers have demonstrated against Uber's entry and petitioned local governments to ban or curtail Uber. For the most part, Uber has fended off these challenges, often working with local governments to develop Uber-friendly municipal ordinances and make local taxis an option for consumers.

How do you compare eBay and Alibaba to Uber and Lyft? What comparisons can you draw between Uber and Airbnb?

Direct competitors include Lyft and Sidecar. Uber has been criticized for shady competitive practices — ordering and canceling rides at competitors — but has exploited first-mover advantages to maintain dominant market share in most cities. Uber has attracted significant venture capital funding and has been valued at $50 billion.

Chapter 20 is the second chapter in Part C of Imperative 4 — Design the Market Offer . Part C focuses on Delivering Customer Value. Chapter 20 deepens discussion of distribution — Chapter 19 — by focusing on Retailing and Wholesaling. We commence with retailing.

Retailing is the sale of goods and services from individuals or organizations to consumers/end users.[1] Wholesalers are important intermediaries, sitting between suppliers and retailers or end users. In Chapter 19, we showed the firm may reach consumers and/or end users via a *direct* channel or through an *indirect* channel system.[2] With a direct channel, the firm is solely responsible for all channel operations, especially the interface with consumers/end users. With an indirect channel system, firm performance rests on the success of channel intermediaries, especially retailers.

Recalling Table 15.2 (p. 400), the subcomponent manufacturer (SM) can only be successful if the component manufacturer (CM), finished goods manufacturer, distributor, and retailer are each successful. Each intermediary must persuade customers to purchase products containing its subcomponents. If just one entity fails, consumers do not purchase finished goods containing SM subcomponents.

Although all channel entities are important for success, retailers have pride of place. Retailers have direct day-by-day interaction with consumers. Retailers are not only important for making sales, they may also be valuable information sources. After all, in addition to consumers, retailers also interface with the supplier's competitors and complementers.

THE CHANGING VIEW

OLD WAY	NEW WAY
Mostly bricks & mortar	Online retailing increasing rapidly
Bricks & mortar retailers focus domestically	Increasing global presence by leading retailers
Small retailers seek revenues close to home	Small retailers going global via the Internet
Payment by cash and credit card	New payment systems gaining traction
Retailer data about consumers is limited	Explosion of data about consumers
Peer-to-peer business relationships limited	Internet apps driving peer-to-peer commerce
Consumer data relatively safe	Consumer data increasingly at risk from hackers

VALUE RETAILERS OFFER

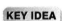

Retailers are very different entities from producers and other intermediaries; nonetheless, their success drivers are similar. Each entity must deliver value to customers. The important differences are in types of value. Typically, producer value relates to product and service attributes, communications, and availability (through intermediaries to retailers). Retailers do not typically *design* nor *produce* products. But, by interfacing with consumers, retailers deliver product and service values provided by producers.

Retailers offer three broad types of value:

- Product assortment
- Customer experience
- Accessibility

At some level, the value producers offer consumers is irrelevant to distribution channel entities. The value consumers/end users receive is not the most important issue for distributors, wholesalers, or retailers. What mostly concerns these intermediaries is achieving their own objectives, typically stated in financial terms — revenues, profits, return on investment. The value producers offer consumers is only relevant inasmuch as it motivates consumers to purchase, and so enables intermediaries to reach their goals.

Retailers offer consumers value in several ways:

- **Product assortment.** Retailers choose the set of goods and services to offer consumers, hence providing choice value. Regardless of store type (pp. 514–518), retailer assortments may be *broad* — spanning many product forms/classes as in department stores and Amazon — or *narrow* — a single or few product forms as in specialty stores. A retailer may feature many products of a certain type — *deep* — or just a few — *shallow* — Figure 20.1. Products offered by retailers may derive from a range of suppliers or as few as one — direct distribution.

....
FIGURE 20.1
*Product Assortment
Types — Exemplars*

- **Customer experience.** Retailing is a service, conforming to various service characteristics — Chapter 13. But retail service elements vary widely. Shopping in a physical location is quite different from shopping at home via direct marketing or the Internet. Physical stores differ on multiple dimensions like external/internal appearance, personal service, product display and selection, payment systems. The consumer experience may include *extras* — like playgrounds (McDonald's) — and the ability to try products before purchase, like built-in driving ranges associated with golf products retailing. Internet shopping cannot offer these types of additional services, but can provide unique virtual experiences like rotating, interactive product displays and dynamic personalization.

Groupon creates online experiences similar in look and feel to physical stores. Groupon personalizes the shopping experience, enhances product views, and highlights key product offerings. All the while, vibrant *SALE* signs attract customers. The online shopping process is easy and intuitive.

In some physical stores, IKEA demonstrates furniture in complete rooms. IKEA's catalog uses a mobile app to provide a similar but virtual experience online.

- **Accessibility.** Ease of accessing the store is often critical for consumers. *Time* and *place* convenience are watchwords. *Time convenience* concerns hours of operation. Of course, online stores are open 24/7/365, as are aptly named convenience stores like 7-Eleven. Physical stores generally have limited operating hours. *Place convenience* concerns the effort consumers must make to reach the store from residences and workplaces. Physical distance and travel routes are key elements for location, but superior transportation and parking alternatives may make more distant retailers quite convenient. Indeed, growth of the U.S. interstate highway system allowed Walmart to be successful building stores in low-cost rural areas. An important convenience element may also be the presence of other stores — complementary and/or competitive.

KEY IDEA

Accessibility — time and place convenience — is critical for physical retail stores. Also important is the presence of other stores — complementary and/or competitive.

ALTERNATIVE RETAIL FORMS

Retailers may interface with consumers in many ways:

TRAVELING RETAIL STORES

This retail form is one of the oldest. Historically in the West and today in many emerging-market countries in Africa and Asia, the peddler carries goods on his/her back or in a cart while traveling from village to village, or house to house. Of necessity, product assortments are highly limited, but consumers may examine goods before purchase. Perhaps the most important value that traveling retailers provide is accessibility: Consumers need not travel to the store; the store comes to them. Despite ancient roots, modern versions of traveling retailers include:

- Avon ladies — sell and deliver cosmetic products to friends and coworkers.
- Bank vans — travel to building sites to cash worker paychecks.
- Clothiers — set up temporary stores in office buildings.
- Food carts — travel to building sites and high traffic locations offering cooked meals.

In Boquete, Panama, Hostel-Plus *Casa Pedro* diversified into the food cart business. Several hours a day, Pedro and wife Marilin serve cooked meals to local residents from their traveling food cart, parked near the town center.

- Pet grooming — specially designed vans visit residential neighborhoods.

KEY IDEA

Major forms of retailing are:
- Traveling retail stores
- Direct marketing
- Internet retailing
- Vending machines
- Fixed-location retail stores

DIRECT MARKETING

Direct-marketing retailers have similarities to the traveling store. The store comes to the consumer with a twist. Differences are twofold:

- **Product examination.** In general, consumers cannot physically examine products before purchase, but some direct marketers build free returns into their value propositions.
- **Time delay.** Typically several days elapse between purchase and receipt of products.

In direct marketing, consumers learn about product offerings via various communications approaches — Chapter 16 (p. 427):

- **Mass media.** Direct marketers advertise in a variety of media — magazines, newspapers, radio, television. In most cases, communication takes the form of regular advertisements, but some television stations present programs entirely devoted to communicating and demonstrating products — Home Shopping Network, QVC. The common feature: The *infomercial* asks consumers to conduct business with the vendor directly.
- **Direct mail.** The firm reaches consumers through the mail. Sometimes communication is personally addressed; other times the addressee is merely *owner/resident*. Direct-mail marketers develop potential customer lists and/or buy targeted lists from list brokers. The key challenge is for consumers to read the communication rather than throw it out. Direct mail is relatively inexpensive, but *response rates* for print-only are low.
- **Telemarketing/telesales** is a form of direct marketing where communication is by telephone. Receiving telephone sales calls at home is highly annoying for many consumers; several countries embrace *opt out* systems. Regardless, many firms targeting small businesses base their communications and distribution efforts on centrally located telesales forces.

Across the various direct-marketing types, product assortments vary from limited — mass media communications/telemarketing — to quite large — direct-mail catalogs. Large assortments are possible since retailers inventory goods in low rent areas, and/or may simply arrange for direct shipment from producers — *drop shipment*. Similar to the traveling retail store, direct marketing allows consumers to make purchases from anywhere.

INTERNET RETAILING

Internet retailing is similar to direct marketing: Consumers make purchase decisions at home or at the office, then wait for delivery. The firm has two core challenges:

- Persuade consumers to visit the website — Chapter 17
- Provide a compelling website experience that encourages purchase.

Major differences from direct marketing are:

- **Assortment.** Product assortments are often very large, much larger that most direct-marketing retailers. Low-cost storage and direct delivery from producers allows Internet retailers to profit from the *long-tail* effect.[3]
- **Product display.** The Internet offers many opportunities for virtual product display — from replicas of physical displays to videos of products in use — that the firm may easily change. Hence, Internet retailers can offer consumers memorable shopping experiences. Clearly, searching an Internet retailer's website is very different from thumbing through a physical catalog. Indeed, some Internet retailers allow consumers to design products directly online, and *try on* different styles and colors virtually.
- **Comparison shopping.** The easy ability to switch from one website to another enables comparison shopping. Search programs help find products/services, and also the best prices for specific goods.

Internet sites provide similar product variety to physical stores. There are multiproduct global chains like Amazon and Alibaba; but also small specialist sites like *www.wessexlearning.com*. Indeed, low-price storage allows Internet retailers to offer greater numbers of products than physical stores; of course, Internet retailers sell products globally — an especially important issue for digital goods.

The critical difference between Internet and physical stores is the inability to see and handle products from Internet sellers. Increasingly, Internet stores attempt to reduce consumer fears of not receiving what they thought they had purchased. Zappos is a good example of enhancing Internet buying experiences:

> Zappos offers a large shoe selection but uses customer service as a differentiator. Delivery is fast; any problem and a friendly agent assists; returning goods is easy; Zappos agents are encouraged to go above and beyond typical service expectations to surprise and delight customers.

On the other hand, compared to physical stores, most Internet retailers provide home delivery. For repeated heavy purchases like bottled water, Internet shopping offers substantial customer value with little risk. (We address P2P retailing — pp. 520–521.)

VENDING MACHINES

Vending machines are important for a few product forms/classes like DVDs, personal products, snacks, soft drinks. They allow retailers to place inexpensive displays and purchase options near potential consumers, frequently for 24/7/365 access. Labor costs relate merely to restocking. Technological advances advise firms when to restock, allow dynamic pricing, and by providing customer data, suggest product assortment changes.

FIXED-LOCATION RETAIL STORES

Physical (bricks & mortar) stores are by far the most widespread retailing form and the largest source of retail activity. Retail stores are responsible for a high percent of GDP in most countries, and employ vast numbers of personnel. Retailing is a major element in the service economy — Chapter 13. All physical retail stores have one element in common: Product displays are real, *not* virtual.**[106v]**

Let's examine the ways fixed-location retail stores vary:

- **Physical product or service.** Retail establishments offer a bewildering variety of physical goods, but many of the physically largest retail operations provide services. Service retailing ranges from hairdressers, nail salons, and restaurants to huge theaters and sport stadiums. Furthermore, when dealing with the public, governments conduct retail operations like hospitals, immigration centers, post offices, and motor vehicle departments.

> Sasa is a large cosmetics retail chain with more than 200 stores and counters across Asia. Sasa carries its own branded cosmetics in its retail shops; these products are not available in other stores. Sasa's exclusivity is one element in its retail strategy. Sasa carries other branded cosmetics and fragrances, prominently displaying the different brands; technically trained in-store brand ambassadors, with in-depth knowledge of cosmetics, fragrances, and lifestyle products promote individual brands, typically displayed at the back of the store. This approach has helped Sasa become the *one-stop cosmetics* store across Asia.

- **Establishment size.** As with services, retail operations for physical goods also range from very small stores — convenience outlets — to massive hypermarkets and superstores. Many large retail chains like Best Buy, Target, and Walmart have been successful with large stores. Regardless, several have opened alternative format smaller stores, often in urban areas — Best Buy Mobile, CityTarget, Walmart Neighborhood Market and Walmart Express.

KEY IDEA

Important characteristics of fixed-location retail stores are:

- Physical product or service
- Establishment size
- Products/service evolution
- Assortment
- Product display
- Service type and level
- Ownership
- Number of stores
- Connection between strategy and operations

- **Products/service evolution.** Consumers purchase all products through some form of retail distribution. Retailers continually add new products and eliminate others.

- **Assortment.** Product assortments range from very *broad* — encompassing many product forms/classes, to very *narrow* — maybe a single product form. Assortments also vary by depth: *deep* assortments — many products per product form/class of a particular type; *shallow* assortments — few options — Figure 20.1 (p. 513). (Generally, assortments are less deep than for Internet retailers.)

- **Product display.** Stores differ widely in product displays. Some warehouse outlets provide only open shipping boxes; other stores spend extensively on display design. Many stores attempt to guide consumers so they come in contact with as much merchandise as possible. Some stores deliberately place cash registers at the back of the store; others, like Stew Leonard's grocery stores (New York) enforce a route on shoppers.

- **Service type and level.** In some retail stores, the only service is receiving payment; other stores offer a high degree of personal attention. *Self-service* generally means less service, but consumer ability to co-create with retailers like airline check-in has considerable value — checking in via automatic kiosk is better than standing in a long line at a ticket counter.

MARKETING QUESTION

Research Ron Johnson's tenure as JCPenney CEO. After such a successful career at Apple, why did Johnson fail at JCP? How would you advise Mr. Ullman?

> Ron Johnson was the architect of Apple's highly successful retail strategy; JCPenney (JCP) appointed Johnson as CEO. Johnson made many changes at JCP, notably in merchandising, pricing — reduced frequency and extent of *sales* — and store design. Typically, Johnson did not conduct small-scale tests prior to action. Following the changes, store traffic declined; sales fell; losses exceeded $1 billion in Johnson's one full year; JCP's share price dropped 50 percent. After 16 months as CEO, JCP fired Johnson and reappointed Myron Ullman, Johnson's predecessor.

- **Ownership.** Individuals, families, and small groups own the vast majority of retail outlets — mostly small establishments and typically a single store. Corporations often own large numbers of a specific type of retail establishment.

- **Number of stores.** When individuals, families, and groups own retail operations, the median number of establishments owned and operated is one. Multiple establishments — chains — generally require corporate ownership (but see following item). Chains may be local, regional (within a country), national, regional (multicountry), or global. A critical decision for chain stores is degree of autonomy granted individual stores and store groupings to adapt to local conditions, versus greater efficiency with centralized decision-making.

> A few years ago, Best Buy's drive for procurement efficiency left many stores without locally popular products. By contrast, the ability of KFC franchisees around the world to offer locally popular food items has been very successful.

- **Connection between strategy and operations.** In most cases, retail owners — individuals, families, small groups, corporations — develop retail strategies *and* execute retail operations. But strategy and operations may be separated, as in franchising. Brand owners like Burger King, Jollibee, KFC, Pizza Hut, Subway, Sushi King (fast food) and Hilton, Holiday

PLANOGRAMS

Consumers make many purchase choices in stores; hence, display is critical. The strategic retail decision concerns product form/class selection and space allocation. The planogram is a visual diagram specifying physical placement of products/brands within a product class, most often used by supermarkets. Seemingly minor issues like high/low and right/left shelf positions may make a big difference: Consumers infer high shelf position as a quality indicator.[4] The retailer (corporate) and/or category captain — Chapter 23 — develops planograms; store managers are responsible for implementation. Sophisticated retailers develop multiple planograms per product form/class to account for local market variation; *planogram police* from headquarters ensure compliance.

Inn, Tune Hotels (hospitality) decide *strategy*, but other entities own individual retail establishments and conduct day-to-day *operations*.

Illegal activity is a significant problem for physical stores and Internet retailers. The core problem for physical stores is shoplifting by customers and theft by employees. For Internet retailers, cybercrime is increasing as this retail form becomes increasingly popular. All retailers face challenges of safeguarding customer data. The message for all retailers — increased vigilance.

TYPE OF RETAIL LOCATION

In general, retailers seek to optimize the number of potential customers entering their establishments. Hence, location and target customer accessibility are critical issues. Both Internet and fixed-location retailers face similar challenges.

INTERNET RETAILING

The core challenge is to persuade customers to visit the firm's website. Internet retailers use a variety of mass and digital communications tools (Chapters 15, 16, 17) to increase website traffic. Some retailers, like Amazon, develop *affiliate* programs so others forward customers to their websites.

FIXED-LOCATION RETAIL STORES

Fast-food chains like McDonald's and Starbucks invest heavily to identify traffic patterns — pedestrian and mobile — before choosing sites to open stores. Seemingly minor differences like side of the street/corners can have a large impact on success or failure.

MARKETING QUESTION

Location, location, location is a well-known adage for successful fixed-location retailers. What criteria would inform your location decision for a new store — Main Street, indoor mall, outdoor mall?

Neighborhood stores serve local residents, but in many cases, location per se maybe less important than the type and number of neighboring stores. In the 1930s, inspired by the formula for gravity, economist William Reilly proposed the *Law of Retail Gravitation* — large concentrations of stores attract greater numbers of shoppers than smaller concentrations.

The combination of ease of access and retail concentration has driven many forms of retail infrastructure:

Main Street. Main Street retail infrastructures (including central business districts and strip malls) combine ease of access and retail concentration. Many stores are noncompetitive and may even be complementary. The presence of several complementary stores offering a wide variety of goods and services is attractive for consumers with shopping lists. In many cities around the world, local merchants form trade associations to encourage shoppers to visit their stores:

In Singapore, the Orchard Road Business Association (ORBA) hosts numerous events to encourage visitors. ORBA partnered with Samsung to present *Fashion Steps Out 2013* (FSO). FSO featured models wearing the latest fashions, paired with the newly launched Samsung Galaxy S4 smartphones — the perfect *life companions*.

Outdoor malls. Frequently, outdoor malls derive from Main Street infrastructures. Many cities globally have improved shopping experiences by closing streets to traffic. Major examples include Clis Road — Sendai, Japan; Ala Moana Center — Hawaii; Sawgrass Mills — Florida; Nanjing Road — Shanghai. But some malls like Woodbury Commons, New York — a tourist favorite — were constructed specifically to ban automobiles.

Indoor malls. Indoor malls extend the purpose of outdoor malls by protecting shoppers from the physical environment. The Minneapolis Mall of America primarily protects against winter cold and storms; elsewhere, many malls protect shoppers from heat and humidity. Indeed, Jakarta (Indonesia) has more than 80 indoor malls; Singapore has around 160. Many indoor malls are so pleasant, they are destinations for many families and individuals regardless of shopping needs.[5]

Ancient indoor markets include huge structures like the Grand Bazaar, Istanbul. Similarly, most modern malls comprise an eclectic variety of stores and restaurants, but some malls focus on specific product classes, like clothing or electronics, where many competitors vie for business.

CONTEMPORARY RETAILING TRENDS

The retail industry is ever changing. Here are some modern retailing trends.

GROWTH OF INTERNET SHOPPING

Increasingly, people around the world secure products/services via the Internet. The convenience that Internet shopping affords and the greater ability to visualize options are key drivers. Mobile devices and social media are supportive; they enhance communications and consumer ability to act on recommendations quickly. Low prices; broader product assortments — like supermarket products; and improved logistic systems — including home-delivery alternatives like neighborhood retailers as distribution points and locker systems — are all positive factors.[6]

TRACKING SHOPPING BEHAVIOR

Driven by technology, firm understanding of customer behavior at retail continues to grow.**[994v]** Most consumers accept *cookies* that allow Internet behavior tracking, specifically progress through websites. Internet retailers profile shoppers, then make personalized offers. Physical stores — especially supermarkets — make similar offers; they use store cards to profile customers via shopping basket analysis. Physical stores will improve tracking behavior by evolving security cameras into marketing research devices. Tracking store and aisle entry and departure can aid staff scheduling and shelf display. Cameras assessing age, gender, and ethnicity offer greater possibilities, though such devices raise serious privacy issues.

PRODUCT RETURNS

In several product forms/classes — especially clothing — *returns* are high and increasing. As an inducement to purchase, many retailers employ no-cost return policies; but when consumers return goods, costs mount quickly and margins shrink. Returns are significantly higher for Internet versus in-store shopping, and rise in holiday periods. Retailers are increasingly employing virtual methodologies to improve consumer choices to reduce returns.

CHANGING FACE OF SHOPPING AREAS

As Internet shopping grows, bricks & mortar stores suffer and many will go out of business. Shopping districts will continue to evolve as offerings shift to services that consumers cannot secure on the Internet. Gyms, hairdressers, nail salons, restaurants, frozen yogurt stores, and other personal service establishment are taking the place of many traditional stores selling physical goods. Consider, for example, store closings by Barnes & Noble, Gap, Office Depot.

OPERATIONS OF INTERNET AND PHYSICAL STORES INCREASINGLY INTERTWINED

Retailers are combining positive features of Internet shopping and bricks & mortar stores to enhance customer value.[371v] Recognizing inventory limitations, physical stores are installing Internet terminals so consumers may search more broadly. Internet shopping has the problem of delayed delivery, but firms that combine Internet and physical locations increasingly allow pickup, or deliver Internet orders the same day. Barnes & Noble, Macy's, Target, and Walmart offer this service option in certain cities.

A related evolving trend is the self-managed Internet shopping experience with real-time personal interaction. Many Internet stores now offer *instant chat* with a representative, and sometimes a *live* conversation. As GPS-enhanced smartphones proliferate, retailers can send messages to close consumers based on their locations — at home, in town, in the mall, even in the store. Such targeted communications promise to enhance store traffic by personalizing the shopping experience.

> During the year-end festive season (2013), the Kuala Lumpur City Centre (KLCC) shopping mall used social media to attract shoppers. For 12 days, KLCC invited shoppers to take photos with themed props at the mall's center court, and encouraged uploading to Facebook, Instagram, and Twitter. During the campaign, KLCC garnered 10,000 Facebook *likes*; Instagram followers increased by 400 percent!

Many physical-store retailers already make Internet sales through their own websites or via store fronts on established sites like Amazon or eBay. But Internet retailers may reverse the process by using their brand strength to open physical stores. Internet eyeglass specialist Warby Parker (WB) has opened several stores in Boston, Los Angeles, New York, and San Francisco. WB's physical stores incur greater overhead and must hire and train sales staff; but WB saves shipping costs and offers more personal service. Even Amazon has a physical store — in Seattle. Such personalization is, of course a two-way street. The physical-store shopper may receive text messages from an Internet retailer: "Now that you are in store XXX, just scan the barcode on the item you are considering purchasing, and we'll give you a better price."

MARKETING QUESTION

The chapter identifies several retail trends. Which of these trends is present in your country? What other trends can you identify?

In a related trend, many independent merchants engage in *retail arbitrage*. Internet prices are often lower than physical-store prices, but physical-store prices may be lower than the Internet — excess inventory, *loss leaders*, and other reasons. Arbitrageurs search physical stores for these situations, purchase products, then resell on Amazon or eBay.

GLOBALIZATION OF RETAILING

Compared to other industries, retailing has been slow to globalize.[7] Many large retail organization focus only on their home countries. But retailing is now globalizing quickly. Major chains like Carrefour, Metro, Tesco, and Walmart now operate in many countries around the world. German grocery discounters Aldi and Metro each have a significant global presence: For example, Aldi operates in 18 countries including the U.S. (Trader Joe's).[8] Many fast-food and snack brands have become ubiquitous via franchising. But locally entrenched retailers may outperform foreign entrants; Walmart withdrew from Germany and South Korea; Tesco abandoned its *Fresh and Easy* U.S. entry.[9]

PEER-TO-PEER (P2P) TRANSACTIONS

Essentially, retail operators sell products/services to consumers. But we should not forget that many retail transactions involve just individuals. For eons, people have sold goods to (or exchanged goods with) one another. Historically, products were goats, horses, sheep, swine; today

KEY IDEA

Retailing trends include:

- Growth of Internet shopping
- Tracking shopping behavior
- Product returns
- Changing face of shopping areas
- Operations of Internet and physical stores increasingly intertwined
- Globalization of retailing
- P2P transactions
- Evolution in purchasing and payment systems
- Onsite production
- Continued retail evolution
- Customer privacy

they are more likely to be secondhand cars, sports equipment, apartments/houses. In many cases, buyers and sellers find each other; in other cases, agents and brokers fulfill the matching function. Today, the Internet provides the infrastructure for increased P2P transactions. Alibaba and eBay, Angie's List and Craigslist, allow people with things or services to sell to find and make deals with people who want to buy. EHarmony, Match.com, OkCupid, and Tinder help people find each other.

More recently, focused approaches have seen enormous success in the *sharing* economy.

In the U.S. and around the world, Airbnb links people with rooms, apartments, or houses to rent with people looking for short-term accommodation. Uber, Lyft, and Sidecar are transforming taxi service by linking people who require transportation with cars and drivers. Of course, in P2P transactions, both buyers and sellers face risks: Airbnb accommodations may not be *as advertised*, and renters may trash an apartment; Uber must deal with potential improper behavior by drivers. Both Airbnb and Uber face entrenched interests: Governments are concerned that Airbnb causes losses in tax revenues; the taxi industry objects to competition from Uber.

Some women borrow clothes from each other. They may have items in their closets they've barely worn but don't want to sell or discard. Conversely, women sometimes have anxious moments when they have *nothing to wear*. Closet Collective is a P2P community where women rent clothes from each other. Closet Collective brokers the relationship, and makes the process hassle free by handling dry cleaning, shipping, and insurance.

MARKETING QUESTION

Ask a retail store owner/ manager:

1. How have expanded purchasing and payment options impacted their business?

2. Has the impact been positive or negative on cash flow, costs, store traffic?

3. In what ways?

EVOLUTION IN PURCHASING AND PAYMENT SYSTEMS

Gone are the days when all consumers paid cash for products. During the past half century, credit cards have become ubiquitous — American Express, Discover, MasterCard, and Visa lead the industry. Debit and prepaid cards account for over $1 trillion purchases annually. Although back-office credit card systems continue to evolve, they are unseen by consumers. Nonetheless, technology is driving significant changes that improve the customer experience. *Swiping* the card is giving way to optical scanning; small transponders (perhaps attached to a key chain) take the place of physical cards; payments by smartphone and various Apple devices (Apple Pay) are growing quickly.

In Internet shopping, services like PayPal safeguard consumer credit card data and make payment faster. And one-click purchasing at sites like Amazon and Groupon simplify the buying process even more. Relatedly, for frequently purchased products like groceries, websites retain purchase histories to simplify consumer selection.

Bitcoin is a virtual currency for making payments over the Internet without transaction fees or financial institution involvement. No central authority issues new money nor tracks transactions. Created anonymously, Bitcoin can be *mined* (like gold) by solving complex mathematical problems; but the process is highly complex, and consumes enormous amounts of processing power (and electricity), so most people purchase from Bitcoin agents. The network collectively manages payment tasks, P2P networking, and proof-of-work to process and verify payments. Bitcoins are sent (assigned) from one Internet address to another; each user potentially has many addresses. Each payment transaction is broadcast to the network and included in the blockchain so a person cannot spend the included bitcoins twice. After an hour or two, the massive amount of processing power locks each transaction in time, and continues to extend the blockchain. Bitcoin provides a fast and reliable payment network that anyone can use. A growing number of merchants accept Bitcoin — like content aggregator Reddit.com and dating site OkCupid — and increasing numbers of bricks & mortar businesses.

ONSITE PRODUCTION

Developing technologies may allow onsite production of certain products. Print-on-demand technology in bookstores enables consumers to select books and have them produced while they wait. And 3-D printing may allow retail stores to produce a variety of different-shaped products.

CONTINUED RETAIL EVOLUTION

The previous segments provide some ideas about the future of retailing. We do not pretend to be able to predict the future retail landscape — but it will surely be different as time passes. In recent years, not only has the Internet introduced an entirely new retailing form that will continue to evolve, but traditional bricks & mortar retailing has seen many innovations as entrepreneurs and established firms continually seek new ways of serving evolving customer needs. National brands were dominant in supermarkets for decades, but private-label/store brands are winning in some product forms — even Amazon is developing private brands. A few years ago there was no Apple store, Brandy Melville, Chipotle, Whole Foods, Airbnb, or Uber.

We cannot tell what will emerge in the next 10–20 years but technology will no doubt play a major role. Retailers will learn to adapt to location-based service made possible by smartphones — outside and inside physical stores (p. 520). Indeed, Tesco's use of QR codes to bring the shopping experience to subway platforms offers many interesting opportunities. Virtual shopping will continue to advance, and in-store experiences will be more customer-experience focused. Together, virtual and physical experiences will provide greater customer value. **[636v]**

CUSTOMER PRIVACY

A special issue of increasing concern is confidentiality of customer data. In recent years, hackers have broken into credit card databases at Home Depot, Target, and many other retailers. Relatedly, JPMorgan Chase suffered a 76-million-customer data breach. Safeguarding customer data must be a high retailer priority.

RETAIL PROFITABILITY

Retailers use many different performance measures — some are intermediate measures; others are output measures — Chapter 24. We note some of these in Table 20.1 (p. 523). Perhaps the most significant measure is retail profitability. Many people are confused about definitions of profit margins and the *right* performance metrics. We attempt to clear up misunderstandings.

MARGINS

KEY IDEA

Retailers typically express margins as a percentage of their selling price.

Retailers make profit margins on the goods they sell. Typically we express retail margins as a percentage in one of two ways. Both ways are correct, but when we discuss retail margins we must know which way we are talking about. In this simple illustration, the unit margin is $20.

Retail Price   = $100
Retailer's Cost = $ 80
Unit margin   = $ 20

The critical question: What is the retailer's percentage margin? The options are: percent markup on *cost*, and percent margin on *retail price*:

• Percent markup on cost = (20/80) × 100 = (1/4) × 100 = **25%**

• Percent retail margin = (20/100) × 100 = (1/5) × 100 = **20%**

Although percent markup on cost seems more intuitively reasonable, retailers typically express their margins as a percentage of the retail selling price. Of course, margin percentages expressed in this manner are always lower!

Intermediate Measures	Output Measures
Number of shoppers	Sales per square foot
Length of visit	Sales per linear foot (supermarkets)
Average purchases per customer visit	Same-store sales growth
Number of customers per day	Sales per average inventory (inventory turns)

KEY IDEA

The retailer may measure store performance via several intermediate and output measures.

SETTING RETAIL PRICE

The retailer must set the retail price; key inputs are product cost and required percent retail margin. Suppose product cost to the retailer = $50; and required retail margin = 40 percent.

Let:

C = Product Cost to the retailer ($)

P = Retail Selling Price ($)

M = Retail Margin, expressed as percent of Retail Selling Price (stated as a decimal)

Then:

$P = C + (P \times M)$

$P - (P \times M) = C$

$P (1 - M) = C$

$P = C/(1 - M)$

In the illustration:

$C = $50; M = 40\%$ or 0.4,

$P = $50/(1 - 0.4) = $50/0.6 = $**$83.33**

Mechanically applying the 40 percent retail margin indicates a retail selling price of $83.33. Frequently, the retailer selects a more conventional price, perhaps $79.50 or $84.95.

PROFITABILITY

Building on the retail margin discussion, we must be sure to choose the correct metric for measuring retail profit performance. Another way to state percent retail margin is return on sales — profit/sales. Regardless, in many firms, the fundamental profitability measure across products and businesses is return on investment (ROI) — profit/investment.

To calculate ROI, we must supplement the retail margin concept with inventory turnover. We may find a 50 percent retail margin product is less profitable than a 10 percent retail margin product, if inventory turnover for the 50 percent margin items product is far slower.

Inventory turnover (stockturn) is the number of times the firm sells its average product inventory during the year. There are three ways to calculate turnover. The results are approximately the same:

- Cost of Goods Sold/Average Inventory at Cost
- Net Sales/Average Inventory at Retail Selling Price
- Sales (in units)/Average Inventory (in units)

Suppose cost of goods sold for one year = $1.0 million. Beginning-year inventory at cost = $250,000. End-year inventory at cost = $150,000.

Average Inventory = ($250,000 + $150,000)/2 = $200,000

Inventory Turnover = $1,000,000/$200,000 = 5

Turnover is an especially important control measure in retailing and wholesaling. A jeweler's turnover may be one or two times per year; a supermarket's produce department selling fresh fruit and vegetables could easily exceed 50 times per year. ROI is the fundamental profitability measure for many businesses.

Return on Investment

ROI = Profit/Investment

As we saw in Chapter 12, p. 321, we modify this equation by inserting sales on both the top and bottom lines of the equation.

ROI = Profit/Sales × Sales/Investment

For businesses like retailing and wholesaling, inventory is a large component of total investment. If inventory is the focus, the components of the ROI equation can be restated in more familiar terms:

Profit/Sales = Retail Margin; Sales/Investment = Inventory Turns

Thus:

ROI = Retail Margin x Inventory Turns

Consider a business (like a supermarket), where average retail margin = 2 percent and inventory turns = 25 times per year. Although retail margin is extremely low (2 percent), ROI is much healthier:

ROI = 2% × 25 = 50%

For retailers with high inventory costs, the firm must consider both retail margin and inventory turns.

WHOLESALING

Wholesalers sit between suppliers — producers and other intermediaries — and customers — retailers and industrial firms. Retailers and industrial firms secure products from wholesalers. To be effective, wholesalers conduct many activities. Table 20.2 shows the functions of several intermediary types, including wholesalers.

TABLE 20.2
Selected Intermediaries and Functions

Distribution Entity	Description of Distribution Entity
Agents, brokers, manufacturers' representatives	These entities have similar functions. Generally, they sell products but do not take title or physically handle goods. They may work for the supplier or the customer, or be impartial between supplier and customer.
Distributors	Provide promotional support for suppliers, especially for selective or exclusive distribution. Often a synonym for wholesaler.
Warehouse operators	Receive and inventory products, arrange product pickup, often break bulk.
Wholesalers	Primarily buy, take title to, store, and physically handle goods in large quantities. Usually break bulk — resell to retailers or industrial businesses.

The wholesaler must provide value to both suppliers and customers. Figure 20.2 (p. 525) shows the fundamental basis of wholesaler value. In the absence of a wholesaler, each supplier must develop a relationship with each retailer/end user, and vice versa — 8 × 4 = 32 connections in the illustration. When a wholesaler sits between suppliers and retailers/end users, each supplier and each customer requires only one relationship — with the wholesaler — 4 + 8 = 12 connections.[10]

FIGURE 20.2
The Value of Wholesalers

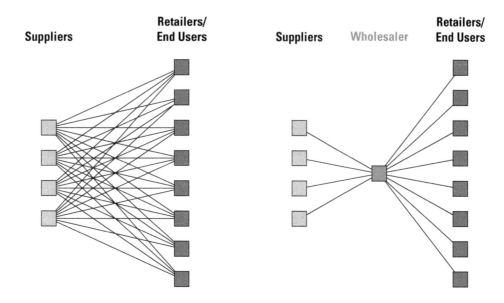

VALUE TO SUPPLIERS

Wholesalers offer two main values to suppliers:

- **Market access.** The core value wholesalers provide suppliers is market access. Reaching retailers/end users is difficult if not impossible for many small suppliers — wholesalers know which retailers are appropriate for supplier products and maintain necessary relationships.

- **Information on customer requirements.** By virtue of direct retailer/end-user relationships, wholesalers learn what products are selling and what consumers/end users require. Wholesalers may feed these data to suppliers for product modification and new product development.

> Etsy Wholesale is an Internet site for handmade, vintage, and other artisan items. Small-scale producers secure access to thousands of retailers; retailers secure access to thousands of suppliers. Etsy's low 3.5 percent markup and customer service helps retain suppliers and keeps prices low for retailers. **[780v]**

VALUE TO RETAILERS/END USERS

Wholesalers offer several values to retailers/end users:

- **One-stop shopping.** Rather than develop relationships with multiple suppliers, retailers/end users focus on one — the wholesaler. Reducing the number of connections offers numerous cost-saving advantages — fewer salespeople calling, reduced deliveries, lower transportation costs, fewer invoices.

- **More effective procurement.** The more cutting-edge wholesalers continually reduce lead times and drive down procurement costs for their customers. These wholesalers offer sophisticated online ordering systems, including automatic reordering processes for frequently purchased items.

- **Enhanced assortments.** Over and above value inherent in individual products, wholesalers provide value in the entire product assortment. Indeed, wholesalers may develop special assortments that add value. Systems integrators combine many different product to provide end-user solutions.

KEY IDEA

Wholesalers offer various types of value.

To suppliers:
- Market access
- Information on customer requirements

To retailers/end users:
- One-stop shopping
- More effective procurement
- Enhanced assortments
- Consulting

- **Consulting.** Some wholesalers provide business advice to retail customers like location, store design, product assortment, and inventory and financial management. Others advise on pricing and additional service offerings.

> Leading U.S. industrial wholesaler Grainger provides a broad and deep assortment of maintenance, repair, operations (MRO) products. But Grainger also offers solutions on MRO issues including procurement, inventory management, and warehouse operation. Indeed, Grainger account managers even identify problems their industrial customers had not considered, then solve them.

DEVELOPING MARKET STRATEGY FOR RETAILERS AND WHOLESALERS

The fundamental basis of developing and implementing market strategy is no different for retailers and wholesalers than for firms in other industries. Regardless, we outline a few critical issues.

MISSION

Having decided on the retailing or wholesaling industry, the firm must decide its broad approach to product assortment:

- **Type of product.** From which product forms/classes will the firm select products?
- **Breadth of product assortment.** The firm must choose between many or few product forms/classes — *broad* or *narrow*.
- **Depth of product assortment.** The firm can choose to have many or few products per product form — *deep* or *shallow*.

Essentially the firms must decide what type of enterprise to become. We now focus on retailing.

MARKET SEGMENTS

Having decided on the type of retail enterprise, the firm should have a good idea of customer needs it aims to satisfy and the types of customers it hopes to serve.

MARKET STRATEGY

The retailer should identify its objectives, then construct a well-defined positioning statement.

OBJECTIVES. Strategic and operational objectives. Positioning comprises:

- **Customer targets.** Decision makers and influencers for retailer products.
- **Competitor targets.** Various options for customers to purchase similar products to firm offers.
- **Value proposition.** Why customers should buy from the retailer rather than competitors. The value proposition embraces the breadth and depth of product assortment, but also the retailer's general approach to pricing — Walmart positions itself as a low-price store; Ritz-Carlton offers luxury accommodations. Differentiators often concern the type and degree of experience value the retailer offers consumers in the form of extra services.
- **Reasons to believe.** Why consumers should believe the retailer can deliver promised value.

Select a retailer with which you are familiar. Identify the market segment(s) this retailer targets. What is the retailer's positioning statement for its most important market segment?

- customer targets
- competitor targets
- value proposition
- reasons to believe

MARKET IMPLEMENTATION

PRODUCT

Assortment. What specific assortment of products/services will the retailer offer?

Product turnover. How frequently will the product assortment change? Polar opposites are:

- **Slow change.** Some stores change product assortments rarely. Convenience stores and hardware stores attract shoppers who know they can always purchase certain products at that store. Certainty of product assortment provides significant value in some product forms/classes.

- **Fast change.** Zara is a great example of a fast-change store. Zara's value proposition focuses on new choices; hence, it deliberately turns over its assortment every two or three weeks.

Most firms operate between these extremes. Stores offering *fashion* goods tend toward lots of change. Many stores vary product assortments by season, even though their products may be similar year by year. Of course, the retailer's approach to product change drives many organizational decisions. Slow-change stores require efficient inventory control systems with automatic reorder points. By contrast, Zara requires a complex production and supply-chain system, and a process for dealing with unsold products.[663v]

> Leading global clothes retailers Zara and H&M (Europe) are facing tough competition from Japan's *Fast Retailing (FR)* under the *Uniqlo* brand. FR is now Asia's largest clothes retailer with well over 1,000 stores, mostly in Japan. FR is shifting focus to the U.S. and China (including Hong Kong and Taiwan).

PROMOTION

The retailer must persuade customers to visit its store(s) — physical or online. Essentially the retailer has two promotional tasks:

- **Get consumers to the store.** Promotional activities are similar to those for most other firms but with a different objective. Differences include shop windows to attract customers and even salespeople to encourage people to enter the store. for Internet retailers, the task is to secure website visitors.

- **Help consumers around the store.** This is a very different challenge. For physical stores, the tools are display, layout, lighting, music, signage, and other devices to move shoppers from area to area. For Internet retailers, the task focuses on website design.

Of course, these challenges are quite separate; different organizational units are typically responsible. Internet retailers typically also assign responsibility to separate departments. Amazon has one department dedicated to attracting consumers to its website; a second department helps consumers around the website.

> Brandy Melville (BM) is the U.S.'s fastest-growing tween and teen girl retailer — branches in the U.S., Canada, and Europe, and a popular website. But BM does not advertise. BM bases virtually its entire communication on social media: Instagram — two million followers; Facebook — 200,000 likes; Twitter — 60,000 followers.

DISTRIBUTION

How will firm products reach customer homes/offices. Delivery options are important. Unfortunately, some durable goods physical-store retailers outsource delivery to third parties — a poor delivery experience may cancel out a good store experience. Of course, efficient package delivery services like FedEx and UPS enable Internet retailing.

PRICE

How will the firm price individual products? The store develops a general approach to price in its value proposition, but must decide issues like when to put products on sale. Executing these decisions for a single store is relatively straightforward; ensuring consistency across a multiple-store chain requires significant systems sophistication.

KEY MESSAGES

- Retailing is a critical component of national economies.
- Core values retailers offer customers are product assortments, customer experiences, and accessibility.
- Consumers may choose among many different retailing forms.
- Different types of fixed-location retail operations vary on several dimensions.
- The success of a fixed-location retail store depends in part on neighboring stores and the overall physical environment.
- Retailing continues to evolve along several dimensions.
- Retailers should choose carefully among available performance measures.
- Successful wholesalers offer significant value to suppliers and retailers/end users.

What other messages did you glean from this chapter?

VIDEOS AND AUDIOS

For complimentary material, see Axcess Capon codes at www.axcessvids.com

Shopping   198v 🌐   Devora Rogers   TEDx WakeForestU

QUESTIONS FOR STUDY AND DISCUSSION

Can you answer the questions implied by this chapter's learning outcomes? Check!

1. Every country has its own retailing issues. Suppose you were designing an expansion strategy for a well-financed restaurant chain, what would be your major considerations?

2. As a hitherto successful retailer, you are facing Internet competition. Consumers entering your stores compare your prices to other options via smartphone. Some consumers even receive texts from Internet retailers offering to beat your prices. What actions will you take to chart a profitable future?

3. The central business district in your town has shuttered stores because retailers have failed. As mayor, faced with declining tax revenues, what actions will you take to turn the situation around?

4. As a long-standing domestic U.S. retailer, you are concerned about well-financed Asian and European retailers entering the U.S. How will you address the potential challenge from foreign entrants?

5. Uniqlo aspires to be the world's leading fashion retailer by 2020. Uniqlo has strong principles like *Global One* — use the world's best practices as one united corporate group across the globe; and *Something for (almost) Everyone*. What challenges does Uniqlo face in maintaining a strong culture while pursuing aggressive global growth?

TRUE/FALSE QUESTIONS
Answers on page A2 and at www.axcessvids.com — 911p

1. Retailers offer consumers choice value through product assortments. ❑ **TRUE** ❑ **FALSE**

2. Retailers typically state margins as a percentage of costs. ❑ **TRUE** ❑ **FALSE**

3. Wholesalers sit between suppliers, producers, and other intermediaries. ❑ **TRUE** ❑ **FALSE**

4. A slow-change store requires an efficient inventory control system. ❑ **TRUE** ❑ **FALSE**

5. According to Reilly's Law of Retail Gravitation, consumers living near large store concentrations prefer to shop where concentration is lower. ❑ **TRUE** ❑ **FALSE**

MULTIPLE CHOICE QUESTIONS
Answers on page A2 and at www.axcessvids.com — 128p

1. Which of the following is NOT a characteristic of Internet retailing?
   a. Purchase decisions can be made from home.
   b. Limited opportunities for real product display.
   c. Easy ability for comparison shopping.
   d. Retailers benefit from the *long-tail* effect.

2. Which of the following is NOT a typical characteristic for distinguishing among different types of retail operations?
   a. relation between strategy and operations
   b. service level
   c. time delay in receiving purchased goods
   d. physical closeness to other stores
   e. ownership
   f. product assortment

3. Similarities between Internet retailing and physical stores do NOT include:
   a. illegal activity
   b. optimizing the number of potential customers
   c. convenience
   d. physical inspection of products

4. Retail profitability metrics do NOT typically include:
   a. inventory turnover
   b. retail profit margin
   c. return per linear/square foot
   d. Net Present Value

5. Wholesaler value to customers does NOT include:
   a. dealing with complex supply chain systems
   b. effective procurement
   c. breadth and depth of product assortments
   d. consulting advice

CHAPTER 21

CRITICAL UNDERPINNINGS OF PRICING DECISIONS

For complimentary material, see Axcess Capon codes at www.axcessvids.com

LEARNING OUTCOMES

When you have completed this chapter, you will be able to:

- Discriminate between pricing strategy and pricing tactics.
- Recognize the key role of price in capturing customer value.
- Analyze the role of costs in pricing decisions.
- Incorporate competitor objectives and strategies in determining prices.
- Relate strategic objectives to pricing decisions.

OPENING CASE: SOUTHWEST AIRLINES

Southwest Airlines (SWA) is a major U.S. domestic airline. But in 1973, SWA was a puny upstart battling Braniff, a significant national/international carrier (based in Texas). That SWA survived a harrowing period was due in no small part to astute pricing decisions by CEO Lamar Muse.[1]

SWA was formed in the mid-1960s to fly among three major Texas cities — Dallas, Houston, and San Antonio. Flight distances ranged from 190 to 250 miles; flight times were about 45 minutes. Because SWA's proposed routes were within Texas, the Texas Railroad Commission, rather than the Civil Aeronautics Board, was its regulator. To start flying, SWA fought an extensive legal battle with Braniff and Texas International Airlines (TI) that went to the U.S. Supreme Court, but SWA prevailed.

In June 1971, SWA started flying from Dallas to Houston and San Antonio. Initial advertising positioned SWA as The Love Machine. SWA had new Boeing 737s, attractive hostesses in hot pants, and quick ticketing. Braniff and TI fares from Dallas were: Houston — $27; San Antonio — $28. SWA entered at $20 on both routes. Braniff and TI immediately met SWA prices. In November 1971, SWA added San Antonio–Houston, also $20, and shifted some flights from Houston Intercontinental airport (HI) to the close-in Hobby airport (HH). In late 1972, SWA abandoned HI altogether.

During the next few months, SWA made several pricing moves. In November 1971, SWA experimented with $10 on weekend evening flights; in May 1972, SWA extended the $10 fare to all flights after 9 p.m. Passenger load factors were higher than full-fare flights. In July 1972, facing a deteriorating financial condition, SWA raised the basic fare to $26, increased leg room, and provided free drinks. Within one week, TI matched SWA fares; Braniff followed two days later and increased onboard service. Now flying into Hobby (as well as HI), Braniff started a $10 evening fare at 7:30 p.m.

SWA devised numerous publicity stunts — SWA held onboard parties, decorated aircraft cabins, and hung posters in lounges and on aircraft. By end July 1972, SWA's market share on the important Dallas–Houston route was 40 percent. Braniff's share dropped from 75 to 48 percent; TI's share dropped from 25 to 11 percent. But Braniff's passenger load was roughly the same as before SWA's entry.

In October 1972, SWA replaced its $10 fares with $13 fares after 8 p.m. on weekdays and all weekend, supported with heavy advertising; traffic increased. SWA was now profitable on Dallas–Houston, but was unprofitable on Dallas–San Antonio where Braniff had four times as many flights. On January 22, 1973, SWA announced a 60-Day Half-Price Sale from Dallas to San Antonio. Passenger loads increased threefold almost immediately and SWA reached 85 percent load factor. On February 1, Braniff responded with a 60-day half-price Get Acquainted *sale at $13 for all Dallas–HH (but not HI) flights.*

CEO Muse reported his initial reaction to Braniff's price move: "Them bastards." He said Braniff knew that Dallas to Houston was SWA's one profitable route; he thought Braniff expected SWA to eliminate its $13 Dallas–San Antonio fares. Muse also believed Braniff's move was a predatory action, designed to put SWA out of business. If Braniff were successful, Muse believed it would raise prices back to $26 or higher, close HH, and force passengers back to HI.

Case Question

How do you assess Southwest Airlines' pricing actions? How do you assess Braniff's pricing actions? Could similar price actions occur in today's airline industry?

Muse said he believed the public should realize that SWA's highly reliable hourly service was worth $26, and that it should be disgusted at Braniff's action. SWA ran double-truck (facing pages) advertisements in Dallas and Houston newspapers with a picture of Muse, a statement — "Nobody's Goin' to Shoot Southwest Airlines Out of the Sky for a Lousy $13" — and all the reasons the public should not let that happen. SWA also printed 50,000 brochures with even stronger language. SWA gave these to all passengers; off-duty hostesses handed them out at lunch hour in downtown Dallas and Houston.

SWA also offered a premium. SWA told passengers that the flight was worth $26; SWA would like them to pay $26. But if they felt they had to fly Braniff because of the $13 price, Southwest would also take them for $13. Those who paid the full fare received a gift — a fifth of Chivas Regal or Crown Royal, or a nice leather ice bucket. These items cost SWA around $7 to $8, but each had a retail value of around $13. According to Muse: "Businessmen, in particular, put $26 on their expense reports and took a fifth of Chivas Regal home!" On April 1, Braniff ended its Get Acquainted *sale; SWA also went back to $26. February 1973 was SWA's best month, and in March it made its first profit. By 2015, SWA was the U.S.'s largest domestic airline: 2014 revenue — $18.6 billion: net income — $1.1 billion.[2]*

© age fotostock / SuperStock

Chapter 21 is the first of two chapters in Part D of Imperative 4 — *Design the Market Offer*. Part D focuses on *Getting Paid for Customer Value*. Chapter 21 addresses *Critical Underpinnings of Pricing Decisions*.

Pricing is critical for earning profits and creating shareholder value.[3] Pricing is also pivotal for entering new markets, introducing new products, and changing firm objectives and/or strategy. Figure 21.1 shows that price decisions have greater profit impact than any other lever. Reasons include:

- Price affects profit margin — profit margin equals price *less* cost.
- Price affects unit volume — via the demand curve.
- Because price affects volume — price also affects unit costs via economies of scale.
- Price often affects customer quality and value perceptions.

Henry Ford understood the critical role of price. Ford's vision was *a car in every garage*; the challenge was to design, build, and distribute a $250 car at a profit. Ford's *Model T* assembly line kept costs down and brought automobiles to the masses. Ford became the leading U.S. car firm by understanding what customers valued and pricing accordingly.

FIGURE 21.1
How Pricing and Other Levers Affect Profits[4]

1% improvement in:	Creates operating profit improvement of:
Price	11.0%
Variable cost	7.8%
Volume	3.3%
Fixed cost	2.3%

KEY IDEA

Price has a larger impact on profits than any other lever. Price affects:

- Margins
- Unit volumes
- Costs
- Customer quality and value perceptions (often)

Table 21.1 shows how price could affect International Paper (IP), a leading *Fortune* 500 firm. Let's make the assumption for this illustration that IP's unit sales remain constant while overall prices go up or down by 1 percent.[5] (Since unit sales are constant, none of the cost items change.)

- **1 percent price increase.** Profits *increase* 42 percent, to $791 million.
- **1 percent price decrease.** Profits *drop* 42 percent, to $315 million.

TABLE 21.1
How Pricing Affects Profits at International Paper

	Year 2014	1% price increase	1% price decrease
Net Sales ($millions)	$23,617	$23,853	$23,381
Net Income ($millions)	$ 555	$ 791	$ 319

THE CHANGING VIEW

OLD WAY	NEW WAY
Customers are ill-informed	Customers are well-informed
Focus on costs	Focus on perceived customer value
Full-cost systems pervasive	Activity-based costing becoming prevalent
Inflation permitted easy price increases	Low inflation/foreign competition hold prices down
Perceived customer value ignored	Perceived customer value measured and tracked
Prestige sometimes ahead of value perceptions	Value consciousness pervasive among customers

Chapter 21 focuses on the fundamental underpinnings for developing price strategy. In Chapter 22, you learn how to set actual prices.

Pricing strategy is the firm's overall approach to setting price. Figure 21.2 shows four critical underpinnings of pricing decisions: *perceived customer value, costs, competition,* and *strategic objectives*. Too much emphasis on a single element leads to suboptimal pricing, like the destructive, downward pricing spiral that can follow from an excessive focus on competitors. Skilled pricing executives assess all factors before developing pricing strategy.[6]

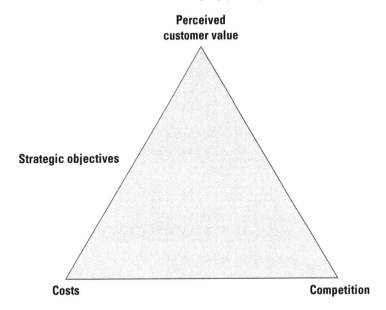

Perceived customer value

Strategic objectives

Costs

Competition

FIGURE 21.2
Critical Considerations in Setting Pricing Strategy

KEY IDEA

In setting prices, the firm should consider:

• Perceived customer value
• Costs
• Competition
• Strategic objectives

Excessive focus on a single element leads to suboptimal pricing decisions.

PERCEIVED CUSTOMER VALUE

When increased competition brings more options, customers invariably seek lower prices. As customers turn elsewhere, the firm may believe it has a pricing problem. More likely, it has a *perceived value* problem — the firm delivers insufficient value, or has not established a good price/value relationship. We focus on three value-related issues — creating, measuring, and capturing value. Then we turn to a closely associated issue — price sensitivity.

KEY IDEA

What seems to be a pricing problem may more likely be a perceived value problem.

CREATING VALUE

Chapter 9 shows that the value proposition is central to market strategy. The firm creates value in its offer primarily through nonprice elements in the marketing mix — Chapters 12–20:

• **Product.** Typically delivers the major portion of the value proposition.
• **Service.** Adds additional value to the core product.
• **Promotion.** Conveys information about value, but sometimes provides value in its own right — like reassuring customers they made a good purchase.
• **Distribution.** Provides value through time and place convenience.

Price may also create value by contributing to brand image. Products like Bentley, Ferrari, and Rolls-Royce automobiles; Rolex; and Apple's iPod are all perceived as quality brands. Factors outside the firm's control also affect customer-value perceptions. On a hot day, you may value a can of Coke at $3 if that is your only option, but if you could also obtain Pepsi and 7-Up, Coke value would be less.

KEY IDEA

The firm creates value for customers primarily via nonprice elements in its offer — the marketing mix.

Many factors affect the value customers perceive in firm offers.

MARKETING QUESTION

The price for *Managing Marketing in the 21st Century* is 80 percent less than the price of competitor textbooks. How should Wessex Press address a concern with price/quality perceptions?

MEASURING VALUE

Measuring the value customers perceive in firm and competitor offers is critical. If you don't know *customer-value* perceptions, you'll never make good pricing decisions. Some approaches are:

DIRECT VALUE ASSESSMENT. The firm simply asks customers what they would pay for various products. Downward response bias is a concern, but carefully phrased questions can provide helpful data. In launching the original Ford Mustang, Lee Iacocca asked customers to estimate its price. Estimates were much higher than Ford's planned price, so Iacocca knew the Mustang would be a winner. The Mustang is the best-selling new U.S. car ever.

DOLLARMETRIC METHOD. This method compares each option with the others. For each pair of options, customers say which they prefer and how much extra they would pay. Summing positive and negative differences reveals the relative value of the options. Table 21.2 shows the responses for four products — A, B, C, D.

TABLE 21.2

Illustrative Data from the Dollarmetric Method

Options Compared	Preferred Option	Extra Price for Preferred Option
A and B	B	$10
A and C	C	$13
A and D	A	$5
B and C	C	$3
B and D	B	$8
C and D	C	$12

MARKETING QUESTION

Managing Marketing in the 21st Century (700+ pages) and *Capon's Marketing Framework* (450+ pages) have identical prices. Prices for black & white printed books are slightly more expensive than PDF versions. Prices for printed color versions are considerably more expensive. Do you agree with this pricing decision? Why or why not?

We calculate customer relative value for these options:

- *Extra price* is positive for the preferred option, negative for the nonpreferred option.
- Each option has three comparisons. Sum the *extra prices* for each option.
- Divide the sums of *extra prices* by three to calculate average *extra prices*.

  The average extra prices customers are prepared to pay for the four options are:

  $$A = -10 - 13 + 5 = -18/3 = \mathbf{-6} \qquad B = 10 - 3 + 8 = 15/3 = \mathbf{+5}$$
  $$C = + 13 + 3 + 12 = 28/3 = \mathbf{+9.3} \qquad D = -5 - 8 - 12 = -25/3 = \mathbf{-8.3}$$

- Using the least valued option as the base, find the difference between the base and the average *extra price* for each option. This figure is what the customer would pay over the base.

  D is the least valued option, so the base is –8.3. The *extra prices* for the other options are:

  $$A = (-6) - (-8.3) = \mathbf{\$2.3} \qquad B = 5 - (-8.3) = \mathbf{\$13.3} \qquad C = 9.3 - (-8.3) = \mathbf{\$17.6}$$

PERCEIVED VALUE ANALYSIS. Table 21.3 identifies five steps for measuring an offer's perceived value. Data are best secured directly from customers, but sometimes experienced managers provide *best-guess* data that marketing research can validate.

TABLE 21.3

Measuring an Offer's Perceived Value

Step	Description
1. Identify customer-required benefits/values	Identify the key benefits/values customers require — typically 5 to 8 — but exclude price.
2. *Weight* relative value of benefits/values to customers	Weight each benefit/value by allocating 100 points based on its importance to customers. Weights sum to 100.
3. *Rate* each offer from the various suppliers	Rate each offer based on how well customers believe it delivers the required benefit/value (1 = poor; 10 = excellent).
4. Develop benefit/value scores	For each offer, form individual benefit/value scores by multiplying the results of step 2 and step 3 for each benefit/value. Benefit/Value score = Weighting × Rating.
5. Develop the perceived value scores	For each offer, sum the individual benefit/value scores.

KEY IDEA

Critical topics in perceived customer value are:

- Creating value
- Measuring value
- Capturing value

The perceived value scores, Step 5 in Table 21.3, are a measure of each supplier's value, as perceived by customers. Note that price does *not* enter into the analysis, but is important for interpretation. Table 21.4 shows a numeric illustration: A, B, C represent three different suppliers of easy chairs. (We note prices in the table.) The results and interpretation are:

- **Perceived value.** Supplier B — 820 — offers the greatest perceived value, followed by A — 665; C — 580.
- **Price.** Supplier A has the highest price — $500; followed by B — $450; and C — $300.

Supplier C has the lowest perceived value and the lowest price, but A and B are misordered. Supplier B has the greatest perceived value — 820 versus supplier A — 665. But supplier A's price is higher — $500 versus supplier B — $450. Since supplier B provides greater value for a lower price, it should be gaining market share.

Benefits Required	Relative Importance Weighting	Supplier A Price = $500		Supplier B Price = $450		Supplier C Price = $300	
		Rating (1–10)	Total	Rating (1–10)	Total	Rating (1–10)	Total
Chair design	20	5	100	7	140	6	120
Comfort	30	6	180	8	240	4	120
Fabric quality	15	10	150	9	135	8	120
Fabric design	15	5	75	7	105	4	60
Ease of purchase	20	8	160	10	200	8	160
Grand Total	**100**		**665**		**820**		**580**

TABLE 21.4
Illustration: Perceived Value Analysis for Easy Chair Suppliers

The *customer-value map* is a useful approach for displaying value/price (V/P) positions — Figure 21.3.[7] These positions relate directly to Table 21.4 and are good predictors of likely market-share changes in most products/markets. Exceptions are markets where higher prices lead to greater sales, like prestige products or luxury goods. Other exceptions are inefficient markets, like new product forms, and complex products like insurance.

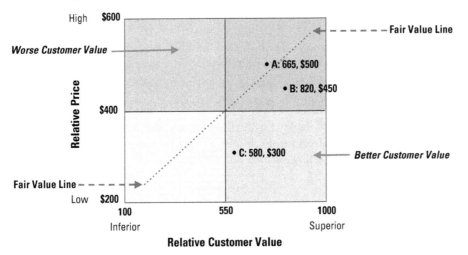

FIGURE 21.3
Customer-Value Map

ECONOMIC ANALYSIS — ECONOMIC VALUE FOR THE CUSTOMER (EVC). Many B2B firms use EVC — the maximum price customers will pay — to calculate the economic value of new products. EVC analysis depends critically on competitive products in the customer's choice set.[8] EVC helps clarify firm options: Should the firm add more value for a higher price or provide less value for a lower price? Chapter 4, pp. 101–102, shows an EVC calculation.

Value/Price Options

Higher value for higher price. Alcoa's new press makes very wide metal and alloy sheets. For customers building airplane wings, wide sheets mean less time and fewer materials (rivets). Rivets add weight, so fewer rivets mean lower fuel costs. Fewer rivets also mean lower inspection and maintenance costs. Alcoa has lead market share for aircraft wings and enjoys premium prices.[9]

Lower value for lower price. ChemX (disguised) supplied chemicals for extracting oil from wells; it also studied customer operations and advised on usage quantities. A small customer did not follow ChemX's advice; it simply pumped a few gallons of chemicals into each well when ChemX's truck came by. By mutual agreement, the customer discontinued the monitoring service. ChemX reduced prices to that customer by 7 percent, but profitability increased from minus 6 percent to plus 32 percent because it no longer provided monitoring![10]

MARKETING QUESTION

Wessex Press sells several print and PDF versions of *Managing Marketing in the 21st Century*: black & white PDF version — less than $50; hard cover, color version — more than $200; soft cover, color — intermediate price. Color book purchasers receive a free PDF version. How do you assess this pricing approach?

PRICE EXPERIMENT. The firm offers the test product at different prices in different market areas, like geographic locations — A/B testing. Sales levels at different prices reflect customer value. The Internet offers many possibilities for systematically changing price when customers visit the firm's website. The experimental approach has the advantage of securing real market data, but higher-paying customers may be upset if they discover the experiment! Several years ago, Amazon received negative publicity for a price experiment and immediately stopped the practice.[11,12]

CAPTURING VALUE

The firm incurs many costs to develop an offer; it creates value if costs are less than perceived customer value. Figure 21.4 shows how price apportions created value: The firm retains some value; customers receive some value. High prices imply the firm retains most value; low prices imply the firm transfers most value to customers. A critical firm decision is the degree to which it retains/transfers value. Table 21.5 suggests conditions that favor retaining and transferring value.

FIGURE 21.4
Price as Value Sharing

TABLE 21.5
Conditions for the Firm to Retain and Transfer Value

Criteria	Transfer Value	Retain Value
Competitors	Strong and aggressive	Weak or lax
Firm objectives	Growth and market share	Profit and cash flow
Market conditions	Growth market — firm well positioned	Mature or declining
Potential competitive entry	Likely	Unlikely
Response to price changes	Customers highly responsive	Customers nonresponsive

KEY IDEA

Price shares value — some to the firm, some to customers.

Most firms develop new products, then set prices based on costs or some value estimate using a method like we just discussed. By contrast, Avon starts with the value it wants a new product to deliver to customers, then sets a target price. Avon translates this price into cost parameters that enable it to meet profit targets. Engineering and manufacturing must then design a product/production process that delivers desired customer value within the cost parameters.[13] P&G used this approach to develop Naturella (feminine hygiene pads) for the Mexican market[14]; Zara (fashion retailer) operates similarly.

CUSTOMER PRICE SENSITIVITY

Sometimes, reducing price a little (increasing customer value a little) may lead to a major increase in customer purchase volume. Other times, customers may only buy more if the price reduction is substantial — major increase in customer value. (Equivalent effects hold for price increases.) Sometimes customers are *price sensitive*; other times they are *price insensitive*. Classical microeconomics focuses on price sensitivity at the market level; we also discuss individual price sensitivity.

MARKET-LEVEL PRICE SENSITIVITY. Figure 21.5 shows elastic and inelastic *demand curves*:

- **Price elasticity.** When price goes down a little, volume increases significantly. When price goes up a little, volume decreases significantly. Many grocery items are price elastic.
- **Price inelasticity.** Volume does not change much, even with significant price changes.[15] Products like critical raw materials, electricity, and heart pacemakers are price inelastic.

Price Elastic   **Price Inelastic**

We quantify price sensitivity via the *price elasticity of demand*.

Price elasticity of demand (PED) = Percentage change in demand/percentage change in price.

Because volume typically increases when price decreases, PED has a negative sign. Conventionally, when PED's absolute value (ignoring the minus sign) is less than one, the market is *price inelastic*; when PED is greater than one, the market is *price elastic*.

Table 21.6 shows illustrative PED calculations for three products — A, B, C; in each case, current demand = 1,000 units; current price = $100. The markets for B and C are *price inelastic*; the market for A is *price elastic*. Table 21.7 shows how to estimate the effect of price changes on sales volume for products X, Y, and Z, knowing current sales and price elasticity.

New Price ($)	Absolute Price Change ($)	Percent Price Change (%)	Sales Volume (units)	Absolute Volume Change (units)	Percent Volume Change (%)	Price Elasticity Calculation	Price Elasticity (PED)
A $ 99	−$1	−1%	1030	+30	+3%	+3%/−1%	−3.0
B $ 98	−$2	−2%	1010	+10	+1%	+1%/−2%	−0.5
C $105	+$5	+5%	990	−10	−1%	−1%/+5%	−0.2

Original Price ($)	Original Sales Volume (units)	New Price ($)	Percent Price Change (%)	Price Elasticity	Sales Volume Calculation	Percent Sales Volume Change (%)	Sales Volume Change (units)	New Sales Volume (units)
X $50	300	$55	+10%	− 4.0	+10% X − 4.0 =	− 40%	−120	180
Y $80	200	$75	−6.3%	− 0.3	−6.3% X − 0.3 =	+ 1.9%	+ 3.8	204
Z $90	150	$95	+5.6%	− 2.0	+5.6% X − 2.0 =	−11.2%	−16.8	133

A final related item: Pundits often advise marketers to set prices at what *the market will bear*. This advice is *useless*. All markets *bear* many prices; each price produces a different volume. The firm should decide what volume it wants to sell, then set the appropriate price. Understanding customer value and price sensitivity helps the firm do just that.

MARKETING QUESTION

How should firm marketing efforts differ between price-elastic versus price-inelastic markets?

FIGURE 21.5
Market Demand Curves

MARKETING QUESTION

Are airline tickets, theater tickets, health club memberships, milk, and HIV medication price elastic or price inelastic? How did you decide?

KEY IDEA

Price elasticity of demand (PED) helps estimate market demand when price changes.

TABLE 21.6
Calculating Price Elasticity

TABLE 21.7
Calculating Sales Volume from Price Elasticity

KEY IDEA

Pricing at *what the market will bear* is not useful advice; the market *will bear* many prices.

INDIVIDUAL CUSTOMER PRICE SENSITIVITY. Markets are rarely homogeneous. Some customers place high value on an offer; other customers value the offer less. Some consumers are price sensitive because disposable income is low, and/or they face financial demands. Some B2B customers are price sensitive because competitors are cutting prices, and profits are under pressure. Customers with full information on alternatives, benefits/values, and prices tend to be more price sensitive than those with less information. Other factors affecting willingness to pay include brand loyalty, frequency of use, past experience, product availability, and seasonality. Timing may also be important: Customers are generally less price sensitive for unplanned, immediately required services, than for planned purchases — hence, higher same-day and rush-order prices. Table 21.8 provides a comprehensive list of factors affecting price sensitivity.

....
TABLE 21.8
Factors Affecting
Individual Customer
Price Sensitivity

Factors	Related Questions
Competitive comparison	Can customers easily and fairly compare alternative offers? Without purchasing? Are experts required? Do customers know how to use firm and competitor products? Are prices directly comparable, or must customers make calculations to understand differences?
Education	Do firms educate customers to focus on price by fierce price competition?
End benefit/value	For components of final products, what end benefit/value does the offer deliver? How price sensitive are end users? What percentage of the end product's price does the firm's offer represent? Can the firm reposition its offer to deliver an end benefit to price-insensitive customers?
Expenditures	How significant are absolute purchase expenditures? What percentage of annual spending/income/wealth does the purchase represent?
Fairness	How does the current price compare to customer experience with similar products? What do customers expect to pay? Is the price justified?
Inventory	Do buyers hold inventory? Do buyers expect current prices to be temporary?
Nonmonetary costs	What effort, time, and/or risk must customers expend to make a purchase?
Perceived substitutes	What competitive offers and prices do customers consider? Can the firm influence customer price expectations via positioning decisions?
Price/quality	Are price and quality related for competitor products?
Shared cost	Do customers pay the full cost? If not, what portion do they pay?
Switching costs	What costs/investments would customers incur if they switched suppliers? Are customers locked into current suppliers? For how long? Can the firm encourage switching?
Terms	Are financing options available and clearly communicated?
Unique value	How do customers weigh elements of the firm's offer that influence their decisions? Is the firms' offer differentiated from competitors? Can the firm persuade customers some offer elements are more important than others?

MARKETING QUESTION

You are chief marketing officer for a firm selling automobile headlights; your firm is sole supplier for a car model that sells relatively well globally. Your CEO suggests the firm lower prices to increase demand. How will you respond?

MARKETING QUESTION

As the newly appointed marketing director for a chain of movie houses, you find that prices are identical for all seats, for all movies. How might you improve profits by adopting a different pricing approach?

MARKETING QUESTION

Mike caused Bill to become sensitive to price. What industries or firms *educate* customers to be sensitive to price?

MARKETING ENRICHMENT 21.1

Customer Value and Price Pain **155p**

Mike Smith is a salesman for component supplier MachinCo; Mike earns a low salary but can make a high bonus based on quarterly sales versus quota. In mid-March, Mike realizes he will not make quota for Q1 (quarter 1), but he knows that Bill typically places a major order early in each quarter. Mike calls Bill:

Mike: "Bill, how would you like to place your regular order next week, instead of mid-April?" Bill demurs — he is concerned about inventory and payment timing. Mike calls again: "Bill, I've got you a great deal. If you place your order next week, I can get you $18 per unit instead of the regular $20 and you can defer payment by a couple of weeks." Bill places the order. In mid-June, and mid-September, Mike and Bill play out the same scenario. In early December, Bill calls Mike.

Bill: "I've been thinking about my quarterly order: I'm ready to place an order for mid-December delivery. I'll pay $16 per unit!"

Price-sensitive customers feel pain when prices are high; Marketing Enrichment 21.1 **[155p]** shows four scenarios formed from customer-value assessments in the context of price *pain*.

COSTS

Costs are important for setting prices.[16] After all, costs represent one half of the profit equation: *Profit = sales revenues – costs*. In practice, many firms use costs for setting prices, but often do so inappropriately. Because you must understand these issues, we start with them. Then we show how the firm *should* use costs in pricing decisions.

THE INAPPROPRIATE ROLE FOR COSTS: COST-PLUS PRICING

Cost-plus pricing is a pricing methodology that many firms use, harkening back to our earlier discussion of *internal* orientation — Chapter 1. Despite its popularity, *cost-plus* is the *wrong* way to set prices.[17] Cost-plus pricing proceeds simply by identifying product costs, then adding a predetermined profit margin (markup). Table 21.9 shows how this works:

Variable costs	$400,000
Total fixed costs	$300,000
Total costs	$700,000
Standard markup: 15% of costs	$105,000
Price	**$805,000**

TABLE 21.9
Illustration: Cost-Plus Pricing for Capital Equipment item

Advantages of cost-plus pricing are:

- **Profitability.** All sales seem profitable as price must, by definition, be above cost.
- **Simplicity.** If the firm knows its costs, pricing is simple. Anyone can do the math.[18]
- **Defensibility.** Legally acceptable and often required for government and other cost-plus contracts.

Regardless, cost-plus pricing has four main disadvantages:

PROFIT LIMITATIONS. Customer value has no role in price setting:

- **Prices are too low.** Customers value the offer at more than the cost-plus price. Table 21.9: Suppose customers value the product at $900,000. By setting price at $805,000, the firm forgoes $95,000 profit on each item sold: $900,000 less $805,000 = $95,000.
- **Prices are too high.** Customers value the offer at less than the cost-plus price. Table 21.9: Suppose customers value the product at $750,000; they will not purchase at $805,000. The firm forgoes $50,000 profit on each item it could have sold at $750,000: $750,000 – $700,000 = $50,000.

In both cases, the firm sets prices incorrectly — it has not assessed customer value. Cost-plus pricing leads to overpricing in price-sensitive markets and underpricing in price-insensitive markets. Cost-plus pricing also leaves the firm vulnerable to competitors. By estimating firm costs, competitors can predict firm prices.

INAPPROPRIATE TREATMENT OF FIXED COSTS. Firms frequently classify costs as fixed and variable — Table 21.9[19]:

- **Variable costs.** Vary directly with the volume of sales and production. Variable costs increase as volume increases, and decrease as volume decreases. What costs are variable depends on the specific product and technology. For manufactured products, variable costs usually include direct labor, raw materials, sales commissions, and utilities to power production machines.
- **Fixed costs.** Do not vary with the volume of sales or production, over a reasonable range. Fixed costs include overhead and allocated items like depreciation, rent, salaries, and SG&A (selling, general, and administrative).

KEY IDEA

In cost-plus pricing, the firm identifies costs, then adds a profit margin.

Cost-plus pricing does not consider customer value.

KEY IDEA

Disadvantages of cost-plus pricing include:

- Profit limitations
- Inappropriate treatment of fixed costs
- Arbitrary overhead calculations
- Mismatch with market realities

Firms often determine fixed costs per unit arbitrarily by assuming some level of sales and/or production.

MARKETING ENRICHMENT 01

Financial Analysis for Marketing Decisions **308p**

MARKETING QUESTION

What would be the implications for Apple and Verizon if they based prices for the iPod and smartphone service, respectively, on cost?

As noted, the cost-plus price equals costs plus a predetermined margin. Using the fixed and variable cost distinction:

Cost per unit = *variable* cost per unit plus *fixed* cost per unit

Variable cost per unit is relatively straightforward, but calculating fixed cost per unit is *illogical*:

1. Fixed cost per unit equals fixed costs divided by number of units sold.
2. But the number of units varies with the price.
3. Hence, to set the price, price is an input to the calculation; this makes no sense!

In practice, many firms arbitrarily assume some sales level to calculate fixed costs per unit.

ARBITRARY OVERHEAD ALLOCATIONS. Suppose the firm has two business units, A and B; A is comfortably profitable but B is not. Corporate may reduce overhead allocations to B, and increase overhead allocations to A. Corporate reduces B's fixed costs, but increases A's fixed costs. Such financial machinations are typical of firms striving to even out profits across products. But such actions are highly demotivating to A's managers! (Activity-based costing [ABC] systems mitigate this problem: Marketing Enrichment 01 **[308p, p. 10]**.)

Industrial parts maker Parker Hannifin (PH) traditionally set prices based on cost (manufacturing and delivery) plus a target markup (35 percent). Following an extensive study, PH classified products based on degree of competition: A — at least one large competitor helps shape prices; through B and C to D — *specials* and *classics* that only PH produced. PH raised many prices, some as much as 60 percent, but reduced several A product prices. In three years, net income rose from $130 million to $673 million; return on invested capital increased from 14 to 21 percent; and PH's share price doubled.

MISMATCH WITH MARKET REALITIES. When demand falls, logic suggests the firm should lower prices. Pure cost-plus pricing does not allow such action. As sales fall, and the firm spreads fixed costs over lower volumes, fixed costs per unit increase — and so must price! When demand surges, logic suggests the firm should raise prices. But the firm spreads fixed costs over larger volumes, and fixed costs per unit decrease. And so must price! Variable markups based on demand can partially solve this problem.

APPROPRIATE ROLES FOR COSTS

Cost-plus pricing is the lazy way to set prices. But we should not underestimate the role costs play in price setting. Costs are important in three critical situations:

BIRTH CONTROL. Costs are particularly important for new product introduction. Typically, forecast return for a new product must meet or exceed financial criteria like the firm's *hurdle rate* — minimum return for a new investment (typically related to cost of capital) to receive go-ahead approval. The firm bases cash-flow estimates on target prices, unit sales, and costs. The relevant costs are *fully loaded costs*, meaning they include all incremental costs related to the new product, *including* incremental overhead.

DEATH CONTROL. Costs are also important when the firm is considering dropping a product. The relevant cost is the *marginal cost* — the cost to make and sell one additional unit. Marginal cost includes all variable costs plus some incremental fixed costs,[20] but *excludes* all allocated overhead. Suppose product Z's costs are:

Marginal cost (to produce and sell each unit) = $4 per unit
Overhead allocation = $2 per unit
Fully loaded cost = $6 per unit

Let's examine two situations:

- **Situation A.** Price = $7. Product Z makes a bottom-line *profit* of $1 (7 − 6 = 1).

- **Situation B.** Price = $5. Product Z makes a bottom-line *loss* of $1 (5 – 6 = –1). Many would consider dropping the product; after all a *loss* is a *loss*. But if we consider only the marginal cost, product Z makes a $1 profit contribution (5 – 4 = 1). This *contribution* helps cover overhead costs like rent, top manager salaries, and the corporate jet. The firm incurs these costs anyway; if the firm dropped product Z, other products would have to carry this burden.

KEY IDEA

Costs have three important price-setting roles:
- Birth control
- Death control
- Profit planning

The marginal cost is the *floor price*; only in rare circumstances should the firm set prices below the floor price.[21] Returning to the illustration; at prices less than $4, the firm loses money on every unit it makes and sells — it should drop the product. At prices greater than $6, the firm earns bottom-line profit — it should retain the product. At prices between $4 and $6, the product makes a positive contribution to covering fixed costs; if this price range is sustainable, generally the firm should continue with the product, at least in the short run.

PROFIT PLANNING. Birth control and death control are special cases; the major role for costs is profit planning. Table 21.10 shows a simple illustration. The firm explores various possible prices, and estimates unit sales and unit costs. The firm uses these data to forecast sales revenues and profits at different prices, then selects the price that optimizes profits. In the illustration, the optimal price is $12.

Price a	Estimated Unit Sales Volume b	Sales Revenues c = a x b	Estimated Costs d	Profits e = c – d
$ 8	650	$5,200	$4,800	$400
$10	500	$5,000	$4,500	$500
$12	400	$4,800	$4,100	$700
$14	300	$4,200	$3,700	$500

(Marketing Enrichment 21.2 [691p] for the relationship between customer value and firm costs.)

TABLE 21.10
Role of Costs in Profit Planning

MARKETING ENRICHMENT 21.2
The Relationship between Customer Value and Firm Costs 691p

COMPETITION

The firm should always consider competitor prices. Basing price on competitor prices is legal and ensures price parity, but focusing too heavily on competitor pricing strategies has distinct disadvantages:

- *Price parity* with competitors devalues attributes/features and benefits/values; such pricing tends to *commoditize* products. Customers then focus buying decisions on price.
- *Excessive price focus* may lead to losses for everyone, both the firm and competitors.

Generally, the firm should not focus on beating competitor *prices*. Rather, the firm should beat competitor *offers* — product, service, and other marketing-mix elements. The firm should attempt to make offers with greater value per unit price than competitors. *Offer* superiority is crucial, not *price* superiority. Of course, price plays a critical balancing role. Two issues are crucial:

KEY IDEA

The firm should seek *offer* superiority, not *price* superiority.

- How will competitors respond to firm price changes?
- How should the firm respond to competitor price reductions?

HOW WILL COMPETITORS RESPOND TO FIRM PRICE CHANGES?

When making price changes, the firm should always consider likely competitor responses. Although pricing tactics can be quite complicated, basically competitors have three pricing options — *raise*, *hold*, or *lower*. Whether or not firm price moves are successful depends on competitor choices. Table 21.11 summarizes common scenarios, firm actions, and likely competitor responses. We revisit some questions the firm should answer:

- Has the competitor been raising or lowering prices?
- How comparable are the various competitive offers in terms of perceived customer value?
- How many firms are competing? What are their market shares?
- What are competitor costs and profits?
- How are competitor products positioned relative to the firm's product(s)?

TABLE 21.11

Likely Competitive Responses to Firm Actions under Various Scenarios

Current Situation	Firm Action	Likely Competitor Response
Few competitors and marginal profits Firm is market-share leader Market demand inelastic	Raise prices	Accept the firm's price leadership; also raise prices
All competitors make similar offers Market demand moderately elastic No competitor dominant	Lower prices	Follow suit
Competitors profitable Market demand moderately elastic Market offers highly differentiated	Raise prices	Hold prices constant (High-quality restaurants do not typically raise prices to follow other restaurants.)

KEY IDEA

In high fixed cost/low variable cost oligopolies, competitors often cut prices to gain extra volume. Prices can spiral downward and profits vanish.

Assessing likely competitor response is always important, but is vital in oligopolies with few major competitors, high fixed costs, and low variable costs (airlines, many highly capital-intensive industries). When several competitors have poor profits, sometimes one firm cuts price to gain volume and better cover fixed costs. Competitors follow and prices spiral downward. Sometimes firms launch *trial balloons*, strategic preannounced price intentions to gauge likely competitor response. Warnings and other signals — Chapter 5 — may preempt competitors, but can raise antitrust issues. Successful and unsuccessful price leadership examples are:

Oligopoly Pricing

Successful price leadership. Coca-Cola raised concentrate price by 7 percent, twice the usual rate. Two weeks later, PepsiCo announced a similar increase.

Successful price leadership. British Aluminum Company (BACO) competed fiercely against Alcoa and Alcan in the low-growth, barely profitable British aluminum oligopoly. BACO divided the market into three parts: BACO long-term contract customers — *ours*; competitor long-term contract customers — *theirs*; switchers — *up-for-grabs*. BACO resolved not to lose any *our* business on price. If it did lose, BACO *punished* the competitor by pricing low at one of *theirs*. BACO effectively executed this *tit-for-tat* strategy; Alcoa and Alcan *got the message*.[22]

Unsuccessful price leadership. American Airlines (AA) attempted to change the pricing structure for domestic U.S. airlines. American West, Continental, Delta, Northwest, United, and USAir quickly followed AA's lead. But TWA undercut AA's prices by 10 to 20 percent, and the attempt failed.[23]

RESPONDING TO COMPETITOR PRICE REDUCTIONS

Firm response depends on market position. Generally, strong firms should match price cuts *only after* exhausting other options. But weak firms with minimal sustainable differential advantage may have to respond right away. Only the low-cost producer wins when price cutting is rampant; how that firm uses its cost advantage determines competitor fates. (Of course, the firm may also have to decide how to respond to competitor price increases.)

Firms with dominant market shares often face severe price competition from small competitors and/or new entrants. These competitors may believe the leader:

- Has not carefully managed costs, and assumes its own costs are lower.

- Does not know individual product costs because of difficulties allocating overhead.
- Will not retaliate directly because it would sacrifice profits on its much larger volume.

Unless demand is *price elastic*, the firm should minimize direct price-cutting responses.[24] The nature of competitive price reductions governs price and nonprice options:

PRICE OPTIONS. Price retaliation ranges among indirect and direct actions:

- **Indirect price retaliation.** The firm signals disapproval by cutting prices in the competitor's strong markets. Suppose firm A is a strong supplier in segment 1, and firm B is a strong supplier in segment 2. Firm A enters segment 2 with low prices that significantly undercut firm B. In response, firm B visits firm A's loyal customers in segment 1, presents its offer, and the following conversation ensues:

  > *Firm B:* "Thanks for listening to our offer, but we know you can't buy from us."
  >
  > *Firm A's loyal customer:* "Why not?"
  >
  > *Firm B:* "Firm A just visited some of our customers and we can't meet its low prices."
  >
  > *Firm A's loyal customer:* "We'll have to have a conversation with firm A!"

  This scenario was played out by InfoX (disguised): InfoX provided premium data services to select private universities. InfoY (disguised) made similar offerings to public universities. In an aggressive move, InfoY offered low prices to InfoX's customers (private universities). InfoX responded like firm B (above); InfoY withdrew its offers.[25] Similarly, America West's (AW) (now part of American Airlines) hub was in Phoenix. AW introduced new low-fare flights from Houston. Continental (then the dominant Houston airline) cut prices on flights from Phoenix. AW withdrew its low fares in Houston; Continental withdrew its low fares in Phoenix.[26]

- **Selective price competition.** If the competitor attacks part of the firm's product line with low prices, the firm has two sorts of options:

  - **Selective price cuts.** The firm may cut prices directly against the attack and/or offer lower prices in select channels like the Internet. Siebel Systems (owned by Oracle) sells discounted software; hotels and airlines distribute low-price products via Priceline.com, cheapOair, and other consolidators.

  - **Introduce a *fighter* brand.** The firm cuts prices against the attack but with a specially designed *fighter* brand. To compete with store brands, P&G offers low-price brands to supermarkets meeting strict volume-based criteria — like *Tide Basic* in 100 southern U.S. stores where market share was poor. Delta and United Airlines introduced Song and Ted, respectively (now abandoned) to compete with low-price carriers like jetBlue and Southwest Airlines.

- **Cut prices across the board.** Ultimately the firm may have to cut prices broadly.[27] But this approach will not succeed unless the firm also cuts costs, especially variable costs. Typically, the highest variable-cost producer *blinks first* when prices fall. Some firms, notably U.S. airlines, use bankruptcy filings to reduce costs.

NONPRICE OPTIONS. The firm exercises creativity to compete in areas other than price. Alternatives for defending market positions include:

- **Change the basis of competition.** The firm changes the type of competition. For example, the firm may bundle products to remove competitor price advantage, like McDonald's successful *Value Meals*.

- **Clarify and reinforce the price/value relationship.** Goodyear prices tires based on expected miles driven; Orica prices explosives based on degree of rock fragmentation.[28] The firm may be able to sensitize customers to the value it offers by creating price/value expectations — higher/lower prices imply higher/lower value. By stressing that packages *absolutely positively* get there overnight, FedEx implies superiority to other carriers. This approach is especially important when product failure is a major concern.

KEY IDEA

Rampant price-cutting is disastrous for all but the low-cost producer.

MARKETING QUESTION

Select a product form, then search the Internet for different prices. Do prices vary across products? Why? If you were to purchase, which supplier would you choose? Why?

MARKETING QUESTION

Identify several examples of nonprice actions that firms took when competitors cut prices. Were these actions successful? Why or why not? What was the rationale for firm actions?

MARKETING
QUESTION

Examine pricing plans from
several cell phone service
providers. Is it easy to
compare plans?

- **Invest in fixed-cost marketing expenditures.** The firm reinforces its position and builds switching costs by making marketing expenditures like advertising, customer service, better product quality and delivery, and loyalty programs. The firm spreads these fixed costs over large volumes. During Asian economic crises, some luxury Malaysian hotels compete on price; by contrast, Ritz-Carlton increases service. Each hotel's general manager greets arriving guests with music, drinks, and personalized items; occupancy rates improved. Relatedly, major airlines use loyalty programs to defend against low-price airlines.
- **Make pricing opaque.** Price transparency increases customer bargaining power, so the firm may make pricing opaque. The firm shifts from traditional schemes, like pricing by the yard to pricing by the meter; or uses discounts/rebates without changing list prices.[29]
- **Signal market position.** Communicate firm capabilities and/or intentions — Chapter 5. Sara Lee (SL) is low-cost supplier for several products, but sets prices relatively high. SL lets competitors know its low-cost position to deter price cutting.

If none of these actions work and the firm is in severe trouble, it may seek help. U.S. airlines regularly appeal to unions for wage reductions and simplified work rules. Firms facing foreign competition lobby governments for tariff protection. Britain's sugar giant Tate & Lyle receives large government subsidies for export competition; U.S. steel firms frequently seek protection.

KEY IDEA

The firm has various price
and nonprice actions
for responding to price
competition.

If the firm cannot withstand competitive attack, it may have to withdraw:

- **Partial withdrawal.** The crucial decision is which market segment(s) to cede to competitors and which to retain. The firm must develop a razor-sharp focus on *retained* segments and take appropriate actions — redesign products, add services, and/or offer long-term contracts.
- **Total withdrawal.** When facing a competitor with significant cost advantage pursuing a low-price strategy, *discretion may be the better part of valor*. The firm withdraws and plays a different game. Faced with intense Taiwanese price competition, Intel withdrew from memory chips but successfully refocused on microprocessors.

STRATEGIC OBJECTIVES

KEY IDEA

The firm should link pricing
strategy to strategic objectives.

Choosing strategic objectives is a major component of developing market strategy. The firm has three major options for optimizing performance — *sales volume and/or market-share growth*, *profits*, *cash flow*. Generally, each strategic objective relates to a particular pricing strategy:

SALES VOLUME AND/OR MARKET-SHARE GROWTH. The firm offers high customer value — value/price (V/P) ratio superior to competitors. Appropriate conditions are:

- Deep pockets to absorb initially low profit margins
- Desire to deter competitors
- Good ability to cut costs in the future
- Price-elastic market
- Sufficient capacity to fulfill increased demand

Ryanair's price leadership in European air travel and P&G's aggressive price strategy in disposable diapers follow this *penetration-pricing* approach.

KEY IDEA

The firm has three major
options for optimizing
performance:
- Sales volume and/or
  market-share growth
- Profits
- Cash flow

To improve U.S. market shares, European luxury automobile brands have gone down market: Mercedes CLA sedan — less than $30,000 — at least 50 percent lower price than flagship products; Audi A3 — manufacturer suggested retail price $29,900; BMW X1 price — $30,900.

PROFITS. When the paramount objective is maximizing profits, the firm provides less value to customers and retains more value for itself as profit. Firms use this *skim-pricing* approach when products have patent protection — like pharmaceuticals — or offer high value, like pioneering high technology products.

Penetration Pricing and Skim Pricing

Here we review *penetration pricing* and *skim pricing*, introduced in Chapter 10. These price strategies correspond to different strategic objectives: maximizing growth and/or market share, and maximizing profits, respectively.

Penetration pricing. The firm provides significant customer value by setting prices close to costs. Volume increases; unit costs fall; the firm reduces price; and volume increases ... in a virtuous spiral. The firm forgoes high profits today in favor of achieving high volumes, and ultimately earning profits from high unit volumes, but low profit margins. **[553v]**

Skim pricing. The firm retains value by pricing high. The firm earns high profit margins, but provides less value to its relatively few customers. The firm reduces prices periodically — sequential skimming — to attract increasing numbers of customers. These customers experience greater value in part because of the original higher-price framing.[30]

Apple used a skim-pricing strategy for the iPhone launch. Introduced at $599, Apple reduced price to $399 after just two months.[31] Less than one year later, Apple priced the new iPhone 3G at $199.

CASH FLOW. If the firm plans market withdrawal, maximizing cash flow is often a good short-term strategic objective. In Chapter 10, we discuss *harvesting* products as the approach to short-term cash-flow maximization.[32]

KEY MESSAGES

- Pricing is a big deal. Pricing decisions have a major impact on profits.
- Four critical considerations should enter firm pricing decisions:
  - *Perceived customer value.* The firm must make key decisions about creating, measuring, and capturing value. The firm must understand customer price sensitivity.
  - *Costs.* Many firms use cost inappropriately by implementing cost-plus approaches to setting prices. Costs have three proper roles — birth control, death control, profit planning.
  - *Competition.* Critical firm issues are predicting how competitors will respond to firm price changes and deciding how to respond to competitor price reductions (increases). The firm has available several price and nonprice actions.
  - *Strategic objectives.* The firm has three major options for optimizing performance — sales volume and/or market-share growth, profits, cash flow.

MARKETING QUESTION

What other messages did you glean from this chapter?

VIDEOS AND AUDIOS

For complimentary material, see Axcess Capon codes at www.axcessvids.com

Pricing	**365v**	Reed Holden	Holden Advisors
Pricing	**982v**	Spencer Lum	ground-glass.com
The Pain of Paying	**422v**	Dan Ariely	Fuqua School of Business, Duke University

QUESTIONS FOR STUDY AND DISCUSSION

Can you answer the questions implied by this chapter's learning outcomes? Check!

1. Merck priced prescription hair-growth drug Propecia — $50 per month's supply. Over-the-counter competitor Rogaine (topical liquid) — about $30 per month. Merck's drug for enlarged prostate, Proscar, has the same active ingredient — finasteride — as Propecia. Merck's price for 30 Proscar tablets — $70 — one Proscar tablet equals five daily doses of Propecia. Some physicians write Proscar prescriptions for balding men; they slice the pills into five parts. Hence, they pay about $14 per month ($70/5) for hair-loss treatment, versus $50 for Propecia. Merck defends Propecia's price premium by citing research costs including clinical trials — $450 million. Most insurance policies cover Proscar, but not Propecia. The makers of Rogaine launched an $80 million advertising campaign for extra-strength Rogaine, applied twice daily. An Italian website offers Proscar tablets for U.S. delivery at $63 per 36 tablets. Suggest actions for:

   • Merck's director of marketing
   • Compliance director for a national HMO
   • Rogaine's marketing director

2. Develop a customer-value map for soft drinks (or a product form of your choice). Interpret the map. What pricing options do the several competitors have?

3. Market leaders frequently have cost structures with a high proportion of fixed costs. Why? What pricing alternatives would you recommend to one of their small competitors? Why?

4. In 1958, Kaplan, Dirlam, and Lanzillotti showed that cost-plus pricing was the most common pricing method. In 1995, Shim and Sudit found essentially the same result. This chapter argues that cost-plus pricing is deeply flawed. Why does this apparent incongruity exist? What should firms do about it?

TRUE/FALSE QUESTIONS

Answers on page A2 and at www.axcessvids.com — 444p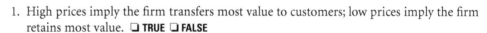

1. High prices imply the firm transfers most value to customers; low prices imply the firm retains most value. ❏ **TRUE** ❏ **FALSE**

2. Price-elastic items include products where volume does not change much, even with significant price changes. ❏ **TRUE** ❏ **FALSE**

3. Cost-plus pricing is a pricing methodology used by many firms. This approach proceeds by identifying product costs, then adding a predetermined profit margin. ❏ **TRUE** ❏ **FALSE**

4. Marginal cost includes all variable costs and some incremental fixed costs, but excludes all allocated overhead costs. ❏ **TRUE** ❏ **FALSE**

5. When demand is price inelastic, the firm should maximize direct price-cutting responses to gain additional market share. ❏ **TRUE** ❏ **FALSE**

MULTIPLE CHOICE QUESTIONS

Answers on page A2 and at www.axcessvids.com — 388p

1. Which of the following is NOT a method used to measure the value that customers perceive on firm and competitor offers?

   a. direct value assessment
   b. dollarmetric method
   c. price experiment
   d. factor analysis

2. In the _____ approach to measuring value, the firm offers the test product at different prices in different market areas, like different geographic locations. The firm bases its measure of customer value on sales levels at different prices.

   a. direct value assessment
   b. dollarmetric method
   c. price experiment
   d. factor analysis

3. Which of the following is the correct formula to calculate the price elasticity of demand?

   a. percentage change in price / percentage change in demand
   b. percentage change in demand / percentage change in price
   c. percentage change in price minus percentage change in demand
   d. percentage change in demand minus percentage change in price

4. All of the following are nonprice options a firm can use to defend its position against competition EXCEPT:

   a. Clarify and reinforce the price/value relationship.
   b. Make pricing opaque.
   c. Signal the firm's position.
   d. Invest in variable-cost marketing expenditures.

5. All of the following represent conditions for a high value/price strategy EXCEPT:

   a. good ability to cut costs in the future
   b. sufficient capacity to fulfill demand increases
   c. desire to deter competitors
   d. price-inelastic market

PART D – GETTING PAID FOR CUSTOMER VALUE

CHAPTER 22

SETTING PRICES

For complimentary material, see Axcess Capon codes at www.axcessvids.com

LEARNING OUTCOMES

When you have completed this chapter, you will be able to:

- Set price for a new product.
- Change price for an existing product.
- Manage and monitor pricing tactics.
- Use the pricing-toolkit and price-waterfall concepts for setting prices.
- Assess several approaches to setting prices.
- Address several pricing issues.
- Design a system for price management.
- Integrate pricing with other marketing implementation elements.

OPENING CASE: ORACLE CORPORATION

Led by its famously aggressive CEO, Larry Ellison (pictured next page), Oracle is a world leader in enterprise software, and the second-largest cloud SaaS (software as a service) and PaaS (platform as a service) firm.[237v] Oracle develops, manufactures, distributes, and supports databases and middleware software, application software, and cloud systems worldwide. Oracle's 2014 revenues, close to $40 billion, and back-to-back years of 20 percent-plus net profit margins were a sharp improvement from a decade earlier.

In the early 2000s, Oracle competed strongly with Microsoft and IBM in the small- and medium-size business (SMB) software market. Oracle pursued a clear pricing strategy, placing list prices online for customers, implying pricing rigidity and fair pricing for all. But later, IBM and Microsoft lowered enterprise database prices for SMB customers. Oracle reacted strongly by offering large discounts to close deals. Oracle's price aggressiveness became well known in the industry. Many customers delayed purchase commitments until the end of the quarter, anticipating heavily discounted prices from Oracle salespeople to make their numbers. As competition between IBM, Microsoft, and Oracle heated up, Oracle adopted price competition as a strategic weapon. Jacqueline Woods, Oracle vice president of global practices and pricing, stated: "Now we are saying that it is time to lower our prices to penetrate broader markets." But Oracle's pricing actions led to significant margin erosion, and did not impede IBM and Microsoft's determination to fight for revenues.

To address decreasing margins, Oracle pursued an aggressive acquisition strategy so as to offer customers more compelling value propositions. Between 2005 and 2009, Oracle acquired more than 50 software firms (2005 — 13; 2006 — 13; 2007 — 11; 2008 — 13; 2009 — 5), including BEA, Hyperion, PeopleSoft, and Siebel, together with server manufacturer Sun Microsystems. Oracle invested more than $30 billion in these efforts.[177v]

By pursuing acquisition in the context of a deep understanding of customer needs, Oracle could offer customers very attractive product bundles (especially software), and incentivize the purchase of additional software for integration with database software. These acquisitions also brought Oracle an extensive customer base to which it offered integrated solutions. Oracle secured innovation and revenue growth, and constructed a software ecosystem whose constituent products worked well together.

Case Question

In addition to offering integrated solutions, Oracle's ecosystem created high customer-switching costs and allowed it to escape the price war with IBM and Microsoft. Oracle's new strategy even allowed price increases of 20 percent in the 2009 economic slowdown. Oracle became a one-stop shop for many customers, keen to avoid the high financial and organizational costs and risks of migrating databases from one software supplier to another. Correspondingly, Oracle secures significant revenues from maintenance and service contracts.

Oracle's financial results demonstrate the success of its strategy. Revenues increased from less than $10 billion in 2002 to $38 billion in 2014; net income — $10 billion. The stock market reacted favorably: Oracle's stock price increased from $11 in 2003 to $45 in late 2014.

How do you assess Oracle's strategy and performance? What other options did Oracle have in the early 2000s? As an Oracle customer, how do you feel about Oracle's strategy? Is Oracle's strategy sustainable?

THE CHANGING VIEW

OLD WAY	NEW WAY
Antitrust considerations are minimal	Growing enforcement in U.S. and European Union
Destructive pricing tactics common	Growing sophistication in using the pricing toolkit
Inefficient product markets	Efficient product markets — role of the Internet
List-price mentality	Varied pricing tactics
Price and offer homogeneity	Price and offer heterogeneity
Pricing complexity limited by human factors	Pricing complexity driven by software
Pricing decisions disorganized	Intellectual capital development in pricing
Standard pricing	Customized pricing

When Ryanair launched Ireland-to-Britain routes in the 1980s, it chose a low-price strategy. Ryanair was initially successful because incumbents British Airways and Aer Lingus held a *price umbrella* over the market. In the early 1990s, Aer Lingus cut prices and almost forced Ryanair into bankruptcy. Ryanair then buttressed its low-price strategy with a sustained effort to cut costs. Ryanair considerably expanded its route structure. Today, Ryanair is a leading European airline and is comfortably profitable (Chapter 21 Opening Case).

Chapter 22 is the second of two chapters in Part D of Imperative 4 — *Design the Market Offer.* Part D focuses on *Getting Paid for Customer Value.* Chapter 22 addresses *Setting Prices.*

Using Chapter 21 as background, Chapter 22 shows price-setting mechanics.**[924v]** The firm should use the four factors we discussed — *perceived customer value, costs, competitors, strategic objectives* — to approach price setting holistically. The firm starts with perceived customer value, considers costs, then factors in competitors and its strategic objectives. Chapter 22 shows how to approach strategic price setting for a new product, change price for an existing product, and avoid price changes. Then we turn to several issues in tactical pricing decisions; we conclude by discussing pricing management.

SETTING PRICE FOR A NEW PRODUCT

Ace Furnace (Ace) (fictional) is setting price for a new manufacturing furnace. Ace believes the furnace offers superior value versus competitor Beta. Table 22.1 shows data that Ace collected. Customer startup costs and postpurchase costs are the same for both Ace and Beta. To frame the *right* approach for setting price, we first show improper methods — cost-plus and competitive-equivalence approaches. Then we introduce the correct method:

TABLE 22.1
Data for Price Setting Collected by Ace Furnace

Beta	Furnace price	$260,000
Ace	Economic value to the customer (EVC)	$360,000
Ace	Direct out-of-pocket cost: variable and fixed	$100,000
Ace	Fully loaded cost, including overhead allocations	$160,000

IMPROPER APPROACHES

COST-PLUS. Since the pricing decision concerns a new product, Ace must consider the fully loaded cost — $160,000. Commonly used markups in the furnace industry are 75 percent and 50 percent. Price options are:

  75 percent markup: Price = $160,000 × 1.75   = **$280,000**

  50 percent markup: Price = $160,000 × 1.5   = **$240,000**

Note: At 75 percent markup, Ace price exceeds Beta — $280,000 versus $260,000.
    At 50 percent markup, Ace price is less than Beta — $240,000 versus $260,000.

We have no way to know which price is *better* for Ace.

COMPETITIVE EQUIVALENCE. Strict competitive equivalence suggests that Ace set a $260,000 price — same as Beta. But Ace offers considerable extra value. If Ace sets price at $260,000, it should sell lots of furnaces. But does a $260,000 price represent appropriate value-sharing between Ace and its customers? Note: This approach does not consider Beta's response.

THE *RIGHT* WAY TO SET PRICE

KEY IDEA

Figure 22.1 diagrams the recommended three-step approach:

- **Step 1: Determine maximum price.** The maximum price is the EVC from Ace's furnace — $360,000.[1] At $360,000, rational customers should be indifferent between furnaces from Ace and Beta. (Of course, customers may believe Ace's furnace poses a greater risk because the new product has no track record — we ignore this factor in the illustration.)

- **Step 2: Determine minimum price.** The minimum price is Ace's fully loaded cost — $160,000. (Ace earns profit contribution at any price above direct out-of-pocket cost — $100,000, but this is an incorrect figure for the minimum price of a new product.)

- **Step 3: Set price based on Ace's strategic objectives and Beta's likely competitive response.** From steps 1 and 2, Ace's price should be between $360,000 and $160,000 — the crucial question is where. Ace should consider its strategic objectives and its forecast of Beta's likely response — probably correlated factors. Possible strategic objectives are:

  - **Toehold.** Ace wants a market presence but has little other ambition. Perhaps Ace identified a small high-price segment. Ace sets price around **$320,000**. Sales will be low, but profit margins will be high. Beta is unlikely to respond.

  - **Profit.** Ace has greater ambition than the toehold option, so price is closer to Beta's $260,000. Because Ace offers greater customer value, it may set the price between $260,000 and, say, $280,000. Ace will probably take some market share from Beta — the closer Ace's price is to $260,000, the more likely Beta will reduce price. Prices significantly above $260,000 signal to Beta that Ace wishes to avoid price competition.

  - **Market share.** Ace is ready to battle Beta for market share. At $260,000 and below, Ace offers customers significantly greater value than Beta. Between $200,000 and $220,000, Ace may sell many furnaces with good profit margins. But these prices will encourage a strong response from Beta. Ace must plan how to address Beta's likely actions.

When setting price, Ace should also consider potential customer lifetime value (CLV). Ace should ask several questions. Is this a one-time purchase, or will customers purchase more furnaces? Can Ace sell furnace parts and accessories and/or multiyear service contracts? Can Ace sell complementary products/services? Will customers recommend Ace to others? Responses should influence Ace's price-setting decisions.

Setting Price for a New Product

Incorrect approaches:
- Cost-plus
- Competitive equivalence

Correct approach:
1. Determine maximum price
2. Determine minimum price
3. Set price based on:
   - Strategic objectives
   - Likely competitive response

FIGURE 22.1
Pricing Analysis for New Capital Equipment Item

KEY IDEA

Changing Price for an Existing Product
The firm must calculate required sales at the new price to make the same profit as at the current price.

CHANGING PRICE FOR AN EXISTING PRODUCT

The firm has many reasons to change price. Sometimes external competitive pressures are critical; other pressures may be internal. Financial managers want increased profit margins by raising prices. Or, seeking increased sales, the sales force lobbies for price decreases. Critical questions are:

- Can the firm *increase price* without losing significant sales volume? How much volume will the firm lose? Will incremental profit margin offset lost sales?

- If the firm *decreases price*, will it gain significant sales volume? How much volume will the firm gain? Will extra sales offset reduced profit margin?

To answer these questions, the firm must calculate the sales volume necessary — at the proposed price — for the firm to make the same profit as it earns at the current price. Figure 22.2 shows a five-step process for considering price changes. Before tackling this section, you should become familiar with Marketing Enrichment FM.1. **[308p]**

MARKETING ENRICHMENT FM.1
Financial Analysis for Marketing Decisions **308p**

....
FIGURE 22.2
Process for Determining Price Changes

Step 1: Reconfigure the traditional income statement. We partition costs into two categories — variable costs and fixed costs.[2] Table 22.2 is a simplified version of Marketing Enrichment FM.1 **[308p]** Table FM.4 (derived from the traditional income statement — Table FM.2).

....
TABLE 22.2
Illustration: Product Income Statement ($000s)

Sales Revenues (SR) (40 million lbs. @ 50 cents/lb. selling price [SP])	$20,000
Variable Costs (VC)	$12,000
Contribution Margin (CM)	$ 8,000
Fixed Costs (FC)	$ 6,600
Net Profit before Taxes (NP)	$ 1,400

Step 2: Calculate current contribution margin per unit. *Contribution margin* (CM) is an important concept. CM must cover fixed costs— any remainder is profit. CM equals (is identical to) sales revenues (SR) less variable costs (VC). (Hence, variable costs do not enter future CM calculations.)

Restated: $CM \equiv SR - VC$ On a per-unit basis, $SP - VCU \equiv CMU$

And: $SR \equiv CM + VC$ On a per-unit basis, $SP \equiv CMU + VCU$

Table 22.3 shows that *contribution margin per unit (CMU)* is simply CM on a per-unit basis — similarly for *variable cost per unit (VCU)*:

....
TABLE 22.3
Illustration: Contribution Margin per Unit (CMU) Calculation

	Totals ($000s)	Unit Sales (000s)*	Per Unit (lbs.)	Units (cents)
Sales revenue (SR) *less*	$20,000	40,000	Price per unit (SP)	50 cents
Variable costs (VC) *equals*	$12,000	40,000	Variable cost per unit (VCU)	30 cents
Contribution margin (CM)	$ 8,000	40,000	**Contribution margin per unit (CMU)**	**20 cents**

* lbs.

Step 3: Proposed price change: Calculate new contribution margin per unit. Suppose the firm is considering two options: raise price by 5 cents; lower price by 5 cents. VCU does not change. But:

- **Decrease price.** A price reduction from 50 cents to 45 cents *decreases* CMU:

  $SP \equiv VCU + CMU$ so that:

     45 cents $\equiv$ 30 cents + 15 cents
     Hence, new CMU = **15 cents/lb.**

- **Increase price.** A price increase from 50 cents to 55 cents *increases* CMU:

SP ≡ VCU + CMU   so that:

  55 cents ≡ 30 cents + 25 cents
  Hence, new CMU = **25 cents/lb.**

Step 4: Determine new sales targets. Determine what sales volumes are necessary — at the proposed 45 cents/lb. and 55 cents/lb. prices — to make the same profit — $1.4 million — as at the current 50-cent/lb. price. These are minimum requirements:

- **Decrease price.** Unit sales volume for $1.4 million profit when price = 45 cents/lb.:

Target sales volume (lbs.)	= (Fixed costs + profit objective)/CMU
	= ($6.6 million + $1.4 million)/15 cents
	= $8 million/15 cents
	= **53.3 million lbs.**
Percent sales volume increase	= (53.3 – 40 million) × 100 /40 million
	= **33.25%**
Target sales revenue ($)	= 53.3 million lbs. × 45 cents/lb.
	= **$24 million**

If the firm *reduces* price to 45 cents/lb., it must sell at least 53.3 million pounds (33.25% increase) — $24 million — to make the same profit as previously.

- **Increase price.** Unit sales volume for $1.4 million profit when price = 55 cents/lb.:

Target sales volume (units)	= (Fixed costs + profit objective)/CMU
	= ($6.6 million + $1.4 million)/25 cents
	= $8 million/25 cents
	= **32 million lbs.**
Percent sales volume decrease	= (32 – 40 million) × 100 /40 million
	= **20%**
Target sales revenue ($)	= 32 million lbs. × 55 cents
	= **$17.6 million**

If the firm *increases* price to 55 cents/lb., it must sell at least 32 million pounds (20% decrease) — $17.6 million — to make the same profit as previously.

We summarize these results in Table 22.4.

Price	CMU	Target Volume (lbs.)	Sales Volume Percentage Change	Target Revenues
50 cents	20 cents	40 million	—	$20 million
45 cents	15 cents	53.3 million	+ 32.5%	$24 million
55 cents	25 cents	32 million	– 20%	$17.6 million

Step 5: Assess the risk/reward trade-off. The results from Step 4 *do not make* the pricing decision. The firm must assess the likelihood it can meet (or exceed) the new volume targets: 53.3 million lbs. ($24 million) @ 45 cents/lb.; or 32 million lbs. ($17.6 million) @ 55 cents/lb. The decision depends, in part, on competitive response. Considering all factors, the firm must decide whether or not to change price and take the chance of meeting or exceeding sales volume targets. (Marketing Enrichment 22.1 **[307p]** for a short-cut approach to assessing price changes.)

Isos is a small European computer services firm that priced its services at £75 per hour. Isos decided to raise prices but was concerned about potential negative customer reaction. Isos advised customers that prices would rise to £85 per hour in 30 days, but customers who paid in advance would remain at £75 per hour.

MARKETING QUESTION

The sales force is pressuring you to cut prices, so they can increase sales. Finance pushes for price increases to raise profit margins. What calculations would you complete before responding?

TABLE 22.4
Illustration: Summary of Pricing Calculations

MARKETING ENRICHMENT 22.1
A Short-Cut Approach to Assessing Price Changes **307p**

AVOIDING PRICE CHANGES

KEY IDEA

Many firms make a fixed offer, then vary price when under pressure. The firm may avoid price changes via a price menu — variable offers with fixed prices.

Many firms address pricing issues by assessing the value they offer customers, and then decide on the price. This approach often leads to considerable customer pressure for price reductions — *fixed offer, variable price*. An alternative approach for mitigating this pressure is to design several offers, each at a fixed price — *variable offer, fixed price*. The firm presents a *price menu*, including two or more product alternatives, and different delivery and/or service options like employee training, guaranteed supply, special packaging. Table 22.5 illustrates five separate price-menu options. IBM and Oracle each have web-based à la carte menus that salespeople and customers can access through password-protected portals.

The price-menu approach has two significant benefits. First, firms often add services to a base product and then charge higher prices. The price menu tests the value of extra services; if customers do not value the extra service, they will continue to buy the base product. Second, by pricing the product and service together in a single offer, the firm averages; some customers overpay (don't want services) and some underpay (use services). With a price menu, each customer selects the offer that best meets its needs. Information technology facilitates managing price menus, but the firm should ensure customers understand its price menu.

ChemX (disguised) sold additives for improving factory productivity, together with employee training and technical support. Sophisticated customers resented paying for unneeded services and purchased from low-price, low-service suppliers. Other customers bought sufficient additives to qualify for supplier support, but purchased large volumes from low-price suppliers. ChemX developed an à la carte price menu with services priced separately (except for long-term contracts). ChemX also cut prices to be more competitive with lower-priced suppliers.[3]

TABLE 22.5
Illustration: Price Menu

	Offer 1	Offer 2	Offer 3	Offer 4	Offer 5
Product version 1	*	*			*
Product version 2			*	*	
Delivery option 1	*	*	*		
Delivery option 2				*	*
Service 1		*	*	*	*
Service 2			*	*	*
Service 3					*
Price	$150	$155	$165	$175	$180

TACTICAL PRICING

Tactical pricing is the ongoing stream of pricing decisions the firm makes on a daily basis. Generally, robust strategic pricing drives good tactical pricing, but tactical pricing has a major impact on firm performance. One common misconception is that each product has a single price; in fact, single prices are rare. Table 22.6 shows the *pricing toolkit*, the variety of tools the firm can use to make price adjustments, often for individual customers. Undisciplined use of the toolkit can lead to *price-waterfall* problems (pp. 556–557).

TABLE 22.6
Selected Tools in the Pricing Toolkit

Acceptable currency	Company shares	Guarantees and warranties	Price stability
Allowances	Credit	Inventory carrying costs	Returns
Barter	Credit terms	Leasing	Slotting fees**
Bundling and unbundling	Discounts	List price	
Buy-backs	Freight	Markdown money*	

* Agreements by suppliers to make payments to retail customers if they offer discounts to consumers
** Payments by suppliers to retailers for shelf space in stores

THE PRICING TOOLKIT

Sometimes the firm wants price changes to be highly visible to customers and competitors; other times, the firm wants to keep price changes secret. Firms often set highly visible list prices (rate cards, rack rates), but make minimal sales at list price. Rather, list price is the basis for discounts and rebates; actual prices may be 20 or 30 percent off list. The firm can base discounts on many factors like firm/customer relationship, inventory, matching competitors, quantity, selling effort, timing.[4] Less visible ways to change price include allowances — for advertising, selling effort, trade-ins, and returns. Credit availability and terms (time to pay, interest rates) can be potent pricing tools, especially during inflation. This approach is very popular for FMCG firms.

Freight/shipping charges are important price-changing mechanisms. For CIF (cost, insurance, freight) prices, the supplier pays; for FOB (free on board) prices, the customer pays.[5] The firm can change price by modifying customer inventory arrangements: JIT (just-in-time) systems cut customer inventory holding costs; selling on consignment (pay when used) reduces inventory costs to zero. Leasing versus purchasing offers customers the ability to reduce capital employed; product guarantees and warranties reduce prices by protecting customers from repair costs. The firm should recognize that *toolkit* elements are differentially important across customers. For an equivalent price reduction, some customers may prefer larger discounts; others may prefer advertising allowances. In B2B, the reward system for purchasing staff may be important: Some customers incentivize staff based on price reductions off the invoice price. A cash discount applied when the firm receives the order may be very attractive! Sometimes firms and customers prefer buy-backs and barter to money transactions. Indeed, some firms providing services to startups accept payment in firm equity.

MARKETING QUESTION

Identify six specific pricing tools you have observed. Why do you think the supplier used them?

KEY IDEA

Single product prices are rare in the real world.

Price actions vary between highly visible and opaque.

Barter

• BAE Systems earned $20 billion revenues from Saudi Arabia for Tornado fighters, Hawk trainers, and backup services. Most payments were in oil.

• During an Argentinian recession, consumers acquired food and clothing, psychological counseling, and dental work, all by barter.

• In Siberia's Altai territory, over 50 percent of economic transactions are bartered; some large firms transact 90 percent of business by barter.

• Sloty (disguised) (Polish firm) contracted with Norton to erect a turn-key grinding wheel factory. Partial payment to Norton was a *buyback* of products made in the plant.[6]

• Travelers purchase products in low-price countries — Gucci/Louis Vuitton handbags, iPhones (U.S.) — then secure the arbitrage by bartering (or reselling) for goods and services at home.

The firm can also modify prices by shifting between *unbundling* — pricing items separately (like an à la carte restaurant meal), and *bundling* — each offer has a single price (like a prix-fixe meal). *Mixed bundling* combines bundled and unbundled prices — Chapter 12. Amazon Prime is an interesting example of a bundled offer — unlimited shipping for a fixed price, bundled with any and all purchases.

POCKET PRICES AND PRICE WATERFALLS

Some firms use toolkit items appropriately, but many firms have poor systems for tracking use. List price and invoice price are transparent, but other pricing elements are often deeply buried in myriad financial accounts: early payment discounts — interest-expense account; cooperative advertising allowances — promotion and advertising accounts.[7] Hence, these firms do not know their *pocket prices* — the money they actually receive (in their pockets). When firms conduct pocket-price analysis, they are often surprised to find a broad price range, but little rationale — Figure 22.3 (p. 557). Small-volume customers may receive large discounts; high-volume customers do not. The most aggressive, clever, and/or persistent customers get the best prices, aka *squeaky wheel* syndrome. These customers manipulate supplier management systems for extra discounts; firm salespeople often cooperate:

> Knowing Oracle's concern with end-of-quarter results, customers waited for salespeople to offer larger discounts. Oracle booked most sales at end of quarter. To address this problem, Oracle rejected some last-minute deals with large discounts (Opening Case).

FIGURE 22.3
Hypothetical Pocket-Price Band for Industrial Parts Manufacturer

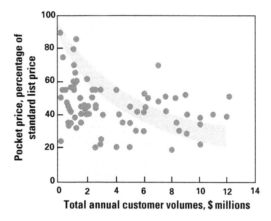

The *price waterfall* — Figure 22.4 — illustrates how pricing-toolkit elements cumulate to produce the pocket price.**[166v]** Customers can earn 27.6 percent reductions from four separate discounts (1 to 4) to make the invoice price 72.4 percent of standard list price. They can also earn 15.3 percent reductions from seven other toolkit items (5 to 11) to make the pocket price 57.1 percent of list price.[8]

FIGURE 22.4
Hypothetical Price Waterfall for Consumer Durables Manufacturer Averaged over All Accounts. Average Discount from Standard List Price (percent)[9]

To optimize pricing, the firm must understand the pocket price for each customer, and the way these prices develop. This task may not be easy; the firm may have to modify its accounting systems. Agricultural firm Syngenta's Brazilian subsidiary built a software program to estimate currency shifts, employee commissions, freight charges, and other costs for calculating pocket prices for proposed sales. Soton (disguised) took several initiatives to address price-waterfall problems:

- Acted aggressively to bring overdiscounted customers into line with other customers.
- Delivered specific benefits/values to profitable customers to increase sales volumes.
- Brought price setting under control by improving the accounting system.
- Tightened up discounts and based sales force compensation on the pocket price.

KEY IDEA

The firm requires good systems to track pricing-toolkit elements.

Pricing-toolkit elements produce the pocket price via the price waterfall.

Pricing-toolkit elements are differentially important to customers.

DESIGNING PRICING APPROACHES

Several pricing methods are available for managers with pricing responsibility:

PRICE DISCRIMINATION — VARIABLE PRICING

The firm optimizes profits by setting different prices for different customers and market segments — some pay more, others pay less.[10] The firm can amplify this effect by designing multiple offers with different values: AmEx offers several personal credit cards — green, gold, platinum, black — at successively higher prices. The core benefit — charging payments — is identical, but extra services differentiate the offers. Consider an historical illustration from 19th-century French railroads:

> An 18th-century economist explained the rationale for price discrimination: "It is not because of the few thousand francs which would have to be spent to put a roof over the third-class carriages or to upholster the third-class seats that some company or other has open carriages with wooden benches ... What the company is trying to do is to prevent the passengers who can pay the first-class fare from traveling third-class: it hits the poor, not because it wants to hurt them, but to frighten the rich ... And it is again for the same reason that companies, having proved almost cruel to the third-class passengers and mean to the second-class one, become lavish in dealing with first-class passengers. Having refused the poor what is necessary, they give the rich what is superfluous."[11]
> (For a contemporary example.[593p])

Regardless, the firm may benefit from an inflexible single price. When salespeople have no *price discretion*, aggressive customers cannot negotiate price discounts (Oracle boxed insert, p. 557). Also, a single price is simpler to understand and provides a perception of fairness, like CarMax's *no haggle* pricing policy for automobiles.

DYNAMIC PRICING

Dynamic pricing is a special case of *price discrimination* when demand varies over time. Some prices change *predictably*, like cities setting road and bridge tolls higher during rush hours and/or on weekdays, lower on weekends.[12] Electric utilities, movie theaters, and telecommunications firms price by time of day; hotels price by day of the week and season. Some firms advertise special prices and/or offer products for limited time periods to create a sense of urgency; when time is up, they raise prices significantly, and/or withdraw the product.

Airlines use dynamic pricing continuously and *less predictably* via *yield management* systems — algorithms adjust fares based on demand and available seat capacity. European discount airlines like easyJet and Ryanair set low fares weeks before the flight, then raise prices as seats fill and flight time approaches. Other services like hotels and Broadway shows employ similar processes to optimize revenues, but in reverse — prices start high, then reduce as the date/start time approaches. The San Francisco Giants (major league baseball) uses data like past ticket sales, day and time of game, team record, pitching match-up, weather, and secondary market prices to set prices for individual games.

More recently, e-commerce firms use dynamic pricing for physical goods, often changing prices several times daily in response to competitive offers. Customers seem to accept dynamic pricing but sometimes believe it is unfair. Coke announced the pending installation of new vending machines: prices would increase as temperatures rose; the storm of protest led Coke to back off.[13]

> United Airlines (UA) personalizes dynamic pricing online. Suppose a customer uses a PC to search for a specific route and day, selects a flight, then returns later for booking. UA's *booking* price may be higher than the original *search* price. Relatedly, if that customer were to use a different PC, UA would offer the original lower price — cookies!

MARKETING QUESTION

Compare and contrast pricing in 19th-century French railroads with 21st-century passenger air travel.

MARKETING QUESTION

Next time you fly, ask fellow travelers what fare they paid. What is the basis for price differences? Be prepared for them — or you — to be disgruntled!

KEY IDEA

Important approaches to pricing include:

- Price discrimination — variable pricing
- Dynamic pricing
- Variable-rate versus flat-rate pricing
- Customer-driven pricing
- Auction pricing

MARKETING
QUESTION

In your educational institution, the most popular courses are oversubscribed; some students must take less popular courses. In an attempt to solve this problem, CasU (disguised) introduced a two-tier pricing system: More popular courses had a higher price. How do you react to this approach?

VARIABLE-RATE VERSUS FLAT-RATE PRICING

Firms selling services can price by use — *variable rate*; or by time period — *flat rate*. Variable prices may earn greater revenues, but flat-rate prices are generally easier (and less costly) to administer.[14] Previously, ski resorts charged for chair lifts by the ride — variable rate; but today, most charge per day, week, or season — flat rate. Commuter rail travelers and season ticket holders for sporting and cultural events pay a flat-rate price; others pay by the trip/event. Some firms combine flat rates and usage fees, like smartphone service providers.

CUSTOMER-DRIVEN PRICING

In many markets, sellers set a price; buyers accept the seller's price, or they do not.[15] In customer-driven pricing, the customer names the price; the firm can accept or not. At Priceline.com, customers *name their own price* for automobiles, hotel reservations, mortgages, and airplane tickets. If the product/service is available, customers *must* complete the purchase. Customer-driven pricing has significant potential in service businesses where suppliers cannot inventory their offers.

AUCTION PRICING

Auction pricing is a form of customer-driven pricing where customers compete with each other to purchase products. Auctions are increasingly popular in e-commerce. Alternative types of auction are:

ENGLISH AUCTION. Used especially for secondhand items. Prices start low; potential buyers bid up the price. Auctioneers seek the buyer willing to pay the highest price. Typically, the seller sets a *reserve price*; if the price does not reach the reserve, the seller withdraws the product. eBay and Amazon.com use English auctions; similarly, Ticketmaster auctions the best seats to concerts.

VICKREY AUCTION. A *sealed-bid* English auction where the winning bidder pays the price of the second-highest bid.[16] eBay employs Vickrey auctions; so does Google for online advertising.

DUTCH AUCTION. Prices start high; the seller reduces price until a buyer bids. Originally used in flower auctions in The Netherlands, Google used a Dutch auction for its IPO.

INTERNET AUCTIONS. Typically, Internet auctions use either the English or Vickrey approach. But in contrast to traditional auctions — single location and completed in one hour or less — bidders in Internet auctions are highly dispersed geographically. Furthermore, Internet auctions may continue for several days, hence imposing significant monitoring costs.

REVERSE AUCTION. This type of auction is for suppliers. The customer states requirements; suppliers bid to provide the product. Prices go down and the lowest bidder wins the business[17]:

Car Inc. (CI) (disguised) authorized 25 suppliers to bid in a 20-minute reverse auction for plastic automobile parts. The benchmark (starting) price was the most recent price — $745,000. The first bid was $738,000; after 10 minutes the price was $612,000. Thirty seconds before planned auction closing, the price was $585,000; each extra bid added one minute of bidding. After 13 more minutes, bidding concluded; CI paid $518,000.

MARKETING
QUESTION

Why did the Chilean firm come off so badly? What makes for a successful reverse auction for the customer? For the supplier?

Many suppliers worry that reverse auctions lead to lower prices, but exceptions occur. A Chilean firm used a reverse auction to purchase a mining chemical. Two profitable suppliers competed. Each roughly knew the other's costs, but neither had sufficient capacity to satisfy the full requirement. Also, each supplier had a *most-favored-nation* clause with its major customer; these customers received the lowest price offered to any other customer. The reverse auction took five minutes; the final price was 45 percent above the previous price. The Chilean firm tried to nullify the auction, but the suppliers refused.

SETTING THE ACTUAL PRICE

Setting the actual price raises several important issues:

MARKETING
QUESTION

Suppose your revenue goal for a service offering is $50. Various managers have suggested the following communications and pricing approaches:

- Advertise and price the service at $50.
- Advertise a $45 price, then add a $5 surcharge at the time of purchase.
- Advertise a $55 price with a $5 discount.

Which option will you choose? Why?

FEES AND SURCHARGES

Many firms use *fees and surcharges* to increase pocket prices, especially in difficult economic times. Banks charge for ATM use and bounced checks; telecoms charge fees for directory assistance, setup, change of service, number portability, and service termination; airlines charge fees and surcharges for checked bags, flight changes, fuel, pillows, and preferred seats (aisle, extra legroom [exit rows], and front of plane). Revenues and profits increase, but overly aggressive fees may lead customers to go elsewhere — they don't like being nickel-and-dimed.

Several Internet banks and Virgin Mobile USA (cell phone service) are examples of successful firms that make pricing simple and transparent.[18]

PROMOTIONAL PRICING VERSUS STEADY PRICING

In many situations, sales are sensitive to short-term price promotions — Chapter 16. Firms often execute price promotions by comparing the sale price with the regular (reference) price — the *anchor*. In *loss-leader pricing*, retailers deliberately take losses on some products to build customer traffic and sell other products. Despite sales increases, promotions can have negative effects:

- **Brand image.** The promotion negatively affects brand image, especially upscale and luxury brands.
- **Diversion.** Retailers and/or distributors *divert* products to noncompeting outlets, often in different geographies.
- **Hidden costs.** Frequent price promotions can be difficult and costly to administer. Relatedly, addressing competitor price promotions via price-matching guarantees is difficult to implement consistently across many selling outlets, leading to customer dissatisfaction.
- **Poor forecasting.** Demand exceeds forecast and customers are upset. Hong Kong Disneyland's one-day discount tickets were not valid on *special days* like Chinese New Year. Chinese New Year was four days in Hong Kong but longer in mainland China. When Chinese New Year was over in Hong Kong, but still continued on the mainland, mainlanders flooded into Hong Kong. Disneyland had to close its gates.
- **Time-shifting.** Customers buy for inventory to avoid paying the full price later.

KEY IDEA

Considerations in setting actual prices include:

- Fees and surcharges
- Promotional pricing versus steady pricing
- Psychological pricing
- Pricing bases

Some firms have abandoned promotional pricing. P&G introduced *everyday low pricing*; Burger King stopped using promotional devices like coupons and discounts. JCPenney abandoned sales promotions, but revenues dropped substantially; customers who found value in the *thrill of the chase* for the best deal went elsewhere. JCPenney reintroduced promotions, having failed to *retrain* customers! Groupon price promotions require minimum buyer numbers to form a *group*, hence fueling word of mouth among anxious buyers to avoid cancellation.

PSYCHOLOGICAL PRICING

For many customers, the psychological distance from $9.95 to $10.00 is greater than from $10.00 to $10.05; hence, many firms set prices to end with 95 cents.[19] Price framing is also important. Customers typically view an $8 product discounted to $7 more favorably than a $6 product with a $1 surcharge.[20] Indeed, firms use price to *frame* offers. Apple framed the iPhone's value with a $599 initial price; the subsequent $399 price seemed like a great deal. Relatedly,

Nook, a neighborhood restaurant in Manhattan's Hell's Kitchen, added an expensive filet mignon dish to its menu.

Louis Vuitton (LV) creates high-price, limited-edition *products of the year;* LV priced the *Theda* bag at US$5,550. Said factory director Stephen Fallon, "The aim of the fashion bags isn't to make money, but to make envy." Compared to the *product of the year,* LV's other bags are inexpensive, so they seem like bargains.[21]

PRICING BASES

Most industries have accepted bases for setting prices, typically by individual product. Changing the *price basis* may offer advantage. Some firms sell individual medical diagnoses rather than diagnostic machines; some software firms price per use rather than by software package. Japan's Viking chain of buffet restaurants sets prices in *yen per minute* to increase customer turns; Zipcar prices by annual membership fee plus a per hour charge versus daily or weekly prices at most car-rental firms. Relatedly, customers pay $99 annually for Amazon Prime, then receive unlimited free two-day shipping and other benefits. In Africa, Asia, and Latin America, fast-growing Millicom International Cellular charges customers per second (versus per minute). Some B2B firms share risk with customers by *gain sharing* — receiving partial payment in customer profits earned with their products; customers pay advertising agencies by results rather than percentage of billings (traditional).[22] Auction firms Christie's and Sotheby's offer customers price guarantees for artwork, but share differences in price above the guarantee (plus sales commissions).

TelServ (TS) (disguised) sold, installed, and maintained telephone switch boxes containing various numbers of switches; installation costs drove prices for maintenance service. TS found customer value was more related to number of maintained switches. TS then priced per switch, lowering some prices and raising others; profitability improved.

SPECIAL TOPICS IN SETTING PRICES

We examine several special pricing topics:

COMPLEMENTARY PRODUCT PRICING

Complementary products are used together — hot dogs and buns, automobiles and spare parts, vacuum cleaners and bags, printers and cartridges, movies and popcorn. The firm must make a two-part pricing decision. Gillette is well known for pricing razors low and blades high, but strong differential advantage from recent innovations lets Gillette price each component high. HP Inc. prices printers low and cartridges high, but faces strong competition from low-price cartridge refills. In the U.S., wireless carriers heavily subsidize cell phones in exchange for multiyear service contracts.

KEY IDEA

Special pricing topics include:
- Complementary product pricing
- Gray market pricing
- Pay-what-you-want pricing
- Topsy-turvy pricing
- Transfer pricing

Timing can be critical. Sometimes it makes sense to lock in customers with an initial sale, then upsell later — like selling a car and later offering a special-deal options package. Other times, it may be more advantageous to offer additional items simultaneously with the main purchase.[23]

FREE. Sometimes firms set a zero price — FREE. FREE may be useful in several situations[24]:

- *Cross-subsidies.* One product is FREE; a second product is not free. To encourage increased purchases, Amazon provides FREE shipping for orders more than $35; cell phone carriers provide FREE phones for multiyear-subscription contracts. Some clubs offer FREE entry to women, but men must pay.

- *Multiple versions.* The firm offers a limited product version FREE. The firm hopes some portion of FREE customers will upgrade to enhanced versions and pay. FREE is common for software and on the Internet: Monty Python launched a free channel on YouTube; sales of movies and TV shows increased by 23,000 percent. Earlier, the Grateful Dead allowed fans to tape concerts free; merchandise and ticket sales increased.

- *Nonfinancial goals.* Psychological motives like personal achievement and altruism may drive organizational member goals. Craigslist, Wikipedia, and Linux fall into this category.

- *Public image.* Many people and organizations criticize prescription drug firms for high prices. Merck's long-standing program provides FREE drugs to combat river blindness (endemic in parts of Africa and Latin America); in the recession, Pfizer provided drugs FREE to people who lost jobs.

- *Trial.* The firm provides free samples, or allows service access for a limited time, so customers enjoy the experience. Many FMCG firms and retailers use this approach.

- *Two-sided markets.* The firm offers products FREE in one market — *subsidy side*; then secures revenues from the second market — *money side*. Consumers enjoy Internet search, radio, TV, and websites FREE; advertisers pay for consumer attention. Relatedly, employers pay, job seekers do not; home sellers pay agents, home buyers do not.[25] Google provides Android FREE to handset makers (more than 300), and software development kits FREE to app makers; Google earns revenues from increased advertising on mobile devices.[26]

GRAY MARKET PRICING

Gray markets undercut firm strategy.[27] Gray markets develop when the firm sells similar products in different markets at different prices. Customers purchase products in low-price markets, then ship for resale to high-price markets — *diversion*. Suppliers can avoid gray markets by reducing price dispersion.[28] Goodyear gave large discounts to regional tire distributors; some resold tires in other regions; Goodyear reduced discounts to stop the practice. Of course, when products are in short supply, resellers may set prices higher than the original price.**[824v]**

PAY-WHAT-YOU-WANT PRICING

In a pricing innovation, British rock band Radiohead released *In Rainbows* as a digital download; customers chose their own prices! Many charitable organizations traditionally offer services on this basis, and restaurants in several countries have adopted similar pricing approaches.[29] These organizations rely on customers' sense of fairness and satisfaction to earn revenues.[30] Wessex Press, publisher of *Managing Marketing in the 21st Century* and other textbooks, previously offered read-online versions, but discontinued the practice.

TOPSY-TURVY PRICING

Typically, airlines pay airport authorities for gate access and other services. But Ryanair makes agreements with small cities it selects as destinations. These cities often pay Ryanair significant subsidies for landing and ground-handling fees, funds for hiring staff, marketing new routes, office space, and hotel accommodations.[31]

MARKETING QUESTION

How do you assess the previously used pay-what-you-think-it's-worth (pay what you want) pricing approach for *Managing Marketing in the 21st Century*? Why do you think Wessex Press stopped this practice? As incoming marketing director, what prices would you set for print and PDF versions of *Managing Marketing in the 21st Century*? Why? How does the secondary market affect your decision?

Suppliers and customers exchange value. The firm provides product/service value; the customer provides monetary value via the price. But sometimes the customer provides additional value and the supplier, not the customer, pays the price — *topsy-turvy pricing*. Sports teams typically pay medical practitioners to treat players, but some hospitals and medical practices receive value by calling themselves *official medical providers*. They pay sports teams up to $1.5 million annually to treat players.

Relatedly, sometimes patent holders make *reverse* payments to potential competitors — *pay for delay* — to extend monopoly positions, especially in pharmaceuticals.

TRANSFER PRICING

Firms set *transfer prices* among business units and geographic subsidiaries — like a firm in Australia shipping to a sister subsidiary in Italy. Of course, transfer prices affect subsidiary profits and, internationally, firm tariff and tax liabilities. Thousands of U.S. firms legally avoid income taxes by converting U.S. sales to paper profits in countries with lower tax rates.[32]

PRICING MANAGEMENT

"At Alcoa, we have pricing responsibility clearly delineated by customer. For example, Airbus pricing comes through a system. It doesn't matter where the product is made; individual plants do not quote prices. The same is true for automotive. We assign one individual to make sure we offer the best price, best cost, best delivery, best everything — at any given time. The most senior marketing manager for mill products is responsible for pricing all aerospace products anywhere in the world. But he cannot offer Airbus a contract without a few of us reviewing it at the market sector/lead team level."[33]

Now that you have learned about critical underpinnings of pricing decisions — Chapter 21 — and actually setting prices — Chapter 22 — you probably have several questions. How should the firm create a *price management* structure? How should the firm set prices? Who should be responsible? Generally, centralized pricing provides greater control; decentralized pricing offers greater market sensitivity. But decentralized pricing may also have long-run negative effects[34]:

KEY IDEA

The firm should develop pricing policies at high managerial levels.

Price setting can be a strategic capability.

- **Information sharing.** Customers talk to each other about prices; those paying higher prices exert pressure for price reductions.
- **Limited perspective.** Local decision-makers like salespeople are unlikely to consider the potential long-run impact of local price reductions on the entire firm customer base.
- **Negotiation.** Customers learn to place end-of-period orders when suppliers are anxious about revenues and may reduce prices. They also learn to play off multiple vendors against each other.

For these reasons, many firms develop pricing policies via a governance process that addresses long-run strategic questions like pricing new products, as well as short-term tactical decisions. These policies set guidelines for price discounts by product and channel, often across thousands of products. These guidelines include *escalation* processes to more senior managers that decentralized salespeople/sales managers may employ in special situations. They also set guidelines for multiperson buying decisions like those involving purchasing agents (tend to focus on price), and engineers, operations, and marketing personnel (other concerns). To enforce strategic pricing (and avoid slippage to cost-plus behavior), Parker Hannifin (PH) (Chapter 21 boxed insert, p. 541) appointed a series of divisional pricing specialists.

Some experts argue that price setting is a strategic capability, comparable to new product development and advertising.[35] Most firms have significant capabilities for *creating* customer value, but less expertise in *measuring* and *capturing* value. Far too often, managers with pricing responsibility do not understand price-volume-profit trade-offs. These managers lack good analytic skills; they rely instead on gut instinct, hearsay, response to competitors, and *rules of thumb*. Polaroid failed to exploit an early lead in digital-imaging technology because it was unable to capture value.[36] When Sun Country Airlines temporarily suspended operations, the CEO complained it had insufficient expertise to price routes effectively. Even GE Chairman Jeffrey Immelt fessed up; "[we] did an analysis of our pricing in appliances and found that about $5 billion is discretionary [by the sales force] ... with the prices we charge, we're too sloppy."[37]

As competition increases globally and earning profits becomes more difficult, successful firms develop human, systems, and social capital for improving pricing decisions — Roche Marketing University (below). Igoods (IG) industrial goods firm (disguised) set up a *war room* with wall charts and complex graphs. IG cross-functional teams met daily to monitor the flow of leads, quotes, and signed deals; target customers; and watch the win rate. Teams updated a dashboard weekly so IG executives had a clear view on sales revenues, discounting trends, and key account behavior. The war room helps the firm price competitively and gives the sales force the best possible advantage when bidding against competitors.[38] Firms that develop the appropriate capabilities and focus significant effort on pricing make better pricing decisions.

Roche Marketing University

Pharmaceuticals giant Roche builds pricing knowledge and teaches three areas of pricing capability:

- *Human capital.* Broad pricing knowledge at decision makers' command.
- *Social capital.* Ability to negotiate agreements on prices among firm decision-makers. Marketing may want *low steady* prices to demonstrate *good value*; salespeople may want high prices with discount flexibility so they can make sales and be heroes, and/or if they know buyers earn rewards for securing discounts off list price.
- *Systems capital.* Supports pricing decisions by:
  - Assembling accurate information on customer purchase history, including actual prices paid.
  - Managing price changes.[39]
  - Providing product and customer profitability.
  - Quickly responding to requests for price quotations.
  - Testing different prices.
  - Tracking competitor prices and discounts.
  - Tracking firm prices, discounts, and reasons for different customer discounts.

KEY MESSAGES

- To set price for a new product, the firm should start with perceived customer value; consider costs; then factor in competitors, and its strategic objectives.
- When contemplating changing price for an existing product, the firm should use a contribution margin approach to assess volumes required to meet various profit targets, then assess risk/return trade-offs at the various prices.
- The firm may avoid frequent price changes by implementing a price-menu system.
- Many pricing-toolkit elements are available for setting the actual price.
- Undisciplined use of pricing-toolkit elements leads to price-waterfall problems. Appropriate systems and pricing discipline address these problems.
- The firm should consider many issues in designing pricing approaches and setting actual prices.
- To set prices well, the firm must invest in human, systems, and social capital.

MARKETING QUESTION

What other messages did you glean from this chapter?

Summary questions for making better pricing decisions — Table 22.7.[40]

1. What is the pricing objective as per the market strategy?
2. What value do customers perceive in the firm's product/service?
3. Is there variation in customer-value perceptions? Search for segments.
4. How price sensitive are customers?
5. How are competitors likely to respond to firm prices?
6. What is the optimal approach to setting prices — variable pricing, dynamic pricing, variable-rate pricing, flat-rate pricing, customer-driven pricing, auction pricing?
7. What pocket price does the firm receive?
8. What emotional reactions do customers have to prices?
9. How do factors like brand preferences, demand shifts, and seasonality affect price?
10. Which customers are profitable to serve?[41]

VIDEOS AND AUDIOS

For complimentary material, see Axcess Capon codes at www.axcessvids.com

Segmented Pricing   **256v** 🌐   Hitendra Wadhwa   Columbia Business School

QUESTIONS FOR STUDY AND DISCUSSION

Can you answer the questions implied by this chapter's learning outcomes? Check!

1. Should movie theaters charge variable prices like live theaters? Why or why not?

2. Select a product that interests you. What price would you set? Why? Does your recommended price differ from the current price? Why or why not?

3. Table 22.8 shows Printfirm (disguised) inkjet printer and cartridge prices:

	Price	Variable Cost	Unit Sales	Price Elasticity
Printer	$400	$300	100,000	−2.5
Cartridges	$ 25	$ 10	10 per printer	−1.0

Printfirm is considering three pricing options:
- Increase printer price by 10 percent
- Increase cartridge price by 10 percent
- Reduce printer price by 5 percent and increase cartridge price by 10 percent

What advice would you offer Printfirm?

4. How would you go about setting price for a subscription-based online specialized news site, automobile repair shop, accounting service?

5. Canon distributes digital cameras to many retail chains. These chains compete, in part by differentiating on price. What are the implications for a retail chain, and for Canon?

TRUE/FALSE QUESTIONS

Answers on page A2 and at www.axcessvids.com — 703p

1. Tactical pricing is the ongoing stream of pricing decisions that firms make on a daily basis.
   ❏ **TRUE** ❏ **FALSE**

2. Common misconception: A product has multiple prices; in fact, single prices are most common. ❏ **TRUE** ❏ **FALSE**

3. In an English auction, the customer states its requirements and suppliers bid to provide the product. Prices go down and the lowest bidder wins the business. ❏ **TRUE** ❏ **FALSE**

4. Three important areas of pricing capability are human capital, social capital, and systems capital. ❏ **TRUE** ❏ **FALSE**

5. The price waterfall refers to the fact that because the firm provides customers with discounts and allowances, the pocket price is often considerably less than the list price. ❏ **TRUE** ❏ **FALSE**

MULTIPLE CHOICE QUESTIONS

Answers on page A2 and at www.axcessvids.com — 451p

1. A _____ is the variety of tools the firms can use to make price adjustments, often for individual customers.
   a. pricing toolkit
   b. product portfolio
   c. perceptual map
   d. factor portfolio

2. Pricing services by use is referred to as _____.
   a. fixed-rate pricing
   b. penetration pricing
   c. marginal pricing
   d. variable-rate pricing

3. A sealed-bid auction where the winning bidder pays the price of the second-highest bidder is called a(n) _____.
   a. English auction
   b. Dutch auction
   c. reverse auction
   d. Vickrey auction

4. Which of the following develop when the manufacturer sells similar products to multiple geographic markets at significantly different prices?
   a. gray markets
   b. black markets
   c. blue markets
   d. green markets

5. *Topsy-turvy* pricing occurs when:
   a. The supplier sets prices at a fixed percentage above competitor prices.
   b. The supplier raises then lowers prices at regular intervals.
   c. The supplier pays the customer, rather than the customer paying the supplier.
   d. The customer switches suppliers at regular intervals to secure the lowest prices.

CHAPTER 23

ENSURING THE FIRM IMPLEMENTS THE MARKET OFFER AS PLANNED

For complimentary material, see Axcess Capon codes at www.axcessvids.com

It is amazing what you can accomplish if you do not care who gets the credit.

— Harry S. Truman

LEARNING OUTCOMES

When you have completed this chapter, you will be able to:

- Understand how several externally oriented firms became successful via functional excellence.
- Examine how individual functional areas can create differential advantage.
- Recognize the challenges of creating an externally oriented firm.
- Deploy an organizational development model to facilitate becoming externally oriented.
- Explain the pros and cons of traditional and newer approaches of organizing for marketing.
- Appreciate the critical role of systems and processes, and human resources, in developing and implementing market strategy.
- Realize the importance of other functions in contributing to marketing as a philosophy.
- Understand the importance of integrating many organizational functions and business units.
- Take steps to ensure your firm maintains an external orientation.

OPENING CASE: BRISTOL-MYERS SQUIBB

Senior executives at Bristol-Myers Squibb (BMS) (multinational pharmaceutical/healthcare) concluded BMS needed greater market focus and greater consistency in marketing processes and application among therapeutic franchises and across the firm. The chief marketing officer, senior vice president for Marketing, and senior marketing leaders formulated and implemented a Marketing

Excellence *initiative with two main elements:* Marketing system — *a systematic and analytic approach to marketing;* Talent system — *an approach to career and talent development for all marketers. BMS also implemented a formal development program to educate and train marketers worldwide so as to embed marketing excellence within the culture.*

NEW MARKETING APPROACH. *The new vision reflected the importance of marketing to BMS. Marketers should strive and aspire to create a premier marketing firm, not just a premier pharmaceutical marketing firm. To achieve the vision, BMS studied marketing programs/frameworks at successful marketing firms like P&G and Starbucks.*

The primary impact of Marketing Excellence *was implementation of a specific marketing process across BMS. Previously, brand managers planned in an* ad hoc *fashion; senior management presentations reflected this individuality. Hence, making comparisons across brands, pharmaceutical franchises, and geographic regions, was difficult.* Marketing Excellence *provided a disciplined, systematic, and analytic approach that gave BMS a philosophy, consistent framework, and application tools to enable and empower marketers. The new approach facilitated better performance measurement and cross-brand comparisons.*

- **Marketing principles.** *BMS wanted to guide marketer thinking in three areas: customer focus, value and brand creation, and their collective strategic implementation. To illustrate,* principle 1: Marketers should secure deeper insights into customers and their interactions. *This principle was critical to BMS because of the many customer types it faced.* Principle 3: BMS should anticipate and out-maneuver competitors' activities. *This principle reflected increasing competition and the relatively short time to establish differential advantage.*

- **Brand-management choices.** *To be successful, marketers must make strategic choices from a set of options. BMS created a set of choices categorized as strategic, planning, and execution. Strategic choices: Deciding what the market definition is now and will be in the future; how BMS will differentiate the brand; what specific business opportunities are available for the brand; what future data are needed to support those opportunities. Planning and execution choices: How to implement the strategic choices by considering customer segmentation and messaging; specific brand tactics; measurement systems for plans and tactics. Marketers also had to establish alternative strategies and plans.*

- **Marketing application tools.** *BMS supported each choice with a specific set of tools, guiding questions, and worksheets to assist BMS marketers' thought processes.*

ENHANCE MARKETING COMPETENCE. *BMS believed embedding* Marketing Excellence *worldwide would require a sustainable infrastructure to develop and train marketers. In the first three years, around 400 BMS marketing executives of all levels attended programs directed and taught by Columbia Business School marketing faculty, approximately 25 participants per program.*

BMS marketers gained experience with the principles and choices; BMS developed a unique, innovative, and sustainable training program. The program comprised a mix of delivery methods to train new marketers and those transitioning into marketing. The curriculum was delivered via interactive case-driven learning accessed online, and through workshops facilitated by experienced BMS marketers designated as coaches.

RESULTS. Marketing Excellence *benefited BMS in three important areas:*

- **Cross-functional integration.** *The new approach encourages cross-functional teamwork and strongly recommends that marketers consult, inform, and align with functions like R&D, market research, medical affairs. The common framework provides a way to educate nonmarketers on marketing fundamentals, and provides a familiar approach across brands.*

- **International operations.** *BMS substantially changed its approach to international operations. Previously, regional and country heads had significant autonomy. Local executives made positioning decisions for new pharmaceuticals, including choice of brand names; BMS might position a specific product in several different ways, including different brand names. BMS placed core positioning decisions for new drugs centrally; local executives cannot change positioning.*

Case Question

How do you assess BMS' *Marketing Excellence* initiative? Do you think the design is applicable to firms in other industries?

Bristol-Myers Squibb

• **Marketing culture.** Marketing Excellence *fostered a strong marketing culture within BMS. Brand managers around the world follow the same process, and vocabulary is common. Plans are easily shared for cross-brand comparisons and best-practice sharing.*

Marketing Excellence *has embedded a sustainable and consistent approach to marketing within BMS; industry experts rate three consecutive product launches among the top 10 in pharmaceuticals.*

In previous chapters, we focused on gaining insight into markets, customers, competitors, complementers, the company; developing market strategy; and designing implementation programs around product, service, promotion, distribution, price. People with marketing titles tend to do much, but not all, of this work. By contrast, executing implementation programs involves many people throughout the firm, across several functional areas.

To execute well, the firm must practice the Principle of Integration, and seamlessly align various implementation programs with its market strategies. All employees must recognize that customers are central to firm success and act accordingly. Vision, mission, strategy form the superstructure within which employees do their jobs; firm values underpin its culture. Much of the difficult execution effort relates to organization structure, systems and processes, and human resource practices. Unfortunately, these elements tend to evolve slowly and lag both environmental changes and the firm's market strategies.

Chapter 1 shows that securing appropriate alignment is much easier when the firm has customer-focused values leading to a true external orientation. Chapter 23 presents a model for creating and maintaining an external orientation, including specific action steps. To frame the chapter, we show how several externally oriented firms became successful by achieving excellence in particular functional areas. We should all try to emulate these exemplars.

THE CHANGING VIEW

OLD WAY	NEW WAY
Customer satisfaction and loyalty are low priority	Customer satisfaction and loyalty are high priority
Hierarchy-based organization	Knowledge-based organization
Human resource factors are neglected	Human resource factors are highlighted
Internally oriented structures, systems, and processes	Externally oriented structures, systems, and processes
Marketing as a separate function	Marketing as everybody's business
Marketing seen as a department	Marketing seen as a philosophy
Market-share oriented	Shareholder and customer-value oriented
No customer information systems	Highly developed customer information systems
Operational focus	Strategic focus
Rigid, inflexible structures	Flexible, adaptive structures
Rules-driven	Values-driven
Sales and marketing are discrete	Sales and marketing are merging
Selection, training, rewards driven by bureaucracy	Selection, training, rewards driven by strategy

FUNCTIONAL EXCELLENCE IN SUCCESSFUL EXTERNALLY ORIENTED FIRMS

What does it take to deliver customer value and secure differential advantage? Successful firms deploy various resources and expertise to build core competence. Functional expertise includes customer service, finance, human resources, operations and the supply chain, research and development, and sales. Table 23.1 shows firms that leveraged such expertise for success.[1]

Functional Area	Company	Capability	Customer Benefit
Customer Service	Amazon	Collaborative filtering; one-click	Ease purchasing
	Fidelity	24/7/365 availability	Convenience
	Nordstrom	Values and reward system	Attentive personalized service
Finance	Monsanto	Accepts barter payment	Able to purchase without cash
	Praxair	Flexible billing system	Site-based bills to facilitate project management
	ComplyFirst	Accounts receivable function	Eliminate tedious activities
Human Resources	Google	Employee quality of life	Innovative products/services
	In-N-Out Burger	Training and benefits	Superior service
	Ritz-Carlton; Singapore Airlines	Selection and training	Superior service
Operations and the Supply Chain	Alcoa	Integrated operations and supply chain	Just-in-time delivery
	FedEx	System ownership	Reliability
	Walmart	Logistics and inventory management	Low prices
Research and Development	3M	Many new technologies	Innovative products
	Apple; Samsung	Design skills	Aesthetically pleasing, functional, trendy products
	DuPont; Monsanto	Research skills in chemistry	Productivity increases
Sales	Avon	*Avon Lady* sales force	Close personal relationships between buyer and seller
	Direct Line	Direct sales of insurance	Lower prices
	IBM	Global account management program	Partnership relationship with leading technology firm

TABLE 23.1
Delivering Customer Value and Securing Differential Advantage via Functional Excellence

MARKETING QUESTION

When you place an order online, many supplier functions are involved in getting the product to you. Chart out supplier processes.

MARKETING QUESTION

Think about your smartphone service provider. With what functions or departments have you had contact — mail, e-mail, retail store, customer-service representative? Did one area provide a good experience? Is this part of the supplier's differential advantage?

MARKETING QUESTION

Select three firms from Table 23.1. What resource investments are they making to maintain differential advantages?

CUSTOMER SERVICE

We previously discussed key dimensions of customer service — Chapter 13. Increased competition has made customer service strategically important for delivering customer value; securing differential advantage; and attracting, retaining, and growing customers. Yet, in many firms, customer service does not report to marketing. This may not matter when an external orientation is the firm's dominant philosophy and everyone is on the same page. But we have witnessed many cases where the *customer service* job focused on collecting payments against invoices, or when customers desiring service had long telephone waits (forced to hear Musak or an endlessly repeated message), then finally reached a clueless employee — *noncustomer service*. Poor customer service generates significant customer dissatisfaction, especially if expectations are high, and can destroy an otherwise effective market strategy.

Amazon CEO Jeff Bezos is dedicated to Amazon customers. Without follow-through and superlative service, Amazon could have suffered the fate of so many Internet startup failures. Amazon's website is easy to navigate, acknowledges orders immediately, personalizes the customer experience, remembers basic ordering information, and makes purchasing suggestions

What firm provided you personally with the best customer service? What was so great? How could your selected firm improve performance?

based on past behavior. Delivery performance is also excellent. Amazon's expansion well beyond books is fulfilling Bezos' vision of being the leading Internet retailer.

Mutual fund leader Fidelity is a fine example of customer-service excellence. Fidelity's key insight was that investors preferred to interact with brokers on their personal schedules, not just when the market was open. Fidelity's innovation was to become the first financial services firm open 24/7/365. Many other factors contributed to Fidelity's leadership, but the Fidelity Greenline Forum exemplifies customer confidence and trust in Fidelity. This online community comprises Fidelity investors who are passionate about smart investing and value highly the customer-service convenience Fidelity offers.

Some externally oriented firms differentiate their offers from tough competitors via customer-service excellence. Nordstrom (department store) is rightly famous for employees' customer-service zeal. Careful employee selection, enlightened management, and supportive incentive systems encourage the *right* behavior. Nordstrom accepts returned goods without question, sometimes from competitor stores! Recall our earlier message: Competitors eventually eliminate virtually all advantages. The quest for differential advantage must be central and ongoing.

FINANCE

Clearly, technical financial skills are a key success factor in finance departments, but financial decisions and controls play a critical role in managing the broader operations of any successful firm. Financial engineering is central to marketing major capital goods and services — from aircraft and earth-moving equipment to business systems. Externally oriented firms galvanize their finance and accounting functions; they contribute to marketing efforts in many ways, like helping to assess and quantify market opportunities.

Getting paid is a critical element in any business model, but sometimes the firm must be creative. Monsanto provides genetically modified seeds to large growers in many countries. When growers have difficulty paying cash, Monsanto accepts finished crops (barter); later, Monsanto sells these crops at market prices.

Which firms have finance operations that make doing business with them easier? What specifically do they do? How could they improve?

Invoicing and billing systems can be a major customer problem, but a good place to seek differential advantage. After all, the bill is one supplier communication customers always read! Praxair (industrial gases) has many construction customers that work simultaneously on different projects; they must account for costs by site and project. Praxair created a flexible billing system that offers customers this service.

ComplyFirst is a third-party administrator providing certification services for truckers. (Federal regulations require biannual certification.) Jack's Trucking (JT) (disguised) used a competitor service for all trucker-testing arrangements, but paid all physician and laboratory testing invoices directly. ComplyFirst agreed to pay all individual invoices and send JT a single monthly invoice. JT switched its entire trucker-certification business to ComplyFirst.

HUMAN RESOURCES

Human resources (HR) is a vital function for any business, but some firms create differential advantage by developing and motivating their workforces to achieve high levels of excellence. Many consulting firms claim HR advantages are the most sustainable since excellence in recruiting, selecting, onboarding, and *talent management* is difficult to copy. GE and IBM are well known for developing successive generations of business leaders; many former GE executives become CEOs of major corporations.

Google encourages an innovative culture via employee benefits. Many are free — Wi-Fi-equipped shuttles to/from San Francisco and its Mountain View campus, doctors, meals, clothes washers and driers (and detergent), flu shots. Other conveniences include car wash, oil change, climbing wall, lap pool, volley ball, ping pong (and other table games), massages, scooters, language study, lecture series, notaries, and an annual ski trip (all expenses paid). Google also makes payments for referring hires, having babies, and buying hybrid cars.

Firms as different as HCL Technologies (outsourced software developer) and In-N-Out Burger (INOB) (200+ outlets/southwest U.S.) succeed by putting employees first. INOB emphasizes employee training; above-market pay; retirement, and healthcare, and other benefits to earn greater per-store sales than McDonald's and Burger King.

Managing human resources is especially important in services firms, where employee/customer interaction is constant and ongoing. Major hotel chains like Four Seasons, Marriott, Ritz-Carlton place particular emphasis on employees at every organizational level.[2] Singapore Airlines' 40-year leading reputation among long-distance air travelers is primarily based on cabin service delivered by *Singapore Girls*. Virgin Atlantic has a similar capability and has achieved considerable success on North Atlantic routes. CEO Sir Richard Branson firmly believes that employees come first; if Virgin treats its employees right, they will treat Virgin customers right.

OPERATIONS AND THE SUPPLY CHAIN

Internal operations and *supply-chain* management are important areas for improving external focus, especially in services where firm/customer interactions are ubiquitous. All contemporary approaches to teaching operations start with firm strategy, then design systems by working backward from the marketplace. The operations system is a great place for securing differential advantage.[3] Of course, efficient operations and supply chain systems drive down costs and provide greater flexibility in pricing decisions.

Alcoa continuously introduces innovation into operating processes, including forecasting customer needs, and created advantages unlike other sheet metal providers. A senior executive explained how Alcoa integrates operations and the supply chain:

> "We spent a great deal of time trying to get accurate bills of material from our customers. It's very difficult in aerospace because customers don't think of airplanes in terms of extruded feet or pieces of sheet [metal]. They think in terms of tail assemblies, or speed brakes, or section 39 on a fuselage. After four years, we now have a bill of materials that is probably 80 percent accurate. So I can push a button and tell you how much product goes into a 757. We can tell the revenues and profitability. We supplement with an array of outside data to get a handle on billed rates and forecasting. We use five different sources, and supplement with a couple of good consultants to alert us to potential changes in the bills of materials. Airplanes are not static. Even if they are specified and the airworthiness certificate is built on a certain structure, the structure can change. We then pull together a five-year estimate by quarter — volume, product types, Alcoa share, and so forth. Then we can do facilities planning and capacity planning and get ahead on investments. Our investment cycle is rarely less than 12 to 24 months.
>
> "To make the system work day by day, we bring customer personnel into our plant, and we go to their plant. We see how their process is constructed and what information they're using. We usually do a lot of work to match the systems. We use a combination of electronic and paper kanbans. Our best illustration is the system we constructed for Ford, American Axle, General Motors, Dana for drive shafts for rear-wheel drive cars. They give us a piece-by-piece pull signal Monday morning. We build the requirement in truckload quantities. They send trucks in, starting at 2:00 on Wednesday. We have the exact piece of every spec; there could be 30, 40, 50 specs in 48 hours. Their truck can't wait more than 30 minutes. We're the only guys in the world that can do it. It used to take us 29 operations and about 9 weeks. Now we do it in 48 hours or less."[4]

FedEx constructed a unique model for shipping time-sensitive packages by forming its own airline and constructing a giant sorting facility in Memphis. The result: Consistent overnight package delivery in the continental U.S.

MARKETING QUESTION

Which firms do the best job of managing human resources? How does this translate into marketplace success criteria? Define key objectives and success criteria for HR. How do you assess jetBlue's approach?**[584v]**

KEY IDEA

The most successful externally oriented firms seek functional excellence in:

- Customer service
- Finance
- Human resources
- Operations and the supply chain
- Research and development
- Sales

  Integrating these efforts helps implement market strategy.

Walmart became the world's largest firm by offering everyday low prices, built on maintaining low costs throughout the supply chain. Walmart partners with suppliers to transmit point-of-sale data to improve forecasting. Walmart benefits from purchasing, manufacturing, and packaging efficiencies, and reduced inventory. Walmart also introduced *cross-docking*: The supplier drives its truck through a facility containing many Walmart store-delivery trucks and loads them directly. Systems for receiving goods and managing receivables and payables are paperless and highly efficient. Walmart is renowned for high stock-turns in most product categories and earns significant profits, despite low prices.[5]

RESEARCH AND DEVELOPMENT

R&D breakthroughs have given birth to many great firms. 3M, Apple, DuPont, GlaxoSmithKline (GSK), HP, Intel, Medtronics, Monsanto, Xerox are just a few that achieved and maintained pre-eminence based on technological strengths. When the firm manages the R&D/Marketing interface well, the impact can be dramatic.

3M has a formidable record for innovation combined with successful, even ingenious, marketing; 3M survived a period of excessive focus on internal process improvement, and has ratcheted up its innovation performance. Apple is the world's most valuable brand based on a continuous innovation culture. Macintosh computers have long offered elegant design and functionality. More recently, Apple's innovation process has produced game-changing products like the iPod, iTunes, iPhone, iPad. Over the years, DuPont and Monsanto have demonstrated consistent ability to build markets for many chemical industry products. Today, they compete vigorously in high-growth, genetically modified seeds.

SALES

The sales function rarely reports to marketing yet, as with customer service, selling is critical for implementing the market strategy. In Chapter 18, we discuss many aspects of the sales function and showed how innovation in sales can be the key to success. In B2C, several firms have gained differential advantage via innovative selling efforts or sales channels. Avon sells cosmetics differently from most cosmetics firms. *Avon Ladies* are independent businesswomen with close personal relationships to customers. These women consult on cosmetics issues, help customers select the most relevant products, and personally deliver orders. The traditional agency system for selling insurance products is very costly; in Britain, Direct Line's direct-selling Internet approach for automobile, business, home, and pet insurance allowed it to capture large market shares. Concerning B2B, we learned that firms like IBM and DHL are driving successful growth by innovating with key/strategic/global account programs. Better and faster data from customer relationship management (CRM) systems like SAP and salesforce.com can also provide differential advantage by enabling salespeople to offer customers greater value.

INTEGRATED SYSTEMS

Specific functional areas bring success to externally oriented firms. These firms succeed, not because of a single strong suit, but because they integrate efforts from many functions. Toyota is an outstanding example of high performance based on three integrated systems:
- **Research and development.** Toyota's process begins with extensive research into customer demographics and lifestyle trends. These data feed into four research and design studios in Japan, U.S. (2), and Europe. These studios compete for the best design in a target market.
- **Manufacturing.** Toyota's process is perhaps the world's best-known, most-discussed, and most-praised industrial operation. The Toyota system has spawned many books and is a model of Total Quality Management (TQM) — Chapter 14. Boeing and Airbus copied the Toyota system.

- **Dealer management and customer service.** Toyota invests heavily in dealers and customer service. All Toyota franchised dealers must adhere to a strong set of guidelines; if not, Toyota does not renew agreements. When Toyota introduced the Lexus, it installed a completely independent dealer system. The first Lexus cars had a minor quality problem; Toyota fixed the problem, filled the gas tank, and returned a clean car. For the first 10 years, each management employee telephoned four customers per month to gain real-time data on the car and dealer.[6]

Notwithstanding problems with unexpected acceleration in some cars, Toyota's excellence on multiple integrated dimensions made it the world's most profitable carmaker. Toyota products span the entire range of automotive offerings.

Transforming the Organization to Become Externally Oriented

Culture eats strategy for breakfast. — Peter F. Drucker

To achieve success in increasingly competitive markets, the firm must focus resources to deliver customer value and secure differential advantage. In the final analysis, nothing else matters. Continual realignment with the ever-changing environment is difficult but necessary; some firms do better than others. The most successful firms develop an *external orientation* culture.

Chapter 1 introduces the idea of organizational orientations; we described the external orientation and various *internal orientations*.[7] Firms with internal orientations focus on various internal functional needs, and are often excessively regimented and rule-based. But externally oriented firms look outward, focusing on customers, competitors, complementers, and broader environmental variables. These firms know that current products and processes are the key reasons for past and present success. But they also know the external environment is always changing; they must be sufficiently flexible to make internal changes — organization structure, systems and processes, human resources — to adjust to new market realities.[8] Rather than fearing change, externally oriented firms know change is inevitable; they welcome change as a challenge and understand new opportunities are the firm's *lifeblood*.

It's one thing to recognize the value of an external orientation; it's quite another to change the *status quo*. To make the transformation requires committed leadership, typically fewer management layers, new systems and processes and ways of working (like empowering customers in product development),[9] building new capabilities, and changes in mind-sets and behavior.[10] Top management exhortations are insufficient; successful implementation of an external orientation demands middle management support and work-group experts with informal power.[11]

> **KEY IDEA**
>
> Any model/framework for developing an external orientation must focus on customers.

Some successful corporate leaders believe instilling an external orientation is a critical part of their jobs; they institute *change-management* processes to accomplish this task. Intel owes its success to addressing environmental discontinuities, like legal and regulatory issues, and competitive challenges. When asked about his most important achievement, former CEO Andy Grove said: "It's that I've played a significant part in developing the work environment and culture at the company and with the directors."[12,13]

External Orientation. A senior executive of Valeo (French car-parts manufacturer) stated: "Customers expect seamless delivery, and they don't care how we are organized. We have to work as more of a team and forget our internal battles." Crossing divisional lines, Valeo developed seven principal *domains* — product areas broadly related to automobile functions. Valeo's new organization provides customer coherence in a highly complex structure.[14]

continues

MARKETING QUESTION

If you had been on the U.S. healthcare firm's management team, how would you have made this initiative succeed?

Internal Orientation. Three decentralized business units of a major U.S. healthcare firm separately sold products for use in hospital operating rooms. A corporate group decided the firm should develop a single integrated offer to better satisfy customer needs. Senior business-unit managers agreed with the rationale but could not make it work — too many entrenched interests, especially around pricing.

We demonstrate how to develop an external orientation. Figure 23.1 shows the standard inverted pyramid used by externally oriented firms like SAS and Nordstrom. This framework places customers at the top of the pyramid to reinforce their critical role in firm success.

....
FIGURE 23.1
Framework for Developing an External Orientation

MARKETING QUESTION

Select your two favorite firms; identify their values. Are these firms living up to their values? If not, where are they failing? What is the marketing significance of communicating these values?

KEY IDEA

An external orientation framework comprises:

Values
↓
Vision, Mission, Strategy
↓
Organizing the Firm's Marketing Efforts
↓
Systems and Processes
↓
Managing Human Resources

VALUES

A company's values — what it stands for and what it believes in — are crucial to its competitive success.

— Robert Haas, Chairman and former CEO Levi Strauss[15]

Values are a common set of beliefs that guide the behavior of all organization members, in all functions. Some values are *hard* — easily measured like profitability and market share; other values are *soft* — customer preeminence, integrity, respect for others, trust. Many firms use customer-focused value statements to emphasize the importance of building a customer-focused culture.

Values can be integral to firm success: Investment firm KKR (Kohlberg, Kravis, Roberts) employs accountability, excellence, fortitude, innovation, integrity, respect, sharing, teamwork. Certainly, misplaced (or absent) values can lead to failure. Arthur Andersen, Enron, Galleon, HealthSouth, Madoff Investments, Tyco, Worldcom are recent examples of firms losing their way. Previously, firm values were often unstated; today, many firms are rethinking corporate values and making them explicit and public (advertising, annual reports, websites). Many firms' values explicitly emphasize customers[16]:

- **Apple.** *Apple values are the qualities, customs, standards, and principles that the company believes will help it and its employees succeed. They are the basis for what we do and how we do it. Taken together, they identify Apple as a unique company. The values that govern our business conduct [are]: Empathy for Customers/Users, Aggressiveness/ Achievement, Positive Social Contribution, Innovation/Vision, Individual Performance, Team Spirit, Quality/ Excellence, Individual Reward, Good Management.*[494v]

- **Procter & Gamble.** *We show respect for all individuals; the interests of the company and the individual are inseparable; we are strategically focused in our work; innovation is the cornerstone of our success; we are externally focused; we value personal mastery; we seek to be the best; mutual interdependency is a way of life.*[17]

- **Seagate.** *People, customer success, excellence, innovation, teamwork, openness, social responsibility and sustained profitability — focus on our long-term perspective for leadership and prosperity. These values should inspire us to a level of excellence that maximizes value for customers, business partners, and shareholders, while supporting our employees and the communities in which our employees live and work. These values are intended to be a foundation to guide our decisions. They are reflected in our business objectives and they represent the global standard by which all of our individual and collective actions will be measured.*

- **Williams-Sonoma.** *We are in the business of enhancing the quality of our customers' life at home. To succeed, we live by a short, but important list of values — people first, customers, quality, shareholders.*

KEY IDEA

Organizational values are a common set of beliefs that guide the behavior of firm members. They are often integral to firm success.

Values statements are worthwhile only if the entire firm embraces them.

Merrill Lynch and L'Oreal show the importance of values, but with different results.

> Winthrop H. Smith Jr., son of a Merrill Lynch founder, blames Merrill's billions of dollars in subprime related losses on CEO Stan O'Neal's failure to embrace/articulate five core principles underlying Merrill's culture — primacy of client interests, respect for colleagues, teamwork, responsibility to the community, integrity.[18]

> L'Oreal is highly successful: "At L'Oreal, everyone shares a few common values — that's the heart of our culture. Everyone is passionate. We obsess with product, like touching products, feeling products. We're all very flexible, because we really change. We say that everyone's a product manager, even the CEO. The product only becomes successful by confronting opinions ... and changing the concept 25 times and the packaging 25 times. If you're not flexible, you'll be miserable here. We all share the same values but there's a very high premium placed on diversity, of different personality types and quirks. Our people are not stamped out of a mold."[19]

Values statements are more likely to *stick* if employees actively participate in their development; they are worthwhile only if the entire firm embraces them. Figure 23.2 (p. 577) shows J&J's credo: The credo epitomizes an external orientation that focuses on customer well-being and drives executive behavior. When Tylenol capsules were laced with cyanide (1982), J&J followed its credo by immediately withdrawing Tylenol capsules to protect customers from potential harm.[20]

An important component for installing an external orientation is developing *artifacts* that exemplify an external orientation like:

- Stories — examples of employees performing exceptional behavior like providing *over-the-top* customer service
- Arrangements — like an open and friendly entrance and welcome area
- Rituals — like customer events and awards for employee customer-oriented behavior
- Language — externally versus internally focused[21]

FIGURE 23.2
Johnson & Johnson Credo

**MARKETING
QUESTION**

In the 1982 cyanide-lacing crisis, J&J received many plaudits for acting consistently with its credo by withdrawing all Tylenol capsules from U.S. drugstores and supermarkets.

J&J's credo is alive and well, but in recent years, some J&J actions have fallen short of behavior required by the credo. What specific actions can you identify? Why did they occur? How should J&J proceed to secure full adherence with its credo?

> We believe our first responsibility is to the doctors, nurses and patients,
> to mothers and fathers and all others who use our products and services.
> In meeting their needs everything we do must be of high quality.
> We must constantly strive to reduce our costs
> in order to maintain reasonable prices.
> Customers' orders must be serviced promptly and accurately.
> Our suppliers and distributors must have an opportunity to make a fair profit.
>
> We are responsible to our employees,
> the men and women who work with us throughout the world.
> Everyone must be considered as an individual.
> We must respect their dignity and recognize their merit.
> They must have a sense of security in their jobs.
> Compensation must be fair and adequate,
> and working conditions clean, orderly and safe.
> We must be mindful of ways to help our employees
> fulfill their family responsibilities.
> Employees must feel free to make suggestions and complaints.
> There must be equal opportunity for employment, development
> and advancement for those qualified.
> We must provide competent management,
> and their actions must be just and ethical.
>
> We are responsible to the communities in which we live and work
> and to the world community as well.
> We must be good citizens — support good works and charities
> and bear our fair share of taxes.
> We must encourage civic improvements and better health and education.
> We must maintain in good order the property we are privileged to use,
> protecting the environment and natural resources.
>
> Our final responsibility is to our stockholders.
> Business must make a sound profit.
> We must experiment with new ideas.
> Research must be carried on, innovative programs developed
> and mistakes paid for.
> New equipment must be purchased, new facilities provided
> and new products launched.
> Reserves must be created to provide for adverse times.
> When we operate according to these principles,
> the stockholders should realize a fair return.

VISION, MISSION, STRATEGY

Beginning with a values statement emphasizing customer preeminence, all framework elements must reflect and reinforce company commitment to an external orientation. Many organizational transformations start at the bottom of the pyramid, developing/reworking external elements we discuss in Chapter 7:

KEY IDEA

Well-thought-through vision, mission, and strategy are critical for developing an external orientation.

- **Vision.** A description of the firm's ideal future state — an impressionistic picture of what the future should be. Good vision statements set a broad direction — they should inspire employees for the long run. A good vision statement is not too broad, nor too specific, nor easily achievable.

- **Mission.** Guides the firm's search for market opportunities more directly. A well-developed mission keeps the firm focused in a limited arena where success is likely.
- **Strategy.** The firm's game plan for the market, pointing the way to firm actions. The market strategy specifies objectives, target market segments, and positioning statements.

Decisions about vision, mission, and strategy are very important; hence, *Managing Marketing in the 21st Century* has spent considerable space discussing them. Active involvement and/or communications about change sends powerful signals throughout the firm. But communication is one thing; behavior is another. Senior managers must exercise leadership with their behavior — *talk the talk*, but also *walk the walk*. Firm integrity and credibility are at stake; managers must follow through or employees will see hypocrisy.[22]

The more difficult work of culture change lies in aligning the firm's *internal architecture* — organization structure, systems and processes, HR practices — with vision, mission, strategy. Customer-oriented values are a good start; unless the culture is externally focused, desire for the status quo undermines firm efforts. Architectural elements must also reflect and shape the culture, but alignment must be systemic. Changing one element, say organization structure, is insufficient; change must pervade all areas. Bob Joss, a serious marketer and former Westpac (large Australian firm) CEO, said: "Too often the popular conception is that strategy and vision are all that matters, 'just get the strategy right and success follows.' Nothing could be further from the truth. In business, execution is the major management challenge. Disciplined daily execution of myriad details must be done correctly to deliver a strategy."[23]

KEY IDEA

An external orientation framework comprises:

Values
↓
Vision, Mission, Strategy
↓
Organizing the Firm's Marketing Efforts
↓
Systems and Processes
↓
Managing Human Resources

ORGANIZING THE FIRM'S MARKETING EFFORTS

To execute the market strategy, the firm must design the marketing organization's *internal architecture* so it can make effective and timely decisions. Some traditional structures still have great value, but contemporary approaches are breaking new ground.[24] Table 23.2 is a guide to figures showing traditional and newer approaches.

Traditional Approaches	Figure	Newer Approaches	Figure
Functional	23.3	Inclusion	23.7
Product/brand management	23.4	Business process	23.8
Segment-based	23.5	Customer management	23.9
Combined product/brand management and market segment	23.6		

TABLE 23.2
Traditional and Newer Approaches to Organizing Marketing

TRADITIONAL ORGANIZATIONAL MODELS

FUNCTIONAL MARKETING ORGANIZATION. The firm places activities like advertising and promotion, distribution, marketing administration, marketing research, and new product development in a marketing department — Figure 23.3 (p. 579). Marketing is usually separate from the sales force and functions like accounting, human resources, production, R&D.

Reporting relationships vary by firm and industry. Most commonly, heads of sales and marketing report to a Marketing and Sales SVP. One variant is separate sales and marketing VPs reporting to a more senior level. But conflict between marketing — long-term focus — and sales — short-term focus — may occur, and only be resolved at high organizational level (C-Suite). One CEO commented: "The trouble with this company is that the functional elevators don't stop until they reach the 20th floor. I'm going to make sure that they stop much lower down!"

KEY IDEA

Several traditional and newer organizational forms are available for organizing marketing efforts.

Functional organizations tend to work best when markets and products are homogeneous (like many small firms). Sometimes, functional organizations linger too long in growing firms. As firms become more complex, they require specialized responsibility for either products or markets. Product/brand-management and market-segment organizations (below) attempt to solve this problem.

FIGURE 23.3
Functional Marketing Organization

KEY IDEA

An external orientation framework comprises:

Values

↓

Vision, Mission, Strategy

↓

Organizing the Firm's Marketing Efforts

↓

Systems and Processes

↓

Managing Human Resources

PRODUCT/BRAND-MANAGEMENT ORGANIZATION. P&G developed the original product management organization to provide product/brand focus.[25] Figure 23.4 shows a well-documented example at General Foods (Altria). Product/brand managers develop market plans for products and brands; they are responsible for volume, market share, and/or profits, but do not control all resource inputs. In many FMCG firms, product/brand managers compete for resources like promotional dollars and sales force time. Internal brand manager competition spurs extra effort, but may undermine coherent product line strategy.

FIGURE 23.4[26]
Product/Brand Management Marketing Organization

KEY IDEA

Traditional marketing organizations include:

• Functional
• Product/brand management
• Category management
• Market segment
• Combined product/brand management and market segment

Brand manager turnover is a second critical issue. Many firms move brand managers rapidly so they gain experience; also, well-trained brand managers are attractive hires for many firms. But incoming brand managers often want to *make their mark* by modifying brand strategy. Lack of coherence and a disjointed long-run strategy may result:

> In a single year, P&G's *Bounty* (paper towel) lost 1.8 market-share points — $49 million revenues across supermarkets, drugstores, major discounters. Newly aggressive Kimberly Clark (KC) introduced softer, more absorbent Scott *with ridges*. KC increased advertising in target markets — Bounty reduced advertising by 30 percent. KC prices increased 6 percent; Bounty increased prices by 9 percent. KC ran more frequent price promotions and had greater salesperson presence in supermarkets. The core problem (acknowledged by P&G): Bounty had four brand managers in 18 months.

Regardless, the general management orientation provides a clear career path.

CATEGORY-MANAGEMENT ORGANIZATION. This approach attempts to address problems with the product/brand-management organization, in part by leveraging success from strong brands to weaker brands. The *category-management* organization directs multiple brands in a complementary manner. P&G category manager for laundry products is responsible for Bounce, Cheer, Downy, Dryel, Febreze, Gain, Ivory, Tide.

New Meaning to Category Management

Increasing retailer power in FMCG has given a new meaning to *category management*. Major supermarkets now manage operations on a category-by-category basis. Sophisticated data analysis allows for more granular determination of individual product profitability — by region, state, city, and even individual store. Retailers add new products and brands only if they help achieve category goals.

Some U.S. retailers outsource product category management to suppliers. Retailers direct the chosen supplier to increase category revenues and profits. Mostly (but not always) retailers appoint the market-leading supplier as *category captain*. This supplier gains privileged access to retail sales data for all category suppliers, including competitors. Appointments are typically for several years.[27]

MARKET-SEGMENT ORGANIZATION. This organization is more externally focused than preceding options; managers are responsible for individual market segments. The market-segment organization may overlie other marketing and sales functions (typically, functionally organized). IBM organizes by industry: Business sector managers are responsible for broad industry categories like manufacturing, banking and financial services, transportation, retailing. For Ciba Chemicals' evolution from a product-management organization to a market-segment organization — Figure 23.5.

FIGURE 23.5
Market-Segment Organization

COMBINED PRODUCT/BRAND MANAGEMENT AND MARKET-SEGMENT ORGANIZATION.

Product/brand and market-segment organizations each omit a crucial dimension. In product/brand organizations, no one is specifically responsible for market segments; in market-segment organizations, no one is specifically responsible for individual products/ brands. For a synthetic fibers firm incorporating both dimensions — Figure 23.6. Segment managers are responsible for end-use markets like household textiles, apparel, industrial products. Product managers are responsible for individual product lines like nylon, polyester, new fibers.[28]

FIGURE 23.6
Combined Product/Brand Management and Market-Segment Organization

NEWER NONTRADITIONAL ORGANIZATIONAL MODELS

INCLUSION ORGANIZATION. In the inclusion organization, the firm groups many activities under marketing — Figure 23.7. As one marketing practitioner asserted: "Marketing is everything, and everything is marketing." Pillsbury adopted this organization early, but found *brute force* unsatisfactory for developing an external perspective.[29] British Airways (BA) introduced a similar approach: BA recognized that Operations controlled two critical customer requirements — safety and schedule reliability. BA restructured — Operations reported to Marketing; indeed, 80 percent of employees reported through Marketing. The *inclusion organization* may work well in service businesses, where marketing and operations are difficult to distinguish, but is not appropriate for all firms.

FIGURE 23.7
Inclusion Organization

BUSINESS PROCESS ORGANIZATION. The reengineering movement spurred some firm attempts to organize around *business processes.*[30] The firm retains a classic functional structure, but much organizational output results from cross-functional teams. A British-based Unilever subsidiary reorganized on this basis — Figure 23.8. Marketing's major responsibilities are brand development, innovation, and related strategic tasks. The sales force conducts operational marketing tasks like trade promotions. The core thrust of this organizational approach is greater organizational ability to address changing customer requirements. Cross-functional teams facilitate a heightened external orientation throughout the organization.[31]

FIGURE 23.8
*Business Process Organization —
Example from a
Unilever Subsidiary*

Statements by senior executives at leading firms[32]:

Consumer durables. "The key to our organizational transformation has been the reorganization of our business units around distinct teams that serve our various customer segments. Each team is cross-functional and has full P&L responsibility. ... it hasn't been easy, but ... it has meant the difference between failure and success."

Global package goods. "Getting cross-functional coordination right has been our biggest go-to-market objective. We managed around key processes ... then we embedded those processes into our organization's culture. All our incentives are aligned around one strategic plan. When you work in silos, it's tough to be nimble. You need to build your organization around core processes rather than core functions."

CUSTOMER-MANAGEMENT ORGANIZATION. This organization focuses specifically on customers. We expect customer-management organizations to become more popular as the customer lifetime value (CLV) concept and the strategic importance of customer retention become more widespread — Chapter 2. CRM systems that allow firms to identify customers by name, buying patterns, and history support this organizational form.[33]

The customer-management organization (CMO) turns the product/brand-management organization (PBMO) on its side — Figure 23.9 (p. 583).[34] In PBMO, brands (B1 ... B4 ... Bn) are pillars; all other functional activities serve the brands. In CMO, customer portfolios (CP1 ... CP4 ... CPn) are pillars; brands and other functions like customer service, marketing research, R&D serve customer portfolios. Customer managers, reporting to a chief customer officer (CCO), have responsibility and authority for customer portfolios; brand management is almost a staff function.[35] Product/brand managers continue to manage brand assets, but support customer managers by developing products/brands to increase CLV. In CMO, traditional metrics shift: Product profitability to customer profitability; current sales to CLV; brand equity to customer equity; market share to customer equity share.[36]

KEY IDEA

Newer marketing organizations include:

• Inclusion
• Business process
• Customer management

A specific CMO advantage is increased customer contact; hence, customer managers gain significant customer insight. The blinders that occur in PBMOs diminish,[37] but implementing CMO typically requires significant organizational change[38]:

ABB restructured so as to respond more quickly to customer needs. ABB replaced four industrial divisions with four new customer segments — process industries; manufacturing and consumer industries; utilities; oil, gas, and petrochemicals — two product-based divisions, and a new organization to manage the corporate transformation. Based on a vision of *collaborative commerce* between suppliers, manufacturers, and customers, ABB's goal was to achieve "highly flexible mass customization," by creating flexible links with customers, through the Internet and traditional channels. ABB also strove for a seamless and coherent flow of internal information-technology systems.[39]

Faced with a serious performance crisis, British Gas (BG) found significant profitability variation by customer; BG formed a new segment-driven organization. *Premier Energy* focused on good paying, heavy users by offering additional services and relocation assistance. *Energy First* addressed cost reduction in serving lower-use customers who settled bills with prepaid cards. *Pay-As-You-Go Energy* served late payers by developing expertise in managing receivables. BG improved financial performance by increasing customer retention and reducing bad debts.[40]

Microsoft faced several problems — slow decision-making, defection of talented employees, increasingly tough competition. Microsoft redeveloped its vision and shifted to a customer-focused organization. Individual organizational units became responsible for customer groups — corporate customers, knowledge workers, home PC buyers, game players, software developers, web surfers, cybershoppers. Said founder Bill Gates: "The new structure puts the customer at the center of everything we do by reorganizing our business divisions by customer segment rather than along product lines."[41]

MARKETING QUESTION

As a current or potential customer, how does Microsoft classify you? Call the customer-service department or go to Microsoft's website to find out. How do you assess IBM's approach?**[562v]**

....
FIGURE 23.9
Transition from Brand Management to Customer Management

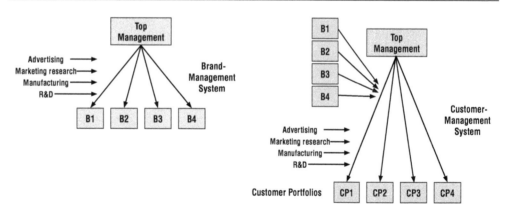

KEY IDEA

Organizational structure should support an integrated marketing approach.

As they become able to identify and understand individual customers, more B2C firms will adopt CMO. Most B2B firms already identify customers; hence, customer management is becoming more widespread. Many firms build key/strategic account management programs; key/strategic account managers (KAMs/SAMs) develop and manage relationships with the most important current and potential customers — Chapter 18. Initially these programs were domestic.[42] Today, firms with global customers are developing global account programs; global account managers (GAMs) develop and manage relationships with key global customers.[43]

The firm may implement CMO at the corporate level or in individual business units, but there are trade-offs. At corporate, customer management may be ineffective because account managers do not possess deep understanding across the corporate business portfolio. Focus at the business level only, and the firm may be unable to develop an integrated corporate-wide offer:

Lucent's (now Alcatel-Lucent, owned by Nokia) business-unit organization pushed authority and responsibility deep in the firm. But getting business units to cooperate was difficult. Several businesses developed variations of the *softswitch* telecommunications product.[44] One customer said he was "confused on what Lucent is actually offering, because I've heard different descriptions of the same solution from different Lucent teams."[45]

SYSTEMS AND PROCESSES

All firms use systems and processes to produce organizational outputs; we can array them along a continuum from *hard systems* to *soft systems*. Hard systems typically require capital equipment, and are often computer-based like automatic teller machines, Internet portals, auction sites. *Soft systems* are human-resource-intensive, like retail customer-service desks. Many customer interactions involve combinations of hard and soft systems. Although customer-facing systems are generally getting better, there are many options for improvement.

HARD SYSTEMS. Hard systems improve operational efficiency and reduce costs. But they can also contribute to creating an external orientation, improve marketing effectiveness, optimize sales force efforts, and help secure differential advantage. Perhaps the most popular hard systems in major firms are enterprise resource planning (ERP). ERP software contains customer-focused modules and attempts to integrate data from many departments and functions across the firm. ERP uses a single computer platform serving individual departmental needs and makes information available to others. Hard systems are also the core of supply-chain management, leading to better supply/demand matching, reduced inventories, fewer stockouts, and less customer disappointment. Benefits from hard systems are:

- **Customer information.** Customer information is more readily available and widely distributed; hence, employees better understand customer needs. At insurance firms like USAA, hard systems are essential to success. USAA service associates have full access to client records and are prompted to ask customers about other financial services. A customer telephone call about homeowner insurance for a new home triggers a change of address for auto insurance and a profile update.

- **Customer intimacy.** Customer relationship management (CRM) systems — Chapter 2 — provide significant information about customers, including purchase histories, buying patterns, and firm interactions. These data sources alleviate the soul-less anonymity of transaction-based markets. Large firms can emulate the high-touch personal service that small firms offer, like the local grocer who knew customers by name and built his business on that basis.

- **Customer effort.** User-friendly computer systems are not just for employees. Many firms use externally facing systems for customers to access product information and order online; customers save time, effort, and risk in purchasing. These systems help the firm get closer to customers and reinforce the brand. Examples include FedEx/UPS package tracking and customer portals, and customer-managed check-in kiosks and personal travel portals for many major airlines.

> Dell was an innovator in using its website for product design and fulfillment. Customers use a *choiceboard* to design their computers. Dell builds-to-order then delivers promptly. Apple, HP Inc., and others have emulated Dell's system.

SOFT SYSTEMS. People-based soft systems can also help the firm be more externally oriented. Consider the planning process.[46] Good planning is externally driven: Planning commences by emphasizing insight into the market, customers, competitors, complementers, and the environment in general. Well-developed situation analyses, based on precepts in Chapters 3, 4, 5, force an external orientation and help deliver solid planning assumptions — Transition to Strategic Marketing (pp. 173–174). Firms building market strategy using the Chapter 9 framework become more externally focused. Try it yourself: Use *The Virgin Marketer: Create Your Market Plan* (companion volume) to develop market strategy for your choice of a firm/brand.

Good planning is collaborative and participative; it involves cross-functional involvement at several managerial levels. Planning brings people across the firm face-to-face with external realities. Outputs from market planning set firm direction; they also play a critical role driving an external orientation via monitor-and-control processes — Chapter 24. A good planning system produces measures that encourage organizational members to look beyond their narrow

---

KEY IDEA

Systems and processes help produce organizational outputs and provide consistency to customers.

KEY IDEA

Good hard systems improve operational efficiency. Hard systems also improve marketing effectiveness and help secure differential advantage.

Soft systems can help make firms more externally oriented.

KEY IDEA

An external orientation framework comprises:

  Values
   ↓
  Vision, Mission, Strategy
   ↓
  Organizing the Firm's Marketing Efforts
   ↓
  Systems and Processes
   ↓
  Managing Human Resources

silos. Marketing executives have a major responsibility to be sensitive to issues concerning sister organizational functions, and behave accordingly. To illustrate, many departments are sometimes extremely frustrated with marketing: "Marketing is hesitant to make predictions and/or makes inaccurate predictions; marketing provides poor customer feedback; marketing makes unrealistic customer promises — about delivery, product features, new product introductions; marketing seems indifferent to costs, manufacturing loads, and working capital requirements." Such complaints do not auger well for interfunctional collaboration; if these complaints are justified, marketing must shape up.[47]

MAKING FIRM SYSTEMS AND PROCESSES THE BEST THEY CAN BE. More important than any individual system/process are methodologies for evolving and integrating systems and processes to drive an external orientation[48]:

> **KEY IDEA**
> _____
>
> Approaches for improving systems and processes include:
> • Best-practice transfer
> • Benchmarking
> • Reengineering

- **Best-practice transfer.** For any process, some business units, departments, or functions are probably more effective than others. Unfortunately, lateral communication within firms is generally poor: Underperforming units may know little about their more effective cousins. A *best-practice* system helps identify and transmit superior expertise, knowledge, and processes across the firm. Multibusiness, multinational firms offer rich terrain for identifying best practices. Samsung's system communicates hundreds of best-practice examples company-wide. An extensive annual evaluation process identifies *best of the best*; the winners personally receive awards from Samsung's CEO.

> Starbucks shares best practices among U.S. operations and international partners. Founder and CEO Howard Schultz opines, "In some cases the international partners are better than we are, and they're teaching us some things. At our first global conference, 30 countries were represented. We had a mini controlled Starbucks trade show where each country set up a booth to show its best practice."[49]
>
> Pantene entered P&G's portfolio as a shampoo. Later, P&G Taiwan made several product changes and successfully repositioned Pantene as a high-end beauty product. Sales took off in Asia Pacific, Latin America, Europe, and the U.S. as P&G geographic regions adopted Taiwan's best practice. Pantene is now a $3 billion brand.[50]

Some firms assign specific employees as *thought leaders* to identify and promote best practices throughout the organization. Xerox Services gives COI (continuous operating improvement) awards to employees at all levels to encourage identifying best practices and promoting sharing across the firm. At Intel, the *data czar* identifies best-known methods and places them in a knowledge repository. Bain employees write up consultancy projects as *knowledge modules* — stored electronically to avoid *reinventing the wheel* when faced with similar challenges. Each market success/failure is an opportunity to identify best practices/best-practice barriers — aka *win/loss* analysis.[51]

Disseminating best practices, expertise, and knowledge across the firm can be a major challenge. Contemporary methods include specially tagged databases for easy search, and collaborative *communities of practice* where experts share information. Other options include regular e-mail communications, *virtual meeting technology* for spur-of-the-moment knowledge-sharing, and meetings designed to break down barriers and facilitate transfer. Other ways to encourage internal communications are workspace arrangements and frequent personnel transfer from one organizational unit to another.

> Chevron's best-practices discovery team identifies groups of people sharing best practices in grassroots networks; the team publicizes these efforts using a *best-practice resource map*. Process masters (PMs) identify and disseminate best practices. PMs have no formal authority, but broad experience generally commands respect.[52]
>
> Xerox shares knowledge through an online intellicenter — *Knowledge Universe* — housing a research catalog and best-practices infobank. Xerox uses blogs, chat rooms, podcasts, and webcasts to disseminate information. Xerox publishes a *Xerox Yellow Pages* to facilitate employee interaction.

MARKETING QUESTION

Identify a specific customer-service process — like buying a product in a store. Visit several establishments to examine their processes. What improvement suggestions do you have?

- **Benchmarking.** Best practices frequently occur in other firms. *Benchmarking* competitors, customers, suppliers, and firms in other industries, like Xerox's *best-in-class* concept, can improve firm processes.[53] Global fast-food firm Yum! Brands (KFC, Pizza Hut, Taco Bell) identified internal best practice and benchmarked its fierce rival McDonald's. Yum!'s three improvement areas were more healthy food, greater drink variety, and menus matched to time of day. Target implemented *Horizontal Councils* in each merchandising and functional area. Council members meet regularly to share best and worst practices, but senior managers always ask them: "What did you find out from other firms about this?" They must have answers to these questions! The Columbia Initiative for Managing Global Accounts enabled 3M, Citibank, Deloitte & Touche, HP, Lucent, Milliken, Saatchi and Saatchi, Schneider Electric to benchmark one another's programs.

- **Reengineering.** The *reengineering* approach examines fundamental assumptions about firm systems and processes, then seeks alternative approaches for redesign and improvement. Many organizational processes have long histories, but changes in customers, competitors, complementers, and broad environmental factors may obsolete them. The critical question is: Can a new process reduce costs and/or increase customer value? The Internet has driven change in many business processes, like supplier-customer relationships — online communication has superseded telephone calls/faxes for purchase orders, invoices, shipping notices. Most successful firms have made major commitments to process-based reengineering:

IBM Credit's (IBMC) process for financing major computer system sales traditionally involved several steps: A salesperson provided purchase and customer data to a *logger* — created a file and sent it onward; credit specialist — conduct credit check; business practices — request changes in standard loan covenants; pricer — decide the interest rate; administrator — develop formal quote, sent overnight to the salesperson for presentation to the client.

To deliver a quote averaged six days, but sometimes took two weeks. Salespeople could not access application status, and anxious customers switched to competitors. IBMC researched actual work time per application — average, 90 minutes! The file spent much time at in- and out-boxes. IBMC's new *deal structurers* averaged four hours for 90 percent of requests; specialists did the rest. Today, customers input data online; credit scoring, agreeing on terms and conditions, setting the interest rate and payment terms, and sending out contracts takes a few minutes.[54]

MANAGING HUMAN RESOURCES

Many firms trying to be more externally oriented believe the simple mantra — *Happy employees make happy customers. Human resource management* (HRM) conducts activities like recruiting, selecting, training, measuring and rewarding, career developing, and talent managing. HR processes provide many opportunities for emphasizing an organization-wide external focus. An external orientation should follow from hiring the *right* people to the *right* positions. The firm requires different skills as it evolves its target markets and adopts new technologies. Indeed, embracing *big data* and shifting investment to digital media and e-commerce requires totally new skill sets. Many firms, like Kimberly Clark and SAP, appoint chief marketing technologists to manage these transitions.[55] HRM systems should support high performance, and develop and manage career transitions effectively. Chapter 18 discusses HRM tools in the sales management context. Here we focus on two additional areas — marketing executives and non-marketing employees whose responsibilities require critical customer interactions.

KEY IDEA

Hiring experienced marketers, including those at the highest levels, can play a major role in developing an external orientation.

Marketing education helps marketers learn new behaviors that can instill an external perspective.

MARKETING EXECUTIVES. The ideal marketer is multifaceted, possessing a blend of analytic, creative, and leadership skills — committed, energetic, hardworking, talented. Senior marketing

KEY IDEA

If the firm hires the *right* people and develops and manages them appropriately, an external orientation should follow.

KEY IDEA

An external orientation framework comprises:

Values

↓

Vision, Mission, Strategy

↓

Organizing the Firm's Marketing Efforts

↓

Systems and Processes

↓

Managing Human Resources

MARKETING QUESTION

What firms should have customer-focused training for employees? What sort of training should they have?

leaders must be passionate about serving customers, and inspiring to their teams. They should also be capable of influencing CEOs and top managers in resource allocation decisions. And, they must be able to drive the serving-customers message deep into their organizations. McKinsey identified several undesirable traits — expensive, faddish, inconsistent, narrow, self-important, uncommercial, undisciplined, not accountable.[56] Ways to enlarge marketing talent pools include:

- **Recruiting and selecting.** Successful hires can play a major role in developing an external orientation. Many internally oriented firms striving for change use this approach. Citibank hired experienced marketing professionals from well-known FMCG firms like P&G and General Mills; these hires had a major impact on Citibank. Intel hired Eric Kim, architect of Samsung's enhanced brand equity; Vodafone hired Lance Batchelor, Amazon's chief marketing officer (Domino's Pizza later hired Batchelor as CEO); Prudential hired Rodger Lawson, responsible for Fidelity's growth; HP hired Marty Homlish, architect of SAP's brand improvement; Barnes & Noble hired Ron Boire, former senior executive at Sony Electronics, Best Buy, Toys "R" Us, Brookstone, Sears. Hiring from direct competitors can be advantageous, but the firm must be concerned about noncompete clauses in executive contracts.

Chief marketing officers (CMOs) typically have broad decision-making authority, but face high performance expectations and increasingly active boards of directors. Whereas internally promoted CMOs are typically familiar with firm culture, organization, and systems and processes, outside hires face steep learning curves. Outside hires may also face internal resistance when they attempt to change the status quo. The most effective new CMOs *hit the ground running* with a clear sense of strategic direction (if not fully worked out plans), new team, and good understanding of potential internal challenges.[57]

For many years, GE marketing comprised (at best) advertising and promotional materials, sales support, and trade shows — marketing was not involved in strategic discussions. In the 2000s, seeking internal growth, GE developed a new marketing framework comprising principles, people, process. GE recognized four key roles for marketing leaders: *instigator* — think strategically and challenge the status quo; *innovator* — identify opportunities to move GE forward; *integrator* — work across multiple organizations and functions; and *implementer* — make stuff happen (typically without line authority). GE established CMO positions in all businesses and at corporate, sourced CMOs from within and outside GE, and doubled the number of marketers to 5,000. GE identified eight major capability areas for marketing — strategy & innovation, branding & communications, sales force effectiveness, new world skills, market knowledge, segmentation & targeting, value creation & pricing, commercial activation — each with detailed definitions requiring specific skills. Each marketing team completes an annual self-assessment on 35 skills, embracing 140 definitions, to identify areas of strength and improvement opportunities.[58]

- **Training and developing.** In-depth marketing education, for new hires and the full cadre of senior and middle managers, can help embed an external orientation throughout the firm — BMS (Opening Case). Well-designed professional education helps build and embed new behaviors, orients executives to firm culture, and facilitates team building. The author has directed many *action-learning* programs for marketing executives; participants bring their marketing problems, then hammer through analysis, alternatives, and solutions in a collaborative atmosphere.

Pfizer augments education and leadership training via a sophisticated computer-based human relations information system including a learning-management component accessible through an easy-to-use portal. Any marketer (new/experienced), regardless of location, can access a personal development plan comprising job roles, competencies, online tools. The plan offers recommended training about Pfizer's many marketing processes — from *How do I execute a plan of action for sales material?* to *How do I do DTC [direct-to-consumer] advertising?* Pfizer employees can access the full set of guidance, learning, principles, and prophecies. (And managers can check progress!)[59]

> Advice to a new CMO from Alex Myers, Senior Vice President, Carlsberg: "Measurement and accountability, not creativity, should be at the core. And before you talk, listen to other functions, to other people internally, to consumers, to customers. Before you start driving in a new direction, make sure the fact base is solid. But don't forget to be passionate about brands and about what the consumer wants."[60]

NONMARKETING PROFESSIONALS. To become a truly externally oriented organization, all employees (not only marketers) must become externally focused. Customer-responsive employees are critical for managing the customer experience, especially in services:

• **Recruiting and selecting.** Firms as diverse as L.L. Bean, Hyatt, Nordstrom, Singapore Airlines, Walmart work hard at selecting and *onboarding* new employees. Southwest Airlines even includes loyal customers in the new-hire interview process. Some B2B firms allow customers to choose their strategic account managers from several qualified candidates; others regularly recruit customer employees to gain greater customer insight.

• **Training and developing.** Training and developing present great opportunities for shaping employee perspectives, including addressing customer concerns and complaints. SAS and British Airways were widely praised for educating *all* employees on how to treat customers. Better employee/customer interaction improved market share and profits; when each firm's focus shifted to cost reduction, performance deteriorated on both measures. Yum! broke down barriers among brands and implemented three initiatives (p. 586) by training top managers, then subordinates, right down the chain of command. Many firms modify training courses to include customer participation; others implement internal branding programs — Chapter 11. Customers serve as participants, speakers, and/or facilitators in the learning process; they may even participate in annual employee reviews.[61] More broadly, Google and P&G employees participate in each other's training programs.

> In-N-Out Burger exceeds Burger King and McDonald's in per-store sales. In-N-Out pays employees more than the going rate; managers earn over $100,000 annually. Employees with over one year's service are eligible to attend In-N-Out University.[62]

• **Measuring and rewarding.** Measurement and reward systems are critical for aligning employees to an external thrust. Asking employees to be externally oriented is insufficient; the firm must hold them accountable. Nordstrom entered the Cleveland market and was immediately successful, mainly because it outshone competitors in customer service. But many employees had previously worked for competitors like Dillard's, Kaufman's, JCPenney, Sears! A major part of Nordstrom's success is an HRM development model that inculcates values and sets high standards for employee behavior.

Workforce measurement systems should be tightly linked to reward systems. When customer-focused measures drive incentive compensation, the external orientation effort has real teeth. Managers are often skeptical about basing take-home pay on survey findings, but Microsoft and Xerox each report excellent results using customer satisfaction measures. Good survey design, rigorously tested items, competent and independent data collectors reduce skepticism. At Bloomberg, every employee, including the janitor and person who stocks the kitchen, receives incentive compensation based on terminal installations. *Equity equivalence certificates* get everyone's attention; they all know Bloomberg's core objective is placing terminals with customers.

KEY IDEA

Critical human resource
practices for developing an
external orientation include:
- Recruiting and selecting
- Training and developing
- Measuring and rewarding
- Work processes

Caution: Required performance must be attainable. If targets are set too high, executives may engage in unethical and possibly illegal actions:

> Sunbeam chairman *Chainsaw* Al Dunlap was widely criticized for setting excessively high performance targets. Required revenues and profits were *so outrageous, they were ridiculous.* To retain their jobs and stock options, managers used several types of aberrant behavior — withheld commissions from independent sales representatives; did not pay bills; forced vendors to accept partial payment. Managers also booked future orders early by offering heavily discounted prices and extended credit.[63] Dunlap was fired and settled SEC charges for $700K.

- **Work processes.** Except for very small organizations, most firms specialize by function. Some managers making critical customer-based decisions are far removed from the market, like financial managers deciding on credit. Service firms like Avis, Disney, Hyatt instill a learning culture; they ensure all executives retain customer focus by planning consistent and regular customer contact, regardless of function and position. Some bankers spend one half-day per month as tellers; insurance executives answer policyholder inquiries. Some firms participate in short- and long-term job exchange with customers, like shipping department employees working in customer receiving departments. Many firms sponsor user groups/customer advisory boards where executives hear directly from customers; customers talk to each other; and the firm provides data on strategy and product planning decisions. Some firms creatively seek insight into customer lives. At Unilever, cross-functional teams gain simultaneous exposure to customers. Gessy-Lever (Brazil) uses ethnographic research; employees live for several weeks in Rio de Janeiro's favelas (shantytowns).

KEY IDEA

Managers at all functions
and levels should have
consistent and regular
customer contact.

Top management exposure to customers is especially important. Sir Terry Leahy, former Tesco CEO had a hands-on approach. Two days per week, Leahy visited branches, often unannounced. One week a year, Leahy and other senior executives spent time in stores, working checkouts and stocking shelves. Many B2B firms are introducing *executive-sponsor* programs so senior executive interface with major customers. Of course, employees must *work* for the firm to deliver products/services to customers. Strikes, job stoppages, working to rule, and other job-related actions play havoc with firm ability to deliver value to customers. In manufacturing industries, inventories may cushion the impact. The damage is often most severe in service firms; customers may be severely inconvenienced — like airline travel. Even if aircraft fly, *unhappy* employees do not make *happy* customers!

Sustaining an External Orientation

KEY IDEA

The firm must clearly understand the implications for
developing and sustaining an
external orientation. Many
elements can get in the way.

Many industry leaders have stumbled badly and lost preeminent positions. Why? The stories are strikingly similar: The firm originally gained industry leadership by delivering customer value and securing differential advantage. The firm developed and focused resources, core competencies, and expertise toward this goal. The firm was externally oriented ... but then things changed. Past success began to hold the firm back; it could not sustain an external orientation and adjust to the new reality. We can find old and new leaders in many industries: air freight — Emery/FedEx; automobiles — General Motors/Toyota; book sellers — Barnes & Noble/Amazon; smartphones — Nokia/Apple, Samsung; home video — Blockbuster/Netflix; imaging systems — Xerox/Canon; PCs — IBM, Dell/Lenovo. The original leader had superior technology, and/or scale economies, and/or substantial buying power, and/or well-established brands. But the new leader changed the rules — new business model, and/or product design, and/or technology.

Getting everything right is difficult: Remember, *a chain is only as strong as its weakest link.* For perfect integration of the entire market offer, the firm should execute every *moment of truth* flawlessly — not merely satisfy customers, but delight them. Poor performance on some dimensions can overwhelm world-class performance on others. When it was PC market leader, even Dell had problems:

Dell sells notebook computers to incoming college students, preconfigured to institutional specifications. One year, a demand spike caught Dell unprepared. Dell broke delivery promises and could not provide accurate delivery information. The recorded voice at customer service insisted Dell was really concerned about the caller's time. Maybe once or twice, but 40 times?

Sustaining an external orientation is a little easier if the firm understands its challenges:

- **Accounting systems.** The firm must produce data in a form that supports an external perspective. Despite advances in business intelligence and analytics, many firms measure profits only by product; they should also measure profits by customer and/or customer group.

- **Bureaucracy.** As firms grow, departmentalization and task specialization are efficient ways to complete repetitive tasks. But rules and behaviors, reinforced by day-to-day work pressures, become embedded in the organization.[64] As customers, we have all dealt with employees who tell us, "That's not my department" or "You'll have to talk to XYZ about that." Firms must complete day-by-day tasks, but they must also build the agility to serve customers well. Flattening organization structures, increasing employee empowerment, and introducing sensing mechanisms to identify and address market opportunities are proven ways to defeat bureaucracy.

- **Centralization versus decentralization.** Centralizing and standardizing can have great value, especially for cost reduction. But excessive centralization leads to standardized actions, rather than *customer responsiveness*. Key decision-makers are distant from customers; employees with detailed market, customer, competitor, and complementer insight play less significant decision-making roles. Conversely, excessive decentralization can leave the firm lacking clear focus. Deciding which activities are better centralized and which are better decentralized (closer to the customer) is a critical firm challenge.[65]

  Multibusiness and/or multiproduct firms like Sony face a special challenge. Sony's myriad units often act like *warring tribes*, each pursuing its agenda, rather than cooperating as *Sony United* to better serve customers. Broadly speaking, three complementary ways to break down silos and improve customer focus are: *Coordination* — establish internal structural mechanisms and processes; *cooperation* — use cultural means, incentives, and power allocation; and *capability* — encourage skill development and define clear career paths.[66]

Home Depot secured a dominant position in home-improvement retailing by addressing customer needs, but the incoming CEO consolidated nine regional purchasing centers into one centralized buying operation. Costs reduced, but customer needs and store-level inventory were often mismatched. Home Depot later recreated regional merchandising teams, scattered throughout the U.S., to consider local requirements in store-level buying.

- **Excessive focus on organizational efficiency.** Many firms work hard to reduce costs by improving organizational efficiency. They use techniques like *six sigma* to make continuous incremental process improvements — operations and customer service. An organizational culture dominated by six sigma can become internally focused, less innovative, and drive out behaviors that address external changes.

- **Functional divisions.** Firms develop specialized functions to increase expertise in key areas. But specialization can lead to silo thinking and divisiveness among specialties. Functional heads must recognize the importance of cross-functional cooperation. Merck's recovery after the Vioxx scandal owes much to *One Merck*, introduced by CEO Clarke. Said Clarke: "We need a more integrated approach. From the time we begin talking about a particular drug franchise, I want researchers, marketers, and manufacturing people sitting in the same room."[67]

- **Functional view of marketing.** The firm must distinguish between marketing as a *philosophy* and marketing as a *department*. The firm that delegates all marketing problems to a

MARKETING QUESTION

How do you assess your college/school/university on degree of external orientation? Are some parts more externally focused than others? If yes, what accounts for these differences?

marketing department will neither create nor deliver fully integrated offers. Achieving integration demands coordination among many different functional departments.

- **Internal politics.** The CEO and/or business head must actively support instituting an external orientation, and frequently communicate this support. If this does not occur, some functions will be suspicious of customer-focused initiatives. Jockeying for power and position occurs in all firms; leaders must not allow political concerns to override customer centricity.

- **Inward-oriented marketing departments.** Marketing departments are sometimes their own worst enemies. They implement a not-invented-here syndrome that quashes *foreign* ideas and initiatives to *protect their turf*. This problem tends to be most serious in firms with good reputations for marketing expertise, and where the marketing department has great political power.

- **Misaligned incentives.** As noted earlier, people in organizations do what is *inspected* of them, not what is *expected* of them! People behave in ways that earn rewards. Conflicting and function-specific performance objectives and rewards make integrating across functional boundaries very difficult. The result: Internal conflict and division.

- **Social fabric of institutions.** Firm employees know each other and interact daily. Customers, competitors, suppliers are occasional *intruders* who interrupt daily life! How often have employees ignored you — the customer — as they chat together, seemingly oblivious of your presence? And how often do they interrupt their conversation with you to answer a telephone call?

KEY IDEA

Yesterday's and today's success sow the seeds of tomorrow's defeat.

For long-run success, the firm must be responsive yet dynamic, learning but not forgetting, understanding of human behavior yet demanding of high performance, customer-sensitive yet competitive, and shareholder-value-creating but not short-sighted. As CEO, Jack Welch lifted performance at an already highly regarded GE to an entirely new level. In one of his more famous exhortations, he stated: "I want managers who manage with their face to the customer and their backside to the CEO!" Jeff Bezos, Amazon founder and CEO, described himself and Amazon as "customer obsessed!" And at IBM, customer-focused Lou Gerstner restored the fallen computer giant to its former glory with a *services* vision. Leadership counts! Leaders must spread an external orientation throughout the firm.

MARKETING QUESTION

What other messages did you glean from this chapter?

KEY MESSAGES

- For long-run success, the firm must develop and sustain an external orientation.
- Firms with an external orientation often build success on functional excellence — customer service, finance, human resources, operations and the supply chain, research and development, sales.
- The model for developing an external orientation contains external elements — vision, mission, strategy; and internal architectural elements — organization structure, systems and processes, HRM practices. Customer-focused values help achieve necessary alignment.
- The firm can achieve an external orientation only if all employees do their jobs with a keen understanding that customers are central to success.
- Most action in developing an external orientation rests in the firm's internal architecture.
- Sustaining an external orientation can be very difficult. Past and current success contains the seeds of future failure. Inability to adapt leads many previously successful firms to fail.
- The firm must beware several impediments to sustaining an external orientation: accounting systems, bureaucracy, centralization versus decentralization, excessive focus on organizational efficiency, functional divisions, functional view of marketing, internal politics, inward-oriented marketing departments, misaligned incentives, the social fabric of institutions.

VIDEOS AND AUDIOS

For complimentary material, see Axcess Capon codes at www.axcessvids.com

Developing the Marketing Organization	**557v** 🔊	Samuel Moed	Bristol-Myers Squibb
Marketing at GE	**220v** 🔊	Steve Liquori	Columbia Business School
Leading the Marketing Organization	**943v** 🔊	William Klepper	Columbia Business School
Marketing Careers	**364v** 🔊	Stanford Business School	
Developing and Implementing Strategy	**766v** 🔊	Robynne Berg	
Marketing Imperative 5	**131a** 🔊	Noel Capon	Columbia Business School

QUESTIONS FOR STUDY AND DISCUSSION

Can you answer the questions implied by this chapter's learning outcomes? Check!

1. Identify three firms that do a great job of being externally oriented — what makes you think they really are externally oriented?

2. Identify three internally oriented firms — what makes you think they really are internally oriented? What recommendations do you have for these firms?

3. Think about a time when you decided to no longer be a firm's customer. Why did you quit? How could the firm have saved you as a customer? What changes would the firm have to make for you to return?

4. What markets does your school/college/university address? How does your school/college/ university organize to address these markets? Is the organization structure appropriate? What would you change?

5. Go to a local restaurant. Map the process for addressing customers. Reengineer this process and develop a better one. Alternatively, complete this task for *Managing Marketing in the 21st Century*.

TRUE/FALSE QUESTIONS

Answers on page A2 and at www.axcessvids.com — 490p 🔊

1. The category-management organization attempts to address problems with the product/ brand-management organization and to leverage success from strong brands to weaker brands. ❏ **TRUE** ❏ **FALSE**

2. The business process organization retains a classic functional structure, with much organizational output resulting from cross-functional teams. ❏ **TRUE** ❏ **FALSE**

3. Soft systems improve operational efficiency and reduce costs. ❏ **TRUE** ❏ **FALSE**

4. The reengineering approach examines fundamental assumptions about firm systems and processes and seeks alternative approaches for redesign and improvement. ❏ **TRUE** ❏ **FALSE**

5. To become a truly externally oriented organization, all employees, not only marketers, must become externally focused. ❏ **TRUE** ❏ **FALSE**

MULTIPLE CHOICE QUESTIONS

Answers on page A2 and at www.axcessvids.com — 249p

1. Which of the following represents a description of the firm's ideal future or an impressionistic picture of what the future should be?

   a. vision
   b. mission
   c. strategy
   d. objective

2. Which of the following types of organizational structures places activities like marketing research, distribution, advertising and promotion, marketing administration, and new product development in what is traditionally called a marketing department?

   a. product/brand management
   b. functional marketing
   c. category management
   d. market segment

3. The _____ organization retains a classic functional structure, but much organizational output results from cross-functional teams.

   a. product/brand management
   b. functional marketing
   c. business process
   d. market segment

4. A specific advantage of the _____ structure is that customer contact increases, and customer portfolio managers gain significant customer insight.

   a. product/brand-management
   b. functional-marketing
   c. category-management
   d. customer-management

5. All of the following represent challenges for a firm working toward sustaining an external orientation EXCEPT:

   a. bureaucracy
   b. accounting systems
   c. functional divisions
   d. All selections represent challenges.

CHAPTER 24

MONITORING AND CONTROLLING FIRM PERFORMANCE AND FUNCTIONING

For complimentary material, see Axcess Capon codes at www.axcessvids.com

LEARNING OUTCOMES

When you have completed this chapter, you will be able to:

- Describe critical elements in the monitor-and-control process.
- Implement key principles of monitor and control.
- Measure input, intermediate, and output variables.
- Monitor and control firm performance versus objectives.
- Monitor and control firm functioning.
- Understand and recognize organizational success factors.

OPENING CASE: SONY ELECTRONICS

Sony has been a consumer electronics leader for many years. Ron Boire, then President of Sony Electronics Sales, talked about Sony's careful focus on well-chosen measures and how it uses them to secure the behavior it requires. "Sony is really driven by the concept of, 'If you can't measure it, you can't do it.' Sometimes that's straightforward; sometimes it's very complicated. Interactions that Sony salespeople have with our retail trade channel customers are a good example.

"With national customers like Best Buy, Sears, Target, and Walmart or a strategically important regional chain, we used to do classic sales compensation. Each salesperson had a sales budget, and we measured salespeople performance against budget. If you had a budget target of $1 million for a product category, and you sold at $1.1 million, you did a great job and you made a good bonus. Regardless of what was stuck in the barn at the end of the month or the end of the year. Regardless of whether or not they could pay for it. Regardless of whether you delivered it to them on time.

"Today, we base up to 70 percent of our inventory management/asset management group's compensation, and 50 percent of our salespeople's compensation, on customer scorecards. We agree on metrics individually with each national and strategic customer. Most focus on simple things like on-

time delivery, percent in stock, forecast accuracy, and gross margin return on inventory — the key retail performance metric. To set these metrics we ask each customer: 'What's important to you? What are your targets? What are your strategic concerns?' Best Buy's current target is 90 percent on-time delivery, plus or minus one day, and 95 percent in stock. We may or may not hit that metric due to a variety of reasons, but everybody has the same goal in mind. Depending on their size, we track retailers either monthly or weekly. And our salespeople are bonus compensated twice a year based on their customer scorecards.

"As the saying goes, 'People do what they're paid to do.' When you change the basis of people's paychecks, it really is remarkable how fast they change their behavior. We've seen a tremendous shift in the behavior of the organization, and a very positive reaction from the marketplace. No one else in the consumer electronics industry is doing this. And in most industries that our customers do business in — appliances, software, consumer electronics, or computers — all sales forces are compensated on sell-in. It's revolutionary in consumer electronics for a salesperson to say, 'No, I won't take your purchase order, because you have too much inventory.' Everybody talks about aligning with your customers, but if you're paying your salespeople to stuff the box you can't be aligned — it's impossible."

Sony wants to know customer profitability. Boire continued, "We measure customer profitability from a contribution margin perspective. Once you get past that sell-in mentality, you can focus on simple measurements like contribution margin; incremental contribution margin is the best ongoing measure of a marketing relationship with our trade channel customers. Marketing holds the P&Ls on these major customer accounts, but the only thing we load in are direct costs attributable to that customer; we include the sales team and all its funding, but we take nothing from headquarters. We look at the contribution margin in dollars per customer; we project midrange contributions some years ahead, and we calculate a net present value [NPV] with a conservative termination value.

"Sometimes we have one or two customers that are in financial difficulties. And we ask, what's the contribution margin of this customer? If they go away, the fixed cost at headquarters doesn't go away. But there may be $30 million in contribution margin that goes away. The contribution dollars and the NPV give you the measures to say, 'What should we invest in this customer to try to help them stay healthy?' We have one of those customers now. We've hired outside consultants to go in as a crisis management team to work with them on process reengineering. We're working with them on inventory and supply-chain management. We're working with them on advertising productivity. And the at-risk number in our minds is this annual contribution margin. If we invest up to that point and the customer turns the corner, we're not going to claim sole credit for saving them, but we certainly didn't help them go down, right? On a day-to-day basis, this grounds management as to the relative value of any customer. Because we can say, 'You know what? The net present value of this customer is $600 million. That's what this relationship is worth.'

"Outside the consumer electronics channel we have less influence. A major national multicategory retailer that's in difficulties, we're such a small percentage of their total business that it wouldn't matter what we did. What we can do in those cases is manage our risk well, as we did with Kmart. We called the day Kmart would file for bankruptcy protection. We predicted it well in advance. We took some losses, but we managed our receivables with Kmart probably better than anyone in the trade."[1] **[163v]**

Case Question

Compare and contrast Sony's old monitor-and-control system with the new system. Suppose a firm with which you are familiar made this sort of change. What implementation problems would you anticipate? How would you deal with them?

SONY

Lack of a monitor-and-control system can put the most successful firm at risk. In the early 2000s, Starbucks (Chapter 1 Opening Case) was a highly successful fast-growing firm. Then profits dropped by 50 percent; share price dropped by 75 percent. Said a Starbucks executive, "When the numbers went south, we couldn't even make an educated guess about why. We had no way to get details about sales, no way to capture customer opinion, no good way to get information from the baristas."

In recent years, the Marketing Science Institute placed marketing measurement on its agenda.[2] For many years, most firms measured brand, marketing, and product managers solely on sales, market share, and/or profit contribution. Firms generally did not explore factors driving these results, nor question whether the firm was securing sales and profits today at the expense of long-term harm to brand equity. Today, many firms use brand-health-check measures — Chapter 11 — but monitoring and controlling marketing performance is a broader issue.

Marketing and business managers take many actions — enter new markets/segments, introduce new products, increase/reduce advertising, add/cut salespeople, shift distribution channels, raise/lower prices. Typically, the firm hopes to increase sales, market share, and/or profits, and create shareholder value. But the firm must also know whether or not its actions lead to intended results. A good monitor-and-control system reveals if firm actions — individually and collectively — improved performance. Leading indicators help assess whether the firm is on track, or if it should change direction.

THE CHANGING VIEW

OLD WAY	NEW WAY
Accounting profit	Shareholder value creation
Backward looking	Forward looking
Bottom-line oriented	Variety of measures
Fact finding	Learning and improvement
Financial focus	Business focus
Focus on firm success	Focus on firm and customer success
Internally oriented	Externally oriented
Measurement and control based on accounting performance measures	Measurement and control based on marketing performance measures
Output measures only	Emphasis also on input and intermediate measures
Postaction control	Steering control
Punitive philosophy	Analytic philosophy
Unbalanced scorecard	Balanced scorecard

MARKETING QUESTION

Consider your personal objectives and strategy: Have you thought through these rigorously? Are you achieving your planned objectives? Are you functioning well in trying to achieve your objectives?

KEY PRINCIPLES OF MONITOR-AND-CONTROL PROCESSES

You have likely heard this popular management saying: *If you can't measure it, you can't manage it.* People in organizations tend to do what is *inspected* of them, not what is *expected* of them. Hence, good monitor-and-control processes are critical for ensuring that people do what they are supposed to do, so the *right* actions lead to the *right* results. *Monitoring* focuses on measuring how well the firm is conducting various business aspects. *Control* is concerned with making changes/adjustments so the firm improves performance. Monitor-and-control processes are the most powerful means of changing individual behavior and enhancing long-term results.[3] Chapter 24 focuses on two complementary areas — firm performance and firm functioning:

KEY IDEA

- **Firm performance.** *Is the firm achieving planned results?* Planned results are the *standards* against which the firm measures actual results. All things equal, if actual results meet or exceed standards, performance is satisfactory and the firm continues to operate as planned. If actual results are below standards, the firm should modify its actions.[4]

- **Firm functioning.** To achieve desired results, the firm allocates resources and takes actions. *Is the firm functioning well?* For greater insight, we drill down into three aspects:
  - *Implementation.* Did the firm implement planned actions?
  - *Strategy.* Is the market strategy well conceived and on target?
  - *Managerial processes.* Are managerial processes the best they can be?

Monitor and control should not occur at managerial whim; the firm should build a monitor-and-control philosophy into its DNA. This is not a simple matter; it may take considerable time and effort to assemble the infrastructure for an effective system. Measurement is crucial; in this chapter we discuss many types of measures. But the best-designed measures have no impact unless the firm also implements a process for developing standards, and assessing results against those standards. Effective monitor-and-control processes rest on five core principles:

- Focus on market levers and develop alternative plans.
- Implement steering control rather than postaction control.
- Use the right performance measures at the right organizational levels.
- Model the relationship between input, intermediate, output measures.
- Tie compensation to performance.

Monitor-and-control processes are the most powerful means of changing individual behavior in firms.

Monitor-and-control processes focus on two complementary areas:
- Is the firm achieving planned results?
- Is the firm functioning well?

FOCUS ON MARKET LEVERS AND DEVELOP ALTERNATIVE PLANS

Market levers flow from the market strategy and implementation plans; they include actions like introducing new products, increasing/decreasing advertising, adding/replacing salespeople, and enhancing training. The firm allocates resources and takes actions to achieve planned performance. Actual performance versus standards tells if firm resource allocations and actions were successful. Monitor-and-control efforts should focus on market levers. If actual results fall below standards, the firm should be ready with alternative plans.

KEY IDEA

The firm should plan contingent actions for when actual performance falls below standards.

> Pfizer built experimentation with marketing levers into its DNA. Pfizer continually tests different advertising and promotion strategies, and ways of allocating selling effort. Pfizer spends millions of dollars on experiments as it searches for optimal actions. Said a senior Pfizer executive: "We're measurement-intense. So 'metrics are us.' We believe in it. We measure everything. That is the root of our business."[5]

> Historically, Samsung focused on low-price, high-volume products so production managers could optimize capacity utilization. Samsung's monitor-and-control system now measures *market price position* and encourages sales of higher-price products.

IMPLEMENT STEERING CONTROL RATHER THAN POSTACTION CONTROL

Steering control and *postaction control* are different *monitor-and-control approaches*. Firms using *postaction control* wait a preset time period, then compare actual results against standards. If results are unsatisfactory, they take corrective action. Firms exercising postaction control typically develop annual market plans and set standards by quarter, but increased environmental change and complexity are driving reduced time periods.

KEY IDEA

Postaction control means waiting a *preset* time before comparing actual results against performance standards.

KEY IDEA

Steering control allows the firm to be market responsive. Steering control *continually* compares firm results to performance standards.

In contrast, *steering control* is dynamic, continuous, anticipatory. Firms using steering control set standards for measures like sales, market share, profit, then calendarize by month, week, or even day. These firms set control limits for performance and continually compare actual results against standards.[6] Because they also track leading indicators, these firms are more market responsive.

Amazon employs A/B testing extensively.[221v] For its web-based promotions, Amazon sends millions of e-mails during two or three days. Early on, Amazon tests multiple legs of each message for click-throughs and sales. Within a couple of hours, Amazon knows what's working/what's not, then sends only those messages providing the best results.[7]

Historically, Gillette consolidated sales each quarter; now these figures are available daily. Cisco can close its books in a single day by converting 50 different ledgers in a single global system. Managers can view data like revenues, margins, backlog, expenses — by region, business unit, channel, account manager — daily, and take appropriate actions.[8] Dell focuses heavily on short feedback cycles. Discussing salespeople, a senior Dell executive opined, "We drive to develop a meritocratic environment where people have a profit-per-minute mentality."[9] At Zara's Spanish headquarters, sales managers sit at terminals monitoring sales at every store around the world, thus enabling twice-per-week restocking.

Based on early data from many stores, by 8 a.m. on one Friday after Thanksgiving Walmart knew sales would not reach expectations. Between Friday and Sunday, Walmart executives decided which items to mark down. New prices took effect nationwide on Tuesday; on Thursday Walmart broadcast a video promoting the newly discounted items. New advertising began on Friday with revamped displays in all stores. Walmart sales rebounded, and quarterly earnings were within the expected range.

KEY IDEA

Feedback cycles — time between firm actions and decisions on measured results — should not be too short.

Internet-related technology and analytics systems have made frequent performance monitoring more viable. But *feedback cycles* — time between firm action and decisions on measured results — should not be too short. The firm must guard against taking action based on random fluctuations. A leading pharmaceutical firm made major changes in a new product launch four weeks after introduction, long before it could make a decent assessment of results. Relatedly, on returning as Starbucks CEO, Howard Schultz stopped reporting monthly growth in same-store sales; Schultz believed this measure drove short-term thinking by store managers.

USE THE RIGHT PERFORMANCE MEASURES AT THE RIGHT ORGANIZATIONAL LEVELS

If possible, monitor-and-control processes should employ objective measures like sales, market share, profits.[10] When less concrete measures like customer satisfaction are appropriate, the firm should use validated scales.[11] Regardless, the firm should use the *right* measures:

Kellogg's CEO introduced a *volume-to-value* strategy to shift resources to higher-margin products. He altered Kellogg's daily tracking systems to record dollar sales — not sales by weight — and overhauled bonus plans to reward profits and cash flow — not volume. In meetings, the CEO interrupted executives who gave results in weight sold rather than dollars.

Many life insurance firms compensate agents on number and value of new policies. But agents often receive little/no compensation for maintaining existing policies. Hence, agents *roll over* existing policyholders into new policies. But new policies must be in force for several years before the firm profits. Failure to measure and reward agents for serving existing policyholders creates serious profit problems.

The firm should measure performance at multiple organizational levels — like corporate, geographic region, business unit, market segment, marketing function, customer, sales region, sales district, sales territory. Alcoa measures profitability by market sector, business, customer and, in its aerospace division, by airplane program.[12] *De-averaging* performance via finer-grained analysis may allow the firm to identify particularly well-performing areas that warrant greater investment, and poorly performing units whose problems need addressing.

Bowen (boxed insert) illustrates the *iceberg principle* — Figure 24.1 — opportunities and problems may lie hidden beneath the surface. Organizational position should largely drive the data employees receive. Senior managers do not typically require performance variances by salesperson, but they should have the ability to make *deep dives*. Salespeople do not need to know performance variances of peers in other sales regions.

KEY IDEA

The firm should use objective measures for monitor-and-control purposes; if scales are appropriate, these should be validated.

FIGURE 24.1
The Iceberg Principle

1/7

Waterline   Above the surface

Below the surface

6/7

Bowen

Bowen (disguised) sells tools through retail stores. We illustrate the *iceberg principle* via Bowen's sales force — national, regional, district, territory — Figure 24.2. Bowen performs satisfactorily nationally, and in each geographic region. But Northeast region results comprise strong performance in the New York and New Jersey/Pennsylvania districts, and very poor performance in Capitol (New England performance is acceptable). In Capitol, two salespeople — Mapes and Hornig — perform exceptionally well, but Grant and Canatos pull the district down.

MARKETING QUESTION

As incoming sales manager for the Capitol district, what actions would you contemplate for turning the situation around?

FIGURE 24.2
The Iceberg Principle in a National Sales Force

Key

| Excellent | Superior | Acceptable |
| Needs Improvement | Unacceptable |

National

Sales Regions

Northeast   South   Midwest   West

Sales Districts

Capitol   New York   New Jersey/Pennsylvania   New England

Sales Territories

Williams   Busch   Grant   Mapes   Canatos   Hornig

KEY IDEA

The firm should measure performance at multiple organizational levels.

Good performance in a unit or subunit can hide poor performance elsewhere. The firm must isolate problem areas.

MODEL RELATIONSHIPS AMONG INPUT, INTERMEDIATE, AND OUTPUT MEASURES

Monitor-and-control systems must distinguish between cause and effect to gain insight. Suppose we observe that advertising spending increases and sales also increase. One interpretation: Advertising was effective — increased advertising spending caused increased sales. An alternative interpretation: Increased sales caused increased advertising spending — advertising budget is a fixed percentage of sales! To ensure the firm makes valid inferences, it must distinguish among:

- **Input measures** — actions the firm takes
- **Intermediate measures** — customer actions or state-of-mind changes
- **Output measures** — performance variables like sales and profits[13]

Figure 24.3 shows the flowchart of input measures leading to intermediate measures; in turn, intermediate measures lead to output measures in a cause-and-effect relationship. Market levers provide input measures; inputs affect intermediate steps that must occur before customers purchase products and provide the firm with outputs. Generally, collecting data on input and output measures is relatively easy; securing data on intermediate measures is often more resource-intensive.

Regarding numbers of measures, the firm is generally better off choosing a limited number of *good* measures, rather than just a lot of measures. Home Depot's CEO used an excessive 30 store-manager measures (since reduced to eight) but omitted customer satisfaction! The firm must have confidence in the presumed relationships between inputs and intermediates, and between intermediates and outputs. Many marketing researchers spend significant effort investigating these relationships.[14] To illustrate, when the firm takes advertising and sales force actions, input, intermediate, and output measures may be as follows:

- **Input measures** — financial resources spent on advertising, number of sales calls per day
- **Intermediate measures:**
  - *Customer actions* — number of customers agreeing to product trial, number of customers placing deposits for future purchases
  - *Customer mental states* — product awareness, associations, attitudes, product interest, intention to purchase
- **Output measures** — sales, market share, profits

Output measures are *lagging indicators — rearview mirror —* what has happened. Intermediate and input measures are *leading indicators — dashboards —* what should happen.[15]

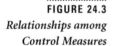

KEY IDEA

Critical control variables are:

   Input measures
      ↓
   Intermediate measures
      ↓
   Output measures

FIGURE 24.3
*Relationships among
Control Measures*

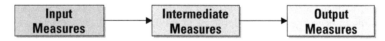

TIE COMPENSATION TO PERFORMANCE

The performance-to-compensation linkage is the final but critical piece of the monitor-and-control puzzle. In the Opening Case, we saw how Sony dramatically changed sales force behavior by linking compensation to a new set of performance measures. From a loss situation in the early 2000s, Lego made a significant profit in the following recession. An important contributing factor to the turnaround was tying employee pay to newly developed key performance indicators.

KEY IDEA

Generally, people in organizations do what they are paid to do.

Developing the performance-to-compensation linkage is not easy. When compensation design is poor, employees optimize individual performance and compensation. As a result, they take actions that may harm the firm, frequently by failing to cooperate across functional boundaries and business units — Chapter 23.

CRITICAL ELEMENTS OF THE MONITOR-AND-CONTROL PROCESS

McDonald's customer satisfaction rankings dropped considerably; it suffered the first quarterly loss in 40 years; share price hovered around a ten-year low. A major factor: To avoid bothering powerful franchisees, McDonald's did not seek detailed store-by-store information. McDonald's lacked a good system to monitor performance against outlet standards.

Former Coach CEO Lew Frankfort receives many reports: daily and weekly sales by product class/ form and store (more than 1,000 full-price and factory outlets); number of people entering the store; percentage purchasing; actual purchases; dollars spent.

Figure 24.4 (p. 603) shows nine repeatable yet distinct stages for any monitor-and-control process[16]:

1. **Identify the process to control.** Clarify the control system's focus.

2. **Decide and define measures.** Options include input, intermediate, output variables. The firm must also decide *when* to measure, and devise a process for developing standards.

3. **Develop measurement system.** Figure out a system to collect, integrate, analyze relevant data, and distribute results.

4. **Set standards.** Decide which standards to apply for each measure. Generally, standards flow from action programs related to the market strategy. Of course, standards likely differ by market segment.

5. **Measure results.** Using the measurement system from step 3, collect, integrate, analyze, and distribute results.

6. **Compare results against standards; identify gaps and variances.** Compare results — step 5 — against standards — step 4 — to identify *performance gaps* and *variances*.

7. **Understand and communicate performance gaps.** Communicate data and interpretation of performance gaps to executives responsible for taking action. Some gaps will be positive — results exceed standards. Other gaps will be negative — results are inferior to standards.

8. **Generate and evaluate alternatives.** Executives identify alternative corrective actions to close negative gaps. Large positive gaps may indicate a requirement for higher performance standards. Executives should always question appropriateness of the original standards.

9. **Select alternatives and take action.** Executives select courses of action, then develop and implement action plans.

Monitor-and-control processes are not one-time events. After completing the nine stages, the firm should confirm that stages 1, 2, 3 are well developed. Then, completing step 9 leads directly to step 4 — confirm or reset standards. Table 24.1 (p. 603) illustrates for individual salespeople.

The firm must recognize the impact of monitor-and-control systems on employee motivation. The firm optimizes motivated behavior when standards are moderately challenging. Participation in standard setting also enhances motivation. Standards that are too easy or too difficult to achieve reduce motivation. Perceived fairness in setting standards is very important.[17]

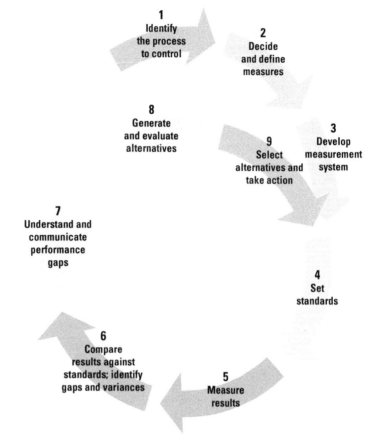

FIGURE 24.4
The Monitor-and-Control Process

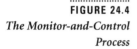

Select your favorite/least favorite class. Develop a monitor-and-control system designed to enhance the performance of all students in the class. Present your system to, and discuss with, the professor.

TABLE 24.1
Illustrating the Monitor-and-Control Process for Individual Salespeople

Process Step	Managerial Focus
1. Identify the process to control	Actions and performance of individual salespeople
2. Decide and define measures	What measures? • Input measures: total number of calls per day, number of calls to new accounts per day, sales expenses per call • Intermediate measures: number of factory trials, number of formal customer planning meetings • Output measures: sales revenues, profits, sales revenues from new accounts When to measure: monthly How to develop standards: individual salesperson with district sales manager; regional sales manager approves standards
3. Develop measurement system	Develop coding system for existing/new accounts. Develop systems to secure data for individual salespeople: • Call data and intermediate measures from salesperson call reports • Sales expense data from travel and entertainment (T&E) reports • Sales revenue data from order entry process • Profit data from accounting department Develop system to aggregate data at district, regional, and national levels.
4. Set standards	Specific input, intermediate, output standards vary by salesperson experience and sales territory characteristics (sales opportunity and workload).
5. Measure results	Collect data. Secured from the system developed in step 3

continues

Process Step	Managerial Focus	
6. Compare results against standards; identify gaps and variances	Seek discrepancies between standards and results. To illustrate: • Calls per day are at standard — no gap • Sales expenses exceed standard — negative gap • Sales exceed standard — positive gap • Profits below standard — negative gap	**TABLE 24.1** *continued*
7. Understand and communicate performance gaps	To illustrate, sales expenses exceed standard: • Investigate travel requirements, customer density in relevant territory, customer contact level • Assess appropriateness of each input, intermediate, output standard • Establish reason(s) for discrepancies: Perhaps expense budget is too low for territory size and customer contact level; perhaps the salesperson plans trips poorly and/or has overly expensive tastes in hotels/restaurants • Communicate findings to responsible individuals	
8. Generate and evaluate alternatives	Based on the analysis in step 7	
9. Select alternatives and take action	Based on alternatives developed in step 8	

Monitoring and Controlling Firm Performance

What performance should the firm monitor and control? The Figure 24.3 framework — *input* → *intermediate* → *output* — helps answer this question. We address this topic in reverse order.[18]

OUTPUT MEASURES

Recall that *output measures* are the *final* results the firm wants to achieve. These measures can be *hard* — objectively assessed; or *soft* — like rating scales requiring more interpretation. *Internal* hard measures include sales units/dollars, product profitability, and customer profitability; *external* (market-based) hard measures include market share, relative market share, *market occupancy ratio*. Soft measures include brand health checks, customer satisfaction.[19]

KEY IDEA

Critical control variables are:
Input measures
↓
Intermediate measures
↓
Output measures

INTERNAL HARD MEASURES — SALES VOLUME

Sales volume includes sales units, sales revenues, and their growth rates.[20] Overall measures are important, but breaking these down to identify components provides greater insight. Two alternative revenue breakdowns are:

REVENUE PREDICTABILITY. We may classify revenue in three ways:

• **Continuous.** Revenue the firm expects to receive on a regular week-by-week or month-by-month basis. Examples — raw material sales, long-term contractual payments.

• **Periodic.** Sales are infrequent but can be forecast — capital equipment sales, seasonal goods.

• **Episodic.** Occur because of unanticipated events and cannot be forecast, like building materials sales following a hurricane.

Some firms develop strategies to shift *periodic* revenues to *continuous*, like technology firms replacing product sales by service sales on a usage basis.

PENETRATION VERSUS GROWTH. Many firms want to distinguish between sales based on current business — *penetration* — and sales from new business — *growth*. Retail organizations gain

KEY IDEA

Important internal *hard* measures are:
• Sales – units and revenues
• Product profitability
• Customer profitability

THE SALES INFORMATION SYSTEM

The sales information system is fundamental to managing a business. In good systems, the firm captures each sale on multiple dimensions like customer; product item; order, delivery, and payment date; price; terms; delivery location. When the firm enjoys such disaggregated data, it can develop summary reports by aggregating across products, customers, and other variables. Some firms develop their own proprietary systems to address specific issues, other firms use publicly available software from firms like Oracle, SAP. Developing a sales information system may seem conceptually straightforward, but can be difficult in practice. Issues include:

• *Timing.* The frequency with which managers require information depends on decisions they have to make. When Amazon sends an e-mail blast, it requires reports every few minutes so it can improve message effectiveness. Walmart shares sales data with suppliers every 24 hours so as to optimize store delivery; Cisco closes its books every 24 hours. For other firms, hourly or daily data may be overkill and weekly or even monthly data may be sufficient. The firm must select the *right* periodicity, based on the decisions it has to make.

• *Organizational complexity.* Many firms comprise multiple businesses. Each business may have a sales information system sufficient for its own activities, but system incompatibility makes integrating across businesses difficult, if not impossible. For many multinational firms, aggregating product sales data across countries and geographic regions is a real problem. Relatedly, aggregating sales by customer across product divisions and/or geographic regions is similarly challenging.

> When Lou Gerstner arrived as IBM's new CEO, he asked a senior executive: "How much business do we do annually with Ford around the world?" The response: "Give us a couple of days and we'll get back to you." IBM had no system to capture global sales by customer (much less profitability). Today, IBM has a sophisticated system that produces this information.

• *Distribution.* Typically, sales information systems capture sales to direct customers, but the firm may be more interested in sales to distributor customers/end users. The firm must seek these data from distributors, but they may not wish to share. Many firms must be content with estimates of end-user purchases.

• *Profitability.* Sales information systems provide sales data, *not* profitability data. To secure product and customer profitability, the firm must take the extra steps of subtracting out variable costs and various fixed-cost allocations. This process can be quite complicated.

MARKETING ENRICHMENT 24.1
Monitoring and Controlling Sales Revenues **702p**

deeper insight by partitioning sales into *same-store sales* (penetration) and *new-store sales* (growth). Figure 24.5 (boxed insert, p. 606) illustrates the iceberg approach to monitoring and controlling sales revenues. We examine firm performance in each cell of the 2x2 matrix formed from current and new products, and current and new markets.[21] (For a deeper analysis, Marketing Enrichment 24.1 [702p].)

ISSUES WITH SALES MEASURES. We consider three topics:

KEY IDEA

The firm should measure both sales units and sales revenues.

The firm must ensure sales measures are accurate and consistently derived.

• **Different sales volume measures.** At a minimum, the firm should measure both sales units and sales revenues. Both measures are necessary to distinguish between revenue growth based on sales units and revenue growth based on price increases.

• **Sales quality.** Some firms focus on specific types of sales. General Mills measures sales of products meeting certain nutritional targets, and sets goals on that basis.

• **Accuracy and consistency of sales volume measures.** The firm must ensure sales units and sales revenue measures are accurate, and are derived consistently from period to period. Sometimes growth-seeking firms abuse these sound business practices, forcing the SEC to demand earnings restatements:

As a senior MicroStrategy manager, what measures could you have taken to identify and control questionable practices?

Are Sales Real?

• Software firm MicroStrategy booked incomplete sales as revenues.
• BMS booked sales to wholesalers early to meet quarterly targets.
• Several firms heavily discount prices, effectively shifting future sales to the current period. *Channel stuffing* (*loading*) created trouble for Brocade, Coca-Cola, Computer Associates, Dial, PepsiCo, Peregrine Systems, Symbol Technologies, Warnaco.

Used in moderation and tightly managed, *vendor financing* is a sound business practice. But some firms abuse vendor financing by excessive lending to customers; effectively, they purchase from themselves to meet unrealistic sales goals. *Factoring* (selling) firm accounts receivable is also acceptable practice, but inconsistent factoring practice to *improve* financial statements is not. Finally, retailers do not typically account for *slotting fees* separately from product revenues, yet slotting fee revenues often rival overall profits.[22] Lack of transparency can easily lead to unsound decision-making.

THE ICEBERG PRINCIPLE IN PRACTICE

Gross analysis. Figure 24.5: Overall sales revenue standard — $160 million; actual sales revenues — $150 million; sales performance — $10 million below standard (total/total). This comparison provides zero information about reasons for the discrepancy, nor options for solving the problem.

Markets

		Current	**New**	**Total**
Products	**New**	Standard: $20 million Actual: $10 million	Standard: $15 million Actual: $5 million	Standard: $35 million Actual: $15 million
	Current	Standard: $100 million Actual: $120 million	Standard: $25 million Actual: $15 million	Standard: $125 million Actual: $135 million
	Total	Standard: $120 million Actual: $130 million	Standard: $40 million Actual: $20 million	Standard: $160 million Actual: $150 million

FIGURE 24.5
Illustrating Monitoring and Controlling Sales Revenues

First-level breakdown (marginals). We examine firm performance by product and market.

- *Product analysis:*
  - Current products did fine: $135 million actual versus $125 million standard — + $10 million.
  - New products did poorly: $15 million actual versus $35 million standard — – $20 million.
- *Market analysis:*
  - Current markets did fine: $130 million actual versus $120 million standard — + $10 million
  - New markets performed poorly: $20 million actual versus $40 million standard — – $20 million.
- *Conclusion:* The firm has problems with new products and new markets.

Second-level breakdown.

- Good performance — current products and current markets: $120 million actual versus $100 million standard (+ $20 million).
- Poor performance — all other market/product combinations:
  - current markets/new products: $10 million actual versus $20 million standard — – $10 million.
  - current products/new markets: $15 million actual versus $25 million standard — – $10 million.
  - new products/new markets: $5 million actual versus $15 million standard — – $10 million.

Assuming standards were well set, these performance gaps are very troubling; the firm is failing with new products and new markets. These results demand even deeper analysis. Breakdowns by market segment or sales region/district/ territory may provide clues to causes of poor performance.

Finally, suppose overall actual sales revenue total had been $161 million versus the $160 million standard. Despite this apparently satisfactory performance, some product/market combinations would probably have performed below standard. The firm must always consider the *iceberg principle*; overperformance in one area often masks underperformance somewhere else. Only by isolating underperforming areas and taking appropriate action can the firm improve overall performance.

INTERNAL HARD MEASURES — PRODUCT PROFITABILITY

MARKETING ENRICHMENT 24.2

The Overhead Allocation Problem **566p**

What is the overhead allocation problem? Why do firms face this issue?

Achieving good sales performance is important, but management is generally more interested in profits. Unfortunately, the most common profit measure — *bottom-line profit* — may not be terribly useful for assessing marketing effectiveness. Failure to meet profit targets may result from lack of promised resources or *unfair* corporate overhead allocations, rather than poor marketing. (Marketing Enrichment 24.2 **[566p]** illustrates the overhead allocation problem, and a solution.)

The firm should focus on measures that exclude allocations — like *profit contribution* and *direct product profit.*

PROFIT CONTRIBUTION equals sales revenues less variable costs. To earn positive net profits, profit contribution must exceed fixed costs.

DIRECT PRODUCT PROFIT assesses profit performance after taking into account fixed costs. The firm separates fixed costs into two parts: costs *directly related* to the product — *direct fixed costs* (would disappear if the product were dropped); and *allocated* costs — *indirect fixed costs* (would remain if the product were dropped). Direct product profit equals profit contribution less direct fixed costs.[23]

Direct product profit is an excellent measure for marketers:

- Sales revenue is a key determinant of profit contribution.
- Marketing expenses — advertising, promotion, field sales — are a major portion of direct fixed costs. Marketers must ensure individual marketing expenses help the firm achieve sales volume, market share, and profit targets.

PROFIT RETURN MEASURES. Some firms prefer *profit return* measures to *absolute* measures like profit contribution or direct product profit. Two popular measures are *return on sales (ROS)* and *return on investment (ROI).*[24] But an exclusive focus on either, especially ROS, can lead to poor decisions.[25]

KEY IDEA

Be careful with return on sales (ROS) as a performance measure.

Illustrating the ROS/ROI Problem

At VW, the key brand performance measure was ROS. VW marketed Seat and Skoda as strategically low-price brands, but meeting ROS targets was difficult. To improve ROS, Seat and Skoda introduced larger, higher-price (higher profit) cars. But these cars destroyed VW's low-cost strategic positioning. VW switched to ROI measures.

INTERNAL HARD MEASURES — CUSTOMER PROFITABILITY

KEY IDEA

Most firms measure product profitability; fewer firms measure customer profitability.

Most firms have systems to measure product profitability; some are rudimentary, others are highly sophisticated. DHL places customers into actionable segments and measures profit by segment. By contrast, relatively few firms measure customer profitability. Yet customers provide firm revenues and are its core assets — Chapter 1. Hence, the firm should understand the profitability dynamics of individual customers, market segments, and distribution channels. Conceptually, translating product profitability to customer profitability is straightforward, but financial system design and implementation may be challenging and expensive. When firms do secure customer profitability (fully accounting for direct service and shipping costs), they often identify unprofitable customers.

Table 24.2 (p. 608) shows an income statement comprising three products; Table 24.3 (p. 608) shows the same economic reality presented as an income statement comprising three customers.[26]

	Product X	Product Y	Product Z	Total
Sales Revenues	$4,330	$6,400	$7,001	$17,731
less Cost of Goods Sold	3,175	4,120	5,213	12,508
Gross Margin	1,155	2,280	1,788	5,223
less Other Operating Costs				4,023
Net Profit				1,200

....
TABLE 24.2
Product Income Statements ($000s)

	Customer* A	Customer* B	Customer* C	Total
Sales Revenues	$9,380	$4,351	$4,000	$17,731
less Cost of Goods Sold	4,452	4,353	3,703	12,508
Gross Margin	4,928	(2)	297	5,223
less Other Operating Costs:				
Sales Force	425	225	225	875
Field Service	224	325	224	773
Technical Assistance	285	285	380	950
Order Processing	275	162.5	112.5	550
Delivery	437	233	205	875
Other Operating Costs	1,646	1,230.5	1,146.5	4,023
Net Profit	3,282	(1,232.5)	(849.5)	1,200

....
TABLE 24.3
Customer Income Statements ($000s)

* Instead of customers, the column headings could equally well be market segments or distribution channels.

When customers purchase directly from the firm, the accounting system provides sales revenues and cost assignments. Difficulties arise when individual product data reside on different systems, and these systems do not *talk to each other*; similarly for customer profitability.

KEY IDEA

Sales and profit measures have serious shortcomings; they don't show firm performance relative to competitors.

> An experienced marketing executive reported: "We measure profitability by customer, geographic territory, and lines of service (products). We don't get every piece of data on every customer, but we get 70–80 percent of global data so we get a very good indication of profit contribution. Achieving customer profitability is very important to us. Some countries don't have the data, some don't put product codes in their systems, and some don't care if it's right or wrong. So we must deal with data capture and data quality issues."

Sales and profit measures provide good data on firm performance, but lack an external benchmark. Firm sales and profits may be happily growing at 10 percent per annum, but simultaneous 20 percent market or competitor growth would suggest a serious problem. Market-based measures address this issue.[27]

EXTERNAL HARD MEASURES — MARKET SHARE

Market share compares firm performance directly with competitors and is the most common *market-based* measure. The firm should measure market share in both units and revenues. These measures are identical when firm price equals the market average. When firm price exceeds the market average, revenue share exceeds unit share (and vice versa). When he became GE's CEO, Jack Welch required each business be No. 1 or No. 2 in its market.[28] *Relative market share* assesses firm market share versus competitors — BCG portfolio matrix — Chapter 12. *Market occupancy ratio* measures the firm's breadth of market activity. MTV has an important 60-country *footprint*, even though many countries operate at breakeven. Table 24.4 shows several market-based measures.

KEY IDEA

Important external *hard* measures are:
- Market share
- Relative market share
- Market occupancy ratio

Measure	Calculation	Information Provided
Market share (MS) (%)	Firm sales/Sales of all competitors	Market position versus all competitors
Relative market share (RMS) (%)	Firm sales/Sales of major competitor(s)	Market position versus major competitor(s)
Market occupancy ratio (MOR) (%)	Number of firm customers/ Total number of customers	Fraction of potential customers with which the firm does business

SOFT MEASURES

KEY IDEA

Customer satisfaction and attitudes are widely used *soft* measures.

The firm should regularly take the customer pulse. Customer satisfaction and attitudes are widely employed *soft* output measures. Soft measures help track how customers are responding to the firm and competitors. Because many soft measures are tied to hard measures — like customer satisfaction to sales — they can be valuable intermediate measures.[29]

> IBM's chief marketing intelligence officer said: "IBM hired me because the CEO couldn't get reliable marketing information. Each business unit invented its own customer satisfaction survey, chose its own sample, executed its own survey, and reported results. Guess what? Every customer was totally satisfied — no dissatisfaction! Meanwhile, market shares were falling like a rock. Marketing played the role of honest broker. We had incredible battles to get consistent measures that people would believe in. Remember, people get paid on these numbers, so they would *game* the system."[30]

KEY IDEA

A well-structured, validated, independently administered customer survey provides the best soft data.

MARKETING QUESTION

Why is Net Promoter Score so popular? What are the pros and cons for this performance measure?

A well-structured, validated, independently administered customer survey provides the best soft data. Generally, the firm seeks measures of the firm and competitors. At Siebel Systems (owned by Oracle), each six months, an independent firm measures satisfaction with Siebel departments and personnel at 400–500 customers (around 20 percent). Siebel bases salespeople bonuses and commissions on these results. Salespeople don't receive full commissions until one year after the sale, and then only if satisfaction scores are up to par. Microsoft employs performance-based stock awards for the top 600 managers, mainly based on customer satisfaction ratings.[31]

POPULAR SOFT MEASURES

Net Promoter Score (NPS). The firm derives its NPS from answers to a single question measured on a 0 to 10 scale:

"How likely is it that you would recommend XXXX to a friend or colleague?"

0 = not at all likely; 5 = neutral; 10 = extremely likely.

Net Promoter Score = percentage of customers scoring 9 or 10 (promoters) minus percentage of customers scoring 0 to 6 (detractors).

Leading U.S. scores (2015): USAA — 80; Costco — 78; Nordstrom — 75; Apple — 70; Amazon — 69; Southwest Airlines — 66

Firms using NPS also probe for the reasons behind the score.[32]

Burke's Secure Customer Index (SCI). Five equally weighted components are:

- Overall *customer satisfaction* with the firm
- Likelihood of *repeat business* for the firm
- Likelihood to *recommend* the firm to others
- *Preference* for the firm versus others
- Extent to which the firm has *earned loyalty*

Burke measures customer responses on five-point scales: *agree completely — disagree completely*: Scores range from 0 to 100. Burke recommends tracking the SCI index over time and making comparisons with competitors and best-in-class performers.[33]

Enterprise car rental surveys one in every 15 customers for the Enterprise Service Quality Index (ESQi). Enterprise aggregates responses to just two questions:

- On a scale ranging from *completely satisfied* to *completely unsatisfied*, how would you rate your last Enterprise experience?
- Would you rent from Enterprise again?

Each Enterprise branch office receives ESQi scores; branch managers scoring under the company average are not promoted. Similarly, GE (and many other firms) use *Net Promoter Score* to gauge customer sentiment.**[521v]**[34] Marketing research provider Burke developed a customer loyalty index; brand health checks are another popular soft measure — Chapter 11, p. 298.

INTERMEDIATE MEASURES

The firm takes actions — *inputs* — to improve *outputs*. *Intermediate* measures sit between inputs and outputs. Success on intermediate measures *does not guarantee* output performance. But the firm only achieves good output performance *by securing good intermediate performance*. Intermediate measures have two key characteristics:

- **Input effect.** The firm's marketing effort must affect the intermediate measure.
- **Output effect.** The intermediate measure must influence another intermediate measure and/or an important output measure(s).

The distributor of inexpensive Fleischmann's gin developed a new retail distribution strategy; shelve products next to high-quality Gordon's and Gilbey's. The theory: Consumers would reach Gordon's and Gilbey's displays, see less-expensive Fleischmann bottles, then select Fleischmann's. The key intermediate measure: number of stores accepting Fleischmann's shelf placement.

The sales cycle for Jostens high school yearbooks (delivered June) starts early fall. Salespeople ask high school decision-makers to agree to a formal presentation. Jostens' predictive sales model estimates the probability of a sale, conditional on a presentation. Number of signed agreement cards is an important intermediate measure for Jostens.

The best intermediate measures are leading indicators of output performance; they should result from a tested customer purchase model: inputs → intermediates → outputs. For open-enrollment programs, Columbia Business School Executive Education models promotional spend — *input*; number of enquires — *intermediate*; number of participants — *output*. Pfizer's marketing-process model for prescription pharmaceuticals comprises 32 distinct steps. Marketers indicate the type of return Pfizer needs from each specific marketing input. Pfizer's extensive historical database provides good information on relationships among input measures and intermediate measures. Pfizer knows a given type and amount of advertising — *input* — will generate a certain number of physician requests — *intermediate* — and those requests will lead to a certain number of prescriptions — *output*.

Intermediate measures are particularly important in long-cycle sales processes, as for major capital goods. Many months or even years may elapse between initial customer contact and actual sale. Many firms manage sales pipelines — Chapter 18 — using intermediate measures. Pipeline management can help sales managers close unfavorable intermediate performance gaps by requiring salespeople to change input actions.[35] We discuss intermediate sales force and advertising measures.

INTERMEDIATE SALES FORCE MEASURES

The firm should base these measures on a sales pipeline model. Intermediate sales force measures differ from firm to firm. For one firm, factory trials may be a good measure; for another firm, dollars of co-op advertising agreed — Table 24.5 (p. 611).

KEY IDEA

Critical control variables are:

Input measures
↓
Intermediate measures
↓
Output measures

KEY IDEA

Success on intermediate measures *does not guarantee* firm output performance. But the firm can only achieve good output performance *by securing good intermediate performance.*

MARKETING QUESTION

BMS introduced Abilify for people suffering from schizophrenia and bipolar disorder. BMS promotional strategy was twofold:

- Sales representatives detailed Abilify to physicians
- Consumer advertising

What output measures would you suggest for Abilify? What intermediate measures would you suggest?

KEY IDEA

Intermediate objectives are particularly important for long-cycle sales.

Measure	Rationale
Commitments to co-op advertising	Customers place resources at risk and make best efforts
Customer's subjective impression of salesperson interaction — telesales	Indicator of future sales
Distribution breadth for products	Securing distribution is necessary for end-user purchases
Entry on approved supplier list	Customers purchase only from fully qualified suppliers
Factory trials agreed	Customers will not buy without factory use experience
Proposals accepted	Necessary step to win business
Retail displays accepted	Good shelf positioning leads to sales

INTERMEDIATE ADVERTISING MEASURES

The firm should base measures on an advertising effectiveness model geared to the market situation. For a newly launched product, *awareness* may be appropriate; for an established product, *quality perception* may be better — Table 24.6.

TABLE 24.6
Possible Intermediate Measures for Advertising

Measure	Information Provided
Awareness	Degree of product/brand awareness
Liking	Indicates positive feeling toward the product/brand
Interest	Indicates likelihood of product/brand purchase
Product quality perception	Perception of product/brand quality
Number of press mentions	Indicates customer awareness
Message recall	Indicates advertising effectiveness

KEY IDEA

Critical control variables are:

Input measures

↓

Intermediate measures

↓

Output measures

KEY IDEA

Monitoring and controlling firm functioning comprises:
- Implementation control
- Strategy control
- Managerial process control

Monitoring and Controlling Firm Functioning

In a well-developed monitor-and-control system, input measures are closely and explicitly linked to intermediate measures. In turn, intermediate measures are closely and explicitly related to output measures.

INPUT MEASURES

Input measure performance depends on three aspects of firm functioning:
- **Implementation control.** Did the firm implement planned actions?
- **Strategy control.** Is the market strategy well conceived and on target?
- **Managerial process control.** Are firm processes the best they can be?

IMPLEMENTATION CONTROL

The firm's market strategy spawns many implementation programs; these programs generate action plans in marketing-mix areas like product, service, promotion, distribution, and price. The market strategy may also generate action plans in functional areas like engineering, operations, R&D, technical service. Marketing and other functional managers are typically responsible for ensuring the firm executes these action plans. Table 24.7 (p. 612) and Table 24.8 (p. 612) respectively illustrate possible input measures for the sales force and new product development.

Measure	Measure Focus
Implementation of sales planning system	Ensure sales force plans time allocations
New product knowledge training	Ensure sales force is competent to sell new products
Sales calls per day	Ensure sales force is working hard
Sales calls on new accounts	Ensure sales force spends time with target accounts
Sales territories vacant	Ensure sales managers plan for attrition
Total expenses	Manage sales force discretionary costs

TABLE 24.7
Possible Input Measures —
Sales Force

Measure	Measure Focus
Qualified new product ideas generated	Creativity in generating high-quality ideas
New concepts tested	Success in developing new ideas
Licenses/technology purchases checked out	Success in looking for ideas outside the firm
Products completing beta tests	Success in moving ideas through the new product development system
Test markets conducted	Success in developing products for market readiness
New products launched	Entire new product development process

TABLE 24.8
Possible Input Measures —
New Product Development

Home Depot (HD) measures store associate time use. HD reschedules tasks that take associates away from customers; HD receives deliveries at night. HD schedules demonstrations of pneumatic nail guns on Mondays and Tuesdays from 7 a.m. to 9 a.m. when sales are highest. A senior ExxonMobil executive is very clear: "Operationally, you've got to start with measuring, monitoring, and helping your own employees. Because, unless your employees *get it*, they can't deliver on your brand promise. If they *get it*, then you can reach through them to customers."[36]

KEY IDEA

Implementation control: Did the firm implement planned actions?

STRATEGY CONTROL

Strategy control answers the question: *Is the firm's market strategy well conceived and on target?* The firm typically sets strategy for the medium or long run; it should not overreact to poor output performance by making hasty changes. For strategy control, *postaction control* is generally superior to *steering control.*

Figure 24.6 (p. 613) shows how to integrate strategy control and implementation control to isolate causes of firm output performance.[37] Performance is good in Cell A — less so in other cells:

MARKET STRATEGY GOOD/IMPLEMENTATION GOOD (CELL A). A well-developed and well-implemented strategy should drive good output performance. The firm must monitor customers, competitors, and the general environment to ensure the strategy remains on track.

MARKET STRATEGY GOOD/IMPLEMENTATION POOR (CELL B). Poor implementation of a good strategy will probably generate poor output performance. Sometimes an especially robust strategy can survive poor implementation, but this is unusual. Cole National (CN) targeted hardware and other small stores for key-making machines and key blanks; CN succeeded despite poor sales force execution. The firm should focus on improving execution.

MARKET STRATEGY POOR/IMPLEMENTATION GOOD (CELL C). Rarely does excellent implementation overcome a poor strategy. If the firm fails to provide customer value, successfully implementing other marketing elements will not compensate. Some years ago, Frito-Lay failed with a new cookie despite legendary sales force implementation.

MARKET STRATEGY POOR/IMPLEMENTATION POOR (CELL D). Output performance is likely disastrous. The challenge is to isolate the cause — poor strategy or poor implementation?

KEY IDEA

Strategy control: Is the firm's market strategy well conceived and on target?

Postaction approaches are generally superior for strategy control.

FIGURE 24.6
Integrating Strategy and Implementation Control

MARKETING
QUESTION

Consider your personal work experience. Which Figure 24.6 quadrant best describes the organization's situation you experienced? Why?

This framework explicitly recognizes that good output performance requires both good strategy *and* good implementation. Poor output performance has many authors; the management challenge is isolating the cause. The firm should conduct deep analysis across many business aspects:

- **Market-strategy foundations** — market, customer, competitor, company, complementer insight — Chapters 3, 4, 5, 6
- **Market segmentation and market strategy** — Chapters 8, 9, 10, 11
- **Action plans** — Chapter 9
- **Measures for monitoring and controlling implementation** — Chapter 24
- **Actual performance versus input, intermediate, and output standards** — Chapter 24 (Marketing Enrichment 24.3 **[383p]** shows how to separate out planning and performance variances.)

MARKETING
ENRICHMENT 24.3

Separate Planning and Performance Variances **383p**

KEY IDEA

Distinguishing between strategy and implementation problems is crucial.

No matter where the firm isolates problems — strategy or implementation — some things must change. Regardless, changes are more difficult to make than others. Change can be a special problem when the environment evolves quickly and managers cling to outdated strategies; and implementation programs outlive their usefulness. Advertising is relatively easy to modify; indeed, most firms undertake reviews annually if not more frequently. Distribution arrangements are more difficult to alter due to logistical, contractual, and interpersonal relationships. Figure 24.7 suggests inertia levels for different marketing-mix implementation areas.[38]

FIGURE 24.7
Inertia in Marketing-Mix Implementation

MANAGERIAL PROCESS CONTROL

Are the firm's processes the best they can be? We addressed this question in Chapter 23. Three broad approaches to *managerial process control* and process improvement are *best-practice transfer, benchmarking, reengineering*. Here, we focus explicitly on improving marketing functioning — the *marketing audit*.[39]

MARKETING AUDIT. The *marketing audit* is a comprehensive process for evaluating marketing practices — market strategy, systems and processes, activities, organization. To ensure confidences are kept and findings are unbiased, outsiders typically conduct the audit. Auditors meet with managers, customers, industry experts; they collect and analyze internal financial, sales, and operating data, plus competitive and industry data. A useful auditing framework has six parts, each spawning several questions[40]:

- **Marketing environment.** What changes are occurring at customers, competitors, complementers, and suppliers? What PESTLE trends — Chapter 3 — affect the industry? How do these changes/trends affect the firm? What are performance implications?

- **Market objectives and strategy.** Are the firm's market objectives and strategy realistic given the environment and firm strengths? Do managers understand objectives and strategy?

- **Marketing implementation.** How do firm offers compare to competitor offers — product, service, promotion, distribution, price? Does the marketing mix implement the market strategy? Are they mutually consistent?

- **Marketing organization.** Are job roles and responsibilities clear and consistent? Is recruiting, hiring, training, and development on track? Is senior management engaged with major customers? Do measurement and reward systems motivate performance?

- **Marketing systems.** How effective are firm marketing systems — brand monitoring, competitor intelligence, customer advisory boards, customer database design and updates, marketing research, measuring customer satisfaction, new product development, sales forecasting and pipeline management, sales lead generation, tapping into social media?

- **Marketing productivity.** How profitable are firm product lines? How profitable are firm customers/segments? Do some products/customers merit additional effort? Should the firm reprice/discontinue some products? Should the firm drop some customers? Should the firm pursue other customers more vigorously? Is firm focus appropriate, given the market environment? How should the firm allocate resources across the marketing mix? Does the firm need more or less product improvements, trade incentives, and/or sales/service personnel?

Marketing audits can be very effective as a diagnostic tool. The firm should look out for[41]:

- **Considering marketing only as the marketing department's job.** Customers are critical firm assets. Marketing is everybody's business, not just a marketing department responsibility.[42]

- **Cutting prices rather than increasing value.** The sales force complains and the firm cuts prices. The firm earns insufficient profit to enhance customer value.

- **Failure to invest for the future, especially in human resources.** The firm views marketing and HR as expenses, not as investments. The firm underfunds marketing, training and development.

- **Failure to segment markets effectively.** Firms form simple geographic or demographic segments; they do not probe sufficiently deeply to gain good insight.

- **Insufficient knowledge of customer attitudes and behavior.** Firms collect customer data too infrequently. Even with frequent collection, senior managers are often ill-informed and data do not drive marketing decision-making.

- **New product development delegated to developers.** Technical employees develop new products with little marketing input and insufficient customer insight.

KEY IDEA

Managerial process control: Are the firm's processes the best they can be?

KEY IDEA

The marketing audit is a comprehensive process for evaluating marketing practices.

Many of these concerns mirror issues we discuss in Section I — Marketing and the Firm. We reinforce them here because firms find it so difficult to be truly externally oriented. No matter how noble the intentions, following through requires attention to detail, hard work, and the right mind-set. The marketing audit is a useful tool to keep the firm on track.

THE BALANCED SCORECARD

KEY IDEA

The balanced scorecard reflects a *steering control* philosophy, balancing input, intermediate, and output marketing measures.

The *balanced scorecard* is an increasingly widespread approach for monitoring and controlling firm performance and firm functioning.[462v] The balanced scorecard seeks a middle ground between using too few measures and too many. Each extreme leads to problems:

TOO FEW MEASURES. Managers may *game* the system to optimize performance on those measures, especially whether they drive compensation. Such behavior may cause unintended consequences. When short-term profit is the only standard, performing well is very easy: Just cut advertising and R&D for a couple of quarters. Of course, such actions hurt the firm in the long run. Previously, U.S. airlines competed by advertising shorter flight times; when on-time performance data became widely available, airlines lengthened advertised flight times and improved *on-time* performance! When the incoming Home Depot CEO focused on *inventory velocity* (inventory turns), some managers ordered fewer products; inventory velocity improved, but customers couldn't find products they wanted.

TOO MANY MEASURES. Multiple measures cause problems if they are unclear or conflicting. Employees have difficulty discerning required behavior; they may focus efforts on actions that impede reaching firm goals.[43]

Many firms address these problems via the balanced scorecard.[44] Well-balanced scorecards reflect a *steering control* philosophy by *balancing* input, intermediate, and output measures. PepsiCo's marketplace profit and loss system, the basis for managerial bonuses, includes:

- Customer attitudes
- Employee motivation
- Financial profit and loss
- Market share
- Quality

Perhaps the most commonly used measures for balanced scorecards are:

- **Market share** — external hard output measure
- **Customer satisfaction relative to competition** — external soft output measure
- **Customer retention versus industry averages** — external hard output measure
- **Investment as a percentage of sales** — hard input measure
- **Employee attitudes and retention** (especially customer-facing employees) — soft and hard input measures

Many balanced scorecards focus on four measurement categories — financial, customer, internal business processes, learning and growth. Table 24.9 shows candidate measures for a global account management program. Table 24.10 (p. 616) shows key elements in a balanced scorecard for gasoline marketing.[45] This particular scorecard is noteworthy for many *soft* measures; financial measures are weighted 10 percent versus 90 percent for nonfinancial measures.

TABLE 24.9
Candidate Variables for Balanced Scorecard Approach: Measuring the Global Account Program

Financial
- Year-on-year revenue and profit growth
- Sales expense as a percentage of revenues

Customer
- Customer satisfaction and loyalty
- Access to customer at C-level — CEO, CFO, CIO, COO

Internal Business Process
- Percentage of customers with long-term contracts
- Percentage of customers with *solutions* contracts
- Process improvements from collaboration — summary billing, product development

Learning and Growth
- Number of best-practices adopters
- Improved management practices

Perspective	Weighting	Objective	Measure
Financial	10%	Service operating efficiency	Budget variance
Client	30%	Evaluate organizational effectiveness	Client satisfaction service agreement feedback (5-point scale) • Gasoline marketing • Retail dealer operations • Franchise reengineering • Training • Retail dealer operations • Fuels support • Leadership development • Real estate • Strategy implementation
Internal	40%	Excel in channel management	Tracking versus channel strategy • Retail • Wholesale • Fuels support • Training • Real estate
		Optimize sales force management development	Area manager development index
		Service integration/alignment	Quality service forums
Learning and Growth	20%	Core competencies and skills	Personnel development • 360 feedback on all employees • Competency plan on employees executed
		Organizational involvement/ scorecard understanding	Idea generation index Quarterly climate survey

TABLE 24.10
Balanced Scorecard: Mobil Gasoline Marketing

The firm should closely align scorecards for different functional areas and managerial levels — brand, category managers; district, regional, national sales managers. Carefully designed and aligned sets of measures improve firm chances of securing high performance. Well-designed scorecards help minimize deviant behavior — accounting manipulation, channel loading — that may cause significant problems.

MARKETING QUESTION

In your educational institution, each instructor has his/her own way of measuring student performance. Can you suggest a balanced-scorecard framework for all instructors to use that would measure student performance?

KEY MESSAGES

MARKETING QUESTION

What other messages did you glean from this chapter?

The purpose of monitor-and-control systems is to improve firm performance. Four key principles are:

- Focus on market levers and develop alternative plans.
- Mostly implement steering control rather than postaction control.
- Use the *right* performance measures at the *right* organizational levels.
- Model relationships among input, intermediate, output measures.

Critical stages in developing a monitor-and-control process are:

- Identify the process to control.
- Decide and define measures.
- Develop measurement system.
- Set standards.
- Measure results.
- Compare results against standards; identify gaps and variances.
- Understand and communicate performance gaps.
- Generate and evaluate alternatives.
- Select alternatives and take action.

The firm should monitor and control three types of measure:
- *Output measures* — final results the firm wants to achieve; can be *hard* or *soft*.
- *Intermediate measures* — sit between input and output measures; affect other intermediate measures and/or output measures.
- *Input measures* — concerned with firm functioning; explicitly linked to intermediate measures. Input measures concern three types of control:
  - Implementation control
  - Strategy control
  - Managerial process control
- The marketing audit is a useful approach for evaluating marketing systems and processes.
- The balanced scorecard typically embraces input, intermediate, and output measures.

VIDEOS AND AUDIOS

For complimentary material, see Axcess Capon codes at www.axcessvids.com

Monitor and Control	**452v**	Alan Fortier	Fortier & Associates
Monitor and Control	**302v**	Ron Boire	Toys "R" Us
Marketing Imperative 6	**973a**	Noel Capon	Columbia Business School

QUESTIONS FOR STUDY AND DISCUSSION

Can you answer the questions implied by this chapter's learning outcomes? Check!

1. Chapter 24 discusses several output measures. Develop six other output measures a firm could use. How did you choose these measures? Why is each measure valuable? What does each measure add to output measures discussed in the chapter?

2. Many managers are distrustful of *soft* measures like customer satisfaction. How would you convince these managers that *soft* measures have value?

3. Use the input → intermediate → output framework to identify alternative measures for the marketing executive responsible for Apple's iPad. Using these measures, develop a balanced scorecard to assess executive performance. Alternatively, complete this task for *Managing Marketing in the 21st Century*.

4. How can a marketing audit enhance brand value? What do you expect to learn from the audit process?

5. How would you justify the investment in capturing timely customer data?

TRUE/FALSE QUESTIONS

Answers on page A2 and at www.axcessvids.com — 117p

1. Firms using steering control wait for a preset amount of time, then compare actual results against standards. ❏ **TRUE** ❏ **FALSE**

2. Internal hard measures include market share and market occupancy ratio. ❏ **TRUE** ❏ **FALSE**

3. Direct product profit assesses product profit performance after taking into account fixed costs incurred by the product. ❏ **TRUE** ❏ **FALSE**

4. Customer satisfaction is the most common market-based measure, comparing the firm's performance directly with competitors. ❏ **TRUE** ❏ **FALSE**

5. Strategy control asks the question: *Is the firm's market strategy well conceived and on target?* ❏ **TRUE** ❏ **FALSE**

MULTIPLE CHOICE QUESTIONS

Answers on page A2 and at www.axcessvids.com — 567p

1. Which of the following is NOT one of the key principles on which a firm should build its monitor-and-control processes?

   a. Focus on market levers and develop alternative plans.
   b. Implement postaction control rather than steering controls.
   c. Use the right performance measures at the right organizational levels.
   d. Model the relationship between input, intermediate, and output measures.

2. Which of the following is NOT an example of an internal hard measure?

   a. sales revenues
   b. product profitability
   c. customer profitability
   d. market share

3. Which of the following is NOT a basic aspect of firm functioning to enhance performance on input measures?

   a. implementation control
   b. strategy control
   c. managerial process control
   d. vision control

4. All of the following are important parts of an auditing framework EXCEPT:

   a. marketing environment
   b. marketing systems and processes
   c. marketing productivity
   d. marketing demographics

5. All of the following are commonly used measures for balanced scorecards EXCEPT:

   a. market share
   b. debt-to-equity ratio
   c. customer retention versus industry averages
   d. employee attitudes and retention

SECTION V

SPECIAL
MARKETING TOPICS

For complimentary material, see Axcess Capon codes at www.axcessvids.com

SPECIAL MARKETING TOPICS comprises two chapters. Chapter 25 focuses on a topic appearing in various places throughout *Managing Marketing in the 21st Century* — International, Regional, and Global Marketing. Globalization is one of the major trends facing practically all firms in practically all industries. Chapter 25 helps firms decide whether or not to enter foreign markets, which foreign markets to enter, and which entry options to choose. Further, the chapter discusses designing, implementing, and organizing for international, regional, and global marketing. Chapter 26 concerns ethical, legal, and socially responsible decisions in marketing. Marketers face many challenges in making marketing decisions, not the least of which is making them appropriately.

Managing Marketing in the 21st Century

SECTION I: MARKETING AND THE FIRM

CHAPTER 1
Introduction to Managing Marketing

CHAPTER 2
The Value of Customers

SECTION II: FUNDAMENTAL INSIGHTS FOR STRATEGIC MARKETING

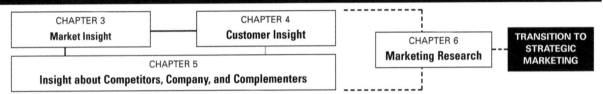

CHAPTER 3
Market Insight

CHAPTER 4
Customer Insight

CHAPTER 5
Insight about Competitors, Company, and Complementers

CHAPTER 6
Marketing Research

TRANSITION TO STRATEGIC MARKETING

SECTION III: STRATEGIC MARKETING

IMPERATIVE 1
Determine and Recommend Which Markets to Address

IMPERATIVE 2
Identify and Target Market Segments

CHAPTER 7
Identifying and Choosing Opportunities

CHAPTER 8
Market Segmentation and Targeting

IMPERATIVE 3
Set Strategic Direction and Positioning

CHAPTER 9
Market Strategy – Integrating Firm Efforts for Marketing Success

CHAPTER 10
Managing through the Life Cycle

CHAPTER 11
Managing Brands

SECTION IV: IMPLEMENTING THE MARKET STRATEGY

IMPERATIVE 4
Design the Market Offer

PART A: PROVIDING CUSTOMER VALUE

PART B: COMMUNICATING CUSTOMER VALUE

PART C: DELIVERING CUSTOMER VALUE

PART D: GETTING PAID FOR CUSTOMER VALUE

CHAPTER 12
Managing the Product Line

CHAPTER 15
Integrated Marketing Communications

CHAPTER 19
Distribution Decisions

CHAPTER 21
Critical Underpinnings of Pricing Decisions

CHAPTER 13
Managing Services and Customer Service

CHAPTER 16
Mass Communications

CHAPTER 20
Retailing and Wholesaling

CHAPTER 22
Setting Prices

CHAPTER 14
Developing New Products

CHAPTER 17
Digital Marketing

CHAPTER 18
Directing and Managing the Field Sales Effort

IMPERATIVE 5
Secure Support from Other Functions

IMPERATIVE 6
Monitor and Control Execution and Performance

CHAPTER 23
Ensuring the Firm Implements the Market Offer as Planned: Becoming an Externally Oriented Firm

CHAPTER 24
Monitoring and Controlling Firm Performance and Functioning

SECTION V: SPECIAL MARKETING TOPICS

CHAPTER 25
International, Regional, and Global Marketing

CHAPTER 26
Ethical, Legal, and Socially Responsible Decisions in Marketing

CHAPTER 25

INTERNATIONAL, REGIONAL, AND GLOBAL MARKETING

For complimentary material, see Axcess Capon codes at www.axcessvids.com

LEARNING OUTCOMES

When you have completed this chapter, you will be able to:

- Decide whether or not to enter foreign markets.
- Assess alternative foreign markets and decide which to enter.
- Become familiar with global and regional government-type organizations aspiring to enhance foreign trade and investment.
- Decide how to enter foreign markets.
- Develop market strategy for approaching international, regional, global markets.
- Segment global markets and develop global branding strategies.
- Implement international, regional, and global market strategies.
- Develop the *right* organization for managing firm activities in foreign markets.
- Manage global customers.

OPENING CASE: DHL

DHL (Dalsey, Hillblom, and Lynn) was founded in 1969 as a document courier in the Asia Pacific region several years before Federal Express (now FedEx).[1] During the next 30 years, DHL expanded throughout Asia Pacific, Europe, and the Americas. In 2002, Deutsche Post (DP) acquired DHL. Subsequently, DP acquired more than 100 firms in related fields, including Danzas-AEI (Europe's largest freight forwarder) and leading domestic parcel firms in Britain, France, Spain, and the Benelux countries. (In 2008, DHL withdrew from the U.S. domestic market.) By 2009, DHL had annual revenues around $70 billion and employed more than 300,000 people worldwide.

DHL serves the express delivery and logistics business segments for its parent DP. DHL's express service links 120,000 destinations in more than 220 countries and territories. DHL provides delivery services from a network of 5,000 offices with a fleet of more than 70,000 vehicles and 400 aircraft.

DHL maintains 3.5 million square meters of warehouse space at over 1,000 distribution centers and provides freight forwarding, logistics, and supply-chain-management services.

DHL's vision states: Customers trust DHL as the preferred global express and logistics partner, leading the industry in terms of quality, profitability, and market share. DHL enhances the business of our customers by offering highest quality express and logistics solutions based on strong local expertise combined with the most extensive global network presence.

To serve customers, DHL's four major brands (businesses) have profit and loss responsibility:

- *DHL Express: same-day, time-definite, day-definite express delivery services*
- *DHL Supply Chain CIS: contract logistics and industry solutions — supply-chain management, warehousing, distribution, value-added services, logistics outsourcing, lead logistics supplier*
- *Global Forwarding Freight Air Freight and Ocean Freight Services: air freight, ocean freight, industrial projects, customer program management*
- *Global Forwarding Freight Road and Rail Freight: flexible and customized road and intermodal transport network*

DHL customers comprise three tiers:

- *Tier 1 — top 100 customers, managed by Global Customer Solutions (GCS) globally.*
- *Tier 2 — other multinational customers, managed by individual business units globally.*
- *Tier 3 — thousands of local customers, managed by individual business units locally.*

Global Customer Solutions. *DHL organizes GCS by nine industry sectors (Aerospace; Automotive; Chemical; Consulting; Fashion; Industrial, Engineering, and Manufacturing; Life Sciences; Retail; Technology). Each Tier 1 customer has a dedicated global customer manager (GCM) who reports into an industry sector. GCMs are responsible for global revenues and profits of their customers. They enjoy three types of support:*

How do you assess DHL's approach to addressing increased globalization?

- *Local Key Account Managers (KAMs). Individual KAMs work for one of the brands in a specific country but are assigned to GCMs on a dotted-line basis.*
- *Regional Customer Managers (RCMs). RCMs are responsible for certain areas of the world — Asia Pacific; Europe, Middle East, Africa; and the Americas. They report to GCMs but have more direct everyday contact with KAMs.*
- *Staff Support. Various types including program management, supply-chain consultants, pricing, information technology, tender management, and legal/risk expertise.* [600v]

The world is being flattened. I didn't start it and you can't stop it, except at great cost to human development and your own future. But we can manage it, for better or worse.

— Thomas L. Friedman, *New York Times* correspondent, author *The World is Flat*[2]

Opportunities for firms to engage in international, regional, and global marketing are large and growing.[3] Since the 1950s, intercountry trade has increased dramatically — Figure 25.1. One trend is critical: Individual firms increasingly seek opportunities beyond their domestic markets. The purpose of this chapter is to help you think through critical issues approaching foreign markets.

Note that Chapter 25's title is deliberate — international, regional, and global marketing. One size does not fit all. Some firms engage in *global marketing* by entering many foreign markets in different continents; some focus on specific geographic regions — *regional marketing*; and others on just a few foreign countries — *international marketing*. But venturing abroad into unfamiliar territory is not for everyone; many firms prefer to focus on their domestic markets.

In this chapter you will learn to assess international markets, develop market strategy, implement market offers, and manage the marketing process anywhere in the world.

FIGURE 25.1
Global Merchandise Trade ($ billions)[4]

Source: World Trade Organization

Growing international trade offers many opportunities for firms venturing abroad.

Chapter 25 focuses on key marketing issues for expanding geographically. We draw on the marketing imperatives, principles, and philosophy from previous chapters as we ask and answer several important questions:

- Should the firm engage in marketing outside its domestic borders?
- How should the firm choose which foreign markets to enter?
- What foreign-market-entry options are available?
- What market strategy should the firm choose for foreign markets?
- What global market-strategy issues must the firm address, and how should it do so?
- How should the firm organize for global markets?
- How should the firm address global customers?

THE CHANGING VIEW

OLD WAY	NEW WAY
Brand decisions made locally and regionally; supported by myriad advertising and PR agencies	Strategic brand decisions made centrally; single agency acts as global partner
Firms conduct international trade in multiple languages	English emerging as the lingua franca of international and global business
Firms make many international marketing decisions at country and regional levels	Firms struggle over which decisions to centralize at head office and which to place in countries and regions
Intercountry agreements on economic issues fragmented and limited in scope	Intercountry agreements on economic issues becoming the norm
International and global marketing mainly for large firms	International and global marketing an increasing option for small- and medium-size firms
Most firms group countries by geographic proximity for international and global marketing	Leading firms group countries in ways other than geographic proximity
Product and geography dominate organizational design for international marketing	Global customer organizations are increasingly important
Technology is not a major factor in international, regional, and global marketing	Global package delivery and the Internet are critical growth drivers for international, regional, and global marketing

SHOULD YOU ENTER FOREIGN MARKETS?

KEY IDEA

Before entering foreign markets, the firm should make sure it has good reasons for venturing abroad.

Historically, large firms were more likely to venture abroad than medium-size and small firms. Firms like Citibank, Ford, General Motors, Heinz, IBM, Nestlé, Shell, and many others have operated overseas for decades. Today, firms of all sizes contemplate taking the plunge into foreign markets. IBM earns two thirds of revenues outside the U.S.; the much younger Google earns over 50 percent. But, before going abroad, the firm should be very clear about its reasons. Why should the firm trade home-market familiarity for the uncertainties and risks of venturing overseas?[5] Unless it has a good answer to this question, the firm probably shouldn't bother.

Generally, firms go abroad for a variety of different reasons:

- **Diversify risk.** Domestic firms spread risk by seeking revenues in countries with different local and regional business cycles. But they assume currency, foreign government, and other risks.

- **Follow customers.** When an important customer enters a foreign market, the firm may have little choice but to follow, like Toyota suppliers. Following customers is especially common when transportation costs are high: Van Leer (The Netherlands) places facilities for making storage drums (oil/chemicals) close to oil-company customer refineries.

- **Gain knowledge.** Foreign-market entry may be the best way to enhance intellectual capital, especially if the industry's most demanding customers are abroad. The firm may also learn serendipitously: Cemex adopted English as a common language, rotates managers internationally, and gained access to international consultants.

In recent years, many Indian firms entered foreign markets (often via acquisition) to enhance scale, gain technology, and improve competitiveness, as foreign competitors entered India. Tata Motors acquired Jaguar Land Rover; by purchasing European steelmaker Corus, Tata Steel gained 80 U.S. patents and 1,000 researchers. Chinese firms are also expanding abroad: Lenovo acquired IBM's PC business; Geely acquired Volvo (from Ford); Haier invested in several domestic appliance firms.

- **Growth opportunities.** Revenue and profit opportunities may seem greater abroad than at home. An attractive opportunity may arrive randomly, like an unsolicited request for firm products from a foreign market, or result from a broad search process the firm conducts. Fierce home-market competition can drive such a search: Many small Italian firms, like wedding-dress maker Giovanna Sbiroli, lost business to Asian imports, but successfully entered foreign markets with distinctively Italian products.
- **Keep competitors honest.** Sometimes a foreign competitor subsidizes entry in the firm's domestic market with profits earned at home. To *keep the competitor honest* and deny it such funding, the firm may enter the aggressor's home market.

To enter the U.S. market, European home appliance leader Electrolux acquired third-place White Consolidated. Then, U.S. market leader Whirlpool acquired Philips' home appliance business (Europe No. 2); GE (U.S. No. 2) acquired a stake in Britain's GEC. Later, Maytag (U.S. No. 4) acquired Hoover, and Whirlpool acquired Maytag.

When leading European cement producer Holcim invested in Mexico, Mexican cement maker Cemex entered Spain where Holcim had significant investments.

- **Reduce costs.** Sometimes firms derive success from low-cost operations that allow low prices. By entering foreign markets, the firm may be able to tap international capital markets and secure lower capital costs. It may also enhance scale economies and secure access to low-cost labor. (Sometimes venturing abroad increases costs, like bringing employee pay up to international standards.)
- **Small home market.** For firms based in small countries, going abroad may be the only reasonable way to grow — like many Hong Kong, Singapore, Swiss and Scandinavian firms.

When the firm enters foreign markets, the many unknowns increase risks. The firm should only go abroad if it believes that profits from foreign-market entry outweigh the risks. Conversely, the firm should not hesitate to withdraw from a foreign market(s) if entry is unprofitable — like Carrefour exiting Southeast Asia, and Walmart leaving Germany and Korea. Of course, never venturing abroad, but rather competing with aggressive domestic and foreign competitors, may be even more risky!

HOW TO CHOOSE WHICH FOREIGN MARKETS TO ENTER

As with domestic markets, the choice of which foreign markets to enter depends on market attractiveness and the firm's ability to compete. Key considerations are appropriate financial return, risk, and timing of profit flows — Chapter 7. These factors depend on foreign-market attractiveness for firm products/services and the firm's ability to compete.

....
FOREIGN-MARKET ATTRACTIVENESS

KEY IDEA

Considerations in assessing foreign-market attractiveness include:

- Economic, political, legal/regulatory issues:
  - Domestic
  - International
- Sociocultural and geographic distance

To assess foreign-market attractiveness, we adapt the PESTLE framework — Chapter 3. PESTLE factors affect market attractiveness in different ways. For international markets, we examine several dimensions that factor heavily in assessing market attractiveness — economic, political, legal/regulatory, and sociocultural and geographic distance.

ECONOMIC, POLITICAL, LEGAL/REGULATORY

Economic. The crucial economic issue is current and potential market size for firm products/ services. A critical determinant is often country wealth: Wealthier countries' greater spending power implies larger markets for many products/services but some firms target low-income consumers and societies. The most important wealth measures are *gross domestic product* (GDP) and *GDP per capita*.[6]

GDP is the annual market value of all final goods and services made within national borders. For intercountry comparisons, economists typically convert local-currency GDP into U.S. dollars using one of two approaches — *current currency exchange rate (nominal)* or *purchasing power parity (PPP)*. Economists often prefer PPP because it better indicates living standards in less-developed countries.[7] Marketing Enrichment 25.1 **[502p]** shows individual country data for population and GDP (PPP) per capita organized by various regions (mainly geographic). Despite widespread use, GDP measures ignore potentially important economic factors, especially for less-developed countries:

- Barter
- Gifts, loans, and debt forgiveness from international organizations and wealthy countries
- Nonmarket transactions — like subsistence farming
- Remittances from country nationals living abroad[8]
- Underground economy — includes tax-avoiding activities like undocumented immigrant labor, home business, freelancing,[9] illegal trade like drug trafficking — and other criminal businesses
- Uneven wealth distribution — significant concentration among a small elite group

In less-developed countries, the population exceeding certain thresholds may be better market potential measures for some products than GDP per capita. At US$1,000 annually, family diets shift from vegetables to meat; at US$10,000 annually, people purchase automobiles. Indeed, as the global middle class grows, especially in emerging markets like many Asian countries, both local and multinational firms seek opportunities outside traditional markets. Many firms keep a close watch on thresholds, especially in the large emerging BRICI countries — Brazil, Russia, India, China, Indonesia.[10]

Political. The political environment often has an important impact on market attractiveness. Many countries develop governmental and institutional processes to benefit local firms. Some give exporters financing and tax advantages; others impose tariffs and quotas on imported goods. Sometimes countries get into spats: The U.S. imposed a 25 percent tariff on tires imported from China; the following year, China responded with increased import duties on U.S.-sourced chicken parts. Governments may use administrative procedures like inspections, delayed approvals, and the courts to restrict foreign firm products. Of course, restricting imports negatively affects consumers, but on safety issues governments often act to protect citizens; in pharmaceuticals, some countries ignore patents; Thailand invoked compulsory drug licensing.

Many Western firms complain that China uses unfair standards, conflicting regulations, and buy-local policies to discriminate against foreign firms — both exporters to China and local subsidiaries. Some standards effectively eliminate foreign products; China's indigenous-innovation policy gives preference to local firms for state contracts.

International marketers sometimes adapt systems and processes to address disadvantageous decisions by foreign governments. Many firms avoid high tariffs on finished products by importing parts for local assembly — like the Segway personal transporter. **[570v]** *Commercial vans* imported to the U.S. face a 25 percent tariff, so auto firms import *wagons* from Asian factories, then remove the seats and windows before sale.

Increasingly, firms with international aspirations target emerging markets, especially BRICI. As these economies grow, many consumers previously living at subsistence levels become able to afford higher-value products.[11] PepsiCo is making major multibillion-dollar investments in China and Russia (acquiring Russia's largest juice maker, OAO Lebedyansky — $2 billion) and India — $500 million. Of course, the firm may have to conduct significant marketing research to understand these markets. In China and Russia (accounting for over half of all global soup consumption — mostly homemade), where tastes vary by region, Campbell's conducted thousands of consumer interviews and offers many soup varieties.

MARKETING ENRICHMENT 25.1

Population, GDP/Capita, and Corruption Index for Countries on Planet Earth **502p**

Ease of Doing Business **138p**

MARKETING QUESTION

In Kenya, sugar was sold in 50 and 100 kg. bags for both industrial and consumer markets. Trade liberalization and common market protocols led to severe price competition from imported sugar. How should Kensug Inc. (disguised), a major Kenyan sugar producer, address this challenge?

MARKETING QUESTION

Segway is considering additional investment in Asia. On which countries should Segway focus? Why? What additional data would you require to appropriately advise Segway?

Legal/Regulatory. Regulation is often a critical entry variable. Many French entrepreneurs start businesses in Britain because the regulatory environment is friendlier; in Germany, firms must abide by strict environmental laws. Britain's largest train operator, First Group, entered the U.S. market (by acquiring the largest operator of yellow school buses and Greyhound intercity coaches). First Group believed geographically proximate countries like France and Germany were too tightly regulated. Corruption is a serious problem in many countries — Marketing Enrichment 25.1 **[502p]** (p. 626).

Several major global organizations have missions to enhance foreign-market attractiveness by securing intercountry agreements to increase trade and investment:

- **International Monetary Fund (IMF)** — 188 member countries. The *IMF* works to foster global monetary cooperation, secure financial stability, facilitate international trade, promote high employment and sustainable economic growth, and reduce poverty.

- **World Bank (WB)** — 188 member countries. The *WB* provides financial and technical assistance to developing countries via the *International Bank for Reconstruction and Development (IBRD)* and the *International Development Association (IDA)*. The IBRD concentrates on middle income and creditworthy poor countries; the IDA focuses on the world's poorest countries.[12]

- **World Trade Organization (WTO)** — 155 member countries. The *WTO* succeeded the General Agreement on Tariffs and Trade (*GATT*). Formed after World War 2, GATT sought agreements to reduce trade barriers around the world. The WTO encompasses GATT but addresses a broader scope of international agreements to liberalize trade via trade rules and dispute resolutions. The WTO is working on trade-barrier reductions from the Doha (Qatar) negotiations, begun in 2001.

Relatedly, many governments cooperate in investigating and prosecuting bribery. German prosecutors received significant help from other countries in their successful prosecution of Siemens AG (fined more than $250 million) for bribing customers around the world.

Several regional organizations focus on increasing member-country trade, and reducing administrative barriers to investment. Some organizations are free-trade areas and customs unions; others aspire to substantial economic and political integration — Table 25.1 (p. 628). The most important country groupings include[13]:

- **European Union (EU)** — 28 member countries. The EU is an economic and political union of 500 million people, generating 30 percent of global world product. Only six individual countries have a larger territory size; the EU has the world's second longest coastline, and borders 21 nonmember states. People, goods, services, and capital move freely; all EU countries apply a common external tariff. EU citizens elect the European Parliament every five years. Most EU countries use the euro; Great Britain and Denmark opted out and some newly admitted countries have yet to qualify. The EU faces an immigration crisis related to Middle East instability.

- **NAFTA** — 3 member countries. NAFTA is a trade agreement among Canada, Mexico, and the U.S. NAFTA focuses almost exclusively on trade and investment. NAFTA's 450 million population generates similar economic activity to the EU.

- **Mercosur** — 5 member countries. Mercosur comprises Brazil, Argentina, Paraguay, Uruguay, Venezuela, along with several associate members. Like NAFTA, Mercosur is a free-trade zone; population exceeds 260 million.

- **ASEAN** — 10 member countries. The ASEAN promotes economic growth and cultural development in Southeast Asia. All ASEA members are also members of the ASEAN Free Trade Area (AFTA), dedicated to reducing tariffs among members. ASEAN's population is 600 million; unlike the EU, AFTA does not have a common external tariff.

In addition, many countries form bilateral trade agreements. Australia has free-trade agreements with New Zealand, and the U.S. with Peru.[14]

KEY IDEA

Important global organizations impacting international trade include:

- International Monetary Fund (IMF)
- World Bank (WB)
- World Trade Organization (WTO)

KEY IDEA

Important regional organizations impacting international trade include:

- European Union (EU)
- NAFTA
- Mercosur
- ASEAN

When contemplating foreign-market entry, the firm should understand the type and scope of the target country's international relationships — with individual countries, regional groups, global institutions. The firm should also become familiar with the scope, rules, and regulations of relevant regional and global organizations, and predict how these may evolve. Today's bilateral trade relationships may form the basis of tomorrow's free-trade areas or economic/political unions.

Intercountry relationships can have a major impact on foreign-market attractiveness. Exports to a free-trade-group country enter other countries duty free, so the firm can make logistics decisions regionally. Political unions allowing free movement of labor and capital affect production-facility and many other decisions.

KEY IDEA

A country's economic and political relationships with other countries influence the economic attractiveness of that country's markets.

....
TABLE 25.1
Selected Common Markets and Trade Zones

Organization	Current Members
Americas	
North American Free Trade Agreement (NAFTA)	3: Canada, Mexico, U.S.
Andean Community (CAN)	5: Bolivia, Columbia, Ecuador, Peru, Venezuela
Common Market of the South (MERCOSUR)[15]	4: Argentina, Brazil, Paraguay, Uruguay
Caribbean Community (CARICOM)[16]	15: Antigua and Barbuda, Bahamas,[17] Barbados, Belize, Dominica, Grenada, Guyana, Haiti, Jamaica, Montserrat, St Kitts and Nevis, St. Lucia, St. Vincent and the Grenadines, Suriname, Trinidad and Tobago
Asia Pacific	
Asia Pacific Economic Indonesia, Japan, Cooperation (APEC)	21: Australia, Brunei Darussalam, Canada, Chile, China, Hong Kong, Malaysia, Mexico, New Zealand, Papua New Guinea, Peru, Philippines, Russia, Singapore, South Korea, Taiwan, Thailand, U.S., Vietnam
Association of Southeast Philippines, Asian Nations (ASEAN)	10: Brunei Darussalam, Cambodia, Indonesia, Laos, Malaysia, Myanmar, Singapore, Thailand, Vietnam
Europe	
European Union (EU)	28: Austria, Belgium, Bulgaria, Croatia, Cyprus, Czech Republic, Denmark, Estonia, Finland, France, Germany, Great Britain, Greece, Hungary, Ireland, Italy, Latvia, Lithuania, Luxembourg, Malta, Netherlands, Poland, Portugal, Romania, Slovakia, Slovenia, Spain, Sweden
European Economic Area (EEA)	EU members plus Iceland, Liechtenstein, Norway[18]
Africa	
Common Market for Eastern and Southern Africa (COMESA)	20: Angola, Burundi, Comoros, Democratic Republic of the Congo, Djibouti, Egypt, Eritrea, Ethiopia, Kenya, Madagascar, Malawi, Mauritius, Namibia, Rwanda, Seychelles, Sudan, Swaziland, Uganda, Zambia, Zimbabwe
Council of Arab Economic Unity Syria, (CAEU)	12: Egypt, Iraq, Jordan, Kuwait, Libya, Mauritania, Palestine, Somalia, Sudan, United Arab Emirates, Yemen
East African Community (EAC)	5: Burundi, Kenya, Rwanda, Tanzania, Uganda
Economic Community of Central African States (ECCAS)	10: Angola, Burundi, Cameroon, Central African Republic, Chad, Democratic Republic of the Congo, Equatorial Guinea, Gabon, Republic of the Congo, Sao Tome and Principe
Economic Organization of West African States (ECOWAS)	15: Benin, Burkina Faso, Cape Verde, Ivory Coast, Gambia, Ghana, Guinea, Guinea-Bissau, Liberia, Mali, Niger, Nigeria, Senegal, Sierra Leone, Togo

MARKETING QUESTION

Your firm manufactures inexpensive consumer goods. Management has asked you to identify the most attractive country markets to enter, taking intergovernmental multicountry regional organizations into account. How would you proceed?

SOCIOCULTURAL AND GEOGRAPHIC DISTANCE

Sociocultural. Countries often differ from each other on multiple dimensions — aesthetics, education, language, law, politics, religion, social organization, technical and material, and values and attitudes — Table 3.6, p. 79. Hofstede's five-dimensional framework is a useful approach for assessing culture[19]: **[212v]**

- **Individualism versus collectivism.** The extent to which people develop and display individual personalities; versus conducting themselves primarily as members of family or religious groups. **[956v]**

- **Long-term versus short-term orientation.** The extent to which people value attitudes and actions that affect the future — persistence, thrift; versus attitudes and actions that are affected by the past or present — stability, tradition, and reciprocity. **[222v]**

- **Masculinity versus femininity.** The relative value placed on competitiveness, assertiveness, ambition, wealth accumulation — *masculinity*; versus relationships, quality of life — *femininity*. **[497v]**

- **Small versus large power distance.** The extent to which people accept and expect power relations to be consultative; versus based on formal hierarchies. **[288v]**

- **Strong versus weak uncertainty avoidance.** The extent to which people are anxious about the unknown and prefer explicit rules and formally structured activities; versus preferring flexible rules, guidelines, and informal activities. **[372v]**

Sociocultural distance varies widely from one country pair to another. Typically, low sociocultural distance occurs among colonizing and colonized nations — Britain/British Commonwealth countries; France/many African countries; Spain/Spanish Latin America; Portugal/Angola, Brazil; the Netherlands/Indonesia. Foreign diasporas also display small sociocultural distance from their home countries, like Irish, Italian, and Mexican Americans; Turks in Germany; Chinese in southeast Asian countries.[20]

Low sociocultural distance between the home and target countries implies reduced risk; high sociocultural distance can lead to failure despite other promising factors. When sociocultural distance is high, the firm may improve its chances of success by hiring people and organizations from the target country; and seeking common ground among various sociocultural imperatives. Anecdotes about cultural insensitivity and business failure are legion:

UST (disguised), a technology firm, was well placed to win a major contract in a Chinese firm. But, at a banquet given by the Chinese firm, a senior U.S. manager started eating before the host — a cultural *no-no*. A French firm won the contract: Its technology was inferior, but the Chinese felt more comfortable.

Firms can get in trouble with seemingly straightforward dimensions like language. The firm should work hard to avoid such mistakes as Chevrolet launching the *Chevy Nova* in Spanish Latin America — *no va* — doesn't go! Rigorous and independent back translation can avoid this sort of problem. Because translation mistakes are easy to make, leading firms typically work with established language service providers.

Geographic. *Geographic distance* concerns the ease/difficulty of transportation and communications between home and target countries. Technology and the physical environment are also key issues. In addition to physical distance, important factors include climate, presence/absence of physical land borders, separation by land/water, time zones, topography, and transportation and communication alternatives. Reduced geographic distance implies increased market-entry attractiveness. Of course, within-country geographic dimensions are also important.

BALANCING COUNTRY ATTRACTIVENESS FACTORS

When assessing foreign-market attractiveness, the firm must consider various political, economic, sociocultural, technological, legal/regulatory, environmental (physical) (PESTLE) forces.[21] In general, positive political, economic, and legal/regulatory factors, and low sociocultural and geographic distance imply attractive opportunities, but typically the firm must balance positives and negatives. Consider a U.S. firm evaluating Australia: Many political, legal, and sociocultural factors are positive, but the relatively small population and large geographic distance may be negatives. Relatedly, South Korean firms conduct little business with North Korea despite geographic proximity and a common language!

Table 25.2 illustrates a simple approach for securing an attractiveness score for several individual countries. Possible scores range from 100 — very low attractiveness, to 1,000 — highly attractive.

Criteria	Rating (1–10 scale) Importance Weight (I)	Great Britain (RA)	Australia (RB)	Mexico (RC)	Great Britain I × RA	Australia I × RB	Mexico I × RC
1 Market size	30	8	3	5	240	90	150
2 Growth potential	20	5	7	8	100	140	160
3 Communications ease	10	10	10	3	100	100	30
4 Travel ease	10	5	2	9	50	20	90
5 Currency stability	10	7	7	4	70	70	40
6 Firm learning	10	3	3	8	30	30	80
7 Degree of corruption	10	8	8	5	80	80	50
	100				670	530	600

TABLE 25.2
Assessing Country Attractiveness –
Illustration for a U.S. firm

ASSESSING THE FIRM'S ABILITY TO COMPETE

Foreign-market attractiveness is important but the firm must also consider its ability to compete. Put starkly, what are the firm's chances of attracting, retaining, and growing customers in the face of current and potential competitors, in a proposed foreign market? A new market entrant may secure differential advantage on the basis of technological expertise or brand strength, but also from an ability to execute projects and political and networking skills.

Bus-service firm Automóviles Luarca SA (ALSA) grew in Spain's highly regulated transportation market. ALSA became adept at navigating the often highly complex process of securing licenses by forging personal connections and managing relationships with local officials. In the 1980s, ALSA became a minority partner in a joint venture offering taxi service near Hong Kong, and started building relationships in China. In 1990, when regulations allowed, ALSA formed a joint venture offering bus service from Beijing to Tianjin. Many other joint ventures followed: providing bus services (regular schedules and modern comfortable coaches — innovations in China), building bus stations, assembling buses, and managing maintenance facilities. ALSA's success derived from political skill and expertise in licenses.[22]

The firm should pay close attention to strong domestic competitors and other foreign entrants. Generally, local firms are effective in catering to local tastes, use local resources efficiently, and know how to address local obstacles. In less-developed countries, local competitors often enjoy low labor costs and technological parity with new entrants. Baidu (China) — search engine, Bharti-Airtel (India) — cell phone service, Ctrip (China) — online travel service, Focus Media (China) — out-of-home advertising, Gol (Brazil) — budget airline, Grupo Positivo (Brazil) — PCs, Titan Industries (India) — wristwatches, Wimm-Bill-Dann Foods (Russia) — dairy products, and many others succeed at home despite facing strong multinational competitors.[23]

KEY IDEA

Regardless of foreign-market attractiveness, before entry, the firm should assess its ability to compete.

Increasingly, firms from less-developed countries are making significant inroads in mature advanced-economy markets. Frequently, domestic firms seek high profit margins by adding customer value and targeting upmarket segments. But these firms are often less effective in cost control. A foreign entrant may serve an unfilled market need for a basic low-price product, then later add higher-value, higher-price products. In the 1980s, Japanese automobile firms secured high market shares in many developed countries using this approach. More recently, Giant (bicycles) took advantage of low-cost labor in Taiwan (later mainland China) to enter the global bicycle market. Giant has moved upmarket and now offers bicycles at many different quality and price levels.

Today, many firms from low-wage Asian countries offer outsourcing services in developed countries, often competing with their customers' internal organizations. Indian technology firms like Tata Infotech and Wipro are major technology players; Indian firms run many customer service operations, and Indian law firms secure significant revenues from developed countries.

OPTIONS FOR ENTERING FOREIGN MARKETS

A firm with regional or global ambitions may have already entered several foreign markets and have significant international experience, perhaps with different entry approaches. By contrast, a domestic firm going abroad for the first time starts from scratch.

In this section, we focus on alternative ways to enter foreign markets. For *all* foreign-entry decisions, the core marketing issue concerns planned investment and involvement in the target country. We distinguish between *passive* entry and *active* entry: The firm may enter some markets *passively* and others *actively* — it may also switch from *passive* to *active* as it achieves success and/or learns about the new foreign market. Of course, the firm must also make important decisions about finance, human resources, location, and production, but we focus on customer-facing marketing issues.

The firm must decide how many foreign markets to enter, how quickly, and in what order. More entries expand opportunities and permit better fixed-cost amortization; but they also require greater resources and increase risk. Speed of entry involves several trade-offs; simultaneous or fast-sequential entries earn profits more quickly, preempt competition, and erect entry barriers. When Citibank launched credit cards in Asia Pacific, it entered, in order, Indonesia, Singapore, Taiwan, Thailand, Australia, India, Malaysia — within 18 months. Uber (Chapter 20 Opening Case) moved very fast with its global expansion. Going more slowly is less risky and allows the firm to learn; later entries may be more effective, and place less strain on managerial talent. When the firm makes sequential entries, order is important; early failure may cause the firm to push back, or even abort, other planned foreign-market entries.

PASSIVE ENTRY

These approaches allow the firm to leverage another firm's skills/resources for market entry. This organization does all or most of the work; hence, the firm has little control over marketing and sales efforts. Risk and financial return are lower than for active entry. Two of the most common passive entry modes are:

EXPORTING

The firm exports products but outsources most in-country activities in foreign markets by [749v]:

- Simply responding to orders arriving from abroad.
- Appointing an export agent to sell products in foreign markets.[24] The firm may not know (or care about) destination countries; it simply fills export orders.
- Deciding which foreign markets to address, then appointing local sales agents and/or distributors (exclusive/nonexclusive) to conduct marketing and sales efforts.

> Wessex Press entered the Asia Pacific, Indian, and Russian markets via *passive entry*. S.J. Learning (Malaysia), Wiley (India), and Piter Publishing (Russia) print, sell, and distribute local versions of Wessex's marketing and other textbooks.

KEY IDEA

When entering foreign markets, the firm can choose among several *passive* and *active* entry modes.

KEY IDEA

Major options for *passive* entry into foreign markets are:
- Exporting
- Licensing

LICENSING

The firm has an asset — product/process technology (patent, trade secret), brand name, trademark — with value in foreign markets. The firm (licensor) agrees that another firm (licensee) can use the asset commercially; in return, the licensee typically pays *minimum* royalties (right to use the asset) and/or *earned* royalties (based on sales or profits) to the licensor. *Brand licensing* is very common in B2C: Product scope includes clothing; food; movie-, comic-, and sports-related merchandise; and toys. In B2B markets, international licensing agreements are largely technology based. The licensee is typically responsible for marketing, production, sales. The licensor gains foreign-market access and financial returns with minimal short-term risk. But licensing is no panacea; the licensor must consider:

- **Brand image.** Are licensee products/services consistent with brand vision?
- **Potential competitor.** Well-managed licensees become very familiar with licensor operations. Aggressive licensees have the potential to become serious competitors in the licensor's home or other markets. This problem is significant for patent-based licenses when the patent expires. Licensors can minimize potential competition by continually providing new and additional value to licensees.

ACTIVE ENTRY

In these approaches, the firm plays an active role in marketing and sales — greater profit potential but higher risk. The firm should be especially careful projecting from domestic experience but can reduce uncertainty via marketing research. Many foreign countries, especially emerging markets, lack local market research infrastructure, but this should not be a barrier. By conducting research directly, the firm may secure differential advantage. Essentially, the firm has three major active-entry options:

IMPORTING

Traditional. Products enter foreign markets as imports from the firm's home country and/or third countries.[25] The firm actively participates in marketing and selling products via traveling home-based sales representatives, and local salespeople/distributors. Both Boeing (U.S.) and Airbus (France) conduct vigorous marketing and direct selling efforts: Airlines around the world import finished airplanes. Zara designs and produces most products in Spain, then imports goods into foreign markets. Zara markets and sells to local consumers via wholly owned stores.

Many firms earn significant revenues from foreign markets by supplying raw materials, parts, or finished products. Some firms even outsource production, then import goods into target countries. Have you heard of Foxconn? If you own an Apple iPod or iPhone, Sony PlayStation, or Dell/HP Inc. PC, Foxconn probably made it. At factories in China and Taiwan, Foxconn's one-million-plus employees produce and send branded electronic products to many countries around the world.

> Many firms address foreign markets by importing products *from* their home country and/or third countries. By contrast, many services firms *import* customers to their home countries. Tourism is a classic example. Today, *medical tourism* is a fast-growing facet of both the medical and tourism industries. Low prices, state-of-the-art hospitals, and well-trained physicians in countries like Brunei, China, Hungary, India, Mexico, Singapore, Thailand, and Turkey attract North American and Western European patients for a wide range of medical procedures. Some U.S. firms even offer employees reduced insurance premiums for accepting treatment abroad. [293v]

Facilitated by the Internet. The Internet and growth in air-courier transportation have changed the game for many firms, helping them identify and serve customers in many foreign markets. The firm sells products online; buyers pay for products and shipping by credit card or other online payment system. An air courier or other transportation service delivers the purchase.

MARKETING QUESTION

Tasks Everyday (TED), **[642p]** based in Mumbai, India, offers *virtual assistants* for small, midsize, and large firms and busy professionals. TED has a ready supply of university-graduate assistants and is seeking rapid expansion. How would you advise TED?

KEY IDEA

Major options for *active* entry into foreign markets are:

- Importing
- Local production
- Franchising

MARKETING QUESTION

On opening day of the 2008 baseball season, the Boston Red Sox beat the Oakland Athletics by six to five. But they did not play in Massachusetts or California; the game was played in Japan. Develop an international market strategy for Major League Baseball.

For many years, Boston-based Lobster Trap (LT) sold live lobsters to U.S. restaurants and European wholesalers. After working with government officials, LT entered China. LT ships specially packed lobsters via FedEx.

Extreme Outdoors, a Florida provider of elaborate outdoor kitchens, lists products on eBay and sells to customers in Canada, France, Germany, Israel, Norway, and Sweden.

Wessex Press reaches foreign-market customers via *www.wessexlearning.com*. Many firms host foreign language websites. Consider Amazon: Canada — amazon.ca; China — amazon.cn; France — amazon.fr; Germany — amazon.de; Great Britain — amazon.co.uk; Japan — amazon.co.jp; Spain — amazon.es.

Even better, the firm can *export* any digital product — book, movie, recorded music, video game — without traditional import arrangements. Wessex offers all products as PDF e-books; customers pay by credit card and can *import* to any geography. Airbnb provides an online booking and payment platform for guests and hosts to arrange international (and domestic) accommodations. TutorVista (India) uses voice-over-Internet telephony, instant messaging, and electronic blackboards to provide online tutoring and educational content in more than 30 subjects to students in many foreign countries.

LOCAL PRODUCTION

KEY IDEA

Firms that set up production in a foreign country may choose among:

- Acquisition
- Greenfield
- Joint venture

Sometimes host countries insist that foreign firms form joint ventures with local firms.

For success in many country markets, local presence is at least desirable and may be necessary. The firm has several options for producing products locally:

Acquisition. The firm acquires a firm/business unit in the foreign market. Marketing, sales, distribution, operations, and other functions are already in place. The firm leverages local management and customer relationships, and surmounts many political, sociocultural, legal/regulatory barriers. Entry can be fast, but acquisition may be more expensive than *greenfield* investment. Further, governmental bodies may delay, modify,[26] or even prohibit some acquisitions, like the EU blocking GE's Honeywell purchase.

Greenfield. In a *greenfield* project, the firm constructs local facilities from scratch. Factors driving this option include high tariff barriers, high transportation costs, local content rules, and wanting to be close to customers. Some firms enter foreign markets via imports and build local marketing and sales organizations. When revenues reach a threshold, they switch to local production. Trade liberalization, transportation-cost reductions, and outsourcing have reduced greenfield's attraction but it remains a popular approach.

Greenfield Market Entry is Tough

Tesco is the world's third-largest supermarket, Britain's largest and most successful retail chain, and the global leader in Internet grocery. Tesco entered the U.S. in 2007 — Sainsbury's and Marks & Spencer (Britain), Carrefour (France), and many European food retailers had failed. Years of marketing research and planning preceded Tesco's entry. Tesco conducted many focus groups and surveys and a senior executive team lived with 60 U.S. families for two weeks; Tesco even built a mock store in a California warehouse. Tesco opened several *Fresh & Easy* stores in Phoenix neighborhoods to gain more data. At 10,000 square feet, *Fresh & Easy* supermarket/convenience store hybrids were quite different from Tesco's mammoth British stores. But they similarly promise *Every Day Low Price* and build on Tesco's British convenience store experience in product assortment and operational efficiency. *Fresh & Easy* stores offered wider food selection (including ready meals) than typical U.S. convenience stores. Using customer data from its Clubcard loyalty program, Tesco modified product assortments and sent customers discount offers tailored to shopping behavior. Within three years, Tesco was operating 150 *Fresh & Easy* stores in Arizona, California, and Nevada. In 2013, citing inadequate financial results, Tesco announced it would exit the U.S. market.

> Local relationships are important for various aspects of foreign-market entry. Cemex and other Mexican producers used various import-blocking tactics to prevent the *Mary Nour* from unloading 27,000 tons of Russian cement at Mexican ports. After six frustrating months, the *Mary Nour* left Mexican waters.

Local production requires host-country investment but strengthens local institutional and customer ties. The firm becomes part of the host country's administrative and cultural fabric as supplier, customer, employer, taxpayer. Local production also avoids quotas and tariffs — Toyota and Nissan initially produced automobiles in the U.S. to avoid quotas. Challenges for firms producing in foreign markets are exposure to local labor laws, safety and security, and currency and expropriation risks.

Increasingly, firms make production-location decisions regionally or globally; they may shift operations to low-wage countries or outsource to third parties. Many U.S. service firms place call centers in India, Malaysia, Pakistan, and African English-speaking countries. Some firms site production to gain marketing and sales advantage. Boeing enhances Dreamliner sales efforts to Japanese airlines by securing complete wing assemblies from Japan's Fuji Heavy Industries.

> Swedish/Swiss engineering firm ABB's various country subsidiaries specialize in producing certain products, then ship them to sister subsidiaries. ABB's specialization increases efficiency, lowers production costs, and vastly offsets increased transportation costs.

Joint Venture. A joint venture with a local partner helps the firm reduce political, sociocultural, legal/regulatory risks, but degree of ownership can be a critical issue. Some governments require foreign entrants to have domestic partners, and may limit percentage ownership — U.S. airlines must have majority U.S. ownership. Some foreign entrants demand majority control, but they may be surprised: GE's wholly owned Korean subsidiary was unsuccessful, but a newer minority-stake joint venture with Hyundai Motors is very successful. Overall, results from international joint ventures are mixed; problems arise when investment requirements and results differ from expectations, partner objectives change, and parent-firm problems negatively affect the joint venture.

FRANCHISING

As discussed for domestic markets — Chapter 19 — *franchising* is a popular foreign-entry mode when the firm's value proposition requires local production and/or delivery. Fast food is the most prevalent example; brands like Burger King, KFC, McDonalds, Pizza Hut, Subway, and Wendy's have expanded into foreign markets via franchising. Other international franchises include hotel brands like Hilton, Holiday Inn, Hyatt, Sheraton; Curves (women's fitness centers); and Home Instead (senior care). The franchisor secures franchisees, conducts marketing and brand building, enforces standards, and may supply raw materials. The franchisee invests in local operations, directs local marketing and sales, and pays fees to the franchisor.

Because many franchisees are local entrepreneurs, market entry can be fast and profitable. Franchisors often appoint master franchisees for a country or geographic region. These established businesses are knowledgeable about local laws, customs, consumer needs; they often act as minifranchisors in their geographic areas. For the franchisor, securing strict adherence to standards from independent franchisees can be difficult; failure or inconsistency may negatively affect the brand. In the hotel market, customers expect brand consistency from property to property, yet many different hotel operators manage individual global brands.

Sometimes franchisors allow local market variation to better address local needs — KFC offers egg sandwiches for breakfast in Japan, chickpea burgers in India, and the *Twister* in Australia.

STRATEGIES FOR INTERNATIONAL, REGIONAL, AND GLOBAL MARKETING

Globalization is driving increased numbers of firms to expand outside their home countries. The firm must decide on the scope of foreign activities, then make serious strategic international and global marketing and investment decisions. The basis for these decisions should be the six marketing imperatives at the heart of *Managing Marketing in the 21st Century*. Specifically, the firm must decide about objectives, market segmentation, and branding.

SCOPE

Firms engage in *international marketing* when they expand outside their domestic markets. *Global marketing* involves expansion into multiple countries and continents around the world. The distinction involves *scope*: how many and which foreign markets to address, and the challenges they face in each — Figure 25.2:

FIGURE 25.2
Approaches to Addressing Foreign Markets

LIMITED INTERNATIONAL MARKETING

Typical exemplars are firms that limit operations outside their domestic markets to a few geographically proximate countries. Good examples are U.S. firms in Canada, Mexico, and Caribbean countries — State Farm (insurance) and Alaska Airlines; Belgian firms in Holland and Luxembourg; New Zealand firms in Australia. These firms generally face five core challenges:

- Which countries to enter
- In what order
- How to enter
- What market strategy to employ
- How to implement the market strategy

REGIONAL MARKETING

These experienced international marketers focus their efforts on a relatively large group of countries, typically (but not always) within a single continent or geographic area — like Europe, Latin America, or portions of Asia Pacific. Many airlines fly between geographically proximate countries, like Ryanair and easyJet — Europe. By contrast, Brazilian bus maker Marcopolo concentrates on a *region* comprising noncontiguous less-developed markets — Argentina, China, Colombia, Egypt, India, Mexico, South Africa. The regional marketer's strategic anchor may be its domestic market, but the firm allocates resources and optimize performance broadly across several countries.

MARKETING QUESTION

You have been appointed Tata Motors' Marketing Vice President for North America. Your immediate task is to launch the *Nano*, a four-door, four-passenger vehicle that sells in India for about $2,200. What will be the core elements in your three-year launch plan? Make sure you ask and answer critical strategic questions.

GLOBAL MARKETING

Global marketers have also extensive international experience, but set their sights more broadly. Rather than focus on a single region, they seek opportunities globally. The typical global marketer has multicountry presence in several continents, and faces the challenge of optimizing global performance.

Both regional and global marketers are serious about foreign markets; each firm type must carefully manage and adjust its country portfolio via vigilant assessment and performance measurement. Sometimes the firm *fills out* geographic scope by adding countries; other times it withdraws — some country markets may be less attractive than they previously appeared. Walmart's stated goal is to be a global retailer yet it withdrew from Germany and South Korea (but entered Africa by acquiring Massmart). Regional marketers may contemplate forging global strategies, and enter countries in new continents/regions.

KEY IDEA

When firms expand internationally, they often follow a trajectory:
- Limited international marketing
- Regional marketing
- Global marketing

PRODUCT INNOVATION AND INTERNATIONAL GROWTH: THE INTERNATIONAL PRODUCT LIFE CYCLE

The international product life cycle (IPLC) model dates to the 1960s. The four-stage, time-bound, IPLC attempted to describe the international trade cycle for most products. Stage 1: U.S.-developed products launched domestically, then beyond the U.S. to dominate the world market. In stages 2, 3, 4, producers from other developed countries became stronger in their markets, then in third-country markets and, finally, in the U.S.[27]

The IPLC was a useful descriptive device in the mid-20th century and may still describe some product evolution today. But many changes have decreased its utility[28]:

- *Innovation locus.* The IPLC assumed innovation occurred in the U.S. Although the U.S. is responsible for much global innovation, many firms in other advanced economies — Western Europe, Japan, Korea — also produce significant innovation.

- *Global launch.* Enhanced global competition means product innovators can no longer wait months and years to go abroad. Increasingly, innovative firms launch simultaneously in many countries and regions. Easily copied digital products like movies are a special case: Three weeks after release, *Avatar*'s $1 billion box-office revenues made it the all-time most successful movie — international revenues approached $700 million.[29]

- *New products and developing economies.* The IPLC assumed that developing economies received the product last and never innovated. But as multinationals mature, they transfer ideas and products among subsidiaries, even bypassing head office. Walmart's international failures relate to local insensitivity, but it is evolving. In India, Walmart modeled *Best Price Modern Wholesale* stores for small merchants on successful *Maxxi* stores (Brazil); in China, *Smart Choice* discount supermarkets derive from *Todo Dia* stores (Brazil); Walmart is successful in Japan with private-label wines, cookies, and other products developed by *Asda* (Britain). McDonald's Australia pioneered McCafé; *Big Tasty* burger was developed in Germany and test marketed in Sweden; sales are high in Europe, Latin America, Australia.[835v]

GE, John Deere, P&G, Unilever, and others now develop products for customers in low-income countries.[30] GE Healthcare developed the MAC 800 electrocardiograph for doctors in China and India. Reversing the *hand-me-down* IPLC, GE pursued a *hand-me-up* strategy by launching MAC 800 in the U.S. Nestlé sells low-cost South Asian Maggi noodles in Australia.

Emerging markets can act as idea generators. Obopay (Silicon Valley startup) offers consumers and small businesses money transfer via cell phone.[31] Millions of Africans and Indians now have access to financial services; Obopay's system is also available in the U.S. Worldwide estimates of one billion bank accounts and four billion cell phones suggest a large potential global market.

- *Emerging market multinationals.* Until recently, virtually all multinationals were based in the U.S., Western Europe, Japan. But as emerging economies spawn strong domestic firms, many are becoming multinationals (by organic growth and acquisition).[32] China's Hisense and Haier compete in the global home appliance market; Lenovo and Taiwan's Acer are PC leaders[33]; BYD is world leader in nickel-cadmium batteries. Brazil's Embraer is a world leader in regional jet aircraft; Sadia and Perdigão are global players in pork, poultry, grain; Anheuser-Busch InBev is a global beer leader. Mexico's Cemex is a world leader in ready-mix concrete. India's Tata is a global conglomerate; ArcelorMittal (steel), Wipro (information services) and Ranbaxy (generic drugs), are also major players. Frequently these firms have cost advantages from domestic labor and economies of scale from large home markets; also, they may not have costly *legacy* systems. They may have strong local competencies like addressing hard-to-reach, price-sensitive customers, and standardize these approaches for foreign markets.[34,35]

OBJECTIVES

The firm should consider objectives at two levels: international business overall, and selectivity by region and country. In general, relevant measures are similar to those for domestic markets — revenues, profits, and market share — Chapter 24. The firm should also set goals for the speed with which it ramps up international activity.

SEGMENTING MULTIPLE COUNTRY MARKETS

International and global marketers should answer two critical questions:

- How should we form segments for developing international market strategy? The firm can either group countries or form across-country segments.
- How should we decide which segments to address?

Segmentation also has important implications for organizing for international and global markets.

SEGMENTATION BY GROUPING COUNTRIES

This approach examines markets by country groupings:

- **Common markets and trade zones.** Groupings are related to geographic proximity, but omit nonmember geographically proximate countries. Examples: AFTA, EU, Mercosur, NAFTA.[36]
- **Cultural closeness.** The firm groups countries based on attitudinal dimensions. A synthesis of research studies shows country clusters — Table 25.3.[37]

TABLE 25.3
Clustering Countries by Attitudinal Dimensions

Anglo	Arab	Far Eastern	Germanic	Latin American	Latin European	Near Eastern	Nordic	Independents
Australia	Bahrain	Indonesia	Austria	Argentina	Belgium	Greece	Denmark	Brazil
Canada	Kuwait	Hong Kong	Germany	Chile	France	Iran	Finland	India
Great Britain	Oman	Malaysia	Switzerland	Colombia	Italy	Turkey	Norway	Israel
Ireland	United Arab Emirates	Philippines		Mexico	Portugal		Sweden	Japan
New Zealand	Saudi Arabia	Singapore		Peru	Spain			
South Africa		Taiwan		Venezuela				
United States								

- **Geographic proximity.** Options include grouping by continent — Africa, Asia, Australasia, Europe, North America, South America; or by subcontinent — Scandinavia, Central America, Southeast Asia, Indian subcontinent.[38] Reduced physical distance has many logistical benefits.
- **Historical relationships.** Examples include: British Commonwealth (former British possessions), Commonwealth of Independent States (CIS) (formerly members of the Soviet Union), Spain and Spanish Latin America, Portugal and Brazil.
- **Income.** Groupings based on the income dimension of consumer demographics[39]:
  - *Organisation for Economic Co-operation and Development (OECD) members (high income):* 34 countries — includes Australia, Italy, U.S.
  - *Other high income:* 39 countries — includes Andorra, Israel, United Arab Emirates
  - *Upper middle income:* 46 countries — includes Algeria, Lithuania, Venezuela
  - *Lower middle income:* 55 countries — includes Albania, Kosovo, West Bank and Gaza
  - *Low income:* 43 countries — includes Afghanistan, Madagascar, Zimbabwe

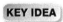

KEY IDEA

Many firms form segments by grouping countries. Geographic proximity is the most common method but other approaches may be more useful.

- **Language.** These groupings comprise elements of geographic proximity and historical relationships but focus specifically on language, like English- or Spanish-speaking countries.
- **Market maturity.** Geographically proximate countries may differ markedly in stage of economic and market development. McDonald's addresses four separate multicountry segments: U.S.; International Lead Markets (Australia, Canada, France, Germany, Great Britain); high growth markets (China, Italy, Poland, Russia, South Korea, Spain, Switzerland and the Netherlands) and Foundation Markets (all other countries).
- **Specific purpose.** Examples include OPEC (oil production), NATO (defense).

ACROSS-COUNTRY SEGMENTATION

KEY IDEA

Some firms form segments that cross country boundaries.

This approach forms market segments, regardless of geographic location by focusing on customer attributes:

- **Demographic characteristics.** Traditional demographic variables alone or in combination — Chapter 8 — can form segments. B2C attributes include age, education, gender, income, religion. B2B attributes include firm size, growth, industry, profitability. In the Opening Case, DHL employs a fairly typical B2B global segmentation:
  - *Tier 1* — top 100 customers
  - *Tier 2* — other multinational customers
  - *Tier 3* — thousands of local customers
- **Values.** Roper Starch Worldwide identified six global B2C segments by interviewing 1,000 consumers in 35 countries about core values. Generally, consumers in different segments had different activities, media use, product purchases[40]:
  - *Strivers* — place greater emphasis on material and professional goals than other groups
  - *Devouts* — tradition and duty very important
  - *Altruists* — interested in social issues, society welfare
  - *Intimates* — value close personal family relationships
  - *Fun seekers* — frequent restaurants, bars, movies
  - *Creatives* — strong interest in education, knowledge, technology

Good examples of targeting market segments regardless of geographic location are:

- Phonak (Switzerland) — personal communication assistants (hearing aids) to baby boomers
- Clinique — products for particular skin types and skin tones
- P&G — Always/Whisper brands to teenage girls; same questions about puberty, regardless of location

MARKETING QUESTION

Toyota earned an enviable reputation for high-quality products. But Toyota was forced to recall more than seven million automobiles because of unintended acceleration. What actions would you suggest Toyota take to repair damage to its brand?

In the automobile industry, firms like BMW and Toyota make automobiles for specific market segments regardless of geographic location. By contrast, Ford traditionally made separate models for regional markets like the U.S. and Europe, in part because differing managerial perspectives made global collaboration difficult. Today, the *One Ford* initiative is a global approach, starting with the Ford Fiesta. To support Ford's global efforts, advertising agency WPP formed regional hubs for North America (Detroit), Asia Pacific (Shanghai), Europe, and Latin America comprising individual WPP agencies. Team Detroit includes JWT, Mindshare, Ogilvy & Mather Worldwide, Wunderman, Y&R; a senior WPP executive signs off on all Ford global launches.

BRANDING IN GLOBAL MARKETS

The firm's first branding choice is between *local* and *global*. When the firm provides the same or similar products in multiple countries, should it offer a single brand — *global branding* — or multiple *local brands*? The branding decision follows directly from the firm's segmentation choices. Global brands are now ubiquitous. Arguments for a global branding strategy include:

- **Cross-border travel.** Increased travel drives demand as consumers seek out their favorite brands while traveling. Beverages and hotels are two good examples.
- **Growth.** The firm may be able to leverage brand equity in new geographic markets.
- **Homogeneity of customer tastes across countries.** Global media and global product availability shape consumer tastes for global brands. Sweden's H&M operates 500 stores in 12 European countries — 80 percent outside Sweden. H&M attributes its success to global fashion trends driven by satellite television, movies, music, and the Internet. Relatedly, many B2B firms are standardizing global purchases for parts and raw materials.
- **Increased global media reach and lower costs.** Television — like Star TV (Asia), CNN, ESPN, BBCWorld News — and the Internet cross country borders to reach multinational audiences. The firm can achieve scale economies in advertising, perhaps by dubbing in different languages.

Global brands offer specific advantages:

- **Aspirational values.** Global brands deliver aspirational values for products like cosmetics and sports drinks by association with global events — Olympic Games, World Cup.
- **Brand image.** A global brand promotes a consistent brand image.
- **Best practice.** Global branding eases best-practice transfer across geographies.
- **Differential advantage.** Global brands often signify quality and innovation.
- **Global appeal.** Some brands like Apple, BMW, Google, Rolex, and Rolls-Royce have global appeal from many years of international exposure.
- **Human capital.** A global brand can help recruit and retain better quality human resources worldwide. Ernst & Young, IBM, and Siemens invest heavily in using brands for global recruiting.

Firms that adopt global branding make branding decisions at corporate headquarters.[41] Typically, global branding is an affirmative decision traditionally, many firms make branding decisions locally, almost by default. Most multinational firms vest substantial decision-making authority and performance responsibility in country managers and regional vice presidents. Hence, firms may brand products quite differently from one country/region to another.

MARKETING QUESTION

Ford was not successful with its acquisitions of British brands Land Rover and Jaguar. Now owned by Tata Motors (India), both brands are enjoying sales and profit growth. What accounts for this turnaround?

Unilever is the second-largest detergent firm globally (after P&G) — brands include ALA, OMO, Persil, and Skip. Traditionally, these brands operated as a loose confederation embracing 25 different positionings, names, and packaging designs in various countries. Unilever's *Dirt Is Good* (DIG) umbrella provides a single global positioning for its brands by invoking the universal social mission of human development focused on children. The underlying notion: *When children are learning and developing sometimes their clothes get dirty — DIG takes care of the dirt.* To develop this positioning, Unilever embraced several core principles the DIG team implemented:

- *Build.* Unilever dramatically increased resources to the global approach. Unilever provides tools and practical tips to operating teams around the world.
- *Connect.* Each brand stakeholder had a voice in developing a new vision that emphasized similarities (not differences) across geographic markets.
- *Focus.* Address underlying differences but make clear choices.
- *Inspire.* Inspire consumers, customers, and internal stakeholders with the new positioning.
- *Organize.* Demonstrate new ways of working by agreeing to new roles.

Unilever achieved double-digit growth and market-share increases in key markets.[42]

For many years, Samsung and LG located branding responsibility with dozens of individual country agencies. In shifting to global branding, Samsung ($600 million) and LG ($350 million) placed their entire advertising budgets with single global agencies. Sometimes internal roadblocks inhibit this evolution: Unilever decided to manage its Dove soap brand globally — but only top management intervention secured cooperation from German and French subsidiaries.

Global branding does not imply identical implementation programs across countries.[43] Differing national tastes often drive product design variations; MTV is a global brand with local and regional adaptations. Pricing should reflect what local customers can pay; promotional activities should be appropriate for the market, and distribution decisions reflect local options. *Think global, act local* — *glocal* — is a mantra that guides many firms. Petit Bateau (PB) is a good example:

> PB makes and sells high-quality clothing for babies and children. PB's consistent global brand image emphasizes comfort and quality. Designs and fabrics are fairly standard; all products bear PB's trademark blue-and-yellow logo. PB's websites, posters, and hangtags are identical except for text translations. Yet in the U.S., young women (20s and 30s) wear PB's tee-shirts. PB raises prices and dedicates the front half of stores to *Les Grands* (for adults); posters depict young women wearing PB products.

In practice, global firms have global, regional, and local brands. Coca-Cola offers 500 brands in 200 countries: Four brands are global — Classic Coca-Cola/Coca-Cola, Diet Coke/Coke Light, Sprite, Fanta. Many soft drink brands — fruit juice, bottled water, and sports drinks — are only available regionally, sometimes in a single country. Local bottlers support these brands; they often outsell global brands. Table 25.4 displays selected Coke brands.

Americas		Europe, Middle East, Africa		Asia Pacific
Barq's	Mello Yellow	Cherry Coke	Sensun	Ambasa
Cherry Coke	Minute Maid	Kinley	Tab	Kin Cider
Citra	Mr. Pibb	Lilt	Tab X-tra	Krest
Delaware Punch	Nordic Ginger Ale	Mezzo Mix	Urge	Lemon & Paeroa
Fresca	Quatro	Schizan		Lift
Kinley	Surge			Mello
Kuat	Tai			Sarsi

Nestlé has 10 worldwide corporate brands, 45 worldwide strategic brands, 140 regional strategic brands, and 7,500 local brands. Nestlé continually evolves its brand portfolio. Nestlé redefined Chambourcy and Findus from worldwide strategic brands to regional strategic brands, and used the German Maggi brand to expand into Eastern Europe with prepared foods. See Nestlé's branding tree — Figure 25.3 (p. 641).

Building a Company without Borders: Reckitt Benckiser[44]

Reckitt Coleman (Britain) and Benckiser (Netherlands) merged to form Reckitt Benckiser (RB) — postmerger performance has exceeded expectations. RB deliberately placed top managers in new territories; most country managers and many direct reports are foreigners. All 400 top managers have the same employment contract and compensation structure; hence, relocation is relatively easy. RB's global mobility supports taking a successful product from one country to another, like Dettol (British antiseptic disinfectant) to Chile. RB seeks ideas in all markets, supports minority positions, and takes risks. A Korean brand manager identified a potential new air freshener; most evaluating group members believed it would fail in Europe. Two members were passionate advocates and RB went ahead — the Air Wick Freshmatic, launched in 85 countries, is RB's most successful new product ever. RB acquired SSL International; Durex (condoms) and Scholl's (foot products) brands offer good expansion opportunities in China and Russia.

KEY IDEA

Alternative approaches to international marketing include:

- Global — focus on consistency and efficiency across multiple countries
- Local — focus on serving specific customer needs in individual countries
- *Glocal* — marries global and local via global market strategy and local implementation

TABLE 25.4
Selected Coca-Cola Soft Drink Brands by Region

FIGURE 25.3
The Nestlé Branding Tree[45]

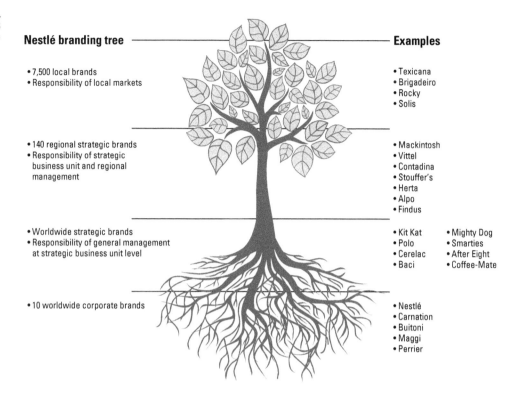

Nestlé branding tree ——————————————— **Examples**

• 7,500 local brands
• Responsibility of local markets

• Texicana
• Brigadeiro
• Rocky
• Solis

• 140 regional strategic brands
• Responsibility of strategic business unit and regional management

• Mackintosh
• Vittel
• Contadina
• Stouffer's
• Herta
• Alpo
• Findus

• Worldwide strategic brands
• Responsibility of general management at strategic business unit level

• Kit Kat   • Mighty Dog
• Polo   • Smarties
• Cerelac   • After Eight
• Baci   • Coffee-Mate

• 10 worldwide corporate brands

• Nestlé
• Carnation
• Buitoni
• Maggi
• Perrier

COUNTRY OF ORIGIN

Our final area of strategy assessment is country of origin (COO): The firm's origin may add to (or subtract from) firm brands in forming customer attitudes and intentions, and securing purchase.[46] Three possible effects are[47]:

- **Cognitive.** COO signals product quality — positive or negative. German engineering and French wine — positive; French cars and computers — negative.

- **Affective.** COO has symbolic and emotional meaning for customers; it confers attributes like authenticity, exoticness, status. Many second-generation Italian-American women are strongly attached to Italian products, especially food-related — *Italy* has a strong emotional and symbolic connotation for these consumers. Relatedly, many Asian consumers have positive attitudes toward Western brands.

- **Normative.** Customers view purchasing from certain countries as the *right* thing to do — domestic products to help the national economy[48] or products from a developing country to help alleviate poverty. Or the *wrong* thing to do — British consumers avoiding Argentine beef during the Falklands/Malvinas war; European antiwar consumers avoiding U.S. products after the Iraq invasion; Chinese consumers boycotting Japanese products because of economic and military rivalry.[49]

The extent of cognitive, affective, and normative effects varies across products, across countries, and across evaluators.[50] Some COO effects are long lasting, like individualism and democracy — U.S. — but others change over time. South Africa's image improved dramatically when it abolished apartheid and adopted majority rule; perceptions of Japanese goods evolved from *cheap and nasty* —1940s–1950s — to high quality today.

COO-related branding issues and differential national tariffs make country-of-origin markings a critical issue. When the final product comprises parts made in different countries, courts use various tests to assess the appropriate *Made in XXX* mark.[51]

MARKETING QUESTION

In the aftermath of WWII, Western customers viewed Japanese goods as *cheap and nasty*; today, many customers have positive associations with Japanese products. How would you advise a Russian firm seeking to export to the U.S.?

IMPLEMENTING INTERNATIONAL, REGIONAL, AND GLOBAL MARKET STRATEGIES

The core challenge for international and global marketers is balancing efficiency benefits from centralized corporate control versus addressing local market needs. Core problems are:

- **Excessive control.** The firm makes most decisions at corporate. Local managers must sell standard products, at standard prices, using standard communications and distribution systems. Lack of flexibility in meeting customer needs causes problems.

- **Excessive flexibility.** The firm offers a core product in multiple countries, but country managers make most other decisions. The firm gains few benefits from being multi-national, perhaps branding, cost economies, intellectual capital transfer. Country-specific approaches may cause problems when individual customers purchase in several countries.

Today, most serious international and global marketers try to balance control and flexibility benefits. These firms typically set market strategy centrally, but allow significant discretion for local implementation. BMS offers a good example:

> Historically, BMS individual country managers made strategic and operational marketing decisions for new drugs after securing local regulatory approval. Different countries positioned the same drug differently, often with locally chosen brand names, and made local pricing decisions. Regulatory approval and implementation is still local, but BMS imposes a single brand vision and a single brand name for each new drug. Successful examples include Abilify (schizophrenia, bipolar disorder) and Reyataz (HIV).

For marketing mix implementation decisions, we assume the firm has set market strategy centrally but provides significant autonomy to meet local needs.

PRODUCT

Degree of product standardization is the critical *product* decision for international, regional, and global marketers. Product standardization across national markets reduces costs and may permit lower prices. But standardization ignores local requirements and eases *gray market* formation — shipping standard products across national borders by firm customers. Alternatively, the firm may develop a core product appropriate for many foreign markets, then allow local variations. Some variations are trivial — local language translation for books, movies, packaging — but others are more substantial. Firms offering food and body care products frequently use different formulations to match local requirements; FMCG firms should select packaging colors and shapes sensitively.[453v]

> Disney understands localization. Hong Kong's Disneyland sells local food and gifts; Main Street parades focus on Chinese themes and music; Mickey and Minnie dress in red Chinese outfits; visitors take photos with Cai Shen Ye, the bearded Chinese god of wealth.

In large foreign markets, customer needs may differ by geographic region. China — coastal cities versus interior cities; India — large cities like Delhi, Kolkata, Mumbai versus rural areas. To address Indian disparities, some cell phones double as flashlights (for power outages) and are for sharing. In B2B markets, many multinational customers are shifting to global procurement; suppliers often standardize product lines to reduce costs.

Frequently, firms with successful domestic products enter foreign markets by focusing on the diaspora. Coca-Cola Russia created a new version of a traditional Russian drink — *kvass*; Krushka & Bochka now sells in New York targeting Russian immigrants.

MARKETING QUESTION

Middle East news organization Al Jazeera entered the U.S. in 2013, but withdrew in 2016. What went wrong? Why did Al Jazeera leave after less than three years?

MARKETING QUESTION

Successful Spanish restaurant chain 100 Montaditos (inexpensive sandwiches, beer) entered the U.S. with a goal of opening 4,000 outlets in five years, via a combination of company-owned and franchised stores. Do you think 100 Montaditos will be successful? Why or why not? How would you advise 100 Montaditos?

COMMUNICATIONS

Firms expanding internationally may have to adapt communications and messaging approaches to local conditions. In rural India, several firms secure consumer mobile phone numbers, then periodically call with 15-minute segments of prerecorded music or soap-opera episodes interspersed with advertising. In Brazil, Nestlé's barge, *Nestlé Até Voce a Bordo* (*Nestlé Takes You on Board*), travels the Amazon to showcase Nestlé products to river-port inhabitants. Citibank launched credit cards in India using door-to-door salespeople — unthinkable in developed economies. Hindustan Lever's *Shakti Amma* program trains rural women as entrepreneurial salespeople (and distributors) of consumer products in small villages.

Concerning messaging, in cricket-loving, India, Pakistan, and Sri Lanka, Pepsi advertisements regularly feature cricket players. Language differences across countries imply different communications approaches. But the firm must be careful about translations; poor translations can cause problems — Table 25.2 (p. 630). In low-literacy countries, the firm should emphasize visuals, including graphs and diagrams, rather than words. But the firm must be careful how customers interpret images and symbols (including logos). Color is an important issue: In Western Europe and the U.S., white implies birth, peace, and purity; in China, death, mourning, and spirits. In Western Europe and the U.S., blue implies authority, coldness, and conservatism; in Islamic countries, honesty, trust, virtue, wealth. Of course, media decisions depend on local options.

Exxon gains globalization benefits while localizing messages. Typically, Exxon develops TV advertising campaigns with expensive visuals, but uses multiple groups of local actors to tailor these campaigns to local markets.

Communications are also critical in face-to-face situations. Different negotiating styles are more or less successful in different cultures. *Individualistic* cultures like the U.S. favor direct *to-the-point* approaches; *collectivist* cultures like China favor an emphasis on developing personal relationships. Furthermore, English is fast becoming the lingua franca of international business, but true bilingual fluency is relatively rare. Both customer and internal firm communications can pose significant problems. An Indonesian national may give a competent English *presentation*, but be unable to understand and implement decisions *proposed* in English.

DISTRIBUTION

Firm distribution efforts should be appropriate to the local market. In China, Gucci and Louis Vuitton prosper with large stores that offer wide product variety with prices as low as a few hundred dollars — attracting luxury entrants and gift buyers. By contrast, Tiffany is less successful with small stores and limited high-end product selection. In the U.S., Walmart focuses distribution in very large stores — Supercenters and Sam's Clubs; but in Mexico it also operates small convenience stores — *Bodega Aurrera Express.*

Distribution systems common in developed countries may not be available in foreign markets, so creativity is critical. In Russia, P&G secured distribution to 80 percent of the population by funding 30 regional distributors and 70 subdistributors. In Eastern Europe, P&G's *McVan* model provides significant competitive advantage by funding distributors to secure information technology, training, vans, working capital. Coca-Cola distributes products in over 200 countries by doing *whatever it takes.* In less-developed countries, individuals deliver Coke using handcarts, motorcycles, and small boats, depending on topography. In Russia, Coke vehicles stock half a million stores.

PRICE

The basic framework for setting prices — Chapters 21, 22 — applies equally well in global markets. Regardless, the firm should pay particular attention to gearing prices to target market segment(s) in specific countries. Firms may successfully offer mass-market products at similar prices in several developed countries. But in less-developed countries, similar product/price combinations may only address wealthy elites. To reach broader market segments with the same products, the firm may have to reduce prices.

When setting prices for multiple countries, the firm must consider arbitrage and *gray markets*. If price differences between two countries are significantly greater than transportation, import duty, and other costs, entrepreneurs may purchase in Country A for resale in Country B. Such gray market activity typically plays havoc with marketing efforts in foreign markets. Of course, the firm must keep its eye on exchange rates as actual prices necessarily diverge from planned prices as currency values evolve.[52]

When exporting products, the firm should be alert to antidumping regulations. *Dumping* occurs when foreign-market prices are less than fair market value, below home-market prices, and often below average costs. Typically, governments initiate *antidumping* investigations to protect local industries. The U.S. government initiated an antidumping investigation of aluminum extrusions from China; in retaliation, China imposed antidumping duties on U.S. chicken products. The EU initiates roughly 30 antidumping investigations annually.

When the firm targets multinational B2B customers, price differences by country are a special problem. Historically, many firms set markedly different prices for similar products in different countries. These differential prices did not pose a serious problem when multinationals made procurement decisions locally. Today, many multinationals use global procurement systems. They do not understand why they should pay widely different prices from country to country; they pressure suppliers for price equivalence around the world.[53] Transfer pricing is becoming a significant political issue as U.S. firms seek to minimize U.S. tax liabilities.

Transfer pricing is a special issue for international marketers. Transfer prices are internal to the firm — between one subsidiary and another. Many firms set high transfer prices when exporting from low-tax-rate countries (low transfer prices when exporting from high-tax-rate countries). Taxes are lower, but high transfer prices may imply higher import duties.

ORGANIZING FOR INTERNATIONAL, REGIONAL, AND GLOBAL MARKETS

Thus far we have discussed how to analyze options, design strategy, and select implementation approaches for addressing foreign markets. In this final section we address critical organizational decisions that can make or break international, regional, and global initiatives. In part, organization structure depends on the number of foreign markets the firm enters and its investment. Many international efforts start with export departments and international divisions, then evolve to more advanced forms — Figure 25.4.[54]

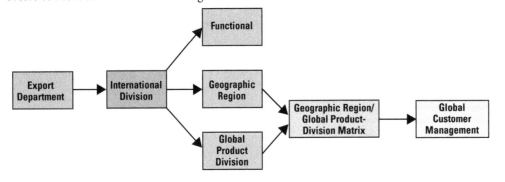

FIGURE 25.4
Organizational Approaches to International, Regional, and Global Markets

KEY IDEA

As firms increase participation in foreign markets, they typically evolve organization structures.

EXPORT DEPARTMENT

Typically, an export department at head office directs initial firm efforts in foreign markets. This department interfaces with agents and brokers, and develops intellectual capital about international marketing and sales. When the firm transitions to local marketing and sales directed by country managers, the export department often continues as the key organizational link to head office.

INTERNATIONAL DIVISION

As foreign sales increase, the firm replaces the export department with an international division — country managers report to the international-division head. The relationship between country managers and corporate varies widely — from significant corporate control to significant local autonomy. Local autonomy promotes entrepreneurship, initiative, and speedy adaptation to local needs. Kraft successfully introduced Vegemite iSnack 2.0 in Australia and New Zealand — from concept to launch in 10 months! Between the control/autonomy extremes, corporate may allow local autonomy within a broad corporate policy framework.[55]

Many firms augment local marketing and sales with additional functions like production, technical service, finance, even R&D. Country manager responsibility morphs from marketing and sales to general management, with P&L responsibility. Country managers often become very powerful individuals within the firm. Using this model, IBM local country operations were, for many years, a series of mini-IBM fiefdoms.

Export departments and international divisions are appropriate organizational devices when the firm has limited entry in foreign markets. At some point, when international revenues become significant and/or the firm enters multiple foreign markets, more advanced organizational forms are appropriate.

GEOGRAPHIC REGION

MARKETING QUESTION

How do you assess Starbucks' organizational shift?

In this form, the firm places individual countries in a regional structure, typically based on geographic proximity. Country managers are responsible for country performance, reporting to regional VPs with region-wide responsibilities. A typical structure comprises four regions: U.S. and Canada; Latin America; Europe, Middle East, Africa (EMEA); and Asia Pacific.[56] There are many variations: Some firms split the Indian subcontinent from the rest of Asia Pacific; BMS treats Japan as a region; previously, the French electrical firm Schneider treated France as a region; Starbucks evolved from an international division to three geographic regions — Asia, Americas, EMEA. Some firms develop strategy based on different market-development stages and organize similarly. For several years, Cisco grouped many developing countries into a single geographic division; McDonald's segmentation approach requires four noncontiguous geographic regions (p. 638).

Advantages of the geographic-region organization over the international division are:

- Allows the firm to integrate functions across countries, within regions
- Avoids duplication costs
- Offers greater ability to manage performance across several countries
- Provides promotion opportunities for upwardly mobile executives.

The geographic (and international) division structure is appropriate when customer needs are *heterogeneous* across geography; country managers have significant autonomy.[57] Observers attribute McDonald's success to country franchises' ability to tailor offerings to local tastes. In Vienna, McCafés offer blended coffee; in Indonesia, customers may order French fries or rice; one option in South Korea is roast pork on a bun with garlicky soy sauce.

Swiss packaging firm Tetrapak operates globally through 40 market companies and 80 sales offices. Tetrapak manages global marketing efforts via 11 geographically proximate country clusters: North America, Central and South America, North Europe, Central Europe, South Europe, East Europe & Central Asia, Greater Middle East, Sub-Saharan Africa, Greater China, South & Southeast Asia, and Northeast Asia & Oceania. Each cluster head is country manager for Tetrapak's most important country in that cluster. Hence, Tetrapak's Japanese country manager heads the Northeast Asia & Oceania cluster encompassing Japan, Korea, Australia, and New Zealand.

GLOBAL PRODUCT DIVISION

The international-division and geographic-region structures place heavy focus on geographic diversity. By contrast, the global product-division (GPD) (brand, business unit) structure focuses on global consistency and cost efficiency. The GPD is appropriate when customer needs are *homogeneous* across geography.[58] The GPD structure promotes production rationalization and is popular among FMCG firms with large product lines. GPD usually overlies a geographic structure where regional and/or country organizations have sales and distribution responsibility. Corporate provides regions with standardized advertising programs for adaptation to local markets. The firm manages P&L at the product-division level; because it concentrates organization expertise by product, making global product variations is relatively straightforward. Conversely, the GPD fragments international expertise, and product managers tend to favor large developed-country markets over emerging markets.

"L'Oreal is the most amazing global company. It's really global in the truest sense of the word. Inherent in our structure for the past 15 years has been a desire to truly integrate global development and have global brands. We have a system called the Affair d'Marc, according to the brand's origin. So, L'Oreal and Lancôme are Parisian brands; Redken and Maybelline are U.S. brands. In those countries, each Affair d'Marc has a development team for the basic brand strategy, brand image, and brand health, globally. Now L'Oreal is a Paris brand, so it has an Affair d'Marc in Paris, a 60-person group responsible for the L'Oreal brand. But because the U.S. is the largest and most competitive country for L'Oreal business, in spite of that structure, we must be 100 percent integrated into L'Oreal development. So we are considered co-developers; we have video-conferences every week, meetings once a month, and we debate a lot. We're the lead on several projects. We have a lot of ownership on practically all hair color projects. For the latest hair color launch we were the lead country. We had many meetings with the international team in France, working on brand international expansion. If we took a U.S. brand to Latin America, we would work with that team."[59] **[914v]**

GEOGRAPHIC REGION/PRODUCT DIVISION MATRIX

Advanced organization structures typically focus on a single dimension — Figure 25.4 (p. 644). Geographic-region organizations emphasize customer diversity in national markets; GPD organizations emphasize consistency, efficiency, cost reduction. Matrix organizations attempt to balance both geographic and product concerns.[60] Some firms, like P&G, have moved beyond the matrix:

KEY IDEA

Firms operating in many countries often develop geography/product matrix organizations.

P&G evolved slowly from a geographic-regional structure to a product/geographic matrix, but found this structure too unwieldy. In the current structure, product and geographic axes have different roles:
- *Product.* Global business units (GBUs) have P&L responsibility.
- *Geography.* Geographic market-development organizations (MDOs) develop local go-to-market strategies and direct local sales forces — shared across GBUs.

This organization works via a series of tables that produce protocols for deciding GBU/MDO conflicts, an elaborate review system, and flexibility to treat distinct areas like emerging markets outside the framework.

FUNCTIONAL

In the functional structure, all firm functions globally report directly to corporate; corporate controls decision making around the world. The downside may be unresponsiveness to local conditions like offering inappropriate products, pricing, and service in various countries. Toyota had been very successful with a functional structure, but was unresponsive to local-U.S. dealer complaints about unintended acceleration, leading to a recall crisis. Complaints were adjudicated by a special committee in Japan, then routed back to the U.S.!

"Consistent with managing the ExxonMobil (EM) brand globally, we changed our organizational structure. We went from a geographic organization to a global functional organization. Previously, EM was organized as six geographically based operating companies held together by a logo. Each operating company was largely autonomous, had its own marketing staff, and developed its own advertising campaigns. Now, all the strategy development occurs at corporate. EM develops advertising campaigns globally; it operates with three guiding principles — consistency, improve communications quality, efficiency. The operating companies execute locally. Corporate provides all advertising material and allows local variation in music background."[61]

GLOBAL CUSTOMER MANAGEMENT

When firms expand operations to multiple countries they often evolve procurement operations to better enable global contracts, manage global supplier relationships, secure better prices, and optimize customer service. Global procurement is often more effective and efficient than sourcing locally. Hence, B2B suppliers must develop organizational structures that interface effectively with their global customers. In the *global customer management* structure, customer becomes a major organizational design axis — Figure 25.5. The centerpiece of global customer management is the *global account manager* (GAM). GAMs have full customer responsibility, but balancing customer priorities with product-division and geographic imperatives is often difficult.[62] Marketing Enrichment 25.2 **[338p]** provides a primer on managing global customers.

MARKETING ENRICHMENT 25.2
A Primer on Managing Global Customers **338p**

Previously, IBM had strong country managers reporting to powerful regional executives. Today, IBM operates with an industry-based structure where senior executives head up customer industries — financial services, manufacturing, retail. In each industry organization, GAMs manage IBM relationships with major global customers. Domestic salespeople report through the industry organization.[63] Geographic organizational structures remain intact for government relations, corporate advertising, *care* and feeding of locally employed personnel, but country heads no longer have budget responsibility.

FIGURE 25.5
Organizational Design Dimensions for Global Marketing

KEY IDEA

Many B2B firms adopt global customer management organizations to address multinational customers.

What other messages did you glean from this chapter?

KEY MESSAGES

- Before your firm enters one or more foreign markets, make sure you have a good answer to the question — why are we going abroad?

- In assessing country attractiveness for market entry, you should consider political, economic, sociocultural, legal/regulatory, and geographic factors.

- Many international organizations take actions that affect foreign markets. Some organizations are global — WTO, World Bank; others are regional — EU, NAFTA, ASEAN. The firm should monitor these organizations' activities, and individual bilateral agreements between countries.

- Passive entry strategies for entering foreign markets include exporting and licensing.

- Active entry strategies for entering foreign markets include importing — traditional and Internet-facilitated; local production — greenfield, acquisition, joint venture; and franchising.

- Many firms follow a strategy of progressive commitment to international markets — limited commitment, regional marketing, global marketing.

- When firms address the global market, they may segment by country group or identify across-country segments.

- Many factors drive firms to develop global market strategies.

- Many firms offering products globally also provide products/brands for specific regions and individual countries.

- A *glocal* approach combines global strategy and local implementation.

- International and global marketers may choose among various organizational forms.

VIDEOS AND AUDIOS

For complimentary material, see Axcess Capon codes at www.axcessvids.com

Global Marketing	**125v**	Spencer Pingel	Colgate-Palmolive
Entering Foreign Markets	**410v**	Eric Knudsen	Zoll Medical

QUESTIONS FOR STUDY AND DISCUSSION

Can you answer the questions implied by this chapter's learning outcomes? Check!

1. Wessex Press secured a manuscript titled *The Song of Hiroshima* by Atsuhiro Ozaki. Ozaki was working at the Hiroshima radio station on August 6, 1945, the day the atom bomb dropped. *The Song of Hiroshima* is a personal account of his experience on that day and the following few days. How would you advise Wessex Press to distribute, promote, and sell *The Song of Hiroshima*?

2. Suppose you recently joined Maxpleasure Inc., the well-known European condom manufacturer, as regional marketing manager for Africa. CEO Jennifer Major selected you from several well-qualified candidates. Major believes growing desire for family planning and the ravages of AIDS offer Maxpleasure an important opportunity to improve sales and profits in Africa. (USAID and the EU heavily subsidize condom production.) How will you approach this new assignment? What decisions must you make within the first 100 days?

3. As CEO of a successful U.S. budget-hotel chain, you have decided to expand operations to Central and Eastern Asia. All U.S. hotels are company run but you are willing to contemplate a franchise business model. Either way, entry costs for any new foreign market are significant, and you must choose countries very carefully. How will you go about developing an ordered list of countries by market attractiveness? Pick half a dozen countries to test your approach.

4. To fill an unexpected vacancy, Citibank has promoted you from regional sales manager in the midwest U.S. to be global account manager (GAM) for Siemens, an important Citibank customer. You will be based in Munich, Germany. On Monday morning you are due to meet with your new boss, the global account director, for the first time. Prepare a list of questions.

5. Select a product in which you are interested. Alternatively, consider *Managing Marketing in the 21st Century*. Develop a strategy and action plans for improving global sales of your selected product, or the global sales of all Wessex Press books.

TRUE/FALSE QUESTIONS

Answers on page A2 and at www.axcessvids.com — 804p

1. Gross domestic product is the annual market value of all final goods and services made within a country's borders. ❏ **TRUE** ❏ **FALSE**

2. NAFTA is a free-trade zone comprising Brazil, Argentina, Paraguay, Uruguay — and several associate members. ❏ **TRUE** ❏ **FALSE**

3. Major options for active entry into foreign markets include exporting, local production, and franchising. ❏ **TRUE** ❏ **FALSE**

4. A firm constructs local facilities from scratch in a greenfield project. ❏ **TRUE** ❏ **FALSE**

5. Heterogeneity of consumer tastes across countries is a strong supporting argument for global branding. ❏ **TRUE** ❏ **FALSE**

MULTIPLE CHOICE QUESTIONS

Answers on page A2 and at www.axcessvids.com — 415p

1. The annual market value of all final goods and services made within a country's borders is referred to as _____.

   a. gross national product
   b. gross domestic product
   c. gross national income
   d. purchasing power parity

2. The _____ is an organization comprising nearly 200 member countries that works together to foster global monetary cooperation, secure financial stability, facilitate international trade, promote high employment and sustainable economic growth and reduce poverty.

   a. World Bank
   b. World Trade Organization
   c. International Monetary Fund
   d. NAFTA

3. All of the following represent forms of active entry for entering a foreign market EXCEPT:

   a. licensing
   b. importing
   c. local production
   d. franchising

4. All of the following are options that firms can use to set up production operations in a foreign country locally EXCEPT:

a. exporting
b. greenfield
c. acquisition
d. joint venture

5. The organizational structure that focuses on global consistency and cost efficiency and is appropriate when customer needs are homogeneous across geography is referred to as

_____.

a. functional
b. international division
c. global customer management
d. global product division

CHAPTER 26

ETHICAL, LEGAL, AND SOCIALLY RESPONSIBLE DECISIONS IN MARKETING*

For complimentary material, see Axcess Capon codes at www.axcessvids.com

LEARNING OUTCOMES

When you have completed this chapter, you will be able to:

• Understand and analyze the scope of marketing ethics.
• Realize the difference between ethical and legal implications for marketers.
• Distinguish between business ethics and marketing ethics.
• Be aware of various ethical and legal issues in implementing marketing decisions.
• Understand practical areas of social responsibility in marketing.
• Review the role of marketing ethics within corporate social responsibility.

OPENING CASE: OLYMPUS CORPORATION

Olympus Corporation (OC) (Japan) manufactures optics and reprography products. Established in 1919, OC initially specialized in microscopes and thermometers. OC enjoyed 70 percent global market share for gastrointestinal endoscopes — US$2.5 billion — and employed more than 40,000 people globally.

In October 2011, OC's British-born CEO Michael Woodford, who had recently been promoted to his position after a six-month stint as OC president, caused a furor in Japan. Woodford exposed OC's deep involvement in one of the biggest and longest-running loss-hiding arrangements in Japanese corporate history.[1] Woodford was immediately fired; board chair Tsuyoshi Kikukawa, OC's previous president and CEO, resumed these positions. The incident raised concern about tobashi (concealment) schemes and corporate governance in Japan. The facts concerning apparent irregular payments for acquisitions exposed by Japanese financial magazine Facta had come to Woodford's attention. As a result, OC assumed significant asset impairment charges. The Japanese press speculated on OC connections to yakuza (Japanese organized crime syndicates). OC denied allegations of impropriety.

---

* Nicholas Grigoriou, Lecturer in Marketing, School of Business, Monash University, Malaysia, participated in preparing this chapter.

Despite OC denials, the matter quickly snowballed into a scandal over tobashi *schemes involving more than ¥120 billion ($1.5 billion) investment losses, dubious fees, and other payments dating to the late 1980s; and suspicion of covert payments to criminal organizations. On October 26, 2011, OC replaced Kikukawa; Shuichi Takayama became chairman, president, and CEO. On November 8, 2011, OC admitted its accounting practices were* inappropriate; *OC agreed it had used corporate funds to cover investment losses for more than 20 years. OC blamed these accounting lapses on former president Kikukawa, auditor Hideo Yamada, and executive vice president Hisashi Mori.*

By 2012 the OC affair had developed into one of the largest and longest-lived loss-concealing financial scandals in Japanese corporate history. OC's market value dropped by 80 percent; most board members resigned. Criminal investigations in Japan, Britain, and the U.S. led to the arrest of 11 past and present OC Japanese directors, senior managers, auditors, and bankers for alleged criminal activities and/or cover-ups. The Olympus *affair raised considerable concern over Japan's prevailing corporate governance and transparency in financial markets. In 2012, Woodford reportedly received £10 million (US$16 m) damages from OC for defamation and wrongful dismissal. OC announced 2,700 layoffs (7 percent of the workforce), and closed 40 percent of its 30 manufacturing plants.*[2]

Case Question

What are the ethical and legal issues involved in the Olympus scandal? What are some of the takeaways regarding ethical decision-making? Faced with the information Woodford received, how would you have acted?

OLYMPUS®

We divide Chapter 26 into two parts: ethical and legal decisions, and social responsibility in marketing. Initially, we focus on decisions that marketers must make. The objective is ensuring marketers make these strategy and implementation decisions — product, promotion, distribution, price — in an ethical and legal manner. In a sense, this view of marketing is reactive: Marketers must make these decisions; let's make sure they make them appropriately. The social responsibility philosophy is more forward looking: What decision can marketers make that go beyond the broad goal of ethical and legal decision-making in pursuit of economic profit?

THE CHANGING VIEW

OLD WAY	NEW WAY
Physical environment taken for granted	Increased *green* environmental concerns
Governments largely ignored physical environmental issues	Governments increasingly involved in setting environmental standards and monitoring performance
Unethical behavior in some business organizations	Unethical behavior in some business organizations
Illegal behavior in some business organizations	Illegal behavior in some business organizations
Sanctions for illegal corporate behavior modest	Sanctions for illegal corporate behavior increasingly harsh
Business education focus on ethical behavior practically nonexistent	Business education focus on ethical behavior increasing modestly
Concerns for personal privacy modest	Concerns for personal privacy increasing marketedly
Hacker attacks on corporate databases modest	Hacker attacks increasingly sophisticated
Corporate perspectives on ethical behavior assumed	Corporate behavior on ethical behavior increasingly formalized
Fewer temptations for unethical behavior present	Heightened global competition raises temptations for unethical behavior

KEY IDEA

Marketers must consider
three different types of issue
in making decisions:

- ethical
- legal
- socially responsible

**MARKETING
QUESTION**

Many business executives
argue that their firms are
at a competitive disadvantage
in certain countries unless
they pay bribes. Suppose you
were asked to pay a bribe to
ensure your firm won an
important contract. How
would you respond?

ETHICAL AND LEGAL DECISIONS IN MARKETING

Marketing is a pervasive area of business activity; hence, marketers have a significant responsibility when conducting everyday business activities. Marketers must balance societal expectations like environmental concerns, safe products, communications honesty, and fair pricing with organizational values, stakeholder — customer, employee, supplier — relationships, and corporate goals like revenues and profits. Marketers influence the way myriad people and organizations perceive the firm and its offerings.[3]

As a single window on ethical and legal decisions, consider how people view CEOs, other senior executives, and their organizations. Positive: Jack Ma — Alibaba; Tim Cook — Apple; David Tang — Shanghai Tang; Howard Schultz — Starbucks; Richard Branson — Virgin. Negative: Bernie Madoff; Jeffrey Fastow, Kenneth Lay, Jeffrey Skilling — Enron; senior executives at GlaxoSmithKline (bribery and corruption in China); Ramalinga Raju — Chairman, Satyam Computer Services (financial accounts manipulation). The securities-fraud conviction of Bernie Ebbers (2002) — WorldCom — led directly to passage of the Sarbanes-Oxley Act, the most sweeping U.S. regulatory change since the 1930s.

Unfortunately, negative examples are not rare and isolated. Rather, breaches of legal and ethical standards are far more common than we like to think. Indeed, some observers insist that corruption and fraud is one of the top five challenges for American companies abroad.[4] Many law-breaking cases never make mainstream media, and many ethical breaches never rise to the law-breaking level. Indeed, we cannot begin to assess the ethical breaches committed in business firms on a daily basis. What we attempt in this chapter is to give you insight into ethical behavior so you do not embark on a journey that could land you in serious trouble, and cause many casualties along the way. Because unethical and illegal actions are closely linked, we address these topics together.

Marketers can go beyond just making *good* decisions. Do you as a marketer aspire to higher goals? Perhaps your decisions can *improve* societal well-being while earning profits for your firm. Perhaps your firm's products can provide benefits to unserved market segments; or are especially good for the environment; or provide employment and income for otherwise disadvantage individuals.

In 2014, the Ethisphere Institute named SingTel (Singapore telecom firm) as the world's most ethical company for the fourth time. SingTel Human Resources Director Aileen Tan said: "Environmental, social, and governance issues; and performance are integral to our corporate sustainability and responsibility strategy. At SingTel, we are committed to an ongoing process to better understand our internal and external drivers as we strive to differentiate ourselves in this highly competitive market. This is a journey and we will continue to work harder."

Said Ethisphere CEO Timothy Erblich: "The entire community of World's Most Ethical Companies believes that customers, employees, investors, and regulators place a high premium on trust and that ethics and good governance are key in earning it. SingTel joins an exclusive community committed to driving performance through leading business practices."[5]

As a marketer or an executive in another function, you will have responsibility for managing firm business activities and spending financial resources wisely. To achieve company objectives, you should make your decisions with an ethical mind-set and avoid legal problems. To help you make decisions that avoid pitfalls, we begin with several definitions of ethics. To a large extent, ethical principles are universal. Indeed, many internationally active firms are converging on appropriate corporate behavior regardless of location. By contrast, what is legal and illegal often varies from jurisdiction to jurisdiction; actions that are illegal in Western countries may be quite acceptable in other parts of the world, and vice versa.

DEFINITIONS OF ETHICS

Marketing (along with finance) may be the organizational function most often cited for ethics abuse. But before focusing on marketing ethics, we consider some broader ethics definitions:

- Ethics is *the inquiry into the nature and grounds of morality where the term* morality *is taken to mean moral judgments, standards, and rules of conduct.*[6] **[655v]**

- Business ethics are *actions that require the organization or individual to behave in accordance with carefully thought out rules of moral philosophy.*[7]

Extending this definition:

- Business ethics are the *rules, standards, codes, or principles that provide guidelines for morally right behavior and truthfulness in specific situations.*[8]

And

- Marketing ethics is *an inquiry into the nature and grounds of moral judgments, standards, and rules of conduct relating to marketing decisions and marketing situations.*[9]

Figure 26.1 illustrates the relationship among the three ethics types.

KEY IDEA

Marketers should consider ethical issues at three levels:
- general ethics
- business ethics
- marketing ethics

General Ethics

Business Ethics

Marketing Ethics

FIGURE 26.1
Relationship among Ethics Types

FRAMEWORK FOR ETHICAL AND LEGAL MARKETING DECISIONS

The general goal for marketing decision-making is to offer value to customers so they purchase, and/or recommend to others, firm products/services rather than competitor offers. Marketers make many decisions in securing insight, developing value propositions, designing market offers, and executing implementation decisions. In each area, marketers should be ready to address, appropriately, the many ethical dilemmas they may face.

The firm secures several types of insight — particularly customer insight.* Marketing Imperative 3 — *Set strategic direction and positioning* — concerns developing the market strategy. Marketing Imperative 4 — *Design the market offer* — focuses on implementing the market strategy. Execution of implementation decisions has the most direct effect on customers. We examine the potential for unethical decision-making in *product*-related areas — including packaging and labeling; *promotion* — embracing advertising and personal selling; *distribution*; and three areas of *pricing* decisions — Figure 26.2 (p. 656).

SECURING CUSTOMER INSIGHT

To develop and evolve market strategy and implementation programs, the firm should secure insight about the market, customers, competitors, complementers — Chapters 3, 4, 5, 6. The firm has many options available for collecting data and securing insight in an ethical manner.

MARKETING QUESTION

In 2015, Volkswagen admitted installing software to fake emission test results for millions of diesel-engine powered automobiles — regular emissions were up to 40 times greater than U.S. standards. The CEO resigned, Volkswagen received highly negative publicity globally — share price declined more than 40 percent. Why do you think such deplorable behavior occurred? Suppose you had been a Volkswagen middle manager several years earlier and accidentally discovered this practice, what would you have done? Why?

---

* We address issues in competitor information gathering in Chapter 5.

KEY IDEA

Marketers should be wary of the many ethical pitfalls in conducting marketing research and act accordingly.

But, there are also many unethical approaches. We commence our discussion of marketing decision-making by focusing on the insight-development process.

To secure customer insight, marketing organizations frequently secure data from customers. By caring about ethics and by acting on those concerns, organizations promote the integrity of marketing research. Since much data collection occurs without direct managerial supervision, there is ample scope to conduct research improperly. Many firms outsource data collection to third-party suppliers; hence, behavior of both firm employees and employees at outsourced providers may cause concerns. At a basic level, management must ensure that collectors do their jobs — actually collect data from respondents versus filling in questionnaires at home while watching television!

Marketing organizations must carefully consider research study design to ensure respondents are not harmed — physically or emotionally — during the research process. Data-collection personnel should be well-trained and well-briefed for the research study. In particular, the firm should ensure its marketing research studies avoid unethical practices like:

- failing to provide respondents with anonymity;
- misrepresenting and/or omitting pertinent information about the research;
- conducting selling or fundraising under the guise of marketing research;
- treating respondents unfairly.

A more common unethical practice in marketing research is failure to obtain *informed consent* from respondents. Informed consent involves securing prior respondent permission to participate in the study. Informed consent is fundamental for pharmaceutical trials and medical research, but also has application in marketing research. Respondents should know the:

- names of organization(s) commissioning and conducting research, and researcher/data collector — confirmed by appropriate identification;
- aims and general purposes of research;
- benefit to respondent for participating;
- nature of respondent involvement — time commitment, question types;
- data-collection method — computer entry, audio/video recording;
- details regarding confidentiality guarantees;
- process for withdrawing from the study and discarding data;
- procedures for making complaints and/or securing information about research.

Privacy. A key element of *informed consent* guidelines focuses on protecting respondent privacy. We saw earlier the growth of *big data* for marketing research. Companies secure consumer data from many sources and *fish* for insight using powerful analytic tools. Not so many years ago, consumers with product needs walked into stores, paid cash, and left with their purchases, anonymously. Today, most readers of this book select products from Internet websites and stores, and pay by credit card directly or via an online payment system. Many organizations know who you are — product suppliers, credit card firms, package delivery services. Furthermore, one or more of these organizations may sell data about you to third parties; and they may harass you by mail, e-mail, and/or telephone. Personal data about your shopping habits is stored in *cookies* on your electronic devices. The level of anonymity your parents and grandparents enjoyed no longer applies.

One ethical decision for marketers is how to use the data it collects on individual consumers in the normal course of commerce. A second issue concerns the extent to which the firm protects data about you from hackers. Banks, major retailers, and the adultery promoting *Ashley Madison* website have been subject to attacks and loss of personal data on millions of consumers causing significant personal harm.

FIGURE 26.2
*Framework for
Marketing Ethics*

PRODUCT DECISIONS

PRODUCTS AND SERVICES

Marketers have an absolute obligation to design, produce, and deliver products and services that do not endanger customer health and well-being. As we show in Chapter 12, industry after industry has too many examples of customer injury or death due to product deficiencies and/or customer use.

Some products should be absolutely safe regardless of how customers consume and/or use them — food, clothing, and children's items fall into this category. Other products may be perfectly safe if customers use them appropriately, but can cause injury or death if used improperly — automobiles, motorcycles, pharmaceuticals. In some cases, products cause harm; in other cases, a service may be inherently dangerous — bungee jumping, jet skiing, paragliding. The firm has different responsibilities in each case:

- **Absolutely safe products.** The process for providing absolutely safe products begins in the design stage of the new product development process. Safety should be central to design.
  - *Food products.* The firm should ensure all ingredients are absolutely safe and that the production process does not introduce safety concerns. Safety failures in manufactured products are all too common. In Anhui province (China), 13 babies died from contaminated milk powder. Fonterra (New Zealand dairy supplier) identified bacteria causing botulism in infant formula and sports-drink ingredients.
  - *Manufactured products generally.* From time to time, design flaws become evident. The firm has an absolute responsibility to withdraw the product and advise interested parties as soon as possible. J&J knew 40 percent of its hip implants failed, yet hid these data and continued to supply for several years. A related concern is ongoing design evolution. As customer needs evolve and/or cost pressures mount, ingredient substitution and modified production processes may introduce problems. Marketers must be sufficiently involved with design and production activities that they intercept incipient safety problems.

In the early 1960s, hydrofluorocarbons (HFCs) were hailed as breakthrough products for use in aerosols and refrigerator coolants. Subsequent research demonstrated these ingredients destroyed the earth's ozone layer. Today, manufacturers have replaced HFCs with more eco-friendly substitutes.

KEY IDEA

To develop and implement market strategy, the firm must address many ethical dilemmas. Dilemmas include securing insight and making decisions concerning:

- Product — including packaging and labeling
- Promotions — including advertising and personal selling
- Distribution
- Price

Relatedly, the seller has a responsibility not to sell consumers inappropriate products like alcohol to the inebriated — especially potential drivers — nor hand guns to the mentally ill. The most serious cases are pharmaceutical firms promoting drugs for unauthorized uses — Glaxo-SmithKline paid $3 billion in fines for promoting antidepressants for unapproved uses.

- **Safe products if used appropriately.** The firm should be concerned with two quite separate safety issues:

  - *Design failure* — the firm must build safety into product design. The automobile industry provides a sobering example. Every few months we hear of a product recall like Toyota — steering; General Motors — ignition switches; Honda — airbags. Safety concerns may be unexpected: Debenhams (major British retailer) recalled snowsuits and jackets for babies and small children because of faulty zippers. Ongoing alerts about car-seat safety persist. A related services example concerns *safe* mortgage-backed securities constructed from *highly risky* individual mortgages — a major cause of the 2008/9 recession.

  - *Use failure* — Design and manufacturing quality is excellent, but customer use causes problems. Automobiles, motorcycles, and snowmobiles are safe if used properly. But they may cause injury and death if used inappropriately, both to customers and others. Similarly, electrical appliances may cause electric shocks.

MARKETING QUESTION

Suppose manufacturers designed cars and trucks with built-in speed limits. What kind of legal and ethical issues would they face?

- **Products that cause harm.** Many products are legal to make and sell, yet cause harm. Furthermore, consumers know they are harmful yet purchase and consume them nonetheless. Consider: Cigarettes cause lung cancer and heart disease leading to death; sugary drinks cause diabetes and obesity; red meat can cause heart disease. Conversely, some firms strive to improve consumer health: Au Bon Pain and other food chains are reducing salt and sugar in their products; General Mills increased the percentage of healthy whole grains in its cereals; McDonald's added apples to *Happy Meals*.

Services may cause other types of harm. On Wall Street and in other financial areas, financial institutions sometimes put the firm's interests far above those of customers, even to the extent of swindling them.[10] Potential legal jeopardy can also be an issue. Many financial institutions offer financial products that assist customers in evading taxation. Under pressure from the U.S. government, many Swiss banks and other financial institutions no longer offer such products.

MARKETING QUESTION

Following a series of take-overs and organizational realignments, senior management at your conglomerate firm has appointed you brand manager for its leading cigarette brand. Your salary will increase substantially. Will you accept the position? How would your answer change if your father, a long-time smoker, had died of lung cancer? How do you assess proposals to introduce e-cigarettes, and enter the marijuana market?

- **Unsafe products/services.** Many consumers love thrills — bungee jumping, mountain climbing, paragliding, roller coasters. The firm's responsibility is to minimize the inherent danger to human health. The railroad shipping dangerous chemicals should ensure its track bed is solid and drivers are competent and well-trained. Fairgrounds should ensure their rides are well designed, well maintained, and well operated, and that customers behave appropriately.

> Synthes (later acquired by J&J —$20 billion) conducted illegal clinical trials, essentially experimenting on humans. Spine surgeons injected Norian XR in patients; at least five died from blood clots. Four senior executives took responsibility for Synthes actions and pled guilty to criminal charges.

Regardless of its particular set of products/services, the firm has an absolute and ongoing responsibility to place customer safety first. The firm should *do what it takes* to protect customers and others.

PACKAGING AND LABELING

Packaging and labeling are common domains for unethical marketing practice, especially in FMCG. Drivers for unethical behavior are desires for cost savings and/or increased revenues. Packaging's two basic functions are product protection and communications. Firms are sometimes tempted to cut costs on packaging material; hence, products are improperly protected and may be defective when customers receive them.

Packaging may be the single most important factor for purchasing decisions made at point of sale. Proper packaging helps products gain shelf space and stand out from competition. Relatedly, packaging can directly influence consumer-purchasing decisions. Packaging should protect products; packaging should also protect consumers!

Unethical (and maybe illegal) packaging actions are various:

- **Package size.** Placing products in large packages to convey the false impression the amount of product is also large.

- **Package shape.** Using odd-shaped packages to make price comparisons difficult, and to convey incorrect impressions of product quantity.

- **Package labeling.** Untrue statements like false third-party endorsements — *approved by the U.S. Dietician's Association*; impossible claims — *Domino's sugar is carbon free.*

- **Packaging graphics.** Packaging designs and visuals that inaccurately reflect package contents.

Many FMCG and other products remain in their packages until used. The firm must take special care to avoid unauthorized use, especially by children. Pharmaceutical firms now provide products in tamper-proof containers; P&G redesigned Tide Pods detergent packaging after children mistook the pods for candy.

PROMOTION DECISIONS

We examine ethical issues in advertising and personal selling.

ADVERTISING

Many consumers consider advertising the most visible marketing element. Today, consumers are inundated by advertising messages from many media channels. The core ethical issue for advertisers is *truth* in messaging. Absolute truth in advertising is not a legal issue but is an ethical issue. Many advertisers must decide what level of exaggeration is acceptable — *the best product for solving your problem* or *beats all competitors.* Typically, the legal system allows exaggeration — *puffery* — so long as claims are not deceptive.

For many people, *deceptive advertising* has become synonymous with deceptive business practice. Deceptive advertising is *any act, claim, or message that:*

- *causes at least some consumers acting reasonably to make decisions they would not otherwise make;*

- *leads at least some consumers acting reasonably to believe something about the product, brand, or manufacturer that is not verifiably true; or*

- *has the potential to foster distrust of any kind, general or specific, or in other ways cause an erosion of ethical values deemed desirable in society.*[11]

Most deceptive advertising centers around false claims about product content, performance, and/or quality. Examples are legion:

- Korean automobile firms Kia and Hyundai made miles-per-gallon claims in U.S. advertising — overstated by up to six miles per gallon (on average one to two miles per gallon). Kia and Hyundai reimbursed drivers for incorrect mileage claims with prepaid debit cards.

- Danone (France) claimed its *Activia* yogurt was *scientifically* proven to have certain health and nutritional benefits. No such *scientific* study existed; a U.S. court forced Danone to

MARKETING QUESTION

Suppose you were the head marketing executive for a firm that distributes several brands of gin, scotch whisky, and vodka. Under government pressure, your trade association has publicly agreed to halt advertising on television. But you believe that a limited amount of television advertising will increase sales significantly. What decision will you make about television advertising?

> limit promotional messages to factual claims.
>
> - Ferrero's advertising claimed its *Nutella* brand — rich in saturated fats —was a healthy breakfast option. A U.S. court compelled Ferrero to change Nutella health claims in subsequent promotional campaigns.

Promoting products in the media without stating they were paid *advertorials* is an ethical problem. Marketers should be especially concerned with advertising to *at-risk* groups, like bereaved or ill consumers, or products linked to those events. Children are a special case as their cognitive processes are not fully developed. Many information types — like advertising messages — may be not only be harmful, they may also cause family dissention.

Is Pranking Ethical?

Fear has long been an element in marketers' promotional arsenal – Chapter 16, p. 416. Deodorant firms often use fear of body odor to promote their products. Today, fear of aging drives the multibillion-dollar cosmetics industry. Question: Are some uses of fear overstepping ethical boundaries? In particular, how do you as a current/future marketer assess the rising popularity of *prank-vertising*? Examples:

- To promote the movie *Carrie*, marketers constructed special effects at a New York City coffee house. Remote-controlled tables, chairs, and bookshelves moved around as though a café patron were a real-life *Carrie* — an angry teenage girl with telekinetic powers. Many patrons received a good fright!

- LG created several stunts to demonstrate the lifelike displays of its televisions. One stunt occurred in an elevator. As the elevator reached the top level, the floor appeared to fall away — many riders panicked.

- Toronto-based John Street agency parodied the prank-vertising trend by producing a video in which babies were stolen from a park and criminals raided homes after midnight.

MARKETING QUESTION

Is *prank-vertising* unethical? As a marketing director, would you invest in *prank-vertising*? Would you draw an acceptable/ unacceptable line? Where would you draw that line?

Not only must the firm decide *what* to say, it must also decide *where* to say it. Typically, placing advertising in mainstream media is noncontroversial, but many countries support various special interest media appealing to narrow audience segments. Suppose the particular interest offends a significant portion of the population; should the firm nonetheless advertise in such media and, implicitly, support the special interest? Or, should the firm avoid controversy by not advertising in such media?

> Ford decided to advertise several automobile brands in gay and lesbian magazines. Ford's decision provoked an uproar among individuals and groups opposed to gay rights. Ford withdrew the advertisements; the withdrawal generated a comparable uproar from gay-rights groups. Ford reversed its earlier decisions and ran the advertisements.

SALES PRACTICES

The sales force is the organizational function most likely to face ethical dilemmas. Salespeople conduct their jobs with little supervision and are typically highly trusted by their firms. Some ethical decisions are personal: Should I use the company car on personal business? Is this a legitimate item to put on my expense account?

The greater ethical challenges concern interactions with customers. Typically, the firm invests salespeople with great responsibility for their behavior and performance. Indeed, to many customers, the salesperson *is* the firm. Salespeople may face temptations to profit personally by behaving unethically.

Unethical selling practice takes many forms:

- **Omission.** The salesperson focuses on positive aspects of the offer but does not share information on issues that might reasonably concern customers — product features, delivery, pricing.
- **Commission.** The salesperson lies about product features and/or product availability and delivery.
- **Individual pressure.** The salesperson calls and/or visits potential customers frequently and/or pressures them to buy immediately rather than allow time for consideration.
- **Inertia selling.** The salesperson demands payment for products delivered to customers who did not request them.
- **Social pressure.** The salesperson falsely tells the customer that others have purchased the product.
- **Mismatch between customer needs and product features.** The sales person tries to persuade customers to buy, knowing the product does not meet their needs.
- **Bribery.** In B2B, people make purchasing decisions to benefit their organizations; they may also secure personal benefit, often with salesperson assistance. Some pharmaceutical firms lavish gifts and trips on doctors (illegally) to encourage prescribing their drugs. Taking a procurement executive to lunch or sending a holiday gift may be harmless (but prohibited in some buying organizations). Paying a multimillion-dollar bribe is not. Salespeople must be clear where the line is drawn and should not overstep. Passage of the U.S. Foreign Corrupt Practices Act led to many prosecutions around the world.

DISTRIBUTION DECISIONS

Distributors deciding which products to offer may face ethical challenges; CVS (drugstore chain) stopped selling cigarettes despite forgoing $2 billion annual revenues. Nonetheless, many difficult distribution issues have less to do with ethical decisions and more with legal issues. Actions like falsely stating products will be available for only a short period; refusing to show customers advertised products; and staging *liquidation sales* when shops are not closing are clearly problematic.

Other than pricing, distribution issues are more subject to legal concerns than any other marketing-implementation variable. Jurisdiction plays an important role in distribution, especially internationally. What is legal in one country may be normal business practice in another. Marketers must address the regulatory environment country by country.

As marketing executives, you have the responsibility to become familiar with distribution rules in countries where you operate. But before you make serious decisions, be sure to consult with a knowledgeable attorney. Of course, international marketers may have to deal with many different legal structures. Regardless, several distribution issues are common:

- **Exclusive territories.** Many courts look unfavorably on arrangements that give distributors exclusive territories when this reduces competition.
- **Price discrimination.** Many countries prohibit suppliers from colluding with competitors. Setting different prices for different buyers where this would reduce competition is also frequently illegal.
- **Resale price maintenance (RPM).** Under RPM, suppliers set *retail* prices. In some countries, RPM is illegal; in other countries, RPM is quite legal.
- **Selecting and terminating distributors.** Generally, suppliers are free to select and terminate distributors, but suppliers may have to follow acceptable practices.

MARKETING QUESTION

Tesla is pioneering electric-powered automobiles. Tesla attempts to distribute products through its own showrooms but has run afoul of state laws requiring automobile sales be made through franchised dealerships. How would you advise Tesla?

- **State and local laws.** Over and above national laws, the U.S. has state and local laws concerning distribution. Such laws may define opening and closing hours/days, and what products retailers may sell.
- **Tying agreements.** Sometimes, strong suppliers force resellers to sell their entire product lines. The U.S. bans such *full-line forcing* if it reduces competition. Relatedly, bundling is controversial: Viacom provides bundles of popular and less popular channels to customers — Cablevision has sued Viacom on antitrust grounds.

In 2013, the U.S. Supreme Court provided U.S. students with a major victory. As a Thai student in the U.S., Supap Kirtsaeng realized that prices for English-language, international-edition textbooks (mainly paperbacks) sold in developing countries were far lower than equivalent domestic U.S. textbooks (mainly hardbacks). Kirtsaeng arbitraged by buying books outside the U.S., then reselling to U.S. students on eBay. Major U.S. publisher Wiley sued Kirtsaeng on copyright grounds; Kirtsaeng prevailed on the *first-sale* principle — once he purchased a book, it was his to resell. The *Thai* decision had major repercussions for textbook publishers.

PRICING DECISIONS

As with distribution decisions, many firms engage professionals or analysts to advise on legal implications of pricing decisions. Although a complex area, marketers should have a working knowledge of three broad pricing topics embracing both ethical and legal issues.[12]

KEY IDEA

Important legal and ethical pricing issues include:

- Anticompetitive pricing, including:
  - Discriminatory pricing
  - Predatory pricing
  - Price conspiracies
- Dumping
- Fairness in consumer pricing, including:
  - Bait and switch
  - Deceptive pricing

ANTICOMPETITIVE PRICING

Several pricing approaches are anticompetitive:

- **Discriminatory pricing.** In many jurisdictions, firms may not sell identical products to different customers at different prices, when the effect is to lessen competition or create a monopoly. The main defense against such laws is cost-justification and meeting a competitive threat.
- **Predatory pricing.** Predatory pricing is typically defined as pricing below average variable costs, with the intention of putting a competitor out of business. Dominant firms sometimes engage in predatory pricing by temporarily pricing very low to thwart competitors.
- **Price conspiracies.** A scenario when a firm and competitors overtly collude to fix prices, make implicit agreements to price in parallel, and/or exchange price information. Higher prices and customer harm typically occur. Over a two-year period, executives from South Korean giants Samsung and LG held secret meetings to fix prices for flat-panel televisions, laptop computers, washing machines. Samsung paid 26 billion won (US$21 million) in fines; LG paid 19 billion won (US$16 million). In financial services, U.S. and British regulators imposed many multimillion-dollar fines on leading global banks for conspiring to fix Libor and the euro interbank rate; Deutsche Bank pleaded guilty to criminal charges and paid $2.5 billion fines (also $1.6 billion legal costs).

DUMPING

Dumping is a form of price discrimination specific to international marketing. Some firms *dump* products in foreign markets at less than fair market value, below home-market prices, and often below average costs. Dumping prices are often higher than variable costs, so the firm earns positive contribution margin. Dumping may be illegal in the receiving country if it causes or threatens material harm to the domestic industry.

SolarWorld (SW) filed a complaint with the U.S. Commerce Department alleging Chinese firms violated trade laws by *dumping* solar panels in the U.S. SW claimed Chinese firms were able to gain market share because of unfair Chinese government subsidies. U.S. authorities imposed average duties exceeding 30 percent on Chinese-made solar panels.

FAIRNESS IN CONSUMER PRICING

Two important fairness issues for consumers are:

- **Bait and switch.** Retailers advertise a low-price product — the *bait* — but have only limited availability. The *bait* sells quickly and retailers offer most customers a higher-price and higher-profit product — the *switch*. Many consumers complain about bait-and-switch tactics in booking airline flights online at third-party travel websites; consumers often complain camera and computer stores practice such tactics.

- **Deceptive pricing.** False prices or prices that may confuse or mislead customers are deceptive. If the firm advertises a product at price = $X, but the product cannot function without other critical elements, the $X price is deceptive. (Hence, many electrical products carry the disclaimer *batteries not included*.)

    Other types of deception include making former-price comparisons like — *was* $XX, but *now* only $2.50 — when $2.50 was the *former* price! Or, making discounts conditional on other purchases — *buy one, get one free* or *two for the price of* one. This strategy is only ethical if the item's initial price had been the *regular* price, and not inflated to offset cost of the discount.

> **KEY IDEA**
>
> Many governments scrutinize prices for illegal activity.

> **MARKETING QUESTION**
>
> Turing Pharmaceuticals acquired a 60-year-old drug for treating life-threatening parasitic infections — *Daraprim* — and raised the price from $13.50 to $750 per tablet. How do you assess Turing's action?

SOCIAL RESPONSIBILITY IN MARKETING

Many writers argue the firm has a single responsibility — to maximize profits and enhance shareholder value.[919v][13] A more modern position acknowledges this economic goal but believes that as an integral member of society, business firms should also have a broader perspective — corporate social responsibility (CSR). Google's vision — *don't be evil* — embraces one approach.

As the organizational function charged with interfacing with society, marketing has a major role to play both in terms of directing company resources toward *doing good*. In practice, CSR approaches are highly varied. Initially introduced in the U.S., many firms around the world incorporate CSR approaches to promote ethical behavior. Central to the notion of corporate social responsibility is the *triple bottom line* (TBL/3BL).

TBL incorporates the idea of *sustainability* into business decisions. TBL is an accounting framework comprising three dimensions — social, environmental/ecological, financial — aka 3Ps — people, planet, profits. Did you know the *Dow Jones Sustainability Indexes* (DJSI) are a family of indexes for evaluating sustainability performance of the 2,500 largest companies on the Dow Jones Global Total Stock Market Index? DJSI considers economic, environmental, and social performance. Key issues embrace corporate governance, risk management, branding, climate change mitigation, supply-chain standards, and labor practices. The DJSI rejects firms that do not operate in a sustainable and ethical manner. The DJSI family contains one global index — DJSI World — and various regional geographic indexes like Asia Pacific, Europe, and North America.[14]

For many firms, taking environmentally friendly actions like saving energy and/or cutting waste are minimally positive, but simultaneously increase short-term profits. Deeper and more serious approaches, like Unilever embracing the entire supply chain, include increasing customer demand for *green* products. Such environmental commitment are long-term investments for more fundamentally sound and sustainable businesses.

> **KEY IDEA**
>
> Socially responsible approaches for marketers cut across four areas:
> - workplace and employees
> - products
> - customers
> - philanthropy

WORKPLACE AND EMPLOYEES

The firm has a special and absolute responsibility to provide safe workplaces and working conditions for employees. Unfortunately, around the world, we see too many instances of unsafe workplaces, notably in Bangladesh where more than 1,000 textile workers died in fires.

Workplaces and employees are not just issues for firms and their at-risk employees. B2B customers and their brands — major European and U.S. retailers in the Bangladesh case — increasingly receive significant negative publicity for apparent indifference to working conditions at their suppliers. Even Apple has received significant criticism for working conditions at Chinese electronics supplier Foxconn. Many garment retailers have enacted new policies following the Bangladesh incident; some industry leaders, like H&M, work with local governments on safety, minimum wages, and related issues.

Safe workplaces are minimum conditions; the firm must make decisions about employee benefits over and above payment for work performance. Google is perhaps the poster child for positive working conditions: Benefits include child care, meals, medical services, sports facilities, and transportation. Starbucks pays for employees' online college education.

Many firms also make organizational arrangements to help employees give back to society on their own time, often in support of local causes. These firms encourage employees to work with local schools and religious groups to provide educational experiences for young people. At many business schools and universities, senior executives make presentations to classes and/or teach courses as adjunct professors.

MARKETING QUESTION

How would you advise Coca-Cola's CEO to address the *water-rights* issue? **[284v]**

Increasingly, firms are also concerned about the ecological impact of their decisions, particularly global warming, carbon emissions, and other environmental hazards. In 1984, the release of methyl isocyanate (MIC) gas from Union Carbide's Bhopal, India, plant killed more than 3,000 people. More recently, Coca-Cola (and the Indian government) was widely criticized for causing immense water-shortages in areas with volatile water supplies, especially in summer. The U.S. coal and fracking industries face similar scrutiny. Many firms now design energy efficient workplaces using *green* products, even generating electricity from roof-top solar panels; or have active programs to improve their environmental footprints, and may appoint top-level executives as chief sustainability officers.

PRODUCTS

For many years, the dominant business mantra was *buyer beware* — after purchase, the product was the customer's problem. Today, firms have many more product-related concerns, notably environmental impact. Core issues are:

- **Product composition.** Individual components are important factors in product use and disposal. Some components degrade naturally; others become environmental hazards. As environmental-friendly laws proliferate, firms are examining raw materials more seriously. Some firms are designing products to be more environmentally friendly. Levi's offers *Waste<Less* jeans comprising at least 20 percent recycled plastic; Patagonia makes wet suits from natural rubber rather than neoprene (made from oil feedstock). P&G's laundry detergents increasingly clean clothes effectively in cold water (saves energy); P&G also sells *Tide Pods* — fixed detergent amount per wash — to counter consumer tendencies to use more than recommended amounts. Audi is pioneering an aluminum sustainability standard for lighter-weight automobiles, and LED headlights that emit less carbon dioxide than halogens. Finally, in addition to redesigning packaging to reduce cardboard consumption, Lego can verify it sources all 2,000 raw material items from sustainable forests.

  Remanufacturing is growing in popularity — firms make new products with parts from discarded products. Good examples include automobiles, car batteries, computers, and toner cartridges. Remanufacturing is a $50 billion industry — some firms build remanufacturing into their product development processes.

- **Product use.** Some products harm the environment during use. Perhaps the firm designed the product many years previously with a now-obsolete technology — like gas-guzzling automobiles — when environmental concerns were more limited. Both producer and customer face important questions. Should the firm embark on a program to persuade customers to scrap their obsolete products? Should customers scrap their product regardless of inducements to do so? To address this problem with automobiles, the U.S. government initiated a *cash-for-clunkers* program to retire fuel-inefficient automobiles.

- **Product and packaging disposal.** Traditionally, customers were responsible for disposing of packaging and used products. But governments, particularly European, have passed environmentally friendly laws focused on disposal. Increasingly, firms develop programs to take back products ready for discard. Several electronics firms like HP Inc. take back electronics products; H&M places recycled clothes bins in its stores. BASF and other chemical firms are developing environmentally friendly biodegradable plastics as replacements for environmentally unfriendly plastic packaging.

CUSTOMERS

The mantra for treating customers in socially responsible ways is *doing well by doing good*. Making products/services available to underserved populations is a critical issue for many firms. Grameen Bank pioneered microfinance in Asia, providing small loans to individuals and organizations to start and run businesses. Microfinance has expanded from its Bangladeshi origins to many countries in Asia, Africa, and the U.S.

> In India, Hindustan Unilever's (HUL) Project Shakti targets villages with populations less than 2,000. HUL partners with women's self-help groups. HUL selects entrepreneurs — Shakti ammas — as door-to-door salespeople. Each Shakti amma serves 6–10 villages; across India 45,000 Shakti ammas reach three million homes in 15 states. HUL has extended Project Shakti to 26,000 male members of Shakti amma families and to more distant villages via bicycles.

Other successful examples of *doing well by doing good* include:

- HUL's Lifebuoy hand-wash awareness campaign to improve hygiene reached more than 120 million Indians.
- ITC delivers information on weather, scientific farming, and risk management — in local languages — to mostly illiterate farmers. ITC's system also supports the sale of products farmers require, and sales of farmers' produce.

PHILANTHROPY

Across the world, myriad political and social causes seek resources to achieve their goals. Firms may donate to political campaigns — to elect politicians favorable to their perspectives — or to promote social causes like education, eliminating discrimination, gender equality, workplace safety. Support for such causes typically reflects the values of owners and/or organizational leaders.

Relatedly, the firm may donate to organizations that deliver services to particular groups like caregivers to destitute and low income families — Red Cross — or arts and social organizations. Sometimes, corporate foundations make these donations; other times, firms make donations in local communities. Some firms donate in kind, like pharmaceutical firms that provide low-price or free drugs to developing countries, or even perform R&D on rare diseases from which they will never make profits.

When donating, the firm should consider two issues — the donation itself and information about the donation. Making the donation helps fulfill the firm's social goals. But, the fact of

---

MARKETING QUESTION

You are the new CEO of a low-cost regional Asian airline. Your expansion plans require the purchase of 50 aircraft. You must choose between a deal with Airbus for new planes, or purchasing previous generation aircraft at much lower prices. The older aircraft are less fuel efficient and more highly polluting, but can be refurbished like new. Total anticipated lifetime costs of purchase and use is 10 percent lower for the older aircraft. What decision will you make? How would this change if the savings were 25 percent? Or, 5 percent?

MARKETING QUESTION

What opportunities can you identify for *doing well by doing good*?

making the donation may bring favorable or unfavorable publicity. Indeed, favorable publicity and enhancing the firm's brand(s) may mitigate complaints from shareholders that management is *wasting my money*.

NATIONAL RESPONSIBILITIES

In our increasingly globalized world, national boundaries are becoming less important, but nation states are nonetheless a fact of life. Governments around the world fulfill a host of responsibilities by securing resources via taxation. But corporate tax rates differ from country to country; hence, many multinational firms are tempted to arrange their affairs, by transfer pricing and legal tax avoidance strategies, to accumulate profits in low-tax countries (tax havens) and avoid making profits in high-tax countries. Each firm must make serious decisions on its responsibilities to the countries in which it does business. Pressures to act more responsibly are growing as consumer groups increasingly protest nonresponsible tax behavior: A British group targeted Starbucks; Starbucks made several million dollars in voluntary ex gratia payments to the British tax authorities.

Relatedly, some U.S. firms shift corporate headquarters to other countries — *inversions* — also for tax avoidance. Accenture moved corporate headquarters to Ireland; Burger King acquired Canadian chain Tim Horton; Pfizer acquired Ireland-based Allergan. Shifting headquarters is a significant political issue in the U.S.

BEHAVING APPROPRIATELY AS MARKETERS

In this chapter, we identified a variety of legal and ethical issues you may confront as you develop your career. We also highlighted some proactive options for organizations. Individually, we all should, at a minimum, behave legally and ethically. And if we can *do well by doing good*, so much the better. Additionally, management has a responsibility — starting from the CEO and senior functional leaders like head of marketing and head of sales — to take four sorts of action:

- **Transparent commitment** — make very clear, in written and public statements, company commitment to ethical behavior. Many firms publish vision and values statements about ethical practices and concern for employees, local communities, and the physical environment.

- **Lead by example** — by their behavior, personally demonstrate leadership commitment to ethical principles and sustainability.

- **Develop and sustain a transparent culture** — have open lines of communication so employees are not punished when they identify and report — *whistle-blowers* — instances of unethical or illegal behavior.

- **Educate employees** — provide training for employees in addressing ethical dilemmas.

As the 21st century evolves, business challenges are intensifying in depth and scope. Increasing competition places ever-greater pressure on employees to reach and exceed performance objectives. Temptations to cut corners and behave unethically will not diminish, but may increase. Now, at the dawn of your careers, you must develop an ethical framework that works for you and helps you make tough calls. At the end of the day, you have to live with yourself and your decisions.

KEY MESSAGES

- Your personal ethical framework for making marketing decisions should derive from an understanding of ethical behavior in general and business ethics in particular.

- To a large extent, ethical principles are universal; by contrast, many legal issues are jurisdictionally determined.

- Marketers face a variety of legal and ethical challenges in making product, promotion, distribution, and price decisions.

- Marketers should develop personal ethical frameworks for decisions they face on a daily basis; they should also explore opportunities for *doing well by doing good*.

- Social responsible decisions embrace workplace and employees, products, customers, and philanthropy.

MARKETING QUESTION

What other messages did you glean from this chapter?

QUESTIONS FOR STUDY AND DISCUSSION

Can you answer the questions implied by this chapter's learning outcomes? Check!

1. You've just joined a well-known telecom firm as a senior executive in China with responsibility for winning projects. You are aware of corruption scandals involved in bidding for such projects. What steps can you take to ensure your behavior is legally and ethically correct, without compromising your success?

2. Suppose you are marketing executive for a beverage firm that sells and distributes a full line of soda products. What legal and ethical issues would concern you when designing a market strategy for your new orange-flavored soda?

3. In Malaysia, some company executives want to support a *pro-Muslim* interest group; you have been assigned responsibility for organizing an inaugural event. You are aware that many international clients will likely be uncomfortable with this support. How will you manage your internal and external constituencies?

TRUE/FALSE QUESTIONS

Answers on page A2 and at www.axcessvids.com — 120p

1. Ethics are largely universal but legal frameworks may vary across markets and countries.
   ❏ TRUE ❏ FALSE

2. Business ethics is actions that require individuals to behave in accordance with carefully thought out rules of moral philosophy. ❏ TRUE ❏ FALSE

3. Dumping may be illegal in the receiving country if it causes or threatens material harm to the domestic industry. ❏ TRUE ❏ FALSE

4. The 3Ps of the triple bottom line are *product, promotion,* and *price.* ❏ TRUE ❏ FALSE

5. Corporate social responsibility approaches include the workplace and employees, products, customers, and philanthropy. ❏ TRUE ❏ FALSE

MULTIPLE CHOICE QUESTIONS

Answers on page A2 and at www.axcessvids.com — 548p

1. Marketing ethics does NOT include:

    a. ensuring shareholders are treated appropriately
    b. avoiding the setting of deceptive prices
    c. banning untoward advertisements
    d. making products for underserved populations
    e. creating rules of conduct relating to marketing decisions

2. Key elements of privacy do NOT include:

    a. informed consent
    b. data protection
    c. ensuring customers behave appropriately
    d. permission to use personal data
    e. preventing hackers

3. Unethical sales practices do NOT include:

    a. a salesperson focusing only on positive aspects of the offer and not sharing information on other customer issues
    b. a salesperson lying about product features and/or product availability and delivery
    c. a salesperson bringing her manager on the initial customer call
    d. bribery
    e. a salesperson falsely telling the customer that others have purchased the product

4. Illegal issues in distribution do NOT include:

    a. exclusive territories
    b. price discrimination
    c. buyer beware
    d. setting different prices for different buyers
    e. resale price maintenance (RPM)
    f. selecting and terminating distributors

CONCLUDING

COMMENT

MANY READERS OF *MANAGING MARKETING IN THE 21ST CENTURY* have no doubt visited Genting, Las Vegas, Monte Carlo, Macau, or a similar location. If not, you must be familiar with the way gambling establishments work. You may win a lot of money, or you may lose a lot of money, but the gambling house always wins. Even if you do win once or twice, the odds are stacked against you, and you will almost certainly lose over the long run — the laws of probability govern your performance. Essentially, you play games of chance; if you attempt to change the odds by counting cards or by some other means, the casino will eject you.

In business, you are also gamblers. You make bets on markets, market segments, and products. Sometimes you win; other times you may lose. In many respects you are just like the patrons of gambling establishments. But there is one big difference. As you address markets in North America and around the world, you have the ability to shift the odds in your favor. That's what *Managing Marketing in the 21st Century* is all about — shifting the odds. Two matters are crucial — data, information, and insight; and frameworks to help organize your thinking and your approaches. In *Managing Marketing in the 21st Century*, we show you how to secure data, information, insight — and we provide many useful frameworks. You now have the ability to improve your chances of success. Good luck!

ENDNOTES

For complimentary material, see Axcess Capon codes at www.axcessvids.com

CHAPTER 1

1 Based in part on an interview with Howard Schultz; N. Capon, *The Marketing Mavens*, New York: Crown Business, 2007.

2 Stephan Haeckel, Director of IBM's Advanced Business Institute, summed up the marketing philosophy: "Marketing's future is not as a function of business, but as the function of business." S.H. Haeckel, "Adaptive Enterprise Design: The Sense-and-Respond Model," *Planning Review*, (May–June 1995).

3 A.G. Lafley, "What Only the CEO Can Do," *Harvard Business Review*, 87 (May 2009), pp. 54–62, at p. 57.

4 For a new chief marketing officer's (CMO) experience, F.M. Jacques, "Even Commodities Have Customers," *Harvard Business Review*, 85 (May 2007), pp. 110–119.

5 Many marketing researchers try to show positive relationships between marketing, profit, and shareholder value: Kumar and Shah find a direct relationship between customer equity — total value of all firm customers ($\sum$CLV Chapter 2) — and market capitalization. R.T. Rust, T. Ambler, G.S. Carpenter, V. Kumar, and R.K. Srivastava, "Measuring Marketing Productivity: Current Knowledge and Future Directions," *Journal of Marketing*, 68 (October 2004), pp. 76–89; D. O'Sullivan and A.V. Abela, "Marketing Performance Measurement Ability and Firm Performance," *Journal of Marketing*, 71 (April 2007), pp. 79–93; S. Srinivasan and D.M. Hanssens, "Marketing and Firm Value: Metrics, Methods, Findings, and Future Directions," *Journal of Marketing Research*, 46 (June 2009), pp. 293–312; and "Commentaries and Rejoinder," pp. 313–329.

6 Marketing ideas and concepts have broad applicability. We focus on for-profit firms but other domains include: public and not-for-profit organizations — for customers and funders; politicians — for votes; nations, states, and cities — for tourists and business investment; ideas and causes — for individuals to exert political pressure. At some level, marketing is a technology to encourage people to behave in a desired fashion; hence, marketing relates to the exercise of power — reward, coercive, legitimate, referent, and expert power. J.R.P. French and B. Raven, "The Bases of Social Power," in D. Cartwright and A. Zander, *Group Dynamics*, New York: Harper & Row, 1959 .

7 Some firms extend the customer-value/shareholder-value link to employees. A senior Citibank executive described his firm's customer relationship managers: "Our critical assets walk in the door at 9:00 A.M. and walk out at 6:00 P.M."

8 R. Martin, "The Age of Customer Capitalism," *Harvard Business Review*, 88 (January–February 2010), pp. 58–65, makes important distinctions among managerial capitalism (A.A. Berle and G.C. Means, *The Modern Corporation and Private Property*, New York: Macmillan, 1932), shareholder-value capitalism (M.C. Jensen and W.H. Meckling, "Theory of the Firm: Managerial Behavior, Agency Costs, and Ownership Structure," *Journal of Financial Economics*, 3 (October 1976), pp. 305–360), and customer-driven capitalism. Customer-driven capitalism focuses on delivering customer value and satisfaction.

9 In *CFO* magazine. Also Martin, *op. cit.*

10 "At Alibaba, Investors Come Last," *BusinessWeek*, August 17, 2009, p. 49.

11 IBM's earnings were: 1990 — $6.02 billion; 1991 — $2.82 billion; 1992 — ($4.96 billion); and 1993 — ($8.10 billion). L.V. Gerstner, *Who Says Elephants Can't Dance?* New York: Harper Business, 2002.

12 P.F. Drucker, *The Practice of Management*, New York, Harper and Row, 1954, pp. 37–38.

13 "The customer is the most important in our business. The customer is not dependent on us; we are dependent on him. The customer is not an interruption of our work; he is the purpose of it. A customer does us a favor when he comes to see us; we aren't doing him a favor by waiting on him. A customer is part of our business, not an outsider. He is not just

money in the cash register; he is a human being with feelings like our own. He comes to us with his needs and wants; it's our job to fill them. A customer deserves the most courtesy we can give him. He is the life-blood of this and every business. He pays your salary. Without him we would have to close our doors. Don't ever forget it." Reputedly developed by Mahatma Gandhi and hung in his South African law office.

14 W.I. Huyett and S.P. Viguerie, "Extreme Competition," *The McKinsey Quarterly*, 1 (2005), pp. 47–57.

15 For marketing's historical development, see R.S Tedlow, *New and Improved: The Story of Mass Marketing in America*, New York: Basic, 1990; F.E. Webster, "The Changing Role of Marketing in the Corporation," *Journal of Marketing*, 58 (October 1992), pp. 1–17.

16 Returns to shareholders combine dividends and capital gains from increasing share prices.

17 Cost of capital combines cost of equity and cost of debt. Multibusiness firms should make appropriate adjustments for risk and may set different target rates of return for each business. Many firms, like Herman Miller (office furniture), have adopted Economic Value Added (EVA) to manage and measure investment success. EVA is operating net income on a cash basis (or operating net income excluding amortization of goodwill and certain intangibles) less an explicit capital charge (debt plus equity): G. B. Stewart III, "EVA: Fact, and Fantasy," *Journal of Applied Corporate Finance*, 7 (Summer 1994), pp. 72–84. Also A.K. Sharma and S. Kumar, "Economic Value Added (EVA) — Literature Review and Relevant Issues," *International Journal of Economics and Finance*, 2 (May 2010), pp. 200–220. Three ways to increase EVA are: (1) increase profits without increasing capital, (2) invest in projects that earn more than the cost of capital, (3) withdraw from projects earning unattractive returns; Marketing Enrichment FM.1 **[308p]**.

18 M.W. Johnson, C.M. Christensen, and H. Kagerman, "Reinventing Your Business Model," *Harvard Business Review*, 86 (December 2008), pp. 51–59, identifies four business-model components — customer value proposition, profit formula, key resources, and key processes.

19 P.F. Drucker, *Management: Tasks, Responsibilities, Practices*, New York, Harper & Row, 1973, p. 63.

20 Personal communication from David Haines, former Director of Global Branding, Vodafone.

21 Gerstner, *op. cit.*, p. 72.

22 *Ibid*, p. 189.

23 This term is taken from military usage.

24 A.J. Slywotsky and B.P. Shapiro, "Leveraging to Beat the Odds: The New Marketing Mind-Set," *Harvard Business Review*, 71 (September–October 1993), pp. 97–107. Rahm Emmanuel, President Obama's first chief of staff, captured this perspective cogently by paraphrasing Niccolò Machiavelli (*The Prince*): "You never want a serious crisis to go to waste."

25 "The World's Most Admired Companies," *Fortune*, March 16, 2009, p. 77.

26 "As Antidote to Slowdown, Intel Will Spend, Not Cut," *The New York Times*, February 28, 2001.

27 "Don't Cut Back on Innovation," *Fortune*, April 22, 2009, p. 69.

28 "Wachovia Bank and Trust Company," in N. Capon, *The Marketing of Financial Services*, Englewood Cliffs, NJ: Prentice Hall, 1992.

29 Personal communication from Pat Kelly, former Senior Vice President Worldwide Marketing, Pfizer Pharmaceuticals.

30 Many researchers found positive correlations between external orientation and organizational performance: C.R. Cano, F.A. Carrillat, and F. Jaramillo, "A Meta-Analysis of the Relationship between Market Orientation and Business Performance: Evidence from Five Continents," *International Journal of Research in Marketing*, 21 (2004), pp. 179–200.

31 Haeckel, *op. cit.*, and S.H. Haeckel, *Adaptive Enterprise: Creating and Leading Sense-and-Respond Organizations*, Cambridge, MA: HBS Press, 1999.

32 D. Brass, "Microsoft's Creative Destruction," *The New York Times*, February 4 2010, p. A27.

33 Personal communication from a senior Nabisco executive.

34 J. A. Byrne, *Chainsaw: The Notorious Career of Al Dunlap in the Era of Profit-at-Any-Price*, New York: Harper Business, 1999.

35 "CMOs and CEOs Can Work Better Together," *HBR Blog Network*, June 20, 2014.

36 FMCG firms understand this value — far too many executives see only marketing communication expenses.

37 "Less Than the Sum of Its Parts," *The Economist*, June 23, 2001.

38 K. Simmonds, "Removing the Chains from Product Strategy," *Journal of Management Studies*, 5 (1968), pp. 29–40.

39 J. Welch, *Jack: Straight from the Gut*, Warner: New York, 2001.

40 Personal communication from Pat Kelly, *op. cit.*

41 This principle is also fundamental to military strategy: "The secret of strategy is concentration of firepower on the right battlefield" (Napoleon); "The heart of all strategy is concentration of strength" (Von Clausewitz); "The essence of strategy is concentration of strength against enemy weakness" (Liddell-Hart). Important examples are the Inchon landings in the Korean War and Allied use of air power and mobility in the first Gulf War.

42 Other important selectivity dimensions are product portfolio choices; distribution system decisions; whether to focus on nonusers, current customers, or competitors' customers; and which members of customer decision-making groups to target.

43 The firm should not discard market opportunities because it does not currently possess the required competencies; perhaps it can secure them.

44 Personal communication from Eric Kim, former Executive Vice President, Global Marketing Operations, Samsung Inc.

45 Personal communication from Michael George, former Chief Marketing Officer and Vice President, Corporate Strategy, Dell.

46 "A Cheerleader, for a Company in a Midlife Funk," *The New York Times*, June 23, 2002.

47 In the 1992 U.S. presidential election, a critical statement was, "It's the economy, stupid."

48 Personal communication from Stew McHie, former Global Brand Manager, Exxon Mobil Fuels Marketing.

49 J. Collins, *Good to Great: Why Some Companies Make the Leap ... and Others Don't*, New York: Collins, 2001. Also J.R. Williams, "How Sustainable Is Your Competitive Advantage?," *California Management Review*, 34 (Spring 1992), pp. 29–52; P. Ghemawat, "Sustainable Advantage," *Harvard Business Review*, 64 (September–October 1986), pp. 53–94.

50 For other approaches to developing differential advantage: G. Stalk, P. Evans, and L.E. Shulman, "Competing on Capabilities: The New Rules of Corporate Strategy," *Harvard Business Review*, 70 (March–April 1992), pp. 57–69; D.J. Collis and C.A. Montgomery, "Competing on Resources: Strategy in the 1990s," *Harvard Business Review*, 73 (July–August) 1995, pp. 118–128; M. Reeves and M.S. Deimler, "New Bases of Competitive Advantage: The Adaptive Imperative," *The Boston Consulting Group*, 2009. For knowledge assets in securing competitive advantage, see D.J. Teece, "Capturing Value from Knowledge Assets," *California Management Review*, 40 (Spring 1998), pp. 55–78.

51 R. D'Aveni, *Hypercompetition*, New York: The Free Press, 1994.

52 R.L. Foster, *Innovation: The Attacker's Advantage*, New York: Summit, 1986.

53 Some data suggest any difference may have value: G.S. Carpenter, R. Glazer, and K. Nakamoto, *Readings on Market-Driving Strategies: Towards a New Theory of Competitive Advantage*, New York: Addison Wesley Longman, 1997.

54 Personal communication from Michael Francis, former Senior Vice President of Marketing, Target Stores.

55 Personal communication from Marty Homlish, former senior marketing executive, Sony Electronics. Also H. Krohmer, C. Homburg, and J.P. Workman, "Should Marketing Be Cross-Functional? Conceptual Development and International Empirical Evidence," *Journal of Business Research*, 55 (2002), pp. 451–465, for a study of functional integration.

CHAPTER 2

1 L. Selden and G. Colvin, *Angel Customers & Demon Customers*, New York: Portfolio, 2003; used by permission.

2 This chapter benefited considerably from discussions with colleagues Sunil Gupta and Don Lehmann: S. Gupta, D.R. Lehmann, and J. Ames Stuart, "Valuing Customers," *Journal of Marketing Research*, 41 (February 2004), pp. 7–19; S. Gupta and D.R. Lehmann, "Customers as Assets," *Journal of Interactive Marketing*, 17 (Winter 2003), pp. 9–24; and S. Gupta and D.R. Lehmann, *Managing Customers as Investments*, Philadelphia, PA: Wharton, 2004.

3 Personal communication from Ron Boire, former President Consumer Sales, Sony Electronics — CEO Barnes & Noble (2015).

4 The firm applies the sum of net margins across all customers to its fixed costs to identify overall gross margin. Net margin equals gross margin less specific costs for retaining customers.

5 In each successive year, the value of money decreases — $100 earned next year is worth less than $100 earned this year. Hence, we discount all future margins to the present as in net present value (NPV) calculations. We treat the original acquisition cost for current customers as a sunk cost. Also P.D. Berger and N.I. Nasr, "Customer Lifetime Value: Marketing Models and Applications," *Journal of Interactive Marketing*, 12 (Winter 1998), pp. 17–30.

6 Margin = revenues less costs; most firms do not track costs by customer. Marketing Enrichment FM.1 **[308p]** shows customer profitability calculations.

7 Strictly speaking, the margin-multiple formula applies to a series of terms summed to infinity. Hence, we avoid arbitrary assumptions about actual customer lifetime. Assuming reasonable values for retention rate (r) and discount rate (d), after a few years the impact of all terms is very small. You can check this out for yourself.

8 Note that the term *discount* in *discount rate* has a quite different meaning from selling at a *discount* from list price.

9 R. G. McGrath, "How the Growth Outliers Do It," *Harvard Business Review*, 90 (January–February 2012), pp. 111–116, shows that 10 growth-outlier firms (5 percent growth in revenues and net profits, each year for 10 years) (from a 4,793 sample) reported customer satisfaction and customer retention in excess of 90 percent.

10 S. Gupta and C.F. Mela, "What Is a Free Customer Worth," *Harvard Business Review*, 86 (November 2008), pp. 102–109.

11 *Customer Referral Value* (CRV) measures the value of customer referrals, V. Kumar, J.A. Petersen, and R.P. Leone, "Driving Profitability by Encouraging Customer Referrals: Who, When, and How," *Journal of Marketing*, 74 (September 2010), pp. 1–17. Intention to recommend (refer) is central to Net Promoter Score — Chapter 24.

12 I. Garnefeld, A. Eggert, S.V. Helm, and S.S. Tax, "Growing Existing Customers' Revenue Streams through Customer Referral Programs," *Journal of Marketing*, 77 (July 2013), pp. 17–32.

13 F.F. Reicheld, *The Loyalty Effect*, Boston, MA: Harvard Business School Press, 1996, p. 51.

14 Reicheld, *op. cit.*, p. 38.

15 Empirical studies on customer profitability relationships show mixed results. Reicheld, *op. cit.* supports the propositions in this chapter. W.J. Reinhartz and V. Kumar, "On the Profitability of Long-Life Customers in a Noncontractual Setting: An Empirical Investigation and Implications for Marketing," *Journal of Marketing*, 64 (October 2000), pp. 17–35; W. Reinartz and V. Kumar, "The Mismanagement of Customer Loyalty," *Harvard Business Review*, 80 (July 2002), pp. 86–94; and W. Reinartz and V. Kumar, "The Impact of Customer Relationship Characteristics on Profitable Lifetime Duration," *Journal of Marketing*, 67 (January 2003), pp. 77–99, report some contrary findings.

16 Gupta and Lehmann, *op. cit.*, pp. 35–39, also show the impact on CLV when: (a) Margins grow at a decreasing rate, (b) Retention rates increase with length of customer tenure, (c) Time horizon is finite versus infinite.

17 Reicheld, *op. cit.*, p. 36. Also F.F. Reicheld, *Loyalty Rules*, Boston, MA: Harvard Business School Press, 2001; B.J. Pine II, D. Peppers, and M. Rogers, "Do You Want to Keep Your Customers Forever?," *Harvard Business Review*, 73 (March–April 1995), pp. 103–154; R.C. Blattberg and J. Deighton, "Manage Marketing by the Customer Equity Test," *Harvard Business Review*, 74 (July–August 1996), pp. 136–144; R.C. Blattberg, G. Getz, and J.S. Thomas, *Customer Equity*, Boston, MA: Harvard Business School Press, 2001; and R.T. Rust, V.A. Zeithaml, and K.N. Lemon, *Driving Customer Equity*, New York: Free Press, 2000.

18 Steady-state market shares are independent of starting positions. Jane's and Joe's initial division of the 1,000 customers does not affect the long run.

19 Reicheld's work also demonstrates the importance of employee and shareholder loyalty.

20 "Customer Acquisition Cost — A Key Marketing Metric," *National Petroleum News*, April 2003. These costs are averages and may vary widely depending on complexity of the selling process.

21 In the credit card industry, a good response rate for new-customer direct mail campaigns is 2 to 3 percent. To secure 1,000 applications, the firm must send 30,000 to 50,000 solicitations. Factoring in costs for credit evaluation, card issuance, and entering customer data into its system, the cost to acquire each new customer ranges from $50 to $100.

22 Adapted from Table 3.2, pp 54–55, S. Gupta and D.R. Lehmann, *Managing Customers as Investments*, Philadelphia, PA: Wharton, 2005.

23 To maximize CLV, marketing must calculate optimal budget allocations across different spending categories, D.M. Hanssens, D. Thorpe, and C. Finkbeiner, "Marketing When Customer Equity Matters," *Harvard Business Review*, (May 2008), pp. 117–123.

24 For empirical studies: W. Reinartz, J. Thomas, and V. Kumar, "Balancing Acquisition and Retention Resources to Maximize Customer Profitability," *Journal of Marketing*, 69 (January 2005), pp. 63–79 and J. Thomas, W. Reinartz, and V. Kumar, "Getting the Most out of All Your Customers," *Harvard Business Review*, 82 (July–August 2004), pp. 116–123.

25 V. Mittal and W.A. Kamakura, "Satisfaction, Repurchase Intent, and Repurchase Behavior: Investigating the Moderating Effect of Customer Characteristics," *Journal of Marketing Research*, 38 (February 2001), pp. 131–142.

26 Also, B. Cooil, T.L. Keiningham, L. Askoy, and M. Hsu, "A Longitudinal Analysis of Customer Satisfaction and Share of Wallet: Investigating the Moderating Effect of Customer Characteristics," *Journal of Marketing*, 7 (January 2007), pp. 67–83.

27 In B2C industries like banking, credit cards, and retailing, and in much B2B, customers frequently patronize multiple suppliers. The critical issue is often not loyalty *versus* defection, but *share* of wallet.

28 Personal communication from Dave Goudge, former senior vice president for marketing, Boise Office Solutions (now OfficeMax).

29 Some firms use CLV to make decisions on the most effective way of communicating with customers: V. Kumar, R. Venkatesan, T. Bohling, and D. Beckmann, "The Power of CLV: Managing Customer Lifetime Value at IBM," *Marketing Science*, 27 (July–August 2008), pp. 585–599. Also R. Venkatesan, V. Kumar, and T. Bohling, "Optimal Customer Relationship Management Using Bayesian Decision Theory: An Application for Customer Selection," *Journal of Marketing Research*, 44 (November 2007), pp. 579–594.

30 When evaluating customer acquisition efforts, the firm should estimate potential CLV, including the option value of abandoning customers that become unprofitable, M. Haenlein, A.M. Kaplan, and D. Schoder, "Valuing the Real Option of Abandoning Unprofitable Customers When Calculating Customer Lifetime Value," *Journal of Marketing*, 70 (July 2006) pp. 5–20.

31 Firms that minimize credit losses reject many customers that would have repaid their credit. Credit card firms must strike a balance, recognizing they must accept many customers who won't pay!

32 Also Selden and Colvin, *op. cit.*

33 Many firms have adopted activity-based costing (ABC) to secure more precise answers to these types of question.

34 Also *Kanthal (A)*, 9-190-002, Harvard Business School.

35 We ignore the value of the customer in covering fixed manufacturing costs (part of cost of goods sold). We assume that a thorough activity-based costing (ABC) system generated selling, service, and additional expenses. Of course, in some situations, selling and service are shared activities across businesses. For a more detailed example of assessing customer profitability, Marketing Enrichment FM.1 **[308p]**.

36 Selden and Colvin, *op. cit.*, pp. 54–55. Selden and Colvin suggest the profit skew is even more extreme than we suggest — 150 percent of profit from 20 percent of customers.

37 V. Kumar and D. Shah, "Expanding the Role of Marketing: From Customer Equity to Market Capitalization," *Journal of Marketing*, 73 (November 2009), pp. 119–136. Also R. Niraj, M. Gupta, and C. Narasimhan, "Customer Profitability in a Supply Chain," *Journal of Marketing*, 65 (July 2001), pp. 1–16.

38 For this discussion, overhead comprises costs not directly assigned to customers, like long-run R&D and corporate assessments for advertising, legal services, and government relations.

39 M. Hanlin and A.M. Kaplan, "Unprofitable Customers and Their Management," *Business Horizons*, 52 (2009), pp. 89–97 and V. Mittal, M. Sarkees, and F. Murshed, "The Right Way to Manage Unprofitable Customers," *Harvard Business Review*, 86 (April 2008), pp. 95–101. Of course, predicting future customer profitability may be difficult: E.C. Malthouse and R.C. Blattberg, "Can We predict Customer Lifetime Value?," *Journal of Interactive Marketing*, 19 (Winter 2005), pp. 2–16.

40 "Minding the Store: Analyzing Customers, Best Buy Decides Not All Are Welcome," *The Wall Street Journal*, November 8, 2004. Relatedly, *wardrobers* purchase garments for events, then return them afterward; *closeters* purchase products like tools, computers, or video cameras for a specific use, then return them after completing the task.

41 Mittal, Sarkees, and Murshed, *op. cit.*, suggest a *reassess, educate, renegotiate, migrate* process with customers prior to termination.

42 The fast growth of blogs and Twitter is raising this concern to new levels.

43 An important factor in PepsiCo's divestiture of Kentucky Fried Chicken, Taco Bell, and Pizza Hut was Coca-Cola's success in persuading many fast-food chains that selling PepsiCo drinks was aiding a competitor.

44 These customer types and nonpayers (deadbeats) are *jaycustomers*: C. Lovelock and J. Wirtz, *Service Marketing: People, Technology, Strategy* (7th ed.), Upper Saddle River, NJ: Prentice-Hall, 2011.

45 I. Gordon, *Relationship Marketing: New Strategies, Techniques and Technologies to Win the Customers You Want and Keep Them Forever*, Ontario: Wiley, 1998, p. 9.

46 "Every Little Helps Tesco to £1.6 Billion Record," *The Daily Telegraph*, April 21, 2004. For background on Tesco, see *Tesco PLC: Getting to the Top... Staying at the Top?* Fontainebleau, France: INSEAD, 1999.

47 Chapter 23 shows how to build this type of organization.

48 M. Ebner, A. Hu, D. Levitt, and J. McCrory, "How to Rescue CRM," *The McKinsey Quarterly*, 4 (2002), pp. 49–57; also D.K. Rigby, F.F. Reichheld, and P. Schefter, "Avoid the Four Perils of CRM," *Harvard Business Review*, 80 (February 2002), pp. 101–109.

49 Peter Heffring, former President CRM Division, Teradata, 2002.

50 Gordon, *op. cit.*, p. 30.

51 R. Glazer, "Strategy and Structure in Information-Intensive Markets: The Relationship between Marketing and IT," *Journal of Market-Focused Management*, 2, (1997), pp. 65–81. Glazer believes firms should organize key IT functions — information acquisition, distribution and interpretation, and organizational memory — into *departments* within decision teams. Also R. Winer, "A Framework of Customer Relationship Management," *California Management Review*, 43 (2001), pp. 89–105.

52 From granular database modeling, BlackRock discovered that people living near IBM offices frequently prepaid mortgages early (for company relocation).

53 Also A. Agarwal, D.P. Harding, and J.R. Schumacher, "Organizing for CRM," *The McKinsey Quarterly*, 3 (2004), pp. 81–91.

54 Personal communication from Lance Batchelor, former Head Worldwide Marketing, Amazon.com.

55 Do not confuse *event-driven* marketing with event marketing. Event marketing comprises promotional activities like trade shows that firms design and implement for current and potential customers.

56 Thanks to Mark Holtom, Eventricity, for insight on events.

57 Immediacy is critical for Austra; sales drop dramatically for even a two- or three-day delay in making customer contact.

58 J. Fox-Greene, A.J. McCarthy, and P.S. Simone, "How U.S. Banks Can Attract Middle-Market Customers," *McKinsey on Corporate & Investment Banking*, 7 (September 2008), pp. 9–15.

59 S. Coyles and T.C. Gokey, "Customer Retention Is Not Enough," *The McKinsey Quarterly*, 2 (2002), pp. 81–89, distinguish among different types of loyalty: *emotive loyalists* — committed customers who rarely reassess chosen suppliers; *inertial loyalists* — rarely reassess due to high switching costs or low involvement, and *deliberative loyalists* — frequently reassess on rational criteria. A loyalty ladder in B2B markets embraces: *cynic* — won't buy; *skeptic* — willing to be convinced; *switcher* — will buy if the price is right; buys a bundle of products; invests in the relationship; actively seeks to expand the relationship; *enthusiastic advocate*; and willing to pay a premium, D. Narayandas, *Customer Management Strategy in Business Markets*, N9-503-060, 2003, Harvard Business School. An alternative loyalty scheme identifies: *negative advocates* — strongly negative and persuade others not to buy; *negative status* — strong negative, would never use; *occasional users* — buy very occasionally; *switchers nonpreferred* — purchase from time to time; *switchers-preferred* — prefer the product but will buy others with sufficient inducement; *truly loyal* — will always purchase if available; *super loyal* — undertake significant search cost to find and purchase; *ultra loyal* — like *super loyal* but also enthusiastic advocates to others.

60 T. Wagner, T. Hennig-Thurau and T. Rudolph, "Does Customer Demotion Jeopardize Loyalty?" *Journal of Marketing*, 73 (May 2009), pp. 69–85.

61 *Hilton Honors Worldwide: Loyalty Wars*, 9-501-010, Harvard Business School.

62 G.R. Dowling and M. Uncles, "Do Customer Loyalty Programs Really Work?," *Sloan Management Review*, (Summer 1997), pp. 71–82; L. O'Brien and C. Jones, "Do Rewards Really Create Loyalty?," *Harvard Business Review*, 73 (May–June 1995), pp. 75–82; J.C. Nune and X. Drèze, "Your Loyalty Program Is Betraying You," *Harvard Business Review*, 84 (April 2006), pp. 124–131.

63 R. Kivetz, O. Urminsky, and Y. Zheng, "The Goal-Gradient Hypothesis Resurrected: Purchase Acceleration, Illusionary Goal Progress, and Customer Retention," *Journal of Marketing Research*, 43 (February 2006), pp 39-58.

64 Loyalty programs are a vigorous research area in marketing: R. Kivetz and I. Simonson, "The Idiosyncratic Fit Heuristic: Effort Advantage as a Determinant of Consumer Response to Loyalty Programs," *Journal of Marketing Research*, 40 (November 2003), pp. 454–467; R. Kivetz and I. Simonson, "Earning the Right to Indulge: Effort as a Determinant of Customer Preferences Toward Frequency Program Rewards," *Journal of Marketing Research*, 39 (May 2003), pp. 155–170; R. Kivetz, "The Effects of Effort and Intrinsic Motivation on Risky Choice," *Marketing Science*, 22 (2003), pp. 477–502; R. Kivetz, "Promotion Reactance: The Role of Effort-Reward Congruity," *Journal of Consumer Research*, 31 (March 2005), pp. 725–736. For a review, see T.H.A. Bijmolt, M. Dorotic, and P.C. Verhoer, "Loyalty Programs: Generalizations on Their Adoption, Effectiveness, and Design," *Foundations and Trends in Marketing*, 5 (2010), pp. 197–258.

65 These data from *Sonik CD: Future Growth Strategy*, Columbia Business School, by permission of Professor Sunil Gupta. Ignore differences in fixed costs across alternatives.

CHAPTER 3

1 For a good discussion of market definition, see *Note on Market Definition and Segmentation*, 9-579-083, Harvard Business School.

2 T. Levitt, "Marketing Myopia," *Harvard Business Review*, 53 (September–October 1975), pp. 26 *et seq*.

3 R.K. Srivastava, M.I. Alpert, and A.D. Shocker, "A Customer-Oriented Approach for Determining Market Structures," *Journal of Marketing*, 48 (Spring 1984), pp. 32–45.

4 Some use *product category* instead of *product class*; *product subcategory* instead of *product form*.

5 Since B2C market demand drives B2B market demand, we focus on key indicators of B2C market size.

6 India's population growth rate — 1.31 percent — is more than twice China's — 0.48 percent, CIA Factbook 2012.

7 The required fertility rate to sustain the population globally is 2.3 — 2.1 in advanced countries. More than 70 countries have fertility rates less than 2.1 — up from 24 in the 1970s.

8 Data from U.S. Census Bureau, International Data Base, 2012.

9 Migration data from the United Nations.

10 *Ad Budget Alignment: Maximizing Impact in the Hispanic Market*, Washington, DC: Association of Hispanic Advertising Agencies (AHAA), 2004.

11 Wikipedia. Derived from IMF data; figures in current Geary–Khamis dollars, aka International dollars.

12 The *Gini* coefficient, measuring the inequality of a distribution, provides similar results to EPIR.

13 United Nations Population Database. Estimates of population percentages over age 65 in 2050 from *The Economist*: Italy and Spain — 70 percent, Germany — 57 percent, France — 53 percent, Sweden and Britain — 49 percent, and Ireland — 48 percent.

14 The related *technology life cycle* encompasses many product classes — usually presented as an S-curve of technological performance versus time. A technology may take a considerable time to get off the ground, but once established, performance increases rapidly. Then the technology reaches its limits. Successive technologies follow similar patterns.

15 For an excellent review of product life cycle research, S. Klepper, "Entry, Exit, Growth, and Innovation over the Product Life Cycle," *American Economic Review*, 86 (June 1996), pp. 562–583.

16 S.L. Holak and Y.E. Tang, "Advertising's Effect on the Product Evolutionary Cycle," *Journal of Marketing*, 54 (July 1990), pp. 16–29.

17 The first hybrids were built between 1899 and 1920. The Electric and Hybrid Vehicle Research, Development and Demonstration Act of 1976 spurred development of gas-electric hybrid cars. Development accelerated when California adopted *zero emission vehicle* (ZEV) rules in 1990. The first commercial prototypes were built in 1996. The first commercially available hybrid was the 2000 Honda Insight, followed by the 2000 Toyota Prius. L.E. Hall, *Back to the Past: The History of Hybrids*.

18 E.M. Rogers, *Diffusion of Innovations*, 5th Ed., New York: Free Press, 2003. We address this topic in Chapter 12.

19 Andy Grove (former Intel CEO) initially dismissed the Macintosh computer as a toy. He believed the graphical interface was a nuisance and absence of a hard disk a severe limitation. A.S. Grove, *Only the Paranoid Survive*, New York, Doubleday, 1996.

20 *Xerox Corporation: The Customer Satisfaction Program*, 9-591-055, Harvard Business School.

21 The U.S. banking industry restructured in the 1980s and 1990s. A combination of federal and state regulation had led to considerable overbanking. The U.S. still has several thousand banks. By comparison, Great Britain (about one-fifth the U.S. population) had four major banks until deregulation increased the number somewhat.

22 Fragmentation and concentration is often in the eye of the beholder. A British firm examining its home market may identify just a few major competitors — a concentrated oligopoly. Similar markets in various European countries may also appear to be oligopolies. But a European perspective would see a single fragmented market. What appears as an oligopoly at the lower level seems fragmented at a higher level. This perspective change has important strategic implications.

23 R.W. Olshavsky, "Time and the Rate of Adoption of Innovations," *Journal of Consumer Research*, 6 (March 1980), pp. 425–428; W. Qualls, R. W. Olshavsky, and R.E. Michaels, "Shortening of the PLC–An Empirical Test," *Journal of Marketing*, 45 (Fall 1981), pp. 76–80. Some life cycles, like fads, start and end quickly; when product use changes — like bicycles and motorcycles from transportation to recreation — the life cycle has multiple distinct elements.

24 M. E. Porter, *Competitor Strategy: Techniques for Analyzing Industries and Competitors*, New York: Free Press, 1980. B. Greenwald and J. Kahn, *Competition Demystified*, New York: Portfolio, 2005, builds on Porter's model but focuses attention on barriers to entry.

25 Bankruptcy laws often prolong marginal players and negatively affect industry profitability.

26 Historically, many industries comprised relatively insulated national oligopolies. As national barriers fall, global oligopolies are developing in several industries.

27 AmBev (Brazil), Interbrew (Belgium) and Anheuser-Busch (U.S.) joined to become Anheuser-Busch InBev (ABI), the leading global brewer. In 2015, SABMiller agreed to be acquired by ABI.

28 Management buyouts (MBOs) are a special case of LBOs; existing management executes the purchase. In recent years, LBOs have rebranded as *private equity*.

29 C. Zook with J. Allen, *Profit from the Core: Growth Strategy in an Era of Turbulence*, Boston, MA: Harvard Business School Press, 2001, pp. 26–28.

30 M. Corstjens and J. Merrihue, "Optimal Marketing," *Harvard Business Review*, 81 (October 2003), pp. 114–121, for Samsung's decisions to invest in various global product/markets.

31 R.M. Kanter, "Collaborative Advantage: The Art of Alliances," *Harvard Business Review*, 72 (July–August 1994), pp. 96–108.

32 In pyramid sales forces, salespeople earn commissions from direct sales. They also earn *overrides* on sales of salespeople they recruit. They may also earn overrides on sales from their recruits' recruits, and so on.

33 When indirect competitive threats are high, political forces may impel governments to remove/amend offending regulations.

34 Some firms address large commodity price swings by *hedging* purchases. Some multinationals, like Caterpillar, strive to match production and sales by country to avoid currency swing problems.

35 K. Harrigan, *Strategies for Vertical Integration*, Lexington, MA: Lexington Books, 1983.

36 H. Simon, *Hidden Champions: Lessons from 500 of the World's Best Unknown Companies*, Boston, MA: Harvard Business School Press, 1996; also *Hidden Champions of the Twenty-First Century: The Success Strategies of Unknown World Market Leaders*, New York: Springer-Science+Business Media, 2009.

37 Pricing is crucial in two-sided markets — Chapter 22; T. Eisenmann, G. Parker, and M.W. Van Alstyne, "Strategies for Two-Sided Markets," *Harvard Business Review*, 84 (October 2006), pp. 92–101.

38 This section draws on P. Fitzroy, A. Ghobadian, and J.M. Hulbert, *Strategic Management: The Challenge of Creating Value*, London: Routledge, 2012.

39 For tips on dealing with different cultures, R.E. Axtell (ed.), *Do's and Taboos around the World*, New York: Wiley, 1993.

40 J. Garreau, *The Nine Nations of North America*, Boston, MA: Houghton-Mifflin, 1981, classifies North America (Canada and U.S.) into nine sub-cultures.

41 Taken in part, and modified, from V. Terpstra, *The Cultural Environment of International Business*, Cincinnati, OH: Southwestern Publishing, 1978, Figure 1. Also V. Terpstra and K. David, *The Cultural Environment of International Business*, 3rd Ed. Cincinnati, OH: Southwestern, 1991.

42 *Baby boomers* — 77 million persons born in the U.S. between 1946 and 1965; *generation X* — 50 million persons born between 1966 and 1980; *millenials* — 77 million persons born between 1981 and 1999.

43 United Nations' membership: End 1940s — 59; end 1960s — 126; 2011 — 192 (total number of countries — 196).

44 Thanks to Alan Fortier for this demonstration.

45 C. M. Christensen, *The Innovator's Dilemma: When New Technologies Cause Great Firms to Fail*, Boston, MA: Harvard Business School Press, 1997.

46 D. A. Beck, J. N. Fraser, A. C. Reuter-Domenech, and P. Sidebottom, "Personal Financial Services Goes Global," *The McKinsey Quarterly*, 3 1999, pp. 39–47.

47 L. Downes and C. Mui, *Unleashing the Killer App: Digital Strategies for Market Dominance,* Boston, MA: Harvard Business School Press, 1998, pp. xix, 243. George Washington University Forecast of Emerging Technologies identified several future technologies and dates: 2005 — fuel-cell-powered cars introduced; 2008 — virtual assistants common and genetically modified food widely accepted; 2010 — smart robots in homes and factories; 2012 — children genetically designed; 2030 — average life span 100 years; 2050 — humans travel to nearby star systems. Also The World Future Society.

48 C. M. Christensen, *op. cit.* Disruptive technologies that damaged incumbents include: handheld calculators — slide rule manufacturers; overnight package delivery — freight forwarders; TV — radio, jet aircraft — turbo-props and ocean liners.

49 J.H. Dessauer, *My Years with Xerox: The Billions Nobody Wanted*, Garden City, NJ: Doubleday, 1971.

50 *Doing a Dyson (A), (B), (C)*, 599-051-1BW, European Case Clearing House. Most major vacuum cleaner manufacturers have since copied Dyson's invention.

51 Batteries are too expensive for the world's poor; the impact has been dramatic.

52 K. O'Neill Packard and F. Reinhardt, "What Every Executive Needs to Know About Global Warming," *Harvard Business Review*, 78 (July–August 2000), pp. 129–135.

53 For P&G's struggles to address environmental issues in Germany, see *Procter & Gamble Company: Lenor Refill Package*, 9-592-016, Harvard Business School.

54 J. Elkington, *Cannibals with Forks: The Triple Bottom Line of 21st Century Business*, Oxford, UK: Capstone, 1997, pp. xiv, 402, believes firms should adopt the triple bottom line and pursue social, environmental, and economic objectives.

55 Over two-thirds of South Korean households subscribe versus U.S. — 15 percent — and Western Europe — 8 percent.

56 Paradoxically, many consider GE, one of the world's most successful firms, a conglomerate.

57 Some highly successful private equity firms like the Blackstone Group and Kohlberg Kravis Roberts (KKR) resemble conglomerates.

58 N. Capon, J.U. Farley, and J. Hulbert, "International Diffusion of Corporate and Strategic Planning Processes," *Columbia Journal of World Business*, 15 (Fall 1980), pp. 5–13.

59 N. Capon, J.U. Farley, and J.M. Hulbert, *Corporate Strategic Planning*, New York: Columbia University Press, 1987.

60 I. Nonaka and H. Takeuchi, *The Knowledge-Creating Company*, New York: Oxford University Press, 1995.

61 F. Broetzmann and J. Goetz, "The Revival of Scenario Planning: An Integral Part of Reliable Corporate Management," Ernst & Young, 2010; and C. Roxburgh, "The Use and Abuse of Scenarios," *The McKinsey Quarterly*, (November 2009), pp 1–10.

CHAPTER 4

1 This and the preceding example are from *Selling Power*.

2 In advanced Western societies, individual, family, and organizational customers increasingly avoid purchase — they often prefer to rent or lease. We use the term *purchase* loosely to encompass these methods.

3 Typically, indirect customers are all customers in the customer channel beyond direct customers.

4 Firms with both *paying* and *free* customers must decide how to balance marketing efforts among them. Firms must consider both *direct* and *indirect* network effects and assess whether they are positive or negative. For an auction house, *direct* effects concern how buyers attract (or not) more buyers and how sellers attract (or not) more sellers. *Indirect* effects concern how buyers attract (or not) more sellers and how sellers attract (or not) more buyers. S. Gupta and C. Mela, "What Is a Free Customer Worth," *Harvard Business Review*, 86 (November 2008), pp. 102–109, shows how to value *free* customers.

5 In many nation states, government is the largest organizational purchaser. The annual budget for the U.S. Defense department is between $600 billion and $700 billion.

6 T.V. Bonoma, "Major Sales: Who Really Does the Buying?," *Harvard Business Review*, 60 (May–June 1982), pp. 111–120.

7 M.H. Morris, P. Berthon, and L.F. Pitt, "Assessing the Structure of Industrial Buying Centers with Multivariate Tools," *Industrial Marketing Management*, 28 (1999), pp. 263–276, for a study of role structure in organizational buying.

8 University of Washington, University of Southern California, Georgia Tech, MIT, and Purdue.

9 Personal communication from Richard L. Melville Jr., former Vice Chairman, Aerospace Market Sector Lead Team, Alcoa Inc.

10 This example shows the importance of branding. Without a brand, the product has no identity — indirect customers see it as generic. Consider: If Intel's product works, the indirect customer never sees it!

11 Personal communication from Dale Hayes, former Vice President Brand Management and Customer Communications, UPS.

12 Sometimes the firm wants customers to purchase products; sometimes to influence other customers. Some marketing seeks other behavioral responses like voting. We focus on mainstream marketing. Some influence techniques, such as force and threats of force, are not part of marketing — organizations, like protection rackets, specialize in these techniques to encourage purchase of their services!

13 In addition to *communicating* value, the communications process may also *create* value.

14 This watermelon has a thin rind, no seeds, and tastes delicious.

15 From the president of Stanley Works.

16 Personal communication.

17 A. Maslow, *Motivation and Personality*, New York: Harper, 1954. Maslow's framework raises the question, discussed extensively by Freud: Are all needs fully conscious?

18 Related work from J. Guttman, "A Means-End Chain Model Based on Consumer Categorization Processes," *Journal of Marketing*, 46 (Spring 1982), pp. 60–72; B.A. Walker and J.C. Olson, "Means-End Chains: Connecting Products with Self," *Journal of Business Research*, 22 (1991), pp. 111–118; T.R. Graeff, "Comprehending Product Attributes and Benefits: The Role of Product Knowledge and Means-End Chain Inferences," *Psychology and Marketing*, 14 (March 1997), pp. 163–183; J.C. Olson and T.J. Reynolds, "The Means-End Approach to Understanding Consumer Decision Making," in *Understanding Consumer Decision Making: The Means-End Approach to Marketing and Advertising Strategy*, T.J. Reynolds and J.C. Olson, Eds., Hillsdale, NJ: Erlbaum, 2001, pp. 3–20.

19 For customer-based definitions of competition: G.S. Day and R. Wensley, "Assessing Advantage: A Framework for Diagnosing Competitive Superiority," *Journal of Marketing*, 52 (April 1988), pp. 1–20.

20 A separate system has two categories: *rational* — subsuming functional and economic; and *emotional* — psychological. These value-laden terms may obscure the often vital importance of psychological benefits.

21 Example from Systematic Inventive Thinking (SIT).

22 Alternative value models embrace more value types — conditional, emotional, epistemic, functional, social: J.N. Sheth, B.I. Newman, and B.L. Gross, "Why We Buy What We Buy: A Theory of Consumption Value," *Journal of Business Research*, 22 (1991), pp. 159–170; emotional, price/value for money, quality/performance, social: J.C. Sweeney and G.N. Soutar, "Consumer Perceived Value: The Development of a Multiple Item Scale," *Journal of Retailing*, 77 (2001), pp. 203–220. Also S.E. Beatty, L.R. Kahle, P. Homer, and S. Misra, "Alternative Measurement Approaches to Consumer Values: The List of Values and the Rokeach Value Survey," *Psychology and Marketing*, 2 (Fall 1985), pp. 181–200. Of course, the firm must assess which value type — functional, psychological, or economic — is most important in the specific purchase decision.

23 R. Friedmann, "Psychological Meaning of Products: Identification and Marketing Applications," *Psychology and Marketing*, 3 (Spring 1986), pp. 1–15.

24 Personal communication from Jackson's (disguised) regional sales manager. Chapter 21 includes further discussion of economic value. *Value-in-use* captures the same idea.

25 GE's *at-the-customer, for-the-customer* initiative sends six-sigma squads to improve processes at customers like Southwest Airlines.

26 Transactions costs derive from search, information, bargaining, decision, policing, and enforcement: L. Downes and C. Mui, *Unleashing the Killer App: Digital Strategies for Market Dominance*, Boston, MA: Harvard Business School Press, 1998; based on R.H. Coase, "The Nature of the Firm: Origin," *Economica*, 4 (1937), pp. 368–405.

27 J.L. Forbis and N.T. Mehta, "Value-Based Strategies for Industrial Products," *Business Horizons*, 24 (1981), pp. 32–42.

28 This calculation does not include savings from avoiding costs to repair cotton-based conveyor belts, nor downtime costs of more frequently replacing cotton conveyor belts.

29 Customers may receive some value items over time; hence, time value may be important.

30 In *Wild Man Blues*, Woody Allen explains his love for New York City: He can always get duck wonton soup at 3:30 A.M., but would never want to!

31 For value in scarcity, secrecy, amplification, entertainment, and tricksterism: S. Brown, "Torment Your Customers (They'll Love It)," *Harvard Business Review* 79 (October 2001), pp. 83–88.

32 A. Pettigrew, *Politics of Organizational Decision Making*, London: Tavistock, 1973, p. 266.

33 C. Meyer and A. Schwager, "Understanding Customer Experience," *Harvard Business Review*, 85 (February 2007), pp. 117–126.

34 Outside's Go: Travel & Style for Men.

35 B.J. Pine II and J.H. Gilmore, *The Experience Economy*, Boston, MA: Harvard Business School Press, 1999.

36 B. Schmitt, *Experiential Marketing: How to Get Customers to Sense, Feel, Think, Act and Relate to Your Company and Brands*: New York: Free Press, 1999; and B. Schmitt, "Experience Marketing: Concepts, Frameworks, and Consumer Insights," *Foundations and Trends in Marketing*, 5 (2010), pp. 55–112, for a review. Also B.J. Pine II and J.H. Gilmore, "Welcome to the Experience Economy," *Harvard Business Review*, 76 (July–August 1998), pp. 97–105.

37 H. Stern, "The Significance of Impulse Buying Today," *Journal of Marketing*, 26 (April 1962) pp. 59–62.

38 Other purchase-decision process models include: J.A. Howard and J. Sheth, *The Theory of Buyer Behavior*, New York: Wiley, 1969. Mapping the purchase decision is similar to process mapping in reengineering — Chapter 23.

39 Marketing scholars have paid more attention to evaluating alternatives than any other stage.

40 Thanks to Paul Capon and Peter Capon for help with this illustration.

41 Formally,

$$\text{Value of an alternative} = \sum_{i=1}^{i=n} A_i B_i$$

A_i = importance weight for attribute "i"; B_i = belief that the alternative possesses attribute "i"; and n = the number of salient attributes.

42 For *cognitive algebra* research: J.R. Bettman, N. Capon, and R.J. Lutz, "Multi-attribute Measurement Models and Multi-attribute Attitude Theory: A Test of Construct Validity," *Journal of Consumer Research*, 1 (March 1975), pp. 1–15; J.R. Bettman, N. Capon, and R.J. Lutz, "Cognitive Algebra in Multi-attribute Attitude Models," *Journal of Marketing Research*, 12 (May 1975), pp. 151–164; and J.R. Bettman, N. Capon, and R.J. Lutz, "Information Processing in Attitude Formation and Change," *Communication Research*, 2 (Fall 1975), pp. 267–278.

43 B2B customers use similar processes to evaluate suppliers.

44 E.J. Johnson and D.G. Goldstein, "Do Defaults Save Lives?," *Science*, 302 [2003], pp. 1338-1339. Defaults can be *mass* — presented to all customers, or *personalized* — tailored to individuals. D.G. Goldstein, E.T. Johnson, A. Herrmann, and M. Heitman, "Nudge Your Customers toward Better Choices," *Harvard Business Review*, 86 (December 2008), pp. 99–105.

45 Consumers who travel for the book but not the home-entertainment system are probably making proportional judgments, consistent with the Weber-Fechner law of psychophysics: R. Thaler, "Toward a Positive Theory of Consumer Choice," *Journal of Economic Behavior and Organization*, 1 (1980), pp. 39–60.

46 This section relies heavily on I. Simonson, "Get Closer to Your Customers by Understanding How They Make Choices," *California Management Review*, (Summer 1993), pp. 74–84.

47 I. Simonson and A. Tversky, "Choice in Context: Tradeoff Contrast and Extremeness Aversion," *Journal of Marketing Research*, 29 (1992), pp. 281–295; also R. Kivetz, O. Netzer, and V. Srinivasan, "Alternative Models for Capturing the Compromise Effect," *Journal of Marketing Research*, 41 (August 2004), pp. 237–257, and G.E. Smith and T.T. Nagle, "Frames of Reference and Buyers' Perception of Price and Value," *California Management Review*, 38 (1995), pp. 98–116.

48 J. Huber, J. W. Payne, and C. Puto, "Adding Asymmetrically Dominated Alternatives: Violations of Regularity and the Similarity Hypothesis," *Journal of Consumer Research* 9 (1982), pp. 90–98.

49 I.P. Levin and G.J. Gaeth, "How Consumers Are Affected by the Framing of Attribute Information Before and After Consuming the Product," *Journal of Consumer Research*, 15 (1988), pp. 374–378.

50 R. Dhar and I. Simonson, "The Effect of the Focus of Comparison on Consumer Preferences," *Journal of Marketing Research*, 29 (November 1992), pp. 430–440.

51 I. Simonson, S. Nowlis, and K. Lemon, "The Effect of Local Consideration Sets on Global Choice Between Lower Price and Higher Quality," *Marketing Science*, 12 (Fall 1993), pp. 357–377; also J. Gourville and D. Soman, "Pricing and the Psychology of Consumption," *Harvard Business Review*, 80 (September 2002), pp. 90–99.

52 T. Levitt, "After the Sale Is Over," *Harvard Business Review*, 61 (September–October 1983), pp. 87–93.

53 D.C. Edelman, "Branding in the Digital Age," *Harvard Business Review*, 88 (December 2010), pp. 62–69, shows that 60 percent of facial-skin-care customers sought information online *after* purchase.

54 Firm responses include: Ignore, try to address customer concerns, buy the sites, build sites to refute charges, supply data to competitor hate-site sponsors, and/or register sites like IhatefirmX.com or FirmXsucks.com before disgruntled customers can do so.

55 The firm may use a few well-chosen questions to gain customer insight like: Who are they? What, where, when, and how do they buy? Why do they buy? How do they choose?

56 A.J. Slywotzky, D.J. Morrison, and B. Andelman, *The Profit Zone*, New York: Times Business, 2002.

57 Based in part on Howard and Sheth, *op. cit.*, Columbia Business School, and Robinson, Faris, and Wind (RFW), Wharton: P.J. Robinson, C.W. Faris and Y. Wind, *Industrial Buying and Creative Marketing*, Boston, MA: Allyn and Bacon, 1967. RFW use different terms: routinized-response behavior — *straight rebuy*; limited problem-solving — *modified rebuy*; extended problem-solving — *new buy*.

58 R.D. Blackwell, P.W. Miniard, and J.F. Engel, *Consumer Behavior*, 10th Ed., Ft. Worth, TX: Thomson/South-Western, 2005, for psychological processes in consumer behavior.

59 E. Hall, *The Silent Language*, Garden City, NY: Anchor, 1973.

60 500 companies produce more than 2,000 kretek brands.

61 W. Chan Kim and R. Mauborgne, *Blue Ocean Strategy*, Boston, MA: Harvard Business School Press, 2005, pp. 71–74.

62 A condensed version of Coleman-Rainwater: R.P. Coleman and L.P. Rainwater, with K.A. McClelland, *Social Standing in America: New Dimensions of Class*, New York: Basic Books, from Blackwell, Engel, and Miniard, *op. cit.*

63 Groups an individual consciously wants to avoid — *dissociative* groups.

64 Typically, buying books at Amazon.co.uk and shipping to the U.S. is less expensive than buying from Amazon.com!

65 K.L. Milkman, T. Rogers, and M.H. Bazerman, "Harnessing Our Inner Angels and Demons," *Perspectives on Psychological Science*, 3 (2008), pp. 324–338.

66 Table 4.10 summarizes VALS2 — SRI International, Menlo Park, CA. Name changes from the previous version include: Innovators — formerly Actualizers; Thinkers — formerly Fulfilleds; and Survivors — formerly Strugglers.

67 For discussion of organizational politics: P. Block, *The Empowered Manager: Positive Political Skills at Work*: San Francisco, CA: Jossey Bass, 1991.

68 Chapter 3 discusses broad environmental influences — globalization, industry concentration, and increased competition. This section is based on N. Capon, *Key Account Management and Planning*, New York: The Free Press, 2001, and N. Capon, D. Potter, and F. Schindler, *Managing Global Accounts*, Bronxville, NY: Wessex, 2008.

69 Personal communication.

70 Marriott Corporation has highly sophisticated sourcing systems and significant procurement expertise. Marriott performs over half its purchasing and distribution activities for non-Marriott clients!

71 When Jose Lopez, GM procurement czar, joined Volkswagen, GM alleged he took a 3,350-page printout listing 60,000 parts and suppliers for GM Europe, exact prices, and delivery schedules.

72 Xerox uses a fivefold *customer relationship triangle* — supplier, authorized supplier, preferred supplier, sole supplier, and quality partner.

73 J.D. Burdett, "A Model for Customer-Supplier Alliances," *Logistics Information Management*, 5 (1992), pp. 25–31, for contrasting approaches to buyer/seller relationships.

CHAPTER 5

1 Based on material from Boeing and Airbus websites and Wikipedia.

2 Boeing switched from traditional in-house manufacture to an out-sourced model, assembling components from other manufacturers. Boeing lost control of the process and purchased some subcontractors.

3 Personal communication from Michael George, former Chief Marketing Officer and Vice President, Corporate Strategy, Dell.

4 "Detroit Motor Show," *Telegraph Motoring*, January 15, 2005. Ford since sold Jaguar to Tata Motors.

5 S. Rattner, *Overhaul: An Insider's Account of the Obama Administration's Emergency Rescue of the Auto Industry*, New York: Houghton Mifflin Harcourt, 2010.

6 *Groupthink* refers to drawing conclusions based on the shared, and poorly examined, assumptions of group members: Wikipedia; I.L. Janis, *Groupthink: Psychological Studies of Policy Decisions and Fiascoes* (2nd ed.), Boston: Wadsworth, 1972.

7 J. Urbany, D.B. Montgomery, and M. Moore, "Competitive Reactions and Modes of Competitive Reasoning," Cambridge, MA: Marketing Science Institute, 2001. Also B.H. Clark and D.B. Montgomery, "Managerial Identification of Competitors," *Journal of Marketing*, 63 (July 1999), pp. 67–83.

8 For this example and more on *strategic intuition*: W. Duggan, *Strategic Intuition: The Creative Spark in Human Achievement*, New York: Columbia Business School, 2007, p. 94.

9 In *Winning*, New York: HarperBusiness, 2005, former GE CEO J. Welch and S. Welch focus on five competitively oriented sets of questions as the basis for developing strategy: 1. What does the playing field look like now? — identifying and describing competitors; 2. What has the competition been up to? — strategy and actions; 3. What have you been up to? — the firm's strategy and actions; 4. What's around the corner? — potential competitor actions; 5. What's your winning move? — actions the firm can take.

10 Of course, firms may use legal, political, and/or regulatory means to remove (or weaken) competitors.

11 Prepared in part by Françoise Simon, SDC Group. Reproduced with permission.

12 *Citibank N.A.*, in N. Capon, *The Marketing of Financial Services: A Book of Cases*, Englewood Cliffs, NJ: Prentice Hall, 1992.

13 M. Tushman and C. O'Reilly, "Ambidextrous Organizations: Managing Evolutionary and Revolutionary Change," *California Management Review*, 38 (1996), pp. 8–30.

14 For a good source, L.M. Fuld, *Competitor Intelligence: How to Get It — How to Use It*, New York: Wiley, 1985.

15 L.M. Fuld, *The Secret Language of Competitive Intelligence*, New York: Crown Business, 2006, pp. 40–41. For a good example of gaining insight from a competitor's production process, pp. 123–134.

16 Fuld 2006, *op. cit.* pp. 51–56.

17 "How Companies Respond to Competitors: A McKinsey Global Survey," *The McKinsey Quarterly*, 2008.

18 Based on L. Fahey, *Outwitting, Outmaneuvering and Outperforming Competitors*, New York: Wiley, 1999, Table 5.3, p. 133, with permission.

19 For a good description of a war game, Fuld 2006, *op. cit.*, pp. 69–118.

20 "A Pretext for Revenge," *Fortune*, June 11, 2007, p. 103. HP was involved in a pretexting scandal when its agents investigated information leaks from the board of directors; HP's chairman and several board members resigned.

21 When the author proctored a graduate-school standardized test at Columbia Business School (as a Ph.D. student), he identified Stanley Kaplan writing questions on scraps of paper, presumably to improve his test-prep products.

22 Based on a competitor analysis framework in Fahey, *op. cit.*, by permission.

23 M.E. Porter, *Competitive Advantage: Creating and Sustaining Superior Performance*, New York: Free Press, 1985.

24 To reinforce this point, around 500 B.C., Chinese warrior Sun Tzu said: "All men see the tactics whereby I conquer, but none see the strategy out of which victory evolved." *The Art of War*, Wikipedia; Oxford; Oxford University Press, 1963.

25 Reproduced from Fahey, *op. cit.*, Table 4.1, p. 90, with permission.

26 Nobel Prize-winner John Nash was a pioneer of game theory — Academy Award-winning film, *A Beautiful Mind*. Other influential pioneers were: J. von Neumann and O. Morgenstern, *Theory of Games and Economic Behavior*, New York: Wiley, 1964 [c1944].

27 This illustration is the prisoner's dilemma. Two persons are alleged to have committed a crime but the police have insufficient evidence to convict either without a confession. The police separate the prisoners and offer each a deal. If both confess, each receives a medium-length sentence; if neither confesses, each receives a short sentence; if only one confesses and implicates the other, the confessor goes free but the implicated prisoner receives a long sentence. Should a prisoner confess or not? Marketing applications often involve pricing, but also new product introduction, service delivery, and advertising.

28 Personal communication from a former J&J executive.

29 This section based on Fahey, *op. cit.*, Chapter 16, with permission.

30 For an excellent discussion of signaling, Fahey, *op. cit.*, Chapter 4.

31 "AMD Sets a Course for 2008," *ZDNet News*, June 1, 2006.

32 H. Gatignon and D. Reibstein, "Formulating Competitive Strategies," *Wharton on Dynamic Competitive Strategies*, G. Day and D. Reibstein (eds.), New York: Wiley, 1997.

33 This section based in part on A. Brandenburger and B.J. Nalebuff, *Co-opetition*, New York: Doubleday, 1996. Broadly, complementarity includes relationships by which the firm secures needed resources. Formal agreements include co-branding; joint production, marketing,

and distribution; joint ventures; R&D partnerships; and supply agreements; but formality is not a requirement for complementarity.

34 These products are not strictly competitors. General Mills has several such delivery arrangements.

35 A major exception is Southwest Airlines — it has no interline agreements.

36 Reilly's Law of Retail Gravitation formalized the power of stores to draw consumers; Wikipedia — Chapter 20.

CHAPTER 6

1 Note: *Data* is a plural word; *datum* is singular.

2 Case material from Client Insight, LLC, Boston.

3 Personal communication.

4 Personal communication.

5 Personal communication from Michael Francis, former Executive Vice President of Marketing, Target Stores.

6 *Stratified random sampling:* Draw random samples from each group. *Cluster sampling:* Randomly select groups; *area (geographical cluster)* sampling is a special case for groups selected by geography.

7 *Boston Fights Drugs (A)*, 9-588-031, Harvard Business School.

8 For a good review, J. Manyika, M. Chui, B. Brown, J. Bughin, R. Dobbs, C. Roxburgh, and A. Hung Byers, "Big Data: The Next Frontier for Innovation, Competition, and Productivity," *McKinsey Global Institute*, May 2011.

9 A. McAfee and E. Brynjolfsson, "Big Data: The Management Revolution," *Harvard Business Review*, 90 (October 2012), pp. 60–67.

10 S. Madden, "How Companies Like Amazon Use Big Data to Make You Love Them," *fastcodesign.com*, 2013.

11 A.C. Micu, K. Dedeker, I. Lewis, O. Netzer, J. Plummer, and J. Rubinson, "The Shape of Marketing Research in 2021," *Journal of Advertising Research*, 51 (March 2011), pp. 1–9.

12 T.H. Davenport and D.J. Patil, "Data Scientist: The Sexiest Job in the 21st Century," *Harvard Business Review*, 90 (October 2012), pp. 70–76.

13 O. Netzer, R. Feldman, J. Goldenburg, and M. Fresco, "Mine Your Own Business: Market-Structure Surveillance though Text Mining," *Marketing Science*, 31 (May–June 2012), pp. 521–543.

14 Micu, Dedeker, Lewis, Netzer, Plummer, and J. Rubinson, *op. cit.*

15 For the impact on scientific research — **478v.**

16 Personal communication from Stephen Cunliffe, former President, Nestlé Prepared Foods, U.S.

17 "Vince Camuto: Nine West's Founder Looks Back," *Fortune*, June 29, 2011.

18 C.M. Christensen, S.D. Anthony, G. Berstelll, and D. Nitterhouse, "Finding the Right Job for Your Product," *Sloan Management Review*, 48 (Spring 2007), pp. 38–47.

19 Thanks to Andrew Gershoff for this example.

20 G. Zaltman and R.A. Higie, "Seeing the Voice of the Customer: The Zaltman Metaphor Elicitation Technique," Working Paper 93-114, Cambridge, MA: Marketing Science Institute, 1994. Patent.

21 The picture approach derives from the Thematic Apperception Test (TAT), widely used in psychology.

22 Attributed to Yogi Berra, baseball player and manager — New York Yankees and New York Mets.

23 Mystery shopping is a form of observational research where the researcher participates in the behavior being studied.

24 Technological innovations, like tracking in-store shopping behavior with eye cameras, add rigor to the observational methodology.

25 Example from The Michael Allen Company.

26 F. Gouillart and F. Sturdivant, "Spend a Day in the Life of Your Customers," *Harvard Business Review*, 72 (January–February 1994), pp. 116–125.

27 As Kellogg's CEO, Carlos Gutierrez used to spend an hour each Sunday morning watching consumers buy cereal in supermarkets.

28 A.G. Laffley and R. Charan, *The Game-Changer: How You Can Drive Revenue and Profit Growth with Innovation*, New York: Crown Business, 2008. Also R.J. Harrington and A.K. Tjan, "Transforming Strategy One Customer at a Time," *Harvard Business Review*, 86 (March 2008), pp. 62–72.

29 Probability sampling approaches include simple random, stratified random, multistage clustering, and systematic. Convenience sampling is not recommended for projecting results to the population. For a good overview: N.K. Malhotra, *Marketing Research: An Applied Orientation*, Upper Saddle River, NJ: Pearson, 2006, Chapter 11.

30 E. Ofek and O. Toubia, "Marketing and Innovation Management: An Integrated Perspective," *Foundations and Trends in Marketing*, 4(2009), pp. 77–128, reports a professionally administered online survey in which more than 50 percent of respondents reported awareness of at least one *fictitious* oral-care brand.

31 Closed-end response questions typically allow for "other."

32 Ordinal scales measure rank order; interview scales measure differences among scale points; ration scales possess a nonarbitrary zero value.

33 Chapter 8 uses these scales to assess market segments on market attractiveness and business strengths criteria.

34 Numbers of brands/comparisons are: 3 brands/3 comparisons; 4 brands/ 6 comparisons; 5 brands/10 comparisons; 6 brands/15 comparisons; 7 brands/21 comparisons; etc.

35 Panel members may be subject to the Hawthorne effect. Because someone is observing, they behave differently.

36 *Repeated measures* on the same individuals is a problem for panel data. Special statistical techniques typically take care of this issue.

37 Scanner data have largely superseded other services to secure sales data, like audits for retail store sales and warehouse withdrawals.

38 S.A. Brasel and J. Gipps, "Breaking through Fast Forwarding: Brand Information and Visual Attention," *Journal of Marketing*, 72 (November 2008), pp 31–48.

39 S.M. McClure, J. Li, D. Tomlin, K.S. Cypert, L.M. Montagu, and P.R. Montague, "Neural Correlates of Behavioral Preferences for Culturally Familiar Drinks," *Neuron*, 44 (October 2004), 379–387.

40 T.H. Davenport, "How to Design Smart Business Experiments," *Harvard Business Review*, 87 (February 2009), pp. 69-76.

41 D.T. Campbell and J.C. Stanley, *Experimental and Quasi-Experimental Designs for Research*, New York: Houghton Mifflin, 1963.

42 J. Surowiecki, *The Wisdom of Crowds*, New York: Doubleday, 2004.

43 For a glossary of marketing research terms.

44 Attributed to Yogi Berra, *op. cit.*

45 More fine-grained analyses use a segment-by-segment approach.

46 Other forecasting methods include BASES and ASSESSOR — Chapter 14. The classic non-durable forecasting model is L.A. Fourt and J.N. Woodlock, "Early Prediction of Market Success for New Grocery Products," *Journal of Marketing*, 25 (October 1960), pp. 31–38. For a review of the seminal Bass model for consumer durables and other new product forecasting models: V. Mahajan, E. Muller, and F.M. Bass, "New Product Diffusion Models in Marketing: A Review and Directions for Research," *Journal of Marketing*, 54 (January 1990), pp. 1–28. For a more contemporary application: F.M. Bass, K. Gordon, T.L. Ferguson, and M.L. Githens, "DirecTV: Forecasting Diffusion of a New Product Technology Prior to Product Launch," *Interfaces*, 31 (May–June 2001), pp. 582–593. Also Marketing Enrichment 14.1 **[143p]**.

CHAPTER 7

1 Response to a question asked by R. Rumelt (1998). D. Lovallo and L.T. Mendonca, "Strategy's Strategist: An Interview with Richard Rumelt," *The McKinsey Quarterly*, August 2007.

2 Zipcar and Flexcar commenced in the mid-2000s with similar business models; they merged as Zipcar in late 2007.

3 Relatedly, many European cities provide bicycle sharing. For a $30 membership fee, customers access bicycles from bike stands around the city. Paris — 20,000 bicycles, 1,450 stations — has the largest system. In 2011, Paris introduced electric car rental.

4 C. Zook with J. Allen, *Profit from the Core*, Boston, MA: Harvard Business School, 2001; C. Zook, *Beyond the Core*, Boston, MA: Harvard Business School, 2004; and C. Zook, *Unstoppable*, Boston, MA: Harvard Business School, 2007. For a shortened version of the 2007 book: C. Zook, "Finding Your Next Core Business," *Harvard Business Review*, 85 (April 2007), pp. 66–75.

5 O. Gadiesh and J.M. Gilbert, "Profit Pools: A Fresh Look at Strategy," *Harvard Business Review*, 76 (May–June 1998), pp. 139–147.

6 *White space* is also called *blue ocean*. W.C. Kim and R. Mauborgne, *Blue Ocean Strategy: How to Create Uncontested Market Space and Make the Competition Irrelevant*, Boston, MA: Harvard Business School Press, 2005.

7 B. Chakravortu, "Finding Competitive Advantage in Adversity," *Harvard Business Review*, 88 (November 2010), pp, 103–108.

8 A.S. Grove, *Only the Paranoid Survive*, New York: Doubleday, 1996.

9 In May 1961, President John Kennedy developed a vision for NASA. "Achieving the goal, before this decade is out, of landing a man on the moon and returning him safely to Earth."

10 J.C. Collins and J.I. Porras, "Building Your Company's Vision," *Harvard Business Review*, 74 (September–October 1996), pp. 65–77 — *vision* is closely related to *BHAGs* — Big Hairy Audacious Goals. Terms like *vision*, *mission*, and *strategic objective* (Chapter 9) often have multiple definitions and confuse managers; readers should clarify each author's definition. Specifically, *mission* is neither a firm/business-unit charter or motherhood statement, nor *strategic objectives*. Also D.J. Collis and M.G. Rukstad, "Can You Say What Your Strategy Is?" *Harvard Business Review*, 86 (April 2008), pp. 82–90.

11 Google CEO Eric Schmidt estimated this vision will take 300 years to achieve.

12 Quoted by Hazel Stewart, Managing Director, Wilson Learning Australia, "Want Successful Change Management? Get Employee Buy-In!," Internet, July, 2012.

13 J.B. Quinn, *The Intelligent Enterprise: A New Paradigm*, New York: Free Press, 1992.

14 A focused mission is contrary to conglomeration. Conglomerates diversify risk by operating multiple different businesses. In the West, conglomerates have generally lost favor, but current exemplars are VEBA (Germany), GE (U.S.), Keiretsu (Japan), Chaebol (Korea), and large family-owned firms in smaller Asian countries.

15 *BYD Company, Ltd.*, 9-606-139, Harvard Business School. Berkshire Hathaway (Warren Buffett) purchased 10 percent ownership in BYD.

16 This insight underlay the famous article: T. Levitt, "Marketing Myopia," *Harvard Business Review*, 53 (September–October 1975), p. 26 *et seq.*

17 T. Levitt, *op. cit.*

18 J.M. Brion, *Corporate Marketing Planning*, New York: Wiley, 1967, pp. 155–156. For a simpler version: H. I. Ansoff, *Corporate Strategy*, New York: McGraw-Hill, 1965, p. 109. Ansoff labels the four cells in his 2×2 matrix — market penetration, market development, product development, and diversification.

19 Day shows that Cell A entries have a 25–40 percent failure probability; Cells C, F, and I have 75–90 percent. In general, Cells D and G have

higher failure probabilities than Cells B and C. G.S. Day, "Is It Real? Can We Win? Is It Worth Doing? Managing Risk and Reward in an Innovation Portfolio," *Harvard Business Review*, (December 2007), pp. 110–120.

20 Zook, 2007, *op. cit.*

21 Research suggests that interrelationships among market opportunities may be more important than technological competencies and synergies. N. Capon, J.U. Farley, J. Hulbert, and L.E. Martin, "Corporate Diversity and Economic Performance: The Impact of Market Specialization," *Strategic Management Journal*, 9 (January–February 1988), pp. 61–74.

22 Quaker's Snapple acquisition is probably better viewed as a business extension. Cadbury Schweppes purchased Snapple (plus Mistic [teas and soft drinks] and Stewart's root beer) for $1.03 billion plus assuming $400 million debt. In 2010, Kraft Foods acquired Cadbury Schweppes.

23 Based in part on H.I. Ansoff and J.M. Stewart, "Strategies for a Technologically-Based Business," *Harvard Business Review*, 45 (November–December 1967), pp. 71–83.

24 T. Levitt, *Marketing for Business Growth*, New York: McGraw-Hill, 1974.

25 G.J. Tellis and P.N. Golder, *Will and Vision: How Latecomers Grow to Dominate Markets*, New York: McGraw-Hill, 2006.

26 Tellis and Golder, *op. cit.*

27 *We've Got Rhythm! Medtronic Corporation's Cardiac Pacemaker Business*, 9-698-004, Harvard Business School.

28 R.G. McGrath and I.C. MacMillan, *Discovery-Driven Growth*, Boston: Harvard Business School, 2009.

29 Dell holds more than 500 patents on business processes.

30 Chapter 10 discusses strategic options in evolving markets. For capability development — *dynamic capabilities*; P. Fitzroy and J.M. Hulbert, *Strategic Management: Creating Value in Turbulent Times*, Hoboken, NJ: Wiley, 2005.

31 T. Kuczmarski, *Managing New Products* (3rd ed.), Englewood Cliffs, NJ: Prentice Hall, 2000. Most firms base financial return calculations on discounted cash flow analyses, using higher discount rates for higher risk ventures. More recently, firms also use *real options* analysis to account for large potential upsides and the ability to abandon a venture before making the entire investment; A.B. van Putten and I.C. MacMillan, "Making Real Options Really Work," *Harvard Business Review*, 82 (December 2004), pp. 134–141.

32 Management fashion plays a role in selecting growth paths. In the late 1960s and early 1970s, many U.S. firms chose *conglomeration*; today, firms generally prefer more-focused approaches. Research shows that *related growth strategies* — markets/customers or products/technologies — are generally more successful; R.P. Rumelt, *Strategy, Structure, and Economic Performance*, Cambridge, MA: Harvard University Press, 1974; R.P. Rumelt, "Diversification and the Market Share Effect," *Strategic Management Journal*, 3 (October–December 1982), pp. 359–369; and C.H. Christensen and C.A. Montgomery, "Corporate Economic Performance: Diversification Strategy versus Market Structure," *Strategic Management Journal*, (October–December 1981), pp. 327–343.

33 Losses from the CAT scanner were largely responsible for EMI's subsequent merger with Thorn PLC. *EMI and the CT Scanner (A) and (B)*, 9-383-194/195, Harvard Business School. Innovator Geoffrey Hounsfield received the Nobel Prize. (Thorn later divested EMI.)

34 F. Webster, "The Changing Role of Marketing," *Journal of Marketing*, 56 (1992), pp. 1–17.

35 The seminal article: C.K. Prahalad and G. Hamel, "Core Competence of the Corporation," *Harvard Business Review*, 68 (May–June 1990), pp. 79–91. K.P. Coyne, S.J.D. Hall, and P.G. Clifford, "Is Your Core Competence a Mirage?," *The McKinsey Quarterly*, 1 (1997), pp. 40–54, proposes a formal definition: "A core competence is a combination of complementary skills and knowledge bases embedded in a group or team that results in the ability to execute one or more critical processes

to a world-class standard" (p. 43). Also P. Leinwand and C. Mainardi, "The Coherence Premium," *Harvard Business Review*, 88 (June 2010), pp. 86–92.

36 The Carlyle Group (private equity) grew by acquiring disparate businesses from "larger companies that were looking [to pare their holdings] to find their core competencies"; "Carlyle Changes Its Stripes," *BusinessWeek*, February 12, 2007, at p. 58.

37 "Virgin in the Oil Patch," *Fortune*, February 6, 2006.

38 Ansoff, *op. cit.*; M. Goold and A. Campbell, "Desperately Seeking Synergy," *Harvard Business Review*, 76 (September–October 1998), pp. 131–143.

39 G.E. Blau, J.F. Pekny, V.A. Varma, and P.R. Bunch, "Managing a Portfolio of Interdependent New Product Candidates in the Pharmaceutical Industry," *Journal of Product Innovation Management*, 21 (2004), pp. 227–245.

40 A contributing factor to Enron's collapse was the absence of a risk assessment for the entire venture portfolio, K. Eichenwald, *A Conspiracy of Fools*, New York: Broadway, 2004.

41 N. Capon and R. Glazer, "Marketing and Technology: A Strategic Co-Alignment," *Journal of Marketing*, 51 (July 1987), pp. 1–14. Pharmaceutical giant Merck focuses largely on internal development but has had problems with product failure.

42 N. Capon, J. U. Farley, and J. Hulbert, *Corporate Strategic Planning*, New York: Columbia University Press, 1988; and N. Capon, J.U. Farley, and S. Hoenig, *Toward an Integrative Explanation of Corporate Financial Performance*, Norwell, MA: Kluwer Academic Publishers, 1997.

43 Personal communication from Pat Kelly, former Senior Vice President, Worldwide Marketing, Pfizer Pharmaceuticals.

44 Some firms post research problems on Eli Lilly's InnoCentive website — problem solvers earn cash payments.

45 A.J. Slywotzky and D.J. Morrison, *Value Migration*, New York: Times Business, 1996; and *The Profit Zone*, Times Business: New York, 1998. Also R. Wise and P. Baumgartner, "Go Downstream: The New Profit Imperative in Manufacturing," *Harvard Business Review*, 77 (September–October 1999), pp. 133–141.

46 Offshoring is a controversial political issue in the U.S.

47 B. Arruñada and X.H. Vázquez, "When Your Contract Manufacturer Becomes Your Competitor," *Harvard Business Review*, 84 (September 2006), pp. 135–144.

48 McKinsey showed that successful acquirer goals are: adding capabilities, expanding geographically, and buying growth; rarely is diversification a goal. *The McKinsey Quarterly* Chart Focus Newsletter, July 2007.

49 L.V. Gerstner, Jr., *Who Says Elephants Can't Dance?*, New York: HarperBusiness, 2003, p. 222. Gerstner adds that IBM often accelerated technology development through highly focused acquisitions.

50 eBay's Skype acquisition was widely considered a failure; in 2010, eBay sold most of its Skype investment to an investor group, since acquired by Microsoft.

51 Personal communication from Pat Kelly, *op. cit.*

52 M.A. Hayward and D.C. Hambrick, "Explaining the Premiums Paid for Large Acquisitions: Evidence of CEO Hubris," *Administrative Science Quarterly*, 42 (1997), pp. 103–127.

53 M. Bradley, A. Desai, and E.H. Kim, "Synergistic Gains from Acquisitions and Their Division between the Stockholders of Target and Acquiring Firms," *Journal of Financial Economics*, 21 (1988), pp. 3–40; E. Berkovitch and M.P. Narayanan, "Motives for Take-overs: An Empirical Investigation," *Journal of Financial and Quantitative Analysis*, 28 (1993), pp. 347–362; M.L. Sirower, *The Synergy Trap: How Companies Lose the Acquisition Game*, New York: Free Press, 1997.

54 Capon, Farley, and Hoenig, *op. cit.*

55 Gerstner, *op. cit.*

56 W.H. Bergquist, *Building Strategic Relationships: How to Extend Your Organization's Reach through Partnerships, Alliances and Joint Ventures*, San Francisco, CA: Jossey-Bass, 1995.

57 For licensing issues, *Amicon Corporation (A,B,C,D)*, 9-574-093/4/5/6, Harvard Business School.

58 At PARC, Xerox pioneered the Ethernet, the graphical user interface, the mouse, and Alto, an early personal computer.

59 P.A. Gompers and J. Lerner, "Can Corporate Venture Capital Work?," Working Paper, Harvard Business School, 1998. Xerox replaced XTV with Xerox New Enterprise (XNE) (mid-1990s) and took a more aggressive ownership approach. Xerox closed XNE in 1999. Internal corporate venturing seems to follow a cycle of 10 years or less; typically, the firm closes the program and later restarts in a different form: R.A. Burgelman and L. Välikangas, "Managing Internal Corporate Venturing Cycles," *Sloan Management Review*, (Summer 2005), pp. 26–34.

60 M. Tushman and C.A. O'Reilly III, "Ambidextrous Organizations: Managing Evolutionary and Revolutionary Change," *California Management Review*, 38 (Summer 1996), pp. 8–30.

CHAPTER 8

1 Marriott-brand properties include Marriott Hotels & Resorts, JW Marriott, and Marriott Vacation Club.

2 By contrast, when Cendant added Budget to its Avis subsidiary, it combined back-office operations like accounting and maintenance, but kept front offices separate. Similarly, upscale handbag-maker Coach factory outlets are normally one hour's drive from full-price stores.

3 Ideally, segments are mutually exclusive and collectively exhaustive.

4 Segmentation is a way of escaping the commodity trap. F.M. Jacques, "Even Commodities Have Customers," *Harvard Business Review*, 85 (May 2007), pp. 110–119.

5 SMSA is a Bureau of the Census definition of urban agglomerations, regardless of political boundaries.

6 *Daypart* — like morning, afternoon, evening — is an oft-employed *use occasion* variable.

7 For a life-stage segmentation scheme based on birthdates: baby boomers — 1946 to 1965; generation X — 1966 to 1980; millennials — 1981 to 1999. As one senior marketing executive confided, "If you want to know where the next profitable client base is going to be, just watch that pig moving through the python!"

8 Y. Atsmon, A. Keretsz, and I. Vittal, "Is Your Emerging Market Strategy Local Enough," *The McKinsey Quarterly* (April 2011), advocates addressing the China market via 22 geographically proximate and relatively demographically homogeneous urban clusters.

9 "Taxonomy at the Pump: Mobil's Five Types of Gasoline Buyers," *The Wall Street Journal*, January 30, 1995.

10 R.J. Harrington and A.K. Tjan, "Transforming Strategy One Customer at a Time," *Harvard Business Review*, 86 (March 2008), pp. 62–72.

11 "Mirabella Told Summer Issue to Be Its Last," *The New York Times*, April 28, 2000.

12 An Internet-shopper study identified eight segments — shopping lovers (11.1 percent), adventurous shoppers (8.9 percent), suspicious learners (9.6 percent), business users (12.4 percent), fearful browsers (10.7 percent), fun seekers (12.1 percent), technology muddlers (19.6 percent), and shopping avoiders (15.6 percent).

13 Macy's identifies four female lifestyles among core customers (it also has male lifestyles): Katherine — traditional, classy dresser, takes risks, likes quality; Julie — neo-traditional, slightly more edgy, but still classic; Erin — contemporary, loves newness, shops by brand; and Alex — fashion consumer, wants the latest and greatest. Walmart also identified a handful of segments like *loyalist*, *selective shopper*, and *skeptic*; it addresses segments by modifying skus and department placement by store.

14 *The Wall Street Journal, op. cit.* A two cents price increase would have led to a 20 percent increase in Mobil's profits.

15 A *lifestage* formulation has 11 groups: Midlife Success, Young Achievers, Striving Singles, Accumulated Wealth, Young Accumulators, Mainstream Families, Sustaining Families, Affluent Empty Nesters, Conservative Classics, Cautious Couples, and Sustaining Seniors. An alternative approach based on technology adoption, income, and children in the household has 53 clusters comprising 11 groups. Other commercially available segmentation schemes include VALS (Chapter 4), Mosaic (Experian), Acorn (ESRI), and PSYTE (MapInfo).

16 C.K. Prahalad, *The Fortune at the Bottom of the Pyramid*, Philadelphia PA: Wharton School, 2004. Of course, the base of the pyramid should also be segmented: V.K. Rangan, M. Chu, and D. Petkoski, "Segmenting the Base of the Pyramid," *Harvard Business Review*, 89 (June 2011), pp. 113–117.

17 C.P. Beshouri, "A Grassroots Approach to Emerging-Market Consumers," *The McKinsey Quarterly*, 4 (2006), pp. 61–71.

18 M. Yunus, *Banker to the Poor: Micro-Lending and the Battle against World Poverty*, Jackson TN: PublicAffairs, 1999.

19 E. Simanis and D. Duke, "Profits at the Bottom of the Pyramid," *Harvard Business Review*, XY (October 2014), pp. 87–93.

20 *op. cit.*

21 In addition to segmenting product markets, the firm may also segment the investor market. Shareholder Relations departments use descriptor variables like current/previous firm and/or competitor holdings, assets under management, average holding period, and investment style.

22 D.K. Rigby and V. Vishwanath, "Localization: The Revolution in Consumer Markets," *Harvard Business Review*, 84 (April 2006), pp. 82–92.

23 B.J. Pine II, B. Victor, and A.C. Boyton, "Making Mass Customization Work," *Harvard Business Review*, 71 (September–October 1993), pp. 108–119; B.J. Pine II, D. Peppers, and M. Rogers, "Do You Want to Keep Your Customers Forever?," *Harvard Business Review*, 73 (March–April 1995), pp. 103–114; and E. Feitzinger and H.L. Lee, "Mass Customization at Hewlett-Packard: The Power of Postponement," *Harvard Business Review*, 75 (January–February 1997), pp. 116–121.

24 A.J. Slywotzky, "The Age of the Choiceboard," *Harvard Business Review*, 78 (January–February 2000), pp. 40–41.

25 Some heavy users in the single-male segment visit fast-food restaurants upward of 20 times per month, spending in excess of $40 per day!

26 M.J.A. Berry and G. Linoff, *Data Mining Techniques for Marketing, Sales and Customer Support*, New York: Wiley, 1997.

27 *TESCO PLC: Getting to the Top … Staying at the Top?* 599-037-1BW, European Case Clearing House. Tesco's loyalty card comes in gold, silver, and bronze tiers, reflecting customer profitability. G.S. Linoff and M.J.A. Berry, *Data Mining Techniques: For Marketing, Sales, and Customer Relationship Management*. Indianapolis, IN: Wiley, 2011.

28 The firm may also evaluate segment opportunities via financial analysis (FA). FA typically embeds assumptions about the segment and the firm. The multifactor analysis makes assumptions explicit and is an excellent complement to financial analysis.

29 H. Simon, *Hidden Champions: Lessons from 500 of the World's Best Unknown Companies*, Boston, MA: Harvard Business School Press, 1996; also *Hidden Champions of the Twenty-First Century: The Success Strategies of Unknown World Market Leaders*, New York: Springer-Science+Business Media, 2009.

30 We use a linear compensatory model with correlated variables — at best, the variables have interval-scale properties. In practice, these theoretical concerns cause little difficulty. Parallel analyses typically report high

convergence of relative positions. But the firm should be careful not to attach too much importance to absolute (versus relative) factor scores.

31 When all rating scores are 1, the total factor score is 100 ; when all rating scores are 10, the total factor score is 1,000.

32 We assume market segments are independent — targeting one segment has no effect on targeting others. If the firm contemplates targeting multiple segments, it should consider potential synergies among segments. The firm must also consider the complexity of designing and delivering individual market offers. Chapter 9 addresses this issue.

33 O. Netzer, R. Feldman, J. Goldenburg, and M. Fresko, "Mine Your Own Business: Market-Structure Surveillance Through Text Mining," *Marketing Science*, 31 (May–June 2012), pp. 521–543.

34 The firm typically develops dimensions from customer survey data and an analytic process like multidimensional scaling — Marketing Enrichment 6.1 **[710p]**. For scaling procedures to develop perceptual maps, see any good marketing research text — for example, D.R. Lehmann, J. Steckel, and S. Gupta, *Marketing Research*, Reading, MA: Addison-Wesley, 1997. Most firms use two-dimensional maps, but three dimensions may be useful. If three dimensions (A, B, C) best describe the market, three separate two-dimensional maps (AB, AC, BC) typically suffice.

35 This map does not capture other possibly important customer-need dimensions like toy size or willingness to pay.

36 An ideal point is the *center of gravity* of customer needs. *High* is not necessarily better than *low*, *more* is not necessarily better than *less*! Consider aero-engines for a 50-seat aircraft. Low-power engines cannot fly the airplane; high-power engines are too heavy. *Ideal* power is between high and low. Also, the perceptual map shows segment size, but neither growth nor potential size.

37 The firm may also shift segment ideal points by persuading customers to modify their needs — this tends to be difficult.

38 Whirlpool based all design variations on extensive consumer research.

39 Stockbroker Edward D. Jones grew with a focused strategy — offering personal service in rural areas and small towns.

40 "Wish I'd Thought of That!" *Fortune*, May 15, 2000.

41 Sometimes the large company elects to acquire rather than fight; small firm owners may reap large financial rewards.

42 Aquilisa Quartz: Simply a Better Shower, Harvard Business School, 9-502-030.

....
CHAPTER 9

1 Personal communication.

2 For more on Mayo Clinic: L.L. Berry and N. Bendapudi, "Clueing in Customers," *Harvard Business Review*, 81 (February 2003), pp. 2–7.

3 Note: *market* strategy, not *marketing* strategy. Many functional areas, not just marketing, should help develop and implement the strategy.

4 Strategies do not always exist before the fact. Sometimes a firm is successful, then after-the-fact analysis reveals a pattern of actions. Someone designates this pattern as a strategy. Generally, researchers cannot tell whether a pattern existed as an idea or concept before the fact; H. Mintzberg, *The Rise and Fall of Strategic Planning*, New York: Free Press, 1994. Also N. Capon, "Review of *The Rise and Fall of Strategic Planning* by Henry Mintzberg," *Academy of Management Review*, (January 1996), pp. 298–301.

5 For an interesting perspective on strategy: B.D. Henderson, "The Origin of Strategy," *Harvard Business Review*, 67 (November–December 1989), pp. 139–143. Also *Marketing Strategy — An Overview*, 9-579-054, Harvard Business School.

6 J.R. Williams, "How Sustainable Is Your Competitive Advantage?," *California Management Review*, 34 (Spring 1992), pp. 29–52; P.

Ghemawat, "Sustainable Advantage," *Harvard Business Review*, 64 (September–October 1986), pp. 53–94; and M.E. Porter and V.E. Millar, "How Information Gives You Competitive Advantage," *Harvard Business Review*, 63 (July–August 1985), pp. 149–159.

7 To ensure the firm seriously considers competition, relabel *Market Strategy* as *Competitive Market Strategy*.

8 Sometimes the firm must work closely with third-party organizations like joint-venture partners.

9 Behavioral economics suggests several reasons firms may develop poor strategies: *overconfidence* — unrealistic belief in their abilities; *mental accounting* — categorizing money differently depending on its origin, where it's kept, and how it's spent; *status quo bias* — keeping things the way they are; *anchoring* — basing actions on what is known; *sunk cost* — throwing good money after bad; *herding instinct* — following others; *misestimating hedonic states* — inability to estimate pleasure/pain if things change quickly; and *false consensus* — overestimating the extent to which others share views: C. Roxburgh, "Hidden Flaws in Strategy," *The McKinsey Quarterly*, 2 (2003), pp. 1–9. D.P. Lovallo and O. Sibony, "Distortions and Deceptions in Strategic Decisions," *The McKinsey Quarterly*, 1 (2006), pp. 19–29, identify three cognitive distortions — overoptimism, loss aversion, and overconfidence; and four deceptions resulting from organizational interactions — misaligned time horizons, misaligned risk aversion profiles, overacceptance of the champion's views (champion bias), and overacceptance of top management's views (*sunflower* management).

10 R.D. Buzzell, B.T. Gale, and R.G.M. Sultan, "Market Share — a Key to Profitability," *Harvard Business Review*, 53 (January–February 1975), pp. 97–106, was the first paper in a stream of research on the relationship between market share and profitability. In general, the relationship is positive, but may break down at high market share levels.

11 If the firm is well positioned in a growing market segment, short-term profits (or cash flow) could be the appropriate strategic objective: A.J. Slywotsky and B.P. Shapiro, "Leveraging to Beat the Odds: The New Marketing Mind-Set," *Harvard Business Review*, 71 (September–October 1993), pp. 97–107.

12 We present a detailed exposition of *cash cows* and other product portfolio members — Chapter 12.

13 PIMS (Profit Impact of Market Strategy) measures the relationship between business actions and results. PIMS was developed at GE in the mid-1960s; in the early 1970s, PIMS moved to the Marketing Science Institute. The Strategic Planning Institute has maintained this research since 1975.

14 Generally, operational objectives set in real numbers — units, dollars, are more useful than objectives stated as percentages. Units have direct capacity implications, and the firm takes dollars to the bank, not percentages. Further, the *base* for percentage calculations is often disputable.

15 The strategic-focus-alternatives tree is loosely based on the famous DuPont formula; Wikipedia.

16 Pepsi offered large soft-drink bottles to remove Coke's *hourglass* bottle advantage in supermarkets: J. Sculley with J.A. Byrne, *Odyssey: Pepsi to Apple . . . A Journey of Adventure, Ideas and the Future*, New York: Harper & Row, 1987.

17 Some price promotions merely time-shift purchases without securing product-use increases.

18 Citibank also reduced costs as fewer customers called for explanations.

19 Working capital = accounts receivable *plus* cash *plus* inventories *less* accounts payable.

20 End users are individuals, family, or formal organizations.

21 H. Evans, *They Made America*, New York: Little Brown, 2004, pp. 391–392.

22 College Savings Bank (A) and (B) in N. Capon, *The Marketing of Financial Services: A Book of Cases*, Englewood Cliffs, NJ: Prentice Hall, 1992.

23 P. M. Nattermann, "Best Practice Does Not Equal Best Strategy," *The McKinsey Quarterly*, August 18, 2004.

24 In B2B marketing argot — a *specification sell*. By tightly specifying product/service attributes, the purchaser has little choice of suppliers.

25 Generally, the firm should avoid head-to-head competition with stronger competitors — who may respond strongly, and concentrate on weaker firms. But competing against strong competitors may lead to a more adept organization, better equipped to face competition elsewhere. Porter showed that countries whose firms together earned the highest global market shares in many product classes experienced fierce domestic competition: M. E. Porter, *The Competitive Advantage of Nations*, New York: Free Press, 1990.

26 In the U.S., the firm can use comparative claims in advertising if supported statistically — not so in other countries.

27 "Achieving Market Focus," Chapter 7, in F.J. Gouillart and J.N. Kelly, *Transforming the Organization*, New York: McGraw-Hill, 1996.

28 Thanks to Mary Murphy, Impact Planning Group, for this acronym.

29 A. Ries, J. Trout, and P. Kotler, *Positioning: The Battle for Your Mind*, New York: McGraw-Hill, 2000.

30 Robert Christian, formerly of Impact Planning Group, Old Greenwich, CT, developed this structure.

31 Developed by the author from published data.

32 With these capabilities, Cemex saves on fuel, maintenance, and payroll, and uses 35 percent fewer trucks. Cemex secures higher prices by delivering a perishable item within minutes of receiving an order. Customers use the Internet to place orders, secure delivery information, and check payment records.

33 In Britain and Ireland, doctors frequently recommend Guinness for pregnant women!

34 Based on an earlier version developed by the Impact Planning Group.

CHAPTER 10

1 Michael O'Leary, Ryanair's CEO, specializes in four-letter-word abuse against anyone who comes in range. O'Leary notes that "Business books are bullshit and are usually written by wankers." A. Ruddock, *Michael O'Leary: A Life in Full Flight*, London: Penguin, 2007.

2 Note the slope differences between older inventions like the automobile and the telephone, and newer inventions like web access and the cell phone. Some analysts measure life-cycle duration from birth to death. An alternative is from take-off until the onset of maturity — the critical strategic period when firms often establish long-run competitive positions. Well-supported products entering maturity in dominant position are difficult to dislodge. Most observers believe life cycles are shortening: R. Olshavsky, "Time and the Rate of Adoption of Innovations," *Journal of Consumer Research*, 6 (March 1980), pp. 425–428; and W. Qualls, R. Olshavsky, and R. Michaels, "Shortening of the PLC — an Empirical Test," *Journal of Marketing*, 45 (Fall 1981), pp. 76–80. Other observers dispute this view; B.L. Bayus, "Are Product Life Cycles Really Getting Shorter," *Journal of Product Innovation Management*, 11 (1994), pp. 300–308: B.L. Bayus, "An Analysis of Product Lifetimes in a Technologically Dynamic Industry," *Management Science*, 44 (June 1998), pp. 763–775; and R. Agarwal and B.L. Bayus, "The Market Evolution and Sales Take-Off of Product Innovations," *Management Science*, 48 (August 2002), pp. 1024–1041.

3 Other approaches to developing competitive strategy include three generic strategies — low cost, focus, and differentiation: M.E. Porter, *Competitive Advantage: Creating and Sustaining Superior Performance*, New York: Free Press, 1985; and three value disciplines — *operational excellence, customer intimacy,* and *product leadership*, M. Treacy and F. Wiersema, *The Discipline of Market Leaders*, Reading, MA: Addison-Wesley, 1997. Other strategy literature has focused on more internally focused perspectives like core competencies and strategic resources: G. Hamel and C.K. Prahalad, "The Core Competence of the Corporation," *Harvard Business Review*, 68 (May–June 1990), pp. 79–91. In Chapter 10, these approaches appear in different forms as strategies at various life-cycle stages. Despite some merit, prescriptions from the approaches noted here are too simplistic for today's competitive, complex, and global environments. An external focus should play a major role in strategy development — the scenario approach does just that.

4 Many observers associate the U.S. high level of new firm formation with its historically strong venture capital market.

5 Classically, RCA licensed color TV patents to spread the *catch-22* market-development burden: Demand for color TV sets was weak without large numbers of color TV programs; production of color TV programs was difficult to spur without a large installed base of color TVs!

6 GSM is the standard wireless phone technology in Europe and many other countries, but not the U.S. Because the U.S. has multiple incompatible technologies, European cell phones and services are more advanced.

7 Entry barriers retard firm market *entry*; exit barriers retard firm market *exit*. The general term for inhibiting firm movement is *mobility barriers*. For entry barriers: T.S. Gruca and D. Sudharshan, "A Framework for Entry Deterrence Strategy: The Competitive Environment, Choices, and Consequences," *Journal of Marketing*, 59 (July 1995), pp. 44–55; and B. Greenwald and J. Kahn, *Competition Demystified: A Radically Simplified Approach to Business Strategy*, New York: Portfolio Hardcover, 2005.

8 For theoretical underpinnings of the experience curve: *Perspectives on Experience*, Boston, MA: Boston Consulting Group, 1972.

9 Penetration pricing relies on three simple relationships. When demand is price-elastic, low prices drive high volumes; high volumes reduce unit costs; lower unit costs permit price reductions, *et seq.*

10 7-Eleven Japan was so successful, it acquired 7-Eleven US, the original parent!

11 In the 1980s, Pepsi displaced Coke as the leading cola in supermarkets by introducing large plastic bottles and aggressively tying up bottle-producing capacity. J. Sculley and J.A. Byrne, *Odyssey*, New York: Harper & Row, 1988.

12 G.S. Carpenter and K. Nakamoto, "Consumer Preference Formation and Pioneering Advantage," *Journal of Marketing Research*, 26 (August 1989), pp. 285–298. Research supporting the success of pioneering firms includes: G. Urban, T. Carter, S. Gaskin, and Z. Mucha, "Market Share Rewards to Pioneering Brands: An Empirical Analysis and Strategic Implications," *Management Science*, 32 (June 1986), pp. 645–659; and M. Song, C.A. DiBenedetto, and Y. L. Zhao, "Pioneering Advantages in Manufacturing and Service Industries: Empirical Evidence from Nine Countries," *Strategic Management Journal*, 20 (1999), pp. 811–836.

13 The term *price skimming* is derived from the practice of skimming the cream from unhomogenized milk.

14 J. Dean, "Pricing Policies for New Products," *Harvard Business Review*, 28 (November–December 1950), pp. 28–36.

15 Peter Drucker famously posed the question: "If we were to decide now, would we still enter the businesses we are in today? And if not, what are we going to do about it?" P. Drucker, *Managing for the Future*, New York: Truman Talley/Dutton, 1992.

16 R. Buaron, "New Game Strategies," *The McKinsey Quarterly* (Spring 1981), pp. 24–30.

17 Hence the sobriquet *Neutron Jack*, referring to empty buildings after GE sold businesses in number *three* position or below.

18 Frequently, the U.S. leader does not lead abroad. Outside the U.S., Ford and Heinz are larger than GM and Campbell's, respectively. Followers often target foreign geographic segments early in the product life cycle.

19 Patients receive Taxol (paclitaxel) intravenously. Because it is not water-soluble, doctors mix Taxol with castor oil and alcohol (Cremophor).

20 G. Stalk Jr., D.K. Pecaut, and B. Burnett, "Breaking Compromises, Breakaway Growth," *Harvard Business Review*, 74 (September–October 1996), pp. 131–139; and Y. Moon, "Break Free from the Product Life Cycle," *Harvard Business Review*, 83 (May 2005), pp. 77–94.

21 Price elasticity = percentage change in quantity demanded divided by percentage change in price = $dQ/Q \div dP/P$.

22 Productive ways to identify creative opportunities include — analogous situations in other industries, deep insight into customer purchase and use, industry diseconomies, latent dissatisfactions, and performance anomalies; Stalk, Pecaut, and Burnett, *op. cit.*

23 An informal survey of plumbers revealed that clean dishes require less than 50 percent of the amount of dishwashing soap recommended by dishwasher manufacturers.

24 For interesting approaches to securing growth in mature markets: W.C. Kim and R. Mauborgne, "Creating New Market Space," *Harvard Business Review*, 77 (January–February 1999), pp. 83–93; and *Blue Ocean Strategy*, Boston, MA: Harvard Business School, 2005 (same authors).

25 M. Baghai, S. Smit, and P. Viguerie, "Is Your Growth Strategy Flying Blind?" *Harvard Business Review*, 87 (May 2009), pp. 86–96.

26 J.S. Brown and J. Hagel III, "Innovation Blowback: Disruptive Management Practices from Asia," *The McKinsey Quarterly*, 1 (2005), pp. 35–45.

27 Economists refer to concentrated markets as oligopolies. J.N. Sheth and R.S. Sisodia, *The Rule of Three: Thriving and Surviving in Competitive Markets*, New York: Free Press, 2002, suggest many mature industries follow *The Rule of Three* — three generalist firms have most market share. Empirically, leading firms and small specialists are more profitable than those *stuck in the middle*: C. Uslay, Z.A. Altintig, and R.D. Winsor, "An Empirical Examination of the "Rule of Three": Strategy Implications for Top Management, Marketers, and Investors," *Journal of Marketing*, 74 (March 2010), pp. 20–39.

28 I.C. Macmillan and L. Selden, "The Incumbent's Advantage," *Harvard Business Review*, 86 (October 2008), pp. 111–121.

29 Managers often confuse *harvesting* with *milking*. Milking focuses on securing resources for use elsewhere in the firm — *the cow must be fed so the milk continues to flow.* Harvesting implies a decision to exit, sooner or later.

30 For maintaining current business while preparing for discontinuous change: M.L. Tushman and C.A. O'Reilly III, "Ambidextrous Organizations: Managing Evolutionary and Revolutionary Change," *California Management Review*, 28 (Summer 1996), pp. 8–30.

31 For further discussion — Chapter 19 and *Norton Company (A)*, 9-570-001, Harvard Business School.

32 Based in part on N. Kumar, "Strategies to Fight Low-Cost Rivals," *Harvard Business Review* 84 (December 2006), pp. 104–112.

33 D.J. Bryce and J.H. Dyer, "Strategies to Crack Well-Guarded Markets," *Harvard Business Review*, 85 (May 2007), pp. 84–92.

34 In the 1980s and 1990s, BancOne (later Bank One) grew by acquiring many Midwestern banks.

35 A.J. Slywotsky and D.J. Morrison, *The Profit Zone*, New York: Times Business, 1997; also A.J. Slywotsky and B.P. Shapiro, "Leveraging to Beat the Odds: The New Marketing Mind-Set," *Harvard Business Review*, 71 (September–October 1993), pp. 97–107.

36 Viable options are similar to long-run market leadership.

37 Many firms hang on too long before exiting: J.T. Horn, D.P. Lovallo, and S.P. Viguerie, "Learning to Let Go: Making Better Exit Decisions," *The McKinsey Quarterly*, 2 (2006), pp. 65–75.

38 Personal communication from former W. A. Taylor executive.

39 K. Harrigan, "Strategies for Declining Industries," *Journal of Business Strategy*, 1 (Fall 1980), pp. 20–34. Of course, investment may be extremely low if the firm has depreciated most capital equipment.

40 R. Adner and D.C. Snow, "Bold Retreat: A New Strategy for Old Technologies," *Harvard Business Review*, 88 (March 2010), pp. 77–81.

41 R. Gulati, N. Nohria, and F. Wohlgezogen, "Roaring out of Recession," *Harvard Business Review*, 88 (March 2010), pp. 63–69.

CHAPTER 11

1 J. Sampson, "Brand Valuation: Today and Tomorrow," Chapter 20 in *Brand Valuation*, R. Perrier and P. Stobart (eds.), London: Premier Books, 1997.

2 Adapted from B.H. Schmitt and D. Rogers, "SAP: Building a Leading Technology Brand," Center on Global Brand Leadership, Columbia Business School, and personal communication from Marty Homlish. In 2011, Homlish joined HP as executive vice president and chief marketing officer.

3 S. King, *Developing New Brands*, London: J. Walter Thompson Co. Ltd., 1984.

4 American Marketing Association, from K.L. Keller, *Strategic Brand Management*, Upper Saddle River, NJ: Prentice Hall, 2003, Chapter 1.

5 In Romeo and Juliet (ll, 11, 1-2), Juliet says, "What's in a name — that which we call a rose by any other name would smell as sweet." In *Positioning: The Battle for Your Mind*, New York: McGraw Hill, 2001, Ries and Trout say: "Shakespeare was wrong. A rose by any other name would not smell as sweet ... which is why the single most important decision in the marketing of perfume is the name."

6 The shape of a fragrance bottle was critical to Calvin Klein's trademark-infringement lawsuit against Ralph Lauren.

7 Apparently *irrelevant attributes* may have important differentiating properties. G.S. Carpenter, R. Glazer, and K. Nakamoto, "Meaningful Brands from Meaningless Differentiation: The Dependence on Irrelevant Attributes," *Journal of Marketing Research*, 31 (August 1994), pp. 339–350.

8 J. M. Hulbert, N. Capon, and N. Piercy, *Total Integrated Marketing: Breaking the Bounds of the Function*, New York: Free Press, 2003.

9 B.H. Schmitt, *Experiential Marketing*, New York: Free Press, 1999; and *Customer Experience Management*, Hoboken, NJ: Wiley, 2003.

10 Most retailers outsource manufacturing, typically to producers of product brands — 20 percent of U.S. retail goods are store-branded.

11 T. Peters. *The Brand Called You: Or: Fifty Ways to Transform Yourself from an 'Employee' into a Brand That Shouts Distinction, Commitment, and Passion!*, New York: Fast Company, 1997.

12 Thanks to David James, Henley Management College.

13 Under trademark law, a brand's registration may be revoked if the brand name is judged to have become generic.

14 A. Muniz, Jr. and T.C. O'Guinn, "Brand Community," *Journal of Consumer Research*, 27 (March 2001), pp. 412–432. Also S. Fournier and L. Lee, "Getting Brand Communities Right," *Harvard Business Review*, 87 (April 2009), pp. 105-110.

15 D.A. Aaker, *Brand Portfolio Strategy*, New York: Free Press, 2004.

16 J. Aaker, "Dimensions of Brand Personality," *Journal of Marketing Research*, 34 (August 1997), pp. 334–356. Based on data from 1,000 U.S. respondents: 60 well-known brands and 114 personality traits.

17 D.A. Aaker, *Managing Brand Equity*, New York: Free Press, 1991 pp. 114–128, identifies 11 types of associations — product attributes, intangibles, customer benefits, relative price, use/application, user/customer, celebrity/person, life style/personality, product class, competitors, and country/geographic area.

18 From the top left — Sir Richard Branson (Virgin), Henry Kravis (KKR), Sergey Brin (Google), Jamie Dimon (JPMorgan Chase), Nancy McKinstry (Wolters Kluwer); second row — Meg Whitman (Hewlett Packard

Enterprise), Michael Dell (Dell), Mark Zuckerberg (Facebook), Philippe Wolgen (Clinuvel), Warren Buffett (Berkshire Hathaway).

19 G. Ghislanzoni and J. Shearn, "Leading Change: An Interview with the CEO of Banca Intesa," *The McKinsey Quarterly*, 3 (2005), pp. 73–80.

20 Aaker, 1991, *op. cit.*, p. 15; *Building Strong Brands*, New York: Free Press, 1995; and *Brand Leadership* (with E. Joachimsthaler), New York: Free Press, 2000.

21 L. de Chematony and M.H.B. McDonald, *Creating Powerful Brands*, Oxford: Butterworth-Heinemann, 1992.

22 Reputedly, the majority of *Star Wars'* $20 billion revenues resulted from nonmovie merchandise. For more on customer brand equity: K.L. Keller, "Conceptualizing, Measuring, and Managing Customer-Based Brand Equity," *Journal of Marketing*, 57 (1993), pp. 1–22.

23 T.S. Wurster, "The Leading Brands," Perspectives, Boston, MA: The Boston Consulting Group, 1987; and research by Ting Wu, Columbia University. Also G.J. Tellis and P.N. Golder, *Will and Vision: How Latecomers Grow to Dominate Markets*, New York: McGraw-Hill, 2002, Chapters 1 and 11.

24 Aaker's 1991 *op. cit.* original brand equity notion encompassed brand awareness, brand associations, perceived quality, brand loyalty, and other proprietary brand assets. FBE components are not necessarily positive for customers: Brand loyalty may impede the search for more attractive options, and branded products have higher prices than generics.

25 F. Stahl, M. Heitmann, D.R. Lehmann, and S. Neslin, "The Impact of Brand Equity on Customer Acquisition, Retention, and Profit Margins," *Journal of Marketing*, 76 (July 2012), pp. 44–63.

26 "Big Blue," *Fortune*, April 14, 1997.

27 P. Berthon, J.M. Hulbert, and L.F. Pitt, "Brand Management Prognostications," *Sloan Management Review*, 40 (Winter 1999), pp. 53–65.

28 Triarc returned Snapple to its roots; Cadbury Schweppes acquired Snapple for $1 billion.

29 Aaker, 1991, *op. cit.*, pp. 80–85.

30 For a detailed examination of *brand resilience*: J.R. Copulsky, *Brand Resilience: Managing Risk and Recovery in a High-Speed World*, New York: Palgrave Macmillan, 2011.

31 Sears created KCD IP (Kenmore, Craftsman, DieHard) to issue $1.8 billion worth of bonds backed by the intellectual property of its three largest brands. Sears pays KCD royalty fees to license the brands; KCD uses the fees to pay interest on the bonds.

32 D.A. Ailawadi, D.R. Lehmann, and S.A. Neslin, "Revenue Premium as an Outcome Measure of Brand Equity," *Journal of Marketing*, 67 (October 2003), pp. 1–17.

33 The cost to create a successful mid-size B2C brand is about $100 million. At a 15 percent success rate, brand value = $670 million (100/0.15).

34 Boston Consulting Group (John Lindquist), reported in "What's in a Name?," *The Economist*, January 6, 1996 — profit figures not discounted. In Britain, Hitachi and General Electric (GEC) (British, since acquired) jointly owned a factory that made TV sets. Hitachi sold twice as many identical TVs at a $75 premium over GEC sets: P.H. Farquhar, "Managing Brand Equity," *Marketing Research*, (September 1989), pp. 24–33.

35 From NUMMI, GM learned important lessons about automobile manufacturing. Key metrics and performance at GM, NUMMI, and Toyota, respectively, were: assembly hours per vehicle — 31, 19, 16; defects per 100 vehicles — 130, 45, 45; assembly space per vehicle (sq. feet/vehicle/year) — 8.1, 7.0, 4.8; average parts inventory — 2 weeks, 2 days, 2 hours.

36 From P. Berthon, M.B. Holbrook, and J.M. Hulbert, "Understanding and Managing the Brandspace," *Sloan Management Review*, 44 (2003), pp. 49–55, by permission.

37 Developed from G. Gordon, A. di Benedetto, and R. Calantone, "Brand Equity as an Evolutionary Process," *The Journal of Brand Management*, 2 (1994), pp. 47–56.

38 "Bringing a Corporate Brand to Life Using the Principles of Experiential Marketing," Presentation by C.P. Lange and S. Tollefson at True Love or One-Night Stand?: Conference on Brand Relationships and Experiences. Columbia Business School, May 29-30, 2001.

39 Personal communication from David Haines, former Director of Global Branding, Vodafone.

40 L.M. Lodish and C. Mela, "If Brands Are Built over Years, Why Are They Managed over Quarters?," *Harvard Business Review*, 85 (July–August 2007), pp. 104–112.

41 Repeat purchasers often act with significant intentionality (brand loyalty), but may exhibit habitual behavior with little or no connection to the brand. For an ethnographic brand loyalty study: S. Fournier and J.L Lao, "Reviving Brand Loyalty: A Reconceptualization within the Framework of Consumer-Brand Relationships," *International Journal of Research in Marketing*, 14 (1997), pp. 451–472.

42 K.L. Keller, "Conceptualizing, Measuring, and Managing Customer-Based Brand Equity," *Journal of Marketing*, 57 (January 1993), pp. 1–22; and "The Brand Report Card," *Harvard Business Review*, 78 (January–February 2000), pp. 147–157.

43 S.J. Carlotti Jr., M.E. Coe, and J. Perrey, "Making Brand Portfolios Work," *The McKinsey Quarterly*, 4 (2000). Many remaining P&G brands are market leaders; 21 have annual revenues in excess of $1 billion.

44 Aaker, 1991, *op. cit.*

45 M.J. Hatch and M. Schultz, "Are the Strategic Stars Aligned for Your Corporate Brand?," *Harvard Business Review*, 79 (February 2001), pp. 129–134.

46 In one study, 80 percent of all new grocery products extended or leveraged existing brands; E. Tauber, "Brand Leverage: Strategy for Growth in a Cost Conscious World," *Journal of Advertising Research*, (August–September 1988), pp. 26–30.

47 S. Jayachandran, P. Kaufman, and K. Hewett, "Brand Licensing:What Drives Royalty Rates," *Journal of Marketing*, 77 (September 2013), pp. 108–122.

48 V.R. Lane, "Brand Leverage Power: The Critical Role of Brand Balance," *Business Horizons*, (January–February 1998), pp. 75–84; and D.A. Aaker, "Brand Extensions: The Good, The Bad and The Ugly," *Sloan Management Review*, (Summer 1990), pp. 47–56.

49 S. K. Reddy, S. L. Holak, and S. Bhat, "To Extend or Not to Extend: Success Determinants of Line Extensions," *Journal of Marketing Research*, 31 (May 1994), pp. 243–262.

50 FMCG firms build and manage brands for the long run. By contrast, pharmaceutical firms must build a brand for each new drug, M. Corstjens and M. Carpenter, "From Managing Pills to Managing Brands," *Harvard Business Review*, 78 (March–April 2000), pp. 20–21.

51 R. Batra, P. Lenk, and M. Wedel, "Brand Extension Strategy Planning: Empirical Estimation of Brand-Category Personality Fit and Atypicality," *Journal of Marketing Research*, 47 (April 2010), pp. 335–347, develop an approach to measure brand fit.

52 Retailers typically merchandise products by category rather than by brand — hence, consumers may face higher search costs for new products.

53 D.A. Aaker and K.L. Keller, "Consumer Evaluation of Brand Extensions," *Journal of Marketing*, 54 (January 1990), pp. 27–41; S.M. Broniarczyk and J.W. Alba, "The Importance of the Brand in Brand Extension," *Journal of Marketing Research*, 31 (May 1994), pp. 214–228; S.J. Milberg, C.W. Park, and M.S. McCarthy, "Managing Negative Feedback Effects Associated With Brand Extensions: The Impact of Alternative Branding Strategies," *Journal of Consumer Psychology*, 6 (1997), pp. 119–140; D.R. John, B. Loken, and C. Joiner, "The Negative Impact of Extensions: Can Flagship Products Be Diluted?," *Journal of Marketing*, 62 (January 1998), pp. 19–

32; and V. Swaminathan, R.J. Fox, and S.K. Reddy, "The Impact of Brand Extension Introduction on Choice," *Journal of Marketing*, 65 (October 2001), pp. 1–15.

54 E.M. Tauber, "Brand Franchise Extension: New Product Benefits from Existing Brand Names," *Business Horizons*, 24 (March–April 1981), pp. 36–41.

55 For brand revitalization: D. Desmet, L. Finskud, M. Glucksman, N.H. Marshall, M.J. Reyner, and K. Warren, "The End of Voodoo Brand Management," *The McKinsey Quarterly*, 2 (1998), pp. 107–117.

56 M. Ritson, "Should You Launch a Fighter Brand?," *Harvard Business Review*, 87 (October 2009), pp. 87–94.

57 Personal communication from David Haines, *op. cit.*

58 Formerly BHP Steel (Australia) and British Steel, respectively.

59 Polaroid filed for bankruptcy in 2001. Polaroid still has a multimillion-dollar instant photography business with some pockets of growth, and is the fourth-largest seller of portable DVD players and plasma TVs, with outsourced production.

CHAPTER 12

1 We use *product* to include both physical products and intangible services.

2 ABC faced a late-night television crisis. ABC's serious news program *Nightline* did not attract the younger viewers most desired by advertisers. Hence, ABC bid for the David Letterman show to replace *Nightline* in the crucial 11.35 p.m. weekday slot. This crisis reflected a long-running battle between ABC's news and entertainment divisions for resources for their respective programs (products).

3 J.L. Bower, *Managing the Resource Allocation Process*, Boston, MA: Harvard Business School Press, 1970 showed that real-world behavior did not conform to academics' convenient, simplifying assumptions. Today, *behavioral finance* examines how actual behavior often differs from simplistic assumptions.

4 For a detailed treatment of financial analysis techniques: J.C. Van Horne and J.M. Wachowicz, Jr., *Fundamentals of Financial Management* (13th ed.), Englewood Cliffs, NJ: Prentice Hall, 2008.

5 Most firms try to maximize shareholder value by improving return on shareholder equity (ROE). They often use return-on-investment (ROI) as a proxy for ROE, N. Capon, J.U. Farley, and J. Hulbert, *Corporate Strategic Planning*, New York: Columbia University Press, 1988.

6 Stern Stewart trademarked EVA; J. M. Stern, J. S. Shiely, and I. Ross, *The EVA Challenge*, New York: Wiley, 2001. Also Marketing Enrichment FM.1 **[308p, pp. 16–17]**.

7 R.L. Foster, *Innovation: The Attacker's Advantage*, New York: Summit, 1986.

8 P. Haspeslagh, "Portfolio Planning: Uses and Limits," *Harvard Business Review*, 60 (January–February 1982), pp. 58–74.

9 The visual appearance of portfolio matrices — 2×2, 3×3 — is arbitrary. Regardless, by placing products in the matrix, the firm can assess potential return and risk and gain insight into strategic options. "A picture is worth 1,000 words" captures much of portfolio models' appeal — senior managers can assess the firm's products in two simple dimensions.

10 Typically, firms use a linear scale for market growth, and a logarithmic scale for RMS. Further, the RMS scale is typically high to low, versus the more common low-to-high x-axis scaling.

11 This framework focuses on internal cash flows; it does not consider cash inflows from, or outflows to, external constituencies.

12 R. Vernon, "Gone Are the Cash Cows of Yesteryear," *Harvard Business Review*, 58 (November–December 1980), pp. 150–155.

13 Firms typically expense capital investments over several years. Hence, a profitable growth product may be cash flow negative.

14 A less common error is overinvestment to drive out all competitors; this approach rarely succeeds.

15 Top management often focuses greater than average attention on *dogs*; and managerial turnover is high. GE's former CEO Jack Welch required that each GE business be No. 1 or No. 2 in their market. Welch recognized that strong No. 2s could reach GE's demanding profit performance standards, but less competitively placed product lines could not!

16 Also, generally in accord with growth/share matrix predictions, cash flows are not always accurate, D.C. Hambrick, I.C. MacMillan, and D.L. Day, "Strategic Attributes and Performance in the BCG Matrix — A PIMS-Based Analysis of Industrial Product Business," *Academy of Management Journal*, 25 (September 1982), pp. 510–531. PIMS' own studies produced similar results, B.T. Gale and B. Branch, "Cash Flow Analysis: More Important Than Ever," *Harvard Business Review*, 59 (July–August 1981), pp. 131–136.

17 Key issues are market segmentation and geographic-market boundaries. Choice of market boundary should be strategically significant for the firm and revisited periodically.

18 Examples include Arthur D. Little's *stage of industry maturity* (embryonic, growth, mature, aging) versus *competitive position* (dominant, strong, favorable, tenable, weak); the Shell Chemical Directional Policy Matrix, D.C. Hussey, "Portfolio Analysis: Practical Experience with the Directional Policy Matrix," *Long Range Planning* 11 (August 1978), pp. 2–8; and Mead Paper's system, C.W. Hofer and D.E. Schendel, *Strategy Formulation: Analytical Concepts*, St. Paul, MN: West, 1978. In each case, matrix position indicates an investment strategy.

19 Note we define the x-axis as low to high, different from the growth-share matrix.

20 Of course, this statement does not apply to new products the firm gains from acquisitions.

21 For an extension of these ideas: N. Capon and R. Glazer, "Marketing and Technology: A Strategic Coalignment," *Journal of Marketing*, 51 (July 1987), pp. 1–14.

22 Personal communication from Judith Czelusniak, former Head of Global Public Relations, Bloomberg LP.

23 Chapter 5 discusses complementarity with competitors, customers, and suppliers. For an approach to product policy: *Principles of Product Policy*, 9-506-018, Harvard Business School.

24 T. Gallagher, M.M. Mitchke, and M.C. Rogers, "Profiting from Spare Parts," *The McKinsey Quarterly*, (February 2005), pp. 1–6.

25 A.J. Slywotzky, D.J. Morrison, and B. Andelman, *The Profit Zone*, New York: Times Business, 2002.

26 Best Buy bases simple product innovations on customer feedback.

27 Firewall (fighter, fighting) brands are sometimes called *flankers* — Chapter 11. C.M. Christensen, *The Innovator's Dilemma: When New Technologies Cause Great Firms to Fail*, New York: Harper Business Essentials, 2004; and C.M. Christensen and M.E. Raynor, *The Innovator's Solution: Creating and Sustaining Successful Growth*, Boston, MA: Harvard Business School Press, 2003.

28 C. Shapiro and H.R. Varian, *Information Rules*, Boston, MA: Harvard Business School Press, 1999.

29 Also R. Deneckere and P. McAfee, "Damaged Goods," *Journal of Economics and Management Strategy*, 5 (1996), pp. 149–174; and G. Taguchi and D. Clausing, "Robust Quality," *Harvard Business Review*, 68 (January–February 1990), pp. 65–75. Do not confuse deliberate product degradation with low product quality.

30 Shapiro and Varian, *op. cit.*, p. 59.

31 C. Anderson, *The Long Tail*, New York: Hyperion, 2006; and A. Elbese, "Should You Invest in the Long Tail," *Harvard Business Review*, 86 (July–August 2008), pp. 88–96.

32 J.A. Howard and J.N. Sheth, *The Theory of Buyer Behavior*, New York: Wiley, 1969.

33 J.T. Horn, D.P. Lovallo, and S.P. Viguerie "Learning to Let Go: Making Better Exit Decisions," *McKinsey Quarterly*, (2006), pp. 65–75.

34 G.J. Avlonitis, "'Project Dropstrat': Product Elimination and the Product Life Cycle Concept," *European Journal of Marketing*, (September 1990), pp. 55–67. Also S.J. Hart, "Product Deletion and the Effects of Strategy," *European Journal of Marketing*, (October 1989), pp. 6–17; D.M. Lambert and J.U. Sterling, "The Product Abandonment Decision, *Management Accounting*, (August 1998), pp. 8–27; and M.A. Mitchell, R.D. Taylor, and F. Tanyel, "Product Elimination Decisions: A Comparison of American and British Manufacturing Firms," *International Journal of Commerce & Management*, (1998), pp. 8–27. For classic articles: R.S. Alexander, "The Death and Burial of Sick Products," *Journal of Marketing*, 28 (April 1964), pp. 1–7; P. Kotler, "Phasing Out Weak Products," *Harvard Business Review*, 43, (March–April 1965), pp. 108–118; and P.W. Hamelman and E.M. Mazze, "Improving Product Abandonment Decisions," *Journal of Marketing*, 36 (April 1972), pp. 20–26.

35 Personal communication from Bob Bridden, former Group Vice President, Global Marketing, Avon.

36 "The Joy of Bundling," The Boston Consulting Group, 2008.

37 The OECD estimates that international trade in counterfeit and pirated goods exceeds $250 billion annually. Domestic trade may rival this figure.

38 In 2011, a blogger identified several counterfeit Apple stores in Chinese cities.

39 R.F. Maruca, "Is Your Brand at Risk?," *Harvard Business Review*, 77 (November–December 1999), pp. 22, 25. For a case study on counterfeiting: P.F. Nunes and N.P. Mulani, "Can Knockoffs Knock Out Your Business?", *Harvard Business Review*, 86 (October 2008), pp. 41–50. Commercial brand protection services are proliferating.

40 China's Tomato Garden was a major Microsoft pirate. In 2009, CEO Hong Lei received a three-and-one-half-year prison term for piracy; three partners also received jail terms.

41 R. Foster and S. Kaplan, *Creative Destruction: Why Companies That Are Built to Last Underperform the Market — and How to Successfully Transform Them*, New York: Currency/Doubleday, 2001.

42 "The Dream Phone," *Fortune*, November 15, 2010, pp. 129–140 @ p. 131.

43 Some pharma firms whose drugs are going off patent collaborate in introducing *authorized generics* to compete with independent generic producers. Examples include Pfizer's Zoloft (antidepressant) and Merck's Zocor (cholesterol lowering).

44 The American Customer Satisfaction Index (ACSI) measures customer satisfaction with hundreds of products/services annually — National Quality Research Center, Ross School of Business, University of Michigan.

45 B. T. Gale, *Managing Customer Value*, New York: Free Press, 1994, Exhibit 1-3, p. 16.

46 Gale, *op. cit*, taken from Exhibit 1-1, p. 9.

47 *The New York Times'* experience with lying journalist Jayson Blair, Wikipedia, and *The New Republic's* experience with Stephen Glass (*Shattered Glass*), Wikipedia, are good examples for information products.

48 R. Nader, *Unsafe at Any Speed: The Designed-In Dangers of the American Automobile*, New York: Pocket Books, 1966.

49 *The Procter & Gamble Company: Lenor Refill Package*, 9-592-016, Harvard Business School.

50 Personal communication from Ron Boire.

CHAPTER 13

1 From *The Economist*.

2 C.H. Lovelock and J. Wirtz, *Services Marketing* (7th ed.), Upper Saddle River, NJ: Prentice Hall, 2011, distinguish between services directed at people's bodies — healthcare and transportation, and services directed at people's minds — education, radio, TV.

3 Lovelock and Wirtz, *op. cit.*; C.H. Lovelock, *Product Plus: How Product + Service = Competitive Advantage*, New York: McGraw-Hill, 1994. Government statistics typically count manufacturers' in-house activities as value-added manufacturing. Identical outsourced activity is mostly counted as a service. This statistical quirk has helped fuel reported service growth.

4 From inception, the *Fortune* 500 contained only manufacturing firms; in the mid-1990s, the *Fortune* 500 expanded to include service firms.

5 Automobile firms finance car purchases; Boeing finances aircraft.

6 Offered by The Franchise Company, *www.thefranchisecompany.com* — Chapter 20. *Franchisors* develop strategy; *franchisees* provide capital and entrepreneurial energy.

7 B.G. Auguste, E.P. Harmon, and V. Pandit, "The Right Service Strategies for Product Companies," *The McKinsey Quarterly*, 1 (2006), pp. 41–51.

8 Manufacturers offering services compete with value-added resellers (VARs). VARs assert that manufacturers cannot make impartial product recommendations. Manufacturers disagree.

9 For elaboration of services trends: Lovelock and Wirtz, *op. cit.*

10 M.J. Bitner, "Evaluating Service Encounters: The Effects of Physical Surroundings and Employee Responses," *Journal of Marketing*, 54 (April 1990), pp. 69–82, offers an alternative framework: *physical evidence* — surroundings and tangible cues; *participants* — human actors like supplier personnel and customers; and *process* — procedures, mechanisms, and activity flow.

11 E. Goffman, *The Presentation of Self in Everyday Life*, New York: Doubleday Anchor, 1959. In financial services, onstage — front office; offstage — back office.

12 J. Carlzon, *Moments of Truth*, Cambridge, MA: Ballinger, 1987.

13 C.W.L. Hart, "The Power of Unconditional Service Guarantees," *Harvard Business Review*, 66 (July–August 1988), pp. 54–62.

14 P. Kotler and S.J. Levy, "Demarketing, Yes, Demarketing," *Harvard Business Review*, 49 (November–December 1971), pp. 74–80.

15 "The Mass Transit Railroad in Hong Kong," in N. Capon and W. Van Honacker, *The Asian Marketing Case Book*, Singapore: Prentice Hall, 1999, addresses supply/demand imbalances.

16 D. Koushik, J.A. Higbie, and C. Eister, "Retail Price Optimization at Inter-Continental Hotels Group," *Interfaces*, 42 (January 2012), pp. 42–57.

17 Firms like Allied Signal, GE, and Motorola adopted six-sigma DMAIC — define, measure, analyze, improve, control — to improve processes. The related DMADV process focuses on product design — Chapter 14.

18 This relationship is fundamental to the service-profit chain: J.L. Heskett, T.O. Jones, G.W. Loveman, W.E. Sasser Jr., and L. Schlesinger, "Putting the Service-Profit Chain to Work," *Harvard Business Review*, 72 (March–April 1994), pp. 164–174; and G.W. Loveman, "Employee Satisfaction, Customer Loyalty, and Financial Performance: An Empirical Examination of the Service Profit Chain in Retail Banking," *Journal of Service Research*, 1 (August 1998), pp. 18–31.

19 M. Gilbert, "A Culture that Recognizes the Contributions Made by Unsung Heroes," *Workforce Management*, 83 (November 2004), pp. 82–84.

20 Or reduce prices to specific segments; the challenge is identifying these customers. For many years, the Saturday night stopover fulfilled this function.

21 Compared to major airlines, easyJet sets low fares that generally increase as departure approaches. O. Koenigsberg, E. Muller, and N.J. Vilcassim, "Should easyJet Offer Last-Minute Deals?," *Quantitative Marketing and Economics*, 6 (2008), pp. 279–297.

22 *Shouldice Hospital Ltd.*, 9-683-068, Harvard Business School. Note how this one physician/multiple customer model differs from the one patient/multiple physician model at Mayo Clinic (Chapter 9 Opening

Case). Also K. Ramdas, E. Teisberg, and A.L. Tucker, "4 Ways to Reinvent Service Delivery," *Harvard Business Review*, 90 (December 2012, pp. 99–106.

23 Developed by Columbia Business School MBA student Cory Linton from R. Schachter and C.H. Lovelock, "The Boston Adult Education Center," in C.H. Lovelock, *Services Marketing*, 3rd. ed., Upper Saddle River, NJ: Prentice Hall, 1996, pp. 254–267.

24 G.L. Shostack, "Service Positioning Through Structural Change," *Journal of Marketing*, 51 (January 1987), pp. 33–34.

25 E.W. Anderson, C. Fornell, and S.K. Mazvancheryl, "Customer Satisfaction and Shareholder Value," *Journal of Marketing*, 68 (October 2004), pp. 172–186; L. Askoy, B. Cooil, C. Groening, T.L. Keiningham, and A. Yalçin, "The Long-Term Stock Market Valuation of Customer Satisfaction," *Journal of Marketing*, 72 (July 2008), pp. 105–122.

26 *Not* perceived quality alone. A. Parasuraman, V.A. Zeithaml, and L.L Berry, "A Conceptual Model of Service Quality and Its Implications for Future Research," *Journal of Marketing*, (Fall 1985), pp. 41–50, and V.A. Zeithaml, A. Parasuraman, and L.L. Berry, *Delivering Quality Service: Balancing Customer Expectations and Perceptions*, Free Press, 1990. Some expectations' models include a *tolerance zone*: Service quality below expectations but still acceptable.

27 V.A. Zeithaml, A. Parasuraman, and L.L. Berry, "Ten Lessons for Improving Service Quality," Boston, MA: Marketing Science Institute, 2003, pp. 61–77, expand five key variables into ten lessons for improving service quality. Reliability and listening overarch eight items: basic service, service design, service recovery, surprising customers, fair play, teamwork, employee research, and servant leadership.

28 The firm must be very clear about what these terms mean for individual customers. High responsiveness may mean two hours for some customers but two minutes for others. Related service quality dimensions include access, communication, courtesy, and competence.

29 V.A. Zeithaml, L.L. Berry, and A. Parasuraman, "The Behavioral Consequences of Service Quality," *Journal of Marketing*, 60 (April 1996), pp. 31–46.

30 Ogilvy and Mather data show that 85 percent of automobile purchasers are satisfied, but only 40 percent repurchase the brand; two-thirds of consumers identifying a favorite packaged goods brand purchased another brand most recently; and 65 percent to 85 percent of B2B defectors were satisfied/very satisfied with former suppliers.

31 T.O. Jones and W.E. Sasser, "Why Satisfied Customers Defect," *Harvard Business Review*, 73 (November–December 1995), pp. 88–99.

32 R.T. Rust and M-H Huang, *Service Marketing*, Boston, MA: Marketing Science Institute, 2011.

33 Personal communications from Lisa Gray, former MBA student, Columbia University, and Captain Paul Capon (USAF); also F.F. Reicheld, *The Loyalty Effect*, Boston, MA: Harvard Business School Press, 1996, p. 71.

34 B.J. Pine II, D. Peppers, and M. Rogers, "Do You Want to Keep Your Customers Forever?," *Harvard Business Review*, 73 (March–April 1995), pp. 103–114.

35 To achieve ground efficiency, Southwest Airlines benchmarked Indy 500 pit crews.

36 W. Whitt, "Improving Service by Informing Customers about Anticipated Delays," *Management Science*, 45 (February 1999), pp. 192–207.

37 I. Roos, "Methods of Investigating Critical Incidents: A Comparative Review" *Journal of Service Research* (February 2002), pp. 193–204.

38 J. van Doorn and P. C. Veroef, "Critical Incidents and the Impact of Satisfaction on Customer Share," *Journal of Marketing*, 72 (July 2008), pp. 123–142.

39 C.W.L. Hart, J.L. Heskett, and W.E. Sasser Jr., "The Profitable Art of Service Recovery," *Harvard Business Review*, 68 (July–August 1990), pp. 148–156.

40 Technical Assistance Research Program (TARP), Consumer Complaint Handling in America: An Update Study, Parts I and II, Washington, DC: TARP and U.S. Office of Consumer Affairs, April 1986. Consumer reasons for not complaining include: They don't think it's worth the time or effort; no one would be concerned about (or act upon) the problem; and/or they don't know how or where to complain. G. Knox and R. van Oest, "Customer Complaints and Recovery Effectiveness: A Customer Base Approach," *Journal of Marketing*, 78 (September 2014), pp. 42–57.

41 Some web devices allow unhappy customers to secure e-mail addresses and personal phone numbers of senior executives.

42 Excerpted and abridged from M.J. Tucker, "Poppin' Fresh Dough," *Datamation*, (May 1997), pp. 50–58.

43 For poor customer service and commentaries: D. Ariely, "The Customers' Revenge," *Harvard Business Review*, 85 (December 2007), pp. 31–43.

44 Personal communication from Judith Czelusniak, former Head Global Public Relations, Bloomberg L.P.

45 TARP and Blockbuster video-store chain respectively. E.W. Anderson, "Customer Satisfaction and Word of Mouth," *Journal of Service Research*, 1 (August 1998), pp. 5–17, finds only slightly greater word of mouth from highly dissatisfied customers than from highly satisfied customers, contrary to popular belief.

46 Also social media — Chapter 17.

47 Lovelock and Wirtz, *op. cit.*

48 H. Takeuchi and J.A. Quelch, "Quality Is More than Making a Good Product," *Harvard Business Review*, 61 (July–August 1983), pp. 139–145. We can decompose extended purchase decisions into finer-grained prepurchase customer service.

49 M.M. Lele and U.S. Karmarkar, "Good Product Support Is Smart Marketing," *Harvard Business Review*, 61 (November–December 1983), pp. 124–132; I.C. MacMillan and R.G. McGrath, "Discovering New Points of Differentiation," *Harvard Business Review*, 75 (July–August 1997), pp. 133–145.

50 R.G. Bundschuh and T.M. Dezvane, "How to Make After-Sales Services Pay Off," *The McKinsey Quarterly*, 4 (2003), pp. 116–127.

51 Personal communication from Judith Czelusniak, former Head Global Public Relations, Bloomberg L.P.

52 W.H. Davidow and B. Uttal, *Total Customer Service*, New York: Harper & Row, 1989 focuses on six elements — leadership, strategy, personnel, design, infrastructure, and metrics — for delivering outstanding customer service. Also Heskett, Jones, Loveman, Sasser, and Schlesinger, *op. cit.*, and R.T. Rust, A.J. Zahorik, and T.L. Keiningham, "Return on Quality (ROQ): Making Service Quality Financially Accountable," *Journal of Marketing*, 59 (April 1995), pp. 58–70.

53 QT's employee turnover is less than 15 percent (average retail turnover exceeds 100 percent) and financial performance is stellar. Wawa (500 stores, five U.S. states) has similar results. N. Bendapudi and V. Bendapudi, "Creating the Living Brand," *Harvard Business Review*, 83 (May 2005), pp. 124–132.

54 Personal communication from Hal Cramer, former President Fuels Marketing, ExxonMobil.

55 Davidow and Uttal, *op. cit.*

56 T. Baumgartner, R.H. John, and T. Nauclér, "Transforming Sales and Service," *The McKinsey Quarterly*, 4 (2005), pp. 81–91.

57 B. Donaldson and T. O'Toole, *Strategic Market Relationships: From Strategy to Implementation*, Chichester, UK: Wiley, 2002.

58 "American Express: Happy Workers Mean Happy Customers," *Fortune*, August 16, 2010, p. 14.

59 *Accor: Global Excellence Through People*, Lausanne, Switzerland: IMD for an excellent example.

60 L.L. Berry and A. Parasuraman, *Marketing Services: Competing through Quality*, New York: Free Press, 1991, p. 16, and K.A. Gibson and D.K.

Khandelwal, "Getting More from Call Centers," *The McKinsey Quarterly*, April 2005.

61 A. Braff, Z.H.M. Gaibi, and J.C. Garcia, "A Call Center's Last Line of Defense," *The McKinsey Quarterly*, (2006), pp. 12–14.

62 *The Ritz-Carlton: Using Information Systems to Better Serve the Customer*, 9-395-064, Harvard Business School, for Ritz-Carlton's legendary service.

63 Many Vietnamese wear sandals; Ho considered sandals a driving danger.

64 "Vinataxi," in N. Capon and W. Van Honacker, *The Asian Marketing Case Book*, Singapore: Prentice Hall, 1999.

65 *Xerox Corporation: The Customer Satisfaction Program*, 9-591-055, Harvard Business School.

66 F.F. Reicheld and W.E Sasser Jr., "Zero Defections: Quality Comes to Services," *Harvard Business Review*, 68 (September–October 1990), pp. 105–111; T.O. Jones and W.E Sasser Jr., "Why Satisfied Customers Defect," *Harvard Business Review*, 73 (November–December 1995), pp. 88–99; and F.F. Reicheld, "Learning from Customer Defections," *Harvard Business Review*, 74 (March–April 1996), pp. 56–69. Some firms use net-promoter score: the percentage of people who would recommend the firm, minus those who wouldn't. F.F. Reicheld, "The One Number You Need to Grow," *Harvard Business Review*, 81 (December 2003), pp. 46–54. Also Chapter 24.

67 D. McGarry and F. Heller, "Agile to Adaptive: Making Organizations More Responsive to Customers — A Xerox Case Study," Chapter 9 in N. Pal and D. Pantaleo (eds.), *The Agile Enterprise: Reinventing Your Organization for Success in an On-Demand World*, New York: Springer, 2005.

CHAPTER 14

1 Based on material provided by Client Insight (CI), LLC, Boston, MA. CI principals work extensively with Thomson businesses.

2 Marketing *really new products* is high on The Marketing Science Institute's placed research priority list.

3 P.F. Drucker, *The Practice of Management*, New York: Harper and Row, 1956, pp. 65–67.

4 W. Duggan, *Strategic Intuition*, New York: Columbia Business School, 2007.

5 As reported in *Harper's Monthly Magazine*, September 1932.

6 Duggan, *op. cit.* p. 102. In a different field, T.S. Elliot said, "Immature poets imitate. Mature poets steal." Duggan, *op. cit.*, pp. 101–102.

7 Disruptive technologies (existing) include personal computers (mainframes and mini computers), small off-road motorcycles (powerful on-road bikes), and transistors (vacuum tubes). Henry Ford's assembly line was a disruptive process innovation; previously, many small firms produced automobiles one by one. Ford's low costs put them out of business.

8 R. Foster and S. Kaplan, *Creative Destruction: Why Companies That Are Built to Last Underperform the Market — and How to Successfully Transform Them*, New York: Currency/Doubleday, 2001.

9 C.M. Christensen, *The Innovator's Dilemma: When New Technologies Cause Great Firms to Fail*, Boston, MA: Harvard Business School Press, 1997; New York: Harper Business Essentials, 2004.

10 A midlevel employee pushed IBM's entry into the Internet against significant internal resistance. G. Hamel, "Waking Up IBM: How a Gang of Unlikely Rebels Transformed Big Blue," *Harvard Business Review*, 78 (July–August 2000), pp. 137–146.

11 Christensen, *op. cit.* Also M. Tushman and C. O'Reilly, "Ambidextrous Organizations: Managing Evolutionary and Revolutionary Change," *California Management Review*, 38 (1996), pp. 8–30; and C.A. O'Reilly and M.L. Tushman, "The Ambidextrous Organization," *Harvard Business Review*, 82 (April 2004), pp. 74–81.

12 Innovation leader 3M's new product performance reportedly suffered when incoming CEO James McNerney rigorously implemented *six sigma*.

13 N. Capon, J.U. Farley, D.R. Lehmann, and J.M. Hulbert, "Profiles of Product Innovators Among Large U.S. Manufacturers," *Management Science*, 38 (February 1992), pp. 157–169. Also Synectics Corporation, *Succeeding at Innovation*, Cambridge, MA, 1993; and *Managing Innovation: A Primer*, Stamford, CT: Gartner, 2006. Individual firms develop their own approaches to innovation. Amazon measures everything, keeps development teams small, is unafraid of weird ideas, opens up to outsiders, and watches customers rather than competitors.

14 Conventional wisdom argues that competition spurs innovation. Research at Columbia Business School suggests that in some industries monopoly generates greater innovation: Increased profits provide greater resources for R&D, and advancing technology spurs demand. R. Goettler and B. R. Gordon, "Does AMD Spur Intel to Innovate More?," *Journal of Political Economy*, forthcoming, 2012.

15 Also *Change at Whirlpool Corporation (A), (B), (C)*, 9-705-463, Harvard Business School.

16 U.S. supermarkets introduce 20,000 to 40,000 new skus annually.

17 At 3M, Art Fry developed Post-It notes in this system.

18 One successful commercial development process has five stages: 1. *Observation* — cognitive psychologists, anthropologists, and sociologists try to understand the customer experience. 2. *Brainstorming* — intense idea-generating sessions analyzing data gathered in stage 1. 3. *Rapid Prototyping* — Mocking up working models to help visualize possible solutions. 4. *Refining* — narrowing down choices to a few possibilities. 5. *Implementation* — use engineering, design, and social-science capabilities to create an actual product/service. "The Power of Design," *BusinessWeek*, May 17, 2004, pp. 86–94.

19 D.L. Liebermann and D.B. Montgomery, "First-Mover Advantages," *Strategic Management Journal*, 9 (1988), pp. 41–58.

20 "Chevy Builds a Hybrid to Haul," *The New York Times*, April 26, 2009.

21 E.A. Roth and K.D. Sneader, "Reinventing Innovation at Consumer Goods Companies," *The McKinsey Quarterly*, 2006, report that less than 7 percent of new U.S.-launched FMCGs offer significant new or added benefits. The authors argue that firms should concentrate insight gathering on focus groups, rely on internal resources, and secure as many ideas as possible.

22 "Chaos by Design," *Fortune*, October 2, 2006.

23 From Booz Allen Hamilton. Some development projects lead to cost reductions. New-to-the-world products — aka *really new products* — let customers do new things, but at the cost of greater uncertainty about benefits and cost-benefit trade-offs, and requiring greater behavior changes for successful use. Also, W. Riggs and E. von Hippel, "The Impact of Scientific and Commercial Values on the Sources of Scientific Instrument Innovation," *Research Policy*, 23 (July 1994), pp. 459-469.

24 "Back to the Future at Apple," *BusinessWeek*, May 24, 1998.

25 Research at Columbia Business School suggests that market-based synergies may be as important as technological synergy; N. Capon, J.U. Farley, J. Hulbert, and L.E. Martin, "Corporate Diversity and Economic Performance: The Impact of Market Specialization," *Strategic Management Journal*, 9 (January–February 1988), pp. 61–74.

26 M.T. Hansen and J. Birkenshaw, "The Innovation Value Chain," *Harvard Business Review*, 85 (June 2007), pp. 121–130.

27 I. Royer, "Why Bad Projects Are so Hard to Kill," *Harvard Business Review*, 81 (February 2003), pp. 48–56.

28 For discussion of stage-gate process issues, G.L. Urban and J.R. Hauser, *Design and Marketing of New Products*, Englewood Cliffs, NJ: Prentice Hall, 1993; www.prod-dev.com/stage-gate.shtml; and *Product Development: A Customer-Driven Approach*, Harvard Business School. Some research suggests too rigorously applying the stage-gate process may restrict organizational learning and negatively affect development of

novel products; R. Sethi and Z. Iqbal, "Stage-Gate Controls, Learning Failure and Adverse Effect on Novel New Products," *Journal of Marketing*, 72 (January 2008), pp. 118–134.

29　Generally, new *service* development receives less funding than new *product* development, but some service firms invest significantly. S. Thomke, "R&D Comes to Services," *Harvard Business Review*, 81 (April 2003), pp. 71–79.

30　Sony's honorary chairman Masaru Ibuka had the original Walkman idea; CEO Akio Morita championed development despite internal opposition. The Walkman was not successful with its initial teenager target — initial customers were yuppies for jogging and commuting. J. Mingo, *How the Cadillac Got Its Fins*, New York: Harper Business, 1994.

31　G.A. Stevens and J. Burley, "3000 Raw Ideas = 1 Commercial Success," *Research Technology Management*, 40 (May–June 1997), pp. 16–27.

32　From Booz Allen and Hamilton — improved performance relates to attention to core competence and focused innovation.

33　Jack Welch (GE) had a simple mantra: "The operative assumption is that someone, somewhere, has a better idea, and the operative compulsion is to find out who has that better idea, learn it, and put it into action."

34　L. Huston and N. Sakkab, "Inside Procter & Gamble's New Model for Innovation," *Harvard Business Review*, 84 (March 2006), pp. 58–86.

35　O. Toubia, "Idea Generation, Creativity, and Incentives," *Marketing Science*, 25 (September–October 2006), pp. 411–42, shows the positive impact of financial incentives on the number and quality of new ideas.

36　J.I. Cash, Jr., M.J. Earl, and R. Morison, "Teaming Up to Crack Enterprise Innovation: Enterprise Integration," *Harvard Business Review*, 86 (November 2008), pp. 90–100.

37　E. von Hippel, *The Sources of Innovation*, New York: Oxford University Press, 1988.

38　O. Shenkar, "Imitation Is More Valuable than Innovation," *Harvard Business Review*, (April 2010), pp. 28–29.

39　In Cisco's sophisticated creation-net process, individual innovators often formed teams to improve on one individual's idea. G. Jouret, "Inside Cisco's Search for the Next Big Idea," *Harvard Business Review*, 87 (September 2009), pp. 43–45; and J.S. Brown and J. Hagel III, "Creation Nets: Getting the Most from Open Innovation," *The McKinsey Quarterly*, (2006), pp. 41–51.

40　Formed after the Netflix contest, Kaggle runs similar contests for firms that supply data sets and prize money. Also F. Gouillart and D. Billings, "Community Powered Problem Solving," *Harvard Business Review*, 91 (April 2013), pp. 71–77).

41　E. von Hippel, S. Thomke, and M. Sonnack, "Creating Breakthroughs at 3M," *Harvard Business Review*, 77 (September–October 1999), pp. 47–57, at p. 54, and E. von Hippel, *Democratizing Innovation*, Cambridge, MA: MIT Press, 2005. Free download at **667p**. The author was a lead user for gas phase chromatography.

42　Von Hippel, Thomke, and Sonnack, *op. cit.*

43　O. Shenkar, *Copycats*, Boston, MA: Harvard Business School, 2010.

44　L. Downes and C. Mui, *Unleashing the Killer App: Digital Strategies for Market Dominance*, Boston, MA: Harvard Business School Press, 1998.

45　S.D. Anthony, *The Silver Lining: An Innovation Playbook for Uncertain Times*, Boston, MA: Harvard Business School Press, 2009.

46　Independent consulting organizations like Synectics (Cambridge, MA) have proprietary idea-generation processes. Research shows that creativity training (visualization) plus extrinsic rewards increase creativity in new product development. J.E. Burroughs, D.W. Dahl, C.P. Moreau, A. Chattopadhyay, and G.J. Corn, "Facilitating and Rewarding Creativity During New Product Development," *Journal of Marketing*, 78 (July 2011), pp. 53–67.

47　Based in part on *www.mindtools.com*; also J. Goldenberg, *Creativity in Product Innovation*, Cambridge, UK: Cambridge University Press, 2002.

48　J. Goldenberg, R. Horowitz, A. Levav, and D. Mazursky, "Finding Your Innovation Sweet Spot," *Harvard Business Review*, 81 (March 2003), pp. 3–10. Goldenberg et al.'s work is the basis for this section.

49　A.F. Osborn, *Applied Imagination: Principles and Procedures of Creative Problem Solving*, New York: Scribner, 1953.

50　A different type of *reverse brainstorming* focuses on group process. Rather than generate ideas in groups, participants meet periodically but bring with them ideas they generated between meetings.

51　Also E. De Bono, *Lateral Thinking: Creativity Step by Step*: New York, Harper & Row, 1970.

52　E. De Bono, *Six Thinking Hats: An Essential Approach to Business Management from the Creator of Lateral Thinking*, Boston, MA: Little Brown, 1985.

53　From Nobel prize-winning (twice) scientist Linus Pauling.

54　*New-to-the-firm* products are generally riskier — but are more important if successful, T.D. Kuczmarski, *Managing New Products: Competing through Excellence*, Englewood Cliffs, NJ: Prentice Hall, 1988.

55　O. Toubia and L Florès, "Adaptive Idea Screening Using Consumers," *Marketing Science*, 26 (2007), pp. 342–361.

56　The firm may earn royalty income from attractive screened-out ideas (incompatible with its mission) by securing patents.

57　G.L. Urban, J.R. Hauser, and J.H. Roberts, "Prelaunch Forecasting of New Automobiles," *Management Science*, 36, No. 4 (April 1990), pp. 401–421.

58　BASES, the **B**ooz **A**llen **S**ales **E**stimation **S**ystem, from A.C. Nielsen.

59　Allied Signal, GE, Motorola, and other major firms embrace the five step six-sigma-DMADV approach — define, measure, analyze, design, verify. The related DMAIC process focuses on process improvement.

60　W.H. Davidow and B. Uttal, *Total Customer Service: The Ultimate Weapon*, New York: Harper & Row, 1989.

61　The 777 is a favorite example: All Regional Project Directors attended Columbia Business School's executive *Marketing Management* Program, like previous generations of Boeing executives.

62　D.K. Sobek II, J.K. Liker, and A.C. Ward, "Another Look at How Toyota Integrates Product Development," *Harvard Business Review*, 76 (July–August 1998), pp. 36–49.

63　Quotation and boxed insert: Personal communication from Ron Boire, then President Consumer Sales Company, Sony Electronics.

64　Personal communication from Eric Kim, former Executive Vice President Global Marketing Operations, Samsung Electronics, and "Samsung: Design Strategy at Samsung Electronics: Becoming a Top-Tier Company," Boston, MA: Design Management Institute 2008. Samsung has six design centers around the world; in 2010, Samsung was 19 on Interbrand's global brand valuation (versus Sony, 34). For insight on design, R. Verganti, "Innovating through Design," *Harvard Business Review*, 84 (December 2006), pp. 114–122.

65　Some firms design using the cradle-to-cradle (C2C) philosophy; Steelcase's new *Think* chair is 99 percent recyclable: W. McDonough and M. Braungart, *Cradle to Cradle: Remaking the Way We Make Things*, New York: North Point, 2002.

66　A.J. Slywotzky and D.J. Morrison, *The Profit Zone*, New York: Times Business, 1997.

67　From the QFD Institute website, *www.qfdi.org*.

68　J.R. Hauser and D. Clausing, "The House of Quality," *Harvard Business Review*, 66 (May–June 1988), pp. 63–73; and J.R. Hauser, "How Puritan-Bennett Used the House of Quality," *Sloan Management Review*, 34 (Spring 1993), pp. 61–70.

69　From consumers, distributors, and/or regulators.

70　For simplicity, we omit other primary CAs like *good appearance*.

71 A. Ward, "The Second Toyota Paradox: How Delaying Decisions Can Make Better Cars Faster," *Sloan Management Review*, 36 (Spring 1995), pp. 43–61.

72 S. Thomke and E. von Hippel, "Customers as Innovators: A New Way to Create Value," *Harvard Business Review*, 80 (April 2002), pp. 74–81.

72 G.P. Pisano and R. Verganti, "Which Kind of Collaboration Is Right for You?," *Harvard Business Review*, 86 (December 2008), pp. 78–86; V. Ramaswamy and F. Gouillart, "Building the Co-Creative Enterprise," *Harvard Business Review*, 88 (October 2010), pp. 100–109 and *The Power of Co-Creation*, New York: Free Press, 2010; J. Grönlund, D.R. Sjödin, and J. Fishammar, "Open Innovation and the Stage-Gate Process," *California Management Review*, 52 (Spring 2010), pp. 106–131.

74 B. Nagji and G. Tuff, "Managing Your Innovation Portfolio," *Harvard Business Review*, 90 (May 2012), pp. 67–74 make similar balancing arguments. They note differing allocations among core, adjacent, and transformational investments are appropriate for different firms.

75 R.G. Cooper, S.J. Edgett, and E.J. Kleinschmidt, "Portfolio Management for New Product Development: Results of an Industry Practices Study," *R&D Management*, 31 (2001), pp. 361–380; R.G. Cooper and S.J. Edgett, "Portfolio Management for New Products: Picking the Winners," Product Development Institute, Reference Paper 11, 2008; and S. Kavadias and R.O. Chao, "Resource Allocation and Product Portfolio Management," in C.H. Loch and S. Kavadias (eds.), *Handbook of New Product Development Management*, Oxford: Elsevier/ Butterworth, 2007, Chapter 6, pp. 135–163.

76 Coinstar (Redbox video rental) consistently places primitive versions of new kiosk concepts in public spaces to assess customer reaction.

77 Gleevec (Novartis) addresses chronic myeloid leukemia by halting the body's production of the abnormal "Philadelphia chromosome." Gleevec's clinical trials took half the normal time and was the fastest-ever FDA approval — 72 days. *Gleevec: Success by Design in Oncology*, Columbia Business School.

78 More on ASSESSOR, G.L. Urban and J.R. Hauser, *Design and Marketing of New Products*, Englewood Cliffs, NJ: Prentice Hall, 1993, pp. 461–467; and *www.mktgeng.com*. Both BASES and ASSESSOR may be useful for concept testing and prior to product launch. The Bass model (endnote 79, **143p**) is another valuable tool.

79 F. Bass, "A New Product Growth Model for Consumer Durables," *Management Science*, 15 (1969), pp. 215–227, and/or later formulations to forecast new product sales.

80 R.R. Burke, "Virtual Shopping: Breakthrough in Marketing Research," *Harvard Business Review*, 74 (March–April 1996), pp. 120–131.

81 N.D. Cadbury, "When, Where, and How to Test Market," *Harvard Business Review*, 52 (May–June 1975), pp. 96–103.

82 Also *New Product Commercialization: Common Mistakes*, 9-594-127, Harvard Business School.

83 Scholastic worked hard to avoid early availability of Harry Potter novels.

84 Also J. Schneider and J. Hall, "Why Most Product Launches Fail," *Harvard Business Review*, 89 (April 2011), pp. 21–23.

85 Some authors even advocate making deliberate mistakes. P.J.H. Schoemaker and R.E. Gunther, "The Wisdom of Deliberate Mistakes," *Harvard Business Review*, 84 (June 2006), pp. 109–115.

86 E.M. Rogers, *Diffusion of Innovations* (5th Ed.), New York: Free Press, 2003; E. Ofek and O. Toubia, "Marketing and Innovation Management: An Integrated Perspective," *Foundations and Trends in Marketing*, 4 (2009), pp. 77–128.

87 Size percentages, based on standard deviations from the mean, have not been empirically validated.

88 G.A. Moore, *Crossing the Chasm — Marketing & Selling High-Tech Products to Mainstream Customers*, New York: HarperBusiness, 2002.

89 J.T. Gourville, "Eager Sellers, Stony Buyers," *Harvard Business Review*, 84 (June 2006), pp 99-106, argues that several factors may slow new prod-

uct adoption: *Status quo bias* — the tendency to continue with current products; *endowment effect* — valuing products they already possess; and *loss aversion* — a focus on potential loss in benefits from adopting a new product versus potential gains from new benefits (Prospect Theory).

CHAPTER 15

1 H. Schultz and D.J. Yang, *Pour Your Heart Into It*, New York: Hyperion, 1997, p. 245. Aka McDonald's for yuppies.

2 Information from independent tests led Mercedes to redesign the A Class; Suzuki withdrew the Samurai; and Toyota recalled the 2010 Lexus GX 460.

3 Some physician spokespeople place *shills* in the audience to ask questions about off-label uses.

4 Many local TV stations continue to air liquor ads.

5 The U.S. allows *puffery* — unbelievable exaggerated claims.

6 Judges and juries play important roles in lawsuits for false or misleading advertising. Relatedly, U.S. consumers can sign up to avoid telemarketing calls.

7 Alternative categories are: *broadcast media* — television, radio, newspapers; and *addressable media* — e-mail, direct mail, telephone; *Note on Marketing and the World Wide Web*, Harvard Business School.

8 G.E. Belch and M.A. Belch, *Advertising and Promotion: An Integrated Marketing Communications Perspective* (9th ed.), Homewood, IL: McGraw-Hill/Irwin, 2011.

9 Welch's grape juice print ads tapped into a different sense by incorporating lickable strips to stimulate taste buds.

10 J. Hulbert and N. Capon, "Interpersonal Communication in Marketing: An Overview," *Journal of Marketing Research*, 9 (February 1972), pp. 27–34.

11 Product placement addresses the problem of consumers skipping TV advertisements using DVR technology. Virtual placement allows the firm to insert different communications in different geographic areas; C.A. Russell and M. Belch, "A Managerial Investigation into the Product Placement Industry," *Journal of Advertising Research*, 45 (March 2005), pp. 73–92.

12 *Branded entertainment* derives from product placement; the content provider and advertiser jointly develop content.

13 S. Gopalakrishna, G.L. Lilien, J.D. Williams, and I.K. Sequeira, "Do Trade Shows Pay Off?," *Journal of Marketing*, 59 (July 1995), pp. 75–83 report an interesting study.

14 Word of mouth can be highly valuable; it comes in various forms:
• *Persuasive* — explicit person-to-person recommendation
• *Casual* — positive mention but not an explicit recommendation, typically oral
• *Visual* — unconscious nonverbal recommendation based on behavior, like wearing clothes with a designer label
• *Artificial* — produced by computer algorithms like Amazon and Netflix recommendations
V. Kumar, J.A. Petersen, and R.P. Leone, "How Valuable is Word of Mouth?," *Harvard Business Review*, 85 (October 2007), pp. 139–146.

15 *Buzz marketing* focuses on getting people talking about the firm's products. *Guerrilla marketing* is a subset of buzz marketing that typically uses stunts. Buzz marketing relies on the six buttons of buzz — taboo (sex, lies, bathroom humor), unusual, outrageous, hilarious, remarkable, and secrets (kept and revealed) — to get people talking. Five popular types of media story enhance *buzz* — David & Goliath, unusual and outrageous, controversy, celebrities, and what's currently hot in the media; M. Hughes, *Buzz Marketing*, New York: Portfolio, 2005. BzzAgent and

Buzzador use social networking to pair consumers with products and give them Internet tools to share opinions.

16 C. Locke, "Smart Customers, Dumb Customers," *Harvard Business Review*, 78 (November–December 2000), pp. 187–191.

17 Hughes, *op. cit.* Within six months of launch, eBay acquired Half.com for $300 million.

18 R. Iyengar, C. Van den Bulte, and T.W. Valente, "Opinion Leadership and Social Contagion in New Product Diffusion," *Marketing Science*, 30 (2011), pp. 195–212.

19 "The Big Benioff," *Fortune*, December 13, 2004.

20 Film producers used similar strategies for *Crouching Tiger, Hidden Dragon* and *X-Men: The Movie*.

21 Also *Communications Policy*, 9-576-086; *Integrated Marketing Communications*, 9-599-087; *Marketing Promotions*, 9-506-028, Harvard Business School.

22 Berkshire Hathaway shares trade at over $100,000 per share. CEO Warren Buffett (Columbia Business School alumnus) refuses to split the stock; he believes the high share price generates a more stable shareholder base.

23 The purpose of corporate advertising is not always clear: Options include umbrella for marketing activities, persuading investors to become shareholders, and CEO self-aggrandizement.

CHAPTER 16

1 Visa rejected several banks' requests to place bank logos on its cards; they switched all new card acquisitions (and replacements) to MasterCard.

2 Founder of Wanamaker department store, Philadelphia, 1875. Statement also attributed to Lord Leverhume, founder of Unilever.

3 Newspapers like *Financial Times*, *The New York Times*, and *Wall Street Journal* have dropped this model for web versions and charge directly for content.

4 H.E. Krugman, "What Makes Advertising Effective?," *Harvard Business Review*, 53 (March–April 1975), pp. 96–103, is the classic advertising effectiveness article.

5 For a fine discussion of hierarchy-of-effects models: G.E. Belch and M.A. Belch, *Advertising and Promotion: An Integrated Marketing and Communications Perspective*, 8th ed., Homewood, IL: McGraw-Hill/Irwin, 2011.

6 Customers exhibit differing (self-explanatory) awareness levels. In order, recall dominance, top of the mind, unaided recall, aided recall, and recognition (from a list).

7 D. Vakratsas and T. Ambler, "How Advertising Works: What Do We Really Know?," *Journal of Marketing*, 63 (January 1999), pp. 26–43.

8 Although advertising effects are generally short-term, researchers also observe long-term effects; R.P. Leone, "Generalizing What Is Known about Temporal Aggregation and Advertising Carryover," *Marketing Science*, 14 (1995), G141–150; L.M. Lodish, M. Abraham, S. Kalmenson, J. Livelsberger, B. Lubetkin, B. Richardson, and M.E. Stevens, "How Advertising Works: A Meta-Analysis of 389 Real World Split Cable TV Advertising Experiments," *Journal of Marketing Research*, 32 (May 1995), pp. 125–139; and "A Summary of Fifty-Five In-Market Experimental Estimates of the Long-Term Effects of Advertising," *Marketing Science*, 14 (1995), G133–140.

9 Several high-involvement models are based on a learning hierarchy; Belch and Belch, *op. cit.*

10 Sampling customers to induce trial is more cost-effective than advertising in some product categories.

11 Some use different terminology: awareness and knowledge — *think*; liking — *feel*; trial — *act*. The two hierarchies then become: high-involvement: *think → feel → act*; low involvement: *think → act → feel*.

12 For classic work on advertising objectives: R.H. Colley, *Defining Advertising Goals for Measured Advertising Results*, New York: Association of National Advertisers, 1961.

13 Thanks to Columbia Business School Professor Gita Johar for this example.

14 Chapter 25, p. 629.

15 Both campaigns were dropped within weeks of introduction.

16 B.H. Schmitt, "Advertising and Mass Communications," in N. Capon (Ed.), Section 7, *Marketing*, in AMA Management Handbook (3rd ed.), J. Hampton (Ed.), AMACOM, 1994, 2-108 – 2-115, p. 2-112. Creativity is different from impact. Advertising campaigns may earn creativity awards yet fail to achieve objectives.

17 More recently, Absolut lost market share to other imported vodkas.

18 "Elida Returns to Its Youth to Find Secrets of Success," *Financial Times*, November 5, 1999. PlayStation ads mostly show different games, demonstrating that Sony had the broadest variety.

19 Some countries ban comparative advertising. B. Buchanan and D. Goldman, "Us vs. Them: The Minefield of Comparative Ads," *Harvard Business Review*, 67 (May–June 1989), pp. 38–50, reviews the legal status. For *deceptive advertising*: G.V. Johar, "Consumer Involvement and Deception from Implied Advertising Claims," *Journal of Marketing Research*, 32 (August 1995), pp. 267–279.

20 Humor, often using exaggeration, can make a demonstration advertisement more effective.

21 E.J. Faison, "Effectiveness of One-Sided and Two-Sided Mass Communications in Advertising," *Public Opinion Quarterly*, 25 (Fall 1961), pp. 468–469; R.E. Settle and L.L. Golden, "Attribution Theory and Advertiser Credibility," *Journal of Marketing Research*, 11 (May 1974), pp. 181–185.

22 H.E. Krugman, "On Application of Learning Theory to TV Copy Testing," *Public Opinion Quarterly*, 26 (1962), pp. 626–639.

23 A.G. Sawyer, "The Effects of Repetition of Refutational and Supportive Advertising Appeals," *Journal of Marketing Research*, 10 (February 1973), pp. 23–37; G.J. Szybillo and R. Heslin, "Resistance to Persuasion: Inoculation Theory in a Marketing Context," *Journal of Marketing Research*, 10 (November 1973), pp. 396–403.

24 Cosmetic companies use many celebrities. Ms. Spears ceased being effective when she shaved her head!

25 In a six-year period, Salton sold more than 40 million George Foreman grills — revenues increased twelvefold. Venus and Serena Williams annually earned $20 million and $16 million, respectively, promoting brands like Avon, Nortel Networks, Reebok, Sega, and Wilson's The Leather Experts. Muhammad Ali sold an 80 percent stake in his name, image, and likeness for $50 million.

26 The Davie Brown celebrity index evaluates awareness, appeal, and relevance of a celebrity to brand image. The seven key attributes are appeal, notice, trendsetter, influence, trust, endorsement, and aspiration.

27 M.L. Ray and W.L. Wilkie, "Fear: The Potential of an Appeal Neglected by Marketing," *Journal of Marketing*, 34 (January 1970), pp. 54–62; and B. Sternthal and C.S. Craig, "Fear Appeals Revisited and Revised," *Journal of Consumer Research*, 1 (December 1974), pp. 12–18.

28 GoDaddy is an Internet domain registry. For other banned ads, **811v**.

29 For more on humor: B. Sternthal and C.S. Craig, "Humor in Advertising," *Journal of Marketing*, 37 (October 1973), pp. 12–18; and T.J. Madden and M.C. Weinberger, "Humor in Advertising: A Practitioner View," *Journal of Advertising Research*, 24 (August–September 1984), pp. 23–26. For a taxonomy: P.S. Speck, "The Humorous Message Taxonomy: A Framework for the Study of Humorous Ads," *Journal of Current Issues and Research in Advertising*, 22 (1993), pp. 1–44.

30 Insider's Report, McCann Worldgroup.

31 Source: *ZenithOptimedia*. Advertising expenditure breakdown by geographic area ($billions): North America — 165; Western Europe — 104; Asia Pacific — 121; Central/Eastern Europe — 25; Latin America — 33; Middle East/North Africa — 4; rest of world — 11.

32 In somewhat of an overstatement, Robin Kerr, former chairman of media giant Universal McCann, said: "The media planner is becoming the most important person on the planet." *The Economist*, April 2, 2005.

33 Belch and Belch, *op. cit.*

34 Ai Jia pays $1,200 per month for a 15-person team (excluding uniforms and bicycles). By contrast, a one-time 15-second commercial on local TV costs $2,800; a large, prominently located billboard costs $3,000 to $8,000 per month.

35 Advertisers must exercise caution regarding audited figures as media companies may try to artificially enhance their viewership/readership. Concerning TV: In a low-viewership week, ABC labeled several days of *Good Morning America*, as specials — *Good Morning America*, so they wouldn't count in the ratings. Conversely, other networks run popular shows one or two minutes after the hour/half hour, so the weaker following show gains the advantage of high ratings from the strong show.

36 Audience certification is crucial for establishing good comparable cost data. Independent agencies like Mediamark Research Inc. (MRI), Nielsen, and Simmons Market Research Bureau certify audiences for various advertising vehicles. Total circulation typically provides print media data; projections from samples provide radio and TV data. Paper-and-pencil diaries for estimating listeners/viewers has largely given way to electronic measurement systems, but simple on/off measures do not capture who or how many listeners/viewers; DVR use poses special challenges for TV advertising measurement.

37 The firm should adjust circulation by proportion of target audience — a better measure is *CPM target customer*, but this is difficult to calculate. The *M* in CPM represents thousand; MM represents million.

38 "In Vogue," *The Economist*, September 21, 2002. Some firms build program-engagement measures based on survey data.

39 The classic paper is H.A. Zielske, "The Remembering and Forgetting of Advertising," *Journal of Marketing*, 23 (January 1959), pp. 239–243. Also J.A. Simon, "What Do Zielske's Real Data Show about Pulsing," *Journal of Marketing Research*, 23 (March 1979) pp. 415–420; and L.M. Lodish, Empirical Studies on Individual Responses to Exposure Patterns," *Journal of Marketing Research*, 8 (May 1971), pp. 214–216.

40 The firm should also consider the timing of competitive advertising.

41 K.S. Palda, *The Measurement of Cumulative Advertising*, Upper Saddle River, NJ: Prentice Hall, 1964.

42 J.A. Simon and J. Arndt, "The Shape of the Advertising Response Function," *Journal of Advertising Research*, 20 (1980), pp. 11–28; P.B. Luchsinger, V.S. Mullen, and P.T. Jannuzzo, "How Many Advertising Dollars Are Enough," *Media Decisions*, 12 (1977), p. 59. Also D.A. Aaker and J.M. Carman, "Are You Overadvertising?," *Journal of Advertising Research*, 22 (1982), pp. 57–70; and G. Assmus, J.U. Farley, and D.R. Lehmann, "How Advertising Affects Sales: Meta Analysis of Econometric Results," *Journal of Marketing Research*, 21 (1984), pp. 65–74.

43 J.D.C. Little, "Models and Managers: The Concept of a Decision Calculus," *Management Science*, 50 (December 2004), pp. 1841–1853.

44 J.N. Sheth and R.J. Sisodia, "Feeling the Heat," *Marketing Management*, 4 (1995), pp. 8–23. Direct marketing more precisely measures results.

45 According to Schmitt, *op. cit.*, two-thirds of major advertisers use this method. Our colleague Joe Plummer estimates that 85 percent of marketers use last year's sales to budget current year's spending.

46 The underlying model is: Share of spend → share of voice → share of mind → market share. Firms like TNS Media and ComScore help firms benchmark advertising spending versus competitors.

47 For advertising budgeting models: Little, *op. cit.*; M.L. Vidale and R.H. Wolfe, "An Operations Research Study of Sales Response to Advertising,

Operations Research (June 1957), pp. 370–381; J.D.C. Little, "A Model of Adaptive Control of Promotional Spending," *Operations Research*, (November 1966), pp. 1075–1097; G.L. Lillien, P. Kotler, and K.S. Morthy, *Marketing Models*, Upper Saddle River, NJ: Prentice Hall, 1992, Chapter 6.

48 Split-cable TV systems show identical programming in a confined geography — different ads appear on each half.

49 Commercial entities offering this service are Information Resources Inc. (IRI), Burke Marketing Research (the Burke day-after recall test), and ASI Market Research.

50 IRI's BehaviorScan service uses customer panels in 25 U.S. markets in conjunction with split-cable TV systems.

51 R.I. Haley, J. Stafforini, and A. Fox, "The Missing Measures of Copy Testing," *Journal of Advertising Research*, (May–June 1994), pp. 46–56.

52 The firm may also use recognition and recall measures in conjunction with overall advertising program analysis.

53 Thanks to colleague Gita Johar for this example, Quirk's Marketing Research Review, 1988.

54 The top five U.S. agencies account for 60 percent of advertising expenditures, up from 30 percent in 2000. Several agencies, like WPP, earn more fee revenue from marketing services than advertising.

55 A recent trend for advertising agencies is to form separate departments focused on social media and analytics. In some agencies, project managers coordinate internal matters, then interface with account/relationship managers.

56 Absolut and HSBC (earlier) are good examples of a campaign idea and various executions of that idea.

57 For a synopsis: M. Kalter and E. Stearns, "Direct Marketing," in N. Capon (Ed.), Section 2, Marketing, in *AMA Management Handbook* (3rd ed.), J. Hampton (Ed.), New York: AMACOM, 1994, 2-116–2-121.

58 Bernays, Sigmund Freud's nephew, is often known as the *father* of public relations. L. Tye, *The Father of Spin: Edward L. Bernays and the Birth of Public Relations*, New York: Random House, 1998.

59 Successful P&PR campaigns are legion. James Sterling Moran hatched out an ostrich egg to publicize *The Egg and I*, a best-selling book. He opened a Washington embassy for a mythical country to publicize the movie *The Mouse that Roared*. To promote a Broadway show, he rigged a taxi so a chimpanzee seemed to be driving.

60 *College Savings Bank (A) and (B)* in N. Capon, *The Marketing of Financial Services: A Book of Cases*, Englewood Cliffs, NJ: Prentice Hall, 1992, pp. 93–121.

61 "The New Pitch," *The New Yorker*, March 28, 2005.

62 The author believes that in crisis, the firm's decision makers should reject arguments from legal (admitting guilt attracts lawsuits) and finance (repair actions reduce profits) in favor of doing what is right!

63 "Bad for You," *The Economist*, June 19, 1999. Two bottling-system failures emerged: "bad" carbon dioxide at one plant and fungicide contamination from wooden pallets at another.

64 *Spiffs* are direct cash payments from a firm to customer salespeople, contingent on sales success.

65 The producers earned $120 million in sponsored advertising, product tie-ins, promotions, and sweepstakes. Relatedly, Bulgari paid Fay Weldon for highlighting the firm in her novel.

66 Chapter 15, endnote 11. Product placement ranges from background items to an integral part of the storyline. Using TV, some firms integrate product placement with product advertising in commercial breaks. Products placed more than 1,000 annually in U.S. TV shows include Coca-Cola Classic, Everlast (apparel and sporting equipment), Nike (apparel) and Gatorade. For contrasting views on product placement: E.M. Peebles, "And Now, a Word from Our Sponsor," *Harvard Business Review*, (October 2003), pp. 31–41.

67 Philips placed video monitors throughout the arena and created a retail showroom. For research on sponsorship effectiveness: G.V. Johar and M.T. Pham, "Relatedness, Prominence and Constructive Sponsor Identification," *Journal of Marketing Research*, 36 (August 1999), pp. 299–312. Stadium owners have problems when they make bad partner choices. New England Patriots — CMGI (failed dot-com); Tennessee Titans — Adelphi Communications (former CEO jailed for corporate looting and accounting fraud); Houston Astros — Enron Field!

68 FMCG firms' spending on consumer and trade promotion often exceeds 50 percent of total marketing budgets.

69 C.F. Mela, S. Gupta, and D.R. Lehmann, "The Long-Term Impact of Promotion and Advertising on Consumer Brand Choice," *Journal of Marketing Research*, 34 (May 1997), pp. 248–261. M. Tsiros and D.M. Hardesty, "Ending a Price Promotion: Retracting It in One Step or Phasing It Out Gradually," *Journal of Marketing*, 74 (January 2010), pp 49–64 shows that *steadily decreasing discounting* (SDD) is more effective than returning to the prediscounted price in one step.

70 To divert is to resell products to other retailers, typically in a different geographic area.

71 "Maybe Maytag Should Give Away Cash?," *The New York Times*, March 31, 1993; and S. Gupta and D.R. Lehmann, *Managing Customers as Investments*, Philadelphia: Wharton, 2005, pp. 3–4. Hoover is a Maytag subsidiary. *The Times* commented: "In the United States, top executives lose their jobs when their companies sell too little. In Britain, it can happen when their companies sell too much." The promotion was such a good deal that many consumers used their airline tickets, but sold their Hoovers! Relatedly, P&G underestimated the popularity of its sales promotion, "Pampers Perks" — Fisher-Price toys for consumers who collected *points* on diaper packages. After two months, consumers had not received their toys.

CHAPTER 17

1 Thanks to Jeremy Kagan, Lyn Maize, Peter Propp, and Judy Strauss for assistance in preparing this chapter.

2 Based on data secured from the Internet and Harvard Business School case study, *Facebook*, 9-808-128.

3 B. Halligan and D. Shah, *Inbound Marketing*, 2014 Paperback, Hoboken, NJ: Wiley.

4 Click fraud is an ongoing problem for paid search — the paid-search advertising network simulates clicks on the ads it features. Of course, all major search engines work hard to detect and combat click fraud. A second problem is inflated measures from search engine robots and other automated software.

5 For the vast majority of search engines, *paid* search payments do not affect *organic* search results. But in China, advertising payments to Baidu — leading search engine — improves *organic* search results. D. Rowles, *Mobile Marketing*, London: Kogan Page, 2014, p.148.

6 Some writers address *blogs* under the rubric of social media. We prefer to consider blogs separately, inasmuch as they are hosted independently of social media platforms like Facebook, Instagram, LinkedIn, and Twitter.

7 "Blogs: Fad or Marketing Medium of the Future?," *Brandweek*, November 24, 2004.

8 BzzAgent (U.S.), Buzzador (Scandinavia), TRND (Germany) are word-of-mouth media networks. They pair consumers with products and give them digital tools to share opinions.

9 J. Strauss, "Marketing Communication Strategies," in *The Handbook of Technology Management*, Vol. 2, H. Bidgoli (Ed.), Hoboken, NJ: Wiley, 2010, pp. 449–461.

10 A. Beale and J. Strauss, *Radically Transparent: Monitoring and Managing Reputations Online*, Indianapolis, IN: Wiley, 2008.

11 Some writers refer to Twitter as a *microblogging* service.

12 Secured from the Internet; some figures may be inflated; figure out of date by the time you read this table!

13 P. Manchanda, G.M. Packard, and A. Pattabhiramaiah, "Social Dollars: The Economic Impact of Customer Participation in a Firm-Sponsored Online Community," January 12, 2012. Available at SSRN.

14 Success factors for a viral marketing campaign are: memorable message; structure of the social network; behavioral characteristics of recipients and incentives to share the message; and a seeding strategy that determines the initial set of target consumers; O. Hinz, B. Skiera, C. Barrot, and J.U. Becker, "Seeding Strategies for Viral Marketing: An Empirical Comparison," *Journal of Marketing*, 75 (November–December 2011), pp. 55–71.

15 I. Nitzan and S.B. Libal, "Social Effects on Customer Retention," *Journal of Marketing*, 75 (November 2011), pp. 24–38.

16 Some evidence suggests that comments about service experiences made on mobile devices (temporally close to the event) are more negative than those made with greater reflection on nonportable devices. N. Lurie, H. Liu, and S. Ransbotham, "The Characteristics and Perceived Value of Mobile Word-of-Mouth," *MSI Report*, No. 14–109.

17 Ad sizes in pixels (wide × tall) are: standard banner – 468 × 60; skyscraper – 160 × 600; medium rectangle – 300 × 250.

18 Based, in part on, Rocket Fuel, "What's Under the Hood of Programmatic?" [685v]

19 White Ops and Association of National Advertisers, *The Bot Baseline: Fraud in Digital Advertising*, 2014. [370p]

20 op. cit.

21 D. Peppers and M. Rogers, *The One-to-One Future: Building Relationships One Customer at a Time*, New York: Currency Doubleday, 1993.

22 "Your Train Will Be Late, She Says Cheerily: Voice of Amtrak Computer Works on Frayed Nerves," *The New York Times*, November 24, 2004.

CHAPTER 18

1 Sales force costs are a large part of Pfizer's marketing and sales expenses — around 40 percent of sales revenues. Thomas Friedman (*New York Times* columnist) labels professional service workers who bring in business as the new *untouchables* — will not be laid off.

2 U.S. Bureau of Labor Statistics.

3 G. Sabnis, S.C. Chatterjee, R. Grewal, and G. Lilien, "The Sales Lead Black Hole: On Sales Reps Follow Up of Marketing Leads," *Journal of Marketing*, 77 (January 2013), pp. 52–67.

4 C. Homburg and O. Jensen, "The Thought Worlds of Marketing and Sales: Which Differences Make a Difference?" *Journal of Marketing*, 71 (july 2007), pp. 124–142.

5 Part of the problem may be historic: Marketing evolved from the sales force to become its own entity. Marketing and sales may also lack effective interpersonal and conflict-resolution skills.

6 The author of a well-known psychology textbook attended her publisher's annual sales conference. In explaining their books to the sales force, individual editors (product managers) focused on securing more sales effort on their books than on colleagues' books. Also, marketing may mislead sales by inflating objectives on certain products as a way to secure greater sales force effort. W.M. Strahle, R.L. Spiro, and F. Acito, "Marketing and Sales: Strategic Alignment and Functional Implementation," *Journal of Personal Selling & Sales Management*, 16 (Winter 1996), pp. 1–20.

7 D. Rouzies, E. Anderson, A.K. Kohli, R.E. Michaels, B.A. Weiss, and A.A. Zoltners, "Sales and Marketing Integration: A Proposed Framework," *Journal of Personal Selling and Sales Management*, 25 (Spring 2005), pp. 113–122. P. Kotler, N. Rackham, and S. Krishnaswamy, "Ending the War between Sales & Marketing," *Harvard Business Review*, 84 (July–August

2006), pp. 68–78, contains a multi-item scale for measuring marketing and sales alignment and integration.

8 Five specific planning problems we have come across are:
   • The sales force receives the finished marketing plan late, far beyond end-of-period deadlines.
   • The sales force starts and finishes its planning early, before marketing delivers its plans.
   • Sales and marketing do not share either plans or *voice of the customer* feedback.
   • The sales force has no input into marketing and views marketing as irrelevant to daily issues.
   • Marketing believes the sales force is *sandbagging* the sales forecasts to make it easier to earn incentive compensation.

9 C. Homburg, O. Jensen, and H. Krohmer, "Configurations of Marketing and Sales: A Taxonomy," *Journal of Marketing*, 72 (March 2008), pp. 133–154, identifies five empirical archetypes of the marketing-sales interface. The most successful archetypes demonstrate strong structural linkages between marketing and sales.

10 Material sourced from N. Capon and G. Tubridy, *Sales Eats First*, Bronxville, NY: Wessex, 2011.

11 Fred Hassan (Schering-Plough CEO) in T.A. Stewart and D. Champion, "Leading Change from the Top Line," *Harvard Business Review*, 84 (July–August 2006), pp. 90–97.

12 Seven of IBM's nine CEOs, including current CEO Virginia Rometty, had sales backgrounds.

13 *www.sellingpower.com/video* for a series of short videos about selling.

14 R.C. Dudley and D. Narayandas, "A Portfolio Approach to Sales," *Harvard Business Review*, 84 (July–August 2006), pp. 16–18, classify sales but omit retention. The authors split *new business* into two categories: *expansion* — serve customer needs not currently being satisfied; and *innovation* — identify and serve new-customer needs.

15 Direct costs typically include sales force costs, but exclude costs not controllable by sales managers — plant overhead and R&D allocations. For a detailed discussion of financial analysis, Marketing Enrichment FM.1 **[308p]**.

16 We use fictional firm Essex throughout the chapter.

17 If marketing and sales objectives are not integrated, sales is likely to set its own objectives disconnected from marketing; Strahle, Spiro, and Acito, *op. cit.*

18 Where *not to* allocate resources may be as important as where *to* allocate. Marketing should advise the sales force on *go* and *no-go* areas.

19 Calendarization is especially important when sales patterns are seasonal.

20 Physicians can use approved drugs for any indication (disease state) but the FDA prohibits promoting drugs for nonapproved indications. Allergan, Astra Zeneca, Bristol-Myers Squibb, Eli Lilly, Forest Laboratories, and Novartis each made settlements with the U.S. Justice Department concerning unapproved uses and other infractions.

21 The firm may assume alternative sales response functions; viz. advertising response functions — Chapter 16.

22 For an alternative but more complex process: A.A. Zoltners, P. Sinha, and S.E. Lorimer, "Match Your Sales Force Structure to Your Business Cycle," *Harvard Business Review*, 84 (July–August 2006), pp. 81–89.

23 When store traffic is heaviest, Home Depot employees cease all non-customer-facing activities; many airlines are following Ryanair's innovation of making sales to *captive* airline passengers.

24 Cisco CEO John Chambers reputedly made 200 CEO sales calls in one month using TelePresence.

25 In Table 17.3, cells IIA and IIIC have zero revenue objectives and zero effort. Sometimes firms allocate zero effort, yet set positive revenue objectives — like a declining product with a core of loyal customers. Conversely, the firm may place selling effort on a segment but not expect sales revenues in the current period.

26 This table contains rounding errors.

27 Many firms incorrectly use current revenue-based classes (ignoring potential) to allocate effort. Decision calculus models use managerial judgment of likely sales responses, then solve for optimal allocations; L.M. Lodish, "CALLPLAN: An Interactive Salesman's Call Planning System," *Management Science*, 18, Part II. (December 1971b), pp. 25–40.

28 Of course, some salespeople thrive on seeking new opportunities — we are speaking of general *comfort* tendencies.

29 V. Kumar, R. Venkatesan, and W. Reinhart, "Performance Implications of Adopting a Customer-Focused Sales Campaign," *Journal of Marketing*, 72 (September 2008), pp. 50–68, found that multiproduct firms that orchestrated selling efforts across products secured better results than those focusing on products individually.

30 P. Lay, T. Hewlin, and G. Moore, "In a Downturn, Provoke Your Customers," *Harvard Business Review*, 87 (March 2009), pp. 48–56.

31 Much psychological research suggests people use relatively few criteria to process information and make decisions. G.A. Miller, "The Magical Number Seven, Plus or Minus Two," *Psychological Review*, 63 (March 1956), pp. 81–97; J.M. Hulbert, "Information Processing Capacity and Attitude Management," *Journal of Marketing Research*, 12 (February 1975), pp. 104–106. Incorporating too many benefits in a sales approach may confuse customers and/or create credibility gaps.

32 Boeing's sales approach to airlines includes attractive pricing, financing and leasing arrangements, and service and training packages.

33 Many *how-to-sell* books on consultative selling and other systems teach these procedures.

34 Like primacy/recency decisions: Should the salesperson present more powerful arguments earlier or later in the sales call?

35 M. Dixon and B. Adamson, *The Challenger Sale: Taking Control of the Customer Conversation*, New York: Portfolio, 2011.

36 For outsourced sales forces: E. Anderson and B. Trinkle, *Outsourcing the Sales Function*, Mason, OH: Thomson, 2005.

37 D. Ledingham, M. Kovac, and H. Locke Simon, "The New Science of Sales Force Productivity," *Harvard Business Review*, 84 (September 2006), pp. 124–133.

38 The firm must trade off efficiency gains from standardization and transformational change.

39 *Front office/back office* distinction from HP.

40 We focus on employee-based sales forces.

41 Actual ratios deviate for operational reasons like workload.

42 N. Adams, J. Gillibrand, D. Treinish, K. Woodberry, and B. Zaldivar, "British Aerospace Regional Aircraft: Addressing the Need for Key Account Management," Term Paper for Developing and Managing Strategic Customers, B8699-02, New York: Graduate School of Business, Columbia University.

43 Wachovia deliberately understaffed product specialist functions to motivate account managers to understand their products; Wachovia Bank and Trust Company in N. Capon, *The Marketing of Financial Services: A Book of Cases*, Englewood Cliffs, NJ: Prentice Hall, 1992.

44 Some pharmaceutical firms abandoned this organization under pressure from physician organizations.

45 Stuart Dean instituted a process to avoid multiple calling on individual customers.

46 "Steve Jobs: The Graying Prince of a Shrinking Kingdom," *Fortune*, May 14, 2001.

47 This is not simple; HP took three years to secure organizational agreement for its global pipeline system.

48 Like Siebel Systems and www.salesforce.com.

49 HP does not credit salespeople for sales resulting from opportunities *not* entered into the pipeline.

50 Based on the expectancy/value model for securing motivated behavior; J.W. Atkinson, "Motivational Determinants of Risk Taking Behavior," *Psychological Review*, 64 (1957), pp. 359–372.

51 Other motivators include special bonuses, prizes, evaluation points, stamp schemes, and training awards.

52 Two potential problems relate to bonuses: Successful salespeople may slack off after earning the bonus; and salespeople who believe they will not earn the bonus may shift sales to a subsequent period. Over-achievement commissions address the first problem; calendarizing the bonus addresses the second. Notwithstanding mixed perspectives and empirical results on the value of bonuses, T.J. Steenburgh, "Effort or Timing: The Effect of Lump-Sum Bonuses." *Quantitative Marketing and Economics*, 6 (2008), pp. 235–256, shows that bonuses drive greater salesperson effort.

53 At Microsoft, a salesperson and customer escalated the decision for significant discounting on a potential sale several managerial levels. Robert Youngjohns, President North America Sales, said: "I asked one question. What is the impact of this sale on the salesperson's attainment of quota?" The answer: "Without this sale the salesperson is at 98.2 percent of quota: with the sale, the sales person is at 102.2 percent of quota!"

54 Some firms employ product-mix incentives to avoid a narrow focus on easy-to-sell products.

55 P. R. Sinha, "Premium Marketing to the Masses: An Interview with LG Electronics India's Managing Director," *The McKinsey Quarterly*, (Special Edition 2005), pp. 52–61.

56 *BusinessWeek*, November 27, 1989.

57 Sears Auto Centers (A), (B), and (C), 9-394-009/10/11, Harvard Business School.

58 A. Miller, *Death of a Salesman*, 1949; D. Mamet, *Glengarry Glen Ross*, 1984.

59 Personal communication.

60 Some firms reward salespeople for recruiting new salespeople.

61 M.E. Elling, H.J. Fogle, C.S. McKhann, and C. Simon, "Making More of Pharma's Sales Force," *The McKinsey Quarterly*, (2002), pp. 86–95, suggests pharmaceutical reps are inadequately trained!

62 The firm should use validated psychometric tests for salesperson selection.

63 Empathy and ego drive (need to persuade) from D. Mayer and H.M. Greenberg, "What Makes a Good Salesman," *Harvard Business Review*, 42 (July–August 1964), pp. 119–125. Ego strength embraces the self-confidence and ability to handle rejection, accept criticism, and *bounce back*.

64 Capon and Tubridy, *op. cit.*, pp. 36–37.

65 In order: Don't follow the customer buying process; don't listen to customer needs; don't follow up; be pushy, aggressive, or disrespectful; don't explain solutions adequately; make exaggerated or inaccurate claims; don't understand the customer's business; act too familiar; and don't know or respect the competition; T. Atkinson and R. Koprowski, "Sales Rep's Biggest Mistakes," *Harvard Business Review*, 84 (July–August 2006), p. 20.

66 E. Anderson and V. Onyemah, "How Right Should the Customer Be?," *Harvard Business Review*, 84 (July–August 2006), pp. 59–67.

67 Gaining access is critical. Of 100 pharmaceutical reps calling on physicians, only eight see the doctor and are remembered! Elling, Fogle, McKhann, and Simon, *op. cit*.

68 T. Üstüner and D. Godes, "Better Sales Networks," *Harvard Business Review*, 84 (July–August 2006), pp. 102–112.

69 The firm can develop alternative career tracks for career salespeople, involving increased responsibility, income, and recognition.

70 Personal communication.

71 *Key* and *strategic* are interchangeable. Generally, European use is *key*; U.S. use is *strategic*. Firms making excessive price concessions to large customers may find smaller customers are more profitable.

72 For critical factors driving key/strategic account management: N. Capon, *Key Account Management*, New York: Free Press, 2001, Chapter 2.

73 D. Narayandas and V.K. Rangan, "Building and Sustaining Buyer-Seller Relationships in Mature Industrial Markets," *Journal of Marketing*, 68 (July 2004), pp. 63–77.

74 "IBM's All-Star Salesman," *Fortune*, September 29, 2008. For building sales networks: T. Üstüner and D. Godes, "Better Sales Networks," *Harvard Business Review*, 84 (July–August 2006), pp. 102–112.

75 Walmart has a large percentage share of some suppliers' sales — Playtex (28%), Clorox (27%), Hasbro (24%), Revlon (24%), Tootsie Roll Ind. (24%), Spectrum Brands (18%), Russell (18%), P&G (16%), General Mills (16%), and J. M. Smucker (16%).

76 N. Capon, D. Potter, and F. Schindler, *Managing Global Accounts* (2nd ed.), Bronxville, NY: Wessex, 2008.

CHAPTER 19

1 From interviews with Cisco executives and data from V.K. Rangan, *Transforming Your Go-To-Market Strategy*, Boston, MA: Harvard Business School Press, 2006.

2 Some observers believe that P&G acquired Gillette to improve its power position versus large supermarket chains.

3 An end user is where the product loses its identity; both consumers and firms can be end users. Consumer advertising may push end users down the channel. Previously, end users for microprocessors were PC manufacturers; *intel inside* turned consumers into end users.

4 The broad view includes *concentration* and *dispersion*. Inputs are concentrated in Korea, and prefabricated steel beams are dispersed to Argentina. Relatedly, natural resources are randomly distributed — *meaningless heterogeneity*; customers require disparate resource bundles — *meaningful heterogeneity*. All distribution systems transform *meaningless heterogeneity* into *meaningful heterogeneity*. For example, a New York restaurant serves patrons a delicious salad of California lettuce, Mexican tomatoes, and Arizona carrots.

5 C.B. Bucklin, S.P. DeFalco, J.R. DeVincentis, and J.P. Levis III, "Are You Tough Enough to Manage Your Channels?," *The McKinsey Quarterly*, (1996), pp. 105–114.

6 *Distribution* encompasses all these functions — *logistics* is about getting the product from A to B.

7 When increasing numbers of consumers began shopping online, Sears dropped its catalog; D.V. Fites, "Make Your Dealers Your Partners," *Harvard Business Review*, 74 (March–April 1996), pp. 84–95.

8 Many supply chains have global scope via technological advances in communications and transportation, and reduced trade barriers. Hides from Argentinean cows are tanned in China, sewn into flight jackets in Korea, then sold in Japan.

9 *Going to Market*, 9-599-078, Harvard Business School.

10 Many *physical distribution* functions are irrelevant for services and information products.

11 Developing a product range to satisfy customers; especially important for wholesalers and retailers.

12 Aka outbound logistics. *Drop shipping* — manufacturer ships products direct to customers, often in retailer packaging — has grown along with direct marketing and Internet commerce. Products needing repair are returned via inbound (reverse) logistics. Annually, suppliers spend $40 billion handling over $60 billion returned goods; personal communication from John Beystehner, former senior VP Worldwide Sales and Marketing, UPS.

13 Includes finishing, fitting, shaping, and sizing — also, paint-mixing and product assembly.

14 Includes data on financing, inventory, ownership changes, product availability, product location, and sales.

15 When purchases are difficult and complex, advisors, agents, and brokers often provide impartiality.

16 Channel members often shift risks relating to title transfer and financing via insurance, warranties, and guarantees.

17 Chapter 2 — customer relationship management.

18 Some direct sales approaches involve pyramid schemes. Salespeople earn commissions on their own sales; they also earn commissions on the sales of salespeople they recruit, sometimes ad infinitum. Handtech.com reps earn 10 percent commission on their sales, half the $145 fee of salespeople they recruit, and 2–5 percent of recruits' sales.

19 For factors driving direct marketing growth; pros and cons — Chapter 16.

20 D. Rigby, "The Future of Shopping," *Harvard Business Review*, 89 (December 2011), pp. 64–73.

21 *Christian Science Monitor, Kentucky Post, Seattle-Post Intelligencer.*

22 Most Internet action is from startup firms and traditional retailers adding Internet capability; some successful Internet startups like T-shirt firm Threadless build on their brand equity to open retail stores.

23 Firms that sell products through multiple websites (third-party and their own) should take care to ensure consistency in product availability, model numbers, product reviews, and visuals.

24 Disputes between franchisees and the franchisor are not uncommon; they typically concern high fees and insufficient customer demand.

25 Franchising does not imply the presence of physical retail outlets.

26 Similarly, Ford traditionally distributed products through franchised dealerships but purchased its Salt Lake City franchises. Ford superstores offer Ford, Lincoln, and Mazda brands.

27 Banco Popular is the largest U.S. Hispanic bank.

28 These customers account for 80 percent of Haiti's economy. Sogebank is Haiti's leading commercial bank.

29 Some department stores emphasize *store brands* — Kohl's (U.S.) and Marks & Spencer (Britain). *Showcase* stores focus on manufacturer brands — vendors are responsible for inventory, staff, and selling space.

30 J.A. Narus and J.C. Anderson, "Rethinking Distribution," *Harvard Business Review*, 74 (July–August 1996), pp. 112–120.

31 J.D. Hlavacek and T.J. McCuistion, "Industrial Distributors — When, Who and How?," *Harvard Business Review*, 61 (March–April 1983), pp. 96–101.

32 Narus and Anderson, *op. cit.*

33 Ekornes also changed salesperson pay from commission to salary plus bonus — based on retailer-service; N. Kumar, "The Power of Trust in Manufacturer-Retailer Relationships," *Harvard Business Review*, 74 (November–December 1996), pp. 92–106.

34 P.F. Nunes and F.V. Cespedes, "The Customer Has Escaped," *Harvard Business Review*, 81 (November 2003), pp. 96–105. In response to *showrooming*, in 2012 Target stopped distributing Amazon's Kindle.

35 Among WD-40's more esoteric uses are: Freeing a person's tongue stuck to cold metal, cleaning ostrich eggs for craft uses, preventing squirrels from climbing into a birdhouse, and removing a python coiled around an Asian bus undercarriage.

36 Distributor agreements involve preferred credit terms, cash payments, and other benefits; sometimes distributors forgo exclusivity in favor of new opportunities.

37 Coke denied allegations of abusive practices.

38 From Pegram, *Selecting and Evaluating Distributors*, reproduced in B. Rosenbloom, *Marketing Channels: A Management View* (8th ed.), Stamford, CT: Cengage Learning, 2013.

39 L.W. Stern and F.D. Sturdivant, "Customer-Driven Distribution Systems," *Harvard Business Review*, 65 (July–August 1987), pp. 34–41; V.K. Rangan, A.J. Menzes, and E. Maier, "Channel Selection for New Industrial Products: A Framework, Method and Application," *Journal of Marketing*, 56 (July 1992), pp. 69–82; V.K. Rangan, *Designing Channels of Distribution*, Boston, MA: Harvard Business School, 1994, 9-594-116; J.M. Hulbert, *Marketing: A Strategic Perspective*, Katonah, NY: Impact Publishing, 1985; E. Anderson, G.S. Day, and V.K. Rangan, "Strategic Channel Design," *Sloan Management Review*, (Summer 1997), pp. 59–69.

40 Factoring firms buy accounts receivable at a discount.

41 FOB (free on board) — price at the factory/warehouse; CIF (carriage, insurance and freight) — price delivered to the customer.

42 Atlas Honda Ltd.: Communication Plan 1993; N. Capon and W. Van Honacker, *The Asian Marketing Casebook*, Singapore: Prentice Hall, 1998. Anticompetitive practices, like Honda's, are illegal in many countries.

43 In the U.S., *functional-discount* structures must be objectively measurable to ensure they are fair and nondiscriminatory. The Supreme Court condemned discounts that create exclusivity, or promote anticompetitive behavior. D. A. Balto "Networks and Exclusivity: Antitrust Analysis to Promote Network Competition," *George Mason Law Review*, 7 (Spring 1999), pp. 523–576.

44 Also Rosenbloom, *op. cit.* and A. Coughlan, E. Anderson, L.W. Stern, and A. El-Ansary, *Marketing Channels* (8th ed.), Englewood Cliffs: Prentice Hall, 2011.

45 Reproduced with permission from Rosenbloom, *op. cit.*

46 Some suppliers require extensive information on each sale — by product item, customer, and delivery and billing location.

47 In *U-boat* diversion, the *diverter* loads merchandise purchased for export onto a cargo ship. The ship sails but returns to the same or neighboring port; the diverter resells products in the home (higher-price) market.

48 This section benefited from D. Ford, L.E. Gadde, H. Hakansson, A. Lundgren, I. Snehota, P. Turnbull, and D. Wilson, *Managing Business Relationships*, Chichester, UK: Wiley, 1988. The seminal work on power identified five bases — coercive, reward, legitimate, referent, and expert; J.R.P. French and B. Raven, "The Bases of Social Power," in D. Cartwright and A. Zander, *Group Dynamics*. New York: Harper & Row, 1959.

49 A.P. Chandler, Jr., *The Visible Hand: The Managerial Revolution in American Business*, Cambridge, MA: Harvard University Press, 1977.

50 Amazon works with tens of thousands of commissioned affiliates who direct traffic to its website.

51 Of course, mutual fund suppliers no longer have direct contact with investors; A. J. Slywotzky and D. J. Morrison, *The Profit Zone*, New York: Times Business, 1997.

52 A 2002 Financial Accounting Standards Board (FASB) rule required that manufacturers restate 2001 revenues by subtracting incentive payments from reported sales. This one-time event revealed these payments.

53 Shelf position is important for both bricks & mortar and virtual displays; A. Valenzuela and P. Raghubir, "Position-based Beliefs: The Center-Stage Effect," *Journal of Consumer Psychology*, 19 (2009), pp. 185–196.

54 *Norton Company (A) and (B)*, 9-570-001/2, Harvard Business School.

55 In the 1990s, the U.S. had more than 15,000 car dealerships. Today, the top 250 firms sell over 50 percent of industry volume.

56 C.B. Bucklin, P.A. Thomas-Graham, and E.A. Webster, "Channel Conflict: When Is It Dangerous?," *The McKinsey Quarterly*, (1997), pp. 36–43.

57 Bucklin, Thomas-Graham, and Webster, *op. cit.*

58 Bucklin, Thomas-Graham, and Webster, *op. cit.*

59 The *Merck Manual* comprises 3,000 pages on disorders and suggested therapies. Parker Hannifin's "O-Ring Handbook" helps design engineers specify solutions for preventing oil/air system leakage, Hlavacek and McCuistion, *op. cit.*

60 Suppliers learn about distribution challenges and opportunities — hence, the firm can better serve third-party distributors. This action also sends distributors a message about supplier options. Dealer concentration led Ford and GM to acquire equity positions in some automobile dealers. Power equipment manufacturer Cummins acquired many distributors. Global leader Claas sells combine harvesters to farmers through local distributors; in each major country, Claas owns at least one retail outlet to gain first-hand experience of farmer problems/needs. H. Simon, *Hidden Champions: Lessons from 500 of the World's Best Unknown Companies*, Boston, MA: Harvard Business School Press, 1996.

61 Heinz (U.S.) placed food, pet food, and food service into a single unit — distribution improved and Heinz secured greater bargaining power with retail chains.

62 Armstrong World Industries offers educational benefits to distributors that place 100 percent of business with Armstrong.

63 For trust in partnership relationships: J.C. Anderson and J.A. Narus, "A Model of Distributor Firm and Manufacturing Firm Working Partnerships," *Journal of Marketing*, 54 (January 1990), pp. 42–58; and Kumar, *op. cit.* Also J. Lewis, *Trusted Partners: How Companies Build Mutual Trust and Win Together*, New York: Free Press, 1999.

64 *Cross-docking* removes the need for regional warehouses.

65 G. Stalk, P. Evans, and L.E. Shulman, "Competing on Capabilities: The New Rules of Corporate Strategy," *Harvard Business Review*, 70 (March–April 1992), pp. 57–69.

66 JCPenney previously held up to nine months' inventory. M.L. Fisher, A. Ramam, and A.S. McClelland, "Rocket Science Retailing Is Almost Here — Are You Ready?," *Harvard Business Review*, 78 (July–August 2000), pp. 115–124, for a thoughtful article on getting the *right product* in the *right place* at the *right time* at the *right price*. Based on research at Japan-based World Company and Spain-based Zara fashion retailers.

67 J.D. Sterman, "Modeling Managerial Behavior: Misperceptions of Feedback in a Dynamic Decision Making Experiment," *Management Science*, 35 (March 1989), pp. 321–339, addresses trade-offs in *beer-game* simulations.

68 M. Hammer and J. Champy, *Re-engineering the Corporation: A Manifesto for Business Revolution*, New York: Harper Business, 1994. A narrow view of supply-chain management focuses on product flow. A broad view includes customer relationship management, customer service management, demand management, order fulfillment, manufacturing flow management, procurement, product development, commercialization, and returns, M.C. Cooper, D.M. Lambert, J.D. Pagh, "Supply Chain Management: More Than a New Name for Logistics," *The International Journal of Logistics Management*, 8 (1997), pp. 1–13.

CHAPTER 20

1 Adapted from Wikipedia.

2 For the remainder of this chapter we employ the term *consumer* for B2C and B2B contexts.

3 C. Anderson, *The Long Tail*, New York: Hyperion, 2006.

4 A. Valenzuela and P. Raghubir, "Position-Based Beliefs: The Center Stage Effect," *Journal of Consumer Psychology*, 19 (2009), pp. 185–196.

5 An Indonesian study found that fewer than 20 percent of mall visitors actually purchased anything!

6 U.S. Internet sales are roughly 10 percent of total retail sales; mobile devices account for 20 percent of online sales.

7 M. Corstjens and R. Lal, "Retail Doesn't Cross Borders," *Harvard Business Review*, 90 (April 2012), pp. 104–111.

8 J-B E.M. Steenkamp and N. Kumar, "Don't Be Undersold," *Harvard Business Review*, 87 (December 2009), pp. 91–95.

9 Corstjens and Lal, *op. cit.*

10 Sometimes intermediaries actually remove value from both suppliers and customer; the case of high-frequency traders, M. Lewis, *Flash Boys: A Wall Street Revolt*, New York: Norton, 2014.

CHAPTER 21

1 Personal communication from Lamar Muse. Also J.H. Gittell, *The Southwest Airlines Way*, New York: McGraw Hill, 2003, and *Southwest Airlines (A)*, 9-575-060, Harvard Business School.

2 By 2011, Southwest Airlines operated 550 Boeing 737 jet aircraft serving 75 cities in 40 states, making more than 3,100 flights daily. SWA was the largest U.S. domestic airline. Annual revenues exceeded $12 billion and SWA had been consistently profitable for almost 40 years. In 2011, SWA acquired AirTran.

3 Good pricing texts include T.T. Nagle, J. Hogan, and J. Hale, *The Strategy and Tactics of Pricing: Growing More Profitably*, 5th ed. Upper Saddle River, NJ: Pearson Prentice Hall, 2010; and R. Holden and M. Burton, *Pricing with Confidence: 10 Ways to Stop Leaving Money on the Table*, Hoboken, NJ: Wiley, 2008. Important articles include P.E. Green and Y. Wind, "New Way to Measure Consumers' Judgments," *Harvard Business Review*, 53 (July–August 1975), pp. 107–118; R.J. Dolan and A.P. Jeuland, "Experience Curves and Dynamic Demand Models: Implications for Optimal Pricing Strategies," *Journal of Marketing*, 45 (Winter 1981), pp. 52–73. For classic pricing works, A.D.H. Kaplan, J.B. Dirlam, and R.F. Lanzillotti, *Pricing in Big Business*, Washington, DC: Brookings Institution, 1958; and J. Dean, "Pricing Policies for New Products," *Harvard Business Review*, 28 (November–December 1950), pp. 28–36.

4 Based on 2,463 companies in the Compustat database; M.V. Marn and R.L. Rosiello, "Managing Price, Gaining Profit," *Harvard Business Review*, 70 (September–October 1992), pp. 84–94. More recently, percentage reductions in operating profit from a 1 percent price decrease were: food and drug stores — 23.7 percent; airlines — 12.9 percent; computers and office equipment — 11 percent; tobacco — 4.9 percent; semiconductors — 3.9 percent; and diversified financial — 2.4 percent, *Fortune*, May 14, 2001. Fortier & Associates report similar findings for a 2 percent improvement: price — 20 percent; variable costs — 11 percent; volume — 9 percent; fixed costs — 7 percent.

5 Of course, we expect unit volume to change with price — the illustration just shows the magnitude of the effect.

6 *Principles of Pricing*, 9-506-021, Harvard Business School.

7 Also B.T. Gale, "How Much Is Your Product *Really* Worth?," Boston: Customer Value Inc., 2002; and B.T. Gale, *Managing Customer Value*, New York: Free Press, 1994.

8 Aka *value in use* (VIU). Industry-specific terms include: *systems cost analysis* — defense; *outcomes research* — healthcare; *total distribution cost analysis* — logistics and transportation; and *total cost of ownership* — electronics.

9 J. Zale and W. Wise, "Pricing When Sales Slow," *The Professional Pricing Society Journal*, 10 (3rd Quarter 2001), pp. 1–9. Note that many aircraft components are now bonded rather than riveted — indirect competition!

10 J.C. Anderson and J.A. Narus, "Business Marketing: Understand What Customers Value," *Harvard Business Review*, 76 (November–December 1998), pp. 5–15.

11 Personal communication from Lance Batchelor, former Head of Worldwide Marketing, Amazon.com.

12 Conjoint analysis is a powerful method for measuring the perceived value (*utility*) of various product attributes and the *disutility of price*. Marketing Enrichment 6.1 **[710p]** shows a research design including product attributes and three price levels — current price, and 125 percent and 150 percent of current price.

13 P.C. Browne, N. Capon, T.S. Harris, H.N. Mantel, C.A. Newland, and A.H. Walsh, *The Ratemaking Process for the United States Postal Service*, New York: Institute of Public Administration, 1991. Also R. Cooper and R. Slagmulder, "Develop Profitable New Products with Target Costing," *Sloan Management Review*, 40 (Summer 1999), pp. 23–33.

14 A.O. Laffley and R. Charan, *Game-Changer*, New York: Crown Business, 2008, pp. 88–90.

15 *Positive sloping* demand curves are relatively rare — volume increases as price increases! They occur with luxury products like perfumes and fragrances. Price conveys information about product and/or service quality.

16 Before tackling this section, students should become familiar with Marketing Enrichment FM.1 **[308p]**, Section 1.

17 E. Shim and E.F. Sudit, "How Manufacturers Price Products," *Management Accounting*, (February 1995), pp. 37–39 report that more than 80 percent of U.S. manufacturers use cost-plus pricing — 7 percent use *fully allocated costs* (Marketing Enrichment FM.1 **[308p]**).

18 Cost-plus pricing can be useful when the firm must set prices for many products, like in supermarkets.

19 Advances in activity-based costing (ABC) provide firms with superior knowledge of cost dynamics.

20 For example, if the firm adds fixed capacity or a new shift.

21 A price below $4 may be acceptable when demand is cyclical and stopping and starting production is very costly.

22 N. Capon, J.U. Farley, and J. Hulbert, "Pricing and Forecasting in an Oligopoly Firm," *Journal of Management Studies*, 12 (1975), pp. 133–156.

23 American Airlines attempted to simplify the complex pricing system by combining price increases and reductions; *American Airlines (A) and (B)*, 9-594-001 and 9-594-019, Harvard Business School.

24 This section draws on A.K. Rao, M.E. Bergen, and S. Davis, "How to Fight a Price War," *Harvard Business Review*, 78 (March–April 2000), pp. 107–116.

25 Zale and Wise, *op. cit.*

26 S. Jayachandran, J. Gimeno, and P.R. Varadarjan, "The Theory of Multimarket Competition: A Synthesis and Implications for Marketing Strategy," *Journal of Marketing*, 63 (July 1999), pp. 49–66.

27 H.J. Van Heerde, E. Gijsbrechts, and K. Pauwels, "Winners and Losers in a Major Price War," *Journal of Marketing*, 45 (October 2008), pp. 499–518, show how a retail market leader stopped market share losses and increased share price when forced to initiate a price war.

28 M. Bertini and L. Wathieu, "How to Stop Customers from Fixating on Price," *Harvard Business Review*, 88 (May 2010), pp. 84–91.

29 Forty percent of consumer rebates are never redeemed, in part because some firms make redemption difficult.

30 *Polaroid, The First Thirty Years, 1948–1978: A Chronology of Polaroid Photographic Products*, Cambridge, MA: Polaroid Corporation, 1979, provides a classic description of sequential skimming.

31 Steve Jobs apologized for such a swift price reduction; affected customers received $100 store credit.

32 For problems of inappropriate actions, *We've Got Rhythm! Medtronic Corporation's Cardiac Pacemaker Business*, 9-698-004, Harvard Business School.

CHAPTER 22

1 We omit time value of money issues to simplify the illustration.

2 Traditional income statements partitions are cost of goods sold (COGS) and all other costs — mostly marketing and SG&A. Table 20.2 gathers variable costs and fixed costs from these traditional categories:
- *Variable costs* — raw materials, direct labor, electricity (for production), freight, and sales commissions.
- *Fixed costs* — indirect labor, manufacturing overhead, and depreciation; also advertising, field sales (salary, expenses), and product and marketing management.

We assume variable costs per unit and fixed costs are constant over the volume range we consider.

3 T. Nagle, "How to Pull It Off," *Across the Board*, (March 1999), pp. 53–56.

4 Annual volume discounts based on matching/exceeding last year's volume may repel aggressive new competitors.

5 For more on these terms, **544p** and **568p**.

6 *Norton Company*, 9-581-046, Harvard Business School.

7 M.V. Marn and R.L. Rosiello, "Managing Price, Gaining Profit," *Harvard Business Review*, 70 (September–October 1992), pp. 84–94.

8 More detailed analysis calculates the pocket margin for each account: hence, a *pocket-margin* distribution and *pocket-margin* waterfall; M. V. Marn, E.V. Roegner, and C.C. Zawada, "The Power of Pricing," *The McKinsey Quarterly*, (2003), pp. 1–8.

9 For real examples of a price band and price waterfalls, Marn, Roegner, and Zawada, *op. cit.*.

10 Similar products sold to different customers at different prices may run afoul of anti-price-discrimination legislation — like the U.S. Robinson-Patman Act.

11 18th-century economist quoted in R.B. Ekelund, "Price Discrimination and Product Differentiation in Economic Theory: An Early Analysis," *Quarterly Journal of Economics*, 84 (1970), pp. 268–278. Question: Is this analysis applicable to contemporary airline travel?

12 Examples include Singapore, Sweden (Trondheim, Bergen, Oslo), Netherlands (Amsterdam, Rotterdam, Utrecht, The Hague), and London.

13 When commodities represent a significant portion of product cost, the firm may link price to commodity price indices. Customers may secure price predictability by hedging the relevant commodity.

14 Some electric utilities are shifting to hourly pricing and installing smart meters so customers can monitor use and time-shift activities.

15 The profusion of price information on the Internet is encouraging consumers to haggle with retailers. National stores like Best Buy, The Home Depot, and Ralph Lauren allow salespeople to negotiate prices.

16 Bidders avoid the *winner's curse* of paying far too much.

17 S.D. Yap, "An Exploratory Study of the Introduction of Online Reverse Auctions," *Journal of Marketing*, 67 (July 2003), pp. 96–107.

18 G. McGovern and Y. Moon, "Companies and the Customers Who Hate Them," *Harvard Business Review*, 85 (June 2007), pp. 78–84.

19 E. Anderson and D. Simester, "Mind Your Pricing Cuts," *Harvard Business Review*, 81 (September 2003), pp. 97–103.

20 G.E. Smith and T.T. Nagle, "Frames of Reference and Buyers' Perception of Price and Value," *California Management Review*, 38 (1995), pp. 98–116.

21 "The Magic Touch," *Fortune*, September 6, 2004.

22 Some law firms are shifting from prices based on billable hours to flat payments plus success fees. In American Express' winning case against MasterCard and Visa, winning lawyer fees exceeded $150 million.

23 G. Antorcha and J. Schürmann, "Just-in-Time Pricing," *The Boston Consulting Group*, 2010.

24 C. Anderson, *FREE*, New York: Hyperion, 2009. K. Pauwels and A. Weiss, "Moving from Free to Fee: How Online Firms Market to Change Their Business Model Successfully," *Journal of Marketing*, 72 (May 2008), pp. 14–31, discuss the challenges of shifting from FREE to a nonzero price on the Internet.

25 Sometimes the subsidy implies a zero price — like network TV; other times the subsidy side pays something — like most newspapers.

26 Ways to respond to competition from FREE offerings include: Introduce a FREE basic product, gain widespread use, then: a. Charge for a premium version; b. Sell other products; c. Charge third parties for access to customers; and/or d: Offer a FREE product with a paid offering; D.J. Bryce, J.H. Dyer, and N.W. Hatch, "Competing against FREE," *Harvard Business Review*, 89 (June 2011), pp. 104–111.

27 *Black markets* occur when demand is greater than supply. Buyers resell products at higher prices. Tickets for popular concerts/sporting events are often *scalped* at prices higher than list. Producers of the hit Broadway show *The Producers* (top price $100) offered 50 seats per night at $480 per ticket.

28 Some jurisdictions prohibit imports of *gray market* products.

29 Der Wiener Deewan — Vienna; Just Around the Corner — London; Lentil as Anything — Melbourne; One World Café — Salt Lake City. Also Potager, Arlington, TX, but after two months they had to return to menu pricing.

30 J-Y. Kim M. Natter, and M. Spann, "Pay What You Want: A New Participative Pricing Mechanism," *Journal of Marketing*, 73 (January 2009), pp. 44–58, and Y. Chen, O. Koenigsberg, and Z.J. Zhang, "Pay-as-You-Wish-Pricing," Working Paper, Columbia Business School, 2011.

31 Ryanair has fallen afoul of European Union regulators who view such arrangements as illegal subsidies. Small U.S. cities make guaranteed-revenue arrangements with airlines in exchange for air service.

32 The firm should set transfer prices at *arms' length* to avoid potential legal entanglements. In 2006, Britain's GSK settled a transfer-pricing case with the U.S. for $3.6 billion.

33 Personal communication from Dick Melville, former vice chairman of Alcoa's Aerospace Market Sector Lead Team.

34 J. Zale and W. Wise, "Pricing When Sales Slow," *The Professional Pricing Society Journal*, 10 (3rd Quarter 2001), pp. 1–9.

35 S. Dutta, M. Bergen, D. Levy, M. Ritson, and M. Zbaracki, "Pricing as a Strategic Capability," *Sloan Management Review*, 43 (Spring 2002), pp. 61–66; and S. Dutta, M. Zbaracki, and M. Bergen, "Pricing Process as a Capability: A Resource-Based Perspective," *Strategic Management Journal*, 24 (2003), pp. 615–630. Also *Organizing for Pricing*, Perspectives, Boston Consulting Group, 2002.

36 Dutta, Bergen, Levy, Ritson; and Zbaracki, *op. cit.*; Dutta, Zbaracki, and Bergen, *op. cit.*; and M. Tripsas and G. Gavetti, "Capabilities, Cognition, and Inertia: Evidence from Digital Imaging," *Strategic Management Journal*, 21 (2000), pp. 1147–1161.

37 J.R. Immelt interviewed by T.A. Stewart, "Growth as a Process," *Harvard Business Review*, 84 (June 2006), pp. 60–70, at pp. 64–65.

38 S. Duranton and J-M. Izaret, "Crisis Pricing for the Downturn and After," Boston: *The Boston Consulting Group*, 2009.

39 Traditionally, firm data on orders, promotions, revenues, and inventory levels were kept in separate locations. Some firms now collect these data in a single place and use complex algorithms to modify prices. The Internet allows instant price changes; without automation, the cost to change prices can be significant. And it can take months for price adjustments to filter down to distributors, retailers, and salespeople — hence, suboptimal pricing. An Internet problem is pricing accuracy. An incorrect price can lead to high sales volume before a mistake is identified. For example, $588 Hitachi computer monitors listed at $164, a $299 MP3 player listed for $26.89, and United Airlines offered $27 U.S.-to-Paris flights!

40 Also R.J. Dolan, "How Do You Know When the Price Is Right?," *Harvard Business Review*, 74 (September–October 1995), pp. 4–11.

41 To conclude this chapter, a pricing anecdote. When George Bernard Shaw first visited the U.S., several New York society women, knowing his reputation for wit, sought to outwit him. Said one, "Mr. Shaw, would you sleep with me for one million dollars?" Shaw responded, "How about ten dollars?" The woman was taken aback, "Mr. Shaw, what do you take me for? A whore?" Shaw replied, "Madam, we've already established what you are, we're just trying to figure out the price."

CHAPTER 23

1 J. M. Hulbert, N. Capon, and N. Piercy, *Total Integrated Marketing: Breaking the Bounds of the Function*, NY: Free Press, 2003.

2 Ritz-Carlton's CEO even carried bags as a bellhop — a fellow employee admonished him for turning down a tip!

3 B.F. Shapiro, "Can Marketing and Manufacturing Coexist?," *Harvard Business Review*, 55 (September–October 1977), pp. 104–112.

4 Personal communication from Richard L. Melville Jr., former Vice Chairman Aerospace Market Sector Lead Team, Alcoa.

5 Similarly, Apple considers its supply chain a critical success factor for the iPod, iPhone, and iPad.

6 New York City mayor Mike Bloomberg received this call regarding his new Lexus — he introduced the customer-calling system for Bloomberg terminals.

7 For important work on market orientation: B. J. Jaworski and A.J. Kohli, "Market Orientation: Antecedents and Consequences," *Journal of Marketing*, 57 (July 1993), pp. 53–70; S. F. Slater and J. C. Narver, "Market Orientation and the Learning Organization," *Journal of Marketing*, 59 (July 1995), pp. 63–74, and other work by these authors.

8 Also G.S. Day, "The Capabilities of Market-Driven Organizations," *Journal of Marketing*, 58 (October 1994), pp. 37–52.

9 C. Fuschs and M. Schrier, "Customer Empowerment in New Product Development," *Journal of Product Innovation Management*, 28 (2011), pp. 17–32.

10 J. Claret, P. Mauger, and E.V. Roegner, "Profiting from Proliferation: Managing a Marketing and Sales Transformation," *The McKinsey Quarterly*, (2006), pp. 111–121.

11 S.K. Lam, F. Krauss, and M. Ahearne, "The Diffusion of Market Orientation Throughout the Organization: A Social Learning Perspective," *Journal of Marketing*, 74 (September 2010), pp. 61–79.

12 J. Garten, "Andy Grove Made the Elephant Dance," *BusinessWeek*, April 11, 2005, p. 26.

13 J.P. Kotter, *Leading Change*, Boston: Harvard Business School Press, 1996, identifies eight principles of change management: Establish a sense of urgency, form a powerful guiding coalition, create a vision, communicate the vision, empower others to act on the vision, plan for and create short-term wins, consolidate improvements and produce still more change, and institutionalize new approaches .

14 "Less Than the Sum of its Parts," *The Economist*, June 23, 2001, pp. 73–74.

15 R.R. Ellsworth, *Leading with Purpose*, Stanford, CA.: Stanford University Press, 2002, p.115.

16 *www.amanet.org/research/pdfs/2002_corp_value.pdf. Satisfying customers* was essential in 77 percent of firms' value statements.

17 From P&G's *Purpose*: "We will provide branded products and services of superior quality and value that improve the lives of the world's consumers, now and for generations to come. As a result, consumers will reward us with leadership sales, profit and value creation, allowing our people, our shareholders, and the communities in which we live and

work to prosper" — and *Values*: integrity, leadership, ownership, passion for winning, trust.

18 "Win Smith on the Exit of Merrill CEO Stan O'Neal," *BusinessWeek*, November 12, 2007, pp. 25–26. Bank of America acquired Merrill as losses increased, less than one year after O'Neal's 2009 ouster.

19 Personal communication from Michael Tangui, former Senior Vice President of Marketing for the L'Oreal Paris brand in the U.S.

20 Senior employees affirm that J&J frequently resolves difficult management decisions by reference to the credo. Regardless, recent problems at J&J, including significant fines, suggest that continued vigilance is critical or values may take second place to business pressures.

21 C. Homburg and C. Pflesser, "A Multiple-Layer Model of Market-Oriented Organizational Culture: Measurement Issues and Performance Outcomes," *Journal of Marketing Research*, 37 (November 2000), pp. 449–462.

22 P.F. Drucker, "The Coming of the New Organization," *Harvard Business Review*, 76 (January–February 1998), pp. 45–53; J.B. Quinn, *Intelligent Enterprise*, New York: Free Press, 1992.

23 B. Costock, R. Gulati, and S. Liguori, "Unleashing the Power of Marketing," *Harvard Business Review*, 88 (October 2010), pp. 90–98 for developing the marketing function at GE.

24 R.S. Achrol, "Evolution of the Marketing Organization," *Journal of Marketing*, 55 (October 1991), pp. 77–93. J.P. Workman Jr., C. Homburg, and K. Gruner, "Marketing Organization: An Integrative Framework of Dimensions and Determinants," *Journal of Marketing*, 62 (July 1998), pp. 21–41; L.P. Katsanis, "Some Effects of Changes in Brand Management Systems: Issues and Implications," *International Marketing Review*, 16 (1999), pp. 518–532. C. Homburg. J.P. Workman Jr., and O. Jensen, "Fundamental Changes in Marketing Organization: The Movement Toward a Customer-Focused Structure," *Journal of the Academy of Marketing Science*, 28 (2000), pp. 459–478.

25 P&G is organized into business areas like Personal Beauty, House & Home, Health & Wellness, Baby & Family, and Pet Nutrition & Care. The brand management organization is essentially a *matrix*. Individuals charged with marketing activities, like salespeople, execute various brand manager plans, yet report to their sales organizations.

26 From *General Foods Corporation: The Product Management System*, 5-587-053, Harvard Business School. Also J.A. Quelch, P.W. Farris, and J.M. Olver, "The Product Management Audit: Design and Survey Findings," *Harvard Business Review*, 65 (March–April 1987), pp. 30, 32, 36; also *Journal of Consumer Marketing*, 4 (1987), pp. 45–58.

27 Research shows that both retailers and category captains gain from this relationship, and that category captains do not discriminate against competitors; R.A. Gooner, N.A. Morgan, and W.D. Perreault, "Is Retail Category Management Worth the Effort (and Does a Category Captain Help or Hinder)?" *Journal of Marketing*, 75 (September 2011), pp.18–33.

28 When an individual product targets a single end-use market, product/brand and market-segment managers overlap.

29 R.J. Keith, "The Marketing Revolution," *Journal of Marketing*, 24 (January 1960), pp. 35–38.

30 M. Hammer and J. Champy, *Reengineering the Corporation: A Manifesto for Business Revolution*, New York: Nicholas Brealy, 1993.

31 M. de Swaan Arons, F. van den Driest, and K. Weed, "The Ultimate Marketing Machine," *Harvard Business Review*, 91 (July–August 2014). pp. 55–63.

32 "Go-to-Market Advantage: The New Battlefield for Consumer Companies," *The Boston Consulting Group*, 2007. J.M. Hulbert and L. Pitt, "Exit Left Center Stage? The Future of Functional Marketing," *European Management Journal*, 14 (1996), pp. 47–60.

33 R.C. Blattberg and J. Deighton, "Interactive Marketing: Exploiting the Age of Addressability," *Sloan Management Review*, 33 (Fall 1991), pp. 5–14; D. Peppers and M. Rogers, *The One-to-One Future: Building Relationships One Customer at a Time*, New York: Century Doubleday, 1993.

34 Like Tom Peters' suggestion to turn the organization on its head; T. Peters, *Thriving on Chaos*, New York: Bantam, 1987.

35 This thinking has influenced terminology in Blattberg and Deighton, *op. cit.* and Peppers and Rogers, *op. cit.* Wachovia Bank (merger of First Union and Wachovia) has long managed retail customers like this. N. Capon, "Wachovia Bank and Trust Company," *The Marketing of Financial Services*, Englewood Cliffs, NJ: Prentice Hall, 1992.

36 R.T. Rust, C. Moorman, and G. Bhalla, "Rethinking Marketing," *Harvard Business Review*, 88 (January–February 2010), pp. 94–101, notes that such diverse firms as Chrysler, Oracle, Samsung, Sears, United Airlines, and Wachovia have CCOs.

37 J.K. Johansson and I. Nonaka, "Market Research the Japanese Way," *Harvard Business Review*, 65 (May–June 1987), pp. 16–19; L.P. Carbone and S.H. Haeckel, "Engineering Customer Experience," *Marketing Management*, 3 (1994), pp. 8–19; G.A. Churchill, R.H. Collins, and W.A. Strang, "Should Retail Salespersons Be Similar to Their Customers?," *Journal of Retailing*, 51 (Fall 1975), pp. 29–42; A.G. Woodside and W.J. Davenport, "The Effect of Salesman Similarity and Expertise on Consumer Purchasing Behavior," *Journal of Marketing*, 11 (May 1974), pp. 198–202.

38 Peppers and Rogers, *op. cit.* For research on aligning the organization with the market, G.S. Day, "Aligning Organizational Structure to the Market," *Business Strategy Review*, 10 (1999), pp. 33–46, and G.S. Day, "Aligning the Organization with the Market," *MIT Sloan Management Review* (Fall 2006), pp. 41–49. AMEX has separate marketing groups focused of different customer types: *acquisition* — secures new cardmembers; *early engagement* — focuses specifically on different aspects of new membership (activation; day 1 post activation to day 90; day 91 to day 180; day 180 to day 360); *loyalty* — increase spend and cardmember engagement; *retention* — monitor cardmembers close to attrition.

39 "A Great Leap, Preferably Forward," *The Economist*, January 20, 2001.

40 M.W. Blenko, M.C. Mankins, and P. Rogers, "The Decision-Driven Organization," *Harvard Business Review*, 88 (June 2010), pp. 54–62.

41 "Visionary-in-Chief," *BusinessWeek*, May 17, 1999.

42 N. Capon, *Key Account Management and Planning*, New York: Free Press, 2001.

43 N. Capon, D. Potter, and F. Schindler, *Managing Global Accounts*, (2nd ed.), Bronxville, NY: Wessex, 2008.

44 A communications switch programmable by outsiders.

45 "The Genesis of a Giant's Stumble," *The New York Times*, January 21, 2001. In 2006, Lucent merged with Alcatel; in 2016, Nokia acquired Alcatel-Lucent.

46 N. Capon, J.U. Farley, and J. Hulbert, *Corporate Strategic Planning*, New York: Columbia University Press, 1988.

47 Shapiro, *op. cit.*

48 J&J's *process excellence* approach rests on six principles — customer focus, fact-based management, alignment to strategy, process management across functions, continuous assessment and renewal, and innovative improvement. *Process excellence* rests on a set of structured methodologies and tools — lean thinking, six sigma (DMAIC), design excellence (DMADV), business assessment, dashboards (scorecards), and preferred (best) practices. J&J has trained process improvement professionals to coach or lead applications of these techniques. Note: Six sigma processes have less than 3.4 defects per million.

49 Personal communication from Howard Schultz.

50 A.O. Laffley and R. Charan, *Game-Changer*, New York: Crown Business, 2008, pp. 112–113.

51 "I Think of My Failures as a Gift," Interview with A.G. Lafley, former P&G CEO, *Harvard Business Review*, 89 (April 2011), pp. 86–89; and R.

G. McGrath, "Failing by Design," *Harvard Business Review*, 89 (April 2011), pp. 76–83.

52 ExxonMobil has Centers of Excellence/Expertise (COE) responsible for sharing best practices around the world via meetings and an automated e-mail system. COE personnel are available to address specific problems.

53 R.C. Camp, *Benchmarking: The Search for Industry Best Practices that Lead to Superior Performance*, Milwaukee, WI: American Society for Quality, 1989.

54 Hammer and Champy, *op. cit.* Business processes often cut across existing functional departments. Internal *political opposition* to change may be widespread, contributing to the failure of many well-intended re-engineering projects.

55 S. Brinker and L. McLellan, "The Rise of the Chief Marketing Technologist," *Harvard Business Review*, 91 (July–August 2014), pp. 83–85.

56 F. Cassidy, A. Freeling, and D. Kiewell, "Credibility Gap for Marketers," *The McKinsey Quarterly*, 2005, no. 2.

57 Executive-search firm Spencer Stuart reports average tenure for CMOs as less than two years.

58 B. Comstock, R. Gualati, and S. Liguori, "Unleashing the Power of Marketing," *Harvard Business Review*, 88 (October 2010), pp. 1800–1808.

59 Personal communication from Pat Kelly, former Senior Vice President, Worldwide Marketing, Pfizer Pharmaceuticals.

60 T.R. Knudsen, "Confronting Proliferation ... in Beer. An Interview with Carlsberg's Alex Myers," *The McKinsey Quarterly*, (May 2007).

61 R.W. Revans, *Developing Effective Managers: A New Approach to Business Education*, New York: Praeger, 1971. L. Fortini-Campbell, *Hitting the Sweet Spot*, Chicago: The Copy Workshop, 1992; and F.J. Gouillart and F.D. Sturdivant, "A Day in the Life of Your Customers," *Harvard Business Review*, 72 (January–February 1994), pp. 116–125.

62 S. Perman, *In-N-Out Burger*, San Francisco: Collins, 2009.

63 J.A. Byrne, *Chainsaw: The Notorious Career of Al Dunlap in the Era of Profit-at-Any Price*, New York: HarperBusiness, 1999.

64 Weber's original bureaucracy concept was much more positive. M. C. Weber, C. Wright Mills (ed.), and H. H. Gerth (ed.), from M. Weber: *Essays in Sociology*, Oxford, UK: Oxford University Press, 1958.

65 Additional organizational dimensions requiring decisions are: *Formalization* — the extent to which the firm enacts formal rules and procedures for decisions and working relationships, and *specialization* — the degree to which the firm divides up tasks and activities.

66 R. Gulati, "Silo Busting: How to Execute on the Promise of Customer Focus," *Harvard Business Review*, 85 (May 2007), pp. 98–108.

67 "From Scandal to Stardom: How Merck Healed Itself," *Fortune*, February 18, 2008, p. 96.

CHAPTER 24

1 Personal communication from Ron Boire.

2 The Marketing Science Institute (MSI) is a research-based, industry/academic collaboration headquartered in Cambridge, MA.

3 The reward system should reinforce appropriate behavior if performance meets or exceeds standards; it should change behavior if performance fails to reach standards. Former Columbia professor J.O. Whitney identifies several inappropriate behaviors leading to poor performance: vacillation, paralysis, bravado, intransigence, impatience, hand-wringing, breast-beating, rage, withdrawal, and flight!

4 Note the use of *performance* in this chapter. Suppose the performance measure is sales dollars; actual sales were $12 million versus a standard of $10 million. Performance refers to the variance between actual sales and the standard, in this case a positive $2 million (12–10). Performance does *not* refer to the actual sales, $12 million.

5 Personal communication from Pat Kelly, former Senior Vice President, Worldwide Marketing, Pfizer Pharmaceuticals.

6 Control limits ensure that random fluctuations do not cause firms to act too hastily.

7 Personal communication from Lance Batchelor, former Head of Worldwide Marketing, Amazon. Amazon feeds sales data directly to its supply chain. Suppliers dispatch products within hours.

8 A side benefit is happier, more motivated salespeople. Previously, salespeople complained about the time to fill out expense reports and the long wait for reimbursement. Cisco now calculates and pays sales commissions in real time, as orders arrive.

9 Personal communication from Steve Larned, former VP of Marketing, Dell Americas.

10 A nontrivial issue is standardization of terms across business units and across the firm. Profit numbers can vary widely depending on when the firm recognizes revenues and how it allocates costs. For effective analysis, the firm should compare *apples with apples*.

11 For a comprehensive set of performance measures: P.W. Faris, N.T. Bendle, P.E. Pfeifer, and D.J. Reibstein, *Marketing Metrics: 50+ Metrics Every Executive Should Master*, Upper Saddle River, NJ: Pearson, 2006.

12 Said Dick Melville, Vice Chairman Alcoa's Aerospace Market Sector Lead Team, "If you want to push a button and say, 'What does the entire Alcoa profit look like on a Canadaire CRJ-70?' or 'What is the profitability of all of our castings in the new Pratt & Whitney jet engine?' we can tell you." Personal communication.

13 Sometimes it may be valuable to measure the results of actions the firm did not take — like an investment bank that measures the outcomes of deals it turned down and counts as successes those that failed!

14 D. Bowman and H. Gatignon, "Market Response and Marketing Mix Models: Trends and Research Opportunities," *Foundations and Trends in Marketing*, 4 (2009), pp. 129–207.

15 P. Lapoint, *Marketing by the Dashboard Light*, New York: Association of National Advertisers, 2005.

16 W. Edwards Deming is widely credited as the founder of the Quality movement. The famous Japanese quality prize is named after Deming. An anecdote: In the early 1990s, the author attended a small meeting of Columbia faculty with then 90-year-old Deming. During the conversation, some of us were surprised to hear Deming say, "When I turned around Japan. ..." Then we thought about it. He actually did! The following system elaborates the Deming Cycle:
   Plan. Design/revise business process components to improve results.
   Do. Implement the plan and measure performance.
   Check. Assess measurements; report results to decision makers.
   Act. Decide on changes needed to improve the process.

17 R. Simons, *Levers of Control*, Boston, MA: Harvard Business School Press, 1994.

18 Note that this framework is equally effective for overall performance, and for subelements like advertising, innovation, and sales force.

19 Marketers have typically lacked the political power or technical ability to question traditional performance measures like sales and profits. Fortunately, leading thinkers in accounting and finance are increasingly moving toward more appropriate measures that look outward and forward rather than inward and backward. Activity-based costing is making a significant dent in traditional costing approaches. Kaplan has called for measures that include stock market, operations, and customer data. R.S. Kaplan and D.P. Norton, "Putting the Balanced Scorecard to Work," *Harvard Business Review*, 71 (September–October 1993), pp. 134–142. Some firms set social and/or environmental measures — GE requires business units to cut carbon dioxide (CO_2) emissions, each with different targets.

20 Attempting to focus employee attention on innovation, some firms adopt related business-unit measures. These measures often focus on

percentage of operating period sales revenues derived from products not in the product line several years previously, along with customer retention and its opposite — customer churn.

21 M. Treacy and J. Sims, "Take Command of Your Growth," *Harvard Business Review*, 82 (April 2004), pp. 127–133.

22 Illustrative supplier payments/profit margins as a percentage of sales are: Albertsons — 6.2 percent/5.0 percent, Kroger — 5.3 percent/5.2 percent, and Safeway — 6.5 percent/5.2 percent, "Accounting Games in the Grocer's Aisle," *BusinessWeek*, April 14, 2003.

23 After subtracting indirect fixed costs from direct product profit, the residual is bottom-line profit.

24 Return on equity (ROE) derives from ROI by focusing on the equity portion of the firm's capital structure. In good times, the firm can increase ROE by increasing debt and decreasing equity, but in bad times profits may be insufficient to make interest payments on debt. Bankruptcy may ensue, as with Lehman Brothers.

25 Some firms assess various marketing programs via return on marketing investment (ROMI) — incremental revenue (profit) generated by the program divided by the program's cost. For a critique of these and other return measures: T. Ambler and J. Roberts, "Assessing Marketing Performance: Don't Settle for a Silver Metric," *Journal of Marketing Management*, 24 (2008), pp. 733–750.

26 Activity-based costing (ABC) — Marketing Enrichment FM.1 **[308p]** is very helpful in making the conversion.

27 To measure and reward senior managers, P&G uses operating TSR (total shareholder return) comprising sales growth, profit margin growth, and increased capital efficiency. P&G believes improved operating TSR leads to increased stock price.

28 Later, when Welch became concerned about growth, he told business leaders they had *low market share*. Hence, a business leader's job was to identify growth opportunities — Chapter 3, p. 63.

29 E.W. Anderson, C.G. Fornell, and D.R. Lehmann, "Customer Satisfaction, Market Share, and Profitability," *Journal of Marketing*, 58 (July 1994), pp. 53–66. Brand health checks (Chapter 11) fall into this category.

30 Personal communication.

31 Previously, Microsoft based stock-bonus awards on meeting sales and profit targets.

32 Research on 400 companies in 28 industries showed a median Net Promoter Score of 16 percent. Leading companies like Amazon, eBay, and USAA scored from 75 percent to 80 percent; F.F. Reicheld, "The One Number You Need to Grow," *Harvard Business Review*, 81 (December 2003), pp. 46–54. Although it is widely used, writers have criticized the simplicity of Net Promoter Score and whether a single *recommendation* measure can fully predict loyalty behavior; N.A. Morgan and L.L. Rego, "The Value of Different Customer Satisfaction and Loyalty Metrics in Predicting Business Performance," *Marketing Science*, 25 (September–October 2006), pp. 426–439; T.L. Keiningham, B. Cooil, T.W. Andreassen, and L. Askoy, "A Longitudinal Examination of Net Promoter and Firm Revenue Growth," *Journal of Marketing*, 71 (July 2007), pp. 39–51.

33 *www.burke.com/Services*

34 J.R. Immelt interviewed by T.A. Stewart, "Growth as a Process," *Harvard Business Review*, 84 (June 2006), pp. 60–70.

35 As digital media has increased in importance, many web-based intermediate measures have been developed, like *hits*, *page views*, and *unique visitors*.

36 Personal communication from Hal Cramer, former President Fuels Marketing, ExxonMobil.

37 T.V. Bonoma, "Making Your Strategy Work," *Harvard Business Review*, 62 (March–April 1984), pp. 68–78.

38 T.V. Bonoma, "Market Success Can Breed 'Marketing Inertia,'" *Harvard Business Review*, 59 (September–October 1981), pp. 115–121.

39 Former Columbia Business School professor Abe Shuchman, mentor to the author, was one of the first writers on the marketing audit. A. Shuchman, "The Marketing Audit: Its Nature, Purposes and Problems," Management Report No. 32, *Analyzing and Improving Marketing Performance*, New York: American Management Association, 1959.

40 W.H. Rodgers, G.A. Osborne, and P. Kotler, "Auditing the Marketing Function," in N. Capon (Ed.), Section 7, *Marketing*, in AMA Management Handbook (3rd ed.), J. Hampton (Ed.), AMACOM, 1994. This section is heavily based on this material. Also P. Kotler, W.T. Gregor, and W.H. Rodgers III, "The Marketing Audit Comes of Age," *Sloan Management Review*, 30 (Winter 1989), pp. 49–62.

41 Rodgers, Osborne, and Kotler, *op. cit.*

42 For detailed discussion of functional integration to serve customers, J. Hulbert, N. Capon, and N. Piercy, *Total Integrated Marketing*, New York: Free Press, 2003.

43 Other performance measurement problems include only comparing against internal referents like prior years' performance. A. Likierman, "The Five Traps of Performance Measurement," *Harvard Business Review*, 87 (October 2009), pp. 96–101.

44 Kaplan and Norton, *op. cit.* For a more thorough and recent treatment: R.S. Kaplan and D.P. Norton, *Strategy Maps: Converting Intangible Assets into Tangible Outcomes*, Boston, MA: Harvard Business School Press, 2004.

45 Reproduced with permission from *Mobil USM&R (D): Gasoline Marketing*, N9-196-151, Harvard Business School; Anderson, Fornel, and Lehmann, *op. cit.* Brand health checks (Chapter 11) fall into this category.

....

CHAPTER 25

1 For DHL's founding and biography of the *H* (Larry Lee Hillblom): J.D. Scurlock, *King Larry: The Life and Ruins of a Billionaire Genius*, New York: Simon & Schuster, 2012.

2 T.L. Friedman, *The World is Flat*, New York: Farrar, Strauss and Giroux, 2005.

3 Source: World Trade Organization: International Trade Statistics 2007.

4 For a thoughtful analysis of globalization: T.L. Friedman, *The World Is Flat: A Brief History of the Twenty-First Century* (*expanded edition*), New York: Farrar, Strauss & Giroux, 2006.

5 W.J. Henisz and B.A. Zelner, "The Hidden Risks in Emerging Markets," *Harvard Business Review*, 88 (April 2010), pp. 2–8.

6 GDP per capita source: Wikipedia, from The World Bank.

7 PPP accounts for currency weakness in world markets. For example, India ranks 12th by nominal GDP but 4th by PPP, *Wikipedia*.

8 Annual remittances globally are about $300 billion. Leading recipients: India — $45 billion; China — $34 billion; Mexico — $26 billion; the Philippines — $18 billion; and Poland — $12 billion. Source: The World Bank.

9 Estimates of percent GDP range from U.S. — 9 percent to Bolivia and Georgia — 70 percent.

10 Goldman Sachs originally coined the term *BRIC*; it also identified the *Next 11 (N11)* — Bangladesh, Egypt, Indonesia, Iran, Korea, Mexico, Nigeria, Pakistan, Philippines, Turkey, and Vietnam, poised to rival the G7 — Canada, France, Germany, Great Britain, Italy, Japan, United Kingdom, and United States (adding Russia formed the G8), in economic influence in the 21st century. In 2010, Indonesia received a *promotion*: BRIC became BRICI.

11 The Boston Consulting Group, "Decoding the Next Billion Consumers," Boston, MA: The Boston Consulting Group, 2007.

12 Additionally, leaders of the world's wealthiest countries meet annually to discuss global economic issues. The G8 comprises the following countries:

	Population (millions)	GDP per capita (US $billions)
Canada	32	29.3
France	60	26.0
Germany	82	26.2
Great Britain	60	25.5
Italy	58	25.1
Japan	127	28.7
Russia	145	9.7
U.S.	290	36.3

A.K. Vaidya, Ed., *Globalization: Encyclopedia of Trade, Labor, and Politics*, 2006, p. 600. The G20 is an outgrowth of the G8 and comprises 19 nations plus the EU — 85 percent of global GDP, 80 percent of global trade, and two thirds world population. Member countries are Argentina, Australia, Brazil, Canada, China, France, Germany, Great Britain, India, Indonesia, Italy, Japan, Mexico, Russia, Saudi Arabia, South Africa, Korea, Turkey, and the U.S.

13 GDPs of these regional groups are roughly: EU — $16 trillion; NAFTA — $17 trillion; Mercosur — $3 trillion; ASEAN — $1 trillion.

14 Some economists argue that growth in bilateral arrangements hinders prospects for global agreements.

15 Venezuela has applied for full membership; Bolivia, Chile, Columbia, Ecuador, and Peru are associate members.

16 Associate members: Anguilla, Bermuda, British Virgin Islands, Cayman Islands, Turks and Caicos Islands.

17 The Bahamas is a member of the Community but not of the Common Market.

18 Formerly members of the European Free Trade Area; Switzerland declined to join.

19 G. Hofstede, *Culture's Consequences: Comparing Values, Behaviors, Institutions and Organizations across Nations* (2nd ed.), Thousand Oaks, CA.: Sage, 2001. An alternative framework embraces seven dimensions: *Universalism* versus *particularism*, *collectivism* versus *individualism*, *affective* versus *neutral* relationships, *specificity* versus *diffuseness*, *achievement* versus *ascription*, *orientation toward time*, and *internal* versus *external control*; F. Trompenaars, "Resolving International Conflict," *Business Strategy Review*, 7 (1996), pp. 51–68.

20 Of course, many countries also harbor subcultures; in China, vast cultural differences exist between coastal and inland cities, and between urban and rural populations.

21 Adapted from the CAGE framework in P. Ghemawat, *Redefining Global Strategy: Crossing Borders in a World Where Differences Still Matter*, Boston, MA: Harvard Business School Press, 2007.

22 M.F. Guillén and E. Garcia-Canai, "How to Conquer New Markets with Old Skills," *Harvard Business Review*, 88 (November 2010), pp. 118–112. ALSA expanded into Europe in the 1960s; today, an ALSA subsidiary helps multinationals operate in China.

23 A.K. Bhattacharya and D.C. Michael, "How Local Companies Keep Multinationals at Bay," *Harvard Business Review*, 86 (March 2008), pp. 85–95.

24 Some agent organizations, like Japanese trading houses, are huge and represent many producers.

25 The firm exports, customers import. Because increasing numbers of firms are outsourcing production activities abroad, we believe it makes more sense to focus the discussion on imports by customers rather than on exports by the firm.

26 A typical government concern is to preserve competition. Sometimes governments allow acquisitions to proceed only if the acquiring firm divests one or more competitive business units.

27 R. Vernon, "International Investment and International Trade in the Product Life Cycle," *Quarterly Journal of Economics*, 80 (May 1966), pp. 190–207; and L.T. Wells, "A Product Life Cycle for International Trade," *Journal of Marketing*, 5 (July 1968), pp. 1–6.

28 I. Ayal, "International Product Life Cycle: A Reassessment and Product Policy Implications," *Journal of Marketing*, 45 (Fall 1981), pp. 91–96.

29 D.J. Isenberg, "The Global Entrepreneur," *Harvard Business Review*, 86 (December 2008), pp. 107–111.

30 J.R Immelt, V. Govindarajan, and C. Trimble, "How GE Is Disrupting Itself," *Harvard Business Review*, 87 (October 2009), pp. 56–65.

31 N.T. Washburn and B.T. Hunsaker, "Finding Great Ideas in Emerging Markets," *Harvard Business Review*, 89 (September 2011), pp. 115–120.

32 Bhattacharya and Michael, *op. cit.* Also The Boston Consulting Group's biennial publication on the 100 New Global Challengers.

33 For Haier's approach to foreign markets: Y. Wu., "China's Refrigerator Magnate," *The McKinsey Quarterly*, 3 (2003) pp. 107–115; and H. Liu and K. Li, "Strategic Implications of Emerging Chinese Multinationals: The Haier Case Study," *European Management Journal*, 20 (December 2002), pp. 699–706.

34 Some observers believe that competition from emerging-market multinationals will increase: The markets for managerial talent and capital are increasingly liquid; emerging markets are very large; ever-stronger domestic firms are developing international and global ambitions; and Western firms are dispersing R&D to these countries. *The Economist*, Special Report on Innovation in Emerging Markets, April 2010.

35 Ghemawat's AAA Triangle framework embraces *Adaptation* — focus on local customer needs, *Arbitrage* — focus on global economies, and *Aggregation* — achieving scale and scope economies via international standardization: P. Ghemawat, "Managing Differences: The Central Challenge of Global Strategy," *Harvard Business Review*, 85 (March 2007), pp. 58–68.

36 Several European countries like Iceland, Lichtenstein, Norway, and Switzerland are not members of the EU.

37 Studies of country clusters are limited by the number included and their variation across studies; many parts of the world seem to be ignored, especially Africa. Table 25.3 is based on eight studies, mostly completed in the 1970s: S. Ronen and O. Shenker, "Clustering Countries on Attitudinal Dimensions," *The Academy of Management Review*, 10 (July 1985), pp. 435–454.

38 For organizational purposes, many multinationals group Europe, the Middle East, Africa as the EMEA region.

39 Source: The World Bank.

40 Young & Rubican (Y&R) developed a western-European based 4Cs (Cross Cultural Consumer Characterization) lifestyle segmentation from several basic values — survival, escape, security, status, control, discovery, and enlightenment. Y&R labeled its segments Resigned, Struggler, Mainstream, Aspirer, Succeeder, Explorer, and Reformer.

41 M. Schultz and M.J. Hatch, "The Cycles of Corporate Branding: The Case of the LEGO Company," *California Management Review*, 46 (Fall 2003), pp. 6–26.

42 Based on an online bulletin from EffectiveBrands.

43 D.A. Aaker and E. Joachimsthaler, "The Lure of Global Branding," *Harvard Business Review*, 77 (November–December 1999), pp. 137–144.

44 B. Becht, "Building a Company without Borders," *Harvard Business Review*, 88 (April 2010), pp. 103–106.

45 A.J. Parsons, "Nestlé: The Visions of Local Managers," *The McKinsey Quarterly*, (1966-2), pp. 5–29.

46 P. Kotler and D. Gertner, "Country as Brand, Product, and Beyond: A Place Marketing and Brand Marketing Perspective," *Brand Management*, 9 (April 2002), pp. 249–261; and N. Papadopoulos and L. Heslop, "Country Equity and Country Branding: Problems and Opportunities," *Brand Management*, 9 (April 2002), pp. 294–314.

47 P.W.J. Verlegh and J.-B. E.M. Steenkamp, "A Review and Meta-Analysis of Country of Origin Research," *Journal of Economic Psychology*, 20 (1999), pp. 521–546.

48 Likely driven by ethnocentrism: T.A. Shimp and S. Sharma, "Consumer Ethnocentrism: Construction and Validation of the CETSCALE," *Journal of Marketing Research*, 24 (August 1987), pp. 220–289.

49 J.G. Klein, R. Ettenson, and M.D. Morris, "The Animosity Model of Foreign Product Purchase: An Empirical Test in the People's Republic of China," *Journal of Marketing*, 62 (January 1998), pp. 89–100.

50 Z. Gürhan-Canli and D. Maheswaran, "Cultural Variations in Country of Origin Effects," *Journal of Marketing Research*, 37 (August 2000), pp. 309–317.

51 I. Clarke III, M. Owens, and J.B. Ford, "Integrating Country of Origin into Global Marketing Strategy: A Review of U.S. Marketing Statutes," *International Marketing Review*, 17 (2000), pp. 114–126.

52 The firm may be able to fix its selling price by hedging foreign currencies and other financing mechanisms.

53 Contract terms are an important issue: FOB (free on board) — customer responsible for shipping; CIF (carriage, insurance, freight) — supplier responsible for shipping.

54 N. Capon, J.U. Farley, and J. Hulbert, *Corporate Strategic Planning*, New York: Columbia University Press, 1988, for empirical data concerning organization structure for international business.

55 G. Ghislanzoni, R. Penttinen, and D. Turnbull, "The Multi-local Challenge: Managing Cross-Border Functions," *The McKinsey Quarterly*, 2008.

56 A geographic-region arrangement within the international division may precede birth of the full-scale geographic-region structure.

57 S. Douglas and Y. Wind, "The Myth of Globalization," *Columbia Journal of World Business*, (Winter 1987), pp. 19–29.

58 T. Levitt, "The Globalization of Markets," *Harvard Business Review*, 61 (May–June 1983), pp. 92–102. J.A. Quelch and E.J. Hoff, "Customizing Global Marketing," *Harvard Business Review*, 64 (May–June 1986), pp. 59–68 provides a more integrative view.

59 Personal communication from Carol Hamilton, President, L'Oreal Paris USA.

60 Some corporations base one branch of their matrix organizations on a functional structure.

61 Personal communication from Stewart McHie, former Global Brand Manager, ExxonMobil Fuel Marketing Company.

62 N. Capon, D. Potter, and F. Schindler, *Managing Global Accounts* (2nd ed.), Bronxville, NY: Wessex, 2008; and N. Capon and C. Senn, "Global Customer Management Programs: How to Make Them Really Work," *California Management Review*, 52 (Winter 2010), pp. 32–55. For alternative approaches: P. Cheverton, *Global Account Management: A Complete Action Kit of Tools and Techniques for Managing Key Global Customers*, London: Kogan Page, 2008; and G. Yip and A.J.M. Brink, *Managing Global Customers*, Oxford: Oxford University Press, 2007.

63 This organization is matrixed with a brand management organization focused on IBM products.

CHAPTER 26

1 *Wall Street Journal*, November 8, 2011.

2 Source: *Wikipedia*.

3 G. Svensson and G. Wood, "A Model of Business Ethics," *Journal of Business Ethics*, 77 (2008), pp. 303–322.

4 "China Business Report 2013-2014," U.S. Chamber of Commerce; Dexter Roberts, "American Companies in China Cite Corruption Challenges in Survey," *Shanghai Businessweek*, February 26, 2014, *http://www.bloomberg.com/bw/articles/2014-02-26/american-companies-in-china-cite-corruption-challenges-in-survey*.

5 J. Mont, "Ethisphere Institute Lauds the World's Most Ethical Companies," *Compliance Week*, March 20, 2014. **[397p]**

6 P. Taylor, *Principles of Ethics: An Introduction to Ethics* (2nd Ed.), Encino, California: Dickinson, 1975.

7 D.P. Robin and R.E. Reidenbach,"Social Responsibility, Ethics, and Marketing Strategy: Closing the Gap between Concept and Application," *Journal of Marketing*, 51 (1987), pp. 44–58.

8 P.V. Lewis, "Defining 'Business Ethics': Like Nailing Jello to a Wall," *Journal of Business Ethics*, 4 (1985), pp. 377–383.

9 S. J. Vitell, K. C. Rallapalli, and A. Singhapakdi, "Marketing Norms: The Influence of Personal Moral Philosophies and Organizational Ethical Culture," *Journal of the Academy of Marketing Science*, 21 (1993), pp. 331–337.

10 M. Lewis, *Flash Boys: A Wall Street Revolt*, New York: Norton, 2014.

11 R.N. Aditya, "The Psychology of Deception in Marketing: A Conceptual Framework for Research and Practice," *Psychology and Marketing*, 7 (2001), pp. 735–762.

12 For a fuller discussion and bibliography: G.W. Ortmeyer, "Ethical Issues in Pricing," in N.C. Smith and J.A. Quelch, *Ethics in Marketing*, New York: McGraw Hill, 1993, Chapter 5.1. If unsure about pricing actions, consult a knowledgeable attorney.

13 M. Friedman, *Capitalism and Freedom*, Chicago: University of Chicago Press, 1962.

14 Source: *Wikipedia*.

ANSWERS

CHAPTER 1

TRUE/FALSE QUESTIONS
1. True
2. True
3. False
4. True
5. False

MULTIPLE CHOICE QUESTIONS
1. c
2. a
3. c
4. c

CHAPTER 2

TRUE/FALSE QUESTIONS
1. True
2. False
3. True
4. True
5. False
6. False

MULTIPLE CHOICE QUESTIONS
1. a
2. d
3. d
4. a
5. a
6. b

CHAPTER 3

TRUE/FALSE QUESTIONS
1. True
2. False
3. True
4. False
5. True

MULTIPLE CHOICE QUESTIONS
1. b
2. a
3. c
4. b
5. e

CHAPTER 4

TRUE/FALSE QUESTIONS
1. True
2. False
3. False
4. True
5. False

MULTIPLE CHOICE QUESTIONS
1. a
2. c
3. d
4. c
5. a

CHAPTER 5

TRUE/FALSE QUESTIONS
1. False
2. True
3. True
4. True
5. False

MULTIPLE CHOICE QUESTIONS
1. a
2. d
3. d
4. b
5. c

CHAPTER 6

TRUE/FALSE QUESTIONS
1. False
2. True
3. False
4. True
5. True

MULTIPLE CHOICE QUESTIONS
1. c
2. d
3. a
4. b
5. d

CHAPTER 7

TRUE/FALSE QUESTIONS
1. True
2. False
3. True
4. True
5. False

MULTIPLE CHOICE QUESTIONS
1. a
2. c
3. a
4. a

CHAPTER 8

TRUE/FALSE QUESTIONS
1. True
2. True
3. False
4. True
5. True

MULTIPLE CHOICE QUESTIONS
1. d
2. c
3. a
4. d
5. d

CHAPTER 9

TRUE/FALSE QUESTIONS
1. True
2. True
3. False
4. True
5. False

MULTIPLE CHOICE QUESTIONS
1. d
2. b
3. a
4. b
5. d

CHAPTER 10

TRUE/FALSE QUESTIONS
1. True
2. False
3. True
4. True
5. False

MULTIPLE CHOICE QUESTIONS
1. c
2. b
3. b
4. d
5. d

CHAPTER 11

TRUE/FALSE QUESTIONS
1. True
2. True
3. False
4. False
5. True

MULTIPLE CHOICE QUESTIONS
1. d
2. d
3. a
4. a
5. d

CHAPTER 12

TRUE/FALSE QUESTIONS
1. True
2. False
3. False
4. True
5. True

MULTIPLE CHOICE QUESTIONS
1. d
2. b
3. b
4. d
5. d

CHAPTER 13

TRUE/FALSE QUESTIONS
1. True
2. False
3. True
4. False

MULTIPLE CHOICE QUESTIONS
1. d
2. a
3. c
4. a

CHAPTER 14

TRUE/FALSE QUESTIONS
1. False
2. True
3. False
4. False
5. True

MULTIPLE CHOICE QUESTIONS
1. a
2. d
3. c
4. c

CHAPTER 15

TRUE/FALSE QUESTIONS
1. True
2. False
3. True
4. False
5. True

MULTIPLE CHOICE QUESTIONS
1. d
2. c
3. a
4. d

CHAPTER 16

TRUE/FALSE QUESTIONS
1. False
2. False
3. True
4. False
5. True

MULTIPLE CHOICE QUESTIONS
1. b
2. c
3. d
4. c
5. b

CHAPTER 17

TRUE/FALSE QUESTIONS
1. False
2. False
3. False
4. True
5. True

MULTIPLE CHOICE QUESTIONS
1. b
2. a
3. a
4. d
5. d

CHAPTER 18

TRUE/FALSE QUESTIONS
1. True
2. True
3. True
4. False
5. False

MULTIPLE CHOICE QUESTIONS
1. a
2. c
3. d
4. d
5. a

CHAPTER 19

TRUE/FALSE QUESTIONS
1. False
2. True
3. True
4. False
5. False

MULTIPLE CHOICE QUESTIONS
1. c
2. a
3. d
4. d

CHAPTER 20

TRUE/FALSE QUESTIONS
1. True
2. False
3. True
4. True
5. False

MULTIPLE CHOICE QUESTIONS
1. b
2. d
3. d
4. d
5. a

CHAPTER 21

TRUE/FALSE QUESTIONS
1. False
2. False
3. True
4. True
5. False

MULTIPLE CHOICE QUESTIONS
1. d
2. c
3. b
4. d
5. d

CHAPTER 22

TRUE/FALSE QUESTIONS
1. True
2. False
3. False
4. True
5. True

MULTIPLE CHOICE QUESTIONS
1. a
2. d
3. d
4. a
5. c

CHAPTER 23

TRUE/FALSE QUESTIONS
1. True
2. True
3. False
4. True
5. True

MULTIPLE CHOICE QUESTIONS
1. a
2. b
3. c
4. d
5. d

CHAPTER 24

TRUE/FALSE QUESTIONS
1. False
2. False
3. True
4. False
5. True

MULTIPLE CHOICE QUESTIONS
1. b
2. d
3. d
4. d
5. b

CHAPTER 25

TRUE/FALSE QUESTIONS
1. True
2. False
3. False
4. True
5. False

MULTIPLE CHOICE QUESTIONS
1. b
2. c
3. a
4. a
5. d

CHAPTER 26

TRUE/FALSE QUESTIONS
1. True
2. True
3. True
4. False
5. True

MULTIPLE CHOICE QUESTIONS
1. a
2. c
3. c
4. c

GLOSSARY

80:20 rule. 80 percent of a firm's revenues come from 20 percent of its customers. An extension is the **80:20:120 rule** — these 20 percent of customers earn the firm 120 percent of its profits.

20:80 rule. This rule follows directly from the 80:20 rule: 20 percent of a firm's revenues come from 80 percent of its customers. An extension is the **20:80:20 rule** — these 80 percent of customers are responsible for reducing the firm's profits by 20 percent.

ACCORD. An acronym for factors that affect the speed of new product adoption: **A**dvantage, **C**ompatibility, **C**omplexity, **O**bservability, **R**isk, and **D**ivisibility.

Acquisition. A firm purchases another firm or business.

Acquisition cost (AC). The cost of attracting a new customer to the firm.

Action-learning. An approach to organizational development that focuses on learning by doing.

Activity-based costing (ABC). A costing system based on identifying the causes of cost behavior and associating each cost with its cause.

Adoption categories. Describe consumer behavior in adopting innovations — innovators, early adopters, early majority, late majority, and laggards.

Adoption curve. The sales trajectory for a new product or product form.

Advertising. Paid communications directed at a mass audience.

Advertising agency. A third-party organization to which many firms outsource the development and execution of their advertising.

Advertising budget. The monetary amount to be spent on advertising. Approaches to budget setting are:

Objective and task. A *bottom-up* approach focusing on advertising objectives and the tasks to be accomplished.

Percentage of sales. A rule-of-thumb approach that sets the budget as a percentage of sales: current sales, anticipated next-year sales, or some combination.

Competitive parity. An approach that bases the budget on competitors' spending.

Advertising effectiveness measures. Used to test advertising effectiveness. Options include:

Recognition. Advertising that respondents recognize.

Aided recall. Advertising that respondents remember with prompting.

Unaided recall. Advertising that respondents remember without prompting.

Advertising objectives. What the firm is trying to achieve with its advertising:

Intermediate objectives relate to the hierarchy-of-effects models and include awareness, knowledge, liking or preference, trial, and emotional commitment (to a brand).

Output objectives. What the firm ultimately wants to achieve, like sales, repeat purchase, market share, and brand loyalty.

Advertising response function (ARF). Relates advertising spending to an objective like sales.

Advertising strategy. Specifies how the firm will spend resources to achieve advertising objectives and includes decisions about target audience, advertising objectives, messaging, execution, media selections and timing, advertising budget, and program evaluation.

Alliances. Formal economic relationships between the firm and other entities (partners) — suppliers, customers, and distributors.

Alpha test. A new product test within the firm by company employees.

Angel investors. Wealthy individuals who provide funding for new business ventures at a very early stage. Angel investors typically invest before venture capitalists.

Antitrust. U.S. laws that prohibit actions to reduce competition.

ASSESSOR. A new-product-forecasting model based on trial and repeat.

Auction pricing. A product's price resulting from competition among potential buyers:

Dutch auction. Prices start high; the seller reduces price until a buyer bids.

English auction. Prices start low and potential buyers bid up the price.

Reverse auction. The buyer states product requirements; suppliers bid to provide the product, and prices go down.

Vickrey auction. A form of **sealed-bid** English auction where the winning bidder pays the price of the second-highest bid.

B2B — Business-to-business. This acronym generally describes marketing where customers are other organizations — business, public, and not-for-profit.

B2C — Business-to-consumer. This acronym generally describes marketing where customers are consumers.

Backward integration. A customer undertakes activities currently performed by its suppliers.

Bait and switch. Retailers advertise a low price for a product with limited availability. The *bait* sells quickly. Retailers offer most customers a higher-priced product — the *switch*.

Balanced scorecard. A performance measurement system that balances input, intermediary, and output variables.

BASES. A new-product-forecasting model that uses an historical database to improve forecast accuracy.

BDI. See brand development index.

Beacons. Retailers use Beacons, *Bluetooth* technology, and the shopper's smartphone to identify location within the store for communication and data gathering.

Behavioral targeting. An Internet-based technique that uses information collected from a users online activity to present (on a website visit) or send by e-mail specific messages to motivate purchase or other goals.

Benchmarking. The practice of securing best practices from outside the firm at other organizations.

Benefits and values, categories of:

Economic. Result from financial considerations of purchasing a product or service.

Functional. Follow from the product's design.

Psychological. Satisfy customer needs like status, affiliation, reassurance, risk, and security.

Search. Customers can gain good information before they purchase.

Use. Customers do not know the value at the time of purchase.

Credence. Customers do not know the value until long after the purchase.

Best practice transfer. An approach to identifying and transmitting superior processes across the firm.

Beta test. A new product test by cooperating customers.

Big data. Collections of large and complex data sets that offer the possibility of gaining insight.

Blog. An Internet vehicle for individuals to offer opinions and receive feedback from others.

Brand. The traditional definition is: *a name, term, sign, symbol, or design (or letter, number, or character), or a combination of them intended to identify the goods and services of one seller or group of sellers and to differentiate them from competition.* A more customer-focused definition is: *a collection of perceptions and associations that customers hold about a product, a service, or a company. This collection embodies values that create meaning for customers that represent a promise of the experience customers expect when they have contact with the brand.*

Brand architecture. The organizing structure for the firm's brand portfolio.

Brand associations. The meanings the brand has for customers.

Brand attachment. The strength of the bond connecting the brand with the self (cognitive and emotional) including positive feelings and memories (related to brand attitude strength).[1]

Brand attitude strength. Positive or negative feeling (valence) about the brand factored by the confidence that the feeling is valid (related to brand attachment).

Brand awareness. The extent to which customers know that the brand exists.

Brand broadening/leveraging. A branding approach for extending an existing brand into a new product form/class.

Brand coherence. The extent of agreement between brand identity and the experience a customer has with the brand.

Brand commitment. Often used as a synonym for brand loyalty.

Brand development index (BDI). A U.S.-based measure of brand strength used in B2C. BDI in a specific geographic area is percentage of brand sales divided by percentage of the U.S. population, converted to a percentage.

Brand earnings. That portion of a firm's earnings that is attributable to the brand.

Brand equity. The classic definition is: *a set of brand assets and liabilities linked to a brand, its name, and symbol that add to (or subtract from) the value provided by a product or service to a firm and/or that firm's customers.* There are two types of brand equity:

> **Customer brand equity** is the value customers receive from a brand, less the value they receive from a generic product. Customer brand equity comprises value received before purchase — **prepurchase equity**, and value received after purchase — **postpurchase equity**.

> **Firm brand equity** derives directly from customer brand equity when the firm secures in its customers brand awareness, positive attitudes, high perceived quality, positive word-of-mouth, intentions to purchase, purchase, brand loyalty, positive brand image and associations (or brand personality), and satisfaction.

Brand equity protection. Actions the firm takes to reduce the negative effects on its brand(s) from actions like counterfeiting, diversion, tampering, and theft.

Brand essence. The brand's fundamental promise reflected in its brand identity.

Brand experience. Customers' subjective internal (sensations, feelings, cognitions) and behavioral responses evoked by brand-related stimuli that are part of its design and identity, packaging, communications, and environment.[2]

Brand extension. Broadening (leveraging) the brand to a new product form/class.

Brand harmonization. The extent to which the firm positions the brand consistently in different product/markets.

Brand health check. A way of measuring the overall health of the brand.

Brand identity. What the firm wants the brand to mean to customers, including brand personality and the brand promise.

Brand image. The overall meaning that the brand has to customers.

Brand licensing. The practice of making agreements with third-party organizations to attach the brand to their products.

Brand loyalty. The extent to which customers are predisposed to make repeat purchases of the brand.

Brand management. The practice of developing and/or sustaining brand identity by designing and executing marketing actions.

Brand migration. The process of transferring the equity in a brand being retired to a surviving brand.

Brand parity. The extent of similarity or difference of various brands (typically in a product form/class).

Brand personality. A set of enduring and distinct human characteristics associated with a brand.

Brand positioning. The process by which the firm attempts to align brand image with brand identity.

Brand prominence. The extent to which the brand is top of mind; the ease and frequency with which the brand and feelings about the brand are brought to mind.

Brand promise. A synonym for brand essence.

Brand resilience. The ability of a brand to recover from negative information.

Brand revitalization. An approach designed to rejuvenate underperforming brands.

Brand strategy. The firm's game plan for developing and achieving objectives for the brand.

Brand trust. The willingness of the average customer to rely on the ability of the brand to perform its stated function.

---

1   C.W. Park, D.J. MacInnis, J. Priester, A.B. Eisingerich, and D. Iacobucci, "Brand Attachment and Brand Attitude Strength: Conceptual and Empirical Differentiation of Two Critical Brand Equity Drivers," *Journal of Marketing*, 74 (November 2010), pp. 1–17. **[eg1]**

2   J.J. Brakus, B.H. Schmitt, and L. Zarantonello, "Brand Experience: What Is It? How Is It Measured? Does It Affect Loyalty?" *Journal of Marketing*, 73 (May 2009), pp. 52–68. **[eg2]**

Brand valuation. The process of putting a monetary value on brand equity, typically firm brand equity (FBE).

Branding. The attachment of a symbol to a product, service, and/or organization that uniquely identifies the supplier and/or owner. The symbol may consist of words, a concept, or an auditory or visual signal.

Breakeven analysis. The approach for calculating the breakeven point.

Breakeven point (BE). The level of sales required to cover fixed costs.

Bundling. The firm sells a product and sets a price only in combination with other products and/or services. *Unbundling* — the firm sells products and sets prices for each item individually; *Mixed bundling* — the firm offers its products as part of a bundle, but also individually.

Business-case analysis. Assesses the financial viability of a project, including various risk factors.

Business model. The way the firm creates value, generates revenues, and incurs costs.

Business strengths. Capabilities, competences, and resources the firm needs to be successful.

Buzz marketing. A communications approach designed to secure positive word of mouth — *buzz* — about the firm's products.

CAD. An acronym for computer-aided design. CAD uses computer systems to design detailed two- or three-dimensional models of physical objects like mechanical parts, buildings, and molecules.

Calendarize. Partitioning sales objectives by time period like quarter, month, or week.

CAM. An acronym for computer-aided manufacturing: CAM is a manufacturing process that uses specialized computers to control, monitor, and adjust tools and machinery in manufacturing.

Candidate descriptor variables — segmentation variables. Used to identify segments; typically fall into one of four categories: geography, demography, behavioral, and socio-psychological.

Capabilities, resources, competences. Three related terms that embrace several factors the firm can use as the basis for securing differential advantage. Often called business strengths.

Category development index (CDI). A U.S.-based measure of category strength used in B2C. CDI in a specific geographic area is percentage of category sales divided by percentage of U.S. population, converted to a percentage.

CDI. See category development index.

CLV. See customer lifetime value.

Channel stuffing. The firm overloads distributors and hence overstates its revenues. Can lead to legal problems.

Chasm. The transition between making sales to innovating and early-adopting customers, and to the mainstream market. Products failing to *cross the chasm* do not realize their potential.

Co-branding. An approach to branding typically involving cooperation between two brands from different firms.

Cognitive algebra. Embraces various mental approaches customers might use to integrate information about alternatives to make purchase decisions. These include:

Linear compensatory. The customer chooses the alternative with the highest value. An alternative's value comprises the values from each attribute such that high value on one attribute balances out poor value on another.

Lexicographic. The customer chooses the alternative that performs best on the most important attribute. To resolve ties, the customer moves to the second most important attribute.

Conjunctive. The customer sets a performance cut-off for each attribute. The chosen alternative must meet or exceed each cut-off.

Disjunctive. The customer sets a performance cut-off for each attribute. The chosen alternative must meet or exceed a cut-off for at least one attribute.

Cognitive resources. Describe the decision maker's ability to process information. Key features are:

Direction. Are they paying attention?

Intensity. Can they process the information?

Commercialization. The final step in bringing a new product to market.

Commodity brand. A brand with little brand equity. Customers believe the firm's offer has little or no additional value over competitive offers.

Communication process. The activities involved in sending and receiving information.

Communications tipping point. The level above which communications generate customer resentment.

Competitive assessment analysis. A way of mapping customer needs, required benefits, and values, with the required resources, to assess the competitive position of various suppliers.

Competitive data:

Level of. The organizational level for collecting data — corporate, business unit, market, and market segment.

Type of. The sorts of quantitative and qualitative data the firm can collect.

Secondary. Data that have been collected for another purpose.

Primary. Data that require a focused acquisition effort.

Competitive intelligence department. An organizational unit that collects, analyzes, and distributes competitive information.

Competitive intelligence system. A process to collect, analyze, and distribute competitive information.

Competitor. Any organization whose products and services provide similar or superior benefits and values to the same customers that the firm seeks to attract and retain. They may be:

Current. Competitors that the firm faces *today*.

Potential. Competitors that the firm may face *tomorrow*.

Direct. Offer similar benefits with similar products, technologies, or business models.

Indirect. Offer similar benefits with alternative products, technologies, or business models.

Competitor target. The organizational entity against which the firm decides to compete.

Complementary products. Products that are used together like razors and razor blades, vacuum cleaners and bags, and printers and toner cartridges.

Complementer. Any organization like independents and competitors whose actions can affect the firm's sales.

Concentrated market. A market with few substantial competitors.

Concept definition. See product concept.

Contextual advertising (targeting). A type of advertising used on the Internet in which the user receives an advertisement related to the content s/he is viewing. Hence, a person on a travel-oriented website may see an ad for hotels or travel packages.

Contribution margin (CM). Sales revenues less variable costs, and:

Contribution margin per unit (CMU). Contribution margin stated on a per-unit basis.

Contribution margin rate (CMR). Contribution stated per monetary unit of sales revenues.

Control, types of:

Firm functioning. Asks the question, "Is the firm functioning well?" Three subareas are:

Implementation. Did the firm implement its planned actions?

Strategy. Is the firm's market strategy well conceived and on target?

Managerial process. Are the firm's managerial processes the best they can be?

Performance control. Did the firm achieve its desired results?

Postaction. The firm waits until a preset time, then compares actual results against standards.

Steering. A dynamic, continuous, and anticipatory system. The firm sets control limits for performance standards and compares results against standards on an ongoing basis.

Control unit. An element of the sales force for monitoring and controlling sales activities and performance, like a sales region, sales district, or sales territory.

Cookie. A piece of text stored by a user's web browser for identification and authentication.

Cooperation with competitors:

Backoffice. Competitors work together in non-customer-facing activities to reduce costs and improve efficiency for all firms.

Marketplace or frontoffice. Competitors work together to better satisfy customer needs like developing a new technology standard.

Core product. The central element in the firm's offer of a physical product, like an automobile.

Core service. The central element in the firm's service offer, like overnight package delivery.

Cost of capital. The financial return the firm must earn to recover its capital outlay. The cost of capital is a weighted average of the firm's cost of equity and debt. In evaluating investment opportunities, the firm discounts expected future cash flows at its cost of capital.

Cost per action (CPA). A measure of advertising cost in digital media. CPA is the cost charged to the advertiser when an online customer takes a particular action. Examples:

Cost per registration (CPR). The advertiser pays the website host for each new customer registration.

Cost per sale (CPS). The advertiser pays the website host, by percentage or flat fee, for each sale generated by the advertisement.

Cost per click (CPC). A measure of advertising cost in digital media. With CPC, the website owner charges the advertiser each time a viewer clicks on the advertisement.

Cost per 1000 (CPM). A measure of the advertising cost. CPM = Absolute Cost of Advertising Space × 1000/Circulation.

Costs, types of:

Direct. Occur because a particular product, organizational unit, or activity exists or is being contemplated. Can be identified with, or directly linked to, a product, sales territory, or function. Include all variable costs and at least some fixed costs.

Direct fixed costs. Costs directly related to the product. These costs do not vary directly with the number of units sold, but are associated with individual products.

Fixed. Do not vary with the volume of sales or production over a reasonable range. Usually comprise overhead items like managerial salaries, depreciation, and selling, general, and administrative expenses (SG&A).

Fully loaded. Incremental costs plus overhead charges.

Indirect. Relate to several products, organizational units, or activities. Cannot be identified with a single product, sales territory, or activity. Are always fixed costs.

Marginal. The cost to make and sell one additional unit. Includes all variable costs and some incremental fixed costs, but *excludes* overhead charges.

Programmed. Set and controlled by managers for a planning period.

Standby. Do not change significantly without a major change in operations.

Variable. Vary directly with the volume of sales and production. Increase as volume increases and decrease as volume decreases.

Counterfeiting. Illegal copying of a firm's products.

CPA. See cost per action.

CPC. See cost per click.

CPM. See cost per 1000.

Creative brief. A *contract* between the firm and its advertising agency that provides parameters and information for translating the firm's market strategy into an advertising message.

Cross-docking. The logistics practice of unloading materials from an incoming truck/railroad car and reloading directly onto outbound trucks/rail cars, with minimal (or zero) storage.

Cross-selling. Selling different products to a customer who has already purchased from the firm.

Customer. Any person or organization in the channel of distribution or decision (other than competitors) whose actions can affect the purchase of the firm's products and services. Categories of customers include:

Current (today). The firm does business with these customers today.

Potential (tomorrow). The firm hopes to do business with these customers in the future.

Direct. Exchange money or other resources with the firm for its products.

Indirect. Secure the firm's products from intermediaries like manufacturers or distributors.

Macro-level. Organizational units like manufacturers, wholesalers, retailers, government entities, and families.

Micro-level. Individuals with influence or decision-making authority within the macro-level customer.

Customer attribute (CA). A characteristic, function, or property of the seller's offer.

Customer audience targeting. Used on the Internet. The advertiser provides a list of people it wants, or does not want, to receive its advertisements.

Customer experience. A state, condition, or event that consciously affects a customer.

Customer insight. A deep and unique understanding of customers' needs and required benefits and values.

Customer lifetime. The estimated length of time a firm's customer will remain a customer.

Customer lifetime value (CLV). The economic value to the firm from a customer over the lifetime of its relationship. CLV is the discounted future stream of profits the customer generates.

Customer needs. A basis for identifying market segments.

Customer needs, types of:

Latent. The customer is not consciously aware of these needs.

Recognized. The customer is consciously aware of these needs; they may be *expressed* to others, or *nonexpressed*.

Customer profitability. The profit the firm earns from an individual customer or group of customers.

Customer relationship management (CRM). The ongoing process of identifying and creating new value with individual customers and sharing these benefits over a lifetime of association with them.

Customer segment. A finer-grained group of customers than a market segment. Within a market segment, the firm might identify several customer segments.

Customer service. Any act, performance, or information that enhances the firm's core product or service.

Customer service strategy. An approach to delivering customer service based on understanding customers' needs for customer service.

Customer target. Individuals and/organizations that the firm tries to make its customers.

Customer tiers. A term for classifying customers in terms of importance to the firm. For example:

Tier I (platinum). The firm's most important current and potential customers.

Tier II (gold). Important current and potential customers but less so than Tier I.

Tier III (bronze). Important current and potential customers but less so than Tiers I and II.

Customer value. The utility a customer receives from purchasing the firm's product or service. Value is a higher-level construct embracing several benefits the product offers.

Customer value map. A method of assessing a product's price/value position by plotting relative customer value versus relative price for various competitive products.

Customer value, methods of assessing:

Dollarmetric method. A method for assessing customer value. For several pairs of alternatives, the customer states which alternative she prefers and how much extra she would pay.

Direct value assessment. The firm simply asks customers what they would pay for various products.

Economic value for the customer (EVC). The price the customer pays for a competitive product, plus the net additional value the firm's product provides. EVC is an upper bound for price.

Perceived value analysis. The firm secures data directly from customers, but sometimes experienced managers provide *best-guess* data that can be validated later by marketing research.

Price experiment. The firm offers the test product at different prices in different market areas, like geographic locations.

Data mining. A quantitative approach to gain insight into customers' purchasing behavior as the basis for making specialized offers.

Data warehouse. A place to store data on an individual customer's characteristics and purchase transactions.

Decision making. Deviations from rationality:

Hyperbolic discounting. As decision time approaches, individuals reverse their preferences from larger rewards received later to smaller rewards received earlier.

Mental accounting. Consumers categorize funds and resources in separate mental accounts and spend differently from these accounts.

Prospect theory. Individuals place greater weight on potential losses than on equivalent value potential gains.

Decision-making process (DMP). The individual stages that members of the decision-making unit complete in making a purchase.

Decision-making unit (DMU). The individuals involved in a purchase decision.

Defection rate (1–r). The rate at which the firm loses customers from one time period to the next (also called *churn*). Sometimes calculated as a probability. The opposite of retention rate.

Demand curve. A graph of the relationship between price and volume showing price sensitivity.

Demarketing. Firm efforts to reduce demand, typically because of a supply/demand imbalance.

Demonstration ad. Shows the product in use and focuses on its performance.

Development. The process of turning a product concept into an actual product.

Digital communication. The electronic transmission of digitally encoded information.

Direct marketing. A communications tool embracing many ways of requesting a direct customer response. Includes traditional print and broadcast advertising as well as newer digital options like e-mail and the Internet.

Direct product profit. Assesses profit performance after taking into account the fixed costs the product incurs.

Discount rate (d). The rate at which the firm discounts future earnings so as to calculate customer lifetime value. The discount factor is typically set equal to the firm's cost of capital.

Disintermediation. The removal of a layer in a distribution system.

Distribution channel or Distribution. Encompasses the entities, interrelationships, and functions that members perform, so that the supplier's products reach customers.

Distribution channel breadth. The number of members at a particular level in the channel system:

Exclusive. A distribution strategy that focuses on a few well-chosen outlets.

Intensive. A distribution strategy that maximizes the number of outlets.

Selective. A sort of compromise between intensive and exclusive distribution.

Distribution conflict:

   Operational. Focuses on day-to-day issues like late shipments, invoicing errors, unfulfilled salesperson promises, unacceptable product quality, supplier attempts to load channels, and price and margin disputes.

   Strategic. May change the relationships among distribution channel members.

Distribution exclusivity:

   Geographic. The supplier gives the distributor a monopoly on selling products in its territory.

   Product. The supplier gives the distributor exclusivity to sell a group of products.

   Supplier. The intermediary agrees to distribute only the supplier's products.

Distribution functions. The activities that the distribution channel must perform. Concerned with the physical product, information, and/or ownership.

Distribution, method:

   Direct. The supplier supplies products directly to consumers and end users.

   Indirect. Intermediaries like distributors, wholesalers, and retailers play a major role in transferring products to consumers and end users.

Distribution, view of:

   Broad view. Encompasses changes in *state, physical location,* and *time.*

   Narrow view. Encompasses mainly changes in *physical location* and *time.*

Disutility of price. Refers to the fact that whereas customers receive value (utility) from a product's features/attributes, they must *give up* economic resources. Price has negative value or disutility.

Diversion. The practice of purchasing the firm's products ostensibly for sale to one set of customers, then reselling (diverting) those products to a different set of customers. Typically, the firm's strategy is negatively affected.

Divest. Selling a business to another firm.

Dollarmetric method. A method for estimating the monetary value of customer brand equity.

Downstream. The firm's customers and its customers' customers, etc.

Drop shipping. A retailer makes the sale but the manufacturer ships the product direct to the retailer's customer.

Dumping. Selling products in foreign markets below home market prices at "less than fair market value" and often below average costs.

Duration effect. The relationship between customer retention rate and customer lifetime. As customer retention rate increases, customer lifetime increases.

Dynamic pricing. A special case of price discrimination where the price varies over time.

Economic value for the customer (EVC). The price the customer pays for a competitive product, plus the net additional value the firm's product provides. EVC is an upper bound for price.

Efficient consumer response (ECR). An approach to drive out excess inventory by focusing on consumer demand-pull versus supplier-push. Developed by food manufacturers and distributors.

Endorsed brand. The firm uses one firm brand to support — endorse — another.

Engineering characteristics (EC). Engineering parameters to design and modify a product.

Entry barrier. Something that forestalls or slows a firm's entry into a market.

Environmental influences. Factors external to the consumer that affect decision making, embracing culture, social class, other people, family, and the situation.

Ethnographic research. An observational research technique derived from anthropology.

Exchange. The firm and its customers exchange value. Through its products and services, the firm offers value to customers. Customers typically offer value to the firm via their financial resources. If the firm and customer each accept the value offered by the other, an exchange occurs.

Executional style. The way the firm turns the core message into effective advertising:

   Rational-style advertising appeals to people's sense of logic.

   Emotional-style advertising appeals to the emotions.

Expectations disconfirmation. A key feature of the SERVQUAL model. Customer satisfaction is the *difference* between expected quality and perceived quality.

Experience curve. An empirical relationship between unit product cost and the firm's experience in making and distributing the product.

Experiment. A research approach where the researcher manipulates one or more independent variables to assess the impact on a dependent variable.

External orientation. A firm with this orientation focuses on customers, competitors, complementers, and factors in the external environment that could affect its future health.

Face time. The time a salesperson spends face-to-face with customers.

Factoring. A process by which the firm sells its accounts receivable for cash.

Family or masterbrand. The brand for a group of closely related products serving a similar function.

Feature or attribute. A characteristic, function, or property of the seller's offer.

Feature/benefit/value ladder. A hierarchy that joins the product's features with the benefits and values those features deliver to customers.

Features of services:

Divisibility. A feature of services emphasizing that they often comprise a sequence of activities.

Inseparability. A feature of services emphasizing that production and consumption occur simultaneously.

Intangibility. A feature of services emphasizing that they have no physical presence. They cannot be touched, driven, flown, worn, kicked, batted, squashed, or sat upon.

Perishability. A feature of services relating to *inseparability*. Services cannot be inventoried.

Variability. A feature of services emphasizing a lack of consistency because of human involvement in service delivery.

Feedback cycle. The time period between the firm's actions and its measured results.

Fighter/fighting brand. See firewall brand.

Financial analysis approaches. Methods for making resource decisions.

Economic profit or economic value added (EVA). The firm's annual profit less an explicit charge for capital.

Internal rate of return (IRR). A method of evaluating investment opportunities using future cash flows. IRR is the discount rate that equalizes cash inflows and cash outflows.

Net present value (NPV). A method of evaluating investment opportunities using future cash flows. **NPV** is the monetary value from discounting cash flows at a predetermined rate, typically the firm's cost of capital.

Payback. Payback is the forecast time to pay back the investment. In general, shorter paybacks are better than longer paybacks.

Return on investment (ROI). ROI calculations project future accounting data. They compare the product's forecast rate of return with a target (or *hurdle*) rate.

Financial analysis perspective. Making resource allocations based on financial analysis.

Firewall brand. Brand that defends the firm's profitable products, sometimes termed *fighter (fighting) brand*.

First-mover advantage. An advantage gained simply by being first. The firm may earn a leading reputation for quality and/or gain superior market knowledge.

Five-forces model. A set of forces impinging on the firm:

Current direct competitors. Satisfy customer needs by offering similar benefits with similar products, technology, or business models.

New direct entrants. Offer similar products, but were not previously competitors.

Indirect competitors. Satisfy similar customer needs by offering alternative products, technologies, or business models.

Suppliers. Provide the firm's inputs.

Buyers. Purchase the firm's products.

Flanker brand. A brand introduced to protect an important brand from competition.

Floor price. The price below which a firm should never sell a product, typically the marginal cost.

Flower of customer service. Eight elements of customer service: safekeeping, order-taking, information, consultation, billing, payment, exceptions, and hospitality.

Focus group. A small number of people, typically eight to 12, assembled by a marketing researcher to secure insight into customers' needs and motivations.

Follower. A firm that enters after the pioneer has created a new market.

Forecasts, types of:

Market. The predicted market-level sales in a future time period.

Sales. The firm's predicted sales in a future time period:
Bottom-up. A forecast that starts with customer-by-customer forecasts.
Synthetic. A forecast that combines top-down and bottom-up forecasts.
Top-down. A forecast that starts with a market-size forecast.

Forward integration. A supplier undertakes activities currently performed by its customers.

Fragmented market. A market with many competitors.

Franchising. A distribution strategy in which the franchisor develops a business model. Franchisees agree to implement the franchisor's model and typically pay an initiation fee and ongoing fees.

Full-line forcing. See tying agreements.

Game theory. A process that helps marketers think through options available to the firm and its competitors and how pursuing these options may affect these parties.

Global account manager (GAM). A person responsible for the firm's most important global customers.

Global branding. A branding approach that uses a common brand around the world.

***Good* market segments.** Segments that satisfy five criteria: differentiated, identifiable, stable, appropriate size, and accessible.

Gray markets. A reseller offers the firm's product in a market at a price lower than the firm's price in that market.

Gross domestic product (GDP). A measure of the nation's economy based on its production of goods and services.

Gross profit. Sales revenues less cost of goods sold.

Gross rating points (GRPs) Combines reach and frequency. GRP = Reach × Frequency.

Growth path. Describes the route the firm or business unit takes to achieve its growth objectives. Nine individual approaches reduce to four basic options:

Market growth. Engage related and new customers with existing products.

Market penetration. Focus on existing products in existing markets.

Product and market diversification. Bring new products to new customers.

Product growth. Bring related and new products to existing customers.

Growth-share matrix. BCG's portfolio analysis system; dimensions are forecast long-run market growth rate and relative market share. Product types in the growth-share matrix are:

Cash cows. High market shares in low growth markets; should generate cash.

Dogs. Low market shares in low growth markets; many *dog* products have poor financial performance, but some are respectable.

Stars. High market shares in high growth markets; comparatively rare. Many *stars* consume significant cash, but should create generous returns later.

Problem children, question marks, lottery tickets, or wildcats. Low market shares in high growth markets. Need a lot of investment and are high risk.

Guerilla marketing. Word-of-mouth communication stimulated by the firm.

Harvest. The firm seeks short-term cash flow at the expense of sales and market share.

Hierarchy-of-effects models. Describes how advertising works for different types of products:

High-involvement products. The purchase involves financial and/or psychosocial risks.

Low-involvement products. The purchase involves little risk.

Hierarchy of needs. Developed by psychologist Maslow; needs are in five groups, ordered low to high — physiological, safety and security, social, ego, and self-actualization.

Hockey stick. A forecasting practice in which managers make overly optimistic estimates about future revenues and costs so that their projects achieve the required returns.

Hospitable market. A market that is attractive to the firm.

House of Quality. A popular graphical representation of the quality functional deployment process — links customers attributes and engineering characteristics.

Human resource management (HRM). Processes for managing people including recruiting, selecting, training and development, work processes, talent management and career paths, and recognition and reward.

Hurdle rate. A minimum return that any investment opportunity must exceed.

Iconic brand. A brand with high customer brand equity and high firm brand equity.

Iceberg principle. An analogy to the iceberg whereby good aggregate performance in a unit or subunit can *hide* poor performance elsewhere in the same unit.

Idea library. A storage medium for ideas that were suggested and/or discussed but not used.

Imitation. Copying a competitor's strategy; often used in early-growth markets to surpass leaders.

Implementation (of growth strategy). Alternative approaches for the firm to achieve its objectives:

Acquisition. The firm acquires another firm or a business unit.

Equity investment. The firm takes an ownership position.

Insourcing. The firm undertakes activities currently done by others.

Internal development. The firm develops the opportunity in-house.

Licensing and technology purchase. The firm secures access to technology developed by others. License — the original firm maintains ownership. Technology purchase — the firm gains ownership.

Outsourcing. The firm secures other firms to undertake activities it previously conducted in-house so it can focus on higher return opportunities.

Strategic alliance. Two firms join together to develop a stronger combined entity.

Implementation programs. Alternative approaches for the firm to achieve its objectives. In the context of market strategy, these include the marketing mix and other functional programs.

Independent inventors. Innovators working independently outside any corporate umbrella.

Indicators, types of:

Leading. Help managers assess if they are on track to achieve planned results.

Lagging. Measure what has already occurred.

Inhospitable market. A market that is unattractive to the firm.

Initial public offering (IPO). A company's first sale of stock to the public. Venture capitalists often sell equity stakes in an IPO.

Innovation. Endowing human and material resources with new and greater wealth-producing capacity.

Innovation, types of:

Disruptive innovations. Developed from a new technology offering new and very different value propositions, initially for new applications and a limited number of new-to-the-market customers.

Sustaining innovations. An innovation that improves the performance of established products along dimensions valued by mainstream customers.

Insight. Securing understanding of strengths and weaknesses in order to gain strategic perspectives. Three important types are:

Competitive insight is the ability to describe, evaluate, project, and manage competitors.

Company insight is the firm's understanding of itself — its advantages and disadvantages compared to the competition.

Complementer insight is insight into any organization whose actions affect the firm's sales.

Integrated marketing communications. The integration of the firm's various communications efforts, using various tools, for various communications targets.

Interdependence of opportunities. The extent to which the needed resources and/or the success or failure of one opportunity are related to one or more other opportunities.

Intermediation. The introduction of a layer in a distribution system.

Internal architecture. The firm's organizational structure, systems and processes, and HRM practices.

Internal orientation. A firm with this orientation looks inward. It focuses on internal functions like finance, operations, sales, and technology (R&D), rather than external factors.

Intrafirm competition. A type of competition where different firm units compete with each other.

IPO. See initial public offering.

Just-in-time (JIT). An approach to reducing inventory by making raw materials and parts deliveries shortly before use in the production line.

Kenneling. The practice of purchasing low-share businesses in low growth markets and placing them together. The acquirer typically makes profits by rationalizing operations to achieve lower costs.

Kill point. A point where the firm must decide to proceed or drop the project.

Lead users. Organizations and individuals who think up, and may even prototype, new products.

Leapfrog. A way of surpassing the market leader by developing innovative and superior products, and/or entering emerging market segments; often used in early growth markets.

Leveraged buyout (LBO). Formation of a new firm when an existing firm spins off a business to a group of investors and/or management — a management buyout (MBO).

Life cycles. A common means for describing the evolution of markets and products. Product-class and product-form life cycles are typically partitioned into several stages:

Introduction. The period from product launch until sales take off and grow at an accelerating rate. Total sales during introduction are generally low.

Early growth. The period from sales take-off until the growth rate begins to slow.

Late growth. Sales are still growing, but the rate of growth is slowing.

Maturity. The sales growth rate ranges from flat to growth in gross national product (GNP).

Decline. Overall sales decrease year by year.

Liquidate. Closing down a business and selling its assets.

Lock-in. The situation when customers are committed to buying from the firm. Lock-in customers have high **switching costs**.

Logistics. The process of moving a product from point A to point B:

Outbound. Getting the product from the supplier to the customer.

Inbound (reverse). Getting the product from the customer back to the producer.

Loyalty programs. Methods that firms use to enhance customer retention.

> **Hard rewards.** Denominated in dollars and cents, or translatable points.
>
> **Soft rewards.** Include toll-free information numbers, restaurant seating, theater ticket availability, hotel room and airline seat upgrades.
>
> **Probabilistic rewards.** The customer wins a large reward, or zero.
>
> **Deterministic rewards.** The customer accumulates points, then collects the reward.

Maintenance expenses. Expenses specifically designed to enhance customer retention.

Managerial process environment. The received wisdom that executives use to lead and manage their firms — their intellectual capital.

Margin. Embraces many specific definitions based on revenues less costs.

Margin multiple. A quick way to calculate CLV if customer margin, customer retention rate, and discount rate are constant from time period to time period. CLV equals customer margin multiplied by the margin multiple.

Margins, types of:

> **Unit margin.** A term used by retailers and wholesalers that measures the difference between the product's selling price and its unit cost.
>
> **Percent margin on cost.** The product's margin divided by the cost, stated as a percentage (not generally used by wholesalers and retailers).
>
> **Percent margin on selling price.** The product's margin divided by the selling price, stated as a percentage. Wholesalers and retailers generally use this term.
>
> **Inventory turnover (stockturn).** The number of times the firm sells average product inventory during the year.
>
> **Customer margin.** Sales revenues less all attributable customer costs.

Market. Customers — people and organizations — who require goods and services to satisfy their needs. Customers must have sufficient purchasing power and a willingness to pay for the products that suppliers offer.

Market-factor testing. A process for exploring the effect of one or more marketing-mix elements on expected sales. Typically performed in a simulated environment.

Market insight. The understanding firms secure about future market changes that lead to an appreciation of opportunities and threats.

Market levers. The actions the firm takes to achieve its performance standards.

Market occupancy ratio. A performance measure defined as the ratio of firm's number of customers to the total number of customers.

Market offer. The package of benefits and values the firm offers to customers.

Market-segment attractiveness. How attractive a segment is to the firm. An individual segment may be differentially attractive to different firms.

Market segmentation. A conceptual and analytic process for grouping actual and potential customers into market segments.

Market share. The most common market-based performance measure; compares the firm's sales units or revenues directly with competitors.

Market strategy. The firm's game plan for addressing the market.

Market structure. The market, products serving the market, and suppliers offering these products.

Market tinkering. An approach to new product development in which a firm makes minor modifications to its current products.

Marketing. There are several related meanings:

> **Philosophy.** Marketing as a guiding philosophy for the entire organization embraces an external orientation. It recognizes that revenues from customers are the critical source of cash flows.
>
> **Imperatives.** Marketing as six imperatives describes the specifics of the marketing job. These are the *must dos* of marketing.
>
> **Principles.** The firm must apply four marketing principles to do the marketing job well. They act as guidelines for making good marketing decisions based on the six imperatives.
>
> **American Marketing Association (AMA).** The AMA periodically redefines *marketing*. The 2004 definition stated, "Marketing is an organizational function and a set of processes for creating, communicating, and delivering value to customers and for managing customer relationships in ways that benefit the organization and its stakeholders." In 2007, the definition became, "Marketing is the activity, set of institutions, and processes for creating, communicating, delivering, and exchanging offerings that have value for customers, clients, partners, and society at large."

Marketing audit. A comprehensive process for evaluating the firm's marketing practices.

Marketing mix. The traditional description of the tools marketers use to construct an offer. They are often called the 4Ps—product, place (distribution), promotion, and price. Today, service is often treated separately to form 4Ps and an **S**.

Marketing myopia. The tendency for firms to have such an overly narrow view of their market that they miss opportunities and/or fail to recognize threats.

Marketing principles. Guidelines for making good marketing decisions:

Selectivity and concentration. Because resources are scarce, the firm should be selective in its choice of market and market segment. It should concentrate its resources against its chosen targets.

Customer value. Success in target market segments depends on the firm's ability to provide customers with value.

Differential advantage. To be profitable, the firm must provide a net benefit, or cluster of benefits, to a sizable group of customers, that they value and are willing to pay for, but cannot get, or believe they cannot get, elsewhere. Competition eventually erodes away any differential advantage—the firm must continually renew its differential advantage.

Integration. The firm must carefully integrate and coordinate all elements in the design and execution of its market strategy. Integration includes elements of the marketing mix and the activities of all functions that play a role in delivering promised benefits.

Marketing research, types of:

Primary. The firm collects data for the specific purpose of the study.

Secondary. Based on data that has already been collected for another purpose.

Qualitative. A flexible and versatile approach comprising several techniques that is not concerned with numbers. Often used for exploratory studies.

Quantitative. A research approach that uses numerical data to test hypotheses.

Marketing research process. A rigorous methodology for improving the probability that investments in marketing research will produce actionable insights.

Mass communication. Communications intended to reach a large audience via mass media.

Mass customization. Related to segments-of-one. The firm customizes its products to individual requirements on a large scale.

Mass-market brand. A brand the firm targets at the mass market.

Means/ends tree. A diagrammatic method for outlining, assessing, and choosing among various alternatives.

Measures, types of:

Input. Focus on actions taken by the firm — leading indicators.

Intermediate. Focus on actions that customers take — leading indicators.

Output. Focus on performance variables like sales and profits — lagging indicators.

Hard. Objectively measured like sales volume, profit, and market performance.

Soft. Rating scale measures like customer satisfaction or attitudes.

Media class. A group of closely related media — newspapers, TV, and billboards are each media classes.

Media objectives. What the firm wants to accomplish with its media strategy:

Frequency. The average number of times a targeted individual is exposed to the advertising.

Impact. The effect of an advertising message on the target audience: Impact results from a combination of frequency, reach, and creativity.

Reach. The number of targeted individuals exposed to the advertising message at least once.

Duplicated reach. The portion of the target audience exposed to the advertising message from multiple media sources.

Unduplicated reach. The portion of the target audience exposed to the advertising message from a single source.

Media schedule. The placement and timing of advertisements for the advertising program.

Media vehicle. A specific exemplar of a media class — *The New York Times* and *60 Minutes* are each media vehicles.

Merger. Two firms join together to form a new entity.

Miscommunication. Misperception and/or misunderstanding by a *receiver* of a message the *sender* intended to send. Problems may occur in:

Encoding. Translating and interpreting the intended message into the actual sent message.

Distortion. Receiving a different message from the message that was sent.

Decoding. Misperceiving and/or misunderstanding the received message because of selective attention, distortion, and/or retention.

Mission. Guides the firm's search for opportunity so it can focus on a limited number of areas where it is likely to be successful.

Modularity. A design approach in which the firm uses common components (modules) to produce a broad product line.

Moment of truth. An interaction between a service customer and service personnel.

Monitor-and-control system. A process for measuring whether the firm's actions, individually and collectively, are consistent with its plan. Forms the basis for making adjustments.

Monolithic brand. The brand for a group of products fulfilling many different functions. A **corporate brand** — for the firm as a whole — is a special case of a monolithic brand.

Multibranding. A brand architecture approach in which the firm uses multiple brands for its entries in various product classes.

Multifactor matrix. A portfolio analysis system that helps the firm decide which segments to target by assessing the attractiveness of market segments and the extent to which the firm possesses the business strengths to succeed.

Native advertising. A form of online advertising in which the advertisement is matched to the surrounding material — like an article seemingly written by an editor.

Negative complementarity. The negative effect on sales of one product caused by customer dissatisfaction with another product.

Negative working capital. Working capital equals current assets minus current liabilities. Negative working capital implies that the firm's suppliers and/or customers are financing its operations.

Net Promoter Score (NPS). Widely used measure of customer satisfaction derived from a single question measured on a 0 to 10 scale: "How likely is it that you would recommend XXXX to a friend or colleague?"

New idea processes. Methods for generating new ideas:
  Structured thinking. Logical ways to create new product ideas.
  Unstructured thinking. A family of approaches that attempt to *break the mold* and develop totally new ideas by thinking *outside the box.*

Noncompete agreement. An employee agrees not to work for a direct competitor for a specified period of time after he or she leaves the company.

Nondisclosure agreement (NDA). Aka a confidentiality agreement; a contract promising to protect confidential data disclosed during employment or other business transaction.[3]

One-on-one interviews. A marketing research approach conducted by interviewing respondents individually.

One-sided advertising. Advertising that focuses only on the product's positive attributes.

Opportunity costs. Costs incurred by not taking a course of action. They are not out-of-pocket costs but represent forgone profits due to inaction.

Organization structures, types of:
  Business process. An outgrowth of reengineering movement, the firm organizes around business processes.
  Category management. An evolutionary development of a product/brand management structure in which the firm manages multiple brands in a complementary manner.
  Combined product/brand management/market segment. Combines a product/brand focus with a market-segment focus.
  Customer management. An organization focused specifically on customers.
  Functional marketing. The firm places activities like marketing research, distribution, advertising and promotion, marketing administration, and new product development in a marketing department. Other major functional areas are likewise in separate departments.
  Inclusion. The firm groups many activities together under marketing.
  Market segment. Managers are responsible for individual market segments.
  Traditional product/brand management. Product and brand managers develop market plans for their products and brands. They are responsible for volume, share, and/or profit — they compete for resources like advertising dollars and sales force time.

Organizational orientations, types of:
  External. A firm with this orientation focuses on customers, competitors, complementers, and factors in the external environment that could affect its future health.
  Internal. A firm with this orientation looks inward. It focuses on internal functions like finance, operations, sales, and technology (R&D), rather than external factors.
  Financial. This firm is *run by the numbers* with scant regard for strategic issues. It avoids expenses with long-term payoff like R&D and marketing, in favor of increasing short-term profits. It often minimizes capital investment.

Operations. This firm's culture revolves around operational efficiency; there is typically a shared belief that cost reduction and volume maximization will ensure success. The firm does not have a deep understanding of customers' needs.

Sales. Maximizing short-term sales volume is the overarching goal. This firm often cuts prices to secure orders, but does little forward planning. As markets evolve, broadly acceptable new products are not available.

Technological (R&D). "Have technology, will travel— our technology will sell itself." This firm is often technologically sophisticated but rarely understands marketing and makes new product decisions with little or no customer input.

Outsourcing. When the firm engages a supplier to conduct an activity previously done in-house.

Packaging communication. Communication delivered by the package containing the product.

Paid search. Online advertisers pay to appear next to and be associated with search results based on keywords. For example, an electronics retailer might pay to appear next to searches for HDTVs.

Panel. A group of respondents who agree to provide data over time.

Partnership model. An approach to distribution channel members that involves building cooperation and trust.

Penetration pricing. A long-run low-price strategy to grow a market and secure high market share.

Perceived customer value. The value the customer believes the firm is delivering.

Perceptual map. A way of plotting the various products and market-segment ideal points (and sizes) into a two-dimensional (sometimes three) space defined by the most important customer needs.

Performance gap (variance[4]). The difference between performance standards and actual performance.

Performance objectives. Describe the business results the firm hopes to achieve. A performance objective has two components:

Strategic. The qualitative and directional results the firm wants to achieve. Strategic objectives typically fall into three categories: growth and market share, profitability, and cash flow.

Operational. Quantitative statements of business results the firm hopes to achieve that relate directly to the strategic objectives. How much is required and by when.

Permission marketing. Presenting marketing messages only to people who agree to receive them; the firm receives permission by asking people to *opt in*. When firms do not have permission they frequently allow people to *opt out* of future messages.

Personal communication. Face-to-face communications with targeted individuals or groups.

PESTLE model. An acronym for identifying the environmental forces acting on an industry — **P**olitical, **E**conomic, **S**ociocultural, **T**echnological, **L**egal, and **E**nvironmental (Physical).

Pioneer. A firm that creates new markets and is the first, or among the first, with a new product form.

Pipeline analysis. A method for tracking the firm's performance at different selling process stages.

Pocket price. The amount of money the firm actually receives — in its pocket.

Portfolio analysis. A method of evaluating investment opportunities that arrays the firm's products in two dimensions.

Portfolio approach. Individual products play different roles in the firm's portfolio. Some products generate growth and market share, some products earn profits, and some deliver cash flow.

Positioning. The heart of the market strategy that should create a unique and favorable image in the minds of target customers. Positioning requires four key decisions: select customer targets, frame competitor targets, design the value proposition, and articulate the reasons to believe.

Potentials, types of:

Market. The maximum market-level sales that the firm expects in a future time period.

Sales. The maximum sales that the firm could achieve in a future time period.

Power. The ability of one channel member to get another to do what it wants it to do.

Predatory pricing. Pricing below cost with the intent to eliminate a competitor.

Preemptive. Acting before competitors.

Preliminary screening. The first stage for eliminating new product ideas.

Price bases. The ways in which a firm can set prices such as by individual product, by use, or by results.

---

4 Not to be confused with the statistical term *variance*, as in mean and variance.

Price discretion. The firm's ability to use several pricing approaches. Firms that offer high value but also have low costs enjoy the most price discretion.

Price discrimination. Setting different prices for the same product to different segments or customers.

Price elasticity of demand (PED). PED = % change in demand/% change in price.

Price fixing. Competitors collude to set prices.

Price management. Organizing the firm to make its strategic and tactical pricing decisions.

Price sensitivity. Degree of change in volume related to change in price:

Price-elastic market. Volume *increases/decreases* significantly as price *decreases/increases*.

Price-inelastic market. Volume is *relatively insensitive* to price changes.

Price setting, types of:

Competitive-driven pricing. Pricing based on competitors' prices.

Cost-plus pricing. Setting price by identifying costs and adding a *satisfactory* profit margin.

Customer-driven pricing. Customers name the prices they are prepared to pay. If the product is available, they must complete the purchase.

Deceptive pricing. False prices and prices that might confuse or mislead customers.

Fees and surcharges. Extra charges such as bank fees for ATM use or airline fees for checked bags.

Flat-rate pricing. Pricing for a fixed time period. **Variable-rate pricing.** Pricing by use.

Loss-leader pricing. Retailers deliberately take losses to build customer traffic.

Psychological pricing. A common retail practice of pricing just below a *benchmark* number, like $9.95 or $9.99 versus $10.00.

Topsy-turvy pricing. The supplier receives additional value from a customer so that suppliers pay a price, rather than customers.

Transfer pricing. A price set for transactions among a firm's business units.

Variable pricing. Setting different prices for different customers/segments.

Price skimming. A strategy of setting high prices even though costs are falling. Often used in the early stages of the product life cycle.

Price umbrella. By setting a high price, a firm relieves competitors of pricing pressure.

Price waterfall. The reduction, by discounts and allowances, from list price to pocket price.

Pricing, and transportation:

CIF (carriage, insurance, freight). The supplier pays the cost, insurance, and freight.

FOB (free on board). The customer pays freight, insurance, and other charges.

Pricing information systems. Methods to provide decision makers with detailed price information.

Pricing menu. An approach to pricing in which the firm designs multiple offers, each at a fixed price.

Pricing strategy. The firm's overall approach to setting prices; should be based on four considerations — perceived customer value, costs, competition, and strategic objectives:

Penetration pricing. The firm sets prices close to costs as it seeks growth and market share.

Skim pricing. The firm keeps prices high to secure high margins.

Pricing toolkit. A set of pricing tactics for the firm to change a product's price.

Product. Sometimes *product* refers to the core offer, both *physical products* and *services*. We use this shorthand in much of the book. But tangible physical products can be touched, worn, kicked, or sat upon; a service cannot.

Product, types of:

Product class. A set of products offered by competing suppliers that serve a set of customer needs in a roughly similar manner.

Product form. A group of products offered by competing suppliers that are more closely similar in the way they meet customer needs than products in a product class.

Product item. A uniquely identified product offered by the firm.

Product line. A group of related products offered by the firm.

Product cannibalization. Sales of the firm's lower margin product decrease sales of a higher margin product.

Product complementarity. Relationships among the firm's products. *Positive complementarity* occurs when one product helps another; *negative complementarity* when one product hurts another.

Product concept. A description of a product idea that details the benefits and values the product should deliver to customers.

Product portfolio. Describes the set of products that the firm or business unit offers.

Product portfolio imbalance. The firm's products are mis-balanced between resource generating and resource consuming. In the growth/share matrix, this imbalance refers to cash flows.

Product proliferation. The firm offers a large number of products. Often viewed as undesirable, but can act as a barrier against competitive entry. Sometimes confused with market segmentation.

Profit contribution. The extent to which the product's sales revenues exceed variable costs.

Programmatic advertising (media) (marketing). The firm automates buying and placing advertisements based on rules and filters to optimize reaching a desired audience — much used in digital communications.

Publicity. Communication for which the firm does not pay, typically via the press.

Public relations (PR). Communication that embraces publicity but is broader — includes other ways of managing the firm's image to gain favorable responses.

Pull. A communications approach that focuses on indirect customers.

Purchase decision categories:

  Routinized-response behavior. A straightforward purchase decision; purchase criteria are well-established, and the alternatives are well known. Aka *straight rebuy.*

  Limited problem-solving. Purchase criteria are well-established, but a new alternative and/or supplier is available; more difficult than a straight rebuy. Aka *modified rebuy.*

  Extended problem-solving. Purchase criteria are not well-developed, and the alternatives are not well known; more difficult than a modified rebuy. Aka *new buy.*

Pure-form sales organization. Specialized and unspecialized ways to organize the selling effort.

Push. A communications approach that focuses on direct customers.

Quality function deployment (QFD). Maps customer needs into design, development, engineering, manufacturing, and service functions. Helps firms seek out both spoken and unspoken customer needs and translate these needs into actions and designs.

Quantitative analyses, types of:

  Cluster. A way of grouping a large number of items, people, or organizations into a small number of groups; popular for forming market segments.

Conjoint. A way of assessing the value that customers put on individual product attributes.

Discriminant. A way of identifying variables that discriminate between two or more groups.

Factor. A way of reducing a large number of variables into a manageable number of factors.

Multidimensional scaling. A way of developing a perceptual map of a market for use in segmentation and targeting.

Regression. A research technique for assessing the relationship between one or more independent variables and a dependent variable.

Quasi-personal communication (QPC). Interaction and feedback without human involvement, usually via artificial intelligence software.

Reasons to believe. Claims that support the firm's value proposition. Should provide compelling evidence to make the firm's claims believable.

Recommendation systems. Software that enables a firm to make personal recommendations to customers based on their prior purchases or browsing behavior on the Internet, or personal or social characteristics.

Reengineering. Examines fundamental assumptions about the way the firm conducts its activities. Seeks alternative approaches for redesigning and improving the firm's processes.

Reference groups. Individuals and groups that influence customers in their decision making:

  Primary. Include family members and organizational work groups.

  Secondary. Include club and church members and professional organizations.

  Aspirational. Those to which the customer would like to belong.

Relative market share (RMS). A dimensionless ratio used in the growth-share matrix; the firm's market share divided by the nearest competitor's market share.

Retail price maintenance (RPM). A distribution practice where suppliers set the prices at which retailers can sell their products. Following a 2007 Supreme Court decision, RPM is legal in the U.S., but is illegal in many other countries.

Retention rate (r). The rate at which the firm retains customers from one time period to the next. Sometimes calculated as a probability. The opposite of defection rate.

Return measures, types of:

  Return on sales (ROS). Profit expressed as a percentage of sales revenues; may be calculated for net or gross profit.

Return on investment (ROI). Profit expressed as a percentage of investment; may be calculated for gross or operating profit or net profit.

Return on stockholder equity (ROE). Profit expressed as a percentage of stockholder equity.

Return per linear foot (ROLF). Profit divided by the linear feet of shelf space.

Reverse logistics. The process of returning used goods/equipment from the point of use for disposal, refurbishing, or remanufacturing.

Reward system. The way to compensate salespeople for their efforts and performance. Includes elements like financial compensation, recognition, and promotions and work assignments.

RPS. An acronym for rapid prototyping system. RPS is a method for turning three-dimensional computer models into three-dimensional physical objects.

Safety factor. Indicates the extent to which the product's revenues exceed the breakeven point.

Sales approach. The essential message that the salesperson delivers to customers.

Sales force management tasks. Six related jobs that sales managers must complete to be effective.

Task 1. Set and achieve sales objectives.

Task 2. Determine and allocate selling effort.

Task 3. Develop sales approaches.

Task 4. Design the sales organization.

Task 5. Create critical organizational processes.

Task 6. Staff the sales organization.

Sales forecast. The firm's predicted sales in a future time period:

Bottom-up. A forecast that starts with customer-by-customer forecasts.

Top-down. A forecast that starts with a market-size forecast.

Sales objectives. The firm's desired results — typically stated in terms of sales revenues, sales units, or profit contribution.

Sales potential. The maximum sales that the firm could achieve in a future time period.

Sales promotion (SP). Activities providing extra customer value, often for immediate sales. Includes:

Trade shows. Products displayed to large numbers of customers at one time.

Product placement. Products placed in movies and TV shows.

Sales quotas. Sales objectives stated in terms of specific performance requirements.

Sales response function. The relationship between selling effort and sales results.

Sales territory. A set of customers or geographic area assigned to an individual salesperson.

Salesperson workload. The effort a salesperson must expend to complete assigned activities; a key variable for designing sales territories.

Scanner data. Purchase data collected electronically at point of sale, typically from bar codes (product/service identifiers).

Scenario. A descriptive narrative of how the future may evolve for a plausible option.

Screening criteria. Aids for evaluating and selecting opportunities. Important screening criteria are:

Objectives. What does the firm seek to achieve by investing in the opportunity?

Compatibility (or fit). Can the firm successfully address the opportunity?

Core competence. Can the firm use its core competencies or gain new core competencies?

Synergy. Can the firm use existing resources and earn greater returns than a standalone entry?

Contribution to the venture portfolio. Does the opportunity add positively to the set of opportunities the firm is pursuing?

Search engine optimization. An element of search marketing strategy whose goal is to move the firm's website link as high up the ranking list as possible.

Secondary market. Resale of a product or service. Most financial markets are secondary markets.

Segment-of-one. The firm addresses customers individually by developing customized offers.

Selling effort. The demands of the sales job. Methods to estimate required selling effort include:

Single-factor model. Uses a simple classification of customer importance.

Portfolio model. A more complex approach for estimating required selling effort.

Sentiment analysis. The analysis of text to determine its polarity. Used by firms to examine comments about their brands in social media.

Service. Any act or performance that one party can offer another that is essentially intangible and does not result in the ownership of anything. Anything that cannot be dropped on your foot.

Service equipment. Physical products needed to perform the service.

Service facilities. Where the firm produces the service. These facilities can be:

Offstage. Out of the customers' sight.

Onstage. Where customers experience deeds, performances, or efforts.

Service guarantee. A promise about the service experience that includes elements of value if the firm does not keep its promise.

Service personnel. People who provide the service.

Service quality. The extent to which the firm's service performance exceeds customers' expectations.

SERVQUAL. A popular model and measurement device for service quality based on several *gaps*.

Shadow system. Securing competitive information by having executives *shadow* specific competitors.

Shareholder value. The total value to shareholders—market capitalization—is measured by the market price of the firm's shares times the number of shares outstanding. Increasing shareholder value has become a mantra for many firms.

Shareholder-value perspective. Management's job is to maximize returns for shareholders. The shareholder-value perspective is prevalent in many capitalist countries—particularly in the U.S.

Signal. Information the firm sends to competitors, hoping they will process the information and act accordingly.

Six Sigma. A data-driven methodology for eliminating defects in any process.

SKU. See stock-keeping unit.

Slotting fees. Payments that suppliers make to retailers for providing shelf space for their products.

SMART goals. Goals that are **s**pecific, **m**easurable, **a**chievable, **r**ealistic, and **t**imely.

Social media. Online tools and platforms that allow Internet users to collaborate on content, share insights and experiences, and connect for business or pleasure. Involves multimedia and includes blogs, wikis, photo and video sharing, forums, and networks for meeting like-minded people.

Spam. Unsolicited and unwanted e-mail messages.

Span of control. The ratio of subordinates to supervisors. For example, a sales manager supervising 10 salespeople would be a span of 10 to 1.

Special relationships. Informal economic relationships between the firm and other entities such as government agencies, political parties, and public interest groups, as well as suppliers and customers.

Specialty brand. A brand providing high customer brand equity but relatively low firm sales.

Stage-gate approach. A systematic process for condensing a large number of ideas to a few products the firm can successfully launch. After each *stage*, the idea or project must pass through a *gate* (meet or exceed a standard) to continue. Each gate is a *kill point* where the firm must decide whether to proceed or drop the project.

Standalone brand. An individual brand with no apparent relationship to any other firm brand.

Standardized segments. Commercially available customer groupings that many firms find useful.

Standards. The firm's planned results; criteria against which the firm measures its performance.

Stock-keeping unit (sku). A unique identifier assigned to a specific product or service.

Strategic account manager (SAM). A person responsible for the firm's most important customers.

Strategic (or key) accounts. Customers that provide the highest levels of current and/or potential sales and profits.

Strategic alliance. A cooperative arrangement that pools the strengths of individual partner firms. Strategic alliances range in formality from a new joint-venture firm to temporary, informal arrangements.

Strategic focus. Selected from a tree of alternatives and states broadly how the firm will achieve its performance objectives.

Strategic options. A variety of alternatives, each requiring significant investment, among which the firm must choose.

Strategic sourcing. A discipline of specially designed systems and processes for reducing the costs of purchased materials and services.

Strategy for growth. A set of frameworks that helps the firm decide which businesses to be in and which businesses not to be in. Includes vision, mission, growth path, and timing of entry.

Supply chain. A coordinated system of organizations, people, activities, information, and resources that move a product or service, physically or virtually, from supplier to customer.

Survey. A common technique for securing data by asking respondents questions.

Switching costs. The costs that a customer must incur to switch from one supplier to another. Customers with high switching costs experience *lock-in.*

Synergy. Occurs when the combined effect of two or more elements is greater than the sum of their separate effects — *positive synergy.* If the combined effect is less than the sum of the separate effects, there is *negative synergy.*

Systems, types of:

Hard. Based on information technology.

Soft. Based on employees.

Systems integrators. Firms that install, service, and integrate software from many vendors.

Tactical pricing. The ongoing stream of pricing decisions the firm makes on a daily basis.

Target audience. The audience that the firm is trying to reach with its advertising.

Targeting. Deciding the market segments against which the firm should concentrate its resources.

Technology, types of:

Disruptive technology. A new technology offering new and very different value propositions, initially for new applications and a limited number of new-to-the-market customers.

Sustaining technology. A new technology that improves the performance of established products along dimensions valued by mainstream customers.

Telemarketing/Telesales. Communication by telephone, usually viewed as a subset of personal communication:

Inbound. Initiated by the customer.

Outbound. Initiated by the firm.

Test marketing. Tests a full-scale product launch on a limited basis.

Timing of entry. Denotes alternative entry stages in the product form life cycle:

Pioneer. Creates new markets.

Follow-the-leader. Enters markets when they are growing rapidly.

Segmenter. Enters in the late-growth stage by matching offers to emerging customer needs.

Me-too. Enters mature markets.

Timing pattern. When the advertising will appear. The major options are:

Continuous. A regular periodic advertising pattern.

Flighting. Repeated high advertising levels followed by low (or no) advertising.

Pulsing. Continuous and flighting advertising combined, within a single media vehicle or class or across multiple media vehicles and classes.

Tracking study. A method of securing research data. In a tracking study, aka a longitudinal study, a panel of individuals agrees to provide responses periodically over time.

Two-sided advertising. Presents both pro and con messages for a product as a way of gaining credibility.

Tying agreements. Strong suppliers *force* resellers to sell their entire product line. This practice is illegal in the U.S. if it reduces competition.

Type I error. A false positive error like investing in a project that fails or hiring a salesperson who performs poorly.

Type II error. A false negative error like rejecting a project that would have succeeded or not hiring a salesperson who would have performed well.

Umbrella branding. A brand architecture approach in which the firm uses a monolithic brand for several products, like a corporate brand.

Upstream. The firm's suppliers and its suppliers' suppliers, etc.

VALS2. This framework groups customers based on their *self-orientation* and *resources*:

Self-orientation. How they pursue and acquire products, services, and experiences to give their identities "shape, substance, and character."

Resources. The full range of their psychological, physical, demographic, and material assets.

Value-added resellers (VARs). Firms that build additional software modules onto other firms' platforms and modify hardware for niche markets.

Value proposition. The heart of positioning that provides a convincing answer to a deceptively simple question: Why should target customers prefer the firm's offer to competitors' offers?

Values, types of. A common set of beliefs that guide the behavior of the firm's employees. Values can be:

Hard, like profitability and market share.

Soft, like integrity, respect for others, trust, and customer preeminence.

Vendor financing. The supplier finances the customer's purchase of its products.

Venture capitalists. Individuals and firms that provide funds for new early-stage businesses.

Venture portfolio. The set of opportunities the firm decides to pursue.

Viral marketing. Marketing techniques that use preexisting social networks to convey marketing messages.

Virtual testing. A new approach to customer testing in which the firm creates an online shopping display that it can modify and secure results from quickly. Customers shop as in a real store with all the distracting clutter.

Vision. A description of an ideal future state; an impressionistic picture of what the future should be:

    Corporate vision. Focuses on the firm

    Business-unit vision. Focuses on the business.

Wiki. A website that allows user to easily create and edit interlinked websites. Uses include creating collaborative websites, powering community websites, and for knowledge management systems.

Winback. Securing sales from a customer that previously defected.

Word-of-mouth (WOM) communication. Communication between and among current and potential customers.

Yield management. Continuous price adjustments based on demand and available capacity.

INDEX

Locators with an *E* indicate an endnote. When business processes occur in a given order, or have a logical order, subentries may be force sorted to reflect that order, particularly when the process spans a chapter. Case studies are often force sorted to the top.

CPSIA information can be obtained
at www.ICGtesting.com
Printed in the USA
LVHW011556291221
707397LV00003B/5